DOCUMENTS
ON
AMERICAN FOREIGN
RELATIONS

VOL. XI

JANUARY 1 – DECEMBER 31, 1949

Edited by RAYMOND DENNETT

and ROBERT K. TURNER

PUBLISHED FOR

WORLD PEACE FOUNDATION

BY

PRINCETON UNIVERSITY PRESS

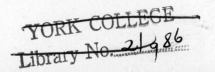

Copyright, 1950, by
Princeton University Press

London: Geoffrey Cumberlege
Oxford University Press

PRINTED IN THE UNITED STATES OF AMERICA BY
THE HILDRETH PRESS, INC., BRISTOL, CONNECTICUT

WORLD PEACE FOUNDATION
40 Mt. Vernon Street, Boston, Massachusetts
Founded in 1910

The World Peace Foundation is a non-profit organization which was founded in 1910 by Edwin Ginn, the educational publisher, for the purpose of promoting peace, justice and goodwill among nations. For many years the Foundation has sought to increase public understanding of international problems by an objective presentation of the facts of international relations. This purpose is accomplished principally through its publications and through the maintenance of a Documents and Reference Collection open without restriction to students and scholars in the field of international affairs. Particular attention has been focused on the field of international cooperation through the publication of the quarterly periodical, *International Organization,* and on the field of United States foreign policy through the publication of an annual series, *Documents on American Foreign Relations.*

Preface

With the publication of the present volume, the eleventh in a series published by World Peace Foundation as a part of its contribution to a better understanding of international affairs, the editors have achieved their goal of placing before the public within a year of the period to which they pertain the documents of major significance in the field of United States foreign relations. This objective could not have been accomplished without the generous financial support of the Rockefeller Foundation nor in the absence of the unstinting cooperation and assistance of other members of the Staff of World Peace Foundation.

Acknowledgment is made to Miss Margaret L. Bates who contributed the chapter on international peace and security; to Miss Anne M. Griswold who prepared the sections on dependent areas, and on agriculture and natural resources; to Mrs. Katherine D. Durant for her work on national defense, and on labor and social problems; and to Miss Amelia Leiss for the drafting of the chapters on cultural relations and on relations with the western hemisphere. Miss Margaret A. McCarthy and Miss Jane M. Walsh undertook the formidable task of typing and proofreading the manuscript.

The organization evolved through Volumes IX and X of the series has been followed in the present volume, although those familiar with the series will note the new topical arrangement adopted for the chapter on *Labor and Social Problems* which completes the revision of the format for succeeding volumes. Editorial notes, liberally documented for reference, have again been supplied where the large bulk of pertinent material prevented its republication in full. Where official documentation and data were not available (as, for example, in the section of Chapter III dealing with the year's negotiations on the Austrian state treaty), the editors have been forced to rely upon press reports and other unofficial sources for their information. This practice has, however, been kept to a minimum and applied only as a last resort.

RAYMOND DENNETT
ROBERT K. TURNER

September 1, 1950

CONTENTS

III. OCCUPATION POLICY

IV. ECONOMIC RECONSTRUCTION AND DEVELOPMENT

CONTENTS

CHAPTER I

Principles and Policy: General Statements

(1) *Annual Message of the President (Truman) to the Congress on the State of the Union, January 5, 1949.*[1]

[EXCERPTS]

Mr. President, Mr. Speaker, Members of the Congress, I am happy to report to this Eighty-first Congress that the state of the Union is good. Our Nation is better able than ever before to meet the needs of the American people and to give them their fair chance in the pursuit of happiness. It is foremost among the nations of the world in the search for peace.

During the last 16 years the American people have been creating a society which offers new opportunities for every man to enjoy his share of the good things of life.

In this society we are conservative about the values and principles which we cherish; but we are forward-looking in protecting those values and principles and in extending their benefits. We have rejected the discredited theory that the fortunes of the Nation should be in the hands of a privileged few. We have abandoned the "trickle down" concept of national prosperity. Instead we believe that our economic system should rest on a democratic foundation and that wealth should be created for the benefit of all.

. . . .

Our domestic programs are the foundation of our foreign policy. The world today looks to us for leadership because we have so largely realized, within our borders, those benefits of democracy for which most of the peoples of the world are yearning.

We are following a foreign policy which is the outward expression of the democratic faith we profess. We are doing what we can to encourage free states and free peoples throughout the world, to aid the suffering and afflicted in foreign lands, and to strengthen democratic nations against aggression.

The heart of our foreign policy is peace. We are supporting a world organization to keep peace and a world economic policy to create prosperity for mankind. Our guiding star is the principle of international cooperation. To this concept we have made a national commitment as profound as anything in history. To it we have pledged our resources and our honor.

Until a system of world security is established upon which we can safely rely, we cannot escape the burden of creating and maintaining armed forces sufficient to deter aggression. We have made great progress in the last year in the effective organization of our armed forces, but further improvements in

[1] *Congressional Record*, 95, p. 66 (Daily edition, January 5, 1949); Department of State, *Bulletin*, XX, p. 75.

our national security legislation are necessary. Universal training is essential to the security of the United States.

During the course of this session I shall have occasion to ask the Congress to consider several measures in the field of foreign policy. At this time I recommend that we restore the Reciprocal Trade Agreements Act to full effectiveness, and extend it for 3 years. We should also open our doors to displaced persons without unfair discrimination.

It should be clear by now to all nations that we are not seeking to freeze the status quo. We have no intention of preserving the injustices of the past. We welcome the constructive efforts being made by many nations to achieve a better life for their citizens. In the European recovery program, in our good-neighbor policy, and in the United Nations we have begun to batter down those national walls which block the economic growth and the social advancement of the peoples of the world.

We believe that if we hold resolutely to this course, the principle of international cooperation will eventually command the approval even of those nations which are now seeking to weaken or subvert it.

We stand at the opening of an era which can mean either great achievement or terrible catastrophe for ourselves and for all mankind.

The strength of our Nation must continue to be used in the interest of all our people rather than a privileged few. It must continue to be used unselfishly in the struggle for world peace and the betterment of mankind the world over.

.   .   .   .

(2) *Message of the President (Truman) to the Congress Transmitting Recommendations for the Budget for the Fiscal Year 1950, January 10, 1949.*[2]

[EXCERPTS]

I am transmitting my recommendations for the Budget of the United States for the fiscal year ending June 30, 1950.

Under the laws of our country, the Budget, when approved by the Congress, becomes the plan of action for the Federal Government. It thus embodies decisions of tremendous importance, particularly in these times, to the American people and to the entire world. The preparation of the Budget is one of the most important duties of the President. It represents a carefully prepared plan for carrying out the many activities and services of Government which the Congress has authorized, and others which I am recommending, in response to the needs and desires of the American people.

This is the fourth Budget prepared since the close of World War II. The character of the postwar world still presents many complex problems and unanswered questions. This Budget is the clearest expression that can be given at this time to the program which the Government of the United States should follow in the world today.

2 *Ibid.,* p. 108; *New York Times,* January 11, 1949, p. C–19.

It is founded on the conviction that the United States must continue to exert strong, positive effort to achieve peace in the world and growing prosperity at home. Substantial direct assistance is provided for other members of the family of nations, and expenditures in support of our armed forces are materially increased. Funds are included for the necessary strengthening of our economy through the development and conservation of the Nation's productive resources. Increased emphasis is placed on the provision of badly needed measures to promote the education, health, and security of our people.

To support this program, the Budget provides for expenditures of 41.9 billion dollars for the fiscal year 1950, about 1.7 billion dollars above the requirements for the present year. Under existing law and with continuing high levels of economic activity, revenues for the fiscal year would be 41 billion dollars. This would result in an estimated deficit of 873 million dollars.

. . . .

The 1950 Budget, like all those since the end of the war, is dominated by our international and national defense programs. Together, they are expected to amount to 21 billion dollars, or half of all Budget expenditures.

International affairs and finance account for 6.7 billion dollars of expenditures in the fiscal year 1950, compared with 7.2 billion dollars in 1949. Most of these funds will be spent as part of the strong economic support we are extending to the free nations of Western Europe, whose recovery is the key to continued independence and to safeguarding freedom in many other parts of the world. Our investment in European recovery will repay us many times in terms of increased strength and improved organization for peace.

But in existing circumstances, economic strength is not enough to assure continued independence to free peoples. Under the Charter of the United Nations, therefore, we have been discussing with some of the Western European countries measures designed to increase the security of the North Atlantic area. To further this objective, I expect later to request funds for providing military supplies to those countries and to certain other countries where the provision of such assistance is important to our national security. It is not possible now to predict accurately what will be needed, and I have therefore included no allowance in the Budget. The fact that additional funds will be required to meet the demands of this program emphasizes even more strongly the need for increased revenues in the years ahead.

While we believe that active participation in the work of the United Nations and support for the economic recovery and growing strength of free nations are the most important steps we can take toward peace, we must also maintain adequate national defense forces. In this Budget, expenditures for national defense are estimated to total 14.3 billion dollars in 1950, compared to 11.8 billion dollars for 1949. New authorizations recommended for national defense in 1950 total 15.9 billion dollars. Defense expenditures to maintain the present program are expected to be higher in 1951, as a result of expanding programs now under way and the large orders already placed for aircraft, ships, and other material and equipment, which will be delivered and paid for in the next few years.

The military forces recommended in this Budget are the most powerful this Nation has ever maintained in peacetime. The principal objective we should have in mind in planning for our national defense at this time is to build a foundation of military strength which can be sustained for a period of years without excessive strain on our productive resources, and which will permit rapid expansion should the need arise. The recommendations in this Budget move toward this objective. I believe that they will permit this Nation to maintain a proper military preparedness in the present uncertain period.

. . . .

The following sections describe in broad outline the Government programs in each of the major functional areas and the principal changes proposed in this Budget.

International Affairs and Finance

Two world wars and the years between have convinced the people of the United States that their security and well-being depend on conditions of peace and stability in the world. The complexity of the international postwar recovery problem and the tensions which make the transition to peace more difficult have deepened this conviction.

The fundamental objective of United States foreign policy is to achieve world peace and international security resting on the strength, mutual interests, and cooperation of free nations. The Budget reflects this policy in the funds provided for our participation in the United Nations and for the regular operations of the State Department and other agencies. But the instruments of our policy requiring the largest measure of budgetary support are the extraordinary programs of economic and military aid to those nations and peoples who share our international objectives and our determination to make them effective. Through all these means, we are acting to strengthen the great moral force of freedom on which we believe the advancement of people everywhere depends.

Total expenditures for international activities, exclusive of possible expenditures for a new program of providing military supplies to certain countries, are expected to be 6.7 billion dollars in the fiscal year 1950 — a drop from the 7.2 billion dollars estimated for the fiscal year 1949. Expenditures for economic assistance may be expected to decline in subsequent years with continued progress toward world economic recovery. But any forward estimate of our international expenditures must be highly tentative in view of the present uncertain world situation.

Reconstruction and military aid. — Our aid to European recovery is the major program of economic assistance in which we are now engaged. Begun in April 1948, this program is expected to result in 4.6 billion dollars of expenditures in the present fiscal year, and 4.5 billion dollars in the fiscal year 1950 — nearly 70 percent of our 1950 expenditures for international activities.

United States aid to western European countries and the mutual self-help which it has stimulated among them are already resulting in substantial progress toward economic recovery and political stability. The volume of production — both agricultural and industrial — is increasing as the months go by. This momentum must be maintained if the European economy is to become independent of extraordinary outside assistance by the target date of July 1952. To meet this objective, it is also extremely important for this Nation to undertake through such means as an extended and less restrictive reciprocal trade act, those adjustments in our foreign trade pattern which will help to bring about a higher level and a better balance of world trade.

Further authorizing legislation by the Congress will be necessary before the end of the current fiscal year in order to carry the European recovery program forward without interruption. By the end of December, authorizations issued to the European countries for procurement had nearly reached the limit set by the presently available Economic Cooperation Administration funds. The bulk of the commodities involved will be shipped by the end of March. This Budget accordingly anticipates a supplemental appropriation request for 1,250 million dollars for the remainder of the current fiscal year, in addition to the 4.3 billion dollar appropriation requested for the fiscal year 1950.

I recommend that, in extending the Economic Cooperation Act, the Congress eliminate the present legal requirement which in effect charges 3 billion dollars of the fiscal year 1949 expenditures for European aid against the fiscal year 1948 surplus. This wholly artificial bookkeeping shift in no way affects the Government's actual financial operations, but it does result in a distorted picture of the Budget surplus or deficit in these 2 years.

I have already referred to the prospective North Atlantic arrangements, now under discussion. In addition, we are considering furnishing military supplies to certain countries in furtherance of our national security. As with the European recovery program, military aid will call for a large measure of mutual aid and self-help among the participating countries. Because of present uncertainty as to cost and timing, no amounts are included for this program in the Budget.

The scope and magnitude of several of our other current assistance programs cannot be accurately foreseen at this time. These now include aid to Greece, Turkey, China, and Korea. Funds are provided for assistance programs of this character in the Budget under "other proposed aid legislation," with appropriations tentatively estimated at 600 million dollars and expenditures at 355 million dollars for the fiscal year 1950. I shall recommend specific legislation and appropriations to the Congress at a later date.

The Export-Import Bank will continue to make loans in fiscal year 1950 for promoting international trade and economic development, particularly in Latin America. Net expenditures of the Bank in the fiscal year 1950 are expected to be relatively low because of rising collections on earlier loans and because our aid to Europe is now financed almost entirely from ECA funds.

Mainly because of a large Canadian repayment, the Bank is expected to show no net expenditures in the current fiscal year.

Foreign relief. — Our principal foreign relief activities at the present time are those under the Army's program of government and relief in occupied areas — primarily Germany and Japan. Tentative estimates of about 1 billion dollars of appropriations and expenditures for fiscal year 1950 are included in this Budget — a substantial decline from 1949. These estimates include funds to continue the rehabilitation program now under way in Japan. With these additional sums for rehabilitation and with further ECA recovery aid for Germany in the next fiscal year, progress toward economic recovery in the occupied areas should continue, with a resulting further decline in expenditures in subsequent years.

Foreign relations. — The principal change contemplated in the program of the Department of State is the planned expansion of information and education activities. Expenditures for Foreign Service buildings are expected to decline, so that total expenditures for foreign relations activities are expected to be about the same in the fiscal year 1950 as in 1949. As part of our general program for improved Federal administration, provision is made for increased flexibility in management for the Secretary of State through the consolidation of appropriations. Amounts are included in this Budget to cover the cost of proposed legislation granting Foreign Service personnel pay raises similar to those given most employees under the Federal Employees Salary Act of 1948.

I am requesting legislation authorizing the payment of 17 million dollars in the fiscal year 1949 for payment of war-damage claims of neutral European countries.

Philippine aid. — Our assistance to the Philippine Republic in its recovery from war devastation is now at a peak level. Total expenditures for rehabilitation and for payment of war-damage claims are expected to decline slightly in the fiscal year 1950 and to fall much more sharply in the fiscal year 1951. In our veterans' program we are continuing to give compensation to disabled Philippine veterans who fought in our joint efforts against the Japanese. Provision for financing veterans' hospitals and medical services, authorized by recent legislation, are included in the reserve for contingencies, pending the development with the Philippine Republic of detailed plans for carrying out this program.

International organizations. — Our contribution to the International Refugee Organization is estimated at 70 million dollars in the fiscal year 1950, approximately the same as in 1949. With the expected migration of refugees to the United States and other areas, the IRO program should be substantially completed by June 30, 1950. It is my hope that the present Displaced Persons Act will be speedily stripped of its restrictive and discriminatory provisions in order that we may make a contribution to this program more worthy of our best traditions. A tentative estimate of 16 million dollars for the fiscal year 1949 is also included in this Budget for our contribution to the United Nations' program of relief for Arab and other refugees from Palestine.

Outlays for our participation in other international organizations, including the United Nations, will continue in the fiscal year 1950 at about the same level as in 1949. A 1949 supplemental appropriation of 65 million dollars is included for the loan for the United Nations' headquarters construction. Tentative estimates are included in 1950 for a loan to the Food and Agriculture Organization for construction of a headquarters building, and for our contribution to the International Trade Organization.

. . . .

(3) *Inaugural Address of the President (Truman), January 20, 1949.*[3]

Mr. Vice President, Mr. Chief Justice, and fellow citizens: I accept with humility the honor which the American people have conferred upon me. I accept it with a deep resolve to do all that I can for the welfare of this Nation and for the peace of the world.

In performing the duties of my office, I need the help and prayers of every one of you. I ask for your encouragement and your support. The tasks we face are difficult, and we can accomplish them only if we work together.

Each period of our national history has had its special challenges. Those that confront us now are as momentous as any in the past. Today marks the beginning not only of a new administration, but of a period that will be eventful, perhaps decisive, for us and for the world.

It may be our lot to experience, and in large measure to bring about, a major turning point in the long history of the human race. The first half of this century has been marked by unprecedented and brutal attacks on the rights of man, and by the two most frightful wars in history. The supreme need of our time is for men to learn to live together in peace and harmony.

The peoples of the earth face the future with grave uncertainty, composed almost equally of great hopes and great fears. In this time of doubt, they look to the United States as never before for good will, strength, and wise leadership.

It is fitting, therefore, that we take this occasion to proclaim to the world the essential principles of the faith by which we live, and to declare our aims to all peoples.

The American people stand firm in the faith which has inspired this Nation from the beginning. We believe that all men have a right to equal justice under law and equal opportunity to share in the common good. We believe that all men have the right to freedom of thought and expression. We believe that all men are created equal because they are created in the image of God.

From this faith we will not be moved.

The American people desire, and are determined to work for, a world in which all nations and all peoples are free to govern themselves as they see fit and to achieve a decent and satisfying life. Above all else, our people desire, and are determined to work for, peace on earth — a just and lasting peace — based on genuine agreement freely arrived at by equals.

3 Department of State Publication 3653; Senate Document 5, 81st Cong., 1st sess.; Department of State, *Bulletin*, XX, p. 123; *New York Times*, January 21, 1949.

In the pursuit of these aims, the United States and other like-minded nations find themselves directly opposed by a regime with contrary aims and a totally different concept of life.

That regime adheres to a false philosophy which purports to offer freedom, security, and greater opportunity to mankind. Misled by this philosophy, many peoples have sacrificed their liberties only to learn to their sorrow that deceit and mockery, poverty and tyranny, are their reward.

That false philosophy is communism.

Communism is based on the belief that man is so weak and inadequate that he is unable to govern himself, and therefore requires the rule of strong masters.

Democracy is based on the conviction that man has the moral and intellectual capacity, as well as the inalienable right, to govern himself with reason and justice.

Communism subjects the individual to arrest without lawful cause, punishment without trial, and forced labor as the chattel of the state. It decrees what information he shall receive, what art he shall produce, what leaders he shall follow, and what thoughts he shall think.

Democracy maintains that government is established for the benefit of the individual, and is charged with the responsibility of protecting the rights of the individual and his freedom in the exercise of his abilities.

Communism maintains that social wrongs can be corrected only by violence.

Democracy has proved that social justice can be achieved through peaceful change.

Communism holds that the world is so deeply divided into opposing classes that war is inevitable.

Democracy holds that free nations can settle differences justly and maintain lasting peace.

These differences between communism and democracy do not concern the United States alone. People everywhere are coming to realize that what is involved is material well-being, human dignity, and the right to believe in and worship God.

I state these differences, not to draw issues of belief as such, but because the actions resulting from the communist philosophy are a threat to the efforts of free nations to bring about world recovery and lasting peace.

Since the end of hostilities, the United States has invested its substance and its energy in a great constructive effort to restore peace, stability, and freedom to the world.

We have sought no territory and we have imposed our will on none. We have asked for no privileges we would not extend to others.

We have constantly and vigorously supported the United Nations and related agencies as a means of applying democratic principles to international relations. We have consistently advocated and relied upon peaceful settlement of disputes among nations.

We have made every effort to secure agreement on effective international control of our most powerful weapon, and we have worked steadily for the limitation and control of all armaments.

We have encouraged, by precept and example, the expansion of world trade on a sound and fair basis.

Almost a year ago, in company with sixteen free nations of Europe, we launched the greatest cooperative economic program in history. The purpose of that unprecedented effort is to invigorate and strengthen democracy in Europe, so that the free people of that continent can resume their rightful place in the forefront of civilization and can contribute once more to the security and welfare of the world.

Our efforts have brought new hope to all mankind. We have beaten back despair and defeatism. We have saved a number of countries from losing their liberty. Hundreds of millions of people all over the world now agree with us, that we need not have war — that we can have peace.

The initiative is ours.

We are moving on with other nations to build an even stronger structure of international order and justice. We shall have as our partners countries which, no longer solely concerned with the problem of national survival, are now working to improve the standards of living of all their people. We are ready to undertake new projects to strengthen the free world.

In the coming years, our program for peace and freedom will emphasize four major courses of action.

First, we will continue to give unfaltering support to the United Nations and related agencies, and we will continue to search for ways to strengthen their authority and increase their effectiveness. We believe that the United Nations will be strengthened by the new nations which are being formed in lands now advancing toward self-government under democratic principles.

Second, we will continue our programs for world economic recovery.

This means, first of all, that we must keep our full weight behind the European Recovery Program. We are confident of the success of this major venture in world recovery. We believe that our partners in this effort will achieve the status of self-supportiong nations once again.

In addition, we must carry out our plans for reducing the barriers to world trade and increasing its volume. Economic recovery and peace itself depend on increased world trade.

Third, we will strengthen freedom-loving nations against the dangers of aggression.

We are now working out with a number of countries a joint agreement designed to strengthen the security of the North Atlantic area. Such an agreement would take the form of a collective defense arrangement within the terms of the United Nations Charter.

We have already established such a defense pact for the Western Hemisphere by the treaty of Rio de Janeiro.

The primary purpose of these agreements is to provide unmistakable proof of the joint determination of the free countries to resist armed attack from any quarter. Each country participating in these arrangements must contribute all it can to the common defense.

If we can make it sufficiently clear, in advance, that any armed attack affecting our national security would be met with overwhelming force, the armed attack might never occur.

I hope soon to send to the Senate a treaty respecting the North Atlantic security plan.

In addition, we will provide military advice and equipment to free nations which will cooperate with us in the maintenance of peace and security.

Fourth, we must embark on a bold new program for making the benefits of our scientific advances and industrial progress available for the improvement and growth of underdeveloped areas.

More than half the people of the world are living in conditions approaching misery. Their food is inadequate. They are victims of disease. Their economic life is primitive and stagnant. Their poverty is a handicap and a threat both to them and to more prosperous areas.

For the first time in history, humanity possesses the knowledge and the skill to relieve the suffering of these people.

The United States is preeminent among nations in the development of industrial and scientific techniques. The material resources which we can afford to use for the assistance of other peoples are limited. But our imponderable resources in technical knowledge are constantly growing and are inexhaustible.

I believe that we should make available to peace-loving peoples the benefits of our store of technical knowledge in order to help them realize their aspirations for a better life. And, in cooperation with other nations, we should foster capital investment in areas needing development.

Our aim should be to help the free peoples of the world, through their own efforts, to produce more food, more clothing, more materials for housing, and more mechanical power to lighten their burdens.

We invite other countries to pool their technological resources in this undertaking. Their contributions will be warmly welcomed. This should be a cooperative enterprise in which all nations work together through the United Nations and its specialized agencies wherever practicable. It must be a worldwide effort for the achievement of peace, plenty, and freedom.

With the cooperation of business, private capital, agriculture, and labor in this country, this program can greatly increase the industrial activity in other nations and can raise substantially their standards of living.

Such new economic developments must be devised and controlled to benefit the peoples of the areas in which they are established. Guaranties to the investor must be balanced by guaranties in the interest of the people whose resources and whose labor go into these developments.

The old imperialism — exploitation for foreign profit — has no place in our plans. What we envisage is a program of development based on the concepts of democratic fair-dealing.

All countries, including our own, will greatly benefit from a constructive program for the better use of the world's human and natural resources. Experience shows that our commerce with other countries expands as they progress industrially and economically.

Greater production is the key to prosperity and peace. And the key to greater production is a wider and more vigorous application of modern scientific and technical knowledge.

Only by helping the least fortunate of its members to help themselves can the human family achieve the decent, satisfying life that is the right of all people.

Democracy alone can supply the vitalizing force to stir the peoples of the world into triumphant action, not only against their human oppressors, but also against their ancient enemies — hunger, misery, and despair.

On the basis of these four major courses of action we hope to help create the conditions that will lead eventually to personal freedom and happiness for all mankind.

If we are to be successful in carrying out these policies, it is clear that we must have continued prosperity in this country and we must keep ourselves strong.

Slowly but surely we are weaving a world fabric of international security and growing prosperity.

We are aided by all who wish to live in freedom from fear — even by those who live today in fear under their own governments.

We are aided by all who want relief from the lies of propaganda — who desire truth and sincerity.

We are aided by all who desire self-government and a voice in deciding their own affairs.

We are aided by all who long for economic security — for the security and abundance that men in free societies can enjoy.

We are aided by all who desire freedom of speech, freedom of religion, and freedom to live their own lives for useful ends.

Our allies are the millions who hunger and thirst after righteousness.

In due time, as our stability becomes manifest, as more and more nations come to know the benefits of democracy and to participate in growing abundance, I believe that those countries which now oppose us will abandon their delusions and join with the free nations of the world in a just settlement of international differences.

Events have brought our American democracy to new influence and new responsibilities. They will test our courage, our devotion to duty, and our concept of liberty.

But I say to all men, what we have achieved in liberty, we will surpass in greater liberty.

Steadfast in our faith in the Almighty, we will advance toward a world where man's freedom is secure.

To that end we will devote our strength, our resources, and our firmness of resolve. With God's help, the future of mankind will be assured in a world of justice, harmony, and peace.

(4) *Address by the Counselor of the Department of State (Bohlen) before the New York Bar Association, New York, January 28, 1949.*[4]

We are now well into a new year and a little past the customary time for stock-taking in the commercial sense. Yet the inauguration of a new national administration, and the concurrent assumption of duties by a new Secretary of State, make this an opportune time for us to re-examine the position of the United States in world affairs.

Mr. Acheson is the fifth Secretary of State to take office in little more than four years, yet, as one who has served under all of them, I can testify to the continuity and consistency of our basic foreign policy. That this is true is a tribute to the high qualities of character and ability of the men who have filled the office. It is also confirmation of the fact that our foreign policy transcends personalities and is rooted in our American traditions and in the requirements of the national interest. This is inevitably true, because ours is a democratic society and our informed public opinion will not long support or tolerate any policy that does not square with the convictions of our people and serve their best interest.

It would seem that a little reflection on this truth would reveal the error and the futility of attempting to identify a policy, or those charged with carrying it out, by the use of such stereotyped labels as "hard" or "soft". The use of such terms is much more likely to reflect the subjective attitude of those who use them than to describe those policies or persons to whom they are applied.

Foreign policy simply does not fall into such easy classifications. Responsible government officials just don't single out a certain country and decide that our policy toward that country will be "hard" or "soft."

Our government is engaged in thousands of contacts and negotiations with other governments every day, and a marked degree of open-mindedness and flexibility is required. Within the limits of certain fundamental principles, which we can never compromise, we must be prepared to carry on the give-and-take of human relationships in international affairs, just as we all do in our personal affairs. Each case must be judged on its own merits, though always by the criterion of what is best for the United States.

Obviously we learn by experience the approaches and methods that work best in dealing with particular countries. We learn how much confidence can be placed in the pledges of individual governments, and conduct ourselves accordingly in dealing with them. But it's a poor diplomat who permits his emotional reaction to congeal his attitude toward a government into a "hard" or "soft" category, when the security and well-being of his country may depend on his remaining alert and objective.

4 Department of State Press Release 61, January 28, 1949.

Moreover, no nation, no matter how powerful, can make or carry out its policies toward other countries exactly as it desires. Every government must take into account the policies and actions of other governments, and must be ready to adapt itself to the rapid changes that occur in its global environment. An inflexible policy, either "hard" or "soft" or any other kind, does not comport with national security and satisfactory economic conditions in the imperfect world in which all nations live.

I am convinced that an objective appraisal of our policies during and since the war will show that they have been determined on the basis of these general principles — that is, fidelity to our fundamental convictions, flexibility as to methods and details.

The compulsion to win unconditional victory was certainly the overriding consideration during the war. Failure of the Allied coalition to be guided by that all-compelling purpose — any wavering in the determination to maintain an unbroken front against the enemy — would have benefited no one but Hitler and his Axis partners.

With the end of hostilities, it was necessary to ascertain whether the same unity of purpose and action could be maintained to overcome the many serious problems resulting from the war and to restore stability and some degree of prosperity to the world. The United States and the western democracies proceeded to make the test and to make it honestly and sincerely.

It is inconceivable, even from the vantage point of hindsight, to suppose that we could have done otherwise. Our moral standing in the eyes of the world, to single out one consideration, required that we try to find a solid basis for continued understanding and cooperation with our wartime Allies. We could not have done otherwise than make every effort to reach such an understanding and make it fully effective.

It is eternally to the credit of the United States that the effort was made. In large measure, the record of that endeavor is the basis of our moral position in the world today. That applies also to the other nations of the West, for they too made the same effort.

It has become fashionable to criticize the agreements arrived at during the wartime conferences and to condemn those who made them on behalf of the western Allies.

The basic deficiency in the series of Allied agreements, and the peace treaties with the satellite countries as well, has been and is the failure of the Soviet Government and the Governments it dominates to live up to international commitments formally assumed. Until that defect is remedied, it is difficult to see how the agreements already made can be expected to accomplish their purpose. Until a fundamental change is made in that respect, it is difficult to see what useful purpose would be served by acceding to pressure for compromises on our part in order to achieve agreements of doubtful validity. This is a matter that goes to the root of the differences of philosophy and moral values that now divide the world.

In our democratic society the function of the state is to preserve and promote human rights and fundamental freedoms. The state exists for the benefit of man, not man for the benefit of the state. Each individual must have as much liberty for the conduct of his life as is compatible with the rights of others. These are the essential purposes of our laws. Freedom and dignity of the individual can be attained only under a system of law which protects the rights of individuals.

This moral concept which lies behind our laws makes for the acceptability of the principle that in international affairs there should reign the rule of law rather than force and anarchy.

The Soviet concept of law is diametrically opposed. They vigorously deny that there is any moral concept involved and denounce as bourgeois hypocrisy the belief that there is such a thing as truth and justice. To them, law is an instrument of the state and not a protection for the individual. No less an authority than Mr. Vyshinsky whose book, "The law of the Soviet State", has recently been published in this country leaves no doubt on this subject. He asserts that "legal relationships (and, consequently, law itself) are rooted in the material conditions of life, and that law is merely the will of the dominant class, elevated into a statute. . . ."

He is no less explicit on the subject of Soviet justice:

> The task of justice in the USSR is to assure the precise and unswerving fulfillment of Soviet laws by all the institutions, organizations, officials, and citizens of the USSR.
> This the court accomplishes by destroying without pity all the foes of the people in whatsoever form they manifest their criminal encroachments upon socialism. . . ;

nor is he any less so in his description of bourgeois justice and civil rights:

> Bourgeois theorists strive to depict the court as an organ above classes and apart from politics, acting, supposedly, in the interests of all society and guided by commands of law and justice common to all mankind, instead of by the interests of the dominant class. Such a conception of the court's essence and tasks is, of course, radically false. It has always been an instrument in the hands of the dominant class, assuring the strengthening of its dominance and the protection of its interests. . .
> In our state, naturally, there is and can be no place for freedom of speech, press, and so on for the foes of socialism. Every sort of attempt on their part to utilize to the detriment of the state — that is to say, to the detriment of all the toilers — these freedoms granted to the toilers must be classified as a counter-revolutionary crime to which Article 58, Paragraph 10, or one of the corresponding articles of the Criminal Code is applicable.

It is not difficult to imagine how any government holding as a matter of profound doctrine such concepts of law within the state would view the concept of the rule of law in international affairs.

It logically and obviously follows that, from the Soviet point of view, international law would merely be an instrument for the furtherance of the purposes of the Soviet state and not as a universal concept applicable to all nations.

It is this fundamental difference in concept which accounts for the deep cleavage between the Soviet Union and the countries it dominates on the one hand and the rest of the world on the other. With this in mind, it is obvious that the differences which separate these two worlds are not due to disputes between nations, in the customary sense of that term, nor in a clash of interests which traditionally lead to disputes and quarrels between nations.

Because of this fact the problem is not exclusively one of international relations or relations between states. It is far wider than that. It is not susceptible of being bridged by the magic of an agreement. This does not mean that the practical unresolved questions of the postwar world may not be progressively settled. But we must clearly recognize that such agreements on practical questions as may be reached will not in themselves bring about a fundamental solution. We have to look forward to a long period of struggle and effort before we achieve a stable and tranquil world.

Our course in foreign affairs since the defeat of the Axis powers falls into three more or less distinct periods.

The first was the period in which we were giving a fair test to the assumption that in the immediate postwar period great power cooperation could be continued as a basis for reconstruction and reorganization. The fact that Soviet conduct gradually rendered that assumption invalid does not mean that the degree of cooperation that did exist then was futile or that time was lost. During that period the United Nations got under way, and immediate relief and rehabilitation needs were met by UNRRA and other means.

Next came the period in which the true intentions of the Soviets and international communism became unmistakably clear and were fully recognized as a threat to world peace and the integrity of the free nations. That period, the stage of "holding the line", began with President Truman's message to Congress on March 12, 1947, which set in motion the aid programs for Greece and Turkey.

The third period began a short time later, with the adoption and operation of the Marshall Plan. This was the response of the democracies to the realization that the European nations struggling for recovery and a return to tolerable standards of living could expect neither help nor mercy from the Soviet Union. It became apparent that the great task of recovery and reconstruction would have to be done regardless of the Soviet attitude.

It was also in this period that it became clear that while the Marshall Plan would in fact make possible the economic recovery of western Europe, the fear of aggression was a heavy burden on the cooperative effort. The psychological handicaps under which the Europeans are working are severe enough without the added fear that the fruits of their hard labor might be taken over by an alien army. Whether such fears are in fact fully justified or not, probably no man this side of the Iron Curtain and not many behind it can say with certainty. That they do exist is sufficient cause to do everything in our power to remove them.

The negotiation of a collective defense arrangement for the North Atlantic area, under the United Nations Charter, is designed for this purpose. These negotiations, which are still proceeding, envision an association of the United States, Canada, the Brussels Pact nations and possibly other western European countries for purposes of common defense against aggression. As the President stated in his inaugural address, this agreement will take the form of a treaty which will be submitted to the Senate for ratification.

It is important to note that while this step is taken to assure western Europe against the immediate threat of aggression and to allay fears that might impede recovery, it is not less an attempt to safeguard the long-term security of the United States. History in two world catastrophes has driven home to us the lesson that the security of the North Atlantic area is vital to the security of the United States. It is our intention to carry out the provisions of the Vandenberg Resolution for participation of this country in collective defense arrangements where the security of the United States is affected and in conformity with the UN Charter.

Irrespective of the present situation of western Europe, the proposed North Atlantic pact is necessary and desirable. In two great wars, the democracies of North America and western Europe, brought together by mutual devotion to their common heritage, joined forces in defense of western civilization. Both times this common interest and purpose found expression in an association formed after the event. The negotiation of a treaty for the cooperative strengthening of security in the North Atlantic area represents an agreed effort to formalize this natural association before it becomes necessary to improvise it once again under the pressure of threatened catastrophe. This agreement is primarily, but not purely, for military security. It opens the way for other forms of cooperation in the common interest.

The North Atlantic pact, if put into effect along the lines now indicated, will serve as a deterrent to potential aggressors only to the extent that the participating nations possess the strength to resist aggression. It is obvious that the western European countries, still struggling to regain their economic health, cannot now bear the double burden of both recovery and rearmament. The recovery effort must be given priority. Therefore, the United States proposes to provide the military supplies and equipment, above the quantities the other countries can supply themselves, in order to put teeth in the pact. Each of the other countries, however, will be expected to meet its own needs to the greatest practical extent, and to contribute what it can to the common cause. This country also proposes to supply military assistance to other free nations which will cooperate in the common effort to preserve and promote peace and security. This must be done with primary regard to maintaining the economic strength of the United States.

The stabilizing influence of the Marshall Plan, supplementing the courage and diligence of the people of western Europe, has started the participating nations to the recovery of their rightful place in the world community.

We will continue to encourage and promote reconstruction and progress in every possible way. We will press forward with our efforts to expand world trade as a material factor in establishing a peaceful and orderly world society. We will utilize the Reciprocal Trade Agreements program to the fullest possible extent and will seek to make the International Trade Organization a going and effective concern.

In addition, we will make available our immense technological resources to other people to assist them in their efforts to achieve better conditions of life. This objective itself is fundamental to the preservation of peace and the extension of freedom in the world.

This fourth point mentioned in the President's inaugural address has aroused the greatest speculation.

As the Secretary of State said at his first press conference, this means the use of material means to non-material ends. Material objects are the means by which people can attain freedom — freedom from the pressure of those other human beings who would restrict their freedom, and help in the ancient struggle of man to earn his living and to get his bread from the soil.

Much has been done on such a program. Much more can be done. What will be done will vary from country to country depending on the resources of the country, its own pool of skills, its needs.

Sometimes the United States may provide the necessary training or personnel. Such skills and techniques could be made available through the UN and the specialized agencies and this effort can be expanded.

If the proper conditions are created, private capital will flow into these areas and skills and techniques will go with such investments. The efforts of the UN and some other countries and of the United States can be brought together and intensified.

We are willing and anxious to work with every country that wishes to enter into a cooperative effort to this end. This is not a program requiring a tremendous effort for a brief time. It is a long run program requiring sustained and imaginative effort.

By such broad and fundamental approaches to the problems of the world we not only facilitate the settlement of immediate outstanding issues, but build toward a more tranquil world. This is a long and difficult process. It is a matter of day-to-day effort, of disposing of each problem as it arises, within the limits of our abilities and powers. There is no magic formula or panacea. It is, in the last analysis, good common sense and plain, hard work in which each of us must do his share.

(5) *Address by the President (Truman) on the Requirements for a Lasting Peace, Delivered at the Dedication of World War Memorial Park, Little Rock, Arkansas, June 11, 1949.*[5]

We are not a militaristic country. We do not glorify the military way of life. Some nations have taken greater pride in their military victories than in any other national achievements, but it has never been so with us. When we think of war, it is with a prayer that the sacrifices our dead have made will never have to be repeated.

5 Department of State Publication 3653; *ibid.*, 3553; Department of State, *Bulletin*, XX, p. 771; *New York Times*, June 12, 1949, p. 4.

After every war we have solemnly resolved to prevent future wars. We have learned, however, that it is not enough to make resolutions. It is not enough to utter them in speeches or to engrave them on monuments. We have learned that we must devote the best efforts of our whole Nation to make those resolutions come true.

We entered the first World War to restore peace and to preserve human freedom; but when that war was finished, we turned aside from the task we had begun. We turned our backs upon the League of Nations — the international organization which was established to maintain peace. We ignored the economic problems of the world, and adopted a tariff policy which only made them worse. We let our domestic affairs fall into the hands of selfish interests.

We failed to join with others to take the steps which might have prevented a second world war.

This time we are fully aware of the mistakes that were made in the past. We are on guard against the indifference and isolationism which can only lead to the tragedy of war. This time we will not let our decisions be made for us by a little group of men who are concerned only with their own special interests.

This time we have taken vigorous and far-seeing measures to preserve peace and restore prosperity throughout the world. We have assumed the responsibility that I believe God intended this great Republic to assume after the first World War. We have shouldered the enormous responsibilities that go with our tremendous strength.

We have been fortunate in having many public servants of ability and vision who have devoted themselves to the problems of foreign affairs and national defense. We have able leaders in the Congress, who have mastered the complex details of our relations with other nations. They have made themselves familiar with the effects of our policies in all parts of the globe. They have labored painstakingly to enact a body of legislation to carry out the responsibilities we have assumed.

Most significant of all, the people of this country understand the supreme importance of our foreign policy and the great objectives toward which we are moving. Public debate has threshed out the basic questions of our foreign policy. The people have made up their minds. They have supported, and will continue to support, the measures necessary to maintain peace.

We have had to work for peace in the face of troubled conditions and against Communist pressures. But because we have been united in our determination to use our strength and our substance, we have already turned the tide in favor of freedom and peace. The disintegration of the democracies of Europe has been halted. Free peoples in many parts of the world have been given new hope and new confidence. The restoration of a system of world trade has begun. And all this has been accomplished without closing the door to peaceful negotiation of the differences between the free nations and the Soviet Union.

But we are only midway in carrying out our policy. We have a long way to go before we can make the free world secure against the social and political evils on which Communism thrives. The cause of peace and freedom is still threatened.

Yet there are some who have grown weary of the effort we are making. There are voices which claim that because our policy has been successful so far, we can now afford to relax. There are some who want to slash the aid we are giving to the economic recovery of other nations; there are some who want to reject the measures that are necessary for defense against aggression; there are some who wish to abandon our efforts toward the revival of world trade. These are the same voices that misled us in the 1920's. They are misguided by short-run considerations. They refuse to face the plain facts. They try to convince us that we cannot afford to pay the price of peace.

But the people of the United States will not be misled a second time. We know that the short-sighted course, the easy way, is not the path to peace. The task is difficult, and requires firm determination and steadfast effort.

We know that if we are to build a lasting peace in the world we must achieve three essential conditions.

First, this Nation must be strong and prosperous.

Second, other nations devoted to the cause of peace and freedom must also be strong and prosperous.

Third, there must be an international structure capable of adjusting international differences and maintaining peace.

The first condition is our own strength and prosperity.

It is unusual for this Nation to maintain substantial armed forces in time of peace. Yet, so long as there is a threat to the principles of peace — the principles on which the United Nations is founded — we must maintain strong armed forces. Any uncertainty as to the ability or the willingness of the free nations of the world to defend themselves is an invitation to aggression. We have seen the truth of this statement in the outbreak of two world wars.

Our national strength is not, however, simply a matter of weapons and trained men. Even more important are our economic growth and continued prosperity.

Our economy is the center of a world economy. The hope of economic revival throughout the world depends in large measure upon the prosperity of the United States. If our production and purchasing power are badly impaired, if the buying and selling and investing that we do in other parts of the world are cut off, other nations will be plunged into chaos and despair.

It is a prime belief of the Communist philosophy that our kind of economy is doomed to failure. The Communists predict that our prosperity will collapse — bringing the rest of the free world down with it. But they are wrong — wrong as they can be.

We know more today about keeping our economy strong than we have ever known before. We know how to strengthen our economy through the expansion of production and purchasing power and the improvement of standards of living. We understand that constantly rising national output, increasing real wages, and a fair income for farmers are basic elements of our economic strength.

To maintain these elements of prosperity, it is not sufficient to drift with the tide. We must take advantage of the new opportunities, the increased demands which result from the natural growth of our population. We must develop our natural resources and restore those we have depleted or wasted. We must establish a fair distribution of business opportunity; we must have a free labor movement able to hold its own at the bargaining table; we must protect the purchasing power of Americans against the hazards and misfortunes of life.

These steps are necessary if we are to continue strong and prosperous. That is why our domestic programs for the development of resources, for protection against economic hazards, for the improvement of social conditions, are fundamental to our national effort for peace.

The second condition essential to peace is that other nations, as well as our own, must be strong and prosperous.

We need other nations as our allies in the cause of human freedom. We have seen free nations lost to the democratic way of life because of economic disaster. We know that despair over economic conditions will turn men away from freedom and into the hands of dictators.

It is to our interest, therefore, to aid other nations to restore and maintain their economic health. Our aim is not only to help other nations to help themselves, but also to encourage economic cooperation among them.

We have taken the lead in cooperating with other nations to restore a mutually beneficial system of world trade. No nation today can achieve prosperity in isolation. Only through participation in the trade of the world can a country raise its own standards of living and contribute to the welfare of other nations.

For years before the war, world trade was crippled by high tariffs, import quotas, exchange manipulation, and other artificial devices for securing commercial advantages. These practices were a symptom of international anarchy. They resulted, ultimately, in idle ships, idle men, and economic chaos.

We have come a long way toward correcting these evils. Since 1934, we have worked out a multitude of agreements with other countries to reduce specific tariff barriers. In the general agreement on trade and tariffs of 1948, we struck a world-wide blow at these obstacles to trade.

But this work is not yet finished. If we are to succeed it is vital that the authority to negotiate reciprocal trade agreements be extended. We should then go on to establish a permanent international trade organization to apply standards of fair dealing in the commerce among nations.

The same cooperative principle has been applied in our great undertaking to restore the economies of the Western European nations to a self-sustaining basis. The food, fuel and equipment which we have sent to Europe have been matched by the efforts which these nations have made to restore their own economies and to cooperate with one another in increasing their production and raising their standards of living.

It is fair to say that the European Recovery Program has halted the social and economic disintegration which threatened the countries of Western Europe with Communism and civil strife.

Nevertheless, the European Recovery Program is still in its early stages. At the outset it was estimated that it would take four years before these countries could again become independent of special economic aid. Only a little more than one year has passed since we began.

If we were to falter now and cut down our aid, the momentum of recovery would be destroyed. The people of these countries would be thrown into confusion and their advance toward economic self-reliance would be blocked. A slash in the funds available for European recovery at this time would be the worst kind of false economy. It would cancel the hopes and the plans of the Western European nations. It would be a great gain for Communism.

I am confident we shall not make this mistake.

Our concern with the economic health of the world also extends to its underdeveloped regions. The prospects for peace will be immeasurably brighter if we can offer a future of hope and a better life to the people of these regions. In these areas there are millions who for centuries have known nothing but exploitation and poverty, and whose economic life is still primitive.

I have offered a program for bringing these people the benefits of our modern civilization. It is not a program of relief. While it is intended ultimately to bring about a great movement of capital through the channels of private investment for the development of these poverty-stricken regions, it is not a program of imperialism. The development of these areas offers enormous potential benefits to a growing world economy.

We have to lay the foundations for this program with care. I expect shortly to send to the Congress recommendations for initial legislation. This will be but the first step of many that we shall take, over the years to come, in this cooperative effort to better the living standards and to unlock the human skills and the natural resources of the underdeveloped parts of the globe.

The third condition essential for peace is an international structure capable of suppressing international violence. However well conceived our economic programs may be, they cannot succeed unless there is some assurance against the outbreak of aggression. Neither our own prosperity nor the prosperity of other nations can survive unless we can protect the operations of economic life from the threat of war.

Such protection depends on two factors. First, there must be constant efforts by all nations to adjust their differences peacefully. Second, there must be an agreement among nations to employ overwhelming force against armed aggression.

The United Nations is a valuable instrument for accomplishing these ends. It has already achieved the peaceful settlement of difficult issues. It has stopped hostilities in the Near East and in Indonesia. It has done a great deal to explore and find solutions for many of the economic and social problems which afflict the world.

Much remains to be done, however, to carry out the principles of the United Nations. Within the terms of the United Nations Charter, we and certain other countries have undertaken to provide greater assurance against the danger of armed conflict. That is the purpose of the North Atlantic Treaty. The idea behind this treaty — the association of democratic nations for mutual defense — is well understood in this country. Perhaps we do not understand, however, the importance of this pact in the eyes of the other democratic nations which are parties to it. They have been greatly weakened by the war. They have been haunted by the fear of again becoming the scene of conflict. By assuring them of our support the pact goes a long way to dispel their fears.

I have been greatly heartened by the unanimous report of the Foreign Relations Committee of the Senate this past week in favor of the North Atlantic Treaty. I believe that it will soon be passed by an overwhelming majority in the Senate. The effect of this action will be immediate and far-reaching in allaying the fears which have retarded economic recovery in Europe.

It is of vital importance that the Atlantic pact be followed by a program of military aid to increase the effective strength of the free nations against aggression. This military assistance program — based upon mutual help — will give additional confidence to the people of those nations as they continue to rebuild their economies.

These measures will bring a stability to the democratic nations of Europe which has not existed since the end of the war. They will at the same time contribute directly to the security of the United States.

I have discussed the three essential elements of lasting peace — a strong and prosperous United States; a strong and prosperous community of free nations; an international organization capable of preventing aggression.

We have given greatly of our effort and our strength to build a firm and enduring foreign policy upon these essentials. The burdens we have had to assume in this enterprise have been unusual. The size of the national budget shows that we are engaged in an undertaking without parallel in the history of our country or of the world.

But the goal we seek is a great one, and worth the price. Never has a nation had the opportunity which we have today to do so much for the peace and prosperity of mankind. Never has a nation had a better chance of reaching this high goal.

We must not falter now.

We must not defeat our own efforts by doing only half the job that lies before us.

The brave men whose memory we honor here did all that was required of them. They did not fail us. We must not fail them in our efforts to reach the goal for which they died.

We must press on in the confidence that we will succeed in the mission a divine Providence has assigned to us.

(6) Address by the President (Truman) before the Imperial Council of the Shrine of North America, Chicago, Illinois, July 19, 1949.[6]

[EXCERPT]

. . . .

During the war, we established warm ties of comradeship and common purpose between ourselves and other peoples in the struggle against tyranny. We hoped that an enduring peace could be built on these ties of friendship. In part, these high hopes have not been realized. Leaders of some nations have cut off communications and built barriers of suspicion between their people and the outside world.

But, in spite of this, there persists in this country a sincere feeling of friendship and sympathy for those peoples who have been cut off from us by force or political intrigue. We are convinced that if they were permitted to know the facts they would return our friendship.

We shall, therefore, continue in our efforts to help them learn the facts. We believe that the people of the world should have the facts, not only about ourselves, but about all the things that concern them most deeply. Only if men know the truth are they in a position to work for a stable and peaceful world.

In this country, where the facts are readily available, we have a special obligation to inform ourselves concerning world affairs and important international issues.

This is vitally important if our country is to carry out the responsibilities of world leadership that it has today. For, in this Nation, foreign policy is not made by the decisions of a few. It is the result of the democratic process, and represents the collective judgment of the people. Our foreign policy is founded upon an enlightened public opinion.

The importance of public opinion in the United States is not always understood or properly evaluated. Public opinion in a country such as ours cannot be ignored or manipulated to suit the occasion. It cannot be stampeded. Its formation is necessarily a slow process, because the people must be given ample opportunity to discuss the issues and reach a reasoned conclusion. But once a democratic decision is made, it represents the collective will of the Nation and can be depended upon to endure.

Those who rule by arbitrary power in other nations do not understand these things. For this reason, they do not realize the strength behind our foreign policy.

The major decisions in our foreign policy since the war have been made on the basis of an informed public opinion and overwhelming public support.

For example, in 1945, the people of our country were almost unanimously in favor of our participation in the United Nations. The Senate reflected that public sentiment when it approved the Charter by a vote of 87 to 2.

In 1948, after almost a year of discussion and debate, it was clear that a substantial majority of the people of this Nation approved our participation in the

6 Department of State Publication 3653; Department of State, *Bulletin*, XXI, p. 145; *New York Times*. July 20, 1949, p. 3.

European Recovery Program. The Congress translated that approval into legislative action by a vote of approximately four to one.

Our people continue to support the United Nations as fully as they did four years ago, in spite of the fact that some nations have obstructed its work through the misuse of the veto. We want to improve the United Nations. This desire was expressed in Senate Resolution 239, which called for the strengthening of the United Nations and the development of regional and other arrangements for the mutual defense of the free nations. This resolution was approved by the Senate last year by a vote of sixty-four to four.

As a means of carrying out these desires of the people for stronger support of the principles of the United Nations, the North Atlantic Treaty has been negotiated and is before the Senate. The Senate is now engaged in discussing the treaty with the deliberation and close attention that is part of the democratic process. All points of view have been made known. Public opinion among our people is overwhelmingly in favor of ratification of the treaty, and I am sure that the Senate will give its approval.

These momentous decisions are the decisions not of the Government alone, but of the people of the United States. For this reason, it is clear that this country will steadfastly continue, together with other nations of like purpose, along the path we have chosen toward peace and freedom for the world.

The formation of foreign policy on the part of the democratic nations may be a slow and painful process, but the results endure.

It is only in the totalitarian states, where all decisions are made by a few men at the top, that foreign policies can be reversed or radically altered in secrecy, or changed abruptly without warning. Between totalitarian states, disagreements can suddenly become open conflicts, and allies can change into enemies over night. The democratic nations, by contrast, because they rely on the collective judgment of their people, are dependable and stable in their foreign relations.

Today, the great quest of mankind is for a world order capable of maintaining world peace.

Just as the democratic nations formulate their foreign policies after due consideration for the opinions of their citizens, so they formulate their plans for international order with due regard for the independence and the sovereignty of other nations.

The kind of world organization for which this nation and the other democratic nations are striving is a world organization based on the voluntary agreement of independent states.

We are familiar, in our own history, with this kind of organization. Our country began as a federation — an association of local democratic sovereignties within a larger whole. The existing states, whether large or small, were brought together on the basis of voluntary agreement.

This principle of mutual respect and voluntary agreement is essential to the creation of a strong world organization for maintaining a just peace. In this respect, associations of nations are like associations of individuals — they will not survive and prosper unless the rights and the integrity of the members are respected.

This is the principle on which the United Nations is based. The United Nations is designed to give every nation a share in forming decisions on world issues. Such an organization will have its difficulties. We all know, from our experience in business, in unions, cooperatives, or fraternal groups, how much hard work and honest give and take is required to make this kind of organization successful. But we also know that in the long run an organization based on voluntary agreement among its members will command greater loyalty, speak with greater authority, and have a greater chance for success than any other kind. We must therefore continue to support and continue to improve the United Nations, as the way to lasting peace.

In contrast to the United Nations is the concept of a world order based on the rule of force. In the past, attempts to organize the world by force have always failed. The most recent failure was the attempt of Nazi Germany to establish European unity through the rule of force. This attempt to create an empire by conquest lasted only a few years.

In spite of the record of history, the leaders of some nations today appear still to be relying on force as a method of world organization. Their doctrine calls for the destruction of free governments through the use of force and the effort to create class warfare. To achieve their aims, they make a false appeal to men's sense of justice; they play upon the common desire of men to improve their condition of life.

But, in practice, this system of world organization is no better than the old tyrannies that have failed. It is incapable of satisfying the needs and desires of men for a better life. In its inner structure, it manifests the fatal weaknesses of all dictatorships. Within the circle of its control today, tensions and conflicts appear to be increasing. It may have temporary triumphs, but in the long run it must either destroy itself, or abandon its attempt to force other nations into its pattern.

Some people would have us believe that war is inevitable between the nations which are devoted to our concept of international organization and the concept which now bears the name of Communism. This is not the case. I am optimistic as I look toward the future, because I believe in the superior attraction for men's minds and hearts of the democratic principles which have been tried and tested in free nations, and which are now winning the allegiance of men throughout the world.

In the battle for men's minds our faith is more appealing, more dynamic, and stronger than any totalitarian force. The world longs for the kind of tolerance and mutual adjustment which is represented by democratic principles.

This country has had a revolutionary effect in the world since it was founded. Our democracy was born in a world of absolute monarchies. The idea which we made a living reality spread throughout the world and brought the day of the absolute monarch to an end. We have always been a challenge to tyranny of any kind. We are such a challenge today.

Our idea prevailed against the absolute monarchies of the nineteenth century. It is prevailing against the new and more terrible dictatorships of the twentieth century.

The reason is clear. Our idea of democracy speaks in terms which men can understand. It speaks of opportunity and tolerance and self-government. It speaks of the dignity of the individual, his freedom of conscience and the right to worship as he pleases. It does not exact blind loyalty to false ideas or improbable theories. It does not make a god out of the state, or out of man, or out of any human creation.

The world is tired of political fanaticism. It is weary of the lies, propaganda and hysteria created by dictatorships. It is disgusted by the practice of torture and political assassination. It is sick of the kind of political allegiance which is inspired solely by fear.

Men want to live together in peace. They want to have useful work. They want to feel themselves united in brotherly affection. They want to enjoy that great privilege — a privilege denied to millions throughout the world today — the right to think their own thoughts and to have their own convictions.

These desires of mankind are satisfied by the democratic principles which we have put into practice. These principles are at work today as they were in the past. In the conflict that exists throughout the world, these are our greatest advantages. They should give us confidence that we shall eventually succeed in establishing the kind of international organization to preserve the peace for which men yearn.

In working toward this goal, we must act wisely and steadfastly. We must realize that many dangers yet lie ahead, and that there are many tasks and problems which will be difficult to master. We must also preserve in this country full enjoyment of those basic democratic principles which are our greatest assets.

In this period of history when our country bears the major responsibility of world leadership, our domestic and foreign policies are inseparable. We must maintain a strong and stable economy as the basis of our own well-being and as the primary source of strength of the free world. We must also support economic health and democratic ideals in other countries, if we ourselves are to remain strong and prosperous.

Both these objectives require action now.

We must take proper steps to see that our economy moves safely through the present transition period, and that employment and production start expanding again. If we were to make our plans on the assumption that employment and production will get smaller, we would only make matters worse, and waste much of our potential economic strength. What we must do, instead, is to make all our plans, private and public, in such a way as to give us more jobs and more output. This is the way toward a stronger economy.

Furthermore, we must take action to insure that the hard-won economic recovery of other free nations does not revert to stagnation and despair. One of the most foolish things we could do right now would be to slash our appropriations for European recovery. If we did that, we would be deliberately throwing away gains for peace and freedom that we have painfully made. Only the Communists would profit if we took such a short-sighted course.

We have been making progress in working toward peace and freedom because we have been willing to make the investment that was necessary. It would be disastrous now to change our policy and settle for halfway measures.

It would be disastrous to lose or impair the understanding and support we have gained among the other democratic peoples. These are priceless assets in the great task of constructing a peaceful and orderly world.

The kind of peace we seek cannot be won at a single stroke or by a single nation. Peace worthy of the name can be assured only by the combined effort of many peoples willing to make sacrifices in the cause of freedom.

The peoples of the world look to the United States for the leadership of this great crusade for peace. We have not taken up this task lightly, and we will not lay it down.

We must go resolutely forward, step by step, toward the creation of a world in which we, and all people, can live and prosper in peace.

(7) *Address by the President (Truman) on Collective Security and Freedom from Aggression, Delivered before the Convention of the Veterans of Foreign Wars, Miami, Florida, August 22, 1949.[7]*

[EXCERPT]

All the countries that signed the [North Atlantic] Treaty have learned the tragic cost of war. All of us have learned how weakness invites aggression — how democratic countries, unless they stand together, can be taken over one by one. And now, all of us are determined that, by joint efforts and a common defense, we shall become strong enough to prevent another terrible conflict.

Four years ago, when the war ended, the world entered a new phase of human history. There were many who believed that the world would quickly return to its old ways. Many believed that the countries of the world would work their way, peacefully and in cooperation, back to conditions of stability and prosperity.

But the effects of this last war were too far-reaching to permit such an easy adjustment. The destruction had been too great to allow a quick recovery. The accumulated wealth of generations had been poured out and lost in the conflict. Conditions of world trade had been fundamentally altered. As a result of the upheaval, many peoples demanded new rights and new responsibilities. Men who had lived for centuries in economic or political servitude asked for independence and a fair share of the good things of life.

The war against tyranny was sustained by belief in the Four Freedoms. Men refused to yield to dictatorship because they desired and believed they could secure conditions of material and spiritual freedom. When the war ended, they demanded to be treated as free men. They demanded a world in which they could attain security and liberty.

7 Department of State Publication 3653, p. 43.

This demand cannot be suppressed. It must not be frustrated. It presents a challenge to us and to the values of our civilization which will require all our energies and wisdom to satisfy.

One pretended answer to this demand of mankind is offered by organized Communism. But that answer is a false one. Communism claims to satisfy the universal desire for a better life. But, in fact, it lures men by false promises back to tyranny and slavery — and more and more people, all over the world, are learning that fact.

The free nations of the world offer a different answer to the demand of mankind for security and liberty. Our answer is based upon voluntary association among free nations, mutual adjustment of our common problems, and combined economic effort. We are convinced that through these means the world can achieve economic progress and at the same time maintain and expand democratic freedoms. We are convinced that our answer will prevail.

The people of the United States have been meeting this challenge. In four short years they have done more in the cause of world peace and world recovery than any nation has ever before been called upon to do.

We are not alone in this effort. Many nations which share our democratic values and our traditions are working with us. Without these allies in the cause of peace, our task would be hopeless. We can win a permanent peace only through the joint efforts of free nations striving toward the same objectives.

To achieve a better world we must prevent international violence. Unless protection against war can be secured, all efforts for the advancement of mankind will fail. One of the most important aspects of our foreign policy, therefore, is our effort to establish international order.

To this end, we have joined with other nations in creating a world organization which would outlaw aggression and establish a means of settling international disputes.

The principles of the United Nations are still our goal. We have undertaken to defend and preserve them. We will keep that pledge.

Shortly after the end of the war, however, it became apparent that the United Nations could not live up to all our hopes for it until all nations were united in the desire for peace. It became necessary, therefore, for the free countries to take action to defend the principles of that organization and to preserve it.

By an overwhelming bipartisan vote, the Congress approved my recommendation early in 1947 that the United States help Greece and Turkey resist Communist pressures. Our prompt action preserved the integrity of both countries.

By an equally overwhelming vote in 1948, the Congress approved our joint enterprise with sixteen European nations to achieve economic recovery. The European Recovery Program has prevented general collapse in Europe, and has given hope to all countries who want to see the world resume the course of economic progress.

While we are working with our friends in Europe, we are also working with our friends and neighbors in this hemisphere. The Pact of Rio de Janeiro, signed in September 1947, binds the nations of North and South America together in a defensive alliance.

The United States and eleven other nations have now joined in the North Atlantic Treaty. Like the Rio pact, this is a pledge of mutual assistance by nations which are determined to protect their independence. It is based on the principle that an armed attack on one member nation is an attack on all.

The next task is to back up this principle with military assistance to European nations, and to certain other nations, which are unable to build up their defenses without outside help.

I have recommended to the Congress that the United States supply three kinds of military assistance to friendly democratic nations in need of our help. First, we should help them increase their own military production. Second, we should transfer to them some essential items of military equipment. Third, we should send some of our experts abroad to help train and equip their military forces.

Some people who do not understand the state of the world very well have tried to make the Military Assistance Program seem a difficult and confused issue. On the contrary, it is very simple.

The purpose of the Military Assistance Program is to prevent aggression. Our European partners in the North Atlantic Treaty are not strong enough today to defend themselves effectively. Since the end of the war they have been concentrating on rebuilding their war-torn economies. We can strengthen them, and ourselves, by transferring some military means to them, and by joining with them in a common defense plan. The Military Assistance Program is based on the same principle of self-help and mutual aid that is the cornerstone of the European Recovery Program and the North Atlantic Treaty.

We are not arming ourselves and our friends to start a fight with anybody. We are building defenses so that we won't have to fight.

Our aid will be limited to the material necessary to equip mobile defense forces. These forces will constitute no threat to the independence of other nations. The democratic nations have no desire for aggression; they only want to be able to defend their homes.

Most of our assistance under this program will go to Atlantic Treaty countries, but we will also help certain other nations whose security is important to world peace. We must continue our aid to Greece and Turkey. We should help Iran maintain its firm stand against Soviet pressure. And, in the Far East, two young republics — the Philippines and Korea — need military assistance if they are to maintain their national security.

If it were possible, we would prefer that these bulwarks against aggression be established by the United Nations. We hope the peace of the world will some day be enforced by security forces under the control and direction of the United Nations.

We have been working for that.

But the Soviet Union has blocked every effort to establish an effective international police force and to free the world from the fear of aggression. For that reason, we have had to join other friendly nations in forming regional defense pacts.

The United Nations Charter was wisely drawn to permit these regional defense pacts and other collective security arrangements which are consistent with the great principles of the Charter. The Military Assistance Program will help the United Nations to operate more effectively by increasing the collective as well as the individual ability of free countries to resist aggression.

The Military Assistance Program and the European Recovery Program are part and parcel of the same policy. There is the closest relationship between economic recovery and military defense. On the one hand, economic recovery will lag if the haunting fear of military aggression is widespread. Such fear will prevent new investments from being made and new industries from being established. On the other hand, if protection against aggression is assured, economic recovery will move forward more rapidly. Sound economic recovery and adequate military defense must be carried forward together in balance. That is exactly what we propose to do.

Great progress has been made in economic recovery in Europe. The production of the Western nations of Europe has been rising steadily. To continue the momentum of this economic advance it is necessary now to remove the obstacles created by the fear of military aggression.

We should therefore undertake a program of military assistance without delay. The cost of such a program is considerable, but it represents an investment in security that will be worth many times its cost. It is part of the price of peace.

Peace with freedom and justice cannot be bought cheaply. No single program can bring it about, nor can any single nation. It can only be assured by the combined efforts of the multitudes of people throughout the world who want a secure peace. They are our friends and they are friends worth having. We must keep them our friends if the world is to be a decent place for our children and their children to live in.

We must face the fact that we have forever put behind us the false security of isolationism. We have done so because we have learned — learned the hard way — that, in the world of today, isolationism is a futile and vulnerable shield. We have learned that the defense of the United States and the defense of other freedom-loving nations are indivisible. We have learned that we can serve our country best by joining in the common defense of the rights of all mankind. . . .

(8) *Address by the Ambassador at Large (Jessup) on the Foreign Policy of a Free Democracy, Delivered before the Convention of the Veterans of Foreign Wars, Miami, Florida, August 24, 1949.*[8]

[EXCERPTS]

. . . .

I should be very happy if I could report to you that peace is safe and secure, but it is not. Peace is being maintained by the United States and a large group of like-minded nations. We are fighting for a just and permanent peace on the Atlantic and Pacific fronts today just as much as we were between Pearl Harbor and V-E and V-J days. We cannot relax our efforts for a day, for an hour.

. . . .

We know that the job of winning the war included not only military effort but also scientific, economic, and financial effort. Keeping the peace also requires a multiple effort. If the United States weakens its military strength, the peace is not secure. The same is true if we weaken our foreign policy. It is also true, if we do not remain strong economically, financially, and morally.

It is not bombast to say the United States is the most powerful country in the world. Some people in some nations may state that fact with envy; most people in most nations say it with hope. Only those who do not want peace say it with fear. Our national program has been clearly stated. It is based on national strength to be used in cooperation with other nations through the United Nations in the interest and for the well-being of all the world. That is the program laid down in the inaugural address of the President of the United States. Every Department and agency of the government has a part to play in carrying out that program. Every citizen has a vital stake in its success.

I am not going to talk about the elements of our economic, financial, and military strength. I do want to speak of our moral strength and our foreign policy.

It is not an American habit to talk much about moral strength, or those things which are called spiritual values. I make no apology for raising that theme. We know that the Communists are fighting all over the world to capture the mind and the spirit of men so that they can then enslave them by the ruthless totalitarian methods which kill the spirit, darken the mind, and torture the body. They begin with beautiful promises. They have cunning and skillful agents trained in corrupting the mind. They have the greatest success where there is ignorance or despair. Our job is to dispel the ignorance and to replace despair with hope.

On the Atlantic front our chief problem was the weary despair which the war and its ruin inevitably brought. The Marshall Plan, the Atlantic pact, and the Military Aid Program are bringing back hope.

On the Pacific front they need hope also, but the great problem is the vast ignorance of hundreds of millions of people on which Communism feeds. These people do not know that in countries ruled by Communists there is no freedom. They do not know that the prophets of Communism have publicly proclaimed that they will encourage national independence merely as a stepping stone to a new and terrible slavery. They do not know what our civilization and political principles have produced in the way of a free and prosperous life for the people of a great country.

Our idea of freedom and the good life is something we have for export. If we don't export it, the people who do not know it exists will buy the cheap shoddy promises of Communism. To back our export we need to have the fire of conviction which established this country and which in this generation has brought us to victory in two world wars. That same fire of conviction can keep us at peace.

Our peace strategy is global. The Atlantic and Pacific fronts are only illustrative. As in the war we have our allies, and our strategy must be a joint strategy. With our allies we have preponderant peace forces. We must be constantly alert that no trickery on the part of those who do not seek peace and that no error on our own part, brings us to the loss, or to the abuse, of that great power.

It is true today as it was when spoken 40 years ago by a great Secretary of War and Secretary of State — Elihu Root — that "We wish for no victories but those of peace; for no territory except our own; for no sovereignty except the sovereignty over ourselves."

That is our fundamental strength. Unlike the Soviet Union, we do not want more territory or subject peoples. We want all peoples to be free and prosperous because we believe that progress means a united move upward rather than climbing on the backs of others who are pushed down. We have acted on that belief, and we are putting it into practice through the United Nations, the symbol of international cooperation.

. . . .

Let us frankly acknowledge that many of the actions and much of the effort of the United States in international affairs in recent months have been directed toward countering the clear threat to ourselves and other free peoples. We could not have done otherwise without betraying all that we stand for. Let us also frankly admit that self-interest, if we had taken that as the sole guide, would have dictated the same course.

The realities of the situation have required us to develop new methods and measures to meet them successfully, but they have not diverted us from our long-range, primary objectives. We still seek a just and enduring peace, in which all peoples will be free to achieve better living conditions and a wider enjoyment of human rights. We still firmly support the United Nations as the most feasible and effective means by which the nations of the world can work together to keep the peace and promote the welfare of their peoples.

The United Nations should not be judged by utopian standards, but by the world as it is. As long as deep-seated differences among its members persist, the United Nations is bound to be affected by that division. Nevertheless, the fact of primary importance is that the United Nations continues to function in spite of the East-West conflict, even though its effectiveness is diminished. It provides a common meeting ground for all the nations which genuinely seek the solution of problems by consultation and collaboration. By the continuity of its operations, the United Nations strengthens the habit of working together. Above all, it contains the contending forces within a recognized forum and requires them to justify their actions to the world in terms of the purposes ond provisions of the Charter. The United Nations looms larger and larger as the manifest conscience of mankind.

Within the limits of the matters with which the United Nations was expected to deal, it has gradually and painstakingly achieved a record of real accomplishment. A look at that record should caution us against taking an unduly pessimistic view of the ability of the United Nations to deal with particular cases. If the representatives of the United Nations had been as easily discouraged as some observers, they would not have manifested the patience and perseverance that eventually brings success.

.   .   .   .

The United States has never been afraid to face the future. Times of peace and prosperity as well as those of danger and distress need forethought. If we did not plan ahead for peace, we would be less likely to reach the goal and less likely to retain the gains when they are made. It is Communist, and not American doctrine, that enmity and war are inevitable.

Consistent with our faith and with our word pledged through the ratification of the United Nations Charter, we have cooperated in the efforts of the United Nations to work toward disarmament. Little progress has yet been made because the Soviet Union has refused to accept the conclusions of the majority in the Commission for Conventional Armaments regarding the essential features of an effective plan of regulation. The Soviet Union tried to shift the blame for this lack of progress, but the other members recognized their proposals as a mere propaganda maneuver and rejected them.

The General Assembly requested the Commission to give highest priority to the development of a plan for a census of armaments and armed forces, with a control organization for verifying the information to be submitted to the states subscribing to the plan. This request reflected the belief, shared by the United States, that disarmament cannot be based on promises alone but only on duly certified knowledge of the facts: This means that the whole international community must have full information about armaments and armed forces, checked and double-checked by neutral observers, as a necessary prerequisite to any actual reduction and regulation of conventional arms.

It must be emphasized that the plan for an arms census and verification of the figures will not go into effect even for those countries which have supported it unless and until it has been approved in the Security Council and the General Assembly and has been subscribed to by the United States and other governments. In other words, the plan will become a reality only after each member of the United Nations has had an opportunity to review it and decide whether it wishes to accept the plan. We are not going to exchange arms for empty promises.

We have gone forward also in the search for safe control of the most dangerous weapon. The majority of the United Nations Atomic Energy Commission has developed a plan for international control of atomic energy, based largely on proposals made by the United States. We offered to give up atomic weapons and to transfer to an international authority atomic activities dangerous to international security, but only upon the absolutely essential condition that a system of effective and enforceable safeguards has first been established and is in actual operation.

The plan of the majority of the Commission, incorporating this condition, has been approved by the General Assembly as providing "the necessary basis" for a system which would safeguard international security. The Commission, however, is unable to proceed further because the Soviet Union has refused to accept the plan approved by the majority of the Commission and by the General Assembly. In accordance with the provisions of the General Assembly resolution and our standard policy, we have begun talks among the six sponsoring powers. We have never closed the door to the Soviet Union for a discussion of any international problem.

One of the plain facts in the present situation is that the Soviet Union is contemptuous of weakness but respects strength. It was the strength of the West which led the Soviet Union to abandon the Berlin blockade and to make at least some moves toward agreement in the recent meeting of the Council of Foreign Ministers in Paris. Our strength is made up of unity with the free peoples of the world; of industrial power; of military power; and of calm confidence in the soundness of our domestic system and our peaceful foreign policy.

We had revealed that strength in several ways. There was the Berlin airlift. That great operation saved the people of Berlin from the starvation with which the Berlin blockade threatened them. I want to pay tribute to the men who organized it and operated it.

Then there was the steady progress toward the organization of a Western German Government. Here the basic unity of purpose and of policy between France, the United Kingdom, and the United States was a most potent factor. That is a unity we must preserve, strengthen, and extend.

We have other friends and allies for peace in all parts of the world. We are closely bound to our good neighbors south of the Rio Grande and have formalized that unity in the defensive pact of Rio de Janeiro, which was concluded within the framework of the United Nations Charter. We have similarly concluded the North Atlantic Treaty with eleven nations who form the North Atlantic community, again acting in conformity with the Charter. We are working closely with other members of the United Nations for our mutual benefit and strength to promote the common purpose of maintaining peace and the good life.

These close associations are not and cannot be the result of domination and dictation. The Soviet Union believes in that method as did Hitler. We do not believe in it. There are always differences of opinion between the closest of friends. Those differences can be resolved by mutual understanding and accommodation because the common purpose is basic. When the Soviet Union comes to realize the soundness of that common purpose and the method of achieving it we stand ready to work equally with them. It must not be forgotten that we are as friendly to the Russian people as to other people. We are not trying to conquer Russia. We are not rivals for the domination of the world because we do not want to dominate the world. If their government will abandon the dream of world domination which throughout history has destroyed such blind dreamers, a full share in international cooperation will be theirs.

At this moment in history we must continue the process of helping Western Europe to rebuild itself in economic stability and in the sense of safety which comes from a well-planned common defense if any state should again be misled into contemplating the fatal step of committing aggression against the democratic forces of the world.

The only way the Western European members of the pact can rapidly acquire an effective defense is for the United States to supplement what they are doing for themselves and each other by supplying arms and equipment from this country, as proposed in the Military Assistance Program. This aid will enable the pact members in Europe to turn their shadow armies into effective forces that will become the nucleus of the integrated defense essential to the maintenance of peace in the North Atlantic area. The development of an actual defense-in-being in Western Europe will give the people of those countries the reassurance that they require for further economic and social progress, and will prove to be a stabilizing influence in Europe and the world.

No one regrets more than do the government and people of the United States that we must devote to arms and other defense measures part of our substance and energy, which we would prefer to use for more productive purposes.

The menace of aggressive Communism to the liberties and rights of free peoples is the immediate and pressing problem that must be overcome. We are confident that the concerted effort of the free nations will succeed in overcoming it. But we are well aware that this is not the only problem, nor in the long perspective of history perhaps, the most significant. We will not hesitate to do what is necessary to help the free nations preserve their independence and integrity. Neither will we lose sight of the constructive and humane tasks which we set ourselves while the war was being fought.

.   .   .   .

(9) Address by the President (Truman) on the Occasion of the Laying of the Cornerstone of the Secretariat Building of the Permanent Headquarters of the United Nations, New York, October 24, 1949.[9]

President Romulo, Mr. Lie, distinguished representatives, and fellow guests: We have come together to lay the cornerstone of the permanent head-

9 *Ibid.*, p. 643; United Nations General Assembly, Document A/PV.237 October 31, 1949.

quarters of the United Nations. These are the most important buildings in the world, for they are the center of man's hope for peace and a better life. This is the place where the nations of the world will work together to make that hope a reality.

This occasion is a source of special pride to the people of the United States. We are deeply conscious of the honor of having the permanent headquarters of the United Nations in this country. At the same time, we know how important it is that the people of other nations should come to know at first hand the work of this world organization. We consider it appropriate, therefore, that the United Nations should hold meetings from time to time in other countries when that can be done. For the United Nations must draw its inspiration from the people of every land; it must be truly representative of and responsive to the peoples of the world whom it was created to serve.

This ceremony marks a new stage in the growth of the United Nations. It is fitting that it should take place on United Nations Day, the fourth anniversary of the day the Charter entered into effect. During the four years of its existence, this organization has become a powerful force for promoting peace and friendship among the peoples of the world. The construction of this new headquarters is tangible proof of the steadfast faith of the members in the vitality and strength of the organization, and of our determination that it shall become more and more effective in the years ahead.

The Charter embodies the hopes and ideals of men everywhere. Hopes and ideals are not static. They are dynamic, and they give life and vigor to the United Nations. We look forward to a continuing growth and evolution of the organization to meet the changing needs of the world's peoples. We hope that eventually every nation on earth will be a fully qualified and loyal member.

We who are close to the United Nations sometimes forget that it is more than the procedures, the councils, and the debates, through which it operates. We tend to overlook the fact that the organization is the living embodiment of the principles of the Charter — the renunciation of aggression and the joint determination to build a better life.

But if we overlook this fact, we will fail to realize the strength and power of the United Nations. We will fail to understand the true nature of this new force that has been created in the affairs of our time.

The United Nations is essentially an expression of the moral nature of man's aspirations. The Charter clearly shows our determination that international problems must be settled on a basis acceptable to the conscience of mankind.

Because the United Nations is the dynamic expression of what all the peoples of the world desire, because it sets up a standard of right and justice for all nations, it is greater than any of its members. The compact that underlies the United Nations cannot be ignored — and it cannot be infringed or dissolved.

We in the United States, in the course of our own history, have learned what it means to set up an organization to give expression to the common desire for peace and unity. Our Constitution expressed the will of the people that there should be a United States. And through toil and struggle the people made their will prevail.

In the same way, I think, the Charter and the organization served by these buildings express the will of the people of the world that there shall be a United Nations.

This does not mean that all the member countries are of one mind on all issues. The controversies which divide us go very deep. We should understand that these buildings are not a monument to the unanimous agreement of nations on all things. But they signify one new and important fact. They signify that the peoples of the world are of one mind in their determination to solve their common problems by working together.

Our success in the United Nations will be measured not only in terms of our ability to meet and master political controversies. We have learned that political controversies grow out of social and economic problems. If the people of the world are to live together in peace, we must work together to establish the conditions that will provide a firm foundation for peace.

For this reason, our success will also be measured by the extent to which the rights of individual human beings are realized. And it will be measured by the extent of our economic and social progress.

These fundamental facts are recognized both in the language of the Charter and in the activities in which the United Nations has been engaged during the past four years. The Charter plainly makes respect for human rights by nations a matter of international concern. The member nations have learned from bitter experience that regard for human rights is indispensable to political, economic, and social progress. They have learned that disregard of human rights is the beginning of tyranny and, too often, the beginning of war.

For these reasons, the United Nations has devoted much of its time to fostering respect for human rights. The General Assembly has adopted the Universal Declaration of Human Rights and the Convention on Genocide. Other important measures in this field are under study.

I am confident that this great work will go steadily forward. The preparation of a Covenant on Human Rights by the Human Rights Commission is a task with which the United States is deeply concerned. We believe strongly that the attainment of basic civil and political rights for men and women everywhere — without regard to race, language, or religion — is essential to the peace we are seeking. We hope that the Covenant on Human Rights will contain effective provisions regarding freedom of information. The minds of men must be free from artificial and arbitrary restraints in order that they may seek the truth and apply their intelligence to the making of a better world.

Another field in which the United Nations is undertaking to build the foundations of a peaceful world is that of economic development. Today, at least half of mankind lives in dire poverty. Hundreds of millions of men, women, and children lack adequate food, clothing, and shelter. We cannot achieve permanent peace and prosperity in the world until the standard of living in underdeveloped areas is raised.

It is for this reason that I have urged the launching of a vigorous and concerted effort to apply modern technology and capital investment to improve the lot of these peoples. These areas need a large expansion of investment and trade. In order for this to take place, they also need the application of scientific knowledge and technical skills to their basic problems — producing more food, improving health and sanitation, making use of their natural resources, and educating their people.

To meet these needs, the United Nations and its agencies are preparing a detailed program for technical assistance to underdeveloped areas.

The Economic and Social Council last summer defined the basic principles which should underlie this program. The General Assembly is now completing and perfecting the initial plans. The fact that the Economic Committee of the Assembly voted unanimously for the resolution on technical assistance shows that this is a common cause which commands united support. Although differences may arise over details of the program, I fervently hope that the members of the United Nations will remain unanimous in their determination to raise the standards of living of the less fortunate members of the human family.

The United States intends to play its full part in this great enterprise. We are already carrying on a number of activities in this field. I shall urge the Congress, when it reconvenes in January, to give high priority to proposals which will make possible additional technical assistance and capital investment.

I should like to speak of one other problem which is of major concern to the United Nations. That is the control of atomic energy.

Ever since the first atomic weapon was developed, a major objective of United States policy has been a system of international control of atomic energy that would assure effective prohibition of atomic weapons, and at the same time would promote the peaceful use of atomic energy by all nations.

In November 1945, Prime Minister Attlee of the United Kingdom, Prime Minister King of Canada, and I agreed that the problem of international control of atomic energy should be referred to the United Nations. The establishment of the United Nations Atomic Energy Commission was one of the first acts of the first session of the General Assembly.

That Commission worked for three years on the problem. It developed a plan of control which reflected valuable contributions by almost every country represented on the Commission. This plan of control was overwhelmingly approved by the General Assembly on November 4, 1948.

This is a good plan. It is a plan that can work, and more important, it is a plan that can be effective in accomplishing its purpose. It is the only plan so far developed that would meet the technical requirements of control, that would make prohibition of atomic weapons effective, and at the same time promote the peaceful development of atomic energy on a cooperative basis.

We support this plan and will continue to support it unless and until a better and more effective plan is put forward. To assure that atomic energy will be devoted to man's welfare and not to his destruction is a continuing challenge to all nations and all peoples. The United States is now, and will remain, ready to do its full share in meeting this challenge.

Respect for human rights, promotion of economic development, and a system for control of weapons are requisites to the kind of world we seek. We cannot solve these problems overnight, but we must keep everlastingly working at them in order to reach our goal.

No single nation can always have its own way, for these are human problems, and the solution of human problems is to be found in negotiation and mutual adjustment.

The challenge of the twentieth century is the challenge of human relations, and not of impersonal natural forces. The real dangers confronting us today have their origins in outmoded habits of thought, in the inertia of human nature, and in preoccupation with supposed national interests to the detriment of the common good.

As members of the United Nations, we are convinced that patience, the spirit of reasonableness, and hard work will solve the most stubborn political problems. We are convinced that individual rights and social and economic progress can be advanced through international cooperation.

Our faith is in the betterment of human relations. Our vision is of a better world in which men and nations can live together, respecting one another's rights and cooperating in building a better life for all. Our efforts are made in the belief that men and nations can cooperate, that there are no international problems which men of good will cannot solve or adjust.

Mr. President, Mr. Lie, the laying of this cornerstone is an act of faith — our unshakable faith that the United Nations will succeed in accomplishing the great tasks for which it was created.

But "faith without works is dead." We must make our devotion to the ideals of the Charter as strong as the steel in this building. We must pursue the objectives of the Charter with resolution as firm as the rock on which this building rests. We must conduct our affairs foursquare with the Charter, in terms as true as this cornerstone.

If we do these things, the United Nations will endure and will bring the blessings of peace and well-being to mankind.

CHAPTER II

Conduct of Foreign Relations

1. FORMULATION OF FOREIGN POLICY

Pursuant to Public Law 162 (80th Cong.), approved July 7, 1947, the Commission on Organization of the Executive Branch of the Government appointed in January 1948 a Task Force on Foreign Affairs charged with the responsibility of analyzing the "present-day problems confronting the Government in the conduct of foreign affairs."[1] The Task Force, composed of Harvey H. Bundy, partner in Choate, Hall and Stewart, attorneys, of Boston, and James Grafton Rogers, president of the Foreign Bondholders Council and former Deputy Director of the Office of Strategic Services, with Henry L. Stimson, former Secretary of State, as advisor, submitted its conclusions and recommendations on the "Organization of the Government for the Conduct of Foreign Affairs" in January, 1949.[2] The Task Force analysis served in turn as a basis for the commission's report on foreign affairs, submitted to the Congress on February 21, 1949.[3]

A. General

(1) Report to the Chairman of the Commission on Organization of the Executive Branch of the Government (Hoover) by the Task Force on Foreign Affairs, Submitted, January, 1949.[4]

[EXCERPT]

SUMMARY STATEMENT

Your Foreign Affairs Task Force, after completion of comprehensive studies by ourselves and our staff, has been impressed by the drastic changes in the conduct of foreign affairs over the last 15 years, not only in the character and magnitude of the problems but also in the accelerated tempo of the operations and the complicated nature of the governmental activities and procedures.

In approaching the question of solutions for the problems presented, the task force has considered it no part of its duties to appraise the capacity or performance of any individual, but rather to deal only with the type of personnel and the machinery best adapted in the long run to make it easier for whatever persons may be in office to carry out their duties effectively.

It is of course true that the effectiveness of any operation, whether in government or in private business, depends primarily on the quality of the men and women who occupy positions of responsibility, and in this matter of the conduct of foreign affairs there is a strong temptation to say that all that is necessary is to obtain the services of a sufficient number of the ablest men and

---

[1] House Document 79, 81st Cong., 1st sess., p. 1.
[2] Commission on Organization of the Executive Branch of the Government. *Task Force Report on Foreign Affairs* [Appendix H], Washington, 1949.
[3] House Document 79, cited above.
[4] *Task Force Report on Foreign Affairs* . . ., cited above.

women in the United States and let them determine the machinery best suited to their own operations.

A report to this effect would hardly be helpful. Furthermore, it is believed that the form of the machinery used is of great importance in aiding or hampering any public servant in the performance of his duties. There are certain principles and certain procedures which in the light of experience can be utilized to improve materially the present unsatisfactory situation. These principles and procedures, it is hoped, will commend themselves to the Congress, to the President, and to the executive departments and agencies as valuable in making the United States activities in foreign affairs more consistent, more efficient, and in fact more wise.

A number of facts have struck us with great force:

FIRST

a. The traditional line of demarcation between domestic and foreign problems has completely disappeared, and the governmental organization must be shaped to formulate and execute national policies which have both domestic and foreign aspects.

b. The activities of departments and agencies other than the State Department affect to an extraordinary degree the conduct of foreign affairs, and these other departments and agencies show an increasing tendency to establish policies or make policy interpretations in the foreign affairs area which are not coordinated with the foreign policies or interpretations of the State Department. The policies or interpretations of the State Department, in turn, are not always coordinated with over-all United States national policies.

c. As a result the conduct of foreign affairs within the executive branch more than ever requires action, supervision, and coordination from the office of the President and cannot be solely the special province of the State Department.

d. In partial response to this situation, specialized inter-departmental bodies have appeared at the cabinet level to advise the President on the conduct of foreign affairs in certain areas, such as national security and international finance. There is a complete absence of such mechanisms to advise the President in other important or potentially important areas.

Recommendation

To meet these problems we recommend that the President should establish cabinet-level committees to advise him on both the domestic and foreign aspects of matters affecting foreign affairs and involving more than one department or agency of the executive branch. They should be on a regular or *ad hoc* basis as the occasion demands. Specific committees should not be established by statute, but general enabling legislation should afford a flexible framework within which the President can act and should provide for specific institutional aids, including an executive secretary with purely procedural and no substantive powers. The executive secretary should not build up a large secretariat but should meet the bulk of his personnel needs by calling upon the various departments and agencies.

SECOND

a. The State Department has expanded enormously due, in part at least, to the absorption of certain war agencies of the government, such as the Foreign Economic Administration (FEA), the Office of Strategic Services (OSS), and the Office of War Information (OWI).

b. There have been built up in the State Department organizational units which to some extent, at least, duplicate or parallel activities which are or should be appropriate functions of other departments and agencies of the government.

c. The activities of the State Department have extended into fields of program operation, such as propaganda, surplus property disposition, and foreign economic assistance, which had never before been part of the functions of the State Department.

Recommendation

To meet this situation we recommend that the State Department's general responsibilities in foreign affairs should consist of obtaining definition of proposed objectives of the United States, of formulating proposed policies to achieve United States objectives (in conjunction with other departments and agencies where their interests are involved or where they have experience to contribute), and of recommending the choice and timing of the various means and instruments of carrying out United States foreign policies, as well as its traditional responsibilities in connection with representation abroad, collection and distribution of information, and negotiation. As a corollary, the State Department should not have responsibility for operation of programs such as those relating to foreign economic assistance and propaganda except in very unusual instances. The other departments and agencies, when called upon by the President or the Congress, should administer specific means or instruments of carrying out United States foreign policies (under the observation and with the advice of the State Department) in a manner consistent with other United States foreign policies and with over-all United States objectives.

THIRD

a. An appalling burden has fallen on the Secretary and Under Secretary of State and no human being has the time or energy to carry on the duties they have been attempting to perform. At the present time and under present conditions, this situation is intolerable.

b. There are many delays and much confusion in the coordination of the activities of the various major organizational units within the State Department, largely resulting from a lack of operational responsibility below the level of the office of the Secretary or Under Secretary.

Recommendation

We recommend that the internal organization of the State Department should be recast as follows:

a. The structure for policy and action should be regional to the fullest possible extent with four regional Assistant Secretaries responsible for the four traditional geographic areas of the world, but supplemented by an Assistant Secretary for multilateral affairs who should be responsible for matters transcending the spheres of the regional Assistant Secretaries, and who should be responsible for our policy with respect to international organizations, for interdepartmental coordination and for supervision of certain small groups of functional specialists.

b. The Secretary should delegate to the four regional Assistant Secretaries responsibility to take action in their respective areas within broad policies previously defined by him, and he should decentralize to them the day-to-day tools of administration.

c. The Secretary, in exercising supervision, should be aided by an Under Secretary who, as at present, can act for him as his alter ego, and by a Deputy Under Secretary who will be responsible for the planning and coordinating process and, in particular, for overseeing a high-level operational policy committee and an executive secretariat which are to insure thorough consideration of all aspects of policy matters and to enforce orderly procedure.

d. The administration and management of the State Department and its missions overseas should be made the responsibility of a Deputy Under Secretary for Administration who in personnel, budget, and other managerial problems, can invoke and rely upon the active attention and direction of the Secretary and Under Secretary.

e. The responsibility for recommending action should be assigned in each case to a single officer below the rank of Assistant Secretary who is in either the regional or multilateral system (depending on where the decision is to be effectuated) who must consult (but never be required to secure concurrence of) the other regional desks and multilateral or advisory groups affected, and then report their consultation and comment with his recommendation. Final action on such recommendations should be restricted to the five Assistant Secretaries, the Deputy Under Secretaries, the Under Secretary, or the Secretary.

f. The present economic and other functional staffs should be reduced to (*i*) a small group of specialists (mentioned above) who do not duplicate the informational and advising functions of other departments or agencies but act as liaison with them and serve as staff consultants within the State Department and (*ii*) functional specialists attached to the regional offices. The Department should rely primarily upon the other departments and agencies for information and experience within their fields, insisting upon their being organized to supply these needs.

FOURTH

a. There is serious unrest in the relations between the Foreign Service and the State Department personnel of the civil service.

b. The personnel of both the State Department and the Foreign Service, in general, have been of high quality and have demonstrated a devotion to duty during a most confused and difficult period. Both services have been kept out of politics.

Recommendation

We recommend that the personnel in the permanent State Department establishment in Washington and the personnel of the Foreign Service above certain levels should be amalgamated over a short period of years into a single foreign affairs service, divided into grades and divisions, obligated to serve at home or overseas and constituting a safeguarded career group administered separately from the general civil service as it now exists.

FIFTH

There has been growing distrust of the State Department and its operations by members of the Congress, and to some extent also by the public. This produces serious, and in some cases disastrous, effects upon the maintenance of the continuous operation of sound foreign policies, with the ever present danger of withdrawal of vital congressional approval and financial support.

Recommendation

The recommendations made above will, we believe, materially improve this situation. We further recommend that the State Department should place congressional relations in the hands of an Assistant Secretary on a full-time basis who should be responsible for supervising and give direction to all State Department relationships with the Congress.

We recognize the confusion that has resulted from constant changes in the principal officers of the State Department and also of other departments and agencies, and the added confusion in the State Department which has come from repeated threats of major reorganizations and from constant minor organizational changes and reassignments of duties. We, therefore, emphasize the importance of continuity in office, and we recommend that any reorganization which may be determined upon be carried through as rapidly as possible. And we also recognize that some of our recommendations may already have been adopted or are already under consideration.

· · · · ·

(2) **Report to the Congress by the Commission on Organization of the Executive Branch of the Government, Submitted, February 21, 1949.**[5]

[EXCERPTS]

· · · · ·

5 House Document 79, cited above, p.3.

II The Complexities of the Present Situation

The time is particularly appropriate to appraise the machinery of the Government for the conduct of foreign affairs. The United States emerged from the recent World War with a radically new role in world affairs. As a result, today's organizational requirements are drastically different from those of the prewar era. The executive branch today finds itself forced to develop positive foreign policies and programs, involving not merely the State Department but many other departments and agencies as well, and to deal cooperatively with other nations on a multilateral as well as a bilateral basis. The Congress, in addition, finds that the exercise of its traditional powers in the domestic as well as in the international field has made it a participant in the conduct of foreign affairs on an unprecedented scale.

The problems of Government organization for the conduct of foreign affairs are, therefore, not confined to the State Department alone but involve the organization of the Presidency, the State Department and the Foreign Service, the department and agencies other than the State Department, the interdepartmental relationships, and the relationships between the executive and legislative branches. The special problems in each of these cases will be discussed separately at a subsequent point. Accompanying the involvement of all these elements and contributing to the complexities of the situation is the increased size of the Government as a whole and of the State Department in particular.

Tangible manifestations of the foregoing are found on all sides. In the Presidency new factors affecting the conduct of foreign affairs include the Chief of Staff to the President and statutory interdepartmental bodies such as the National Security Council. The State Department itself, in terms of appropriations is 12 times larger and in terms of personnel almost 5 times larger in 1948 than it was in 1938. In the interdepartmental field there are more than 30 committees concerned with economic, social, military, and other aspects of foreign affairs. Of 59 major departments and agencies in the executive branch,[6] at least 46 are drawn into foreign affairs to a greater or lesser extent. Certain units are deeply involved, such as the National Military Establishment in connection with the administration of occupied areas abroad, the Economic Cooperation Administration in connection with financial assistance overseas, the Treasury Department in international financial matters, and the Commerce Department in connection with export control. Finally, Congressional participation in the conduct of foreign affairs has become particularly evident in the enhancement of the role of the House of Representatives in connection with appropriations for foreign programs.

A. The Executive-Legislative Relationship Under the Constitution in the Conduct of Foreign Affairs

The organization of the executive branch for the conduct of foreign affairs must necessarily be shaped to accord with the over-all governmental frame-

6 These 59 departments and agencies are exclusive of nonstatutory interdepartmental committees and certain temporary bodies which, if included, would raise the total to 74.

work provided by the Constitution. The constitutional doctrine of separation of powers between executive and legislative branches results in a duality of authority over foreign affairs which complicates the machinery of Government in that area, especially in contrast with the machinery of countries operating under the parliamentary system of government.

The difficulty caused by this duality of authority has been sharpened by the new position of the United States in world affairs. Prior to the recent World War, the Congress at times had considerable influence, of course, on foreign relations, but not on any continuous basis. The President, on the other hand, possessing relatively greater powers than in domestic affairs, largely controlled foreign affairs with only occasional reference to the Congress. Recent events have changed the situation and made the Congress a much more significant and regular participant in foreign affairs. As a consequence, the solutions of today's problems require joint legislative-executive cooperation on a scale heretofore unknown in American history.

The Constitution is not at all precise in its allocation of foreign affairs powers between the two branches. The President has the power to negotiate treaties, but only subject to confirmation by two-thirds vote of the Senate. The Constitution gives the President the power to appoint ambassadors and ministers, again subject to Senate confirmation. In addition, he is specifically empowered to receive ambassadors and ministers of other nations. Except for such powers, however, the executive authority must be derived from general constitutional provisions.

On the other hand, the Constitution gives the Congress certain explicit authority in the international field, including the powers to regulate foreign commerce, to fix import duties, and to declare war. Most important of all is its control over appropriation of funds. As the United States has assumed its new role in world affairs, and as domestic and foreign problems have involved more and more the same or closely related issues, all these congressional powers have assumed greater significance than in the prewar era.

It is one thing to suggest the need for the executive and legislative branches to cooperate in the conduct of foreign affairs and another to achieve such cooperation. One particular obstacle which should be frankly faced is the traditionally suspicious attitude of the Congress toward foreign affairs and toward the segment of the executive branch concerned with it.

This attitude appears to stem from three principal sources:

1. The fact that the State Department is the channel of communications between the United States and foreign nations. In that sense, the State Department represents foreigners. Furthermore, foreign affairs problems are usually troublesome and irritating, and they involve dollars or other commitments to other than the American electorate. In seeking to solve these problems the State Department is handicapped by the lack of any domestic constituency which will give the Congress credit for action taken or which will rise to the State Department's defense against congressional criticism.

2. The fact that the conduct of foreign affairs of necessity must frequently be on a secret and confidential basis. This is particularly true in the preliminary stages of a given matter where announcement of the intentions of the United States prior to consultation with other nations would result in embarrassments which would make it impossible to deal with those nations. This secrecy is resented by the Congress, which feels that secrecy is too often used to avoid congressional interference and control. The result is to afford a breeding ground for constant conflict.

3. The fact that up to about 1924 social prestige and protocol considerations were paramount in the minds and actions of the bulk of Americans concerned with foreign affairs. From this grew the conception of State Department and Foreign Service personnel as being primarily concerned with tea parties and striped pants. Today, as a result of the Rogers Act of 1924 and the Foreign Service Act of 1946, and as a result of foreign affairs being injected as never before into the main stream of American life, this fact is no longer true, but the memory lingers on and will persist for at least another generation.

Given the present constitutional framework and the attitude of the legislative branch toward foreign affairs, the situation calls for mutual cooperation and restraint. The executive branch must appreciate the role of the Congress and the propriety of its participation in foreign affairs where *legislative* decisions are required. Similarly, the Congress should appreciate that leadership in the conduct of foreign affairs can come only from the executive side of the Government and that the Congress should not attempt to participate in *executive* decisions in the international field.

One serious procedural impediment to achieving satisfactory legislative-executive cooperation is the constitutional requirement of a two-thirds Senate vote for the confirmation of treaties. No thoughtful student of the conduct of foreign affairs can ignore the consequences of this provision. It is a serious trouble breeder between the executive branch and the Senate in that such an inherently rigid rule encourages circumvention by the executive by resort to the procedures of executive agreements and joint resolutions. Attempts to use these procedures, in turn, involve friction between the Senate and the House of Representatives. An especially bad result is that the emphasis is directed to the question of whether the proper procedure is being employed, instead of to the substance of the issues before the Congress. The question of a change in the present requirement of a two-thirds Senate vote is deemed, however, to be outside the province of this Commission.

B. The Organization Within the Executive Branch for the Conduct of Foreign Affairs

The problem of organization within the executive branch for the conduct of foreign affairs is, in the final analysis, the same problem as in the Government as a whole. First, despite the relatively greater authority assigned by the Constitution to the President in the foreign affairs field, authority or the power of command over the foreign affairs activities of the entire executive branch is not satisfactorily vested in the President. Similarly, at the departmental level, including the State Department, full authority is not placed in the departmental or agency heads. Second, the line of command and supervision over foreign affairs activities from the President to the department and agency heads, and through them to their subordinate units, is far from clear. Third, the staff services for foreign affairs activities of the President, the Secretary of State, and the other department and agency heads are utterly inadequate.

III. Organizational Concepts

The conduct of foreign affairs today involves almost the entire executive branch — the President, the President's executive offices, the State Department, numerous other departments and agencies, and intricate interdepartmental machinery. In addition, it involves constant cooperation between the executive branch and the Congress. As a consequence the problems of organization are equally government-wide in scope, and organization reforms must be based on definite concepts of the part to be played by each segment of the Government.

The concepts for organization within the executive branch are, in summary, the following:

1. The decisions within the executive branch on the objectives of the United States in world affairs are ultimately decisions for the President only to make. He may, of course, delegate this power, but, as the sole elected member of the executive branch, he cannot divest himself of his final responsibility. When the President does delegate the power to make decisions, it must be recognized that it is impractical to make a blanket delegation to the State Department alone or to any other single department or agency.

2. The executive responsibility for the formulation and carrying out of foreign policies to achieve objectives is today that of the President with staff assistance from his executive office and the State Department. Under the President this responsibility is shared in various degrees by numerous departments and agencies throughout the executive establishment.

3. The responsibility for coordinating all the foreign affairs activities of the State Department and the other departments and agencies, whether in the decision-making process or in the processes of policy formulation and execution, ultimately is also that of the President. In delegating this responsibility the President may turn to the State Department, which is the specialist in foreign affairs, as, for example, to provide chairmen for interdepartmental committees, or he may turn elsewhere, depending on the balance of foreign and domestic implications in a particular problem.

4. The conduct of foreign affairs today involves the use of many means and instruments. Financial assistance, force or potential force, and propaganda are a few of the major ones. The utilization of these instruments similarly involves the performance of numerous supporting functions. A few examples are collection of information, evaluation of information through analysis and research, dissemination of information, employment of personnel, disburse-

ment of funds, making of contracts, issuance of rules and regulations, and drafting of legislation.

5. The responsibility today for a decision as to which of several instruments to employ in the conduct of foreign affairs, together with the accompanying decisions as to when to employ them and as to the purposes to be accomplished thereby, carries with it two additional responsibilities. The first is for coordination throughout the executive branch in the choice of the instrument, the time of its use, and the purposes to be accomplished thereby. The second is for loyal teamwork between the State Department and other departments and agencies instead of the evasion and backbiting that characterized these relationships during the recent war.

It is essential to recognize that in the discharge of this multifold responsibility, two different segments of the executive branch may perform functions which appear similar, but there should not and need not be duplication in the performance of identical functions in two parts of the Government. For example, if it is deemed to be of advantage to the United States that a democratic rather than a communistic government be in power in a foreign country, it may be found desirable to employ many instruments, including those of public information or propaganda, financial assistance, or other aids against outside interference. The medium of information may be in the State Department, the financial assistance instrument in the Economic Cooperation Administration, the Export-Import Bank and elsewhere, and other instruments may be in other branches of the Government.

All of these instruments, for example, involve the function of research and analysis of information. The State Department's research and analysis would relate to the state of public opinion of the country in question and the factors influential in forming public opinion; the Economic Cooperation Administration's research and analysis would be directed to the economic condition of the foreign country and the balance of international trade; and the military establishment's research and analysis would pertain to the status of communist military power on the borders of the country in question and the strategic disposition of United States forces in occupied areas nearby to strengthen the democratic elements in power in the country in question. Yet the performance of these functions involves no inevitable duplication of effort. For example, no duplication would occur in the case of financial assistance so long as the State Department economic and research units do not go over the same economic ground as those of Economic Cooperation Administration.

6. The effective discharge of the executive responsibilities in the conduct of foreign affairs (including the formulation of policies, employment of instruments to carry out policies, and coordination in both the formulation and execution stages) requires that authority be vested in the President and descend from him through a clear line of command to responsible department and agency heads with subordinate authority over cohesive executive agencies.

7. Decisions as to the conduct of foreign affairs today inevitably are decisions affecting our whole political, economic, and social life. The problem of organization for the conduct of foreign affairs is, therefore, but a segment of the

larger problem of organization for the conduct of national affairs. Hence, governmental organization for the conduct of foreign affairs cannot be treated as a separate mechanism but must be regarded as an integral part of a larger mechanism.

These general concepts provide the foundation for the recommendations which follow. In some measure these recommendations are geared to the immediate future. Times change, however, and organizational forms must be adjusted accordingly. Organization cannot be immutable and the recommendations herein cannot be regarded as having indefinite validity.

B. Role of the President

(1) Report and Recommendations to the Congress by the Commission on Organization of the Executive Branch of the Government Concerning the Role of the President in the Formulation of Foreign Policy, Submitted, February 21, 1949.[7]

[EXCERPTS]

The President, as the single member of the executive branch answerable to the electorate, is ultimately responsible to the American people for the formulation, execution, and coordination of foreign policies. The emphasis is on "ultimately," because the President, either personally or institutionally, can attempt to control only the very top and crucial problems of foreign policy formulation, execution and coordination.

Today the authority of the President over the foreign affairs activities of the executive branch is seriously hampered by both legal and practical impediments. The legislative creation of new agencies and specific coordinative bodies with foreign affairs powers, the existence of independent regulatory agencies with executive functions, and the grant of foreign affairs authority and funds to bureaus and offices below the level of the department or agency head, all serve to lessen the efficiency of the executive branch as a whole. Likewise these factors detract from the President's ability to correct administrative weaknesses. They lessen the capabilities of the departments and agencies to provide "self-coordination" and correspondingly throw a greater burden on the executive office of the President. They also prevent the establishment of a direct and effective chain of command from the Chief Executive down through the numerous segments of the executive branch.

The Presidency, furthermore, is only casually organized to furnish staff assistance to the President in the conduct of foreign affairs. Better machinery is badly needed to bring competent and better rounded foreign affairs advice to the President and to force prompt resolution of interdepartmental disputes which, if left unsettled at lower levels, may impair the foreign relations of the United States. The Cabinet, moreover, it must be recognized, is not and cannot become an effective deliberative council of advisers to the President.

7 *Ibid.*, p. 10.

Recommendation No. 4

Cabinet level committees, with their memberships and assignments fixed by the President, are necessary in crucial areas in the conduct of foreign affairs where the issues transcend the responsibility of any single department and where Presidential consideration or decision is necessary.

The foreign affairs requirements are but a part of the national requirements of the United States. In the formulation, execution, and coordination of the policies to meet these requirements, the ultimate responsibility lies with the President. In the main, this process takes place at the department and agency level, but on certain crucial problems Presidential consideration and often Presidential decision will be necessary.

In our first report, Part Two, the Executive Office of the President, attention is called to the desirability of the establishment of cabinet level national policy committees to advise the President in the instances where his consideration or decision is necessary. These committees, on a regular or ad hoc basis as required, will serve as a systematic means of providing the President with balanced advice on the critical international problems of the day which transcend the responsibilities of the State Department or any other single department.

Likewise, as recommended in our first report, the President should be free to select the membership of the Cabinet-level committees dealing with foreign affairs, and to determine their assignments and the scope of their authority. Since the President cannot be compelled to follow, or even listen to the advice of any particular body, no attempt should be made to legislate specifically on this subject. Instead, general enabling legislation should provide a flexible framework within which the President may act.

The need for Cabinet-level committees on the conduct of foreign affairs, as emphasized above, exists only where Presidential consideration or decision is required on matters transcending the responsibilites of a single department. In a great number of foreign affairs matters this requirement will not be present. The Cabinet-level committees should not, therefore, supplant the State Department as a staff arm of the President, and the State Department in this role should be the major coordinating force within the executive branch on foreign affairs matters. Likewise, the Cabinet-level committee device must be carefully controlled so that the committees confine themselves to producing integrated advice to the President and do not become additional foreign affairs agencies in the executive branch which themselves have to be coordinated.

Recommendation No. 5

The successful functioning of Cabinet-level and other interdepartmental committees in the foreign affairs area should be facilitated by the assistance of specific institutional aids in the Executive Office and the State Department.

The Cabinet-level and interdepartmental committees cannot function successfully without specific institutional aids. The staff secretary to the President, whose appointment is recommended in our report, General Management of the Executive Branch, should keep the President advised of policy issues being considered by the principal Cabinet-level committees, and of any overlapping of assignments or conflicts which may exist. Each permanent or semi-permanent Cabinet-level committee, moreover, such as the present National Security Council and National Advisory Council, will ordinarily require a full-time executive secretary, and a small nucleus of staff supplemented by additional staff drawn from the regular policy units of the departments and agencies participating in the work of the various committees. By this means the essential secretariat service and staff work will be furnished. Through these institutional aids coordination of high-level foreign affairs matters should be greatly facilitated and, indeed, the issues for Presidential consideration should be so narrowed as to relieve the President in practice of what would otherwise be a heavy burden.

Similarly, staff and secretariat assistance should be provided for interdepartmental committees below the Cabinet level. In most instances this assistance should be provided by the State Department, which at present is doing considerable work of this kind. In special cases, however, other departments or agencies may furnish these aids. The activities of these interdepartmental committees should also be subject to scrutiny by the President's staff secretary.

·   ·   ·   ·   ·   ·   ·

C. Role of the Department of State

(1) Report and Recommendations to the Congress by the Commission on Organization of the Executive Branch of the Government Concerning the Role of the Department of State in the Formulation of Foreign Policy, Submitted, February 21, 1949.[8]

[EXCERPTS]

·   ·   ·   ·   ·   ·   ·

2. THE RELATIONSHIP OF THE STATE DEPARTMENT TO THE OTHER DEPARTMENTS AND AGENCIES

Active participation of the departments and agencies other than the State Department in all phases of present-day foreign affairs imposes severe strains on the organizational structure of the Government. These other departments and agencies display an increasing tendency to establish policies or to make policy interpretations which are not coordinated with the foreign policies and interpretations of the State Department. The State Department, in turn, does not always coordinate its policies with over-all United States national policies. With the conduct of foreign affairs no longer the exclusive province of the State Department, coordinated action by the State Department and some 45 other units with foreign affairs activities is a sine qua non for efficient and effective dispatch of business. Until such action is achieved, the line of command and supervision from the President down through the department heads to subordinate levels will remain unclear, indecisive, and ineffective.

This new situation in the foreign affairs field does not mean, however, that

8 *Ibid.*, p. 11.

the State Department has become just another executive department. Its statutory authority, basically unchanged since 1789, definitely fixes its role as a staff specialist and arm of the President in the conduct of foreign affairs and leaves its duties flexible and elastic. The other departments and agencies, in contrast, derive their foreign affairs authority through direct grants from the Congress which spell out the substantive tasks to be accomplished, usually in considerable detail. In essence, the State Department functions can be described as relating to the means or procedures of conducting foreign relations, whereas the organic statutes of the other departments and agencies pertain more to substantive matters, e.g. powers over fissionable materials, loans, communications, aviation, exports, imports, and the like. Coordination of all these varied activities obviously cannot be directed from the Presidential level. A large part must be delegated by the President to the State Department as his staff agency.

On certain crucial issues, however, coordination of foreign policy formulation and execution must come from the President or his executive office. To date the principal response to this need for high-level integration has been the development of specialized interdepartmental bodies at the cabinet level to advise the President on certain aspects of foreign affairs, such as national security and international finance. The absence of similar mechanisms in other important areas, particularly where foreign affairs touch upon domestic affairs, tends to give the President a partial and limited perspective in reaching decisions and to leave a substantial amount of policy execution to be coordinated on a "hit or miss" basis.

A final complicating factor in present-day governmental organization for the conduct of foreign affairs is the looseness and variation in organization of foreign affairs activities in the other departments and agencies. Some important departments have more than one bureau or office involved in foreign affairs but have no mechanism whereby the department head is able to coordinate the international activities of his own department. This results not only in confusion within a particular department but also places an added administrative burden upon the State Department which must seek not only to coordinate interdepartmental activity but activity within another department as well. Thus once again an important requirement of clear power of command and a clear chain of command is reemphasized.

3. THE INTERNAL ORGANIZATION OF THE STATE DEPARTMENT

The organizational difficulties of the State Department and the Foreign Service stem more from practical than legal sources. By and large the Secretary of State in legal theory is in command of the Department itself. In the case of the Foreign Service the Secretary's theoretical power in substantive matters is also clear. On the administrative side, however, ambiguous language in the Foreign Service Act of 1946 has tended to strengthen the traditional status of the career service as a semi-independent organization.

The practical difficulties in the main relate to impediments in the Secretary's chain of command and to his need for more adequate staff assistance and procedures. As a result, the Secretary and the Under-Secretary have an intolerable burden and little time for thoughtful and considered reflection on foreign affairs problems. The frequent and continued absences of the Secretary from the Department since the end of World War II, moreover, sets apart the job of head of the State Department from that of the usual department chief.

Numerous factors contribute to the existence of the present impediments in the Secretary's chain of command. One major factor is the existence of two personnel systems, one for the Foreign Service and the other for the Department, each separately administered. Serious unrest and bad feeling exist between the members of these two services and make effective administration an impossible job.

A second major impediment is the system whereby coordinate authority at the substantive policy action level is vested in two different types of units, geographic and economic, each of which reports to different heads who, in turn, report only to the Secretary and Under Secretary. This coordinate authority arrangement necessitates an elaborate and time-consuming system of lateral clearance (in part through excessive use of the committee device), prevents the fixing of responsibility, and tends to foster undesirable duplication of work.

Other significant and disturbing factors, less comprehensive in character, which tend to fragmentize the Department and thereby weaken the internal chain of command, include the following:

a. The Lack of Adequate Utilization of Staff Aids and Procedures

The heavy demands on the time of the Secretary and Under Secretary make it particularly essential that smooth working procedures exist for assembling and correlating staff advice on important policy matters and, conversely, for keeping the heads of action and other units informed of top level decisions and the reasons therefor. The postwar establishment of the Executive Secretariat and the Policy Planning Staff represents steps in the right direction, and both should be strengthened and more effective use made of their resources.

b. The Need at the Top Command Level for Better Public Relations and Utilization of Public Opinion

Today, American and foreign public opinion are both vital factors in the conduct of foreign affairs. At present the Assistant Secretary, Public Affairs, is burdened with operational duties of the foreign information and educational exchange programs and is not a participant in high-level policy formulation. Furthermore, the State Department's relationships with the press and other media of public information are extremely weak.

c. The Need for an Effective Intelligence Organization in the State Department

The weakest and least effective unit in the State Department today is the one known as Research and Intelligence. This situation arises largely because of non-acceptance of the intelligence personnel by certain influential segments of the Department, particularly the geographic offices, and from a basic misconception on all sides, including the intelligence unit itself, of the intelligence needs of the State Department. At present there appears to be an overemphasis on pure research, the bulk of which is not utilized within the Department. The relationships with the Central Intelligence Agency, moreover, which at present partake of rivalry rather than cooperation, require correction.

d. The Imposition on the State Department of Program Operational Responsibility

In the years since the recent World War the State Department has tended more and more to assume responsibility for program operations, either as the direct operator or as an active coordinator. In some instances these responsibilities have been given the State Department because of the absence of any other agency in the Government to do the job. This situation throws needless burdens on the Secretary and Under Secretary. The regular units of the State Department, however, are not presently equipped or oriented to handle such programs. Finally, the creation of new and separate units inside the State Department to operate these programs increases the difficulties of internal and interdepartmental coordination.

All these factors, taken together, contribute to the low esteem in which the State Department is held in the eyes of the Congress, the press, the general public, and, indeed, of many of its own personnel. Organizational reforms, while not a panacea for the State Department's ills, can as a minimum, chart for it a truer course in these difficult times.

. . . .

C. Recommendations Relating to the State Department and the Foreign Service

These recommendations, based on the organizational concepts previously set forth, fall into two general categories. First, general recommendations defining the role of the State Department in the conduct of foreign affairs and, second, specific recommendations of internal organizational reforms.

1. Recommendations Relating to the Role of the State Department

Recommendation No. 6

The State Department should concentrate on obtaining definition of proposed objectives for the United States in foreign affairs, on formulating proposed policies in conjunction with other departments and agencies to achieve those objectives, and on recommending the choice and timing of the use of various instruments to carry out foreign policies so formulated.

The ultimate responsibility within the executive branch in the determination of United States objectives and in formulating, executing, and coordinating foreign policies lies with the President. Under him, the State Department is cast in the role of the staff specialist in foreign affairs, and, pursuant to Presidential delegation, its role will involve leadership in defining and developing United States foreign policies, in determining the means and timing of their accomplishment through employment of the available instruments, in the recording of such policies, and in seeing to it that such policies are explained at home and abroad. These responsibilities necessarily will mean that, except for coordination in crucial areas where Cabinet-level committees are involved, the State Department will be the focal point for coordination of foreign affairs activities throughout the Government.

The State Department is not, however, the sole unit of the executive branch for determination of the objectives of the United States in world affairs or for formulating and executing foreign policies to achieve those objectives. Many other governmental departments and agencies, by reason of the present-day blending of the domestic and foreign aspects of national problems and by reason of operations abroad, are sources of policy considerations in the conduct of foreign affairs. The State Department should consult with and advise these other departments and agencies for the purpose of bringing their experience to bear in the formulation of foreign policies and of assisting them in administering particular instruments of foreign policy so as to achieve desired objectives in a consistent manner. The agency charged with responsibility for action should not, however, be required to obtain the concurrence of other agencies prior to taking action.

It is sound to adopt the principle that the department or agency with the power to exercise an instrument of foreign policy should be looked to, and relied upon, by the State Department to gather the necessary facts within the special competence of the particular department or agency on a world-wide basis; to evaluate those facts; to propose policies or programs within its power to execute; and to execute the programs agreed upon in accordance with established policy. These other departments and agencies must be organized internally so as to be able to meet the State Department's requests promptly and, if they are still unable to render these services adequately, the President should take measures to ensure the correction of their shortcomings. The State Department then would be free to concentrate on coordination within the executive branch, particularly on seeing that conflicts are resolved, making sure for the President that other departments and agencies do not, as in the past, slide out of their responsibilities, and exercising general guidance so that all the Government's foreign affairs activities are conducted in consonance.

In this manner, the State Department will be able to discontinue the bulk of the specialized functions it has recently been, or now is, performing in the fields of foodstuffs, petroleum and other fuels, aviation, shipping, labor, welfare, and the like. It will, however, have to retain a small group of specialists in these fields as expert advisers and as the focal point for consultation and coordination with other agencies. Furthermore, insofar as certain other departments and agencies are oriented to act only in terms of domestic interests and pressures, the State Department on occasion may still have to assume more positive leadership, but it should do so only after the particular failure has been brought to the Chief Executive's attention.

Recommendation No. 7

The State Department as a general rule should not be given responsibility for the operation of specific programs, whether overseas or at home.

This proposition as a general rule is desirable. Difficulties in application, however, exist, especially in that the sudden thrusting on the executive branch of responsibility for new world-wide programs found it with little or nothing in the way of machinery to carry out such programs. As a consequence the State Department has had to assume responsibility for activities such as liquidation of surplus property abroad, the foreign information program, and the educational exchange program.

The recent creation of the Economic Cooperation Administration to handle the economic assistance program in Europe and in the Far East prevented the placing of this additional program burden on the State Department. In this instance the advantages in creating a new agency appear to have been overwhelming and the solution is in accord with the principle of this recommendation.

The Government's responsibilities for occupied areas in Germany, Austria and the Far East are divided,[9] with the State Department being assigned responsibility for formulation of policy and the Army Department for execution and administration of policy. From the outset, serious frictions have existed in this arrangement. The basic difficulty has been the uncertainty and delay in the preparation and enunciation of policy and the consequent tendency of the administrative agency, through its daily decisions, to make its own policy. Other factors have been the attempt to handle occupied-areas problems below the secretarial level, without clear definition of responsibility and without clear channels for the transmission of policy guidance from the State Department to the theater commanders.

The transfer of responsibility for the civil or non-military aspects of administration of occupied areas from the Army Department to the State Department, leaving the garrison or other military functions to the Army Department, has been under frequent consideration during recent years. In the instant recommendation, it is proposed that the State Department not undertake operational programs unless unusual circumstances exist. The present circumstances do not appear to be sufficiently unusual to call for an assumption of occupied areas responsibility by the State Department.

The machinery for administration of occupied areas, as well as that of logistical support, is presently supplied by the military establishment. It is wholly consistent with the concepts underlying this report that this adminis-

[9] Commissioners Acheson and Forrestal, by reason of the positions they occupy in the executive branch and their consequent direct relationship to certain immediate occupied areas questions, have abstained from participation in the views expressed in this and the two following paragraphs dealing with occupied areas. This nonparticipation relates only to the occupied areas discussion and not to the balance of the recommendations or to the other portions of the report.

trative machinery be located outside the State Department, as, for example, in the military establishment or in new administration of overseas affairs, but that it receive its instructions from, and report to, the Secretary of State. Thus a direct channel of communication would exist between the theater commanders, as high commissioners or otherwise, and the Secretary of State, who in turn is directly under the President, who is the Commander in Chief. Likewise, the State Department would not have to build up, by transfer from the Army Department or otherwise, a self-sufficient group within its own organization responsible for the non-military administrative phases of occupied areas.

In certain other areas, governmental agencies are now in existence to which the State Department's present operation responsibilities for engineering, rehabilitation, and like programs could be transferred. Likewise, the functions of visa control and munitions export control should be transferred from the State Department to the Justice and Commerce Departments, respectively.

In two instances it appears that operational responsibility, for the present at least, must remain in the State Department in default of any other satisfactory location in the executive branch. The one is the educational exchange program which the task force report recommended be transferred to the Federal Security Agency. The Federal Security Agency does not have the orientation, experience, or skills to carry on work in this broad cultural field, and therefore the State Department should continue to administer this program.

The second instance is the foreign information program with its heavy load of operational and technical duties in connection with the radio broadcasting activities of the "Voice of America." Here, the task force recommended transfer to a Government corporation which would make it possible to keep the operation responsive to State Department policy guidance. A strong motivation behind this suggestion is the urgent need for freeing the Assistant Secretary, Public Affairs, from devoting his personal attention to details of an operational nature and for making him available as a high-level staff adviser and chief of press and other public relations for the Secretary of State. This end can be equally well attained, however, by reorganization within the public affairs area. One possibility is the creation of a new post under the Assistant Secretary of a "general manager" to whom would be assigned full operational authority and responsibility for the "Voice of America" and such other portions of the foreign information program as are primarily operational in character.

Recommendation No. 8

The State Department should continue to discharge its traditional responsibilities of representation, reporting, and negotiation.

The State Department's principal duties under presidential direction should be:

a. To establish, man, maintain, and conduct the machinery of diplomatic relations, correspondence, conversations, negotiation, and agreement with other governments except where, in technical or special cases, parts of these activities are assigned to other departments or agencies, and even then the State Department should observe and counsel their conduct.

b. To recruit and maintain personnel adequate for its tasks at home and abroad, protected as a career service by tradition as well as law from invasion by political or other demoralizing influence.

c. To give guidance and direction to our diplomatic missions and delegations abroad, to review and distribute to other interested agencies the intelligence gathered by the State Department, to see to it that the recommendations of the missions are acknowledged and considered but leaving to them, wherever possible, ways and means of accomplishment.

d. To aid the President in the selection of qualified persons other than career servants whenever he or the Congress determines they should be drawn from the public at large for particular purposes or particular missions.

e. To assume primary responsibility for foreign relations aspects of general policies followed by all peacetime missions overseas, including occupation forces and special missions and programs, and to this end to see that the activities of all American officers abroad are reported to, and are observed and counseled by, the chief of the American diplomatic mission if such officers are temporary, and if permanent and not involving operational programs, that such officers are made part of the diplomatic mission itself.

f. To recommend to the President any participation and the extent of our participation in international bodies and conferences and to supervise our delegations when established except as the President or Congress otherwise determines in special cases. This involves consultation and coordination with other departments and agencies.

g. To preserve with the Senate and House a continuous working system of liaison and intercommunication on all matters affecting foreign affairs, in order to reach mutual comprehension, confidence, and agreement.

2. RECOMMENDATIONS RELATING TO INTERNAL ORGANIZATION

Recommendation No. 9

The State Department should be organized so that the Secretary of State, legally and practically, is in command of the Department and the Foreign Service, so that the line of command from the Secretary of State through the Under and Assistant Secretaries to the lowest level is clear and unencumbered, and so that the Secretary of State is provided with adequate staff services at the top level. The Department should also have authority and funds to equip itself with persons of the highest capacity to represent this country at international organizations and conferences.

This recommendation is fundamental. Its objectives, in terms of the internal organization of the State Department, are to simplify the structure, clarify the Secretary's authority, make his lines of command clear and free from interference, separate staff responsibility from action or line responsibility, and relieve the Secretary and Under Secretary from the burdensome details which now come to them, and thereby afford them an opportunity for thoughtful study of major policy problems.

Representation of the United States at international organizations and conferences by individuals with special abilities for the peculiar type of task involved will relieve the Secretary and other top Departmental officials from the additional heavy burdens which have been imposed on them since the end of the recent war. While the United Nations Participation Act — with the amendments currently proposed — equips the Government with permanent representatives and staff at the United Nations headquarters, problems still remain in regard to departmental assistance at meetings of the General Assembly. Similar problems arise in connection with the greatly increased need for representation at such meetings as the Council of Foreign Ministers, Council of Foreign Ministers of the American Republics, and the like. Furthermore, a need exists for providing State Department representation at conferences dealing with telecommunications, aviation, shipping, agriculture, labor, and many other matters.

The only present means of providing representatives is to tear the Department apart to meet each individual situation. At one time in the past year, for example, the Secretary of State and all but one of the Assistant Secretaries were absent from the Department on missions to international meetings. The burden on those left behind was excessive and the functioning of the Department was seriously impaired.

The Secretary of State and his principal assistants are needed in Washington. The Government should be able to send high level officials, with adequate staffs, to represent the United States at international organizations and conferences. When not so engaged, these men should, in part at least, be able to spend their time in the Department advising and aiding the Secretary in the formation of the policies which they may have to handle. In this way they can be fully informed of all facets of United States policies.

This over-all recommendation will be amplified in various respects by the recommendations which follow. In reaching these conclusions the Commission and its task force have kept in close touch with the organizational plans for the State Department developed under Secretary Marshall and Under Secretary Lovett. The Commission is happy to say that its thinking and that of the State Department are in complete accord on principles, and, except for certain particulars in which the Commission's recommendations are more far-reaching than those of the State Department, the conclusions of both on specific changes are in agreement.

By way of preface to these recommendations it is first desirable to outline the general pattern of internal organization which will facilitate achievement of the objectives of the over-all recommendation. This pattern, shown graphically on pages 42 and 43 together with the present top level organization, is as follows:

1. The strengthening of the Secretary and Under Secretary level by the addi-

tion of two Deputy Under Secretaries, the one to act in matters of substance, and the other, as "general manager," to administer the Department and the overseas service.

2. The fixing of responsibility for action in five line units under five Assistant Secretaries. Four of these Assistant Secretaries would head up regional units, with the responsibility for the four traditional geographic segments of the world. A fifth would be in charge of relationships with international organizations, including the United Nations and its affiliated organizations.

Both the regional and international organization Assistant Secretaries would *at the action level* be responsible for and be equipped, in terms of personnel, to deal with not solely "political" aspects of foreign affairs, as is the basic conception of the duties of the existing geographic office directors, but for all aspects, whether they be political, economic, public opinion, intelligence, or administration.

The Assistant Secretary, Public Affairs, would also have top, but not immediate, responsibility for action in connection with the operations of the foreign information programs and of the educational exchange programs. Action in these public affairs fields, however, is not of the same character as that required of the regional and international organization Assistant Secretaries and, moreover, the Assistant Secretary, Public Affairs, should organize his unit, by the "general manager" device referred to earlier or otherwise, so that he can devote the bulk of his own time to his staff duties at the top level of the State Department.

3. The provision of adequate *staff* services to the Secretary and Under Secretary and to the line units consisting of:

a. An Assistant Secretary, Economic and Social Affairs, with the dual function of supervising a staff group who would afford a source of expert advice from a a global instead of a regional point of view on economic, social, and other specialized aspects of foreign affairs and who would be the channel of communication and the point of coordination on interdepartmental relations within the executive branch in the foreign affairs field.

b. An Assistant Secretary for congressional relations on a full-time basis.

c. An Assistant Secretary, Public Affairs, referred to previously, who would serve as the high-level adviser on domestic and foreign public opinion and as the chief of press and other media of public relations.

d. The Legal Adviser as at present.

e. An active high-level Operations Committee, under the direct supervision of the Deputy Under Secretary for substantive matters, assisted by the Executive Secretariat to insure coordination between the staff and action levels. This Committee is not to be an additional layer in the line of command but a device to facilitate communication of information, coordination of related activities, and generally to promote teamwork between the action and staff units.

f. A Planning Adviser supported by a broad-gauge staff to function as an anticipator of the problems which will arise tomorrow because of today's policies.

g. A Special Assistant, Intelligence, who, as chief of intelligence, would supervise the centralized intelligence activities of the Department, serve as a source of guidance to the decentralized intelligence arms of the regional units, and provide the focal point for coordination with the Central Intelligence Agency.

This pattern of organization means that the State Department would have a Secretary, Under Secretary, two Deputy Under Secretaries, eight Assistant Secretaries, and three senior officials of rank equivalent to that of Assistant Secretary. It contemplates abolition of the posts of Counselor, Assistant Secretary, Occupied Areas, and Assistant Secretary, Transportation and Communications. The net increase in senior officials over the present scheme of organization is three, namely the two Deputy Under Secretaries and one additional Assistant Secretary. It will further have the effect of eliminating the Director General of the Foreign Service and the Special Assistant, Press Relations.

The office level as an additional "layer" in the Department's structure will also disappear except possibly on the administrative side, thus removing a blockage point in the Secretary's line of command. Deputies to the various Assistant Secretaries on the substantive side, equivalent in experience and stature to the present office directors, will, of course, still be required.

Finally, the pattern of organization set forth above can succeed only on the fundamental premise, set forth in Recommendation No. 20 hereinafter, that the two personnel services — the Foreign Service and the Department Service — be amalgamated into a single service responsive to the Secretary.

a. RECOMMENDATIONS PERTAINING TO ACTION RESPONSIBILITIES

Recommendation No. 10

The fundamental world objectives and foreign policies of the United States should be continuously defined so as to permit delegation of authority to the line units to take action within the objectives and policies so defined.

The State Department, since the war, has at all levels been too much concerned with "details" and not enough with "policy." The Secretary-Under Secretary top command is overburdened by being drawn down into participation in too many daily decisions with the consequence that the entire Department lives day-to-day, and policies tend to be determined in terms of short-range decisions.

The State Department began in recent years to endeavor to reduce the United States objectives and foreign policies to writing. Continued emphasis on this admittedly difficult task, and on making such written statements available to all concerned, will provide the means by which the regional Assistant Secretaries and the international organization Assistant Secretary may assume responsibility for all but the most crucial decisions and afford the top command time for reflection and long-range thinking. Furthermore, this process will make possible the relation of objectives within and between countries and regions and between regions and international organizations, thereby leading to greater consistency of policy. Likewise, it will furnish a means for more intelligent guidance to chiefs of missions abroad and relieve them of the necessity of referring all details to Washington.

Recommendation No. 11

Within the action units responsibility for decisions should be clearly fixed with adequate machinery by which the decision-maker can consult but never be required to obtain the concurrence of staff advisory units or other action units.

The responsibility for the formulation of foreign policy proposals and for action in line with approved policies should be placed on the four regional Assistant Secretaries and the international organization Assistant Secretary. Instances of unclear jurisdiction should be resolved at the top level through the Deputy Under Secretary on the substantive side, particularly through the Operations Committee, of which he would be deputy chairman. Each Assistant Secretary will have, as an integral part of his line operation, the functional advisers on economic and social problems, who are now under the Assistant Secretary, Economic Affairs. Likewise, each Assistant Secretary should have a very small group of intelligence research personnel and information specialists.

Within the regional and the international organization systems the responsibility for recommending action in a given case should be assigned to a single officer below the Assistant Secretary level. The present intolerable system of coordinate authority whereby concurrences in different chains of command within the Department are required should be eliminated. The action officer should, however, consult staff advisory groups or other action units and report the results of such recommendations with his recommended action. Adequate machinery to enforce this consultation process should be developed through the Eexecutive Secretariat. Every consultant should be allowed to attach to any document his comment of protest if he dissents, after his views have been considered. The action on such recommendations should be restricted to the five Assistant Secretaries concerned, the Deputy Under Secretaries, the Under Secretary, and the Secretary. By this means the present evils of the geographic-functional conflict can be materially reduced.

The role of the Assistant Secretary, International Organizations, is different from that of the four regional Assistant Secretaries in one important respect. While participating in the formulation of foreign policy he should not be an additional agent in this field, but should, so far as possible, obtain his policy guidance from the various regional units, the Planning Adviser, and from other staff advisers, probably largely through the Operations Committee. This difference lends emphasis to the conclusion that a properly conceived and executed regional scheme of organization can operate adequately to arrive at policies for multilateral dealings.

Recommendation No. 12

The five Assistant Secretaries with action responsibilities should serve as the focal points of contact between the Department and the overseas and international organization missions in both substantive and administrative matters.

The delegation of substantive authority to the four regional Assistant Secretaries and to one international organization Assistant Secretary should result in their being able to handle the bulk of substantive matters coming into the Department from missions at overseas points and at international organizations without reference to the top command of the Department. Concurrently, the Deputy Under Secretary for Administration should delegate to them adequate tools of administration with which to meet the needs of these missions. While the Deputy Under Secretary on the administrative side must at all times retain firm control over the determination and carrying out of administrative policies, particularly with respect to inspections, much of the day-to-day work in connection with personnel administration, organizational planning, budgetary and other matters with respect to overseas and other missions can be more efficiently performed on a decentralized basis in the action units. Within the State Department, however, the administrative aspects of the action units should be decentralized only to the extent the Secretary, acting through the Deputy Under Secretary for Administration, deems it advisable.

The delegation of authority to act and the decentralization of tools of administration to the line Assistant Secretaries can, moreover, be advantageously carried one step further by giving greater authority (but not autonomy) to the missions abroad and at international organizations, both in regard to substantive action and administration. This further delegation and decentralization must, of course, be a matter of secretarial policy and must depend upon the capacity of the various chiefs of missions. Progress in this direction is essential, however, because at the present time the officers in the Department in Washington tend to ride the field missions with much too tight a rein and endeavor to give them much too meticulous guidance.

Recommendation No. 13

The chief of each United States foreign mission should be the responsible American spokesman for the area or country to which he is assigned. He should observe and counsel all United States activities therein, and he should be responsible for administration of his mission.

In its new role in the conduct of foreign affairs, the United States frequently engages in two general types of activity in foreign countries. The one is the traditional representation and reporting activities of the diplomatic missions; the other, the special operational activities of various economic, social, and other programs.

As to the traditional representation and reporting activities, it is desirable not only to have all personnel responsible to the chief of the mission but also part of the mission. There has been less serious question of this proposition since the 1939 consolidation of the Commerce and Agriculture overseas services with the Foreign Service. In subsequent recommendations herein, however, it is proposed that a small number of specialist attachés who, as part of their work, fill the information needs of the other departments and agencies, be designated by those other departments and agencies. These specialists while on overseas service should, as temporary or reserve officers, be a part of the Foreign Affairs Service and should be responsible to the chief of the mission for their work, deportment, and for purposes of administration. They should, moreover, be an integral part of the mission to which they are assigned and their services would be utilized by the chief of mission and the State Department as well as by the department by which they are appointed. This line relationship to the chief of the mission is essential and his authority should include:

a. The power to return to the United States any specialist on duty for reasons related to improper deportment or for unsatisfactory work performance, subject always to final decision by the Secretary of State.
b. The right to object to assigning a given individual to the mission, subject always to the Secretary of State having the final word.
c. The right to express disagreement with (but not to prevent transmission of) reports of specialists designated by the other agencies.
d. The ultimate authority overseas with respect to foreign affairs aspects of programs operations, such as those currently being performed by Economic Cooperation Administration.

In the case of operational activities abroad, where they are directly under the State Department, the personnel involved should also be part of the mission. Where such tasks are assigned to other departments or agencies, whether they be economic, social, technical, or otherwise, they may be separately headed and administered at home. It is unworkable and dangerous, however, to have American spokesmen and operators abroad dealing with foreign nations who are independent of the ambassadors or ministers and who are not responsible to them for supervision and coordination.

b. RECOMMENDATIONS PERTAINING TO STAFF
RESPONSIBILITIES

Recommendation No. 14

The Assistant Secretary, Economic and Social Affairs, should concentrate on providing a source of economic, social, and other advice from a global standpoint and upon serving as a channel of communication and focal point of coordination with the other departments and agencies in the executive branch.

The staff advisers under the Assistant Secretary, Economic and Social Affairs, must be *consulted* by the action units, but their *concurrence* in proposed action should *not* be required. A very small group of functional advisers should suffice for these purposes and they should not seek to duplicate as at present the staffs of other departments and agencies or the functional specialists assigned to the State Department's regional action units. The other departments and agencies should, in the main, be relied upon for information within their special competences, both domestic and foreign.

At the same time, it must be recognized that the division between the action and staff units heretofore drawn has in certain respects a delusive simplicity. There are limited occasions when the action requirements of the Department will transcend the four regional and the one international organization units and where action with respect to individual countries must be taken on a global basis. An example is the handling of trade agreements. To this limited extent this staff unit is a hybrid organization with some action responsibilities. The top command of the State Department must take particular care that this limited action responsibility does not afford an "empire-building" device whereby the unit headed by the Assistant Secretary, Economic and Social Affairs again seeks to have coordinate authority with the actions units, and that the geographic versus functional conflict does not again cripple the Department. The overseeing of this particular problem is one which the Deputy Under Secretary on the substantive side must keep under his direct and continuous surveillance.

Recommendation No. 15

The Assistant Secretary, Congressional Affairs, should be responsible on a full-time basis for establishing a coordinated program of two-way liaison with the Congress.

The recent experience of endeavoring to take care of congressional relations on a part-time basis has demonstrated the need for full-time, high-level direction in this field. The Assistant Secretary, Congressional Relations, should participate actively in top-level policy formulation in the State Department. He should be able to marshal personnel from anywhere within the Department to present to the Congress special phases of foreign affairs problems. Conversely, he should be able to arrange to bring to the Department the views of congressional leaders on international matters.

It is not intended that this Assistant Secretary should serve as the exclusive channel of communication between the State Department and the Congress. On frequent occasions the Secretary and the Under Secretary will be called upon to consult with congressional leaders. In addition, the Assistant Secretary will have to be able to call upon various specialists within the Department to provide information on technical phases of foreign affairs activities. He will also have to work with the budget officers of the State Department in connection with appropriation matters. Where congressional contacts are made directly by other departmental officials, the Assistant Secretary should be kept informed. Finally, as a minor but significant part of his work, the Assistant Secretary should be the medium whereby the State Department provides helpful services to the members of Congress. In all these duties the Assistant Secretary must have adequate staff to aid in the preparation of material, in following important issues, and in performing various services.

Recommendation No. 16

The Assistant Secretary, Public Affairs, should concentrate on serving as a high-level staff adviser on domestic and foreign public opinion, and as chief of press relations and other media of public relations for the State Department.

Today American public opinion is a vital factor in the conduct of foreign affairs, and the State Department must not only estimate and evaluate the views of the American public in foreign affairs matters but also must win its acceptance and support on the paramount issues. Furthermore, the opinions of the peoples of foreign countries, as contrasted with their governments, also bear upon the conduct of American foreign relations.

The weakest link with the American public is the absence in the State Department of a single high official responsible for the vital contacts with the press and other media of public information. The Assistant Secretary, Public Affairs, should fill this void. Furthermore, he should be the staff officer advising the Secretary and Under Secretary, and also the action units, on the public opinion aspects of any problem. Finally, he should observe and give policy guidance to foreign information and educational exchange programs, the operational responsibility for which should be in a "general manager" reporting to the Assistant Secretary. A precedent for the relationship envisaged between the Assistant Secretary and the "general manager" is that which recently existed between the Under Secretary and the Coordinator for Aid to Greece and Turkey where the latter, with effective backing from the Under Secretary, ran the operational program without interference from other segments of the Department.

Recommendation No. 17

The Secretary of State should continue the present high-level planning activity under a Planning Adviser, with special emphasis on freeing him and his staff of current problems, upon providing him with broad-gauge staff, and upon utilization by him of competent advice from inside and outside the Government.

The present Policy Planning Staff has been a valuable aid to the top command of the State Department, especially as an "anticipator" of problems. At present, however, its effectiveness appears to have been lessened by a tendency of the top command to utilize it on day-to-day problems, by its almost exclusive reliance for its staff on individuals with Foreign Service backgrounds, and by its reluctance to draw sufficiently upon the resources of other departments and agencies except possibly those of the National Military Establishment. These weaknesses should be corrected.

In addition, the Secretary of State should endeavor to bring together a small group of highly competent and reliable individuals from outside the Government to counsel the Planning Adviser. This group should not, either on request or on its own initiative, give affirmative advice as to what the world objectives and foreign policies of the United States should be, but it should concentrate on problems submitted to it by the Planning Adviser and in advising him on the probable consequences of various proposed courses of action. This group might include former ambassadors, other Government officials, leaders from business, commerce and labor, and educators.

Recommendation No. 18

The centralized intelligence unit in the State Department should be reorganized and reoriented, and intelligence advisers should be assigned to the regional action units.

The present misconception of the intelligence needs of the State Department must be eradicated. The creation of revitalized regional units on the action side should tend to correct the current deplorable attitude of the existing geographic officers toward intelligence. The reorientation of the centralized intelligence activities by de-emphasis of academic research and increased attention on current estimates and evaluations and to serving and making use of the Central Intelligence Agency is required. At present, except for the Special Projects Staff, the Biographic Information Division, and the routine library, reference and collection functions, the existing intelligence unit appears to expend too much of its energies on projects which do not contribute sufficiently to the main work of the State Department.

The task force report contemplates the decentralization of the present area research personnel as intact units to the four new regional action units. This move would involve almost 5 percent of the personnel of the entire Department.

The Commission is not in favor of this step.

It is recognized, however, that the new regional units, as self-contained line organizations, will need intelligence advisers just as they also need economic and social advisers. These regional intelligence advisers should perform staff functions within the action units and should not themselves engage in research work. Their responsibilities should be to understand the foreign policy problems of the action units, to recommend particular intelligence research projects to the central intelligence unit, and to follow up on the performance of such research by the central unit. In addition, they should assist the central unit in the preparation of "political" estimates for the Central Intelligence Agency and for other departments. It is recommended that these regional intelligence advisers be assigned to the regional units from the present research divisions.

The really significant intelligence needs of the Department must be met on a centralized basis. This central unit, under a Special Assistant to the Secretary as at present, should occupy a dual position. In relation to the intelligence advisers in the regional units, the central unit should be both a source of general intelligence guidance and a channel of communication with the Central Intelligence Agency and the intelligence organizations of other departments. As an intelligence unit itself it should be a device by which the Secretary and Under Secretary can obtain expert evaluations and check on information coming from the action units.

The Planning Adviser in particular should make full use of the Special Assistant and of his central staff in connection with his planning activities. For this task the Special Assistant should build up a group of mature individuals with high talent in analysis and evaluation, who should have full access to all information coming into the Department. This group must be supported by a body of skilled researchers.

The central unit should not, however, seek to monitor all information coming into the State Department from abroad, but should concentrate on tasks assigned to it by the Secretary, the Under Secretary, and the Planning Adviser, and on issues raised through its relations with the Central Intelligence Agency. It should continue to include, of course, the library, reference and collection functions, but should be organized internally so that the Special Assistant does not have to devote the bulk of his time to administrative and supervisory duties.

A prime responsibility of the chief of the intelligence unit is in relation to the Central Intelligence Agency and the intelligence units of other departments. He should be responsible for setting up effective machinery by which the Central Intelligence Agency and the other departments can obtain "political" estimates from the State Department. Conversely, he must see to it that the State Department gets evaluations and other data from the Central Intelligence Agency and the other departments which are useful to the State Department in formulating its policies and programs. In part he should be able to do this through membership on the Intelligence Advisory Committee. In these various ways he will be better able to make evaluations for the top command of the State Department and, in particular, to check on the recommendations of the regional units.

Recommendation No. 19

The Operations Committee, with the Under Secretary or Deputy Under Secretary for substantive matters as chairman, and staffed by the Executive Secretariat, should be made the coordinating link between the action and staff segments and between the various units within each segment.

Serious present weaknesses are the lack of any systematic means of bringing problems to the top command level and, conversely, of ensuring that the various Assistant Secretaries are advised of what takes place at the top level.

High-level committees have been suggested on past occasions, but the efforts to place them in operation have proved abortive largely because of inadequate top-level support; the absence of any secretariat and staff assistance; and the inclusion of too many individuals as participants in the meetings. Failure to overcome the individualistic tradition of the Department whereby senior career officers insist upon direct access to the Secretary and Under Secretary has also been a factor.

The Operations Committee should meet frequently, perhaps daily. The Under Secretary, when present, should preside, although as a general rule the Deputy Under Secretary on the substantive side, as a kind of combined deputy chairman and executive secretary, would probably carry the bulk of the responsibility. The present Executive Secretariat should provide "secretarial" and "staff assistance." This assistance would include maintenance of a file on pending problems, preparation of agenda and organization of documentation for meetings, preparation of post-meeting reports and transmission of decisions to the heads of action units, and following up to make sure that action is actually taken.

The provision of a top-level head for the Operations Committee, particularly by making it the primary responsibility of the Deputy Under Secretary, plus the selection of a man for that post with the will to make the Committee work, and the provision of staff assistance by the Executive Secretariat, should meet two of the past difficulties which defeated less ambitious attempts. Confining the participants to Assistant Secretaries and other senior officials of equivalent rank, moreover, would reduce the membership of the Committee to workable size (approximately 12), thereby removing another objectionable feature. Finally, other recommendations, particularly the delineation of line and staff responsibilities and the amalgamation of the Foreign Service and Department personnel systems, should in time help break down the individualistic tradition and the atmosphere of distrust which have prevented similar committees from functioning successfully in the past.

C. RECOMMENDATIONS RELATING TO PERSONNEL

Recommendation No. 20

The personnel in the permanent State Department establishment in Washington and the personnel of the Foreign Service above certain levels should be amalgamated over a short period of years into a single foreign affairs service obligated to serve at home or overseas and constituting a safeguarded career group administered separately from the general Civil Service.

The State Department and the American embassies, legations, and consulates abroad, which together make up the diplomatic and consular machinery of the Nation, are now served by two separate groups of men and women, one "The Foreign Service of the United States" and the other enrolled under the ordinary Civil Service system. The two groups, in terms of American citizens, are approximately equal in size. This division of forces between a Foreign Service centering on a separate corps of officers, mostly stationed abroad but partly in key positions in Washington, and a group of employees who work chiefly at home is a source of serious friction and increasing inefficiency. Such a division of personnel in foreign affairs has been abandoned in all but a handful of countries. Among those in which it still exists, the United States is the only great power.

The division leads to jealousies and to inequality of compensation among people doing much the same work. The Foreign Service, through long periods of service abroad, undoubtedly looses contact with American domestic conditions. The Civil Service employees, who seldom or never serve abroad for any long period, fail often to understand other nations and appreciate foreign conditions.

The present conditions also lead to the existence of two administrative offices, one for each body of public servants, but both in the same household and dealing frequently with the same personnel questions. The Foreign Service is in law and practice largely self-administered, and is to some degree even independent of the Secretary of State.

In recommending the consolidation of the Foreign Service and the State Department Service into a single new Foreign Affairs Service, it is believed that for the present the consolidated service should be separate from the general Civil Service. The Commission's recommendations on the general Civil Service, in our report on Personnel Management, contemplate sweeping changes in the entire Civil Service personnel system. These changes will necessarily involve adjustments and experimentation extending over a period of years. Similarly, the consolidation of the Foreign Service and the State Department Service will also require the gradual solution of numerous problems in terms of practical circumstances. Consequently it is believed that the two reorganizations should for the present proceed on separate bases but that the top officials in both systems should keep in close touch with each other so that the guiding principles in both readjustments are not at variance.

Certain general principles for carrying out this consolidation are set forth in the task force report, Recommendation 15. The Commission is generally in accord with those principles. The list below reiterates some of those principles which warrant special emphasis, and restates others with certain modifications:

a. The members of the single new foreign affairs service should all be pledged to serve at home or abroad.

b. The consolidation should be *mandatory* but should be carried out *gradually* over a short period of years.

c. The consolidated service should include all personnel except (I) at the top level the Secretary, the Under Secretary, the Deputy Under Secretaries, the Assistant Secretaries, and others of comparable rank, and ambassadors and ministers, (II) certain technical personnel in programs such as foreign information, for whom the existence of comparable overseas assignments seems improbable, (III) at the lower levels, mechanical or subsidiary employees such as janitors, engineers, guards, and messengers, and all alien employees of whatever rank.

d. The consolidation should receive the continuous attention and support of the Secretary and the Under Secretary, with the direct execution being entrusted to the Deputy Under Secretary for Administration. Over-all policies and standards governing entrance, transfer, classification, examination, promotion, and retirement should be established by the Secretary, perhaps after consultation with a temporary advisory board with a membership such as that suggested by the task force report. Particular attention should be given to equalizing the time spent in the field with that at home.

e. The assignment of personnel within the consolidated system requires a flexible system of personnel administration so that the Secretary is free to draw upon not only the various talents within the service as he needs them, but also on qualified personnel from elsewhere in the executive branch and from outside the Government. This flexible system should also make it possible for members of the foreign affairs service to transfer to positions elsewhere in the executive branch for which they have the necessary qualifications. Under this principle the general, special, and staff personnel categories suggested in the task force report should be utilized as tools in personnel administration and not as rigid compartments to which considerations of caste and perquisites become attached.

f. The present Civil Service personnel of the State Department should enter the consolidated service on application and oral examination. This process must take into account the needs of the single service for personnel with special as well as general aptitudes, including certain aptitudes of primary importance in the Department at home as contrasted with the missions overseas. Departmental personnel who are unwilling to enter the new service but who are qualified for their present duties might be continued in their present posts on some special "limited service" basis or be given opportunities elsewhere in the government.

g. All members of the consolidated service of the same grade should have equal status in every respect, including compensation and retirement rights.

h. Recruitment and promotion policies should be varied and flexible so as to obtain and keep individuals with the different required qualifications, including especially resourcefulness and executive ability. Administration should be geared so as to place more responsibility on young men in the first 15 years of service. In the case of members with special aptitudes, they should be enlisted and promoted without reference to the versatility and elasticity expected of others with more general talents. This will necessarily involve recruitment of personnel at all levels and not merely at the bottom or present Class 6 level.

i. A temporary or reserve officer classification should be continued and should be open to (I) representatives of other departments and agencies nominated by them and acceptable to the State Department on personal and similar grounds who will serve abroad as technical reporters and attachés in the small number of cases where this service cannot be adequately performed by the new corps; (II) personnel to implement special programs such as the European Recovery Program or in other temporary capacities; and (III) applicants for admission to the general or special officer classifications who have passed the necessary examinations but who are awaiting appointment. These temporary or reserve officers should have status identical with the general and special officers of corresponding grade and should be paid and supported like other members of the corps, the funds, in the case of representatives of other departments and agencies, to come from grants to the single service from appropriations of the other departments and agencies.

j. The consolidated service should not be self-administered but subject to direction and inspection of the Secretary. For purposes of recruitment, examination, promotion, retirement, and inspection, the Secretary should have authority to set up special boards to assist him in an advisory capacity.

The departments and agencies other than the State Department will continue to have heavy requirements for information from overseas points. In the main these needs should be filled by the single foreign affairs service which should take active measures to recruit specialists from the other segments of the executive branch and from business, labor, and other sources. The Secretary of State should obtain advice from the other departments and agencies through interdepartmental consultation, but the existing Board of the Foreign Service, which represents the undesirable practice of administration by a committee, should be abolished.

In the limited number of cases where specialized technical reporting, or an unusual quantity of reporting or other special requirements exist, the other departments and agencies should designate and obtain appropriations for personnel for their overseas work. These individuals would be sent abroad as temporary or reserve officers in the single service (see subparagraph (*i*) above). While on such assignments they should constitute an integral part of the missions to which they are assigned and should serve the chiefs of mission and the State Department as well as the department or agency by which they are appointed and in which their career lies.

· · · · · · ·

D. Role of the Congress

(1) *Recommendations to the Congress by the Commission on Organization of the Executive Branch of the Government Concerning the Role of the Congress in the Formulation of Foreign Policy, Submitted, February 21, 1949.*[10]

[EXCERPT]

· · · · · ·

---

10 *Ibid.*, p. 23.

Recommendation No. 1

Legislation which grants new foreign affairs powers of an executive nature otherwise than to the President or to an established executive department or agency will normally cause serious difficulty in efficient administration. Such legislation should not be adopted unless there are overwhelming advantages in creating a new agency.

Each time the Congress creates a new agency with the power to employ a specified instrument of foreign policy, it weakens the executive establishment as a whole. Jurisdictional conflicts are immediately set in motion which increase the possibility of duplication and the burden of coordination. The latter is already so heavy on the President that many problems of coordination must be left untouched.

By giving the new powers to the President, the Congress would strengthen his executive power to integrate this new authority with already existing authority. By giving it to an existing department or agency, the burden of coordination would be transferred in large measure from the President to the head of the department or agency. Particular care, moreover, should be taken not to confer executive powers on independent commissions which are not responsible to the President. While the creation of independent bodies to discharge quasi-judicial and quasi-legislative functions will always be necessary, the grant to them of executive powers is contrary to the principles of sound organization and impedes the efficient conduct of foreign affairs.

Recommendation No. 2

Effective administration is not achieved by establishing by legislation the precise functions and membership of coordinating and advisory bodies within the executive branch.

The recent legislative practice of establishing interdepartment bodies with defined responsibilities over foreign affairs — e.g. National Security Council or National Advisory Council — tends to obscure the responsibility for making executive decisions, to make each of the bodies acquire the aspects of a new agency, and to encourage other interdepartmental groups to seek formal congressional sanction. All of these tendencies add up to weakening the power of the Chief Executive, a circumstance which in turn reduces his responsibility and complicates the administration of the executive branch. Such legislation does not assure better coordination in the executive branch, nor can it require the President to use the advice received. The Congress can, however, facilitate executive creation of coordinating and advisory bodies by enactment of general enabling legislation which will provide a flexible framework within which the President can act.

Recommendation No. 3

Legislation making specific grants of foreign affairs powers and of supporting funds below the level of the appropriate department or agency head should be avoided.

In the past the Congress on occasion has granted specific power and appropriated specific funds below the department or agency head level, as in the cases of the foreign affairs activities of the Civil Aeronautics Administration and the Bureau of Labor Statistics. This practice tends to free the grantee from executive control and encourages him to establish independent channels of communication with the Congress. It aggravates the problem of coordinating foreign relations activities both within individual departments and agencies and between different units of the executive branch.

The practice of appropriating funds directly to a constituent unit of a department or agency further limits the ability of the department or agency head to adjust the foreign affairs programs of his several bureaus or offices to meet changing international conditions and to reduce internal overlapping or duplication of effort.

.   .   .   .

2. DEPARTMENT OF STATE

A. Organization

1. GENERAL

In a message to the Congress on March 4, 1949, President Truman requested the enactment of legislation providing for modifications and improvements in the internal structure of the Department of State similar to the general recommendations of the Commission on Organization of the Executive Branch of the Government.[1] The Senate Committee on Foreign Relations, following hearings held during March and April, approved the text of its own bill (S.1704) which was reported to the Senate on April 26[2] and approved by the Senate on May 6.[3] The House of Representatives on May 16 amended the Senate bill by substituting a text reported by the House Committee on Foreign Affairs (H.R.3559).[4] The Senate concurred in the House amendments on May 16 and the bill was signed into law by the President on May 26, 1949.[5]

As a result of reorganization measures commenced on May 27, the Department was organized into five Bureaus (United Nations Affairs, European Affairs, Inter-American Affairs, Near Eastern, South Asian, and African Affairs, and Far Eastern Affairs), two Areas (Public Affairs and Economic Affairs), and the Office of the Assistant Secretary for Congressional Relations. The former offices of the Department were abolished and the functions, personnel and records of each were transferred to the corresponding new Bureau or Area.[6]

(1) *An Act to Strengthen and Improve the Organization and Administration of the Department of State, Approved, May 26, 1949.*[7]

Be it enacted by the Senate and House of Representatives of the United States of America in Congress assembled, That there shall be in the Depart-

---

1 For the text of President Truman's message, see *Congressional Record*, 95, p. 1915 (Daily edition, March 4, 1949); Department of State, *Bulletin*, XX, p. 333. For further information regarding the recommendations of the Commission on Organization of the Executive Branch of the Government with reference to the Department of State see this volume, p. 52.
2 Senate Report 304, 81st Cong., 1st sess.
3 *Congressional Record*, p. 5933 (Daily edition, May 6, 1949).
4 *Ibid.*, p. 6263 (Daily edition, May 12, 1949).
5 Public Law 73, 81st Cong., 1st sess.
6 For information regarding reorganization of particular offices of the Department, see this volume, p. 76.
7 Public Law 73, 81st Cong., 1st sess.

ment of State in addition to the Secretary of State an Under Secretary of State and ten Assistant Secretaries of State.

SEC. 2. The Secretary of State and the officers referred to in section 1 of this Act shall be appointed by the President, by and with the advice and consent of the Senate. The Counselor of the Department of State and the Legal Advisor, who are required to be appointed by the President, by and with the advice and consent of the Senate, shall rank equally with the Assistant Secretaries of State. Any such officer holding office at the time the provisions of this Act become effective shall not be required to be reappointed by reason of the enactment of this Act. The Secretary may designate two of the Assistant Secretaries as Deputy Under Secretaries.

SEC. 3. The Secretary of State, or such person or persons designated by him, notwithstanding the provisions of the Foreign Service Act of 1946 (60 Stat. 999) or any other law, except where authority is inherent in or vested in the President of the United States, shall administer, coordinate, and direct the Foreign Service of the United States and the personnel of the State Department. Any provisions in the Foreign Service Act of 1946, or in any other law, vesting authority in the "Assistant Secretary of State for Administration", the "Assistant Secretary of State in Charge of the Administration of the Department", the "Director General", or any other reference with respect thereto, are hereby amended to vest such authority in the Secretary of State.

SEC. 4. The Secretary of State may promulgate such rules and regulations as may be necessary to carry out the functions now or hereafter vested in the Secretary of State or the Department of State, and he may delegate authority to perform any of such functions to officers and employees under his direction and supervision.

SEC. 5. The following statutes or parts of statutes are hereby repealed:

Section 200 of the Revised Statutes, as amended and amplified by the Acts authorizing the establishment of additional Assistant Secretaries of State, including section 22 of the Act of May 24, 1924 (ch. 182, and the Act of December 8, 1944, R. S. 200; 43 Stat. 146; 58 Stat. 798; 5 U. S. C. 152, as amended by Public Law 767, Eightieth Congress).

Section 202 of the Foreign Service Act of 1946 (60 Stat. 1000) and any other reference in such Act to the "Deputy Director General".

Section 1041 of the Foreign Service Act of 1946 (60 Stat. 1032).

2. OFFICE OF THE SECRETARY OF STATE

On January 3, 1949, George C. Marshall submitted to the President his resignation from the post of Secretary of State[8] President Truman, on January 7, accepted the resignation, to take effect on January 20.[9] Shortly thereafter, the President submitted for confirmation by the Senate the nomination of Dean G. Acheson, former Assistant Secretary of State, as Secretary Marshall's successor. The nomination, after extensive hearings, was unanimously approved by the Committee on Foreign Relations[10] and confirmed by a vote of 83 to 6 by the Senate on January 18.[11] Mr. Acheson took the oath of office as Secretary of State on January 21[12] and served in that capacity throughout the year under review.

8 Department of State, *Bulletin*, XX, p. 86.   9 *Ibid.*
10 *Congressional Record*, 95, p. 470 (Daily edition, January 18, 1949).
11 *Ibid.*, p. 479.   12 Department of State, *Bulletin*, XX, p. 150.

3. OFFICE OF THE UNDER SECRETARY OF STATE

The resignation of Robert A. Lovett from the post of Under Secretary of State was submitted on January 3 and accepted by the President on January 7, to become effective concurrently with Secretary Marshall's resignation.[13] James E. Webb, Director of the Bureau of the Budget since 1946, was nominated to that position and confirmed by the Senate on January 27.[14]

4. DEPUTY UNDER SECRETARIES OF STATE

Pursuant to Public Law 73, the Secretary of State announced on May 27 that he had designated Assistant Secretaries Dean Rusk and John Peurifoy as Deputy Under Secretary for substantive matters and Deputy Under Secretary for Administration respectively.[15] At the time of their appointments, Mr. Rusk and Mr. Peurifoy were serving as Assistant Secretary for United Nations Affairs and Assistant Secretary for Administration.

5. ASSISTANT SECRETARIES OF STATE

Public Law 73, approved by the President on May 26, 1949, provided for the appointment of ten Assistant Secretaries of State to assume direction of the Bureaus of the Department under the supervision of the Under Secretary of State. The reorganization on the Assistant Secretary level is summarized below:

Assistant Secretary of State for United Nations Affairs. Prior to the enactment of legislation calling for the reorganization of the Department, the nomination of Dean Rusk as Assistant Secretary for United Nations Affairs was, on January 31, submitted to the Senate for confirmation.[16] Mr. Rusk's nomination was confirmed on February 7.[17] Reorganization in conformity with Public Law 73 was subsequently undertaken on May 26 with the designation of Assistant Secretary Rusk to the post of Deputy Under Secretary for substantive matters[18] and the nomination as his successor of John D. Hickerson,[19] which nomination was confirmed by the Senate on June 23, 1949.[20]

A State Department announcement of October 27 summarized the reorganization of the Bureau of United Nations Affairs which had become effective on October 3, 1949. The Bureau was composed of the following organization units: Refugees and Displaced Persons Staff, United Nations Planning Staff, Office of Dependent Area Affairs, Office of International Administration and Conferences, Office of United Nations Economic and Social Affairs, and Office of United Nations Political and Security Affairs.[21]

Assistant Secretary of State for Congressional Relations. Nominated prior to the general reorganization of the Department, Ernest A. Gross was confirmed by the Senate on March 1, 1949, as Assistant Secretary for Congressional Relations.[22] Mr. Gross continued in that capacity until his confirmation by the Senate as deputy representative to the United Nations and deputy representative to the Security Council on October 13.[23] On that date, the Senate confirmed Jack K. McFall as his successor.[24]

Assistant Secretary of State for Administration. The post of Assistant Secretary of State for Administration ceased to exist following the appointment of John Peurifoy as Deputy Under Secretary for Administration, a post to which he was named by the Secretary of State on May 27.[25]

Assistant Secretary of State for Inter-American Affairs. Edward G. Miller, Jr., was nominated to the post of Assistant Secretary for Inter-American Affairs on May 26[26] and confirmed by the Senate on June 23.[27] Internal reorganization of the

13 *Ibid.,* p. 86.　　　　14 *Congressional Record,* 95, p. 657 (Daily edition, January 27, 1949).
15 Department of State, *Bulletin,* XX, p. 734.
16 *Congressional Record,* 95, p. 736 (Daily edition, January 31, 1949).
17 *Ibid.,* p. 894 (Daily edition, February 7, 1949).
18 Department of State, *Bulletin,* XX, p. 734.
19 *Ibid.,* p. 735.
20 *Congressional Record,* 95, p. 8377 (Daily edition, June 23, 1949).
21 Department of State, *Bulletin,* XXI, p. 713.
22 *Congressional Record,* 95, p. 1697 (Daily edition, March 1, 1949).
23 *Ibid.,* p. 14715 (Daily edition, October 13, 1949).
24 *Ibid.*　　　　25 Department of State, *Bulletin,* XX, p. 734.
26 *Ibid.,* p. 735.　　　　27 *Congressional Record,* 95, p. 13651 (Daily edition, June 23, 1949).

Bureau of Inter-American Affairs was accomplished on October 3, the Bureau consisting of the Office of the Assistant Secretary and offices devoted to east coast affairs, north and west coast affairs, middle American affairs, and regional American affairs.[28]

Assistant Secretary of State for European Affairs. George W. Perkins was nominated to the post of Assistant Secretary for European Affairs on May 26[29] and confirmed by the Senate on June 23.[30] Internal reorganization of the Bureau of European Affairs was announced on October 4, the Bureau consisting of the office of the Assistant Secretary and offices devoted to British Commonwealth and northern European affairs, eastern European affairs, western European affairs, and European regional bureau affairs.[31]

Assistant Secretary of State for Near Eastern, South Asian and African Affairs. George C. McGhee, former Coordinator of Aid for Greece and Turkey, was nominated to the post of Assistant Secretary for Near Eastern and African Affairs on May 26[32] and confirmed by the Senate on June 23.[33] Internal reorganization of the Bureau of Near Eastern, South Asian and African Affairs was accomplished on October 3, the Bureau consisting of the office of the Assistant Secretary and offices devoted to Greek-Turkish-Iranian affairs, African and Near Eastern affairs, and South Asian affairs.[34]

Assistant Secretary of State for Far Eastern Affairs. W. Walton Butterworth was nominated to the post of Assistant Secretary for Far Eastern Affairs on May 26[35] and confirmed by the Senate on September 27, 1949.[36] Internal reorganization of the Bureau of Far Eastern Affairs was announced by the Department on October 4, the Bureau consisting of the office of the Assistant Secretary and offices devoted to Chinese affairs, northeast Asia affairs, and Philippine and southeast Asia affairs.[37]

Assistant Secretary of State for Economic Affairs. With the announcement of nomination of new Assistant Secretaries made by the Department on May 26, the Secretary of State noted that Willard L. Thorp would continue to serve as Assistant Secretary for Economic Affairs.[38] Assistant Secretary Thorp remained in direction of economic affairs throughout the period under review. Internal reorganization of the Area of Economic Affairs was announced by the Department on October 27, the Area consisting of the Office of Assistant Secretary and offices devoted to international trade policy, financing and development policy, and transport and communications policy.[39]

Assistant Secretary of State for Public Affairs. Assistant Secretary for Public Affairs George V. Allen continued the direction Area of Public Affairs following the reorganization of the Department. Mr. Allen resigned his position on November 29 to become Ambassador to Yugoslavia. On December 31, President Truman, subject to confirmation by the Senate, nominated Edward Ware Barrett as Mr. Allen's successor.[40]

6. OFFICE OF THE LEGAL ADVISER

On January 3, 1949, Jack B. Tate assumed the duties of acting Legal Adviser of the Department of State, following the temporary appointment of Ernest A. Gross to the position of Coordinator of Foreign Assistance Programs.[41] With Mr. Gross's permanent appointment as Assistant Secretary for Congressional Relations, Adrian S. Fisher was nominated to the post of Legal Adviser. Mr. Fisher's nomination was submitted to the Senate on May 27[42] and confirmed on June 23.[43]

7. COUNSELOR

George F. Kennan was nominated as Counselor of the Department on May 27, 1949, to succeed Charles Bohlen.[44] The nomination was confirmed by the Senate on June 23.[45]

28 Department of State, *Bulletin*, XXI, p. 677.   29 *Ibid.*, XX, p. 735.
30 *Congressional Record*, 95, p. 8377 (Daily edition, June 23, 1949).
31 Department of State, *Bulletin*, XXI, p. 677.   32 *Ibid.*, XX, p. 735.
33 *Congressional Record*, 95, p. 8377 (Daily edition, June 23, 1949).
34 Department of State, *Bulletin*, XXI, p. 677.   35 *Ibid.*, XX, p. 735.
36 *Congressional Record*, 95, p. 13651 (Daily edition, September 27, 1949).
37 Department of State, *Bulletin*, XXI, p. 677.
38 *Ibid.*, XX, p. 735.   39 *Ibid.*, XXI, p. 713.   40 *Ibid.*, XXII, p. 71.
41 *Ibid.*, XX, p. 150.   42 *Congressional Record*, 95, p. 7113 (Daily edition, May 27, 1949).
43 *Ibid.*, p. 8377 (Daily edition, June 23, 1949).
44 *Ibid.*, p. 7113 (Daily edition, May 27, 1949).   45 *Ibid.*, p. 8377 (Daily edition, June 23, 1949).

8. AMBASSADOR-AT-LARGE

On February 10, 1949, President Truman sent to the Senate for confirmation the nomination of Philip C. Jessup to serve as Ambassador-at-Large.[46] Dr. Jessup's nomination was confirmed on March 1.[47]

B. Appropriations

(1) Comparative Statement of Department of State Appropriations for 1949 and 1950.[1]

Title of Appropriation	Appropriations for 1949	Appropriations for 1950	+ Increase − Decrease for 1950
Departmental and Foreign Service Activities:			
Salaries and Expenses, Department of State			
Domestic Service	$ 22,201,000	$ 24,510,600	+$ 2,309,600
Foreign Service	53,220,000	53,641,500	+ 421,500
	75,421,000	78,152,100	+ 2,731,100
Representation Allowance, Foreign Service	650,000	650,000	——
Foreign Service Retirement and Disability Fund	2,150,000	2,187,000	+ 37,000
Buildings Fund, Department of State	35,000,000	13,000,000	− 22,000,000
Emergencies Arising in Diplomatic and Consular Service	9,750,000	11,400,000	+ 1,650,000
Expenses, North Atlantic Fisheries	25,000	——	− 25,000
Total	122,996,000	105,389,100	− 17,606,900
International Activities:			
Participation in International Organizations	100,966,490	99,663,558	− 1,302,932
United Nations Headquarters Loan	65,000,000	——	− 65,000,000
International Contingencies	3,600,000	3,300,000	− 300,000
United States—Mexican International Boundary and Water Commission:			
Salaries and Expenses	1,014,428	1,120,000	+ 105,572
Construction	1,500,000	900,000	− 600,000
Rio Grande Emergency Flood Protection	100	15,000	+ 14,900
Salaries and Expenses, American Sections, International Commissions	469,130	500,000	+ 30,870
Salaries and Expenses, Philippine Rehabilitation	21,499,000	17,166,398	− 4,332,602
Port-au-Prince Bicentennial Exposition	——	125,000	+ 125,000
Total	194,049,148	122,789,956	− 71,259,192
International Information and Educational Activities:	31,100,000	47,300,000	+ 16,200,000
Claims:			
Payable to the Government of Switzerland	——	14,600,000	+ 14,600,000
Payable to the Government of Finland	——	5,574,740	+ 5,574,740
Total	——	20,174,740	+ 20,174,740
Corporation:			
Institute of Inter-American Affairs	2,500,000	4,751,600	+ 2,251,600
Total:	$350,645,148	$300,405,396	−$50,239,752

46 Department of State, *Bulletin*, XX, p. 185.
47 *Ibid.*, p. 332.
1 From information furnished by the Department of State.

3. INTERNATIONAL ORGANIZATIONS AND CONFERENCES

A. Privileges and Immunities of International Organizations

During the period under review, President Truman, by executive order, extended the privileges and immunities conferred by the International Organization Act of 1945[1] to cover the operations of the South Pacific Commission.[2] By Executive Order 10083, privileges and immunities previously granted the Inter-American Coffee Board, the Intergovernmental Committee on Refugees, and the United States Relief and Rehabilitation Administration were revoked since the organizations in question had ceased to exist.[3]

B. United States Participation in International Organizations

(1) *Report of the Subcommittee on Relations with International Organizations of the Committee of the Senate on Expenditures in the Executive Departments, Submitted, February 11, 1950.*[4]

[EXCERPTS]

* * * * * * *

A. UNITED STATES PARTICIPATION IN INTERNATIONAL ORGANIZATIONS — THE OVER-ALL PICTURE

1. POLICY

The subcommittee made a careful study of the policy of this Government with respect to participation in international organizations and concluded that such participation must be viewed in terms of the manner in which it contributes to the effective achievement of our foreign policy. The official position of the executive branch of the Government, in this respect, is that the United States is seeking to bring about conditions in the world in which democratic government and institutions can survive and flourish. It is difficult, if not impossible, however, to maintain these institutions, either within the United States or elsewhere in the world, unless conditions of peace, freedom, and economic well-being can be brought about in other parts of the world. In order to accomplish these basic objectives, this Government requires the maximum assistance and support from all other like-minded nations, since joint action is far more effective than uncoordinated attempts on the part of individual governments.

The Department of State takes the position that by actively participating in the activities of the international organizations here under consideration, the Government of the United States is taking the most effective possible action, in concert with other freedom-loving nations of the world, in attempting to eliminate the causes and tensions which lead to war, thus effectuating United States foreign policy which is directed basically at international peace and security by means of joint action and cooperation through the United Nations and its specialized agencies.[5]

---

1 For the text of the International Organization Act of 1945, see *Documents*, VIII, 1945–1946, p. 67.
2 Executive Order 10086, *Federal Register*, XIV, p. 7147.　　　　　3 *Ibid.*, p. 6161.
4 Senate Report 1274, 81st Cong., 1st sess. Footnotes, unless quoted, are supplied.
5 "These findings are based upon the testimony of Deputy Under Secretary of State, Dean Rusk, before an executive session of the subcommittee."

2. MEMBERSHIP AND PARTICIPATIONS

(A) General

During the fiscal year ending June 30, 1949, the United States Government held membership and participated in the activities of 47 international organizations.[6] Of these, 39 were either permanent or emergency and fell into three main categories: (1) United Nations and Specialized Agencies; (2) Inter-American Organizations; (3) Other International Organizations. The 8 temporary organizations were of a miscellaneous character and included special commissions, advisory groups, and study groups.

(B) Legal authority for participation

Membership in these organizations has been authorized by Congress, and appropriations covering the costs of participation are made to the Department of State except in a few instances, where they have been made to the Post Office Department, the Department of Commerce, the Department of Agriculture, the Department of the Army, the Department of Justice.[7]

The legal authority for United States participation in these organizations is generally authorized in one of three ways: (1) treaty or convention; (2) specific statute; and (3) general appropriation.

. . . .

3. COST OF PARTICIPATION

(A) General

During the fiscal year ending June 30, 1949, United States participation in the 47 organizations under consideration involved a total outlay of $144,629,-262. Of this amount, $128,734,489 represented actual contributions to the permanent and temporary organizations; $3,290,060 represented the cost of United States missions at the seat of international organizations and the cost of United States participation in meetings of international organizations; $1,138,779 was expended for representation at occasional meetings of miscellaneous international groups and special assignments; and $11,465,934 represented an advance to the United Nations toward the $65,000,000 building loan.[8]

(B) Recapitulation and comparison with fiscal year 1948

In its first report,[9] the subcommittee found that the total United States expenditure for participation in international organizations amounted to $109,-616,644 during the fiscal year June 30, 1948. However, these figures repre-

6 For a listing of international organizations in which the United States participated as of December 31, 1949, see this volume, p. 90.
7 "Appropriations made to Federal departments, other than the Department of State are noted in appendix E [See *ibid.*, p. 88]."
8 ". . . It should be noted that the International Monetary Fund and the International Bank for Reconstruction and Development are not included in this study although they are specialized agencies of the United Nations. They have been omitted because the United States was only required to subscribe an initial share of the capital stock of these organizations when it joined. Current expenses of both agencies are financed from their operating capital and no annual financial contributions are assessed to members."
9 Senate Report 1757 (Preliminary), 80th Cong., 2d sess., p. 3, 21.

sented only an estimate, due to the fact that the report was published prior to the close of that fiscal year. Since then, the Department of State has furnished the subcommittee with the actual total expenditures for that year which amounted to $127,590,347 or $17,973,703 in excess of the original estimates. The subcommittee found that the bulk of this increase was due almost exclusively to additional contributions made by the United States during that period to the International Children's Emergency Fund.[10] The balance represented minor differences between the estimated and actual expenditures.

The subcommittee found that the total outlay of $144,629,262 expended by the United States for participation in international organizations during fiscal year 1949, represents a gross increase of more than $26,000,000 over expenditures for similar purposes during fiscal year 1949 [1948]. This rise is accounted for largely by increased contributions to the United Nations and some of the other international organizations, a new expenditure for Palestine-Arab refugees, and an advance toward the United Nations building loan. However, some of the expenditures made during 1948 were decreased during 1949 to the extent of approximately $9,000,000. Accordingly, the net increase during fiscal 1949 amounted to $17,038,915.

(C) Contributions

(1) *Cost of contributions*[11] — As already indicated, during the fiscal year which ended on June 30, 1949, the United States contributed $128,734,489 to 37 permanent and emergency organizations and to eight temporary organizations. Of this amount, $22,210,257 represented actual contributions to the United Nations and its specialized agencies; $1,889,996 was contributed to the Inter-American Organizations; $200,834 was contributed to the category referred to as "Other International Organizations"; and $277,982 went to the temporary organizations.

. . . .

(D) Cost of United States missions to international organizations[12]

(1) *General.* — During the fiscal year 1949, this Government devoted $1,653,755 to the maintenance of United States missions to international organizations in which it participated. Of this amount, $1,362,630 represents the cost of maintaining six United States missions to permanent international organizations and is financed out of appropriations to the Department of State which are made specifically for that purpose; $291,125 represents the cost of maintaining two United States missions to temporary international organizations and is financed from the Department of State's international contingencies fund.

It is the understanding of the subcommittee that the United States does

---

10 "The United States contributed a total of $32,795,833 to the International Children's Emergency Fund during fiscal 1948, an increase of $17,795,833 over the original estimates."
11 "A tabular break-down of the contributions made by the United States to the permanent and temporary organizations is found in appendix E [See this volume, p. 88]."
12 "A tabular break-down of the cost of United States missions to international organizations is found in appendix G [See *ibid.*, p. 89]."

not maintain permanent missions at the seats of the great bulk of the international organizations in which it participates. With the exception of the eight missions here involved, this Government normally sends regular State Department staff officers and employees to attend meetings and conferences of these organizations when, and if, they occur.

●   ●   ●   ●   ●   ●   ●

4. THE ORGANIZATION OF THE UNITED STATES GOVERNMENT FOR PARTICIPATION IN INTERNATIONAL ORGANIZATIONS

(A) *General*

During recent years, the United States has attained a position of leadership and responsibility in world affairs unprecedented and unparalleled in history. In the course of its studies, the subcommittee was particularly impressed by the tremendous growth in the international organization responsibilities which have been undertaken by this Government since the termination of World War II. This growth is best illustrated by a comparison between appropriations or expenditures for participation in international organizations, conferences, and meetings during the fiscal year 1939, and the fiscal year 1949. Thus, during 1939, the Congress appropriated approximately $835,590 for participation in 23 international organizations as compared with the outlay of $144,629,262 for participation in 47 international organizations during fiscal year 1949. Prior to World War II, this Government participated in less than 75 international conferences each year as compared with approximately 260 conferences involving some 6,000 meetings during the fiscal year ending June 30, 1949.[14]

This tremendous growth appears to be the result of a new method of doing business between the nations of the world. Whereas prior to World War II these nations consulted on common problems on a country-to-country or bilateral basis, the principal international business of most of the governments today is carried on by multilateral negotiations.

These developments have had a tremendous impact upon virtually every agency and department of the United States Government. In recognizing this fact, the Commission on Organization of the Executive Branch of the Government (the Hoover Commission) found, in its recent study, that "the problems of Government organization for the conduct of foreign affairs are * * * not confined to the State Department alone but involve the organization of the Presidency, the State Department, and the Foreign Service, the departments and agencies other than the State Department, the interdepartmental relationships, and the relations between the executive and legislative branches. * * * Of the 59 major departments and agencies in the executive branch, at least 46 are drawn into foreign affairs to a greater or lesser extent."[15]

14 For a partial listing of conferences in which the United States participated during the calendar year 1949, see *ibid.*, p. 92.
15 House Document 79, 81st Cong., 1st sess., p. 3.

It is manifest that this growth in United States participation in foreign affairs generally is directly related to the very great increase by this Government in its participation in international organizations. It is also clear that the greatest burden occasioned by our increased participation has fallen upon the Department of State as the agency primarily responsible for the formulation of policies and positions to be presented by United States representatives in meetings and conference of international organizations.

(B) *The organization of the Department of State for handling its responsibilities with respect to United States participation in international organizations*

(1) *General.* – In order to meet these new responsibilities, the Secretary of State, soon after the creation of the United Nations, established within the Department an Office of Special Political Affairs, to serve primarily as a focal point in the Department for the coordination and integration of matters relating to the United States participation in United Nations.

As the role of the United Nations and other international organizations became increasingly important to this Government, this Office went through a series of reorganizations. The first recognition occurred in 1948 when this Office became the Office of United Nations Affairs. In July 1949, the Secretary of State, in effecting a partial reorganization of the Department, designated an Assistant Secretary of State to head the Office of United Nations Affairs, and in October 1949, a further reorganization of the Department resulted in the designation of that Office as the Bureau of United Nations Affairs.[16]

(2) *The Bureau of United Nations Affairs – Organization and responsibilities.* –

.   .   .   .

The subcommittee found that the Bureau of United Nations Affairs is so organized that problems of a given nature are handled by one staff group, irrespective of the international organization or the United Nations organ or agency involved. Thus, the Office of United Nations Economic and Social Affairs is responsible for all economic and social matters pertaining to international organizations, irrespective of whether they arise in the United Nations Economic and Social Council, the General Assembly, the specialized agencies or any other international organization. The Office of United Nations Political and Security Affairs is concerned with all political problems without regard to whether they arise in the United Nations Security Council, the General Assembly or the Interim Committee of the General Assembly. The Office of Dependent-Area Affairs is responsible for United States policies in the United Nations Trusteeship Council, in the regional organizations concerned with non-self-governing territories[17] and with matters of colonialism and dependent areas in general.

.   .   .   .

16 For further information on the reorganization of the Department of State during 1949, see this volume, p. 75.
17 "The South Pacific Commission and the Caribbean Commission are examples of regional organizations concerned with non-self-governing territories."

(C) *Interdepartmental aspects of United States participation in international organizations*

(1) *General.* — The subcommittee found that there is a serious lack of co-ordination between the various agencies and departments of this Government, with respect to United States participation in international organizations, which may be resulting in waste and duplication and may also be impairing the effective presentation of this Government's policies and position in conferences and meetings of international organizations.

It has already been indicated that the tremendous growth in United States participation in international organizations, on a hitherto unprecedented scale, has had an impact on virtually every department and agency of the United States Government, and includes such fields as politics, economics, health, labor, education, transportation, communication, and finance.

Although the Department of State is the agency primarily responsible for policy formulation and presentation, it is manifest that it must look to the other agencies and departments of the Government for expert advice and technical information in formulating these policies and in determining their effect upon the domestic situation. Accordingly, in the absence of continuous coordination and cooperation between the Department of State and the other governmental agencies, the vital task of attaining this Government's objectives in connection with participation in international organization affairs becomes difficult if not impossible. Equally important is the need for this Government to present a common point of view in the large number of international meetings in which it takes part.

.   .   .   .

(4) *Conclusions.* — It appears that at the present time, there is no single crystallized process for securing interdepartmental coordination in the formulation and presentation of United States policy with respect to international organizations. Furthermore, it is not clear whether the Department of State is making the best use possible of the technical experts of other agencies and departments of the Government thereby eliminating the waste and duplication which might result if the Department maintained its **own** technicians in the various fields. The subcommittee has been informed that efforts are being made by the Department to effect the necessary coordination and to utilize, to the fullest extent, the staffs of other agencies and departments.

.   .   .   .

In the opinion of the subcommittee, three steps are necessary to correct present inadequacies in interdepartmental coordination: (1) The President should, by Executive order, establish guiding principles clearly defining the respective responsibilities of the Department of State and the other departments and agencies of the Government with respect to participation in international organizations; these principles should assign such responsibilities as the preparation of the policy and position to be taken in conferences and meetings of international organizations, the conduct of negotiations and the selection of representatives to attend meetings and conferences; (2) the departments and agencies of the Government, having responsibilities and obligations with respect to the support of United States participation in international organization affairs, should establish adequate internal machinery to handle these obligations; and (3) the President should establish an over-all interdepartmental board or committee with various segments or sections devoted to particular fields, replacing those of the existing interdepartmental committees which are not statutory. Such a board or committee should have both cabinet and lower level representation as well as a permanent secretariat, consisting of technical experts from every agency and department having any appreciable responsibilities in the general field of foreign affairs and in the specific area of international organizations. In such an interdepartmental committee, the traditional position of the Department of State, as the agency responsible for foreign policy, should be given due consideration. This would involve the same personnel now handling these matters and no additional expense would be incurred.

* * * * * * *

C. The Liquidation, Consolidation, and Integration of International Organizations in Which the United States Participates

* * * * * * *

1. ACTION BY THE UNITED STATES

(A) *The need for action*

The subcommittee found, as already indicated, that there has been a steady and astronomical rise in United States expenditures for participation in international organizations during the past 10 years.[18] United States contributions to the United Nations and its specialized agencies alone have risen from $7,443,413 in fiscal year 1946 and $11,592,095 in fiscal year 1947 to $120,565,905 in fiscal year 1948 and $126,345,677 in fiscal year 1949.

* * * * * * *

Accordingly, the subcommittee has reached the conclusion that the astronomical rise in international organization expenditures, referred to above, lends emphasis to the necessity for this Government to take the lead (1) in opposing the creation of new organizations; (2) in attempting to effect a liquidation or consolidation of existing organizations where duplication or overlapping appear to exist; and (3) in assuring that the organizations in which this Government participates are pursuing prudent internal policies with respect to budgetary and auditing procedures, administration, and personnel.

* * * * * * *

[18] "During fiscal year 1939, Congress appropriated $835,590 for participation in 23 international organizations. During fiscal year 1948, participation in 46 international organizations involved an expenditure of $127,590,347. During fiscal year 1949 participation in 47 international organizations involved an outlay of $144,629,262."

(C) Efforts to effect the liquidation, consolidation, and integration of existing organizations

. . . .

(2) *Progress in effecting termination and consolidation.* — The subcommittee noted that some progress has been made in effecting the consolidation and termination of a number of organizations here under consideration. Thus, three organizations have been compelety terminated;[19] three organizations have been terminated and their functions assumed by specialized agencies of the United Nations;[20] the secretariat of three organizations are being taken over by the Pan-American Union;[21] one organization has been reorganized as a nongovernmental agency;[22] and one organization is now serving as a regional office for one of the United Nations specialized agencies.[23]

(3) *Action contemplated in the near future.* — The subcommittee found that at the present time the Department of State is pressing for the following terminations, consolidations, and mergers:

(*a*) Transfer to the United Nations of the functions of the International Penal and Penitentiary Commission;

(*b*) Transfer to the Registrar of the International Court of Justice of the functions of the International Bureau of the Permanent Court of Arbitration;

(*c*) Termination of the Central Bureau of the International Map of the World on the Millionth Scale and transfer of its functions to the United Nations;

(*d*) Integration of the activities of the International Seed Testing Association with the Food and Agriculture Organization;

(*e*) Reorganization of the International Council of Scientific Unions and its Associated Unions into nongovernmental organizations;

(*f*) Integration into the International Trade Organization, upon its full activation, of the International Bureau for the Publication of Customs Tariffs;

(*g*) Integration into the International Trade Organization, upon its full activation, of three commodity groups — the International Cotton Advisory Committee; the International Tin Study Group; and the Rubber Study Group;

(*h*) Integration into the Inter-Governmental Maritime Consultative Organization, upon its full activation, of the International Commission of the Cape Spartel and Tangier Lighthouse and the International Hydrographic Bureau;

19 "Inter-American Committee for Political Defense; Inter-American Development Commission; and Inter-American Coffee Board."
20 "The International Office of Public Health is being absorbed by the World Health Organization; the International Technical Committee of Aerial Legal Experts [CITEJA] has been absorbed by the International Civil Aviation Commission [*sic*]; and the International Institute of Agriculture has been absorbed by the Food and Agriculture Organization."
21 "Inter-American Commission of Women; Inter-American Economic and Social Council; and Inter-American Statistical Institute."
22 "International Statistical Bureau."
23 "The Pan American Sanitary Bureau has become a regional office for the World Health Organization."

(*i*) The possible termination of the International Bureau for the Protection of Industrial Property and the absorption of its functions by one or more of the specialized agencies of the United Nations.

. . . .

APPENDIX E

CONTRIBUTIONS OF THE UNITED STATES TO INTERNATIONAL ORGANIZATIONS DURING FISCAL YEAR 1949[24]

Organization	United States contribution	United States percentage[25]
I. UNITED NATIONS AND SPECIALIZED AGENCIES		
A. Permanent:[26]		
United Nations (including International Court of Justice)	$ 13,841,032	39.89
Food and Agriculture [Organization]	1,250,000	25.00
International Civil Aviation Organization	498,004[27]	18.69
International Labor Organization	1,091,739	19.13
International Telecommunication Union	58,393[28]	7.76
United Nations Educational, Scientific and Cultural Organization	3,601,424	41.88
Universal Postal Union	8,781[29]	4.43
World Health Organization	1,860,884	38.77
Subtotal	22,210,257	35.61
B. Emergency:		
International Refugee Organization	70,643,728	45.57[30]
United Nations International Children's Emergency Fund	25,491,692	72.00
United Nations Relief for Palestine Refugees	8,000,000[31]	54.56[31]
Subtotal	104,135,400	50.77
II. INTER-AMERICAN ORGANIZATIONS		
American International Institute for the Protection of Childhood	2,000	35.97
Inter-American Indian Institute	4,800	15.69
Inter-American Institute of Agricultural Sciences	145,397	51.67
Inter-American Radio Office	5,682	25.51
Inter-American Statistical Institute	29,080	50.20
International Office of Postal Union of Americas and Spain[32]	1,600	8.89
Pan American Institute of Geography and History	10,000	36.23
Pan American Railway Congress	2,500	47.00
Pan American Sanitary Bureau	152,585	53.63
Pan American Union (including Inter-American Defense Board)	1,536,352	72.13
Subtotal	1,889,996	65.78

[24] Unless otherwise indicated, United States participation in international organizations listed is financed from appropriations made or allocated to the Department of State.

[25] Percentage of total scheduled assessments.

[26] Does not include the International Bank for Reconstruction and Development or the International Monetary Fund, which are financed by capital subscriptions from member governments and income from operations rather than by annual contributions.

[27] In addition, $3,750,000 appropriated for ICAO joint support program, of which $385,036 has been expended as of June 30, 1949.

[28] Figure an estimate since actual assessment is not known.

[29] United States participation financed from appropriations made to Post Office Department.

[30] The United States was assessed 39.89 percent of scheduled administrative expenses ($4,797,800) and 45.75 percent of scheduled operational expenses ($150,229,258), or 45.57 percent of total scheduled expenses ($155,027,058).

[31] This amount was contributed out of funds advanced by the Reconstruction Finance Corporation pending an appropriation by the Congress as authorized by Public Law 25, 81st Cong., approved March 24, 1949.

Organization	United States contribution	United States percentage[25]
III. OTHER INTERNATIONAL ORGANIZATIONS		
Bureau of the Interparliamentary Union for the Promotion of International Arbitration	15,000	22.80
Cape Spartel and Tangier Lighthouse	2,000[28]	8.34
Caribbean Commission	131,284	38.40
Central Bureau of the International Map of the World on the Millionth Scale	50	2.04
International Bureau for the Protection of Industrial Property	1,811	5.51
International Bureau for the Publication of Customs Tariffs	2,233	4.30
International Bureau of the Permanent Court of Arbitration	1,546	4.79
International Bureau of Weights and Measures	9,241	17.03
International Council of Scientific Unions and Seven Associated Unions	6,993	9.00[33]
International Criminal Police Commission	3,000[34]	17.97[33]
International Hydrographic Bureau	9,147	14.14
International Meteorological Organization	3,785[35]	4.13
International Penal and Penitentiary Commission	4,837	31.77[33]
International Statistical Bureau at The Hague	2,500[36]	25.66[33]
International Sugar Council	8,089	21.25
Permanent International Association of Navigation Congresses	1,000[37]	23.09[33]
South Pacific Commission	18,318	12.50
Subtotal	220,834	20.65
IV. TEMPORARY ORGANIZATIONS OR ORGANIZATIONS IN WHICH UNITED STATES PARTICIPATION IS TEMPORARY (OTHER THAN THOSE LISTED UNDER I B. ABOVE)		
Central Rhine Commission	8,559	16.66
Inter-Allied Reparation Agency	203,849	28.00
International Authority for the Ruhr	40,000	20.00
International Cotton Advisory Committee	12,000	15.79
International Seed Testing Association	250	7.22
International Tin Study Group	5,440	13.49
International Union of Official Travel Organizations	605[38]	2.70
Rubber Study Group	7,279	18.05
Subtotal	277,982	23.93
Grand total	$128,734,489	47.23

. . . .

APPENDIX G

COST OF UNITED STATES MISSIONS TO INTERNATIONAL ORGANIZATIONS DURING FISCAL YEAR 1949

Permanent organizations:

United Nations	$1,122,183
Economic Commission for Europe (ECE)	117,185
United Nations Educational, Scientific and Cultural Organization (UNESCO)	38,782
International Civil Aviation Organization (ICAO)	71,980

32 Figure an estimate since actual assessment not yet known; United States participation financed from appropriations made to Post Office Department.
33 Percentage an estimate based on past assessments.
34 Figure an estimate since actual assessment not yet known; United States participation financed from appropriations made to Department of Justice.
35 United States participation financed from appropriations made to Department of Commerce.
36 This is the last United States contribution to be made to the Institute.
37 United States participation financed from appropriations made to Department of the Army.
38 United States participation financed from ECA funds. The Department of Commerce applied for membership in January 1949 and membership was accepted on March 30, 1949.

International Refugee Organization (IRO)[39]	7,500
World Health Organization (WHO)[40]	5,000
Temporary organizations:	
Far Eastern Commission	173,825
Inter-Allied Reparation Agency	117,300
Total	1,653,755

* * * * * *

(2) *International Organizations in Which the United States Participates as of December 31, 1949.*[41]

The international organizations listed below are those in which the United States participates through the 1) sending of official government delegations, 2) payment of contributions through specific appropriations or from general or emergency funds, 3) attendance of foreign service officers, or 4) attendance of technical experts. Agencies which are largely inactive, minor technical groups and bilateral organizations have been omitted.

A. General

United Nations (A)[42]

B. Agricultural

Food and Agriculture Organization of the United Nations (A)[43]
International Seed Testing Association (A)

C. Commercial and Financial

Inter-Allied Trade Board for Japan (W)
International Bank for Reconstruction and Development (A)
International Bureau for the Publication of Customs Tariffs (A)
International Monetary Fund (A)
International Trade Organization, Interim Commission (A)
International Union for the Protection of Industrial Property (A)

D. Commodity

International Cotton Advisory Committee (A)
International Sugar Council (A)
International Tin Study Group (A)
International Whaling Commission (A)
International Wheat Council (A)
International Wool Study Group (A)
Rubber Study Group (A)

See end of list for key to symbols used.

39 "This organization is not permanent but is carried here because it is a specialized agency of the United Nations to which the United States sends a permanent delegate during the life of the organization, which is expected to terminate on Mar. 31, 1951."

40 "Although this item is carried as a permanent mission cost, it is more directly a reflection of the cost of backstopping the United States member of the executive board of the World Health Assembly. The United States does not maintain a permanent representative to the World Health Organization and this expenditure is not expected to recur."

41 Compiled from *United States Government Manual*; Senate Report 1274, 81st Cong., 2d sess., Appendix A, p. 50, Appendix B, p. 51; Department of State Publication 3655.

42 Including the International Court of Justice, and such subsidiary bodies as the Drug Supervisory Body (established by the Convention for Limiting the Manufacture and Regulating the Distribution of Narcotic Drugs, 1931), the Permanent Central Opium Board and the United Nations International Children's Emergency Fund.

43 Including the Indo-Pacific Fisheries Council, the International Emergency Food Committee and the International Rice Commission.

E. Educational, Scientific and Cultural

Central Bureau of the International Map of the World on the Millionth Scale (A)

International Bureau of Education (A) (E)

International Bureau of Weights and Measures (A)

International Council of Scientific Unions (A)[44]

International Hydrographic Bureau (A)

International Meteorological Organization (A)

United Nations Educational, Scientific and Cultural Organization (A)

F. Political and Legal

Allied Commission for Austria (W)

Allied Control Council for Germany (W)

Allied Council for Japan (W)

Allied High Commission for Germany (W)

Allied Swiss-German External Assets Liquidation Commission (W)

Committee of Control of the International Zone of Tangier (A)

Council of Foreign Ministers (A)

Far Eastern Commission (W)

Inter-Allied Reparation Agency (W)

International Authority for the Ruhr (T)

Interparliamentary Union for the Promotion of International Arbitration (A)

Mediterranean Zone Board of the International Organization for Mine Clearance of European Waters (W)

Permanent Court of Arbitration (A)

G. Regional

Caribbean Commission (A)

Consultative Council of the North Atlantic Pact

Organization of American States (A)[45]

South Pacific Commission (A)

H. Social and Health

Central International Office for the Control of Liquor Traffic in Africa (A)

International Criminal Police Commission (A)

International Labor Organization (A)

International Penal and Penitentiary Commission (A)

International Refugee Organization (A) (T)

Pan American Sanitary Organization (A)

United Nations Relief and Rehabilitation Administration (A) (T)

World Health Organization (A)

See end of list for key to symbols used.

[44] Including the seven associated unions on chemistry, radio, geography, geology, biological sciences, geodosy and geophysics, and physics.

[45] Including such inter-American specialized agencies and subsidiary bodies as the American Committee on Dependent Territories, the American International Institute for the Protection of Childhood, the Inter-American Commission of Women, the Inter-American Committee on Agriculture, the Inter-American Council of Jurists, the Inter-American Cultural Council, the Inter-American Defense Board, the Inter-American Economic and Social Council, the Inter-American Indian Institute, the Inter-American Institute of Agricultural Sciences, the Inter-American Juridical Committee, the Inter-American Statistical Institute and the Pan American Institute of Geography and History.

I. Transport and Communications

Central Commission of the Rhine (A) (T)

Inter-American Radio Office (A)

Intergovernmental Maritime Consultative Organization, Preparatory Committee (A)

International Civil Aviation Organization (A)

International Commission for the Maintenance of the Lighthouse at Cape Spartel (A)

International Ice Patrol and Ice Observation Service (A)

International Telecommunication Union (A)

Pan American Railway Congress (E)

Permanent International Association of Navigation Congresses (A)

Postal Union of the Americas and Spain (A)

Universal Postal Union (A)

Key to symbols used:
  A — Appropriations and/or contributions
  E — Attendance by technical experts
  T — Temporary organization or participation on temporary basis only
  W — Temporary war agencies

C. International Conferences in Which the United States Participated, January 1 to December 31, 1949.[46]

The following list includes the major international conferences in which the United States participated during the year 1949. Small technical meetings, subcommittee meetings and conferences of limited participation and interest have been omitted.

Date of Meeting	Conference	Place
In continuous session	Atomic Energy Commission, United Nations	Lake Success
In continuous session	Commission on Conventional Armaments, United Nations	Lake Success
In continuous session	Commission on Indonesia, United Nations	Netherlands East Indies
In continuous session	Commission on Korea, United Nations	Seoul, Korea
In continuous session	Conciliation Commission for Palestine, United Nations	Haifa, Jerusalem, Rhodes, Lausanne
In continuous session	Far Eastern Commission	Washington
In continuous session	Inter-American Economic and Social Council	Washington
In continuous session	Inter-Allied Reparation Agency	Brussels
In continuous session	Inter-Allied Trade Board for Japan	Washington
In continuous session	Military Staff Committee, United Nations	Lake Success
In continuous session	Organization of American States, Council	Washington
In continuous session	Provisional Frequency Board, International Telecommunication Union	Geneva
In continuous session	Security Council, United Nations	Lake Success

[46] Compiled from a list prepared by the Department of State, Division of International Conferences.

In continuous session	Security Council Commission on India and Pakistan, United Nations	New Delhi
In continuous session	Special Committee on the Balkans	Athens
January 4–10	Special Teletypewriter Meeting, International Civil Aviation Organization	Montreal
January 9–11	Special Demonstrations of Radio Aids to Air Navigation, International Civil Aviation Organization	Indianapolis
January 10–25	Fiscal Commission, United Nations, Second Session	Lake Success
January 11– February 24	Communications Division, International Civil Aviation Organization, Third Meeting	Montreal
January 13–18	Caribbean Commission, Eighth Meeting	Port-of-Spain
January 13–23	Permanent Committee on Migration, International Labor Organization	Geneva
January 17– February 4	Preliminary Meetings to Discuss Form of Telegraph Regulations, International Telecommunication Union	Geneva
January 18– April 1	Council, International Civil Aviation Organization, Sixth Session	Montreal
January 24– March 25	Trusteeship Council, United Nations, Fourth Session	Lake Success
January 25–28	Executive Committee, International Refugee Organization, Third Meeting	Geneva
January 26– February 8	International Northwest Atlantic Fisheries Conference	Washington
January 31– February 3	Meeting of Experts on Safety in Coal Mines, International Labor Organization	Geneva
February 7–12	Executive Board, United Nations Educational, Scientific and Cultural Organization, Fourteenth Session	Paris
February 7– March 18	Economic and Social Council, United Nations, Eighth Session	Lake Success
February 7– April 5	Council of Foreign Ministers, Deputies for Austria	London
February 8– March 12	Operations Division, International Civil Aviation Organization	Montreal
February 12–20	Meeting on Grain Infestation and Storage, Food and Agriculture Organization	Palmira and Cali, Colombia
February 15–24	Pan American Travel Congress, Third	Buenos Aires
February 16	Committee on Budget and Finance, Executive Board, World Health Organization	Geneva
February 21– March 8	Governing Body, International Labor Organization, 108th Session	Geneva
February 21– March 13	Executive Board, World Health Organization, Third Meeting	Geneva
February 22	Airworthiness Division, International Civil Aviation Organization	Montreal
March 14– April 5	Technical Discussions on Economic Security	London
March 15– May 1	Aeronautical Radio Committee, International Telecommunication Union	Washington
March 16–25	Building, Civil Engineering and Public Works Committee, International Labor Organization	Rome
March 21–30	Transport and Communications Commission, United Nations, Third Session	Lake Success

March 21– April 4	Commission on the Status of Women, United Nations, Third Session	Beirut
March 21– April 11	Subcommission on Economic Development, United Nations, Third Session	Lake Success
March 22– April 12	African-Indian Ocean Regional Air Navigation Meeting, International Civil Aviation Organization	London
March 24–26	Executive Board, United Nations Educational, Scientific and Cultural Organization, Fifteenth Session	Paris
March 24–31	Indo-Pacific Fisheries Council, Food and Agriculture Organization	Singapore
March 24– April 7	Executive Committee, International Refugee Organization, Fourth Meeting	Geneva
March 28– April 2	Rubber Study Group, Sixth Session	London
March 28– April 5	Committee of the Whole, Economic Commission for Asia and the Far East, United Nations	Bangkok
March 28– April 8	Forestry and Timber Utilization Conference for Asia and the Pacific, Food and Agriculture Organization	Mysore, India
March 29– April 8	General Council, International Refugee Organization, Second Session	Geneva
March 30– April 4	North Atlantic Pact Conference	Washington
April 1–2	Council, American International Institute for the Protection of Childhood, Annual Meeting	Montevideo
April 5– May 18	General Assembly, United Nations, Third Session, Second Part	Lake Success
April 8–15	International Congress of Geography, Sixteenth	Lisbon
April 8– August 27	Contracting Parties, General Agreement on Tariffs and Trade, Third Session	Annecy, France
April 11	Subcommission on Employment and Economic Stability, United Nations, Third Session	Lake Success
April 11–14	Special North Atlantic Meteorological Telecommunications Meeting, International Civil Aviation Organization	London
April 11–22	Population Commission, United Nations, Fourth Session	Geneva
April 11– June 9	International Law Commission, United Nations	Lake Success
April 19	Special Meeting on Notices to Airmen (NOTAM), International Civil Aviation Organization	Montreal
April 19–30	Coal Mines Committee, International Labor Organization, Third Session	Pittsburgh
April 20– May 12	Conference on Joint Financing and Operation of Air Navigation Services: Greece and Denmark; International Civil Aviation Organization	London
April 20– May 12	Conference on North Atlantic Ocean Weather Stations, International Civil Aviation Organization	London
April 21– August 12	Diplomatic Conference for Signing Prisoners of War Convention	Geneva
April 25–30	International Cotton Advisory Committee, Eighth Meeting	Brussels

April 25– May 5	Preparatory Conference on Wood Pulp Problems, Food and Agriculture Organization	Montreal
April 25– May 6	Statistical Commission, United Nations, Fourth Session	Geneva
April 25– May 7	Regional Conference of American States, International Labor Organization, Fourth	Montevideo
April 26– May 10	Council of Foreign Ministers, Deputies for Austria	London
April 26– May 14	European Frequency Meeting, International Civil Aviation Organization	Paris
May 1– July 9	Fourth Inter-American Radio Conference, International Telecommunication Union	Washington
May 2–20	Social Commission, United Nations, Fourth Session	Lake Success
May 7–17	South Pacific Commission, Third Session	Noumea, New Caledonia
May 9–18	Economic Commission for Europe, United Nations, Fourth Session	Geneva
May 9–26	Economic and Employment Commission, United Nations, Fourth Session	Lake Success
May 9– June 21	Commission on Human Rights, United Nations, Fourth Session	Lake Success
May 10–24	Four-Power Discussions Regarding Swiss-Allied Accord	Washington
May 16– June 3	Commission on Narcotic Drugs, United Nations, Fourth Session	Lake Success
May 17–28	Inland Transport Committee, International Labor Organization	Brussels
May 17– June 24	Council, International Civil Aviation Organization, Seventh Session	Montreal
May 18–	Region III Frequency Conference, International Telecommunication Union	Geneva
May 18– September 17	Region I Administrative Radio Conference, International Telecommunication Union	Geneva
May 20– June 2	International Authority for the Ruhr, Organizational Meeting for the Council	London
May 23–27	Meeting on Latin American Forestry and Forest Products Conference, Food and Agriculture Organization	Rio de Janeiro
May 23–30	Executive Committee, Pan American Sanitary Organization, Seventh Meeting	Washington
May 23– June 20	Council of Foreign Ministers, Sixth Session	Paris
May 29– June 11	Economic Commission for Latin America, United Nations, Second Session	Havana
May 31– June 16	Subcommission on Freedom of Information and of the Press, United Nations, Third Session	Lake Success
June 1–18	Legal Committee, International Civil Aviation Organization, Fourth Session	Montreal
June 3– July 1	Governing Body, International Labor Organization, 109th Session	Geneva
June 7–9	Ad Hoc Committee on Declaration of Death of Missing Persons, United Nations	Geneva
June 7–20	Assembly, International Civil Aviation Organization, Third Session	Montreal

June 8–29	International Labor Conference, International Labor Organization, 32d Session	Geneva
June 9–15	Executive Board, United Nations Educational, Scientific and Cultural Organization, Sixteenth Session	Paris
June 13–24	Council, Food and Agriculture Organization, Sixth Session	Paris
June 13–July 2	Assembly, World Health Organization, Second Session	Rome
June 14–22	International Tin Study Group, Fourth Meeting	London
June 14–July 19	Trusteeship Council Committee on Higher Education in Trust Territories, United Nations	Lake Success
June 15–July 22	Trusteeship Council, United Nations, Fifth Session	Lake Success
June 20	Drug Supervisory Body, 32d Session	Geneva
June 20–25	International Conference on Science Abstracting, United Nations Educational, Scientific and Cultural Organization	Paris
June 23–December 9	Technical Plan Committee of the International High Frequency Broadcasting Conference, International Telecommunication Union	Paris
June 28–July 8	General Council, International Refugee Organization, Third Special Session	Geneva
June 30–July 8	Executive Committee, International Refugee Organization, Fifth Meeting	Geneva
June 30–September 2	Council of Foreign Ministers, Deputies for Austria	London
July 4–12	International Conference on Public Education, Twelfth	Geneva
July 4–14	International Radio Consultative Committee: Study Group II, International Telecommunication Union	Zurich
July 5–August 15	Economic and Social Council, United Nations, Ninth Session	Geneva
July 6–9	International Wheat Council, First Session	Washington
July 7	International Sugar Council	London
July 8–19	Executive Board, World Health Organization, Fourth Session	Geneva
July 10–20	Third World Forestry Conference, Food and Agriculture Organization	Helsinki
July 11	Executive Committee, International Wheat Council	Washington
July 25–August 3	Commission on Technical Needs in Press, Radio and Films, United Nations Educational, Scientific and Cultural Organization	Paris
July 30–31	Executive Committee, International Penal and Penitentiary Commission	Bern
August 1–7	International Penal and Penitentiary Commission	Bern
August 1–October 14	Administrative Aeronautical Radio Conference, International Telecommunication Union, Second Session	Geneva
August 3	Advisory Committee on Price Equivalents, International Wheat Council	London

August 8	Executive Committee, International Wheat Council	London
August 8–24	Inter-American Commission of Women	Buenos Aires
August 15–October 3	Administrative Council, International Telecommunication Union, Fourth Session	Geneva
August 17–September 6	United Nations Scientific Conference on Conservation and Utilization of Resources	Lake Success
August 22–September 1	International Technical Conference on the Protection of Nature, United Nations Educational, Scientific and Cultural Organization	Lake Success
August 23–25	Constitution Committee, International Seed Testing Association	Belfast
August 23–September 18	United Nations Conference on Road and Motor Transport	Geneva
August 25–27	Technical Committee on Wood Chemistry, Food and Agriculture Organization, Fourth Meeting	Brussels
August 25–September 8	Special Committee on Information Transmitted Under Article 73(e) of the Charter, United Nations	Lake Success
August 26–27	Working Committee, South Pacific Commission, Fifth Meeting	Noumea, New Caledonia
August 27–September 12	Tripartite Economic Discussions	Washington
August 29–September 2	Subcommittee on Iron and Steel, Economic Commission for Asia and the Far East, United Nations, First Meeting	Bangkok
August 29–September 3	Meeting on Herring and Allied Species, Food and Agriculture Organization	The Hague
August 29–September 4	Conference on Mechanical Wood Technology, Food and Agriculture Organization	Geneva
September 1–10	Permanent Agricultural Committee, International Labor Organization, Third Session	Geneva
September 3–16	Executive Board, United Nations Educational, Scientific and Cultural Organization, Seventeenth Session	Paris
September 4–10	International Statistical Institute, 26th Session	Bern
September 10–19	International Navigation Congress, Seventeenth	Lisbon
September 12	Subcommittee on Travel, Economic Commission for Asia and the Far East, United Nations	Singapore
September 12–23	Subcommission on Statistical Sampling, United Nations, Third Session	Geneva
September 12–24	Asian Conference of Experts on Technical Training, International Labor Organization	Singapore
September 12–24	Technical Tripartite Conference on Safety in Coal Mines, International Labor Organization	Geneva
September 13–16	Board of Governors, International Bank for Reconstruction and Development and International Monetary Fund, Fourth Annual Meeting	Washington

September 13– December 9	North American Regional Broadcasting Conference	Montreal
September 17	North Atlantic Council	Washington
September 18–24	Meeting on Outlook and Programs in Latin America, Food and Agriculture Organization	Quito
September 19–24	Mediterranean Fisheries Meeting, Food and Agriculture Organization	Rome
September 19– October 5	General Conference, United Nations Educational, Scientific and Cultural Or- ganization, Fourth Session	Paris
September 20– October 1	Anglo-American-Canadian Atomic Talks	Washington
September 20– December 10	General Assembly, United Nations, Fourth Session	Lake Success
September 23– December 14	Council of Foreign Ministers, Deputies for Austria	New York
September 26– October 1	Meeting on Outlook and Programs in the Far East, Food and Agriculture Organi- gation	Singapore
September 27	Trusteeship Council, United Nations, Special Session	Lake Success
October 3–5	Executive Committee, Pan American Sanitary Organization, Eighth Meeting	Lima
October 5	Drug Supervisory Body, 33d Session	Geneva
October 5–10	Meeting of Inland Transport Experts, Economic Commission for Asia and the Far East, United Nations	Singapore
October 6–12	Directing Council, Pan American Sani- tary Organization, Second Meeting	Lima
October 6–20	Executive Committee, International Ref- ugee Organization, Sixth Meeting	Geneva
October 11–20	General Council, International Refugee Organization, Fourth Session	Geneva
October 12–17	Standing Committee on Industry and Trade, Economic Commission for Asia and the Far East, United Nations	Singapore
October 13–15	Executive Committee, Pan American Sanitary Organization, Ninth Meeting	Lima
October 19–21	Council, International Authority for the Ruhr, Third Meeting	Dusseldorf
October 20–29	Economic Commission for Asia and the Far East, United Nations, Fifth Session	Singapore
October 22– November 5	South Pacific Commission, Fourth Ses- sion	Noumea, New Caledonia
October 24–27	Coal Classification Committee, Economic Commission for Europe, United Nations	Geneva
October 26– November 5	Working Party, International Tin Study Group	The Hague
October 31– November 5	Tripartite Conference on Rhine Navi- gation, International Labor Organization	Geneva
November 1	International Wheat Council, Second Session	London
November 1– December 2	Aerodromes, Air Routes and Ground Aids Division, International Civil Avia- tion Organization, Fourth Session	Montreal
November 2– December 14	International Seminar on Rural and Adult Education, United Nations Edu- cational, Scientific and Cultural Organi- zation	Mysore, India

November 7	International Wool Study Group, Third Meeting	London
November 7	Preparatory Committee for the Annual Conference, Food and Agriculture Organization	Washington
November 7–9	Conference to Consider the Establishment of and International Institute of the Arid Zone, United Nations Educational, Scientific and Cultural Organization	Paris
November 8–19	Metal Trades Committee, International Labor Organization, Third Session	Geneva
November 8– December 9	Special European-Mediterranean Regional Communications Committee Meeting on Aeronautical Fixed Telecommunication Services and the Utilization of Very High Frequencies, International Telecommunication Union	Paris
November 9	Special European-Mediterranean Regional Communications Committee Meeting on Aeronautical Fixed Telecommunication Services, International Civil Aviation Organization	Paris
November 9–10	Tripartite Meeting of Foreign Ministers (France, United Kingdom, United States)	Paris
November 14–17	Council, Food and Agriculture Organization, Seventh Session	Washington
November 14–19	Latin American Forestry and Forest Products Commission, Food and Agriculture Organization, Second Meeting	Lima
November 21– December 7	Conference, Food and Agriculture Organization, Fifth Session	Washington
November 22– December 3	Iron and Steel Committee, International Labor Organization, Third Session	Geneva
November 23–30	International Symposium on High Altitude Biology, United Nations Educational, Scientific and Cultural Organization	Lima
November 23–30	Regional Conference of Latin American Science Experts, United Nations Educational, Scientific and Cultural Organization	Lima
November 24– December 2	Executive Board, United Nations Educational, Scientific and Cultural Organization, Eighteenth Session	Paris
November 28– December 2	Central Rhine Commission, Special Meeting	Strasbourg
November 29	Military Committee, North Atlantic Council	Paris
December 1	Defense Committee, North Atlantic Council	Paris
December 5–10	Caribbean Commission, Ninth Meeting	St. Thomas, Virgin Islands
December 5–16	Social Commission, United Nations, Fifth Session	Lake Success
December 7	Council, Food and Agriculture Organization, Eighth Session	Washington
December 8–22	Trusteeship Council, United Nations, Special Session	Lake Success

4. DIPLOMATIC REPRESENTATION

(1) *Offices Established or Reestablished during the Period from January 1, 1949, to December 31, 1949.*[1]

Post	Rank	Date
Amman, Jordan	L	February 28, 1949
Dacca, Pakistan	C	August 29, 1949
Djakarta, Indonesia	E	December 30, 1949
Medan, Sumatra, Indonesia	C	September 12, 1949
Meshed, Iran	C	July 1, 1949
Salzburg, Austria	C	August 15, 1949
Valletta, Malta	C	November 15, 1949 (R)

(2) *Offices Closed during the Period from January 1, 1949, to December 31, 1949.*[1]

Post	Rank	Date
Batavia, Java, Indonesia	CG	December 30, 1949
Canton, Kwangtung, China	CG	August 24, 1949
Changking, China	C	November 19, 1949
Dairen, Liaoning, China	C	October 21, 1949
Hankow, Hupeh, China	CG	December 5, 1949
Kunming, Yunnan, China	C	December 10, 1949
La Oroya, Peru	CA	September 30, 1949
Limerick, Ireland	C	January 22, 1949
Manzanillo, Cuba	CA	October 29, 1949
Mukden, Liaoning, China	CG	December 6, 1949
Tihwa, Sinkiang, China	C	September 27, 1949

(3) *Changes in Rank of Offices during the Period from January 1, 1949, to December 31, 1949.*[1]

Post	Rank	Changed to	Date
Addis Ababa, Ethiopia	L	E	June 28, 1949
Berlin, Germany	USP	HICOG(B)	September 21, 1949
Bonn, Germany	USP(B)	HICOG(B)	September 21, 1949
Bremerhaven, Germany	VC	C	May 1, 1949
Buenaventura, Colombia	VC	C	April 25, 1949
Camagüey, Cuba[2]	C	CA	March 3, 1949
Dhahran, Saudi Arabia	C	CG	September 7, 1949
Frankfort on the Main, Germany	CG	USP	February 1, 1949[3]
	USP	HICOG	September 21, 1949[4]
Funchal, Madeira, Portugal[5]	C	CA	May 16, 1949
Heidelberg, Germany	USP(B)	HICOG(B)	September 21, 1949
Jidda, Saudi Arabia	L	E	March 18, 1949
Monrovia, Liberia	L	E	May 6, 1949
Poznán, Poland	VC	C	June 15, 1949
Pretoria, Transvaal, Union of South Africa	L	E	March 23, 1949
Puerto la Cruz, Anzoátegui, Venezuela	VC	C	May 16, 1949
Seoul, Korea	USM	E	April 20, 1949
Tel Aviv, Israel	USM	E	March 28, 1949
Tripoli, Lybia	C	CG	July 1, 1949
Vitória, Espírito Santo, Brazil	VC	C	June 20, 1949

1 Compiled from information furnished by the Department of State. Key to symbols used:

B — Branch
C — Consulate
CA — Consular Agency
CG — Consulate Agency
E — Embassy
HICOG — Office of United States High Commissioner for Germany

L — Legation
R — Reestablished
USM — United States Mission
USP — United States Political Adviser
VC — Vice Consulate

2 The consulate was closed on February 7, 1949.
3 The consulate general was combined with the Office of the United States Political Adviser on German Affairs.
4 The Office of the United States Political Adviser was combined with the Office of the United States High Commissioner for Germany.
5 The consulate was closed on May 31, 1949.

CHAPTER III

Occupation Policy

1. GERMANY

[See *Documents*, VIII, 1945–1946, p. 186; IX, 1947, p. 44; X, 1948, p. 78.]

During 1949 little progress was made toward the unification of occupied Germany. Four-power discussions, initiated in a meeting of the Council of Foreign Ministers held in Paris from May 23 to June 10 in an effort to normalize the situation in Berlin and subsequently continued, dealt unsuccessfully with the broad field of German control and occupation, but were ultimately abandoned in September 1949. On the three-power level, French, United Kingdom, and United States negotiations resulted in the fusion of the three western zones into the Federal Republic of Germany with a government operating at Bonn under the provisions of a revised occupation statute and a federal constitution. Military government in the west was replaced by an Allied High Commission to which each of the three western occupation powers designated a commissioner. The dismantling of industrial plants for reparations was curtailed. Western Germany re-entered the field of multilateral and bilateral relations after the western powers permitted the negotiation of an agreement with the Economic Cooperation Administration, participation in the Organization for European Economic Cooperation, application for membership in the International Ruhr Authority, and the re-establishment of consular and commercial relations with certain countries.

A. Four-Power Control

1. COUNCIL OF FOREIGN MINISTERS

As a result of informal consultations between the representatives of the Soviet Union (Malik) and the United States (Jessup) concerning the lifting of the blockade of Berlin,[1] a formal communiqué issued on May 4, 1949, stated that a meeting of the Council of Foreign Ministers would convene in Paris on May 23, 1949, to discuss the broad question of four-power administration of Germany. In addition the agenda of the meeting, which was held from May 23 to June 10, included the resumption of east-west trade and the negotiation of a state treaty with Austria.[2] The United States was represented at these discussions by Dean G. Acheson, Secretary of State, who was accompanied by seventeen advisers including John Foster Dulles, Philip C. Jessup, and Robert D. Murphy.[3] During the meeting of the foreign ministers, the Soviet Union in general proposed the re-establishment, subject to the principle of unanimity, of quadripartite political and economic control over the whole of Germany, requested Soviet membership in the International Ruhr Authority, and insisted upon $10 billion in reparations. The western powers regarded such a program as a return to machinery which in the past had proved ineffective and proposed, in turn, 1) political unification based upon the Bonn constitution;[4] 2) economic unification based upon the termination of wholly Soviet-owned companies, free inter-zonal trade, and cessation of reparations removals; 3) all-German elections to establish a national federal government; and 4) supervisory control of such a government by a four-power body operating on the principle of majority rule.[5] The final communiqué issued by the Council of Foreign Ministers indicated the inability of the ministers to reach agreement on German unification.

---

[1] For further information on negotiations concerning Berlin, see this volume, p. 104.
[2] *New York Times*, May 25, 1949, p. 1. For further information concerning the negotiation of the Austrian treaty, see this volume, p. 167.
[3] Department of State, *Bulletin*, XX, p. 691.
[4] For further information on the constitution of western Germany, see this volume, p. 117.
[5] *New York Times*, May 28, 1949, p. 1.

For further information on the work of the Council of Foreign Ministers concerning the situation in Berlin, see this volume, p. 104.

For a detailed summary of the 1949 meeting of the Council of Foreign Ministers, see *International Organization*, III, p. 561.

(1) *Statement by the Secretary of State (Acheson) on the Problems Facing the Council of Foreign Ministers. Department of State Press Release, May 19, 1949.*[6]

[EXCERPTS]

• • • • • • •

The agreement reached with the Soviet Government on May 4th, which has brought about the lifting of the Berlin blockade and restoration of normal communications with that city and between the zones of occupation in Germany, has made possible this meeting. It has been the obstacle of the Berlin blockade which for the past 10 months has stood in the way of any four-power consideration of the German problem as a whole.

The three Western Powers have repeatedly made clear their willingness to sit down with the representatives of the Soviet Union for a discussion of German problems just as soon as the blockade was removed. We had, since the establishment of the blockade in June of last year, made repeated attempts, by direct negotiation and through the United Nations, to bring this dangerous and, in our view, illegal situation to an end.

While we were not willing to negotiate under pressure of the blockade, we were nonetheless constantly on the alert for any indication which might bring about the adjustment of this situation without impairment of our rights and obligations as an occupying power. As a result of the informal exchanges which occurred in New York, it has been possible to do just that.

We welcome this agreement. It is important, however, to realize that, in itself, this agreement merely restores a situation which existed a year ago and thereby removes an obstacle which for 10 months has stood in the path of further negotiations on Germany. It is not, in itself, a solution or even the beginning of a solution of the vital and difficult problem of the future of Germany. We do not know yet whether this welcome development can be regarded as an encouraging omen for the forthcoming talks until we have come to grips with the realities of the German situation.

• • • • • • •

Much has happened in the world since the last meeting of the Council of Foreign Ministers on this subject. The United States Government and the democracies of western Europe have undertaken a series of steps, the most important of which have been the European Recovery Program and the North Atlantic pact, which have already contributed to a great change for the better in the situation in western Europe. Real progress has been made in the direction of recovery and the resumption of conditions of stability and health throughout this community. Progress has likewise been made, both economic and political, in the parts of Germany which have been the re-

6 Department of State, *Bulletin*, XX, p. 675.

sponsibility of the three Western Powers. The confidence voiced by General Marshall in regard to the vitality of the free countries of western Europe has been fully justified. These countries, with our assistance, have demonstrated their ability to rehabilitate western European civilization with its freedoms intact. It is not our intention, no matter how much we may desire agreement, to accept anything which would tend to undo what has been accomplished or impede future progress along the course we have charted toward the revival of health and strength for the free nations of the world.

. . . .

It remains to be seen whether the present favorable developments have brought about a situation in which workable and effective agreements can be reached with the Soviet Union on the central problem of Germany. I think perhaps we have a better opportunity to do so than we have had before. We most certainly are now in a better position to deal with the consequences of a failure.

I cannot, therefore, honestly state whether or not this new attempt will end in success. No one can tell. The answer will have to await the meeting of the Council of Foreign Ministers itself. I can only say that, as in the past, the United States representatives will approach this meeting with an open mind and with an honest intention to explore all possibilities to arrive at a lasting solution of the problem of Germany. . .

. . . .

(2) *Communiqué Issued by the Sixth Session of the Council of Foreign Ministers. Department of State Press Release, June 21, 1949.*[7]

[EXCERPT]

The sixth session of the Council of Foreign Ministers attended by the Ministers of Foreign Affairs of France, Robert Schuman; of the Union of Soviet Socialist Republics, A. Y. Vyshinsky; of the United Kingdom, Ernest Bevin; and of the United States of America, Dean Acheson, took place in Paris from May 23 to June 20, 1949. During this meeting the German question and the Austrian treaty were discussed. The Council of Foreign Ministers took the following decisions.

I. The German Question

Despite the inability at this session of the Council of Foreign Ministers to reach agreement on the restoration of the economic and political unity of Germany, the Foreign Ministers of France, the Union of Soviet Socialist Republics, the United Kingdom, and the United States will continue their efforts to achieve this result and in particular now agree as follows:

1. During the course of the fourth session of the General Assembly of the United Nations to be convened next September, the four governments, through representatives at the Assembly, will exchange views regarding the

---

7 *Ibid.,* p. 857. For text of that portion of the communiqué dealing with decisions in regard to Austria, see this volume, p. 168.

date and other arrangements for the next session of the Council of Foreign Ministers on the German question.

2. The occupation authorities, in the light of the intention of the Ministers to continue their efforts to achieve the restoration of the economic and political unity of Germany, shall consult together in Berlin on a quadripartite basis.

3. These consultations will have as their purpose, among others, to mitigate the effects of the present administrative division of Germany and of Berlin, notably in the matters listed below:

(A) Expansion of trade and development of the financial and economic relations between the Western zones and the Eastern zone and between Berlin and the zones.

(B) Facilitation of the movement of persons and goods and the exchange of information between the Western zones and the Eastern zone and between Berlin and the zones.

(C) Consideration of questions of common interest relating to the administration of the four sectors in Berlin with a view to normalizing as far as possible the life of the city.

4. In order to assist in the work envisaged in paragraph 3, the respective occupation authorities may call upon German experts and appropriate German organizations in their respective jurisdictions for assistance. The Germans so called upon should exchange pertinent data, prepare reports and, if agreed between them, submit proposals to the occupation authorities.

5. The Governments of France, the Union of Soviet Socialist Republics, the United Kingdom, and the United States agree that the New York agreement of May 4, 1949, shall be maintained. Moreover, in order to promote further the aims set forth in the preceding paragraphs and in order to improve and supplement this and other arrangements and agreements as regards the movement of persons and goods and communications between the Eastern zone and the Western zones and between the zones and Berlin and also in regard to transit, the occupation authorities, each in his own zone, will have an obligation to take the measures necessary to insure the normal functioning and utilization of rail, water, and road transport for such movement of persons and goods and such communications by post, telephone, and telegraph.

6. The occupation authorities will recommend to the leading German economic bodies of the Eastern and Western zones to facilitate the establishment of closer economic ties between the zones and more effective implementation of trade and other economic agreements.

.   .   .   .

2. BERLIN SITUATION

[See *Documents, X, 1948*, p. 81.]

On February 11, 1949, the Technical Committee on Berlin Currency and Trade, appointed by the president of the United Nations Security Council on November

30, 1948, reported that a series of 70 meetings had led to the conclusion that "the present position of the experts of the Four Occupying Powers are so far apart in this matter that further work by the Committee, at this stage, does not appear useful."[8] In the committee's discussions the United States asserted that the lack of any administrative structure upon which to base currency control proved to be the "most serious single obstacle" to agreement. Allegedly distrustful of currency in the hands of the public which established free purchasing power not subject to Soviet manipulation, the Soviet Union submitted proposals which reportedly envisaged such strict controls that the western powers could have obtained relief from the Berlin blockade only by placing themselves under the pressure of Soviet domination over the economic administration of the city. A proposal that the western sectors of the city be given free access to currency subject only to limitations required to protect the Soviet zone from disruptive influences was rejected by the Soviet representatives,[9] who insisted that the proposals of the United States were contrary to the directive issued by the four governments in August 1948[10] and indicated that none of the western powers was interested in solving the problem.[11] Following the failure of the United Nations committee to secure agreement on the currency question, the western powers on March 20, 1949, banned the east mark as legal tender in their sectors of Berlin.[12]

On April 26, 1949, the Department of State revealed that additional negotiations over Berlin were underway. Following Premier Stalin's failure in a press interview of January 30, 1949, with a United States correspondent to make reference to the Berlin currency question, the United States deputy representative to the Security Council (Jessup) as instructed to inquire of the Soviet representative (Malik) as to whether the omission had any significance. On March 15, Mr. Malik replied that, although the currency question was important, the Soviet Union believed that it could be resolved at a meeting of the Council of Foreign Ministers if such a meeting could be arranged.[13] After further exchanges between Mr. Jessup and Mr. Malik and conversations with representatives of France and the United Kingdom, a formal communiqué of May 4 stated that all restrictions imposed on transportation, communications, and trade between Berlin and the western zones would be removed on May 12, and that a meeting of the Council of Foreign Ministers would convene in Paris to consider "questions relating to Germany and problems arising out of the situation in Berlin."[14]

Meeting from May 23 to June 10 the Council of Foreign Ministers found its discussions complicated by a major disruption of transportation within the city from May 21 to June 28, a result of a strike of transport workers in the western sector of the Berlin railway.[15] The final communiqué of the meeting stated that quadripartite consultation towards stabilization of the Berlin situation would be instituted and the agreement which had resulted in the lifting of the blockade would be continued.[16] The transport strike in the city, which had arisen from a decision of the Berlin Railway Administration, which was under Soviet control, to pay all workers in east marks convertible after March 20 into west marks at a ratio of 4:1 rather than 1:1, continued after the adjournment of the foreign ministers meeting and was not settled until agreement was reached whereby the workers were to be paid 60 percent in west marks with the Allied Kommandatura authorizing conversion of the remaining 40 percent into west marks at a 1:1 ratio.[17]

Although quadripartite discussions continued in Berlin after the adjournment of the Council of Foreign Ministers, these were abandoned on September 28, 1949, after charges by the United States that the Berlin Railway Administration had failed to fulfill the agreement with regard to the payment of transport workers.[18]

8 Department of State, *Documents and State Papers*, I, p. 754.
9 Department of State, *Bulletin*, XX, p. 377.   10 See *Documents, X, 1948*, p. 95.
11 *New York Times*, March 17, 1949, p. 3.   12 *Ibid.*, March 21, 1949, p. 1.
13 Department of State, *Bulletin*, XX, p. 590.   14 *Ibid.*, p. 631.
15 Office of Military Government for Germany (U.S.). *Monthly Report of the Military Governor*, May and June 1949, Nos. 47 and 48.
16 *New York Times*, May 25, 1949, p. 1. For further information on the work of the Council of Foreign Ministers, see this volume, p. 101.
17 Office of Military Government for Germany (U.S.). *Monthly Report of the Military Gorvernor*, May and June, Nos. 47 and 48.
18 Office of the United States High Commissioner for Germany. *1st Quarterly Report on Germany, September 21–December 21, 1949*, p. 32.

3. REPATRIATION OF GERMAN WAR PRISONERS

Two exchanges of notes occurred between the United States and Soviet governments on the question of the repatriation of German war prisoners in the Soviet zone in accordance with the terms of the agreement of the Council of Foreign Ministers negotiated in Moscow in April 1947. On January 3, 1949, the United States inquired as to Soviet plans for the final repatriation of the estimated 890,532 war prisoners, of whom only 447,367 had been returned.[19] On March 15, 1949, the United States rejected the charge, made in a Soviet reply of January 24, that it had joined with the French and United Kingdom representatives in preventing the formulation of a comprehensive plan by the Allied Control Council — as specified in the Moscow agreement — and pointed out that a Soviet statement that all war prisoners would be repatriated during 1949 was a unilateral plan the details of which were not available.[20] A final Soviet note of June 4, 1949, repeated the charge that the three western powers had disrupted the preparation of a plan for repatriation of German war prisoners and stated that there was no necessity to enter into further examination of the question.[21]

B. Administration of the Western Zones

[See *Documents, IX, 1947*, p. 65; *X, 1948*, p. 105.]

During 1949 France, the United Kingdom and the United States substantially completed the reorganization of their administrative policies in regard to the three western zones of occupation of Germany. The new program, the principles of which had been agreed upon at a series of meetings during 1948, was implemented by directives resulting from two meetings of the three foreign ministers held during 1949. The first met in Washington from April 1 to April 8, and the second in Paris from November 9 to November 11, 1949. These directives defined changes in policy in three fields: 1) the establishment of civilian administration, under a revised occupation statute, to take the place of military control; 2) the creation of a Federal German Republic under a constitution drafted by German authorities and approved by the occupying powers; and 3) the revision of the plan for reparations payments in accordance with the changed political status and economic needs of the new government and its relation to the rest of western Europe.

1. OCCUPATION MACHINERY

[See *Documents, X, 1948*, p. 137.]

Reorganization of occupation machinery of the three western powers involved three problems: 1) the creation of adequate safeguards to insure security in the event of attempted German rearmament; 2) agreement on the amount of independent authority to be permitted the new western German government; and 3) the nature of the tripartite controls and the method by which they would be applied by each of the three powers when a Federal German Republic composed of a fusion of the three zones was established. The first problem was met by the establishment of a Military Security Board on January 17, 1949, in accordance with agreements reached at London in the meeting of the foreign ministers of Belgium, France, Luxembourg, the Netherlands, the United Kingdom and the United States from November 11 to December 28, 1948.[1] French desire to limit the degree of autonomy to be allowed the new German government and to insure that all important decisions taken by the new control body required unanimous approval ran sharply counter to United States proposals that decisions be by a majority and that in certain types of questions — particularly decisions which might increase occupation costs — France and the United Kingdom give the United States a right to veto.[2] Discussions by representatives of the three governments in London during the first three months of 1949 failed to resolve the differences, which were not composed until the April meeting of the three foreign ministers in Washington.

19 Department of State, *Bulletin*, XX, p. 77.
20 Department of State Press Release 145, March 16, 1949.
21 Department of State, *Bulletin*, XX, p. 824.
1 For details of this meeting, see *Documents, X, 1948*, p. 116.
2 *New York Times*, April 4, 1949, p. 1.

(1) *Directive on the Organization of the Military Security Board for the Western Zones of Germany Issued by the United States, the United Kingdom and France. Department of State Press Release, January 17, 1949.*[3]

[EXCERPTS]

PART I — TERMS OF REFERENCE

1. In accordance with the terms of the London Agreement, a Military Security Board for the Western Zones of Germany will be set up by the Military Governors in order to ensure the maintenance of disarmament and demilitarization in the interests of security.

2. The Board's responsibilities will cover the whole field of disarmament and demilitarization, taking into consideration the laws and directives which have been agreed already on a quadripartite basis. In particular the Board will advise the Military Governors on the maintenance and enforcement of disarmament and demilitarization restrictions. It will carry out the appropriate inspections and will recommend to the Military Governors measures necessary to:

(a) prevent the revival of military or para-military organizations and of the militaristic spirit;

(b) ensure that there shall be no manufacture or import of any arms, war materials or any other materials or equipment which are or may be prohibited;

(c) prevent the infringement by Germans of restrictions in respect of certain industries;

(d) ensure that any military buildings, structures, laboratories, and all shipyards, or factories capable of producing armaments which may be retained are used for peaceful purposes only;

(e) ensure that scientific research is not directed to warlike ends;

(f) ensure that in connection with the construction and operation of merchant shipping and the operation of civil airlines, no war potential is created.

3. In carrying out its task, the Board will:

(a) Study the existing laws and directives, both quadripartite and zonal, and make recommendations if they require additions or amendments, and where advisable produce uniformity throughout the three zones;

(b) Recommend to the Military Governors any laws or regulations to be enacted which may be necessary for the completion of disarmament, or for the prohibition or limitation of specified military, industrial, scientific research or other activities;

(c) Ensure the implementation of the regulations by inspection and ensure that the statistics necessary for the Board are maintained by Germans. The reports of inspections will be presented to the Military Governors, together with the observations of the Board;

(d) Advise the Military Governors on revisions, which may be necessary

3 Department of State, *Bulletin*, XX, p. 195.

from time to time, of the prohibitions of and limitations on capacity or production imposed upon German industry;

(e) Collect, centralize and keep up to date full documentation on the elements which might reconstitute a war potential in the military, industrial and scientific fields.

Part II — Constitution and Functioning

4. *The Military Security Board will be made up of the following elements:*

(a) A Commission
(b) A Committee of Deputies
(c) A Secretariat
(d) Three Divisions: Military, Industrial and Scientific Research
(e) Inspection Groups.

5. *Security in the Ruhr*

The Board will establish such machinery and liaison for co-operation with the International Authority for the Ruhr as may be found necessary.

. . . .

10. *Inspection Groups*

(a) The Divisions will organize, instruct and dispatch inspectors and/or integrated tripartite inspection groups formed from personnel assigned or attached to the Board as often as necessary in order to verify in the three Zones the conditions of execution of the measures ordered by the Military Governors. The Commission may order any special inspections it deems necessary.

(b) Administrative arrangements for these inspections will be made by the Secretariat.

(c) Inspection groups shall have free access at any time to inspect without prior notice for the purposes set forth in paragraph 2 hereof, any place, installation or activity, except that the local Military Government shall be given reasonable advance notice of such intended visits.

11. The creation of the Board implies that disarmament and demilitarization are matters of tripartite responsibility. Until the system of control at Land levels is changed, and as long as unilateral control continues in the Land, the Regional Commissioner (or his equivalent) in each Land will act as the agent of the Military Governors for disarmament and demilitarization. For this purpose he will report to the Military Governors through the Board and will receive his instructions through the same channel. He will provide such information as may be requested and will be responsible for the continuous observation of the execution of prescribed security measures. He will give full facilities for visits by the inspection groups referred to in paragraph 10 above. If he is succeeded by a Tripartite Control Commission, his function will be transferred to that commission. When and if Military Government is no longer adequately represented at Land level, the Board will estab-

lish such tripartite agencies as it deems necessary to ensure control in the Lands.

. . . .

(2) *Occupation Statute for the Western Zones of Germany. Department of State Press Release, April 8, 1949.*[4]

In the exercise of the supreme authority which is retained by the Governments of France, the United States and the United Kingdom,

We, GENERAL PIERRE KOENIG, Military Governor and Commander-in-Chief of the French Zone of Germany,

GENERAL LUCIUS D. CLAY, Military Governor and Commander-in-Chief of the United States Zone of Germany, and

GENERAL SIR BRIAN HUBERT ROBERTSON, Military Governor and Commander-in-Chief of the British Zone of Germany,

DO HEREBY JOINTLY PROCLAIM THE FOLLOWING OCCUPATION STATUTE:

1. During the period in which it is necessary that the occupation continue, the Governments of France, the United States and the United Kingdom desire and intend that the German people shall enjoy self-government to the maximum possible degree consistent with such occupation. The Federal State and the participating Laender shall have, subject only to the limitations in this Instrument, full legislative, executive and judicial powers in accordance with the Basic Law and with their respective constitutions.

2. In order to ensure the accomplishment of the basic purposes of the occupation, powers in the following fields are specifically reserved, including the right to request and verify information and statistics needed by the occupation authorities:

(*a*) disarmament and demilitarization, including related fields of scientific research, prohibitions and restrictions on industry and civil aviation;

(*b*) controls in regard to the Ruhr, restitution, reparations, decartelization, deconcentration, non-discrimination in trade matters, foreign interests in Germany and claims against Germany;

(*c*) foreign affairs, including international agreements made by or on behalf of Germany;

(*d*) displaced persons and the admission of refugees;

(*e*) protection, prestige, and security of Allied forces, dependents, employees, and representatives, their immunities and satisfaction of occupation costs and their other requirements;

(*f*) respect for the Basic Law and the Land constitutions;

(*g*) control over foreign trade and exchange;

(*h*) control over internal action, only to the minimum extent necessary to ensure use of funds, food and other supplies in such manner as to reduce to a minimum the need for external assistance to Germany;

4 *Ibid.*, p. 500.

(*i*) control of the care and treatment in German prisons of persons charged before or sentenced by the courts or tribunals of the occupying powers or occupation authorities; over the carrying out of sentences imposed on them; and over questions of amnesty, pardon or release in relation to them.

3. It is the hope and expectation of the Governments of France, the United States and the United Kingdom that the occupation authorities will not have occasion to take action in fields other than those specifically reserved above. The occupation authorities, however, reserve the right, acting under instructions of their Governments, to resume, in whole or in part, the exercise of full authority if they consider that to do so is essential to security or to preserve democratic government in Germany or in pursuance of the international obligations of their governments. Before so doing, they will formally advise the appropriate German authorities of their decision and of the reasons therefor.

4. The German Federal Government and the governments of the Laender shall have the power, after due notification to the occupation authorities, to legislate and act in the fields reserved to these authorities, except as the occupation authorities otherwise specifically direct, or as such legislation or action would be inconsistent with decisions or actions taken by the occupation authorities themselves.

5. Any amendment of the Basic Law will require the express approval of the occupation authorities before becoming effective. Land constitutions, amendments thereof, all other legislation, and any agreements made between the Federal State and foreign governments, will become effective twenty-one days after official receipt by the occupation authorities unless previously disapproved by them, provisionally or finally. The occupation authorities will not disapprove legislation unless in their opinion it is inconsistent with the Basic Law, a Land Constitution, legislation or other directives of the occupation authorities themselves or the provisions of this Instrument, or unless it constitutes a grave threat to the basic purposes of the occupation.

6. Subject only to the requirements of their security, the occupation authorities guarantee that all agencies of the occupation will respect the civil rights of every person to be protected against arbitrary arrest, search or seizure; to be represented by counsel; to be admitted to bail as circumstances warrant; to communicate with relatives; and to have a fair and prompt trial.

7. Legislation of the occupation authorities enacted before the effective date of the Basic Law shall remain in force until repealed or amended by the occupation authorities in accordance with the following provisions:

(*a*) legislation inconsistent with the foregoing will be repealed or amended to make it consistent herewith;

(*b*) legislation based upon the reserved powers, referred to in paragraph 2 above, will be codified;

(*c*) legislation not referred to in (*a*) and (*b*) will be repealed by the occupation authorities on request from appropriate German authorities.

8. Any action shall be deemed to be the act of the occupation authorities under the powers herein reserved, and effective as such under this Instrument, when taken or evidenced in any manner provided by any agreement between them. The occupation authorities may in their discretion effectuate their decisions either directly or through instructions to the appropriate German authorities.

9. After 12 months and in any event within 18 months of the effective date of this Instrument the occupying powers will undertake a review of its provisions in the light of experience with its operation and with a view to extending the jurisdiction of the German authorities in the legislative, executive and judicial fields.

(3) *Agreement on Tripartite Controls for Western Germany, April 8, 1949. Department of State Press Release, April 25, 1949.*[5]

The Governments of the United Kingdom, France and the United States agree to enter into a trizonal fusion agreement prior to the entry into effect of the Occupation Statute. The representatives of the three occupying powers will make the necessary arrangements to establish tripartite control machinery for the western zones of Germany, which will become effective at the time of the establishment of a provisional German government. The following provisions agreed by the Governments of the United Kingdom, France and the United States shall form the basis of those arrangements:

1. An Allied High Commission composed of one High Commissioner of each occupying power or his representative shall be the supreme Allied agency of control.

2. The nature and extent of controls exercised by the Allied High Commission shall be in harmony with the Occupation Statute and international agreements.

3. In order to permit the German Federal Republic to exercise increased responsibilities over domestic affairs and to reduce the burden of occupation costs, staff personnel shall be kept to a minimum.

4. In the exercise of the powers reserved to the Occupation Authorities to approve amendments to the Federal Constitution, the decisions of the Allied High Commission shall require unanimous agreement.

5. In cases in which the exercise of, or failure to exercise, the powers reserved under paragraph 2 (g) of the Occupation Statute would increase the need for assistance from United States Government appropriated funds, there shall be a system of weighted voting. Under such system the representatives of the Occupation Authorities will have a voting strength proportionate to the funds made available to Germany by their respective governments. This provision shall not, however, reduce the present United States predominant voice in JEIA and JFEA while these organizations, or any successor organization to them, continue in existence and are charged with

[5] Department of State Press Release 287, April 25, 1949.

the performance of any of their present functions. No action taken hereunder shall be contrary to any inter-governmental agreement among the signatories or to the principles of non-discrimination.

6. On all other matters action shall be by majority vote.

7. (a) If a majority decision alters or modifies any inter-governmental agreement which relates to any of the subjects listed in paragraph 2 (a) and 2 (b) of the Occupation Statute, any dissenting High Commissioner may appeal to his Government. This appeal shall serve to suspend the decision pending agreement between the three governments.

(b) If a High Commissioner considers that a majority decision conflicts with any inter-governmental agreement which relates to any of the subjects in paragraph 2 (a) and 2 (b) of the Occupation Statute or with the fundamental principles for the conduct of Germany's external relations or with matters essential to the security, prestige, and requirements of the occupying forces, he may appeal to his Government. Such an appeal shall serve to suspend action for 30 days, and thereafter unless two of the Governments indicate that the grounds do not justify further suspension.

(c) If such appeal is from an action of the Allied High Commission either declining to disapprove or deciding to disapprove German legislation, such legislation shall be provisionally disapproved for the duration of the appeal period.

8. A High Commissioner who considers that a decision made by less than unanimous vote involving any other matter reserved by the Occupation Statute is not in conformity with basic tripartite policies regarding Germany or that a Land constitution, or an amendment thereto, violates the Basic Law, may appeal to his government. An appeal in this case shall serve to suspend action for a period not to exceed twenty-one days from the date of the decision unless all three governments agree otherwise. If such appeal is from an action of the Allied High Commission either declining to disapprove or deciding to disapprove German legislation, such legislation shall be provisionally disapproved for the duration of the appeal period.

9. All powers of the Allied High Commission shall be uniformly exercised in accordance with tripartite policies and directives. To this end in each Land the Allied High Commission shall be represented by a single Land Commissioner who shall be solely responsible to it for all tripartite affairs. In each Land the Land Commissioner shall be a national of the Allied Power in whose zone the Land is situated. Outside his own zone each High Commissioner will delegate an observer to each of the Land Commissioners for purposes of consultation and information. Nothing in this paragraph shall be construed to limit the functions of bodies established pursuant to inter-governmental agreement.

10. To the greatest extent possible, all directives and other instruments of control shall be addressed to the federal and/or Land authorities.

11. The Trizonal Fusion Agreement will continue in force until altered by agreement among the governments.

(4) *Charter of the Allied High Commission for Germany. Department of State Press Release, June 20, 1949.*[6]

I. ESTABLISHMENT OF ALLIED HIGH COMMISSION AND TRANSFER OF CONTROL

1. An Allied High Commission (hereinafter referred to as the High Commission) is hereby established for the exercise of Supreme Allied Authority in the Federal Republic of Germany. The High Commission shall be headed by three High Commissioners, one designated by each of the three powers signatory hereto.

2. As from the date of the entry into force of the Occupation Statute all authority with respect to the control of Germany or over any governmental authority thereof, vested in or exercised by the respective Commanders-in-Chief of the forces of occupation of the three powers in Germany, from whatever source derived and however exercised, will be transferred to the three High Commissioners respectively, to be exercised in accordance with the provisions hereof and of the Occupation Statute.

3. The forces of occupation of the three powers in Germany shall remain stationed in their respective zones of occupation. Command of the forces of occupation in each zone and control of their related military establishments shall remain with the respective Commanders of the forces of occupation in such zones.

4. Legislation of the occupation authorities enacted before the effective date of the Occupation Statute shall remain in force until repealed or amended or otherwise replaced as provided in the Occupation Statute.

II. FUNCTIONS OF THE HIGH COMMISSION

1. The High Commission shall exercise control over the Federal Government and the Governments of its constituent Laender as provided in the Occupation Statute. In the exercise of the powers reserved to the occupation authorities under said Statute, the High Commission shall reach its decisions in accordance with the provisions of the "Agreement as to Tripartite Controls" among the Three Powers dated 8 April 1949 and attached hereto and made a part of this instrument as Annex A. These decisions shall constitute a joint exercise of the authority of all of the three High Commissioners.

2. The High Commission shall act only through the Federal or appropriate Land Government except where direct action or legislation by the High Commission is necessary or appropriate for the due exercise of any of the powers reserved to the occupation authorities under the Occupation Statute.

3. The Headquarters of the High Commission shall be at the seat of the German Federal Government which, together with a surrounding area to be defined, will constitute a special area directly under the High Commission and excluded from any individual zone of occupation. The necessary special arrangements in connection with the definition and administration of this area in as far as they concern the Allies will be determined subsequently by the High Commission.

III. ORGANIZATION OF THE HIGH COMMISSION

1. The organization of the High Commission at its headquarters shall be tripartite in character and shall consist of:

A. An Allied Council (hereinafter referred to as "The Council") composed of the three High Commissioners. Each High Commissioner shall nominate a Deputy or permanent representative who will take his place on the Council in his absence. The Deputies or permanent representatives of the respective High Commissioners acting together may function as an Executive Committee of the Council if the Council so decides;

B. Such committees or bodies as the Council may from time to time establish. These committees and bodies shall advise the Council in their respective spheres and shall exercise such executive functions as the Council may delegate to them. The number, functions, and organization of such committees or bodies may be changed, adjusted, or eliminated entirely by the Council in light of experience. Subject to the above, in order to ensure continuity of operation, the Council ini-

6 Department of State, *Bulletin,* XXI, p. 25.

tially shall be assisted by Committees respectively for Political Affairs, Foreign Trade and Exchange, Finance, Economics, Law and by the Military Security Board. Each Committee shall be assisted by such associated staff as it may require and as the Council approves.

C. Allied General Secretariat.

2. *The Council*

A. The Council shall constitute the supreme authority of the High Commission. The Council shall meet as frequently as it considers necessary and at any time upon the request of any of its members. The Chairmanship of the Council and its various committees shall be held in monthly rotation by each of its members. The Council shall fix the time and place of its meetings and shall establish appropriate rules and procedures for the conduct of its business. Decisions of the Council shall be reached in accordance with Annex A hereof.

3. *Committees*

The composition of each Committee and its terms of reference shall be fixed by the Council. Initially, such Committees, together with their respective terms of reference, shall be as follows:

A. The Political Affairs Committee, consisting of the three Political Advisers to the respective High Commissioners will be concerned with all political and foreign affairs of the German Federal and Land Governments coming with the competence of the Council.

B. A Foreign Trade and Exchange Committee consisting of the respective Economic and Finance Advisers of each of the High Commissioners.

(1) The Committee shall observe the economic, financial and foreign trade policies of the German authorities and shall advise the Council if such policies or any action taken or proposed to be taken pursuant thereto is likely to have such adverse effect on the foreign trade or foreign exchange resources of the German Government as is likely to increase its need for external assistance.

(2) The members of the Committee shall automatically be members of the Board of Directors of the Joint Export-Import Agency (hereinafter referred to as "JEIA") and in conjunction with the other Directors shall be charged with the orderly liquidation of JEIA at the earliest practicable date. The Committee shall assume any control functions presently exercised by JEIA as may warrant retention when the liquidation of JEIA is completed.

(3) It is understood that the German Federal Republic will become party to the convention for European Economic Cooperation and will execute a bilateral agreement with the Government of the United States. It is further understood that thereafter the functions of the High Commission in respect of the matters referred to in (I) will be appropriately modified.

C. The Economics Committee, consisting of the three Economics Advisers to the respective High Commissioners, shall observe the general economic policies of the German authorities and shall advise the Council as to the exercise of its powers in this connection reserved under the Occupation Statute. The Committee shall advise the Council on all matters relating to the Decartelization and Deconcentration of German industry.

D. The Finance Committee, consisting of the three Finance Advisers to the respective High Commissioners, shall observe the general financial policies of the German authorities, and shall advise the Council as to the exercise of its powers in this connection reserved under the Occupation Statute. To the extent necessary within the limits of the provisions of the Occupation Statute the Finance Committee shall succeed to and shall assume the functions heretofore exercised by the Allied Bank Commission.

E. The Law Committee, consisting of the Legal Advisers to the respective High Commissioners, shall advise the Council and its committees on all legal and judicial affairs arising out of the work of the High Commission.

F. The Military Security Board shall deal with all matters of demilitarization, disarmament, industrial prohibitions and limitations, and scientific research, in accordance with its existing terms of reference.

4. *Committee Staffs and Subordinate Groups*

A. Within numerical limitations established by the Council, each of the committees designated pursuant to paragraph 3 of this Article III shall establish such tripartite subordinate committees or other groups as may be necessary to the performance of its functions and as the Council may approve.

B. Except as specifically otherwise provided in subparagraph C of this paragraph 4, personnel for such subordinate committees or groups shall be appointed by each of the High Commissioners on a basis of parity among the three Allied nations. They may include military personnel. The number, functions and organization of such subordinate committees or groups may be changed, adjusted or eliminated entirely by the Council in the light of experience. Each subordinate committee or group shall be answerable to the committee responsible for its creation and shall report to the Council through such committee. Each subordinate agency shall be physically located at the headquarters of the High Commission except as may be otherwise determined by the Council.

C. The subordinate committees and groups established pursuant to subparagraph A of this paragraph 4 shall include:

(1) Joint Export-Import Agency which, until liquidated as provided in subparagraph B of paragraph 3 hereof, shall function under its existing terms of reference with an integrated staff and shall report to the Committee on Foreign Trade and Exchange through its Director General who, together with the Deputy Directors-General, shall be members of the Board of Directors of JEIA.
(2) The Decartelization and Industrial Deconcentration Group, the Coal Control Group and the Steel Control Group, all of which shall report through the Economics Committee.
(3) The Combined Travel Board which shall report through the Political Affairs Committee.
(4) Civil Aviation Board shall report as determined by the Council.
(5) Information and Cultural Affairs Subcommittee which shall report through the Political Affairs Committee.
(6) A subcommittee on foreign interests which shall report as determined by the Council.

5. *Allied General Secretariat*

The High Commission shall be served by a Tripartite General Secretariat. The Secretariat will receive and dispatch all communications to or from the High Commission, prepare the agenda and materials for the meetings of the Council and shall keep the minutes of their meetings. The Secretariat or its appropriate branches shall act as the channel of communication between the High Commission and the agencies of the Federal Government, and between the Council and the several Land Commissioners with respect to matters affecting said Land Governments. The Secretariat shall maintain the records of the High Commission and be responsible for such other tasks as the Council may decide.

IV. LAND COMMISSIONERS

1. All powers of the High Commission shall be uniformly exercised in the constituent Laender of the Federal Republic, in accordance with tripartite policies and the directions of the Council.
2. To achieve uniformity in the exercise of its powers, the High Commission shall be represented at the seat of government of each of the constituent Laender by an Allied Land Commissioner who shall be solely responsible to the Council for ensuring due compliance on the part of the Land authorities with the Council's decisions and directives. The Land Commissioner shall report and be solely responsible to the Council for all matters of tripartite concern in the Land and shall

be the exclusive channel of communication and liaison between the Council and the Land Government with respect to such matters.

3. In particular, each Land Commissioner shall be responsible to the Council for:

A. Initial consideration and prompt transmittal to the Council of Land legislation, together with his recommendations thereon;

B. observing and ensuring due compliance on the part of the Land Government with the provisions of the Federal and Land constitutions, the Occupation Statute and the laws of the occupation authorities in force;

C. providing information as required by the Military Security Board and giving all necessary assistance to the inspectorate of the Military Security Board and such other bodies as may be authorized by the Council;

D. the preparation of such periodic or special reports as the Council may request.

4. Each Land Commissioner and the members of his staff shall be nationals of the Power in whose zone the Land is situated, and shall be appointed by and administratively responsible to the High Commissioner designated by such Power. Each Land Commissioner shall be accountable exclusively to his High Commissioner and shall be his channel of communication and liaison with the Land Government with respect to:

A. All matters which are listed in Article V, paragraph 2;

B. conduct of all relationships between the forces of occupation stationed in the Land and the governmental agencies thereof except to the extent that direct communications and relations may be authorized by him.

5. Each High Commissioner shall designate an observer together with a small personal staff to be agreed in each case by the High Commissioners concerned, to each of the Land Commissioners outside of his own Zone for purposes of consultation and information.

V. INDIVIDUAL RESPONSIBILITIES OF THE HIGH COMMISSIONERS

1. Each High Commissioner shall maintain at the seat of government of each of the Laender in his zone a Land Commissioner with a minimum staff and facilities required for the purposes set forth in Articles IV and V hereof. He shall ensure the due implementation by each of said Land Commissioners of the decisions and directions of the Council. He shall also ensure that all powers of the High Commission are uniformly exercised within said Laender in accordance with tripartite policy and the decisions of the Council.

2. Each High Commissioner shall be responsible to his government with respect to the Laender of his zone for the matters in fields reserved to the occupation authorities listed below. Nevertheless, so far as possible, he shall coordinate the general policies which he may pursue in these fields with those of the other High Commissioners and exercise these powers in accordance with such tripartite legislation or policies as the Council may adopt.

A. Maintenance of law and order if the responsible German authorities are unable to do so;

B. ensuring the protection, prestige, security and immunities of the Allied forces of occupation, of the Allied occupation authorities, their dependents, employees and official representatives;

C. the delivery of reparations and restitutable property;

D. care and administration of displaced persons;

E. the disposition of war criminals;

F. administration of justice in cases falling within the jurisdiction of Allied courts;

G. control of the care and treatment in German prisons of persons charged before or sentenced by the courts or tribunals of the occupation authorities, over the carrying out of sentences imposed on them and over question of amnesty, pardon or release in relation to them.

3. Each High Commissioner shall be individually responsible for the formulation annually in accordance with tripartite policies and criteria, of a budget of occupation costs and other requirements within his zone. Such budget shall be formulated and submitted to the Council on a date to be determined by it for consideration and approval by the Council and for consolidation in a total budget of the occupation authorities for transmission to the German Government. Each High Commissioner shall be responsible to the Council for control of the approved budget for his zone in accordance with accounting standards and procedures established by the Council.

VI. DECISIONS OF THE COUNCIL

1. Formal decisions and directions of the Council affecting the Federal Government or any agency thereof shall be in writing and shall be communicated to the Chancellor by or on behalf of the Council.

2. Formal communications involving matters of lesser import or of a routine character may be addressed to the Minister concerned by the appropriate organ of the Council.

3. Formal decisions or directions of the Council affecting a Land Government or any agency thereof shall be in writing and shall be communicated to its Minister President through the Land Commissioner, in the name of the Council.

4. Formal decisions of the Council shall be recorded in an official gazette maintained by the High Commission at the Allied seat of control in Germany, which shall be published in the English, French, and German languages. Publication of any such decision in the official gazette of the High Commission shall be conclusive evidence that the recorded action or decision was taken pursuant to the powers vested in the occupation authorities under the Occupation Statute.

VII. INTERNATIONAL AUTHORITY FOR THE RUHR

The High Commission shall take all necessary steps to give effect to Article XXII of the agreement establishing the International Authority for the Ruhr of April 28, 1949.

VIII. FOREIGN MISSIONS IN GERMANY

The necessary liaison with the governments of other nations especially interested will be ensured by the appointment by such governments of appropriate missions to the Council of the High Commission having access, by procedures to be determined, to its subordinate bodies and to the German Government.

IX. UNITED NATIONS ORGANIZATIONS IN GERMANY

United Nations organizations and specialized agencies may operate in the Federal Republic of Germany on such terms as may be agreed by the Council.

X. OFFICIAL LANGUAGES

The official languages of the High Commission shall be English and French. Authoritative German texts of documents shall be provided as necessary.

IN WITNESS WHEREOF the foregoing agreement has been duly executed by the respective representatives thereunto duly authorized of the Governments of the United Kingdom of Great Britain, the United States of America and the Republic of France, in triplicate in the French and English languages, each text being equally authentic and shall come into effect on the date of the entry into force of the Occupation Statute.

2. BASIC LAW FOR THE FEDERAL REPUBLIC OF GERMANY

[See *Documents, X, 1948,* p. 127.]

The Military Governors of France, the United Kingdom and the United States approved the Basic Law for the Federal Republic of Germany on May 12, 1949.[7]

7 Office of Military Government (U.S.). *Monthly Report of the Military Governor,* April 1949, No. 46, p. 140. Unless otherwise noted, the information in this section is taken from the *Monthly Report* for the date indicated.

The basic law, in process of drafting during most of 1948, had been approved by the Parliamentary Council on February 10, 1949, and forwarded to the Military Governors, who, on March 2, 1949, transmitted to a delegation of the Parliamentary Council a memorandum pointing out seven particulars in which the draft deviated from the principles laid down in the *aide-mémoire* of November 22, 1948.[8] Failure of a second draft of the disputed articles by a committee of seven of the Parliamentary Council to meet the requirements of the Military Governors led to two statements to the Parliamentary Council from the Council of Foreign Ministers. The first, on April 5, 1949, urged the Council to "give due consideration to the recommendation of the Military Governors." The second, on April 22, 1949, 1) stated that the foreign ministers could not agree to the inclusion of Berlin as a *Land* in the initial organization of the Federal Republic; 2) agreed to give sympathetic consideration to any formulae devised by the Parliamentary Council to secure financial independence for both federal and *Laender* governments as well as to clearly separate the respective functions of the two governmental levels; and 3) indicated a willingness to consider granting the federal government the right to supplement its own revenue by grants from the *Laender* for education, health and welfare purposes.

With the exception of Bavaria, the *Landtag* of which favored a popular referendum but indicated its willingness to approve if the other states did, all of the *Landtage* approved the basic law by May 22, 1949. The first elections for the *Bundestag* were held on August 14, 1949, with 78.5% of the eligible voters participating. On September 12, 1949, the Federal Convention of the German Republic, meeting in Bonn, elected Dr. Theodor Heuss the first Federal President, and, on September 15, Dr. Konrad Adenauer as the first Chancellor of the Republic.

(1) Memorandum Submitted by the Military Governor of the United Kingdom Zone (Robertson) on Behalf of the Military Governors of the Western Zones on the Basic Law of the Federal Republic of Germany, Presented to a Delegation of the Parliamentary Council, March 2, 1949.[9]

1. My colleagues and I have asked you to come here today in order that we might comment to you upon several provisions of your proposed Basic Law as it was passed by the Main Committee of the Parliamentary Council. We have studied this document in light of the Aide-Mémoire which our Liaison Officers delivered to you on 22 November 1948.

2. There are a number of provisions in the Basic Law which deviate from detailed principles set forth in that Aide-Mémoire. However, in viewing the document as a whole, we are prepared to disregard some of these deviations but at the same time feel it necessary again to call your urgent attention to other provisions which, in our opinion, depart too far from these principles.

3. In the first place, we would like to point out that the powers of the federal government as now set forth in Article 36 are not defined with sufficient clarity adequately to safeguard the position of the states in a federal system. To correct this we suggest that you delete present Articles 36 and 36a and substitute therefor a new Article 36 based very largely upon your own language and which might read substantially as follows:

Article 36

(1) The Laender shall retain the right to legislate in the fields hereinafter enumerated except where it is clearly impossible for a single Land to enact effective legislation or where the legislation if enacted would be detrimental to the rights or interests of other Laender. In such cases, and provided that the interests of the several Laender are clearly, directly and integrally affected, the Federation shall have the right to enact such legislation as may be necessary or appropriate.

---

8 For the text of the *aide-mémoire*, see *Documents, X, 1948*, p. 136.
9 Office of Military Government for Germany (U.S.). *Monthly Report of the Military Governor*, February 1949, No. 44, p. 103.

1. Civil law, criminal law and execution of sentences, constitution of courts, court procedure insofar as the Laender are not competent according to Article 112/2, the bar, notaries, and legal advice (Rechtsberatung);
2. Census and registry matters;
3. Associations and assemblies;
4. The right of sojourn and settlement of aliens;
5. The protection of German works of art against removal abroad;
6. Matters relating to refugees and expellees;
7. Public welfare;
8. War damages and compensation (Wiedergutmachung);
9. Provisions for war-disabled persons and surviving dependents, the welfare of former prisoners of war, and the care of war graves;
10. Law relating to the economy (mining, industry, power supply, crafts, trades, commerce, banking and stock exchanges, private insurances);
11. Labor law, including the legal organization of enterprises, protection of workers and provision of employment as well as social insurance including unemployment insurance;
12. The furtherance of scientific research;
13. Expropriation in matters on which the Federation has legislative power;
14. Transfer of land and landed property, natural resources and means of production to public ownership or to other forms of publicly controlled economy;
15. Prevention of the abuse of economic power;
16. Promotion of agricultural and forestry production, safeguarding of food supply, import and export of agricultural and forestry products, deep-sea and coastal fisheries and coastal preservation;
17. Transactions in landed property, law concerning land and agricultural lease, housing, settlements and homesteads;
18. Measures against epidemic and infectious diseases affecting humans and animals, the licensing for medical and other healing professions and the healing trade, and traffic in drugs, medicines, narcotics, and poisons;
19. Protection relating to traffic in food and stimulants as well as in necessities of life, in fodder, in agriculture and forestry, seeds and seedlings, and protection of trees and plants against diseases and pests;
20. Ocean and coastal shipping and aids to navigation, inland shipping, meteorological service, ocean channels, and inland waterways used for general traffic;
21. Road traffic, motor transport, and the construction and maintenance of highways used for long-distance transport;
22. Railways other than federal railways, except mountain railways;
23. Citizenship of the Federation and the Laender;
24. Hunting, protection of nature, and care of the countryside;
25. Land distribution, regional planning, and water conservation;
26. Matters relating to registration and identity cards.

4. In the second place, my colleagues and I would like you to understand that we are ultimately responsible for security and that the powers contained in Article 118c may not be exercised until specifically approved by the Occupation Authorities. This reservation upon the exercise of these police powers will be repeated at the time when you are formally advised of our action with regard to the constitution as a whole.

5. In the third place, we have noted with concern the extent to which the provisions regarding finance powers depart from the criteria agreed upon in London and transmitted to you in paragraph (d) of the Aide-Mémoire. We have already had occasion to advise you that in our opinion substantially the same provisions would result in "the Laender being left without adequate independent sources of revenue for the conduct of their affairs." We would suggest, therefore, several changes, in Articles 122a, 122b, and 123 which would enable these articles more nearly to satisfy the principles of financial organization which we believe to be of primary importance in a federal system. We suggest that these be re-worded to read substantially as follows:

Article 122a

The Federation shall have powers of exclusive legislation in customs and financial monopolies (federal taxes) and of priority legislation on the following taxes (concurrent taxes):

1. Excise taxes and taxes on transactions, with the exception of taxes (Land taxes) with localized application, in particular the taxes on real estate acquisition, incremental value and on fire protection.
2. The taxes on income, property, inheritance and gifts (or donations).
3. "Realsteuern" (taxes on real estate and on businesses), with the exception of the fixing of tax rates.

Article 122b

The Federation shall exercise priority legislation in the field of concurrent taxes only to the extent that it may require the whole or any portion of the proceeds of any concurrent tax or taxes to cover its responsibilities. If the Federation takes over a portion of a concurrent tax the remaining portion shall be retained by the Laender as and where collected.

Article 123

1. The federal taxes shall be administered by federal finance authorities. The Federal Government may, if it so desires, administer, through federal financial authorities, those taxes which it imposes for authorized federal purposes in their entirety, and the tax on income to the extent that such a tax is for federal purposes. The structure of the federal finance authorities and the finance courts and the procedure to be applied by them shall be regulated by federal law. The heads of the finance and customs authorities in the Laender shall be appointed by agreement with the governments of the Laender involved.

2. The Land taxes and concurrent taxes other than those referred to in Article 123 (1) shall be administered by Land finance authorities.

3. The raising of the "Realsteuer" shall be regulated by Land legislation.

To be consistent with what has been said above we wish to call your attention to the need for deleting Article 138c (4) and substituting a detailed specification of Land taxes.

6. In the fourth place, we wish to draw your attention to the fact that Article 129–1(2) is not entirely clear as to the extent to which the independence of the judiciary is ensured. We urge you to give it your thoughtful attention particularly as to the safeguards provided in connection with the dismissal of judges.

7. In the fifth place, we consider that the possibilities for the Federation to establish its own administrative agencies (Articles 112/2 and 116) are wide. We would therefore like to point out that the Military Governors will have to give careful consideration at the time when such agencies are established to ensure that they do not represent too great a centralization of power.

8. In the sixth place we should like to clarify our position with regard to the question of the federal civil service. If principles with regard to the civil service as set out in Articles 27 (b) and 62 are to be embodied in the Constitution they must be modified to conform to the principles enumerated in paragraphs (g) and (h) in our Aide-Mémoire of 22 November 1948.

9. A seventh matter which has concerned us is the question of the reorganization of the territories of the Laender as set out in Articles 25 and 26. In this connection we wish to draw your attention to the statements which we made to the Ministers President on the 20th of July, the pertinent portions of which were as follows:

We wish you to appreciate that the question of Land boundaries is one of great importance to us. We feel that the present is an appropriate time to deal with it, and we are ready to do so. However, it would be much more difficult for us to deal with it later on. It has, for example, reactions with regard to our own zonal boundaries. We do not feel that we should be willing to deal with the subject again at a later date prior to the conclusion of a peace treaty.

Moreover, the fixing of Land boundaries is important in relation to the Constitution itself. We believe that we should recommend to our Governments that the boundaries which were recognized during the drafting of this Constitution should remain unchanged, at least until a peace treaty is signed.

Our position today is the same as it was at that time and we feel we must now advise you that unless we unanimously agree to change this position it must remain so until the peace treaty. In this case also we will remind you of this decision at the time formal action is taken wtih regard to the Constitution as a whole.

10. Finally, my colleagues and I would like you to know that we understand the solicitude which the Parliamentary Council has shown for Berlin. However, in view of the existing situation, that portion of Article 22 which refers to Berlin must be suspended. Nevertheless, there would be not objection to the responsible authorities in Berlin designating a small number of representatives to attend the meetings of the parliament.

(2) *Basic Law for the Federal Republic of Germany, Approved by the Military Governors of the Western Zones of Germany, May 12, 1949.*[10]

Conscious of its responsibility before God and mankind, filled with the resolve to preserve its national and political unity and to serve world peace as an equal partner in a united Europe, the German people
in the Laender Baden, Bavaria, Bremen, Hamburg,
Hesse, Lower Saxony, North Rhine-Westphalia,
Rhineland-Palatinate, Schleswig-Holstein, Wuerttemberg-Baden and Wuerttemberg-Hohenzollern
has, by virtue of its constituent power, enacted this Basic Law of the Federal Republic of Germany to give a new order to political life for a transitional period.

It acted also on behalf of those Germans to whom participation was denied.

The entire German people is called upon to accomplish, by free self-determination, the unity and freedom of Germany.

I. BASIC RIGHTS

Article 1

(1) The dignity of man shall be inviolable. To respect and protect it shall be the duty of all state authority.

(2) The German people therefore acknowledges inviolable and inalienable human rights as the basis of every human community, of peace and of justice in the world.

(3) The following basic rights shall be binding as directly valid law on legislation, administration and judiciary.

Article 2

(1) Everyone shall have the right to the free development of his personality, insofar as he does not infringe the rights of others or offend against the constitutional order or the moral code.

(2) Everyone shall have the right to life and physical inviolability. The freedom of the individual shall be inviolable. These rights may be interfered with only on the basis of a law.

10 Department of State Publication 3526.

Article 3

(1) All men shall be equal before the law.

(2) Men and women shall have equal rights.

(3) No one may be prejudiced or privileged because of his sex, descent, race, language, homeland and origin, faith or his religious and political opinions.

Article 4

(1) Freedom of faith and conscience and freedom of religious and ideological (*weltanschauliche*) profession shall be inviolable.

(2) Undisturbed practice of religion shall be guaranteed.

(3) No one may be compelled against his conscience to perform war service as a combatant. Details shall be regulated by a federal law.

Article 5

(1) Everyone shall have the right freely to express and to disseminate his opinion through speech, writing and illustration and, without hindrance, to instruct himself from generally accessible sources. Freedom of the press and freedom of reporting by radio and motion pictures shall be guaranteed. There shall be no censorship.

(2) These rights shall be limited by the provisions of the general laws, the legal regulations for the protection of juveniles and by the right of personal honour.

(3) Art and science, research and teaching shall be free. Freedom of teaching shall not absolve from loyalty to the constitution.

Article 6

(1) Marriage and family shall be under the special protection of the state.

(2) The care and upbringing of children shall be the natural right of parents and the supreme duty incumbent upon them. The state shall watch over their activity.

(3) Children may be separated from the family against the will of those entitled to bring them up only on a legal basis if those so entitled fail to do their duty or if, on other grounds, a danger of the children being neglected arises.

(4) Every mother shall have a claim to the protection and care of the community.

(5) Illegitimate children shall, through legislation, be given the same conditions for their physical and spiritual development and their position in society as legitimate children.

Article 7

(1) The entire educational system shall be under the supervision of the state.

(2) Those entitled to bring up the child shall have the right to decide whether it shall receive religious instruction.

(3) Religious instruction shall form part of the curriculum in the state schools with the exception of non-confessional schools. Religious instruction shall, without prejudice to the state's right of supervision, be given according to the principles of the religious societies. No teacher may be obliged against his will to give religious instruction.

(4) The right to establish private schools shall be guaranteed. Private schools as substitute for state schools shall require the sanction of the state and shall be subject to Land legislation. The sanction must be given if the private schools, in their educational aims and facilities, as well as in the scholarly training of their teaching personnel, are not inferior to the state schools and if a separation of the pupils according to the means of the parents is not encouraged. The sanction must be withheld if the economic and legal status of the teaching personnel is not sufficiently assured.

(5) A private elementary school shall be permitted only if the educational ad-

ministration recognizes a specific pedagogic interest or, at the request of those entitled to bring up children, if it is to be established as a general community school (*Gemeinschaftsschule*), as a confessional or ideological school or if a state elementary school of this type does not exist in the Gemeinde.

(6) Preparatory schools shall remain abolished.

Article 8

(1) All Germans shall have the right, without prior notification or permission, to assemble peacefully and unarmed.

(2) For open air meetings this right may be restricted by legislation or on the basis of a law.

Article 9

(1) All Germans shall have the right to form associations and societies.

(2) Associations, the objects or activities of which conflict with the criminal laws or which are directed against the constitutional order or the concept of international understanding, shall be prohibited.

(3) The right to form associations to safeguard and improve working and economic conditions shall be guaranteed to everyone and to all professions. Agreements which seek to restrict or hinder this right shall be null and void; measures directed to this end shall be illegal.

Article 10

Secrecy of the mail as well as secrecy of the post and telecommunications shall be inviolable. Restrictions may be ordered only on the basis of a law.

Article 11

(1) All Germans shall enjoy freedom of movement throughout the federal territory.

(2) This right may be restricted only by legislation and only for the cases in which an adequate basis of existence is absent and, as a result, particular burdens would arise for the general public or in which it is necessary for the protection of juveniles from neglect, for combatting the danger of epidemics or in order to prevent criminal acts.

Article 12

(1) All Germans shall have the right freely to choose their occupation, place of work and place of training. The practice of an occupation may be regulated by legislation.

(2) No one may be compelled to perform a particular kind of work except within the framework of an established general compulsory public service equally applicable to everybody.

(3) Forced labour shall be admissible only in the event of imprisonment ordered by a court.

Article 13

(1) The dwelling shall be inviolable.

(2) Searches may be ordered only by a judge or in the event of imminent danger by other authorities provided by law and may be carried out only in the form prescribed therein.

(3) Interventions and restrictions may otherwise be undertaken only to avert a common danger or mortal danger to individuals and, on the basis of a law, also to prevent imminent danger to public safety and order, especially for the relief of the housing shortage, combatting the danger of epidemics or protecting juveniles exposed to dangers.

Article 14

(1) Property and the right of inheritance shall be guaranteed. The contents and limitations shall be determined by legislation.

(2) Property shall involve obligations. Its use shall simultaneously serve the general welfare.

(3) Expropriation shall be admissible only for the wellbeing of the general public. It may be effected only by legislation or on the basis of a law which shall regulate the nature and extent of compensation. The compensation shall be determined after just consideration of the interests of the general public and the participants. Regarding the extent of compensation, appeal may be made to the ordinary courts in case of dispute.

Article 15

Land and landed property, natural resources and means of production may, for the purpose of socialization, be transferred to public ownership or other forms of publicly controlled economy by way of a law which shall regulate the nature and extent of compensation. For the compensation, Article 14, paragraph (3), sentences 3 and 4, shall apply appropriately.

Article 16

(1) No one may be deprived of his German citizenship. The loss of citizenship may occur only on the basis of a law and, against the will of the person concerned, only if the person concerned is not rendered stateless thereby.

(2) No German may be extradited to a foreign country. The politically persecuted shall enjoy the right of asylum.

Article 17

Everyone shall have the right, individually or jointly with others, to address written requests or complaints to the competent authorities and to the popular representative bodies.

Article 18

Whoever abuses the freedom of expression of opinion, in particular the freedom of the press (Article 5, paragraph (1)), the freedom of teaching (Article 5, paragraph (3)), the freedom of assembly (Article 8), the freedom of association, (Article 9), the secrecy of mail, post and telecommunications (Article 10), property (Article 14), or the right of asylum (Article 16, paragraph (2)), in order to attack the free, democratic basic order, shall forefeit these basic rights. The forfeiture and its extent shall be pronounced by the Federal Constitutional Court.

Article 19

(1) Insofar as according to this Basic law a basic right may be restricted by legislation or on the basis of a law, the law must apply in general and not solely to the individual case. Furthermore, the law must name the basic right, indicating the Article.

(2) In no case may a basic right be affected in its basic content.

(3) The basic rights shall also apply to juridical persons within the country insofar as, according to their nature, they may be applied to such persons.

(4) Should any person's rights be infringed by public authority, he may appeal to the courts. Insofar as another authority is not competent, the appeal shall go to the ordinary courts.

II. THE FEDERATION AND THE LAENDER

Article 20

(1) The Federal Republic of Germany is a democratic and social federal state.

(2) All state authority emanates from the people. It shall be exercised by the

people in elections and plebiscites and by means of separate legislative, executive and judicial organs.

(3) Legislation shall be limited by the constitution, the executive and the administration of justice by legislation and the law.

Article 21

(1) The parties shall participate in forming the political will of the people. They can be freely formed. Their internal organization must conform to democratic principles. They must publicly account for the sources of their funds.

(2) Parties which, according to their aims and the behaviour of their members, seek to impair or abolish the free and democratic basic order or to jeopardize the existence of the Federal Republic of Germany, shall be unconstitutional. The Federal Constitutional Court shall decide on the question of unconstitutionality.

(3) Details shall be regulated by federal legislation.

Article 22

The federal flag shall be black-red-gold.

Article 23

For the time being, this Basic Law shall apply in the territory of the Laender Baden, Bavaria, Bremen, Greater Berlin, Hamburg, Hesse, Lower Saxony, North Rhine-Westphalia, Rhineland-Palatinate, Schleswig-Holstein, Wuerttemberg-Baden and Wuerttemberg-Hohenzollern. It shall be put into force for other parts of Germany on their accession.

Article 24

(1) The Federation may, by legislation, transfer soverign powers to international institutions.

(2) In order to preserve peace, the Federation may join a system of mutual collective security; in doing so it will consent to those limitations of its sovereign powers which will bring about and secure a peaceful and lasting order in Europe and among the nations of the world.

(3) For the settlement of international disputes, the Federation will join a general, comprehensive, obligatory system of international arbitration.

Article 25

The general rules of international law shall form part of federal law. They shall take precedence over the laws and create rights and duties directly for the inhabitants of the federal territory.

Article 26

(1) Activities tending to disturb or undertaken with the intention of disturbing the peaceful relations between nations, and especially preparing for aggressive war, shall be unconstitutional. They shall be made subject to punishment.

(2) Weapons designed for warfare may be manufactured, transported or marketed only with the permission of the Federal Government. Details shall be regulated by a federal law.

Article 27

All German merchantmen shall form a unified merchant marine.

Article 28

(1) The constitutional order in the Laender must conform to the principles of the republican, democratic and social state based on the rule of law (*Rechtsstaat*) within the meaning of this Basic Law. In the Laender, Kreise and Gemeinden the

people must have a representative assembly resulting from universal, direct, free, equal and secret elections. In Gemeinden, the Parish Meeting may take the place of an elected body.

(2) The Gemeinden must be guaranteed the right to regulate under their own responsibility all the affairs of the local community in accordance with the laws. The Gemeindeverbände also shall have the right of self-government within the limits of their legal sphere of functions and in accordance with the laws.

(3) The Federation shall guarantee that the constitutional order of the Laender shall correspond to the basic rights and the provisions of paragraphs (1) and (2).

Article 29

(1) The federal territory shall be reorganized by a federal law with due regard to regional unity, historical and cultural connections, economic expediency and social structure. The reorganization shall create Laender which by their size and potentiality are able to fulfil efficiently the functions incumbent upon them.

(2) In areas which, in the reorganization of Laender after 8 May 1945, joined another Land without plebiscite, a certain change in the decision made concerning this subject may be demanded by popular initiative within one year after the coming into force of the Basic Law. The popular initiative shall require the consent of one-tenth of the population qualified to vote in Landtag elections. Should the popular initiative take place, the Federal Government must, in the draft law regarding the reorganization, include a provision determining to which Land the area concerned shall belong.

(3) After adoption of the law, in each area which it is intended should join another Land, that part of the law which concerns this area must be submitted to a referendum. If a popular initiative takes place in accordance with paragraph (2), a referendum must always be carried out in the area concerned.

(4) Insofar as thereby the law is rejected at least in one area, it must be reintroduced in the Bundestag. After re-enactment, it shall require accordingly acceptance by referendum in the entire federal territory.

(5) In a referendum, the majority of the votes cast shall decide.

(6) The procedure shall be regulated by a federal law. The reorganization shall be regulated before the expiry of three years after promulgation of the Basic Law and, should it be necessary in consequence of the accession of another part of Germany, within two years after such accession.

(7) The procedure regarding any other change in the existing territory of the Laender shall be regulated by a federal law, which shall require the approval of the Bundesrat and of the majority of the members of the Bundestag.

Article 30

The exercise of the powers of the state and the performance of state functions shall be the concern of the Laender, insofar as this Basic Law does not otherwise prescribe or permit.

Article 31

Federal law shall supersede Land law.

Article 32

(1) The maintenance of relations with foreign states shall be the affair of the Federation.

(2) Before the conclusion of a treaty affecting the special conditions of a Land, the Land must be consulted sufficiently early.

(3) Insofar as the Laender are competent to legislate, they may, with the approval of the Federal Government, conclude treaties with foreign states.

Article 33

(1) Every German shall have in each Land the same civil (*staatsbürgerliche*) rights and duties.

(2) Every German shall have equal access to any public office in accordance with his suitability, ability and professional achievements.

(3) Enjoyment of municipal and national civil (*bürgerliche und staatsbürgerliche*) rights, access to public offices, as well as the rights acquired in the public service, shall be independent of religious confession. No one may be prejudiced on account of his adherence or non-adherence to a confession or ideology (*Weltanschauung*).

(4) The exercise of state authority (*hoheitsrechtliche Befugnisse*) shall normally be assigned as permanent functions to members of the public service who are in a status of service and loyalty under public law.

(5) Law regarding the public service shall be regulated with due regard to the established principles concerning the legal status of professional officials (*Berufsbeamtentum*).

Article 34

If any person, in exercising the duties of a public office entrusted to him, violates his official obligation towards a third party, liability shall in principle rest with the state or his employing authority. In the case of wilful intent or gross negligence, the right of recourse shall be reserved. In respect to the claim for damages and in respect to the right of recourse, appeal to the ordinary courts must not be excluded.

Article 35

All federal and Land authorities shall render each other mutual legal and official assistance.

Article 36

In the highest federal authorities civil servants (*Beamte*) from all Laender shall be employed in equitable ratio. Persons employed in the other federal offices shall normally be selected from the Land in which they are employed.

Article 37

(1) If a Land fails to fulfil its obligations towards the Federation under the Basic Law or any other federal law, the Federal Government may, with the approval of the Bundesrat, take the necessary measures to force the Land by way of federal compulsion to fulfil its duties.

(2) In order to carry out federal compulsion, the Federal Government or its commissioner shall have the right to give orders to all Laender and their authorities.

III. The Bundestag

Article 38

(1) The deputies of the German Bundestag shall be elected by the people in universal, free, equal, direct and secret elections. They shall be representatives of the whole people, not bound to orders and instructions and subject only to their conscience.

(2) Any person who has reached the age of 21 years shall be eligible to vote and any person who has reached the age of 25 years shall be eligible for election.

(3) Details shall be determined by a federal law.

Article 39

(1) The Bundestag shall be elected for a term of four years. Its electoral period shall end four years after its first assembly or with its dissolution. The new election shall take place in the last three months of the electoral period; in the case of its dissolution, at the latest after 60 days.

(2) The Bundestag shall meet not later than thirty days after the election, nevertheless not before the end of the electoral period of the previous Bundestag.

(3) The Bundestag shall determine the closure and resumption of its sessions. The President of the Bundestag may convene it at an earlier date. He shall be obliged to do so if one-third of the members, the Federal President or the Federal Chancellor so demand.

Article 40

(1) The Bundestag shall elect its President, his deputies and its clerks. It shall draw up its Standing Orders (Rules of Procedure).

(2) The President shall have charge of, and exercise police power in, the Bundestag building. No search or seizure may take place without his permission in the precincts of the Bundestag.

Article 41

(1) The review of elections shall be the responsibility of the Bundestag. It shall decide also whether a deputy has lost his membership in the Bundestag.

(2) An appeal to the Federal Constitutional Court against a decision of the Bundestag shall be admissible.

(3) Details shall be regulated by a federal law.

Article 42

(1) Meetings of the Bundestag shall be public. Upon a motion of one-tenth of its members or upon a motion of the Federal Government the public may, by a two-thirds majority, be excluded. A decision on the motion will be made in a closed meeting.

(2) Decisions of the Bundestag shall require the majority of votes cast insofar as the Basic Law does not determine otherwise. Standing Orders (Rules of Procedure) may admit exceptions in the case of elections to be held by the Bundestag.

(3) Accurate reports of the public meetings of the Bundestag and of its committees shall be privileged.

Article 43

(1) The Bundestag and its committees may demand the presence of any member of the Federal Government.

(2) The members of the Bundesrat and of the Federal Government as well as the persons commissioned by them shall have access to all meetings of the Bundestag and its committees. They must be heard at any time.

Article 44

(1) The Bundestag shall have the right and, upon the motion of one-fourth of its members, the obligation to set up an investigating committee, which shall take the necessary evidence in public proceedings. The public may be excluded.

(2) The provisions relating to criminal procedure shall apply appropriately to the investigations. Secrecy of the mail, post and telecommunications shall remain unaffected.

(3) The courts and administrative authorities shall be obliged to provide legal and official assistance.

(4) The decision of the investigating committees shall not be subjected to judicial review. The courts shall be free to evaluate and judge the facts on which the investigation is based.

Article 45

(1) The Bundestag shall appoint a Standing Committee which shall safeguard the rights of the Bundestag vis-à-vis the Federal Government in the interval between two electoral periods. The Standing Committee shall also have the rights of an investigating committee.

(2) Wider powers, in particular the right to legislate, to elect the Federal Chancellor and to impeach the Federal President, shall not be within the province of the Standing Committee.

Article 46

(1) A deputy may at no time be subject to legal or disciplinary action or otherwise be called to account outside the Bundestag because of his vote or any utterance in the Bundestag or in one of its committees. This shall not apply in the case of defamatory insults.

(2) A deputy may be called to account or arrested for a punishable offence only with the permission of the Bundestag, unless he be apprehended while committing the offence or in the course of the following day.

(3) Furthermore, the permission of the Bundestag shall be required in respect of any other restriction of the personal freedom of a deputy or for the initiating of proceedings against a deputy in accordance with Article 18.

(4) Any criminal proceedings and any proceedings in accordance with Article 18 against a deputy, any detention and any other restriction of his personal freedom shall be suspended upon the demand of the Bundestag.

Article 47

Deputies shall be entitled to refuse to give evidence concerning persons who have entrusted facts to them in their capacity as deputies or to whom they in this capacity have entrusted facts, as well as concerning these facts themselves. Insofar as this right of refusal to give evidence extends, the seizure of documents shall be inadmissible.

Article 48

(1) Any person seeking election to the Bundestag shall have a claim to the leave necessary for his election campaign.

(2) No one may be prevented from assuming or exercising the office of a deputy. Notice of dismissal or dismissal for this reason shall be inadmissible.

(3) Deputies shall have a claim to adequate remuneration, which shall ensure their independence. They shall have the right to free travel in all publicly owned transport. Details shall be regulated by a federal law.

Article 49

Articles 46, 47 and 48 paragraphs (2) and (3) shall apply to the members of the Praesidium and the Standing Committee as well as to their chief deputies also in the interval between two electoral periods.

IV. The Bundesrat

Article 50

The Laender shall participate through the medium of the Bundesrat in the legislation and the administration of the Federation.

Article 51

(1) The Bundesrat shall consist of members of the Governments of the Laender which shall appoint and recall them. They may be represented by other members of their Governments.

(2) Each Land shall have at least three votes; Laender with more than two million inhabitants shall have four, Laender with more than six million inhabitants shall have five votes.

(3) Every Land may delegate as many members as it has votes. The votes of each Land may be given only as a block vote and only by members present or their representatives.

Article 52

(1) The Bundesrat shall elect its President for one year.

(2) The President shall convene the Bundesrat. He must convene it if the representatives of at least two Laender or the Federal Government so demand.

(3) The Bundesrat shall take its decisions with at least the majority of its votes. It shall draw up its Standing Orders (Rules of Procedure). It shall meet in public. The public may be excluded.

(4) Other members or representatives of the Governments of the Laender may belong to the committees of the Bundesrat.

Article 53

The members of the Federal Government shall have the right, and on demand the obligation, to participate in the debates of the Bundesrat and its committees. They must be heard at any time. The Bundesrat must be kept currently informed by the Federal Government on the conduct of federal affairs.

V. THE FEDERAL PRESIDENT

Article 54

(1) The Federal President shall be elected, without discussion, by the Federal Convention. Every German who is eligible to vote in elections for the Bundestag and has reached the age of 40 years shall be eligible for election.

(2) The term of office of the Federal President shall be five years. Immediate re-election shall be admissible only once.

(3) The Federal Convention shall consist of the members of the Bundestag and an equal number of members elected by the popular representative bodies of the Laender according to the principles of proportional representation.

(4) The Federal Convention shall meet not later than thirty days before the expiry of the term of office of the Federal President, in the case of premature termination not later than thirty days after this date. It shall be convened by the President of the Bundestag.

(5) After the expiry of the electoral period, the time limit of paragraph (4), sentence 1, shall begin with the first meeting of the Bundestag.

(6) The person who has received the votes of the majority of the members of the Federal Convention shall be elected. If such majority is not obtained by any candidate in two ballots, the person who receives most votes in a further ballot shall be elected.

(7) Details shall be regulated by a federal law.

Article 55

(1) The Federal President may be a member neither of the Government nor of a legislative body of the Federation or a Land.

(2) The Federal President may not hold any other salaried office, carry on a trade or practise a profession or belong to the management or supervisory board of a profit-making enterprise.

Article 56

On assuming office, the Federal President shall take the following oath in the presence of the assembled members of the Bundestag and the Bundesrat:

> "I swear that I shall dedicate my strength to the well-being of the German people, enhance what is to its advantage, ward off what might harm it, uphold and defend the Basic Law and the laws of the Federation, fulfil my duties conscientiously and do justice to every man. So help me God."

The oath may also be taken without the religious asseveration.

Article 57

In the event of the inability of the Federal President to perform the duties of his office or in the event of a premature vacancy in the office, the functions of the Federal President shall be exercised by the President of the Bundesrat.

Article 58

Orders and instructions of the Federal President shall require for their validity the counter-signature of the Federal Chancellor or the competent Federal Minister. This shall not apply to the appointment and dismissal of the Federal Chancellor, the dissolution of the Bundestag in accordance with Article 63 and a request in accordance with Article 69, paragraph (3).

Article 59

(1) The Federal President shall represent the Federation in matters concerning international law. He shall conclude treaties with foreign states on behalf of the Federation. He shall accredit and receive the envoys.

(2) Treaties which regulate the political relations of the Federation or refer to matters of federal legislation shall require, in the form of a federal law, the approval or the participation of the corporations competent at the time for federal legislation. For administrative agreements the provisions concerning the federal administration shall apply appropriately.

Article 60

(1) The Federal President shall appoint and dismiss the federal judges and the federal officials unless otherwise determined by law.

(2) He shall exercise the right of pardon on behalf of the Federation in individual cases.

(3) He may delegate these powers to other authorities.

(4) Article 46, paragraphs (2) to (4), shall apply appropriately to the Federal President.

Article 61

(1) The Bundestag or the Bundesrat may impeach the Federal President before the Federal Constitutional Court on account of wilful violation of the Basic Law or any other federal law. The motion for impeachment must be brought in by at least one-quarter of the members of the Bundestag or one-quarter of the votes of the Bundesrat. The decision to impeach shall require the majority of two-thirds of the members of the Bundestag or of two-thirds of the votes of the Bundesrat. The prosecution shall be conducted by a person commissioned by the impeaching body.

(2) If the Federal Constitutional Court finds that the Federal President is guilty of a wilful violation of the Basic Law or of any other federal law, it may declare him to have forfeited his office. After the institution of impeachment proceedings, the Federal Constitutional Court may, by interim order, determine that the Federal President is prevented from performing the duties of his office.

VI. The Federal Government

Article 62

The Federal Government shall consist of the Federal Chancellor and the Federal Ministers.

Article 63

(1) The Federal Chancellor shall be elected, without discussion, by the Bundestag on the proposal of the Federal President.

(2) The person who has received the votes of the majority of the members of the Bundestag shall be elected. He shall be appointed by the Federal President.

(3) If the person nominated is not elected, the Bundestag may, within fourteen days after the ballot, elect a Federal Chancellor by more than one half of its members.

(4) If the Federal Chancellor is not elected within this time limit a new ballot shall take place immediately, in which the person who receives most votes shall be elected. If the person elected receives the votes of the majority of the members of the Bundestag the Federal President must, within 7 days after the election, appoint him. If the person elected does not obtain this majority the Federal President must, within seven days, either appoint him or dissolve the Bundestag.

Article 64

(1) The Federal Ministers shall be appointed and dismissed by the Federal President upon the proposal of the Federal Chancellor.

(2) The Federal Chancellor and the Federal Ministers, on assuming office, shall take before the Bundestag the oath provided in Article 56.

Article 65

The Federal Chancellor shall determine and assume responsibility for general policy. Within the limits of this general policy, each Federal Minister shall direct his department individually and on his own responsibility. The Federal Government shall decide on differences of opinion between the Federal Ministers. The Federal Chancellor shall conduct its business in accordance with Standing Orders (Rules of Procedure) adopted by the Federal Government and approved by the Federal President.

Article 66

The Federal Chancellor and the Federal Ministers may not hold any other salaried office, carry on a trade or practise a profession or belong to the management or, without the approval of the Bundestag, to the supervisory board of a profit-making enterprise.

Article 67

(1) The Bundestag may express its lack of confidence in the Federal Chancellor only by electing a successor with the majority of its members and submitting a request to the Federal President for the dismissal of the Federal Chancellor. The Federal President must comply with the request and appoint the person elected.

(2) There must be an interval of 48 hours between the motion and the election.

Article 68

(1) If a motion of the Federal Chancellor to receive a vote of confidence does not obtain the support of the majority of the members of the Bundestag, the Federal President may, upon the proposal of the Federal Chancellor, dissolve the Bundestag within 21 days. The right of dissolution shall lapse as soon as the Bundestag, with the majority of its members, elects another Federal Chancellor.

(2) There must be an interval of 48 hours between the introduction of, and the vote on, the motion.

Article 69

(1) The Federal Chancellor shall appoint a Federal Minister as his deputy.

(2) The office of the Federal Chancellor or of a Federal Minister shall end in any case with the assembly of a new Bundestag, the office of a Federal Minister also with any other termination of the office of the Federal Chancellor.

(3) At the request of the Federal President, the Federal Chancellor, [and] at the request of the Federal Chancellor or of the Federal President a Federal Minister, shall be obliged to carry out the duties of his office until the appointment of his successor.

VII. The Legislation of the Federation

Article 70

(1) The Laender shall have the right of legislation insofar as this Basic Law does not accord legislative powers to the Federation.

(2) The division of competence between the Federation and the Laender shall be determined in accordance with the provisions of this Basic Law concerning exclusive and concurrent legislation.

Article 71

In the field of exclusive legislation of the Federation, the Laender shall have powers of legislation only if, and so far as, they are expressly so empowered in a federal law.

Article 72

(1) In the field of concurrent legislation, the Laender shall have powers of legislation so long and so far as the Federation makes no use of its legislative right.

(2) The Federation shall have legislative rights in this field insofar as a necessity for regulation by federal law exists because:

1. a matter cannot be effectively regulated by the legislation of individual Laender, or
2. the regulation of a matter by a Land law could prejudice the interests of other Laender or of the Laender as a whole, or
3. the preservation of legal or economic unity demands it, in particular the preservation of uniformity of living conditions extending beyond the territory of an individual Land.

Article 73

The Federation shall have exclusive legislation on:

1. foreign affairs;
2. citizenship of the Federation;
3. freedom of movement, passports, immigration, emigration and extradition;
4. currency, money and coinage, weights and measures and regulation of time and calendar;
5. the unity of customs and commercial territory, commercial and navigation agreements, the freedom of traffic in goods and the traffic in goods and payments with foreign countries, including customs and frontier protection;
6. federal railways and air traffic;
7. post and telecommunications;
8. the legal status of persons in the employment of the Federation and of public law corporations under direct supervision of the Federal Government;
9. trade marks, copyright and publishing rights;
10. co-operation of the Federation and the Laender in the criminal police and in matters concerning the protection of the constitution, the establishment of a Federal Office of Criminal Police, as well as the combatting of international crime;
11. statistics for federal purposes.

Article 74

Concurrent legislation shall extend to the following fields:

1. civil law, criminal law and execution of sentences, constitution of courts, court procedure, the bar, notaries and legal advice (*Rechtsberatung*);
2. census and registry matters;
3. association and assemblies;

4. the right of sojourn and settlement of aliens;
5. the protection of German works of art against removal abroad;
6. matters relating to refugees and expellees;
7. public welfare;
8. citizenship of the Laender;
9. war damages and compensation (*Wiedergutmachung*);
10. provisions for war-disabled persons and surviving dependants, the welfare of former prisoners of war and the care of war graves;
11. law relating to the economy (mining, industry, power supply, crafts, trades, commerce, banking and stock exchanges, private insurances);
12. labour law, including the legal organization of enterprises, protection of workers and provision of employment, as well as social insurance including unemployment insurance;
13. the furtherance of scientific research;
14. the law regarding expropriation insofar as it is concerned with the matters enumerated in Articles 73 and 74;
15. transfer of land and landed property, natural resources and means of production to public ownership or to other forms of publicly controlled economy;
16. prevention of the abuse of economic power;
17. promotion of agricultural and forestry production, safeguarding of food supply, import and export of agricultural and forestry products, deep-sea and coastal fisheries and coastal preservation;
18. transactions in landed property, law concerning land and agricultural lease, housing, settlements and homesteads;
19. measures against epidemic and infectious diseases affecting humans and animals, the licensing for medical and other healing professions and the healing trade and traffic in drugs, medicines, narcotics and poisons;
20. protection relating to traffic in food and stimulants as well as in necessities of life, in fodder, in agricultural and forestry seeds and seedlings, and protection of trees and plants against diseases and pests;
21. ocean and coastal shipping and aids to navigation, inland shipping, meteorological service, ocean channels and inland waterways used for general traffic;
22. road traffic, motor transport and the construction and maintenance of highways used for long-distance transport;
23. railways other than federal railways, except mountain railways.

Article 75

The Federation shall have the right on the basis of Article 72 to issue general provisions concerning:
1. the legal status of persons employed in the public service of the Laender, Gemeinden and other public law corporations;
2. the general legal status of the press and motion pictures;
3. hunting, protection of nature and care of the countryside;
4. land distribution, regional planning and water conservation;
5. matters relating to registration and identity cards.

Article 76

(1) Bills shall be introduced in the Bundestag by the Federal Government, by members of the Bundestag or by the Bundesrat.

(2) Federal Government bills shall first be submitted to the Bundesrat. The Bundesrat shall have the right to give its opinion on these bills within three weeks.

(3) Bundesrat bills shall be submitted to the Bundestag by the Federal Government, which must add a statement of its own views.

Article 77

(1) Federal laws shall be passed by the Bundestag. After their adoption, they shall, without delay, be submitted to the Bundesrat by the President of the Bundestag.

(2) The Bundesrat may, within two weeks of the receipt of the adopted bill, demand that a committee composed of members of the Bundestag and Bundesrat be convened to consider the bill jointly. The composition and the procedure of this committee shall be regulated by Standing Orders (Rules of Procedure), which shall be agreed by the Bundestag and shall require the approval of the Bundesrat. The members of the Bundesrat deputed to this committee shall not be bound by instructions. If the approval of the Bundesrat is required for a law, both the Bundestag and the Federal Government may demand that it be convened. Should the committee propose an alteration of the adopted bill, the Bundestag must take a new decision.

(3) Insofar as the approval of the Bundesrat is not required for a law the Bundesrat may, if the procedure in accordance with paragraph (2) is completed, within one week veto a law passed by the Bundestag. The time limit for a veto shall begin in the case of paragraph (2), last sentence, with the receipt of the bill as re-adopted by the Bundestag, in all other cases with the conclusion of the procedure preceding the committee provided for in paragraph (2).

(4) Should the veto be adopted by the majority of the votes of the Bundesrat, it may be rejected by a decision of the majority of the members of the Bundestag. Should the Bundesrat have adopted the veto by a majority of at least two-thirds of its votes, the rejection by the Bundestag shall require a majority of two-thirds, or at least the majority of the members of the Bundestag.

Article 78

A law passed by the Bundestag shall be enacted if the Bundesrat approves, does not bring in a motion in accordance with Article 77, paragraph (2), does not impose a veto within the time limit of Article 77, paragraph (3), withdraws its veto or if the veto is overridden by the Bundestag.

Article 79

(1) The Basic Law may be amended only by a law which expressly alters or adds to the text of the Basic Law.

(2) Such a law shall require the approval of two-thirds of the members of the Bundestag and two-thirds of the votes of the Bundesrat.

(3) An amendment to this Basic Law by which the organization of the Federation into Laender, the basic co-operation of the Laender in legislation or the basic principles laid down in Articles 1 and 20 are affected, shall be inadmissible.

Article 80

(1) By means of a law the Federal Government, a Federal Minister or the Land Governments may be authorized to issue orders (*Rechtsverordnungen*). The contents, purpose and scope of such authorization shall be determined in the law. The legal basis must be cited in the order. If a law provides that an authorization may be further transferred, then the transfer of the authorization shall require an order (*Rechtsverordnung*).

(2) The approval of the Bundesrat shall be required, unless otherwise regulated by federal legislation, for orders (*Rechtsverordnungen*) of the Federal Government or a Federal Minister concerning principles and fees for the use of the facilities of the Federal railways and post and telecommunications, concerning the construction and operation of railways, as well as those issued on the basis of federal laws which require the approval of the Bundesrat or which are executed by the Laender on behalf of the Federation or as their own concern.

Article 81

(1) Should, in the case of Article 68, the Bundestag not be dissolved, the Federal President may, on the request of the Federal Government with the approval of the Bundesrat, declare a state of legislative emergency for a bill, if the Bundestag rejects it despite the fact that the Federal Government has declared it to be urgent. The same shall apply if a bill has been rejected despite the fact that the Federal Chancellor had combined with it the motion described in Article 68.

(2) If the Bundestag, after the state of legislative emergency has been declared, again rejects the bill or passes it in a version stated by the Federal Government to be unacceptable, the bill shall be deemed adopted insofar as the Bundesrat approves it. The same shall apply if the bill has not been passed by the Bundestag within four weeks after its re-submission.

(3) During the term of office of a Federal Chancellor, any other bill rejected by the Bundestag may be passed within a period of six months after the initial declaration of a state of legislative emergency in accordance with paragraphs (1) and (2). After expiry of the period, a further declaration of a state of legislative emergency shall be inadmissible during the term of office of the same Federal Chancellor.

(4) The Basic Law may neither be amended nor wholly or partially repealed or suspended by a law enacted in accordance with paragraph (2).

Article 82

(1) Laws enacted according to the provisions of this Basic Law shall be engrossed by the Federal President with countersignature and published in the Federal Legal Gazette. Orders (*Rechtsverordnungen*) shall be signed by the issuing authority and, unless otherwise regulated by law, published in the Federal Legal Gazette.

(2) Each law and each order (*Rechtsverordnung*) shall specify the date of its coming into force. In the absence of such a provision, they shall come into force on the fourteenth day after the end of the day on which the Federal Legal Gazette has been issued.

VIII. THE EXECUTION OF FEDERAL LAWS AND THE FEDERAL ADMINISTRATION

Article 83

The Laender shall execute the federal laws as their own concern insofar as this Basic Law does not otherwise determine or permit.

Article 84

(1) If the Laender execute the federal laws as their own concern they shall regulate the establishment of the authorities and the administrative procedure insofar as federal laws approved by the Bundesrat do not otherwise determine.

(2) The Federal Government may, with the approval of the Bundesrat, issue general administrative provisions.

(3) The Federal Government shall exercise supervision to ensure that the Laender execute the federal laws in accordance with valid law. For this purpose the Federal Government may send commissioners to the highest Land authorities and, with their approval and, in the case of this approval being refused with the approval of the Bundesrat, also to the subordinate authorities.

(4) Should deficiencies established by the Federal Government in the execution of federal laws in the Laender not be overcome then, on application by the Federal Government or the Land concerned, the Bundesrat shall decide whether the Land has infringed law. Against the decision of the Bundesrat, appeal may be made to the Federal Constitutional Court.

(5) For the execution of federal laws the Federal Government may, by federal legislation which shall require the approval of the Bundesrat, be granted in special cases the power to give individual instructions. They shall, except where the Federal Government considers the case urgent, be directed to the highest Land authorities.

Article 85

(1) Where the execution of federal laws is delegated to the Laender by the Federation, the establishment of the authorities shall remain a concern of the

Laender insofar as Federal legislation approved by the Bundesrat does not determine otherwise.

(2) The Federal Government may issue, with the approval of the Bundesrat, general administrative provisions. It may regulate the uniform training of officials and employees. The heads of the authorities at middle level shall be appointed with its agreement.

(3) The Land authorities shall be subject to the instructions of the highest competent federal authorities. Except where the Federal Government considers it urgent, the instructions shall be directed to the highest Land authorities. Execution of the instructions shall be ensured by the highest Land authority.

(4) Federal supervision shall extend to the legality and suitability of the manner of execution. The Federal Government may for this purpose demand submission of reports and documents and send commissioners to all authorities.

Article 86

If the Federation executes the laws by direct federal administration or by public law corporations or institutions directly supervised by the Federation, the Federal Government shall, insofar as the law does not prescribe details, issue general administrative provisions. It shall regulate, insofar as it is not otherwise determined by the law, the establishment of the authorities.

Article 87

(1) The foreign service, the federal finance administration, the federal railways, the federal postal services and, in accordance with the provisions of Article 89, the administration of the federal waterways and shipping, shall be conducted by a direct federal administration with its own lower level administrative offices. Federal frontier protection authorities and central offices for police information and communications, for the compilation of data for purposes concerning the protection of the constitution and for the criminal police may be established by federal legislation.

(2) Public law corporations directly supervised by the Federation shall be those carriers of social insurance whose sphere of competence extends beyond the territory of a Land.

(3) In addition, independent central federal authorities and new public law corporations and institutions directly supervised by the Federation may be established by federal legislation for matters on which the Federation has the power to legislate. Should the Federation acquire new functions in matters for which it has legislative competence, federal authorities at middle and lower levels may in case of urgent need be established with the approval of the Bundesrat and of the majority of the Bundestag.

Article 88

The Federation shall establish a bank of currency and issue as federal bank.

Article 89

(1) The Federation shall be the owner of the former Reich waterways.

(2) The Federation shall administer the federal waterways through its own authorities. It shall exercise those state functions relating to inland shipping extending beyond the territory of a Land and the functions of ocean-going shipping which are conferred on it by legislation. The Federation may delegate the administration of federal waterways, insofar as they lie within the territory of a Land, to this Land, upon request, to act on its behalf (*Auftragsverwaltung*). Should a waterway touch the territories of several Laender, the Federation may delegate the administration to the Land agreed upon by the Laender concerned.

Article 90

(1) The Federation shall be the owner of the former Reich Autobahnen and Reich highways.

(2) The Laender, or such self-governing corporations under public law as are competent in accordance with Land law, shall administer the federal Autobahnen and other federal highways used for long-distance traffic on behalf of the Federation.

(3) At the request of a Land, the Federation may take over into direct federal administration federal Autobahnen and other federal highways used for long-distance traffic, insofar as they lie within the territory of this Land.

Article 91

(1) In order to avert an imminent danger to the existence or the free democratic basic order of the Federation or a Land, a Land may call in the police forces of other Laender.

(2) If the Land in which the danger is imminent is not itself prepared or in a position to combat the danger, the Federal Government may place the police in that Land or the police forces of other Laender under its instructions. The order (*Anordnung*) shall be rescinded after the danger has been overcome, otherwise at any time on demand from the Bundesrat.

IX. THE ADMINISTRATION OF JUSTICE

Article 92

Judicial authority shall be invested in the judges; it shall be exercised by the Federal Constitutional Court, by the Supreme Federal Court, by the federal courts provided for in this Basic Law and by the courts of the Laender.

Article 93

(1) The Federal Constitutional Court shall decide:

1. on the interpretation of this Basic Law in the event of disputes concerning the extent of the rights and duties of the highest federal organ or of other participants accorded independent rights by this Basic Law or in the Standing Orders (Rules of Procedure) of the highest federal organ;
2. in cases of differences of opinion or doubts on the formal and material compatibility of federal law or Land law with this Basic Law, on the compatibility of Land law ith some other federal law, on the application of the Federal Government, of a Land Government or of one-third of the members of the Bundestag;
3. in cases of differences of opinion on the rights and duties of the Federation and the Laender, particularly in the execution of federal law by the Laender, and in the exercise of federal supervision;
4. on other public law disputes between the Federation and the Laender, between different Laender or within a Land, insofar as appeal to another court is not provided for;
5. in all other cases provided for in this Basic Law.

(2) Furthermore, the Federal Constitutional Court shall act in cases otherwise assigned to it by federal legislation.

Article 94

(1) The Federal Constitutional Court shall consist of federal judges and other members. The members of the Federal Constitutional Court shall be elected half by the Bundestag and half by the Bundesrat. They may not belong to the Bundestag, the Bundesrat, the Federal Government or corresponding bodies of a Land.

(2) A federal law shall regulate its legal constitution and procedure and determine in which cases its decisions shall have the force of law.

Article 95

(1) To preserve the unity of a federal law, a Supreme Federal Court shall be established.

(2) The Supreme Federal Court shall decide in cases where the decision is of fundamental importance for the uniformity of the administration of justice of the higher federal courts.

(3) The appointment of the judges of the Supreme Federal Court shall be decided jointly by the Federal Minister of Justice and a committee for the election of judges consisting of the Land Ministers of Justice and an equal number of members elected by the Bundestag.

(4) Otherwise the constitution of the Supreme Federal Court and its procedure shall be regulated by federal legislation.

Article 96

(1) Higher federal courts shall be established for the spheres of ordinary, administrative, finance, labour and social jurisdiction.

(2) Article 95, paragraph (3), shall apply to the judges of the higher federal courts with the proviso that the place of the Federal Minister of Justice and the Land Ministers of Justice be taken by the Ministers competent for the particular matter. Their conditions of service must be regulated by a special federal law.

(3) The Federation may establish federal disciplinary courts for disciplinary proceedings against federal officials and federal judges.

Article 97

(1) Judges shall be independent and subject only to the law.

(2) Judges who are principally, regularly and definitely employed as such may, against their will, be dismissed before the expiry of their term of office, or permanently or temporarily suspended from office or transferred to another office or be placed on the retired list only through the decision of a court and only on the grounds and in the forms prescribed by legislation. Legislation may set an age limit at which judges who have been appointed for life shall retire. In the case of alterations in the structure of the courts or their districts, judges may be transferred to another court or suspended from office. They must, however, retain their full salary.

Article 98

(1) The legal status of the federal judges must be regulated by a special federal law.

(2) If a federal judge, in his official or unofficial capacity, infringes the principles of the Basic Law or the constitutional order of a Land, the Federal Constitutional Court may on the application of the Bundestag and with a two-thirds majority, order that the judge be transferred to another office or placed on the retired list. In the case of wilful infringement dismissal may also be decided upon.

(3) The legal status of the judges in the Laender must be regulated by special Land legislation. The Federation may issue general provisions.

4) The Laender may determine that the Land Minister of Justice shall, together with a committee for the election of judges, decide on the appointment of judges in the Laender.

(5) The Laender may make an appropriate regulation for Land judges in accordance with paragraph (2). Valid Land constitutional law shall remain unaffected. The Federal Constitutional Court shall decide in the case of impeachment of a judge.

Article 99

By Land legislation the decision on constitutional disputes within a Land may be assigned to the Federal Constitutional Court, and the decision of final instance on matters involving the application of Land law to the higher federal courts.

Article 100

(1) If a court considers unconstitutional a law the validity of which is pertinent to its decision, proceedings must be stayed and, if a violation of a Land Constitu-

tion is involved, the decision of the Land court competent for constitutional disputes shall be obtained and, if a violation of this Basic Law is involved, the decision of the Federal Constitutional Court shall be obtained. This shall also apply if the violation of this Basic Law by Land law or the incompatibility of a Land law with a federal law is involved.

(2) If in litigation it is doubtful whether a rule of international forms part of federal law and whether it creates direct rights and duties for the individual (Article 25), the court shall obtain the decision of the Federal Constitutional Court.

(3) If the court of a Land, in interpreting the Basic Law, intends to deviate from a decision of the Federal Constitutional Court or the constitutional court of another Land, the said constitutional court must obtain the decision of the Federal Constitutional Court. If, in interpreting other federal law, it intends to deviate from the decision of the Supreme Federal Court or a higher federal court, it must obtain the decision of the Supreme Federal Court.

Article 101

(1) Extraordinary courts shall be inadmissible. No one may be prevented from appearing before his lawful judge.

(2) Courts for special matters may be established only by law.

Article 102

The death sentence shall be abolished.

Article 103

(1) Everyone brought before a court shall have a claim to proper legal hearing.

(2) An act may be punished only if it was punishable by law before the act was committed.

(3) No one may be punished more than once on account of the same act in pursuance of the general criminal laws.

Article 104

(1) The freedom of the individual may be restricted only on the basis of a formal law and only with due regard to the forms prescribed therein. Detained persons may be subjected neither to physical nor mental ill-treatment.

(2) Only the judge shall decide on the admissibility and continued duration of a deprivation of liberty. If such deprivation is not based on the order of a judge, a court decision must be obtained without delay. The police may, on its own authority, hold no one in custody beyond the end of the day following the arrest. Details shall be regulated by legislation.

(3) Any person temporarily detained on suspicion of having committed a punishable act must, at the latest on the day following the arrest, be brought before a judge who shall inform him of the reasons for the arrest, interrogate him and give him an opportunity to raise objections. Without delay, the judge must either issue a warrant of arrest, setting out the reasons therefor, or order his release.

(4) A relative of the person detained or a person enjoying his confidence must be notified forthwith of any judicial decision in respect of the ordering or the continued duration of a deprivation of liberty.

X. Finance

Article 105

(1) The Federation shall have exclusive legislation on customs and financial monopolies.

(2) The Federation shall have concurrent legislation on:

   1. excise taxes and taxes on transactions, with the exception of taxes with localized application, in particular the taxes on real estate acquisition, incremental value and on fire protection,

2. the taxes on income, property, inheritance and donations,
3. "Realsteuern" (taxes on real estate and on business) with the exception of the fixing of tax rates.

if it makes a claim on the taxes in their entirety or in part to cover federal expenditures or if the conditions of Article 72, paragraph (2), apply.

(3) Federal legislation on taxes the yield of which accrues in entirety or in part to the Laender or the Gemeinden (*Gemeindeverbände*) shall require the approval of the Bundesrat.

Article 106

(1) Customs, the yield of monopolies, the excise taxes with the exception of the beer tax, the transportation tax, the turnover tax and property dues serving non-recurrent purposes shall accrue to the Federation.

(2) The beer tax, the taxes on transactions with the exception of the transportation tax and turnover tax, the income and corporation taxes, the property tax, the inheritance tax, the "Realsteuern" and the taxes with localized application shall accrue to the Laender and, in accordance with Land legislation, to the Gemeinden (*Gemeindeverbände*).

(3) The Federation may, by means of a federal law which shall require the approval of the Bundesrat, make a claim to a part of the income and corporation taxes to cover its expenditures not covered by other revenues, in particular to cover grants which are to be made to Laender to meet expenditures in the fields of education, public health and welfare.

(4) In order to ensure the working efficiency also of the Laender with low revenues and to equalize the differing burden of expenditure of the Laender, the Federation may make grants and take the funds necessary for this purpose from specific taxes of those accruing to the Laender. A federal law, which shall require the approval of the Bundesrat, shall determine which taxes shall be utilized for this purpose and in what amounts and on what basis the grants shall be distributed among the Laender entitled to equalization; the grants must be handed directly to the Laender.

Article 107

The final distribution of the taxes subject to concurrent legislation between the Federation and the Laender shall be effected not later than 31 December 1952 and by means of a federal law which shall require the approval of the Bundesrat. This shall not apply to the "Realsteuern" and the taxes with localized application. In this, both Federation and Laender shall be given a legal claim to certain taxes or shares in taxes corresponding to their functions.

Article 108

(1) Customs, financial monopolies, the excise taxes subject to concurrent legislation, the transportation tax, the turnover tax and the non-recurrent property dues shall be administered by federal finance authorities. The structure of these authorities and the procedure to be applied by them shall be regulated by federal legislation. The heads of the authorities at middle level shall be appointed by agreement with the Land Governments. The Federation may delegate the administration of the non-recurrent property dues to the Land finance authorities to act on behalf of the Federation (*Auftragsverwaltung*).

(2) Insofar as the Federation makes a claim to a part of the income and corporation taxes it shall have the right to administer them. It may, however, delegate the administration to the Land finance authorities to act on behalf of the Federation.

(3) The remaining taxes shall be administered by Land finance authorities. The Federation may, by means of federal legislation which shall require the approval of the Bundesrat, regulate the structure of these authorities, the procedure to be applied by them and the uniform training of the officials. The heads of the authorities at middle level must be appointed by agreement with the Federal Government.

The administration of the taxes accruing to the Gemeinden (*Gemeindeverbände*) may be transferred by the Laender in entirety or in part to the Gemeinden (*Gemeindeverbände*).

(4) Insofar as the taxes accrue to the Federation, the Land finance authorities shall act on behalf of the Federation. The Laender shall be liable with their revenues for a regular administration of these taxes; the Federal Minister of Finance may supervise the regular administration through federal plenipotentiaries who shall have the right to give instructions to the authorities at middle and lower level.

(5) Finance jurisdiction shall be uniformly regulated by federal legislation.

(6) The general administrative provisions shall be issued by the Federal Government and, insofar as the administration is incumbent upon the Land finance authorities, with the approval of the Bundesrat.

Article 109

The Federation and the Laender shall be self-supporting and independent of each other in their budget economy.

Article 110

(1) All revenues and expenditures of the Federation must be estimated for each fiscal year and included in the budget.

(2) The budget shall be established by law before the commencement of the fiscal year. Revenue and expenditure must be balanced. Expenditures shall as a rule be approved for one year; they may in special cases be approved for a longer period. Otherwise the federal budget law may contain no provisions which extend beyond the fiscal year or which do not concern the revenues and expenditures of the Federation or its administration.

(3) The assets and liabilities shall be indicated in an appendix to the budget.

(4) In the case of federal commercial enterprises, only the final result, and not the detailed revenues and expenditures, need be included in the budget.

Article 111

(1) If by the end of a fiscal year the budget for the following year has not been established by law, the Federal Government shall, until such a law comes into force, be empowered to effect such payments as are necessary:

(a) to maintain legally established institutions and to carry out legally determined measures;

(b) to meet legally established obligations of the Federation;

(c) to continue building projects, procurements and other services or to grant further subsidies for these purposes insofar as funds have already been approved by the budget of a previous year.

(2) Insofar as revenues from taxes, imports and other sources based on special legislation, or working capital reserves, do not cover the expenditures under paragraph (1), the Federal Government may realise by way of credits the funds necessary to conduct current operations up to one-fourth of the final sum contained in the previous budget.

Article 112

Expenditure exceeding the budget and any extraordinary expenditures shall require the approval of the Federal Minister of Finance. They may only be given in case of an unforeseen and irrefutable necessity.

Article 113

Decisions of the Bundestag and Bundesrat which increase the budget expenditure proposed by the Federal Government or include, or imply for the future, new expenditure, shall require the approval of the Federal Government.

Article 114

The Federal Minister of Finance must present to the Bundestag and the Bundesrat an annual statement of all revenues and expenditures as well as of assets and liabilities. The audit thereof shall be carried out by an Audit Office (*Rechnungshof*) the members of which shall possess judicial independence. In order to secure a discharge for the Federal Government, the general statement of account and a survey of the assets and liabilities shall be submitted to the Bundestag and the Bundesrat in the course of the next fiscal year, together with the observations of the Audit Office. The auditing of accounts shall be regulated by a federal law.

Article 115

By way of credits, funds may be obtained only in the case of extraordinary need and as a rule only for expenditure for productive purposes and only on the basis of a federal law. The granting of credits and provision of securities as a charge on the Federation, the effect of which extends beyond the fiscal year, may be undertaken only on the basis of a federal law. The amount of the credits or the extent of the obligation for which the Federation assumes liability must be determined in the law.

XI. TRANSITIONAL AND CONCLUDING PROVISIONS

Article 116

(1) Unless otherwise regulated by law, a German within the meaning of this Basic Law is a person who possesses German nationality or who has been accepted in the territory of the German Reich as at 31 December 1937 as a refugee or expellee of German stock or as the spouse or descendant of such person.

(2) Former German nationals who between 30 January 1933 and 8 May 1945 were deprived of their nationality for political, racial or religious reasons, and their descendants, shall be regranted citizenship on application. They shall not be considered to have lost citizenship insofar as they took up residence in Germany after 8 May 1945 and have not expressed a wish to the contrary.

Article 117

(1) Law which conflicts with Article 3, paragraph (2), shall remain in force until it is adjusted to this provision of the Basic Law, but not beyond 31 March 1953.

(2) Laws which restrict the right of freedom of movement in consideration of the present housing shortage shall remain in force until repealed by federal legislation.

Article 118

The reorganization of the territory comprising the Laender Baden, Wuerttemberg-Baden and Wuerttemberg-Hohenzollern may be accomplished, by agreement between the Laender concerned, in a manner deviating from the provisions of Article 29. Should an agreement not be reached, the reorganization shall be regulated by federal legislation which must provide for a referendum.

Article 119

In matters relating to refugees and expellees, in particular their distribution to the Laender, the Federal Government may, with the approval of the Bundesrat, issue orders (*Verordnungen*) having the force of law pending a regulation by federal legislation. In special cases the Federal Government may be empowered to issue individual instructions. The instructions shall, except in case of imminent danger, be directed to the highest Land authorities.

Article 120

(1) The Federation shall bear the expenses for occupation costs and, in accordance with more detailed provisions by a federal law, the other internal and external

war-induced burdens, and the grants towards the burdens of social insurance, including unemployment insurance and public assistance for the unemployed.

(2) The revenues shall pass to the Federation at the same time at which the Federation assumes the expenditure.

Article 121

The majority of the members of the Bundestag and of the Federal Convention within the meaning of this Basic Law shall be the majority of their statutory number of members.

Article 122

(1) As from the assembly of the Bundestag, laws shall be passed exclusively by the legislative authorities recognized in this Basic Law.

(2) With effect from this date, legislative bodies and bodies acting in an advisory capacity in respect of legislation, the competence of which ends in accordance with paragraph (1), shall be dissolved.

Article 123

(1) Law existing before the assembly of the Bundestag shall remain in force, insofar as it does not conflict with the Basic Law.

(2) The state treaties concluded by the German Reich concerning matters for which, according to this Basic Law, Land legislation is competent, shall remain in force if they are valid and continue to be valid according to general basic principles of law, while reserving all the rights and objections of those concerned, until new state treaties shall have been concluded by the authorities made competent to do so by this Basic Law or until they are otherwise terminated on the grounds of the provisions they contain.

Article 124

Law concerning matters within the exclusive legislative competence of the Federation shall become federal law within the area of its application.

Article 125

Law concerning matters of concurrent federal legislation shall become federal law within the area of its application,

1. insofar as it is uniformly valid within one or more zones of occupation,
2. insofar as it concerns law by which former Reich law has been amended since 8 May 1945.

Article 126

Divergencies of opinion on the continued validity of law as federal law shall be decided by the Federal Constitutional Court.

Article 127

Within one year after promulgation of this Basic Law the Federal Government may, with the approval of the Governments of the Laender concerned, extend law of the Bizonal Economic Administration, insofar as it continues in force as federal law according to Articles 125 or 126, to the Laender Baden, Greater Berlin, Rhineland-Palatinate and Wuerttemberg-Hohenzollern.

Article 128

Insofar as in accordance with still valid law, powers to give instructions within the meaning of Article 84, paragraph (5), still exist, these shall remain in force pending some other legislative regulation.

Article 129

(1) Insofar as legal provisions which continue in force as federal law contain an authorization to issue orders (*Rechtsverordnungen*) or general administrative provisions and to perform administrative acts, this authorization shall pass to the authorities now competent for the subject matter. In doubtful cases the Federal Government shall decide by agreement with the Bundesrat; the decision must be published.

(2) Insofar as legal provisions which continue in force as Land law contain such an authorization, it shall be exercised by the authorities competent according to Land law.

(3) Insofar as legal provisions within the meaning of paragraphs (1) and (2) authorize the alteration or amplification or the issue of legal provisions instead of laws, these authorizations shall lapse.

(4) The provisions of paragraphs (1) and (2) shall apply appropriately insofar as legal provisions refer to regulations no longer valid or to institutions no longer in existence.

Article 130

(1) Administrative organs and other institutions serving the public administration or administration of justice, which are not based on Land law or treaties between Laender, as well as the amalgamated management of the South West German railways and the Administrative Council for the post and telecommunications service of the French Zone of Occupation, shall be under the Federal Government. The latter shall, with the approval of the Bundesrat, regulate the transfer, dissolution, or liquidation of such bodies.

(2) The highest disciplinary authority for the personnel of these administrations and establishments shall be the competent Federal Minister.

(3) Public law corporations and institutions not directly supervised by a Land and not based on treaties between Laender, shall be under the supervision of the competent highest federal authority.

Article 131

The legal status of persons, including the refugees and expellees who were employed in the public service on 8 May 1945 and who have left service for reasons other than those based on civil service or tariff regulations, and who hitherto have not been employed or not in a position corresponding to their former one, shall be regulated by federal legislation. The same shall apply to persons, including the refugees and expellees who were entitled to a pension or other assistance on 8 May 1945, and who no longer receive such or something equivalent for reasons other than those based on civil service or tariff regulations. Without prejudice to other regulations by Land law, legal claims may not be raised until the federal law comes into force.

Article 132

(1) Officials (*Beamte*) and judges who, at the time this Basic Law comes into force, have been appointed for life may, within six months after the first meeting of the Bundestag, be placed on the retired list or waiting list or be transferred to another office with less remuneration, if they are personally or professionally unsuitable for their office. This provision shall apply appropriately also to employees (*Angestellte*) not subject to notice of dismissal. In the case of employees (*Angestellte*) whose conditions of service require notice of dismissal, notice exceeding that required by tariff regulations may be cancelled within the same period.

(2) The provisions shall not apply to members of the public service unaffected by the denazification and demilitarization laws or who are recognized victims of national socialism, insofar as there are no important objections against such persons.

(3) Those affected by the above shall have recourse to the courts in accordance with Article 19, paragraph (4).

(4) Details shall be determined by an order (*Verordnung*) of the Federal Government, which shall require the approval of the Bundesrat.

Article 133

The Federation shall succeed to the rights and obligations of the Bizonal Economic Administration.

Article 134

(1) Reich property shall in principle become federal property.

(2) It shall, without compensation, be transferred to the authorities now competent to carry out the functions, insofar as it was originally destined mainly for administrative functions which according to this Basic Law are not administrative functions of the Federation, and to the Laender insofar as, according to its present, not solely temporary, use, it serves for administrative functions which according to this Basic Law are now to be fulfilled by the Laender. The Federation may also transfer other property to the Laender.

(3) Property which was placed at the disposal of the Reich by the Laender and Gemeinden (*Gemeindeverbände*) shall, without compensation, become once more the property of the Laender and Gemeinden (*Gemeindeverbände*), insofar as the Federation does not require it for its own administrative functions.

(4) Details shall be regulated by a federal law which shall require the approval of the Bundesrat.

Article 135

(1) If, between 8 May 1945 and the coming into force of this Basic Law, a territory has changed from one Land to another, in this territory the property of the Land to which the territory belonged shall be transferred to the Land to which the territory now belongs.

(2) Insofar as it was originally destined mainly for administrative functions, or is at present, and not solely temporarily, mainly used for administrative functions, the property of Laender and other public law corporations and institutions no longer existing shall be transferred to the Land or public law corporation or institution now performing these functions.

(3) Real estate of Laender no longer existing, including appurtenances, shall, insofar as it does not already belong to the property within the meaning of paragraph (1), be transferred to the Land in the territory of which it is situated.

(4) Insofar as an overriding interest of the Federation or the particular interests of a territory require it, a regulation deviating from paragraphs (1) to (3) may be adopted by federal legislation.

(5) Otherwise the legal succession and the settlement of property, insofar as it has not been effected by 1 January 1952 by agreement between the Laender or public law corporations or institutions concerned, shall be regulated by federal legislation which shall require the approval of the Bundesrat.

(6) Participants of the former Land Prussia in civil law enterprises shall pass to the Federation. Details shall be regulated by a federal law which may make provisions deviating from this.

(7) Insofar as property which, according to paragraphs (1) to (3), would accrue to a Land or a public law corporation or institution, has been disposed of by the authority thereby authorized by means of a Land law, on the basis of a Land law or in some other way at the coming into force of the Basic Law, the transfer of property shall be considered as having been effected before the disposal.

Article 136

(1) The Bundesrat shall meet for the first time on the day of the first assembly of the Bundestag.

(2) Until the election of the first Federal President, his functions shall be exercised by the President of the Bundesrat. He shall not have the right to dissolve the Bundestag.

Article 137

(1) The eligibility for election of officials (*Beamte*), employees (*Angestellte*) of the public service and judges of the Federation, of the Laender and of the Gemeinden may be restricted by legislation.

(2) For the election of the first Bundestag, of the first Federal Convention and of the first Federal President of the Federal Republic of Germany the Electoral Law to be adopted by the Parliamentary Council shall apply.

(3) The functions of the Federal Constitutional Court pursuant to Article 41, paragraph (2), shall be exercised, pending its establishment, by the German High Court for the Combined Economic Area which shall decide in accordance with its Standing Orders (Rules of Procedure).

Article 138

Changes in the existing organization of notaries in the Laender Baden, Bavaria, Wuerttemberg-Baden and Wuerttemberg-Hohenzollern shall require the approval of the Governments of these Laender.

Article 139

The legal provisions enacted for the liberation of the German people from national socialism and militarism shall not be affected by the provisions of this Basic Law.

Article 140

The provisions of Articles 136, 137, 138, 139, and 141 of the German Constitution of 11 August 1919 shall be an integral part of this Basic Law.

Article 141

Article 7, paragraph (3), first sentence, shall not apply in a Land in which on 1 January 1949 another legal Land regulation existed.

Article 142

Without prejudice to Article 31, provisions of the Land Constitutions shall also remain in force, insofar as they conform to Articles 1 to 18.

Article 143

(1) Whoever by force or the threat of force changes the constitutional order of the Federation or of a Land, deprives the Federal President of the powers accorded to him by this Basic Law or who by force or the threat of danger compels him to exercise his powers in a specific manner or not at all, or prevents the exercise of his powers, or deprives the Federation or a Land of a territory belonging to them shall be condemned to penal servitude for life or not less than 10 years.

(2) Whoever publicly incites to an action within the meaning of paragraph (1), or plots or otherwise arranges such an action in connivance with another person, shall be condemned to penal servitude up to 10 years.

(3) In less serious cases, a sentence of not less than two years' penal servitude in the cases provided for in paragraph (1), and of not less than one year's imprisonment in the cases provided for in paragraph (2), may be imposed.

(4) Whoever of his own free will gives up his activity or, in case of participation of several persons, prevents a conspiracy, may not be punished in accordance with the provisions of paragraphs (1) to (3).

(5) Insofar as the action is directed exclusively against the constitutional order of a Land, the highest court of the Land shall, in the absence of any other regulation in Land law, be competent to pass judgment. Otherwise the superior court (*Oberlandesgericht*), in the district of which the first Federal Government chooses its seat, shall be competent.

(6) The aforementioned provisions shall be valid pending another regulation by federal law.

Article 144

(1) This Basic Law shall require acceptance by the popular representative bodies in two-thirds of the German Laender in which it shall initially be valid.

(2) Insofar as restrictions are imposed on the application of the Basic Law to one of the Laender enumerated in Article 23, paragraph (1), or to a part of one of these Laender, that Land or a part of that Land shall have the right, in accordance with Article 38, to send representatives to the Bundestag and, in accordance with Article 50, to the Bundesrat.

Article 145

(1) The Parliamentary Council with the participation of the representatives of Greater Berlin shall in a public meeting confirm the adoption of this Basic Law, engross it and promulgate it.

(2) This Basic Law shall come into force at the end of the day of its promulgation.

(3) It shall be published in the Federal Legal Gazette.

Article 146

This Basic Law shall become invalid on the day when a constitution adopted in a free decision by the German people comes into force.

3. RE-INTEGRATION OF WESTERN GERMANY

The re-integration of western Germany into the European community was the topic of a series of discussions between the United Kingdom, France, and the United States during 1949. Discussions begun in London in January on the principles to govern trizonal fusion were supplemented by further consultations among the foreign ministers of the three governments in Washington in the spring which resulted in an announcement in a communiqué of April 8 that "complete agreement" among the three powers had been reached on "the whole range of issues now pending in connection with Germany."[1] In addition to confirming the London recommendations relating to the Occupation Statute[2] and to the international control of the Ruhr[3] the foreign ministers at Washington determined a program of reparations and a schedule of limited and prohibited industries for the western zones. Meeting in Paris on November 9 and 10, the three foreign ministers considered "Germany's relation to Europe, the situation in Germany, and their policy in respect of Germany." Conversations were held on November 11 with the foreign ministers of Belgium, Luxembourg, and the Netherlands on "matters particularly affecting the interests of these three countries." As a result of these meetings, the foreign ministers decided to "support and foster the progressive integration of the German people into the European community" and instructed the Allied High Commission to take steps to that end.[4] The High Commission subsequently conferred at Petersberg on November 15, 17, and 22 with representatives of the western German government on 1) German participation in certain international organizations such as the Organization for European Economic Cooperation, 2) German membership in the International Ruhr Authority, 3) the gradual re-establishment of German consular and commercial relations with other countries, 4) the relaxation of restrictions on German ship-building, and 5) the curtailment of the program of dismantling.

---

[1] Department of State Press Release 233, April 8, 1949. For the text of the three-power communiqué, see *New York Times*, April 9, 1949, p. 2.

[2] For further information on the Occupation Statute for western Germany, see this volume, p. 109.

[3] See *Documents, X, 1948*, p. 115. For further information on the Ruhr authority, see this volume, p. 161.

[4] For the text of the three-power communiqué on the Paris meetings, see Department of State, *Bulletin*, XXI, p. 822.

(1) *German Reparation Program. Department of State Press Release, April 13, 1949.*[5]

The Department of State announced on April 13 that agreement had been reached by the Governments of the United States, United Kingdom, and France, as the powers responsible for occupation of the Western zones of Germany, for the revision of the lists of capital equipment to be removed from Western Germany as reparation. This revision was made in order to bring the reparation dismantling program into harmony with the European Recovery Program. Under it those plants which, if retained in Germany, can contribute most effectively to the coordinated economic revival of the countries participating in the European Recovery Program will be removed from the reparation dismantling list.

In accordance with the agreement reached by the three governments, certain equipment from 159 plants previously scheduled for removal as reparation will be retained in Germany. The amount of equipment which had previously been scheduled for removal from these plants varies from a single piece of equipment in a plant to the entire equipment of an operating factory. The removal of equipment not yet completely dismantled and removed will be completed as quickly as possible.

This agreement, which constitutes a final decision with regard to the removal of those plants originally selected in Western Germany, should enable both the Allied recipients of reparation and responsible authorities in Western Germany to plan promptly for the effective use of the equipment to be removed and that to be retained.

A revised list of plants subject to reparation has been communicated to the Inter-Allied Reparation Agency at Brussels by the three governments.

The equipment which will be retained in Germany is located in 32 plants in the steel industry, 88 metal working plants, 32 chemical plants, and 7 plants in the nonferrous metal industries.

Only 5 of the 32 affected plants in the steel industry produce crude steel. The retention of equipment in this industry will result in a nominal increase in the crude steel-making capacity of Western Germany of 165,000 tons per year beyond the present theoretical capacity of approximately 13,300,000 tons per year. The limitation on crude steel production in the three Western zones of Germany of 11,100,000 tons per year (being a total of 10,700,000 tons per year in the Bizone and 400,000 tons in the French zone) has not been changed. The difference between the actual production of steel under the limitation, and the theoretical capacity of about 13,500,000 tons per year to be left in Western Germany is required for greater flexibility and economy of operation under conditions of changing demand for finished steel products.

These same reasons underlie the decision to retain the equipment in the steel-finishing plants which constitute the remainder of the 32 affected plants or part plants in the steel industry. The steel-finishing capacity in these plants which permits the fabrication of plates, sheets, and tubes, in addition to that

5 *Ibid.,* XX, p. 524; *New York Times,* April 14, 1949, p. 10.

previously permitted, is considered necessary if Germany is to use her crude steel-making capacity most effectively and make as great a contribution to European recovery as possible within the established limitation on production.

The revision of the list of plants was made at the suggestion of the U.S. Government. In proposing such a revision, the United States believed it appropriate that account be taken in the reparation program of the European Recovery Program and the participation of Western Germany in that program. The reparation program was designed to bring about the removal of capital equipment to Allied countries, where it could be usefully employed, when this equipment is in excess of German peaceful needs. The U.S. Government felt that, in view of the possibility which the European Recovery Program offered for meeting the new investment requirements of the Allied countries to an increased extent from new capital equipment, and of the possibility of more effective use of German resources in the interest of the common good of the countries participating in the European Recovery Program, a reexamination of the reparation program would be appropriate. ERP also offered new possibilities of achieving one of the aims of the reparation program, namely the rehabilitation of the economies of the European countries which had been dislocated during the war.

A preliminary examination of the list of plants scheduled for removal led the U.S. Government to select 381 for further study. This study was made by the Humphrey Committee (Industrial Advisory Committee), appointed by Paul Hoffman, Economic Cooperation Administrator. Mr. Hoffman had been charged by the Congress with making such a study in section 115 (f) of the Economic Cooperation Act, reading as follows:

> The Administrator will request the Secretary of State to obtain agreement of those countries concerned that such capital equipment as is scheduled for removal from the three western zones of Germany be retained in Germany if such retention will most effectively serve the purposes of the European recovery program.

This Committee was headed by George M. Humphrey, President of M. A. Hanna Company, and included Frederick V. Geier, President of Cincinnati Milling Machine Company; John L. McCaffrey, President of International Harvester Company; Gwilym A. Price, President of Westinghouse Electric & Manufacturing Company; and Charles E. Wilson, President of General Motors Corporation.

The Committee in turn engaged the services of four leading engineering firms to make a factual review of the chemical, nonferrous metal, and mechanical engineering plants. They also obtained the assistance of George Wolf, president of the United States Steel Export Corporation, and a group of his associates, to review the steel industry of Western Germany and to investigate the particular plants scheduled for reparation.

After a careful examination of the plants and consultation with British and French experts, the Committee submitted a report to the ECA Administrator on January 12, 1949, recommending the retention in Germany of certain equipment in 167 plants of the 381 which it has been requested to examine. The report of the Committee was approved by the Administrator who requested the Secretary of State to seek the agreement of the British and French Governments, as powers in occupation in Western Germany, to the retention of these plants in Germany. The Humphrey Committee report is being made public on April 13 by ECA.

Discussion among the governments resulted in agreement to remove from Germany the equipment in eight plants and part of a ninth which the Humphrey Committee had recommended be retained in Germany.

In addition to certain equipment in the 159 plants to be retained under the present agreement, the French Government, before the Humphrey Committee recommendations had been formulated, decided to retain in the French zone equipment in 40 other plants or parts of plants which had been included in the list of 381 examined by the Humphrey Committee.

The report of the Committee was discussed by the three Governments in conjunction with a report from the Military Governors of the Western zones of Germany on a revised list of prohibitions and restrictions which should be applied to German industry on security grounds. As a result of these discussions, coordinated agreements were reached by the three Governments on these subjects. The revised list of prohibited and restricted industries, which has been furnished to the three military governments for implementation, will be made public shortly.

The Humphrey Committee recommended that the following plants be included among those retained in Germany. However, in the course of discussions among the Governments of France, the United Kingdom, and United States, it was agreed that these plants should be removed from Germany. The list follows:

Bochumer Verein Gusstahlfabrik, Bochum; Deutsche Edelstahlwerke (Tiegelstahl), Bochum; Klockner Werke A.G., Dusseldorf; August Thyssen Hütte, A. G. Niederrheinische, Duisburg; Hoesch A. G., Hohenlimburg; I. G. Farben, buna plant, Ludwigshafen; I. G. Farben, synthetic ammonia plant, Oppau; and I. G. Farben, chlorine and caustic-soda plant, Ludwigshafen. The final decision on the August Thyssen Hütte plant at Hamborn was to retain only the ore sintering and power generation equipment.

(2) *Agreement between the Governments of the United States, France, and the United Kingdom on Prohibited and Limited Industries in the Western Zones of Germany. Department of State Press Release, April 13, 1949.*[6]

Pursuant to instructions received from their respective governments to conclude the agreement hereinafter set forth, concerning prohibited and limited industries in the United States, United Kingdom and French Occupied Areas of Germany (hereinafter referred to for the purposes of this Agreement as Germany), the

6 Department of State Press Release 243, April 13, 1949; Department of State, *Bulletin,* XX, p. 526.

United States, United Kingdom and French Military Governors and Commanders-in-Chief hereby promulgate the following agreement, effective forthwith:

Article I

The prohibitions laid down in this Agreement shall remain in force until the peace settlement.

The limitations laid down in this Agreement shall remain in force until 1st January, 1953, or until the peace settlement, whichever is the earlier, and thereafter as may be agreed.

Should no peace settlement have been concluded by 30th June, 1952, the Military Governors shall forthwith review these limitations in the light of the conditions then prevailing, taking into account the requirements of security of the Allied Powers, the state and effectiveness of the arrangements made to preserve security, and the requirements of European Recovery. Should the Military Governors be unable within 90 days from 30th June, 1952, to reach agreement on the limitations which in the absence of an earlier peace settlement shall be continued after 1st January, 1953, the matter shall be considered forthwith by the three Governments.

Article II

Action within the discretion of the Military Governors under the terms of the Agreement shall be taken by unanimous decision.

Article III

The production or manufacture of the following substances and war materials shall be prohibited, and all plants and equipment for their production or manufacture not already removed or destroyed shall, as soon as possible, be removed from Germany or destroyed.

(a) *The items listed in Schedule A to Control Council Law No. 43 (at Annex A)*
(b) *Primary Magnesium*
(c) *Beryllium*

Article IV

The production, import, export, transport, storage, use and possession of radioactive materials will be the subject of legislation by the Military Governors.

Article V

1. The production of synthetic rubber and butadiene shall be prohibited.
2. In order to give effect to the foregoing prohibitions, facilities for copolymerization, facilities for research and testing of synthetic rubber, and facilities for the production of butadiene at the Huls, Ludwigshafen and Leverkusen plants shall be removed or destroyed.

Article VI

1. The production of petrol, oil and lubricants directly or indirectly from coal or brown coal by the Bergius hydrogenation process, the Fischer-Tropsch synthesis, or analogous processes, shall be prohibited except, temporarily, to the extent inseparable from the production of hydrocarbon waxes for the manufacture of synthetic fatty acids for the production of washing materials.
2. The synthesis of hydrocarbon waxes by the Fischer-Tropsch process shall be permitted only so long as the supply of fats and oils available in Germany is inadequate for the manufacture of sufficient washing materials without the use of synthetic fatty acids, and in any event not beyond 31st December, 1949.
3. The Fischer-Tropsch plants not now engaged in the synthesis of hydrocarbon waxes shall, as soon as possible, be removed from Germany or destroyed. The two Fischer-Tropsch plants engaged in the synthesis of hydrocarbon waxes shall, as soon as possible after production ceases, be removed from Germany or destroyed.
4. All Bergius plants except the Wesseling plant shall, as soon as possible, be re-

moved from Germany or destroyed. The whole Wesseling plant shall be retained, and may be used for the refining of natural petroleum, for the hydrogenation of heavy residues from such refining and for the synthesis of ammonia and methanol.

Article VII

1. The manufacture of electronic valves shall be limited to a list to be drawn up by experts and published by the Military Governors of permitted types that shall not exceed either 10 watts dissipation or 250 megacycles frequency, subject to the authority of the Military Governors, acting upon the advice of the Military Security Board, to permit by license the manufacture of types exceeding 10 watts dissipation (but not exceeding 250 megacycles frequency) in case of necessity.

Article VIII

1. The capacity of the following industries shall be limited as stated below: —

    (a) *Steel,* to that remaining after the removal of reparations;

    (b) *Electric arc and high frequency furnace steel* furnace capacity, to that remaining after the removal of reparations;

    (c) *Primary Aluminum,* to that sufficient to produce 85,000 tons of primary aluminum a year;

    (d) *Shipbuilding,* to that remaining after the removal as reparations of the following yards in addition to those four that have already been made available for reparations: —

        CIND 1206 Germania Werft, Kiel
        CIND 1235 Deutsche Werke, Kiel
        CIND 1287 Deutsche Werft Reihersticg, Hamburg;

    (e) *Ball and Roller Bearings,* to that remaining after the removal as reparations of plant and equipment calculated to leave in Germany capacity sufficient to produce 33 million units a year on a one-shift basis, or present capacity, whichever is the less;

    (f) *Synthetic Ammonia,* to that remaining after the removal of reparations;

    (g) *Chlorine,* to that remaining after the removal of reparations;

    (h) *Styrene,* to 20,000 tons annual working capacity.

2. In order that the total authorized capacity of the industries limited in paragraph 1 above shall not be exceeded, no enterprise shall be permitted, (except under license from the Military Governors, acting upon the advice of the Military Security Board) to increase the productive capacity of any of its plant or equipment that is engaged or partly engaged in any of the industries list in this article, whether it is proposed to effect the increase by the extension of existing facilities, the construction of new facilities, or the addition of new equipment. The construction of new plant and equipment, and the replacement or reconstruction of that removed or destroyed shall likewise be prohibited except under license from the Military Governors, acting upon the advice of the Military Security Board. The Military Security Board will ensure that obsolete or wornout plant or equipment the replacement of which by new has been licensed is removed from Germany or destroyed.

Article IX

1. The production of *steel* shall be limited to 11.1 million ingot tons a year.

2. The production of *primary aluminium* shall be limited to 85,000 tons of primary aluminium a year. No specific limitation shall be placed on imports of bauxite and alumina; they shall, however, be controlled to prevent stock-piling in excess of a number of months' supply, to be determined by the Military Governors.

3. The production of *styrene* shall be limited to 20,000 tons a year.

Article X

1. The manufacture of the following shall be prohibited: —

    (a) *Machine tools* or other manufacturing equipment specifically designed for the production of weapons, ammunition or other implements of war.

(b) Attachments, devices, tools or other objects having no normal, peace-time use and specifically designed to convert or adapt machine tools or other manufacturing equipment to the production of weapons, ammunition or other implements of war.

2. The manufacture of the types of machine tools listed at Annex B shall be prohibited except under license from the Military Governors, acting upon the advice of the Military Security Board, which license will normally be granted unless the Military Governors have reason to think that the tools are not intended for peaceful production.

Article XI

1. The construction of *ships* whose size or speed does not exceed the limits contained in the following table shall be permitted in Germany, provided that no ocean-going ships shall be constructed until a German coastal fleet adequate for the requirements for European and German recovery has been reconstituted. (It has been estimated that Germany will require for this purpose 517,000 G.R.T., including 360,000 G.R.T. of dry cargo ships.)

Dry cargoships	12 knots 7,200 G.R.T.
Tankers	12 knots 7,200 G.R.T.
Small craft	12 knots 650 G.R.T.

(including fishing vessels and ships other than cargo-carrying craft)

Coastal vessels	12 knots 2,700 G.R.T.

2. Notwithstanding the above provisions, Germany shall be permitted during the period of this Agreement to acquire abroad up to 100,000 G.R.T. of tankers of not more than 14 knots speed and 10,700 G.R.T., being not less than 16,000 dwt; and up to 300,000 G.R.T. of dry cargo ships of not more than 12 knots speed and 7,200 G.R.T.

3. In order to provide guidance for the Military Governors, a committee of experts is to be constituted by the Governments of the United States, the United Kingdom and France with instructions to prepare, within three months, a report outlining the types of ships, excluding ships primarily for passengers, which may be required by Germany, although they exceed in one respect or another the limits in paragraph 1 above. The committee shall also determine those features of design, construction, propulsion machinery, etc., which would facilitate use for or conversion for war purposes or which do not conform to normal merchant marine practice and should therefore be prohibited. The recommendations of the committee shall be transmitted to the Military Governors for action in accordance with the procedure outlined in the following paragraph.

4. The Military Governors, acting upon the advice of the Military Security Board, may permit by license the construction or acquisition of ships exceeding in some respects the limitations on speed and tonnage shown in paragraph 1 above, in order to provide for ships having special purposes or functions. The Military Governors shall take into account the requirements of security and the necessity that ships shall be capable of operating economically in the trades or routes for which they are intended.

5. Notwithstanding anything contained herein to the contrary, the Military Governors, acting upon the advice of the Military Security Board, may authorize under license the construction of vessels having a greater speed than 12 knots that are shown to be essential for such purposes as the prevention of smuggling and illegal fishing, frontier control, fire fighting, or for the use of pilots or the civil police.

6. The Military Governors shall promulgate the legislation necessary to give effect to the foregoing provisions; and upon the coming into effect of such legislation the operation of the relevant provisions of Control Council Directives Nos. 33, 37, 44 and 45 shall be suspended. Until the promulgation of such legislation, the building of any ships other than those permitted under the relevant provisions of Control Council Directives Nos. 33, 37, 44 and 45 shall remain prohibited.

Article XII

Nothing in this Agreement shall be interpreted as impairing or reducing the powers with which the Military Security Board is vested.

ANNEX A

SCHEDULE A TO CONTROL COUNCIL LAW NO. 43

Group I

(a) All weapons including atomic means of warfare or apparatus of all calibres and natures capable of projecting lethal or destructive projectiles, liquids, gases or toxic substances, their carriages and mountings.
(b) All projectiles for the above and their means of projection or propulsion. Examples of means of propulsion are cartridges, charges etc.
(c) All military means of destruction such as grenades, bombs, torpedoes, mines, depth mines, depth and demolition charges and self-propelled charges.
(d) All military cutting or piercing weapons (in French: white arms) (in Russian: cold arms), such as bayonets, swords, daggers and lances.

Group II

(a) All vehicles specially equipped or designed for military purposes such as tanks, armoured cars, tank-carrying trailers, armoured railway rolling stock, etc.
(b) Armour of all types for military purposes.
(c) Harness specially designed for military purposes.

Group III

(a) (i) Range-finding apparatus of all kinds for military purposes;
   (ii) Aiming, guiding, and computing devices for fire control;
  (iii) Locating devices of all kinds (particularly all devices for radio direction finding and all devices for radio detention);
  (iv) Instruments for assisting observations of fire or for the remote control of all moving objects.
(b) All signalling and inter-communication equipment and installations specially designed for war purposes; all apparatus for radio interference.
(c) Searchlights with mirror diameter of more than 45 cms.
(d) Optical instruments of all kinds specially designed or intended for war purposes.
(e) Survey and cartographic equipment and instruments of all kinds specially designed for war purposes. Military maps and equipment for using them.
(f) Military engineering tools, machinery and equipment such as special bridging materials.
(g) Personal military equipment and uniforms, and military insignia and decorations.
(h) Cryptographic machines and devices used for cipher purposes.
(i) All camouflage and dazzle devices.

Any of the materials listed in Group III, except for electronic devices such as radar, radiogoniometric and similar equipment, that have a normal peacetime use and are not specially designed for military use, are excluded from the provisions of paragraph 1, Article I of the Law.

Group IV

(a) Warships of all classes. All ships and floating equipment specially designed for servicing warships. All ships with characteristics exceeding those required for normal peacetime uses; or designed or constructed for conversion into warships or for military use.
(b) Special machinery, equipment and installations which in time of peace are normally used solely in warships.
(c) Submersible craft of all kinds; submersible devices of all kinds, designed for military purposes. Special equipment pertaining to these craft and devices.
(d) All military and landing devices.
(e) Material, equipment and installations for the military defense of coasts, harbours etc.

Group V

(a) Aircraft of all types, heavier or lighter than air; with or without means of propulsion, including kites, captive balloons, gliders and model aircraft, and all auxiliary equipment, including aircraft engines and component parts accessories, and spare parts specifically designed for aircraft use.

(b) Ground equipment for servicing, testing or aiding the operation of aircraft, such as catapults, winches and beacons; material for the rapid preparation of airfields such as landing mats; special equipment used in conjunction with air photography; excluding however, from the provisions of paragraph 1, Article I of this Law any such equipment and materials for landing fields and air beacons that have a normal peacetime use and are not specifically designed for military use as listed in Schedule B.

Group VI

All drawings, specifications, designs, models and reproductions directly relating to the development, manufacture, testing, or inspection of the war material, or to experiments or research in connection with war material.

Group VII

Machinery and other manufacturing equipment and tooling used for the development, manufacture, testing or inspection of the war material defined in this Schedule, and not capable of conversion to peacetime production.

Group VIII

(a) The following War Chemicals:

High explosives with the exception of those listed in Schedule B, Group VIIa.
(NOTE: By "high explosives" is meant organic explosives used as fillings for shells, bombs, etc.)
Double-base propellants (i.e. Nitrocellulose propellants containing nitroglycerine, diethyleneglycol dinitrate or analogous substance).
Single-base propellants for any weapons except sporting weapons.
Nitroguanidine.
Poison war gases (including liquids and solids customarily included in this term) with the exception of those listed in Group VIIb of Schedule B.
Rocket fuels:

Hydrogen peroxide of above 37% concentration,
Hydrazine hydrate,
Methyl nitrate.

Highly toxic products from bacteriological or plant sources (with the exception of those bacteriological and plant products which are used for therapeutic purposes).

(b) All special means for individual and collective defense used in peace exclusively by the armed forces, such as protective masks against toxic or lethal devices used for war, detection apparatus etc.

Group IX

All apparatus, devices, and material specially designed for training and instructing personnel in the use, handling, manufacture or maintenance of war material.

Annex B

TYPES OF MACHINE TOOLS THE MANUFACTURE OF WHICH SHALL BE PROHIBITED
EXCEPT UNDER LICENSE FROM THE MILITARY SECURITY BOARD

1. *Spiral bevel gear cutters.*
2. *Broaching machines* of the following kinds:

   (a) Continuous surface type.
   (b) Reciprocating type (bar type cutter) with cutter diameter or equivalent cross section exceeding 2 inches (51 mm), or working stroke exceeding 5 feet (1,524 mm) or pull capacity exceeding 35,000 lbs (15,876 kgs).

3. *General purpose lathes* of the following kinds:
   (a) Lathes of work diameter capacity (swing over carriage) exceeding 56 inches (1,422 mm).
   (b) Lathes of work diameter capacity (swing over carriage) of from 36 inches (914 mm) to 56 inches and with distance between centres (length of work piece) exceeding 14 feet (4,267 mm).
   (c) Lathes of work diameter capacity (swing over carriage) of from 18 inches (457 mm) to 36 inches (914 mm) and with distance between centres exceeding 18 feet (5,486 mm).

4. *Vertical turret lathes* (turret type head, not rotating table) of work diameter capacity exceeding 39 inches (991 mm).

5. *Chucking and facing lathes* of work diameter capacity exceeding 96 inches (2,438 mm) or with travel of carriage exceeding 7 feet (2,134 mm).

6. *Car and locomotive wheel lathes* (machines designed specifically for this work) of work diameter capacity exceeding 96 inches (2,438 mm).

7. *Turret lathes* of chuck capacity exceeding 24 inches (610 mm) or of bar capacity exceeding 3 inches (76 mm).

8. *Milling machines* of general purpose and universal types, horizontal and vertical, any of whose specifications exceed the following limits:
   (a) Maximum overall weight: 4 tons.
   (b) Following rectangular table dimensions:
       (i) Maximum length: 48 inches (1,219 mm).
       (ii) Maximum width: 14 inches (356 mm).
   (c) Following round table dimensions:
       (i) Maximum table diameter: 24 inches (610 mm).
       (ii) Maximum work diameter capacity: 32 inches (813 mm).

9. *Planer milling machines* of distance between housings exceeding 4 feet (1,219 mm) or of length of platen exceeding 12 feet (3,658 mm) or of number of heads exceeding 3.

10. *Grinding machines* of the following kinds:
    (a) Cylindrical general purpose machines of work diameter capacity exceeding 30 inches (762 mm) or of distance between centres exceeding 9 feet (2,743 mm), but not including machines specifically designed for and limited to finishing rolling mill, calendar, printing and other similar machine parts.
    (b) Surface rectangular table machines of platen width exceeding 24 inches (610 mm) or of platen length exceeding 72 inches (1,829 mm).
    (c) Surface round table machines of table diameter exceeding 36 inches (914 mm).

11. *Gear producing machines* of all types whose work diameter capacity exceeds 60 inches (1,524 mm).

12. *Forging hammers* of all types of falling weight exceeding 3½ tons (3.556 metric tons).

13. *Forging machines* of bar stock diameter or equivalent cross section exceeding 3½ inches (89 mm).

14. *Mechanical presses* of an effective operating pressure exceeding 1,000 tons (1,016 metric tons).

15. *Hydraulic presses* of an effective operating pressure exceeding 1,000 tons (1,016 metric tons).

16. *Precision jig boring machines* of a lateral displacement of cutter with reference to work (or displacement of work with reference to cutter) exceeding 24 inches (610 mm).

(3) *Agreement between the Allied High Commission for Germany and the West German Federal Republic on Dismantling and the Incorporation of the Federal Republic into the European Community, Signed at Bonn, November 24, 1949.*[7]

Following upon the meeting of the three foreign ministers in Paris on November 9 and 10 the United Kingdom, French and United States High Commissioners were authorized to discuss with the Federal Chancellor the letters which he had addressed to them on the subject of dismantling a view to a final settlement of this problem. The instructions to the High Commissioners also covered a wider field and required them to examine with the Chancellor other points to be included in a general settlement. Discussions took place accordingly on November 15, 17 and 22 on the Petersberg.

The discussions were animated throughout by the desire and the determination of both parties that their relations should develop progressively upon a basis of mutual confidence. Meanwhile, their primary objective is the incorporation of the Federal Republic as a peaceful member of the European community and to this end German association with the countries of Western Europe in all fields should be diligently pursued by means of her entry into the appropriate international bodies and the exchange of commercial and consular representation with other countries.

Both the High Commissioners and the Chancellor appreciate that progress toward this objective must depend upon the establishment of a true sense of security in Western Europe and they have addressed themselves particularly to this end. In all these matters they have been encouraged to find a wide community of ideas and intention and they have in particular agreed upon the following:

I

The High Commission and the Federal Government are agreed to promote the participation of Germany in all these international organizations through which German experience and support can contribute to the general welfare. They record their satisfaction at the various steps already achieved in this direction citing German participation in OEEC, the desire expressed on both sides that the Federal Republic should be promptly admitted to the Council of Europe as an associate member and the proposed signature of a bilateral agreement with the Government of the United States of America covering ECA assistance.

II

The Federal Government, appreciating the desirability of the closest possible cooperation by Germany in the rehabilitation of Western European economy, declares its intention of applying for membership in the International Authority for the Ruhr in which, at present, the Federal Government is only represented by an observer, it being understood between both parties

7 *New York Times*, November 25, 1949.

that German accession will not be subject to any special conditions under Article 31 of the agreement for the establishment of the authority.

III

The Federal Government further declares its earnest determination to maintain the demilitarization of the Federal territory and to endeavor by all means in its power to prevent the re-creation of armed forces of any kind. To this end the Federal Government will cooperate fully with the High Commission in the work of the military security board.

IV

It is further agreed between them that the Federal Government shall now initiate the gradual re-establishment of consular and commercial relations with those countries where such relations appear advantageous.

V

The Federal Government affirms its resolve as a freely-elected democratic body to pursue unreservedly the principles of freedom, tolerance and humanity which unite the nations of Western Europe and to conduct its affairs according to those principles. The Federal Government is firmly determined to eradicate all traces of nazism from German life and institutions, and to prevent the revival of totalitarianism in this or any form. It will seek to liberalize the structure of government and to exclude authoritarianism.

VI

In the field of decartelization and monopolistic practices the Federal Government will take legislative action corresponding to decisions taken by the High Commission in accordance with Article 2 (B) of the occupation statute.

VII

The High Commission has communicated to the Chancellor the terms of an agreement reached by the three powers for the relaxation of the present restrictions on German shipbuilding.

The main provisions now agreed are as follows:

The construction of ocean-going ships excluding those primarily designed for passengers, and tankers up to 7,200 tons, fishing vessels up to 650 tons and coastal vessels up to 2,700 tons not exceeding twelve knots service speed may begin forthwith. The number of such ships to be constructed shall not be limited.

The Federal Government may, with the approval of the High Commission, acquire or construct before December 31, 1950, six special ships exceeding these limitations of size and speed. Further particulars on this point were communicated to the Chancellor.

The Federal Chancellor raised the question of the construction and repair of ships in German shipyards for export. The High Commissioners informed him that this matter was not discussed by the committee of experts and that they were not in a position to give him a final decision on it. However, they will meanwhile authorize German shipyards to construct for export ships of the types and within such limits of numbers as are applicable to construction for the German economy; they will authorize repair of foreign ships without restriction.

VIII

On the question of dismantling, the High Commission has reviewed the present position in the light of the assurances given by the Federal Government and has agreed to the following modification of the program. The following plants will be removed from the reparations list and dismantling of their equipment will cease forthwith.

A. Synthetic oil and rubber plants. (These plants involving an important security element) — Farbenfabriken Bayer, Leverkusen (except for certain research equipment at Chemische Werke, Huels), Gelsenberg Benzin, A. G.; Hydrierwerke Scholven, A. G.; Ruhroel G. M. B. H., Bottrop; Ruhrchemie, A. G.; Gewerkschaft Victor; Krupp Treibstoff G. M. B. H.; Steinkohlenbergwerke; Dortmunder Parafin; Essener Steinkohle A. G.

B. Steel plants — August Thyssen Hutte, Duisberg, Hamborn; Huttenwerke Siegerland, Charlottenhutte; Deutsche Edelstahlwerke, Krefeld; August Thyssen Hutte, Niederreinische Hutte; Klockner Werke, Duesseldorf; Ruhrstahl A. G. Heinrichshütte, Hattingen; Bochumer Verein Gusstahlwerke, Bochum.

Except that electric furnaces not essential to the functioning of the works will continue to be dismantled or destroyed.

C. Further dismantling at the I. G. Farben plant at Ludwigshafen will not take place except for the removal of the equipment for the production of synthetic ammonia and methanol to the extent provided for in the reparations programme.

D. All dismantling in Berlin will cease and work on the affected plants will be again rendered possible.

It is understood that equipment already dismantled will be made available to IARA [Inter-Allied Reparations Agency] except in the case of Berlin. The present modification of the reparations list will not affect the existing prohibitions and restrictions upon the production of certain materials. Dismantled plants may be reconstructed or re-equipped only as permitted by the Military Security Board and those plants at which dismantling has been stopped will be subject to suitable control to ensure that the limitation on the production of steel [11.1 million tons per annum] is not exceeded.

IX

The question of the termination of the State of war was discussed. Although such termination may be as consistent with the spirit of this protocol, it presents considerable legal and practical difficulties which need to be examined.

X

The High Commissioners and the Federal Chancellor have signed this protocol with the joint determination to carry into effect the purposes stated in the preamble hereof and with the hope that their understandings will constitute a notable contribution to the incorporation of Germany into a peaceful and stable European community of nations.

4. INTERNATIONAL CONTROL OF THE RUHR

[See *Documents, X, 1948*, p. 115.]

Following the announcement of April 8, 1949, that the foreign ministers of the United States, the United Kingdom, and France had approved the London recommendations on the International Authority for the Ruhr, plans were launched for the organization of the authority in order that it might commence operations shortly before the establishment of the western German Government.[1] The agreement establishing the authority was formally signed by the six interested governments in London on April 28[2] and the first organizational meeting of the Council of the authority opened in London on May 20. Wayne G. Jackson, special assistant to the director of the Office of European Affairs, Department of State, represented the United States at those sessions of the Council.[3] Henry Parkman, former governmental affairs adviser to the United States Military Governor, was appointed United States representative to the authority on July 28, 1949.[4] The first meeting of the authority, convened in Dusseldorf on August 8, was reportedly concerned primarily with internal administrative and organizational matters, particularly finance.[5] A German observer, Dr. Walter Bauer, was appointed to the authority by the President of the western German republic (Adenauer) on October 18[6] and a formal application for membership in the authority was transmitted by the west German government to the Allied High Commission early in December 1949.[7]

5. PROVISIONAL RECTIFICATION OF WESTERN GERMAN BOUNDARIES

(1) *Communiqué Issued by the Governments of Belgium, France, Luxembourg, the Netherlands, the United Kingdom, and the United States Regarding the Provisional Rectification of the Western Boundaries of Germany. Department of State Press Release, March 26, 1949.*[1]

In addition to the following communiqué, the Department of State on April 26 announced that French control authorities would maintain jurisdiction over the Kehl port zone until the establishment of the federal German government and the conclusion of negotiations between French and German authorities regarding a joint administration for the port. The city of Kehl was to be returned gradually to German administration and the final disposition of the port zone was to be determined in the peace settlement with Germany. In its announcement the Department of State noted that "if the port authority develops harmoniously, the United States and the United Kingdom will be willing at the time of the peace settlement to bring an attitude of good will toward the establishment of a permanent joint authority."[2]

It was announced at the conclusion of the London talks on Germany on June 7, 1948, that proposals were being submitted to the Governments of the

1 Department of State Press Release 249, April 13, 1949.
2 *Ibid.*, 301, April 28, 1949; Department of State, *Bulletin*, XX, p. 592.
3 *Ibid.*, p. 693.   4 *Ibid.*, XXI, p. 185.
5 *The Times* (London), August 9, 1949, p. 4.
6 *Ibid.*, October 19, 1949, p. 3.   7 *Ibid.*, December 2, 1949, p. 3.
1 Department of State Press Release 191, March 26, 1949; Department of State, *Bulletin*, XX, p. 427.
2 *Ibid.*, p. 590.

United States, France, the United Kingdom, and the BENELUX countries for bringing about provisionally certain minor territorial adjustments in the western boundary of Germany.

The six governments, taking into account the unforeseen delays to which the conclusion of a final peace settlement with Germany has been subjected, consider it necessary to proceed to a preliminary examination of the problem of frontiers and to put into effect the minor adjustments justified by administrative necessities and by conditions affecting communications along Germany's Western frontier. The problem of Germany's frontiers will be re-examined and settled definitively in its entirety at the time of final peace settlement.

After detailed study the six governments have approved the proposals for provisional adjustments of the frontier which have been submitted to them by a working party meeting in Paris.

The six governments have also examined the frontiers of the Saar territory and have agreed that pending confirmation or modification by the terms of the final peace settlement, the present frontier shall be maintained with the minor modifications.

The areas affected by the adjustments will be placed under the administration of the countries adjacent to Germany.

These adjustments may be confirmed or modified by the terms of the final settlement concerning Germany.

The London recommendations fixed a very restricted frame of reference for the working party. Only those proposals might be examined which involved no appreciable loss to the German economy and which, being of minor character only, could be regarded as desirable to eliminate local anomalies and improve communications.

This limited frame of reference did not permit the working party to take into consideration certain major territorial claims of Germany's western neighbors.

Within the limits thus defined, 31 minor rectifications will be effected at a date to be announced later, along the frontier between Germany, on the one hand and the Netherlands, Belgium, Luxembourg, the Saar and France, on the other.

These will affect a total area of approximately 135 square kilometers (approximately 52 square miles) and a population of some 13,500 persons.

These modifications have been defined in general outline. Their exact limits will be fixed by delimitation commissions. These commissions will make their decision after having heard if this appears desirable, the local authorities and persons in the area capable of giving information or explanations necessary for the accomplishment of the commissions' task.

All measures will be taken with a view to safeguarding the interests of the inhabitants, as regards both their personal status and their movable and real property. No one will be forced to accept the nationality of the country to which the area is attached. Persons not desiring to accept this nationality will enjoy the protection accorded to persons and property by the laws of the country and no crimination will be exercised against them. They will have the right to settle in Germany, in which case they will be allowed to take with them their movable property, either retaining ownership of their real property, or selling it and being permitted to transfer the funds to Germany under the special regulations which will be prescribed. They will, on the other hand, have the right to continue to reside in the area concerned, if they so desire.

C. Bizonal Cooperation (Bizonia)

[See *Documents, VIII, 1945–1946,* p. 218; *IX, 1947,* p. 65; *X, 1949,* p. 140.]

By an exchange of notes dated March 31, 1949, the United States and the United Kingdom extended until June 30, 1949, the Fusion Agreement of December 2, 1946, as amended.[1] The agreement of March 31, 1949, provided for earlier termination either by mutual consent or "by the conclusion of a Trizonal Fusion Agreement." The agreement was subsequently amended and extended, subject to similar conditions, until September 30, 1949, by a second exchange of notes dated June 30, 1949.[2]

D. Administration of the United States Zone

On May 3, 1949, President Truman accepted, effective May 15, the resignation of General Lucius Clay as the United States Military Governor in Germany. Pending the appointment of a civilian High Commissioner, the Military Governor's functions were executed by General Clay's military and military government deputies.[1] The nomination of John J. McCloy, then president of the International Bank for Reconstruction and Development, to the post of United States High Commissioner was announced by the President on May 18.[2] The position of the High Commissioner was subsequently established and defined by Executive Order 10062 of June 6, 1949.[3] The High Commissioner was empowered by a further executive order of June 13[4] to serve as the representative of the Administrator for Economic Cooperation in all ECA relations and actions with respect to Germany. The Military Government of the United States Zone of Germany was formally terminated on September 21, 1949, and the Office of the United States Political Adviser was combined with the Office of the United States High Commissioner which, on that date, was authorized to exercise all of the governmental functions of the United States in Germany, with the exception of the command of troops.[5]

(1) *Executive Order 10062, Establishing the Position of United States High Commissioner for Germany, June 6, 1949.*[6]

By virtue of the authority vested in me by the Constitution and the Statutes, including the Foreign Service Act of 1946 (60 Stat. 999), and as President of the United States and Commander in Chief of the Armed Forces of the United States, it is ordered as follows:

1. There is hereby established the position of United States High Commissioner for Germany, which position shall be that of Chief of Mission,

---

1 Department of State, *Treaties and Other International Acts Series* 1959. The Fusion Agreement of 1946 (See *Documents, VIII, 1945–1946,* p. 218) was in turn extended and amended by agreements of December 17, 1947 (See *ibid., IX, 1947,* p. 71) and December 31, 1948 (See *ibid., X, 1948,* p. 141), the latter extension to expire March 31, 1949.
2 Department of State, *Treaties and Other International Acts Series* 1962.
1 Department of State, *Bulletin,* XX, p. 632.　　2 *Ibid.,* p. 730.
3 *Federal Register,* XIV, p. 2965.　　4 Executive Order 10063, *ibid.,* p. 3221.
5 Department of State, *Bulletin,* XXI, p. 513.　　6 *Federal Register,* XIV, p. 2965.

Class 1, in accordance with the provisions of the said Foreign Service Act of 1946.

2. The United States High Commissioner for Germany, hereinafter referred to as the High Commissioner, shall be the supreme United States authority in Germany. The High Commissioner shall have the authority, under the immediate supervision of the Secretary of State (subject, however, to consultation with and ultimate direction by the President), to exercise all of the governmental functions of the United States in Germany (other than the command of troops), including representation of the United States on the Allied High Commission for Germany when established, and the exercise of appropriate functions of a Chief of Mission within the meaning of the Foreign Service Act of 1946.

3. With respect to military matters the Commander of the United States Armed Forces in Germany shall continue to receive instructions directly from the Joint Chiefs of Staff. On request of the High Commissioner, such Commander shall take necessary measures for the maintenance of law and order and such other action as is required to support the policy of the United States in Germany. If major differences arise over policy affecting military matters, necessary reports and recommendations shall be referred to the Department of State and to the National Military Establishment for resolution. In the event of an emergency involving the security of the United States forces in Europe, such Commander may take whatever action he considers essential to safeguard the security of his troops.

4. In the event that the High Commissioner shall assume his duties in accordance with this Executive Order prior to the date that the Military Government of the United States Zone of Germany is terminated, he shall during such interval report to the Secretary of Defense, through the Secretary of the Army, and shall be the United States Military Governor with all the powers thereof including those vested in the United States Military Governor under all international agreements.

2. AUSTRIA

[See *Documents, VIII, 1945–1946*, p. 283; *IX, 1947*, p. 90; *X, 1948*, p. 149.]

A. Occupation and Control

United States occupation policy in Austria during the year under review was, in the main, directed toward increasing the autonomy of the Austrian Government and reducing proportionately the range of controls exercised in civil affairs by the Allied Control Council. The United States paid particular attention to the relaxation of controls of the fields of communications, censorship, internal travel, and civil aviation. Greater autonomy in the conduct of foreign relations was urged by the United States in the form of permitting Austrian membership in various international agencies and adherence to certain international agreements.

The United States expressed the belief that communications control was "one of the most serious problems facing the Allied Council,"[1] and increased its efforts to

---

[1] United States Forces in Austria. *Report of the United States High Commissioner,* May 1949, No. 43, p. 3.

relax controls in the field of communications, proposing that the strict regulations imposed by the Quadripartite Signals Board in September 1947 be replaced by a less rigid system and that quadripartite control be reestablished throughout Austria, "recognizing no special interests for the Soviet Element regarding communications from Vienna."[2] France in general supported the United States efforts; the United Kingdom advocated a more liberal policy ultimately involving the abolition of all communications controls. The United States element reported that, on the other hand, the Soviet Union declined to surrender any "substantial" measures of existing restrictions.[3] The United States was especially concerned with a decision of the QSB placing all communications lines out-going from Vienna under unilateral Soviet control, creating a "communications curtain" which, the United States charged, was designed "to enable the Soviet Union to route all tele-communications through convenient Soviet monitoring stations."[4] At the meeting of the Allied Council on May 27, the Soviet Union took the position that the United Kingdom and United States elements were responsible for the failure of previous attempts to relax communications restrictions, and questioned the sincerity of their desire to relax controls.[5] In a reply on June 10 the United States pointed out that a comparison of the broad measures of relaxation proposed by the United States and the minor and insignificant concessions offered by the Soviet Union refuted the Soviet allegation.[6] Although the issue was again raised during the year, no changes in position of the powers occurred.

Closely related to the question of communications was that of censorship which, for reasons of military security, made it necessary to route all international telephone and telegraph connections through Vienna for screening. The three western powers sought to have censorship either turned over to the respective zonal commanders or abolished. The United States proposal for abolition met with a Soviet counter-proposal that controls be retained on postal, telegraph, and telephone communications from Vienna to Germany, Japan, and Spain. The Soviet proposal was referred to the Executive Committee for further consideration.[7] Although unanimously approved by the Educational Directorate on July 8, a resolution calling for the removal of all censorship over textbooks was defeated in the Executive committee on August 5 when the Soviet Union withdrew its support of the resolution.[8]

Restrictions in the field of internal travel and communication raised in particular the question of the opening of the Danube to traffic by Austrian government craft, with the United States proposing that all controls over such traffic be rescinded. Upon the request of the Austrian Government that river maintenance vessels be permitted complete freedom, the United States sought to raise the whole question of freedom of Danube navigation. Both the United Kingdom and France urged that the Executive Committee look further into this and related United States proposals.[9] Asserting that no restrictions on the river traffic existed, the Soviet Union refused to discuss the question.[10]

Basing its position on the provisions of the Control Agreement by which the occupying powers agreed to the gradual surrender of controls to the Austrian authorities in order to assist them in assuming as quickly as possible jurisdiction over all affairs of state, the United States urged a lessening of restrictions over Austrian civil aviation. The Soviet Union, however, called such a proposal "premature" and maintained that the question should await settlement in the state treaty with Austria. In view of Soviet insistence that the emergence of a coordinated program of Austrian civil aviation would contribute to the strengthening of Austrian "military might," no agreement could be reached on the matter during the year under review.[11]

The question of Austrian accession to various international agreements raised in the control machinery a problem of procedure, with the Soviet Union taking the position that such action by the Austrian Government required the unanimous approval of the Allied Council and the western powers asserting that Austrian accession was effective unless unanimously forbidden by the council.[12] In each case,

2 *Ibid.*, March 1949, No. 41, p. 8.   3 *Ibid.*, p. 9.
4 *Ibid.*, May 1949, No. 43, p. 3.   5 *Ibid.*, p. 8.
6 *Ibid.*, June 1949, No. 44, p. 8.   7 *Ibid.*, August 1949, No. 46, p. 7.
8 *Ibid.*, p. 10.   9 *Ibid.*, April 1949, No. 42, p. 3.
10 *Ibid.*, p. 6.   11 *Ibid.*, May 1949, No. 43, p. 10.
12 *Ibid.*, February 1949, No. 10, p. 14; *ibid.*, March 1949, No. 41, p. 14.

Austrian declarations of accession to two ILO conventions, the UNESCO constitution, the Convention on International Civil Aviation (ICAO), and the Bretton Woods agreements became effective because of the failure of the Allied Council to take any unanimous action on the declarations before the elapse of the 31-day suspension period as provided in Article 6 (a) of the Control Agreement.[13] Austria's accession to the International Wheat Agreement was unanimously approved by all four elements.[14]

On February 11 the Allied Council considered for a fourth time the application of the "Democratic Union" for approval as a political party. Both at this time and in later considerations of the application, the United States, the United Kingdom, and France opposed recognition of the group because its avowed intention to solicit the ex-Nazi vote was, in their opinion, contrary to the Control Council decision of September 11, 1945, on the existence of political parties.[15] The Soviet Union, on the other hand, was favorable to the group's petition. On April 30, the Austrian Minister of the Interior (Helmer) challenged the validity of all decisions taken by the Allied Council prior to the conclusion of the Control Agreement, including the September 1945 decision regulating the existence of political parties. The Executive Committee and the Allied Council unanimously rejected the Minister's charge.[16] On August 26, 1949, the Allied Council received a proposal by the United Kingdom calling for the abolition of all allied control over political parties and the substitution of control by the Austrian Government. The United States Commissioner (Keyes) supported the proposal, asserting that the Austrian people were "politically mature enough to choose their own representatives without interference from anyone."[17] A compromise French proposal which would grant increased but not complete authority to the Austrian Government in the matter of party regulation failed of acceptance when the Soviet Union rejected all such proposals as attempted interference in the forthcoming elections.[18]

The constitutional law establishing the procedures for and regulations of the 1949 elections was discussed by the Executive Committee and the Allied Council in June. In granting approval to the law, both the United Kingdom and France sought to include in the approving resolution of the council a statement reaffirming the authority of the council. Neither the Soviet Union nor the United States felt that such a statement was necessary. As a result the law was approved with the understanding that in so approving the legislation the council was not invalidating previous decisions which had not been rescinded.[19] The coalition of the People's Party and the Socialist Party, which had constituted the previous government, was continued in office as a result of the October elections in which 95 percent of all qualified voters participated. The United States expressed its belief that the results could be regarded as "the democratic expression of the political choice of the Austrian people" and that the elections "were conducted with complete freedom in all occupation zones."[20]

On August 26, 1949, the United States High Commissioner (Keyes) sought the approval of the Allied Council to end the trial of Austrian nationals by military courts, thus restoring to the Austrian Government the maximum degree of sovereignty possible while occupation forces remained in the country. The United Kingdom and France, while endorsing the "desirability" of the United States proposal emphasized the necessity of retaining enough power to fulfill effectively their duties

13 The Soviet Union opposed Austrian accession to UNESCO on the ground that only members of the United Nations were eligible for membership in UNESCO (Ibid., February 1949, No. 40, p. 31). Austrian accession to the ICAO Convention was opposed as a violation of the Allied Control Council decision of August 14, 1947, establishing the Austrian Civil Aviation Department; in addition the Soviet Union declared that due to military occupation commitments Austria would be incapable of implementing ICAO recommendations (Ibid., April 1949, No. 42, p. 33). Austrian accession to the Bretton Woods agreements was opposed by the Soviet Union as "premature" in the absence of an Austrian state treaty (Ibid., May 1949, No. 43, p. 27).
14 Ibid., June 1949, No. 44, p. 11.
15 The decision of September 11, 1945, stipulated that only the Control Council could grant permission for the existence of political parties. Conditions for the organization and regulation of parties, as laid down by the Council, required that they 1) pledge themselves to strengthen and maintain Austrian independence, 2) maintain democratic principles and fight against Nazism in all its forms, and 3) carry on no activity against the occupation authorities or their forces in Austria (Ibid., February 1949, No. 40, p. 9).
16 Ibid., May 1949, No. 43, p. 11.   17 Ibid., August 1949, No. 44, p. 5.
18 Ibid.   19 Ibid., June 1949, No. 44, p. 2.
20 Department of State, Bulletin, XXI, p. 635.

as High Commissioners. The Soviet Union felt that the imminence of an Austrian state treaty made such agreement unnecessary and, therefore, refused to discuss the proposal.[21]

B. Austrian Treaty

[See *Documents, X, 1948*, p. 151.]

During the year under review, representatives of the United States, the United Kingdom, France, and the Soviet Union continued negotiations on the unagreed articles of the Austrian state treaty. Of the 22 articles which were contested when negotiations were resumed on February 8, 1949, agreement had been reached on all but nine when discussions ended for the year on December 15. The principal disputed provisions concerned Yugoslav territorial and reparations claims against Austria and the disposition of German assets in Austria. Treaty negotiations were carried on chiefly by the deputies of the Council of Foreign Ministers in a series of meetings: in London, from February 8 to April 8, from April 25 to May 10, and from June 30 to September 1; and in New York on September 23 and from October 14 to December 15. The treaty was also discussed by the Council of Foreign Ministers in Paris during its meeting from May 21 to June 20, and was later considered in a number of informal meetings among the foreign ministers of the four powers in New York between September 26 and October 6.

The question of Yugoslav claims to the Slovene province of Carinthia and of Yugoslav demands for $190 million in reparations from Austria was raised in an early meeting of the deputies.[1] The deputies received both oral and written statements from the Yugoslav Government in support of its demands, including a somewhat modified proposal for territorial adjustment submitted by the Yugoslav Foreign Minister (Bebler) on February 25. In this latter statement, Mr. Bebler sought the creation within Austria of an autonomous political, economic, and cultural unit for that portion of Carinthia which would remain under Austrian jurisdiction; "substantial reparations;" and an Austrian guarantee of the rights of the Croats and Slovenes in Austria but not included in the autonomous area. Despite speculation in the press as to the Soviet stand regarding the Yugoslav claims, in view of the Cominform's denunciation of Premier Tito, the Soviet deputy (Zarubin) in the early discussions of the deputies supported the Yugoslav proposal. The other deputies opposed the claims, stating that they could agree to no treaty which, contrary to the Potsdam decisions on Austria, failed to reestablish Austria's 1938 frontiers and required payment of reparations by Austria.[2] Later Yugoslav demands sought to include in the treaty provisions by which Austria would 1) prohibit Germanic and anti-United Nations propaganda, 2) demilitarize its frontier with Yugoslavia to a minimum depth of thirteen miles, 3) replace works of art and culture removed from Yugoslavia during the war, 4) renounce all property rights in Yugoslavia, and 5) remove from Austria within three months after the conclusion of the treaty all displaced persons waiving repatriation.[3] The three western deputies declined to consider any of these demands other than that requiring restitution of property.[4] The United States deputy (Reber) rejected the Yugoslav proposal for an autonomous Carinthian province in Austria stating that no ethnic basis existed for such a unit.[5] Soviet support of the Yugoslav claims was withdrawn during the Paris meeting of the Council of Foreign Ministers and a decision was quickly taken to reestablish the Austrian frontiers as those existing prior to January 1, 1938, including in the treaty adequate provisions for the protection of Croat and Slovene minorities in Austria. Drafting of the article on protection of minorities was successfully concluded on August 24.[6]

A second major point of disagreement in the treaty negotiations during 1949 was that of the distribution of German assets in eastern Austria to which the Soviet

---

21 United States Forces in Austria. *Report of the United States High Commissioner*, May 1949, No. 43, p. 10.
1 *New York Times*, February 10, 1949, p. 8.
2 For pertinent sections of the Potsdam decisions, see *Documents, VIII, 1945–1946*, p. 933.
3 *New York Times*, March 8, 1949, p. 8.   4 *Ibid.*, March 9, 1949, p. 10.
5 *Ibid.*, February 13, 1949, p. 31.   6 *Ibid.*, August 25, 1949, p. 9.

Union under the Potsdam decisions laid claim as reparations from Germany. To waive such claims, the Soviet Union demanded a lump sum payment of $150 million together with 60 percent of both Austrian oil production and Austrian oil exploitation rights. To reach agreement on this question, the western deputies proposed the establishment of a special committee which would attempt to arrive at a solution in terms of specific properties involved and to reconcile the Soviet figure of 60 percent with the lower percentage of 58 percent of production and 47 percent of exploitation rights proposed by the western powers. Efforts to obtain more precise data on Austrian oil production and on specific Soviet claims proved futile. When asked by the Soviet Union to agree "in principle" on all aspects of the question of German assets before attempting to discuss specific interests involved, the United States deputy (Reber) replied that the Soviet Union claimed 60 percent of an unknown quantity and that his government could not agree "in principle to an abstraction."[7] On April 7 the United States offered to "increase" its previous proposal of a lump payment of $100 million to the Soviet Union subject to four conditions: 1) that the Austrian Government be permitted to pay the same in convertible currency, in kind, or in both; 2) that Austria's former assets in Bulgaria, Hungary, and Rumania be taken into account;[8] 3) that there be "adequate" settlement concerning Austrian claims for repayment of relief costs; and 4) that there be a "clear-cut" agreement concerning the Austrian industries to which the Soviet Union would relinquish its claims in return for the lump-sum payment.[9] The proposal was rejected by the Soviet deputy (Zarubin) on April 25.[10]

The question of the disposition of Soviet-claimed German assets was resolved by the Council of Foreign Ministers at its Paris meeting when it was agreed that the Soviet Union would receive 60 percent of oil production rights for a thirty-year period and a sum of $150 million payable in freely convertible currency over a six-year period. In return the Soviet Union waived its claims to all other German-held properties.[11] In subsequent meetings of the deputies, the Soviet Union insisted that the $150 million be paid in quarterly instalments of $6.25 million in United States gold dollars, terms which the United States deputy (Reber) charged were excessive in view of the strained Austrian economy.[12] The Soviet deputy (Zarubin) later agreed that profits and other income received from the Soviet concessions in Austria should be determined under Austrian law and exported in convertible currency only if received in that form.[13]

Further negotiations were deadlocked on December 16 when the Soviet deputy informed the three western powers that, although "perfectly willing to go on discussing the treaty," he believed it would be "difficult to reach agreement" until bilateral talks between his government and the Austrian Government concerning payments by the latter for supplies and services delivered since 1945 were completed.[14]

(1) Communiqué Issued by the Sixth Session of the Council of Foreign Ministers. Department of State Press Release, June 21, 1949.[15]

[EXCERPTS]

The sixth session of the Council of Foreign Ministers attended by the Ministers of Foreign Affairs of France, Robert Schuman; of the Union of Soviet Socialist Republics, A. Y. Vyshinsky; of the United Kingdom, Ernest Bevin; and of the United States of America, Dean Acheson, took place in Paris

7 Ibid., April 6, 1949, p. 13.
8 In earlier efforts to reach agreement on the lump-sum payment to be made by Austria for Soviet-claimed German assets in eastern Austria, the United States had suggested $100 million in currency and/or kind and an additional $15 million in the form of Austrian assets in Bulgaria, Hungary, and Rumania (Ibid., February 16, 1949, p. 12).
9 Ibid., April 8, 1949, p. 3.   10 Ibid., April 26, 1949, p. 13.
11 Department of State, Bulletin, XXI, p. 861.   12 New York Times, July 8, 1949, p. 5.
13 Ibid., July 13, 1949, p. 13.   14 Ibid., December 6, 1949, p. 1.
15 Department of State, Bulletin, XXI, p. 857; for the text of the portion dealing with Germany, see this volume p. 103.

from May 23 to June 20, 1949. During this meeting the German question and the Austrian treaty were discussed. The Council of Foreign Ministers took the following decisions.

. . . .

The Foreign Ministers have agreed:

(A) That Austria's frontiers shall be those of January 1, 1938;

(B) That the treaty for Austria shall provide that Austria shall guarantee to protect the rights of the Slovene and Croatian minorities in Austria;

(C) That reparations shall not be exacted from Austria, but that Yugoslavia shall have the right to seize, retain, or liquidate Austrian property, rights and interests within Yugoslav territory;

(D) That the Soviet Union shall receive from Austria $150,000,000 in freely convertible currency to be paid in six years;

(E) That the definitive settlement shall include:

(1) The relinquishment to Austria of all property, rights or interests held or claimed as German assets and of war industrial enterprises, houses, and similar immovable property in Austria held or claimed as war booty, on the understanding that the deputies will be instructed to define more accurately the categories of war booty transferred to Austria (with the exception of those oil assets and DDSG — Danube Shipping Company — properties transferred to the Soviet Union under other paragraphs of article 35 of the treaty indicated in the U.S.S.R. proposals of January 24, 1948, as revised, and retained in general under Austrian jurisdiction). Accordingly the assets of the DDSG in Bulgaria, Hungary, and Rumania as well as 100 percent of the assets of the company in eastern Austria in accordance with a list to be agreed upon by the deputies will be transferred to the U.S.S.R.

(2) That the rights, properties, and interests transferred to the U.S.S.R. as well as the rights, properties, and interests which the U.S.S.R. cedes to Austria shall be transferred without any charges or claims on the part of U.S.S.R. or on the part of Austria. At the same time it is understood that the words "charges or claims" mean not only creditor claims as arising out of the exercise of the Allied control of these rights, properties, and interests after May 8, 1945, but also all other claims including claims in respect of taxes. It is also understood that the reciprocal waivers by the U.S.S.R. and Austria of charges and claims apply to all such charges and claims as exist on the date when Austria formalizes the rights of the U.S.S.R. to the German assets transferred to it and on the date of the actual transfer to Austria of the assets ceded by the U.S.S.R.

(F) That all former German assets which have become the property of the U.S.S.R. shall not be subject to alienation without the consent of the U.S.S.R.

(G) That the deputies shall resume their work promptly for the purpose of reaching agreement not later than September 1, 1949, on the draft treaty as a whole.

3. JAPAN

[See *Documents, VIII, 1945–1946*, p. 266; *IX, 1947*, p. 95; *X, 1948*, p. 153.]

A. General

During 1949, the occupation of Japan continued under the direction of General Douglas MacArthur, as Supreme Commander for the Allied Powers, and the Far Eastern Commission. Membership of the latter organization was increased during the year with the admission, on November 17, 1949, of representatives of the Republic of Burma and the Dominion of Pakistan.[1]

On November 30, 1949, Major General Frank R. McCoy (United States) resigned as chairman and member of the FEC, a capacity in which he had served since February 26, 1946.[2] Maxwell M. Hamilton, appointed by President Truman as General McCoy's successor as chief United States representative on the commission, was elected chairman of the commission on December 8.[3]

(1) Statement by the Supreme Commander for the Allied Powers (MacArthur) on the Fourth Anniversary of the Japanese Surrender, September 2, 1949.[4]

[EXCERPTS]

Today marks the fourth anniversary of that historic event on the battleship Missouri in Tokyo Bay when the warring nations of the Pacific entered into solemn covenants designed to restore the peace. The four years since passed have been fruitful years here in terms of human progress, as the Japanese people have fully and faithfully observed their surrender commitments and advanced steadily and progressively along the road of spiritual regeneration and physical reconstruction.

Today Japan might, indeed, be viewed as a symbol of hope for less fortunate peoples overwhelmed by the despotic rule of coercive force. For, despite the continued presence on Japan's soil of an occupation force from beyond the seas, the Japanese people, in their enjoyment of full personal freedom, know that by their skill and their industry they serve no other cause but their own. They, themselves, plot the ultimate course of Japan's destiny within the family of free nations.

The past year has witnessed accelerated progress in every phase of Japan's reconstruction. True, as elsewhere, there have been assaults upon the integrity of the democratic process by the small existent Communist minority, but these assaults were effectively repulsed — not by the repressive force of police power — but by the weight of an increasingly informed and active Japanese public opinion aroused to meet the threat of their free institutions.

. . . .

Politically, progressive gains have been made in the fabrication of a system of government truly representative in character. The lines of separation between the three great branches, executive, legislative and judicial, as provided by the constitutional design, have found strength in healthy public dis-

---

1 Far Eastern Commission Press Release 58, November 17, 1949.
2 *Ibid.*, 59, November 30, 1949.
3 *Ibid.*, 60, December 8, 1949.
4 Army Department, Civil Affairs Division. *194th Weekly Report on Japan*, Appendix A, p. 7.

cussion of the vital issue of constitutional interpretation, and as a result the affairs of government have advanced with a minimum of overlapping friction and increasing inter-branch cooperation.

The development of the desired autonomous responsibility in the conduct of local affairs has been retarded somewhat by the need for rationalization in the field of government finance to permit local revenues to support local government. A remedy for this difficulty is now being evolved, providing hope that the coming year will produce the legal basis fully to sustain the severance of pre-existing centralized controls and support the development of a political and social system resting upon inter-related and self-sustaining segments at the community level from which the national government may draw its power and direction. Therein will lie the safeguard against the re-emergence of autocracy as the prevailing philosophy of government in Japan.

.   .   .   .

Substantial progress has been made in the building of an effective police system based upon the statutory principle of decentralization in the exercise of the police power. Increasingly the Japanese people are coming to understand that this power rests in their hands, rather than in the hands of any ruling clique, and provides the legal weapon for the preservation of the local security by their direction.

They realize that the maintenance of internal order in the nation as a whole, subject to the safeguards provided by law, is dependent upon the manner in which each community administers the police power corresponding to its local responsibility.

Here, too, difficulties are being experienced, due to the present maladjustment of government finance, but this problem, as pointed out, is in process of solution.

Apart from this, progressive strides have been made toward implementation of the new concepts embodied in the police law, and the police services are being administered with restraint, tolerance and commendable efficiency. The danger that a police state will re-emerge or that the police system as now constituted and manned will fail to maintain reasonable law and order is non-existent.

Progress of trade unionization during the past year, despite a degree of freedom unsurpassed in modern civilization, has been somewhat impeded by the machinations of an irresponsible union leadership, but its rank and file are showing an increasing awareness of this threat to labor's legitimate objectives and are moving to insist upon moderation and objectivity.

.   .   .   .

Economically, Japan is still in transition from an economy of survival to one of health, but the past year has witnessed significant progress along a broad front. Foremost of the gains made lies in the development of a more positive leadership and an increasingly informed public opinion.

Both leaders and people are coming to understand that representative democracy draws its strength from the support of a broad majority of the people imbued with the belief that under it they may attain a standard of living commensurate with the capabilities of modern civilization — that prerequisite to that condition is individual freedom of activity in the field of economic enterprise, for no individual bound in economic thralldom can be politically free.

. . . .

The fruition during the past year of the plans laid down by the Occupation and carried out by the Japanese Government to remove, through the Economic Deconcentration Program, on the one hand, and the Land Reform Program on the other, these barriers to the existence of a free society, has established in Japan the economic basis for the existence of a broad middle class which, having a stake in the economic well-being of the country, will support the ideal of democracy as their way of life and will reject with scorn any will-of-the-wisp economic Utopias which require the surrender of the individual's freedom to the state.

With patience, fortitude and self-discipline the Japanese people withstood the privations of the immediate post-war period. With comparable energy, industry and hope they are now launched on the huge task of making Japan once again self-supporting among the family of nations. On the way to that goal great obstacles have been overcome, although some still remain. Since the summer of 1945, when productive activity of Japan was utterly paralyzed, the production of commodities and goods for home consumption, for industrial use and for export has risen steadily until now it is rapidly approaching the average-level for the years 1930 to 1934, prescribed by the Far Eastern Commission as an interim standard.

. . . .

In the past twelve months two significant decisions to promote the economic rehabilitation of Japan were taken by the Government of the United States. One was that of May, 1949, to cease the removal of industrial plants for reparations.[1] This action dispelled the pall of uncertainty which had previously paralyzed entrepreneurial initiative and restored the incentive to the investment of capital in the rehabilitation and construction of capital plant and equipment.

The second was the authorization by the Congress of the United States of limited budgetary appropriations for financing the importation into Japan of materials needed for rehabilitation purposes in addition to the appropriations previously made for the importation of primary necessities such as food, fertilizer and medicines to protect the Japanese people against widespread suffering and disease.

. . . .

[1] For further information on the United States decision regarding Japanese reparations, see this volume, p. 177.

Since the full employment of Japan's industrial potential requires a vigorous revival of her foreign trade and since among her chief customers in the past were the countries bordering on the Pacific basin, the question as to whether Japan will regain her traditional trade with China, despite the strangle-hold of communism upon that tragic land, has been mooted with increasing frequency.

This question is largely academic. Foreign trade requires production in excess of domestic needs. Human experience demonstrates with striking clarity that the further removed a people becomes from the economic philosophy of free enterprise, in like ratio does its productive capacity deteriorate.

This deterioration proceeds until, as under communism, with incentive completely lost, the human energy and individual initiative which find their expression in production give way to indolence and despair. In such unhealthy climate industry and commerce cannot thrive and realism warns that the potentialities of trade with any people under the structures of a collectivistic system must be discounted accordingly.

For the time being, therefore, and for some time to come, Japan must look elsewhere for the sources of her needed imports and the markets for her manufactures. Against this need Japan has already initiated foreign trade with 113 other countries and territorial areas.

I dare say that no operation in history has been subject to such an extraordinary divergency of opinion carried in the media of public expression than has the Occupation of Japan. Some writers have been extravagant in their praise, others no less extravagant in their criticism. The truth, awaiting the judgment of history, will rest somewhere in between.

Nor has there been any operations subject to such a variety of influences and pressures — the ideological protagonists, the special pleaders, the vindictive and lenient — many seeking to influence public opinion through prevarication of the truth.

In the search for sensationalism, incidents in Japan, elsewhere scarcely worth the public notice, have been exaggerated out of all proportion to their true significance, with the serenity and order and sincerity of purpose normal to post-war Japan all but ignored.

And time and again simultaneous attack has been leveled against Occupation policy, by the leftists as too reactionary and by the conservatives as too liberal. Such an atmosphere, while giving assurance that our moderate course is well charted, does not contribute to an objective public appraisal of the situation.

The great and noble effort by the American people, with the wholehearted support of other Allies, toward the reorientation and reconstruction of the post-war Japan, beyond peradventure of doubt, will prove eminently successful. Long hence history will record of the Occupation that its greatest contribution to the progress of civilization was to introduce into Japan the great concepts of personal liberty and individual dignity and to give the Christian ideal the opportunity to advance into Asia.

Of the Japanese people I can pay no higher tribute than to repeat that they have fully and faithfully fulfilled their surrender commitments and have well earned the freedom and dignity and opportunity which alone can come with the restoration of a formal peace.

B. Political Policies of Occupation

1. JAPANESE FOREIGN RELATIONS

(1) *Announcement by the Department of State on Relaxation of Controls over Japan's Foreign Policy and International Trade Policy. Department of State Press Release, May 6, 1949.*[1]

The Department of State has recommended to the Far Eastern Commission countries that, under SCAP's supervision, Japan be permitted to attend international meetings and conventions and to adhere to and participate in such international arrangements and agreements as other countries may be willing to conclude with Japan.

It is now over three and a half years since Japan surrendered and the Allied Powers began the process of establishing conditions in Japan which would lead finally to the restoration of that country to a normal status in the family of nations. This is the pattern envisaged in the Potsdam Declaration and the Basic Post Surrender Policy for Japan which was approved by the Far Eastern Commission on June 19, 1947. The latter document states in part that one of the objectives to which policies for the post-surrender period for Japan should conform is "to bring about the earliest possible establishment of a democratic and peaceful government which will carry out its international responsibilities, respect the rights of other states, and support the objectives of the United Nations".

It is important from the point of view of developing responsible government in Japan that it should be given increasing direction of its own affairs in the international field as well as in the domestic field as at present. That this process should develop under the guiding hand of the occupation has obvious advantages in developing a healthy international outlook among the Japanese and in averting the confusion that might well arise from any abrupt removal of current restrictions after a peace treaty. The immediate resumption by Japan of some international responsibilities in such fields as trade promotion, citizenship and property problems, cultural relations, technical and scientific arrangements and exchanges would provide a substantial contribution to the economic recovery of Japan.

(2) *Announcement by the Department of State on the Encouragement of Japan's Participation in International Relations, August 18, 1949.*[2]

A basic objective of the occupation in Japan is to foster among the Japanese Government and people a respect for the rights of other nations and

1 Department of State Press Release 331, May 6, 1949.
2 Department of State, *Bulletin,* XXI, p. 307.

governments. It is clear to the United States Government that by facilitating the progressive resumption by Japan of international relationships mutually beneficial to other peoples as well as to the Japanese people, this objective can be materially furthered.

Such international relationships require good will on both sides. Relations between nations are a two-way street. Because Japan is a defeated country under military occuptaion and because the Far Eastern Commission is the international body which formulates the policies, principles, and standards in conformity with which the fulfillment by Japan of its obligations under the terms of surrender may be accomplished, expression of general willingness to enter into even limited relationships with Japan tends to await the leadership of that body.

It was against this background that the United States proposed to the Far Eastern Commission that it take positive action recognizing that SCAP subject to his discretion and continued control has the authority to permit Japan to participate in international relationships such as conventions, meetings, consular arrangements, or other bilateral accords as Japan may be invited to participate in and as SCAP considers to be in the interest of the occupation.

From an examination of the record, it is clear that the Far Eastern Commission has not taken any action denying SCAP the authority to approve Japanese intercourse with the outside world. In fact, under the broad policies of the Far Eastern Commission SCAP is correctly allowing Japanese international relationships of a limited character. Not only will the Japanese through such participation acquire direct experience and knowledge of democratic practices, but also the vestiges of hatred and suspicion of the Japanese left over from the war will tend to be dissipated.

It is not the legal authority of the Far Eastern Commission which is important but rather the assumption of enlightened leadership by the Far Eastern Commission member governments. No matter what position the Far Eastern Commission takes, any government may still refuse to enter into relationships with Japan or deny Japanese access to its territory.

Likewise, the determination of whether or not Japan should be invited to participate in international organizations or conferences lies with the member governments concerned.

Almost 4 years after the war it is obvious that increased participation by Japan in international relationships under the control of SCAP will be a measurable step toward achievement of the Allied objective to foster the growth of a democratic and peaceful Japan.

2. RETENTION OF JAPANESE WAR PRISONERS

In a letter of April 25, 1949, addressed to the Soviet member of the Allied Council for Japan (Derevyanko), the chief of the Diplomatic Section of SCAP (Sebald) stated that it was "a matter of grave concern to the Supreme Commander . . . that the Japanese people be kept informed concerning a matter of vital importance to them": information regarding records of death, disappearance, or illness of Japanese prisoners of war. The note pointed out that there had "at no time been any report whatsover from the Soviet authorities concerning Japanese prisoners of war held in the Soviet Union or in territories under the control of the Soviet Union."[3] A letter from General Derevyanko to the Supreme Commander (MacArthur), dated June 11 and dealing with the "illegal activities and antilabor measures which are practiced at this time by the Japanese Government," contained no reference to the SCAP note of April 25.[4] In commenting on June 13 to the press on the Soviet letter, General MacArthur appraised General Derevyanko's charges as an effort "to screen the Soviet unconscionable failure to abide by the requirements of International Law and specific Potsdam commitments in the return of over 400,000 Japanese citizens, long held in bondage, to their homeland."[5] The question was again raised by the United States in a meeting of the Allied Council for Japan at a meeting on December 21. Subsequently, on December 22, General MacArthur announced that, on the suggestion of the United Kingdom member of the council, he would ask either a neutral nation such as Switzerland or the International Red Cross to gather the fullest possible data concerning 376,000 missing Japanese prisoners.[6]

3. TRIAL OF WAR CRIMINALS

On February 11, 1949, the secretariat of the International Military Tribunal for the Far East ceased operations.[7] In a press release on March 16, 1949, the Far Eastern Commission announced that a policy decision adopted on February 24 had determined that no further trials of Japanese war criminals should be initiated in reference to offenses defined as "planning, preparation, initiation or waging of a war of aggression or a war in violation of international treaties, agreements and assurances, or participation in a common plan of conspiracy for the accomplishment of any of the foregoing."[8] On March 31, the commission recommended that all investigations and trials be completed before June 30 and September 30, respectively, in connection with offenses in the two remaining categories of war crimes: 1) violations of the laws or customs of war; and 2) murder, extermination, enslavement, deportation and other inhumane acts committed against civilian populations on political, racial or religious grounds.[9]

C. Economic Policies of Occupation

1. GENERAL

In its meeting of April 28, 1949, the Far Eastern Commission approved a policy decision endorsing the basic principles of the land reform program then being carried out by the Japanese Government. A program of agrarian reform had been instituted in Japan by SCAP soon after the beginning of the occupation. The FEC policy decision in effect reaffirmed the following major goals of Japanese land reform as determined by legislation and administrative action taken by the Japanese Government: 1) elimination of the system of rents payable in kind and of the exaction of exorbitant rents; 2) large-scale transfer of land ownership to the tenantry, thus creating a large class of independent owner-farmers; and 3) facilitation of credit expansion and education in agricultural techniques to operating farmers.[1] A second major policy decision of the FEC was that taken on July 28, 1949, providing for the restoration to Allied owners of trade-mark rights lost during the war and insuring against Japanese piracy of Allied trade-mark rights and mismarking of goods. Registrations of trade-marks in Japan were, under the policy decision, to be extended from the date of restoration for a period equivalent to the unexpired period at the time of their loss; applications for trade-marks on file at the outbreak of hostilities would automatically be reinstated as pending applications.[2] A third

3 Department of State Press Release 288, April 25, 1949.
4 Army Department. Civil Affairs Division. 183d Weekly Report on Japan, Appendix A, p. 7.
5 Ibid., p. 8.   6 Ibid., 210th Weekly Report on Japan, p. 3.
7 Ibid., 166th Weekly Report on Japan, p. 6.
8 Far Eastern Commission Press Release 51, March 16, 1949.
9 Ibid., 52, April 1, 1949.   1 Far Eastern Commission Press Release 55, May 6, 1949.
2 Ibid., 56, August 16, 1949.

policy decision on March 17, 1949, had dealt with patents, utility models, and designs held by Allied nationals in Japan.[3]

2. REPARATIONS AND LEVEL OF INDUSTRY

In a statement read by General Frank R. McCoy, United States member of the Far Eastern Commission, the United States announced on May 12 that removal of reparations under the advance transfers program instituted by the interim reparations directive of April 4, 1947,[4] would be terminated and that new policy proposals would be submitted to the Far Eastern Commission which, if adopted, would preclude further reparations removals from Japan during the occupation. As explaining this action, the United States pointed out that, since "programs of democratization and reform prescribed by the Far Eastern Commission for Japan could succeed only in a tolerable economic environment" and since "the United States cannot indefinitely bear the burden of Japan's support" in an effort to make such an environment possible, further reparations from the deficit Japanese economy would be inconsistent with the reattainment by Japan of a self-sustaining economy at the earliest possible time. The United States further explained that no "further reparations [are] required for purposes of demilitarization and disarmament."[5] On November 28, 1949, the delivery of all reparations goods under the advance transfers program was completed with the Netherlands. Deliveries remained to be completed to China, the Philippines, and the United Kingdom. At that time SCAP announced that "the movement of undelivered reparations will continue until all present commitments have been completed."[6]

(1) Statement by the United States Member of the Far Eastern Commission (McCoy) on Japanese Reparations and Level of Industry, Made before the Commission, May 12, 1949.[7]

The Japanese reparations problem has been one of the most important and pressing questions with which the Far Eastern Commission and its member countries have had to deal. The United States, on its part, has taken a long and continuing interest in this problem and has been keenly aware of the interest of the other FEC countries in finding a reasonable solution to it. It is to be regretted that this controversial issue which for such a long time has proved incapable of solution by this Commission continues to retard the achievement of economic self-support by Japan, which is so greatly in the interest of our common objectives with respect to that country.

In our discussions of the matter here in the Commission we have proceeded from the agreement contained in the Potsdam Declaration that reparations would be exacted from Japan and that they should be in a form which would not impair the ability of the Japanese people to support themselves. From the earliest days of the Far Eastern Commission the United States has been guided by a desire that the victims of Japanese aggression receive as reparations such of Japan's resources as was possible without jeopardizing Japan's ability to meet its own peaceful needs. The United States has felt, further, that in order that the nations devastated by Japan might receive reparation while their need was greatest, in order that there might be removed from the mind of the Japanese Government and people uncertainty

3 Department of State, Documents and State Papers, I, p. 795.
4 See Documents, IX, 1947, p. 109.   5 Department of State, Bulletin, XX, p. 831.
6 Army Department Civil Affairs Division, 208th Weekly Report on Japan, p. 1.
7 Department of State Press Release 350, May 12, 1949.

regarding the reparations question, and in order that as many as possible of Japan's post-war obligations might be disposed of during the period of the occupation, a reparations program should be worked out and put into effect at the earliest practical moment.

These factors led the United States Government to take the initiative in making a number of policy proposals to the Far Eastern Commission. In April, 1946, the United States submitted to the Far Eastern Commission a pattern of proposals providing that there should be made immediately available for reparations designated quantities of industrial facilities which were at that time considered to be clearly surplus to Japan's peaceful needs. Between May and December of that year the Commission adopted a series of Interim Reparations Policy decisions based upon these U.S. proposals, but the subsequent inability of the Commission to agree on a schedule of shares for division of the facilities among the claimant countries prevented implementation of the decisions. In April, 1947, the U.S. Government offered further proposals, which would have had the effect of making known to Japan precisely, and on a final basis, what industrial capacity should be considered by that country to be immune from removal as reparations and what should be eligible for removal. In the same month, the U.S. because of its desire to work toward a settlement of this matter issued an Advance Transfers interim directive, under authority granted in paragraph III, 3, of the Terms of Reference of the Far Eastern Commission, instructing the Supreme Commander to effect delivery to four of the FEC countries of 30 per cent of the facilities which the Far Eastern Commission itself had previously determined in the Interim Removals decisions to be available for reparations removal. Issuance of this directive was motivated in part by a desire to assist those countries which had in the course of fighting against Japan's aggression on their own territories suffered most grievously, but it was also motivated by a desire to prompt FEC countries to agree upon a reparations program from which all eleven countries might benefit.

In November, 1947, the United States Government took the initiative once more in an effort to end the stalemate within the Commission on the question of reparations shares, a stalemate which continued to make it impossible for any of the Commission's decisions on the reparations problem to take practical effect. This U.S. proposal contained the provision that if the Far Eastern Commission countries would accept the schedule of percentages which had been worked out by the U.S. Government — on the basis of prolonged exchanges of views among Commission members as to the equities involved — the U.S. Government, on its part, would make available an important part of its own share for distribution among the countries which could accept the U.S. proposal as a whole. Sixteen months have passed and this proposal has not been accepted by the Commission.

I should like to emphasize at this point that the action of my Government, and, it is assumed, of the other Member Governments, in participating in the policy decisions which have been taken by the Commission on the question of reparations was predicated upon two basic assumptions, namely, that the resources to be removed from Japan as reparations were clearly excess to the peaceful needs of a self-supporting Japanese economy, and that there would be a shares schedule acceptable to and agreed upon by the Far Eastern Commission countries which would determine in what proportions available reparations should be divided.

As I have already stated, and as the Commission well knows, the second of these assumptions has not been realized and there seems little prospect of its being realized. As regards the first assumption, that reparations removals should be limited to facilities clearly excess to the needs of a self-supporting Japanese economy, successive studies during the past eighteen months of Japan's future industrial requirements have necessitated progressive upward adjustments of earlier estimates of these requirements. The first of these studies was that of Overseas Consultants, Incorporated, whose report was made available to the Commission on March 2, 1948, and the second was that of the so-called Johnston Committee, whose report was made available to the Commission on May 19, 1948. Both of these reports came to the sober conclusion that the quantity of capital equipment in Japan which could be properly considered in excess of Japan's peaceful needs had been greatly overestimated. Both reports indicated that for a variety of reasons the Japanese economy was continuing to operate at a heavy deficit even though living standards remained at a minimum level, and that the end to these deficits is not in sight. The evidence contained in these reports, and the common knowledge of all Far Eastern Commission countries, leads to the inescapable conclusion that the Japanese economy can be made to bear additional economic burdens, beyond those directly related to meeting its own requirements, only by prolonging or increasing the staggering costs borne by the American taxpayer.

The United States has, since the time of the Japanese surrender, carried the burden of preventing such disease and unrest in Japan as might jeopardize the purposes of the occupation. The critical economic conditions with which, it is now apparent, Japan is faced, and the prospect of continuing deficits in Japan's international payments for some years to come, render measures of Japanese economic recovery of utmost importance. It is inescapable that if the basic purposes of the occupation are to be achieved, the Japanese people must be enabled to support themselves at a tolerable standard of living. No one could reasonably suggest that Japan should be abandoned to economic despair. So to abandon Japan would be to undo the costly victory in the Pacific.

I am sure that other Commission countries agree with my Government that the Japanese people themselves must exert maximum efforts for the attainment of recovery. For some months the U.S. Government has explored means whereby this objective could best be achieved. In issuing its directive of December 10 regarding Japan's economic stabilization, the U.S. Government took a major step towards requiring the Japanese people to exert their utmost energies in stabilizing their economy and reducing their dependence for subsistence on foreign subsidy. Under present circumstances in Japan the cost of dismantling, packing, and transporting reparations facilities would conflict with the program of Japan's economic stabilization and would constitute an additional financial burden upon the U.S. Government. I do not wish to emphasize this point unduly, but the U.S. Government would be lacking in candor if it did not point out that the resources at its disposal to meet demands from all parts of the world are limited.

It is now apparent to the U.S. Government that the first as well as the second of the two basic assumptions mentioned earlier, assumptions which underlay the policy decisions of the FEC having to do with reparations and are a precondition for an FEC reparations program, has not been realized. This fact has led my Government to several conclusions. Before stating them, however, I wish to emphasize that the U.S. Government maintains fully and categorically its support of the principle adopted by the Far Eastern Commission that Japan's war-making capacity should be eliminated. As you know, all of Japan's specialized war-making facilities have been destroyed. The U.S. Government believes that all other equipment used for war purposes in the past should, if retained in Japan, be fully converted to the purposes of and utilized in Japan's peaceful economy. Where this cannot be done, the U.S. Government believes that such equipment should be scrapped. The U.S. will not permit difficulties in reaching a solution of the reparations problem to be a means whereby Japan's war capacity might re-emerge.

It may not be amiss at this point to recall that Japan has already been deprived not only of all of its overseas territorial possessions, but also of substantial quantities of real property of Japanese ownership and origin in the former possessions and elsewhere abroad. This property constitutes a large payment which the Japanese have already made towards satisfaction of their reparations obligations. Unfortunately, from the standpoint of equity, some countries have benefited more than others in the reparations that they have obtained in this form. However, from the standpoint of Japan, the loss of these properties, whatever the proportions in which they happen to have been distributed, drastically reduces Japan's ability to support even at a minimum level the needs of its people.

In view of the above considerations, the United States is forced to the following conclusions:

(a) The deficit Japanese economy shows little prospect of being balanced in the near future and, to achieve eventual balance, will require all resources at its disposal.

(b) The burden of removing further reparations from Japan could detract seriously from the occupation objective of stabilizing the Japanese economy and permitting it to move towards self-support.

(c) There is little or no prospect of Far Eastern Commission agreement on a reparations shares schedule despite the repeated initiatives by the United States over the past three years to assist the Commission in reaching such an agreement. Without agreement on a shares schedule the existing Far Eastern Commission policy decisions regarding reparations are incapable of implementation.

(d) Japan has already paid substantial reparations through expropriation of its former overseas assets and in smaller degree, under the Advance Transfer Program.

In light of these conclusions the United States Government is impelled to rescind its interim directive of April 4, 1947, bringing to an end the Advance Transfer Program called for by that directive. It is impelled also to withdraw its proposal of November 6, 1947, on Japanese reparations shares, and I am so informing the Secretary General. Finally, the U.S. Government takes this occasion to announce that it has no intention of taking further unilateral action under its interim directive powers to make possible additional reparations removals from Japan.

I earlier stated my Government's belief that maximum efforts should be exerted by the Japanese themselves for their economic recovery. It is the view of the United States that all facilities, including so-called "primary war facilities," presently designated as available for reparations which can contribute to Japanese recovery should be utilized as necessary in Japan's peaceful economy for recovery purposes.

With regard to "primary war facilities", all of which as I earlier stated were some time ago stripped of their special purpose equipment and thus of their "war facilities" characteristics, it is the view of the U.S. that SCAP, under the authority granted in paragraph 10 of the FEC decision on Reduction of Japanese Industrial War Potential, should as rapidly as practicable require the dismantlement, dispersion or other action for the utilization in Japan's peaceful economy of such of these facilities as are required to meet the needs of the occupation, which needs prominently include economic recovery. Remaining "primary war facilities" should continue to be protected, in the sense of preventing loss or scrapping of individual items, pursuant to the above-mentioned FEC decision requiring their "impounding". Impounding does not, however, include requirement that the facilities be kept in their present locations or that the Japanese devote resources to preserve their value or maintain them in working order.

The United States, it will be recalled, has repeatedly clarified its understanding that the "level of industry" proposals before the Commission, excepting those levels which will lapse by FEC decision on October 1, 1949, had application only to the question of the quantities of industrial facilities which could be spared for reparations, and had no bearing on the matter of future levels of industrial capacity in Japan. Turning now to this latter question, I have already emphasized my Government's support of the principle that Japan's capacity to make war should not be permitted to re-emerge. It is the considered view of the United States Government that this objective does not require that Japan's production for peaceful purposes be limited or that limitations be imposed on levels of Japanese productive capacity in industries devoted to peaceful purposes. This belief, coupled with the evidence of Japan's present economic plight and the difficult problems Japan will face in future in attaining levels of industrial production and foreign trade sufficient to support its people even at minimum levels, render it clearly advisable in my Government's view that Japan be permitted to develop its peaceful industries without limitation. The problem facing us is not one of limitation of Japan's peaceful industries but of reviving these industries to provide the people's barest wants.

The U.S. Government plans shortly to submit to the FEC for its consideration proposals for the rescission or amendment of existing and pending FEC reparations and level of industry policy papers so as to bring FEC policies on these matters, should the proposals be approved by the Commission, into conformity with the position which I have set forth. My Government earnestly hopes that the other Member Governments will appreciate the considerations underlying this position and will be able to concur in the new United States proposals.

3. LABOR POLICY IN JAPAN

(1) *Letter from the Soviet Member of the Allied Council for Japan (Derevyanko) to the Supreme Commander for the Allied Powers (MacArthur) Concerning Labor Policy in Japan, June 11, 1949.*[8]

The ever-increasing pressure on the part of the present Japanese Government upon the democratic rights of the Japanese people, the suppression of the legal activities of trade unions and other democratic organizations, and also the arbitrariness and chastisement committed by the Japanese police in connection with trade union leaders, progressively minded persons, and participants of various labor demonstrations and meetings to the present time have become facts deserving serious attention.

Calling to attention also the fact that the illegal activities of the Government and police organs, intended to forcefully impede the democratization of the nation, are taking place before the eyes of the American occupation authorities. General Headquarters, SCAP does not take any measures to the prevention of these activities flagrantly violating the Potsdam Declaration and the policies of the Far Eastern Commission to the democratization of Japan. These facts explain the increasingly great concern in the broad Japanese public opinion for the fate of democratization of their nation.

The masses of the people are indignant at the activities of the present Japanese Government resorting to the brutal suppression of the democratic movements by analogous methods of violence and repression existing during the period of the militaristic domination of Japan.

The occurrence in Tokyo on 30 and 31 May of the brutal suppression by the Japanese police of the peaceful demonstration consisting of representatives of trade unions, students and other public organizations has aroused a just indignation in the entire nation and beyond its borders.

8 Army Department. Civil Affairs Division. *183d Weekly Report on Japan*, Appendix A, p. 7.

As is known, this suppression was inflicted upon participants of a peaceful demonstration of laborers, employees and students who gathered for the sole purpose of expressing their protest against the new "public safety regulations" which were preconceived for further limiting the rights of labor and public organizations to hold gatherings, meetings and demonstrations.

The Japanese police, attempting to disperse the demonstration, began ruthlessly clubbing them, as a result one member of the Tokyo City Transportation Union, Laborer Kinji Hashimoto was killed by the police. Demonstrators who were headed to the building of the Headquarters Tokyo Metropolitan Police with protests against this bloody suppression and with demands that punitive measures be taken against the ones guilty of the crime were not admitted there and were subjected to new beatings by the police. Gathering on the following day near the Tokyo Metropolitan Assembly Hall, the representatives of numerous trade unions and students organizations, with intentions to demand punishment of those guilty of the killing of the laborer Hashimoto, were again subjected to brutal beating by specially mobilized police numbering about 2,000 policemen. As a result of this one hundred demonstrators received wounds and injuries and more than sixty persons were arrested.

Bringing the above content to your attention I wish to express my hopes that, on your part, proper measures will be taken to prevent illegal activities and antilabor measures which are practiced at this time by the Japanese Government.

At the same time I wish to express my hope that you will take appropriate measures for punishing those guilty of the brutal suppressions of labor demonstrations and killing laborer Hashimoto.

(a) *Comment by the Supreme Commander for the Allied Powers (MacArthur) on the Letter from the Soviet Member of the Allied Council for Japan (Derevyanko). Released to the Press, June 13, 1949.*[9]

The Soviet letter, replete with inaccuracies and misrepresentations of fact, could be disregarded as routine Soviet propaganda did it not so completely unmask the Soviet role as an incitor of disorder and violence in an otherwise orderly Japanese society. The thorough duplicity of its apparent championship of fundamental human rights on the one hand and the Soviet callous indifference to the release for repatriation of Japanese prisoners of war on the other — its talk of greater liberality for Japanese workers and the Soviet practice of labor exploitation, is a shocking demonstration of inconsistent demagoguery.

The purpose of the letter is obviously twofold: To incite irresponsible and unruly minority elements in Japan to violent and disorderly resistance against the duly constituted government of Japan and the lawful orders and processes thereof with a view to creating confusion, unrest and bewilderment in the

9 *Ibid.*, p. 8.

ranks of the law-abiding Japanese masses, and to screen the Soviet unconscionable failure to abide by the requirements of International Law and specific Potsdam commitments in the return of over 400,000 Japanese citizens, long held in bondage, to their homeland.

This failure to meet international commitments and maintain normal standards of human decency in the disposition of captives finds little parallel in the history of modern civilization, and is calculated so to outrage normal sensibilities that even the Japanese Communists have been moved to register a bitter and indignant protest.

The burdened effort at this late date to challenge the number long publicly recorded as held in Soviet hands by charging mathematical error is small solace indeed to the hundreds of thousands of Japanese homes from whom no sophistry can conceal the fact that a family member in Soviet custody has failed to return; and as to whom, contrary to all international covenants respecting prisoners of war, no word whatsoever has been received during the long period of captivity.

For the Soviet to speak in derogation of the status of labor in Japan is hypocrisy compounded. This premise is based upon such fantastic exaggerations as obviously to belie the truth. The Japanese labor laws match the most progressive in their liberality and advanced concept, and the labor movement here, despite its immaturity, has advanced more rapidly and with less friction than has its counterpart in many of the democratic countries of the world.

Incidents of violence have been rare indeed and no segment of Japanese society has made such democratic gains as labor which enjoys rights and liberties and safeguards largely unknown to the peoples of the Soviet Union, which following the totalitarian concept, holds under ruthless suppression individual liberty and personal dignity.

For the Soviet to speak of "democratic rights," "the suppression of legal activities," "arbitrariness and chastisement," is enough to challenge the late lamented Ripley at his imagination's best and leads one to conclude that now there must really be nothing new under the sun.

(2) *Statement by the United States Member of the Far Eastern Commission (McCoy) Concerning Labor Policy in Japan, Made before the Commission, July 13, 1949.*[10]

[EXCERPT]

. . . .

At the meeting of the Commission on June 23 the Soviet member made a series of sweeping, misleading charges against the manner in which SCAP and the Japanese Government are handling the labor situation in Japan. The Soviet member specifically denounced the revisions of the Japanese labor laws enacted at the last Diet session and the action taken by the Japanese authorities in coping with the recent labor demonstrations at the Tokyo Municipal Assembly Building on May 30 and at the Hiroshima plant of the

10 Department of State, *Bulletin*, XXI, p. 107.

Japan Steel Company on June 12. It has not been — nor will it be — the practice of my government to answer charges of this nature which are so clearly of the propaganda variety. However, in order that this Commission may have the full benefit of the facts, there is being circulated to the members of the Commission a memorandum prepared by my government analyzing each of the specific charges made by the Soviet member, as they relate to the revisions of the Japanese labor laws.

I wish to point out at this time that the revisions of the Japanese labor laws enacted in the last Diet session are a direct implementation of FEC–045/5 (Principles for Japanese Trade Unions) which was issued after the original labor laws were enacted. In line with FEC–045/5, the revisions of the laws have strengthened the democratic character of Japanese trade unions through such measures as ensuring that the unions observe direct secret elections, annual general meetings, open financial reports, and protection of individual members against discrimination within the union. Special emphasis was placed on the practical workability of administrative procedures so as to preclude a breakdown which would prevent peaceful settlement of labor disputes. In many instances labor's interests have been further clarified and the rights of individual workers safeguarded.

The Soviet representative has attempted to associate the revisions of these labor laws with the incidents at Tokyo and Hiroshima. However, in neither incident were any labor laws involved and in the Tokyo case no trade union issues of any kind were at stake.

These and other recent incidents of the same nature have been characterized by certain features of disturbing implication. Seizing upon any pretext whatsoever, lawless elements have organized demonstrations for the purpose of exerting mass pressure to intimidate government authorities and others into doing the bidding of the demonstrators. The participants in these affairs have also sought to provoke the authorities into acts of force which could then be denounced as "repressive measures," "police brutality," or, to quote the Soviet member's phrase, "brutal mobbing by the police". In contrast to the acts of violence committed by the demonstrators — including illegal seizures, intimidation, and bodily attacks on company officials — the Japanese authorities have exercised care and restraint. Police have been used only when necessary to clear public buildings so that governmental functions could go on, to protect property and maintain order. Arrests have been made only where demonstrators resisted or even attacked policemen. In the Tokyo incident police action was not taken until after 5 hours of continued disruption of the Tokyo Municipal Assembly proceedings by a militant mob. At Hiroshima, there was no resort to police action until 48 hours after the steel plant had been illegally seized by the demonstrators.

It appears to us that these cases of mob violence are not designed to protect the rights of labor or to advance democratic tendencies, despite the use of democratic phrases by Soviet representatives here and in the Allied Council for Japan. On the contrary, it is clear to us that this is a centrally directed campaign to create fear, social unrest, confusion and disorder, which is intended to undermine the authority of the government, in the hope of creating a condition favorable to the seizure of political power.

It would appear to my government that the primary and central issue raised by the Soviet member at the June 23 meeting of the Commission is whether the legitimate rights and interests of the Japanese people are to be protected by duly constituted authority or to be placed at the mercy of a lawless few.

CHAPTER IV

Economic Reconstruction and Development

During 1949, the work of the United States Government and of the United Nations and its specialized agencies in the economic field was marked by a shift of emphasis from the project of reconstruction to the long-range proposition of economic development. Before the year was out, planning for economic development was being actively promoted in various organizations of the United Nations system and, as a result of President Truman's pronouncement in his inaugural address of a "bold new program" of development of backward areas,[1] in departments and agencies of the United States Government. Concurrently with this newer phase of economic activity, the United States in cooperation with the countries of western Europe continued its economic assistance program under the Economic Cooperation Administration.

1. UNITED NATIONS REGIONAL ECONOMIC COMMISSIONS

The United States continued for the year under review its participation in the three existing United Nations regional economic commissions: for Europe, for Asia and the far east, and for Latin America. Pending clarification of the situation in the middle east resulting in part from the Palestine question, progress toward the creation of the proposed Economic Commission for the Middle East[2] was largely suspended.

A. Economic Commission for Asia and the Far East

[See *Documents, IX, 1947*, p. 153; *X, 1948*, p. 180.]

The United States participated in two meetings of the Economic Commission for Asia and the Far East in 1949: the first at Bangkok from March 28 to April 5 when the commission met as the Committee of the Whole, and the second at Singapore from October 20 to 29 when ECAFE met for its fifth regular session. Edwin F. Stanton, United States Ambassador to Siam, and Philip H. Trezise attended the Bangkok session of the Committee of the Whole of ECAFE while Myron M. Cowen, ambassador to the Philippines, headed the United States delegation to the fifth session.[3] Questions of particular interest to the United States which were discussed in these meetings included that of industrial and economic development in the ECAFE region and of intra-regional trade promotion, particularly with respect to trade between the ECAFE countries and Japan.

On the motion of the United States, the committee on April 5 adopted a resolution recognizing the essential role of investment and of the full utilization of domestic capital resources in the promotion of industrial development. Pursuant to this resolution the ECAFE secretariat was instructed to undertake an exhaustive inquiry into the region's facilities for the mobilization of financial and monetary sources in the encouragement of productive investment.[4] On the same date, the committee approved a joint United States-United Kingdom-Indian resolution recommending the establishment by the commission of a Committee on Industry and Trade and emphasizing the necessity that ECAFE itself give "primary attention to those industries and to those aspects of trade which are of urgent importance to the economy of

1 For the text of the President's inaugural address, see this volume, p. 7.
2 See *Documents, X, 1948*, p. 192.
3 United Nations Economic and Social Council, Document E/CN.11/AC.11/SR.1, March 28, 1949; *ibid.*, Document E/CN.11/AC.11/SR.2, March 29, 1949; Department of State, *Bulletin* XXI, p. 628.
4 United Nations Economic and Social Council, Document E/CN.11/AC.11/Sub.1/1/Rev.1, April 4, 1949; *ibid.*, Document E/CN.11/AC.11/1, April 5, 1949.

the region."[5] During discussions at the fifth session of ECAFE of the development of intra-regional trade, Mr. Cowen (United States) denied Soviet allegations that his government was attempting to stifle industrial competition from Japan and other far eastern nations.[6] The United States voted in support of a resolution on trade promotion which the commission adopted on October 27.[7] The United States also participated in the adoption on October 26 of a resolution on industrial development which called for the initiation of preliminary technical studies as a sound basis for the work of development, and close cooperation with the International Bank for Reconstruction and Development in studying the Bank's loan requirements in respect of several categories of projects of an important character common to most of the ECAFE countries.[8] On October 29, the United States joined with the majority of the members of the commission in accepting a resolution relating to the general question of technical assistance for the economic development of the ECAFE region.[9]

(1) *Resolution on Trade in Asia and the Far East, Approved by the United Nations Economic Commission for Asia and the Far East, October 27, 1949.*[10]

THE ECONOMIC COMMISSION FOR ASIA AND THE FAR EAST

HAVING CONSIDERED the Report of the Committee on Industry and Trade.[11]

APPROVES generally the conclusions of the Committee in respect of trade and

WARMLY ENDORSES the commendation expressed almost unanimously by the Committee for the work already done by the Trade Promotion Division and in particular for the technique of inquiry adopted by the Division; and

RECOGNIZING the importance of promoting intra-regional trade between ECAFE countries as a means of enhancing their economic reconstruction and the development of the national industries of these countries, improving the level of living of their peoples, and strengthening their economic relations; and

RECOGNIZING further that the expansion of such trade is an important factor in bringing about a fuller development of the resources of the region; and

NOTING that closer trade relations will help foster better understanding with a view of promoting world peace;

APPROVES in general the future programme of work, leaving it to the Executive Secretary in the light of the opinions expressed in the Committee to determine priorities;

RECOMMENDS that where practicable countries contemplating changes in policy governing trade and exchange controls should make available advance information for circulation through the Trade Promotion Division; and

RECOMMENDS that member countries be urged to establish permanent trade promotion agencies in the different countries of the region and to exchange trade delegations;

RECOMMENDS FURTHER that adequate staff should be provided as soon as possible to enable the Division to continue to expand its valuable activities;

5 *Ibid.*, Document E/CN.11/AC.11/Sub.1/5, April 4, 1949; *ibid.*, Document E/CN.11/AC.11/8, April 5, 1949.
6 *Ibid.*, Document E/CN.11/SR.65, October 26, 1949, p. 4.
7 *Ibid.*, Document E/CN.11/221, October 28, 1949.
8 *Ibid.*, Document E/CN.11/216, October 28, 1949.
9 *Ibid.*, Document E/CN.11/231, October 29, 1949.
10 *Ibid.*, Document E/CN.11/221, October 28, 1949.
11 *Ibid.*, Document E/CN.11/206–E/CN.11/I&T/11, October 19, 1949.

BEARING IN MIND that the reconstruction of Japan should not be allowed to prejudice the peace and economic progress of the ECAFE region;

NOTING however that the trade between Japan and ECAFE countries is at present complementary and that its expansion would be beneficial to the region as a whole;

CONSIDERING also that the expansion of food production in the region would tend to expand trade and alleviate dollar shortage;

RECOMMENDS that studies of trade with Japan and in the region generally should be intensified, special attention being devoted to identifying the factors impeding trade and the causes of changes in the volume and patterns of trade; and

TAKING NOTE of the progress so far made by the International Monetary Fund in its study of balance of payments;

RECOMMENDS that the Secretariat and the International Monetary Fund in conjunction should make every effort to complete their study in time to submit a full report to the next meeting of the Committee on Industry and Trade.

(2) Resolution on Technical Assistance for Asia and the Far East, Approved by the United Nations Economic Commission for Asia and the Far East, October 29, 1949.[12]

THE ECONOMIC COMMISSION FOR ASIA AND THE FAR EAST

NOTING the paper E/CN.11/200 prepared by the Executive Secretary summarising technical assistance activities in the region to date and the present position in respect of increased technical assistance services to be made available in 1950 under Resolution 200 (III) of the General Assembly;[13]

NOTING also that the Economic and Social Council at its Ninth Session considered the whole question of technical assistance[14] and that the Fourth Session of the General Assembly is now considering the recommendations made by the Council;

NOTING further the proposals of the Secretary-General "to make full use of the resources not only of the Secretariat at Headquarters but also of the Secretariats of the Regional Economic Commissions" (page 52 of E/1327/Add.1);[15]

BEARING IN MIND the terms of Resolution E/CN.11/180/Rev.1, Annex B of the Fourth Session of the Commission on the importance of preparation of integrated programmes of economic development;

RECOMMENDS to the Governments of the region

1. that they make full use of the facilities to be made available under Resolution 200 (III) with respect to the different services offered under this resolution;

2. that in anticipation of the expanded technical assistance programme

12 *Ibid.*, Document E/CN.11/231, October 29, 1949.
13 For further information on consideration by the General Assembly of technical assistance to under-developed areas, see this volume, p. 251.
14 For further information on consideration by the Economic and Social Council of technical assistance to under-developed areas, see *ibid.*, p. 251.
15 For further information on these proposals, see *ibid.*, p. 251.

they should so plan the stages of their schemes of economic development as to enable them to make use on a systematic and well co-ordinated basis of these additional facilities as they become available;

3. that in preparing requests under this resolution they should attach great importance to the proper selection of projects so that only those of high priority are submitted and that these are in every way adequately documented;

4. that in carrying out these recommendations they make full use of the facilities afforded by the ECAFE Secretariat;

REQUESTS the Secretariat

(a) to expedite its Report on "Fields of Economic Development Handicapped by Lack of Trained Personnel";

(b) to make available its facilities to assist the Governments of the Member and Associate Member countries to prepare their technical assistance projects and schemes;

REQUESTS the Economic and Social Council

(a) to consider in what ways the Commission and its Secretariat may with advantage participate in the specific aspects of the technical assistance programme under the administration of the Secretary-General of the United Nations; in such ways as receiving and forwarding applications for assistance, if Governments so desire, and in being associated in any appropriate manner with such arrangements as may be made by the Secretary-General for the provision of assistance and in any other suitable ways;

(b) to take the necessary action to ensure that the Secretariat is adequately staffed to carry out such functions as may be assigned to it;

REQUESTS the Secretary-General to bring this resolution to the notice of the General Assembly with a view to having it considered, if possible, at the current session of the General Assembly.

B. Economic Commission for Europe

[See *Documents, IX, 1947*, p. 150; *X, 1948*, p. 185.]

The development of east-west trade in Europe, as discussed in the fourth session of the Economic Commission for Europe and in a prior meeting of the commission's Committee on the Development of Trade, was a problem of major interest to the United States in the field of general economic reconstruction and development in Europe. The latter committee met in Geneva from February 14 to 19, 1949; the commission's fourth session was held, also in Geneva, from May 9 to 21. The United States delegation to that session was headed by W. Averell Harriman and Paul R. Porter.[16]

Both in the discussions of the committee and of the commission, general agreement as to the urgent need for and the importance of an expansion of intra-European trade was expressed by all delegates. Wide differences of opinion became obvious, however, during the consideration of obstacles which hampered the development of such trade and of means by which trade between European countries might best be encouraged. On the question of obstacles to trade, the Soviet Union representative to the Committee on Development of Trade (Garaschenko), whose government had taken the initiative in proposing the creation of the committee, made charges of trade discrimination "forced upon eastern Europe" by the inauguration and operation of the European Recovery Program, and contended that so long as the United

16 United Nations Economic and Social Council, Document E/ECE/105, May 14, 1949.

States "bans machinery for the East" no substantial increase in intra-European trade would be possible.[17] Other representatives on the committee also referred to "alleged discriminatory practices of the USA which, in their view, created a major obstacle to the development of European trade."[18] In a working party established by the committee for the consideration of commercial policy, the discussion of trade discrimination brought forth numerous allegations "that the U. S. Government used export licensing as a means of discrimination against certain European countries." To these charges, the United States replied that it did not practice trade discrimination as within the meaning of the Havana Charter for the International Trade Organization.[19] The Soviet representative on the commission itself (Aruntiunian) declared that European trade "was subordinate to western Europe" and that the United States view in imposing restrictive measures on trade from the west to the east was "one-sided and failed to take into account the principle of mutual interests." Citing statistics contained in the *Economic Survey of Europe in 1948*[20] Mr. Aruntiunian stated that eastern exports to western European countries had been 37 per cent higher than western exports to the east, a situation attributable to "the export licensing policy which the United States of America has imposed on the countries of Western Europe" and to "the economic policy applied under the Marshall Plan."[21] Mr. Porter (United States) replied to these charges in a statement of May 16, denying that his government had opposed the creation of the Committee on the Development of Trade, that it forced upon nations cooperating in the European Recovery Program a restrictive system of exports to eastern Europe, and that the United States practiced discrimination in its direct trade with that region.

A proposal submitted to the committee on trade by Czechoslovakia requesting that the Secretariat prepare a full report on the question of discrimination in east-west trade and a Polish amendment to the effect that attention be given particularly in the study to the "differential application of the U.S. export licensing system" resulted in a deadlock in the working party of the committee, the United States taking the view that, since the question raised in the proposal was political in character, it could not be considered in that body.[22] The resolution as amended was accordingly referred to the Committee on the Development of Trade where it was rejected by a recorded vote of 11 to 6.[23]

Methods of stimulating intra-European trade were discussed by a second working party created by the Committee on the Development of Trade. Although recognizing the desirability of an eventual development in the direction of multilateral trade, a point of view which the United States had consistently advocated, the working party agreed that in the near future European governments should concentrate on the promotion of trade within the "existing framework of bilateral agreements." Accordingly, the working party approved a Soviet proposal, also supported by the United Kingdom, calling for bilateral agreements in promotion of trade. The United States opposed the sanctioning of such agreements on the ground that long-term bilateral arrangements in themselves constituted obstacles to eventual multilateral trade and payments.[24] In accordance with the decision of the working party, the committee requested the Secretariat of ECE to study the mechanism and pattern of bilateral agreements, particularly with reference to their duration.[25] On May 21, 1949, the Economic Commission for Europe approved the report of the Committee on the Development of Trade and requested that the committee continue and develop the work which it had already undertaken, thus endorsing the committee's decision to resort to bilateral channels for the expansion of trade between eastern and western Europe.[26]

[17] *Christian Science Monitor*, February 16, 1949, p. 6.
[18] United Nations Economic and Social Council, Document E/ECE/99–E/ECE/TRADE/2, March 17, 1949, p. 2.
[19] *Ibid.*, p. 5.
[20] *Ibid.*, Document E/ECE/91/Rev.1, May 12, 1949.
[21] *Ibid.*, Document E/ECE/SR.4/3, May 18, 1949, p. 13.
[22] *Ibid.*, Document E/ECE/99–E/ECE/TRADE/2, March 17, 1949, p. 5.
[23] *Ibid.*, p. 6.
[24] *New York Times*, February 19, 1949, p. 4.
[25] United Nations Economic and Social Council, Document E/ECE/99–E/ECE/TRADE/2, March 17, 1949, p. 2.
[26] *Ibid.*, Document E/ECE/107, May 23, 1949.

(1) *Statement by the United States Representative on the United Nations Economic Commission for Europe (Harriman) on the Development of Intra-European Trade, Made before the Commission, Geneva, May 9, 1949.* [27]

[EXCERPTS]

In considering the reports which have been submitted to this session by the committees of ECE, I believe that some general remarks are desirable before we proceed to deal with each report separately. We are fortunate in being able to examine these reports against a heartening background. During the last year we have seen, and can draw confidence from, remarkable improvements in large parts of the European economy. The impressive gains in production in 1946 had been checked in 1947. Bilateral trade arrangements had shown themselves unequal to the needs of trade within Europe and lack of foreign exchange threatened to halt essential imports from overseas of food, materials for production, and machinery for reconstruction. These difficulties were intensified by adverse weather conditions throughout most of Europe.

.   .   .   .

I wish to say a few words about trade. At another time in this session we will have before us the matter of approving the terms of reference recommended for the Committee on the Development of Trade. But it is also desirable to comment briefly, during this general review of ECE work, on the question of intra-European trade and on what the new committee on trade may be able to contribute to its expansion. A larger volume of trade between eastern Europe and western Europe can raise standards of living in all Europe and will reduce Europe's need for external aid. These are objectives which the record shows the United States to favor. A significant measure to expand intra-European trade would be an increase in the availability for export from eastern Europe of commodities desired by western Europe. A principal reason why east-west trade has not grown more rapidly since the end of the war has been the failure of the eastern countries, for a variety of causes, to export more of the commodities, which they have traditionally supplied to western Europe.

Before the war, eastern exports to the west consisted mainly of primary products. There is still a wide demand for these products by western countries. Western exports to the east had traditionally consisted of manufactured goods. Since the war, however, the demands of eastern countries for goods from the west have increasingly concentrated on heavy manufactured goods which have been in scarcest world supply. The western countries, though wishing to resume traditional patterns of trade, have been obliged to seek other sources for the primary products formerly available in Europe. Had supplies been available in greater volume from eastern Europe, the western European nations could have obtained them from these traditional sources rather than from the Western Hemisphere, and thus return to a more normal level when eastern Europe resumes large export to the west of the food, timber, coal, and nonferrous metals which western Europe desires. By contributing to the revival of production and export those countries which have joined with us in the European Recovery Program, the United States is giving practical assistance to expanding intra-European trade and intends to continue to do so.

The industrial recovery in the west, which we have aided, has brought with it effective markets for the products of eastern Europe. Increased production has meant that more and more goods which are desired in exchange are becoming available. It is encouraging to note from the economic survey which the secretariat has placed before us that despite the difficulties we have encountered and despite the shifts from prewar trading systems, both total intra-European trade and trade between eastern and western Europe have increased by approximately 25 percent during the past year. It is my hope that the new trade committee will contribute to a sound pattern of expanded production and trade. Its success will depend in large measure on the willingness of countries to make available the necessary statistical information. Without the basic facts of production and trade from all countries of Europe, the committee will lack the essential tools for its work. If intra-European trade is to reach the level required for genuine recovery, there must be an advance from the now prevalent system of bilateral trade to a freer multilateral system. Trading on a multilateral basis, and free trading over increasingly greater areas, is an objective to which my government subscribes most earnestly.

Americans understand through first-hand and intimate experience the part that our own great free-trading area has played in achieving a level of productivity heretofore unapproached. The economic survey which we have at hand has remarked on that productivity in the United States and has drawn attention to the fundamental problem of attaining higher industrial and agricultural productivity in Europe. It notes that the productivity of labor in industry in the United States was in prewar days three times that of labor in Europe taken as a whole, and relatively even greater in agriculture. The survey further points out that in the last decade productivity in American industry has increased 27 percent and in agriculture 54 percent. It ascribes this astounding rise mainly to higher standards of capital equipment and the use of more efficient production techniques. That is, of course, true. But it must be remembered that a basic condition which brought about that higher use of equipment and those more efficient techniques was the existence of a vast trading area uninhibited by artificial barriers and serving as an invitation to the free and economic flow of goods, capital, and people. It provided a market of enormous size for the most efficiently produced goods, wherever produced. It encouraged investment wherever it could be most wisely and economically made. It permitted workers to move where the job opportunities called and where they were most rewarding. The more the nations of Europe can move together toward the establishment of these basic conditions the more effectively can their human and material resources develop ever rising standards of living for their people.

.   .   .   .

(2) Summary Record of Statement by the United States Representative on the United Nations Economic Commission for Europe (Porter) on Obstacles to Intra-European Trade, Made before the Commission, Geneva, May 16, 1949.[28]

[EXCERPTS]

MR. PORTER (United States of America) said the debate had so far revealed three broad areas of agreement: that an expansion of east/west trade was desirable; that a Committee on the Development of Trade should be set up to achieve that end; and that, in spite of differences as to the drafting of its terms of reference, the Committee had made a good start in its work. However, instead of confining themselves to those basic considerations on which all were agreed, the representatives of the USSR and certain other countries had made irrelevant charges against the western countries which had to be refuted for the sake of world opinion.

In the first place, it was untrue that the United Kingdom and United States delegations had opposed the proposal to set up a Committee on the Development of Trade at the Commission's Third Session. They had merely asked for more time to study the question, and had supported the Swedish proposal that an *ad hoc* Committee should be convened to examine the matter further. In the *ad hoc* Committee itself, both delegations had favoured the establishment of a Committee on the Development of Trade.

Furthermore, the restrictions imposed, for security reasons, on the export of certain materials and equipment to Eastern Europe, could easily be removed, if only the USSR would convince world opinion that its intentions were peaceful.

The charge had also been made that the United States engaged in discriminatory practices in its trade with Eastern Europe. Full and complete answers to that charge had been made in various bodies of the United Nations, but the charge had since been repeated and those answers ignored. Such a repetition of accusations coupled with a studied refusal to take note of the replies suggested the technique of a propagandist rather than a genuine attempt to resolve the underlying problems.

A *bona fide* charge of trade discrimination must rest on the acceptance by the accuser of the principles which the guilty party was alleged to have violated. The principles underlying the establishment of mutually beneficial economic relations had been enunciated in the Draft Charter for an International Trade Organization, which was the fruit of much careful effort by countries genuinely interested in the expansion of multi-lateral, non-discriminatory trade. Those principles were simple, and included, first, the establishment and maintenance of a peaceful world community, and secondly, the recognition that the various parts of the world differed in resources, climate,

28 United Nations Economic and Social Council, Document E/ECE/SR.4/13, May 30, 1949, p. 14.

skills and traditions, and were therefore specially placed to produce certain types of goods. The greatest benefit for all would be assured by encouraging each area freely to develop its own special potentialities and to exchange its products with other areas on terms of mutually beneficial economic advantage, unnatural and uneconomic trade barriers being reduced to a minimum.

．　　．　　．　　．　　．　　．　　．

In the field of trade relations, certain Eastern European nations which had not been allowed to trade in the pattern most advantageous to them, had described themselves, in meetings of the Commission, as the relatively underdeveloped countries of Europe. They had solicited the sympathetic interest and assistance of the Commission in fostering their economic development, and had accused the United States of retarding that development. A glance at the real pattern of Eastern European trade, however, would suffice to show how, and by what nation, the tempo of eastern European economic development was being retarded. Available data suggested that, during the current trade year, Eastern European countries would exchange with each other goods to the value of an estimated 2.1 billion dollars, as compared with 1.6 billion dollars in the preceding year, and as compared with something less than 2 billion dollars' worth of goods to be exchanged with countries of Western Europe. Of that total, about 1.2 billion dollars, that was, the predominant share, represented the value of the Soviet Union's imports from and exports to the other countries of Eastern Europe. Only 10% of the total value related to machinery and equipment of the type necessary for economic development, and more than a quarter of that limited quantity consisted of equipment for import into the Soviet Union from the other countries of Eastern Europe. The Soviet Union had indeed furnished some industrial equipment to the other countries, but many complaints had been heard, albeit *sotto voce*, of poor quality and delayed delivery. The bulk of Soviet Union exports to those countries consisted of fuels, raw materials and foodstuffs, which, though useful in many ways, were certainly not conducive to the economic development of under-developed areas, and which in many cases were processed and re-exported to the Soviet Union as finished goods, often as reparations.

Was that the logical trade pattern for the promotion of the economic development of Eastern Europe? Could not more advantageous markets be found for much of the coal, petroleum, timber, grain and potash scheduled for export from the smaller nations of Eastern Europe? If left to themselves, those countries would not consider trading in scarce and important raw materials with countries having substantially similar economies. Exchange under such conditions was not "trade" at all, but merely exploitation, and was far from the type of activity likely to foster economic development. The present time, moreover, was particularly favourable for the sale of the foodstuffs and raw materials available in the smaller countries of Eastern Europe in world markets, since the prices of such eagerly sought-after commodities had risen, in comparison with the pre-war period, to a greater degree than had the prices of the manufactured goods which Eastern Europe would normally import.

Thus, as much as a billion dollars' worth of the goods now traded between Eastern European nations could be directed to other parts of the world, and exchanged for typical exports of the more highly-industrialized countries. Moreover, those exports would be of genuine value in the economic development of the former countries.

．　．　．　．　．　．　．

The usefulness of this artificial trade pattern in achieving political ends was obvious; but it brought numerous other advantages to the Soviet Union. For example, the Soviet Union imported petroleum, timber, aluminum, lead, newsprint, iron and steel in large quantities from some Eastern European countries, and re-exported them in smaller quantities to others. Similarly, available reports showed that the Soviet Union benefited financially by dealing as a middleman in coal and cotton. It had also been frequently reported that the Soviet Union supplied low grade cotton, rancid butter and inferior petrol in return for the most important goods Eastern Europe had available for export. Such practices, benefiting the strong at the expense of the weak, more closely approached the goal of seventeenth-century colonial relations than that of "the economic co-operation and assistance" which the Soviet Union representative had described as characteristic of the economic relations between the countries of Eastern Europe.

The true character of those economic relations was even more strikingly revealed by the discriminatory practices and special privileges embodied in the joint-company agreements concluded between the Soviet Union and certain countries of Eastern Europe. Available data illustrated clearly how the Soviet Union invariably succeeded, by means of such arrangements, in obtaining treatment better than that extended to national enterprises, and vastly superior to that given to the next most-favoured nation.

．　．　．　．　．　．　．

Why did not the smaller countries of Eastern Europe speak out against such practices in such forums as the Commission? Why did they not seek out the real cause of their economic troubles, and why did they talk about principles which did not seem at home in the atmosphere of Eastern Europe? It was only human to complain and to discuss one's grievances, but the only complaints heard from those countries were directed to the wrong address.

In conclusion, he hoped that the commerce of Europe and the world would be conducted with the minimum of restrictions and with the greatest mutual benefit to buyer and seller. By patience and co-operation, by strict adherence to the principles of the Charter of the United Nations, a point should be reached where all nations could abide by such universally accepted rules as those of the Charter for the International Trade Organization. It could confidently be expected that, by that time, which was surely not far off, the evils of discrimination, special privilege and colonial exploitation, would no longer be hampering the free and co-operative economic development of sovereign peoples.

C. Economic Commission for Latin America

[See *Documents, X, 1948,* p. 187.]

Albert Nufer, United States Ambassador to El Salvador, headed the United States delegation to the second session of the United Nations Economic Commission for Latin America which met in Havana, Cuba, from May 29 to June 14, 1949.[29] Topics of particular interest to the United States were the Latin American economic situation and the needs for technical assistance in the area, as well as the regional resources available for that purpose. The session also dealt with the development of agriculture and the expansion of food production, with the problem of multilateral compensation of international payments, and with the questions of immigration, tourism and transport in the ECLA region.[30] On the proposal of the United States, the commission added to its agenda an item concerning coordination of activities between the commission and the Inter-American Economic and Social Council.[31]

In the commission's general discussion of the Latin American economic situation, Mr. Nufer (United States) reviewed his government's policy of encouragement to the Latin American countries and announced that the United States was prepared "to continue such cooperation towards economic development on a broad scale."[32] A representative of the National Association of Manufacturers (Balgooyen) stressed the interests of United States manufacturers and business men in Latin America. He noted, however, that there appeared to be a reluctance on the part of domestic investors to participate in local financial enterprises, apparently because of "the relatively low rate of return obtained, the long term nature of the investment, or because of their preference for liquid funds." In the face of this reluctance, Mr. Balgooyen believed, foreign investors "hesitate before investing their savings in productive enterprises located in countries whose own citizens may not consider the opportunities for such enterprises to be attractive."[33] At the conclusion of general debate on the economic situation, the commission referred the question of technical assistance to an *ad hoc* committee on which the United States was alternately represented by Edmund Kellogg, H. Gerald Smith, and John S. de Beers. On the proposal of Mr. Smith, the committee heard Mr. Balgooyen (N.A.M.) elaborate on the factors preventing a larger flow of United States private capital into Latin America. These factors included a lack of confidence regarding the political stability of some ECLA countries, foreign exchange shortages, uncertainty as to the stability of some local currencies, a fear of nationalization or expropriation in a few countries, and the burdens of double taxation.[34]

Both in the committee and in the meetings of the commission, the United States supported the adoption of four resolutions for technical assistance in the ECLA region: 1) a proposal by Chile on the general subject of technical assistance, adopted by the committee on June 7;[35] 2) a joint proposal by the United States and Brazil urging the promotion of economic research and the training of economists in Latin America, adopted by the committee on June 9;[36] 3) a second Chilean proposal pertaining to economic development, approved by the committee on June 9;[37] and 4) a Uruguayan proposal calling for studies of the conditions affecting capital investments, adopted by the committee on June 9 subject to a United States amendment calling attention to work already undertaken in this field by the Inter-American Economic and Social Council and the Inter-American Development Commission.[38] These resolutions, with only minor amendments, were approved by the Economic Commission for Latin America on June 10, 1949.[39]

29 *Ibid.,* Document E/CN.12/99, September 27, 1949.
30 *Ibid.,* Document E/CN.12/81/Rev. 2, June 13, 1949.
31 *Ibid.,* Document E/CN.12/98, May 31, 1949; *ibid.,* Document E/CN.12/SR.21, August 16, 1949, p. 3.
32 *Ibid.,* p. 6.
33 *Ibid.,* Document E/CN.12/100, May 31, 1949, p. 5.
34 *Ibid.,* Document E/CN.12/AC.3/SR.2, June 3, 1949. p. 6.
35 *Ibid.,* Document E/CN.12/AC.3/SR.3, June 8, 1949, p. 3.
36 *Ibid.,* Document E/CN.12/133, June 8, 1949; *ibid.,* Document E/CN.12/AC.3/SR.4, November 10, 1949, p. 3.
37 *Ibid.,* Document E/CN.12/131, June 10, 1949; *ibid.,* Document E/CN.12/AC.3/SR.4, November 10, 1949, p. 8.
38 *Ibid.,* Document E/CN.132, June 10, 1949; *ibid.,* Document E/CN.12/AC.3/SR.4, November 10, 1949, p. 9.
39 *Ibid.,* Document E/CN.12/SR.24, August 16, 1949.

(1) *Resolution on Technical Assistance for Latin America, Approved by the United Nations Economic Commission for Latin America, June 10, 1949.*[40]

[TRANSLATION]

THE ECONOMIC COMMISSION FOR LATIN AMERICA:

CONSIDERING that the Commission at its First Session adopted the Resolution of 25 June 1948, requesting the Executive Secretary to submit a preliminary study of the needs of the Latin American countries for technical and administrative personnel, means and facilities and their present availability; and also requested him, in addition to such a study which was to be presented to the Second Session, to prepare in due course and submit to the various countries, lists of organizations able to render the necessary technical assistance;

TAKES NOTE of the preliminary study on the needs for technical assistance submitted by the Executive Secretary (E/CN.12/84);

TAKES NOTE of the "Progress Report of the Expert of the International Labour Office on Enquiries Conducted in Vocational and Technical Training Requirements and Facilities in Latin America" (E/CN.12/90), and considers that the International Labour Organization should continue and intensify its ·peration with the Executive Secretary;

TAKES NOTE of the communication (E/CN.12/AC.3/W.5) addressed to the Commission concerning the decision taken by the Governing Body of the International Labour Organization to create within the Organization a Committee for Latin America on manpower, and to authorize the creation of a field office of the International Labour Office in Latin America, designed to implement its programme on manpower in the region;

TAKES NOTE of the offer of technical assistance made by the World Health Organization and by the Panamerican Sanitary Bureau;

REQUESTS the Executive Secretary to complete, as soon as data from the respective governments become available, the tasks entrusted to him by the Commission in Section (b) of the Resolution of 25 June 1948[41] and in cooperation with the Governments and with the Organization of American States to continue collecting information and making studies on the needs for technical assistance; and

INVITES the Governments of the Latin American countries to submit as soon as possible a statement of their needs for technical assistance to the Executive Secretary and to complete those which they may have forwarded already, such statements to be transmitted to the Secretary-General in order that they may be considered in carrying out the "Plan for an expanded co-operative programme through the United Nations and the Specialized Agencies";

CONSIDERING ALSO that in the said Resolution of 25 June 1948 the Commission recognized the important part that technical training and technical assistance play in the economic development of Latin America "for the im-

---

[40] *Ibid.*, Document E/CN.12/130, June 10, 1949.
[41] These tasks included the preparation of "lists containing the names of the organizations able to render the necessary technical assistance" to the region (*ibid.*, Document E/CN.12/75, June 25, 1948).

proved utilization of natural resources and equipment permitting human efforts to become more productive".

EXPRESSES ITS SATISFACTION with regard to Resolution 200 of the General Assembly[42] on technical assistance for economic development, by virtue of which the Secretary-General initiated a programme of services for technical assistance to the Member Governments of the United Nations;

CALLS THE ATTENTION of the Latin American Governments to the technical assistance which can now be extended to them by the Secretary-General in accordance with the said Resolution; and especially calls attention (1) to the sending of comprehensive economic missions or groups of experts of the United Nations and the Specialized Agencies to study on the spot possibilities and plans for economic development and (2) to the availability of fellowships for technicians to improve their knowledge and skills abroad;

EXPRESSES ITS SATISFACTION ALSO, with the statement by the President of the United States of America to the effect that the United States in a co-operative enterprise in which all nations work together through the United Nations and its Specialized Agencies, will place at the disposal of the economically under-developed countries the benefits of their resources of technical knowledge and experience, in order to assist them in raising the standard of living of their peoples;

EXPRESSES THE HOPE that the plan for realizing a broad programme of technical assistance through the United Nations and its Specialized Agencies, which is to be submitted to the Economic and Social Council by the Secretary-General in pursuance of the Council's Resolution 180 (VIII),[43] will obtain sufficient support to enable this plan to be implemented in accordance with the methods and policies which the Economic and Social Council may establish, and thus make possible an effective increase in the technical assistance services of the United Nations and the Specialized Agencies, so that the needs of the Latin American countries may be met;

CALLS THE ATTENTION of the Economic and Social Council to the specific projects requiring technical assistance which have been or may be submitted by the Latin American countries. Some of these projects are mentioned in the Second Part of the Executive Secretary's Preliminary Study on the Needs for Technical Assistance (E/CN.12/84);

REQUESTS the Executive Secretary, in accordance with the methods and policies which the Economic and Social Council of the United Nations may establish, to establish the facilities which will enable him to offer assistance to the Latin American Governments for the appraisal of their most urgent needs for technical assistance for economic development, acting in co-operation with the Specialized Agencies whenever possible.

---

42 For further information on the role of the General Assembly in promoting technical assistance, see this volume, p. 251.
43 For further information on the role of the Economic and Social Council in promoting technical assistance, see *ibid.*, p. 251.

2. FOREIGN ASSISTANCE PROGRAM

A. General

[See *Documents, IX, 1947*, p. 159; *X, 1948*, p. 193.]

(1) *Report of the Joint Congressional Committee on Foreign Economic Cooperation on Progress under the Foreign Assistance Programs, Transmitted to the Congress, January 27, 1949.*[1]

[EXCERPTS]

I. PROBLEMS REQUIRING CONSIDERATION BY CONGRESS

Since the beginning of the foreign-assistance programs, April 3, 1948, Europe has made substantial progress toward economic recovery and in morale. In this report the joint committee is confining itself to suggestions on specific phases of the law's operation and to reporting factual data, but the committee does wish to set down its belief that the workings of the act during the last 9 months have contributed much to the economic rehabilitation and political stability of western Europe.

FUTURE UNITED STATES EXPORTS TO EUROPE

A situation is beginning to emerge which is likely to demand increasing attention from Congress as the foreign-aid program develops. Certain United States exporters who have been selling in Europe for many years are being faced with the fact that the policy of Marshall plan countries is to favor exports and frown on imports, particularly those requiring dollar exchange.

The participating countries are focusing their plans primarily on their dollar deficits with the result that they turn to the United States for imports only as a last resort. In these days of world shortages, the United States is temporarily the principal supplier of many products. Nevertheless, in numerous instances, of which steel is an outstanding example, these scarce items will not find a permanent market in Europe and American suppliers would prefer to dispose of them elsewhere.

European recovery apparently involves more than rebuilding. A considerable amount of remodeling of the economic structure is inevitable. In addition to war damage, the current prostration of Europe can be attributed in part to the loss of eastern European markets and materials and to the drastic curtailment of demand for semiluxury goods particularly in the United Kingdom and in Germany. These conditions appear likely to persist for a considerable period.

If Europe is to attain a position which will permit it to maintain itself without "extraordinary outside assistance," its economic structure must be remodeled to compensate for these fundamental changes.

This remodeling will also reflect any pressures imposed on the economic structure of Europe by the Marshall plan. The current focusing of attention on dollar deficits tends to force Europe to reconstruct its economy so as to get along without certain "normal" exports from the United States.

1 Senate Report 13, 81st Cong., 1st sess.

Congress faces the fact that the economy of Europe will be substantially altered if Europe is to pay its own way in the postwar world. This alteration can be done in such a way that foreign trade with the United States is minimized or maximized. The ECA program can be operated so as to rebuild the European economy to complement American agriculture and industry or so as to erect a barrier between Europe and the United States.

We should make sure that the course we take leads to the destination we desire.

. . . .

GUARANTEES OF AMERICAN INVESTMENTS IN PARTICIPATING COUNTRIES

Encouragement to participation by private capital in European recovery was intended by Public Law 472, section 111 (b) (3), which guarantees the transfer into dollars of foreign currencies received as income or proceeds of sale of approved investments made by Americans in ECA countries. The amount guaranteed is limited to the amount invested.

American business has manifested little interest in this provision. Omitting the guarantees for informational media which involve a different situation, only one guarantee has been made and there have been only 21 applications.

One major technical difficulty has emerged in this connection. The guarantee funds are provided from the $1,000,000,000 authorized for loans. The participating country must approve the project before the guarantee is made. There is a tendency for the European countries to feel that if they do not approve a project submitted by an American investor, they will get the money anyway as a loan without specific limitation as to its use.

The principal difficulty appears to be more fundamental, however. The existing provision is a guaranty of convertibility only and for a limited amount. Since the present-day risks in Europe are so great most investors find more attractive opportunities in the United States.

Congress apparently must choose between providing a much more comprehensive guarantee or waiting until a substantial improvement occurs before private investment will assume an important role in European recovery.

. . . .

II. CHECKLIST REPORT

1. FINDINGS AND DECLARATION OF POLICY

(a) What progress are the participating countries making toward achieving a "joint organization to exert sustained common efforts as set forth in the report of the Committee of European Economic Cooperation signed at Paris on September 22, 1947, which will speedily achieve that economic cooperation in Europe which is essential for lasting peace and prosperity"? (Sec. 102 (a).)[2]

The organization which has been created under the economic cooperation program to constitute "a joint organization to exert sustained common

2 References are to Public Law 472 (See *Documents, X, 1948*, p. 195).

efforts as set forth in the Report of the Committee of European Economic Cooperation signed at Paris on September 22, 1947," is the Organization for European Economic Cooperation, the headquarters for which is in Paris. It is made up of 19 nations and includes all the countries of western Europe with the exception of Spain. Switzerland and Portugal are members but receive no aid. Bizonal Germany, Austria, and Trieste are members, and the French zone of Germany so far participates as though it were a separate country.

These member countries have agreed with each other that they will formulate a common program for European recovery, that they will develop their production, that they will remove restrictions on trade, that they will strive to attain a sound financial status, and that they will exchange information with each other.

The major accomplishments of the OEEC to date have been the division of the funds made available by the ECA among the participating countries, the development of and agreement upon an intra-European payments plan and the preparation and acceptance of a program for the fiscal year 1948–49.

In addition, a program for the fiscal year 1949–50 has been submitted to ECA on which the request for the next appropriation will be based. Substantial progress has also been made on a 4-year program.

The controversy within the organization which has received greatest publicity has been the dispute over the share of ECA assistance to be allocated to bizonal Germany. This difficulty delayed the allocation of funds and the formulation of the annual program for several weeks and was only resolved after the intervention of ECA officials.

The newspapers currently report a disagreement between England and France on the acceptance of luxury exports such as French wines by the United Kingdom, which is barring such products under its austerity program.

To what extent the OEEC organization and accomplishments so far represent a real unification of western Europe is difficult to determine. Mr. Hoffman has emphasized the significance of the fact that representatives of the participating countries have worked together over a period of months debating controversial issues and reaching solutions which it was possible for them all to agree upon in most instances. On the other hand, it should be pointed out that the United Kingdom is charged unofficially by representatives of other participating nations with not going "all-out" to bring about European unification because of her uncertainty as to whether she would be better off to base her future on her leadership of the British Empire or whether she should throw in her lot with western Europe. Furthermore, the political uncertainties within France have made it impossible for that country to play the role in the OEEC which her size and location would indicate she should.

As a consequence of these doubts, it apparently remains to be determined whether the OEEC is to fill the role of the organization established by the nations of western Europe to further economic unification at whatever sacrifice to their own national prestige may be necessary, or whether, on the other hand, the OEEC exists merely because it is necessary to have such an organization if the countries of Europe are to receive the aid made available under the Economic Cooperation Act of 1948.

Consideration is now being given by the participating countries and by the ECA to the structure of the OEEC and its future operations in the expectation that increasing emphasis on European reconstruction as distinct from the supply of commodities, will require a somewhat different approach. The staff of the Joint Committee on Foreign Economic Cooperation is following these developments.

. . . .

(c) What steps have been taken to facilitate the interchange of goods and services among the participating countries and to reduce trade barriers? (Sec. 102 (b) (3) and sec. 115 (b) (3).)

The Benelux countries are in the process of negotiating a joint customs and trade barrier reduction, planned to be effective about the first of 1950.

Each of the bilateral agreements contains an agreement on the part of participating countries to cooperate with each other in facilitating and stimulating increase in the interchange of goods and services, and in reducing public and private barriers to trade among themselves and with other countries. The extent to which the joint organization of participating countries has accomplished agreement in implementation of this provision of the bilaterals awaits further report.

. . . .

8. NATURE AND METHOD OF ASSISTANCE

. . . .

(g) What cooperative steps have been taken with the United Nations? (Sec. 111 (b) (2).)

According to information supplied by ECA, the President has not yet called upon the UN for the use of any of its services or facilities as authorized in section 121 (a). Copies of reports to the Congress, of bilateral agreements executed under the act, etc., have been registered with the UN as required by its charter.

The Economic Commission for Europe, which is a UN organization, has as its United States member Ambassador Harriman, with Paul Porter as his deputy. Liaison is very close between the ECE and OEEC. Personnel from the American staff of the Economic Commission for Europe have been loaned to Harriman's organization in Paris from time to time to assist in its planning work.

. . . .

9. PROTECTION OF DOMESTIC ECONOMY

(a) Have commodities been procured in such a way as to (1) minimize the drain upon the resources of the United States and the impact of such procurement upon the domestic economy, and (2) avoid impairing the fulfillment of the vital needs of the American people?   (Sec. 112 (a).)

Interdepartmental committees constantly reappraise the impact upon the United States economy of ECA procurement, commodity by commodity. Coupled with restrictions written into the act (sec. 112 (g), sec. 177 (d)) dealing with restrictions on the export of goods in short supply and goods scheduled to go into the production of any commodity for delivery to nonparticipating countries who would be refused export licenses in the first instance, ECA's screening processes in furtherance of the mandate in section 112 to minimize the drain upon United States resources and the impact of ECA procurement upon our domestic economy are a continuing procedure.

The Public Advisory Board itself is concerned on a broad basis with anticipated needs, potential deficiencies, and inflationary trends, and meeting once each month keeps the Administrator advised of its views in this regard.

. . . .

11. BILATERAL AND MULTILATERAL AGREEMENTS

(a) **What efforts, individually and collectively, have been taken by the participating countries to accomplish "a joint recovery program based upon self-help and mutual cooperation as embodied in the Report of the Committee of European Economic Cooperation signed at Paris on September 22, 1947"?**   (Sec. 115 (b).)

See 1 (a) above, page 11,[2a] for status of OEEC.

The participating countries have come to grips only recently with the fundamental problems involved in developing an integrated program for western Europe. In preparing the 4-year program designed to make it possible for Europe to continue without extraordinary outside assistance after 1952, the estimates of the individual countries as to planned exports, as well as the availabilities of coal and other materials, were found difficult to reconcile.

Whether it will be possible for the participating countries to develop a "joint recovery program" which is more than a summation of individual programs remains to be determined.

. . . .

(d) **Are the participating countries making "efficient and practical use" of their resources including commodities, facilities, and services furnished them under the act?**   (Sec. 115 (b) (4).)

See 2 (a) above, page 12,[2b] for evidence of trend of production in participating countries.

See 3 (c) above, page 56,[2c] for status of end-use checking by ECA.

The following ECA summary of economic conditions in the participating countries indicates some of the uses that have been made of the commodities, facilities and services that have been furnished under the Act. The summary was dated December 31, 1948.

Industrial production in the participating countries has been rising steadily since the end of the war with the gains continuing into 1948. Total output of factories and mines in the third quarter of 1948 was 10 percent above last

---

2a This volume, p. 201.   2b Not reprinted here.   2c Not reprinted here.

year and nearly equal to the 1938 rate. Outside of the western Germany zones, production in the first 9 months of 1948 is reported at 12 percent above prewar.

Among the heavy industries, the outstanding record has been achieved in steel. Excluding the depressed output of western Germany, steel operations are well above the 1938 rate, and equaled the prewar high of 1937. Although the coal situation has eased partly because of milder weather, tonnage produced is still below prewar in all important areas. The magnitude of the western European reconstruction effort is indicated by the strides made in increasing the output of cement. Production of this basic construction material is far ahead of prewar in every country except Italy and western Germany.

Railway transportation and electric power output have recovered rapidly and have materially assisted the expansion in production. The extent of this contribution may be gaged by the high levels at which these industries are now operating. Total electric power production in countries excluding Germany is 50 percent above prewar and railway freight traffic is up about one-third.

Agricultural production has shown equally impressive gains over the last year, though output is still below prewar. Crop yields in the current year are estimated at 20 percent above last year, largely as a result of improved weather conditions. The domestic output of meat and fats, however, is expected to show little improvement over last year.

The position of the consumer has not, however, improved as much as the overall increase in output might indicate. A larger proportion of available resources are now being channeled into investment than before the war. Consequently, the increases in output have been greater in the capital-goods industries than in the consumer-goods industries. In addition, part of the added farm output is being used to build up depleted herds and to reduce imports.

The supply of food and clothing while greater than last year remains below prewar. In contrast to the gains in such industries as steel and cement, textile output falls short of the prewar average by 25 percent. The food supply has improved over last year but in calorie content is about 5 percent below prewar. In terms of quality and variety the comparison with prewar is still more unfavorable.

While postwar trade recovery has lagged behind production, the ability of western Europe to pay for imports is improving as exports in 1948 have generally increased along with production. Excluding western Germany, the volume of exports and imports now approximate prewar levels.

Exports of the most important trading nation, the United Kingdom, have expanded rapidly over the past year reaching a level 40 percent above prewar in the third quarter. Imports have been held to 18 percent below the prewar volume. In other countries, however, exports have increased less or actually declined and the total remains considerably smaller than before the war. Imports of these countries have generally been falling off over the past year, but are still above prewar levels.

These shifts in trade are reflected, in part, in some reduction in trade deficits thus far this year. An outstanding development was the narrowing of the very large trade deficit with the United States in 1948. This was mostly due to a reduction in imports, but a small increase in much needed exports to the United States helped. Expansion and redirection of trade among the participating countries and with other parts of the world remains a major obstacle to recovery.

Progress toward monetary stability and the more efficient use of manpower have contributed to the improvement in production and trade. With few exceptions, the participating countries have achieved some success in coping with the disruptive effects of inflation. Rises in both prices and the money supply slowed down significantly in most countries during 1948. Improvements in living conditions, transportation, and supplies of materials and fuels are permitting increased output per worker, although productivity has not generally regained prewar levels. The wartime dislocation of the labor force has been largely overcome but scattered labor shortages hinder the expansion in production. On the other hand, unemployment is serious in Italy and Greece and among displaced persons.

The gains achieved by the participating countries in the early phases of the European recovery program must be set against the longer-run task of recovery and stability. To realize this goal, new levels and relationships between production, trade, and consumption are required. While the recovery trends are encouraging, the participating countries still have many difficulties to overcome before a satisfactory balancing of international accounts is achieved.

*   *   *   *   *   *   *

(2) *Report by the Economic Cooperation Administrator (Hoffman) on Recovery Progress and United States Aid, Transmitted to the Congress, February 14, 1949.* [3]

[EXCERPTS]

*   *   *   *   *   *   *

The economic recovery achieved in 1948 is impressive when compared with actual conditions in 1947 and with the conditions which might have developed had the threatened collapse of 1947 been allowed to occur. Had United States assistance not become available, hard currency reserves would have been quickly exhausted; capital equipment intended for the rehabilitation and expansion of European factories would instead have been exported to foreign markets to pay for vital food imports. Even then, hard-currency earnings would have been insufficient to pay for both minimum imports of food and minimum industrial raw-material requirements. Curtailment of imports of industrial raw materials would seriously have affected industrial output, and soon exports would have been inadequate to pay for even the mini-

[3] Economic Cooperation Administration, *European Recovery Program: A Report on Recovery Progress and United States Aid*, Washington, February 1950.

mum food imports. Within a matter of months, considerable parts of Europe would in all probability have faced serious political and economic disorder.

It is against this background that actual conditions at the end of 1948 must be judged. As a result not only of American aid but also of the European action which it reinforced, Western European production in 1948 increased considerably above 1947. Total output of factories and mines in 1948 was 14 percent above 1947 and nearly equal to that of 1938. The countries that had been lagging, notably Germany, Austria, and Italy, narrowed considerably the distance that separated their recovery from that of the other industrial countries of Western Europe.

Among the heavy industries, the outstanding record was achieved in steel. Excluding Western Germany, steel operations were well above the 1938 rate and equal to the high year of 1937. The coal shortage eased; the tonnage produced in 1948 in the Bizone and the United Kingdom remained below that of pre-war, but production in all other important coal fields in Western Europe increased almost to pre-war levels.

The rapid recovery of railway transportation and electric-power output materially assisted in the expansion of production. Total electric-power production in the participating countries, excluding Germany, is 65 percent above pre-war and railway freight traffic is up about one-third.

Crop production in 1948 was considerably above 1947 but was still below pre-war levels, while livestock production was slightly above 1947 and still below pre-war. However, the record of 1948 can in large measure be attributed to the extraordinarily favorable weather conditions which prevailed during the agricultural season.

Food availability from imports as well as from indigenous supplies was much improved over 1947 but was still somewhat below pre-war in caloric content. In terms of quality and variety, the comparison with pre-war is still more unfavorable, largely because of deficiencies in meat, fats, and dairy products. However, the distribution of food among various classes of the population has in many countries been more equitable than before the war.

The progress made in 1948 toward more efficient employment of manpower also assisted in expanding production. Increased supplies of materials and fuels, as well as improvements in food conditions and transportation, permitted gains in output per worker, although productivity in most industries has not recovered fully to pre-war levels. The wartime dislocation of the labor force is being gradually overcome but scattered labor shortages remain. As a result, many countries are attempting to redirect workers to more essential industries. The OEEC Manpower Committee has been investigating the possibility of labor migration from countries with surplus workers, such as Italy and Western Germany, to regions where labor is scarce.

Encouraging progress was made in 1948 toward a better balance between effective supply and demand within many of the participating countries. The upward pressure on prices which had been general in 1947 abated somewhat in these countries during 1948. As a result, many practices adopted by these governments to counteract inflationary pressures, such as rationing, allocation, and price controls, could be relaxed. This has by no means been accomplished just through increased production. It has been the result of wise and, in most cases, difficult fiscal policy decisions. The British budget has been brought into balance and the importance of this accomplishment cannot be over-emphasized. In Italy, the credit restrictions imposed in September 1947 to avert the threat of a runaway inflation have been so drastic that the stabilization produced deflation, which has only recently eased somewhat.

· · · · · ·

The European Recovery Program has made an enormous, quite possibly decisive contribution to the control of inflation in Western Europe. In some small degree the course of financial events has been affected by the ECA's and the OEEC's repeated statements on the matter. There can be no doubt that these exhortations to European governments have influenced their policies. But even where no such influence was exerted, the aid program has had a powerful effect, which is measured, so far as grants-in-aid are concerned, by the accumulation of so-called counterpart funds.

The Economic Cooperation Act wisely provided that the government of each participating country must deposit in a special account amounts of its own currency commensurate with the delivered cost of all goods and services financed by ECA grants in aid. When such goods arrive in the receiving country, they are sold through normal trade channels. The proceeds of these sales are the main source of the funds deposited in the special account, although, in some cases, the deposits have had to be made (under the terms of the ECA's agreements with the country) before the proceeds of the sale of goods have been received.

The operation of this machinery accomplishes two valuable results. In the first place, the people of Western Europe, as private individuals, have to pay for the goods we provide. Businessmen do not receive capital goods or raw materials, and consumers do not receive food or fuel, as gifts. In the second place, amounts of money commensurate with the landed costs of the goods are withdrawn from circulation and held in the special account instead of being automatically paid out again as income. Thus these counterpart funds, so-called because they are the counterparts of the grants-in-aid, constitute a kind of budget surplus and their accumulation has the same deflationary effect that a true budget surplus would have.

The process is relatively painless because the funds are received through the sale of goods instead of having to be collected as taxes. It is deflationary because it soaks up purchasing power which consumers would otherwise be able to spend in other ways. The deflationary effect of accumulating counterpart may, of course, be offset by a budget deficit, or excessive expansion of credit, or other inflationary developments. But the effect is felt nevertheless.

It was not, of course, intended that these deposits of counterpart funds should be immobilized indefinitely, nor has this been the outcome. Where financial balance has been achieved, or where there is a tendency to deflation, the funds can be used subject to the approval of the ECA, to finance public projects or they can be loaned by the government in question to private companies to finance private capital formation. Even in countries where inflation is still a threat, they may have to be released if the only alternative to their use is inflationary borrowing by the government concerned from its central bank. But, under such circumstances, their release may be made the occasion for urging the adoption of more effective fiscal policies.

As a result of stronger fiscal policies as well as of increasing output, the volume of exports has generally risen and the ability of Western Europe to pay for imports improved considerably in 1948. The United Kingdom increased its rate of exports over 1947 and, during 1948, attained a level 37 percent above pre-war. Exports from Belgium, Italy, The Netherlands, and Sweden have also increased as compared with 1947. However, French exports to foreign countries are reported to be at the same volume as in 1947, while the exports of Denmark and Turkey actually declined in 1948 as compared with 1947. The total imports of the participating countries continued below pre-war levels during 1948, but imports from the Western Hemisphere, while less than in 1947, still exceeded pre-war rates.

These changes in the volume of trade resulted in some reductions of the current-account deficits during 1948. Of major importance was the narrowing of the large trade deficit of the participating countries with the United States. During the first 11 months of 1948, imports from the United States declined by $1 billion as compared with 1947, while exports to the United States increased by $223 million. It is expected that total earnings from exports to all areas will pay for more than 50 percent of total imports in 1948/49 as compared with less than 40 per-cent in 1947.

The improvement of Europe's external position has thus been substantial: the total deficit on both capital and current accounts amounted to $7.8 billion in 1947, whereas the figure for 1948/49 is expected to be $5.5 billion. While a heavy drain on European reserves of $2.1 billion took place in 1947, the 1948/49 deficit will be met almost entirely from ECA funds and those spent by the Army for civilian relief.

There will, nevertheless, be a small but manageable drain on gold and dollar resources. Also, during 1948, the participating countries continued to liquidate dollar investments in the United States. Securities worth about $200 million, primarily from France and The Netherlands, were sold during the first nine months of the year.

In accordance with the terms of the Foreign Assistance Act of 1948 and the bilateral agreements, the participating nations have accepted the obligation to take measures, so far as is practicable, to locate, identify, and put to appropriate use assets and earnings therefrom which belong to their citizens and which are situated within the United States. The information resulting from the United States Treasury's census of blocked assets, taken as of June 1, 1948, has been given to the participating nations. The ECA missions have been instructed to discuss with the governments of the participating countries the problems involved in mobilizing and utilizing these assets. However, existing gold and dollar balances of the participating nations are believed to be no greater than necessary to meet minimum needs and the long-term investments of these countries in the United States are a vital factor in recovery objectives. It is not the policy of the United States Government to force further liquidation of necessary gold and dollar balances, or to force the sale or hypothecation of security holdings.

In early 1948, intra-European trade threatened to contract sharply as the result of the exhaustion of gold and dollar reserves and of credits which had been extended on a bilateral basis among the participants at the end of the war. In an effort to find a practicable alternative to strict bilateral balancing of trade at a very reduced level, an Intra-European Payments Plan was established by the OEEC. Under this plan, part of the dollars received from the ECA by any country which is a creditor in its trade with other participants has to be fully matched by grants-in-aid extended by the creditor in its own currency to the debtor countries. Thus Belgium, which is a creditor in its trade with Western Europe, is receiving $247.9 million from the ECA in 1948/49 but is making grants totalling $207.5 million net to other participating countries. The net ERP aid it receives is, therefore, only $40.4 million.

· · · · · · ·

The total use of drawing rights to date is approximately at the anticipated rate. However, some countries have not yet used any of the drawing rights made available to them, while others have already reached the maximum. Both Britain and France have already exhausted their quotas of drawing rights on Belgium and have been forced to resume gold and dollar payments to Belgium or curtail Belgian imports. The OEEC plans study and improvement of the payments agreement this spring.

· · · · · · ·

Much of Europe's recovery in 1948 is directly attributable to American aid—to the food, raw materials and other goods, the purchase of which was financed with aid funds. But American aid did more than this. It stimulated self-help of a magnitude many times greater than the amount of aid given; it encouraged renewed efforts to institute fiscal and monetary reforms and to increase production and expand intra-European trade; and it strengthened the effectiveness of mutual help and cooperation among the participating countries.

Perhaps the most important achievement of the American aid program is that it induced the European countries to embark on the co-operative efforts that are essential for recovery. Coming as they did at the height of a financial emergency, the first operations under the ERP naturally centered on the provision of American aid and its distribution among countries. But as the OEEC grew in strength, the degree of cooperation in Europe steadily increased. The work of the OEEC in drawing up the 1948/49 program and the establishment of the Payments Plan have already been discussed. The OEEC's preliminary analysis of the long-term country programs is a remarkable act of constructive self-criticism, out of which may emerge a truly integrated program of economic development. It is activity of this type which holds the real promise for Western Europe's eventual recovery.

. . . .

(3) *Costs of the European Recovery Program through September 30, 1949.*[4]

		IN MILLIONS OF DOLLARS				
		PROCUREMENT EXPENDITURES				
	PROCURE- MENT AUTHOR- IZED	TOTAL	By UNITED STATES AGENCIES		By TYPE	
			ECA	OTHER	GRANTS	LOANS
Direct program costs:						
Austria	328.9	255.8	82.5	173.3	225.8	—
Belgium-Luxembourg	366.5	252.5	218.1	34.4	201.6	50.9
Denmark	152.9	116.5	107.5	9.0	85.5	31.0
France	1,505.6	1,145.1	1,039.8	105.3	973.1	172.0
Germany, Bizonal Area	567.5	409.8	189.5	220.3	409.8	—
Germany, French Zone	129.6	96.8	46.9	49.9	96.8	—
Greece	236.1	161.3	57.2	104.1	161.3	—
Iceland	9.4	6.2	4.2	2.0	3.9	2.3
Ireland	97.2	51.3	34.7	16.6	—	51.3
Italy	778.6	526.8	393.4	133.4	459.8	67.0
Netherlands	644.0	444.4	377.6	66.8	299.9	144.5
Norway	128.5	82.5	66.6	15.9	47.5	35.0
Sweden	60.6	30.3	30.3	—	30.3	—
Trieste	19.9	14.4	3.5	10.9	14.4	—
Turkey	54.0	10.3	9.6	.7	6.6	3.7
United Kingdom	1,896.9	1,584.5	1,538.6	45.9	1,271.5	313.0
TOTAL, EUROPE	6,976.2	5,188.5	4,200.0	988.5	4,317.8	870.7
China	219.3	167.6	110.9	56.7	167.6	—
Korea	45.9	7.3	2.7	4.6	7.3	—
TOTAL DIRECT PROGRAM COSTS	7,241.4	5,363.4	4,313.6	1,049.8	4,492.7	870.7
Indirect program costs: Technical assistance, requiring deposit of counterpart						
Greece	—	1.7	1.7	—	1.7	—
All other countries[5]	—	.1	.1	—	.1	—
TOTAL	7,241.4	5,365.2	4,315.4	1,049.8	4,494.5	870.7

B. Economic Cooperation Administration

[See *Documents*, X, 1948, p. 227.]

In a report issued to the Congress on January 27, 1949, the Joint Congressional Committee on Foreign Economic Cooperation voiced several criticisms regarding

4 Compiled from House Document 426, 81st Cong., 2d sess., Table F-3, p. 138.
5 Totals $128,691 as follows: Denmark, $18,471; France, $12,577; Netherlands, $8,449; Norway, $10,889; and United Kingdom, $78,305.

the policies under which the Economic Cooperation Administration had functioned during the first year of the foreign assistance program. Empowered to make only recommendations regarding the administration of the Economic Cooperation Act of 1948,[6] the committee suggested that ECA discontinue assistance on a loan basis and resort to the use of extensive grants, with future aid conditioned upon the inauguration by participating nations of financial and monetary reforms. The committee observed that "the imposition on impecunious countries of obligations which they cannot fulfill in the foreseeable future handicaps their recovery . . . and appears to delay the time when these countries might re-enter the market as legitimate borrowers." Financial and monetary reforms seemed desirable since "as long as each participating country relies on a currency that is not desired by its own people and by other nations, there will be a continuous drag on the recovery program." The committee regretted that ECA had taken the position that "German plants should be dismantled unless investigation indicates that a case can be made for their retention," inasmuch as this policy apparently concurred in the view of the western European governments that the entire reparations settlement had been reached on the highest intergovernmental levels in such conferences as Yalta and Potsdam; the committee, on the other hand, felt that a new agreement on the whole reparations question might well have been made a condition of ECA assistance to the European governments holding this view. The committee also criticized ECA for its failure to utilize more than $22 million of the potential $193 million counterpart funds available for the purpose of stockpiling strategic materials, concluding that "ECA would apparently like to be relieved of responsibilities in this field."[7]

The announced intention of the Economic Cooperation Administrator (Hoffman) to divert ECA shipments from United States- to foreign-flag vessels because of a substantial differential between domestic and foreign ocean rates on bulk cargoes became the center of some controversy during the first half of 1949. Hearings by the House Committee on Merchant Marine and Fisheries in January allegedly revealed that recipient nations under the foreign assistance program were applying increasing pressure for the abandonment or modification of the legislative requirement that United States vessels transport at least 50 per cent of all ECA shipments.[8] The problem of interpretation of the pertinent sections of the Economic Cooperation Act of 1948 in which these requirements were contained was resolved in the passage of Public Law 47 which clarified the earlier legislative provisions.[9] Also early in 1949 investigations were launched into the charges made on December 18, 1948, by Howard Bruce, Deputy Economic Cooperation Administrator, that unusually heavy shipments of scrap aluminum and lead were being made to the United States by the nations to which these metals in pure form were being supplied under the foreign assistance program. As a result of these countershipments, planned ECA supplies of these metals were reduced by 34,500 tons pending the results of investigations undertaken first by an ECA mission and later by a joint ECA-Department of Commerce investigation group. The former mission reported late in January that 1) a "major portion" of the scrap consisted of transshipments to the United States through the participating countries, 2) the shortage of aluminum in the United States "would naturally stimulate purchases from Europe" of that metal in scrap form, and 3) with no refining facilities at their disposal, the European nations were forced to ship secondary metals to this country for reprocessing before reuse.[10] The ECA-Commerce investigation confirmed these findings on February 5.[11]

As of December 22, 1948, ECA announced the suspension of further assistance to Indonesia pending clarification of the situation resulting from Dutch military operations there. As of that date, Indonesia had received approximately $57 million in assistance, with some $28 million remaining to be utilized prior to the expiration of fiscal year 1949.[12] Public Law 47 by which the Congress amended and extended the Economic Cooperation Act of 1948 sanctioned this decision of ECA in providing for the suspension of assistance to any participating nations against which the

6 For the text of the Economic Cooperation Act of 1948, see *Documents, X, 1948,* p. 193.
7 Senate Report 13, 81st Cong., 1st sess.
8 *New York Times,* January 19, 1949, p. 2.
9 For the text of Public Law 47, 81st Cong., 1st sess., see this volume, p. 231.
10 *New York Times,* January 28, 1949, p. 3.
11 *Ibid.,* February 6, 1949, p. 1.   12 *Christian Science Monitor,* March 19, 1949, p. 17.

United Nations might be forced to take preventative or enforcement action.[13] Prior to the coming into existence of the Republic of Indonesia on December 27, 1949, the Economic Cooperation Administration made shipments worth roughly $37.5 million to Indonesia in order to expend the ECA allocation for Netherlands colonies before Indonesia, by assuming independence, became ineligible for such assistance.[14]

On December 15, 1949, John J. McCloy, United States High Commissioner for Germany, and Konrad Adenauer, Chancellor of the Federal Republic of Germany, signed at Bonn an economic cooperation agreement embodying the terms and conditions required for the extension of ECA assistance to the western zones.[15]

(1) *An Act to Amend the Economic Cooperation Act of 1948, Approved April 19, 1949.*[16]

On March 7, 1949, identical bills for the amendment of the Economic Cooperation Act of 1948 (H.R. 2362 and S.833) were introduced in the House of Representatives and the Senate by Rep. Sol Bloom (New York) and Senator Tom Connally (Texas), respectively. The major purpose of the bills was to provide authorization for funds for the period from April 3, 1949, when existing appropriations would lapse, and for the fiscal year ending June 30, 1950. For the first period, the bills proposed the authorization of $1,150 million and for the second fiscal year of operation under the foreign assistance program, not more than $4,280 million. Various technical amendments to the Act of 1948 were also provided for. Hearings before the House Committee on Foreign Affairs and the Senate Committee on Foreign Relations resulted in the reporting by both committees of two new bills: S.1209 reported to the Senate unanimously on March 8,[17] and H.R. 3748 reported on March 25, 1949.[18] On the matter of appropriation authorizations the bills differed in the following respects: 1) for the period from April 3 to June 30, S.1209 contained an authorization of $1,150 million, while H.R. 3748 would authorize $1,100 million; 2) for the purposes of forward contracting, the Senate bill authorized up to $150 million while the House bill eliminated this provision entirely; and 3) whereas the Senate bill proposed that the Reconstruction Finance Corporation be permitted to advance $750 million for obligation by ECA 60 days prior to any quarter, the House bill authorized a $1,000 million figure.

Senate debate opened on S.1209 on March 24 and concluded on April 8 with the passage of the bill, with amendments, by a vote of 70 to 7.[19] Attempts to cut the total authorizations under the bill were led by Senator Robert A. Taft (Ohio) who on March 29 proposed a general reduction of approximately 10 per cent, a proposal which the Senate rejected 23 to 54 on April 1.[20] At the same time, the Senate by a vote of 14 to 63 refused to accept an amendment sponsored by Senator Kenneth S. Wherry (Nebraska) which sought to eliminate both the $1,150 million interim period fund and the $150 million forward contracting authorization and to reduce by $642 million the authorization for the second year's program.[21] The Senate accepted amendments relating to increased authority for the Secretary of Agriculture in declaring given commodities in surplus,[22] the protection of small business interests in the procurement operations of ECA,[23] and the suspension of ECA assistance to any participating country against which the United Nations was taking preventative or enforcement action.[24] Amendments were rejected which were designed to place the majority of ECA grants on a loan basis similar to that used by the Recon-

---

13 For the text of Public Law 47, 81st Cong., 1st sess., see below.
14 *New York Times*, December 25, 1949, p. 14.
15 Department of State, *Bulletin*, XXI, p. 982.
16 Public Law 47, 81st Cong., 1st sess. For the text of the Economic Cooperation Act of 1948, see *Documents*, X, 1948, p. 193.
17 Senate Report 100, 81st Cong., 1st sess.; *Congressional Record*, 95, p. 2006 (Daily edition, March 8, 1950).
18 House Report 323, 81st Cong., 1st sess.; *Congressional Record*, 95, p. 3300 (Daily edition, March 25, 1949).
19 *Ibid.*, p. 4230 (Daily edition, April 8, 1949).
20 *Ibid.*, p. 3802 (Daily edition, April 1, 1949).
21 *Ibid.*, p. 3541 (Daily edition, March 30, 1949); *ibid.*, p. 3784 (Daily edition, April 1, 1949).
22 *Ibid.*, p. 4084 (Daily edition, April 8, 1949).
23 *Ibid.*, p. 3261 (Daily edition, March 25, 1949).
24 *Ibid.*, p. 4048 (Daily edition, April 6, 1949).

struction Finance Corporation in its lending operations,[25] to establish an "incentive fund" for the benefit of participating nations contemplating union,[26] and to withhold assistance from any government so controlling its currency that the purchasing power of the monetary unit was not reflected on the world market in terms of United States dollars.[27]

H.R.3748 was brought before the House of Representatives for consideration on April 9.[28] After the adoption of one amendment proposed by Rep. Wright Patman (Texas) and designed to protect the interests of small business in ECA procurement operations, the bill was passed on April 12 by a vote of 354 to 49.[29] The House then amended S.1209 by striking out all after the enacting clause and substituting the approved text of H.R.3748, proceedings for the passage of which the House then vacated. A report on the bill by conferees appointed by the two Houses of the Congress was submitted and approved by the Congress on April 14, 1949.[30] Presidential approval followed on April 19.

Be it enacted by the Senate and House of Representatives of the United States of America in Congress assembled, That the fourth and fifth sentences of section 102 (a) of the Economic Cooperation Act of 1948 are hereby amended to read as follows: "Mindful of the advantages which the United States has enjoyed through the existence of a large domestic market with no internal trade barriers, and believing that similar advantages can accrue to the countries of Europe, it is declared to be the policy of the people of the United States to encourage these countries through their joint organization to exert sustained common efforts to achieve speedily that economic cooperation in Europe which is essential for lasting peace and prosperity. It is further declared to be the policy of the people of the United States to encourage the unification of Europe, and to sustain and strengthen principles of individual liberty, free institutions, and genuine independence in Europe through assistance to those countries of Europe which participate in a joint recovery program based upon self-help and mutual cooperation: *Provided,* That no assistance to the participating countries herein contemplated shall seriously impair the economic stability of the United States."

SEC. 2. The second sentence of section 104 (e) of such Act is hereby amended by striking out "$10,000 per annum" and inserting in lieu thereof "the highest rate authorized by such Act".

SEC. 3. The first sentence of section 105 (c) of such Act is hereby amended by striking out "section 6 of the Act of July 2, 1940 (54 Stat. 714), as amended," and inserting in lieu thereof "the Export Control Act of 1949".

SEC. 4. Section 108 of such Act is hereby amended by adding at the end thereof the following new sentences: "There shall be a Deputy United States Special Representative in Europe who shall (a) be appointed by the President, by and with the advice and consent of the Senate, (b) be entitled to receive the same compensation and allowances as a chief of mission, class 3, within the meaning of the Act of August 13, 1946 (60 Stat. 999), and (c) have the rank of ambassador extraordinary and plenipotentiary. The Deputy United States Special Representative shall perform such functions as the United States Special Representative shall designate, and shall be Acting United States Special Representative during the absence or disability of the United States Special Representative or in the event of a vacancy in the office of United States Special Representative."

SEC. 5. The last sentence of section 109 (a) of such Act is hereby amended by striking out the period and inserting in lieu thereof a semicolon and the following: "and the chief of the special mission shall be entitled to receive the same compensa-

25 *Ibid.,* p. 3543 (Daily edition, March 30, 1949); *ibid.,* p. 4137 (Daily edition, April 7, 1949).
26 *Ibid.,* p. 3958, 3960 (Daily edition, April 5, 1949); *ibid.,* p. 4047 (Daily edition, April 6, 1949).
27 *Ibid.,* p. 4215, 4224 (Daily edition, April 8, 1949).
28 *Ibid.,* p. 4278 (Daily edition, April 9, 1949).
29 *Ibid.,* p. 4504 (Daily edition, April 12, 1949).
30 *Ibid.,* p. 4673, 4676, 4715, 4716 (Daily edition, April 14, 1949).

tion and allowances as a chief of mission, class 3, or a chief of mission, class 4, within the meaning of the Act of August 13, 1946 (60 Stat. 999), or compensation and allowances in accordance with section 110 (a) of this title, as the Administrator shall determine to be necessary or appropriate."

Sec. 6. (a) The last sentence of paragraph (2) of section 111 (a) of such Act is hereby amended to read as follows: "The Administrator shall, in providing for the procurement of commodities under authority of this title, take such steps as may be necessary to assure, as far as is practicable, that at least 50 per centum of the gross tonnage of commodities procured out of funds made available under this title and transported to or from the United States on ocean vessels, computed separately for dry bulk carriers, dry cargo liner and tanker services, is so transported on United States flag vessels to the extent such vessels are available at market rates for United States flag vessels; and, in the administration of this provision, the Administrator shall, insofar as practicable and consistent with the purposes of this title, endeavor to secure a fair and reasonable participation by United States flag vessels in cargoes by geographic area."

(b) Paragraph (3) of section 111 (b) of such Act is hereby amended in the following particulars:

(1) By inserting after "projects" a comma and the following: "including expansion, modernization, or development of existing enterprises" and a comma;

(2) By inserting after "media" the following: "consistent with the national interests of the United States";

(3) By striking out in the first proviso "in the first year after the date of the enactment of this Act does not exceed $15,000,000" and inserting in lieu thereof "made in any fiscal year does not exceed $10,000,000";

(4) By amending subparagraph (i) thereof to read as follows:

"(i) the guaranty to any person shall not exceed the amount of dollars invested in the project by such person with the approval of the Administrator plus actual earnings or profits on said project to the extent provided by such guaranty;";

(5) By inserting after subparagraph (iii) thereof the following new subparagraphs:

"(iv) as used in this paragraph, the term 'investment' includes the furnishing of capital goods items and related services, for use in connection with projects approved by the Administrator, pursuant to a contract providing for payment in whole or in part after June 30, 1950; and

"(v) the guaranty to any person shall be limited to assuring the transfer into United States dollars of other currencies, or credits in such currencies received by such person as earnings or profits from the approved investment, as repayment or return thereof, in whole or in part, or as compensation for the sale or disposition of all or any part thereof. When any payment is made to any person pursuant to a guaranty as hereinbefore described, the currency or credits on account of which such payment is made shall become the property of the United States Government, and the United States Government shall be subrogated to any right, title, claim, or cause of action existing in connection therewith."; and

(6) By amending the next to last sentence thereof to read as follows: "The total amount of the guaranties made under this paragraph (3) shall not exceed $150,000,-000: *Provided*, That any funds allocated to a guaranty and remaining after all liability of the United States assumed in connection therewith has been released, discharged, or otherwise terminated, shall be available for allocation to other guaranties, the foregoing limitation notwithstanding."

(c) Paragraph (2) of section 111 (c) of such Act is hereby amended in the following particulars:

(1) By inserting after the second sentence thereof the following: "In addition to the amount of notes above authorized, the Administrator is authorized, for the purpose of carrying out the provisions of paragraph (3) of subsection (b) of this section, to issue notes from time to time for purchase by the Secretary of the Treasury in an amount not exceeding in the aggregate $150,000,000 less any amount allocated prior to April 3, 1949, for such purpose, until all liabilities arising under guaranties made pursuant to this authorization have expired or been discharged.";

(2) By striking out the first two words, "Such notes" in the third sentence thereof and inserting "The notes hereinabove authorized"; and

(3) By inserting after "Washington" in the sixth sentence thereof "for assistance on credit terms".

SEC. 7. (a) Section 112 (c) of such Act is hereby amended by striking out "25 per centum" and inserting in lieu thereof "12½ per centum".

(b) Section 112 (d) of such Act is hereby amended by adding after the words "any agricultural commodity, or product thereof" the following: "or class, type, or specification thereof".

(c) Section 112 (g) of such Act is hereby amended by striking out "section 6 of the Act of July 2, 1940 (54 Stat. 714), including any amendment thereto," and "section 6 of the Act of July 2, 1940, as amended," and inserting in lieu thereof "the Export Control Act of 1949".

(d) Section 112 of such Act is hereby further amended by adding at the end thereof the following new subsections:

"(i) (1) Insofar as practicable and to the maximum extent consistent with the accomplishment of the purposes of this title, the Administrator shall assist American small business to participate equitably in the furnishing of commodities and services financed with funds authorized under this title by making available or causing to be made available to supplies in the United States, and particularly to small independent enterprises, information, as far in advance as possible, with respect to purchases proposed to be financed with funds authorized under this title, and by making available or causing to be made available to prospective purchasers in the participating countries information as to commodities and services produced by small independent enterprises in the United States, and by otherwise helping to give small business an opportunity to participate in the furnishing of commodities and services financed with funds authorized under this title.

"(2) The Administrator shall appoint a special assistant to advise and assist him in carrying out the foregoing paragraph (1). Each report transmitted to the Congress under section 123 shall include a report of all activities under this subsection.

"(j) The Administrator shall, in providing assistance in the procurement of commodities in the United States, make available United States dollars for marine insurance on such commodities where such insurance is placed on a competitive basis in accordance with normal trade practices prevailing prior to the outbreak of World War II.

"(k) No funds authorized for the purposes of this title shall be used in the United States for advertising foreign products or for advertising foreign travel.

"(1) No funds authorized for the purposes of this title shall be used for the purchase in bulk of any commodities (other than commodities procured by or in the possession of the Commodity Credit Corporation pursuant to price-support programs required by law) at prices higher than the market price prevailing in the United States at the time of the purchase adjusted for differences in the cost of transportation to destination, quality, and terms of payment."

SEC. 8. (a) Section 114 (c) of such Act is hereby amended in the following particulars:

(1) By striking out the period at the end of the first sentence thereof and inserting in lieu thereof a colon and the following: "*Provided further,* That, in addition

to the amount heretofore authorized and appropriated, there are hereby authorized to be appropriated for carrying out the provisions and accomplishing the purposes of this title not to exceed $1,150,000,000 for the period April 3, 1949, through June 30, 1949, and not to exceed $4,280,000,000 for the fiscal year ending June 30, 1950: *Provided further,* That, in addition to the foregoing, any balance, unobligated as of June 30, 1949, or subsequently released from obligation, of funds appropriated for carrying out and accomplishing the purposes of this title for any period ending on or prior to that date is hereby authorized to be made available for obligation through the fiscal year ending June 30, 1950, and to be transferred to and consolidated with any appropriations for carrying out and accomplishing the purposes of this title for said fiscal year."; and

(2) By amending the last sentence of such section 114 (c) to read as follows: "The authorizations in this title are limited to the period ending June 30, 1950, in order that the Congress may pass on any subsequent authorizations."

(b) Section 114 of such Act is hereby further amended by adding at the end thereof the following new subsection:

"(g) Notwithstanding the provisions of any other law, until such time as an appropriation additional to that made by title I of the Foreign Aid Appropriation Act, 1949 (Public Law 793, Eightieth Congress), shall be made pursuant to subsection (c) of this section the Reconstruction Finance Corporation is authorized and directed to make advances not to exceed in the aggregate $1,000,000,000 to carry out the provisions of this title, in such manner, at such times, and in such amounts as the Administrator shall request, and no interest shall be charged on advances made by the Treasury to the Reconstruction Finance Corporation for this purpose. The Reconstruction Finance Corporation shall be repaid without interest for advances made by it hereunder, from funds made available for the purposes of this title."

SEC. 9. (a) Paragraph (6) of section 115 (b) of such Act is hereby amended by striking out the period following the words "grant basis" and inserting in lieu thereof a colon and the following: "*Provided,* That the obligation to make such deposits may be waived, in the discretion of the Administrator, with respect to technical information or assistance furnished under section 111 (a) (3) of this title and with respect to ocean transportation furnished on United States flag vessels under section 111 of this title in an amount not exceeding the amount, as determined by the Administrator, by which the charges for such transportation exceed the cost of such transportation at world market rates."

(b) Such section 115 (b) (6) is hereby further amended by inserting after "or for such other expenditures as may be consistent with" the words "the declaration of policy contained in section 102 and".

(c) Section 115 (d) of such Act is hereby amended to read as follows:

"(d) The Administrator shall encourage each participating country to insure, by an effective follow-up system, that efficient use is made of the commodities, facilities, and services furnished under this title. In order further to insure that each participating country makes efficient use of such commodities, facilities, and services, and of its own resources, the Administrator shall encourage the joint organization of the participating countries referred to in subsection (b) of this section to observe and review the operation of such follow-up systems."

(d) Section 115 of such Act is hereby further amended by adding two new subsections as follows:

"(h) Not less than 5 per centum of each special local currency account established pursuant to paragraph (6) of subsection (b) of this section shall be allocated to the use of the United States Government for expenditure for materials which are required by the United States as a result of deficiencies or potential deficiencies in its own resources or for other local currency requirements of the United States.

"(i) (1) The Administrator shall, to the greatest extent practicable, initiate projects for and assist the appropriate agencies of the United States Government in procuring and stimulating increased production in participating countries of materials which are required by the United States as a result of deficiencies or potential deficiencies in its own resources; and in furtherance of those objectives the Administrator shall, in addition to the local currency allocated pursuant to subsection (h), use such other means available to him under this title as he may deem appropriate.

"(2) In furtherance of such objectives and within the limits of the appropriations and contract authorizations of the Bureau of Federal Supply to procure strategic and critical materials, the Administrator, with the approval of the Director of such Bureau, shall enter into contracts in the name of the United States for the account of such Bureau for the purchase of strategic and critical materials in any participating country. Such contracts may provide for deliveries over definite periods, but not to exceed twenty years in any contract, and may provide for payments in advance of deliveries.

"(3) Nothing in this subsection shall be deemed to restrict or limit in any manner the authority now held by any agency of the United States Government in procuring or stimulating increased production of the materials referred to in paragraphs (1) and (2) in countries other than participating countries."

SEC. 10. (a) The first sentence of section 117 (c) of such Act is hereby amended by striking out the period and inserting in lieu thereof a colon and the following: "*Provided,* That the Administrator shall fix and pay a uniform rate per pound for the ocean transportation of all relief packages of food or other general classification of commodities shipped to any participating foreign country, regardless of methods of shipment and higher rates charged by particular agencies of transportation, but this proviso shall not apply to shipments made by individuals to individuals through the mails."

(b) Section 117 (d) of such Act is hereby amended by striking out "section 6 of the Act of July 2, 1940 (54 Stat. 714), as amended," and inserting in lieu thereof "the Export Control Act of 1949".

(c) Section 117 of such Act is hereby further amended by adding a new subsection to read as follows:

"(e) Whenever the Administrator shall determine that shipping capacity available to Italy is inadequate for such emigration from Italy as may be desirable to further the purposes of this title, the Administrator shall request the United States Maritime Commission to make available to Italy vessels capable of engaging in such service for the purpose of transporting emigrants from Italy to destinations other than the United States, and shall specify the terms and conditions under which such vessels shall thus be made available, and the United States Maritime Commission thereupon shall, notwithstanding any other provisions of law and without reimbursement by the Administrator, make such vessels available to Italy in accordance with such terms and conditions: *Provided,* That the total number of such vessels made available for such purpose shall not at any one time exceed ten: *Provided further,* That title to each such vessel owned by the United States Government shall remain in the United States: *And provided further,* That the terms and conditions under which such vessels are made available to Italy shall obligate Italy to return the vessels forthwith upon demand of the President, and in any event not later than June 30, 1952."

SEC. 11. The second sentence of section 118 of such Act is amended by inserting before the period at the end thereof "or (3) the provision of such assistance would be inconsistent with the obligations of the United States under the Charter of the United Nations to refrain from giving assistance to any State against which the United Nations is taking preventative or enforcement action".

SEC. 12. An amount, equal to any balance, unobligated as of April 2, 1949, or subsequently released from obligation, of funds appropriated by Public Law 793, approved June 28, 1948, for the purposes of the China Aid Act of 1948 is hereby made available to the President for obligation through February 15, 1950, for assistance in areas in China which he may deem to be not under Communist domination, to be furnished in such manner and on such terms and conditions as he may determine.

(2) *An Act Making Appropriations for Foreign Aid for the Fiscal Year Ending June 30, 1950, and for Other Purposes, Approved October 6, 1949.*[31]

After hearings begun on April 27 the House Committee on Appropriations reported to the House on May 23, 1949, H.R.4830, appropriating funds for the second year of the foreign assistance program, for aid to Greece and Turkey, and for government and relief in occupied areas.[32] As reported by the committee the bill included the following major appropriations: 1) for the foreign assistance program during the period from April 3 to June 30, 1949, $1,074 million; 2) for the second fiscal year of the program, $3,568.74 million; 3) for Greek-Turkish aid, $50 million; and 4) for government and relief of occupied areas, $850 million. After accepting an amendment proposed by Rep. J. Vaughn Gary (Virginia) by which the latter appropriation was increased to $925 million,[33] the House passed the bill by a vote of 193 to 27[34] and forwarded it to the Senate where it was, in turn, referred to the Senate Committee on Appropriations from which it was reported, with amendments, on July 12.[35] The bill, as amended by the Senate committee, appropriated as follows: 1) for the foreign assistance program during the period from April 3 to June 30, 1949, $1,000 million; 2) for the second fiscal year of the program, $3,628.38 million; 3) for Greek-Turkish aid, $45 million; and 4) for government and relief of occupied areas, $900 million. Because various amendments to the bill proposed by the Committee on Appropriations were held to be legislative amendments to an appropriation bill, such amendments being prohibited under the Senate rules of procedure, the bill after lengthy debate was recommitted on July 27.[36] Among the amendments offered from the floor and considered in the course of the debate was the requirement proposed by Senator John L. McClellan (Arkansas) that approximately $2,000 million of the foreign assistance appropriation be expended for the purchase of agricultural commodities in surplus in the United States market.

Pending completion of Senate action on H.R.4830 the House of Representatives, in order to assure funds for the operation of ECA and various other government agencies, on July 28 extended temporary appropriations under Public Law 154 (81st Cong., 1st sess.) until August 31, 1949.[37] The Senate approved the resolution with amendments on the same date[38] and the House concurred in the Senate amendments on August 1.[39]

The Senate Committee on Appropriations re-reported H.R.4830 on August 1.[40] Although the committee reported no change in the amounts to be appropriated, three amendments to the House bill were recommended: 1) that $2,000 million of the funds for foreign assistance be obligated for the purchase of surplus agricultural commodities; 2) that $50 million of those funds be earmarked exclusively for assistance to Spain; and 3) that the use of local counterpart funds be denied any participating country failing to comply with the terms of a treaty with the United States. The Vice President (Barkley) ruled that the first two amendments constituted legislative amendments and were therefore not permissible;[41] these rulings

31 Public Law 327, 81st Cong., 1st sess.
32 House Report 657, 81st Cong., 1st sess.; *Congressional Record*, 95, p. 6826 (Daily edition, May 23, 1949).
33 *Ibid.*, p. 7055.   34 *Ibid.*
35 Senate Report 655, 81st Cong., 1st sess.; *Congressional Record*, 95, p. 9461 (Daily edition, July 12, 1949).
36 *Ibid.*, p. 10479 (Daily edition, July 27, 1949).
37 H.J.Res.329, 81st Cong., 1st sess.; *ibid.*, p. 10576 (Daily edition, July 28, 1949).
38 *Ibid.*, p. 10560.
39 *Ibid.*, p. 10693 (Daily edition, August 1, 1949).
40 Senate Report 812, 81st Cong., 1st sess.; *ibid.*, p. 10647.
41 *Ibid.*, p. 10896 (Daily edition, August 1, 1949); *ibid.*, p. 10954 (Daily edition, August 4, 1949).

were confirmed by the Senate by votes of 52 to 32 and 55 to 36.[42] A similar ruling by the Vice President on the third committee amendment[43] was rejected by the Senate[44] which then rejected the amendment itself by a vote of 34 to 46.[45] The bill was passed by the Senate on August 8 by a vote of 63 to 7.[46] Conferees reported to the House on September 28[47] and to the Senate on September 29.[48] On the latter date both Houses accepted the conference report[49] and the bill was signed by President Truman on October 9.

Be it enacted by the Senate and House of Representatives of the United States of America in Congress assembled, That the following sums are appropriated, out of any money in the Treasury not otherwise appropriated, for the fiscal year ending June 30, 1950, namely:

TITLE I

LEGISLATIVE BRANCH

Senate

CONTINGENT EXPENSES OF THE SENATE

Joint Committee on Foreign Economic Cooperation: For salaries and expenses of the Joint Committee on Foreign Economic Cooperation, as authorized by Public Law 472, Eightieth Congress, as amended by Public Law 47, Eighty-first Congress, including per diem and subsistence expenses, without regard to the Travel Expense Act of 1949, approved June 9, 1949, from October 2, 1949, to June 30, 1950, $110,-000: *Provided,* That the amount herein appropriated shall include all expenses necessary to liquidate the affairs of the joint committee not later than June 30, 1950.

FUNDS APPROPRIATED TO THE PRESIDENT

ECONOMIC COOPERATION

For expenses necessary to enable the President to carry out the provisions of the Economic Cooperation Act of 1948, as amended by the Act of April 19, 1949 (Public Law 47), for the period commencing April 3, 1949, through June 30, 1949, including expenses of attendance at meetings concerned with the purposes of this appropriation (not to exceed $6,000); hire of passenger motor vehicles; maintenance and operation and hire of aircraft; payment of damage claims pursuant to law (28 U. S. C. 2672); health service program as authorized by law (5 U. S. C. 150); rents in the District of Columbia; transportation of privately owned automobiles; entertainment (not to exceed $6,000); exchange of funds without regard to section 3651 of the Revised Statutes; and loss by exchange; $1,074,000,000: *Provided,* That not to exceed $4,400,000 in the aggregate shall be available from this appropriation and the appropriation under this head in the Foreign Aid Appropriation Act, 1949, for administrative expenses during the period April 3, 1949, through June 30, 1949.

For expenses necessary to enable the President to carry out the provisions of the Economic Cooperation Act of 1948, as amended by the Act of April 19, 1949 (Public Law 47), for the fiscal year ending June 30, 1950, including expenses of attendance at meetings concerned with the purposes of this appropriation (not to exceed $30,000); purchase (not to exceed two) and hire of passenger motor vehicles; maintenance and operation and hire of aircraft; payment of damage claims pursuant

42 *Ibid.,* p. 10897 (Daily edition, August 1, 1949); *ibid.,* p. 10966 (Daily edition, August 4, 1949).
43 *Ibid.,* p. 10973.   44 *Ibid.,* p. 10978.
45 *Ibid.,* p. 11035 (Daily edition, August 5, 1949).
46 *Ibid.,* p. 11199 (Daily edition, August 8, 1949).
47 House Report 1354, 81st Cong., 1st sess.; *ibid.,* p. 13655 (Daily edition, September 28, 1949).
48 *Ibid.,* p. 13805 (Daily edition, September 29, 1949).
49 *Ibid.,* p. 13806, 13811.

to law 28 U. S. C. 2672); health service program as authorized by law (5 U. S. C. 150); rents in the District of Columbia; transportation of privately owned automobiles; entertainment (not to exceed $25,000); exchange of funds without regard to section 3651 of the Revised Statutes; and loss by exchange; $3,628,380,000, of which not to exceed $350,000 shall be available for expenditures of a confidential character (other than entertainment) under the direction of the Administrator or the Deputy Administrator, who shall make a certificate of the amount of each such expenditure which he may think it advisable not to specify, and every such certificate shall be deemed a sufficient voucher for the amount therein specified: *Provided*, That this appropriation shall be consolidated and merged with appropriations under this head for prior periods, and such consolidated appropriation may be used during the fiscal year 1950 within limitations herein specified: *Provided further*, That not to exceed $16,500,000 of such consolidated appropriation shall be available for administrative expenses during the fiscal year 1950, of which not more than $25,000 shall be available to the Administrator for any further action he may consider advisable to carry out the provisions of section 115 (f) of the Economic Cooperation Act of 1948, as amended by the Act of April 19, 1949 (Public Law 47): *Provided further*, That the Administrator is authorized to issue notes from time to time during the fiscal year 1950 for purchase by the Secretary of the Treasury in an amount not exceeding in the aggregate $150,000,000, for the purpose of allocating funds during such fiscal year to the Export-Import Bank of Washington for assistance on credit terms under the provisions of said Act; and the provisions of paragraph (2) of section 111 (c) of said Act shall, to the extent applicable, be applicable to the notes authorized to be issued in this proviso and to all functions of the Administrator, the Secretary of the Treasury, and the Export-Import Bank of Washington in extending the assistance provided for herein.

The Administrator shall utilize such amounts of the local currency allocated pursuant to section 115 (h) of Public Law 472, Eightieth Congress, as amended, as may be necessary, to give full and continuous publicity through the press, radio, and all other available media, so as to inform the peoples of the participating countries regarding the assistance, including its purpose, source, and character, furnished by the American taxpayer.

ASSISTANCE TO GREECE AND TURKEY

For an additional amount for "Assistance to Greece and Turkey", as authorized by the Act of May 22, 1947 (61 Stat. 103), as amended and supplemented, to be available immediately, $45,000,000, which, together with the amounts heretofore appropriated under this head, shall remain available until June 30, 1950; and the existing limitation under this head in the Foreign Aid Appropriation Act, 1949, on the amount available for administrative expenses, shall continue in effect; and the existing limitation under said head on the amount available for such expenses in the District of Columbia is increased from "$400,000" to "$425,000": *Provided*, That said limitations shall apply only to the administrative expenses of the Department of State.

CHINESE STUDENTS

The President is authorized and directed to allocate to the Secretary of State not to exceed the sum of $4,000,000 out of any unobligated balance of the amount made available under section 12 of the Act entitled "An Act to amend the Economic Cooperation Act of 1948", approved April 19, 1949 (Public Law 47, Eighty-first Congress), to be used, under such regulations as the Secretary of State may prescribe, for necessary expenses of tuition, subsistence, and return passage to China for selected citizens of China to study in accredited colleges, universities, or other educational institutions in the United States approved by the Secretary of State for the purposes of this paragraph; such amount to remain available until expended.

NATIONAL MILITARY ESTABLISHMENT

DEPARTMENT OF THE ARMY—CIVIL FUNCTIONS

GOVERNMENT AND RELIEF IN OCCUPIED AREAS

For expenses, not otherwise provided for, necessary to meet the responsibilities and obligations of the United States in connection with the government or occupation of certain foreign areas, including personal services in the District of Columbia and elsewhere and, subject to such authorizations and limitations as may be prescribed by the head of the department or agency concerned, tuition, personal allowances (not to exceed $10 per day), travel expenses (not to exceed those authorized for like United States military or civilian personnel), and fees incident to instruction in the United States or elsewhere of such persons as may be required to carry out the provisions of this appropriation; travel expenses and transportation; services as authorized by section 15 of the Act of August 2, 1946 (5 U. S. C. 55a), at rates not in excess of $50 per diem for individuals; health service program as authorized by law (5 U. S. C. 150); payment of claims pursuant to law (28 U. S. C. 2672); translation rights, photographic work, educational exhibits, and dissemination of information, including preview and review expenses incident thereto; expenses incident to the operation of schools for American children; printing and binding; purchase and hire of passenger motor vehicles and aircraft; repair and maintenance of buildings, utilities, facilities, and appurtenances; contingencies for the United States commanders, commissioners, or other administrators of foreign areas, to be expended in their respective discretions (not exceeding amounts authorized or approved by the head of the department or agency concerned); such minimum supplies for the civilian populations of such areas as may be essential to prevent starvation, disease, or unrest, prejudicial to the objectives sought to be accomplished; and such supplies, commodities, and equipment as may be essential to carry out the purposes of this appropriation; $912,500,000, of which not to exceed $42,500,000 shall be available for administrative expenses: *Provided,* That the general provisions of the appropriation Act for the fiscal year 1950 for the military functions of the Department of the Army shall apply to expenditures made by that Department from this appropriation: *Provided further,* That expenditures from this appropriation may be made outside continental United States, when necessary to carry out its purposes, without regard to sections 355, 1136, 3648, and 3734, Revised Statutes, as amended, civil service or classification laws, or provisions of law prohibiting payment of any person not a citizen of the United States: *Provided further,* That expenditures from this appropriation may be made, when necessary to carry out its purposes, without regard to section 3709, Revised Statutes, as amended, and the Armed Services Procurment Act of 1947 (Public Law 413, Eightieth Congress): *Provided further,* That expenditures may be made hereunder for the purposes of economic rehabilitation in the occupied areas in such manner as to be consistent with the general objectives of the Economic Cooperation Act of 1948, as amended: *Provided further,* That funds appropriated hereunder and unexpended at the time of the termination of occupation by the United States, of any area for which such funds are made available, may be expended by the President for the procurement of such commodities and technical services, and commodities procured from funds herein or heretofore appropriated for government and relief in occupied areas and not delivered to such an area prior to the time of the termination of occupation, may be utilized by the President, as may be necessary to assist in the maintenance of the political and economic stability of such areas: *Provided further,* That before any such assistance is made available, an agreement shall be entered into between the United States and the recognized government or authority with respect to such area containing such undertakings by such government or authority as the President may determine to be necessary in order to assure the efficient use of such assistance in furtherance of such purposes: *Provided further*, That such agreement shall, when applicable, include requirements and undertakings corresponding to the requirements and undertakings specified in sections 5, 6, and 7 of the Foreign Aid Act of 1947 (Public Law 389, approved December 17, 1947): *Provided further*, That funds appropriated hereunder may be used, insofar as practicable, and under such rules and regulations as may be prescribed by the head of the department or agency concerned, to pay ocean transportation charges from United States ports, including territorial ports, to ports in Japan and the Ryukyus for the movement of supplies donated to, or purchased by, United States voluntary nonprofit relief agencies registered with and recommended by the Advisory Committee on Voluntary Foreign Aid or of relief packages consigned to individuals residing in such countries: *Provided further*, That under the rules and regulations to be prescribed, the head of the department or agency concerned shall fix and pay a uniform rate per pound for the ocean transportation of all relief packages of food or other general classification of commodities shipped to Japan or the Ryukyus regardless of methods of shipment and higher rates charged by particular agencies of transportation, but this proviso shall not apply to shipments made by individuals to individuals: *Provided further*, That the President may transfer to any other department or agency any function or functions provided for under this appropriation, and there shall be transferred to any such department or agency such unobligated balances of this appropriation and, without reimbursement and without regard to the appropriation from which procured, such property as the Director of the Bureau of the Budget shall determine to relate primarily to any function or functions so transferred; and any funds so transferred may be expended either under the authority contained herein or under the authority governing the activities of the department or agency concerned: *Provided further*, That when the Department of the Army, under the authority of the Act of March 3, 1911, as amended (10 U. S. C. 1253), furnishes subsistence supplies to personnel of civilian agencies of the United States Government serving in Germany, payment therefor by such personnel shall be made without regard to the 10 per centum additional charge required by said Act, but payment for subsistence supplies by such personnel shall be at the same rate as is paid by civilian personnel of the Department of the Army serving in Germany.

TITLE II—GENERAL PROVISIONS

SEC. 201. No part of any appropriation contained in this Act shall be used to pay the salary or wages of any person who engages in a strike against the Government of the United States or who is a member of an organization of Government employees that asserts the right to strike against the Government of the United States, or who advocates, or is a member of an organization that advocates, the overthrow of the Government of the United States by force or violence: *Provided*, That for the purposes hereof an affidavit shall be considered prima facie evidence that the person making the affidavit has not contrary to the provisions of this section engaged in a strike against the Government of the United States, is not a member of an organization of Government employees that asserts the right to strike against the Government of the United States, or that such person does not advocate, and is not a member of an organization that advocates, the overthrow of the Government of the United States by force or violence: *Provided further*, That any person who engages in a strike against the Government of the United States or who is a member of an organization of Government employees that asserts the right to strike against the Government of the United States, or who advocates, or who is a member of an organization that advocates, the overthrow of the Government of the United States by force or violence and accepts employment the salary or wages for which are paid from any appropriation contained in this Act shall be guilty of a felony and, upon conviction, shall be fined not more than $1,000 or imprisoned for not more than one year, or both: *Provided further*, That the above penalty clause shall be in addition to, and not in substitution for, any other provisions of existing law.

SEC. 202. During the fiscal year ending June 30, 1950, the Department of the Army is authorized to operate the Morgantown Ordnance Works at Morgantown, West Virginia, the Ohio River Ordnance Works at West Henderson, Kentucky, and the San Jacinto Ordnance Works at San Jacinto, Texas, and to use the appropriation herein made for Government and Relief in Occupied Areas for the production of anhydrous ammonia for the manufacture of nitrogenous fertilizer materials or nitrogenous compounds for its use in the occupied countries and for sale for use in the Republic of South Korea. From the proceeds of materials sold there shall be credited to the appropriation for "Government and relief in occupied areas" an amount equivalent to the cost of production of such materials and any balance to miscellaneous receipts of the Treasury. Section 205 of Public Law 793, Eightieth Congress, and any other laws in conflict herewith, are repealed effective June 30, 1949.

SEC. 203. This Act may be cited as the "Foreign Aid Appropriation Act, 1950".

(3) *Report of the Economic Cooperation Administration-Department of Commerce Mission on Increasing Dollar Earnings of Western Europe, Submitted to the Economic Cooperation Administration, August 29, 1949.*[50]

[EXCERPTS]

A special mission, headed by Wayne C. Taylor, was dispatched jointly by the Department of Commerce and ECA in May 1949 to investigate the possibilities for increased sales of European products in the Western Hemisphere in order to augment collar imports into western Europe. After ten weeks of discussion and investigation in most of the participating nations the mission submitted the following report to Paul G. Hoffman, Economic Cooperation Administrator.

I

The Problem

. . . .

ALTERNATIVE COURSES OF ACTION

A choice now has to be made as to how the United States will deal with the dollar gap problem. By its own actions and the recommendations it makes to other countries the direction of choice will be indicated. There are, generally speaking, four alternatives, plus various combinations of them:

Alternative No. 1. Continuation of Subsidies. We can fail to close the gap and can continue indefinitely to subsidize the participating countries and others with grants of taxpayers' money. This is a policy of drift. It is no solution of the basic problem. While individual countries may need American assistance for specific, sufficient reasons beyond termination of the ECA program in 1952, a general policy based on continued subsidies is undesirable, to say the least.

Alternative No. 2. Reduction of U. S. Exports. We can close the gap by letting our exports come down to the level of our imports. Under pressure to

50 Economic Cooperation Administration, *Report of the ECA-Commerce Mission*. Washington, October 1949.

conserve dollars, the participating countries are now developing policies many of which will, if continued, tend to have that effect. This alternative, so far as it results from exclusion of our goods rather than from fair competition in various markets around the globe, is clearly undesirable. It would damage our export industries. It would cause world trade to stagnate again as in the 1930's, thus defeating our established policy of promoting higher living standards and more cordial international relations through expanded world trade. The whole process would operate through an intensification of restrictive governmental controls.

Alternative No. 3. Expansion of Foreign Investment. We can lend to, or invest in, foreign countries an amount equal to the excess of our exports over our imports. Here a distinction must be drawn between loans (public or private) with fixed interest and repayment provisions, on the one hand, and private investment, on the other. The former cannot be very greatly expanded without imposing an unduly heavy burden on the borrowing countries' balance of payments and standard of living. The record of defaults after World War I tends to establish that point, although additional factors were involved. Expansion of private investment, on the other hand, is highly desirable. However, the gap is much too large to be closed by this method alone.

Alternative No. 4. Expansion of U. S. Imports. We can close the gap by adopting policies that will permit greatly increased purchases of goods and services from the participating countries, from their dependencies (as stabilized relations are reestablished), and from other areas. There is no question here of any obligation on our part to buy from abroad things that are not satisfactory to us — things that we do not want. It is rather a question of stimulating other countries to exert effort and use their inherent resources and capacities in producing and in selling us the things our consumers and businessmen do want; and it is a further question then, on our part, of not maintaining or raising up barriers to prevent these countries from earning their way by selling those desirable goods and services in our market.

Expanded sales in the United States of products from the participating countries, their dependencies, and other areas stand out, in spite of their many difficulties, as the main solution of the dollar gap problem. They will provide the dollars to maintain our own export markets. They will help build our stockpiles of essential raw materials and, over a wider field, retard the depletion of our own natural resources. They will raise living standards here and abroad.

Trade between peoples of different countries flows best and tends to increase naturally in volume when it is freely allowed and encouraged to find its own level. Price, quality, and sales effort determine the direction of that flow. Arbitrary restrictions — whether they be governmental restrictions such as tariffs, exchange controls, multiple exchange rates, administrative rulings, or other export and import controls, or whether they be restrictions instituted by private cartels — hinder increased exchange of goods and services.

Such restrictions, one superimposed upon another, are in evidence to greater or lesser degree in all countries, including the United States. They add to the price of goods sold. Then they have the effect, if not purpose, of channeling and freezing trade at prices higher than world prices.

The answer is to get back to competition. But competition is not a one-sided concept. Our insistence on the opportunity to compete with others carries with it an obligation to let others freely compete with us.

In summary, a weighing of alternative courses of action leads to the conclusion that the present critical lack of balance in world trade should be corrected *primarily by stimulating an expansion of exports of goods and services from other countries to the United States, accompanied by an expansion, as far as feasible, of United States foreign investment.*

III

WHAT EUROPEAN GOVERNMENTS CAN DO

European governments can

develop a more positive attitude toward exporting to the United States. Their ministries of commerce can be strengthened to provide more complete United States market information and reports from their missions here. Publication of lists of possible trade contacts in the United States, specific export opportunities, and educational pamphlets explaining in clear language the general opportunities and advantages of increasing exports to the United States should be part of that effort. To accomplish this purpose foreign government missions in the United States can be enlarged and made more effective by recruiting trade promotion men experienced in the export business.

promote or provide adequate credit facilities to their exporters, with emphasis on the needs of small business. This can be accomplished preferably by a strengthening and liberalization of private credit facilities supported where necessary by government banking.

work through the International Monetary Fund for a return to single rates of exchange realistically evaluated. Multiple rates of exchange penalize exporters on sales to the United States as compared with sales to some other countries. Unrealistic exchange rates wipe out the incentive to export. Uncertainty as to future rates increases the difficulty of selling.

simplify, reduce and as quickly as possible abolish import and export controls. National programs aimed at economic self-sufficiency reduce international trade.

Special import and export taxes and bilateral or other restrictive trade and payments agreements exclude transactions from competitive world markets and cause prices higher than on the free market. They stifle the incentive to sell in competitive world markets, and thus at times limit merchandise available for export to the United States.

encourage increased production, particularly in overseas territories, of basic raw materials and agricultural products now in shot supply. Such encouragement can include facilitation of participation by local as well as metropolitan and foreign capital in the development and utilization of natural resources. It may require stimulation of increased migration of technicians and skilled labor. It can also include the provision to entrepreneurs of research facilities and data similar to that furnished to United States entrepreneurs by the United States Department of Agriculture, by the Coast and Geodetic Survey, and by the Geological Survey.

encourage and participate with private business interests in the development of the travel plant and facilitate to a maximum extent the sales of commodities and services to United States tourists. Entry, visa and currency restrictions can be reduced to a minimum. Currency and export restrictions on tourists' purchases can be removed. Off-season travel at reduced rates can be promoted by the governments in collaboration with transportation and hotel interests. Advertising and publicity campaigns can be undertaken to present to tourists the special features of interest in each country.

IV

WHAT EUROPEAN BUSINESS AND LABOR CAN DO

SALES PROMOTION

European business can

develop aggressive campaigns to sell in the United States market. European businessmen should actively seek buyers, not wait until buyers arrive at their shops or plants.

reexamine their channels of distribution and historical exports in the United States. Modern marketing procedures and improved advertising media pointed toward different market areas should be selected. Many European firms which produce and sell handicraft and specialty products are too small to engage individually in direct distribution. Combinations of such firms which handle noncompetitive but allied products can organize joint export and United States marketing organizations. As part of that effort they could conduct their own market surveys or engage competent marketing counsel to determine price levels and market potentials.

arrange meetings with American buyers and businessmen both in Europe and in the United States, to exchange current information on new market opportunities for their particular products. Some European exporters and industrialists use outmoded and poor sales methods in selling their products to visiting American buyers. American buyers would tend to buy more if they found conditions of buying, selling, and delivery commitments similar to those they experience at home.

personally study United States markets and methods. Their objectives should be: the employment of aggressive and experienced American agents able to secure interior as well as seaboard distribution for their products; the inspection of potential retail outlets — individual stores or leased departments; and the selection of competent advertising agencies which would invest their advertising dollars where they can produce the most profitable sales and repeat orders.

maintain larger inventories in the United States strategically located to service repeat orders and replacements promptly. For this purpose increasing use could be made of foreign trade zones at New York, New Orleans, Los Angeles, San Francisco and elsewhere.

participate in all major trade fairs which may be held in the United States, either as individual firms or in groups. The successful experience in Europe with this marketing technique commends it to the attention of potential sellers to the United States market.

cultivate the full potentialities of the American tourist trade. In addition to maintaining tourist facilities such as hotels, restaurants and transportation, at maximum efficiency and attractiveness, European business should realize to the full the potentialities for direct sale of merchandise to the American tourist.

Special efforts should be made to maintain attractive displays of handicrafts and other consumer goods in European tourist centers. American tourists, now crossing the Atlantic in greater numbers than ever before, are an excellent point of contact between the European economies and the United States dollar market. They are a cross-section of American consumers. Buying the things which individually appeal to them, they often are valuable indicators of what other people in their communities would also buy — if similar merchandise were offered in the United States. American tourists, many of them important businessmen in their own communities, are also first-hand bearers of facts and ideas to the community to which they return. European businessmen should actively cultivate them as protagonists of balanced trade. Both European businessmen and European trade associations can profitably sell them ideas as well as merchandise.

set up trade promotion staffs in the United States to promote exports to this country. They could do this individually as trade associations or other organizations of businessmen. They could be the link between a similar governmental effort and those of specific industries and trade organizations at home.

PRODUCTS DESIGN AND MANUFACTURE

European business can

become more familiar with the requirements of the United States market as to standards and sizes, packaging, colors, and styles. Some of their historical export products which have become outmoded during the past ten years of technological advance in the United States should be restyled and new products should be developed.

make an all out effort to increase management-labor productivity and efficiency, lower production costs and overhead, and reduce prices.

During the war and early post-war years, the productivity and skill of labor declined significantly due to lack of practice, low standards of living and weakened morale. In this way, labor may be said to constitute a war casualty. A concerted effort should be made by labor and management, preferably acting jointly, to raise labor's productivity, to restore and increase its skills, by higher standards of living, improved working conditions, security of employment, training programs, and refresher courses. Toward this end, intensive study should be devoted to techniques of low-cost production as developed in the United States and elsewhere.

The role and interest of labor in a program of increased European export — showing the advantages to labor in this program — should be made clear by management-labor meetings, articles in the labor press and other means. The co-operation of labor is essential to obtain an increased volume of output to sustain a large surplus for export and to maintain the traditionally high standards of quality associated with European products.

develop procedures for subcontracting portions of large orders to firms in other European countries as well as their own. Small industries should where necessary group themselves in productive associations so that they can handle United States orders which may be too large for individual firms.

develop the United States market for the available output of specific factories. European producers have frequently been dismayed at their inability to accept orders from the United States because of the size of the order. This of course should not prevent them from actively exploring the possibilities for distribution in portions of the United States market of the quantities of their product which they are capable of delivering.

INFORMATION

European business can

organize information offices in the regions where their industries are most concentrated. These offices should furnish industry current information on:

    a. How to operate: including the export requirements of European governments, export controls, currency regulations, exchange controls, allocations and other impediments.
    b. United States Customs procedures, tariffs and regulations.
    c. Export packing, new packing techniques and materials.
    d. United States markets for various types of European exports, including data on current prices, styles, designs, quality and other wholesale, retail and consumer requirements.

work with their governments in developing better trade promotional representation in their European government missions in the United States in strategic market centers. Business could lend qualified leaders to their governments for that purpose.

inform and educate itself, labor and the public on the necessity to produce, at a profit but at competitive prices, goods for export to the United States. A sustained public opinion in foreign countries in support of increased exports to the United States is a necessary stimulus to such trade.

FINANCE

European business can

analyze all credit facilities available to it, seek better financial services from private sources for export trade and, if available credit facilities cannot supply necessary assistance at low rates and for sufficiently long terms, approach their governments for additional cooperation. Small business especially requires financial assistance to realize its full potential for exports to the United States.

persuade European banks and financial organizations to take the lead in promoting profitable exports to the United States. They should follow the leadership of those bankers who have grown in importance by establishing both export and import departments for servicing the foreign commerce of their clients.

make permanent associations with United States distributors through financial, long-term participation in joint export-import enterprises.

INVESTMENTS – OVERSEAS TERRITORIES

European business can

explore new opportunities in their overseas territories, possibly in partnerships with United States private enterprise capital, through which exportable commodities can be created for the dollar market. Of utmost importance is the development of production of basic raw materials and agricultural products now in short world supply which business could approach and undertake of its own volition without necessarily waiting for foreign procurement programs or governmental aid. Too often such waiting is the sign of inertia.

V

WHAT U. S. BUSINESS AND LABOR CAN DO

SALES PROMOTION

American business can

search the European markets and industries for new opportunities to obtain semi-finished products or raw materials which can be profitably used in the United States. New inventions purchased on a dollar royalty basis should be part of that effort.

study the costs of distribution within the United States to which foreign imports have been subjected. American merchants, generally, should consider their past policy of insisting on a higher mark-up, and profit, on imported merchandise than on domestic purchases. Few imported products have been sent to the interior markets. Many of these interior shopping centers in the United States have boomed during the war and offer new opportunities for import agencies which previously concentrated their efforts along the Atlantic, Gulf, or Pacific seaboards. The growth of specialty shops throughout the United States can provide, now, a considerable market for imports that, previous to the war, were only to be found in New York, New Orleans, or San Francisco stores.

reexamine European production for specialties which cannot economically be produced by United States mass production techniques. Merchandise of this description is particularly suitable for counter and window display since it tends to extend the coverage of the display and therefore stresses to the prospective customer the variety of choice which is made available to him.

investigate the opportunity for establishing "leased departments" for the display and sale of imported merchandise in department and other stores. For example, connection might be made with selected European manufacturers who, at present, have no direct outlet in the United States.

encourage studies by American transportation companies — sea, rail, truck and air — for opportunities to "feed" their lines with new overseas freight from European countries. They should seek new cargo opportunities to use their seldom-filled capacities.

In many instances American businessmen may find, on studying water vs. rail transportation costs, that they can obtain European exports less expensively than domestic products, particularly if the importers or exporters make efficient use of foreign trade zones of New York, New Orleans, Los Angeles, San Francisco and Seattle, where inventories can be stored, packaged, and assembled prior to the payment of import duties.

attempt to stimulate additional travel volume by organizing facilities for off-season tourist travel. Industrial and agricultural as well as cultural tours might well be arranged for industrialists, farmers and others.

INFORMATION

American business and labor can

publicize as widely as possible in their communities, factories and labor groups the vital importance of imports both to the national economy and to the individual wage-earner and businessman. Export markets are essential to many of the industries which employ the largest amount of labor if they are to maintain full production and full employment. Under present conditions of international trade such exports are maintained by subsidization in the form of international loans and grants. This subsidization is, of course, paid for by the American tax-payer and therefore constitutes a burden upon the individual wage-earner just as surely as it does upon the individual businessman and corporation. Because imports make it possible for exports to be paid for without the necessity of subsidy, each import transaction is a step in the direction of relieving the wage-earner and other American tax-payers from a financial burden.

To the extent that imported goods are barred entry into the United States market by tariffs and other barriers, the competitive influence which they might exert in lowering the prices on goods bought by the wage-earner and other consumers is lacking. It is apparent therefore that tariffs and other barriers to the flow of imports constitute a subsidy to some American producers which is paid in the form of higher prices by the laboring man and other consumers. This is particularly true with reference to certain food products processed from commodities not grown or produced in the United States and with reference to other specialties, whose production by European labor does not directly compete with the production by United States labor of mass-produced merchandise. It is to the interest of both labor and business therefore that they voice and personally promote the philosophy of imports as a primary means of payment for our exports — a method which requires no tax support.

take the educational leadership, individually and through associations, in disseminating, as a part of their institutional advertisements, facts which illustrate the basic importance of imports to the United States national economy and our international strength. We must buy in order to sell. If we do not import we will soon be unable to export.

work closely with foreign business and labor and their trade associations for strengthening private, competitive enterprise. Trade associations should especially work with the small businessman in expediting foreign government priorities and licenses. Frequently these procedures handicap the small European exporter and the United States importer and make it impossible for them to continue in business.

FINANCE

American business can

adopt new procedures for financing specific import transactions. The generally accepted method of financing imports into this country is by means of irrevocable import letters of credit in favor of foreign shippers. On arrival of the goods, the importers are in many instances refinanced on a loan or acceptance basis.

Importers with experience both in this country and in Europe feel that European merchant bankers are more apt to loan money on the strength of the character of the importer and pay greater attention to the collateral put up in the form of goods that are being imported than do the New York bankers. The venture capital and counsel provided by European-type merchant bankers who usually form a very close relationship with their clients is not available here.

In general, inland bankers are little interested in promoting the foreign business of their local customers. If such bankers were more internationally minded and had greater experience in foreign trade financing, they would be in a position to provide counsel to their clients on foreign sources of supply.

OVERSEAS INVESTMENT

American business can

seek active participation in projects in overseas territories of European countries. Direct dollar exports may be produced by these projects or they might increase the economic level of these territories resulting in increased demand for all goods.

Americans, more familiar with American procedures, could aid their European friends in meeting the necessary requisites for profitable investment.

VI

WHAT THE ORGANIZATION FOR EUROPEAN ECONOMIC CO-OPERATION CAN DO

The Organization for European Economic Co-operation should direct its greatest effort toward promoting the elimination of trade barriers in European countries. No cause is more worthy of relentless and sustained effort than freeing trade from shackles fastened during emergencies.

Persistently and doggedly the Organization for European Economic Co-operation should pursue that objective with all European governments and should command the support of all.

C. Organization for European Economic Cooperation

[See *Documents, IX, 1947*, p. 182; *X, 1948*, p. 244.]

For a detailed summary of the work of OEEC during 1949, see *International Organization, III*, p. 382, 566, 739; *ibid., IV*, p. 160.

(1) Second Report of the Organization for European Economic Co-operation on the European Recovery Program, Transmitted to the Economic Cooperation Administration, February 1950.[51]

[EXCERPTS]

INTRODUCTION

THE HALF-WAY MARK

1. This Report is made as the end of the second year of Marshall Aid approaches. Thirty-two months have passed since Mr. Marshall's speech at Harvard from which the European Recovery Programme sprang; twenty-two months since the United States Government enacted the E.R.P. legislation

[51] Organization for European Economic Cooperation, *European Recovery Programme: Second Report of the O.E.E.C.* Paris, February 1950.

and the Organisation for European Economic Co-operation was set up, and the programme began to march.

* * * * * *

4. This threat of bankruptcy and economic dissolution, with the political threats which would follow, was imminent in 1947. It is still there in the background, and will remain there until the structure of world production and trade has found a new equilibrium. Any interruption of the European Recovery Programme, or the onset of world depression, would bring the threat once more to the fore. But the fact remains that the work of these two years in West ern Europe, together with assistance from the United States, has removed the immediate threat and has laid the groundwork for its lasting suppression. On this reckoning — the reckoning of life or death for Western Europe — the first two years of the European Recovery Programme have been unreservedly successful.

5. The recovery programme outlined by the Committee on European Economic Co-operation in the autumn of 1947 was based upon four points:
  (i) A strong production effort by each of the participating countries.
  (ii) The creation and maintenance of internal financial stability.
  (iii) The development of economic co-operation between the participating countries.
  (iv) A solution of the problem of the participating countries' deficit with the American continent, particularly by increased exports.

The course of action to be followed has been restated by the Organisation, but these four points remain the kernel of European recovery.

The Production Effort

6. The Report shows that the production effort is succeeding beyond expectations. In the Interim Report a year ago, the O.E.E.C. felt bound to express doubt whether the countries' estimates at that time of the growth of production would be fulfilled. But the record speaks for itself. The total output of goods and services in 1949 was about 25% above that of 1947, and exceeded the pre-war level; the expansion is continuing, and a further increase of about 10% should be possible by 1952. Both in industry and in agriculture, recovery has gone much faster and farther than in the four years after the 1914–1918 war.

* * * * * *

11. As a result of the general expansion, the production problem in Western Europe is taking a new shape. The expansion has been made possible only by United States assistance; $4–5 billion a year of aid has permitted an expansion of annual output of about $30 billion. The entire structure depended, and still depends, upon imports of food, fuel and raw materials from North America. Now that the main general limitations upon production have been cleared away, the problem is to develop the production of those goods and services which can close the dollar gap by earning dollars or by saving them. This means intensive action in several fields — particularly agriculture, petroleum, tourism, and the range of industries which can supply the North American market. But it also means concentrating on the reduction of costs, the increase of productivity, and the improvement of marketing technique, for the dollar gap will never be closed unless Western European products can compete effectively with American, both in North America itself and in the rest of the world. The emphasis now changes from the growth of total production to the development of dollar-earning and dollar-saving production, and to the increase of productivity and the reduction of costs.

* * * * * *

13. In the production effort, the Overseas Territories have played an important part. The rate of improvement differs widely between territories. In South East Asia, political disturbance has delayed rehabilitation; in the African and other territories, time and supplies were needed to make good the deprivations of the war. As a broad generalisation, it can be said that the volume of exports from the Overseas Territories is as large as it was pre-war, but this conceals big differences between supplies of certain commodities like rubber and phosphates, which have been greatly expanded, and supplies of others, like rice, which are still coming forward in only a trickle. In some territories there is an emergency job of rehabilitation still to be done; in others, the emphasis is upon long-term economic development.

. . . .

Internal Financial Stability

15. Considerable progress has been made since 1947 in the improvement of national finances and the creation and maintenance of internal financial stability. The countries which were facing runaway inflation three years ago have got it under control; in other countries where overt inflation was suppressed by controls, the inflationary pressure has been relieved. In only three out of fifteen O.E.E.C. countries were wholesale prices more than 10% higher in 1949 than in 1948; in four countries wholesale prices were lower. Throughout the participating countries the budgetary position has improved.

16. There is much still to be done. Nearly all the O.E.E.C. countries are still suffering to a greater or less extent from inflationary pressure, which inevitably tends to reduce their exports and increase their imports. This situation can rapidly change; the emergence of deflation and unemployment would be as dangerous to European recovery as renewed inflation, and it is important that the O.E.E.C. countries should be ready to deal with both. It still seems, however, that in many countries the major forces are working to increase inflationary pressure, rather than to reduce it. The devaluations, though necessary for the solution of the dollar problem, increase the costs of imports in European currencies, which in turn reacts upon the cost of living, and tends to raise wages and costs throughout the economy. The rate of increase of production, which contributed so much to internal financial stability in 1948 and 1949, is likely to slow down. There is no less reason than before for a high level of capital expenditure, for the future growth of productivity depends upon this. Much of the future increase in production must be earmarked for this purpose.

17. Inflationary pressure is, therefore, likely to continue in 1950 and later — unless of course conditions of world depression began to appear and confronted Western Europe with a crisis of a rather different (and much more serious) nature. Unless this pressure can be overcome, the O.E.E.C. countries will be unable to right their balances of payments, because the effort to expand exports and reduce imports will be frustrated by the pull exerted by the home market for supplies of all kinds. This is why O.E.E.C. has laid particular weight upon this subject, and has conducted a special investigation of each country's situation and policies in internal finance, and is now embarking upon a further investigation. The solution of the problem rests with the governments themselves; the position is now altogether different from what it was in 1947, and it is appreciably better than in 1948; but this improvement must be relentlessly pressed on, and this is work of high priority during the next two years.

Economic Co-operation

18. The recovery of production and internal finance would have been impossible — and continues to be impossible — without the flow of dollars from E.C.A. But good use has been made, in every one of the O.E.E.C. countries, of the opportunity provided by American aid. Alongside this national action, there has been effective collective action through O.E.E.C., particularly in intra-European trade and payments.

. . . .

22. One of the outstanding features of recent months has been a movement towards balance in intra-European trade. France, for example, which previously had had a deficit with almost every other country, has, in the second half of 1949, been in overall surplus with the other participants. Belgium, whose intra-European surplus had been about twice her dollar deficit, now has a much reduced surplus. The United Kingdom, which previously had been a net exporter to the Continent, has become during the past year a moderate net importer from the other participating countries.

23. With the experience of the past two years to draw upon, the participating countries can now make further progress towards a closer economic integration in Western Europe. This is a step towards the creation of a world-wide multilateral trade and payments system. The objective is clear — it is to secure to the fullest extent possible the advantage of a large competitive market with increased specialisation of production. To gain this objective Western Europe has embarked on the progressive removal of restrictions that hamper the flow of goods and services between the participating counties, and on the creation of a multilateral payments system. In addition, the participating countries are exploring the possibilities in the closely related field of co-ordination of investment. Action on these lines is made possible by the favourable world conditions which now prevail and by the opportunities provided by American aid. Delay would allow interests that flourish at high cost under the shelter of restrictions to entrench themselves; and new investments would be undertaken in the expectation of continued protection.

. . . .

26. During 1949, the participating countries agreed to take an important step towards the removal of quantitative restrictions. They undertook to remove such restrictions on at least 50% of their trade on private account with other participants by 15th December, 1949, both in relation to total trade and to each of the three principal groups of imports: food and feeding-stuffs, raw materials and manufactured goods. These undertakings have, on the whole, been fulfilled. The trend in commercial policy in Western Europe over the past twenty years has thus been reversed.

27. Member countries have now decided to make it their aim to remove, as soon as a satisfactory payments scheme comes into force, quantitative restrictions on at least 60% of their imports on private account from other Member countries. As soon as possible after 30th June, 1950, they will decide what further progress during 1950 they should undertake with a view to attaining a liberalisation of 75% of their imports on private account from other participating countries. This decision will be made in the light of the circumstances then obtaining, including the extent to which practices that may prejudice free competition among European countries have been suppressed. The participating countries have decided that in any event quotas still existing after 31st December, 1950, would have to be justified.

. . . .

The Dollar Deficit

. . . .

35. Progress has been made towards the reduction of the dollar deficit. In 1947, this was more than $8 billion. In 1948, it was reduced to about $5½ billion. In the year 1949–50, it is estimated at slightly below $4½ billion. But this steady improvement from year to year conceals situations of great difficulty which have developed. Throughout 1948 and to the spring of 1949, the reduction was rapid; in the summer of 1949 there was a serious deterioration which lost much of the ground which had been won in the previous twelve months; in the last few months, following the devaluations, there has been a recovery again.

36. The experience of 1949 has shown how vulnerable Western Europe's dollar earnings are to even a small shock coming from outside. On favourable assumptions about the future course of the world economy – and in particular on the assumption that United States business activity does not fall below the level of the middle quarters of 1949 – the Report shows that the O.E.E.C. countries will be able to continue their recovery if they receive aid in the years 1950–51 and 1951–52 at the rate of 75% and 50% of the 1949–50 level respectively.

37. It must be emphasized that failure of the assumption about United States business activity would destroy the basis of the calculations, for dollar earnings cannot expand in face of declining United States demand for raw materials and manufactured goods, and the developing intra-European equilibrium could not survive the struggle for dollars which would result from their renewed scarcity. Moreover, if the assumption about the amount of aid available is not realised, the plans for continued recovery set out in the programmes cannot be fully implemented. There would have to be reductions in essential imports, with cumulative effect upon production. The estimates now made about the availability of supplies from other sources are optimistic, and leave no margin for substitution of non-dollar for dollar imports.

38. The calculations on these assumptions show a reduction in the total dollar deficit from nearly $4½ billion in 1949–50 to $3¼ billion in 1950–51 and $2¼ billion in 1951–52. This leads to a situation in which imports from the United States and Canada are slightly over $3 billion in 1951–52, while E.R.P. Aid is assumed to be $2 billion.

. . . .

The Prospect Ahead

53. It remains to sum up the long-term prospect, and to assess the likelihood that the full objectives of the European Recovery Programme will be reached by the middle of 1952. The progress made in production, internal financial stability, the growth of intra-European trade and the movement towards equilibrium in intra-European payments has been as rapid as any reasonable observer in 1947 would have dared to predict. The Report shows that further progress will be made in the next two years, assuming that aid is available on the scale indicated, and assuming that favourable conditions persist in the world economy.

54. In the last of the four years of E.R.P., the O.E.E.C. countries will still be heavily dependent upon United States aid for their essential imports from North America. After the middle of 1952, Western Europe will in any case have to balance its dollar accounts. The question which arises is whether this balance will be possible at a high enough level of imports from North

America to maintain a healthy economic structure in Western Europe, and to permit trade policies compatible with a growth of world prosperity. For Western Europe and for North America alike, success in maintaining this high level of trade is an imperative need. But success will be possible only if the policies of the countries of Western Europe and of North America are directed towards this objective, on the lines indicated in this Report.

55. The O.E.E.C. countries cannot do this alone, either by their own national efforts, or by collective action. The closer integration of their economies will be a source of strength in the long run but it does not itself contribute decisively to the immediate dollar problem. The balancing of trade between Western Europe and North America, and of both with the rest of the world, is a joint problem, which can be solved only by joint action.

56. The nature of this action is indicated in this Report. The conclusion is that if this action is taken, the problem can become manageable by 1952. The elimination of a dollar deficit of more than $2 billion in 1951–52 will not be easy. However, in 1951–52 some of Western Europe's imports will be financed by 1951–52 E.R.P. funds; the break will not be as sudden as would appear. If speedy measures are taken there will be a strong momentum of dollar earnings. In three years' time, the flow of international investment should have been stimulated. The level of production in countries outside Western Europe should have expanded. The view of the Organisation is that it should be possible, given the assumptions and given the policies, to maintain a flow of imports from North America adequate to the needs of the Western European economy.

57. This does not mean that every one of the O.E.E.C. countries will be in balance; the problems of recovery of some are greater than can be solved in this period. But it does mean that there should be no general Western European crisis; the deficits will be localised rather than general. Indeed, apart from certain countries whose recovery will not be complete, the Western European dollar problem should by then — given the assumptions and the policies — have become part of the problem of general world imbalance, requiring a broader attack, in which it is hoped that the O.E.E.C. countries will be able to participate. The balance of Western Europe will be precarious, and stable equilibrium will not be reached by 1952. To achieve and maintain this equilibrium within a world-wide multilateral trading and financial system, and contribute to further economic progress in Western Europe, will remain the continuing task of the Organisation.

.   .   .   .

3. TECHNICAL ASSISTANCE FOR ECONOMIC DEVELOPMENT

Only the broad range of technical assistance as put forward in the inaugural address of President Truman and as elaborated in general outlines by the United States Government and the United Nations General Assembly and Economic and Social Council is documented in the following section. For other materials and information concerning economic development in specific areas, see this volume as follows: for the work of the Economic Commission for Asia and the Far East, p. 187; for the work of the Economic Commission for Latin America, p. 197.

A. The United States Program

(1) *Message of the President (Truman) to the Congress Recommending the Enactment of Legislation to Authorize an Expanded Program of Technical Assistance for the Underdeveloped Areas of the World, June 24, 1949.*[1]

In order to enable the United States, in cooperation with other countries, to assist the peoples of economically underdeveloped areas to raise their standards of living, I recommend the enactment of legislation to authorize an expanded program of technical assistance for such areas, and an experimental program for encouraging the outflow of private investment beneficial to their economic development. These measures are the essential first steps in an undertaking which will call upon private enterprise and voluntary organizations in the United States, as well as the Government, to take part in a constantly growing effort to improve economic conditions in the less-developed regions of the world.

The grinding poverty and the lack of economic opportunity for many millions of people in the economically underdeveloped parts of Africa, the Near and Far East, and certain regions of Central and South America, constitute one of the greatest challenges of the world today. In spite of their age-old economic and social handicaps, the peoples in these areas have in recent decades been stirred and awakened. The spread of industrial civilization, the growing understanding of modern concepts of government, and the impact of two World Wars have changed their lives and their outlook. They are eager to play a greater part in the community of nations.

All these areas have a common problem. They must create a firm economic base for the democratic aspirations of their citizens. Without such an economic base, they will be unable to meet the expectations which the modern world has aroused in their peoples. If they are frustrated and disappointed, they may turn to false doctrines which hold that the way of progress lies through tyranny.

For the United States the great awakening of these peoples holds tremendous promise. It is not only a promise that new and stronger nations will be associated with us in the cause of human freedom, it is also a promise of new economic strength and growth for ourselves.

With many of the economically underdeveloped areas of the world, we have long had ties of trade and commerce. In many instances today we greatly need the products of their labor and their resources. If the productivity and the purchasing power of these countries are expanded, our own industry and agriculture will benefit. Our experience shows that the volume of our foreign trade is far greater with highly developed countries than it is with countries having a low standard of living and inadequate industry. To increase the output and the national income of the less developed regions is to increase our own economic stability.

In addition, the development of these areas is of utmost importance to our

1 House Document 240, 81st Cong., 1st sess.; Department of State, *Bulletin*, XXI, p. 862; Department of State Publication 2569; *ibid.*, 3653; *New York Times*, June 25, 1949, p. 6.

efforts to restore the economies of the free European nations. As the economies of the underdeveloped areas expand, they will provide needed products for Europe and will offer a better market for European goods. Such expansion is an essential part of the growing system of world trade, which is necessary for European recovery.

Furthermore, the development of these areas will strengthen the United Nations and the fabric of world peace. The preamble to the Charter of the United Nations states that the economic and social advancement of all people is an essential bulwark of peace. Under article 56 of the Charter, we have promised to take separate action and to act jointly with other nations "to promote higher standards of living, full employment, and conditions of economic and social progress and development."

For these various reasons, assistance in the development of the economically underdeveloped areas has become one of the major elements of our foreign policy. In my inaugural address I outlined a program to help the peoples of these areas to attain greater production as a way to prosperity and peace.

The major effort in such a program must be local in character; it must be made by the people of the underdeveloped areas themselves. It is essential, however, to the success of their effort that there be help from abroad. In some cases the peoples of these areas will be unable to begin their part of this great enterprise without initial aid from other countries.

The aid that is needed falls roughly into two categories: The first is the technical, scientific, and managerial knowledge necessary to economic development. This category includes not only medical and educational knowledge, and assistance and advice in such basic fields as sanitation, communications, road building and governmental services, but also, and perhaps most important, assistance in the survey of resources and in planning for long-range economic development.

The second category is production goods — machinery and equipment — and financial assistance in the creation of productive enterprises. The underdeveloped areas need capital for port and harbor development, roads and communications, irrigation and drainage projects, as well as for public utilities and the whole range of extractive, processing, and manufacturing industries. Much of the capital required can be provided by these areas themselves, in spite of their low standards of living. But much must come from abroad.

The two categories of aid are closely related. Technical assistance is necessary to lay the groundwork for productive investment. Investment, in turn, brings with it technical assistance. In general, however, technical surveys of resources and of the possibilities of economic development must precede substantial capital investment. Furthermore, in many of the areas concerned, technical assistance in improving sanitation, communications, or education is required to create conditions in which capital investment can be fruitful.

This country, in recent years, has conducted relatively modest programs of technical cooperation with other countries. In the field of education, channels of exchange and communication have been opened between our citizens and those of other countries. To some extent, the export assistance of a number of Federal agencies, such as the Public Health Service and the Department of Agriculture, has been made available to other countries. We have also participated in the activities of the United Nations, its specialized agencies, and other international organizations to disseminate useful techniques among nations.

Through these various activities we have gained considerable experience in rendering technical assistance to other countries. What is needed now is to expand and integrate these activities and to concentrate them particularly on the economic development of underdeveloped areas.

Much of the aid that is needed can be provided most effectively through the United Nations. Shortly after my inaugural address this Government asked the Economic and Social Council of the United Nations to consider what the United Nations and the specialized international agencies could do in this program.

The Secretary General of the United Nations thereupon asked the United Nations Secretariat and the secretariats of the specialized international agencies to draw up cooperative plans for technical assistance to underdeveloped areas. As a result, a survey was made of technical projects suitable for these agencies in such fields as industry, labor, agriculture, scientific research with respect to natural resources, and fiscal management. The total cost of the program submitted as a result of this survey was estimated to be about $35,000,-000 for the first year. It is expected that the United Nations and the specialized international agencies will shortly adopt programs for carrying out projects of the type included in this survey.

In addition to our participation in this work of the United Nations, much of the technical assistance required can be provided directly by the United States to countries needing it. A careful examination of the existing information concerning the underdeveloped countries shows particular need for technicians and experts with United States training in plant and animal diseases, malaria and typhus control, water supply and sewer systems, metallurgy and mining, and nearly all phases of industry.

It has already been shown that experts in these fields can bring about tremendous improvements. For example, the health of the people of many foreign communities has been greatly improved by the work of United States sanitary engineers in setting up modern water-supply systems. The food supply of many areas has been increased as the result of the advice of United States agricultural experts in the control of animal diseases and the improvement of crops. These are only examples of the wide range of benefits resulting from the careful application of modern techniques to local problems. The benefits which a comprehensive program of expert assistance will make possible can only be revealed by studies and surveys undertaken as a part of the program itself.

To inaugurate the program, I recommend a first-year appropriation of not to exceed $45,000,000. This includes $10,000,000 already requested in the

1950 budget for activities of this character. The sum recommended will cover both our participation in the programs of the international agencies and the assistance to be provided directly by the United States.

In every case, whether the operation is conducted through the United Nations, the other international agencies, or directly by the United States, the country receiving the benefit of the aid will be required to bear a substantial portion of the expense.

The activities necessary to carry out our program of technical aid will be diverse in character and will have to be performed by a number of different Government agencies and private instrumentalities. It will be necessary to utilize not only the resources of international agencies and the United States Government, but also the facilities and the experience of the private business and nonprofit organizations that have long been active in this work.

Since a number of Federal agencies will be involved in the program, I recommend that the administration of the program be vested in the President, with authority to delegate to the Secretary of State and to other Government officers, as may be appropriate. With such administrative flexibility, it will be possible to modify the management of the program as it expands and to meet the practical problems that will arise in its administration in the future.

The second category of outside aid needed by the underdeveloped areas is the provision of capital for the creation of productive enterprises. The International Bank for Reconstruction and Development and the Export-Import Bank have provided some capital for underdeveloped areas, and, as the economic growth of these areas progresses, should be expected to provide a great deal more. In addition, private sources of funds must be encouraged to provide a major part of the capital required.

In view of the present troubled condition of the world — the distortion of world trade, the shortage of dollars, and other aftereffects of the war — the problem of substantially increasing the flow of American capital abroad presents serious difficulties. In all probability novel devices will have to be employed if the investment from this country is to reach proportions sufficient to carry out the objectives of our program.

All countries concerned with the program should work together to bring about conditions favorable to the flow of private capital. To this end we are negotiating agreements with other countries to protect the American investor from unwarranted or discriminatory treatment under the laws of the country in which he makes his investment.

In negotiating such treaties we do not, of course, ask privileges for American capital greater than those granted to other investors in underdeveloped countries or greater than we ourselves grant in this country. We believe that American enterprise should not waste local resources, should provide adequate wages and working conditions for local labor, and should bear an equitable share of the burden of local taxes. At the same time we believe that investors will send their capital abroad on an increasing scale only if they are given assurance against risk of loss through expropriation without compensation, unfair or discriminatory treatment, destruction through war or rebellion, or the inability to convert their earnings into dollars.

Although our investment treaties will be directed at mitigating such risks, they cannot eliminate them entirely. With the best will in the world a foreign country, particularly an underdeveloped country, may not be able to obtain the dollar exchange necessary for the prompt remittance of earnings on dollar capital. Damage or loss resulting from internal and international violence may be beyond the power of our treaty signatories to control.

Many of these conditions of instability in underdeveloped areas which deter foreign investment are themselves a consequence of the lack of economic development which only foreign investment can cure. Therefore, to wait until stable conditions are assured before encouraging the outflow of capital to underdeveloped areas would defer the attainment of our objectives indefinitely. It is necessary to take vigorous action now to break out of this vicious circle.

Since the development of underdeveloped economic areas is of major importance in our foreign policy, it is appropriate to use the resources of the Government to accelerate private efforts toward that end. I recommend, therefore, that the Export-Import Bank be authorized to guarantee United States private capital, invested in productive enterprises abroad which contribute to economic development in underdeveloped areas, against the risks peculiar to those investments.

This guaranty activity will at the outset be largely experimental. Some investments may require only a guaranty against the danger of inconvertibility, others may need protection against the danger of expropriation and other dangers as well. It is impossible at this time to write a standard guaranty. The bank will, of course, be able to require the payment of premiums for such protection, but there is no way now to determine what premium rates will be most appropriate in the long run. Only experience can provide answers to these questions.

The bank has sufficient resources at the present time to begin the guaranty program and to carry on its lending activities as well without any increase in its authorized funds. If the demand for guaranties should prove large, and lending activities continue on the scale expected, it will be necessary to request the Congress at a later date to increase the authorized funds of the bank.

The enactment of these two legislative proposals, the first pertaining to technical assistance and the second to the encouragement of foreign investment, will constitute a national endorsement of a program of major importance in our efforts for world peace and economic stability. Nevertheless, these measures are only the first steps. We are here embarking on a venture that extends far into the future. We are at the beginning of a rising curve of activity, private, governmental, and international, that will continue for many years to come. It is all the more important, therefore, that we start promptly.

In the economically underdeveloped areas of the world today there are new creative energies. We look forward to the time when these countries will be stronger and more independent than they are now, and yet more closely bound to us and to other nations by ties of friendship and commerce, and by kindred ideals. On the other hand, unless we aid the newly awakened spirit in these peoples to find the course of fruitful development, they may fall under the control of those whose philosophy is hostile to human freedom, thereby prolonging the unsettled state of the world and postponing the achievement of permanent peace.

Before the peoples of these areas we hold out the promise of a better future through the democratic way of life. It is vital that we move quickly to bring the meaning of that promise home to them in their daily lives.

Following the President's message of June 24 administration drafts were transmitted to the Congress by the Secretary of State (Acheson) of two bills designed to implement the Point Four Program. One of these bills asked permission for the Export-Import Bank to guarantee investments abroad by United States private enterprise against risks "peculiar to such investments." The second draft dealt with the general program of international exchange of technical knowledge. Legislative drafts of the former bill (S.2197 and H.R.5594) were immediately referred to the Committees on Banking and Currency of the Senate and of the House respectively; and a House draft (H.R.5615) of the second bill and the letter of transmittal from the Secretary of State were referred to the Committee on Foreign Affairs of the House and the Committee on Foreign Relations of the Senate, respectively. Technical assistance became the subject during the remainder of the year of hearings held by the four Congressional committees.

(2) *Statement by the Under Secretary of State (Webb) on Private Investment for Economic Development, Made before the Committee on Banking and Currency of the Senate, August 9, 1949.*[2]

[EXCERPTS]

In large and important areas of the world, poverty and the frustration of hopes for economic betterment are large contributors to instability, political tensions, and violence. Democracy and freedom as we know them cannot grow where widespread disease, illiteracy, and unrest prevail. If democracy is to be a vitalizing force, its economic basis must be secure. Nor can our hopes for an expanding world economy be realized if two-thirds of the world's population are unable to make adequate use of their resources for lack of knowledge and the means to develop them efficiently.

If we can help to accelerate development in underdeveloped areas, political democracy will be strengthened by giving the peoples of those areas hope in a better future; the United Nations and its specialized agencies will be strengthened by participation in continuing positive constructive action for economic development; political tensions can be relieved by demonstrating that development can take place peacefully and with increased personal freedom as the energies of millions of people are devoted to greater production, greater exchange, and greater consumption; our own national security will be strengthened by associating stronger nations with us in the cause of human freedom; a better balance in the world economy can be achieved by

2 Department of State, *Bulletin*, XXI, p. 274.

expanding production and exchange in areas that have advanced too slowly on this front, not for lack of resources but for lack of skills in organizing and developing existing resources; and expanding international trade and increasing markets will contribute to domestic economic stability. Without a positive and effective plan for accelerating the pace of economic development, large areas of the world that are allied with us in the cause of human freedom may be led by the pressures of poverty, social unrest, and hopelessness to give up the fight.

.   .   .   .   .   .

While the bulk of the effort, the planning, the organizing, and the financing of economic development must come from the underdeveloped countries themselves, foreign capital is an essential element. Underdeveloped countries can look to the International Bank and, in appropriate cases, to the Export-Import Bank, for loans to help finance basic development projects for which private financing is not available. Both institutions are expected to continue and to expand their activities in financing undertakings of this character. With assistance from these institutions, underdeveloped countries can expand basic facilities such as power, transportation, and communications and thereby open new areas to development by private capital. It is also hoped that the International Bank and the Export-Import Bank will find increasing opportunities to enter into partnership with private capital in financing projects contributing to economic development abroad.

The Point 4 program puts particular emphasis upon the flow of private investment because United States private capital is potentially the major external source of investment capital for development abroad and because it can contribute not only funds but also the technical skills, managerial experience, and organizational talents that are essential to put capital to effective use. The greater part of our industrial technology has been developed by private organizations. It can be put to work in the development process only through private channels, especially in the form of direct investment where the owner of the technology has the incentive, as well as the skill, to make optimum use of it.

While the outflow of United States private capital has been substantial in the postwar years, it has been low in relation both to its potential volume and to the need for development capital abroad. This is due in part to abnormal conditions. The most significant difficulties appear to be unstable political conditions, balance-of-payments problems leading to limitations on the ability to transfer earnings and capital, and various governmental restrictions imposed on foreign enterprise.

The resumption of large-scale international investment requires a composite of measures to be undertaken cooperatively by capital-importing and capital-exporting countries to reduce present obstacles. The United States is exerting its full influence toward the establishment of more stabilized political conditions and more satisfactory economic relationships throughout the world through participation in the United Nations and its specialized agencies, through the European Recovery Program, and through Reciprocal Trade Agreements and other cooperative measures with individual foreign countries. These efforts to create a sense of security, to secure an expanding and balanced pattern of world trade, and to alleviate economic dislocations arising from the war will, as they bear fruit, help reduce deterrents to the flow of investment capital.

The Department of State recognizes that in a program for the reduction of obstacles to investment abroad it is particularly important to make every effort to improve the climate for private foreign investment. We are constantly working on this problem, particularly through the negotiation of bilateral treaties with foreign governments.

These treaties are designed to assure the potential investor that his property will not be expropriated without prompt, adequate, and effective compensation, that he will be given reasonable opportunity to remit earnings and withdraw his capital, that he will have reasonable freedom to operate, manage, and control his enterprise, and that he will enjoy security in the protection of his person and his property and nondiscriminatory treatment in the conduct of his business affairs. At the same time, foreign countries are entitled to expect that private investments will make a genuine contribution to their national welfare. As stated by the President in his inaugural address —

> . . . Guaranties to the investor must be balanced by guaranties in the interest of the people whose resources and whose labor go into these developments.
> The old imperialism — exploitation for foreign profit — has no place in our plans. What we envisage is a program of development based on the concepts of democratic fair dealing.

The private investor has an obligation to give due regard to the welfare of the persons dependent upon his enterprise, to contribute his fair share of taxes to the local community, to conserve as well as develop local resources, to observe local laws and refrain from interference in the political life of the community, and so to conduct his enterprise that the local economy will derive benefit from his activity.

However, abnormal deterrents to private investment abroad cannot be removed by investment treaties alone. In the present and prospective world economic and political situation certain risks peculiar to investment may for some time remain excessive from the point of view of United States investors. For example, although a treaty may assure no discrimination against United States investors seeking to remit profits, it cannot assure that sufficient dollars for that purpose will actually be available. Similarly, although there may be a completely faithful intention to refrain from expropriation, or in the event that expropriation becomes unavoidable in the public interest, to pay promptly for expropriated property, dollars, may, nevertheless, not be available to permit prompt and adequate payment. Nor can treaties provide assurances against the possibility of confiscation or destruction in the event of internal disturbance or war. Consequently, elimination, or at least a significant reduction of the burden of these risks upon prospective private investors should stimulate a substantial additional flow of private investment funds abroad.

This is the purpose which would be served by the extension of guaranties by the United States Government against risks peculiar to investment in foreign countries.

It is important that we recognize clearly what the proposed legislation is intended to do and what it is not intended to do. The proposed legislation does not guarantee any investor a profit, or protect him against ordinary business risks to which investors everywhere are subject. Guaranties would be limited to risks peculiar to foreign investment, and the investor would have to assume the others. It is not the purpose of the proposed legislation simply to provide an outlet for surplus capital. It is intended to stimulate a flow of productive capital that contributes to economic development abroad. The legislation is specific on this point, and in the administration of the guaranty program, full consideration would be given to the contribution that the investment can be expected to make to economic development. The proposed legislation is not an effort to force particular private enterprises on reluctant countries. Guaranties would be issued only to investments which are acceptable to the government of the recipient country. The proposed legislation is not a program to achieve economic dominion over foreign countries. In accordance with the general spirit of the Point 4 program, it seeks to promote a marriage of economic enterprise with economic opportunities to the mutual advantage of the private investor and the country in which the investment is made.

(3) *Statement by the Under Secretary of State (Webb) on Technical Assistance for Economic Development, Made before the Committee on Foreign Affairs of the House of Representatives, September 27, 1949.*[3]

[EXCERPT]

Two-thirds of the world's population live in underdeveloped areas. For these hundreds of millions of people, economic conditions contrast startlingly with those in the more economically advanced countries. The average per capita income of these people is less than $100 a year. Their life expectancy is some thirty years, or about one-half that in more advanced countries. The incidence of disease is several times greater. Their food supply so meagerly covers their bare subsistence needs, that malnutrition is widespread and actual famine is a constant threat.

The people in the underdeveloped areas are increasingly aware of the possibilities for human advancement through modern technology and economic organization. They have strong aspirations for a better life. They are increasing their pressure on their own governments and in international organizations, for action in the political, social, and economic fields to improve the conditions under which they live. The General Assembly of the United Nations, the Economic and Social Council, and the appropriate specialized agencies have recently been giving greater attention to the insistent appeals for action in the field of economic development.

There are many reasons why the United States should participate in a cooperative effort to supply part of the assistance needed. Our people have traditionally shown a spirit of friendliness and neighborliness toward other peoples. This program gives us a unique opportunity to make available to those peoples who seek them, and without loss to ourselves, the scientific and technical skills which have flourished here and helped to build our strong democratic institutions.

It is important to us, and to the rest of the world, that people in these areas realize that through perseverance, hard work, and a little assistance, they can develop the means for taking care of their material needs and at the same time can preserve and strengthen their individual freedoms. Democracy is most secure where economic conditions are sound. In the interests of world security, as well as world progress, this cooperative technical assistance program holds out great promise.

Another result expected of the program is the strengthening of the United Nations. It is to the United Nations and its specialized agencies that many of the underdeveloped countries are looking for leadership and assistance. The handling of large parts of this program through the United Nations will strengthen its influence and increase its ability to solve other international problems.

There also are many practical economic benefits which will accrue generally from the development of these areas. The flow of capital investment from this country will make available dollars which will be spent here largely for the purchase of capital goods and equipment. This will be more and more important as our programs of emergency foreign aid decline.

In addition to the flow of exports attributable directly to the investment process, the development of productive facilities in these areas will itself have a stimulating and beneficial effect on world trade. These areas cannot acquire the necessary foreign exchange with which to increase their purchases abroad, in the absence of foreign credits or grants, unless they increase their own productive capacity and consequent ability to export. As the productive capacity of these areas is increased, international trade will expand and achieve a better balance. We and other exporting countries will be able to share in a constantly increasing volume of trade.

Our own economy and those of many of the more developed countries are dependent upon the import of many basic minerals and raw materials. The present sources of a number of these commodities are limited and in some cases are approaching exhaustion. The underdeveloped areas have additional sources of supply which, with technical assistance under this program, they would be able to develop. The development of such sources would be of general benefit by increasing the world's supply of important materials and at the same time expanding the purchasing power of the countries of origin.

We all know that the success of the European Recovery Program depends to a great extent upon the opening up of greater markets for European exports and at the same time upon the development of more extensive sources of supply of minerals, raw materials, and other products needed by European countries.

In essence the program laid down by the President as his 4th point of foreign policy involves a cooperative effort with other interested nations to exchange technical knowledge and skills and to foster the international flow of capital investment. The cost to the Government of such a program is very small when we consider the large benefits which it will produce. The exchange of persons and ideas does not require heavy expenditures as do supply programs. Moreover, technical knowledge and skills can be shared without loss to those who now possess them. In fact, those who do share them will themselves learn much through seeing how they can be adapted to different conditions and through learning about the skills developed in other parts of the world. The necessary capital equipment can in large part be procured without the use of Government funds, if efforts to stimulate the flow of private investment are successful.

The idea of exchanging knowledge and skills is not new. We have been participating with other nations in such programs for years. Educational institutions, missionary groups, and a large number of other private agencies have long been engaged in such activities. Participation by the Government in activities of this type has been fostered and coordinated by the Interdepartmental Committee for Scientific and Cultural Cooperation for more than ten years. Under the Smith-Mundt Act and Fulbright Act, citizens of other countries have been coming here and our citizens have gone to other countries, under government auspices, both to learn and to teach. Of particular significance in this field were programs initiated during the war through the Coordinator of Inter-American Affairs. The United Nations, its related specialized agencies, and other international organizations also have been active in helping to develop and impart useful techniques. The new and essential factor in the present proposals is its emphasis on the great importance of economic development in underdeveloped areas and on the concept of an expanded and coordinated approach to the stimulating of technological exchange and capital investment.

Point 4 generally has been received abroad with great enthusiasm. A basic element of the proposal is that wherever practicable, programs shall be carried out through the United Nations and other international agencies. It will be our policy to participate in programs only where they are initiated and approved by the governments concerned. The initiative and the greater part of the work of planning and carrying forward programs of economic development must come from the underdeveloped areas themselves. We and the international agencies can help, but we cannot and should not assume the primary responsibility.

It is intended that the technical assistance programs in which the United States Government participates without the assistance of other international organizations shall be carried on for the most part by the appropriate agencies of the Government rather than by the State Department. One of the most important aims of the proposed program is to integrate closely and maintain a proper balance among various types of development projects. For example, no gain would be achieved if agricultural production in a certain area were increased but no transportation facilities were developed in order to take the food to market. It is considered essential for the success of the effort that there be adequate coordination of the development of programs to be undertaken by the United States Government in cooperation with other countries and that these programs be related specifically to those of the international agencies. It is contemplated, therefore, that the President will delegate to the Secretary of State authority for exercising general direction over and coordination of activities on behalf of the United States. As a member of the National Advisory Council he will work with the Treasury Department and other governmental agencies concerned with the capital investment aspects of the program and can relate technical cooperation activities to our efforts to stimulate the flow of capital.

It is anticipated that in technical cooperation as well as investment, private organizations will play a major role. These organizations, both profit and nonprofit, possess vast stores of knowledge and skill and the ability to teach them to others. Every effort will be put forth to obtain extensive participation by nongovernmental organizations.

Although the bill which is before you makes a general declaration of policy on the part of the United States to promote the development of economically underdeveloped areas of the world, the activities specifically authorized are limited to the technical cooperation aspects of the program. However, technical knowledge and skills must be combined with new capital investment if maximum results are to be achieved. Even though savings are relatively low in underdeveloped countries, we anticipate that a large part of the financing of new capital needed will be obtained in those countries themselves. Most developmental projects involve a large element of local resources and labor which cannot be effectively introduced from outside. Furthermore it would not seem wise from the standpoint either of the borrower or of the lender to encourage the formation of too heavy an external debt by these countries. It is hoped that technical assistance can be given where needed to help them channel domestic savings into productive enterprises.

However, a substantial amount of foreign capital also will be needed. Major emphasis in the program is placed upon stimulating an increased flow of private investment to the underdeveloped areas, although it is recognized that private capital may not be available for certain types of projects such as public utilities, transportation and communications, and that public loans will therefore be required. To supply such funds the International Bank is of course available for sound loans for developmental purposes. We anticipate that the Bank will play an increasingly important role in making loans for developmental projects for which private capital is not available. In many cases, the establishment of basic public services and facilities through such loans is essential before private enterprises can be established. The Export-Import Bank will also continue to make loans to foreign countries for developmental purposes.

The stimulating of private investment not only opens up potentially large sources of capital beyond that which can be made available through public agencies but also has the advantage that private investors bring with their investment an incentive and "know how" for securing the most effective use of the facilities developed.

Our citizens are likely to invest abroad only when they feel that there is an opportunity for a reasonable return on their investment and that the risks involved are not excessive in comparison with similar investments in this country. The assurances which are needed cannot be obtained through one device alone. Cooperative efforts on the part of capital exporting nations and of the underdeveloped countries is needed. We have explored a number of possible methods of approach and have developed several which should be helpful. We propose to familiarize prospective investors with investment opportunities in the underdeveloped areas by expanding existing facilities for disseminating information on economic conditions generally and on specific opportunities for investment in those areas. Technical assistance itself, by making available a healthier and better trained force of workers, and helping to establish more effective government and business practices in underdeveloped areas, opens the way for private investment.

Two general lines of action are now contemplated to reduce the risks not ordinarily encountered in a business enterprise at home, although as the result of experience and further study, other measures may be devised. As a matter of particular significance, we propose to intensify our efforts to secure treaties with other countries which will give greater confidence to investors. These proposed treaties will seek to secure assurance of nondiscriminatory, reasonable, fair, and equitable treatment for our investors, no less favorable than that accorded to the nationals of other countries. Assurances also are sought of reasonable freedom to operate, control, and manage enterprises and of prompt, adequate, and effective compensation in the event of the expropriation of the investor's property. The treaties deal also with the ability of an investor to withdraw earnings and capital investment. They attempt to limit the conditions under which exchange restrictions may be imposed on such withdrawals.

Although these treaties should do much to encourage investment, they can be only a partial solution of the problem. Some of the risks involved, such as the possible inability of the investor to convert the proceeds of his investment into dollars, stem from difficulties which foreign governments may not be able to control despite their most sincere efforts to do so. It is proposed, therefore, that the Export-Import Bank be authorized to guarantee United States private capital newly invested in productive enterprises abroad against risks peculiar to foreign investment. Hearings have been held before both the Senate and the House Banking and Currency Committees on legislation for this purpose.

While we understand that an investor must insist on certain assurances before risking his money abroad, at the same time we recognize that the underdeveloped countries on their part have the right to expect that foreign enterprises will be so conducted as to benefit the area whose resources and labor are involved. Foreign investment like domestic investment should be prepared to bear its fair share of local taxes, should provide adequate wages and working conditions for local labor, should not waste local resources — should, in short, maintain the same standards of conduct which enlightened business is following here at home.

B. The United Nations Program

A limited program of technical assistance under United Nations auspices was in existence at the time President Truman enunciated, as a part of his inaugural address, the "Point Four Program." For the continuation of these activities, the General Assembly had approved, for the fiscal year beginning January 1949, total funds of $288,000 with which the Secretary-General was instructed to undertake assistance projects in fields for which no specialized agency existed. As of January 1, 1949, technical assistance projects, sponsored by the United Nations or by the individual specialized agencies, were being financed in the amount of approximately $5 million annually.

United States proposals for an expanded United Nations program of technical assistance were outlined to the Economic and Social Council by Willard L. Thorp, Assistant Secretary of State for Economic Affairs, on February 25 during the Council's eighth session. On the basis of Mr. Thorp's proposals, the Council on March 5 requested the Secretary-General to prepare a comprehensive program of technical assistance, including methods of financing and of coordinating its planning and execution.[4] The drafting of the report was undertaken from February through April 1949 by the secretariats of the United Nations and of the interested specialized agencies.[5] Simultaneously, the question of financing the program was under discussion in the Subcommission on Economic Development during its third session from March 21 to April 12 and in the Economic and Employment Commission from May 9 to 26.[6]

The report on the expanded program of technical assistance, including separate program plans prepared by the United Nations, FAO, WHO, ILO, UNESCO and ICAO, was transmitted to the members of the Economic and Social Council in May 1949.[7] The cost of the program outlined in the report was placed at approximately $38.5 million for its first year and $50 million for the second, the program to be financed by separate appeals by each participating agency to its respective members for additional voluntary contributions. The report suggested coordinating machinery consisting of a subcommittee established by the ECOSOC Administrative Com-

4 United Nations Economic and Social Council, Document E/1191, February 25, 1949; *ibid.*, Document E/SR.262, March 7, 1949. For a detailed summary of the Council's discussion of technical assistance during its eighth session, see *International Organization*, III, p. 308.

5 The Universal Postal Union and the International Telecommunication Union, because of their highly specialized functions, did not participate in the preparation of the report. The International Bank for Reconstruction and Development and the International Monetary Fund collaborated in the drafting of the program although their existing funds and their incomes from regular operations were such as not to require additional financial contributions in order to continue their work in the field of technical assistance. Provision was made in the report for the future participation in the program of the International Trade Organization and the Intergovernmental Maritime Consultative Organization.

6 For the report of the Subcommission on Economic Development of the question of financing, see United Nations Economic and Social Council, Document E/CN.1/65. The report of the Economic and Employment Commission appears as *ibid.*, Document E/135–E/CN.1/74, May 27, 1949.

7 *Ibid.*, Document E/1327/Add. 1, May 1949 (United Nations Sales No. 1949, II.B.1).

mittee on Coordination to serve as a center for the exchange of information, for joint planning and for the preparation of master reports to the Council. These proposals were debated by the Economic and Social Council at its ninth session held in Geneva during July and August 1949.[8]

The opening speeches of the ECOSOC members revealed various concepts of technical assistance. Whereas some delegates conceived the program as the supplying of food, clothing and shelter, as the furnishing of complete factories, dams and irrigation projects, or as the providing of capital investments without the "strict" restrictions of conventional banking privileges, the United States interpreted the program as the supplying of technical advice, technical training and demonstration equipment to those countries ready to advance their own plans of economic development but lacking resources and technology in some technical phases. In his opening address on July 21, the United States representative (Thorp) urged that the Council make recommendations on the program concerning its content, its method of administration, and its method of financing. Mr. Thorp also expressed the opinion that in the first year of operation under the proposed program the United Nations and the specialized agencies could not effectively spend more than $25 million, or approximately $13.5 million less than the report envisaged. He therefore suggested that the Council produce a coordinated program somewhere within the range of from $15 million to $25 million. The United States further urged that the Council, in consultation with experts, draw up a table of priorities by which the application of technical assistance could be governed. Contrary to the proposal of the United States the Council decided to devote its attention to the establishment of general observations and guiding principles, leaving the assignment of detailed priority ratings within each field of assistance to the participating organizations specializing in that field. The United States supported the report's recommendations concerning administration machinery for the program although it suggested additional coordination of activities with such international organizations as the Organization of American States and the Pan American Sanitary Organization which were not participating directly under the expanded plan. On the question of financing, Mr. Thorp (United States) proposed the adoption of three alternative budgets leaving the final decision on contributions by the agencies and the participating governments for settlement by a general technical assistance conference convened by ECOSOC. Mr. Thorp believed that the bulk of the required capital would necessarily be supplied by private investment, a view with the Polish and Soviet Union representatives (Katz-Suchy and Aruntiunian) opposed on the grounds that most of the under-developed countries were those in which the influence of foreign capital and colonial exploitation had been greatest.

On August 14 and 15 by a vote of 15 to 0 with 3 abstentions (the Soviet Union, Poland and Byelorussia) the Council adopted final resolutions substantially affirming the program and organization recommended in the report. Provision was made for a Technical Assistance Board to coordinate the efforts of the participating countries and agencies, a Technical Assistance Committee to determine general principles and policies by which the program would be developed, and a special account for technical assistance to which contributions from participating countries would be credited.[9] These Council resolutions were then considered by the General Assembly which convened for its fourth session at Lake Success on September 20. After four weeks of debate, the Assembly on November 16 adopted by a vote of 59 to 0 with no abstentions a series of resolutions approving the ECOSOC recommendations with only minor drafting changes.

[8] The Council's discussion of the expanded program of technical assistance is contained in United Nations Economic and Social Council, Documents E/SR.303, E/SR.307–312, E/SR.340–343, from which the following summary, unless otherwise noted, is taken.

[9] For a detailed summary of the discussions of the Council during its ninth session and of the work of the Subcommission on Economic Development and of the Economic and Employment Commission on the question of financing the expanded program, see *International Organization*, III, p. 505–510, 673–674.

(1) Statement by the United States Representative on the United Nations Economic and Social Council (Thorp) on Economic Development and Technical Cooperation, Made before the Council, February 25, 1949.[10]

[EXCERPTS]

In taking up today the question of economic development we are not embarking on a new subject. As a process, economic development has been going on for centuries. It was an early subject for United Nations discussions, at Hot Springs, at Bretton Woods and at San Francisco when the Charter was born. We in the Economic and Social Council have had the question before us since our first meeting, and we devoted particular attention to it during 1948. The Economic and Employment Commission, the Sub-Commission on Economic Development, the regional commissions, and a number of the specialized agencies have discussed it urgently at considerable length. Already, helpful experience has been accumulated by the United Nations and the specialized agencies in connection with various specific projects. Resolutions and recommendations previously adopted contain valuable ideas and suggestions concerning the central problems of economic development, some of its specific aspects, and the possibilities for constructive action.

Economic development was the keynote of the discussions in the Second Committee of the General Assembly in Paris a few months ago. It was obvious that many delegations were greatly concerned with increasing the effectiveness of the United Nations in this field. As a result, two resolutions were adopted by the General Assembly. One, growing out of the general debate in the Committee, recommended that the Economic and Social Council and the specialized agencies give urgent consideration to the whole problem of the economic development of under-developed countries in all of its aspects. The other, proposed by Chile, Peru, Egypt and Burma, expanded the United Nations program of technical assistance.

· · · · · · · ·

The domestic problems of the economic development of a country are numerous and difficult. They may involve basic changes in the economic, political and social institutions and habits. Most of the things that need to be done and that can be done are either wholly or mainly within the control of the individual country and its people.

· · · · · · ·

The bulk of the capital for economic development has to come from the people themselves. There are important reasons for this. In the first place, the amount of funds that can conceivably be made available for foreign investment will fall very far short of the world's capacity to use capital. Larger amounts of capital have been moving across borders since the end of World War II than at any time in the past, but the demands far exceed the supply. Secondly, a country which imported too large a proportion of its capital would be faced for a long time with heavier carrying charges than it can readily

10 Department of State Press Release 111, February 25, 1949; Department of State Publication 3454.

meet in foreign exchange. Many industrialized countries including the United States have been developed in part by foreign capital, but in every case, the bulk of their capital investment is the result of their own savings. These considerations underline the importance for a government to create a climate and devise institutions which will stimulate and mobilize domestic savings, and will channel these savings into productive investment.

．　．　．　．　．　．　．

All this has been succinctly stated as a basic principle in the first report by the Sub-Commission on Economic Development, as follows:

"National development must be based primarily on national resources and must come largely from the effort of the people concerned."

This must be fully understood. The bulk of the effort, the drive, the organization, the planning and much of the financing must come from the people themselves and from their own governments.

Economic development can also be accelerated through international action and cooperation. The freeing of international trade in goods and services from restrictions and discriminations makes possible the expansion of the exchange of the products of the less developed countries for the capital goods needed for development. International migration has been and can still be an important means for bringing skills and needed manpower to less developed areas. The exchange of ideas in the scientific and cultural fields, as well as of information generally, may be in the long run the greatest leaveners of economic development. The United Nations has not been idle in these fields, as witness the Havana Charter for an International Trade Organization and the General Agreement on Tariffs and Trade; the activities of the International Labor Organization and the International Refugee Organization and the forthcoming Conference on the Conservation and Utilization of Resources.

However, the two international factors in economic development which I wish to stress are international flows of capital and international flows of technology.

The receipt of capital from abroad enables countries to acquire more goods and services from abroad than they can pay for with current exports. Irrespective of its source, whether from the proceeds of foreign borrowing or other advances, or from the accumulations arising from past exports, such capital serves to finance the excess foreign requirements of an expanding economy.

All of us are aware of the mistakes that have been made in the past in the use of such capital, not just mistakes of judgment, but improvidence and wastefulness that has actually brought impoverishment rather than enrichment. Both governments and private investors shared in these mistakes in the past. Fortunately, individuals as well as governments now are wiser and more responsible.

American policy does not countenance use of capital investment abroad for the purpose of exploitation. As President Truman said, "The old imperialism — exploitation for foreign profit — has no place in our plans. What we envisage is a program of development based on the concepts of democratic fair-dealing."

The United States has been supplying capital funds to many countries in recent years — through international organizations such as the International Bank for Reconstruction and Development, through government agencies and through private channels. The American economic system is predominantly a private enterprise system and as a result investment, even in many publicly-owned projects, is principally the function of the private capital market, subject to limited public controls and aids. We consider it natural, and desirable, to look to these same private sources to service the foreign field as well. Yet though gross domestic private investment amounted to $38.8 billions in the United States in 1948, private foreign investment amounted to only $0.9 billions. Nearly all this amount took the form of direct investment abroad by American enterprises who were expanding or starting operations in other countries. In light of our present discussion, it is worthy of note that this form of capital flow has certain advantages, since it carries along with the capital a flow of experience and technical knowledge.

The need for a substantial international flow of capital was recognized in the new post-war international machinery. The International Bank for Reconstruction and Development was established to provide an international agency which would gather capital in various markets of the world and facilitate the putting of this capital to work in areas needing such capital. We feel that the Bank has demonstrated that it can perform a useful function and that it has not yet realized its full potentialities.

It seems necessary to find still other means of encouraging the movement of capital from one country to another. President Truman recognized this need when he said that "in cooperation with other nations, we should foster capital investment in areas needing development". For centuries, capital moved in substantial amounts across international boundaries. There was only one requirement — that both the supplier and the recipient must agree. Today, there appear to be many barriers to the flow of private capital in considerable quantities. The suggestion made by the President is that some way be found whereby sufficient assurances be given so that the existing obstacles will be removed.

The importance of this problem and the possibility of its solution are closely related to the development of increased technical cooperation. I now turn, therefore, to my second main point, the international flow of technology, or as it has been called in the United Nations, technical assistance.

. . . .

Here is a field in which genuine international cooperation can expand and flourish. No country has a monopoly of skills, knowledge or available personnel. Certainly the United States has no such monopoly. The amount of technical assistance will begin to approximate the need only if all nations contribute to the joint effort.

There should be no simple division of suppliers and receivers of technical assistance, for often one underdeveloped area will be in a position to furnish useful assistance to still less developed areas. In fact, technical cooperation can be reciprocal and mutually advantageous. It is an enterprise to which all can contribute and from which all may benefit. Technical cooperation is the direct opposite of imperialism. Its aim is the development of intellectual and physical self-reliance, and the conditions of basic economic strength which enable under-developed countries to resist foreign dominance or to cast off oppressive economic ties, if such there are.

There is today a widespread demand in the United Nations and the specialized agencies for increased programs in the field of technical cooperation. We all realize of course that the programs and budgets of these organizations are fixed for the current year and it is obvious that there will be need for planning of such expanded programs and perhaps revision of operating and administrative procedures. Many countries are involved and it will take time if the program is to be developed on the basis of genuine international cooperation. Obviously the program must have multilateral support and participation. It is clearly our hope that there will be general agreement to lift the process of technical cooperation to a new dimension.

For its part the United States is about to embark upon a broad program in the field of technical cooperation in aid of economic development. As an essential part of this program, the United States is prepared to work with other countries, through the United Nations and the Specialized Agencies whenever practicable, in bringing about an expansion of activities in this field.

In order to crystallize discussion in the Council, the United States is submitting a resolution incorporating three proposals.

First, I suggest that the Secretary-General, working through the Administrative Committee on Coordination so that all interested Specialized Agencies can participate, be asked to prepare, for consideration by the Council at its Ninth Session, a concrete program for enlarging the activities of the United Nations and the Specialized Agencies in the field of technical assistance for economic development. The report should also bring to the attention of the Council important problems such as the availability of competent experts and suggestions as to possible priorities among types of projects. In order to avoid overlapping, consultation should be held with the Organization of American States and with those countries or groups of countries which are already carrying on substantial programs in this field.

Second, I suggest that the report cover ways and means for arranging for financial expansion in connection with such projects. The regular budget contributions are based on a fixed percentage. We would hope that there could be some expansion in the regular budget for this type of activity. However, and beyond that, consideration should be given to the establishment of special projects budgets which would permit special contributions for purposes of technical cooperation within the United Nations or within the United Nations and the Specialized Agencies. It is possible that many countries might make their contribution in the form of goods, services and local currency. In order to safeguard the cooperative nature of the enterprise and the international character of the organization sponsoring it, no one country should be expected to assume all or most of the financial burden of the expanded program.

Third, I suggest that the report also include recommendations for the coordination of planning, execution, and control in this field. I have already stressed the importance of concurrent projects. Obviously, there must be some method of assuring comprehensive and coordinated planning and action among the various agencies concerned in carrying out technical assistance programs.

It will be for the ninth Session of our Council to review the documentation to be submitted and, I hope, to formulate recommendations for decisive action by the General Assembly and the Specialized Agencies.

The timetable for the attainment of these objectives of economic development is measured in decades, not in years. The reorientation of the way of life of millions of people can come only gradually. However, with a bold new program of technical cooperation the United Nations can hasten significantly economic development.

There is needless suffering in the world today and discontent and unrest which spring from it. The time is now to embark upon a program which will raise the spirits of men and give them new hope.

(2) Statement by the United States Representative on the United Nations Economic and Social Council (Thorp) on the United Nations Expanded Program of Technical Assistance, Made before the Council, Geneva, July 21, 1949.[11]

[EXCERPTS]

. . . .

At our last session at Lake Success this Council adopted a resolution requesting the Secretary-General, in consultation with the specialized agencies, to prepare a special report proposing an expanded program of technical assistance for economic development. This report was to contain three types of information. First, it was to present a comprehensive plan for the expanded program. Second, it was to suggest methods of financing such a program. Third, it was to recommend ways of coordinating the planning and execution of the program.

The Secretary-General's report was published at the end of May. It is a book of some 300 pages. It lists a great variety of proposals, estimated to cost a total of $35,800,000 the first year. I wish to express our appreciation of the research, preparatory planning, and imagination which this report represents, and particularly the careful statement of objectives in the opening pages of the report.

I shall comment in their order on the three elements of the Secretary-General's report.

11 Department of State, *Bulletin*, XXI, p. 170.

First, the comprehensive plan. The Secretary-General stated in his report that he was in fact presenting not one program but six separate sets of proposals prepared by six different secretariats. The Administrative Committee on Coordination did not find it possible to comment on these proposals. It did not examine them for duplications. It did not suggest omissions. It did not determine whether all these projects would bear directly to economic development. It did not determine whether all these proposals could practically be undertaken in the first year. I think it is a fair statement that this report contains a list of potential projects, but is not a finished program. In defense of the report, I should say that no guidance was given to its authors with respect to any limits within which they should work.

However, there are such limits. The United States believes that an effective and efficient program totaling nearly 36 million dollars could not in fact be carried out by the United Nations and the specialized agencies during the first year. Many delays will be found in expanding the supervisory staff of these agencies, in negotiating agreements with governments, in recruiting the necessary experts, and in organizing the necessary training facilities. The shortage of available technicians and training facilities at the beginning of the program would alone require a substantial reduction in the proposals of the participating agencies for the first year.

. . . . .

My comments are not intended to cast doubt on technical assistance, but rather to urge a careful beginning. I believe this Council should decide what is the range of possibilities for the size of next year's program. Such possibilities are controlled first, by the shortage of technicians and other limiting factors in the operation of technical assistance; and second, by the amounts of money which the member nations are prepared to contribute. I believe we have some notion of the range of possibilities. For myself, I would suggest a range from 15 million to 25 million dollars. The United States believes that the United Nations and the specialized agencies could spend effectively no more than 25 million dollars in the first year. We feel confident that a minimum of 15 million dollars would be available from the member governments for financing the program. This gives us a range of possibilities.

. . . . .

Within this range, the United States suggests that this Council should determine the basic elements in a balanced program, for recommendation to the General Assembly for consideration by a larger audience. The Council should judge the programs put forward in the report on the basis of their contribution to effective economic development. It should determine a 15-million-dollar-program, for example, how much it is prepared to recommend for agriculture, how much for health, how much for education. This same process should be repeated for a 20-million-dollar program and a 25-million-dollar program.

Thus this Council would have obtained from the specialized agencies their best judgment on the technical details of a program, but would have applied its own judgment as to the best use of such resources in a balanced program for economic development, whatever the amount available in the ultimate budget.

·   ·   ·   ·   ·   ·   ·

The United States recognizes, as I am sure we all do, that the specialized agencies are more competent, each in its own technical field, than is this over-all body in the technical field of any one of the agencies. Therefore, the final determination as to the exact projects to be carried out by each agency, within the limits of the funds made available to it, must be made by the agency itself. It is expected, of course, that the agencies will take their decisions in the full light of the Council's recommendations. Only in such way can there be assurance of a balanced program among the agencies which will be technically sound in all aspects and pointed at all times at the single objective of economic development. By thus combining the broader economic judgment of this Council with the technical competence of the specialized agencies, a sound total program can be developed and activated.

·   ·   ·   ·   ·   ·   ·

The second problem relates to the method of establishing and collecting contributions for this program.

·   ·   ·   ·   ·   ·   ·

While I do not believe that it is appropriate to discuss this point in detail until after we have decided on the question of how to deal with the program problem, it may be helpful if I sketch briefly some thoughts on the subject. It has seemed to us that negotiation and commitment of contributions might best be accomplished at a general technical assistance conference sponsored by the United Nations and called by Ecosoc under the General Assembly supplementary rule. The conference might be held during or directly after the General Assembly session, once the report on technical assistance had been adopted. All governments belonging to any agency participating in the program would be invited.

The essential element is to have present at the same time and place representatives of all interested governments to negotiate and commit funds. The conference would take as the basis for its action the reports of Ecosoc and the General Assembly, both as to total over-all program and the proposed proportionate share of each agency. The final act of the conference would record the global amount of all contributions, the total amount of contributions of each agency, the total amount of contribution agreed to be contributed by each participating government, and the undertaking of the participating governments to pay their contributions to the agency to which pledged.

In considering the problem of financial procedure, there are certain considerations which must be kept in mind.

First, the procedure should be the one which would yield the most funds.

Second, it must tend to enforce the basic decisions as to the allocations among the several agencies. Third, it must provide a suitable working relationship between the United Nations and the specialized agencies.

I believe this subject of the appropriate method for determining contributions can best be discussed by this Council, and does not require any preliminary committee work.

I now turn to a third topic in the Secretary-General's report, namely, the method of coordination for this program.

The report recommends that coordination among the various specialized agencies and the United Nations in carrying out the program would be provided by a Technical Assistance Committee, working under the Administrative Committee on Coordination. The TAC, like the present ACC, would be made up of representatives of the various participating agencies. The proposed Technical Assistance Committee has the support of my government.

The United States believes that this committee will be particularly useful in assuring the prompt exchange of information among the United Nations agencies, as well as among individual governments engaged in similar programs. It also affords a continuing point of consultation among the participating agencies.

But the United States is uncertain whether a committee composed only of representatives of participating agencies should be the only group to examine and screen the program before it is presented to this Council. I am not prepared to make any suggestions at this time for a permanent arrangement. But I suspect that the kind of working committee which I am recommending in this Council to review the first-year program will also be helpful in future years.

There is one area of necessary coordination not mentioned in the report, namely, that with other intergovernmental organizations such as the Organization of American States. Already, close working relationships have developed in some fields, notably, between the Pan-American Sanitary Bureau and the World Health Organization. Any definitive plan must provide for this type of coordination as well as those discussed in the report.

· · · · · · · ·

(3) Resolution on the United Nations Expanded Program of Technical Assistance for Economic Development, Adopted by the United Nations Economic and Social Council, August 15, 1949.[12]

The Economic and Social Council

HAVING CONSIDERED the report prepared by the Secretary-General, in consultation with the specialized agencies, on an expanded programme of technical assistance for economic development, pursuant to resolution 180 (VIII)

BEING IMPRESSED with the significant contribution to economic development that can be made by an expansion of the international interchange of technical knowledge through international co-operation among countries,

12 *Ibid.*, p. 325; United Nations Economic and Social Council, Document E/1546, August 17, 1949.

BELIEVING that a sound international programme of this character must combine and make use of the experience of many nations, with different social patterns and cultural traditions and at different stages of development, so as to facilitate progress in the less advanced countries and to help solve their technical and economic problems.

1. *Transmits* to the General Assembly the above-mentioned report together with the observations and guiding principles set out in Annex I of this resolution;

2. *Recommends* that the General Assembly approve the draft resolution in Annex II, which provides for an expanded programme of technical assistance for economic development of under-developed countries;

3. *Requests* the Secretary-General, subject to such decision as may be taken by the General Assembly on the draft resolution in Annex II, to invite the Administrative Committee on Co-ordination to set up a Technical Assistance Board (TAB) which shall consist of the executive heads, or their representatives, of the United Nations and of the specialized agencies which participate in accordance with this paragraph in the expanded programme of technical assistance. The Secretary-General, or his representative, shall be Chairman of the Board. Within the TAB:

(*a*) Each participating organization shall inform the other organizations of requests to it for technical assistance for economic development;

(*b*) Important requests for such assistance shall be promptly discussed;

(*c*) The participating organizations shall discuss their co-ordination efforts under this programme, shall consult before comprehensive missions and programmes of assistance involving several organizations are arranged, and each shall be prepared to co-operate fully with the others in activities involving their common interests;

(*d*) The participating organizations shall exchange information which becomes available to them on current developments in the field of technical assistance, including the progress of technical assistance rendered or projected by them, by Governments and by private organizations;

(*e*) The TAB shall inform the Technical Assistance Committee of the Council (TAC mentioned below of any requests for technical assistance for economic development as soon as they have reached the TAB, so that the TAC shall always be in possession of a list of projects being discussed or reviewed by the TAB or participating organizations;

(*f*) Periodic reports shall be made by the TAB to the TAC; these reports shall include an examination of activities undertaken and results achieved, and a statement on funds received and committed under this expanded programme;

(*g*) Each participating organization shall present annually to the TAB its proposed programme for the next fiscal year in the light of its experience with the expanded programme. The programmes of the several participating organizations shall be examined in relation to each other, and the TAB shall make recommendations concerning them and the total programme to the Council through the TAC;

(*h*) All decisions other than on procedural matters shall be taken by general agreement and, when agreement cannot be reached, the issue in dispute shall be referred for decision to the TAC;

4. *Authorizes* the Secretary-General, after consultation with the other participating organizations, to designate the Executive Secretary of the TAB who shall:

(*a*) Convene and service the TAB and prepare the needed documents;

(*b*) Collect and circulate to members of the TAB:

(*i*) Information regarding enquiries for technical assistance received by the participating organizations;

(*ii*) Programmes of the participating organizations for technical assistance in the fields for which they are responsible;

(*iii*) Information on technical assistance rendered and projected by the participating organizations and any other information which becomes available to them concerning such assistance rendered by Governments or by other public or private bodies;

(*c*) Prepare or arrange for such studies in regard to requests and plans for technical assistance as may be needed by the TAB, and furnish, when required by the TAB, information and analyses relating to the needs and conditions of the various countries requesting assistance;

(*d*) Prepare for the TAB, with the assistance of the organizations concerned and on the basis of information supplied by the Governments concerned, such reports on the operations carried out under the expanded co-operative programme of technical assistance as may be necessary;

(*e*) Perform such other functions as the efficient operation of the TAB may require;

5. *Requests* the Secretary-General to make appropriate arrangements whereby the executive heads of the participating organizations may assign members of their staff to the staff of the TAB as necessary;

6. *Decides* to establish, subject to such decisions as may be taken by the General Assembly on the draft resolution in Annex II and after the conclusion of the Technical Assistance Conference proposed in paragraph 12, a standing Technical Assistance Committee of the Council (TAC), consisting of the members of the Council, which is authorized to sit while the Council is not in session and which shall have the following terms of reference:

(*a*) To make for the Council critical examinations of activities undertaken and results achieved under the expanded programme of technical assistance;

(*b*) To examine each year's programme presented to it by the TAB and report to the Council concerning it, making such recommendations as it may deem necessary;

(*c*) To interpret this resolution in cases of conflicts or questions submitted to it by the TAB, through its chairman, and decide any such conflicts or questions;

(d) To receive reports from the TAB on progress and implementation of, and disbursements of funds under the expanded programme;

(e) To review the working relationships between the participating organizations and the effectiveness of the methods of co-ordination in connection with their technical assistance programmes, making recommendations when appropriate;

(f) To perform such other relevant functions as the Council may assign to it from time to time;

7. *Requests* that the TAB and the TAC, in carrying out their terms of reference, be guided by the "Observations on and Guiding Principles of an Expanded Programme of Technical Assistance for Economic Development" (Annex I) and take into account the records of the debate on the expanded programme which occurred during the ninth session of the Council;

8. *Recommends* to the General Assembly that it authorize the Secretary-General to set up a special account for technical assistance for economic development to which contributions of countries shall be credited and from which transfers shall be made to the participating organizations exclusively for the expanded technical assistance programme to be carried out in the light of the observations and guiding principles contained in Annex I and for administrative expenses connected therewith. The special account may include an evaluation of services or materials on the basis of credits in domestic currencies which Governments are prepared to make available;

9. *Recommends* to the Governments attending the Technical Assistance Conference, provided for in paragraph 12 below, that they approve the following financial arrangements:

(a) Contributions shall be made by Governments in such forms and subject to such conditions as may be agreed between the Secretary-General, after consultation with the TAB, and the contributing Governments, provided that contributions shall be made without limitation as to use by a specific agency or in a specific country or for a specific project;

(b) The Secretary-General shall allot contributions received during the first fiscal year as follows:

(i) The first $10,000,000 in contributions shall be automatically available for distribution to the participating organizations for the expanded technical assistance programme;

(ii) Of the second $10,000,000 of contributions received, 70 per cent shall be automatically available for distribution to the participating organizations and 30 per cent shall be retained for subsequent allocations, bearing in mind the desirability of retaining an appropriate proportion of convertible currencies;

(iii) All contributions above $20,000,000 shall be similarly retained;

(c) Contributions automatically available for distribution to the participating organizations, in accordance with paragraph b (*i*) and (*ii*) above, shall be transferred by the Secretary-General to the organizations in accordance with the following percentages:

	Percent
United Nations	23
International Labour Organization	11
Food and Agriculture Organization	29
United Nations Educational Scientific and Cultural Organization	14
International Civil Aviation Organization	1
World Health Organization	22
TOTAL	100

(*d*) Contributions retained under paragraph b (*ii*) and (*iii*) above shall be allotted by the TAB in such a manner as it may decide and at such time as it may decide, taking into consideration all relevant factors, in particular the amounts and kinds of resources on hand and receivable, the technical assistance requests received which fall within the field of the several participating organizations, the uncommitted balances held by them, and the need for the retention of any reserves to meet unforeseen requests from Governments;

* (*e*) The TAB shall determine the manner in which different currencies and services or materials can be most effectively utilized;

(*f*) The amounts received by the participating organizations shall be available to them for the purpose of assuming obligations or commitments during the fiscal year in which these amounts are received, but actual expenditures shall be allowed to extend over a period of not more than the two ensuing fiscal years;

(*g*) The Secretary-General and the executive heads of the other participating organizations shall, after consultation, make appropriate arrangements for the audit of contributions and expenditures under this programme;

10. *Recommends* that the specialized agencies concerned take such steps as may be necessary to enable them

(*a*) To participate fully under this programme, to adhere to the principles set out in Annex A and to receive monies and other resources from the special account established by paragraph 8;

(*b*) To use these monies and resources for the purposes set out in paragraph 8, to exercise the required controls over the technical assistance activities and the monies and resources received, and to account for their expenditure; and

(*c*) To report to the TAC through the TAB on their technical assistance activities, including those financed from the special account;

11. *Decides* that the financial and allocation arrangements shall be reviewed by the Council not later than its twelfth session in the light of experience during the first year, taking into account the recommendations of the TAB to the TAC;

12. *Decides,* subject to such decision as may be taken by the General Assembly on the draft resolution in Annex II, to call, in accordance with the supplementary rule of procedure of the General Assembly on the calling of international conferences by the Economic and Social Council a Technical Assistance Conference for the purpose of

(*a*) Ascertaining the total amount of contributions available from participating Governments for the execution of the Technical assistance programme of the United Nations and the specialized agencies during the first year of its operation, and

(*b*) Giving final consent to the proportionate shares of the total amount of contributions to be allotted to the various participating organizations and to the other financial arrangements as set out in paragraph 9;

13. *Requests* the Secretary-General:

(*a*) To convene the Technical Assistance Conference at the headquarters of the United Nations at such time as the Secretary-General finds appropriate but, if possible, during or immediately following the fourth session of the General Assembly;

(*b*) To invite the said conference, with the right to vote, all Members of the United Nations and all other Governments members of any specialized agency participating in the programme; and

(*c*) Likewise to invite, without the right to vote, representatives of the specialized agencies.

Annex I

Observations on and Guiding Principles of an Expanded Programme of Technical Assistance for Economic Development

The Council recommends the following principles to serve as guides to the United Nations and specialized agencies participating in the expanded programme of technical assistance, hereinafter called the "participating organizations":

General Principles

The participating organizations should, in extending technical assistance for economic development of underdeveloped countries:

1. Regard it as a primary objective to help those countries to strengthen their national economies through the development of their industries and agriculture with a view to promoting their economic and political independence in the spirit of the Charter of the United Nations and to ensure the attainment of higher levels of economic and social welfare for their entire populations;

2. Observe the following general principles laid down in General Assembly Resolution 200 (III):

(*a*) Technical assistance for economic development of under-developed countries shall be rendered by the participating organizations only in agreement with the Governments concerned and on the basis of requests received from them;

(*b*) The kinds of services to be rendered to each country shall be decided by the Government concerned;

(*c*) The countries desiring assistance should perform, in advance, as much of the work as possible in order to define the nature and scope of the problem involved;

(*d*) The technical assistance furnished shall:

(*i*) not be a means of foreign economic and political interference in the internal affairs of the country concerned and not be accompanied by any considerations of a political nature;

(*ii*) be given only to or through Governments;

(*iii*) be designed to meet the needs of the country concerned; and

(*iv*) be provided as far as possible in the form which that country desires;

3. Avoid distinctions arising from the political structure of the country requesting assistance, or from the race or religion of its population.

Standards of Work and Personnel

1. Highest professional competence should be maintained in all services undertaken by the participating organizations in rendering technical assistance to requesting countries;

2. Experts should be chosen not only for their technical competence but also for their sympathetic understanding of the cultural backgrounds and specific needs of the countries to be assisted and for their capacity to adapt methods of work to local conditions, social and material;

3. Adequate preparation of experts should be provided before assignments are undertaken; such preparation should be designed to give understanding of the broad objectives of the common effort and to encourage open-mindedness and adaptability;

4. Experts and groups of experts visiting a country should not engage in political, commercial, or any activities other than those for which they are sent. The scope of their duties should be strictly defined in each case by agreement between the country requesting assistance and the organizations providing assistance.

5. Even when allocations are committed, projects should not be commenced unless properly qualified experts and assistants are secured and trained;

6. All Governments should be invited to co-operate in the securing and selecting of qualified staff and to facilitate, when necessary, arrangements for their temporary release and for their continued employment on return;

7. Universities, technical schools, foundations, research institutions and other non-governmental sources from which experts may be drawn should be encouraged to release experts for field assignments under the programme, to arrange for their continued employment on return and to undertake special research projects on problems related to economic development.

Participation of Requesting Governments

The requesting Governments should be expected to agree:

1. To facilitate the activities requested from the participating organiza-

tions by assisting them to obtain the necessary information about the problems on which they have been asked to help, such information to be limited strictly to questions directly related to the concrete requests for technical assistance; and, whenever appropriate, facilitate their contacts wih individuals and groups, in addition to Government agencies, concerned with the same or related problems;

2. To give full and prompt consideration to the technical advice they receive as a result of their co-operation with the participating organizations in response to the requests they have initiated;

3. To undertake to maintain or set up as soon as practicable such governmental co-ordination machinery as may be needed to ensure that their own technical, natural and financial resources are mobilized, canalized and utilized in the interest of economic development designed to improve the standard of living of their peoples and through which the effective use of any major international technical assistance resources could be assured;

4. Normally to assume responsibility for a substantial part of the costs of technical services with which they are provided, at least that part which can be paid in their own currencies;

5. To undertake the sustained efforts required for economic development, including continuing support and progressive assumption of financial responsibility for the administration of projects initiated at ther request under international auspices;

6. To publish information or provide for study and analysis material suitable for publication regarding the results of the technical assistance rendered and the experience derived therefrom, so that it may be of value to other countries and to the international organizations rendering technical assistance;

7. To inform the participating organizations, whenever technical assistance is requested, of all assistance which they are already receiving or requesting from other sources in the same field of development;

8. To give publicity to the programme within their countries.

Co-ordination of Effort

1. The projects falling within the competence of participating organizations should be carried out by them and the co-ordination of their work should be effected with due regard to their constitutions and the relations established between them;

2. The work undertaken by the participating organizations under the expanded technical assistance programme should be such as to be suitable for integration with their normal work;

3. Arrangements should be made for requests for assistance within the sphere of two or more organizations to be handled jointly by the organizations concerned; and there should be co-ordination among the participating organizations at the planning level before commitments by them are entered into with Governments;

4. Technical assistance activities which are not at the present time the

special responsibility of any specialized agency, such as certain aspects of industrial development, manufacturing, mining, power and land and water transport, should be undertaken by the Secretary-General of the United Nations;

5. All requests for technical assistance which involve comprehensive or regional development projects falling within the purview of more than one organization should first be submitted to joint examination by the organizations concerned; such requests should be directed to the Secretary-General of the United Nations;

6. Programmes of training should be the subject of co-operative action among participating organizations.

Concentration and Economy

Within the wide range of activities envisaged, the participating organizations should practice, especially at the initial stages of their programmes, concentration of effort and economy. The participating organizations should also ensure the fullest use of any existing facilities.

Selection of Projects

1. The participating organizations, in deciding on a request for assistance, should be guided solely by the Charter of the United Nations, by the principles of the United Nations' programme for technical assistance and by appropriate resolutions of the General Assembly and of the Economic and Social Council. The services envisaged should aim at increased productivity of material and human resources and a wide and equitable distribution of the benefits of such increased productivity, so as to contribute to the realization of higher standards of living for the entire populations. Due attention and respect should be paid to the national sovereignty and national legislation of the under-developed countries and to the social conditions which directly affect their economic development. Requests for technical assistance may therefore be approved which will help Governments to take account of the probable consequences of proposed projects for economic development in terms of the welfare of the population as a whole, including the promotion of full employment, and also to take account of those social conditions, customs and values in a given area which would directly influence the kinds of economic development that may be feasible and desirable. Similarly requests may also be approved for technical assistance to Governments desiring to undertake the specific social improvements that are necessary to permit effective economic development and to mitigate the social problems, particularly problems of dislocation of family and community life, that may arise as a concomitant of economic change. As in any national programme for economic development any increased services undertaken by the Government can be maintained, in the long run, only out of national production, special attention should be given in timing and emphasis to activities tending to bring an early increase in national productivity of material and human resources;

2. The participating organizations, when reviewing and placing in order of priority the requests which they receive, should so far as possible ensure that due regard is paid to the urgency of the needs of the various applicants and their geographical distribution;

3. In response to requests from Governments, especially in connexion with plans for economic development, special consideration should be given to resources and methods of financing the development. It is recommended therefore that participating organizations, before undertaking work of an extensive character involving substantial cost, should assure themselves that Governments requesting such assistance are given full consideration to major capital investment or large continued governmental expenditure which may be needed as a result of this technical assistance. Governments may also require advice concerning conditions and methods of financing appropriate to such projects. Close co-operation among the participating organizations in responding to requests for technical assistance can facilitate the attainment of this objective;

4. Requests for the furnishing of equipment and supplies may be considered insofar as they form an integral part of a project of technical assistance.

Annex II

**Resolution Recommended for Adoption
by the General Assembly**

EXPANDED PROGRAMME OF TECHNICAL ASSISTANCE
FOR ECONOMIC DEVELOPMENT

The General Assembly,

HAVING CONSIDERED the Economic and Social Council's resolution No. 222 (IX) A of 15 August 1949 on an expanded programme of technical assistance for economic development;

Approves the observations and guiding principles set out in Annex I of that resolution and the arrangements made by the Council for the administration of this programme;

Notes the decision of the Council to call a Technical Assistance Conference for the purpose of negotiating contributions to this programme;

Authorizes the Secretary-General to set up a special account for technical assistance for economic development, and approves the recommendations of the Council to Governments participating in the Technical Assistance Conference regarding financial arrangements for administering contributions and authorizes the Secretary-General to fulfil the responsibilities assigned to him in this connexion;

Invites all Governments to make as large voluntary contributions as possible to the special account for technical assistance.

(4) *Resolution on Technical Assistance for Economic Development, Adopted by the United Nations General Assembly, November 16, 1949.*[13]

The General Assembly,

Having considered the Economic and Social Council's resolution 222 (IX) A of 15 August 1949 on an expanded programme of technical assistance for economic development,

1. *Approves* the observations and guiding principles set out in Annex I of that resolution and the arrangements made by the Council for the administration of the programme;

2. *Notes* the decision of the Council to call a Technical Assistance Conference to be convened by the Secretary-General in accordance with the terms of paragraphs 12 and 13 of the Council resolution;

3. *Authorizes* the Secretary-General to set up a special account for technical assistance for economic development, to be available to those organizations which participate in the expanded programme of technical assistance and which accept the observations and guiding principles set out in Annex I of the Council resolution and the arrangements made by the Council for the administration of the programme;

4. *Approves* the recommendations of the Council to Governments participating in the Technical Assistance Conference regarding financial arrangements for administering contributions, and authorizes the Secretary-General to fulfill the responsibilities assigned to him in this connexion;

5. *Invites* all Governments to make as large voluntary contributions as possible to the special account for technical assistance.

13 United Nations General Assembly, Document A/1102, November 17, 1949.

CHAPTER V

National Defense

1. NATIONAL CONTROL OF ATOMIC ENERGY

[See *Documents, X, 1948,* p. 260.]

On May 20, 1949, the Senate confirmed the nominations of Gordon Dean and Dr. Henry De Wolf Smyth to fill vacancies created several months earlier by the resignations of W. W. Waymack and Dr. Robert F. Bacher from the Atomic Energy Commission. Mr. Dean and Dr. Smyth would serve for the remainder of terms expiring on June 30, 1950.[1] Effective December 31, 1949, David E. Lilienthal resigned as chairman of the Atomic Energy Commission in order to return to private life. No successor had been appointed to this post prior to Mr. Lilienthal's retirement.

While the Joint Congressional Committee on Atomic Energy was investigating the Atomic Energy Commission on security matters, Senator Bourke L. Hickenlooper (Iowa) at a press conference on May 22 charged the chairman of the Commission (Lilienthal) with "incredible mismanagement", "maladministration", and "misplaced emphasis" in his administration of the Commission. Due to the seriousness of these charges the Joint Congressional Committee on Atomic Energy undertook a full scale investigation of the Commission. The joint committee opened its investigation on June 1 and devoted a total of 45 meetings to this matter. By a vote of 9 to 6 on October 12 the joint committee absolved the Commission and its chairman of Senator Hickenlooper's accusations and on October 13 filed the majority report with the Congress.[2] During the course of Congressional action on Commission appropriations for the fiscal year 1950, the Senate Committee on Appropriations rejected a subcommittee recommendation that a House approved cut of $77,000,000 in the Commission's $1,167,000,000 budget for the year ending June 30, 1950 be restored.[3] although the Commission had protested to the Congress that this reduction would adversely affect procurement of atomic bomb materials and bomb production. By the terms of this bill (H.R.4177) the Commission could not start construction projects costing more than $500,000 without the prior approval of the Committees on Appropriations of the Senate and House of Representatives and the Joint Congressional Committee on Atomic Energy. With these provisions the bill was signed into law by President Truman on August 24.[4]

In July Senator Brien McMahon (Connecticut), chairman of the joint committee, and Representative Carl T. Durham (North Carolina), vice-chairman of the joint committee, introduced identical bills (S.2215 and H.R.5534) in the Senate and House respectively to require annual legislation for all Commission programs.[5] However, no further action was taken on these measures by Congress during the year under review. A second measure was introduced by Senator McMahon in the Senate on August 3 (S.2372), which provided for the appointment of a chairman of the military liaison committee; the bill also provided for representation of the air force on the military liaison committee.[6] After amendment by the Joint Congressional Committee on Atomic Energy, S.2372 was passed by both houses of the Congress and became law on October 11. Following the announcement by the President of an atomic explosion in the Soviet Union, Senator McMahon introduced on October 11 a bill (S.2668) eliminating the provisions of Public Law 266 (81st Cong., 1st sess.) re-

---

1 For congressional action in 1948 providing for a two-year extension of the initial appointments to the Commission, *see Documents, X, 1948,* p. 260.
2 House Report 1435, 81st Cong., 1st sess.
3 Senate Report 639, 81st Cong., 1st sess.
4 Public Law 266, 81st Cong., 1st sess.
5 *Congressional Record,* 95, p. 9190, 9614 (Daily edition, July 7, 1949).
6 *Ibid.,* p. 10859 (Daily edition, August 3, 1949).

quiring that the Atomic Energy Commission could start no new construction projects for which an estimate was not included in budget for the current fiscal year.[8] After favorable action by both houses, the measure was approved by the President on October 28.[9]

(1) Seventh Semiannual Report of the United States Atomic Energy Commission to the Congress, Covering the Year 1949.[10]

[EXCERPTS]

FOREWORD

In 1949, the Nation's long-range program for the peacetime development of atomic energy set new bench marks of accomplishment.

In November, the Commission authorized the building of the first experimental breeder reactor. With the start of construction of this unit, the program for producing more fissionable material and for generating power for factories and homes and ships from the energy of nuclear fission moved from pencil and paper planning over to the building of full-scale test machines.

. . . .

Weapons development and stock piling moved on at a growing pace during the year. Production of weapons was changed to an industrial type of operation. Design of weapons advanced. Preparation began for future proof-testing at the Eniwetok Proving Ground in the Pacific. AEC activities were coordinated more closely with military activities and military training.

Essential to both the power-production program and the weapons program is an adequate supply of uranium ores. This is being obtained at present. Negotiations abroad and mining and processing plant developments at home during 1949 placed the prospects for continuing supply on a firmer basis.

The construction program of the past two years began to yield its fruit in 1949. New facilities for making feed materials and fissionable materials went into operation. The output of fissionable material set new records. New Laboratories and research machines were put to work and the building of still others advanced. Basic processes for improving chemical separation of fissionable material from fission products were worked out and construction was started on facilities.

The technical and scientific staffs were recruited more nearly to the desired levels both in quantity and quality. Industrial strength was added to the program by new contractors in various fields, but especially in weapons and reactors. Basic research was put upon a broader base with many new university contracts for research.

Some of the problems of labor-management relations became more susceptible of solution. The Atomic Energy Labor Relations Panel assisted in reaching settlements of disputes in which its services were invoked.

This is not to say that the program operated in all its phases without hitch or flaw, or at the speed and with the results desired. Many technical problems await solution through basic and applied research. We have made only a beginning at providing industry with the information service it is entitled to expect. The declassification of scientific and technical information which need no longer be held secret does not proceed at a pace rapid enough to satisfy all of the demands for such data.

Financial controls and reporting were substantially improved during the year. A continuing effort is being made to meet more adequately the require-

8 *Ibid.*, p. 1449 (Daily edition, October 11, 1949).   9 Public Law 422, 81st Cong., 1st sess.
10 Atomic Energy Commission, *Seventh Semiannual Report*, Washington, January 1950.

ments of flexible operation, for keeping account of where projects stand financially at all stages, and for reporting accurately and clearly the financial status of programs at frequent intervals.

To speed its atomic energy program, this Nation requires, above all else, technical men of talent and training. Other vital development programs of industry and government have comparable demands for scientists and technicians. It is important that the Congress and the people of the United States recognize the critical need for fundamental research and the training of scientists, engineers, and technicians.

. . . .

On September 23rd the President announced to the American people that an atomic explosion had occurred in the USSR. The President pointed out that U. S. policy and operations in atomic energy had always taken into account the likelihood that other nations would in time develop atomic weapons. The President's announcement, by its revelation of Russian achievement, emphasizes the importance of the most efficient possible utilization of the resources available for this Nation's atomic energy program.

The Congress in mid-October modified, in the interests of speed, the construction rider in the 1950 appropriations for the national atomic energy program. In early October the President released budgetary reserves so as to advance by some months the start of a quarter-billion dollar expansion program, then at the drawing-board stage and planned for construction in subsequent fiscal years. Some of this work is now actually under way and will require supplemental appropriations at an early date. This action was discussed by the Commission with the Congressional committees concerned.

. . . .

Maintenance of the United States position requires a vigorous, growing program of basic and applied research in nuclear science and engineering. Because of the vital importance of this work, the second part of this Seventh Report to the Congress is devoted to the research program in these fields.

Though successful development of atomic energy depends first of all upon men, it also depends upon information. Policies for the control of atomic energy information are aimed at the basic objective of advancing our own program while giving as little aid as possible to the program of inimical interests. The measures for accomplishnig this obviously need to be adjusted to the presently known facts as to rival development.

. . . .

As in previous years of the Commission's tenure, there has been gratifying and helpful cooperation from all agencies of the Government whose operations touch upon those of the atomic energy program, or which are enlisted under special arrangements to carry on specific tasks. The Commission's relationship with the Military Liaison Committee was further strengthened. The continuous and extensive work on mutual problems by the staffs of the two agencies contributed substantially to effective coordination of Department of Defense and AEC activities.

The General Advisory Committee has continued its diligent and effective work of analyzing the problems of atomic energy development, particularly in the scientific and technical lines, and providing fruitful recommendations for policies and programs in those fields. Other advisory groups appointed by the Commission have made substantial contribution to the progress of 1949.

There was a considerable increase in the exchange between the Joint Committee on Atomic Energy and the Commission. Including the sessions held in connection with a long series of hearings into charges of Commission mis-management, there were during the year, 24 public and 37 executive meetings between the Committee and the Commission dealing with current operational and policy matters. The flow of correspondence and reports from the Commission to the Committee, totalling some 375 reports and communications during 1949, is an indication of the volume of information supplied to members of the Committee. Members of the Committee and the Committee staff visited the sites of operations in the atomic energy program and familiarized themselves in detail with the progress and the problems of the enterprise.

With full awareness of the deficiencies that continue to exist in scope and speed of operations and development of smooth-working relationships throughout the program, the Commission nevertheless feels that at the end of three years of its stewardship, the Nation's atomic energy enterprise is on a sound footing.

PART I

ACTIVITIES AND DEVELOPMENTS IN ATOMIC
ENERGY PROGRAM DURING 1949

I
PRODUCTION

During 1949, advances were made in the main phases of production operations: procurement of raw materials, processing of feed materials for the production plants, and manufacture in these plants of fissionable plutonium and uranium 235 for use in weapons, power development, and research.

RAW MATERIALS

Progress in exploration, ore buying, and ore processing during 1949 helped assure that future ore supplies, both from abroad and from sources in the United States, will be adequate for the operation of the atomic energy program.

Exploration

The Nation-wide search for uranium-bearing ores is carried on both by the Government and private individuals. The Government program is conducted by the Atomic Energy Commission in collaboration with the U. S. Geological Survey, which among other work carries on extensive drilling operations on the Colorado Plateau. Moderate amounts of workable ores have been located that add to the supply for area processing plants. In addition to the drilling program, 3,860 square miles of territory have been mapped and radiometric traverses totaling 28,000 miles made by auto.

II
MILITARY APPLICATION

Progress in the United States program for development of atomic energy was marked during 1949 by significant action in the field of military application, including:

a) Change-over in the weapons production system from a laboratory to an industrial type of operation.

b) Establishment of the branch laboratory at Sandia, near Albuquerque,

New Mexico, as a separate facility and transfer of its operating contract to an industrial contractor.

c) Developments in weapons leading to the requirement for full-scale test operations and improvements to proving ground facilities.

d) Construction of facilities to replace temporary war-built structures at Los Alamos Scientific Laboratory.

e) Improvement of community facilities and services maintained for the personnel of the weapons research center at Los Alamos.

PRODUCTION

The program for establishment of the weapons manufacturing activity on a production basis, reported on previously, was practically completed in 1949. This was, in effect, a change-over from what might be called a laboratory operation, stemming from the "custom built" nature of the original bombs, to a system in which the product as well as the facilities, equipment, and production techniques have been designed and engineered with a view to faster and more efficient production.

Several significant advantages have been gained by this change-over. The Los Alamos Scientific Laboratory has been relieved of a burdensome production operation which interfered, and was inconsistent, with the primary responsibility of the Laboratory in the field of research and development. A strategically important dispersal of the production facilities has been effected, thus reducing the vulnerability of the weapons production chain in event of war. In addition, it permits new developments to be incorporated more rapidly in the finished weapons.

· · · · · · · · · ·

IV

BIOLOGY and MEDICINE

The Atomic Energy Commission continued to sponsor research on medical and biological applications of atomic energy.

As part of its general program for medical research, and to assist in supplying technical information useful in civil defense planning, the Commission has put new emphasis upon diagnosis and treatment of radiation injury. In the field of biology, research includes soils, plant diseases, radiobiology, aquatic biology, genetics, animal pathology, and physiology.

Progress in research in all these fields was reported in some detail in the Sixth Semiannual Report, submitted to the Congress in July 1949, and work with isotopes was covered in a special report issued in October. These findings, and a flow of information distributed in professional circles through many scientific and technical reports (see pp. 161–169), are the results of the research work of some 1,250 scientists in various medical and biological fields.

During the fiscal year 1950, the AEC is investing about 19 million dollars in biological and medical research, distributed 10 million dollars for investigations in major Government-owned installations, 2 million dollars in three major university-owned, atomic energy laboratories, and 7 million dollars for research in private industrial, and educational institutions and in other Government agencies.

· · · · · · · · ·

VI

AEC and CIVIL DEFENSE

The Atomic Energy Commission's chief responsibility in civil defense matters is to provide to the appropriate agencies, and to the public, such technical data as will help in planning in case of an atomic war. Methods, techniques, and areas of knowledge, of interest in this work, particularly knowledge about the effects of atomic weapons, are developed by the AEC in carrying out its primary functions.

The AEC has been designated by the National Security Resources Board as a participant in wartime disaster relief, over-all responsibility for which was assigned to the Government Services Administration.

Within the Atomic Energy Commission, the Division of Biology and Medicine is responsible for coordination of civil defense activities and for necessary liaison outside of the Commission. Other AEC divisions are responsible for preparation of information and for technical consultation in their respective functional areas.

PART II

RESEARCH IN PHYSICAL SCIENCES AND

PROGRESS IN ATOMIC ENERGY

II

MEN, MACHINES, and LABORATORIES for PHYSICAL RESEARCH

The physical research program of the national atomic energy enterprise makes progress only as men of talent and training can be enlisted to work in it, and the unique machines and special and standard laboratory equipment placed at their command.

Employing the broad authorities granted by the Congress in the Atomic Energy Act, the Commission depends upon different means of drawing on the talents of American men of science and technology, training new talent, and furnishing the necessary equipment.

THE LABORATORIES

For carrying on both applied and basic research, the Commission maintains eight major installations at which the land, buildings, and equipment are completely owned or leased by the Government and all costs of staff and supply are reimbursed to the university or industrial contractors who operate them. This group of installations includes:

ARGONNE NATIONAL LABORATORY, operated by the University of Chicago in Du Page County, Illinois.

BROOKHAVEN NATIONAL LABORATORY, operated by Associated Universities, Inc., at Upton, Long Island, N.Y.

KNOLLS ATOMIC POWER LABORATORY, operated by General Electric Company at Schenectady and West Milton, N.Y.

LOS ALAMOS SCIENTIFIC LABORATORY, operated by the University of California at Los Alamos, N. Mex.

MOUND LABORATORY, operated by Monsanto Chemical Co., at Miamisburg, Ohio.

OAK RIDGE NATIONAL LABORATORY, operated by Carbide and Carbon Chemicals Corp., at Oak Ridge, Tenn.

SANDIA LABORATORY, operated by the Sandia Corporation at Albuquerque, N. Mex.

WESTINGHOUSE ATOMIC POWER DIVISION laboratories, Bettis Field, near Pittsburgh, Pa., operated by Westinghouse Electric Corporation.

Four other installations are maintained on university campuses with buildings and equipment financed in large part by the Commission and with staff and supply expenses wholly reimbursed. These are:

AMES LABORATORY, operated by Iowa State College, Ames, Iowa.

RADIATION LABORATORY (including Donner Laboratory of Medical Physics and Crocker Laboratory — Medical Physics) operated by the University of California at Berkeley, Calif.

ROCHESTER ATOMIC ENERGY PROJECT, operated by the University of Rochester, at Rochester, N.Y. (biological and medical research only).

UCLA ATOMIC ENERGY PROJECT, operated by the University of California at Los Angeles (biological and medical research only).

. . . .

MANPOWER AND MONEY FOR RESEARCH

In all, about 8 million dollars is likely to be spent for physical research this year through off-site contracts, compared with about 23 million dollars in the 12 major atomic energy research laboratories. These sums pay only salaries and laboratory operating expenses, plus occasionally the cost of some minor equipment. Construction of facilities and major equipment is budgeted separately. Scientific and technical personnel engaged in the 31-million-dollar physical research program number about 2,150, almost a fourth of the technically trained people employed in all operating phases of the Commission's research and development program.

In reactor development, the operating budget for this fiscal year calls for another 12 million dollars in off-site contracts. This is in addition to about 21 million dollars in Government-owned laboratories.

The table below shows expected dollar costs and scientific employment in the AEC programs in the physical sciences and reactor development in fiscal 1950, compared to the corresponding figures for the biological and medical

Money and manpower for research and development, estimated, 1950

(Approximate figures)

	PHYSICAL SCIENCES		REACTOR DEVELOPMENT		BIOLOGICAL AND MEDICAL SCIENCES		TOTAL	
	Millions of dollars	Numbers of scientists	Millions of dollars	Numbers of scientists	Millions of dollars	Numbers of scientists	Millions of Dollars	Numbers of scientists
8 major Government-owned atomic energy laboratories	18	750	21	900	7	300	46	1,950
4 major university-owned atomic energy laboratories	5	600	....	....	3	350	8	950
Many off-site industrial, educational, research, and Government activities	8	800	12	1,000	7	700	27	2,500
Total	31	2,150	33	1,900	17	1,350	81	5,400

sciences. The 27 million dollars for work outside the 12 major laboratories includes basic research funds in colleges and universities totalling 6.5 million dollars in the physical sciences and 4.3 million dollars in the biological and medical fields. Included also among the 2,500 scientists in this off-site group are over 500 graduate students working on the university contracts. (The AEC training program is discussed in Chapter V.)

The 5,400 total of scientific and technical personnel among these laboratory and off-site groups is more than half of the total employed on the Commission program. Of the others, nearly 4,000 work on the development of new weapons and on research and development projects directly associated with the production of fissionable material. Another 500 are on the Commission's staff in Washington and in the several field offices.

III

ATOMIC ENERGY RESEARCH

. . . .

RESEARCH AND WEAPONS

Nowhere else in the atomic energy program is effectiveness in research and development more vital than in the field of atomic weapons. In order to maintain progress in this field, it is necessary to cover the whole range of activities from fundamental investigations in pure science to applied research, practical development, and production engineering. This includes work in mathematics, physics, chemistry, metallurgy, electronics, and ordnance, and involves specialized equipment and facilities.

For reasons of national security, only a small part of the research story on weapons can be revealed. The following examples will give an indication of some of the types of research carried on.

V

AEC MANAGEMENT FOR RESEARCH

PHYSICAL SECURITY OF RESEARCH OPERATIONS

As of the close of 1949, some 900 research laboratories, institutions, and consultants were under contract with the AEC to conduct scientific research, some aspects of which must be safeguarded in accordance with the Atomic Energy Act of 1946. These range from the extreme security importance of the Los Alamos Scientific Laboratory, employing hundreds of persons on research and development of atomic weapons, to the individual scientist in a university laboratory. Obviously, Los Alamos requires elaborate safeguards, whereas the individual scientists may work with none or with relatively few restrictions.

To monitor the safeguarding requirements of a research program of such magnitude and diversification requires some 3,000 security contacts and inspections a year in practically every state of the Union.

. . . .

PERSONNEL SECURITY IN RESEARCH

Before persons may have access to restricted data or to exclusion areas where the most secret work is carried on, they must be investigated as to character, loyalty, and associations. Under the Atomic Energy Act, individuals who are to be employed by the Atomic Energy Commission or who are to have access to restricted data while employed by an AEC contractor or licensee must be investigated by the FBI and, thereafter, on the basis of this report, the Commission must determine that permitting such an individual to have access to "restricted data" will not endanger the common defense and security.

Even on unclassified research projects the Commission, as a precautionary measure, may often require the principal investigator (or other suitable monitor) to be cleared, to become familiar with the Commission's program, and to have a working knowledge of the classification and declassification requirements. Such projects, while unclassified in their conception, may lead into areas involving restricted data. Adequate security clearance enables such research activities to meet the needs of the AEC and still safeguard restricted data. However, in research projects where the chance of restricted data being discovered is essentially zero, no security requirements are imposed.

The AEC's program for controlling visits to exclusion areas, designed to prevent unauthorized persons from access to restricted data or to areas where classified work is being performed, permits visits with minimum delay between the AEC's various sites where the research employes are engaged in related fields of endeavor. The correlation of such data through visits, symposiums, and through the distribution of reports is controlled so as to retain compartmentalization with respect to production and weapon information and activities.

2. MAINTENANCE OF DEFENSE

A. General Statements

(1) *Budget Message of the President (Truman) to the Congress, January 10, 1949.*[11]

[EXCERPTS]

My budget recommendations for national defense in the fiscal year 1950 are based on a plan for a national defense position of relative military readiness, coupled with a higher degree of mobilization preparedness. This type of military planning will permit us continuously to revise our tactics and develop our weapons to meet modern conditions, but is clearly consistent with our traditional concept of military strength for purposes of defense.

In arriving at my recommendations, I have had the benefit of the considered advice of civilian and military leaders best qualified to evaluate the international, strategic, and economic aspects of our national defense requirements. I believe that these recommendations reflect a proper relationship between our security requirements and our economic and financial resources, and envision an Army, Navy, and Air Force in a condition of relative readiness, all functioning as an integrated team. Moreover, I am convinced that we should plan our military structure at this time so as to insure a balanced

11 *Congressional Record*, 95, p. 139 (Daily edition, January 10, 1949).

military program in the foreseeable future at approximately the level recommended in this budget.

At the same time we must recognize that preparations for defense must be flexible, and not rigid. They must reflect changes in the international situation, changes in technology and in the economic situation. We must be in a position to alter our military programs as circumstances change.

The National Security Act of 1947 established an organizational framework better than we have ever had before and provided for a more flexible control and adjustment of our military program. The establishment of a Weapons Evaluation Board under the Secretary of Defense is an example of the type of development we are continuously making to achieve the best possible assignment of weapons and tasks among the military services. However, we have had enough experience under that act to recognize that further improvements need to be made which cannot be accomplished under existing law. Therefore, I expect to recommend certain changes in the National Security Act which will help to assure readjustments of our defense program as a whole and in all its parts as security requirements change.[12]

The recommendations for the National Military Establishment for the fiscal year 1950 mark a beginning toward a national defense program in which our air, naval, and land forces plan and operate as a team under a unified strategic concept. The 1950 program gives priority to air power and to strengthening the civilian Reserve components, and continues to emphasize research and development and industrial mobilization. The budget provides for maintaining the necessary occupation forces in the former enemy areas for which satisfactory international settlements have not yet been worked out. The budget also provides substantial amounts to continue the matériel improvement programs for which large authorizations were enacted under the augmented fiscal year 1949 budget. Continuing expenditures will be necessary for an orderly replacement program in future years as existing inventories are used up and as matériel wears out or becomes obsolete.

Expenditures by the National Military Establishment for defense purposes in the fiscal year 1950 are expected to amount to somewhat over 13.1 billion dollars, including a tentative estimate of 385 million dollars for programs for which new authorizing legislation will later be requested. The stockpiling of strategic materials and other activities supporting defense are expected to require additional expenditures of about 530 million dollars. Furthermore, a tentative estimate of 600 million dollars has been added for the first year cost of universal training — when in full operation this program may require expenditures of 2 billion dollars annually. In total, the national defense budget I am recommending will require estimated expenditures of slightly less than 14.3 billion dollars in the fiscal year 1950, an increase of 2.5 billion dollars over the 1949 level. Somewhat higher expenditures are likely in subsequent years.

Net new appropriations and other authorizations specifically recom-

12 For the text of the President's recommendations, see this volume p. 294.

National Defense
[Fiscal years. In millions]

PROGRAM OR AGENCY	EXPENDITURES			1950	
	1948 actual	1949 estimated	1950 estimated	Net new appropriations	Other authorizations
National Military Establishment (excluding payments under Armed Forces Leave Act):					
Pay and maintenance of military personnel:					
Pay and allowances of regular personnel	$3,555	$3,434	$3,601	$3,596	....
Pay of retired personnel	148	168	192	191	....
Subsistence, travel, and other	1,192	1,407	1,359	1,488	....
Civilian components	350	590	760	795	....
Research and development	534	557	505	534	....
Aircraft and related procurement	791	1,157	1,718	330	$1,992
Naval ship construction	271	309	406	5	47[14]
Military public works construction	395	286	302	93	20
All other	3,316	3,422	3,908	4,317	....
Tentative estimate for proposed legislation	....	....	385	645	185
Subtotal, National Military Establishment	10,552	11,330	13,136	11,994	2,244
Activities supporting defense:					
Universal training	....	....	600	800	....
Stockpiling of strategic and critical materials (Treasury)	99	350	525	314	211
Payments under Armed Forces Leave Act	269	14	1	....	....
Reconstruction Finance Corporation	−66	−42	−39	....	....
Other	70	93	45	36	....
Total	10,924	11,745	14,268	13,144[13]	2,244

mended in this budget for the National Military Establishment in the fiscal year 1950 are 13.7 billion dollars. This total, however, includes an upward adjustment of 279 million dollars for increased cost of the naval ship construction programs authorized in 1949 and prior years. In addition, 830 million dollars is provided as a tentative estimate for additional public works, for military pay adjustments, and for other special programs, dependent upon the passage of necessary enabling legislation. In all, 14.5 billion dollars of new obligational authority is provided for the National Military Establishment for use in the fiscal year 1950, an increase of 700 million dollars over amounts enacted for the fiscal year 1949.

Of the 13.7 billion dollars of specific recommendations for new obligational authority for the National Military Establishment, 11 million dollars is requested for the Office of the Secretary of Defense, 4.6 billion dollars for the Air Force, 4.5 billion dollars for the Army, and 4.6 billion dollars for the Navy,

---

13 In addition, the budget includes 2,061 million dollars of appropriations recommended to liquidate prior contract authorizations and 75 million dollars to cover other prior year obligations.

14 In addition, 279 million dollars is being made immediately available in the fiscal year 1949 to cover increased cost of completing authorized naval ship construction program.

counting the upward adjustment for ship construction costs mentioned above.

In addition to the new obligational authority for the National Military Establishment, this budget includes 525 million dollars of new authority for procurement of critical and strategic materials, 36 million dollars for other defense-supporting activities, and a tentative appropriation estimate of 800 million dollars for the inauguration of universal training.

In all, new obligational authority for national defense programs of nearly 15.9 billion dollars is included in this budget. This compares with 14.7 billion dollars for the fiscal year 1949, including 2.9 billion dollars made available in 1948, and also including tentative supplemental authorizations of 341 million dollars chiefly for stockpiling.

Of the 15.9 billion dollars, 13.2 billion dollars is requested in the form of appropriations and 2.7 billion dollars in contract authorizations. In addition, appropriations of 2.1 billion dollars are requested to liquidate prior year contract authorizations.

Military strength — summary: The requirements of the various services have been determined, not separately, but in relation to our total security position and the degree of military readiness which is planned. The basic concept upon which my recommendations are based is that this Nation's military security should rest on a nucleus of highly trained and mobile forces — Army, Navy, and Air — backed by ready reserves of trained men, stand-by equipment and productive facilities, and an integrated mobilization plan which relates our national security requirements to the tremendous productive capacity of American industry. Taken as a whole, the amounts recommended in this budget will permit the maintenance and operation in the fiscal year 1950 of the augmented defense forces now reached under the increased 1949 budget program.

Under this budget, the Air Force in fiscal year 1950 will continue at about the present strength of 412,000 officers and men on active duty. It is contemplated that the Air Force will be organized with a minimum of about 48 com-

Military Strength
[In thousands]

	Regulars and Reserves on full-time active duty			Reserves in regular training status		Other Reserves	
	April 1, 1948	Dec. 1, 1948 (est.)	1950 average (est.)	Dec. 1, 1948 (est.)	1950 average (est.)	Dec. 1, 1948 (est.)	1950 average (est.)
Air Force	368	411	412	58	113	400	400
Army	538	662	677	375	555	650	650
Navy and Marine Corps	488	531	527	222	281	900	1,050
Total	1,394	1,604	1,616	655	949	1,950	2,100

NOTE — The recommended strengths for all the services include 18-year-old 1-year enlistees and other personnel in training but exclude cadets and midshipmen at the Military and Naval Academies.

bat groups and 10 squadrons, together with 27 groups of the Air National Guard. Within the limit of the funds provided, it is possible that adjustments in unit structure or strategic planning may at any time require changes in the number of active groups. At the end of fiscal year 1950, the Air Force program contemplates an active inventory of 9,200 aircraft of all types from trainers to heavy bombers. Increased funds in the budget will permit the build-up of supporting forces in the Air National Guard to an average of 45,000 personnel and in the Air Force Reserve to 68,000 personnel in regular training status.

Personnel in the Army will be continued at 677,000 officers and men in order to maintain 10 divisions at increased strengths, together with 59 battalions. The active Army will be backed by the National Guard with an average strength of 325,000 personnel, an Organized Reserve of 230,000 in regular training status, as well as by other reserve personnel and equipment. Continuing responsibilities in the occupation of Germany, Austria, and Japan and in manning outlying bases will engage about 40 percent of the Army strength overseas in fiscal year 1950.

In the naval and marine forces a strength of 527,000 officers and men throughout the fiscal year 1950 is provided. The size of the active naval fleet is planned to be 731 ships, including 288 combatant ships. Its composition will be changed somewhat from the present fleet to accord with assigned functions and presently foreseen defense requirements. The active inventory of regular Navy and Marine Corps aircraft is expected to be 7,450 in the fiscal year 1950.

Under the reserve programs of the Navy and Marine Corps, 281,000 officers and men will be trained in 1950. Stand-by ships and matériel to augment the active Navy will remain available if needed.

Although present recruiting rates indicate that only small inductions, if any, will be necessary under selective service, it is essential that such authority remain available in the event that voluntary enlistments drop. Moreover, it must be recognized that the existence of the Selective Service Act has in itself been a contributing factor to the current results of the recruiting program of the services.

. . . .

Stock piling and other defense activities: The aim of the stock piling program is to provide a basic reserve of materials in which accessible resources are deficient, thereby permitting a rapid and sustained economic mobilization in the event of emergency. Stock pile procurement continues to be hampered by materials shortages and rising prices, since it must meet the competition of current industrial consumption, including that for military purposes. However, the concentration of procurement on the more urgently required materials should permit us to make substantial progress toward our goal of a reasonably adequate stock pile with minimum effect on current consumption.

Toward the stock pile goal, this budget recommends 525 million dollars of new obligational authority for the fiscal year 1950 and supplemental authorizations of 310 million dollars for the present fiscal year. Of these amounts 211 million dollars for 1950 and 270 million dollars for 1949 are in contract authorizations to be used primarily for developmental contracts. A total of 800 million dollars in obligational authority has already been enacted in the last 3 years. In addition, by the end of fiscal year 1950, materials valued at about 700 million dollars will have been transferred to the stock pile from war surplus inventories and from Economic Cooperation Administration operations. Of the total stock pile objective of 3.7 billion dollars, materials and authorizations amounting to 2.3 billion dollars will have been provided.

Deliveries and expenditures, of course, will lag behind authorizations. Expenditures in the fiscal year 1950 are estimated at 525 million dollars, an increase of 175 million dollars in outlays over the current year. By the end of the fiscal year 1950, materials valued at about 1.6 billion dollars are expected to be on hand.

The stock pile represents an addition to the supplies obtainable in an emergency from domestic production and imports from protected sources. The recommended authorizations will permit the stock pile to be built up to the point at which, with the aid of prompt and effective allocations, a comparatively high degree of protection will be afforded to our economy in the event of emergency.

Expenditures for all other defense programs, including expenses of the Selective Service System, maintenance of reserve industrial plants by the Federal Works Agency, and by other agencies, are estimated at 46 million dollars in the fiscal year 1950. On the other hand, net receipts of 39 million dollars are estimated in the Reconstruction Finance Corporation defense program.

.   .   .   .

Atomic energy: To an increasing extent our national welfare and security are linked to our atomic energy program. We must continue to add to our knowledge of this resource and move ahead with practical development. Special emphasis is given to the development of nuclear reactors as an eventual means for converting atomic energy into electricity and into power for propulsion of ships and airplanes.

The 1950 budget provides increased funds for the production of fissionable materials and the development of the science and technology of atomic energy. The present high costs of rapidly accomplishing these purposes must be balanced against the ultimate and far greater costs of failure to move ahead vigorously in this field.

.   .   .   .

B. National Military Establishment
[See *Documents, IX, 1947*, p. 262; *X, 1948*, p. 268.]

During the year under review the movement toward inter-service coordination continued with ranking military officials of the three armed forces presenting their opinions and advice on this subject to the Congress and the nation. On March 5 the President asked the Congress to create an over-all Department of Defense as an executive department of the government; this request followed closely the proposals set forth in the report of the Commission on Organization of the Executive Branch of the Government (Hoover Commission).[15]

Legislation embodying the recommendations of the President to Congress of March 5 and of the Hoover Commission was introduced into the Senate in May (S.1843).[16] S. 1843 was intended to convert the National Military Establishment into an executive department of the government, provide the Secretary of Defense with appropriate responsibility and authority and with civilian and military assistance adequate to fulfill his enlarged responsibility, and convert the Departments of the Army, Navy and Air Force to the status of military departments operating under the Secretary of Defense. After passage of S.1843 by the Senate, the bill was referred to the House, which passed in lieu H.R.5632 on July 18. The House bill provided for reorganization of fiscal management in the National Military Establishment and for the promotion of economy and efficiency.[17] H.R.5632 was approved and signed by the President on August 10 after amendments by the Senate had been considered by a conference of Senate and House members.[18] Shortly thereafter the Senate approved the nomination of General Omar N. Bradley as chairman of the Joint Chiefs of Staff, a position created by Public Law 216 (81st Cong., 1st sess.) which specified that the chairman would neither vote in the councils of the Joint Chiefs nor command any of the forces, but would be the senior military officer under the President and the Secretary of Defense.

Full independence for the air force was achieved with the signing of Transfer Order No. 42 by Secretary of Defense Louis A. Johnson on July 23.[19]

As a result of obvious disagreement within the Department of Defense involving basic subjects affecting national defense, the Committee on Armed Services of the House of Representatives conducted an inquiry into the situation, holding a series of hearings from October 6 to 21. At the conclusion of the hearings, which revealed a bitter dispute as to the role of the navy and naval aviation in the defense organization, the chairman of the committee, Representative Carl Vinson (Georgia), announced that the committee's report would be considered by the Congress when it reconvened in January 1950.[20]

Following congressional approval of a part of the proposals contained in the President's message of March 5, the President on April 2 signed H.R.2216 amending the National Security Act of 1947 to provide for the post of Under Secretary of Defense.[21] On March 23 the Senate confirmed the nomination of Louis A. Johnson as Secretary of Defense, following the resignation of James Forrestal effective April 1.[22] Francis P. Matthews succeeded John L. Sullivan as Secretary of the Navy in May, and the following month Gordon Gray received Congressional approval to assume the post left vacant in April by the resignation of Kenneth C. Royall as Secretary of the Army.

(1) Report of the Commission on Organization of the Executive Branch of the Government to the Congress on the National Security Organization in the Federal Government, February 28, 1949.[23]

[EXCERPTS]

· · · · · · ·

WHAT IS WRONG with the PRESENT ORGANIZATION

The National Security Organization, as legislated in 1947 to establish unification of the armed services and unified national policy on security, has achieved gains. Further improvement may be expected since the organization is still young, but there is evidence that the utmost that can be accomplished under the present statute will fall far short of national needs.

15 *Congressional Record*, 95, p. 1974 (Daily edition, March 7, 1949).
16 *Ibid.*, p. 6205 (Daily edition, May 12, 1949). 17 *Ibid.*, p. 9876 (Daily edition, July 18, 1949).
18 Public Law 216, 81st Cong., 1st sess. 19 *New York Times*, July 24, 1949, p. 28.
20 *London Times*, October 22, 1949, p. 3. 21 Public Law 36, 81st Cong., 1st sess.
22 *Congressional Record*, 95, p. 3071 (Daily edition, March 23, 1949).
23 House Document 86, 81st Cong., 1st sess.

The Commission on Organization of the Executive Branch has had the benefit of an investigation into the National Security Organization by a distinguished committee. The committee found continued disharmony and lack of unified planning. Extravagance in military budgets and waste in military expenditure show a serious lack of understanding of the effect of military costs and spending upon the total economy. True national security depends more upon economic stability and political strength than upon military power.

Interservice rivalries indicate a lack of understanding of the fact that military security depends upon cooperation and balance among the Army, Navy, and Air Force, and upon the creation of a genuinely unified military arm. There is a lack of close working relationships among such important elements as the Research and Development Board and the Joint Chiefs of Staff and the Central Intelligence Agency.

Some part of these weaknesses undoubtedly can be traced to the newness of the operation, but the Commission believes that they show serious organizational defects. The lack of central authority in the direction of the National Military Establishment, the rigid statutory structure established under the act, and divided responsibility, have resulted in a failure to assert clear civilian control over the armed forces.

OVER-ALL DEPARTMENT MANAGEMENT

In our first report we have urged that the foundation of good departmental administration requires that the Secretary have authority from the Congress to organize and contol his organization, and that separate authorities to component subordinates be eliminated.

In our Report on the Budget we propose a new form of "performance" budget for all departments. We also propose that each department or agency keep its own administrative accounts in the manner prescribed by an Accountant General in the Treasury and subject to the approval and audit of the Comptroller General. The Commission also recommends that personnel recruitment be performed by the Department (except possibly in the lower grades), subject to standards and methods of merit selection to be proposed by the Department, but with the approval and enforcement of the Civil Service Commission. The Commission likewise recommends elsewhere that the procurement of supplies peculiar to the Department be decentralized into the Department, under standards and methods established in the Office of General Services. The items of common use would of course be handled by the latter office. Further, we propose that the Department should strengthen its management research unit, working in cooperation with a comparable staff unit under the Office of the Budget.

CIVILIAN CONTROL AND ACCOUNTABILITY

In its study of the executive branch the Commission has established certain principles that must underlie systems of organization in order to assure the three essentials of good Government management: efficiency, economy, and clear accountability to the Congress and the people.

These principles call for centralization of authority and control in the President and the department heads, for clear lines of command and accountability, and for provision of adequate staff for policy formulation and for supervision of operation. Without these, the President and the department heads cannot exercise positive control and hence cannot be held responsible by the Congress and the people for failures or deficiencies of performance.

In the establishment of the present organization for national security, these principles have been repeatedly violated.

a. **The President's authority has been curtailed by statutory stipulation of the membership and duties of both the National Security Council and the National Security Resources Board—the Cabinet committees concerned with vital defense policies.**
b. **The authority of the Secretary of Defense, and hence the control of the President, is weak and heavily qualified by the provisions of the act of 1947 which set up a rigid structure of federation rather than unification.**
c. **In direct proportion to the limitations and confusions of authority among their civilian superiors, the military are left free of civilian control.**

The Commission's report on departmental management has pointed out the weaknesses and fallacies of a department in which statutory authority is delegated to subordinate units, and the department head is left with only the most general supervisory powers over policies, operations, and budgets. In such cases, the department head cannot enforce consistent policies and obtain the necessary efficiency and economy. Nor can he be held strictly accountable since he lacks authority to carry out the mandates of determined policy. The National Military Establishment as set up under the act of 1947, is perilously close to the weakest type of department.

The Secretary of Defense, at present, has only "general" authority over the service departments — the Army, Navy, and Air Force. He cannot hire and fire subordinates except on his immediate staff. Almost all appointive power not in the President's hands is in that of the subordinate service secretaries. The powers of the Secretary of Defense over the budget for the National Military Establishment, and over expenditures, are inadequate. He is inadequately provided with staff and has no authority to reorganize the Establishment, most of whose machinery is rigidly prescribed by statute.

The principle of federation, rather than firm unification, is implicit in the statutory provision that "all powers and duties relating to such departments (the Army, Navy, and Air Force) and not specifically conferred upon the Secretary of Defense" are reserved to the departments. The pattern does not cease at that point. Within the service departments, subordinate units — such as the Corps of Engineers in the Army insofar as its civilian functions are concerned — have direct authority from the Congress exclusive of control even by their own secretaries.

Moreover, the service secretaries are given specific authority to resist the supervision of the Secretary of Defense in budgetary matters by appealing over his head to the President or to the Director of the Budget. The service secretaries sit with the Secretary of Defense on the National Security Council and can "out vote" him in that body's deliberations. They have more staff for planning and execution and, in fact, operate as almost fully autonomous units.

Under these circumstances centralized civilian control scarcely exists. Each military branch follows its own purposes and, due both to the weakness of the Defense Secretary's powers and to the confusion of authority over them, has very much a free hand. In effect, divided responsibility means no responsibility. Civilian control thus depends directly upon the Congress whose chief mechanism is the tightening or loosening of the purse strings. In the present unsatisfactory state of military budget practices and procedure, the effectiveness of this mechanism in the hands of the Congress is highly attenuated.

In the period ahead when national security will demand a large military budget, this time-honored device for subordinating the military to civilian control will be ineffective. The remedy must be sought through organization of the executive branch to establish firm lines of authority and accountability. Otherwise, civilian control will continue to be a label instead of a reality.

What is true of the National Military Establishment is equally true of the operations of the Joint Chiefs of Staff. Three of the four members are spokesmen for separate service arms. The Secretary of Defense, and his viewpoint for the unified Establishment as a whole, is not represented in their deliberations. Thus, though the Secretary of Defense is, under the act, the principal assistant to the President, in military matters, he cannot, as a practical matter, maintain effective civilian control over this most powerful of military units. The Joint Chiefs of Staff, as a unit, report to two officials — the Secretary of Defense and the President. As individuals, they report to the President, the Secretary of Defense, and the service secretaries. Each will tend to answer much more to the service secretary who is his direct superior than to the single policies of a unified Establishment.

Here, too, it is clear that divided responsibility and allegiance are tantamount to an almost complete absence of control. Under this system, the Joint Chiefs of Staff are virtually a law unto themselves, as evidenced in the fact that their activities are not well-coordinated with intra-Military Establishment operations, nor with the policy work of the Cabinet councils. The Joint Chiefs of Staff, like the rest of the National Military Establishment, are not firmly under civilian control.

BUDGET AND EXPENDITURE

The present budget of the armed forces represents about $100 per capita for the Nation, as contrasted with some $2.25 before the First World War. Our task force reports that the current preliminary budget estimates of the three military departments for the fiscal year 1950 were for more than $30,000,000,-000.

Such a budget would be justifiable only if the Nation were actually involved in warfare. It would require a sharp reduction in production for civilian consumption, precipitate the need for controls over the economy and enormously increase inflationary pressures. It reflects a lack of realistic understanding by the three military departments of the economic and social factors of national security.

Moreover, military budgets are not drawn with careful consciousness of cost factors. For example, an examination of the 1950 budget revealed estimates requesting modernization of 102 more tanks of a certain type than the Army actually possessed. In another case, a misplaced figure added some $30,000,000 to budget estimates.

The committee which examined into these matters for the Commission on Organization of the Executive Branch was unable to compare with any degree of accuracy the cost of similar functions in the three services because of varied organizational structures and differing budgetary and accounting classifications and procedures.

Firm control over the budget and over military expenditures, as authorized by the Congress, is of the utmost importance to the national economy. Full control in the hands of the Secretary of Defense, under the authority of the President, would accomplish three main purposes: (a) It would assure budgeting and spending from the standpoint of national welfare, rather than from the standpoint of service rivalries; (b) it would assure clear and direct accountability to the President, the Office of the Budget, and the Congress through a single official, and by these means would assure a budget that conformed to national policy; (c) it would provide the Secretary of Defense with a most effective mechanism for asserting civilian control over the military.

Recommendation No. 1

The Commission, therefore, recommends:

a. **That full power over preparation of the budget and over expenditures as authorized by the Congress be vested in the Secretary of Defense, under the authority of the President.**

b. **That the Secretary of Defense direct and supervise a major overhaul of the entire budget system; that the budget be of a performance type with emphasis on the objectives and purposes to be accomplished rather than upon personnel, supplies, and similar classifications; that uniform terminology, classifications, budgetary, and accounting practices be established throughout all the services along administrative lines of responsibility, so that fiscal and management responsibility go together.**

Under the performance budget system, each major organizational unit with management responsibility would have to prepare, and defend before the Secretary of Defense, complete estimates for its activities on the basis of functions and performance, and therefore could be held responsible for any money it might spend. Accountability would extend to accounting for operating results and to the measurement of performance against standards set through budgetary planning and cost estimates.

Such a system would accomplish a great deal, not only for efficiency, but to establish the authority of the Secretary of Defense and hence to assure civilian control.

c. That the armed services be required, at least in peacetime, to keep complete, accurate, and current inventories.

What Should Be Done To Improve Organization

The Commission calls attention to the findings of its task force report submitted separately to the Congress. The Commission is in general agreement with the conclusions and recommendations of the task force. However, the Commission feels that certain of the measures suggested by the task force for carrying out the policies need strengthening from the broader standpoint of reorganization of the entire executive branch — particularly to insure firm civilian control.

The Commission, in its first report, has recommended that all statutory restrictions on the National Security Council and the National Security Resources Board which limit the authority of the President should be removed and that the President have entire discretion over their membership, assignments, and direction.

The Commission recommends that the post of Chief of Staff to the President be abolished.

Civilian Control

Singleness of control is the essence of efficiency. The present scattering of authority is expensive, promotes rather than curtails service rivalries, and destroys the very principle of unification. Accountability is most strongly enforced when the President and the Congress, in the people's name, can call a single official to book for his conduct of a Government operation.

Recommendation No. 2

Therefore the Commission makes the following recommendations:

a. **That the principle of unified civilian control and accountability be the guiding rule for all legislation concerned with the National Military Establishment and that full authority and accountability be centered in the Secretary of Defense, subject only to the President and the Congress.**

b. **That all statutory authority now vested in the service departments, or their subordinate units, be granted directly to the Secretary of Defense, subject to the authority of the President, with further authority to delegate them as he sees fit and wise.**

c. **That the Secretary of Defense shall have full authority, subject only to the President and the Congress, to establish policies and programs.**

d. That the service secretaries be deprived of their privilege of appeal over the head of the Secretary of Defense; that they be directly and exclusively responsible to him; that the Secretary of Defense be the sole agent reporting to the President; that the service secretaries, to clarify their positions, be designated the Under Secretaries for Army, Navy, and Air Force.[24]

e. That specific provisions be made that the three military services shall be administered by the several under secretaries subject to the full direction and authority of the Secretary of Defense.

f. That there shall be Joint Chiefs of Staff representing the three services, appointed by the President and subject to confirmation by the Senate and that the Secretary of Defense, with the President's approval, shall appoint a chairman to preside over the Joint Chiefs of Staff and to represent, and report to, the Secretary of Defense.

g. That all administrative authority be centered in the Secretary of Defense, subject only to the authority of the President, including full and final authority over preparation of the military budget and over the expenditure of funds appropriated by the Congress.

h. That the Secretary be provided with an Under Secretary of Defense, who shall be his full deputy and act for him in his absence, and three assistant secretaries; and that the Secretary of Defense be empowered to set up such personal assistants to himself as he shall require to relieve him of day-to-day detail, to advise and assist him in planning and carrying out programs, and to organize this staff as he sees fit.

i. That full authority for the procurement and management of supplies and matériel be vested in the Secretary of Defense. The Secretary can delegate this authority to the Munitions Board (or to other officers or agencies as he may determine) with directions to expedite by all possible means the elimination of costly duplication in procurement and waste in utilization among the three services. Our further recommendations regarding the coordination of military with civilian supply management are contained in the Commission's report on the Offices of General Services.

Recommendation No. 3

The following recommendations are made regarding personnel:

a. That, in line with our recommendation below for an integrated system of military personnel administration, military education, training, recruitment, promotion, and transfers among the services be put under the central direction and control of the Secretary of Defense.

b. That the recruitment of civilian employees should be decentralized into

---

24 Commissioners Hoover, Flemming, Manasco, and Mead dissent from the recommendation to to change the designation of the service secretaries to Under Secretaries as they believe that the importance of these positions, the magnitude of the departments, and the danger of diluting civilian control over the military at the departmental level by a change of titles, outweigh considerations favoring a change.

the National Military Establishment under standards and procedures to be approved and enforced by the Civil Service Commission.

c. That full authority be vested in the Secretary of Defense, subject only to policies established by the Congress and the President, to prescribe uniform personnel policies for civilian and military personnel throughout the several services.

TEAMWORK

Recommendation No. 4

Teamwork and coordination throughout the National Military Establishment should be improved. For these purposes, the Commission recommends:

a. That more adequate and effective relations be developed at the working level among the appropriate committees of the Joint Chiefs of Staff on the one hand and the National Security Council, Central Intelligence Agency, Research and Develpment Board, Munitions Board, and the National Security Resources Board on the other hand.

b. That the jurisdiction and activities of the National Security Resources Board be further defined and clarified by the President.

c. That vigorous steps be taken to improve the Central Intelligence Agency and its work.

The present system of military administration does not allow for interchange of military and civilian personnel in administrative positions. Economy and efficiency would be fostered by a flexible system permitting the use of military or civilian skills in the higher posts of military administration and the Secretary should have authority to make such shifts as circumstances dictate.

Supervision over military personnel is now vested in the service department heads and in the President, not in the Secretary of Defense. There are, in addition, many statutory prescriptions of certain administrative services such as promotion boards, retirement boards, and others composed of military personnel, all of which serve to restrict the authority of the Secretary and his top civilian administrators. Moreover, statutory specifications of the numbers and grades of military personnel to be assigned to specific organizational units limit the most economical utilization of available military manpower when conditions require transfers and changes among organizational units.

The Secretary should have full authority to organize personnel management throughout the Military Establishment for greater efficiency and economy, and present hampering restrictions should be removed.

MEDICAL SERVICES

Recommendation No. 5

That steps be instituted to implement the recommendations which the Commission will file later concerning the medical departments of the three services, and their coordination with other medical programs of the Federal Government, as detailed in the Commission's separate report on medical services.

CIVILIAN AND INDUSTRIAL MOBILIZATION

For the security of the Nation, the formulation of plans for civilian and industrial mobilization should be completed at the earliest possible date.

Recommendation No. 6

The Commission therefore makes the following recommendations:

a. That emergency plans for civilian and industrial mobilization be completed promptly and continuously revised.

b. That use of civilian advisory boards should be continued.

c. That full responsibility and authority for formulating stock-pile policy and for its execution be clearly determined and centralized.

d. That further steps be taken immediately under the President's direction to prepare plans for civilian defense. Such an effort will require the participation of many agencies of Government. Similar action should be taken under the President's direction with respect to internal security. No clear allocation of responsibilities has been worked out among the agencies involved. The Commission believes that the problem in this area is one of determining what needs to be done and designating administrative responsibilities.

e. That defenses against unconventional methods of warfare be developed promptly and more vigorous and active attention be given to psychological warfare.

f. That the economic warfare section of the National Security Resources Board develop a comprehensive economic warfare program aimed at supporting national security both in peace and war.

CONCLUSIONS

These provisions should insure the full control and accountability of the National Military Establishment and the full subordination of the military to civilian control by establishing the Secretary of Defense as the principal assistant to the President in military matters, responsible to him and to the Congress for the conduct, efficiency, and economy of the National Military Establishment Lines of command would be clear; interservice rivalries reduced by the fresh emphasis on the singleness of purpose of the total military effort; efficiency promoted and economy achieved through consistent policy and program, and through centralized control.

(2) *Message of the President (Truman) to the Congress on Unification of the Armed Forces, March 5, 1949.*[25]

The maintenance of adequate armed forces has been one of the principal functions of the Federal Government since the establishment of this Nation. Today we maintain our armed forces in support of our primary desire for world peace. They are evidence of our determination to devote our utmost efforts toward achieving that all-important goal.

Throughout our history, the steady advance of science and technology has resulted in constant changes in the means of warfare and the character of our armed forces. In the few years since the cessation of hostilities in World War II, tremendous developments in technology have been made. The speed of aircraft has doubled, the means of undersea warfare have been revolutionized, the range and accuracy of guided missiles have increased, the potentialities of the atom have been more fully revealed.

The development of man's ability to shrink space and time and to control natural forces makes imperative a corresponding development of the means for directing and controlling these new powers. The effective and workable organization of our Government, and especially of our armed forces, is essential in the modern world.

The recent reports of the Commission on Organization of the Executive Branch of the Government have focused attention on the importance of the sound organization of the Federal Government. The Commission has stated that the first essential to the achievement of better government is a general clarification of the lines of authority and responsibility within the executive branch. In its report entitled "National Security Organization," the Commission has specifically applied this principle to the organization of our armed forces. The report states that we now lack adequate civilian authority and control over the military forces, that maximum efficiency and economy is not being realized in defense expenditures, and that interservice relationships must be improved to achieve the most effective defense. The recommendations of the Commission which would strengthen the National Military Establishment and the position of the Secretary of Defense have great merit and present an objective toward which I believe we must continue to move.

I have long been aware of the necessity for keeping our national security organization abreast of our security requirements. To this end I recommended unification of the armed forces to the Congress in December 1945.[26] My desire was to improve our defense organization while the lessons of World War II were still fresh in the minds of all. We must not forget these lessons in evaluating our security position today.

A great deal was learned from those 4 years of war. We learned, among other things, that the organization of our War and Navy Departments, prescribed by detailed statutes, was far too rigid and inflexible for the actual conduct of war. We learned that modern war required the combined use of air,

---

25 *Congressional Record*, 95, p. 1974 (Daily edition, March 7, 1949).
26 For the text of the President's message of December 19, 1945, see *Documents, VIII, 1945–1946*, p. 469.

naval, and land forces welded together under unified commands overseas, and under the strategic direction of the Joint Chiefs of Staff.

Other lessons were also learned. We learned that widely diverse supply policies of the separate services were costly and hampered the total effectiveness of military operations. We learned that there were great differences in training and combat doctrine among the services, and that these differences often provoked sharp conflicts in our theaters of operation.

My message to the Congress of December 1945[27] had a double purpose. It was intended to take advantage of our wartime experience and to prevent a return to the outmoded forms of organization which existed at the outbreak of the war.

Following that message the subject of the proper organization of our armed forces was debated throughout the nation. After the most careful consideration the National Security Act was enacted by the Congress in July 1947.[28]

This act has provided a practical and workable basis for beginning the unification of the military services and for coordinating military policy with foreign and economic policy. A few examples of the progress achieved in the period since the act became effective are evidence of its value.

The efficiency of military purchasing has steadily increased until today more than 75 percent of the matériel of the armed services is procured under coordinated purchasing arrangements.

A number of joint training and education programs have been instituted so that the personnel of each service may gain a greater understanding of the weapons and doctrine of the other services.

A uniform code of military justice has been developed, designed to be applicable to the personnel of all the armed forces. This code is now before the Congress for its consideration.

The coordination of military policy with foreign and economic policies has been greatly improved, principally through the efforts of National Security Council and the National Security Resources Board.

The past 18 months have dispelled any doubt that unification of the armed forces can yield great advantages to the Nation. No one advocates a return to the outmoded organization of the days preceding the National Security Act. On the contrary, the issue today is not whether we should have unification, but how we can make it more effective.

We have now had sufficient experience under the act to be able to identify and correct its weaknesses, without impairing the advantages we have obtained from its strength. We have also had the advantage of a thoroughgoing appraisal by the Commission on the Organization of the Executive Branch of the Government. On the basis of our experience to date, as further borne out by the Commission, we should now proceed to make the needed improvements in the act.

The duties and responsibilities of the Secretary of Defense as now set forth in the act are of too limited a character and are restricted to specified items.

27 See *Documents, VIII, 1945–1946,* p. 469.
28 For the text of the National Security Act of 1947, see *ibid., IX, 1947,* p. 266.

For example, the act expressly provides that all duties not specifically conferred upon the Secretary of Defense are to remain vested in the Secretaries of the Army, the Navy, and the Air Force. While the Secretary of Defense, as head of the National Military Establishment, ought to be ultimately accountable, under the President, for its administration, he is specifically limited by this act in the degree to which he may hold the military departments responsible to him. The departmental Secretaries are specifically authorized to deal directly with higher authority. Furthermore, many of the key responsibilities of the Secretary of Defense have been assigned by this statute, not to the Secretary, but to boards and agencies which derive much of their authority from the military departments themselves.

In short, the act fails to provide for a fully responsible official with authority adequate to meet his responsibility, whom the President and the Congress can hold accountable. The act fails to provide the basis for an organization and a staff adequate to achieve the most efficient and economical defense program and to attain effective and informed civilian control.

I, therefore, recommend that the National Security Act be amended to accomplish two basic purposes: First, to convert the National Military Establishment into an executive department of the Government, to be known as the Department of Defense; and second, to provide the Secretary of Defense with appropriate responsibility and authority, and with civilian and military assistance adequate to fulfill his enlarged responsibility.

Within the new Department of Defense, I recommend that the Departments of the Army, the Navy, and the Air Force be designated as military departments. The responsibility of the Secretary of Defense for exercising direction, authority, and control over the affairs of the Department of Defense should be made clear. Futhermore, the present limitation and restrictions which are inappropriate to his status as head of an executive department should be removed. The Secretary of Defense should be the sole representative of the Department of Defense on the National Security Council.

I am not recommending the blanket transfer of all statutory authority applicable to the Departments of the Army, the Navy, and the Air Force to the Secretary of Defense. Neither am I recommending any change in the statutory assignment of combatant functions to the Army, Navy, and Air Force. I recommend, however, that the Secretaries of the Army, the Navy, and the Air Force administer the respective military departments under the authority, direction, and control of the Secretary of Defense.

To meet these additional responsibilities, the Secretary of Defense needs strengthened civilian and military assistance. This can be provided by the creation of new posts and by the conversion of existing agencies of the National Military Establishment into staff units for the Secretary. I recommend that Congress provide an Under Secretary of Defense and three Assistant Secretaries of Defense.

The duties now placed by statute in the Munitions Board and the Research and Development Board should be recognized as responsibilities of the Secretary of Defense. The act should be amended to make possible the flexible use of both of these agencies, and of the Joint Chiefs of Staff, as staff units for the Secretary of Defense. Finally, I recommend that the Congress provide for a Chairman of the Joint Chiefs of Staff, to be nominated by the President and confirmed by the Senate, to take precedence over all other military personnel, and to be the principal military adviser to the President and the Secretary of Defense, and to perform such other duties as they may prescribe.

In my judgment, these changes will make possible effective organization and management of the Department of Defense. They will provide a responsible official at its head, with strengthened civilian and military assistance, to undertake the immense job of aiding the President and the Congress in determining defense needs and in supervising the administration of our defense activities. These measures are essential to continued and accelerated progress toward unification. I am convinced that only through making steady progress toward this goal can we be assured of serving our major objectives, the most effective organization of our armed forces, a full return on our defense dollar, and strengthened civilian control.

I urge the Congress to give prompt consideration to these recommendations. From the standpoint of present and potential cost to the Nation, there is no more important area in which to work for improved organization and operations. Action on these recommendations will prove beneficial to the Congress, the American people, and the President by providing better means of assuring defense needs and administering the defense program. We should seize this opportunity to strengthen our defense organization which is so vital to the security of this Nation and the peace of the world.

(3) *An Act to Reorganize Fiscal Management and to Promote Economy and Efficiency in the National Military Establishment, Approved August 10, 1949.*[29]

[EXCERPTS]

Be it enacted by the Senate and House of Representatives of the United States of America in Congress assembled,

SHORT TITLE

SECTION 1. This Act may be cited as the "National Security Act Amendments of 1949".

SEC. 2. Section 2 of the National Security Act of 1947 is amended to read as follows

"SEC. 2. In enacting this legislation, it is the intent of Congress to provide a comprehensive program for the future security of the United States; to provide for the establishment of integrated policies and procedures for the departments, agencies, and functions of the Government relating to the national security; to provide three military departments, separately administered, for the operation and administration of the Army, the Navy (including naval aviation and the United States Marine Corps), and the Air Force, with their assigned combat and service components; to provide for their authoritative coordination and unified direction under civilian control of the Secretary of Defense but not to merge them; to provide for the effective

29 Public Law 216, 81st Cong., 1st sess.

strategic direction of the armed forces and for their operation under unified control and for their integration into an efficient team of land, naval, and air forces but not to establish a single Chief of Staff over the armed forces nor an armed forces general staff (but this is not to be interpreted as applying to the Joint Chiefs of Staff or Joint Staff)."

CHANGE IN COMPOSITION OF THE NATIONAL SECURITY COUNCIL

SEC. 3. The fourth paragraph of section 101 (a) of the National Security Act of 1947 is amended to read as follows:
"The Council shall be composed of —
    "(1) the President;
    "(2) the Vice President;
    "(3) the Secretary of State;
    "(4) the Secretary of Defense;
    "(5) the Chairman of the National Security Resources Board; and
    "(6) The Secretaries and Under Secretaries of other executive departments and of the military departments, the Chairman of the Munitions Board, and the Chairman of the Research and Development Board, when appointed by the President by and with the advice and consent of the Senate, to serve at his pleasure."

CONVERSION OF THE NATIONAL MILITARY ESTABLISHMENT INTO AN EXECUTIVE DEPARTMENT

SEC. 4. Section 201 of the National Security Act of 1947 is amended to read as follows:
"SEC. 201. (a) There is hereby established, as an Executive Department of the Government, the Department of Defense, and the Secretary of Defense shall be the head thereof.
"(b) There shall be within the Department of Defense (1) the Department of the Army, the Department of the Navy, and the Department of the Air Force, and each such department shall on and after the date of enactment of the National Security Act Amendments of 1949 be military departments in lieu of their prior status as Executive Departments, and (2) all other agencies created under title II of this Act.
"(c) Section 158 of the Revised Statutes, as amended, is amended to read as follows:
" 'SEC. 158. The provisions of this title shall apply to the following Executive Departments:
    " 'First. The Department of State.
    " 'Second. The Department of Defense.
    " 'Third. The Department of the Treasury.
    " 'Fourth. The Department of Justice.
    " 'Fifth. The Post Office Department.
    " 'Sixth. The Department of the Interior.
    " 'Seventh. The Department of Agriculture.
    " 'Eighth. The Department of Commerce.
    " 'Ninth. The Department of Labor.'
"(d) Except to the extent inconsistent with the provisions of this Act, the provisions of title IV of the Revised Statutes as now or hereafter amended shall be applicable to the Department of Defense."

THE SECRETARY OF DEFENSE

SEC. 5. Section 202 of the National Security Act of 1947, as amended, is further amended to read as follows:
"SEC. 202. (a) There shall be a Secretary of Defense, who shall be appointed from civilian life by the President, by and with the advice and consent of the Senate: *Provided,* That a person who has within ten years been on active duty as a commissioned officer in a Regular component of the armed services shall not be eligible for appointment as Secretary of Defense.

"(b) The Secretary of Defense shall be the principal assistant to the President in all matters relating to the Department of Defense. Under the direction of the President, and subject to the provisions of this Act, he shall have direction, authority, and control over the Department of Defense.

"(c) (1) Notwithstanding any other provision of this Act, the combatant functions assigned to the military services by sections 205 (e), 206 (b), 206 (c), and 208 (f) hereof shall not be transferred, reassigned, abolished, or consolidated.

"(2) Military personnel shall not be so detailed or assigned as to impair such combatant functions.

"(3) The Secretary of Defense shall not direct the use and expenditure of funds of the Department of Defense in such manner as to effect the results prohibited by paragraphs (1) and (2) of this subsection.

"(4) The Departments of the Army, Navy, and Air Force shall be separately administered by their respective Secretaries under the direction, authority, and control of the Secretary of Defense.

"(5) Subject to the provisions of paragraph (1) of this subsection no function which has been or is hereafter authorized by law to be performed by the Department of Defense shall be substantially transferred, reassigned, abolished or consolidated until after a report in regard to all pertinent details shall have been made by the Secretary of Defense to the Committees on Armed Services of the Congress.

"(6) No provision of this Act shall be so construed as to prevent a Secretary of a military department or a member of the Joint Chiefs of Staff from presenting to the Congress, on his own initiative, after first so informing the Secretary of Defense, any recommendation relating to the Department of Defense that he may deem proper.

"(d) The Secretary of Defense shall not less often than semi-annually submit written reports to the President and the Congress covering expenditures, work and accomplishments of the Department of Defense, accompanied by (1) such recommendations as he shall deem appropriate, (2) separate reports from the military departments covering their expenditures, work and accomplishments, and (3) itemized statements showing the savings of public funds and the eliminations of unnecessary duplications and overlappings that have been accomplished pursuant to the provisions of this Act.

"(e) The Secretary of Defense shall cause a seal of office to be made for the Department of Defense, of such design as the President shall approve, and judicial notice shall be taken thereof.

"(f) The Secretary of Defense may, without being relieved of his responsibility therefor, and unless prohibited by some specific provision of this Act or other specific provision of law, perform any function vested in him through or with the aid of such officials or organizational entities of the Department of Defense as he may designate."

DEPUTY SECRETARY OF DEFENSE; ASSISTANT SECRETARIES OF DEFENSE; MILITARY ASSISTANTS; AND CIVILIAN PERSONNEL

SEC. 6. (a) Section 203 of the National Security Act of 1947 is amended to read as follows:

"SEC. 203. (a) There shall be a Deputy Secretary of Defense, who shall be appointed from civilian life by the President, by and with the advice and consent of the Senate: *Provided*, That a person who has within ten years been on active duty as a commissioned officer in a Regular component of the armed services shall not be eligible for appointment as Deputy Secretary of Defense. The Deputy Secretary shall perform such duties and exercise such powers as the Secretary of Defense may prescribe and shall take precedence in the Department of Defense next after the Secretary of Defense. The Deputy Secretary shall act for, and exercise the powers of, the Secretary of Defense during his absence or disability.

"(b) There shall be three Assistant Secretaries of Defense, who shall be appointed from civilian life by the President, by and with the advice and consent of the Senate. The Assistant Secretaries shall perform such duties and exercise such powers as the Secretary of Defense may prescribe and shall take precedence in the Department of Defense after the Secretary of Defense, the Deputy Secretary of Defense, the Secretary of the Army, the Secretary of the Navy, and the Secretary of the Air Force.

"(c) Officers of the armed services may be detailed to duty as assistants and personal aides to the Secretary of Defense, but he shall not establish a military staff other than that provided for by section 211 (a) of this Act."

(b) Section 204 of the National Security Act of 1947 is amended to read as follows:

"SEC. 204. The Secretary of Defense is authorized, subject to the civil-service laws and the Classification Act of 1923, as amended, to appoint and fix the compensation of such civilian personnel as may be necessary for the performance of the functions of the Department of Defense other than those of the Departments of the Army, Navy, and Air Force."

CREATING THE POSITION OF CHAIRMAN OF THE JOINT CHIEFS OF STAFF AND PRESCRIBING HIS POWERS AND DUTIES

SEC. 7. (a) Section 210 of the National Security Act of 1947 is amended to read as follows:

"SEC. 210. There shall be within the Department of Defense an Armed Forces Policy Council composed of the Secretary of Defense, as Chairman, who shall have power of decision; the Deputy Secretary of Defense; the Secretary of the Army; the Secretary of the Navy; the Secretary of the Air Force; the Chairman of the Joint Chiefs of Staff; the Chief of Staff, United States Army; the Chief of Naval Operations; and the Chief of Staff, United States Air Force. The Armed Forces Policy Council shall advise the Secretary of Defense on matters of broad policy relating to the armed forces and shall consider and report on such other matters as the Secretary of Defense may direct."

(b) Section 211 of the National Security Act of 1947 is amended to read as follows:

"SEC. 211. (a) There is hereby established within the Department of Defense the Joint Chiefs of Staff, which shall consist of the Chairman, who shall be the presiding officer thereof but who shall have no vote; the Chief of Staff, United States Army, the Chief of Naval Operations; and the Chief of Staff, United States Air Force. The Joint Chiefs of Staff shall be the principal military advisers to the President, the National Security Council, and the Secretary of Defense.

"(b) Subject to the authority and direction of the President and the Secretary of Defense, the Joint Chiefs of Staff shall perform the following duties, in addition to such other duties as the President or the Secretary of Defense may direct:

"(1) preparation of strategic plans and provision for the strategic direction of the military forces;

"(2) preparation of joint logistic plans and assignment to the military services of logistic responsibilities in accordance with such plans;

"(3) establishment of unified commands in strategic areas;

"(4) review of major material and personnel requirements of the military forces in accordance with strategic and logistic plans;

"(5) formulation of policies for joint training of the military forces;

"(6) formulation of policies for coordinating the military education of members of the military forces; and

"(7) providing United States representation on the Military Staff Committee of the United Nations in accordance with the provisions of the Charter of the United Nations.

"(c) The Chairman of the Joint Chiefs of Staff (hereinafter referred to as the 'Chairman') shall be appointed by the President, by and with the advice and consent of the Senate, from among the Regular officers of the armed services to serve at the pleasure of the President for a term of two years and shall be eligible for one reappointment, by and with the advice and consent of the Senate, except in time of war hereafter declared by the Congress when there shall be no limitation on the number of such reappointments. The Chairman shall receive the basic pay and basic and personal money allowances prescribed by law for the Chief of Staff, United States Army, and such special pays and hazardous duty pays to which he may be entitled under other provisions of law.

"(d) The Chairman, if in the grade of general, shall be additional to the number of officers in the grade of general provided in the third proviso of section 504 (b) of the Officer Personnel Act of 1947 (Public Law 381, Eightieth Congress) or, if in the rank of admiral, shall be additional to the number of officers having the rank of admiral provided in section 413 (a) of such Act. While holding such office he shall take precedence over all other officers of the armed services: *Provided,* That the Chairman shall not exercise military command over the Joint Chiefs of Staff or over any of the military services.

"(e) In addition to participating as a member of the Joint Chiefs of Staff in the performance of the duties assigned in subsection (b) of this section, the Chairman shall, subject to the authority and direction of the President and the Secretary of Defense, perform the following duties:

"(1) serve as the presiding officer of the Joint Chiefs of Staff;

"(2) provide agenda for meetings of the Joint Chiefs of Staff and assist the Joint Chiefs of Staff to prosecute their business as promptly as practicable; and

"(3) inform the Secretary of Defense and, when appropriate as determined by the President of the Secretary of Defense, the President, of those issues upon which agreement among the Joint Chiefs of Staff has not been reached."

(c) Section 212 of the National Security Act of 1947 is amended to read as follows:

"Sec. 212. There shall be, under the Joint Chiefs of Staff, a Joint Staff to consist of not to exceed two hundred and ten officers and to be composed of approximately equal numbers of officers appointed by the Joint Chiefs of Staff from each of the three armed services. The Joint Staff, operating under a Director thereof appointed by the Joint Chiefs of Staff, shall perform such duties as may be directed by the Joint Chiefs of Staff. The Director shall be an officer junior in grade to all members of the Joint Chiefs of Staff."

CHANGING THE RELATIONSHIP OF THE SECRETARY OF DEFENSE TO THE MUNITIONS BOARD

. . . .

CHANGING THE RELATIONSHIPS OF THE SECRETARY OF DEFENSE TO THE RESEARCH AND DEVELOPMENT BOARD

. . . .

COMPENSATION OF SECRETARY OF DEFENSE, DEPUTY SECRETARY OF DEFENSE, SECRETARIES OF MILITARY DEPARTMENTS, AND CONSULTANTS

. . . .

Reorganization of Fiscal Management to Promote Economy and Efficiency

Sec. 11. The National Security Act of 1947 is amended by inserting at the end thereof the following new title:

"TITLE IV

"Promotion of Economy and Efficiency Through Establishment of Uniform Budgetary and Fiscal Procedures and Organizations

"Comptroller of Department of Defense

"Sec. 401. (a) There is hereby established in the Department of Defense the Comptroller of the Department of Defense, who shall be one of the Assistant Secretaries of Defense.

"(b) The Comptroller shall advise and assist the Secretary of Defense in performing such budgetary and fiscal functions as may be required to carry out the Powers conferred upon the Secretary of Defense by this Act, including but not limited to those specified in this subsection. Subject to the authority, direction, and control of the Secretary of Defense, the Comptroller shall —

"(1) supervise and direct the preparation of the budget estimates of the Department of Defense; and

"(2) establish, and supervise the execution of —

"(A) principles, policies, and procedures to be followed in connection with organizational and administrative matters relating to —
"(i) the preparation and execution of the budgets,
"(ii) fiscal, cost, operating, and capital property accounting
"(iii) progress and statistical reporting,
"(iv) internal audit, and
"(B) policies and procedures relating to the expenditure and collection of funds administered by the Department of Defense; and
"(3) establish uniform terminologies, classifications, and procedures in all such matters.

"MILITARY DEPARTMENT BUDGET AND FISCAL ORGANIZATION—DEPARTMENTAL COMPTROLLERS

"SEC. 402. (a) The Secretary of each military department, subject to the authority direction, and control of the Secretary of Defense, shall cause budgeting, accounting, progress and statistical reporting, internal audit and administrative organization structure and managerial procedures relating thereto in the department of which he is the head to be organized and conducted in a manner consistent with the operations of the Office of the Comptroller of the Department of Defense.

"(b) There is hereby established in each of the three military departments a Comptroller of the Army, a Comptroller of the Navy, or a Comptroller of the Air Force, as appropriate in the Department concerned. There shall, in each military department, also be a Deputy Comptroller. Subject to the authority of the respective departmental Secretaries, the comptrollers of the military departments shall be responsible for all budgeting, accounting, progress and statistical reporting, and internal audit in their respective departments and for the administrative organization structure and managerial procedures relating thereto. The Secretaries of the military departments may in their discretion appoint either civilian or military personnel as comptrollers of the military departments. Departmental comptrollers shall be under the direction and supervision of, and directly responsible to, either the Secretary, the Under Secretary, or an Assistant Secretary of the respective military departments: *Provided* That nothing herein shall preclude the comptroller from having concurrent responsibility to a Chief of Staff or a Chief of Naval Operations, a Vice Chief of Staff or a Vice Chief of Naval Operations, or a Deputy Chief of Staff or a Deputy Chief of Naval Operations, if the Secretary of the military department concerned should so prescribe. Where the departmental comptroller is not a civilian, the Secretary of the department concerned shall appoint a civilian as Deputy Comptroller.

"PERFORMANCE BUDGET

"SEC. 403. (a) The budget estimates of the Department of Defense shall be prepared, presented, and justified, where practicable, and authorized programs shall be administered, in such form and manner as the Secretary of Defense, subject to the authority and direction of the President, may determine, so as to account for, and report, the cost of performance of readily identifiable functional programs and activities, with segregation of operating and capital programs. So far as practicable, the budget estimates and authorized programs of the military departments shall be set forth in readily comparable form and shall follow a uniform pattern.

"(b) In order to expedite the conversion from present budget and accounting methods to the cost-of-performance method prescribed in this title, the Secretary of each military department, with the approval of the President and the Secretary of Defense, is authorized and directed, until the end of the second year following the date of enactment of this Act, to make such transfers and adjustments within the military department of which he is the head between appropriations available for obligation by such department in such manner as he deems necessary to cause the obligation and administration of funds and the reports of expenditures to reflect the cost of performance of such programs and activities. Reports of transfers and adjustments made pursuant to the authority of this subsection shall be made currently by the Secretary of Defense to the President and the Congress.

"Obligation of Appropriations

"Sec. 404. In order to prevent overdrafts and deficiencies in any fiscal year for which appropriations are made, on and after the beginning of the next fiscal year following the date of enactment of this Act appropriations made to the Department of Defense or to the military departments, and reimbursements thereto, shall be available for obligation and expenditure only after the Secretary of Defense shall approve scheduled rates of obligation, or modifications thereof: *Provided*, That nothing in this section shall affect the right of the Department of Defense to incur such deficiencies as may be now or hereafter authorized by law to be incurred.

·　　·　　·　　·　　·　　·　　·

MISCELLANEOUS AND TECHNICAL AMENDMENTS AND SAVING PROVISIONS

Sec. 12 (a) The National Security Act of 1947 is amended by striking out the term "National Military Establishment", wherever it appears in such Act, and inserting in lieu thereof "Department of Defense".

(b) Section 207 (a) of the National Security Act of 1947 is amended to read as follows:

"Sec. 207. (a) Within the Department of Defense there is hereby established a military department to be known as the Department of the Air Force, and the Secretary of the Air Force who shall be the head thereof. The Secretary of the Air Force shall be appointed from civilian life by the President by and with the advice and consent of the Senate."

(c) Section 207 (b) of the National Security Act of 1947 is repealed.

(d) The first sentence of section 208 (a) of the National Security Act of 1947 is amended by striking out the word "under" and inserting in lieu thereof the word "within".

(e) Section 308 (b) of the National Security Act of 1947 is amended to read as follows:

"(b) As used in this Act, the term 'Department of Defense' shall be deemed to include the military departments of the Army, the Navy, and the Air Force, and all agencies created under title II of this Act."

(f) The titles of the Secretary of Defense, the Secretary of the Army, the Secretary of the Navy, the Secretary of the Air Force, the Under Secretaries and the Assistant Secretaries of the Departments of the Army, Navy, and Air Force, the Chairman of the Munitions Board, and the Chairman of the Research and Development Board, shall not be changed by virtue of this Act, and the reappointment of the officials holding such titles on the effective date of this Act shall not be required. It is hereby declared to be the intention of Congress that section 203 (a) of the National Security Act of 1947, as amended by section 6 of this Act, shall not be deemed to have created a new office of Deputy Secretary of Defense but shall be deemed to have continued in existence, under a new title, the Office of Under Secretary of Defense which was established by the Act entitled "An Act to amend the National Security Act of 1947 to provide for an Under Secretary of Defense", approved April, 2, 1949 (Public Law 36, Eighty-first Congress). The title of the official holding the Office of Under Secretary of Defense on the effective date of this Act shall be changed to Deputy Secretary of Defense and the reappointment of such official shall not be required.

(g) All laws, orders, regulations, and other actions relating to the National Military Establishment, the Departments of the Army, the Navy, or the Air Force, or to any officer or activity of such establishment or such departments, shall, except to the extent inconsistent with the provisions of this Act, have the same effect as if this Act had not been enacted; but, after the effective date of this Act, any such law, order, regulation, or other action which vested functions in or otherwise related to any officer, department, or establishment, shall be deemed to have vested such function in or relate to the officer or department, executive or military, succeeding the officer, department, or establishment in which such function was vested. For purposes of this subsection the Department of Defense shall be deemed the department succeeding the National Military Establishment, and the military departments of Army,

Navy, and Air Force shall be deemed the departments succeeding the Executive Departments of Army, Navy, and Air Force.

(h) Section 208 (e) of the National Security Act of 1947 is amended by substituting the word "three" for the word "two" appearing therein.

(i) Reorganization Plan Numbered 8 of 1949, which was transmitted to the Congress by the President on July 18, 1949, pursuant to the provisions of the Reorganization Act of 1949, shall not take effect, notwithstanding the provisions of section 6 of such Reorganization Act of 1949.

C. Procurement of Personnel

Senator Millard E. Tydings (Maryland) and Senator George W. Malone (Nevada) introduced legislation (S.66) on January 5, 1949 requiring all qualified young men to undergo a period of training and providing that the National Guard be ordered to active federal service whenever the Congress should deem it necessary for the national security.[30] Hearings on this measure were held in March by the Senate Committee on Armed Services; however, no further action was taken during the year under review.

Also in January Secretary Forrestal announced that the armed forces had reached the personnel strength proposed for them in the President's budget for the 1950 fiscal year — 1,616,000 men.[31] At the end of 1949 the army, navy, air force and marine corps had a total of 1,621,000 officers and men on active duty. During the first month of 1949 the army discontinued use of the draft and the Selective Service Commission ceased to classify registrants as available for duty.

D. Appropriations

In his annual budget message to the Congress President Truman proposed a national defense budget for the 1950 fiscal year of nearly $15,900,000,000.[32] On April 9 Rep. George H. Mahon (Texas) reported to the House of Representatives H.R.4146 making appropriations for the National Security Council, the National Security Resources Board, and for military functions administered by the National Military Establishment for the 1950 fiscal year.[33] During Congressional consideration of this bill a sharp issue developed over the size and power of the air force, with the House three times authorizing a 70-group air force and the Senate approving a 48-group air force, as originally recommended by the President and the Secretary of Defense. Two conferences by joint Congressional committees resulted in final authorization of a 58-group air force.[34] However, what President Truman later called a "major shift in the direction and emphasis" of the defense program occurred with authorization of an increase in air force appropriations of more than $615,000,000 above the original 1950 budget recommendations of President Truman.[35] On October 29 H.R.4146 was signed by the President, after passage by Congress; it provided for military appropriations of $15,585,863,148.[36]

30 *Congressional Record*, 95, p. 35 (Daily edition, January 5, 1949).
31 House Document 17, 81st Cong., 1st sess.
32 For the text of the President's budget message, see this volume, p. 2.
33 *Congressional Record*, 95, p. 4272 (Daily edition, April 9, 1949).
34 House Report 1386, 81st Cong., 1st sess.
35 *New York Times*, October 30, 1949, p. 3.
36 Public Law 434, 81st Cong., 1st sess.

(1) *Comparative Statement of the Appropriations and Contract Authorizations of the National Military Establishment for 1949 and 1950.*[37]

ORGANIZATION UNIT	CONTRACT AUTHORIZATIONS		APPROPRIATIONS	
	1949	1950	1949	1950
Office of the Secretary of Defense			$6,800,000	$191,450,000
Department of the Air Force		$2,045,589,770	939,977,418	4,121,731,000
Department of the Army	$220,000,000	48,363,700	7,828,463,859	6,018,795,188
Department of the Navy	280,000,000[38]	658,960,000[38]	3,768,392,118	4,366,775,794
	$500,000,000[38]	$2,752,913,470[38]	$12,543,633,395	$14,698,751,982

3. MILITARY AND NAVAL MISSIONS TO FOREIGN GOVERNMENTS.

On January 5, 1949 the agreement of October 6, 1947, between the United States and Iran concerning the employment of the United States advisory mission in the Iranian Ministry of War was amended and extended until March 21, 1950.[39]

For information on military and naval assistance to Latin America, see this volume, Chapter XIII. For information on missions to the North Atlantic Powers, see *ibid.*, Chapter XV.

4. FOREIGN INTELLIGENCE ACTIVITIES OF THE FEDERAL GOVERNMENT

In June H.R.2663, designed to maintain the utmost in secrecy for the activities, personnel and expenditures of the Central Intelligence Agency, pursuant to Section 102 of the National Security Act of 1947,[40] was approved and signed by President Truman. It granted to CIA immunity from every ordinary form of congressional supervision and restraint in order to protect the agency.

[37] Compiled from information furnished by the Bureau of the Budget.
[38] Excludes increases in estimated cost of construction from prior years' authorizations under the shipbuilding program.
[39] Department of State,*Treaties and Other International Acts Series* 1924.
[40] For the text of Section 102 of the National Security Act of 1947, see *Documents, IX, 1947, p. 268.*

CHAPTER VI

International Peace and Security

1. GENERAL

(1) *Resolution on the Essentials of Peace, Approved by the United Nations General Assembly, December 1, 1949.*[1]

On September 23, 1949, the Soviet Union submitted to the United Nations General Assembly a draft resolution which 1) called for condemnation of "the preparations for a new war now being conducted in a number of countries and particularly in the United States and the United Kingdom," 2) requested the General Assembly to declare "inadmissable any further delay in the adoption by the United Nations of practical measures for the unconditional prohibition of atomic weapons and the establishment of appropriate strict international control," and 3) requested the conclusion of a "peace pact" by the big five.[2] A counter-draft on the essentials of peace was presented in the Political and Security Committee of the General Assembly by the United States and the United Kingdom in the course of discussions covering the entire field of international relations since 1917, dealing in particular with United States-Soviet relations. On the committee's recommendation, the General Assembly on December 1 approved the United States-United Kingdom proposal by a vote of 53 to 5 with 1 abstention (Yugoslavia). The Soviet resolution was defeated on a paragraph-by-paragraph vote.[3]

The General Assembly,

1. *Declares* that the Charter of the United Nations, the most solemn pact of peace in history, lays down basic principles necessary for an enduring peace; that disregard of these principles is primarily responsible for the continuance of international tension; and that it is urgently necessary for all Members to act in accordance with these principles in the spirit of co-operation on which the United Nations was founded;

Calls upon every nation

2. *To refrain* from threatening or using force contrary to the Charter;

3. *To refrain* from any threats or acts, direct or indirect, aimed at impairing the freedom, independence or integrity of any State, or at fomenting civil strife and subverting the will of the people in any State;

4. *To carry out* in good faith its international agreements;

5. *To afford* all United Nations bodies full co-operation and free access in the performance of the tasks assigned to them under the Charter;

6. *To promote,* in recognition of the paramount importance of preserving the dignity and worth of the human person, full freedom for the peaceful expression of political opposition, full opportunity for the exercise of religious freedom and full respect for all the other fundamental rights expressed in the Universal Declaration of Human Rights;

[1] United Nations General Assembly, *Official Records: Resolutions* (4th session), p. 13.
[2] *Ibid.,* Document A/996, September 24, 1949.
[3] *Ibid., Official Records* (4th session), p. 438.

7. *To promote* nationally and through international co-operation, efforts to achieve and sustain higher standards of living for all peoples;

8. *To remove* the barriers which deny to peoples the free exchange of information and ideas essential to international understanding and peace;

Calls upon every Member

9. *To participate* fully in all the work of the United Nations;

Calls upon the five permanent members of the Security Council

10. *To broaden* progressively their co-operation and to exercise restraint in the use of the veto in order to make the Security Council a more effective instrument for maintaining peace;

Calls upon every nation

11. *To settle* international disputes by peaceful means and to co-operate in supporting United Nations efforts to resolve outstanding problems;

12. *To co-operate* to attain the effective international regulation of conventional armaments; and

13. *To agree* to the exercise of national sovereignty jointly with other nations to the extent necessary to attain international control of atomic energy which would make effective the prohibition of atomic weapons and assure the use of atomic energy for peaceful purposes only.

2. DEVELOPMENT OF UNITED NATIONS MACHINERY
A. General

(1) *Resolutions on the Promotion of International Cooperation in the Political Field, Approved by the United Nations General Assembly, April 28, 1949.*[1]

A series of proposals on the promotion of international cooperation in the political field were studied by the Interim Committee of the General Assembly during 1948, in accordance with its original terms of reference. The committee considered various methods for pacific settlement of disputes, including a Chinese-United States suggestion for the creation of a Panel of Inquiry and Conciliation, and recommended to the General Assembly the adoption of four resolutions to 1) restore to full effect the General Act of 1928 for the pacific settlement of disputes, by opening for accession a new text assigning to the United Nations those functions formerly carried out by the League of Nations; 2) recommend that the Security Council consider appointment of a rapporteur or conciliator for any situation or dispute brought to the Council's attention; 3) assign to the President of the General Assembly or to persons appointed by him the functions of a rapporteur or conciliator; and 4) establish the panel of inquiry and conciliation.[2] The four resolutions were considered at the second part of the third session of the General Assembly, where they were supported by United States, but opposed by the Soviet Union and other eastern European states as usurping the functions of the Security Council in pacific settlement and as the proposals of an illegally constituted group.[3] On April 28, 1949, the Assembly returned to the Interim Committee for further study the proposal assigning conciliatory duties to the President of the General Assembly and approved the other three resolutions.

Members of the Panel of Inquiry and Conciliation later designated by the United

1 United Nations General Assembly, *Official Records: Resolutions,* (3d session, 2d part), p. 10.
2 *Ibid., Official Records* (3d session), Supplement 10, p. 34.
3 *Ibid.,* Document A/809, December 13, 1948; *ibid,* Document A/833, April 12, 1949. The "illegally constituted group" refers to the Interim Committee which the communist states had consistently boycotted.

States were Philip C. Jessup, Ralph J. Bunche, H. Merle Cochran, Frank C. Graham and Mark F. Ethridge.[4]

B

APPOINTMENT OF A RAPPORTEUR OR CONCILIATOR FOR A SITUATION OR DISPUTE BROUGHT TO THE ATTENTION OF THE SECURITY COUNCIL

The General Assembly,

Mindful of its responsibilities, under Articles 13 (1 a) and 11 (1) of the Charter, to promote international co-operation in the political field and to make recommendations with regard to the general principles of the maintenance of international peace and security, and in discharge of its functions under Article 10 of the Charter,

Noting the experience of the League of Nations, which it has caused to be studied, whereby cases were presented to the Council of the League of Nations by a rapporteur who had the function of a conciliator, and that this practice allowed private conversations among the parties and the rapporteur and avoided the crystallization of views that tends to result from taking a stated public position,

Noting that the Security Council has already made use of a similar procedure,

Deeming it desirable that such a practice be developed in the Security Council as an integral part of the system of pacific settlement, and also as a means for the better preparation of cases presented to the Security Council,

Recommends that the Security Council examine the utility and desirability of adopting the following practice:

After a situation or dispute has been brought to the attention of representatives on the Security Council in accordance with rule 6 of the provisional rules of procedure of the Security Council and not later than immediately after the opening statements on behalf of the parties concerned,

(a) The parties shall be invited to meet with the President of the Security Council;

(b) They shall attempt to agree upon a representative on the Security Council to act as rapporteur or conciliator for the case. The representative so agreed upon may be the President or any other representative of the Council who will thereupon be appointed by the President to undertake the function of rapporteur or conciliator. The President shall inform the Security Council whether a rapporteur or conciliator has been appointed;

(c) If a rapporteur or conciliator is appointed, it would be desirable for the Security Council to abstain from further action on the case for a reasonable interval during which actual efforts at conciliation are in progress;

(d) The rapporteur or conciliator so agreed upon and appointed shall attempt to conciliate the situation or dispute, and shall in due course report to the Security Council.

4 United Nations Security Council, Document S/1476, March 30, 1950.

D

CREATION OF A PANEL FOR INQUIRY AND CONCILIATION

The General Assembly

Mindful of its responsibilities, under Article 13 (1 a) and 11 (1) of the Charter, to promote international co-operation in the political field and to make recommendations with regard to the general principles of the maintenance of international peace and security,

Deeming it desirable to facilitate in every practicable way the compliance by Member States with the obligation in Article 33 of the Charter first of all to seek a solution of their disputes by peaceful means of their own choice,

Noting the desirability, as shown by the experience of organs of the United Nations, of having qualified persons readily available to assist those organs in the settlement of disputes and situations by serving on commissions of inquiry or of conciliation,

Concluding that to make provision for a panel of persons having the highest qualifications in this field available to any States involved in controversies and to the General Assembly, the Security Council and their subsidiary organs, when exercising their respective functions in relation to disputes and situations, would promote the use and effectiveness of procedures of inquiry and conciliation,

1. *Invites* each Member State to designate from one to five persons who, by reason of their training, experience, character and standing, are deemed to be well fitted to serve as members of commissions of inquiry or of conciliation and who would be disposed to serve in that capacity;

2. *Directs* the Secretary-General to take charge of the administrative arrangements connected with the composition and use of the panel;

3. *Adopts* the annexed articles relating to the composition and use of the Panel for Inquiry and Conciliation.

ANNEX

ARTICLES RELATING TO THE COMPOSITION AND USE OF THE PANEL FOR INQUIRY AND CONCILIATION

Article 1

The Panel for Inquiry and Conciliation shall consist of persons designated by Member States who, by reason of their training, experience, character and standing, are deemed to be well fitted to serve as members of commissions of inquiry or of conciliation and who would be disposed to serve in that capacity. Each Member State may designate from one to five persons, who may be private persons or government officials. In designating any of its officials, a State shall agree to make every effort to make such person available if his services on a commission are requested. Two or more States may designate the same person. Members of the panel shall be designated for a term of five years and such designations shall be renewable. Members of commissions appointed under these articles shall not, in the performance of their duties, seek or receive instructions from any Government. Membership in the panel shall not, however, render a person ineligible for appointment, as representative of his Government or otherwise, on commissions or other bodies not formed under these articles.

Article 2

The Secretary-General of the United Nations shall have general responsibility for the administrative arrangements connected with the panel. Each Government shall notify him of each designation of a person for inclusion in the panel, including with each notification full pertinent biographical information. Each Government shall inform him when any member of the panel designated by it is no longer available due to death, incapacity or inability to serve.

The Secretary-General shall communicate the panel and any changes which may occur in it from time to time to the Member States, to the Security Council, the General Assembly and the Interim Committee. He shall, where necessary, invite Member States promptly to designate replacements to fill any vacancies on the panel which may occur.

Article 3

The panel shall be available at all times to the organs of the United Nations in case they wish to select from it members of commissions to perform tasks of inquiry or conciliation in connexion with disputes or situations in respect of which the organs are exercising their functions.

Article 4

The panel shall be available at all times to all States, whether or not Members of the United Nations, which are parties to any controversy, for the purpose of selecting from the panel members of commissions to perform tasks of inquiry or conciliation with a view to settlement of the controversy.

Article 5

The method of selecting members of a commission of inquiry or of conciliation from the panel shall be determined in each case by the organ appointing the commission or, in the case of commissions appointed by or at the request of States parties to a controversy, by agreement between the parties.

Whenever the parties to a controversy jointly request the Secretary-General, the President of the General Assembly or the Chairman of the Interim Committee to appoint under these articles a member or members of a commission to perform tasks of inquiry or conciliation in respect of the controversy, or whenever such request is otherwise made pursuant to the provisions of a treaty or agreement registered with the Secretary-General of the United Nations, the officer so requested shall appoint from the panel the number of commissioners required.

Article 6

In connexion with the constituting of any commission under these articles, the Secretary-General shall give the United Nations organ concerned or the parties to the controversy every assistance, by the performance of such tasks as ascertaining the availability of individuals selected from the panel, and making arrangements for the time and place of meeting of the persons so selected.

Article 7

Members of commissions constituted pursuant to these articles by United Nations organs shall have the privileges and immunities specified in the General Convention on the Privileges and Immunities of the United Nations. Members of commissions constituted by States under these articles should, so far as possible, receive the same privileges and immunities.

Article 8

Members of commissions constituted under these articles shall receive appropriate compensation for the period of their service. In the case of commissions constituted under article 4, such compensation shall be provided by the parties to the controversy, each party providing an equal share.

Article 9

Subject to any determinations that may be made by the United Nations organ concerned or by the parties to a controversy in constituting commissions under articles 3 and 4 respectively, commissions constituted under these articles may meet at the seat of the United Nations or at such other places as they may determine to be necessary for the effective performance of their functions.

Article 10

The Secretary-General shall assign to each commission constituted by a United Nations organ under these articles, staff adequate to enable it to perform its duties and shall, as necessary, seek expert assistance from specialized agencies brought into relationship with the United Nations. He shall enter into suitable arrangements with the proper authorities of States in order to assure the commission, so far as it may find it necessary to exercise its functions within their territories, full freedom of movement and all facilities necessary for the performance of its functions. The Secretary-General shall, at the request of any commission appointed by parties to a controversy pursuant to article 4, render this assistance to the commission to the extent possible.

Upon completion of its proceedings each commission appointed by a United Nations organ shall render such reports as may be determined by the appointing organ. Each commission appointed by or at the request of parties to a controversy pursuant to article 4, shall file a report with the Secretary-General. If a settlement of the controversy is reached, such report will normally merely state the terms of settlement.

(2) *Letter from the President (Truman) to the Congress Transmitting the Report on the Participation of the United States in the United Nations for the Year 1949, May 22, 1950.*[5]

I transmit herewith to the Congress, pursuant to the United Nations Participation Act, my fourth annual report on the activities of the United Nations and the participation of the United States. This report for the year 1949 tells an impressive story of accomplishment, much of which we are prone to overlook in the clamor of daily difficulties. I commend it to the careful reading of all our citizens.

The Charter of the United Nations is a contract among the members to settle their disputes peacefully and to promote the economic and social advancement of all peoples for the building and maintenance of a durable world order.

We support the United Nations and keep this contract because the Charter expresses our fundamental aims in the modern world. We know that the fulfillment of the Charter will best advance our own vital interests — to attain peace with justice, to assure freedom, and to bring about economic and social progress, for ourselves and all peoples. It is for this reason that support of the United Nations is and must be Point 1 of our foreign policy.

Most of the nations of the world share these objectives and are working through the United Nations to achieve them. They therefore tend increasingly toward common judgments on the great issues confronting mankind. The decisions of the United Nations in 1949 show to a greater extent than in previous years that the convictions of the world's peoples on matters of fun-

5 Department of State Publication 3765.

damental concern have become clear and firm with the lessons of post war experience.

Relations among nations have never been, and probably never will be, free from difficulties. The intensity of the East-West conflict has obscured the fact that certain critical disputes have arisen from purely local conflicts and that many such problems would continue to confront nations even if relations between the Soviet Union and the rest of the world were far different from what they are today. In a time of swift and profound change like the present, questions of adjustment of views and interests among nations are more numerous and urgent than at any previous period in history. There are few international problems that fail to confront us with the need of making decisions on the policy we should follow or the national attitude we should express in the United Nations and in our direct relations with other states. These problems make daily demands of us for sober judgment and strength of spirit and purpose. They make the same of every nation seeking to carry out the Charter.

The United Nations is an organization to help members resolve international difficulties. It is also a mirror in which the state of world affairs is reflected. We cannot expect from the United Nations immediate solutions of problems as large and complex as many that are before it. But already we have seen how, by its debates and decisions, it is helping to guide the nations into the ways of peace. To the extent that solutions of problems are delayed or are obtained piece-meal, we must be realistically prepared to live with them. Persistent effort through the United Nations is an expression of our faith that these problems can be solved.

This faith is not misplaced. Experience is demonstrating that the United Nations processes of debate, consultation, conciliation, and agreement are capable of bringing about the peaceful settlement of disputes wherever both sides fundamentally respect reason and pledged undertakings above force. The report for 1949 shows how greatly the United Nations has contributed to the settlement of the Indonesian dispute, how it has brought an end to the fighting in Palestine and in Kashmir, and how it continues to work energetically toward further progress in the solution of these disputes. Many lives have been saved through the success of the United Nations in moving such conflicts indoors — from battlegrounds to conference tables.

The power of the United Nations today is that of moral force. Such force gathers its strength slowly, but it does so surely. No nation can ignore the question of how its actions will appear in the world forums of the United Nations. No nation, member or non-member, attending or nonattending, can avoid accountability before the United Nations for actions affecting the peace. The aroused opinion of mankind, when brought to sharp and immediate focus as it often is in the United Nations, is not lightly to be dismissed, even by a nation that has strong battalions.

Much of the useful work of the United Nations is and should be long-range in character. In some of its fields, the tasks are those of development over many years, as in the steady and seemingly prosaic steps toward the building up of international economic and social health through cooperative relations among all nations desiring to help each other. It is in such far-flung and manifold activities no less than in its efforts to handle critical tensions that the United Nations is creating fundamental conditions necessary for the growth of peace. The report I submit this year gives to this work the fuller attention it merits. It shows that in economic and social fields the United Nations is becoming increasingly effective in improving the daily life of millions of people. In 1949 the Economic and Social Council proposed, and the General Assembly unanimously adopted, a program of technical assistance to underdeveloped areas which is directed toward the goal I outlined as Point IV in my inaugural address. This program of the United Nations offers solid promise for world advancement.

By related programs, the United Nations is promoting economic development in regional areas and in various fields of endeavor. Through a program of public works started in the Near East, jobless and homeless refugees can find new homes and the foundation of self-reliance through beneficial employment rather than relief alone. Special training fellowships are being given by the United Nations and the specialized agencies to hundreds of students for study. Upon request, experts are being sent to demonstrate in underdeveloped areas the advanced knowledge and techniques which the local peoples can put to practical use. Expert missions in the fields of public administration and finance, agriculture, medicine and health, social problems, and labor matters have been sent to many countries on request of governments to tackle urgent problems that stand in the way of improved standards of living. All this work will be further intensified as the expanded program of technical assistance is put in operation.

In other fields also, progress is being pressed. The new Field Service and Panel of Field Observers provide specialized help for commissions of peaceful settlement. It has been agreed that two of the former Italian colonies, Libya and Italian Somaliland, are to become independent states. The advancement of trust areas and other non-self-governing territories is steadily being fostered through the cooperation of the administering states and the United Nations. On legal question it is gratifying to observe the gradual increase in the use of the International Court of Justice. Respect for and dependence upon the processes of law are essential in the building of the better world order.

These constructive activities have been overshadowed by the unsolved problems arising from the policies and acts of the Soviet Union which lead to tension and impairment of security in international relations. The United Nations rendered a great service during 1949 by asserting, in the notable resolution of the General Assembly on "Essentials of Peace," the standards of conduct necessary to restore international confidence. Each of the 53 members other than the Communist states represented in the United Nations gave its support to this fundamental call for action to build peace. By this and other steps, the United Nations made it clear that the great issues of security in the postwar period are between the Soviet Union and the rest of the world at large and that these issues arise from failures by the Soviet Union to conform its conduct to the purposes and principles of the Charter.

The international control of atomic energy stands foremost among the urgent matters calling for agreement. Effective international regulation of armaments and armed forces is a related problem of urgency.

Our experience during 1949 in the United Nations provided further demonstration that, as the Secretary of State has recently stated, agreements with the Soviet Union and its satellites are valid only as and when they record existing situations of fact. It is not enough to hope for agreement or to make proposals; it is essential to create the conditions under which it will be to the interest of the Soviet Union to enter into and to keep agreements. All international activities which create moral, economic, and military strength among the nations of the free world will broaden the area of possible agreement and hasten its coming.

We are endeavoring in the United Nations as in our other international actions to make clear to the Soviet Union that we seek to carry out the Charter in deed as in word, and that we ask no more or less from any other member. It will be our plan in the future, as it has been our practice in the past, to do all in our power to strengthen the United Nations as the primary instrument for the maintenance of peace. By our efforts to strengthen it and by our related assistance to other nations under legislation enacted by the Congress, we shall seek to make our utmost contribution to attaining the situation of fact in which agreement can become realistically possible.

The United Nations seeks agreement and the execution in good faith of agreed undertakings. This is the true basis of a world community founded on law and justice. We, for our part, will continue to negotiate and to examine every proposal in our unending effort to achieve security through effective and dependable agreement.

It is a source of encouragement that the United Nations in conducting its work is distinguishing between realities and illusions and is vigilantly insisting, problem by problem, upon solid gains through actual performance. It is striving for real peace, genuine freedom, and actual progress. This fact stands out in its record.

The walkouts of the Soviet Union over Chinese Nationalist representation in the United Nations occurred since the events of 1949 described in this report. In the presence of this willful flouting by the Soviet Government of obligations assumed by it under the Charter, the United Nations has taken the common sense attitude of proceeding with its business as usual.

B. Powers and Procedures

1. CONTINUATION OF THE INTERIM COMMITTEE

[See *Documents, IX, 1947*, p. 325; *X, 1948*, p. 304.]

In its report to the fourth session of the United Nations General Assembly on activities during 1949,[6] the Interim Committee, noting that it had begun a long-

---

[6] United Nations General Assembly, *Official Records* (4th session), Supplement 11.

range program of work in studying the operation and organization of United Nations commissions as well as settlement of disputes and special political problems by the General Assembly, recommended its own continuation for an indefinite period with similar terms of reference. The report was referred to the Ad Hoc Political Committee which approved the Interim Committee's recommendations, despite the opposition of the Soviet Union and the eastern European states on the grounds that the real purpose of the committee was to by-pass the Security Council. On November 21, 1949, the General Assembly extended the life of the committee by 45 votes to 5 with 4 abstentions.[7]

2. VOTING PROCEDURE IN THE SECURITY COUNCIL

[See *Documents, VIII, 1945–46*, p. 56; *IX, 1947*, p. 319; *X, 1948*, p. 311.]

On April 13, 1949, the General Assembly began consideration of a report and recommendations on voting procedure in the Security Council, submitted by its Ad Hoc Political Committee on December 10, 1948.[8] After several days of discussion in plenary session, during which the draft resolution was vigorously condemned by the eastern European states, the resolution was passed by the Assembly by a vote of 43 to 6 with 2 abstentions.[9] A Soviet resolution calling upon members of the United Nations to widen international cooperation on all levels and expressing confidence that the permanent members of the Security Council would when necessary consult prior to important decisions, a resolution which had previously been rejected by the Ad Hoc Committee, was reintroduced in the plenary session of the Assembly and was defeated by 40 votes to 6 with 5 abstentions.[10]

On October 18, 1949 the President of the Security Council (Austin) announced that, in accordance with the General Assembly resolution, the five permanent members of the Council had met to discuss possible decisions which might be exempted from application of the veto and to arrange for consultation before taking important decisions. Mr. Austin stated that since the Soviet Union had not changed its original position, no agreement was currently possible on the use of the veto but that consultation would continue.[11]

(1) *Statement by the United States Representative to the United Nations (Austin) on Voting Procedure in the Security Council, Made before the General Assembly, April 13, 1949.*[12]

[EXCERPTS]

. . . .

The exercise of the veto power on a number of occasions has seriously undermined the confidence of member states in the ability of the Security Council to maintain international peace and security. The chronic disagreement and deadlock in the United Nations is a matter of deepest concern to all those who wish to see this Organization function as it was intended: as an effective instrument to safeguard our common interests in peace and security. The use of the veto and the threat of its use are symptoms of the prevailing disagreement.

. . . .

The practice of the veto is the very reverse of the unanimity principle in the Security Council. Instead of leading to agreement, it aggravates differ-

7 *Ibid., Official Records* (4th session), p. 312.
8 For the text of the report of the Ad Hoc Political Committee and the resolution proposed by it, see *Documents, X, 1948*, p. 313.
9 United Nations General Assembly, *Official Records* (3d session, 2d part), p. 129.
10 *Ibid.*, p. 139.
11 United Nations Security Council, *Official Records* (4th year), No. 48, p. 1.
12 United Nations General Assembly, Document A/P.V.192, April 13, 1949.

ences. It provokes ill-will and undermines friendly relations among states upon which the peace of the world depends. We must reject the idea that if unanimity fails the will of one, however arbitrary, prevails over the will of many, however reasonable. The unanimity principle cannot work where agreement is offered only on condition that the will of the most intransigent member must prevail.

To insist on the exercise of the veto regardless of its effects on the organized international community and to reject any efforts to regulate its application under the Charter, in the light of experience, is to stand in the way of effective progress by the United Nations.

. . . .

In our view the proposals now before us are most moderate. They are designed to be within the limits of what is practicable under prevailing world conditions. We firmly believe that if the members of the United Nations would co-operate in carrying out the programme presented in these proposals we would quickly see substantial improvement in the effectiveness of the Security Council's operations. You will recall that efforts by the Assembly along similar lines in 1946 have resulted in a substantial improvement. I refer to the suggestions made by several members of the Assembly during the debates that abstention of a permanent member of the Security Council should not be considered a veto. That practice was adopted by common consent in the Security Council and has now become a well-accepted Security Council procedure. I believe all of you will agree that the adoption of this practice has substantially added to the effectiveness of the Security Council. For instance, a number of important decisions of the Council during the past two years has been approved with one or more of the permanent members abstaining. At least one Security Council decision under Chapter VII and one decision recommending a State for membership has been approved with a permanent member abstaining.

. . . .

Neither the first nor the second recommendation in the proposed resolution before us violates the spirit of the statement of the four sponsoring Powers at San Francisco. During the debate there upon the voting formula, a questionnaire was addressed to the sponsoring Powers by the smaller Powers. The sponsoring Powers thereupon undertook to make a joint interpretation of the voting formula insofar as such an interpretation of a basic constitutional provision could appropriately be made in advance of its adoption, and in the absence of any practical experience as to the operation of the Organization or of the Security Council. This statement — this Four Power Statement — is not a treaty, nor was it intended to be any part of the treaty which is the Charter of the United Nations. By its own words it is characterized as a "statement of their general attitude toward the whole question of unanimity of permanent members in the decisions of the Security Council." It was connected with the act of agreement upon the Charter and is therefore entitled to great weight in that connexion. It is nevertheless inferior to the Charter and must be subservient to its principles and purposes. Certainly its natural meaning should not be extended by wilful obstruction.

The Four Power Statement contained an expression of hope that there would not arise matters of great importance upon which a decision would have to be made as to whether a procedural vote would apply. Experience since San Francisco has shown that this optimistic expectation has not been realized, and the first recommendation is based on a recognition of this fact. This recommendation should be of assistance to the Security Council in determining whether or not a question is procedural. The Four Power Statement made it clear that the enumeration of procedural questions which it contained was not exclusive. Furthermore, it in no way foreclosed advance agreement as to what questions should be considered procedural. It did not say that a question should be considered nonprocedural simply because one of the permanent members so regards it. The Four Power Statement cannot enjoy a position of supremacy over the Charter.

The Four Power Statement contained another explicit assumption, which has proved contrary to fact, namely, that the permanent members would not use their privileged vote — and I quote this phrase — "wilfully to obstruct the operation of the Council."

The powers participating in the statement thus recognized that self-restraint upon the part of the permanent members was necessary and to be expected if the Security Council was to function as intended. If this be true, it would seem quite proper for the Assembly, in light of experience, to recommend to the permanent members that, if they are unable after genuine effort to achieve unanimity among themselves on certain decisions not immediately concerning their vital interests, they should agree among themselves not to exercise the veto in those decisions. Such agreement among the permanent members is the objective of the second recommendation.

For the reasons I have stated, the Four Power Statement, in the view of my Government, constitutes no barrier to such agreement. The parties to that Statement are free to explore, as this resolution attempts to do, how better voting procedures can be put into operation.

The third recommendation of the draft resolution suggests to the permanent members a "code of conduct" which they should observe in connection with their privileged vote. They are to consult together wherever feasible and to exercise their veto only when they consider a question of vital importance, taking into account the interests of the United Nations as a whole, and to state upon what ground they consider this condition to be present.

All permanent members are on record as favouring consultations. We believe that these consultations should take place whenever there is a possibility of obtaining results. These consultations should take place not only with reference to specific matters before the Council; above all, the method of consultation should be applied as one of the means of implementing the recommendations contained in the draft resolution.

.   .   .   .

3. ADMISSION OF NEW MEMBERS

[See *Documents, VIII, 1945–1946*, p. 524; *IX, 1947*, p. 314; *X, 1948*, p. 318.]

Israel was the one nation admitted to membership in the United Nations during 1949. The Israeli application, which had been submitted and rejected the previous year,[13] was reconsidered by the Security Council on March 4, 1949. The Council, after noting the improved situation in Palestine, decided by a vote of 9 to 1 (Egypt) with 1 abstention (United Kingdom) to recommend Israeli admission to the United Nations.[14] The United States supported Israel's application both in the Council and at the second part of the third session of the General Assembly, where the question was vigorously debated in both the Ad Hoc Political Committee and in plenary session. Israeli admission was at length approved by the Assembly on May 11 by a vote of 37 to 12 with 9 abstentions.[15]

Applications from the Republic of Korea, the People's Democratic Republic of Korea, and Nepal were also considered by the Council during 1949. The application of the Republic of Korea, strongly supported by the United States, was attacked by the Soviet Union as having been submitted by a "puppet" government; and a Chinese resolution recommending Korean admission failed of passage on April 8, 1949, when it received 9 affirmative and 2 negative votes (the Soviet Union and the Ukraine.)[16] The application of Nepal failed of passage by the same vote on September 7.[17] No action was taken on the application of the People's Democratic Republic of Korea since the Council refused to place the matter on its agenda.[18]

The Council on June 16, 1949, began an extensive discussion of the applications for membership which it had so far turned down and its procedure regarding admissions. The Argentine representative (Arce) contended that, since the Security Council made only a "recommendation" as to admission, final decision rested with the General Assembly which might admit states to membership even if their applications had not received a favorable vote in the Council.[19] In the involved legal and procedural debate which followed, the United States representative (Austin) stated that while the United States would not permit its vote to prevent the admission of any state which received seven affirmative votes, it could not support the applications of Albania, Bulgaria, Hungary, Rumania and Mongolia, but would continue to favor other current applications.[20] On September 13 the Council voted on seven proposed Argentinian resolutions urging the admission of Portugal, Transjordan, Italy, Finland, Austria, Ireland, and Ceylon; each resolution received a vote of 9 to 2 and failed of passage through the negative vote of the Soviet Union.[21] Subsequently a Soviet proposal to admit thirteen states to membership (all those currently applying except the Republic of Korea) was rejected by a vote of 2 to 4 with 4 abstentions. The United States abstained on the vote.[22]

At the fourth session of the General Assembly, the United States urged reconsideration of those applicants for admission which fulfilled the conditions laid down in Article 4 of the Charter in accordance with the advisory opinion of the International Court of Justice.[23] The Assembly at length approved 1) nine proposals submitted by Australia calling for reconsideration by the Security Council of the applications of Austria, Ceylon, Finland, Ireland, Italy, Jordan, Republic of Korea, Portugal, and Nepal; 2) an Argentine suggestion requesting an advisory opinion from the International Court of Justice on the Assembly's competence to admit members; and 3) an Iraqi resolution requesting the permanent members to refrain from the use of the veto in connection with membership questions, and asking reconsideration of all pending applications.[24] A Soviet proposal to admit all current applicants except the Republic of Korea was again rejected by 32 votes to 12 with 13 abstentions.[25]

---

13 See *Documents, X, 1948*, p. 319.
14 United Nations Security Council, *Official Records* (4th year), No. 17, p. 14.
15 United Nations General Assembly, *Official Records* (3d session, 2d part), p. 331.
16 United Nations Security Council, *Official Records* (4th year), No. 26, p. 15.
17 *Ibid.*, No. 39, p. 16.   18 *Ibid.*, No. 13, p. 15.
19 *Ibid.*, No. 30, p. 10.   20 *Ibid.*
21 *Ibid.*, No. 41, p. 28.   22 *Ibid.*, No. 42, p. 40.
23 For the text of the advisory opinion, see *Documents, X, 1948*, p. 319.
24 United Nations General Assembly, *Official Records* (4th session), p. 329.
25 *Ibid.*

(1) *Statement by the United States Representative to the United Nations General Assembly (Cooper) on the Admission of Members, Made before the Assembly, November 22, 1949.*[26]

[EXCERPTS]

. . . .

The United States views the United Nations as a universal organization, which should ultimately embrace all states in the world. The President of the United States voiced that hope in his recent speech before the General Assembly. Yet we cannot escape the simple truth that the concept of absolute universality is not applicable. Each Member is obligated to determine, as prerequisites to admission, that each applicant possesses the qualifications set forth in Article 4 of the Charter; that it is a state, that it is peace-loving, that it accepts and is able and willing to carry out the obligations contained in the Charter. These standards should be applied fairly, equitably and tolerantly. But to admit an applicant which does not meet those standards is not in accordance with the Charter. There is no authority granted to a member to impose requirements extraneous to the Charter.

There is no authority, and certainly no moral right, to condition the admission of one applicant upon the acceptance of another applicant. I think all of us are familiar with the advisory opinion of the International Court of Justice, rendered on 28 May 1948, and there is no need to discuss that advisory opinion in detail. The United States adheres to those principles. It is difficult to believe that they are misunderstood by any Member who is genuinely interested in the admission of qualified nations. Yet, in a constant attempt to divert the attention of this body, the applicant states and public opinion, the Soviet Union alleges in monotonous refrain that other Members, and particularly the United States, are practising a discrimination against Albania, Hungary, Bulgaria, Romania and the Mongolian People's Republic, because of their different governmental structure and philosophy. They say that it is this alleged discrimination which is blocking the admission of all applicants for membership.

The delegation of the United States does not intend to engage in a useless debate of denunciation and recrimination, which can serve no useful purpose. Studiously dramatic and sensational as this device may be, it will not bring reason to bear in this discussion. The delegation of the United States prefers to emphasize principles and constructive methods upon which agreement must ultimately be founded if this issue is to be solved.

Nevertheless, [we] will not avoid discussing the state of facts which brings this question before us. We will not fail to point out and lay bare to the General Assembly, and to the states which seek admission, the facts which demonstrate wherein the discrimination lies, and by whom it is being practised. The history of this question shows this clearly. Albania, Hungary, Bulgaria, Romania and the Mongolian People's Republic have submitted themselves to the tests prescribed by Article 4 of the Charter. None has ever been able to secure as many as seven favourable votes in the Security Council.

26 *Ibid.,* Document A/P.V.252, November 22, 1949.

When, in 1947 and 1948, the question was reviewed by the General Assembly, it made favourable recommendations to the Security Council with respect to other applicants, but it did not recommend that the five to which I have referred should be admitted. These repeated findings by the Security Council and the General Assembly do not represent a policy of discrimination against these states. No Member is really deceived or misled concerning the reasons which have prevented their admission thus far. The Soviet Union knows these reasons.

The reasons have been given, and have been spread on the records of this General Assembly. These records make apparent the belief of most Members that, for several concrete reasons, these five applicants have not thus far met the Charter qualifications. The General Assembly, in a resolution adopted only last week, declared that the active assistance given to the Greek guerrillas by Albania in particular, by Bulgaria and by certain other states, including Romania, in disregard of the General Assembly's recommendations, is contrary to the purposes and principles of the United Nations Charter and endangers peace in the Balkans. Just a few weeks ago, the General Assembly decided to request from the International Court of Justice an advisory opinion, which was made necessary by the refusal of Hungary, Romania and Bulgaria to co-operate in efforts toward the peaceful settlement of charges to the effect that these three countries are committing serious violations of their Peace Treaties.

The conduct of these three States — from which the General Assembly discussions arose and arise today — leaves substantially a reasonable doubt of their attitude towards international obligations.

.   .   .   .

The United States holds that its position and the positions taken by other members in the Security Council or in the General Assembly are not discriminatory when they are based objectively upon the terms and requirements of Article 4 of the Charter. The discrimination is being exercised by those who would disregard Article 4 of the Charter by imposing new obstacles to the admission of states now entitled to membership.

The United States submits that the position of the Soviet Union is based neither upon a concept of universality, to which it has made appeal in this debate and which holds the sympathetic interest of some members, nor upon the principle of qualification for membership prescribed by the Charter. The resolution which the Soviet Union offers bears the superficial appearance of supporting universality. But, if that were actually so, the proponent of the resolution would support any applicant, individually as well as in a group, without respect to qualifications. This it refuses to do.

Neither does the Soviet Union support the principle of qualification for membership. Its representatives have stated that it holds serious objections to the qualifications of certain states and considers them unworthy to be members. Without arguing the merit of its objections, it is a decision which it can rightfully make. Yet, by this resolution, it proposes that it is willing to abandon objections which it has contended are serious and sincere, and is now willing to admit states which in its present view are unworthy to be included among the members of the United Nations.

This cannot be called a compromise of reasonable viewpoints. The real purpose of the proposal is to demand that the majority of this body accept as members states which they sincerely believe are not now eligible for membership, their admission to be the price of a relaxation of the Soviet Union veto of other candidates.

. . . .

It has been stated that the present impasse is merely a deadlock of the contending interests of two groups of members. Such a suggestion carries with it a connotation of arbitrary action by both groups which does not take into account the interests of other members of the United Nations and of the Organization itself. The United States rejects this point of view. It is not the true approach to the problem; it simply states a result. It is an easy way to avoid fixing responsibility and to avoid finding the causes which must be understood if, as the United States greatly desires, this question is to be favourably settled. Those members who uphold Article 4 of the Charter and who refuse to admit applicants until they have qualified themselves, and particularly the applicants found by the General Assembly to be acting now against the Charter, are not contributing to a deadlock. They are contributing to the best interests of the United Nations.

. . . .

(2) Resolutions on the Admission of Members to the United Nations, Approved by the United Nations General Assembly, November 22, 1949.[27]

J

The General Assembly,

Keeping in mind the discussion concerning the admission of new Members in the *Ad Hoc* Political Committee at its fourth regular session,

Requests the International Court of Justice to give an advisory opinion on the following question:

"Can the admission of a State to membership in the United Nations, pursuant to Article 4, paragraph 2, of the Charter, be effected by a decision of the General Assembly when the Security Council has made no recommendation for admission by reason of the candidate failing to obtain the requisite majority or of the negative vote of a permanent member upon a resolution so to recommend?"

27 *Ibid., Official Records: Resolutions* (4th session), p. 21.

K

The General Assembly,

Considering the special report of the Security Council on the admission of new Members,

1. *Requests* the States permanent members of the Security Council to refrain from the use of the veto in connexion with the recommendation of States for membership in the United Nations;

2. *Requests* the Security Council to keep under consideration, in the light of Article 4, paragraph 1, of the Charter, the pending applications of all states which so far have not gained admission to the United Nations.

4. LEGAL COMPETENCE OF THE UNITED NATIONS

As a result of the assassination of Count Folke Bernadotte, United Nations Mediator in Palestine, the United Nations General Assembly on December 3, 1948, requested an advisory opinion from the International Court of Justice as to whether the United Nations had the capacity to bring an international claim against a government for injuries to an agent of the United Nations. On February 14, 1949, the United States submitted a written statement to the Court, which on April 11, 1949 delivered its opinion. Subsequently, in accordance with the Court's decision, the General Assembly authorized the Secretary-General to bring such international claims.[28]

(1) **Letter from the Legal Adviser of the Department of State (Tate) to the Registrar of the International Court of Justice (Hambro) Concerning the Legal Competence of the United Nations, February 14, 1949.**[29]

[EXCERPTS]

. . . . . .

Two major problems are posed in the first paragraph of the request for an Advisory Opinion: (1) has the United Nations, as an Organization, the capacity to bring an international claim against a government, *de jure* or *de facto;* and, (2) has the United Nations the capacity to seek reparation for damage caused (*a*) to the United Nations, (*b*) to the victim or to the persons entitled through him? It is on these aspects of the request for an Advisory Opinion that this Government desires to address itself.

(1) Has the United Nations, as an Organization, the capacity to bring an international claim against a government, *de jure* or *de facto?*

In the traditional sense an "international claim" is a claim by the government of one State against that of another seeking reparation for damage either to the interests of the claimant State or to that of a private citizen or a legal entity whose interest the claimant State is entitled to espouse and to represent: whether the emergence of public international organizations of sovereign States requires a re-definition of the concept of "international claim" to include claims by the United Nations and similar international organizations is a question which need not be decided at this time and as to which the United States reserves its views for the purposes of the question

28 *Ibid.*, p. 64.
29 International Court of Justice, *Pleadings, Oral Arguments, Documents, 1949: Reparation for Injuries Suffered in the Service of the United Nations,* p. 19.

before the Court. It is sufficient to point out the established principle of international law any legal entity having legal capacity whether it be a State, an individual, or a public or private entity may present claims against the government of the responsible State for reparation for losses or damages suffered by them as a consequence of acts deemed violative of principles of international law. The United Nations as a public international organization having legal capacity may therefore present claims against the government of a State for reparation for losses or damages sustained by it as a result of such violations nor is there any reason why, as frequently occurs in the case of claims asserted by one State against another, the matter of the settlement of claims on behalf of the United Nations as an organization should not be the subject of direct negotiation between it and the government of the State against which the organization's claim is asserted. Of course there may exist certain local remedies in the tribunals of a respondent State which it may be necessary to exhaust to obtain reparation. Also there is no reason why if the claim is not settled the United Nations might not agree to submit the claim to arbitration under an agreement concluded by the United Nations with the government concerned.

. . . .

It is accordingly the view of this Government that the United Nations, as an Organization, has the capacity to bring a claim against a government. The United Nations, in the view of the United States, cannot "as an Organization" submit a claim to the International Court of Justice for judgment. The Court, under Article 35, is only open to "States," and the United Nations is not, under the Charter, a State, although it may possess certain attributes of a State, as for example "legal capacity" under Article 104.

(2) Has the United Nations the capacity to seek reparation for damage caused (a) to the United Nations, (b) to the victim or to the persons entitled through him?

(a) In view of the Government of the United States the United Nations could present a claim for and recover reparation for direct pecuniary loss sustained by it on account of the act of which complaint is made, responsibility otherwise obtaining.

. . . .

(b) In such a situation as envisaged under (b) of paragraph I of the question submitted to the Court, the United Nations, as an Organization, is without capacity, under ordinary circumstances, to bring an international claim against a government with a view to obtaining the reparation due in respect of the damage caused to the victim or to the persons entitled through him. The basis of an international claim is, in theory, an injury to, or loss suffered by, the State of which the claimant is a national. For that reason it would be appropriate for the government of the State of which the claimant is a national to present the claim to the government of the State causing the injury or loss, and that failing, in an appropriate case, to present it to a proper international forum.

However, Article 100 of the Charter of the United Nations contemplates that officials of the Organizations shall be "international officials responsible only to the organization." Occasionally, such individuals, or those entitled through them, may be stateless and have no government to make claims on their behalf. Under such circumstances, no reason is perceived why the United Nations should not have capacity to intervene to support the claim of the stateless individual.

II.

> In the event of an affirmative reply on point 1 (*b*), how is action by the United Nations to be reconciled with such rights as may be possessed by the State of which the victim is a national?

In view of the character of the answer properly to be given to question 1 (*b*), comment on paragraph II of the question submitted to the Court becomes unnecessary.

(2) *Advisory Opinion of the International Court of Justice Concerning Reparation for Injuries Suffered in the Service of the United Nations, April 11, 1949.*[30]

[EXCERPTS]

. . . .

On December 3rd, 1948, the General Assembly of the United Nations adopted the following Resolution:

> Whereas the series of tragic events which have lately befallen agents of the United Nations engaged in the performance of their duties raises, with greater urgency than ever, the question of the arrangements to be made by the United Nations with a view to ensuring to its agents the fullest measure of protection in the future and ensuring that reparation be made for the injuries suffered; and
>
> Whereas it is highly desirable that the Secretary-General should be able to act without question as efficaciously as possible with a view to obtaining any reparation due; therefore
>
> The General Assembly
>
> Decides to submit the following legal questions to the International Court of Justice for an advisory opinion:
>
> I. In the event of an agent of the United Nations in the performance of his duties suffering injury in circumstances involving the responsibility of a State, has the United Nations, as an Organization, the capacity to bring an international claim against the responsible *de jure* or *de facto* government with a view to obtaining the reparation due in respect of the damage caused (*a*) to the United Nations, (*b*) to the victim or to persons entitled through him?
>
> II. In the event of an affirmative reply on point I (*b*), how is action by the United Nations to be reconciled with such rights as may be possessed by the State of which the victim is a national?
>
> Instructs the Secretary-General, after the Court has given its opinion, to prepare proposals in the light of that opinion, and to submit them to the General Assembly at its next regular session.

. . . .

30 International Court of Justice, *Reparation for Injuries Suffered in the Service of the United Nations: Advisory Opinion of April 11, 1949.*

The questions asked of the Court relate to the "capacity to bring an international claim"; accordingly, we must begin by defining what is meant by that capacity, and consider the characteristics of the Organization, so as to determine whether, in general, these characteristics do, or do not, include for the Organization a right to present an international claim.

Competence to bring an international claim is, for those possessing it, the capacity to resort to the customary methods recognized by international law for the establishment, the presentation and the settlement of claims. Among these methods may be mentioned protest, request for an enquiry, negotiation, and request for submission to an arbitral tribunal or to the Court in so far as this may be authorized by the Statute.

This capacity certainly belongs to the State; a State can bring an international claim against another State. Such a claim takes the form of a claim between two political entities, equal in law, similar in form, and both the direct subjects of international law. It is dealt with by means of negotiation, and cannot, in the present state of the law as to international jurisdiction, be submitted to a tribunal, except with the consent of the States concerned.

When the Organization brings a claim against one of its Members, this claim will be presented in the same manner, and regulated by the same procedure. It may, when necessary, be supported by the political means at the disposal of the Organization. In these ways the Organization would find a method for securing the observance of its rights by the Member against which it has a claim.

But, in the international sphere, has the Organization such a nature as involves the capacity to bring an international claim? In order to answer this question, the Court must first enquire whether the Charter has given the Organization such a position that it possesses, in regard to its Members, rights which it is entitled to ask them to respect. In other words, does the Organization possess international personality? This is no doubt a doctrinal expression, which has sometimes given rise to controversy. But it will be used here to mean that if the Organization is recognized as having that personality, it is an entity capable of availing itself of obligations incumbent upon its Members.

To answer this question, which is not settled by the actual terms of the Charter, we must consider what characteristics it was intended thereby to give the Organization.

The subjects of law in any legal system are not necessarily identical in their nature or in the extent of their rights, and their nature depends upon the needs of the community. Throughout its history, the development of international law has been influenced by the requirements of international life, and the progressive increase in the collective activities of States has already given rise to instances of action upon the international plane by certain entities which are not States. This development culminated in the establishment in June 1945 of an international organization whose purposes and principles are specified in the Charter of the United Nations. But to achieve these ends the attribution of international personality is indispensable.

The Charter has not been content to make the Organization created by it merely a centre "for harmonizing the actions of nations in the attainment of these common ends" (Article I, para. 4). It has equipped that centre with organs, and has given it special tasks. It has defined the position of the Members in relation to the Organization by requiring them to give it every assistance in any action undertaken by it (Article 2, para. 5), and to accept and carry out the decisions of the Security Council; by authorizing the General Assembly to make recommendations to the Members; by giving the Organization legal capacity and privileges and immunities in the territory of each of its Members; and by providing for the conclusion of agreements between the Organization and its Members. Practice — in particular the conclusion of conventions to which the Organization is a party — has confirmed this character of the Organization, which occupies a position in certain respects in detachment from its Members, and which is under a duty to remind them, if need be, of certain obligations. It must be added that the Organization is a political body, charged with political tasks of an important character, and covering a wide field namely, the maintenance of international peace and security, the development of friendly relations among nations, and the achievement of international co-operation in the solution of problems of an economic, social, cultural or humanitarian character (Article I); and in dealing with its Members it employs political means. The "Convention on the Privileges and Immunities of the United Nations" of 1946 create rights and duties between each of the signatories and the Organization (see, in particular, Section 35). It is difficult to see how such a convention could operate except upon the international plane and as between parties possessing international personality.

In the opinion of the Court, the Organization was intended to exercise and enjoy, and is in fact exercising and enjoying, functions and rights which can only be explained on the basis of the possession of a large measure of international personality and the capacity to operate upon an international plane. It is at present the supreme type of international organization, and it could not carry out the intentions of its founders if it was devoid of international personality. It must be acknowledged that its Members, by entrusting certain functions to it, with the attendant duties and responsibilities, have clothed it with the competence required to enable those functions to be effectively discharged.

Accordingly, the Court has come to the conclusion that the Organization is an international person. That is not the same thing as saying that it is a State, which it certainly is not, or that its legal personality and rights and duties are the same as those of a State. Still less is it the same thing as saying that it is "a super-State", whatever that expression may mean. It does not even imply that all its rights and duties must be upon the international plane, any more than all the rights and duties of a State must be upon that plane. What it does mean is that it is a subject of international law and capable of possessing international rights and duties, and that it has capacity to maintain its rights by bringing international claims.

The next question is whether the sum of the international rights of the Organization comprises the right to bring the kind of international claim described in the Request for this Opinion. That is a claim against a State to obtain reparation in respect of the damage caused by the injury of an agent of the Organization in the course of the performance of his duties. Whereas a State possesses the totality of international rights and duties recognized by international law, the rights and duties of an entity such as the Organization must depend upon its purposes and functions as specified or implied in its constituent documents and developed in practice. The functions of the Organization are of such a character that they could not be effectively discharged if they involved the concurrent action, on the international plane, of fifty-eight or more Foreign Offices, and the Court concludes that the Members have endowed the Organization with capacity to bring international claims when necessitated by the discharge of its functions.

What is the position as regards the claims mentioned in the request for an opinion? Question I is divided into two points, which must be considered in turn.

Question I (*a*) is as follows:

> In the event of an agent of the United Nations in the performance of his duties suffering injury in circumstances involving the responsibility of a State, has the United Nations, as an Organization, the capacity to bring an international claim against the responsible *de jure* or *de facto* government with a view to obtaining the reparation due in respect of the damage caused (*a*) to the United Nations . . . ?

The question is concerned solely with the reparation of damage caused to the Organization when one of its agents suffers injury at the same time. It cannot be doubted that the Organization has the capacity to bring an international claim against one of its Members which has caused injury to it by a breach of its international obligations towards it. The damage specified in Question I (*a*) means exclusively damage caused to the interests of the Organization itself, to its administrative machine, to its property and assets, and to the interests of which it is the guardian. It is clear that the Organization has the capacity to bring a claim for this damage. As the claim is based on the breach of an international obligation on the part of the Member held responsible by the Organization, the Member cannot contend that this obligation is governed by municipal law, and the Organization is justified in giving its claim the character of an international claim.

When the Organization has sustained damage resulting from a breach by a Member of its international obligations, it is impossible to see how it can obtain reparation unless it possesses capacity to bring an international claim. It cannot be supposed that in such an event all the Members of the Organization, save the defendant State, must combine to bring a claim against the defendant for the damage suffered by the Organization.

The Court is not called upon to determine the precise extent of the reparation which the Organization would be entitled to recover. It may, however, be said that the measure of the reparation should depend upon the amount of the damage which the Organization has suffered as the result of the wrongful act or omission of the defendant State and should be calculated in accordance with the rules of international law. Amongst other things, this damage would include the reimbursement of any reasonable compensation which the Organization had to pay to its agent or to persons entitled through him. Again, the death or disablement of one of its agents engaged upon a distant mission might involve very considerable expenditure in replacing him. These are mere illustrations, and the Court cannot pretend to forecast all the kinds of damage which the Organization itself might sustain.

Question I (*b*) is as follows:

> . . . has the United Nations, as an Organization, the capacity to bring an international claim . . . in respect of the damage caused . . . (*b*) to the victim or to persons entitled through him?

In dealing with the question of law which arises out of Question I (*b*), it is unnecessary to repeat the considerations which led to an affirmative answer being given to Question I (*a*). It can now be assumed that the Organization has the capacity to bring a claim on the international plane, to negotiate, to conclude a special agreement and to prosecute a claim before an international tribunal. The only legal question which remains to be considered is whether, in the course of bringing an international claim of this kind, the Organization can recover "the reparation due in respect of the damage caused . . . to the victim . . . .".

. . . .

The Charter does not expressly confer upon the Organization the capacity to include, in its claim for reparation, damage caused to the victim or to persons entitled through him. The Court must therefore begin by enquiring whether the provisions of the Charter concerning the functions of the Organization, and the part played by its agents in the performance of those functions, imply for the Organization power to afford its agents the limited protection that would consist in the bringing of a claim on their behalf for reparation for damage suffered in such circumstances. Under international law, the Organization must be deemed to have those powers which, though not expressly provided in the Charter, are conferred upon it by necessary implication as being essential to the performance of its duties. This principle of law was applied by the Permanent Court of International Justice to the International Labour Organization in its Advisory Opinion No. 13 of July 23rd, 1926 (Series B., No. 13, p. 18), and must be applied to the United Nations.

· · · · · · ·

Upon examination of the character of the functions entrusted to the Organization and of the nature of the missions of its agents, it becomes clear that the capacity of the Organization to exercise a measure of functional protection of its agents arises by necessary intendment out of the Charter.

The obligations entered into by States to enable the agents of the Organization to perform their duties are undertaken not in the interest of the agents, but in that of the Organization. When it claims redress for a breach of these obligations, the Organization is invoking its own right, the right that the obligations due to it should be respected. On this ground, it asks for reparation of the injury suffered, for "it is a principle of international law that the breach of an engagement involves an obligation to make reparation in an adequate form"; as was stated by the Permanent Court in its Judgment No. 8 of July 26th, 1927 (Series A., No. 9, p. 21). In claiming reparation based on the injury suffered by its agent, the Organization does not represent the agent, but is asserting its own right, the right to secure respect for undertakings entered into towards the Organization.

Having regard to the foregoing considerations, and to the undeniable right of the Organization to demand that its Members shall fulfill the obligations entered into by them in the interest of the good working of the Organization, the Court is of the opinion that, in the case of a breach of these obligations, the Organization has the capacity to claim adequate reparation, and that in assessing this reparation it is authorized to include the damage suffered by the victim or by persons entitled through him.

· · · · · · ·

Accordingly, the Court arrives at the conclusion that an affirmative answer should be given to Question I (a) and (b) whether or not the defendant State is a Member of the United Nations.

Question II is as follows:

> In the event of an affirmative reply on point I (b), how is action by the United Nations to be reconciled with such rights as may be possessed by the State of which the victim is a national?

The affirmative reply given by the Court on point I (b) obliges it now to examine Question II. When the victim has a nationality, cases can clearly occur in which the injury suffered by him may engage the interest both of his national State and of the Organization. In such an event, competition between the State's right of diplomatic protection and the Organization's right of functional protection might arise, and this is the only case with which the Court is invited to deal.

In such a case, there is no rule of law which assigns priority to the one or to the other, or which compels either the State or the Organization to refrain from bringing an international claim. The Court sees no reason why the parties concerned should not find solutions inspired by goodwill and common sense, and as between the Organization and its Members it draws attention to their duty to render "every assistance" provided by Article 2, paragraph 5, of the Charter.

Although the bases of the two claims are different, that does not mean that the defendant State can be compelled to pay the reparation due in respect of the damage twice over. International tribunals are already familiar with the problem of a claim in which two or more national States are interested, and they know how to protect the defendant State in such a case.

The risk of competition between the Organization and the national State can be reduced or eliminated either by a general convention or by agreements entered into in each particular case. There is no doubt that in due course a practice will be developed, and it is worthy of note that already certain States whose nationals have been injured in the performance of missions undertaken for the Organization have shown a reasonable and co-operative disposition to find a practical solution.

The question of reconciling action by the Organization with the rights of a national State may arise in another way; that is to say, when the agent bears the nationality of the defendant State.

The ordinary practice whereby a State does not exercise protection on behalf of one of its nationals against a State which regards him as its own national, does not constitute a precedent which is relevant here. The action of the Organization is in fact based not upon the nationality of the victim but upon his status as agent of the Organization. Therefore it does not matter whether or not the State to which the claim is addressed regards him as its own national, because the question of nationality is not pertinent to the admissibility of the claim.

In law, therefore, it does not seem that the fact of the possession of the nationality of the defendant State by the agent constitutes any obstacle to a claim brought by the Organization for a breach of obligations towards it occurring in relation to the performance of his mission by that agent.

FOR THESE REASONS,
The Court is of opinion
On Question I (a):

(i) unanimously,
That, in the event of an agent of the United Nations in the performance of his duties suffering injury in circumstances involving the responsibility of a Member State, the United Nations as an Organization has the capacity to bring an international claim against the responsible *de jure* or *de facto* government with a view to obtaining the reparation due in respect of the damage caused to the United Nations.

(ii) unanimously,
That, in the event of an agent of the United Nations in the performance of his duties suffering injury in circumstances involving the responsibility of a State which is not a member, the United Nations as an Organization has the capacity to bring an international claim against the responsible *de jure* or

de facto government with a view to obtaining the reparation due in respect of the damage caused to the United Nations.

On Question I (b):

(i) by eleven votes against four,

That, in the event of an agent of the United Nations in the performance of his duties suffering injury in circumstances involving the responsibility of a Member State, the United Nations as an Organization has the capacity to bring an international claim against the responsible *de jure* or *de facto* government with a view to obtaining the reparation due in respect of the damage caused to the victim or to persons entitled through him.

(ii) by eleven votes against four,

That, in the event of an agent of the United Nations in the performance of his duties suffering injury in circumstances involving the responsibility of a State which is not a member, the United Nations as an Organization has the capacity to bring an international claim against the responsible *de jure* or *de facto* government with a view to obtaining the reparation due in respect of the damage caused to the victim or to persons entitled through him.

On Question II:

By ten votes against five,

When the United Nations as an Organization is bringing a claim for reparation of damage caused to its agent, it can only do so by basing its claim upon a breach of obligations due to itself; respect for this rule will usually prevent a conflict between the action of the United Nations and such rights as the agent's national State may possess, and thus bring about a reconciliation between their claims; moreover, this reconciliation must depend upon considerations applicable to each particular case, and upon agreements to be made between the Organization and individual States, either generally or in each case.

.   .   .   .

5. UNITED NATIONS FIELD SERVICE

A proposal by the Secretary-General of the United Nations (Lie) for the creation of a United Nations Guard was referred by the General Assembly on April 29, 1949, to a fourteen-member special committee on which the United States was represented. The committee met at Lake Success on June 24, 1949, and approved a revised proposal recommending creation of a Field Service to provide technical services and ensure the security of United Nations field missions and the establishment of a Panel of Field Observers, a reserve which might be called upon in connection with truce enforcement, plebiscites, etc.[31] The plan was generally supported by the United States and the United Kingdom, while opposed by Czechoslovakia, Poland and the Soviet Union as establishing an international military force outside the provisions of Article 43 of the Charter and as infringing upon the prerogatives of the Security Council. The creation of the two units was approved by the General Assembly on November 22, 1949, the Field Service by 46 votes to 5 with 3 abstentions and the Panel of Field Observers by 38 votes to 6 with 11 abstentions.[32]

31 United Nations General Assembly, Document A/959, August 24, 1949.
32 *Ibid., Official Records* (4th session), p. 334.

(1) ***Revised Plan for the Establishment of a United Nations Field Service and Field Reserve Panel, Submitted by the Secretary-General (Lie), June 24, 1949.***[33]

United Nations Field Service

Composition and recruitment — The Field Service would be a part of the Secretariat, but would be recruited by secondment from national Governments. It would consist of a maximum of 300 men. Personnel would, as far as possible, be physically fit men between the ages of 22 and 30, with field experience and the necessary technical background. The term of service would be from one to three years, except for a small number of supervisory personnel who would be regular Secretariat members. The Field Service would be stationed at Headquarters for training.

Compensation — The United Nations would provide a daily subsistence allowance, uniforms and equipment. The governments from which individual members of the Service would be seconded would be reimbursed for the amount of the salary of the individual, family allowances, contributions to pension schemes and other emoluments to which the individual is entitled in his own national service.

Functions — The Field Service would provide the following services:

(a) Provision of land transport for missions and such incidental air transport as may be required.

(b) Maintenance of radio communications for missions.

(c) Security of United Nations premises and members of missions.

(d) Safe custody of supplies, records and archives.

(e) Maintenance of order during meetings, hearings and investigations.

(f) Guard duties at Headquarters.

The Field Service would not have any functions of observation of truce terms, of protecting places neutralized during a truce or supply lines incidental to a truce, or of supervising polling places during a plebiscite.

Equipment — The members of the Field Service would wear a United Nations uniform. They would not regularly be supplied with arms of any kind. In isolated instances, where required by the mission and when permitted by the law or authority of the locality, individual members assigned to protecting the security of persons or property would be authorized to carry side-arms. No machine-guns, rifles or any heavier weapons would be used. The Field Service would operate mobile radio equipment and motor vehicles for the transport of personnel. No estimate is made here for the purchase and maintenance of such equipment, since it is believed that it should properly be a charge on the budgets of individual missions.

Field Reserve Panel

It will be noted that the proposed Field Service would not have any func-

---

[33] *Ibid.*, Document A/959, August 24, 1949, p. 14.

tions of observation or protection of truce objectives, nor of supervision of polling in a plebiscite.[34]

Such functions were originally contemplated for the United Nations Guard. In the *Ad Hoc* Political Committee various objections were made to these functions.

During the discussion, several members of the *Ad Hoc* Political Committee suggested consideration of a panel, which might overcome certain of these objections. The Secretary-General has adopted this suggestion and now proposes the establishment of a Field Reserve Panel.

The Panel would consist of the names of men in the national service of Governments and recommended by these Governments. The Bureau of Personnel of the Secretariat would receive these recommendations and would select those who were qualified in accordance with standards of age, physical fitness and experience. A list would then be established, in accordance with the general principles of geographical distribution followed by the Secretariat, and kept current. The members of the Panel would not be called for training and would receive no compensation unless and until called upon for services as hereinafter described.

Functions of the Panel — The purpose of the Panel would be to furnish a reserve of qualified individuals for service as observers, for the guarding of truce objectives and the supervision of polling places. The members of the Panel would be called for service only in response to a specific decision by the General Assembly or Security Council, or an organ authorized by them, requiring such services to be performed and requesting the Secretary-General to make the necessary arrangements. The competent organ could lay down the precise functions to be performed in the particular case, the numbers of men to be utilized and any other necessary conditions, such as the provision of protective weapons, relations with the local authority, wearing of uniforms, etc.

When called into service, the Panel members would receive a daily subsistence allowance, and their Governments would be reimbursed for salaries and family allowances. The expenditures for these purposes would be borne by the budget of the individual missions concerned. The only cost for the establishment of the Panel at this stage would be the incidental expenditure for correspondence and the time spent in scrutinizing applications and maintaining the files.

Size of the Panel — It is not contemplated that members of the Panel would be under any obligation to serve if called upon. Membership in the Panel merely establishes eligibility for service. It is to be assumed that when the necessity for use arises, many of the persons in the Panel would not be available for service. The size of the Panel would therefore have to be fairly large in order to provide a sufficient reservoir. Since the establishment of the

---

34 The members of the Field Service would, of course, be available to render, to any United Nations mission which is authorized to conduct observation or supervise a plebiscite, the services of communication, transportation, security, etc, outlined in the previous section.

Panel involves only incidental expenses, the size of the list may indeed be left indefinite. If the Committee desires to establish a limit, the Secretary-General recommends that he be authorized to list up to 2,000 names in the Panel.

Salient characteristics of the revised proposal

The proposed Field Service is designed to render precisely the same services as are now rendered in a less systematic way by members of the Secretariat. The legal basis for its creation is precisely the same as for any other Secretariat unit, namely, Articles 97, 98, 100 and 101 of the Charter of the United Nations. The legal objections made to the former Guard proposal would therefore not seem to be relevant for the Field Service proposal.

The proposed Field Reserve Panel has assigned to it certain of the functions to which legal objections were made when they were assigned to the proposed Guard. It is to be noted that, in the revised proposal, the members of the Panel would be called upon to perform these functions only in response to a specific decision of a United Nations organ, and the question of legality could be considered by the competent organ at the time the particular decision is made. There can be no doubt that the functions of observation of truce terms and supervision of plebiscites are generally within the authority of the United Nations under the Charter.

Need for the proposed units — The need for the proposed Field Service has already been set forth in the Secretary-General's report to the third regular session of the General Assembly (A/656) and in his remarks at the 200th plenary meeting, on 29 April 1949.

The proposed Field Reserve Panel will enable the organs of the United Nations to have ready to hand the names of qualified personnel from all Member States to fulfil tasks of observation and supervision when desired. Heretofore, the organs have had to rely on emergency recruitment, which has not always been satisfactory as regards individual qualifications, and has been particularly unsatisfactory from the standpoint of equitable geographical participation by Member States in these important tasks of the United Nations.

Cost — The estimated cost of the proposed Field Service is $1,088,500 for the first year (detailed estimates annexed). The cost would be less for succeeding years. This compares with an estimated preliminary estimate of $4,000,000 for the former Guard proposal.

C. United States Participation in the United Nations

A series of amendments to the United Nations Participation Act of 1945[35] became law on October 10, 1949, with the approval by President Truman of Public Law 341. The act, designed principally to add greater flexibility to United States representation in the Security Council and to clarify the President's authority to detail military personnel and equipment for the use of the United Nations was

35 For text of the United Nations Participation Act of 1945, see *Documents, VIII, 1945–1946*, p. 511.

similar to legislation passed by the Senate in the 80th Congress and favorably reported by the House Committee on Foreign Affairs; no action had been taken by the House at that time. The act in the 81st Congress was passed by the House on July 18 and by the Senate on October 6, 1949.

Other administrative and budgetary questions affecting the United States during 1949 centered around the United Nations budget and scale of contributions. On December 9, 1949, the General Assembly adopted a resolution on supplementary estimates for 1949 which reduced authorized appropriations by $283,048; a 1950 budget of $49,641,733 was approved on December 10.[36] The 1950 budget, which included an appropriation of $8,000,000 for the internationalization of Jerusalem, was substantially reduced following currency devaluation in a number of member countries. The scale of assessments approved was in general the same as the 1949 schedule, although the United States contribution was reduced by one-tenth of one-percent, to 39.79 percent of the total. Discussion in the administrative and budgetary committee of the Assembly noted that progress toward the normal ceiling of 33.33 percent on individual contributions was slow.[37]

(1) An Act to Amend the United Nations Participation Act of 1945, Approved October 10, 1949.[38]

Be it enacted by the Senate and House of Representatives of the United States of America in Congress assembled, That subsections (a), (b), (c), and (d) of section 2 of the United Nations Participation Act of 1945 are hereby amended to read as follows:

"(a) The President, by and with the advice and consent of the Senate, shall appoint a representative and a deputy representative of the United States to the United Nations, both of whom shall have the rank and status of envoy extraordinary and ambassador plenipotentiary and shall hold office at the pleasure of the President. Such representative and deputy representative shall represent the United States in the Security Council of the United Nations and may serve ex officio as United States representative on any organ, commission, or other body of the United Nations other than specialized agencies of the United Nations, and shall perform such other functions in connection with the participation of the United States in the United Nations as the President may from time to time direct.

"(b) The President, by and with the advice and consent of the Senate, shall appoint an additional deputy representative of the United States to the Security Council who shall hold office at the pleasure of the President. Such deputy representative shall represent the United States in the Security Council of the United Nations in the event of the absence or disability of both the representative and the deputy representative of the United States to the United Nations.

"(c) The President, by and with the advice and consent of the Senate, shall designate from time to time to attend a specified session or specified sessions of the General Assembly of the United Nations not to exceed five representatives of the United States and such number of alternates as he

36 United Nations General Assembly, *Official Records* (4th session), p. 572, 613.
37 *Ibid.*, p. 105; *ibid.*, Document A/1025, October 18, 1949.
38 Public Law 341, 81st Cong., 1st sess.

may determine consistent with the rules of procedure of the General Assembly. One of the representatives shall be designated as the senior representative.

"(d) The President may also appoint from time to time such other persons as he may deem necessary to represent the United States in the organs and agencies of the United Nations, but the representative of the United States in the Economic and Social Council and in the Trusteeship Council of the United Nations shall be appointed only by and with the advice and consent of the Senate, except that the President may, without the advice and consent of the Senate, designate any officer of the United States to act, without additional compensation, as the representative of the United States in either such Council (A) at any specified session thereof where the position is vacant or in the absence or disability of the regular representative, or (B) in connection with a specified subject matter at any specified session of either such Council in lieu of the regular representative. The President may designate any officer of the Department of State, whose appointment is subject to confirmation by the Senate, to act, without additional compensation, for temporary periods as the representative of the United States in the Security Council of the United Nations in the absence or disability of the representative and deputy representatives appointed under section 2 (a) and (b) or in lieu of such representatives in connection with a specified subject matter. The advice and consent of the Senate shall be required for the appointment by the President of the representative of the United States in any commission that may be formed by the United Nations with respect to atomic energy or in any other commission of the United Nations to which the United States is entitled to appoint a representative."

SEC. 2. Section 2 of such Act is further amended by adding the following new subsection:

"(f) All persons appointed in pursuance of authority contained in this section shall receive compensation at rates determined by the President upon the basis of duties to be performed but not in excess of rates authorized by sections 411 and 412 of the Foreign Service Act of 1946 (Public Law 724, Seventy-ninth Congress) for chiefs of mission and Foreign Service officers occupying positions of equivalent importance, except that no member of the Senate or House of Representatives or officer of the United States who is designated under subsections (c) and (d) of this section as a representative of the United States or as an alternate to attend any specified session or specified sessions of the General Assembly shall be entitled to receive such compensation."

SEC. 3. Subsection (b) of section 5 of such Act is hereby amended by inserting "or aircraft," after "or vehicle,".

SEC. 4. The proviso in section 6 of such Act is hereby amended by inserting that "That" the following: ", except as authorized in section 7 of this Act,".

SEC. 5. Such Act is hereby amended by inserting after section 6 the following new section:

"SEC. 7. (a) Notwithstanding the provisions of any other law, the President, upon the request by the United Nations for cooperative action, and to the extent that he finds that it is consistent with the national interest to comply with such request, may authorize, in support of such activities of the United Nations as are specifically directed to the peaceful settlement of disputes and not involving the employment of armed forces contemplated by chapter VII of the United Nations Charter —

"(1) the detail to the United Nations, under such terms and conditions as the President shall determine, of personnel of the armed forces of the United States to serve as observers, guards, or in any noncombatant capacity, but in no event shall more than a total of one thousand of such personnel be so detailed at any one time: *Provided,* That while so detailed, such personnel shall be considered for all purposes as acting in the line of duty, including the receipt of pay and allowances as personnel of the armed forces of the United States, credit for longevity and retirement, and all other perquisites appertaining to such duty: *Provided further,* That upon authorization or approval by the President, such personnel may accept directly from the United Nations (a) any or all of the allowances or perquisites to which they are entitled under the first proviso hereof, and (b) extraordinary expenses and perquisites incident to such detail;

"(2) the furnishing of facilities, services, or other assistance and the loan of the agreed fair share of the United States of any supplies and equipment to the United Nations by the National Military Establishment, under such terms and conditions as the President shall determine;

"(3) the obligation, insofar as necessary to carry out the purposes of clauses (1) and (2) of this subsection, of any funds appropriated to the National Military Establishment or any department therein, the procurement of such personnel, supplies, equipment, facilities, services, or other assistance as may be made available in accordance with the request of the United Nations, and the replacement of such items, when necessary, where they are furnished from stocks.

"(b) Whenever personnel or assistance is made available pursuant to the authority contained in subsection (a) (1) and (2) of this section, the President shall require reimbursement from the United Nations for the expense thereby incurred by the United States: *Provided,* That in exceptional circumstances, or when the President finds it to be in the national interest, he may waive, in whole or in part, the requirement of such reimbursement: *Provided further,* That when any such reimbursement is made, it shall be credited, at the option of the appropriate department of the National Military Establishment, either to the appropriation, fund, or account utilized in incurring the obligation, or to an appropriate appropriation, fund, or account currently available for the purposes for which expenditures were made.

"(c) In addition to the authorization of appropriations to the Department of State contained in section 8 of this Act, there is hereby authorized to be appropriated to the National Military Establishment, or any department therein, such sums as may be necessary to reimburse such Establishment or department in the event that reimbursement from the United Nations is waived in whole or in part pursuant to authority contained in subsection (b) of this section.

"(d) Nothing in this Act shall authorize the disclosure of any information or knowledge in any case in which such disclosure is prohibited by any other law of the United States."

SEC. 6. Section 7 of such Act is hereby amended to read as follows:

"SEC. 8. There is hereby authorized to be appropriated annually to the Department of State, out of any money in the Treasury not otherwise appropriated, such sums as may be necessary for the payment by the United States of its share of the expenses of the United Nations as apportioned by the General Assembly in accordance with article 17 of the Charter, and for all necessary salaries and expenses of the representatives provided for in section 2 hereof, and of their appropriate staffs, including personal services in the District of Columbia and elsewhere, without regard to the civil-service laws and the Classification Act of 1923, as amended; travel expenses without regard to the Standardized Government Travel Regulations, as amended, the Travel Expense Act of 1949, and section 10 of the Act of March 3, 1933, as amended, and, under such rules and regulations as the Secretary of State may prescribe, travel expenses of families and tranportation of effects of United States representatives and other personnel in going to and returning from their post of duty; allowances for living quarters, including heat, fuel, and light, as authorized by the Act approved June 26, 1930 (5 U. S. C. 118a); cost-of-living allowances for personnel stationed abroad under such rules and regulations as the Secretary of State may prescribe; communications services; stenographic reporting, translating, and other services, by contract; hire of passenger motor vehicles and other local transportation; rent of offices; printing and binding without regard to section 11 of the Act of March 1, 1919 (44 U. S. C. 111); allowances and expenses as provided in section 6 of the Act of July 30, 1946 (Public Law 565, Seventy-ninth Congress), and allowances and expenses equivalent to those provided in section 901 (3) of the Foreign Service Act of 1946 (Public Law 724, Seventy-ninth Congress); the lease or rental (for periods not exceeding ten years) of living quarters for the use of the representative of the United States to the United Nations referred to in paragraph (a) of section 2 hereof, the cost of installation and use of telephones in the same manner as telephone service is provided for use of the Foreign Service pursuant to the Act of August 23, 1912, as amended (31 U. S. C. 679), and the allotment of funds, similar to the allotment authorized by section 902 of the Foreign Service Act of 1946, for unusual expenses incident to the operation and maintenance of such living quarters, to be accounted for in accordance with section 903 of said Act; and such other expenses as may be authorized by the Secretary of State; all without regard to section 3709 of the Revised Statutes, as amended (41 U. S. C. 5)."

D. Proposals for Revision of the United Nations Charter

A series of resolutions calling for revision of the Charter of the United Nations were introduced into the Congress during 1949. On October 12, 1949, the House Committee on Foreign Affairs began hearings on H. Con. Res. 64, sponsored by 102 representatives, which urged support for a world federation of nations; some 35 similar resolutions were also under consideration by the committee. No further action was taken on these proposals in the period under review.

(1) Statement by the Assistant Secretary of State for United Nations Affairs (Rusk) on Revision of the United Nations Charter, Made before the Committee on Foreign Affairs of the House of Representatives, May 12, 1949.[39]

[EXCERPTS]

. . . .

We are not now in favor of going to other governments with formal proposals for major amendments to the Charter except on the question of the removal of the veto for pacific settlement of disputes.

That does not mean we are Brahmins of San Francisco and will not take into account the need for charter amendment.

The real issue there turns on the many proposals now before the public for a significant change in the Charter in the direction of world government or whatever word you want to use to mean restrictions on sovereignty and the throwing of greater responsibility to the international community.

That is a public debate which is absolutely essential between now and the time we come up to take a new look at the Charter, in 1955–56.

It is conceivable that a convention might be called before then but in any event we expect a basic look at the Charter at that time as provided in the Charter itself.

. . . .

When you look at the time schedule on that and the size of the job, a revision of the Charter will require as much study by the public, by the State Department, and by the Congress as did the original Charter.

It is a long, complicated, extremely difficult process. We started the United Nations Charter back in 1939. Studies on postwar organization were started then. We should have, within the next 3 years, some very fundamental ideas of our own about what we think the United Nations ought to look like, if it is to look any different than it does now.

Those 3 years are going to pass much faster than we would like, but we will need to have that time because it will take us a year or two of very care-

39 *To Amend the United Nations Participation Act of 1945. Hearings Before the Committee on Foreign Affairs, House of Representatives, 81st Congress, 1st Session, May 10, 11, 12, and 13, 1949*, p. 55.

ful negotiation with other governments if we are to be concerned with any convention for the consideration of Charter changes.

Now, to a considerable extent the State Department must lag behind the public debate. I do not say that lagging should carry on indefinitely, but this is a question of such fundamental importance that the Congress and the public must debate it out in great detail and with great care before we as a government, the Congress and the executive branch, take a firm international position on any specific proposals.

You have observed during this past year that most of those who have come forward with major changes for Charter revision have begun to realize perhaps more than ever that no different United Nations is likely to come out of the corpse of this one, that we must keep this one intact and energetic and effective as a basis for further discussions with other governments or as an institutional basis for whatever organization or changes we might want to make.

That has been very useful. It is also significant that those who have come forward with such proposals themselves are continuing to adjust, refine, and change and improve their own suggestions.

We hope that they will continue to do that. We hope that the public debate will continue. We hope that the foundations, the universities, the learned societies, the American Society of International Law, and such organizations of technical people will take those issues up and debate them thoroughly during the course of the next few years.

We hope they will keep this public debate going.

However, thus far we have not completed anything like the essential staff work, the basic planning and thinking, the giving of the flesh and blood to the bones, on these proposals to see what we as a government might want to do about it.

We do know that public debate in this country is very far ahead of public debate in other countries on the same issue.

One of the byproducts of a vigorous American debate on this will be a spread of this debate into other countries. If the latter occurs, we will have a basis on which to negotiate with other governments.

. . . .

3. INTERNATIONAL MILITARY CONTROLS

A. Regulation and Reduction of Armaments

[See *Documents, VIII, 1945–46*, p. 330; *IX, 1947*, p. 333; *X, 1948*, p. 324.]

On February 10, 1949, the Security Council transmitted to the Commission on Conventional Armaments "for action according to its terms" a resolution adopted by the General Assembly at its third session concerning the general question of regulation and reduction of armaments.[1] At the same time the Council rejected a Soviet proposal urging the reduction by one-third of the armaments and armed

---

[1] For the text of the resolution, see *Documents, X, 1948*, p. 328.

forces of the permanent members of the Security Council and the simultaneous drafting of a convention for the prohibition and control of atomic energy.[2] The Commission, following a United States proposal, directed its Working Committee to formulate proposals for the receipt, checking, and publication of information submitted by members on their armed forces and armaments; and the Working Committee on May 26 began consideration of a French working paper which outlined principles for collecting and verifying information through the creation of a control authority and an inspectorate empowered to send out international verification terms.[3] The plan was approved by the Working Committee on July 18 by a vote of 8 to 3 and by the Commission on August 1 by the same vote; opposing ballots were cast by the Soviet Union, the Ukraine, and Egypt.[4] In Security Council discussion the census plan received strong support from the United States, Canada, France, United Kingdom and Argentina; the United States representative (Austin) reiterated the willingness of his government to submit to the system of checking and verification envisaged. On October 18, 1949, a French resolution which approved the Commission proposals and transmitted them to the General Assembly received a 9 to 2 vote, and a second French proposal recalling that the principle of submitting information on atomic weapons was "an integral part of the United Nations plan of control and prohibition approved by the General Assembly on 4 November 1948" received a vote of 8 to 2 with 1 abstention; both resolutions failed of passage because of the negative vote of the Soviet Union.[5] The Council rejected by a vote of 3 to 1 with 7 abstentions a Soviet draft which simply recognized as essential the submission by states of information on armed forces, conventional armaments and atomic weapons.[6]

The Soviet resolution was reintroduced in discussion at the fourth session of the General Assembly, together with a Franco-Norwegian suggestion that the Assembly approve the proposals formulated by the Commission on Conventional Armaments and direct the Commission to continue its study of regulation and reduction of armaments. On December 5 the Assembly approved the Franco-Norwegian draft by a vote of 44 to 5 with 5 abstentions; the Soviet proposal was defeated by a vote of 39 to 6 with 9 abstentions.[7]

(1) *Working Paper on Collection and Verification of Information on the Armaments and Armed Forces of the Members of the United Nations, Adopted by the United Nations Commission for Conventional Armaments, August 1, 1949.*[8]

SECTION I

General Consideration

1. *Desire expressed by the General Assembly*

General Assembly resolution 192 (III) of 19 November 1948 expresses the desire that the Commission for Conventional Armaments, "in carrying out its plan of work, will devote its first attention to formulating proposals for the receipt, checking and publication, by an international organ of control within the framework of the Security Council, of full information to be supplied by Member States with regard to their effectives and their conventional armaments."

2 United Nations Security Council, *Official Records* (4th year), No. 11, p. 19.
3 *Ibid.*, Document S/C.3/SC.3/21, May 26, 1949.
4 *Ibid.*, Documents S/C.3/SC.3/SR.25, July 19, 1949; *ibid.*, Document S/C.3/SR.19, August 4, 1949.
5 *Ibid.*, *Official Records* (4th year), No. 48, p. 22.
6 *Ibid.*
7 United Nations General Assembly, *Official Records* (4th session), p. 522.
8 United Nations Security Council, *Official Records* (4th year), Supplement, September – December 1949, p. 2.

2. *Motives for this desire*

This desire is motivated by two considerations:

The first is that "the aim of the reduction of conventional armaments and armed forces can only be attained in an atmosphere of real and lasting improvement in international relations."

The second is that any reduction of armaments implies, as a prerequisite, an exchange between States of exact and authenticated information concerning their conventional armaments and their armed forces.

3. *Aims of the General Assembly resolution*

Accordingly, the General Assembly resolution has two objectives:

In the first place, to encourage the renewal of international confidence, through a relaxation of existing conditions of secrecy, by placing the States "in possession of precise and verified data as to the level of their respective conventional armaments and armed forces."

In the second place, to begin forthwith to prepare the way for a future reduction and regulation of armaments and effectives by introducing in the field of international co-operation precedents likely to become useful in the progress which still remains to be achieved in that direction.

4. *Nature of proposals to be formulated*

Thus are determined two aspects of the proposals to be formulated according to the desire of the General Assembly:

On the one hand, these proposals must be capable of implementation under existing political conditions.

On the other hand, they are not designed to provide of themselves the safeguards which are essential to security, still less to give military advantage to any nation.

5. *Resulting limitations*

Hence the need for interpreting liberally the phrases "exact and authenticated information," "full information" and "precise and verified data," in order to take into account the interests of security as well as the demand for exact data.

This applies particularly to the degree of access by way of inspection for verification purposes which can be agreed to at this time by the participants. As between disclosure of information and adequate verification, the requirements of verification must be paramount.

By virtue of the same premise, the measures to be proposed must also fulfil the following conditions:

As a prerequisite to implementation, they should be accepted by not less than two-thirds of the Member States including all the permanent members of the Security Council.

The information to be made available for census and verification according to such proposals should be purely quantitative, subject only to such qualitative specifications as will be indicated later in this document (section II).

The information will be strictly limited to the existing level of effectives and conventional armaments.

The information will not include data regarding research and experimental material; personnel engaged in the operation of such material will not, as such, be subject to verification, even though they may be subject to census.

6. *Scope of proposals to be formulated*

Proposals to be formulated should, within the above limitations, cover the following points:

(1) Information to be reported, or: scope and nature of census.

(2) Control of such information, or: scope and nature of verification.

(3) Organ of control to be set up: status, rights and duties of the control organ and its agents; organization and administration of the control organ; relations of the control organ to the other organs of the United Nations; rights and obligations of Member States of the United Nations; rights and obligations of other States.

7. *Proposals contained in this document*

Section II of this document only covers points (1) and (2) of the preceding paragraph. The specific proposals or general recommendations which are put forward on those two points are designed to assist in establishing a framework for the international agreement which must eventually sanction the proposals formulated by the Commission for Conventional Armaments.

SECTION II

Proposals and Recommendations on Census and Verification

A. CENSUS

I. *Effectives*

1. *Scope of census*

Elements subject to census should include military and para-military forces, active and reserve, on full-time and part-time basis.

These elements will be designated by name for each State by the control organ.

2. *Nature of census*

(a) *Specifications to be furnished*

The census should indicate the breakdown of total numbers into the following categories:

Ground forces;
Naval forces;
Air forces;

Para-military forces and national police forces;

Active and reserve components of each of the above categories.

(b) Period to be covered

The census should supply the following data to each of the above categories:

Strength on a date to be designated by the control organ;

Daily average strength for the preceding year;

Total effectives released during the preceding year expressed as a percentage of the average strength during the preceding year.

(c) Forms

The above information should be submitted on forms prescribed by the control organ.

(d) Timing

Census reports should be submitted simultaneously by all States.

II. *Conventional armaments*

1. *Scope of census*

(*a*) The census should indicate quantities in the following categories:

Ground forces: Automatic weapons and artillery, classified by type and caliber; Armour, classified by tonnage.

Naval forces: Combatant ships, classified by type and tonnage.

Air forces: Combatant aircraft, classified by type.

(*b*) The census should include total quantities of material both in service and in reserve.

2. *Nature of census*

Provisions applying to the period to be covered, the form, and the timing of "personnel" census, as indicated in 1, 2 (*b*), (*c*), and (*d*) above, should apply to the materiel census.

B. Verification

I. *General recommendations*

1. The control organ should enjoy within the limits indicated above (section I, paragraph 5) the greatest possible freedom of movement and access to data fully depicting the level of conventional armaments and effectives of each State.

2. The activities to be verified should be specified in the international agreement.

3. The control organ should be empowered to direct investigations by international verification teams which will perform all inspections, spot-checks, and physical counts needed for an adequate cross-checking of the reported information.

4. For the purpose of spot-checks, States would be requested to submit reports showing figures as of any date which the control organ might designate, for each or part of the categories of information covered by the census reports.

5. To resolve doubts which may be raised by one or several governments or by the control organ itself, provision should be made for special supplemental inspections.

II. *Scope and nature*

1. *Effectives*

The complete order of battle should be made available to the control organ.

2. *Conventional armaments*

In addition to the inspection of relevant records, verification should be based upon spot-checks of materiel both in service and in reserve wherever stored.

SECTION III

Proposals and Recommendations on the International Organ of Control

I. *Function of the control organ*

The function of the control organ will be to give effect to the census and verification measures concerning conventional armaments and effectives as set out in sections I and II, in accordance with the terms of the international agreement which will sanction the adoption of such measures and in compliance with the directives of the Security Council.

II. *Relationship of the control organ to the other organs of the United Nations*

The control organ will be directly subordinated to the Security Council and will enjoy such relationships to the other organs of the United Nations as result therefrom.

III. *Structure of the control organ*

The control organ will consist of: a central control authority, and inspectorate and a secretariat.

IV. *The central control authority*

1. *Function of the central control authority*

The function of the authority will be to ensure the execution of the census and verification measures, including the following responsibilities:

(a) To interpret the terms of the international agreement concerning these measures and to settle any controversial issue arising therefrom;

(b) To direct the activities of the inspectorate; in particular to determine the organization of the inspectorate according to the specific problems raised by the verification of census reports from each State;

(*c*) To produce and distribute to Member States the standard forms of reports to be returned by Member States;

(*d*) To set dates for the submission of the reports;

(*e*) To submit to the Security Council, for publication, the reports of Member States, the findings of the inspectorate, and the conclusions of the authority;

(*f*) To determine its own rules of procedure, which should include the provision that decisions on all matters which require voting will be adopted by a simple majority;

(*g*) To determine the organization of the secretariat and to direct its activities so as to fulfil the needs of the authority and of the inspectorate·

2. *Composition of the central control authority*

The Member States represented in the authority will be those represented in the Security Council.

Each Member State will be represented by one delegate and one deputy delegate. These delegates may be assisted by technical advisers appointed by each Member State.

V. *The inspectorate*

1. *Function of the inspectorate*

The function of the inspectorate will be to carry out the verification measures in compliance with the directives of the authority, including the following responsibilities:

(*a*) To carry out checks and cross-checks of the appropriate documents, and inspection of bases, depots, and other installations, necessary for the verification of the personnel and materiel census;

(*b*) To adapt verification methods to the specific problems raised in connexion with inspection in each State;

(*c*) To report immediately to the authority all discrepancies found and to carry out all additional cross-checks which may be necessary;

(*d*) To report to the authority any disagreement which may arise during the course of inspection;

(*e*) To report its findings to the authority upon the completion of the verification.

2. *Composition of the inspectorate*

The authority will designate members of the inspectorate by means of selection from lists submitted by each Member State.

This designation should be set up so as to afford the inspectorate a broadly international composition.

The inspectorate for each State will not include any national from the State being inspected. However, when a State is being inspected, it will provide a liaison to facilitate the task of the inspectorate.

3. *Status of the members of the inspectorate*

The members of the inspectorate will enjoy the status and immunities appropriate to the performance of their functions.

VI. *The Secretariat*

1. *Function of the secretariat*

The function of the secretariat will be to assist the authority and the inspectorate in carrying out their tasks.

2. *Staff of the secretariat*

The staff of the secretariat will be provided by the Secretary-General of the United Nations.

(2) *Resolution on the Regulation and Reduction of Armaments and Armed Forces, Approved by the United Nations General Assembly, December 5, 1949.*[9]

The General Assembly,

Recalling its resolution 192 (III) of 19 November 1948, and in particular its recommendation that the Commission for Conventional Armaments, in carrying out its plan of work, devote its first attention to the formulation of proposals for the receipt, checking and publication, by an international organ of control within the framework of the Security Council, of full information to be supplied by Member States with regard to their effectives and their conventional armaments,

Having examined the records of the discussion in the Security Council and in the Commission for Conventional Armaments regarding the implementation of the above-mentioned recommendation,

1. *Approves* the proposals formulated by the Commission for Conventional Armaments for the submission by Member States of full information on their conventional armaments and armed forces and the verification thereof, as constituting the necessary basis for the implementation of the above-mentioned recommendation;

2. *Considers* that the early submission of this information would constitute an essential step towards a substantial reduction of conventional armaments and armed forces and that, on the other hand, no agreement is likely to be reached on this matter so long as each State lacks exact and authenticated information concerning the conventional armaments and armed forces of other States;

3. *Notes* that unanimity among the permanent members of the Security Council, which is essential for the implementation of the above-mentioned proposals, has not yet been achieved;

4. *Recommends* therefore that the Security Council, despite the lack of unanimity among its permanent members on this essential feature of its work, continue its study of the regulation and reduction of conventional

9 United Nations General Assembly, *Official Records: Resolutions* (4th session), p. 22.

armaments and armed forces through the agency of the Commission for Conventional Armaments in accordance with its plan of work, in order to make such progress as may be possible;

5. *Calls upon* all members of the Security Council to co-operate to this end.

B. International Control of Atomic Energy

[See *Documents, VIII, 1945–46*, p. 544; *IX, 1947*, p. 341; *X, 1948*, p. 329.]

After a lapse of nine months, the United Nations Atomic Energy Commission resumed its meetings on February 18, 1949, in accordance with a resolution of the General Assembly.[10] Throughout early 1949 inconclusive debate in the Commission and its Working Committee centered around a series of studies prepared by the Secretariat and a Soviet proposal that work be started simultaneously on two conventions, the first prohibiting atomic weapons and the second providing for the control of atomic energy.[11] A number of representatives pointed out, however, that no new proposals had been offered, and the Commission on July 29 decided to suspend its activities, declaring that no useful purpose would be served by reexamining the Soviet proposals. A second resolution adopted by the Commission, on the proposal of the United States, reported that an impasse on atomic energy existed which could not be solved at the Commission level, and placed the responsibility for this situation on the Soviet Union and the Ukraine. Discussion would be of no practical value, it was stated, until the six sponsoring powers reached a basis for agreement.[12] The Security Council on September 16, 1949, by a vote of 2 to 0 with 9 abstentions defeated a Soviet proposal requesting the Commission to continue its work, and decided by a vote of 9 to 0 with 2 abstentions to transmit the two Commission resolutions to the General Assembly.[13]

The first of a series of meetings of the six sponsoring powers was held at Lake Success on August 9, 1949; an interim report which was submitted to the fourth session of the General Assembly on October 25 merely noted the consultations and forwarded summary records of meetings held. The Soviet position, as noted in the records, was that the Baruch plan was "based on the illusion of a continuing monopoly of the secret of the production of atomic energy",[14] a condition which no longer existed; this statement had been foreshadowed by an announcement by President Truman on September 23 that the United States had evidence that "within recent weeks an atomic explosion occurred in the USSR."[15] A statement by the remaining five sponsoring powers subsequently reported the status of the consultations.[16]

At the dedication ceremonies for the United Nations headquarters on October 24, 1949, President Truman made a new appeal for agreement on international control of atomic energy,[17] and a series of possible solutions were subsequently put forward in the General Assembly. The Assembly president, General Romulo, suggested four lines of negotiation; 1) a short-term armistice on production of atomic weapons, accompanied by an inspection system; 2) interim prohibition of the use of atomic weapons with adequate safeguards; 3) further compromises between the majority and minority plans for atomic energy control; and 4) a new approach to the fundamental problem of control, based on the thesis that the amount of fissionable material currently available was much smaller than previously believed.[18] The Assembly on November 23 approved, by a vote of 49 to 5 with 3 abstentions,

---

10 For the text of the General Assembly resolution, see *Documents, X, 1948*, p. 345.
11 Soviet proposals on control of atomic energy were also considered by the United Nations in connection with regulation of conventional armaments. See this volume, p. 339.
12 For the texts of the two resolutions, see this volume, p. 348.
13 United Nations Security Council, *Official Records* (4th year), No. 43, p. 24 and 28.
14 United Nations General Assembly, Document A/1045, October 24, 1949.
15 Department of State, *Bulletin*, XXI, p. 487.
16 For the text, see *ibid.*, p. 350. 17 *Ibid.*, p. 38.
18 *New York Times*, November 10, 1949, p. 20.

a Franco-Canadian proposal which urged continuance of consultations by the six sponsoring powers and recommended that all nations join in limiting their sovereignty to the extent required for effective international control. Three other resolutions, including the Soviet draft instructing the Atomic Energy Commission to resume its work, were defeated.[19]

(1) **Resolutions on the International Control of Atomic Energy, Approved by the United Nations Atomic Energy Commission, July 29, 1949.**[20]

[A]

The Atomic Energy Commission

Has considered the proposal of the representative of the Union of Soviet Socialist Republics (AEC/37) that the Atomic Energy Commission begin immediately to prepare a draft convention for the prohibition of atomic weapons and a draft convention for the control of atomic energy proceeding from the principle that both conventions must be concluded and put into effect simultaneously;

Has noted the statement of the representative of the Union of Soviet Socialist Republics at the fourth-fifth meeting of the Working Committee on Wednesday, 1 June 1949, that the proposal submitted by the representative of the Union of Soviet Socialist Republics on atomic energy in June 1946 and June 1947 should be taken as a basis for the elaboration of these draft conventions;

Recalls that these same proposals, particularly those of 11 June 1947, have already been analysed in detail and rejected in April 1948 on the grounds that "they ignore the existing technical knowledge of the problem of atomic energy control, do not provide an adequate basis for the effective international control of atomic energy and the elimination from national armaments of atomic weapons, and, therefore, do not conform to the terms of reference of the Atomic Energy Commission";

Recalls that the Union of Soviet Socialist Republics proposal for the preparation of a draft convention for the prohibition of atomic weapons and a draft convention for the control of atomic energy to be concluded and brought into effect simultaneously was rejected by the General Assembly at the 157th plenary meeting in its third session on 4 November 1948, by 40 votes to 6, with 5 abstentions;

And recalls also that at the same time the General Assembly approved the "General Findings" (Part II C) and "Recommendations" (Part III) of the first report and the specific proposals of Part II of the second report of the Commission, as constituting the necessary basis for establishing an effective system of international control of atomic energy to ensure its use only for peaceful purposes and for the elimination from national armaments of atomic weapons in accordance with the terms of reference of the Atomic Energy Commission;

---

19 United Nations General Assembly, *Official Records* (4th session), p. 358.
20 United Nations Atomic Energy Commission, Document AEC/42; *ibid.*, Document AEC/43, August 1, 1949.

The Atomic Energy Commission observes that no material has been presented additional to that previously submitted to the General Assembly, the Commission or the Working Committee;

The Atomic Energy Commission therefore concludes that no useful purpose can be served by further discussions in the Atomic Energy Commission of those proposals which have already been considered and rejected by the appropriate organs of the United Nations. The Atomic Energy Commission reports to the Security Council and the General Assembly accordingly.

[B]

The Atomic Energy Commission
Reports:

That in accordance with the instructions in General Assembly resolution 191 (III) of 4 November 1948, the Atomic Energy Commission has surveyed its programme of work in order to determine whether further work would be practicable and useful;

That the Union of Soviet Socialist Republics and the Ukrainian SSR continue to reject the recommendations of the Commission approved by the General Assembly on 4 November 1948, including those forms of control contained in the plan approved by the General Assembly "as constituting the necessary basis for establishing an effective system of international control of atomic energy to ensure its use only for peaceful purposes and for the elimination from national armaments of atomic weapons in accordance with the terms of reference of the Atomic Energy Commission";

That the Union of Soviet Socialist Republics and the Ukrainian SSR continue to insist on the adoption of the draft resolution (A/C.1/310) proposed by the Union of Soviet Socialist Republics, and rejected by the General Assembly on 4 November 1948, to prepare immediately separate convention based on the proposals of the Soviet Union of June 1946 and June 1947, which provide among other things for national ownership of dangerous and explosive atomic materials, and for national ownership, operation and management of dangerous atomic facilities. This, in the opinion of the majority of the Commission, would not remove causes for suspicion, fear and distrust among nations, would render ineffective the prohibition of atomic weapons, and would continue dangerous national rivalries in the field of atomic energy;

Concludes:

That the impasse as analysed in the third report of the Atomic Energy Commission still exists; that these differences are irreconcilable at the Commission level, and that further discussion in the Atomic Energy Commission would tend to harden these differences and would serve no practicable or useful purpose until such time as the Sponsoring Powers have reported that there exists a basis for agreement.

(2) *Statement by the Representatives of Canada, China, France, the United Kingdom and the United States on the Consultations of the Six Permanent Members of the United Nations Atomic Energy Commission, October 25, 1949.*[21]

On 24 October 1949, the representatives of Canada, China, France, the Union of Soviet Socialist Republics, the United Kingdom and the United States of America agreed to send to the Secretary-General of the United Nations, for transmission to the General Assembly, the following interim report on the consultations of the six permanent members of the Atomic Energy Commission:

"In paragraph 3 of General Assembly resolution 191(III) of 4 November 1948, the representatives of the Sponsoring Powers, who are the Permanent Members of the Atomic Energy Commission, namely, Canada, China, France, the Union of Soviet Socialist Republics, the United Kingdom of Great Britain and Northern Ireland and the United States of America, were requested to hold consultations 'in order to determine if there exists a basis for agreement on the international control of atomic energy to ensure its use only for peaceful purposes, and for the elimination from national armaments of atomic weapons'.

"The first meeting took place on 9 August 1949. The consultations have not yet been concluded and are continuing but, in order to inform the General Assembly of the position which has so far been reached, the six Sponsoring Powers have decided to transmit to it the summary records of the first ten meetings."

It was agreed by the group that any of the representatives of the Governments taking part in these consultations retained the right to submit to the Assembly their observations on the course of the consultations so far. The representatives of Canada, China, France, the United Kingdom and the United States accordingly submit to the General Assembly this statement, which represents their joint views, in the hope that it may assist the Assembly in its consideration of this problem.

Basis of discussion

It was found desirable to approach these consultations from the viewpoint of general principles rather than specific proposals which had been the basis of most of the discussion in the United Nations Atomic Energy Commission. To this end, the representative of the United Kingdom offered a list of topics as a basis for discussion. Included in this paper was a Statement of Principles relating to each topic (Annex I). It was pointed out that the United Kingdom Statement of Principles was based on the plan approved by the General Assembly, but at the same time covered the essential topics with which any plan for the prohibition of atomic weapons and the control of atomic energy would have to deal. The list of topics was then

21 United Nations General Assembly, Document A/1050, October 25, 1949.

adopted as the basis for discussion. The representatives of Canada, China, France, the United Kingdom and the United States made it clear that their Governments accepted the Statement of Principles set forth in this paper and considered them essential to any plan of effective prohibition of atomic weapons and effective control of atomic energy for peaceful purposes. They expressed the readiness of their Governments to consider any alternative proposals which might be put forward, but emphasized that they would continue to support the plan approved by the General Assembly unless and until proposals were made which would provide equally or more effective and workable means of control and prohibition.

Prohibition of atomic weapons

At the request of the Soviet representative, the question of the prohibition of atomic weapons was taken up first. The texts which served as a basis for the discussion were point four of the Statement of Principles, and a Soviet amendment submitted to replace that text (Annex II). In the course of the discussion, the Soviet representative declared that the representatives of all six Sponsoring Powers were in agreement in recognizing that atomic weapons should be prohibited, and he therefore drew the conclusion that his amendment should be accepted. The other representatives pointed out that it had always been agreed that the production, possession or use of atomic weapons by all nations must be prohibited. But it was also agreed that prohibition could only be enforced by means of an effective system of control. This was recognized even in the Soviet amendment, but the remainder of the amendment contained a repetition of the earlier Soviet proposals for control which were deemed inadequate.

The Soviet representative insisted that two separate conventions, one on prohibition and the other on control, should be put into effect simultaneously. The other representatives maintained that the important point to be resolved was what constitutes effective control, and that this control had to embrace all uses of atomic materials in dangerous quantities. In their view the Soviet proposals would not only fail to provide the security required but they would be so inadequate as to be dangerous. They would delude the peoples of the world into thinking that atomic energy was being controlled when in fact it was not. On the other hand, under the approved plan, the prohibition of the use of atomic weapons would rest not only on the pledge of each nation, but no nation would be permitted to possess the materials with which weapons could be made. Furthermore, the Soviet Government took an impracticable stand as regards the question of timing or stages by which prohibition and control would be brought into effect.

Stages for putting into effect prohibition and control

On this topic, the Soviet representative maintained that the entire system of prohibition and control must be put into effect simultaneously over the entire nuclear industry.

The representatives of the other Powers pointed out that this would be physically impossible. The development of atomic energy is the world's newest industry, and already is one of the most complicated. It would not be reasonable to assume that any effective system of control could be introduced and enforced overnight. Control and prohibition must, therefore, go into effect over a period of time and by a series of stages.

The plan approved by the General Assembly on 4 November 1948 does not attempt to define what the stages should be, the order in which they should be put into effect, or the time which the whole process of transition would take. The reason for this is that no detailed provisions on stages could be drawn up until agreement is reached on what the control system should be, and the provisions would also depend on the state of development of atomic energy in the various countries at the time agreement is reached. Until then, detailed study of the question of stages would be unrealistic.

Meanwhile, the approved plan covers the question of stages in so far as it can usefully be carried at present. The plan provides that the schedule of stages of application of control and prohibition over all the many phases of the entire nuclear industry is to be written into the treaty, with the United Nations Atomic Energy Commission as the body to supervise their orderly implementation. No other commitment or position on this question is contained in the approved plan.

Control

(a) Means of Control

The Soviet representative insisted, as in the past, that any plan of control, to be acceptable to the Soviet Union, must be based on the Soviet proposals for control, originally put forward in June 1947 (Document AEC/24, 11 June 1947), which provide for periodic inspection of nationally owned plants producing or using atomic materials, when declared to an international control organ by the Governments concerned.

The representatives of Canada, China, France, the United Kingdom and the United States recalled that the nuclear fuels produced or used in such plants are the very nuclear explosives used in the manufacture of weapons. A new situation therefore was created in the field of armaments where the conversion of a peaceful industry into a war industry could take place rapidly and without warning.

In dealing with such materials a system of control depending merely on inspection would be ineffective. For ordinary chemical or mineral substances and their processing inspection might provide adequate guarantees, but atomic development presented special problems which could not be solved in this way. Materials used in the development of atomic energy were highly radioactive and could not, therefore, be handled except by remote control. The process of measuring atomic fuels was extremely intricate and, at the present stage of our knowledge, subject to appreciable error. It would be impracticable to rely on the inspection of plants and impossible to check the actual amounts of atomic materials inside piles or reactors against the amounts shown in the records.

A system of inspection alone would not prevent the clandestine diversion of atomic materials to war purposes from plants designed for peaceful use and would provide no guarantee that, in spite of any treaty, a nation which was determined to continue the secret manufacture of atomic weapons would be prevented from doing so. A plan based on periodic inspection, on which the Soviet Union insists, would be even less adequate than one based on continuous inspection.

The Soviet representative dismissed these arguments as exaggerated or non-existent.

Since there was evidence that an atomic explosion had been produced in the Soviet Union, the Soviet representative was asked whether he had any new evidence derived from Soviet experience to support his contention that periodic inspection would be sufficient to assure control. No answer has yet been received to this question.

The five Powers remain convinced that any system of inspection alone would be inadequate and that in order to provide security the International Control Agency must itself operate and manage dangerous facilities and must hold dangerous atomic materials and facilities for making or using dangerous quantities of such materials in trust for Member States.

(b) *Ownership*

During the consultations, the question of ownership, which has often been represented as the real obstacle to agreement on control, was the subject of an extended exchange of views.

The Soviet representative argued that international management and operation were equivalent to international ownership; and that neither international ownership nor international management and operation was essential to control. He stated that his Government would not accept either.

The representatives of the other Sponsoring Powers refuted the interpretation put by the Soviet representative on ownership, management and operation. For the reasons given they believed that the management and operation of dangerous facilities must be entrusted to the International Agency. Management and operation were clearly among the more important rights conferred by ownership. Since effective control would be impossible unless these rights were exercised by the Agency, the nations on whose territories such facilities were situated would have to renounce important rights normally conferred by ownership. This did not necessarily mean the complete devolution of the rights of ownership to the Agency; for example, the Agency would not have the right arbitrarily to close atomic power plants; it would have to conform to national legislation as regards public health and working conditions; it could not construct plants at will but only in agreement with the nation concerned. Moreover, the Agency would not be free to determine the production policy for nuclear fuel since this would follow provisions to be laid down in advance in the treaty. The treaty would also determine the quotas for production and consumption of atomic fuel. Finally, the Agency would hold materials and facilities in trust and would not therefore be able to manage or dispose of them arbitrarily or for its own profit but only for the benefit of Member States.

There might well be other rights which would normally be conferred by ownership and which were not specifically mentioned in the approved plan. Their disposition would follow a simple principle. If there were rights, the exercise of which could impair the effectiveness of control, individual nations would be required to renounce them. Otherwise they might retain them.

If individual nations agreed to renounce national ownership of dangerous atomic materials and the right of managing and operating plants making or using them, in favor of an International Agency acting for the international community, such agreement would be on the basic principle, and there would be no need to quarrel over terminology.

(c) *Sovereignty*

A further argument put forward by the Soviet representative was that to confer on any international agency the powers suggested in the Statement of Principles would constitute a gross infringement of national sovereignty and would permit the International Agency to interfere in the internal economy of individual nations.

In answer to this argument it was pointed out that any plan for international prohibition and control must involve some surrender of sovereignty. The representatives of the other Powers argued that it was indefensible to reject a plan for the international control of atomic energy on the purely negative ground that it would infringe national sovereignty. The ideal of international co-operation and, indeed, the whole concept on which the United Nations was based would be meaningless if States insisted on the rigid maintenance of all their sovereign rights. The question was not one of encroachment on sovereignty, but of assuring the security of the world, which could only be attained by the voluntary association of nations in the exercise of certain rights of sovereignty in an open and co-operating world community.

The Soviet representative remarked that, while some representatives had stated that their Governments were prepared to waive sovereignty provided that the majority plan was accepted, the Government of the USSR would not agree to do so.

Basic obstacles in the way of agreement

It appears from these consultations that, as in the past, the Soviet Union will not negotiate except on the basis of the principles set forth in the Soviet proposals of June 1947.

The essential points in the Soviet control proposals, and the reasons for their rejection by the other five Powers, as brought out in the consultations, are as follows:

The Soviet Union proposes that nations should continue to own explosive atomic materials.

The other five Powers feel that under such conditions there would be no effective protection against the sudden use of these materials as atomic weapons.

The Soviet Union proposes that nations continue, as at present, to own, operate and manage facilities making or using dangerous quantities of such materials.

The other five powers believe that, under such conditions, it would be impossible to detect or prevent the diversion of such materials for use in atomic weapons.

The Soviet Union proposes a system of control depending on periodic inspection of facilities the existence of which the national Government concerned reports to the international agency, supplemented by special investigations on suspicion of treaty violations.

The other five Powers believe that periodic inspection would not prevent the diversion of dangerous materials and that the special investigations envisaged would be wholly insufficient to prevent clandestine activities.

Other points of difference, including Soviet insistence on the right to veto the recommendations of the International Control Agency, have not yet been discussed in the consultations.

Conclusions

These consultations have not yet succeeded in bringing about agreement between the USSR and the other five Powers, but they have served to clarify some of the points on which there is disagreement.

It is apparent that there is a fundamental difference not only on methods but also on aims. All of the Sponsoring Powers other than the USSR put world security first and are prepared to accept innovations in traditional concepts of international co-operation, national sovereignty and economic organization where these are necessary for security. The Government of the USSR put its sovereignty first and is unwilling to accept measures which may impinge upon or interfere with its rigid exercise of unimpeded state sovereignty.

If this fundamental difference could be overcome, other differences which have hitherto appeared insurmountable could be seen in true perspective, and reasonable ground might be found for their adjustment.

ANNEX I

List of Topics and Statement of Principles Prepared by the Representative of the United Kingdom of Great Britain and Northern Ireland

1. *International system of control:*

   (a) There should be a strong and comprehensive international system for the control of atomic energy and the prohibition of atomic weapons, aimed at attaining the objectives set forth in the resolution of the General Assembly of 24 January 1946. Such an international system should be established, and its scope and functions defined by an enforceable multilateral treaty in which all nations should participate on fair and equitable terms.

   (b) Policies concerning the production and use of atomic energy which substantially affect world security should be governed by principles established in the treaty. Production and other dangerous facilities should be distributed in accordance with quotas and provisions laid down in the treaty.

2. *International Control Agency:*

   (a) There should be established, within the framework of the Security Council, an international control agency, deriving its powers and status from the treaty under which it is established. The Agency should possess powers and be charged with responsibility necessary and appropriate for the prompt and effective discharge of the duties imposed upon it by the terms of the treaty. Its powers should be sufficiently broad and flexible to enable it to deal with new developments that may hereafter arise in the field of atomic energy.

   (b) The personnel of the Agency should be recruited on an international basis.

   (c) The duly accredited representatives of the Agency should be afforded unimpeded rights of ingress, egress and access for the performance of their inspections and other duties into, from and within the territory of every participating nation, unhindered by national or local authorities.

3. *Exchange of information:*

   (a) The Agency and the participating nations should be guided by the general principle that there should be no secrecy concerning scientific and technical information on atomic energy.

   (b) The Agency should promote among all nations the exchange of basic scientific information on atomic energy for peaceful ends.

4. *Prohibition of atomic weapons:*

   (a) International agreement to outlaw the national production and use of atomic weapons is an essential part of this international system of control.

   (b) The manufacture, possession and use of atomic weapons by all nations and by all persons under their jurisdiction should be forbidden.

   (c) Any existing stocks of atomic weapons should be disposed of, and proper use should be made of nuclear fuel for peaceful purposes.

5. *Development of atomic energy:*

   (a) The development and use of atomic energy even for peaceful purposes are not exclusively matters of domestic concern of individual nations, but rather have predominantly international implications and repercussions. The development of atomic energy must be made an international co-operative enterprise in all its phases.

   (b) The Agency should have positive research and developmental responsibilities in order to remain in the forefront of atomic knowledge so as to render itself more effective in promoting the beneficial uses of atomic energy and in eliminating the destructive ones.

   (c) The Agency should obtain and maintain information as complete and accurate as possible concerning world supplies of source material.

6. *Control over atomic materials and facilities:*

(a) The Agency should hold all atomic source materials, nuclear fuels and dangerous facilities in trust for the participating nations and be responsible for ensuring that the provisions of the treaty in regard to their disposition are executed.
(b) The Agency should have the exclusive right to operate and manage all dangerous atomic facilities.
(c) In any matters affecting security, nations cannot have any proprietary right or rights of decision arising therefrom over atomic source materials, nuclear fuels or dangerous facilities located within their territories.
(d) The Agency must be given indisputable control of the source materials promptly after their separation from their natural deposits, and on taking possession should give fair and equitable compensation determined by agreement with the nation concerned.
(e) Activities related to atomic energy, which are non-dangerous to security, such as mining and milling of source material, and research, may be operated by nations or persons under license from the Agency.

7. *Means of detecting and preventing clandestine activities:*

The Agency should have the duty of seeking out any clandestine activities or facilities involving source material or nuclear fuel; to this end it should have the power to require reports on relevant matters, to verify these reports and obtain such other information as it deems necessary by direct inspection or other means, all subject to appropriate limitations.

8. *Stages:*

The treaty should embrace the entire programme for putting the international system of control into effect, and should provide a schedule for the completion of the transitional process over a period of time, step by step, in an orderly and agreed sequence leading to the full and effective establishment of international control of atomic energy and prohibition of atomic weapons.

ANNEX II

Amendments Submitted by the Representative of the Union of Soviet Socialist Republics to Point 4 of the List of Topics Prepared by the Representative of the United Kingdom of Great Britain and Northern Ireland

4. *Prohibition of atomic weapons:*

(a) An international convention outlawing the production, use and possession of atomic weapons is an essential part of any system of international control of atomic energy. In order to be effective such a convention should be supplemented by the establishment of a universal system of international control, including inspection to ensure that the provisions of the convention are carried out and "to protect States observing the convention from possible violations and evasions".
(b) The Atomic Energy Commission should forthwith proceed to prepare a draft convention for the prohibition of atomic weapons and a draft convention on control of atomic energy, on the understanding that both conventions should be concluded and brought into effect simultaneously.
(c) Atomic weapons should not be used in any circumstances. The production, possession and use of atomic weapons by any State, agency or person whatsoever should be prohibited.
(d) All existing stocks of finished and unfinished atomic weapons should be destroyed within three months of the date of entry into force of the convention for the prohibition of atomic weapons. Nuclear fuel contained in the said atomic weapons should be used for peaceful purposes.

(3) *Resolution on the International Control of Atomic Energy, Approved by the United Nations General Assembly, November 23, 1949.*[22]

The General Assembly,

Recalling its resolutions 1 (I) of 24 January 1946, 41 (I) of 14 December 1946 and 191 (III) of 4 November 1948,

Aware that atomic energy, if used for peace, will lead to the increase of human welfare, but if used for war may bring about the destruction of civilization,

Anxious to free humanity from the dangers which will continue to exist as long as States retain under their individual control the development and operation of atomic energy facilities,

Convinced that an international co-operative effort can avoid these dangers and can hasten the development of the peaceful uses of atomic energy for the benefit of all peoples,

1. *Urges* all nations to join in such a co-operative development and use of atomic energy for peaceful ends;

2. *Calls* upon Governments to do everything in their power to make possible, by the acceptance of effective international control, the effective prohibition and elimination of atomic weapons;

3. *Requests* the permanent members of the United Nations Atomic Energy Commission to continue their consultations, to explore all possible avenues and examine all concrete suggestions with a view to determining whether they might lead to an agreement securing the basic objectives of the General Assembly in this question, and to keep the Atomic Energy Commission and the General Assembly informed of their progress;

4. *Recommends* that all nations, in the use of their rights of sovereignty, join in mutual agreement to limit the individual exercise of those rights in the control of atomic energy to the extent required, in the light of the foregoing considerations, for the promotion of world security and peace, and recommends that all nations agree to exercise such rights jointly.

22 *Ibid., Official Records: Resolutions,* (4th session), p. 22.

CHAPTER VII

Dependent Areas

1. INTERNATIONAL TRUSTEESHIP SYSTEM

A. Trusteeship Council

During 1949 the United Nations Trusteeship Council met four times: for its fourth and fifth regular sessions from January 24 to March 25 and from June 15 to July 22; and in two special sessions convened in December, the first to replace the Mexican representative on the visiting mission to Africa and the second to consider a trusteeship agreement for Italian Somaliland and a Statute for Jerusalem.[1] The United States, represented by Francis B. Sayre and Benjamin Gerig, showed particular interest in the problem of educational and political advancement and of racial discrimination in the trust territories, as well as in the reports on the various areas under trusteeship. The United States also presented its first report on the Trust Territory of the Pacific Islands for the year 1947–1948.

Over the opposition of the United Kingdom, France and Belgium, the Council on March 1 adopted a United States proposal to establish a committee of the Council to consider matters of higher education in trust territories, in particular the establishment of an African university. The committee was empowered to consult with the administering authorities, to call upon such technical experts as it might find desirable, and to ask the assistance of any of the specialized agencies. A report of the findings and recommendations of the committee was to be submitted before the end of the fifth session of the Trusteeship Council.[2] The committee subsequently reported to the fifth session of the Council which incorporated its recommendations in a resolution adopted by 10 votes to 0, the Soviet Union abstaining.

On the basis of a United States resolution approved by the General Assembly, a six-member committee with representatives from France, New Zealand, the United States, China, Mexico, and the Soviet Union was chosen by the Council at its fourth session to make a preliminary study of the question of administrative unions affecting trust territories.[3] The Committee on Administrative Unions submitted its final report to the fifth session on June 21,[4] the Chinese, Mexican, and United States representatives having agreed that the report was not binding in any way. A joint United States-Mexican proposal, adopted on July 18, declared that the Council should study the effects of existing or proposed administrative unions involving trust territories and requested that administering authorities furnish in their reports separate records, statistics and other information in order to safeguard the effective exercise of the Council's supervisory powers.[5]

The United States opposed a Mexican proposal to permit representatives of local groups in trust territories to participate without vote in the Council's discussion of the reports on their territories since the United States representative (Sayre) felt that there existed adequate methods by which the inhabitants of trust territories could inform the Council of their views and because experience had not proved those methods defective.[6] The United States did, however, vote in favor of a measure recommending that Belgium review all legislation involving racial discrimination in Ruanda-Urundi; and a joint Philippine-United States resolution was adopted urging "appropriate legislation or other measures" to end racial discrimination.[7]

---

[1] For discussion in the Trusteeship Council on a trusteeship agreement for Italian Somaliland and a Statute for Jerusalem, see this volume, p. 000.
[2] United Nations Trusteeship Council, Document T/259, February 18, 1949.
[3] *Ibid., Official Records* (4th session), p. 474.   [4] *Ibid.,* Document T/338, June 6, 1949.
[5] *Ibid.,* Document T/373, July 15, 1949. For action by the General Assembly on the question of administrative unions, see this volume, p. 363.
[6] United Nations Trusteeship Council, *Official Records* (4th session), p. 102.
[7] *Ibid.,* p. 498.

The general United States attitude on the reports of the administering authorities of trust territories was one of approval although Mr. Sayre suggested a broadening of the economic base of the territory of Western Samoa, suggested better public health and education facilities in French Togoland and commended 'its administering authority for its plan to permit the people to decide for themselves whether to remain in the French Union. Mr. Sayre congratulated the administering power of the British Cameroons for its development and welfare plans but urged that greater representation be given the Cameroons in the projected legislative council, that wages of workers be increased and that a vigorous effort be made to increase educational facilities.[8]

A four-member mission was appointed to visit British and French administered trust territories leaving November 1, 1949, to which was appointed Mr. Sayre, Pierre Ryckmans (Belgium), Awni Khalidi (Iraq) and Abalardo Ponce-Sotello (Mexico); the latter was replaced by A. Ramos Pedrueza at the first special session. Benjamin Gerig later replaced Mr. Sayre,[9] and Mr. Ryckmans was replaced by Alfred Claeys-Boùùaert.

(1) *Resolution on Higher Education in the Trust Territories of Africa, Adopted by the United Nations Trusteeship Council, July 19, 1949.*[10]

The Council,

(1) HAVING CONSIDERED sub-paragraph (d) of the sixth paragraph of resolution 225 (III) of the General Assembly which recommends that the Council study the financial and technical implications of a further expansion of facilities for higher education of the inhabitants of Trust Territories of Africa,

(2) HAVING ESTABLISHED by its resolution 84 (IV) the Committee on Higher Education in Trust Territories with the following terms of reference:

Having regard to the existing facilities for higher education in Africa already provided by certain Administering Authorities and bearing in mind the plans already made and to be made for their development, to make a preliminary study of the financial and technical implications of a further expansion of these facilities, including the practicability and desirability of establishing in 1952 and maintaining a university to meet the higher educational needs of the inhabitants of Trust Territories in Africa,

(3) HAVING RECEIVED from the Committee a report on the financial and technical implications of a further expansion of facilities for higher education in Africa, and

(4) HAVING EXAMINED the report of the Committee including the statement of the technical expert of the United Nations Educational, Scientific and Cultural Organization, as well as the statements of individual experts heard by the Committee;

I—HIGHER EDUCATION

(5) NOTES that the Government of Belgium has decided to organize the establishment of higher education and classes preparatory to higher edu-

8 Department of State, *Bulletin*, XX, p. 296.
9 United Nations Trusteeship Council, *Official Records* (5th session), p. 19.
10 *Ibid.*, Document T/387, July 22, 1949.

cation in Ruanda-Urundi and in the neighbouring regions of the Belgian Congo and that it has established (a) a School of Humanities (*Collège d'Humanités*) in the Kivu area, accessible to students of Ruanda-Urundi, (b) a humanistic section (*section latine*) and "modern" section (*section moderne*) of secondary education in Ruanda, and that it is preparing to establish (a) a humanistic section (*section latine*) and modern section (*section moderne*) of secondary education in Urundi, (b) a university centre in Ruanda-Urundi which will begin in time to enable it to function regularly in 1955 when the first students have completed their humanistic studies, (c) a university centre at Kisantu in the Belgian Congo which will start its regular functioning as early as 1953, and (d) a university centre at Leopold-ville;

(6) NOTES that the Government of France maintains the Medical College and the newly established College of Science at Dakar in French West Africa and plans to establish by October 1950, a Law School to form part of the projected University of Dakar;

(7) NOTES that the Government of the United Kingdom has established a University College at Ibadan, Nigeria, the University College of the Gold Coast and Makerere College in Uganda which are designed also to serve the three Trust Territories under United Kingdom administration;

(8) COMMENDS the Administering Authorities for the achievements and plans which they have made so far in the field of higher education, and urges the intensification and strengthening of these efforts to the fullest extent possible.

(9) NOTES that some Africans have been appointed to the staffs of certain institutions of higher education in Africa and expresses the hope that the Administering Authorities will increase their efforts to appoint as many qualified Africans as possible to the staffs of institutions of higher education;

(10) CONSIDERING the existing needs and the desirability for the development, expansion or strengthening of institutions of higher education within the Trust Territories themselves, possibly at the initial stage in the form of junior, preparatory or university colleges, university institutes or other post-secondary facilities,

(11) CONSIDERING the necessity of the simultaneous development of higher education with primary, secondary, teacher and technical education,

(12) CONSIDERING the differing educational policies, differences of language and other technical difficulties, which indicate the impracticability of establishing at this time a single university for the six African Trust Territories,

(13) EXPRESSES THE HOPE that the Government of Belgium will proceed as speedily as possible with the implementation of its plans for the establishment of a University Centre in Ruanda-Urundi and recommends that the Government of Belgium consider the initial establishment of suitable preparatory institutions of higher education by 1952:

(14) RECOMMENDS that the Government of France consider the establish-

ment of institutions of higher education for the Trust Territories under its administration if possible by 1952, and expresses the hope that the Government of France will pay particular attention to the higher educational needs of the Trust Territory of Cameroons under French administration, and, specifically, consider the establishment in the Trust Territories of university institutes or university colleges of a technical or professional character which might be integrated with other institutions of higher education in territories under French administration;

(15) RECOMMENDS that the Government of the United Kingdom consider, without prejudice to the normal development of Makerere College, the possibility of establishing in Tanganyika, as soon as possible, facilities for higher education, including vocational and technical education; and, with a view to facilitating the expansion of higher education in Togoland and Cameroons under British administration, recommends that the Government of the United Kingdom take all possible steps to increase the number of scholarships for students from the two Territories;

(16) RECOMMENDS to the Administering Authorities concerned that in the planning and establishment of institutions of higher education particular attention be paid to the technical and cultural needs of the Trust Territories with the objects of advancing human knowledge and of equipping students for responsible citizenship;

II—SCHOLARSHIPS

(17) NOTES that the Governments of France and the United Kingdom provide scholarships for the inhabitants of the Trust Territories under their administration to study in the institutions of higher education in Africa, the United Kingdom and France;

(18) RECOMMENDS that the Administering Authorities consider the possibility of progressively increasing the number of scholarships for higher education in Africa and overseas available to the inhabitants of the African Trust Territories, and to that end

(a) URGES that all possible steps be taken to make available to qualified students from Trust Territories fellowships, scholarships, and internships which have been or may be established by the United Nations or by its specialized agencies,

(b) INVITES the United Nations Educational, Scientific and Cultural Organization to furnish the Administering Authorities with complete information with regard to all fellowships and scholarships and the terms and conditions under which such fellowships or scholarships have been established, and asks the Administering Authorities to collaborate with United Nations Educational, Scientific and Cultural Organization, and other specialized agencies, in the establishment and implementation of scholarship programmes with regard to Trust Territories,

(c) INVITES the Administering Authorities to give full publicity with regard to all fellowships, scholarships, and internships available to the inhabitants of Trust Territories;

III—FINANCIAL CONSIDERATIONS

(19) CONSIDERING the financial difficulties which are at present limiting, according to the statement of the Administering Authorities concerned, the development of education in the African Trust Territories,

(20) INVITES the Economic and Social Council, in consultation with the Trusteeship Council and the Administering Authorities concerned, to take into account the higher educational needs of Trust Territories in its study of programmes of technical assistance for under-developed areas;

(21) SUGGESTS to the Administering Authorities concerned that in financing the expansion of higher education in Africa attempts be made to seek the assistance of such private organizations as may be in a position to give financial support;

IV—REPORTS

(22) REQUESTS the Administering Authorities concerned to make available in the annual reports information with regard to the implementation of the foregoing recommendations.

B. Trusteeship Committee of the General Assembly

In the Trusteeship Committee of the fourth session of the General Assembly and in plenary session, the United States, unlike many of the administering powers, voted in favor of a resolution bringing the supervision of administrative unions more directly under the control of the Trusteeship Council. The resolution as adopted affirmed that the operation of administrative unions between trust territories and other areas should not hamper the free evolution of those territories towards self-government and called on the Trusteeship Council to continue its investigation of such unions, paying particular attention to the desirability of the administering authorities' informing the Council before establishing new unions or extending old ones.[11] Of the resolution concerning political advancement in trust territories[12] the United States voted in committee against two paragraphs: 1) that the Trusteeship Council should express its view that the seat of administration should be inside the territory concerned; and 2) that the Trusteeship Council "should call upon the Administering Authorities to furnish the Council within one year, with general plans and an outline of the ways and means by which they intended to comply with the provisions of the Charter relating to the progressive development of Trust Territories towards self-determination, self-government or independence." As both these paragraphs were accepted in committee the United States voted against the resolution as a whole, but voted for the resolution in plenary session, the paragraphs to which it had objected having been deleted after failing to receive a two-thirds majority vote.[13]

A second resolution of the committee dealing with petitions and visiting missions was accepted by the United States as were the resolutions on economic, social and educational advancement in trust territories and a resolution on the use of the United Nations flag in trust territories.[14]

11 United Nations General Assembly, Document A/P.V.240, November 15, 1949.
12 Ibid., Document A/1028, October 20, 1949.
13 Ibid., Document A/P.V.240, November 15, 1949.
14 For a summary of these further resolutions adopted at the fourth session of the General Assembly, see International Organization, IV, p. 94.

C. Strategic Areas Under Trusteeship

1. UNITED STATES TRUSTEESHIP IN THE PACIFIC

On February 20 the United States submitted its first annual report on the Trust Territory of the Pacific Islands[15] to the Secretary-General of the United Nations (Lie), and on July 8 the report was presented to the Trusteeship Council. While most Council representatives commended the progress made in the territory, the Soviet Union representative (Soldatov) severely criticized several aspects of the administration, asserting that 1) there was no legislative organ in the territory in which the native population could really take part; 2) all authority was in the hands of nationals of the United States; 3) the central organs of administration were not situated within the territory; 4) no steps had been taken to end the primitive tribal system; 5) democratically elected municipalities had not been established; and 6) racial discrimination still existed. The United Kingdom and Belgian representatives agreed that perhaps the administering authority was at fault in establishing a standard of living so high that the indigenous population would not be able to maintain it once the trusteeship had ended. On July 1 a report approving in general the United States administration was adopted by a vote of 8 to 0 with 3 abstentions (New Zealand, the Soviet Union and the United States) and submitted to the Security Council in accordance with Article 83 of the Charter.[16] No action was taken by the Security Council during the period under review.

(1) *Summary Record of Statement by the United States Representative on the United Nations Trusteeship Council (Sayre) on Remarks by the Soviet Union Representative (Soldatov) on United States Administration of the Trust Territory of the Pacific Islands, July 18, 1949.*[17]

[EXCERPTS]

.   .   .   .

. . . In his [the United States representative's] opinion, there were profound differences of outlook and philosophy with regard to the administration of Trust Territories between the USSR and the United States delegations. Three of those differences were fundamental and deserved careful consideration.

The first was illustrated by the frequently discussed problem of how best to bring western forms of democratic government to the inhabitants of Trust Territories still dominated by the tribal system. At a previous meeting of the Council, the USSR representative had said that the Administering Authority was not only retaining but even using the tribal system for its own purposes and that all its reforms had been of a purely bureaucratic character, confined solely to providing new appellations for tribal chiefs. The Administering Authority was criticized for not wiping out the tribal system and replacing it by a western government structure. He could not agree with that USSR philosophy of government as his country believed that real democracy was based upon the desires and consent of the governed. Widespread and popular education was the only sound foundation for a truly democratic government and he therefore felt that the clan or tribal system

---

[15] United Nations Security Council, Document S/1261, February 18, 1949.
[16] United Nations Trusteeship Council, *Official Records*, (5th session), p. 193–229.
[17] *Ibid.*, Document T/SR. 183, July 18, 1949.

under which people had lived for centuries should not be replaced overnight by western forms of government which they neither understood nor desired. The change should be a gradual and progressive development based on education. That process took time and it should be remembered that the Pacific Islands Trusteeship Agreement had been signed only two years previously. The Administering Authority believed that development towards self-government or independence had to be based on the active and intelligent participation of the population; such a constructive participation on a territory-wide basis was currently impracticable because of the primitive condition of the vast majority of the population and the wide divisions and diversities between different cultural groups, caused and accentuated in most instances by their geographical separation. Any attempt to impose political advancement in an arbitrary manner would be a violation of the obligations laid down by article VI of the Trusteeship Agreement which required the Administering Authority to give "due recognition to the customs of the inhabitants in providing a system of law for the Territory".

The second fundamental divergence in thought between the USSR and the United States Governments could be illustrated by the USSR representative's allegation that the introduction of the system of municipalities had been merely a sham reform. The USSR representative apparently believed that the promotion of political advancement required the imposition overnight of a full-fledged government for the whole of the Territory, composed either entirely or at least partially of indigenous inhabitants, and that the institution of municipal organizations was not the right sort of development in that direction. The United States Government could not agree with that view as it held that the development of self-government began with local areas. There had to be development of unity of thought and organization in local communities before there could be any feeling of national consciousness. Clearly, the only practicable way to promote the political advancement of the inhabitants of the Trust Territory and their progressive development towards self-government — an obligation imposed on the Administering Authority by Article 76 of the Charter — was to begin by the organization of municipalities, especially since the Territory covered some three million square miles and its people were separated by wide cultural diversities and had no sense of national unity. It was true that not all municipalities were as yet organized on a representative basis. Many democratic elections had been held, however, and the fact that approximately eighty percent of the indigenous inhabitants of voting age enjoyed some form of suffrage was a clear indication that progress was being made in gradually remoulding the local government. The Administering Authority had started self-government in local municipalities and was expanding it through regional advisory bodies. Its intention was to increase the extent of indigenous participation as the population became prepared to assume such responsibility, and a start had been made by the use of indigenous inhabitants in important regional and district positions, including justice and superior courts. There was clearly no justification for the USSR representative's allegation that the Administering Authority had not taken any steps "to bring the indigenous population of the Territory into the political, legislative and judicial organs of the Territory at all stages and in all posts" or that it did not intend "to introduce any measures which would provide for the participation of the indigenous inhabitants of the Trust Territory in the executive, legislative and judicial organs of the Territory". The plan of the Administering Authority was first to develop self-governing muncipalities, then progressively to increase the powers of regional or district bodies and finally to develop territory-wide organs of self-government in which the indigenous population would play a substantial if not a major part.

Turning to the USSR representative's comments regarding the economic and educational fields, he emphasized again that his Government was seeking from the Islands no financial gain or advantage of any kind, either for itself or for its nationals. The United States Government was deriving no profit whatever from the Islands and on the contrary was spending large sums — which some members even regarded as excessive — for the welfare of the inhabitants.

. . . .

The USSR representative had alleged that "the Administering Authority has not undertaken the necessary measures to bring the indigenous inhabitants into active participation in the economic life of the area and has not taken any steps to develop industry on the basis of local raw material". Facts showed quite clearly that the Administering Authority had, on the contrary, fostered the development of local industries by the indigenous inhabitants.

. . . .

The USSR representative has also criticized the educational system of the Territory alleging that the Administering Authority was not taking "the necessary steps to create conditions which would make it possible for the inhabitants of the Trust Territory to obtain a secondary or higher education". It was clear from page 58 of the Report that since the conclusion of the Trusteeship Agreement the Administering Authority had established a free public school system, that elementary schools were to be found throughout the Territory and that an excellent Teachers' Training School had been set up at Truk. In addition to establishing elementary and intermediate schools and schools for the advanced training of teachers, medical and dental assistants and nurses, the Administering Authority was helping some students to obtain higher education in Hawaii and in the United States. Out of an indigenous population of some 52,000 people, no fewer than 9,300 children were attending school. In that connexion he wished to explain that the apparent discrepancy in figures mentioned by the Iraqi representative at the previous meeting — namely, that according to the Report there seemed to be more children at school than there were children of school age — was due to the fact that only children between six and sixteen years of age had been classified as school children while many who were over that age also attended various schools.

. . . .

The USSR representative had recommended increases in the budget: for education and public health. His Government desired nothing better than improvements in those fields but it had already expended very considerable sums for education and public health, and, in the opinion of many, there was sound basis for the concern expressed in the Council regarding the risk involved in setting up a more expensive governmental structure than the people of the Trust Territory was able to support.

. . . .

Although he did not deny that there was room for further improvement, he made it quite clear that he could not agree with USSR representative's statements impugning the motives of his Government and alleging that it had failed to submit sufficient information regarding the progress of the population.

. . . .

The Administering Authority was also giving careful consideration to the question of transferring the seat of government to the Trust Territory as suggested by the Iraqi representative. The transfer had been prvented so far by housing, transport, communication and other similar difficulties.

. . . .

2. UNITED NATIONS SUPERVISION OF STRATEGIC AREAS

On March 7, 1949, the United Nations Security Council approved by a vote of 8 to 0 with 3 abstentions a resolution recommended by its committee of experts whereby the Trusteeship Council was requested, subject to any decision of the Security Council on security considerations, to perform the functions listed in Articles 87 and 88 of the Charter concerning political, economic, social and educational advancement of the inhabitants of strategic areas. The Trusteeship Council was asked to forward to the Security Council any questionnaire which might be sent the administering authority and to advise the Security Council of all reports and petitions relating to strategic areas, together with any comment or report by the Trusteeship Council.[18] The United States representative (Austin) in supporting the resolution argued that under Article 83 (e) of the Charter the Security Council was obligated to avail itself of the assistance of the Trusteeship Council. The Soviet Union, the Ukraine and Poland, on the other hand, while not objecting to the tasks being turned over to the Trusteeship Council, felt that it was a mistake to define the relations of the Security Council to future strategic areas in the same terms as those for the Pacific Islands. The Trusteeship Council on March 22 adopted without discussion a resolution submitted by its president (Chieh)[19] which accepted the obligations conferred upon it by the Security Council and transmitted to the Security Council a copy of the provisional questionnaire to be sent the United States provided no comments had been received from the Security Council within one month.[20]

18 United Nations Security Council, *Official Records* (4th year), No. 18.
19 United Nations Trusteeship Council, Document T/285, March 21, 1949.
20 *Ibid.*, *Official Records* (4th session), p. 549.

(1) *Statement by the United States Representative to the United Nations Security Council (Austin) on Supervision by the United Nations of Strategic Areas, March 7, 1949.*[21]

The special interest of the United States in this matter is to devise practicable procedures by which the administration of a strategic area — and in particular the Trust Territory of the Pacific Islands under United States administration — can be effectively supervised by the United Nations.

The United States is also interested in maintaining the balance between the General Assembly and Trusteeship Council, on the one hand, and the Security Council and Trusteeship Council, on the other. This is a structural and political balance created by the Charter.

As I advised the Security Council on 15 November 1947 [*220th meeting*], the United States believes that, in accordance with paragraph 3 of Article 83 of the Charter, supervision of this Trust Territory by the Trusteeship Council is provided for in article 13 of the Trusteeship Agreement. This article reads as follows:

> The provisions of Articles 87 and 88 of the Charter shall be applicable to the Trust Territory, provided that the Administering Authority may determine the extent of their applicability to any areas which may from time to time be specified by it as closed for security reasons.

Since these articles of the Charter confer specific powers on the Trusteeship Council, the United States assumed that the Trusteeship Council was already empowered, by virtue of the action of the Security Council in approving the above provision, to supervise the Trust Territory of the Pacific Islands. However, some members of the Security Council felt that the assistance of the Trusteeship Council should be specifically requested by the Security Council. The Committee of Experts of the Security Council accordingly was asked to consider the matter and make recommendations to the Security Council.

We are entirely satisfied with the draft resolution [*S/642*] which the Committee of Experts has recommended to the Security Council and, as the members all know, we supported this recommendation in the Committee. We believe that this proposal is entirely in accordance with the spirit and letter of the Charter and that it represents a wise and practicable division of responsibility and labour between the Security Council and the Trusteeship Council with regard to the supervision of strategic areas. In essence, the Committee of Experts has recommended that the Security Council, while reserving to itself decisions on security matters, should request the Trusteeship Council, acting on behalf of the Security Council, to perform the functions specified in Articles 87 and 88 of the Charter relating to the political, economic, social and educational advancement of the inhabitants of such strategic areas. This seems to us a businesslike arrangement.

The Security Council of course would retain full and ultimate responsibility for all action which the United Nations may take in regard to strategic areas. In so far as the Trusteeship Council would act in this matter, it would act on behalf of the Security Council. The Security Council, if it passed this resolution, would not in any way give up its responsibilities or its right to make further requests or recommendations to the Trusteeship Council in connexion with any matters dealt with in the proposal. It would merely recognize that, in view of the fact that the Trusteeship Council is far better fitted to perform the functions specified in Articles 87 and 88 of the Charter, and in view of the obligation — I say "obligation" — of the Security Council to avail itself in this respect of the assistance of the Trusteeship Council, the most sensible arrangement would be to do so by a general request.

We now have before us the report of the Security Council's Committee which was set up to confer with the Committee of the Trusteeship Council. It gives us a summary of the views of all the members of the Trusteeship Council. That report indicates that the members of the Trusteeship Council, except for the representative of the USSR, were concerned in preserving what they considered the wide freedom of action which the Trusteeship Council has under the Charter and this Trusteeship Agreement, in dealing with all matters — exception questions of security — in relation to strategic areas. A reference to the discussion in the Trusteeship Council on this matter will indicate even more clearly the emphasis which the members of that Council placed on this point.

In our view, the Security Council should take into serious consideration the views expressed by another principal organ of the United Nations as to the latter's responsibilities.

I should like to make clear in more detail our view on the questions before the Security Council.

Article 85 of the Charter gives the General Assembly full and ultimate responsibility with regard to ordinary Trust Territories. Article 83 gives the Security Council full responsibility with regard to strategic Trust Territories. The Charter contemplates that the Trusteeship Council shall assist both the General Assembly in carrying out its functions with relation to ordinary trusteeship agreements, and the Security Council in carrying out certain of its functions in relation to strategic trusteeship agreements.

In the case of the General Assembly, paragraph 2 of Article 85 states that the Trusteeship Council shall assist the General Assembly in carrying out all of its functions. In the case of the Security Council, paragraph 3 of Article 83 states that, subject to certain provisions, the Security Council shall avail itself of the assistance of the Trusteeship Council to perform those functions of the United Nations under the Trusteeship System relating to political, economic, social and educational matters in the strategic areas.

In regard to the disputed point as to whether paragraph 3 of Article 83 obliges the Security Council to avail itself of the assistance of the Trusteeship Council, the United States feels that both the language of that Article and the record of the San Francisco Conference make it clear that the Security Council is under obligation to avail itself of the assistance of the

Trusteeship Council in certain respects and under certain conditions as specified in that Article. The position of the USSR on this disputed point does not appear to have received any support other than that from Poland and the Ukrainian Soviet Socialist Republic.

The acceptance of the principle that the Security Council must avail itself of the assistance of the Trusteeship Council in accordance with the provisions of paragraph 3 of Article 83 does not involve any reduction or limitation of the power of the Security Council in the field of strategic trusteeships. When the Security Council avails itself of the assistance of the Trusteeship Council in accordance with its obligations, that action does not in any way prejudice its full and ultimate responsibility for all functions of the United Nations relating to strategic trusteeships, or deprive it of its jurisdiction to take such further action as it deems appropriate. The resolution of the Committee of Experts recognizes this fact, as well as specifically reserving the exclusive right to the Security Council to make decisions regarding security questions. Thus, the requirements of the Charter and the interests of the Security Council are fully preserved.

If we look at the matter from the point of view of what policy the Security Council should follow in these matters, we find a number of very persuasive reasons for supporting the proposals of the Committee of Experts. The spirit and intent of the Charter call upon the Security Council to create relationships with the Trusteeship Council in the field of strategic trusteeships, similar to those between the General Assembly and the Trusteeship Council in the sphere of non-strategic trusteeships. The Trusteeship Council is the organ of the United Nations specifically designated in the Charter to deal on a day-to-day basis with the problems relating to the political, economic, social and education advancement of the inhabitants of trust territories. The Trusteeship Council is clearly much better qualified than the Security Council to deal with such questions. It is constantly dealing with similar questions in non-strategic areas, and it has personnel specially qualified to deal with these highly technical subjects. On the other hand, the Security Council has no facilities at all to deal with the problems which involve the promotion of the political, economic, social and educational advancement of the inhabitants of trust territories.

It seems to us that it would be much more practicable for the Security Council, under these circumstances, to expedite its own very important work by requesting the Trusteeship Council, in accordance with the resolution of the Committee of Experts, to carry out on its behalf the functions indicated in Articles 87 and 88 of the Charter. This would enable the Trusteeship Council to act in this field as it does on behalf of the General Assembly in non-strategic areas. Such a course of action would be in keeping with the responsibilities of the Trusteeship Council as one of the principal organs of the United Nations, and would avoid that constant friction between the two Councils which we fear would result if, each time a problem arose, we had to decide which organ was to deal with it.

The Committee of Experts' report, while not impinging upon the legitimate responsibilities of the Trusteeship Council under the Charter, and while giving that Council the broad authority which it feels itself entitled to in this field, at the same time fully reserves to the Security Council the right to make final decisions. In this respect, the Security Council is placed in the same position with regard to strategic trusteeships as the General Assembly is placed with regard to non-strategic trusteeships. The Trusteeship Council will keep the Security Council fully informed on all matters relating to the supervision of a strategic area and all its activities with respect thereto.

In the case of the questionnaire, the Trusteeship Council will, in the normal course, prepare and forward it to the Administering Authority. The forwarding of the questionnaire is to be delayed for one month in order to give the Security Council ample time in which to decide on any modifications which it desires made in the questionnaire, thus assuring the Security Council an opportunity to exercise its responsibility in this matter if it so desires. The Security Council will be advised by the Secretary-General [sic] of the receipt of the report of the Administering Authority, and of any petitions relating to the strategic area. These will be transmitted also to the Trusteeship Council for examination and report to the Security Council. Finally, the Security Council will receive from the Trusteeship Council its reports and recommendations on political, economic, social and educational matters affecting a strategic area. Again, on all of these matters, the Trusteeship Council will normally take the initiative and act as it deems appropriate. The Security Council, however, retains its full power to act and the power to make ultimate decisions. Since the Security Council is in continuous session, it would appear that its position in this respect is fully protected as a practical matter by the provisions of the Committee of Experts' resolution.

For these reasons, the United States fully supports the proposed resolution put forward by the Committee of Experts of the Security Council.

(2) *Report by the United Nations Trusteeship Council to the Security Council on Supervision of Strategic Areas, Submitted July 22, 1949.*[22]

[EXCERPTS]

I. INTRODUCTION

In accordance with Article 83 of the Charter, and with the resolution adopted by the Security Council at its 415th meeting on 8 March 1949 and the resolution[23] adopted by the Trusteeship Council at the forty-sixth meeting of its fourth session on 24 March 1949, the Trusteeship Council has carried out on behalf of the Security Council those functions of the United Nations under the International Trusteeship System relating to political,

22 *Ibid.*, Document S/1358, July 29, 1949.
23 United Nations Trusteeship Council, Document T/296, March 30, 1949.

economic, social and educational advancement of the inhabitants of the Trust Territory of the Pacific Islands, designated as a strategic area.

II. Provisional Questionnaire

In accordance with the above-mentioned resolutions of the Security Council and the Trusteeship Council, the Secretary-General, at the request of the Trusteeship Council, had transmitted the Provisional Questionnaire[24] to the Security Council. No observations having been made by that Council within one month, the Secretary-General had transmitted the Provisional Questionnaire to the Government of the United States of America as Administering Authority for the Trust Territory of the Pacific Islands, on 3 May 1949.

III. Examination of the Annual Report

The report of the Government of the United States of America on the administration of the Trust Territory of the Pacific Islands for the period ended 30 June 1948 was transmitted[25] to the members of the Trusteeship Council on 1 April 1949 and was placed on the agenda for the fifth session.

Rear-Admiral Leon S. Fiske, Deputy High Commissioner of the Trust Territory, who had been appointed as the special representative of the Administering Authority, submitted written answers[26] to written questions addressed to him by members of the Council on the report and on the administration of the Territory. During the sixteenth, seventeenth and eighteenth meetings the special representative of the Administering Authority answered oral questions of members of the Council.

During the eighteenth and nineteenth meetings, the Council held a general discussion with a view to formulating conclusions and recommendations relating to the report and to conditions in the Territory, and appointed a Drafting Committee consisting of the representatives of Australia, Costa Rica, Iraq and the United Kingdom to draft a report to form part of the report of the Trusteeship Council to the Security Council on its activities at its fifth session with respect to strategic areas under Trusteeship.

The draft prepared by the Drafting Committee[27] was considered by the Council at the twenty-sixth meeting and adopted with one minor amendment.

.   .   .   .

PART II. CONCLUSIONS AND RECOMMENDATIONS
APPROVED BY THE COUNCIL

1. General

1. The Trusteeship Council, taking into account the comparatively brief period that has elapsed since the Administering Authority assumed responsibility for the administration of the Territory, and recognizing the difficulties arising from the destruction caused by the war, commends the Administering Authority for the progress it has already made in the political, economic, social and educational advancement of the inhabitants, and for the full nature of the information submitted both in the annual report and in the supplementary data provided by the special representative.

2. The Trusteeship Council, recognizing the desirability of the closest pos-

24 *Ibid.*, Document T/44, May 8, 1947.   25 *Ibid.*, Document T/329, April 1, 1949.
26 *Ibid.*, Document T/359, June 30, 1949.   27 *Ibid.*, Document T/378, July 19, 1949.

sible contact between the Administering Authority and the inhabitants, notes that the Administering Authority is giving consideration to the possibility of transferring the seat of government from Guam to a site within the Territory itself, and believes that this will facilitate closer association between the Administering Authority and the indigenous inhabitants.

2. Political Advancement

3. The Trusteeship Council notes with gratification that the Administering Authority has under preparation an organic act for the Trust Territory.

4. The Trusteeship Council, while noting with approval the extent to which purely local forms of self-government have been fostered and encouraged, recommends that the Administering Authority increase its efforts to develop regional governmental organs on a representative and elective basis and that it endeavour to bring representatives of the indigenous population into the territorial government, if only in an advisory capacity in the initial stages.

5. The Trusteeship Council noting that some of the 137 municipal governments established in the Trust Territory enjoy a real measure of autonomy, welcomes the efforts of the Administering Authority to establish democratic organs of purely local government and hopes that further steps may be taken to ensure that the will of the people, rather than hereditary considerations, prevail in the election or appointment of such bodies.

6. The Trusteeship Council, noting that generally speaking the people of the Marianas Islands are relatively advanced, noting also that they do not yet possess a regional council, and noting the willingness of the Administering Authority to consider the possibility of establishing an appropriate regional organ for the Marianas, recommends the Administering Authority to press forward with this measure.

7. The Trusteeship Council welcomes the steps taken by the Administering Authority to effect a real separation of administrative and judicial powers and expresses the hope that, wherever practical, further steps will be taken to effect this separation.

3. Economic Advancement

8. The Trusteeship Council welcomes the declaration of the representative of the Administering Authority that it seeks no profit or aggrandizement from the Trust Territory. It further welcomes the stated policies of the Administering Authority to protect the indigenous inhabitants against loss of their land and institute a sound programme of economic development along lines which will ensure that the profits and benefits accrue to the inhabitants and will assist them in achieving the highest possible level of economic independence.

9. The Trusteeship Council, noting the arrangements at present in force for the purchase of copra by the Island Trading Company, recommends that the Administering Authority keep these arrangements under constant review in order to ensure that the interests of the copra producers are safeguarded by receiving a fair return for their industry.

10. The Trusteeship Council, noting with concern that, in spite of the recommendation of the United States Commercial Company in 1946 that the entire output of the Anguar phosphate mines should be retained as soon as possible for use within the Territory, arrangements to export the entire estimated tonnage of phosphates to Japan are still in force, and noting further that apart from a royalty of 25 cents per ton, the Trust Territory derives no benefit even from a processing tax from the phosphates, recommends that

the Administering Authority subject this arrangement to further review and, in the light of this review, reassure the Council that the interests of the Territory and its inhabitants have been safeguarded.

11. The Trusteeship Council urges the Administering Authority before granting any permits to outside fishing companies to develop the marine resources of the Trust Territory, to explore again the possibility and practicability of developing the fishing industry as a purely indigenous enterprise with assistance from the Administering Authority itself.

12. The Trusteeship Council recommends the Administering Authority to keep the taxation system in the Trust Territory constantly under review with a view to the ultimate abolition of the head tax and its substitution by a more progressive system of taxation based upon the capacity of the individual to pay.

4. Social Advancement

13. The Trusteeship Council, noting that the living standards of the indigenous inhabitants are still below pre-war levels, recommends that the Administering Authority take such steps as may be practicable further to raise the standard of living.

5. Educational Advancement

14. The Trusteeship Council commends the Administering Authority for its achievements in the educational field but recommends that it consider the possibility of establishing secondary schools in the Territory to meet its progressive needs.

15. The Trusteeship Council notes that the Administering Authority is sending promising indigenous students to Hawaii and the continental United States for higher education and urges it to continue doing so.

. . . .

IV. Petitions

No petitions relating to the Trust Territory of the Pacific Islands were received before or during the fifth session of the Council.

V. Visit to the Trust Territory

At the twentieth and twenty-first meetings of its fifth session, the Council decided to appoint a visiting mission of four members to visit all four Trust Territories in the Pacific, which include the Trust Territory of the Pacific Islands. The Council further decided that the mission should begin its work in the spring of 1950 and should spend not more than 110 days on its visit as a whole. At the twenty-third meeting the Council decided that the Governments of the United Kingdom, the Philippines, China and France should be invited to nominate persons for appointment. At the twenty-fifth meeting it appointed as a member of the visiting mission, Sir Alan Burns, who had been nominated by the United Kingdom Government. The appointment of the other members will be made as soon as the nominations of the Governments concerned have been received.

2. UNITED STATES PARTICIPATION IN REGIONAL COMMISSIONS

A. Caribbean Commission

The United States was represented at the eighth session of the Caribbean Commission held at Port-of-Spain from June 13 to 18, 1949 by Ward M. Canaday,

William H. Hastie, Jesús T. Piñero and Dr. Rafael Pico.[1] The four United States Commissioners had met in Washington from May 4 to 6, 1949 to confer with government officials on "matters relating to the work of the Caribbean Commission." They asked the assistance of the United States in improving the transport and communication systems in the area, in promoting industrial development and in utilizing the Caribbean Commission in carrying out the Point Four Program.[2] The United States section, while concurring in the solicitation of the views of the governments on the suggestion to establish a Labor Information Exchange Service, wished it to be placed on record that the United States was strongly in favor of the immediate establishment of such a service. Arising out of discussion of the West Indian Conference resolution on the facilitation of immigration of labor, the Commission noted the legislation being considered by the United States Congress (H.R.199), which if enacted would run counter to the Conference recommendation, and requested the United States section to bring to the attention of the United States Government the adverse effects of such a bill. A United States section working paper on socio-economic surveys in the Caribbean area was examined and endorsed by the Commission which agreed that the proposals in that paper should be accepted as a directive to the Research Branch of the Secretariat. In the light of another paper of the United States section entitled "Technical Cooperation Program," the Commission determined that efforts should be made to bring the Commission territories within the scope of practical benefit of the Point Four Program.[3]

(1) *Address by the United States Co-Chairman on the Caribbean Commission (Canaday) on United States Economic Policy in the Caribbean, Delivered before the Eighth Meeting of the Caribbean Commission, Port-of-Spain, Trinidad, June 15, 1949.*[4]

[EXCERPTS]

* * * * * *

Six months have passed since the third session of the West Indian Conference made its recommendations to the Caribbean Commission. Those recommendations have been studied throughout the various departments of our government.

We have assurance of its desire to take action on those projects which the member governments mutually consider feasible.

* * * * * * *

What we accomplish in the Caribbean now is vital news around the globe.

Only a few weeks ago the United States Commissioners met in Washington to discuss the work of the Commission. We conferred with the President, the Secretary of State, and other high officers of our government.

The President gave renewed emphasis to the declaration made in his January inaugural address. He repeated his hope to make available technical aid to areas such as those coming within the sphere of this Commission. He emphasized his program to help the free peoples of the world through their own efforts to produce more food, more clothing, more materials for housing, and more mechanical power to lighten their burdens. There, in essence, is a projection on the world scene of the purposes and principles of the Caribbean Commission.

1 Department of State, *Bulletin*, XX, p. 816.   2 *Ibid.*, p. 621, 816.
3 Caribbean Commission, *Monthly Bulletin*, July 1949.
4 Department of State, *Bulletin*, XX, p. 813.

He was enthusiastic in the hope that the Caribbean might become a shining example of scientific progress.

Every official with whom we talked showed deep interest in the economic and social progress of this region. We found everywhere the urge to press forward with practical results.

Our Washington discussions confirmed to us that the United States Government has a vigorous interest in the dynamic success of this inspiring enterprise.

There is an increasing realization that the economic and social development of this area is imperative to the security and progress of this hemisphere.

A distinguished former British commissioner aptly said that the influence of an advisory organization such as the Caribbean Commission, rests not on public authority but on public confidence.

Continued public confidence in the work of this Commission can exist only through results — through realism — through action based on sound knowledge of the problems of the region we serve.

By its very nature the Commission must lead the thinking of the member governments through present practice to a practical new world living at a new pace.

Notable achievements have marked the 7 years of the existence of this Commission and of its predecessor the Anglo-American Caribbean Commission. I need not dwell on the wartime accomplishments.

Today the need is that all of us — member governments, territorial governments and commissioners — concentrate similarly on specific programs which can be effected with little delay.

Political stability demands some economic and social progress. For this reason, the United States is interested chiefly in developing the commercial possibilities of the Caribbean.

We are convinced of the necessity of stressing specific plans for industrialization, improvement of communications and transportation, and development of tourist facilities, comparable to its history and magnificent climate.

Let me mention a few key points in which the United States Section is now working to carry forward the Commission's programme.

Industrialization. — The United States Section is gratified that the Central Secretariat has produced for the consideration of the Caribbean Commission detailed proposals for the promotion of primary and secondary industries. We have submitted these draft proposals to a number of authorities both within and outside the United States Government and shall incorporate their views in comments we shall make later in this session.

Communications. — The United States delegation to the Administrative Telephone and Telegraph Conference, which is now being held in Paris, has been requested to emphasize the importance attached by the West Indian Conference to the need for obtaining lower telegraph and telephone tariffs in this area.

Tariffs. — In conveying the recommendation of the West Indian Conference, a committee of experts of the United States Government has already begun assembling basic data on the trade and tariffs of the Caribbean territories and of Cuba, the Dominican Republic, and Haiti.

Tourist Development. — I am happy to report that the United States territories in the Caribbean area, Puerto Rico, and the Virgin Islands have announced their adherence to the Caribbean Tourist Development Association. I am also pleased to inform you that the United States Government has designated Walter C. Reundle, Vice-President of the American Express Company, as its representative on the Tourist Advisory Council of the Association.

Hurricane Warning System. — The United States Weather Bureau and other government agencies have been working together all winter to give effect to the West Indian Conference recommendation concerning improvements in the Caribbean Hurricane Warning System. During the course of this meeting we shall propose a resolution on this subject, recommending that a conference of meteorological and telecommunication experts be convened in the area before the next hurricane season for the purpose of coordinating a uniform hurricane warning system.

Technical Cooperation. — The executive departments of our government have been formulating proposals for the implementation of a programme for technical cooperation envisaged in the President of the United States inaugural address to which I have previously referred. The United States Section proposes that an item on technical cooperation be added to the agenda of this meeting and will submit a paper summarizing the latest information on the subject.

Socio-Economic Survey. — The United States Section has urged consideration by the Research Council at its recent meeting of this vitally important subject and understands that the Research Council has fully endorsed this proposal. We shall propose therefore that these studies be placed on the agenda of the Commission for action at this session. In the consideration of all these matters it is a great pleasure to pay tribute to the excellent work done by the Secretary General and his staff. The Central Secretariat of the Caribbean Commission is composed of men and women representing the peoples of the territories in the area who in their daily lives are familiar with the problems of the Caribbean. They are making a very real and comprehensive contribution to the effective work of the Commission.

There is much work for us to do in the too few days of this meeting.

I pledge the utmost cooperation of the United States commissioners.

It is our earnest hope that this eighth meeting will stand out in the annals of the Commission as one which achieved notable progress in practical action.

We have collected much data, but we strive in this meeting to find ways to put this data to work so that the six million peoples of this area can feel its practical benefit.

.   .   .   .

B. South Pacific Commission

During 1949 the South Pacific Commission held its third and fourth sessions from May 7 to 17 and from October 22 to 31 at Noumea, New Caledonia. The United States was represented at the third session by Dr. Felix M. Keesing and Orson N. Neilson, and at the fourth session by Mr. Neilson and Milton Shalleck. The Commission discussed organizational and work plans and approved a work program for the Research Council in health, economic and social development. Commissioners were invited to consult their governments as to the part which the South Pacific Commission should play in the United Nations program of technical assistance and the Secretary-General (Forsyth) was requested to prepare a report on the type and extent of assistance required by the area.[5] At the fourth session implementation of the annual work program, a study of the technical assistance program and arrangements for the South Pacific Conference to be held in April 1950 were discussed.[6]

3. ADMINISTRATION OF NON-SELF-GOVERNING TERRITORIES

A. United Nations and Non-Self-Governing Territories

One of the most controversial of ten resolutions submitted to the United Nations General Assembly, fourth session, concerned the establishment of the Assembly's Special Committee on Information Transmitted under Article 73 (e) of the Charter and the definition of the term "non-self-governing territory." Regardless of French and United Kingdom statements that the United Nations had no right to comment upon or analyze information submitted to it and that the proposal to establish the Special Committee on a permanent basis was an attempt "to modify the Charter by back door methods"[7] the United States supported a compromise proposal to continue the committee for a period of three years. The United States had proposed substantially the same resolution in the special committee. Against the opposition of France, the United Kingdom and Belgium, who maintained that the right to determine on which territories information should be transmitted rested exclusively with the administering power, the United States supported a resolution requesting the special committee to study the factors to be taken into account in defining a non-self-governing territory.[8] A joint proposal by Mexico and the United States recommending that the special committee concentrate on one functional field each year and suggesting the problem of education for 1950 was accepted in both committee and plenary session.

B. United States Territories and Dependencies

A bill to admit Alaska to statehood (H.R.331) was introduced in the House of Representatives on January 3,[9] reported with amendments from the Committee on Public Lands on March 10,[10] and committed to the Committee of the Whole House on the State of the Union. The bill to admit Hawaii to statehood (H.R.49) was reported from the Committee on Public Lands with amendments on March 10.[11] The bill providing a civil government for Guam (H.R.4499) was favorably reported with an amendment from the Committee on Public Lands[12] and committed to the Committee of the Whole House on the State of the Union on October 3.[13] No further action on any of these bills was taken by the Congress during the period under review.

5 South Pacific Commission, *Proceedings* (3rd session), May 17, 1949.
6 Department of State, *Bulletin,* XXI, p. 547.
7 United Nations General Assembly, Document A/P.V.262.
8 *Ibid.,* Documents A/1159, November 29, 1949; *ibid.,* Document A/P.V.263, December 2, 1949.
9 *Congressional Record,* 95, p. 18 (Daily edition, January 3, 1949).
10 *Ibid.,* p. 2257 (Daily edition, March 10, 1949).
11 *Ibid.*
12 *Ibid.,* p. 5663 (Daily edition, May 3, 1949).
13 *Ibid.,* p. 14004 (Daily edition, October 3, 1949).

(1) *Report of the Committee on Public Lands of the House of Representatives on Statehood for Hawaii, Submitted to the Congress, March 10, 1949.*[14]

[EXCERPT]

. . . .

The islands, one of America's two "incorporated" or fully organized Territories, are governed in much the same manner as are States, but with a number of important differences. The Territory enjoys only the barest modicum of influence in national affairs. The Governor is not elected by the people, but is appointed by the President, as are all Federal officers. Administrative officials, however, are appointed by the Governor. The legislature, bicameral and consisting of 45 members, functions in general like a State legislature, but its every act is subject to Federal repudiation. The "constitution" of the islands remains the Organic Act of April 30, 1900.

Certainly no legitimate objection to statehood can be raised on the ground of economics, for the Territory is not only self-supporting but pays more Federal income tax than does any 1 of 12 States. Hawaii has continually contributed more to the United States Treasury than has been expended by the Federal Government — excluding military appropriations — in the Territory's behalf.

Had Hawaii been a State, it hardly would have been subjected to the indignities which befell it during World War II. Statehood would preclude the discrimination against Hawaii which has been contained in Federal legislation from time to time. It would prevent the continuance of the unwarranted and expensive practice followed by many mainland firms of preparing "export" forms for goods sent to Hawaiian retailers, erroneously regarded as foreigners.

It has been noted by the committee that objection to statehood for Hawaii from some sources revolves around the racial question. Every congressional investigation has disclosed that there is virtually no race problem in the Territory. Almost 90 percent of the people of the Territory today are American citizens. Certainly there is no area under United States jurisdiction where a greater complexity of races lives so harmoniously. Statehood would further enhance this harmonious intermingling of the various racial strains comprising the Hawaiian population, of which the largest percentage is Caucasian.

Public opinion polls of both Hawaiian and mainland sentiment have revealed that a large majority of all those interviewed favored statehood. Both major political parties in the United States included a recommendation of statehood for Hawaii in their party platforms of 1948.

Known as the crossroads of the Pacific, the Hawaiian Islands would be under statehood in an even better position to further the interests of all the Pacific peoples. Statehood would increase immeasurably the prestige of America throughout the Orient.

[14] *Statehood for Hawaii, Hearings Before the Subcommittee on Territorial and Insular Possessions of the Committee on Public Lands House of Representatives, 81st Congress, 1st session,* p. 56.

The prompt enactment of H. R. 49, as amended, is recommended by the Committee on Public Lands.

．　．　．　．　．　．　．

(2) *Report of the Committee on Public Lands of the House of Representatives on Statehood for Alaska, Submitted to the Congress, March 10, 1949.*[15]

[EXCERPTS]

．　．　．　．　．　．

Admitting Alaska to statehood will have great significance from an international standpoint, as indicating that the United States puts into practice what it preaches about self-determination. It will be a clear demonstration of the fulfillment, with respect to Alaska, of the obligation assumed by the United States under the United Nations Charter as an administering power of a non-self-governing Territory, "to develop self-government, to take due account of the political aspirations of the peoples, and to assist them in the progressive development of their free political institutions, according to the particular circumstances of each Territory and its peoples and their varying stages of advancement."

Alaska, by the standards of the Charter, is undeniably ready for statehood. We know that the people of Alaska want it. A Gallup poll dated March 1, 1949, indicated that 68 percent of the voting public on the mainland, from which new settlers will go to Alaska, favored it. As for the development of their free political institutions, and the stage of their advancement. Alaskans have nothing to be ashamed of on this score.

Alaska has served a long period of tutelage in a Territorial status, longer than all but four of the States. It belonged to the United States for 17 years from 1867 to 1884, before even a temporary form of government was provided for it. The first criminal code was not enacted until 1899, and the first civil code was not enacted until 1900. It has been since 1912 only that Alaska has had its own legislature, popularly elected. The powers of that legislature have been restricted by provisions of the Organic Act, enacted in that year and never thoroughly revised to keep pace with changing conditions in the Territory. The legislature may not authorize bonded indebtedness or create any debt; it may not alter, amend, repeal, or modify the fish and game laws passed by Congress; the amount of general property taxes which may be levied is fixed by Congress instead of by local legislature; it may not provide for county government within Alaska without congressional approval. Within the limitations of that act, Alaska has enacted much progressive legislation. It granted women suffrage 6 years before women were permitted to vote in the States. It has many beneficial labor laws on its statute books — an 8-hour workday law, a Workmen's Compensation Act. It has very generous provisions for veterans' benefits. It has tried to speed the development of its resources by creating Territorial agencies designed

15 *Statehood for Alaska, Hearings Before the Subcommittee on Territorial and Insular Possessions of the Committee on Public Lands House of Representatives, 81st Congress, 1st session, p. 38.*

to give advice and assistance to persons interested in settling and investing in Alaska. It has met and dealt as capably as was possible with health and housing problems.

Statehood is not a new notion in connection with Alaska. Alaskans have been asking for it for many, many years in the best frontier tradition. For many years statehood bills have been regularly introduced into Congress without making any headway. In recent years, however, as more and more continental Americans have become conscious of Alaska and as Alaska's population has increased by an influx of settlers from the continental United States, more serious consideration has been given to the possibility of admitting Alaska into the Union. During the first session of the Eightieth Congress, the House Committee on Public Lands held hearings on the subject of statehood in Washington during April 1947, and in Alaska at Anchorage, Seward, Fairbanks, Point Barrow, Nome, Kodiak, Cordova, Juneau, Petersburg, Wrangell, and Ketchikan at the end of August and during September of that year. The hearings served to impress the committee with the importance of Alaska and its resources to the United States, and to convince the committee that only by granting statehood, which Aalska well deserves, can these resources be developed to the fullest in the interests of the United States as a whole.

.   .   .   .

The tradition of self-determination and self-government is a strong American tradition. The people of Alaska, who are citizens of the United States, have asked to be admitted to the Union. The committee is of the opinion that the admission of Alaska will be in the best interests of the United States as a whole.

On the basis of the record compiled at the hearings in Washington and Alaska, the committee has made the following findings of fact, which support the conclusion stated above, that Alaska is ready for statehood and should be granted statehood now.

.   .   .   .

CHAPTER VIII

Trade and Finance

1. GENERAL STATEMENTS OF FOREIGN ECONOMIC POLICY

(1) *Address by the President (Truman) before the Convention of the American Legion, Philadelphia, August 29, 1949.*[1]

[EXCERPTS]

World economic problems are undoubtedly complex. But their importance to us is very clear. World prosperity is necessary to world peace. Furthermore, world prosperity is necessary to our own prosperity in the United States. If these facts are kept in mind, it will be easier to understand what this country is trying to do.

In working for prosperity in the postwar world, the nations of the world face new problems — and greater ones than they have ever faced before. They are suffering from the terrible aftereffects of the war, which caused an almost complete break-down of European industry and of world trade. There is also the rising demand of men all over the world for independence, and for a greater share of the good things of life which only a restored and expanding economic system can bring. Added to these two problems there is a third. That is the attempt of organized Communism to achieve economic and political domination of the world through the misuse of the desires and aspirations of mankind.

These problems require the combined efforts of the free nations. Together, we must repair the damage of war, complete the restoration of the economy of Europe, and revive world trade. We must go forward to establish an expanding world economy in which men everywhere can work to satisfy their desire for freedom and a better life. We must demonstrate that the economic system of the free nations is better than the system of Communism.

The free nations are determined to avoid the mistakes of the past. The roots of the present economic problems go back to the first World War. After that war, the nations of the world made the mistake of following narrow and short-sighted policies of economic nationalism. Each country, working for its own selfish interest, tried to get the best of the others. Each nation erected trade barriers to keep out the products of other nations. Each nation tried to dump its own products in foreign markets.

. . . .

Before the end of World War II, we resolved that the international economic chaos which had led to war should not occur again. We knew that

[1]Department of State Publication 3653; Department of State, *Bulletin*, XXI, p. 400; *New York Times*, August 30, 1949, p. 3.

permanent peace could not exist if the nations of the world resumed the policy of dog-eat-dog.

Consequently, the United States joined with other nations to prepare for a peaceful economic world. The International Monetary Fund was set up to deal with exchange and monetary problems among nations. The International Bank was established to provide investment capital for reconstruction and development. In our proposals for a world trade organization, the United States outlined a method for breaking down the trade barriers which had strangled world commerce in the period between the wars. As the war ended, we made billions of dollars available to relieve suffering and repair the damage of war.

These were good beginnings. Never before in history had nations made such careful, long-range plans for a better economic future.

. . . .

The free nations have overcome the danger of immediate postwar collapse, but we have not yet achieved the sound and expanding world economy that is necessary for lasting prosperity and peace.

This larger task is the one that now confronts us.

The free nations have the resources and the means to accomplish that task.

Together, they have most of the industrial capacity of the world. They have vast supplies of raw materials. They have industrious and skillful populations. The free nations together have all the elements necessary to provide a better way of life for mankind. What is needed is to draw these elements together into a continually expanding and productive international economy.

Such a world economy is vital, not only to the cause of world peace, but also to our own national prosperity and security. We in the United States depend upon foreign countries for many vital minerals and other raw materials. Without foreign trade, many of our industries would suffer. Without foreign trade, for example, it would be difficult, if not impossible, for us to develop atomic energy. Moreover, we need to sell many things abroad. Our cotton, our wheat, and our tobacco, for example, must have foreign markets. Our prosperity would be seriously damaged if the export of our products were cut off.

We cannot, therefore, fall back into economic isolationism. Instead, we must take every action we can to bring about more trade, expanding markets, and growth and development in other countries as well as our own.

. . . .

The first principle which we should clearly understand is that a sound and expanding world economy is essential to world peace. International economic discussions revolve around such prosaic things as tobacco and rubber and rates of interest and the value of currencies. But, behind all these, lie the great objectives of satisfying the material and spiritual needs of mankind and preserving democratic freedom.

The second principle which should be clearly understood is that we are trying to expand the exchange of goods and services among nations. Sound and prosperous relations among nations rest upon the exchange of goods and services on a business basis. We are not engaged in a charitable enterprise. We are not looking for trick solutions to deep-seated problems.

The third principle is that we cannot succeed in creating a sound and expanding world economy unless we keep everlastingly at it. There are times, no doubt, when we shall become impatient or annoyed by delays and obstacles. But we cannot throw in our hand and walk out of the game. Nor can any other nation afford to do so. The path of mutual adjustment and combined economic effort is not an easy one. The economic interests of nations are not easily reconciled. No group can get all it wants. But there is no other way to the solution of our difficulties than the way of mutual concession and cooperation.

The fourth principle is that the democratic nations are not proposing to interfere with one another's internal politics. We know very well how we would feel if some foreign nation tried to tell us how to vote. We recognize that each nation has its own political problems and that it uses different political labels and different slogans from those we use at home. In the same way, nations have different business practices and different governmental devices for achieving the same economic ends.

A community of democratic nations cannot insist on uniformity in matters of politics or business. The only uniformity on which they can insist — and this is what binds them together as free nations — is a firm adherence to democracy, coupled with a common desire to improve the standard of living of all their citizens.

On the basis of these four principles, the free nations of the world can solve the difficulties which confront them. On the basis of these principles, they can achieve their goal of a sound and expanding world economy.

There is one more thing for us, as Americans, to remember. Our country is the most important economic unit in the world today. The future of the world depends upon the continuation of our economic growth and development. If we can continue to increase our national income, and to raise our standards of living, the solution of international economic problems will be far less difficult.

.   .   .   .

(2) *Address by the Secretary of State (Acheson) on the United States as an Importer in the World Economy, Made before the Convention of the National Foreign Trade Council, New York, November 2, 1949.*[2]

[EXCERPTS]

.   .   .   .

The first clear fact of our present economic life that I want to state is that the United States has a serious balance-of-payments problem.

I am sure that all of you here tonight are acquainted with the figures of

2 Department of State, *Bulletin,* XXI, p. 747.

the past year. You know that in 1948 we exported about 13 billion dollars' worth of goods. We imported about 7 billion dollars' worth. The excess of our exports over imports, this dollar gap which we have heard so much about, is thus of the order of 6 billion dollars.

. . . .

Now we have heard a tremendous lot in the past months and years about the balance-of-payments difficulties of other countries and about our own "favorable" balance of trade. I get impatient with this talk about our "favorable" trade balance.

The bald fact is, though many people don't seem to realize it, that we are in real balance-of-payments difficulties. We have been for a long time. I don't see anything "favorable" about the condition I have just described, and I don't see any "balance" in it.

. . . .

It has been fortunate for the world and for us that America's ability to produce was so great that in times of emergency we could permit vast export surpluses. They have served objectives of major national importance. They have not been to our advantage as consumers — for they have reduced the supply of goods which would otherwise have been available to us for consumption. Nor have these export surpluses been to our advantage as taxpayers — for they have necessarily been financed by direct taxation and by government borrowings, the interest on which must come from taxes.

But they have been to our advantage as citizens, for we have learned that the recovery and prosperity of other countries are essential to our national security and prosperity. The question is, what are we going to do about our balance of payments in the future?

I am not for a moment overlooking the many things which other countries must do to help close the gap. Mr. Hoffman spoke to the Council of the Organization for European Economic Cooperation on Monday about some of the measures which we think the European countries need to take to improve their competitive ability and to go forward to new achievements from the high levels of recovery they have reached.

Mr. Hoffman and I see their problems in the same way. The European countries must rise to the needs of the present and future. But allowing for all the progress which can be made by them and other countries, there will still be a large gap to close by increasing our imports.

So, if we hope for effective action on their part, we must ask ourselves what are the courses of action open to us?

In the first place, some countries will probably continue to need our assistance for some years. They will need it so badly and so urgently that I believe we will continue to provide assistance for reasons of our own national interest as well as needs abroad. However, I also believe that we must use this instrument of foreign policy carefully and within the capacity of our resources.

Secondly, I expect that for many years American businessmen will find attractive opportunities for investment abroad. It is a part of the Government's responsibility to do what it can, in cooperation with other governments, to create conditions in which political and other extraordinary risks will not deter investments which on solely economic grounds are promising. To the extent that there is a net outflow of private investment funds, other countries will be enabled to purchase more in this market than they sell.

Thirdly, we might reduce our exports. Some of our exports, it is true, have been abnormal and will be reduced as production recovers abroad. To some extent this has already happened. But if we cut our exports deeply, below the levels needed for the most effective operation of our industries, we shall be doing damage to some of the very industries in which we are most efficient and on which our economic strength importantly depends. This, therefore, is not a sensible alternative for us to adopt.

Finally, we can increase our imports, and allow other countries to pay for a greatly increased portion of our exports to them. It is to this alternative that I want to direct your attention tonight.

For some curious reason, his solution, which seems like a very sensible one, hasn't been very acceptable up to date. For a variety of reasons and in a variety of ways, we have over the past years made it difficult for people to pay us for the goods that we would like to sell them.

Nevertheless, the lesson in national arithmetic is beginning to sink in. There has developed an encouraging and increasing awareness of the good sense and, in fact, the absolute necessity of the United States making it possible for others to pay us for what we sell them.

But there is a vast difference between accepting the idea that we should increase imports into the United States and taking the practical concrete steps that are necessary to increase them. So that we may all have a clearer understanding of what these steps are, let us consider the order of magnitude of the problem and some of the obstacles which stand in the way of our getting increased imports.

I do not wish to speculate on the part the first three alternatives — continued assistance programs, private investment, and reduction of our exports — will play, but it will be a declining part. The major emphasis must in the long run fall on the fourth alternative — increased imports into the United States.

. . . .

The first and perhaps the most important obstacle to imports is fear — fear both here and abroad, working in each case against an increase in our imports.

Manufacturers, producers and exporters abroad look at the extraordinary productive capacity and the amazing productive skill of the United States and of the American people. They see that we here in this country can produce more effectively and with greater skill than almost any other country in the world. They are afraid that they cannot compete effectively in this market. And so they do not really try.

This is a problem for the other countries. They must overcome their fears and meet this obstacle by more efficient production, more skillful management, and more intelligent merchandising methods. In keeping with our whole American tradition of competition, we should not be afraid to see them try to do it. We should encourage them and help them in the effort.

But in this country also there is fear. As you read the hearings before Congress on the trade agreements legislation; as you read the letters which come to the Government about the administration of the trade agreements program, the motif that runs consistently through a large part of them is fear. Fear that to bring into this country a larger volume of things that people in this country want at prices they can afford to pay will be harmful, not beneficial. Fear that if more imports come in, someone in the United States is going to be hurt.

We are faced with perhaps the most important and one of the most difficult problems in human history: the creation of a politically and economically sound community of free nations.

But anyone who read the newspapers during the recent debate about our tariff policy would find that the major part of the discussion was directed to two simple words — "peril-points", and that these peril-points concerned whether a certain number or value of particular products should be admitted to this country.

There are "peril-points" as far as this country is concerned. But they do not have to do with shipments of individual products. One of them lies in the field of military security. Another is the possible economic distress of Western Europe and the American hemisphere. These are the kind of peril-points to which we should be directing our attention.

A familiar obstacle to imports is, of course, the tariff. Over the past 15 years we have made considerable progress in bringing our tariff rates down from the Smoot-Hawley Tariff Act of 1930. But there is still much that can be done. And we propose to do it, within the authority and according to the tested procedures of our Trade Agreements Act.

In this task we must overcome the fears of which I have spoken, and the natural reluctance of those who have long enjoyed a specially favored position to face the prospect of making adjustments and working more effectively, or even differently. But adjustments are being made every day all over this country to new competitive forces in the domestic market place, and adjustments to the competition of increased imports are no different in kind.

Our producers have for the past few years enjoyed a protection over and above the tariff wall through the fact that many foreign exchange rates have been kept at artificially high levels in terms of the dollar. Now, over a wide area, these rates have been changed and this artificial protection has been lessened or removed. The cry goes up from some in this country that we must post-haste raise our tariff barriers to meet this "unfair" competition.

Domestic production of a product may decline because of a change in style, or because a new product has been developed domestically which competes effectively with the old one, or even perhaps because exports have declined. Yet the natural first instinct is to blame the troubles on imports and to try to get at least a temporary relief from those troubles by limitation of imports.

Then we have our customs procedures. I suppose every one of you has at one time or another experienced the apparently inevitable frustrations of dealing with the customs, whether here or abroad. Part of this, as far as we are concerned, is due to the fact that many of our customs regulations are contained in the Tariff Act of 1930, which, as you know, was a highly protective instrument, and which has not yet been revised in this respect in over 10 years.

Under present laws and procedures, it sometimes takes as long as 3 or 5 years before an importer knows exactly what amount of duty he will be required to pay on a given shipment. Sometimes the duty may, after that lapse of years, amount to more than the whole amount of the shipment.

. . . .

I am happy to say that this problem is being vigorously attacked. Secretary Snyder is taking a personal interest in improving and simplifying those aspects of customs administration which lie within the Administrative authority. Real progress has already been made.

When the charter for the International Trade Organization is adopted, as I hope it will be early next session of Congress, its provisions will require substantial changes in some of our customs legislation, which will simplify and facilitate the processes of importation.

Then we have a whole series of regulations which have as their purpose the protection of the public against deception in labeling or against impure and unsanitary foods and drugs. These regulations, for the most part, have good reasons behind them. However, many of them, either because of outmoded legislation or long-established practices which have not been recently re-examined, have a highly protective effect.

. . . .

Another important series of obstacles is created by the existence of our agricultural surpluses, and by the fact that our agricultural price-support systems are so established that in some cases they require limitations upon imports.

Our Federal, and many of our state and local governments, which spend about 10 billion dollars a year for supplies, materials and equipment, are required to "Buy American."

The Federal Government, for example, is prohibited from buying foreign materials, or commodities manufactured from foreign materials, unless these materials are not available in the United States, or unless the prices of corresponding domestic items are "unreasonable." "Unreasonable" is usually interpreted as meaning 25 percent more expensive, duty included in computing the 25 percent.

It would help if these agencies could buy somewhat more freely from abroad.

We have laws and regulations which compel us in many cases to tell the citizens of friendly nations when they offer to carry our goods for us across the seas that we must not employ them because we are obligated to use our own vessels regardless of the quality of service and rate of charge which they may offer us.

I give these illustrations not in a critical sense, but simply to call your attention to the fact that in all these apparently unrelated ways, and in many others, obstacles are being interposed to achievement of this objective of increased imports which we all accept.

And it is important, whenever we encounter examples of each of these particular phenomena, to relate them to our over-all objective and to consider their effect upon that objective; to recognize the validity of that age-old principle that little drops of water can wear away a stone and, conversely, the principle of the homeopaths that repeated little doses of medicine can cure even a malignant disease.

We have made a good start on the economic problems that confront us. Where it has been possible, we have worked through the specialized agencies of the United Nations. In other cases, more limited groups of nations have worked together on common problems. There are many examples of this effort, but I want to call your especial attention to two of them.

First, under the General Agreement on Tariffs and Trade we have negotiated the most comprehensive downward tariff readjustments in history. The most recent was at Annecy this summer, where the 23 nations originally parties to the General Agreement met with 10 other major trading nations of the world. Congress has renewed for the sixth time, this time without amendment, the Trade Agreements Act.

The President has said that he intends to press forward with further negotiations to make the General Agreement, now embracing over 30 nations, an even more effective instrument.

Second, we did not embark upon competitive use of protective quotas and preferential arrangements and other forms of economic warfare. Instead, we got the best brains of the various nations together around the conference table to work out an agreed set of principles, the charter of the International Trade Organization, to govern the conduct of international trade. The organization itself would help to make those principles effective and provide a forum in which the nations of the world could resolve their economic differences.

When this charter is adopted, as I hope it will be early next session of Congress, its provisions will place our foreign trade policy on a more solid footing than we have been able to achieve through the series of temporary reenactments of the Trade Agreements Act.

These are good starts. But in a sense we have covered the easiest part of the road. In times of crisis, needs are recognized and attention and intelligence can be concentrated on the things which most immediately require doing. The test of our wills and wisdom will perhaps be most severe when the challenge seems less, when the exciting war and postwar tasks are followed by more prosaic ones. It will perhaps be less easy then to discern the needs of the day and to concert our actions when we have discerned them.

The key to continued forward movement lies with us. We have looked tonight at just one of the many things that need to be done. But it is a very important one; without it I do not see how the free world structure which we have been building can have a solid economic base. For it is nothing less than finding the solution to our balance-of-payments problem through our role as an importer in the world economy. We cannot start too soon to work out that solution.

In conclusion, I would like to leave with you three simple thoughts which seem to me to provide, if correctly applied, the means to overcome the obstacles to increased imports.

The first thought is this: that for the United States, just as for so many other countries, our basic problem in the field of foreign economic relations is that we are in serious balance-of-payments difficulties. We have an unfavorable balance of trade, unfavorable to the taxpayer and unfavorable to the consumer. It is in the long run a manageable problem, in terms of the magnitudes with which we as a people are accustomed to deal.

The second thought is this: that the solution of this problem is not a simple, single solution. Nor will it come swiftly. It is rather to be found in continuous action along many different lines and in many different fields; in the cumulative effect of a myriad of small actions rather than in any dramatic single measure.

That is why the solution is difficult. Because the campaign will be long, and so often each of the single skirmishes that must be fought and refought to gain a victory in the great campaign doesn't seem important enough to inspire the affirmative attack or the strong and effective defense which may be required. But it is the art of a great general and the test of a good army to develop staying power and see the importance of all the engagements in the light of the grand strategy and the main objective of the campaign. If we lose all the skirmishes, we are likely also in the end to lose the war.

The third and final thought is this: It is fundamental to a solution of this problem that we have a basic change in our traditional attitude of mind. We must become really import-minded. We must want to devote our time and energy to discovering and bringing in imports.

For it will be of little avail for the Government drastically to reduce the barriers we have been discussing, or for other countries greatly to expand their production for export, if the businessmen and people of this country do not really "go after" imports in the good American way.

By and large, people get what they want. If the American people really want imports, imports will come. It's common sense for us to want them and go after them.

(3) *Economic Report of the President (Truman) to the Congress, Transmitted January 6, 1950.*[3]

[EXCERPT]

.   .   .   .

We are now in a transitional stage in the development of our international economic policies. Our short-run programs of aid to friendly countries abroad have begun to bear fruit in increased production, expanding trade, and rising living standards. At the same time, the long-range nature of the problems of world production and trade has emerged more clearly, and the need for the United States to play a continuing role in world development through capital and technical assistance has become evident.

The progress already made toward achieving the objectives of the European recovery program and of other short-run aid programs should prompt the continuation of these programs on a basis commensurate with need. To cripple them now would imperil past progress and risk the waste of expenditures already made. I recommend that these programs be extended on a scale sufficient to accomplish the purposes for which they were established.[4]

In the years ahead, we must lay increasing emphasis upon long-run international economic programs. We need to move vigorously toward a worldwide increase of international trade. This will result in larger imports into our country, which will assist other countries to earn the dollars they need, and will at the same time increase our own standard of living. An immediate step in this direction is to approve promptly the proposed Charter for the International Trade Organization, which has been negotiated to establish a code of fair trade practice and a means for steadily improving international commercial relations.

Even the maximum feasible reduction of barriers to world trade would not alone make possible the continued increases in world production and living standards which are essential to world peace. Such reductions are of little immediate benefit to the underdeveloped areas of the world, which cannot produce enough to achieve an export surplus and build up their productive capital. These areas urgently need improved technical knowledge and increased capital investment. The aim of the Point Four program for assistance to underdeveloped countries is to help meet these needs.[5]

To make the most effective use of invested capital, underdeveloped countries require technical assistance. Hearings have already been held by the Congress on the legislation I have recommended to stimulate the interchange of technical assistance. I urge action on this proposal as soon as possible.

---

[3] *The Economic Report of the President Transmitted to the Congress, January 1950* . . . Washington, 1950, p. 14.
[4] For further information on the European Recovery Program, see this volume, p. 200.
[5] For further information on the program of technical assistance for economic development, see *ibid.*, p. 237.

The United States has sufficient productive strength to provide capital for investment in productive developments abroad. In order to encourage the private investment of United States funds abroad, I urge the Congress to act promptly on the legislation now before it to authorize the Export-Import Bank to guarantee such investments against certain risks peculiar to foreign investment. Through the negotiation of treaties, the Government is moving to improve conditions for investment abroad and assure protection for the legitimate interests of United States investors. It will also continue to be the policy of the Government to encourage American investment abroad only when it is carried on in a way that protects the interests of the people in the foreign countries concerned.

I recommend also that certain provisions of the tax laws governing the taxation of income from foreign investments be revised in order to stimulate the flow of American capital abroad.

In addition to its direct contribution to increased production, the technical assistance program should prepare the way for, and stimulate the preparation of, concrete development projects, on the basis of which an increasing volume of private and public investment can be made. It is unlikely that private funds, including those invested through the International Bank, and the present resources of the Export-Import Bank, will be sufficient to meet the need for investment abroad. It will probably become necessary at a later time to increase the lending authority of the Export-Import Bank.

. . . .

2. IMPLEMENTATION THROUGH INTERNATIONAL MACHINERY

A. International Bank for Reconstruction and Development and International Monetary Fund

[See *Documents, VIII, 1945–1946*, p. 617; *IX, 1947*, p. 413; *X, 1948*, p. 369.]

Following the failure of the 80th Congress to enact legislation amending the Securities Act of 1933 and the Securities Exchange Act of 1934 in order to remove certain technical restrictions which hampered the marketing operations of the International Bank in the United States,[1] legislation to the same effect (H.R.4332 and S.1664) was introduced in the 81st Congress during April 1949.[2] The House bill was reported favorably on May 31[3] and the Senate measure was recommended for approval on June 15.[4] Both Houses passed H.R.4332 on June 21[5] and the bill was signed into law by President Truman on June 29, 1949.[6]

As of September 30, 1949, the International Bank for Reconstruction and Development had made loan commitments totaling $726.16 million, allocated as follows: $250 million to France, $222 million to the Netherlands and to Dutch shipping companies, $75 million to Brazil, $44 million to India, $40 million to Denmark, $34.1 million to Mexico, $16 million to Belgium, $16 million to Chile, $12.5 million to Finland, $12 million to Luxembourg, and $5 million to Colombia. Of the total amount, $541,440,917 had been disbursed.[7] Between April 1, 1947, and September 30, 1949, the International Monetary Fund has sold currency equivalent to

---

1 See *Documents, X, 1948*, p. 369.
2 *Congressional Record*, 95, p. 4923 (Daily edition, April 21, 1949); *ibid.*, p. 5104 (Daily edition, April 25, 1949).
3 House Report 708; *ibid.*, p. 7181 (Daily edition, May 31, 1949).
4 Senate Report 504; *ibid.*, p. 7840 (Daily edition, June 15, 1949).
5 *Ibid.*, p. 8240 (Daily edition, June 21, 1949); *ibid.*, p. 8185.
6 Public Law 182, 81st Cong., 1st sess.   7 House Document 450, 81st Cong., 2d sess., p. 36.

$734.6 million apportioned to purchasing countries as follows: the United Kingdom, $300 million; France, $125 million; the Netherlands, $75.3 million (including $6.8 million in Belgian francs and $6 million in pounds sterling); Belgium, $33 million; Norway, $15.7 million (including $4.6 million in Belgian francs); Denmark, $10.2 million; Turkey, $5 million; India, $100 million; Mexico, $22.5 million; Brazil, $15 million; Union of South Africa, $10 million; Chile, $8.8 million; Czechoslovakia, $6 million; Egypt, $3 million; Yugoslavia, $3 million; Costa Rica, $1.3 million; Nicaragua, $.5 million; and Ethiopia, $.3 million.[8]

For a detailed summary of the activities and operations of the International Bank during 1949, see *International Organization*, III, p. 147, 340, 525, 707; *ibid.*, IV, p. 128. For a detailed summary of the activities and operations of the International Monetary Fund during the year under review, see *ibid.*, III, p. 154, 349 536, 714; *ibid.*, IV, p. 132.

(1) *Report of the National Advisory Council on Its Operations Relating to the International Monetary Fund and the International Bank for Reconstruction and Development, Covering the Period from April 1 to September 30, 1949. Transmitted to the Congress, January 20, 1950.*[9]

[EXCERPTS]

.   .   .   .

The National Advisory Council, in accordance with statutory authority, continued to coordinate the activities of the United States representatives of the Fund and the Bank with those of other agencies of the Government, by consulting and advising with them on major problems arising in administration of the Fund and the Bank. The United States Executive Directors of these institutions, or their alternates, have attended the Council's meetings regularly, and have participated continuously in the work of its Staff Committee.

.   .   .   .

MEMBERSHIP CHANGES IN THE FUND AND THE BANK

During the period under review, one new country, Thailand, was admitted to membership in the Fund and the Bank. At the third annual meetings in Washington in September 1948, the Boards of Governors accepted the request of Thailand for membership, providing for a quota in the Fund of $12,500,000 with a like amount as a subscription to the Bank. Thailand formally became a member of the two organizations on May 3, 1949.

Favorable action by the United States representatives with respect to this application was taken with the approval of the Council.

On September 30, 1949, 48 countries were members of the Fund and the Bank. The members, with their quotas and capital subscriptions as of September 30, 1949, are listed in appendix E.

ORGANIZATIONAL CHANGES

On May 18, 1949, Mr. Eugene R. Black, then United States Executive Director, was elected President of the Bank, succeeding Mr. John J. McCloy,

---

8 *Ibid.*, p. 33.   9 *Ibid.*, p. 28.

who resigned to accept the post of United States High Commissioner for Germany. Mr. Black assumed his new duties on July 1, 1949.

During the period under review, the Fund continued to provide a number of its member countries with technical assistance, as well as, in appropriate instances, necessary foreign currency to meet balance-of-payments deficits on current account. As will be noted in the following section dealing with "par values," the Fund participated actively in the extensive realignment of currencies that occurred in the latter half of September 1949.

Par values

On May 24, 1949, the Fund announced the establishment of an initial par value for the Yugoslav dinar at 50 dinars per United States dollar, the rate proposed by the Government of Yugoslavia. On June 17, 1949, the Fund also announced that it had concurred in the request of the Government of Mexico for the establishment of a new par value for the peso. The new par value of 8.65 pesos per United States dollar replaced the initial par value of 4.855 pesos per United States dollar, established on December 18, 1946, by agreement between Mexico and the Fund. Transactions at this initial parity had been suspended by the Bank of Mexico on July 22, 1948. The United States Executive Director, acting with the approval of the Council, concurred in the Fund action on the proposals of both Yugoslavia and Mexico.

Repurchase of Fund drawings

Article V, section 7 of the Fund's Articles of Agreement provides for the compulsory repurchase of Fund holdings of a member's currency under specified conditions.

During May 1949, Costa Rica became the first country to repurchase some of its own currency from the Fund. This transaction involved Costa Rican colones equivalent to 874,000 dollars, and was effected through a Costa Rican payment to the Fund of 855,000 dollars, and gold to the value of 19,000 dollars. In August 1949, Belgium repurchased from the Fund Belgian francs equivalent to 946,500 dollars, with a payment of 35,000 dollars, and gold to the value of 911,500 dollars. During September 1949, Nicaragua repurchased for 500,000 dollars the total amount of cordobas which it had sold to the Fund in 1948. As a result of this transaction, the Fund's holdings of cordobas reverted to the level in existence prior to the original Nicaraguan drawing.

. . . .

During the 6 months under review, the International Bank made $76,500,-000 in new loan commitments to four of its member countries. The United States Executive Director or his alternate consulted with the Council with respect to each of these loan applications.

Currency readjustments: September 1949

. . . .

TABLE X.—*Changes in currency values, as of Sept. 30, 1949*

COUNTRY	MONETARY UNIT	CURRENCY VALUE: UNITED STATES CENTS PER UNIT OF CURRENCY		REDUC-TION IN VALUE (PERCENT)
		OLD	NEW	
Sterling Area:				
United Kingdom[10]	Pound . .	403.000	280.000	30.5
Iceland	Krona . . .	15.411	10.705	30.5
Ireland	Pound . .	403.000	280.000	30.5
Burma	Rupee . .	30.225	21.000	30.5
Ceylon	Rupee . .	30.225	21.000	30.5
India	Rupee . .	30.225	21.000	30.5
Iraq	Dinar . . .	403.000	280.000	30.5
Australia	Pound . .	322.400	224.000	30.5
New Zealand	Pound . .	403.000	280.000	30.5
South Africa	Pound . .	403.000	280.000	30.5
Canada	Dollar . .	100.000	90.909	9.1
Egypt	Pound . .	413.300	287.156	30.5
Israel:				
Imports[11]	Pound . .	302.000 }	280.000	{ 7.3
Exports	Pound . .	403.000 }		{ 30.5
Jordan	Pound . .	403.000	280.000	30.5
Thailand	Baht . . .	10.075	8.000	20.6
Europe:				
Belgium-Luxembourg[12] . .	Franc . . .	2.282	2.000	12.3
Denmark	Krone . . .	20.838	14.478	30.5
Finland[13]	Markka . .	0.625	0.4348	30.4
France[14]	Franc . . .	0.3669	0.2857	22.1
Germany (western)	Deutsche Mark	30.000	23.810	20.6
Greece[15]	Drachma . .	0.01	0.0067	33.3
Italy[16]	Lira . . .	0.1739	0.1572	9.6
Netherlands[17]	Guilder . .	37.695	26.316	30.2
Norway	Krone . . .	20.150	14.000	30.5
Portugal[18]	Escudo . .	4.000	3.478	13.0
Sweden[19]	Krona . . .	27.816	19.33	30.5

[10] All of the British territorial currencies (except that of British Honduras), were likewise devalued by 30.5 percent.

[11] Free market rate for imports.

[12] The Belgian Congo franc remains at par with the Belgian franc.

[13] The Finnish change shown here followed closely an earlier devaluation (from 0.735 to 0.625 cents per markka), on July 4, 1949, and thus represents a total devaluation of 41 percent during recent months.

[14] Rates shown are those for trade transactions. Under the official free market system used in France, the rates referred to here are technically flexible, though they may be held steady for relatively long periods. All local currencies of French dependencies are pegged to the French franc, except (1) the rupee of French possessions in India, which is maintained at par with the Indian rupee; and (2) the Djibouti franc, which retains its old dollar parity of 0.47 cents.

[15] Under the exchange certificate system used in Greece, the rates referred to here are technically flexible, but for over a year prior to the current devaluation, fluctuations in the old rate had been held to less than 1 percent in either direction.

[16] Under the official free market system used in Italy, the rates referred to here are technically flexible, though they may be held steady for relatively long periods.

[17] The Indonesian guilder remains at par with the Netherlands guilder, but the Surinam guilder retains the old dollar parity of 53 cents.

[18] The change shown here followed closely a minor adjustment (from 4.0124 to 4.0 cents per escudo), on August 8, 1949. Portugal is not a member of the International Monetary Fund and has no par value. Rates shown are mid rates between the official buying and selling rates.

[19] Sweden is not a member of the Fund and has no par value. Rates shown are average rates between the official buying and selling rates.

. . . .

As a further aid to member countries, the International Bank announced an expanded program of technical assistance for economic development. The Bank indicated that it would be prepared to help member countries in making comprehensive surveys of their resources and in working out appropriate long-term investment programs; to work closely with potential borrowers in the analysis and planning of specific projects for Bank financing; and to assist in formulating and putting into effect practical measures to strengthen the financial institutions and practices of its member countries and to encourage productive investment from other sources. The Bank, however, emphasized the importance of action on the part of the less-developed countries to create a sound foundation for economic development.

· · · · · · · ·

Legislation

In June 1949, the United States Congress enacted, and on the 29th day of that month the President approved, legislation amending provisions of the National Bank Act and the Bretton Woods Agreements Act applicable to securities of the International Bank (Public Law 142, Ch. 276, 81st Cong., 1st sess.). This legislation was designed to remove certain requirements which might interfere with the Bank's financing operations and thereby limit its effectiveness in carrying out the purposes for which it was established. The National Bank Act was amended to permit national banks and state member banks of the Federal Reserve System to deal in and underwrite International Bank securities subject to certain prescribed limitations as to amount. The Bretton Woods Agreements Act was amended to provide that any securities issued by the International Bank and any securities guaranteed by the Bank as to both principal and interest shall be deemed exempted securities under the Securities Act of 1933 and the Securities Exchange Act of 1934. Public Law 142 also authorized the Securities and Exchange Commission to require the Bank to file annual and other reports with it and, in consultation with the Council, to suspend these exemptions.

Fiscal operations

For the fiscal year ending June 30, 1949, the International Bank had a net income of about $10,600,000, exclusive of special reserve commissions of $5,000,000. For the three months ending September 30, 1949, the Bank had an income of nearly $3,200,000, exclusive of over $1,300,000 paid into its special reserve. As of September 30, 1949, the Bank had an earned surplus of over $16,800,000, plus about $9,400,000 in its special reserve.

Future lending

On September 30, 1949, the Bank had uncommitted loanable dollar funds amounting to approximately $320,000,000, and was engaged in the investigation of numerous requests for loans throughout the world. After having completed the immediate postwar phase of its activities, the Bank has entered upon a program of developmental loans to assist nations to obtain the fullest utilization of their own resources.

(2) *An Act to Amend the National Bank Act and the Bretton Woods Agreements Act, Approved June 29, 1949.*[20]

Be it enacted by the Senate and House of Representatives of the United States of America in Congress assembled, That paragraph Seventh of section 8 of the National Bank Act, as amended (U. S. C., title 12, sec. 24), is amended by adding to the end thereof the following new sentence: "The limitations and restrictions herein contained as to dealing in and underwriting investment securities shall not apply to obligations issued by the International Bank for Reconstruction and Development which are at the time eligible for purchase by a national bank for its own account: *Provided,* That no association shall hold obligations issued by said bank as a result of underwriting, dealing, or purchasing for its own account (and for this purpose obligations as to which it is under commitment shall be deemed to be held by it) in a total amount exceeding at any one time 10 per centum of its capital stock actually paid in and unimpaired and 10 per centum of its unimpaired surplus fund".

SEC. 2. The Bretton Woods Agreements Act, as amended (U. S. C., title 22, secs. 286–286k), is amended by adding at the end thereof a new section to be numbered section 15 and to read as follows:

"SEC. 15. (a) Any securities issued by International Bank for Reconstruction and Development (including any guaranty by the bank, whether or not limited in scope), and any securities guaranteed by the bank as to both principal and interest, shall be deemed to be exempted securities within the meaning of paragraph (a) (2) of section 3 of the Act of May 27, 1933, as amended (U. S. C., title 15, sec. 77c), and paragraph (a) (12) of section 3 of the Act of June 6, 1934, as amended (U. S. C., title 15, sec. 78c). The bank shall file with the Securities and Exchange Commission such annual and other reports with regard to such securities as the Commission shall determine to be appropriate in view of the special character of the bank and its operations and necessary in the public interest or for the protection of investors.

"(b) The reports of the National Advisory Council provided for in section 4 (a) (6) of the Bretton Woods Agreements Act shall also cover and include the effectiveness of the provisions of section 15 (a) of this Act and the exemption for securities issued by the bank provided by section 8 of the National Bank Act in facilitating the operations of the bank and the extent to which the operations of the bank may assist in financing European recovery and the reconstruction and development of the economic resources of member countries of the bank and the recommendations of the Council as to any modifications it may deem desirable in the provisions of this Act."

20 Public Law 142, 81st Cong., 1st sess.

Sec. 3. The Securities and Exchange Commission acting in consultation with the National Advisory Council on International Monetary and Financial Problems is authorized to suspend the provisions of section 15 (a) of the Bretton Woods Agreements Act at any time as to any or all securities issued or guaranteed by the bank during the period of such suspension. The Commission shall include in its annual reports to Congress such information as it shall deem advisable with regard to the operations and effect of this Act and in connection therewith shall include any views submitted for such purpose by any association of dealers registered with the Commission.

B. International Trade Organization

[See Documents, VIII, 1945–1946, p. 624; IX, 1947, p. 424; X, 1948, p. 375.]

The delay in the ratification of the charter of the International Trade Organization and, accordingly, in the coming into existence of ITO resulted in an emergency session of the Executive Committee of the Interim Commission of ITO at Annecy, France, during July 1949. Two major problems were posed as a result of this situation: 1) the designation of appropriate machinery to continue to exercise, on an interim basis, the functions of ITO in the field of international trade commodities; and 2) the assumption by the Interim Commission of certain responsibilities in the field of barriers to the international transport of goods.[1] The former question was raised in a letter from the Interim Coordinating Committee for International Commodity Arrangements, to which interim responsibility for the administration of ITO's functions in the commodities field had been assigned, stating that in the light of the further delay in the establishment of ITO the Interim Coordinating Committee doubted its ability to continue to exercise these functions effectively and proposing the creation of "an interim body, composed of Government representatives and with more specific responsibilities such, for instance, as those given to the ITO by Chapter VI of the Havana Charter."[2] The second question concerned a request originating with the United Nations Transport and Communications Commission that the Interim Commission, "if it is willing to accept the responsibility of dealing with the matter," receive from member states information and reports relating to various recommendations of the International Chamber of Commerce on the problems of barriers to international transport of goods.[3]

Stating his government's concern lest the Interim Commission's functions be extended beyond its terms of reference and into substantive fields, the United States representative (Lewis) expressed the belief that it would be inadvisable for the Executive Committee to take the initiative in acting upon the ICCICA proposal.[4] A second United States representative (Willoughby) supplemented Mr. Lewis's statement, emphasizing that, while the United States had considerable interest in ensuring that the principles of the Havana charter relating to commodity arrangements were applied and while it was the policy of the administration to seek ratification of the charter as rapidly as possible, the United States could not agree to any step which might be interpreted as placing a part of the charter into effect prior to its approval by the Congress.[5] Ultimately, the Executive Committee notified ICCICA that, in its opinion, no further action need be taken in connection with machinery governing commodity arrangements since the principal trading nations of the world, as contracting parties to the General Agreement on Tariffs and Trade, were under obligation "to observe to the fullest extent of their executive authority the general principles of Chapter VI . . . of the Havana Charter."[6]

---

[1] Interim Commission for the International Trade Organization, Document ICITO/1/16, July 1, 1949.
[2] Ibid., p. 5.
[3] United Nations Economic and Social Council, Document E/C.2/59, October 20, 1949; ibid., Document E/CN.2/65/Rev.1, March 31, 1949.
[4] Interim Commission for the International Trade Organization, Document ICITO/1/17, July 5, 1949, p. 8.
[5] Ibid., Document ICITO/1/18, July 6, 1949.
[6] Ibid., Document ICITO/1/21, August 1, 1949.

Again in the interests of confining the responsibilities of the Interim Commission to administrative matters, the United States representative (Willoughby) opposed the assumption by ICITO of any substantive functions in handling the problem of barriers to the international transport of goods. He suggested, however, that the Interim Commission might properly either 1) request that the United Nations Secretary-General keep such information on the problem as might be obtained from member governments until ITO came into being, or 2) request that the Secretary-General deposit with the Interim Commission information so received to be held until the first conference of ITO met.[7] The Interim Commission decided to place the subject of barriers to international transport of goods on the agenda of the first ITO conference and to assign to the ICITO secretariat the task of receiving and collating information from member governments on items within the terms of reference of ITO which pertained to the subject.[8]

On April 28, 1949, President Truman transmitted to the Congress the charter of the International Trade Organization together with the recommendation that the Congress authorize acceptance of membership in the Organization on behalf of the United States.[9] Prior to the formal transmittal of the charter, Rep. James G. Fulton (Pennsylvania) and Rep. Jacob K. Javits (New York) had, on January 5 and 6, respectively, introduced measures providing for United States participation in ITO and authorizing appropriations for that purpose.[10] Following the President's message of April 28, Rep. John Kee (West Virginia), chairman of the House Committee on Foreign Affairs, introduced a third implementing measure[11] which, along with the two previous bills, was referred to the House Committee on Foreign Affairs. No further action was taken on these measures during 1949.

As of December 31, 1949, only two signatories to the ITO charter, Australia and Liberia, had completed the process of ratification.[12]

(1) Message of the President (Truman) to the Congress, Transmitting the Charter for the International Trade Organization, April 28, 1949.[13]

I submit herewith, for the consideration of the Congress, the Charter for an International Trade Organization, prepared by a conference of the United Nations which met in Habana in 1948, together with a memorandum from the Secretary of State.

The Charter is designed to do two things: to establish a code of international conduct to guide nations in dealing with the fundamental problems of world trade, and to create an agency, within the framework of the United Nations, to help implement this code.

We have learned through bitter experience how necessary it is for nations to approach jointly the task of improving the conditions of world trade.

During the 1930's many nations acted independently, each attempting to gain advantage at the expense of others. The result was a vicious circle — with restrictions by one nation provoking more serious restrictions by other nations in retaliation. The end result was a tremendous drop in the volume of international trade which made the general depression worse and injured all countries.

---

[7] Ibid., p 7.   [8] Ibid.
[9] House Document 61, 81st Cong., 1st sess.; Department of State, Bulletin, XX, p. 601.
[10] Congressional Record, 95, p. 74 (Daily edition, January 5, 1949); ibid., p. 97 (Daily edition, January 6, 1949).
[11] Ibid., p. 5663 (Daily edition, May 5, 1949).
[12] Interim Commission for the International Trade Organization, Document ICITO/1/24, October 31, 1949.
[13] Senate Document 61, 81st Cong., 1st sess., p. 1; Department of State, Bulletin, XX, p. 601.

Since the recent war, though some nations have again acted unilaterally, there has been a general resolve to prevent the vicious circle of restrictions and to achieve progressively freer trade. To gain this objective, action by many nations is necessary. No one nation alone, and no small group of nations, can have enough impact on the network of obstructions that has been built up.

The United States program of reciprocal trade agreements has been a shining beacon of cooperative action to reduce tariff barriers, and it is vitally necessary that the Reciprocal Trade Agreements Act be extended in full force.

But it is clear that trade agreements alone are not enough. These agreements do not touch certain important obstacles to the expansion of world trade. Subsidies, cartels, and many other devices have important effects in limiting trade or creating disadvantages for one country as compared with another. What is needed is cooperative action to attack the whole range of obstacles that stand in the way of broadening international trade.

The Habana Charter is a major step toward achieving that objective. It was agreed upon by the representatives of 54 nations after more than 2 years of preparatory study and negotiation.

The Charter establishes an international organization, which is essential to continuous and effective international cooperation in the field of trade. The nations accepting membership in the International Trade Organization commit themselves to abide by fair and liberal principles of trade. They agree to take no action which may injure another nation without first making a genuine effort to reach a constructive solution through consultation either directly between themselves or through the Organization. They agree to work together continuously to achieve progressively greater trade and to settle differences with respect to national policies that affect the flow of international commerce.

The Charter is the most comprehensive international economic agreement in history. It goes beyond vague generalities and deals with the real nature of the problems confronting us in the present world situation. While it does not include every detail desired by this Nation's representatives, it does provide a practical, realistic method for progressive action toward the goal of expanding world trade.

The United States can be proud of its leadership in this constructive action to help the nations of the world work their way out of the morass of restriction and discrimination that has gripped international trade ever since the First World War. The alternative to the Charter is economic conflict and shrinking international trade.

This Charter is an integral part of the larger program of international economic reconstruction and development. The great objectives of the European recovery program will be only partially realized unless we achieve a vigorous world trading system. The economic advancement of underdeveloped areas likewise depends very largely upon increasing the international exchange of goods and services. Thus the Charter is an effective step toward improved standards of living throughout the world, toward the growth of production, and toward the maintenance of employment and economic stability. It is fundamental to the progressive, expanding world economy so vital to the increasing welfare and prosperity of the people of the United States.

The great structure of international cooperation that is being erected through the United Nations must rest upon a solid foundation of continuous cooperation in economic affairs. The Charter for an International Trade Organization is a necessary part of that foundation, along with the special arrangements that have been made in the fields of money and credit, transportation and communications, food and agriculture, labor and health.

As an essential forward step in our foreign policy, I recommend that the Congress authorize the United States to accept membership in the International Trade Organization.

(a) *Memorandum from the Secretary of State (Acheson) to the President (Truman) on the Charter of the International Trade Organization, April 27, 1949.*[14]

On March 24, 1948, after more than 2 years of public discussion and international negotiation, the representatives of 54 nations, assembled at Habana, completed a Charter for an International Trade Organization for submission to their respective governments. This Charter establishes a code of principles to be accepted in the conduct of international trade and an organization to help make them work. The Organization would take its place with the International Bank and the International Monetary Fund and the Food and Agriculture Organization as a specialized agency of the United Nations.

THE ECONOMIC WORLD TODAY

The world economy is still seriously out of joint. The aftermath of 6 years of struggle, with its depletion of financial and material resources and its distortion of the apparatus for the production and distribution of goods, is still with us. There are pronounced imbalances of trade not only between the United States and most of the rest of the world but between other countries.

Despite constructive efforts to cope with these problems, there is still a widespread feeling in the world of economic and political insecurity. Nations face the problems of increasing production and distribution of goods, of finding ways and means to bring the industrialized nations of the world back into full productivity and stability, and of developing and bringing into the area of productive trade the underdeveloped nations of the world.

In such a situation there is a clear need for a body in which policies in the field of trade can be continually discussed, questioned, explained, adjusted, and harmonious agreement reached. The ITO Charter provides such a body.

ORIGINS OF THE CHARTER

Even while hostilities were still going on, many persons in the United States began to think of how we could reach international agreement after the war which would avoid the mistakes and economic conflict of the interwar period and set the course of international trade along expanding and liberal lines. The Atlantic Charter enunciated the principle of equal access for all to the markets and the raw materials of the world. Article VII of the Mutual Aid Agreements laid down the

14 Senate Document 61, 81st Cong., 1st sess., p. 3; Department of State, *Bulletin*, XX, p. 602; Department of State Press Release 306, April 28, 1949.

principle of negotiation for the reduction of tariffs, for the elimination of preferences, and for the removal of discriminatory practices in international trade. As early as 1943, consultation began with representatives of the British and Canadian Governments to develop agreement on principles which ultimately emerged refined and sharpened in the ITO Charter.

When the Bretton Woods Conference completed its labors, in establishing the Charters of the International Bank and the International Monetary Fund, the delegates recognized that their work was not complete. They realized that action by nations in the field of the international exchanges and in the field of international investment required complementary action in the field of trade. In the final act of that Conference, therefore, they called upon the member nations to continue to work to —

(1) reduce obstacles to international trade and in other ways promote mutually advantageous international commercial relations;

(2) bring about the orderly marketing of staple commodities at prices fair to the producer and consumer alike;

(3) deal with the special problems of international concern which will arise from the cessation of production for war purposes; and

(4) facilitate by cooperative effort the harmonization of national policies of Member States designed to promote and maintain high levels of employment and progressively rising standards of living.

When the Congress accepted membership for the United States in the Bretton Woods organizations, it said:

In the realization that additional measures of international economic cooperation are necessary to facilitate the expansion and balanced growth of international trade and render most effective the operations of the fund and the bank, it is hereby declared to be the policy of the United States to seek to bring about further agreement and cooperation among nations and international bodies, as soon as possible, on ways and means which will best reduce obstacles to and restrictions upon international trade, eliminate unfair trade practices, promote mutually advantageous commercial relations, and otherwise facilitate the expansion and balanced growth of international trade and promote the stability of international economic relations.

Further agreement has now been reached in the ITO Charter.

The basic ideas of the Charter were set forth in the United States Proposals for the Expansion of World Trade and Employment, placed before the peoples of the world for their consideration in December 1945. It was at the suggestion of the United States that the Economic and Social Council of the United Nations at its first meeting in February 1946 appointed a committee to prepare the agenda for an international conference on trade and employment, the Conference which took place at Habana in 1948 and produced the ITO Charter. When that Preparatory Committee met for the first time in London in October 1946 it had before it and adopted as its basic working document a suggested Charter for an International Trade Organization proposed and prepared by the United States. A second meeting of the Committee was held in Geneva in 1947.

After the London meeting, the resulting draft Charter was published. Public hearings were held upon it in seven cities in the United Statees. Extensive hearings were also conducted by the Finance Committee of the United States Senate. Most of the suggestions which were developed at those hearings ultimately found their way into the Charter.

SCOPE OF THE CHARTER

The Charter is comprehensive and detailed. It is a code of principles designed to guide action. It contains commitments covering a wide range of trade relations. It stands in contrast to the resolutions and recommendations of international economic conferences between the two World Wars, which were uniformly in such general terms and so lacking in substantive content as to have little or no practical effect upon the activities of nations. The Charter leaves the world of pious generalities and addresses itself to the more thorny task of providing a guide for action in dealing with specific problems in international trade.

Equally important, the Charter provides a mechanism for continuous consultation between nations on policies affecting world trade. It establishes the obligation and the mechanism of consultation and adjustment before action, rather than retaliation after it.

We are pledged to unfaltering support of the United Nations in the conviction that international differences of opinion can best be composed around the conference table. The International Trade Organization will provide the conference room for discussion of problems of international trade. Its rules for action, its means for consultation, will together provide a method of meeting world trade problems as they arise and of helping to maintain economic peace.

OBJECTIVE OF THE CHARTER

The objective of the Charter can be simply stated. It is to contribute to higher standards of living, to greater production and wider distribution and consumption of goods and services, and thus to economic and political stability throughout the world. It seeks to do this, first, by reducing public and private barriers which restrict and divert trade; second, by establishing the objective of multilateralism and nondiscrimination in international trade and by providing means and fostering conditions under which this objective can be achieved as rapidly as possible; third, by providing a means for dealing with problems arising out of surpluses of primary commodities; fourth, by promoting the economic stability and the maintenance of employment so essential to liberalization of trade policy; and fifth, by advancing the economic development of underdeveloped areas, which have so great a contribution to make to their own welfare and that of the world.

THE SUBSTANTIVE COMMITMENTS OF THE CHARTER

Many of the substantive commitments of the Charter are based on familiar principles of United States policy. Others are of a pioneering character.

(1)

In the first group are:

(a) The commitment that member nations will stand ready to negotiate for the reduction of tariffs and the elimination of tariff preferences. This is simply international acceptance of a policy long followed by the United States under the Hull reciprocal trade agreements program. So far as the United States is concerned, this commitment will be carried out under the authority and procedures of the Reciprocal Trade Agreements Act.

(b) Commitments designed to limit the use of indirect forms of protectionism, such as discriminatory internal taxes, mixing regulations, and arbitrary and concealed barriers in the guise of customs regulations. The principal effect of these commitments will be to concentrate charges upon imports at the customs frontier, to make it widely and definitely known exactly what those charges are, to simplify as much as possible the binding red tape of customs administration and to secure a wider degree of uniformity in such administration. The provisions of the Charter dealing with this subject represent the widest area of detailed agreement yet reached internationally in this complicated and highly important field.

(c) A condemnation in principle of the use of quantitative restrictions, a limitation of their use in practice to specified situations in which all nations are agreed that their use is permissible, and a commitment to keep their use subject to international scrutiny and control.

(d) Acceptance of the basic principle of nondiscrimination and equal opportunity in international trade; the principle of unconditional most-favored-nation treatment.

These principles are familiar in the United States. They have long been incorporated in our trade agreements and commercial treaties. In the Charter they are reaffirmed as objectives in all cases and as rules of immediate and present behavior in cases where that is now possible. Where deviation is required by the exigencies of particular situations, the degree of deviation from the principle, and the conditions under which such deviation will be recognized at legitimate, are specifically laid down.

Some changes in present United States law will be necessary for full compliance with the Charter. These changes, however, are relatively few in number and scope. They will be pointed out in detail to the Congress during the presentation of the Charter and necessary legislation will be presented later.

(2)

The Charter, however, recognizes that governmental trade barriers and discriminations represent only part of the obstacles to increased trade in today's economic world. It therefore goes on to attack problems not hitherto dealt with in broad-scale international agreement.

The Charter contains the first set of international commitments with respect to the restrictive practices of private and public international cartels. In many cases such practices can be as effective and as harmful to the development of international trade as the more familiar restrictions imposed by governments. The Charter defines these harmful practices, and contains commitments by the member nations to take necessary action according to their own constitutional and legal systems to secure the abandonment of practices found to be injurious.

The Charter contains the first set of commitments by governments to guide the operation of their state trading enterprises. The development of state trading has been a phenomenon of increasing importance in the field of international trade. The purpose of the Charter commitments is to subject the conduct of such enterprises, as much as possible, to the same criteria as those which normally govern the operation of private enterprises.

The Charter contains the first set of international rules with respect to the formulation and operation of intergovernmental commodity agreements. Many special problems arise in the field of primary commodities. These are often produced by large numbers of small producers, and surpluses cause widespread hardship. Price fluctuations can be and often are violent.

Intergovernmental action is frequently required to assist in dealing with such problems. In the past such action has normally been by agreement only of the producing countries. The Charter, among other things, would require that in any such agreement consuming countries will have an equal voice with producing countries, a new requirement for commodity agreements.

The Charter contains provisions for consultation between members with respect to their use of subsidies, with a view to limitation of such use when it proves to be harmful to other nations' interests.

The Charter recognizes the importance to international trade of a high and stable level of demand in the member countries. The reduction of barriers to international trade will be of little avail if there is no demand for the products of international trade. The full realization of demand for the products of international trade cannot be achieved if there are unnecessary barriers to the exchange of such products. There are two sides of the same coin. In the Charter member countries would commit themselves to use their best efforts according to their own constitutional procedures, such as our Employment Act of 1946, to achieve and maintain within their borders full and productive employment.

Finally, the Charter recognizes the fundamental importance of the economic development of underdeveloped countries. Vast areas of the world are in very early stages of economic and industrial development, resources are not fully utilized, poverty is widespread, starvation and disease are ever present. Such conditions provide no basis for economic progress or political stability. They are fertile breeding grounds for discontent and unrest.

It is to the common interest of all nations to see such areas brought to a higher stage of economic development. This can be done by the efforts of the people and governments of the areas themselves, by the efforts of private industry, agriculture, and labor in other countries, by the help of other governments, and by the help of international agencies. Therefore, the Charter contains provisions designed to facilitate the flow of technological information and private capital into areas which need and can use them and, at the same time, to safeguard those areas against abuses of foreign investment which have unhappily taken place in the past.

These provisions of the Charter were of deep and primary concern to a large number of the countries represented at Habana. They are of concern to the United States also. For it is in this area that the United States and other highly industrialized and developed countries can make a great contribution to the sound development of other nations and, at the same time, to our own prosperity.

THE EXCEPTIONS IN THE CHARTER

The Charter is designed as a set of principles to be observed in action. It is not just a set of temporary rules to meet the present abnormal and emergency economic situation. It is designed also for the longer term. It will represent agreement as to future objectives as well as to the rules for today's action.

Many of the commitments, such as those dealing with negotiations for the reduction of tariffs and elimination of preferences, the abolition of discriminatory internal taxes and regulations, the simplification and publication of customs regulations, the negotiation and operation of commodity agreements, the limitation of the restrictive practices of cartels, and others, can be, and must be, immediately and fully lived up to.

Other commitments cannot, in the postwar economic world, be fully lived up to by all countries immediately.

For example, the members of the ITO will commit themselves to abandon the use of quantitative restrictions. But during the postwar transition period it is inescapably necessary for many, if not most, countries to budget their foreign purchases. Therefore, the Charter provides that when countries are in real balance-of-payments difficulties they may use quantitative restrictions to limit their expenditures of foreign exchange. When the circumstances which the Charter recognizes as justifying the use of such restrictions have been corrected, members are committed to abandon them.

Under certain circumstances, countries in the process of economic development may have legitimate need to use restrictive measures, which would otherwise be prevented by the Charter, for the development of new industry. Hence, the Charter provides certain cases in which this may be done, provided the Organization is satisfied that carefully specified conditions, agreed to by all the members, have been met.

Under certain circumstances a tariff rate, negotiated under the commitment of members to negotiate for the reduction of their tariffs, may cause or threaten unexpected injury to a domestic industry. The Charter provides that under such circumstances the country granting that concession may withdraw or modify it to the extent necessary to prevent such injury. This provision is patterned on the escape clause which the United States includes in trade agreements negotiated under the Reciprocal Trade Agreements Act.

Under certain circumstances it has been necessary for governments to intervene to prevent the disastrous effects of surpluses of agricultural products by programs restricting domestic production or marketing. In such cases it would be unfair for imports to be exempt from control and they could be limited.

Considerations of national security at times require measures which would not conform to the general principles which would normally be applied under the Charter. An exception is, therefore, provided to permit action to be taken by member countries necessary for their national security.

Without exceptions of this kind, members of the Organization, ourselves included, could not accept the commitments of the Charter. The exceptions are carefully defined and are agreed to by all. Their use is subject to scrutiny by the Organization. Their abuse is subject to complaint by the members.

STRUCTURE AND FUNCTIONS OF THE ORGANIZATION

The International Trade Organization would be a specialized agency of the United Nations. As such, it would enter into relationship with the Economic and

Social Council of the United Nations and with the other specialized agencies in order to insure coordinated action and to avoid duplication of activities and functions.

The structure of the Organization itself is simple. It will have a Conference composed of all the member nations which will be its fundamental governing body. The Conference will meet periodically, but at least once a year.

The executive functions of the Organization will be vested in an Executive Board of 18 countries, of which 8 must be nations of chief economic importance as determined by the Conference. This provision insures a permanent seat for the United States on the Executive Board. Other nations likely to have permanent seats under this test will be the United Kingdom, France, the Benelux Customs Union, and Canada.

Each member country will have one vote in the Conference and on the Executive Board. Decisions of the Conference and of the Executive Board will, except in certain cases where a two-thirds vote is required, be by majority vote.

The Organization will have a Director General, to be appointed by the Conference on recommendation of the Executive Board, who will be responsible for its day-to-day activities under the direction and supervision of the Executive Board.

With one exception, relating to the discriminatory application of restrictions for balance-of-payments reasons, the Organization will have no power to require any member to take any specific action. It will have the power to decide whether a member has lived up to its commitments under the Charter. If it finds that the member has not lived up to a given commitment, it may release other members from certain of their Charter obligations to that member, which, if not satisfied with this decision, may in most cases withdraw from the Organization on 60 days' notice.

Decisions of the Conference of the Organization may be referred to the International Court of Justice for legal opinion.

The Organization will provide a forum where problems may be discussed and conflicting interests reconciled. It provides a means of bringing to bear upon a given problem the force of international public opinion. It provides a means of developing, on a case-by-case basis, international precedents in the field of economic and commercial relations.

The Organization will provide a means for the accumulation and dissemination of trade statistics and information about trade practices of government, e. g., customs regulations, etc., which can be of great service to businessmen.

The Organization will be empowered to make studies in various fields, for example, standardization, uniformity, and simplification of customs regulations. It can be a means for the collection and dissemination of technological information.

The expenditures of the Organization are to be met by contributions from the members. These contributions are to be apportioned among the members in accordance with a scale fixed by the Conference following such principles as may be applied by the United Nations. Should the United Nations place a maximum limit on the proportionate contribution to its budget by any one member, the same limit is to be applied to contributions to the Organization.

PLACE OF THE ITO IN THE STRUCTURE OF INTERNATIONAL COOPERATION

It is apparent that the economic problems facing us today cannot be solved by any one nation, or any few nations, but must be tackled by many nations working together.

We are committed to unfaltering support of the United Nations. We have participated in the building and establishment of the International Monetary Fund to deal with the problems of international exchange. The purpose of the fund is to promote by international action reasonable stability and convertibility of currencies. Clearly, trade must be brought into balance if currencies are ever to be and remain stable. Regulation of exchange controls is futile if nations are free to use quantitative restrictions instead. To solve the problems of international trade, international cooperation with respect to exchange controls and currency valuation must go hand in hand with international cooperation with respect to other forms of trade barriers and the expansion of demand in international trade.

We have participated in the building and operation of the International Bank for Reconstruction and Development. We are interested in foreign private investment. Clearly, loans cannot be repaid or earnings on investments received if international trade is not fostered and freed. International cooperation in provision of capital must go hand in hand with international cooperation in the development of the kind of conditions in which capital can exercise its catalytic and constructive influence.

We are playing a tremendous part in the great work of European recovery. In the development of the European recovery program there has been consistent recognition of the vital importance of increased trade. The participating countries have pledged themselves to cooperate to reduce trade barriers and expand trade in accord with the principles of the draft Charter for an International Trade Organization. Similar pledges are repeated in the convention for European economic cooperation.

Section 115 (b) (3) of the Economic Cooperation Act requires the inclusion in the bilateral aid agreements between each of the participating countries and the United States a general undertaking to cooperate in facilitating and stimulating an increasing interchange of goods and services and in reducing barriers to trade. In accord with this congressional mandate a provision to this effect was included in the bilateral aid agreements with the participating countries.

The European recovery program is designed to help put the European countries on their feet. The ITO Charter provides principles and rules of trade which, if followed over the long term, will give them the best chance of staying on their feet. The problem is one of markets as much as it is one of production. Our investment in the European recovery program can be fully realized only if the participating countries are able and willing to adopt trade policies which will foster multilateral, nondiscriminatory, and expanding international trade, rather than policies of bilateralism, discrimination, limitation, and control. Wide acceptance of the Charter throughout the world would mean that many other nations besides those in western Europe would be marching in the same direction and with the same purpose.

We are deeply interested in assisting in the development of underdeveloped areas of the world. We hope to see these areas develop under political and economic institutions in which human dignity and freedom can be preserved. In particular, we hope to increase the international flow of technical knowledge. This is not something which we can, or would wish, to do alone. Other nations have great reservoirs of knowledge and experience which they, too, can, and will be glad to share. The International Trade Organization will be one means whereby resources of knowledge may be pooled and directed to the areas and projects where they can be most constructive.

CONCLUSION

Thus, the International Trade Organization, like the other specialized agencies of the United Nations, is part of a pattern — the pattern of the great majority of a community of nations cooperating together in various fields of the community's life to provide the services which the community needs.

C. General Agreement on Tariffs and Trade

[See *Documents, IX, 1947*, p. 425; *X, 1948*, p. 375.]

The third session of the Contracting Parties of the General Agreement on Tariffs and Trade met in Annecy, France, from April 8 to August 13, 1949.[1] Concurrently with the session, bilateral tariff negotiations were undertaken between the 23 contracting parties and eleven other countries which had indicated their intention to accede to the General Agreement: Colombia, Denmark, the Dominican

[1] Unless otherwise indicated, information in the following paragraphs is taken from Department of State, *Bulletin*, XXI, p. 774.

Republic, Finland, Greece, Haiti, Italy, Liberia, Nicaragua, Sweden, and Uruguay.[2] The United States delegation was led by Woodbury Willoughby, chief of the Division of Commercial Policy, Department of State, and consisted of members of the Interdepartmental Committee on Trade Agreements.[3]

Two issues involving United States tariff relations with Cuba and one question of United States trade relations with Czechoslovakia and the eastern European countries were dealt with by the Contracting Parties. A working party examined a Cuban application for exemption from certain provisions of the General Agreement in order to permit the execution of measures intended to relieve a crisis in the Cuban textile industry. The measures envisaged involved negotiations with the United States to which Cuba, under the terms of GATT, had granted a number of concessions concerning textiles. The Contracting Parties took no final decision on the matter, but recommended that negotiations be undertaken between the two governments in an effort to reach a mutually satisfactory solution. The second issue between the United States and Cuba concerned the legal status of the preferences which Cuba enjoyed in United States markets by virtue of the General Agreement. The Cuban delegation contended that these preferences could not be reduced or eliminated without the prior consent of the Cuban Government. The United States took the position that, if the Cuban assertion was upheld, negotiations and agreement with the Cuban delegation would have to precede the negotiation by the United States with any acceding country at Annecy of any concessions by which the margin of Cuban preferences in United States markets would be reduced. The United States further maintained that the whole purpose of the General Agreement was the reduction of trade barriers and discriminations, including preferences; therefore, the Cuban position was untenable. After lengthy and unsuccessful efforts to reconcile the two positions, the Contracting Parties, noting that unless some decision on the matter was reached the United States would be unable legally to conclude several negotiations then in progress with the acceding governments, by a vote of 14 to 1 affirmed the United States position. The Cuban delegation then withdrew from the session. When the United States assured the Contracting Parties of its desire to reach agreement with Cuba on this specific issue, the session invited both governments to enter into bilateral negotiations in an effort to resolve the problem.

The Contracting Parties discussed a Czechoslovak complaint that the United States, in the administration of its export licensing system, discriminated against Czechoslovakia and other eastern European states in such manner as to constitute a breach of the General Agreement.[4] In the course of discussion, the United States explained that, in the interests of national security, licenses for export to Czechoslovakia had been denied for the shipment of coal mining drills which appeared to be intended for the mining of strategic materials such as uranium and for the shipment of high quality ball bearings which might easily have been diverted to use in aircraft or for other military purposes.[5] After the chairman of the session (Wilgress) ruled that the only issue to be considered by the Contracting Parties was "whether the United States has failed to carry out its GATT obligations in administering the export license system," the session rejected the Czechoslovak complaint by a vote of 17 to 1.[6]

Of the total budget of $302,000 approved for 1950, the United States share, based upon its volume of foreign trade in 1938 and 1946, was set at $53,000.

The bilateral tariff negotiations with the acceding governments, which continued after the adjournment of the third session of the Contracting Parties, resulted in the conclusion of 147 bilateral agreements, in addition to eighteen of the twenty original Geneva schedules, and in ten new schedules covering the acceding coun-

2 The original contracting parties were Australia, Belgium, Brazil, Burma, Canada, Ceylon, Chile, China, Cuba, Czechoslovakia, France, India, Lebanon, Luxembourg, the Netherlands, New Zealand, Norway, Pakistan, Southern Rhodesia, Syria, the Union of South Africa, the United Kingdom, and the United States.

3 The interdepartmental committee consisted of representatives of the National Military Establishment and of the Departments of Labor, Treasury, and Agriculture. John W. Evans, director of the Commodities Division of the Office of International Trade, Department of State, served as vice-chairman of the delegation (Department of State Press Release 220, April 5, 1949).

4 *New York Times*, March 26, 1949.   5 *Ibid.*, June 3, 1949, p. 8.
6 Department of State, *Bulletin*, XX, p. 750.

tries. The United States engaged in negotiations with each of the eleven delegations. Unable to reach agreement with several of the participating countries, including the United States, the Colombian Government withdrew its application of accession to GATT. While the bilateral negotiations were in progress, the Contracting Parties, in consultation with the acceding governments, drew up a protocol of terms on which the latter governments might adhere to the General Agreement. The protocol, which required separate action on the part of each contracting party with respect to each of the acceding governments, was opened for signature at Lake Success on October 10 and remained opened for signature by the Contracting Parties until November 30 and by acceding governments until April 30, 1950.[7]

Informed that on February 14, 1949, the Chilean Government had signed the protocol of December 14, 1948, providing for Chile's accession to the General Agreement,[8] the United States by Presidential proclamation on March 8, 1949, put into effect as of March 16 those United States concessions initially negotiated with Chile at Geneva but not yet in force.[9] On December 7, 1949, the Department of State announced that the concessions negotiated with Haiti during the Annecy meetings would become effective on January 1, 1950. Thus, Haiti became the first of the ten acceding governments to take the steps required to render these concessions effective.[10]

For further information on the reciprocal trade agreements program under which the Annecy negotiations were conducted on the part of the United States, see this volume, p. 412.

3. IMPLEMENTATION THROUGH NATIONAL MACHINERY

A. Export-Import Bank of Washington

Between August 17 and 24, 1949, hearings were held before the House Committee on Banking and Currency on H.R.5594, a bill to amend the Export-Import Bank Act of 1945[1] to vest in the Export-Import Bank the power to guarantee United States investments abroad. The legislation was designed to implement in part the Point Four Program of technical assistance for economic development.[2] The bill, with amendments, was reported favorably by the committee on October 6, 1949.[3] No further action was taken on the measure during 1949.

7 For the text of the Protocol, see Department of State Publication 3664.
8 See *Documents, X, 1948*, p. 376.
9 Deparmtent of State Press Release 135, March 9, 1949.
10 *Ibid.*, 959, December 7, 1949.
1 See *Documents, VII, 1944–1945*, p. 549.
2 *Export-Import Bank Loan Guaranty Authority. Hearings before the Committee on Banking and Currency, House of Representatives, 81st Congress, 1st session, on H.R.5594* . . . , *August 17, 19, 22, 23, and 24, 1949.* Washington, 1949, p. 2. For further information on United States technical assistance for economic development, see this volume, p. 238.
3 House Report 1384, 81st Cong., 1st sess.

(1) Statement of Loans and Authorizations of the Export-Import Bank of Washington as of December 31, 1949[4]

Country	Authorized Amount	Cancellations and Expirations	Balance Not Yet Disbursed	Amount Disbursed		Principal Repaid on Loans	Principal Outstanding on Loans
				By Eximbank	By Commercial Banks at EIB Risk		
LATIN AMERICA							
Argentina	$93,690,000.00	$93,095,214.80		$594,785.20	—	$420,717.78	$174,067.42
Bolivia	36,998,004.50	48,250.58	$16,070,000.00	20,879,753.92	—	2,225,753.92	18,654,000.00
Brazil	287,502,415.54	114,065,763.65	9,147,588.43	103,804,404.42	$60,484,659.04	64,005,750.85	100,283,312.61
Chile	141,631,007.84	8,566,378.30	43,653,870.10	63,721,651.60	25,689,107.84	32,913,346.16	56,497,413.28
Colombia	65,279,665.44	2,524,629.07	17,430,744.88	23,267,507.30	22,056,784.19	23,021,809.77	22,302,481.72
Costa Rica	8,723,000.00	1,463,392.71	—	7,035,878.62	223,728.67	682,324.97	6,577,282.32
Cuba	90,366,535.31	34,198,061.95	—	30,130,973.36	26,037,500.00	45,601,723.36	10,566,750.00
Dominican Republic	3,300,000.00	16,067.58	—	3,000,000.00	283,932.42	2,929,819.53	354,112.89
Ecuador	27,616,900.00	1,095,829.90	13,201,900.00	13,319,170.10	—	2,486,396.79	10,832,773.31
Haiti	17,350,000.00	2,670,000.00	4,000,000.00	10,680,000.00	—	5,742,500.00	4,937,500.00
Honduras	2,700,000.00	1,700,000.00	—	—	1,000,000.00	677,500.00	322,500.00
Mexico	155,692,631.06	7,498,308.80	28,398,917.35	100,411,723.30	19,383,681.61	42,074,072.61	77,721,332.30
Nicaragua	5,235,000.00	585,000.00	—	4,000,000.00	650,000.00	3,128,500.00	1,521,500.00
Panama	6,500,000.00	2,012,296.12	875,976.65	3,611,727.23	—	2,487,703.88	1,124,023.35
Paraguay	7,800,000.00	1,600,000.00	—	6,000,000.00	200,000.00	2,156,050.00	4,043,950.00
Peru	37,450,000.00	37,005,841.16	—	444,158.84	—	137,827.92	306,330.92
Salvador	1,726,000.00	250,000.00	—	1,476,000.00	—	504,898.69	971,101.31
Uruguay	43,726,600.00	29,211,125.00	206,786.80	220,475.00	14,088,213.20	738,992.68	13,569,695.52
Venezuela	52,496,697.00	36,955,047.83	7,495,697.00	5,347,773.82	2,698,178.35	4,315,578.35	3,730,373.82
Miscellaneous	118,983,198.91	74,766,230.75	19,604,703.00	20,078,226.31	4,534,038.85	24,612,265.16	
TOTAL LATIN AMERICA	1,204,767,655.60	449,327,438.20	160,086,184.21	418,024,209.02	177,329,824.17	260,863,532.42	334,490,500.77
ASIA							
Afghanistan	21,000,000.00	—	21,000,000.00	—	—	—	—
China	221,737,079.99	4,609,410.31	15,390,852.28	191,417,860.35	10,318,957.05	164,756,822.13	36,979,995.27
India	16,000,000.00	16,000,000.00	—	—	—	—	—
Iran	1,130,000.00	667,570.61	—	222,398.75	240,030.64	462,429.39	—
Iraq	100,000.00	100,000.00	—	—	—	—	—
Israel	100,000,000.00	—	92,690,972.46	7,309,027.54	—	—	7,309,027.54
Japan	51,444,978.72	—	21,107,920.84	8,275,411.01	22,061,646.87	25,444,978.72	4,892,079.16
Netherlands Indies	100,000,000.00	100,000,000.00	—	—	—	—	—
Philippine Islands	25,850,000.00	25,600,000.00	250,000.00	—	—	—	—
Saudi Arabia	34,000,000.00	20,000,000.00	4,000,000.00	10,000,000.00	—	2,000,000.00	8,000,000.00
Turkey	46,327,860.00	10,833,129.74	13,266,662.84	22,228,067.42	—	4,868,022.34	17,360,045.08
TOTAL ASIA	617,589,918.71	177,810,110.66	167,706,408.42	239,452,765.07	32,620,634.56	197,532,252.58	74,541,147.05

EUROPE

Country							
Austria	14,255,000.00	1,117,775.00	—	13,137,255.00	—	795,550.00	12,341,675.00
Belgium	132,000,000.00		—	132,000,000.00	—	19,908,472.00	112,091,528.00
Czechoslovakia	23,728,931.61	950,781.01	—	5,384,692.62	17,393,457.98	22,778,150.60	
Denmark	30,000,000.00	10,000,000.00	—	3,400,000.00	16,600,000.00	—	20,000,000.00
Finland	135,105,440.98	7,599,003.63	5,123,841.54	105,461,147.06	16,921,448.75	24,004,015.60	98,378,580.21
France	1,200,000,000.00		—	1,200,000,000.00	—	59,765,500.00	1,140,234,500.00
Germany	7,603,412.93	3,006,750.75	—	4,592,103.18	4,559.00	4,596,662.18	
Greece	25,000,000.00	10,436,687.39	—	14,563,312.61			14,563,312.61
Hungary	2,375,000.00	2,375,000.00	—				
Iceland	1,000,000.00	410,000.00	—	—	590,000.00	590,000.00	—
Italy	151,181,197.91	6,341,628.18	22,643,967.51	81,242,955.30	40,952,646.92	38,015,077.01	84,180,525.21
Latvia	1,903,000.00	1,892,217.97	—		10,782.03	10,782.03	—
Netherlands	209,878,142.50	4,593,596.70	—	204,498,146.60	786,399.20	18,470,407.13	186,814,138.67
Norway	61,000,000.00	10,552,000.21	—	50,221,387.79	226,612.00	1,836,888.64	48,611,111.15
Poland	52,906,742.52	9,359,330.94	—	43,511,233.85	36,177.73	246,471.40	43,300,940.18
Portugal	5,500,000.00	4,229,134.35	—	1,270,865.65	—	1,270,865.65	—
Rumania	50,000.00	50,000.00	—				
Spain	15,072,871.78	1,391,797.89	—	112,333.06	13,568,740.83	13,681,073.89	—
Sweden	17,155,000.00	10,889,000.00	—	2,155,000.00	4,111,000.00	4,649,750.00	1,616,250.00
United Kingdom	22,500,000.00	22,500,000.00	—				
Yugoslavia	20,517,667.00	517,667.00	20,000,000.00	—	—	—	—
Miscellaneous	38,443,732.68		38,443,732.68	—	—	—	—
TOTAL EUROPE	2,167,176,139.91	108,212,371.02	86,211,541.73	1,861,550,402.72	111,201,824.44	210,619,666.13	1,762,132,561.03

OTHER COUNTRIES

Country							
Australia	1,400,000.00	1,400,000.00	—	—	—	—	—
Canada	369,965,000.00	187,550,000.00	4,325,000.00	178,090,000.00	—	177,415,000.00	675,000.00
Egypt	7,100,000.00	—	180,822.22	6,919,177.78	—	—	6,919,177.78
Ethiopia	3,500,000.00	—	2,250,000.00	750,000.00	500,000.00	500,000.00	750,000.00
Jamaica	25,000.00	25,000.00	—	—	—	—	—
Liberia	4,000,000.00	—	4,000,000.00	—	—	—	—
Portuguese West Africa	300,000.00	235,000.00	—	65,000.00	—	33,495.33	31,504.67
Puerto Rico	450,000.00	—	—	450,000.00	—	450,000.00	—
Virgin Islands	250,000.00	250,000.00	—	—	—	—	—
TOTAL OTHER COUNTRIES	386,990,000.00	189,460,000.00	10,755,822.22	186,274,177.78	500,000.00	178,398,495.33	8,375,682.45

VARIOUS COUNTRIES	10,500,000.00	5,000,000.00	5,500,000.00	—	—	—	—

Special Exporter–Importer Credits	4,525,805.15	—	954,618.78	29,915.56	3,541,270.81	3,525,804.15	45,382.22
Total Authorizations	4,391,549,519.37	—	—	—	—	—	—
Add: Advances by Participants	121,383,574.09	—	—	—	—	—	—
GRAND TOTALS	4,512,933,093.46	929,809,919.88	431,214,575.36	2,705,331,470.15	325,193,553.98	850,939,750.61	2,179,585,273.52

4 Compiled from Export-Import Bank of Washington. *Ninth Semiannual Report to Congress for the Period July-December, 1949*, Washington, 1950, Appendix C.

B. Reciprocal Trade Agreements Program

In a letter of January 8, 1949, addressed to Senator Walter F. George (Georgia), chairman of the Senate Committee on Finance, President Truman urged that the Congress promptly enact legislation extending until June 12, 1951 the reciprocal trade agreements program "without the hampering restrictions placed upon it by the last Congress."[1] The President's letter pointed out the close relationship between the program and the negotiations to be conducted by the United States under the General Agreement on Tariffs and Trade, the Contracting Parties of which were to meet in Annecy, France, in April 1949,[2] and stated that "the restrictive provisions and limited extension of the present trade agreements law materially hamper the effectiveness of United States participation in this effort."[3]

Subsequently, on January 10, Rep. Robert L. Doughton (North Carolina) introduced H.R.1211, a bill designed to accomplish the objectives set forth in the President's letter. The bill was favorably reported by the House Committee on Ways and Means on February 7[4] and the House commenced debate on the following day. Following rejection of amendments which would have retained the "peril point" and "escape clause" concepts of the 1948 legislation, and made all agreements negotiated under the act subject to rejection by the Congress, the bill was passed by the House on February 9 by a vote of 319 to 69.[5] The following day the bill was transmitted to the Senate where it became the subject of public hearings held by the Senate Committee on Finance during the period from February 17 to March 8, 1949. Although reported favorably by the committee on March 10,[6] consideration of the measure was delayed in the Senate until September 7 because of the pressure of other unfinished business. In the course of debate amendments were proposed which were designed to 1) suspend agreements negotiated under the measure with such countries as discriminated against United States trade by means of restrictive trade practices, 2) limit imports of oil under such agreements, 3) provide an escape clause in the event that competitive United States products were injured as a result of the provisions of agreements so negotiated, 4) reinstate the "peril point" provision, and 5) reduce the life of the bill from three to two years. These amendments were ultimately defeated, in some instances by extremely narrow margins,[7] and the bill was passed by the Senate by a vote of 62 to 19 on September 15.[8] The measure was signed into law by President Truman on September 26, 1949.[9] New procedures for the administration of the reciprocal trade agreements program were prescribed in Executive Order 10082, issued by President Truman on October 5, 1949.[10]

4. TERMINATION OF WAR-TIME COMMITMENTS

A. Mutual Aid Settlements

[See *Documents, IX, 1947*, p. 445; *X, 1948*, p. 390.]

The twenty-eighth and twenty-ninth reports of the President to the Congress on lend-lease operations, transmitted on July 15, 1949, and January 9, 1950, and covering the period through June 30, 1949,[1] noted that final settlement of lend-lease and mutual aid accounts had been made with Honduras, Canada, the Dominican Republic, and Venezuela. In addition, two agreements with France relating in part to lend-lease matters were signed on March 14, 1949, pursuant to the

---

1 For information concerning the Trade Agreements Extension Act of 1948, see *Documents, X, 1948*, p. 385.

2 For further information on this meeting of the Contracting Parties of GATT, see this volume, p. 407.

3 For the text of the President's letter, see Department of State, *Bulletin*, XX, p. 80.

4 House Report 19, 81st Cong., 1st sess.; *Congressional Record*, 95, p. 954 (Daily edition), February 7, 1949.

5 *Ibid.*, p. 1106 (Daily edition, February 9, 1949).

6 Senate Report 107, 81st Cong., 1st sess.; *ibid.*, p. 2267 (Daily edition, March 10, 1949).

7 The respective votes on these five amendments were 27 to 54, 40 to 41, 29 to 53, 38 to 43, and 33 to 49.

8 *Ibid.*, p. 13179 (Daily edition, September 15, 1949).

9 Public Law 307, 81st Cong., 1st sess.

10 *Federal Register*, XIV, p. 6105.

1 House Document 263, 81st Cong., 1st sess., *ibid.*, 436, 81st Cong., 2d sess. The following note is based upon these reports.

memorandum of understanding of May 28, 1946, between the United States and France,[2] settling a number of residual financial and shipping matters arising out of operations during and immediately after the war. A settlement of lend-lease, reciprocal aid, and financial claims arising out of the war was reached with Ethiopia on May 20, 1949. On September 27, 1949, understandings were reached with the Soviet Union as to the dates and procedures for the return of three icebreakers and 27 frigates of the United States navy which had been transferred to the Soviet Union under lend-lease. Negotiations with the Soviet Union on other lend-lease matters were reported by the President to have made "some progress" but, as of June 30, 1949, there had been no substantial agreement on several of the major issues.

(1) *Defense Aid Provided by Country, Cumulative through June 30, 1949.*[3]

COUNTRY	TOTAL TO JUNE 30, 1949	COUNTRY	TOTAL TO JUNE 30, 1949
AMERICAN REPUBLICS:		Czechoslovakia . . .	$435,446.23
Bolivia	$5,523,017.51	Egypt	2,322,611.92
Brazil	361,393,036.96	Ethiopia	5,151,480.09
Chile	23,244,099.68	Denmark	4,002,032.29
Colombia	8,290,446.18	France and Possessions	3,269,936,471.02
Costa Rica	156,330.15	Greece	81,424,112.31
Cuba	6,551,280.35	Iceland	4,366,404.50
Dominican Republic .	1,617,367.10	Iran	5,303,624.18
Ecuador	7,794,772.09	Iraq	891,469.57
Guatemala	2,653,882.65	Italy	186,726,284.81
Haiti	1,423,147.25	Liberia	15,327,857.52
Honduras	368,364.24	Netherlands and	
Mexico	39,276,246.29	Possessions . . .	246,369,309.96
Nicaragua	887,199.28	Norway	47,023,452.37
Panama	667.33	Poland	12,451,879.69
Paraguay	1,954,442.85	U.S.S.R.	11,054,449,197.21
Peru	18,916,442.85	Saudi Arabia . . .	22,670,314.52
Salvador	878,275.90	Turkey	42,850,057.19
Uruguay	7,132,260.54	Yugoslavia	32,188,847.92
Venezuela	4,528,492.62	TOTAL—OTHER GOVERNMENTS	48,427,747,722.05
TOTAL—AMERICAN REPUBLICS . . .	492,589,800.82	TOTAL—CHARGED TO FOREIGN GOVERNMENTS	48,920,337,522.87
OTHER GOVERNMENTS:		TOTAL—NOT DISTRIBUTED BY FOREIGN GOVERNMENTS	1,308,431,155.34
Belgium	156,254,519.40	GRAND TOTAL	$50,228,768,678.21
British Empire . .	31,610,813,206.15		
China	1,626,789,143.20		

B. Disposal of Surplus Property

The fourteenth and final report of the Department of State on the disposal of United States surplus property in foreign areas was transmitted to the Congress by the Secretary of State on July 29, 1949. During the quarter ending June 30, 1949, all residual balances were either sold by the field offices or returned to the owning agencies because of unsalability. The last remaining field office, that located in Sydney, Australia, was closed on June 7; and the Office of the Foreign Liquidation Commissioner was terminated on June 30, the remaining functions resulting from surplus property disposal then being absorbed within the Department of State itself.[1]

[2] See *Documents, VIII, 1945–1946,* p. 142.
[3] House Document 436, 81st Cong., 2d sess., Statement VI, p. 16.
[1] Department of State Publication 3559.

(1) *Summaries of Foreign Surplus Disposal as of June 30, 1949.*

(a) *By the Office of the Foreign Liquidation Commissioner.*[2]

	ORIGINAL COST	REALIZATION FROM DISPOSAL
Surplus Declarations[3]	$10,440,279,000	—
Sales:		
Major bulk sales	5,836,955,000	$1,007,994,000
Other sales	3,614,213,000	763,850,000
Total sales	9,451,168,000	1,771,844,000
Transfers to UNRRA[4]	121,855,000	84,560,000
Military Program Disposals[5]	412,675,000	35,884,000
Air Service Agreements[6]	4,692,000	—
Other Disposals:		
Donations	50,259,000	—
Abandonments	399,630,000	—
Total Disposals	$10,440,279,000	$1,892,288,000

Total disposals in percent of declarations	100.0%
Realization from sales in percent of declared cost	18.7%

	ORIGINAL COST
Property Sold But Not Delivered:	
Out of Inventory	0
Out of Potential Declarations	$17,000,000
Total	$17,000,000
Property Yet To Be Disposed of:	
Out of Inventory	0
Out of Potential Declarations	0
Total	0

(b) *Total Foreign Surplus Disposal.*[7]

	ORIGINAL COST	REALIZATION FROM DISPOSAL
Disposal by OFLC	$10,440,279,000	$1,892,288,000
Direct sales by Army	234,886,000	72,409,000
Direct sales by Navy	71,946,000	23,540,000
Scrap sales by Army	—	32,107,000
Scrap sales by Navy	—	553,000
Total disposal	$10,747,111,000	$2,020,897,000

[2] *Ibid.*, p. 8.
[3] Includes original cost of surplus property available for sale, property transferred on a nonremunerative basis to UNRRA, and property donated or abandoned. Excludes property withdrawn by owning agencies subsequent to declaration.
[4] Nonremunerative transfers under section 202 of UNRRA Participation Appropriation Act.
[5] Includes property located in the United States.
[6] Represents cost of property transferred under air service agreements.
[7] *Ibid.*, p. 10.

CHAPTER IX
Transport and Communications

1. GENERAL

During the year under review the United States participated in the activities of the following international organizations concerned with specific aspects of international transportation and communications: the International Civil Aviation Organization, the International Telecommunication Union, the Universal Postal Union, the World Meteorological Organization, and the Intergovernmental Maritime Consultative Organization.

Among the international organizations concerned generally with the field of transport and communications was the United Nations Transport and Communications Commission, which met for its third session at Lake Success from March 21 to 30, 1949.[1] The United States was represented by George P. Baker and played a significant part in the adoption by the commission of the following resolutions to the effect that 1) members of the Economic and Social Council should be consulted as to the desirability and practicability of adhering more strictly to uniform standards of maritime tonnage measurement; 2) the Secretary-General was to ascertain views of governments, in order to facilitate commission consideration of the problems of maritime shipping affecting Latin America at its fourth session; and 3) the general measures for assuring coordination of activities in the fields of aviation, shipping, telecommunications and meteorology in regard to safety at sea and in the air proposed by the Preparatory Committee of Experts on Coordination of Safety at Sea and in the Air at London in February 1948 should be followed by international organizations.[2]

2. INTERNATIONAL AIR TRANSPORT

A. Convention on International Civil Aviation, Signed for the United States at Chicago, Illinois, December 7, 1944

(1) *Status of the Convention on International Civil Aviation and the Transit and Transport Agreements, Formulated at Chicago, Illinois, December 7, 1944, as of December 31, 1949.*[1]

COUNTRY	CONVENTION (DATE OF SIGNATURE)	CONVENTION (DATE OF DEPOSIT OF RATIFICATION OR ADHERENCE)	TRANSIT AGREEMENT (TWO FREEDOMS) (DATE OF ACCEPTANCE)	TRANSPORT AGREEMENT (FIVE FREEDOMS) (DATE OF ACCEPTANCE)
Afghanistan	12/7/44	4/4/47	5/17/45	
Argentina		6/4/46[2]	6/4/46	
Australia	12/7/44	3/1/47	8/28/45	
Austria		8/27/48[2]		
Belgium	4/9/45	5/5/47	7/19/45	
Bolivia	12/7/44	4/4/47	4/4/47	4/4/47
Brazil	5/29/45	7/8/46		
Burma		7/8/48[2]		
Canada	12/7/44	2/13/46	2/10/45	

[1] Department of State, *Bulletin,* XX, p. 418.
[2] For a summary of the work of the third session of the Transport and Communications Commission, see *International Organization,* III, p. 514.
[1] Adapted from International Civil Aviation Organization, Document 5495, January 1, 1950 (Revised).
[2] Adherence.

Civil Aviation and Transit (Continued)

Country	Convention (Date of Signature)	Convention (Date of Deposit of Ratification or Adherence)	Transit Agreement (Two Freedoms) (Date of Acceptance)	Transport Agreement (Five Freedoms) (Date of Acceptance)
Ceylon		6/1/48[2]		
Chile	12/7/44	3/11/47		
China	12/7/44	2/20/46		
Colombia	10/31/47	10/31/47		
Cuba	4/20/45	5/11/49	6/20/47	
Czechoslovakia	4/18/45	3/1/47	4/18/45	
Denmark	12/7/44	2/28/47	12/1/48	
Dominican Republic	12/7/44	1/25/46		
Egypt	12/7/44	3/13/47	3/13/47	
El Salvador	5/9/45	6/11/47	6/1/45	6/1/45
Ethiopia		3/1/47	3/22/45	3/22/45
Finland		3/30/49		
France	12/7/44	3/25/47	6/24/48	
Greece	12/7/44	3/13/47	9/21/45	2/28/46[3]
Guatemala	1/30/45	4/28/47	4/28/47	
Haiti	12/7/44	3/25/48		
Honduras	12/7/44		11/13/45	11/13/45
Iceland	12/7/44	3/21/47	3/21/47	
India	12/7/44	3/1/47	5/2/45	
Iraq	12/7/44	6/2/47	6/15/45	
Ireland	12/7/44	10/31/46		
Israel		5/24/49		
Italy	12/7/44	10/31/47		
Jordan		3/18/47[2]	3/18/47	
Lebanon	12/7/44	9/19/49		
Liberia	12/7/44	2/11/47	3/19/45	3/19/45
Luxembourg	7/9/45	4/28/48	4/28/48	
Mexico	12/7/44	6/25/46	6/25/46	
Netherlands	12/7/44	3/26/47	1/12/45	1/12/45
New Zealand	12/7/44	3/7/47	4/19/45	
Nicaragua	12/7/44	12/28/45	12/28/45	
Norway	1/30/45	5/5/47	1/30/45	
Pakistan		11/6/47[2]	8/15/47[4]	
Paraguay	7/27/45	1/21/46	7/27/45	7/27/45
Peru	12/7/44	4/8/46		
Philippines	12/7/44	3/1/47	3/22/46	
Poland	12/7/44	4/6/45	4/6/45	
Portugal	12/7/44	2/27/47		
Siam	12/7/44	4/4/47	3/6/47	3/6/47
Syria	12/7/44	12/21/49		
Spain	12/7/44	3/5/47	7/30/45	
Sweden	12/7/44	11/7/46	11/19/45	11/19/45
Switzerland	7/6/45	2/6/47[5]	7/6/45	
Turkey	12/7/44	12/20/45	6/6/45	6/6/45[6]
Union of South Africa	6/4/45	3/1/47	11/30/45	
United Kingdom	12/7/44	3/1/47	5/31/45[7]	
United States	12/7/44	8/9/46	2/8/45	
Venezuela		4/1/47[2]	3/28/46	3/28/46

[3] Acceptance accompanied by reservations not yet withdrawn.

[4] The Ambassador of Pakistan informed the Secretary of State by note No. F 96/48/1 of March 24, 1948 ". . . . that by virtue of the provisions in clause 4 of the Schedule of the Indian Independence (International Arrangements) Order, 1947 the International Air Services Transit Agreement signed by United India continues to be binding after the partition of the Dominion of Pakistan." The acceptance by India on May 2, 1945, of the Transit Agreement applied also to the territory, then a part of India, which later, on August 15, 1947, became Pakistan.

[5] The Minister of Switzerland made the following statement in the note transmitting the Swiss instrument of ratification: "My government has instructed me to notify you that the authorities of Switzerland have agreed with the authorities in the Principality of Liechtenstein that this Convention will be applicable to the territory of the Principality as well as to that of the Swiss Confederation, as long as the Treaty of March 29, 1923, integrating the whole territory of Liechtenstein with the Swiss customs territory will remain in force."

[6] Acceptance accompanied by reservations not yet withdrawn.

[7] Ibid.

B. International Civil Aviation Organization (ICAO)

The third assembly of the International Civil Aviation Organization met in Montreal from June 7 to 20, 1949, to consider an agenda concerned primarily with financial and administrative matters.[8] The United States delegate, J. Weldon Jones, repeated the position expressed by the United States delegation at the second assembly that the assembly's function was to make policy and not to enter into the details of administration.[9] He recommended that the organization implement the work it had accomplished in air navigation rather than attempt to establish new standards and recommended practices. The United States delegation expressed itself as being prepared to cooperate fully in the promotion of a sound expansion of ICAO and in the search for means of reducing the budget without impairing efficiency or postponing essential work. Many of the immediate problems of the organization could be solved by a further increase in the over-all efficiency of ICAO, the United States maintained. The assembly adopted a budget of $2,810,-607, providing for the operation of the organization during 1950 at approximately the same financial level as during 1949. This permitted continuance of the working program on the same scale as before but at a slower tempo, and allowed no room for expansion.[10]

During the year under review the United States was represented at numerous regional and technical meetings convened by ICAO, including the following: the African-Indian Ocean Regional Air Navigation Meeting, London, March 22; three ICAO Conferences on Joint Financing and Operation of Air Navigation Services, with regard to ocean stations in the North Atlantic and air navigation services in Greenland and the Faroes and in Greece, held concurrently in London beginning April 20; and the Special North Atlantic Meteorological Communications Meeting, London, April 11.

The Convention on the International Recognition of Rights in Aircraft, signed on June 19, 1948 at the second assembly of ICAO in Geneva, was transmitted to the United States Senate on January 13, 1949, and referred to the Committee on Foreign Relations.[11] The chairman of the committee, Senator Tom Connally (Texas) appointed a subcommittee, which reported the convention favorably on July 7. The committee adopted the subcommittee's recommendations and report as its own and recommended that the Senate advise and consent to the ratification of the convention.[12] On August 17 the convention was so acted upon by the Senate.[13] During the year under review the President did not ratify the convention.

C. Bilateral Air-Transport Agreements Concluded by the United States

During 1949 the United States concluded five bilateral air-transport agreements, four of which were of the Bermuda type.[14] The agreement with Canada, replacing the one which had been in effect since February 1945, was signed at a conference on civil aviation between the United States and Canada, which convened on May 23 in New York. Two provisional agreements were concluded with Korea and Yugoslavia, and the agreement of August 3, 1945, with Switzerland was amended.

8 For a summary of the work of the third assembly of ICAO, see *International Organization*, III, p. 710.

9 International Civil Aviation Organization, Document A3–P/26, June 22, 1949.

10 *Ibid., Monthly Bulletin,* July 1949, p. 1.

11 For a description of and approval of this convention at the second assembly of ICAO, see *Documents, X, 1948,* p. 395.

12 Senate Executive Report 9, 81st Cong., 1st sess.

13 *Congressional Record,* 95, p. 11875 (Daily edition, August 17, 1949).

14 For distinction between the "Chicago standard form" agreement and the "Bermuda form" agreement, see *Documents, VIII, 1945–1946,* p. 664.

(1) *Chart of Bilateral Air-Transport Agreements Concluded by the Government of the United States, January 1 to December 31, 1949.*[15]

COUNTRY	DATE OF SIGNATURE	OFFICIAL TEXTS
Burma	September 28, 1949	Department of State Press Release 740, September 27, 1949
Canada	June 4, 1949[16]	*Treaties and Other International Acts Series* 1934.
Dominican Republic	July 19, 1949	Department of State Press Release 615, August 9, 1949.
Finland	March 29, 1949	Department of State Press Release 196, March 29, 1949.
Korea	June 29, 1949[17]	*Treaties and Other International Acts Series* 1979.
Panama	March 31, 1949	*Treaties and Other International Acts Series* 1932.
Switzerland	May 13, 1949[18]	*Treaties and Other International Acts Series* 1929.
Yugoslavia	December 24, 1949[17]	Department of State Press Release 1006, December 24, 1949.

3. MERCHANT SHIPPING

A. Intergovernmental Maritime Consultative Organization

During the year under review the Senate took no final action clearing the way to ratification of the Convention of the Intergovernmental Maritime Consultative Organization, which had been transmitted to it with a recommendation for passage by President Truman in June 1948.[1]

B. United States Merchant Marine Policy

(1) *Report of the United States Maritime Commission to the Congress, Covering the Fiscal Year Ending June 30, 1949.*[2]

[EXCERPTS]

INTRODUCTION

The current maritime position of the United States reflects the retrenchment from war and postwar expansion and the joint efforts of the Government and the industry, during the 1949 fiscal year and since, to build a modern American Merchant Marine closely integrated into the economy of the Nation as a private enterprise and designed as part of the national defense system. To the extent that Government regulation and assistance are required to achieve this purpose, the Maritime Commission has used every means at its disposal to effectuate the national maritime policy expressed in the Merchant Marine Act of 1936 to foster the development and encourage

---

[15] Prepared from information furnished by the Department of State, Aviation Division.
[16] Supersedes United States–Canadian Air Transport Agreement concluded February 17, 1945.
[17] Provisional agreement.
[18] Amends agreement concluded on August 3, 1945.
[1] For a summary of the United Nations Maritime Conference of February–March 1948, which approved the IMCO convention, and the subsequent meetings of the IMCO Preparatory Committee in 1948, see *Documents, X, 1948*, p. 399.
[2] House Document 412, 81st Cong., 1st sess.

the maintenance of a Merchant Marine adequate for both trade and defense.

As the result of a determined policy followed by the Commission since the close of World War II to get the Government out of the shipping business, the Merchant Marine stands very close today to full realization of the ideal of private ownership and operation. Maritime Commission operation has been discontinued. As of June 30, 1949, there was a total of 1,386 vessels in the active American flag fleet, of which 1,025 were privately owned, 3 were operated by the Panama Line, and 358 were on charter from the Maritime Commission. In addition to the 358 chartered vessels active in offshore, coastwise, and intercoastal trades under the American flag, there were under charter as of June 30, 1949, 9 vessels under the Philippine flag, 7 vessels chartered for Great Lakes operations, and 8 inactive vessels. Thus, while the over-all total of Maritime Commission chartered tonnage was 382 vessels at the close of the fiscal year, by September 30, 1949, the total number of Commission vessels under charter had dropped to 225, and it will probably be possible to withdraw substantially all Government-owned war-built vessels from charter operation by June 30, 1950. The Commission believes there will be no need for any general extension of charter authority after that date, although statutory authority may be needed for some exceptional shipping requirements, particularly to supplement privately owned passenger tonnage.

Faced with increasing foreign competition, the privately owned and operated fleet has received assistance from the Government not only through subsidies for part of that fleet, but also through the guaranty of carriage of at least 50 percent of cargoes under the Mutual Defense Assistance Act and 50 percent of cargoes originating in the United States procured through the Economic Cooperation Administration. Despite this aid, however, the shipping situation has tightened, as indicated by the depressed charter market in recent months.

Government assistance to the shipping industry has been accompanied by return revenue to the Government. During the fiscal year 1949 the Commission paid into the United States Treasury a total of $330,920,330.21, including payments of recapture of operating-differential subsidies, proceeds from charter hire, and sales of vessels.

Important steps to remedy the deficiency in passenger vessels under the American flag have been taken with the placing of contracts for the construction of six passenger and combination passenger-cargo vessels for service in the North Atlantic, the Mediterranean, and around the world. These ships, which will make important additions to the presently inadequate troop-carrying potential of the Merchant Marine, are being built under subsidy and defense feature allowances as well as mortgage aid granted to steamship companies under title V of the Merchant Marine Act of 1936, as amended.

While important as marking the beginning of a postwar passenger vessel construction program, the building of these six vessels, and other vessel construction under private contract, will be of only limited help to the American shipbuilding industry. As pointed out recently by the American Bureau of

Shipping, the work currently in progress in the yards which have contracts is expected, with few exceptions, to be completed by the end of 1950. Unless, therefore, additional contracts are placed, the yards will again face the threat of idleness, which will result in the dispersal of skilled and experienced personnel and destroy the stability of the shipbuilding industry.

In this connection, with the concurrence of the Joint Chiefs of Staff, the Commission considers it necessary that a certain minimum number of vessels in the National Defense Reserve Fleet be placed in ready condition against a possible emergency, to augment the national defense force of the Merchant Marine. This will also help the shipbuilding industry maintain its yards and a nucleus of its trained and experienced personnel. The Commission is hopeful, therefore, that an appropriation of $25,000,000 for the repair of 134 vessels in this category will be granted to initiate this program.

In their efforts to cooperate in building more ships for sale to private operators with the aid of construction-differential subsidy allowances and mortgage aid authorized under title V of the Merchant Marine Act of 1936, the industry and the Government have been faced with the problem of foreign currency exchange. In attempting to find the true disparity between American and foreign shipbuilding costs as the basis on which to award construction-differential subsidies, the Commission took into consideration the exchange situations as they existed. The President has requested the Chairman of the Commission to prepare legislation which he will recommend to Congress to amend the Merchant Marine Act of 1936 so as to permit the Commission to allow such subsidies on an actual parity basis, without the present statutory limitation of 50 percent. The Commission stands ready to cooperate with the Congress in providing for the long-range needs of the Merchant Marine.

From the administrative standpoint, the most important development during the fiscal year, and in recent months, concerns reorganization of the Maritime Commission. An active program for promotion of the American Merchant Marine in accordance with the directive contained in the 1936 act has been proposed.

Shipping

The number of United States vessels in operation has continued to decline throughout the year. The active Merchant Marine on June 30, 1949, totaled 1,386 oceangoing vessels of 1,000 gross tons and over aggregating 16,049,000 dead-weight tons (appendix A), compared with 1,723 of 19,552,000 tons on June 30, 1948, and 1,060 of 9,019,000 tons on June 30, 1938. While the total fleet of 3,379 active and inactive vessels of 36,234,000 dead-weight tons was still the world's greatest, the active United States fleet was little more than half the size of the United Kingdom fleet (appendix B).

Government-owned ships under charter (active and inactive, under all authorities of law), decreased from 667 on July 1, 1948, to 382 on July 1, 1949, and to 225 on September 30, 1949. There were no Government-owned vessels active under general agency agreement, and all Government-owned tankers have been sold except for those turned over to the Department of the Navy and a few small coastal type and Liberty tankers in the reserve fleets.

Privately owned vessels in active service numbered 1,025, compared with 1,068 at the beginning of the fiscal year and 1,018 before the war. Including temporarily inactive vessels, the privately owned fleet at the end of the 1949 fiscal year had increased by 32 vessels over the fleet at the beginning of the year. The Maritime Commission has made it a policy to encourage the use of privately owned vessels before Government-owned vessels, and has even refused to permit use of ships chartered from the Government when privately owned vessels were available at equal rates.

· · · · · · ·

Shipbuilding

The fiscal year 1949 marked the start of a long-awaited United States passenger-ship building program. All who have studied the problem since World War II have agreed that the most urgent need of the postwar Merchant Marine was a program for building of new passenger ships. As a culmination of months of planning and negotiation, in August 1948 the Maritime Commission placed contracts for 5 passenger-cargo vessels, 2 of 29,703 displacement tons each for Mediterranean service and 3 of 19,600 displacement tons each for round-the-world service. Keels have been laid for all of these vessels and completion of all of them is expected by the end of 1950. In April 1949 a contract was awarded for a 48,000-gross-ton liner for trans-Atlantic service, designed to be the largest and fastest merchant vessel ever built in an American yard.

· · · · · · ·

A definite start has thus been made on strengthening the inadequate American passenger fleet with modern ships, and on the long-range replacement program for cargo ships, giving consideration to their dual purpose as carriers both in peace and war.

· · · · · · ·

4. INLAND TRANSPORT

From August 23 to September 19 the United Nations held a Conference on Road and Motor Transport at Geneva, at the conclusion of which representatives of 20 nations, including the United States, signed a new convention for the facilitation of international road traffic. The conference met as a result of a recommendation of the second session of the United Nations Transport and Communications Commission in April 1948, which declared that a new global convention was "urgently required."[1] Wayne Coy, Chairman of the Federal Communications Commission, was chairman of the United States delegation to the conference.

Major items in the proposals of the United States delegation at the conference included the elimination of operations involving the carriage of persons for hire or reward, inclusion of annexes as integral rather than separate parts of the conven-

---

1 United Nations Economic and Social Council, Document E/CN.2/45/Rev.1, April 21, 1948, p. 17.

tion, permissibility of requiring an international driver's permit, and certain specifications for maximum permissible dimensions and weights of motor vehicles.[2]

In many respects the Convention on Road Traffic reflected United States practices and recommendations. The effect of the convention would be to simplify and
promote international motoring into and through all nations signatories and to contribute to the convenience and safety of motorists operating under its provisions. It
was intended to bring about eventual reduction in documentation fees, which had
deterred expansion of international travel by automobile.[3] The four main topics
covered by the convention were rules of the road, highway signs and signals, technical conditions for vehicles moving in international traffic, and drivers' documents
and registration requirements.

During the year under review the convention was not submitted to the United
States Senate for its advice and consent. This action was scheduled to be taken
early in 1950.

In November the Secretary of State sent identical notes to the missions in
Washington of the governments of Bulgaria, Czechoslovakia, Hungary, Rumania,
the Union of Soviet Socialist Republics, and Yugoslavia to the effect that the
United States government did not recognize as having any valid effect a convention signed at Belgrade August 18, 1948, establishing a new postwar regime
over navigation on the Danube. Over the objections of the governments of France,
the United States, Austria and the United Kingdom the convention was signed
by the Soviet Union, Bulgaria, Czechoslovakia, Hungary, Rumania, the Ukraine
and Yugoslavia, charged the United States note which listed among the reasons
for non-recognition the facts that the convention contravened the well-established
rights of Belgium, Greece, and Italy; violated the concept of international waterways which had been recognized in Europe for more than 130 years; and, by
failing to provide an adequate basis for freedom of navigation on the Danube,
negated provisions of the peace treaties with Bulgaria, Hungary and Rumania.[4]

5. INTERNATIONAL TELECOMMUNICATIONS

During the year under review the United States was represented at numerous
conferences held under the auspices of the International Telecommunication Union
including: a preparatory meeting to discuss the form of international telegraph
regulations, which convened at Geneva on January 17, 1949 in accordance with a
resolution of the sixth meeting of the International Telegraph Consulting Committee held at Brussels in May 1948; the Special Administrative Conference on Standard Loran (Long Range Radio Navigation Aids), which also convened at Geneva
on January 17; the joint meeting of the International Telecommunication Union
Region 2 and fourth Inter-American Radio Conference, which met in Washington
from April 25 through July 9; and the International Telephone and Telegraph Conference, which convened on May 19 in Paris. Other conferences sponsored by ITU
in which the United States participated were the Administrative Radio Conferences
for Regions 1 and 3 of ITU, which convened simultaneously on May 18 in Geneva,
and the second session of the International Administrative Aeronautical Radio Conference, which convened in Geneva on August 1 to conclude a global plan for the
assignment of channels in the high-frequency bands allocated exclusively to the
aeronautical mobile service by the Atlantic City Radio Conference of 1947.[1] The
United States was also represented at the fourth session of the ITU Administrative
Council held in Geneva from August 15 to October 3.[2]

The Inter-American Radio Agreement of 1949, including the first complete radio-
frequency-assignment plan under the provisions of the international radio regulations of Atlantic City, 1947, for any region of the world, was adopted at the joint
meeting of the International Telecommunication Union Region 2 and the fourth

2 *Ibid.*, Document E/CONF.8/26, August 18, 1949; *ibid.*, Document E/CONF.8/29, August 24, 1949.
3 For the text of the Convention on Road Traffic, see *ibid.*, Document E/CONF.8/47, September 16,
1949; for the final act of the conference, see *ibid.*, Document E/CONF.8/48, September 16, 1949.
4 Department of State, *Bulletin*, XXI, p. 832.
1 Department of State, *Bulletin*, XXI, p. 144.
2 International Telecommunication Union, *Journal des Télécommunications*, November 1949, p. 486.

Inter-American Radio Conference. The conference also adopted a strong declaration of principles on freedom of information in the American region and prepared an ITU Region 2 report to the second session of the International Administrative Aeronautical Radio Conference.[3]

An important result of the International Telephone and Telegraph Conference was the signature of the International Telegraph Regulations by the United States, with certain specific reservations; previously the United States had not become a party to these regulations. Prior to the opening of the conference the United States had forwarded to the Secretary-General of ITU the text of its proposals, formulated by the Federal Communications Commission, for revising the Cairo Regulations of 1938. They included provisions regarding the classifications of telegrams and rates and proposed a unification of the rates for ordinary telegrams composed of plain language, cipher language, code language or any mixture thereof; this unification would take place initially at 75 percent of the prevailing rates for ordinary full-rate messages.[4] The deferred rate and code rate for international cablegrams and telegrams would be abolished.

The Administrative Radio Conference for Region 1 — Europe, the Asiatic part of the Soviet Union and Africa — elaborated new rules of procedure and resolved to make provision in its frequency assignment plan for the operation of the service provided by the North-East Atlantic Standard Loran Chain in certain bands.[5] One of the important projects discussed at the Administrative Radio Conference for Region 3 — Asia (except the Soviet Union, the Mongolian People's Republic, Turkey, Israel, Saudi Arabia, Iraq, Lebanon, Syria, and Yemen) and Australia — was the assignment of frequencies to some 6000 requirements.[6]

Important projects in which the United States was interested in the field of telecommunications were approved at the fourth session of the Administrative Council of ITU; these included approval of the results of the Special Administrative Conference for the Northeast Atlantic (Loran), continuation of the Provisional Frequency Board, restrictions placed on languages used by ITU, and the admission of Japan as a member of the Union.[7]

Because of increases in wages, altered operational practices and changes to be effected as a result of the decisions of the International Telegraph and Telephone Conference held in May at Paris, the United States requested the convening of a conference for the revision of the Bermuda Telecommunications Agreement of 1945. The conference was held at London from August 8 to 12 under the chairmanship of Wayne Coy, chairman of the Federal Communications Commission.[8] The revised agreement adopted by the conference included new ceiling rates for telegrams between the United States and countries of the British Commonwealth (excepting Canada) and recommended general conditions which should govern the retention of existing radiotelegraph circuits between these countries and establishment of new or additional circuits.

6. METEOROLOGY

On January 13, 1949, the Convention of the World Meteorological Organization, which had been opened for signature at Washington on October 11, 1947, was transmitted to the Senate and then referred to the Committee on Foreign Relations. A subcommittee of five members was appointed to study the matter and hold hearings. On April 19 the committee accepted the subcommittee's favorable report, and the following day the Senate gave its advice and consent to ratification of the convention.[1] With presidential action on May 4 the United States became the seventeenth government to deposit its instrument of ratification or accession.[2] The

3 Department of State, *Bulletin*, XXI, p. 258.
4 Department of State Press Release 180, March 23, 1949.
5 For a summary of this conference, see *International Organization*, IV, p. 135.
6 International Telecommunication Union, *Journal des Télécommunications*, December 1949, p. 526.
7 For a summary of the work of this session, see *ibid.*, p. 136.
8 Department of State, *Bulletin*, XXI, p. 509.
1 Senate Executive Report 5, 81st Cong., 1st sess.; *Congressional Record*, 95, p. 4916 (Daily edition, April 20, 1949). For information on the Conference of Directors of the International Meteorological Organization of September-October 1947 at which this convention was concluded, see *Documents, IX*, 1947, p. 475.
2 Department of State Press Release 324, May 5, 1949.

report of the Senate Committee on Foreign Relations revealed that the contributions of the United States to the support of IMO had not exceeded a few thousand dollars per year — $4,100 during 1948 — and estimated that the United States' percentage of the total world contribution would continue at approximately its present figure of four percent.[3]

(1) Convention of the World Meteorological Organization, Signed October 11, 1947. Ratified by the Government of the United States, May 4, 1949.[4]

[EXCERPTS]

With a view to coordinating, standardizing, and improving world meteorological activities and to encouraging an efficient exchange of meteorological information between countries in the aid of human activities the contracting States agree to the present Convention, as follows:

PART I

ESTABLISHMENT

Article 1

The World Meteorological Organization (hereinafter called the Organization) is hereby established.

PART II

Article 2: Purposes

The purposes of the Organization shall be:

(a) To facilitate worldwide cooperation in the establishment of networks of stations for the making of meteorological observations or other geophysical observations related to meteorology and to promote the establishment and maintenance of meteorological centers charged with the provision of meteorological services;

(b) To promote the establishment and maintenance of systems for the rapid exchange of weather information;

(c) To promote standardization of meteorological observations and to ensure the uniform publication of observations and statistics;

(d) To further the application of meteorology to aviation, shipping, agriculture, and other human activities; and

(e) To encourage research and training in meteorology and to assist in coordinating the international aspects of such research and training.

PART III

MEMBERSHIP

Article 3: Members

The following may become Members of the Organization by the procedure set forth in the present Convention:

(a) Any State represented at the Conference of Directors of the International Meteorological Organization convened at Washington, D. C., on September 22, 1947, as listed in Annex I attached hereto, and which signs the present Convention and ratifies it in accordance with Article 32, or which accedes thereto, in accordance with Article 33;

(b) Any Member of the United Nations having a meteorological service by acceding to the present Convention in accordance with Article 33;

(c) Any State, fully responsible for the conduct of its international relations and having a meteorological service, not listed in Annex I of the present Convention and not a Member of the United Nations, after the submission of a request for

---

[3] Senate Executive Report 5, 81st Cong., 1st sess.
[4] International Meteorological Organization, Convention of the World Meteorological Organization, Lausanne, n. d.

membership to the Secretariat of the Organization and after its approval by two-thirds of the Members of the Organization as specified in paragraphs (a), (b) and (c) of this Article by acceding to the present Convention in accordance with Article 33;

(d) Any territory or group of territories maintaining its own meteorological service and listed in Annex II attached hereto, upon application of the present Convention on its behalf, in accordance with paragraph (a) of Article 34, by the State or States responsible for its international relations and represented at the Conference of Directors of the International Meteorological Organization convened at Washington, D.C., on September 22, 1947, as listed in Annex I of the present Convention;

(e) Any territory or group of territories, not listed in Annex II of the present Convention, maintaining its own meteorological service but not responsible for the conduct of its international relations, on behalf of which the present Convention is applied in accordance with paragraph (b) of Article 34, provided that the request for membership is presented by the Member responsible for its international relations, and secures approval by two-thirds of the Members of the Organization as specified in paragraphs (a), (b) and (c) of this Article;

(f) Any trust territory or group of trust territories maintaining its own meteorological service and administered by the United Nations to which the United Nations applies the present Convention in accordance with Article 34.

Any request for membership in the Organization shall state in accordance with which paragraph of this Article membership is sought.

PART IV

Organization

Article 4

(a) The Organization shall comprise:
  (1) The World Meteorological Congress (hereinafter called the Congress);
  (2) The Executive Committee;
  (3) Regional Meteorological Associations (hereinafter called the Regional Associations;
  (4) Technical Commissions;
  (5) The Secretariat.

(b) There shall be a President and two Vice-Presidents of the Organization who shall also be President and Vice-Presidents of the Congress and of the Executive Committee.

PART V

Eligibility

Article 5

(a) Eligibility for election to the offices of President and Vice-President of the Organization, of President and Vice-President of the Regional Associations, and for membership, subject to the provisions of Article 13(c) of the present Convention, on the Executive Committee should be confined to the Directors of Meteorological Services of Members of the Organization.

(b) In the performance of their duties, the officers of the Organization and the members of the Executive Committee should regard themselves as representatives of the Organization rather than as representatives of particular Members thereof.

PART VI

The World Meteorological Congress

Article 6: Composition

(a) The Congress is the supreme body of the Organization and shall be composed of delegates representing Members. Each Member shall designate one of its delegates, who should be the director of its meteorological service, as its principal delegate.

(b) With a view to securing the widest possible technical representation, any director of a meteorological service or any other individual may be invited by the President to be present at and participate in the discussions of the Congress.

Article 7: Functions

The functions of the Congress shall be:

(a) To determine general regulations, subject to the provisions of the present Convention, prescribing the constitution and the functions of the various bodies of the Organization;

(b) To determine its own rules of procedure;

(c) To elect the President and Vice-Presidents of the Organization, and other Members of the Executive Committee, in accordance with the provisions of Article 10 (a) (4) of the present Convention. Presidents and Vice-Presidents of Regional Associations and Technical Commissions shall be elected in accordance with the provisions of Articles 18 (e) and 19 (c), respectively, of the present Convention;

(d) To adopt technical regulations covering meteorological practices and procedures;

(e) To determine general policies for the fulfilment of the purposes of the Organization as set forth in Article 2 of the present Convention;

(f) To make recommendations to members on matters within the purposes of the Organization;

(g) To refer to any other body of the Organization any matter within the provisions of the present Convention upon which such body is empowered to act;

(h) To consider the reports and activities of the Executive Committee and to take such action in regard thereto as the Congress may determine;

(i) To establish Regional Associations in accordance with the provisions of Article 18; to determine their geographical limits, coordinate their activities, and consider their recommendations;

(j) To establish Technical Commissions in accordance with the provisions of Article 19; to define their terms of reference, coordinate their activities, and consider their recommendations;

(k) To determine the location of the Secretariat of the Organization;

(l) To take any other appropriate action to further the purposes of the Organization.

Article 8: Execution of Congress Decisions

(a) All Members shall do their utmost to implement the decisions of the Congress.

(b) If, however, any Member finds it impracticable to give effect to some requirement in a technical resolution adopted by Congress, such Member shall inform the Secretary General of the Organization whether its inability to give effect to it is provisional or final, and state its reasons therefore.

Article 9: Meetings

Meetings of the Congress shall be convened by decision of the Congress or of the Executive Committee at intervals not exceeding four years.

Article 10: Voting

(a) Each Member shall have one vote in decisions of the Congress, except that only Members of the Organization which are States, as specified in paragraphs (a), (b) and (c) of Article 3 of the present Convention (hereinafter referred to as "Members which are States"), shall be entitled to vote on any of the following subjects:

(1) Amendment or interpretation of the present Convention or proposals for a new Convention;

(2) Membership of the Organization;

(3) Relations with the United Nations and other intergovernmental organizations;

(4) Election of the President and Vice-Presidents of the Organization and of the members of the Executive Committee other than the Presidents and Vice-Presidents of the Regional Associations.

(b) Decisions of the Congress shall be by two-thirds majority of the votes cast for and against, except that elections of individuals to serve in any capacity in the Organization shall be by simple majority of the votes cast. The provisions of this paragraph, however, shall not apply to decisions taken in accordance with Articles 3, 25, 26, and 28 of the present Convention.

Article 11: Quorum

A majority of the Members shall be required to constitute a quorum for meetings of the Congress. For those meetings of the Congress at which decisions are taken on the subjects enumerated in paragraph (a) of Article 10, a majority of the Members which are States shall be required to constitute a quorum.

Article 12: First Meeting of the Congress

The first meeting of the Congress shall be convened by the President of the International Meteorological Committee of the International Meteorological Organization as soon as practicable after the coming into force of the present Convention.

PART VII

THE EXECUTIVE COMMITTEE

Article 13: Composition

The Executive Committee shall consist of:
(a) The President and Vice-Presidents of the Organization;
(b) The Presidents of Regional Associations, or in the event that Presidents cannot attend, alternates as provided for in the general regulations;
(c) Directors of Meteorological Services of Members of the Organization or their alternates, equal in number to the number of Regions, provided that not more than one-third of the members of the Executive Committee, including the President and Vice-Presidents of the Organization, shall come from one region.

Article 14: Functions

The Executive Committee is the executive body of the Congress and its functions shall be:
(a) To supervise the execution of the resolutions of the Congress;
(b) To adopt resolutions arising out of recommendations of the Technical Commissions on matters of urgency affecting the technical regulations, provided that all Regional Associations concerned are given an opportunity to express their approval or disapproval before adoption by the Executive Committee;
(c) To provide technical information, counsel, and assistance in the field of meteorology;
(d) To study and make recommendations on any matter affecting international meteorology and the operation of meteorological services;
(e) To prepare the agenda for the Congress and to give guidance to the Regional Associations and Technical Commissions in the preparation of their agenda;
(f) To report on its activities to each session of the Congress;
(g) To administer the finances of the Organization in accordance with the provisions of Part XI of the present Convention;
(h) To perform such other functions as may be conferred on it by the Congress or by the present Convention.

PART VIII

REGIONAL ASSOCIATIONS

Article 18

(a) Regional Associations shall be composed of the Members of the Organization, the networks of which lie in or extend into the Region.
(b) Members of the Organization shall be entitled to attend the meetings of Regional Associations to which they do not belong, take part in the discussions,

present their views upon questions affecting their own Meteorological Service, but shall not have the right to vote.

(c) Regional Associations shall meet as often as necessary. The time and place of the meeting shall be determined by the Presidents of the Regional Associations in agreement with the President of the Organization.

(d) The functions of the Regional Associations shall be:
  (i) To promote the execution of the resolutions of Congress and the Executive Committee in their respective regions;
  (ii) To consider matters brought to their attention by the Executive Committee;
  (iii) To discuss matters of general meteorological interest and to coordinate meteorological and associated activities in their respective regions;
  (iv) To make recommendations to Congress and the Executive Committee on matters within the purposes of the Organization;
  (v) To perform such other functions as may be conferred on them by the Congress.

(e) Each Regional Association shall elect its President and Vice-President.

PART IX

TECHNICAL COMMISSIONS

Article 19

(a) Commissions consisting of technical experts may be established by the Congress to study and make recommendations to the Congress and the Executive Committee on any subject within the purposes of the Organization.

(b) Members of the Organization have the right to be represented on the Technical Commissions.

(c) Each Technical Commission shall elect its President and Vice-President.

(d) Presidents of Technical Commissions may participate without vote in the meetings of the Congress and of the Executive Committee.

PART X

THE SECRETARIAT

PART XI

FINANCES

Article 23

(a) The Congress shall determine the maximum expenditures which may be incurred by the Organization on the basis of estimates submitted by the Secretary General and recommended by the Executive Committee.

(b) The Congress shall delegate to the Executive Committee such authority as may be required to approve the annual expenditures of the Organization within the limitations determined by the Congress.

Article 24

The expenditures of the Organization shall be apportioned among the Members of the Organization in the proportions determined by the Congress.

PART XII

RELATIONS WITH THE UNITED NATIONS

Article 25

The Organization shall be brought into relationship with the United Nations pursuant to Article 57 of the Charter of the United Nations, subject to the approval of the terms of the agreement by two-thirds of the Members which are States.

PART XIII

RELATIONS WITH OTHER ORGANIZATIONS

. . . .

PART XIV

LEGAL STATUS, PRIVILEGES AND IMMUNITIES

. . . .

PART XV

AMENDMENTS

. . . .

PART XVI

INTERPRETATION AND DISPUTES

Article 29

Any question or dispute concerning the interpretation or application of the present Convention which is not settled by negotiation or by the Congress shall be referred to an independent arbitrator appointed by the President of the International Court of Justice, unless the parties concerned agree on another mode of settlement.

PART XVII

WITHDRAWAL

Article 30

(a) Any Member may withdraw from the Organization on twelve months' notice in writing given by it to the Secretary General of the Organization, who shall at once inform all the Members of the Organization of such notice of withdrawal.

(b) Any Member of the Organization not responsible for its own international relations may be withdrawn from the Organization on twelve months' notice in writing given by the Member or other authority responsible for its international relations to the Secretary General of the Organization, who shall at once inform all the Members of the Organization of such notice of withdrawal.

PART XVIII

SUSPENSION

Article 31

If any Member fails to meet its financial obligations to the Organization or otherwise fails in its obligations under the present Convention, the Congress may by resolution suspend it from exercising its rights and enjoying privileges as a Member of the Organization until it has met such financial or other obligations.

PART XIX

RATIFICATION AND ACCESSION

. . . .

PART XX

ENTRY INTO FORCE

Article 35

The present Convention shall come into force on the thirtieth day after the date of the deposit of the thirtieth instrument of ratification or accession. The present Convention shall come into force for each State ratifying or acceding after that date on the thirtieth day after the deposit of its instrument of ratification or accession.

The present Convention shall bear the date on which it is opened for signature and shall remain open for signature for a period of 120 days thereafter.

IN WITNESS WHEREOF the undersigned, having been duly authorized by their respective Governments, have signed the present Convention.

DONE at Washington this eleventh day of October 1947, in the English and French languages, each equally authentic, the original of which shall be deposited in the archives of the Government of the United States of America. The Government of the United States of America shall transmit certified copies thereof to all the signatory and acceding States.

7. PASSPORT AND FRONTIER FORMALITIES

Continuation of the reduction, simplification and unification of passports and frontier formalities was sought in a resolution passed at the third session of the United Nations Transport and Communications Commission in March.[1] Also at this session a resolution was adopted recommending that the United Nations Economic and Social Council instruct the Secretary-General to transmit to Members of the United Nations the Secretariat's report, "Barriers to the International Transport of Goods" and the report of the International Chamber of Commerce considered by the second session of the commission and requesting Members to report their views on the ICC's recommendations relating to the reduction of the number of documents required in international transport of goods and to the abolition of the transit manifest.[2]

On May 11, 1949 Senator McCarran (Nevada) introduced into the Senate a bill (S.1832) to amend the Immigration Act of October 16, 1918 as amended.[3] S.1832 proposed to create three new classes of aliens who might not be granted visas or admitted into the United States; they were: 1) persons seeking to enter the country to obtain or transmit information, not available to the public, respecting the national security; 2) persons seeking to enter to engage in activity to control or overthrow the government by force or violence; and 3) persons seeking to enter to organize, aid, join or associate with any association or group designated by the Attorney General as subversive to the national security. It eliminated the discretionary power of the Attorney General to admit an otherwise inadmissible alien. No further action was taken on this measure following the expression of strong disapproval by the Secretary of State (Acheson), who felt that the primary effect of the bill would be to interfere drastically with the Department of State's conduct of foreign relations and would contravene the program of President Truman.

---

1 United Nations Economic and Social Council, Document E/CN.2/65/Rev.1, March 31, 1949, p. 15.
2 *Ibid.*, p. 8. For information on the work of the Interim Commission of the International Trade Organization on this subject, see this volume, p. 398.
3 *Congressional Record*, 95, p. 6113 (Daily edition, May 11, 1949).

CHAPTER X

Agriculture and Natural Resources

1. GENERAL

A. Food and Agriculture Organization

[See *Documents, VI, 1943–1944*, p. 415; *VII, 1944–1945*, p. 657; *VIII, 1945–1946*, p. 697; *IX, 1947*, p. 476; *X, 1948*, p. 403.]

During 1949 the United States participated in the following major meetings and conferences convened under the sponsorship of the Food and Agriculture Organization: Council, sixth session, Paris, June 13 to 24, and seventh and eighth sessions, Washington, November 14 to 17, and December 7; FAO Conference, fifth session, Washington, November 21 to December 6; International Rice Commission, first meeting, opening March 7, in Bangkok; Indo-Pacific Fisheries Council, first session, Singapore, March 24 to 31.

1. COUNCIL

The United States was represented at the sixth session of the FAO Council by Albert J. Loveland, Under Secretary of Agriculture, and Edward G. Cale, associate chief of the Division of International Resources, Department of State;[1] at the seventh session by Mr. Loveland, Fred J. Rossiter, associate director of the Office of Foreign Agricultural Relations, Department of Agriculture, and John W. Evans, chief of the Economic Resources and Security Staff, Department of State; and at the eighth session by Mr. Rossiter and Mr. Evans.[2] Among the topics discussed by the Council during the year were recommendations for increased food production, the question of increased technical assistance for economic development, the maintenance and expansion of high levels of agricultural production and consumption in the face of current financial disequilibrium and balances of payments difficulties, and the distribution of surpluses and commodities. The Council reviewed a report on FAO participation in the expanded program of technical assistance prepared by the United Nations and the specialized agencies[3] and discussed the advisability of requesting a special session of the United Nations General Assembly to deal with international investment and technical aid. The United States representative (Cale) agreed that such a meeting might be necessary before the Food and Agriculture Organization took final action on the program.[4] Among other action taken by the sixth session of the Council were its decisions to abolish the International Emergency Food Committee since the need for it no longer existed, and to instruct the Director General to prepare a report for submission not later than September 30, 1949, analyzing the circumstances which had led to the existence of surpluses, with recommendations for any appropriate action for their disposal.[5]

The Council received a proposal from the International Federation of Agricultural Producers for the creation of an international commodity clearing house to be financed by the importing and exporting nations of agricultural commodities. This agency was designed to channel surpluses from hard currency areas into soft currency countries, thus permitting surplus producing nations to maintain high levels of agricultural production without resorting to restrictive measures, the destruction of crops, or dumping devices.[6] The Director General endorsed the proposal and

---

1 Food and Agriculture Organization. *Report of the Council, Sixth Session, June 13 to 24, 1949*, p. 23.
2 *Ibid., Report of the Council, Seventh Session, November 14 to 17, 1949*, p. 27.
3 For further information concerning the action of the FAO Conference on the proposal, see this volume, p. 432.
4 Food and Agriculture Organization, Document CL/6/9, n. d.
5 *New York Times*, June 21, 1949, p. 8.
6 Food and Agriculture Organization, Document C49/24, November 7, 1949.

strongly urged its acceptance by the fifth session of the FAO Conference. At the conclusion of the seventh session of the Council the report on commodity problems, prepared by the Director General, was submitted to the Conference together with a review of the report on that subject submitted by a working party of the Council.[7] The working party had recommended as an alternative to the proposed clearing house, the study of other methods of achieving the same ends which would not "impair the existing volume of international trade or unduly postpone achievement of currency convertibility, and restoration of competitive unilateral trade."[8] Following rejection by the Conference of the proposal for the commodity clearing house, the United States at the eighth session of the Council was named to membership on the Committee on Commodity Problems established by the Conference. Mr. Rossiter expressed the hope that the committee would begin work immediately as his government attached very great importance to its work and expected it to prepare concrete proposals for the solution of problems of surpluses and shortages.[9]

2. CONFERENCE

The fifth annual session of the FAO Conference opened in Washington on November 21, 1949. Charles F. Brannan, Secretary of Agriculture, headed the United States delegation which included Albert J. Loveland, John M. Evans, Durward V. Sandifer, Stanley Andrews, Philip V. Cardon and Ralph S. Roberts.[10] In meetings of the commission concerned with a review of the world food outlook, the United States representative (Andrews) discounted the proposal of a commodity clearing house both as a short term solution to the problems of trade imbalance and inconvertibility and as a long term solution to the problems of food production and distribution. In his opinion a permanent solution would depend upon the helping of food deficit countries to help themselves.[11] In press reports it was indicated that the United States did not support the clearing house proposal due to the need for United States acreage reduction as a soil conservation measure and because of the objections of soft currency countries which had indicated that fiscal operations under the international commodity clearing house would jeopardize their own efforts to regain a trade balance and currency convertibility.[12] Following the defeat of the clearing house proposal the Conference established a fourteen member committee under the Council to consider the needs of deficit countries, to study distribution schemes proposed by surplus nations, and to investigate general methods of surplus disposal.[13] Mr. Brannan pledged the wholehearted cooperation of the United States in the work of the committee.[14]

The Conference unanimously approved the United Nations plan for technical assistance to underdeveloped areas.[15] FAO planned to direct its technical assistance to two groups: small producers and governments. Assistance to producers was to consist of 1) the training of instructors; 2) facilitation of supplies and adoption of better materials; and 3) organization of demonstration projects. To assist governments FAO was to 1) provide experts; 2) organize the training of personnel; 3) organize exchange visits of experts; 4) provide technical and scientific information; 5) assist in establishing or improving research institutions; and 6) assist in organization of pilot development projects.[16]

Following discussion by the Conference of financial questions, the United States representative (Roberts) agreed to accept 27.1 percent as the United States share in the cost of the organization but asked for an understanding that an effort would be made to establish as soon as possible the previously agreed ceiling of 25 percent. A bill (H.J.Res.344) to increase the United States contribution from $1,250,000 to $2,000,000 was reported by the House Foreign Affairs Committee "with the distinct understanding that the increase will be used to contribute to larger programs,

7 *Ibid.*, Document C49/10, n. d. 8 *Ibid.*, Document C49/24, November 7, 1949.
9 *Ibid.*, Document C18/SR.1, December 7, 1949. 10 Department of State. *Bulletin*, XXI, p. 823.
11 Food and Agriculture Organization. Documents C/49/I/SR.4–C/49/I/SR.6, November 24, 25; 1949: *New York Times*, November 25, 1949, p. 1.
12 *Ibid.*
13 *Ibid.*, Document C49/I/18/Add., December 2, 1949; *ibid.*, Document C49/46/Add., December 2, 1949.
14 *Ibid.*, Document C49/I/SR.15, December 5, 1949.
15 Department of State, *Bulletin*, XXI, p. 906.
16 Food and Agriculture Organization, Document C49/11/34.

not to contribute a larger share to the present program."[17] No further action was taken on the bill by the Congress during the period under review.

(1) Address by the President (Truman) before the Fifth Session of the Conference of the Food and Agriculture Organization, Washington, November 22, 1949.[18]

The Food and Agriculture Organization has an inspiring task, for you are working to increase the food supply of the people of the world. That task is central to the whole broad effort to raise living standards and achieve greater freedom for all mankind. All the work of the United Nations and its many associated organizations is important in building a peaceful world, but none is of more significance than yours. If by working together in this organization, we can create an abundance of food for all countries, we shall bring better health, longer lives, and greater happiness to mankind everywhere.

For this reason, it was most appropriate that the Nobel peace prize this year should have been awarded to your former Director-General Lord Boyd Orr, that great pioneer in international cooperation in food and agriculture. You delegates to this organization can properly share in this recognition of the importance of your work to world peace.

We have all learned in recent years that if we are to achieve peace we must have a positive, forward-looking program to satisfy the physical needs and spiritual aspirations of mankind. Your organization is primarily concerned with meeting the need of hundreds of millions of people for more and better food. To achieve this, your work centers around two major problems. The first is to increase the production of food stuffs and other agricultural commodities. The second is to see that those commodities reach the peoples and countries which need them.

We all know there are immense possibilities of increasing agricultural production throughout the world. The United States, for example, had a high agricultural production before the war—and yet during the war we were able to increase the production of many commodities tremendously by using new and better techniques. New hybrid varieties of field crops, better livestock, better fertilizers, amazing new weed and insect killers—these and many more advances in agricultural techniques are opening up new horizons of production. It is no exaggeration to say that, as a result, an agricultural revolution has been taking place in the United States.

If this can be done in our country, think of what can be done to increase production in those parts of the world where modern methods and modern machinery are relatively unknown. This is one of the great opportunities toward which I pointed in my inaugural address last January, when I spoke of the need for a bold new program for making the benefits of our scientific advance and industrial progress available for the improvement and growth of underdeveloped areas.

In the beginning, the greatest advance will probably result from the most

17 Department of State, *Bulletin*, XXI, p. 935.   18 *Ibid.*, p. 857a.

elementary improvements. The control of animal diseases and the improvement of simple tools, such as plows and threshing equipment, would greatly increase production and better the lot of millions of small farmers in many parts of the world.

I know that the FAO understands these great possibilities. I am glad that your organization has worked out a specific program as your part of the United Nations' effort along these lines. The United States will continue to look to the FAO for leadership in the international cooperative effort to increase food and agricultural production throughout the world. Our experience, our knowledge, our technical experts are all available to you, and I hope that you will continue to call upon them as needed.

Because your organization is concerned with raising the living standards of people throughout the world, you are properly concerned not only with production but also with the distribution of food and agricultural commodities. You understand the imperative necessity that the nations work together toward a system of international trade which will contribute to an expanding world economy.

The nations of the world have taken a number of progressive steps in this direction. The European Recovery Program is essentially an international effort to restore Western Europe as a vital force in a progressive world economy. The International Wheat Agreement is a practical means for achieving better distribution of world wheat supplies. Most of the trading nations have joined in agreements to reduce barriers to world trade.

As the nations regain the productive capacity destroyed during the war and as new productive capacity is added by the growth of underdeveloped areas, we should find it easier to develop lasting patterns for the international exchange of goods and services. I hope that the International Trade Organization will soon be established to help expand world trade by carrying on a continuous and systematic attack on trade barriers.

At the present time, there is still need for resourcefulness in meeting certain immediate problems. I know that, at this session, the FAO will be considering ways and means of moving temporary surpluses of certain commodities from countries where they are not needed to countries where they are badly needed. The United States welcomes the initiative of this organization in seeking a solution to this problem. We pledge ourselves to work wholeheartedly with the other members in attempting to devise practical and effective methods for solving it.

As our Thanksgiving season again approaches, we should all be reminded that the harvest has a twofold significance. It is one mark of civilization to be able to produce abundantly, but it is a more important mark to be able to use abundance for the welfare of mankind. The United States is glad to work with the Food and Agriculture Organization toward the goal of increasing the production of food and improving its distribution. We regard this as a major cooperative endeavor toward our common objective of a stable and peaceful world.

B. Conservation of Natural Resources

The United Nations Scientific Conference on the Conservation and Utilization of Resources met from August 17 to September 6, 1949, at Lake Success, New York, as a result of a United States proposal adopted by the Economic and Social Council in 1947.[1] As defined in the Economic and Social Council resolution of 1947, the purpose of the conference was to exchange information on techniques, economic costs, and benefits of resource conservation and utilization, and was "devoted solely to the exchange of ideas and experience on these matters among engineers, resource technicians, economists and other experts in related fields." The conference had no power to formulate resolutions or recommendations or to commit governments to any policy.[2]

Carter Goodrich, professor of economics at Columbia University, was designated chairman of the preparatory commission[3] while Julius A. Krug, Secretary of the Interior, served as chairman of the United States delegation to the Conference.[4] The agenda included the discussion of forests, mineral resources, fuels and energy, water, land resources, and wildlife and fisheries. At the request of the United States the peaceful utilization of atomic energy was not discussed.[5] After the close of the conference, delegates were conducted on field trips to outstanding industrial centers and conservation activities in the United States, such as the Tennessee Valley Authority.[6] Secretary Krug emphasized that the world could take new hope and courage from the conference which had served to demonstrate that it was possible to overcome differences in cultural background to reach better understanding.[7]

(1) *Address by the Secretary of the Interior (Krug) before the United Nations Scientific Conference on the Conservation and Utilization of Resources, Lake Success, August 17, 1949.*[8]

[EXCERPTS]

. . . .

This conference is meeting to deal with concrete, physical facts and new ideas. You are bringing together outstanding specialists in many resource fields to exchange knowledge and share wisdom in a common cause. That cause is the improvement of man's standard of living, particularly in the underdeveloped areas of the world, through the protection and wise use of man's common heritage of natural wealth, wherever it may be.

This is no selfish purpose. It is a step along the road of freeing millions of people from the grinding burden of toil and hardship. It is a step in the direction of using the world's resources for the benefit of all its people. It is a great stride toward international team-work on a high plane of knowledge and skill. I think that you are participating in one of the greatest adventures of the human will and mind in this century.

When President Truman invited the Economic and Social Council to hold this meeting in this country he was aiming at the very heart of the problem of world peace. Real conservation can remove economic pressures and fears of scarcity which have always played a large part in bringing on wars.

Conservation touches not only the ability of people to live well; it touches their ability to live at all. Conservation and wise development of our resources would help insure world peace.

1 United Nations Economic and Social Council, *Official Records* (4th session), p. 262–274; see *Documents, IX,* 1947, p. 482.
2 United Nations Economic and Social Council, Document E/CONF.7/4, March 1949.
3 *New York Times,* March 12, 1949, p. 5.   4 *Ibid.,* August 6, 1949, p. 7.
5 *Ibid.,* September 7, 1949, p. 16.   6 *Ibid.,* August 17, 1949, p. 25.
7 *Ibid.,* September 7, 1949, p. 16.   8 *Ibid.,* August 18, 1949, p. 14.

The world is interested in everything you do which stimulates the economic progress of large areas that have been by-passed in the world's industrial growth. The President of this country has indicated to you his great hopes in this regard. He intends, when programs are ready, to obtain substantial help for those areas, both in technology and in investment. They need help, and the entire world will benefit if they receive it.

. . . .

I think it is time that we start a new era in conservation, an era consecrated to the development and wise use of what is available to the people of the world. There is not the slightest question in my mind that scientists and engineers can find and develop food, fuels and materials to meet the demands of the world's increasing population with a greatly improved standard of living. I do not side with those who "view with alarm" the increasing world population and the decreasing reserves of some things which now appear to be essential in our way of living. But to meet the serious problems, we must start in time.

Certainly the greatest problem facing the world today is that of raising the standard of living of the people, not just maintaining it. This necessary objective cannot be accomplished by "locking up" our natural wealth. It can be accomplished, and steady future progress can be assured, by the intensive concentration of the world's scientific and engineering know-how on the basic problem of making the most of what we have. You all know of dozens of examples of the opportunities for using this "know-how." To mention just a few, I would list:

1. The peacetime application of atomic energy.

2. More effective utilization of solar energy.

3. Development of synthetic fuels, particularly from oil shales.

4. Development of substitute materials for those in short supply. For example, aluminum, magnesium and glass can be produced in almost limitless quantities. With improved technology they can be substituted for many uses of steel, copper and lead, which many people feel may at some future date be in short supply.

5. Improved agricultural methods, including the development of new plants which will require less water and less nutrition from the soil and absorb more energy perhaps from the sun and better ways of checking soil erosion and restoring soil productivity.

6. Increased use of sea water for the growth of food fishes and other food materials for extracting chemicals and minerals, and for conversion to fresh water for irrigation and industrial purposes.

7. Improved utilization of metals and other materials to eliminate the waste presently experienced, particularly in the construction of homes and office buildings and consumers' durable goods, such as automobiles.

8. Development of hydro-electric power to conserve soil, gas and coal.

9. Development of improved use of foods and feeds for human and animal nutrition.

10. Further development of improved space heating in cold weather and cooling in warm weather.

These are just a few of the ideas for raising the world's living standards which deserve the attention of all of us.

Your work here will begin to tell us what can and should happen in this world. It is perfectly possible that the destruction of the last war will be wiped out in the memory of men by scientific progress and service in these peaceful, constructive fields.

. . . .

2. AGRICULTURAL COMMODITIES

A. Rice

(1) Constitution of the International Rice Commission, Entered into Force, January 4, 1949. Instrument of Acceptance Deposited by the United States, February 28, 1949.[1]

The following constitution of the International Rice Commission, formulated at the International Rice Meeting held at Baguio, Philippines, from March 1 to 13, 1948,[2] was approved at the fourth session of the FAO Conference in November 1948. With the deposit of instruments of acceptance by twelve nations, the aggregate rice production of which was sufficient to meet the requirements of Article XI of the Constitution, the Constitution entered into force on January 4, 1949. Acceptance by the United States was completed on February 28. The first meeting of the commission was held in Bangkok on March 7, 1949, and was devoted primarily to the drafting of the first year's program.[3]

PREAMBLE

The Council of the Food and Agriculture Organization of the United Nations, having regard to the deliberations of the Rice Study Group which met at Trivandrum, of the Third Session of the Conference of the Organization, and of the International Rice Meeting held at Baguio, and with a view to co-operative action in matters relating to the production, conservation, distribution, and consumption of rice (excepting matters relating to international trade) hereby establishes an International Rice Commission in accordance with the following Constitution.

ARTICLE I

THE COMMISSION

There shall be a Commission, known as the International Rice Commission, with the functions set forth in Article IV of this Constitution.

ARTICLE II

MEMBERSHIP

The members of the Commission shall be such of the governments members of the Food and Agriculture Organization of the United Nations as may accept this Constitution in accordance with the provisions of Article VII hereof.

---

1 Department of State, *Treaties and Other International Act Series* 1938.
2 See *Documents, X, 1948*, p. 410.
3 Food and Agriculture Organization, Document C49/8, October 1949.

ARTICLE III

ORGANIZATION

1. Each government that becomes a member of the Commission as defined in Article II hereof (hereinafter called a "member government") shall have the right to be represented at meetings of the Commission by a single delegate, who may be accompanied by an alternate and by experts and advisers. Alternates, experts, and advisers shall be entitled to take part in the proceedings of the Commission but not to vote, except in the case of an alternate who is duly authorized to act for a delegate.

2. Each member government shall have one vote. Decisions of the Commission shall be taken by a simple majority of votes cast except as otherwise provided by this Constitution. A majority of the members of the Commission shall constitute a quorum.

3. The Commission shall elect a Chairman from among the delegates, who shall serve for a period of one year, without prejudice to the right of re-election.

4. Subject to the provisions of paragraphs 2 and 5 of this Article, the Commission shall, with the concurrence of the Director-General of the Food and Agriculture Organization, establish its own rules of procedure and determine the time and place of its meetings.

5. The Chairman shall call a meeting of the Commission at least once a year, unless otherwise directed by a majority of member governments. The initial meeting shall be called by the Director-General of the Food and Agriculture Organization within six months after the entry into force of this Constitution and at such place as he may designate.

6. Any member government shall have the right, with the concurrence of the Director-General of the Food and Agriculture Organization, to call for a special meeting of the Commission.

7. The seat of the commission shall be the same place as the seat of the Far Eastern regional office of the Food and Agriculture Organization.

8. The Director-General of the Food and Agriculture Organization shall appoint a Secretary to the Commission and shall provide its secretariat from the staff of the Far Eastern regional office.

ARTICLE IV

FUNCTIONS

The Commission shall, except in matters relating to international trade, have the functions of:

    (a) formulating and keeping under review the scientific, technical, and economic problems involved in the production, conservation, distribution, and consumption of rice;

    (b) promoting and co-ordinating research into those problems and its application to the development and adoption of improved methods in everyday practice;

    (c) encouraging and assisting the mobilization and use of scientifically and technically trained persons in such a way as to secure the greatest common benefit to member countries in matters relating to the production, conservation, distribution, and consumption of rice;

    (d) undertaking, where necessary and appropriate, co-operative projects directed to the solution of the above-mentioned problems;

    (e) assembling, collating, and disseminating, through the publications of the Food and Agriculture Organization and otherwise, information relating to the production, conservation, distribution, and consumption of rice;

(f) establishing such committees and calling such meetings of experts as the Commission may consider desirable for the performance of the foregoing functions;

(g) recommending to member governments, through the Food and Agriculture Organization, such national and international action as may appear to the Commission to be necessary or desirable for the solution of the above-mentioned problems;

(h) recommending to the Food and Agriculture Organization the provision of technical assistance to member governments in measures directed to that end;

(i) extending its good offices in assisting member governments to secure materials and equipment necessary for improvement of the production, conservation, distribution, or consumption of rice;

(j) reporting annually on its activities to the Council of the Food and Agriculture Organization, and making such other reports to the Food and Agriculture Organization on matters relating to the production, conservation, distribution, and consumption of rice as the Commission itself may consider expedient or the Council of the Food and Agriculture Organization may require.

ARTICLE V

CO-OPERATION WITH INTERNATIONAL ORGANIZATIONS

The Commission shall maintain, through the Food and Agriculture Organization, close liaison with the United Nations and its specialized agencies in matters of mutual interest.

ARTICLE VI

EXPENSES

1. Expenses incurred by delegates and their alternates, experts, and advisers in attending meetings of the Commission and expenses incurred by experts under paragraph (f) of Article IV hereof shall be determined and paid by their respective governments.

2. The expenses of the secretariat of the Commission and any expenses incurred by the chairman of the Commission in performing duties connected with its work in intervals between meetings of the Commission shall be determined and paid by the Food and Agriculture Organization within the limits of an annual budget prepared and approved in accordance with the Rules of Procedure and Financial Regulations of that Organization for the time being in force.

3. Expenses incurred by the Commission in undertaking any co-operative project in accordance with paragraph (d) of Article IV hereof shall, unless they are met by the Food and Agriculture Organization or from any other source, be determined and paid by member governments in such manner and proportions as they may mutually agree.

ARTICLE VII

ACCEPTANCE AND WITHDRAWAL

1. Acceptance of this Constitution by any member government of the Food and Agriculture Organization shall be effected by the deposit of a notification of acceptance with the Director-General of the Organization and shall take effect on receipt of such notification by the Director-General, who shall forthwith inform each of the member governments of the Organization

2. Any member government may withdraw from the Commission at any time after the expiration of one year from the date on which its acceptance takes effect, or this Constitution comes into force, whichever is the later, by giving written notice of such withdrawal to the Director-General of the Food and Agriculture Organization, who shall forthwith inform all member governments of the Commission. Any such notice of withdrawal shall become effective six months after the date of its receipt by the Director-General.

ARTICLE VIII

AMENDMENTS

This Constitution may be amended by the vote of a two-thirds majority of all the members of the Commission, with the concurrence of the Council of the Food and Agriculture Organization.

ARTICLE IX

ENTRY INTO FORCE

This Constitution shall enter into force as soon as notifications of acceptance have been received from the governments of at least ten countries members of the Food and Agriculture Organization representing in the aggregate not less than half of the world production of rice in the crop year 1947/48 as shown by official statistics.

B. Rubber

The Rubber Study Group held its sixth meeting at London from March 28 to April 1, 1949. Chairman of the United States delegation was Donald D. Kennedy, chief of the Division of International Resources, Department of State.[4] The meeting examined the world rubber situation regarding production and consumption in the light of changes since the fifth meeting of the study group in April 1948, and considered measures for the expansion of world consumption of rubber.[5]

C. Sugar

The President (Truman) on December 20, 1949, proclaimed the protocol of August 31, 1948, prolonging for one year after that date the agreement on the regulation of the production and marketing of sugar, signed at London on May 6, 1937. Ratification of the protocol was advised by the Senate on October 18 and effected by President Truman on November 1, 1949. The protocol, similar to the one of the previous year,[6] stated that a revision of the agreement was necessary, and that in any such revision account should be taken of any principles of commodity policy agreed to under the auspices of the United Nations.[7] The Senate report stated that failure to come to a satisfactory solution of international sugar problems would tend to render domestic sugar conditions difficult, and it emphasized that a sound world sugar economy was necessary to avoid a repetition of the serious world sugar surplus condition.[8]

---

4 Department of State, *Bulletin*, XX, p. 398.
5 *Ibid.*, p. 521.   6 See *Documents, X, 1948*, p. 410.
7 For text of the protocol, see Department of State, *Treaties and Other International Acts Series* 1997.
8 Senate Report 13, 81st Cong., 1st sess.

D. Wheat

In accordance with the decision of the preparatory committee for the International Wheat Agreement,[9] an international wheat conference composed of representatives of fifty nations opened in Washington on January 26, 1949, to negotiate a new agreement to replace that of 1948 which had failed of ratification by the United States. The United States delegation to the conference was headed by Charles F. Brannan, Secretary of Agriculture, and included Albert J. Loveland, Edward G. Cale, Elmer F. Kruse, Loring K. Macy, Fred J. Rossiter and Leroy K. Smith.[10] Secretary Brannan, subsequently served as chairman of the conference The new agreement was opened for signature between March 23 and April 15, 1949. Neither the Soviet Union nor Argentina accepted the new text, the former because of dissatisfaction with the proposed Soviet export allowance and the latter because of the absence of a companion pact requiring the exchange of capital goods for wheat sold or purchased under the agreement.[11]

On June 13, 1949, the United States Senate advised and consented to ratification of the agreement.[12] Ratification was accomplished by the President on June 17, 1949. The agreement entered into force with respect to Parts 1, 3, 4 and 5 on July 1, 1949, and with respect to Part 2 on August 1.

Following discussions by a preparatory committee which had met in Washington since June 27, the International Wheat Council which was to execute the agreement convened in Washington on July 6. The United States delegation consisted of Albert J. Loveland, Ralph S. Trigg, Fred J. Rossiter, Edward G. Cale, and James C. Foster.[13] The first session of the council was concerned for the most part with administrative matters and established two committees upon both of which the United States was represented: the Advisory Committee on Price Equivalents which convened in London on August 3, 1949; and the Executive Committee which met in London on August 8.[14]

National measures designed to implement the International Wheat Agreement were announced by the Department of Agriculture on July 29, 1949. On that date, the Department disclosed that the selling price for transactions under the agreement would range from forty to fifty cents a bushel below current market prices, the difference to be borne by the government from funds available to the Department of Agriculture for the disposal of farm surpluses. Countries purchasing wheat with ECA funds were not eligible to participate in purchases under the agreement.[15] On October 27, the President signed into law legislation (H.R.6305) authorizing the absorption by the Commodity Credit Corporation of all losses resulting from wheat shipments under the agreement.[16] The same legislation made it possible for nations participating in the European Recovery Program to purchase wheat at prices below the current market levels.

(1) International Wheat Agreement, Signed at Washington March 23 to April 15, 1949. Entered into Force July 1, 1949.[17]

[EXCERPTS]

The Governments parties to this Agreement,

Intending to overcome the serious hardship caused to producers and consumers by burdensome surpluses and critical shortages of wheat, and

Having resolved that it is desirable to conclude an international wheat agreement for this purpose,

Have agreed as follows:

9 See *Documents, X, 1948*, p. 411. 10 Department of State, *Bulletin*, XX, p. 167.
11 *Christian Science Monitor*, March 19. 1949, p. 17.
12 *Congressional Record*, 95, p. 7753 (Daily edition, June 13, 1949).
13 Department of State, *Bulletin*, XXI, p. 52. 14 *Ibid*., p. 228.
15 *New York Times*, July 30, 1949, p. 20. 16 Public Law 421, 81st Cong., 1st sess.
17 Department of State, *Treaties and Other International Acts Series* 1957.

Article I: Objectives

The objectives of this Agreement are to assure supplies of wheat to importing countries and markets for wheat to exporting countries at equitable and stable prices.

Article II: Definitions

.   .   .   .

PART 2 — RIGHTS AND OBLIGATIONS

Article III: Guaranteed Purchases and Guaranteed Sales

1. The quantities of wheat set out in Annex A to this Article for each importing country represent, subject to any increase or reduction made in accordance with the provisions of Part 3 of this Agreement, the guaranteed purchases of that country for each of the four crop-years covered by this Agreement.

2. The quantities of wheat set out in Annex B to this Article for each exporting country represent, subject to any increase or reduction made in accordance with the provisions of Part 3 of this Agreement, the guaranteed sales of that country for each of the four crop-years covered by this Agreement.

3. The guaranteed purchases of an importing country represent the maximum quantity of wheat which, subject to deduction of the amount of the transactions entered in the Council's records in accordance with Article IV against those guaranteed purchases,

(a) that importing country may be required by the Council, as provided in Article V, to purchase from the exporting countries at prices consistent with the minimum prices specified in or determined under Article VI, or

(b) the exporting countries may be required by the Council, as provided in Article V, to sell to that importing country at prices consistent with the maximum prices specified in or determined under Article VI.

4. The guaranteed sales of an exporting country represent the maximum quantity of wheat which, subject to deduction of the amount of the transactions entered in the Council's records in accordance with Article IV against those guaranteed sales,

(a) that exporting country may be required by the Council, as provided in Article V, to sell to the importing countries at prices consistent with the maximum prices specified in or determined under Article VI, or

(b) the importing countries may be required by the Council, as provided in Article V, to purchase from that exporting country at prices consistent with the minimum prices specified in or determined under Article VI.

5. If an importing country finds difficulty in exercising its right to purchase its unfulfilled guaranteed quantities at prices consistent with the maximum prices specified in or determined under Article VI or an exporting country finds difficulty in exercising its right to sell its unfulfilled guaranteed quantities at prices consistent with the minimum prices so specified or determined, it may have resort to the procedure in Article V.

6. Exporting countries are under no obligation to sell any wheat under this Agreement unless required to do so as provided in Article V at prices consistent with the maximum prices specified in or determined under Article VI. Importing countries are under no obligation to purchase any wheat under this Agreement unless required to do so as provided in Article V at prices consistent with the minimum prices specified in or determined under Article VI.

7. The quantity, if any, of wheat-flour to be supplied by the exporting country and accepted by the importing country against their respective guaranteed quantities shall, subject to the provisions of Article V, be determined by agreement between the buyer and seller in each transaction.

8. Exporting and importing countries shall be free to fulfill their guaranteed quantities through private trade channels or otherwise. Nothing in this Agreement shall be construed to exempt any private trader from any laws or regulations to which he is otherwise subject.

ANNEX A TO ARTICLE III

Guaranteed Purchases

Crop-year August 1 to July 31	1949/50	1950/51	1951/52	1952/53	Equivalent in bushels for each crop-year
	.... thousands of metric tons[18]				
Austria	300	300	300	300	11,023,113
Belgium	550	550	550	550	20,209,040
Bolivia	75	75	75	75	2,755,778
Brazil	360	360	360	360	13,227,736
Ceylon	80	80	80	80	2,939,497
China	200	200	200	200	7,348,742
Colombia	20	20	20	20	734,874
Cuba	202	202	202	202	7,422,229
Denmark	44	44	44	44	1,616,723
Dominican Republic	20	20	20	20	734,874
Ecuador	30	30	30	30	1,102,311
Egypt	190	190	190	190	6,981,305
El Salvador	11	11	11	11	404,181
Greece	428	428	428	428	15,726,308
Guatemala	10	10	10	10	367,437
India	1,042	1,042	1,042	1,042	38,286,946
Ireland	275	275	275	275	10,104,520
Israel	100	100	100	100	3,674,371
Italy	1,100	1,100	1,100	1,100	40,418,081
Lebanon	65	65	65	65	2,388,341
Liberia	1	1	1	1	36,744
Mexico	170	170	170	170	6,246,431
Netherlands[19]	700	700	700	700	25,720,597
New Zealand	125	125	125	125	4,592,964
Nicaragua	8	8	8	8	293,950
Norway	210	210	210	210	7,716,179
Panama	17	17	17	17	624,643
Paraguay	60	60	60	60	2,204,623
Peru	200	200	200	200	7,348,742
Philippines	196	196	196	196	7,201,767
Portugal	120	120	120	120	4,409,245
Saudi Arabia	50	50	50	50	1,837,185
Sweden	75	75	75	75	2,755,778
Switzerland	175	175	175	175	6,430,149
Union of South Africa	300	300	300	300	11,023,113
United Kingdom	4,819	4,819	4,819	4,819	177,067,938
Venezuela	90	90	90	90	3,306,934
Total (37 countries)	12,418	12,418	12,418	12,418	456,283,389

[18] Unless the Council decides otherwise, 72 metric tons of wheat-flour shall be deemed equivalent to 100 metric tons of wheat for the purpose of relating quantities of wheat-flour to the quantities specified in this Annex.

[19] Quantity listed for the Netherlands includes for each crop-year 75,000 metric tons or 2,755,778 bushels for Indonesia.

ANNEX B TO ARTICLE III

Guaranteed Sales

Crop-year August 1 to July 31	1949/50	1950/51	1951/52	1952/53	Equivalent in bushels for each crop-year
	.... thousands of metric tons 20				
Australia	2,177	2,177	2,177	2,177	80,000,000
Canada	5,527	5,527	5,527	5,527	203,069,635
France	90	90	90	90	3,306,934
United States of America[21]	4,574	4,574	4,574	4,574	168,069,635
Uruguay	50	50	50	50	1,837,185
Total	12,418	12,418	12,418	12,418	456,283,389

Article IV: Recording of Transactions Against Guaranteed Quantities

1. The Council shall keep records for each crop-year of those transactions and parts of transactions in wheat which are part of the guaranteed quantities in Annexes A and B to Article III.

2. A transaction or part of a transaction in wheat grain between an exporting country and an importing country shall be entered in the Council's records against the guaranteed quantities of those countries for a crop-year:

(a) provided that (i) it is at a price not higher than the maximum nor lower than the minimum specified in or determined under Article VI for that crop-year, and (ii) the exporting country and the importing country have not agreed that it shall not be entered against their guaranteed quantities; and

(b) to the extent that (i) both the exporting and the importing country concerned have unfulfilled guaranteed quantities for that crop-year, and (ii) the loading period specified in the transaction falls within that crop-year.

3. If the exporting country and the importing country concerned so agree, a transaction or part of a transaction made under an agreement for the purchase and sale of wheat entered into prior to the entry into force of Part 2 of this Agreement shall, irrespective of price but subject to the conditions in (b) of paragraph 2 of this Article, also be entered in the Council's records against the guaranteed quantities of those countries.

4. If a commercial contract or governmental agreement on the sale and purchase of wheat-flour contains a statement, or if the exporting country and the importing country concerned inform the Council that they are agreed, that the price of such wheat-flour is consistent with the prices specified in or determined under Article VI, the wheat grain equivalent of such wheat-flour shall, subject to the conditions prescribed in (a) (ii) and (b) of paragraph 2 of this Article, be entered in the Council's records against the guaranteed quantities of those countries. If the commercial contract or governmental agreement does not contain a statement of the nature referred to above and the exporting country and the importing country concerned do not agree that the price of the wheat-flour is consistent with the prices specified in or determined under Article VI, either of those countries may, unless they have agreed that the wheat grain equivalent of that wheat-flour shall not be entered in the Council's records against their guaranteed quantities, request the Council to decide the issue. Should the Council, on consideration of such a request, decide that the price of such wheat-flour is consistent with the prices specified in or determined under Article VI, the wheat grain equivalent of the wheat-flour shall be entered against the guaranteed quantities of the exporting and importing countries concerned, subject to the conditions prescribed in (b) of paragraph 2 of this Article.

20 Unless the Council decides otherwise, 72 metric tons of wheat-flour shall be deemed equivalent to 100 metric tons of wheat for the purpose of relating quantities of wheat-flour to the quantities specified in this Annex.

21 In the event of the provisions of Article X being invoked by reason of a short crop it will be recognized that these guaranteed sales do not include the minimum requirements of wheat of any Occupied Area for which the United States of America has, or may assume, supply responsibility, and that the necessity of meeting these requirements will be one of the factors considered in determining the ability of the United States of America to deliver its guaranteed sales under this Agreement.

Should the Council, on consideration of such a request, decide that the price of such wheat-flour is inconsistent with the prices specified in or determined under Article VI, the wheat grain equivalent of the wheat-flour shall not be so entered.

5. The Council shall prescribe rules of procedure, in accordance with the following provisions, for the reporting and recording of transactions which are part of the guaranteed quantities:

(a) Any transaction or part of a transaction, between an exporting country and an importing country, qualifying under paragraph 2, 3, or 4 of this Article to form part of the guaranteed quantities of those countries shall be reported to the Council within such period and in such detail and by one or both of those countries as the Council shall lay down in its rules of procedure.

(b) Any transaction or part of a transaction reported in accordance with the provisions of subparagraph (a) shall be entered in the Council's records against the guaranteed quantities of the exporting country and the importing country between which the transaction is made.

(c) The order in which transactions and parts of transactions shall be entered in the Council's records against the guaranteed quantities shall be prescribed by the Council in its rules of procedure.

(d) The Council shall, within a time to be prescribed in its rules of procedure, notify each exporting country and each importing country of the entry of any transaction or part of a transaction in the Council's records against the guaranteed quantities of that country.

(e) If, within a period which the Council shall prescribe in its rules of procedure, the importing country or the exporting country concerned objects in any respect to the entry of a transaction or part of a transaction in the Council's records against its guaranteed quantities, the Council shall review the matter and, if it decides that the objection is well founded, shall amend its records accordingly.

(f) If any exporting or importing country considers it probable that the full amount of wheat already entered in the Council's records against its guaranteed quantity for the current crop-year will not be loaded within that crop-year, that country may request the Council to make appropriate reductions in the amounts entered in its records. The Council shall consider the matter and, if it decides that the request is justified, shall amend its records accordingly.

(g) Any wheat purchased by an importing country from an exporting country and resold to another importing country may, by agreement of the importing countries concerned, be entered against the unfulfilled guaranteed purchases of the importing country to which the wheat is finally resold provided that a corresponding reduction is made in the amount entered against the guaranteed purchases of the first importing country.

(h) The Council shall send to all exporting and importing countries, weekly or at such other interval as the Council may prescribe in its rules of procedure, a statement of the amounts entered in its records against guaranteed quantities.

(i) The Council shall notify all exporting and importing countries immediately when the guaranteed quantity of any exporting or importing country for any crop-year has been fulfilled.

6. Each exporting country and each importing country may be permitted, in the fulfillment of its guaranteed quantities, a degree of tolerance to be prescribed by the Council for that country on the basis of the size of its guaranteed quantities and other relevant factors.

Article V: Enforcement of Rights

1. (a) Any importing country which finds difficulty in purchasing its unfulfilled guaranteed quantity for any crop-year at prices consistent with the maxi-

mum prices specified in or determined under Article VI may request the Council's help in making the desired purchases.

(b) Within three days of the receipt of a request under sub-paragraph (a) the Secretary of the Council shall notify those exporting countries which have unfulfilled guaranteed quantities for the relevant crop-year of the amount of the unfulfilled guaranteed quantity of the importing country which has requested the Council's help and invite them to offer to sell wheat at prices consistent with the maximum prices specified in or determined under Article VI.

(c) If within fourteen days of the notification by the Secretary of the Council under subparagraph (b) the whole of the unfulfilled guaranteed quantity of the importing country concerned, or such part thereof as in the opinion of the Council is reasonable at the time the request is made, has not been offered for sale, the Council, having regard to any circumstances which the exporting and the importing countries may wish to submit for consideration and in particular to the industrial programs of any country as well as to the normal traditional volume and ratio of imports of wheat-flour and wheat grain imported by the importing country concerned, shall, within seven days, decide the quantities, and also if requested to do so the quality and grade, of wheat grain and/or wheat-flour which it is appropriate for each or any of the exporting countries to sell to that importing country for loading during the relevant crop-year.

(d) Each exporting country required by the Council's decision under sub-paragraph (c) to offer quantities of wheat grain and/or wheat-flour for sale to the importing country shall, within thirty days from the date of that decision, offer to sell those quantities to such importing country for loading during the relevant crop-year at prices consistent with the maximum prices specified in or determined under Article VI and, unless those countries agree otherwise, on the same conditions regarding the currency in which payment is to be made as prevail generally between them at that time. If no trade relations have hitherto existed between the exporting country and the importing country concerned and if those countries fail to agree on the currency in which payment is to be made, the Council shall decide the issue.

(e) In case of disagreement between an exporting country and an importing country on the quantity of wheat-flour to be included in a particular transaction being negotiated in compliance with the Council's decision under subparagraph (c), or on the relation of the price of such wheat-flour to the maximum prices of wheat grain specified in or determined under Article VI, or on the conditions on which the wheat grain and/or wheat-flour shall be bought and sold, the matter shall be referred to the Council for decision.

2. (a) Any exporting country which finds difficulty in selling its unfulfilled guaranteed quantity for any crop-year at prices consistent with the minimum prices specified in or determined under Article VI may request the Council's help in making the desired sales.

(b) Within three days of the receipt of a request under sub-paragraph (a) the Secretary of the Council shall notify those importing countries which have unfulfilled guaranteed quantities for the relevant crop-year of the amount of the unfulfilled guaranteed quantity of the exporting country which has requested the Council's help and invite them to offer to purchase wheat at prices consistent with the minimum prices specified in or determined under Article VI.

(c) If within fourteen days of the notification by the Secretary of the Council under subparagraph (b) the whole of the unfulfilled guaranteed quantity of the exporting country concerned, or such part thereof as in the opinion of the Council is reasonable at the time the request is made, has not been purchased, the Council, having regard to any circumstances which the exporting and the importing countries may wish to submit for consideration and in particular to the industrial programs of any country as well as to the normal traditional volume and ratio of imports of wheat-flour and wheat grain imported by the importing countries concerned, shall, within seven days, decide the quantities, and also if requested to do so the quality and grade, of wheat grain and/or wheat-flour which it is appropriate for each or any of the importing countries to purchase from that exporting country for loading during the relevant crop-year.

(d) Each importing country required by the Council's decision under subparagraph (c) to offer to purchase quantities of wheat grain and/or wheat-flour from the exporting country shall, within thirty days from the date of that decision, offer to purchase those quantities from such exporting country for loading during the relevant crop-year at prices consistent with the minimum prices specified in or determined under Article VI and, unless those countries agree otherwise, on the same conditions regarding the currency in which payment is to be made as prevail generally between them at that time. If no trade relations have hitherto existed between the exporting country and the importing country concerned and if those countries fail to agree on the currency in which payment is to be made, the Council shall decide the issue.

(e) In case of disagreement between an exporting country and an importing country on the quantity of wheat-flour to be included in a particular transaction being negotiated in compliance with the Council's decision under subparagraph (c), or on the relation of the price of such wheat-flour to the minimum prices of wheat grain specified in or determined under Article VI, or on the conditions on which the wheat grain and/or wheat-flour shall be bought and sold, the matter shall be referred to the Council for decision.

Article VI: Prices

1. The basic minimum and maximum prices for the duration of this Agreement shall be:

Crop-year	Minimum	Maximum
1949/50	$1.50	$1.80
1950/51	$1.40	$1.80
1951/52	$1.30	$1.80
1952/53	$1.20	$1.80

Canadian currency per bushel at the parity for the Canadian dollar, determined for the purposes of the International Monetary Fund as at March 1, 1949 for No. 1 Manitoba Northern wheat in bulk in store Fort William/Port Arthur. The basic minimum and maximum prices, and the equivalents thereof hereafter referred to, shall exclude such carrying charges and marketing costs as may be agreed between the buyer and the seller.

. . . .

Article VII: Stocks

1. In order to assure supplies of wheat to importing countries, each exporting country shall endeavor to maintain stocks of old crop wheat at the end of its crop-year at a level adequate to ensure that it will fulfill its guaranteed sales under this Agreement in each subsequent crop-year.

2. In the event of a short crop being harvested by an exporting country, particular consideration shall be given by the Council to the efforts made by that exporting country to maintain adequate stocks as required by paragraph 1 of this Article before that country is relieved of any of its obligations under Article X.

3. In order to avoid disproportionate purchases of wheat at the beginning and end of a crop-year, which might prejudice the stabilization of prices under this

Agreement and render difficult the fulfillment of the obligations of all exporting and importing countries, importing countries shall endeavor to maintain adequate stocks at all times.

4. In the event of an appeal by an importing country under Article XII, particular consideration shall be given by the Council to the efforts made by that importing country to maintain adequate stocks as required by paragraph 3 of this Article before it decides in favor of such an appeal.

Article VIII: Information to be Supplied to the Council

The exporting and importing countries shall report to the Council, within the time prescribed by it, such information as the Council may request in connection with the administration of this Agreement.

PART 3 — ADJUSTMENT OF GUARANTEED QUANTITIES

Article IX: Adjustments in Case of Nonparticipation or Withdrawal of Countries

1. In the event of any difference occurring between the total of the guaranteed purchases in Annex A to Article III and the total of the guaranteed sales in Annex B to Article III as a result of any country or countries listed in Annex A or Annex B (a) not signing or (b) not depositing an instrument of acceptance of or (c) withdrawing under paragraph 5, 6, or 7 of Article XXII from or (d) being expelled under Article XIX from or (e) being found by the Council under Article XIX to be in default of the whole or part of its guaranteed quantities under this Agreement, the Council shall, without prejudice to the right of any country to withdraw from this Agreement under paragraph 6 of Article XXII, adjust the remaining guaranteed quantities so as to make the total in the one Annex equal to the total in the other Annex.

2. The adjustment under this Article shall, unless the Council decides otherwise by two-thirds of the votes cast by the exporting countries and two-thirds of the votes cast by the importing countries, be made by reducing pro rata the guaranteed quantities in Annex A or Annex B, as the case may be, by the amount necessary to make the total in the one Annex equal to the total in the other Annex.

3. In making adjustments under this Article, the Council shall keep in mind the general desirability of maintaining the total guaranteed purchases and the total guaranteed sales at the highest possible level.

Article X: Adjustment in Case of Short Crop or Necessity to Safeguard Balance of Payments or Monetary Reserves

1. Any exporting or importing country which fears that it may be prevented, by a short crop in the case of an exporting country or the necessity to safeguard its balance of payments or monetary reserves in the case of an importing country, from carrying out its obligations under this Agreement in respect of a particular crop-year shall report the matter to the Council.

2. If the matter reported relates to balance of payments or monetary reserves, the Council shall seek and take into account, together with all facts which it considers relevant, the opinion of the International Monetary Fund, as far as the matter concerns a country which is a member of the Fund, on the existence and extent of the necessity referred to in paragraph 1 of this Article.

3. The Council shall discuss with the reporting country the matter reported under paragraph 1 of this Article and shall decide whether such country's representations are well founded. If it finds that they are well-founded, it shall decide whether and to what extent and on what conditions the reporting country shall be relieved of its guaranteed quantity for the crop-year concerned. The Council shall inform the reporting country of its decision.

4. If the Council decides that the reporting country shall be relieved of the whole or part of its guaranteed quantity for the crop-year concerned, the following procedure shall apply:

(a) The Council shall, if the reporting country is an importing country, invite the other importing countries, or, if the reporting country is an exporting country, invite the other exporting countries, to increase their guaranteed quantities for the crop-year concerned up to the amount of the guaranteed quantity of which the reporting country is relieved; provided that an increase in the guaranteed quantities of an exporting country shall require approval by the Council by two-thirds of the votes cast by the exporting countries and two-thirds of the votes cast by the importing countries if any importing country, within such period as the Council shall prescribe, objects to such increase on the ground that it will have the effect of making the balance of payments problems of that importing country more difficult.

(b) If the amount of which the importing country is relieved cannot be fully offset in the manner provided in (a) of this paragraph, the Council shall invite the exporting countries, if the reporting country is an importing country, or the importing countries, if the reporting country is an exporting country, to accept a reduction of their guaranteed quantities for the crop-year concerned up to the amount of the guaranteed quantity of which the reporting country is relieved, after taking account of any adjustments made under (a) of this paragraph.

(c) If the total offers received by the Council from the exporting and importing countries to increase their guaranteed quantities under (a) of this paragraph or to reduce their guaranteed quantities under (b) of this paragraph exceed the amount of the guaranteed quantity of which the reporting country is relieved, their guaranteed quantities shall, unless the Council decides otherwise, be increased or reduced, as the case may be, on a pro rata basis, provided that the increase or reduction of the guaranteed quantity of any such country shall not exceed its offer.

(d) If the amount of the guaranteed quantity of which the reporting country is relieved cannot be fully offset in the manner provided in (a) and (b) of this paragraph, the Council shall reduce the guaranteed quantities in Annex A to Article III, if the reporting country is an exporting country, or in Annex B to Article III, if the reporting country is an importing country, for the crop-year concerned by the amount necessary to make the total in the one Annex equal to the total in the other Annex. Unless the exporting countries, in the case of a reduction in Annex B, or the importing countries, in the case of a reduction in Annex A, agree otherwise, the reduction shall be made on a pro rata basis, account being taken of any reduction already made under (b) of this paragraph.

Article XI: Increase of Guaranteed Quantities by Consent

The Council may at any time, upon request by an exporting or importing country, approve an increase in the figures in one Annex for the remaining period of this Agreement if an equal increase is made in the other Annex for that period, provided that the exporting and importing countries whose figures would thereby be changed consent.

Article XII: Additional Purchases in Case of Critical Need

In order to meet a critical need which has arisen or threatens to arise in its territory, an importing country may appeal to the Council for assistance in obtaining supplies of wheat in addition to its guaranteed purchases. On consideration of such an appeal the Council may reduce pro rata the guaranteed quantities of the other importing countries in order to provide the quantity of wheat which it determines to be necessary to relieve the emergency created by the critical need, provided that it considers that such emergency cannot be met in any other manner. Two-thirds of the votes cast by the exporting countries and two-thirds of the votes cast by the importing countries shall be required for any reduction of guaranteed purchases under this paragraph.

PART 4 — ADMINISTRATION

Article XIII: The Council

A. Constitution

1. An International Wheat Council is hereby established to administer this Agreement.

2. Each exporting country and each importing country shall be a voting member of the Council and may be represented at its meetings by one delegate, one alternate, and advisers.

3. Any country which the Council recognizes as an irregular exporter or an irregular importer of wheat may become a non-voting member of the Council, provided that it accepts the obligations prescribed in Article VIII and agrees to pay such membership fees as shall be determined by the Council. Each country which is a non-voting member of the Council shall be entitled to have one representative at its meetings.

4. The Food and Agriculture Organization of the United Nations, the International Trade Organization, the Interim Coordinating Committee for International Commodity Arrangements, and such other intergovernmental organizations as the Council may decide, shall each be entitled to have one non-voting representative at meetings of the Council.

5. The Council shall elect for each crop-year a Chairman and a Vice Chairman.

B. Powers and Functions

6. The Council shall establish its rules of procedure.

7. The Council shall keep such records as are required by the terms of this Agreement and may keep such other records as it considers desirable.

8. The Council shall publish an annual report and may publish any other information concerning matters within the scope of this Agreement.

9. The Council, after consultation with the International Wheat Council established under the Memorandum of Agreement approved in June 1942[22] and amended in June 1946,[23] may take over the records, assets and liabilities of that body.

10. The Council shall have such other powers and perform such other functions as it may deem necessary to carry out the terms of this Agreement.

11. The Council may, by two-thirds of the votes cast by the exporting countries and two-thirds of the votes cast by the importing countries, delegate the exercise of any of its powers or functions. The Council may at any time revoke such delegation by a majority of the votes cast. Any decision made under any powers or functions delegated by the Council in accordance with this paragraph shall be subject to review by the Council at the request of any exporting or importing country made within a period which the Council shall prescribe. Any decision, in respect of which no request for review has been made within the prescribed period, shall be binding on all exporting and importing countries.

C. Voting

12. The importing countries shall hold 1,000 votes, which shall be distributed between them in the proportions which their respective guaranteed purchases for the current crop-year bear to the total of the guaranteed purchases for that crop-year. The exporting countries shall also hold 1,000 votes, which shall be distributed between them in the proportions which their respective guaranteed sales for the current crop-year bear to the total of the guaranteed sales for that crop-year. No exporting country or importing country shall have less than one vote and there shall be no fractional votes.

13. The Council shall redistribute the votes in accordance with the provisions of paragraph 12 of this Article whenever there is any change in the guaranteed purchases or guaranteed sales for the current crop-year.

14. If an exporting or an importing country forfeits its votes under paragraph 5

[22] Department of State, *Executive Agreement Series* 384.
[23] *Ibid., Treaties and Other International Acts Series* 1540.

of Article XVII or is deprived of its votes under paragraph 3 of Article XIX, the Council shall redistribute the votes as if that country had no guaranteed quantity for the current crop-year.

15. Except where otherwise specified in this Agreement, decisions of the Council shall be by a majority of the total votes cast.

16. Any exporting country may authorize any other exporting country, and any importing country may authorize any other importing country, to represent its interests and to exercise its votes at any meeting or meetings of the Council. Evidence of such authorization satisfactory to the Council shall be submitted to the Council.

D. Sessions

17. The Council shall meet at least once during each half of each crop-year and at such other times as the Chairman may decide.

18. The Chairman shall convene a Session of the Council if so requested by (a) any five delegates of the exporting and importing countries or (b) the delegate or delegates of any of the exporting and importing countries holding a total of not less than ten per cent of the total votes or (c) the Executive Committee.

E. Quorum

19. The presence of delegates with a majority of the votes held by the exporting countries and a majority of the votes held by the importing countries shall be necessary to constitute a quorum at any meeting of the Council.

F. Seat

20. The Council shall select in July 1949 its temporary seat. The Council shall select, so soon as it deems the time propitious, its permanent seat after consultation with the appropriate organs and specialized agencies of the United Nations.

G. Legal Capacity

21. The Council shall have in the territory of each exporting and importing country such legal capacity as may be necessary for the exercise of its functions under this Agreement.

H. Decisions

22. Each exporting and importing country undertakes to accept as binding all decisions of the Council under the provisions of this Agreement.

Article XIV: Executive Committee

1. The Council shall establish an Executive Committee. The members of the Executive Committee shall be three exporting countries elected annually by the exporting countries and not more than seven importing countries elected annually by the importing countries. The Council shall appoint the Chairman of the Executive Committee and may appoint a Vice Chairman.

2. The Executive Committee shall be responsible to and work under the general direction of the Council. It shall have such powers and functions as are expressly assigned to it under this Agreement and such other powers and functions as the Council may delegate to it under paragraph 11 of Article XIII.

3. The exporting countries on the Executive Committee shall have the same total number of votes as the importing countries. The votes of the exporting countries shall be divided among them as they shall decide, provided that no exporting country shall have more than forty per cent of the total votes of the exporting countries. The votes of the importing countries shall be divided among them as they shall decide, provided that no importing country shall have more than forty per cent of the total votes of the importing countries.

4. The Council shall prescribe rules of procedure regarding voting in the Executive Committee, and may make such other provisions regarding rules of procedure in the Executive Committee as it thinks fit. A decision of the Executive Committee shall require the same majority of votes as this Agreement prescribes for the Council when making a decision on a similar matter.

5. Any exporting or importing country which is not a member of the Executive Committee may participate, without voting, in the discussion of any question before the Executive Committee whenever the latter considers that the interests of that country are affected.

Article XV: Advisory Committee on Price Equivalents

The Council shall establish an Advisory Committee on Price Equivalents consisting of representatives of three exporting countries and of three importing countries. The Committee shall advise the Council and the Executive Committee on the matters referred to in paragraphs 4, 5, and 6 of Article VI and on such other questions as the Council or the Executive Committee may refer to it. The Chairman of the Committee shall be appointed by the Council.

Article XVI: The Secretariat

1. The Council shall have a Secretariat consisting of a Secretary and such staff as may be required for the work of the Council and of its committees.
2. The Council shall appoint the Secretary and determine his duties.
3. The staff shall be appointed by the Secretary in accordance with regulations established by the Council.

Article XVII: Finance

1. The expenses of delegations to the Council, of representatives on the Executive Committee, and of representatives on the Advisory Committee on Price Equivalents shall be met by their respective Governments. The other expenses necessary for the administration of this Agreement, including those of the Secretariat and any remuneration which the Council may decide to pay to its Chairman or its Vice Chairman, shall be met by annual contributions from the exporting and importing countries. The contribution of each such country for each crop-year shall be proportionate to the number of votes held by it when the budget for that crop-year is settled.

. . . .

Article XVIII: Cooperation With Other Intergovernmental Organizations

. . . .

Article XIX: Disputes and Complaints

1. Any dispute concerning the interpretation or application of this Agreement which is not settled by negotiation and any complaint that any exporting or importing country has failed to fulfill its obligations under this Agreement, shall, at the request of any exporting or importing country party to the dispute or making the complaint, be referred to the Council which shall make a decision on the matter.
2. No exporting or importing country shall be found to have committed a breach of this Agreement except by a majority of the votes held by the exporting countries and a majority of the votes held by the importing countries. Any finding that an exporting or importing country is in breach of this Agreement shall specify the nature of the breach and, if the breach involves default by that country in its guaranteed quantities, the extent of such default.
3. If the Council finds that an exporting country or an importing country has committed a breach of this Agreement, it may, by a majority of the votes held by the exporting countries and a majority of the votes held by the importing countries, deprive the country concerned of its voting rights until it fulfills its obligations or expel that country from the Agreement.
4. If any exporting or importing country is deprived of its votes under this Article, the votes shall be redistributed as provided in paragraph 14 of Article XIII. If any exporting or importing country is found in default of the whole or part of its guaranteed quantities or is expelled from this Agreement, the remaining guaranteed quantities shall be adjusted as provided in Article IX.

PART 5 — FINAL PROVISIONS

Article XX: Signature, Acceptance, and Entry into Force

·   ·   ·   ·   ·   ·

Article XXI: Accession

·   ·   ·   ·   ·

Article XXII: Duration, Amendment, Withdrawal and Termination

·   ·   ·   ·   ·   ·

Article XXIII: Territorial Application

·   ·   ·   ·   ·

3. NATURAL RESOURCES

A. Fisheries

The United States was host to the governments which participated in the International Northwest Atlantic Fisheries Conference held at Washington from January 26 to February 8, 1949, to conclude the International Convention for the Northwest Atlantic Fisheries. The convention provided for a commission for the collection and dissemination of scientific information on which all contracting governments were represented, and separate panels for each sub-area, composed of the governments with particular fishing interests in each area. The treaty was signed at Washington, February 8, 1949 by Canada, Denmark, France, Iceland, Italy, Norway, Portugal, Spain, the United Kingdom for itself and Newfoundland, and the United States.[1]

During 1949 the United States Senate conducted hearings on three fisheries treaties, favorably reported all three, and on July 25, 1949 advised ratification.[2] Two of these treaties involved the tuna fisheries of the Eastern Pacific Ocean: the Convention with Mexico for the Establishment of an International Commission for the Scientific Investigation of Tuna, signed at Mexico City, January 25, 1949;[3] and the Convention for the Establishment of an Inter-American Tuna Commission signed at Washington, May 31, 1949,[4] between Costa Rica and the United States with provision for adherence of governments whose nationals operated in the fisheries involved.

At a meeting held at Singapore from March 24 to 31, 1949, a United States delegation participated in the establishment of the Indo-Pacific Fisheries Council, first of a number of proposed regional councils of the Food and Agriculture Organization to deal with fisheries. The council set up permanent working committees to formulate programs for the study of the fish resources of the region and of the problems of their preservation and marketing.[5]

B. Timber

During 1949 the United States participated in the Preparatory Conference on World Pulp Problems on April 25, 1949 at Montreal; the first FAO World Conference on Mechanical Wood Technology, held at Geneva in September 1949; and the first session of the FAO Latin American Commission for Forestry and Forest Products, held at Rio de Janeiro during the last week of May. Recommendations of the conference on World Pulp Problems largely concerned to a review of the world situation and the collection and standardization of statistics.[6] The Geneva Conference reached agreement on international standardization of basic timber tests while the FAO Forestry Commission at Rio de Janeiro examined a report on

1 For the text of the convention, see Department of State, *Documents and State Papers*, I, p. 707.
2 Senate Report 10, 81st Cong., 1st sess.; Senate Report 11, 81st Cong., 1st sess.
3 For text of the convention, see Department of State Press Release 53, January 25, 1949.
4 For text of the convention, see *ibid.*, 400, May 31, 1949.
5 Food and Agriculture Organization Press Release 1/R/244, March 1949.
6 Food and Agriculture Organization, Document C49/8, n. d.

the utilization of Latin American forest resources and equipment requirements for such utilization.[7]

C. Tin

The International Tin Study Group held its fourth meeting at London during June 1949. The meeting had been called to consider the world tin position and to discuss proposal for an intergovernmental agreement on tin. The United States was represented on a working party established by the Tin Study Group to prepare a statement on the position and prospects of the tin industry and to draft an international control agreement. The group was scheduled to consider the statement and agreement at its next meeting in 1950.[8]

[7] *Ibid.*
[8] Department of State, *Bulletin,* XXI, p. 47, 701.

CHAPTER XI

Labor and Social Problems

1. INTERNATIONAL LABOR COOPERATION

A. General

The 32d session of the International Labor Conference met at Geneva from June 8 to July 2, 1949. Philip M. Kaiser, director of the Office of International Labor Affairs, Department of Labor, and Senator Herbert R. O'Conor (Maryland) headed the United States government delegation; other members were Charles P. McCormick, president of McCormick and Company, for the employers and George P. Delaney, international representatives of the American Federation of Labor, for the workers.[1] The conference adopted three new international labor conventions, revised five others, approved three recommendations, revised one other, and voted several resolutions on ILO policy. One of the conventions complementing the Convention on Freedom of Association and Protection of the Rights to Organize adopted at the previous session, required ratifying countries to assure workers the right to organize into trade unions without interference and to bargain collectively. The other two new conventions were designed to assure workers employed in the execution of contracts entered into by public authorities, wages, hours of work and working conditions not less favorable than those generally prevailing in the industry and to protect wages by assuring that they were paid promptly, in cash, in full, and directly to the workers. The conference also approved a budget of $5,983,526 to finance ILO's operations in 1950 and examined the manner in which countries were applying the ILO conventions which they had ratified.[2]

During the year under review the United States participated in the following activities of subordinate bodies of the International Labor Organization: the third session of the Permanent Migration Committee, Geneva, January 13; the second session of the Building, Civil Engineering and Public Works Committee, Rome, March 15; the third session of the Coal Mines Committee, Pittsburgh, April 19; the Fourth Regional Conference of American States Members of ILO, Montevideo, April 25; the third session of the Inland Transport Committee, Brussels, May 17; the Technical Tripartite Conference on Safety in Coal Mines, Geneva, September 12; the Asian Conference of Experts on Technical Training, Singapore, September 12; the Seventh International Conference of Labor Statisticians, Geneva, September 26; and the third session of the Metal Trade Committee, Geneva, November 8. The Governing Body of ILO upon which the United States was represented held its 108th, 109th and 110th meetings during 1949.

B. Freedom of Association

At its ninth session, which met at Geneva from July 5 to August 15, the United Nations Economic and Social Council discussed at length three proposals concerning the establishment of a commission on freedom of association. Acting upon a recommendation of the Social Committee concerning trade union rights the Council adopted a joint United States-United Kingdom resolution requesting that ILO proceed with the establishment of a fact-finding and conciliation commission on freedom of association and that the Secretary-General and the Director General of ILO formulate a procedure for making the commission's services available to the appropriate organs of the United Nations with respect to members which were not members of ILO.[3] In presenting this measure to the Social Committee the United States emphasized that the question of trade union rights was one of the most important

1 Department of State, *Bulletin*, XX, p. 815.　　　　2 *Ibid.*, XXI, p. 103.
3 United Nations Economic and Social Council, Document E/SR.318, August 2, 1949, p. 15.

ever brought before the Economic and Social Council. Because the International Labor Organization had particular responsibility in the field of labor and long experience with such problems, it in close cooperation with the Economic and Social Council was the appropriate body to deal with trade union rights. One of the main problems facing the United Nations was how to make the most effective use of the specialized agencies; this measure was designed to utilize the services and the special experience of ILO, the United States maintained.[4]

C. Forced Labor and Slavery

The demand of the American Federation of Labor for an investigation of forced labor in eastern European countries was acted upon by the eighth session of the United Nations Economic and Social Council, which met at Lake Success from February 7 to March 18, 1949, after the matter had been deferred from the sixth and seventh sessions. Lengthy debate, filled with charges and counter-charges, centered around the assertion by the United States delegate (Thorp) that 8 to 14 million persons in the Soviet Union were forced to work under slave-labor conditions. The Council approved a United States resolution, as amended, that the nature and extent of forced labor be considered by the International Labor Organization, in cooperation with the Secretary-General, who was to inquire of governments the extent to which they would cooperate in an impartial inquiry in their countries on the charges made in the Council, and that the matter be referred to the Commission on Human Rights for examination in connection with the drafting of the Covenant on Human Rights.[5] The United States subsequently replied to the inquiry of the Secretary-General that it would cooperate fully in such an inquiry. In June the Director General of ILO, David A. Morse, transmitted to the Economic and Social Council certain conclusions approved by the ILO Governing Body at its 109th session implementing the ECOSOC resolution of March 7 calling for an investigation of the question of forced labor. The Governing Body concluded that the Director General should establish close contact with the Secretary-General in order to establish an impartial commission of inquiry into this matter.[6]

At the ninth session of the Economic and Social Council the United States introduced a resolution proposing the establishment of a commission of inquiry of eleven members serving in their personal capacities, five members of which were to be chosen by the Council, five by ILO and the eleven elected by the other ten members.[7] At the end of the debate the Council adopted the United States resolution with major amendments which deleted the part concerning the constitution of a commission of inquiry and substituted a clause stating that replies to the Secretary-General's inquiries so far received from governments did not provide the conditions under which a commission could operate effectively, and instructing the Secretary-General to request governments which had not yet stated their willingness to cooperate in an impartial inquiry to consider whether they could reply before the next session of the Council.[8]

D. Full Employment and Economic Stability

The United States was represented by Isador Lubin at the fourth session of the United Nations Economic and Employment Commission, which was held at Lake Success from May 9 to 26, 1949. As it had during the third session of the commission the United States strongly criticized the reports of the Subcommissions on Economic Development and on Employment and Economic Stability, emphasizing that the subcommission should indicate specific measures for the improvement of underdeveloped areas and methods of carrying out such measures.[9] A joint resolution submitted by the United States, France and the United Kingdom inviting the Secretary-General to appoint a group of experts to prepare a report on national and

---

4 *Ibid.*, Document E/AC.7/SR.108, August 3, 1949, p. 5.
5 *Ibid.*, Document E/SR.263, March 7, 1949, p. 5.
6 *Ibid.*, Document E/1337/Add.7, June 21, 1949.
7 *Ibid.*, Document E/1484, August 3, 1949.
8 *Ibid.*, Document E/SR.324, August 11, 1949, p. 22.
9 *Ibid.*, Document E/CN.1/SR.69, May 12, 1949, p. 5. For action by the fourth session of the United Nations General Assembly on the problems of unemployment and full employment, see *International Organization*, IV, p. 83.

international measures to achieve and maintain full employment and asking the Economic and Employment Commission to examine the report and submit to the next session of the Council comments and recommendations for action was adopted at the ninth session of the Economic and Social Council.[10]

2. INTERNATIONAL SOCIAL COOPERATION

A. General

The United States was represented by A. J. Altmeyer at the fourth and fifth sessions of the United Nations Social Commission, which met at Lake Success from May 2 to 20 and from December 5 to 15 respectively. Included among the subjects acted upon by the earlier session were traffic in persons and the suppression of the prostitution of others; advisory social welfare services; housing, town and country planning with special reference to tropical housing problems; and the prevention of crime and the treatment of offenders. The agenda for the fifth session included the latter three topics, problems of social rehabilitation of the physically handicapped and a study of the interrelationship of the economic and social activities of the United Nations.

B. Human Rights

[See *Documents, VIII, 1945–1946,* p. 722; *IX, 1947,* p. 497; *X, 1948,* p. 428.]

Mrs. Eleanor Roosevelt represented the United States at the fifth session of the United Nations Commission on Human Rights, which met at Lake Success from May 9 to June 20, to examine the draft International Covenant on Human Rights, which had been in preparation since December 1947. Taking the view that the covenant was essentially a document intended to safeguard human rights and freedoms against state action, the United States introduced proposals following along the lines of familiar, traditional safeguards in United States constitutional and statutory law and court decisions and urged that each of the rights in the covenant be stated in clear and concise language and in terms of limitations on state action.[1] The United States opposed inclusion in the covenant of a detailed listing of specific limitations on each right on the grounds that such enumerations would be provisional and incomplete and would give the impression that the limitations were being emphasized rather than the right itself and favored instead inclusion of a general limitation clause, pointing out that this course had been followed with respect to the Universal Declaration of Human Rights, which contained a general restriction applying to the whole Declaration.[2]

Three views in regard to international machinery for implementation of the covenant emerged during lengthy debate on this matter, with the United States supporting the view that at that time provision should be made only for the filing of complaints by states against states with respect to violations under the covenant. It felt that further experience was needed before developing provisions for petitions from private individuals, groups and organizations.[3] The United States and the United Kingdom jointly proposed that the covenant provide for the establishment by the Secretary-General of a panel of persons designated by signatory states and serving in their individual capacities; from this panel a Human Rights Committee would be selected to consider disputes between states relating to observance of the covenant. This and other draft texts on implementation of the covenant were referred to governments for comment. Because the commission did not have sufficient time to complete both the covenant and measures for its implementation, it was decided to complete preliminary revision of the covenant. The draft covenant was then submitted to member states for comments.

10 United Nations Economic and Social Council, Document E/SR.336, August 24, 1949, p. 15.
1 United States Mission to the United Nations Press Release 626, May 10, 1949.
2 United Nations Economic and Social Council, Documents E/CN.4/SR.88, May 19, 1949, p. 10; E/CN.4/SR.90, May 20, 1949, p. 9; E/CN.4/SR.91, May 31, 1949, p. 5; and E/CN.4/SR.93, May 27, 1949, p. 8.
3 Department of State, *Bulletin,* XXI, p. 7.

(1) *Statement by the United States Representative on the United Nations Commission on Human Rights, (Mrs. Eleanor Roosevelt) on the Draft International Covenant on Human Rights.   Released to the Press, January 3, 1950.*[4]

[EXCERPTS]

The United States is today making public the letter it has sent to Secretary General Trygve Lie containing its comments on the draft International Covenant on Human Rights together with a number of suggested revisions. The Human Rights Commission last June transmitted a suggested draft Covenant to all United Nations Member States, requesting their comments by January 1, 1950.

. . . .

There are several aspects of the United States proposals that I would like to point out. The first is that the United States has offered for the first time a comprehensive article on the implementation of the Covenant.

The essentials of this article are that it provides that any State party to the Covenant may raise a question of violation of the Covenant "if (it) considers that another State Party is not giving effect to a provision of that Covenant . . ."

The implementation mechanism proposed contemplates that the States involved in an alleged violation shall initially undertake a settlement between them. If this should fail, the plan provides a method for setting up a Human Rights Committee of five persons chosen "for their high moral character and suitable ability" to serve in their personal capacities. The Committee would have authority to call for relevant information from any State concerned, request advisory opinions from the International Court of Justice, through the Human Rights Commission, and report its findings of fact not later than two years after its first meeting.

. . . .

The second article I would like to point out is Article 17 on Freedom of Information. As you will see, it is a very simple, straight-forward article worded so as to protect from governmental interference the right to hold opinions, to seek, receive and impart information, opinions and ideas, regardless of frontiers. In restricting the protection to the area of governmental interference, the proposed draft follows the articles previously proposed by the Sub-Commission on Freedom of Information and by the 1947 Geneva Conference on Freedom of Information.

You will note in connection with this article that the United States has suggested a general limitation clause, instead of listing in detail the specific exceptions which might enable countries to restrict freedom of information. It seems to us that a general limitation clause is the only practicable way of handling the question of limitation on freedom. For example, when the Conference on Freedom of Information drafted a proposed article it initially listed eight such exceptions or limitations. In addition, the drafting com-

4 United States Mission to the United Nations Press Release 785, January 3, 1950.

mittee on the Covenant forwarded to the Commission a list of 25 other possible limitations.

. . . .

Another important article is Article 24 which contains what is known as the federal state provision. A number of Member States, including the United States, have a form of constitutional government which reserves to their constituent states certain powers of government wherein the federal or national government does not operate. Under the federal state provision proposed for the Covenant, the obligation of the United States would be limited under the Covenant to matters within the federal government's sphere of jurisdiction. Where it is determined by appropriate constitutional processes that the Covenant involves matters purely the concern of the constituent states, the federal government undertakes to recommend favorably to those states the incorporation of the provisions of the Covenant in their basic law.

. . . .

The United States feels that the economic and social proposals should not be included in the Covenant on Human Rights since their inclusion would seriously prejudice the completion of the Covenant at the next session of the Commission. Proposals in the economic and social spheres should be taken up only after the most careful consideration and the fullest possible exploration. Economic and social development is progressing at varying rates and finds itself at widely divergent levels in the various countries of the world. The difficulty of quickly drafting effective, acceptable articles at the next session of the Commission under these circumstances seems obvious. Study and exploration of these questions inevitably would take a great deal of time.

. . . .

The Commission on Human Rights convenes for its next session on March 27, 1950, and the United States attaches great importance to the completion of the draft International Covenant on Human Rights at that session in order that it may be forwarded to the Economic and Social Council and to the 1950 Session of the General Assembly for its consideration and final approval.

1. GENOCIDE
[See *Documents, X, 1948*, p. 429.]

On June 16 President Truman sent to the Senate for its advice and consent with respect to ratification the Convention on the Prevention and Punishment of the Crime of Genocide adopted unanimously by the General Assembly on December 9, 1948.[5] No further action was taken by the United States on the convention during the year under review.

(1) *Message of the President (Truman) Transmitting to the Senate the Convention on the Prevention and Punishment of the Crime of Genocide, June 16, 1949.*[6]

With a view to receiving the advice and consent of the Senate to ratification, I transmit herewith a certified copy of the Convention on the Prevention

---

5 *Congressional Record*, 95, p. 7980 (Daily edition, June 16, 1949).   6 *Ibid.*

and Punishment of the Crime of Genocide, adopted unanimously by the General Assembly of the United Nations in Paris on December 9, 1948, and signed on behalf of the United States on December 11, 1948.

The character of the convention is explained in the enclosed report of the Acting Secretary of State. I endorse the recommendations of the Acting Secretary of State in his report and urge that the Senate advise and consent to my ratification of this convention.

In my letter of February 5, 1947, transmitting to the Congress my first annual report on the activities of the United Nations and the participation of the United States therein, I pointed out that one of the important achievements of the General Assembly's first session was the agreement of the members of the United Nations that genocide constitutes a crime under international law. I also emphasize that America has long been a symbol of freedom and democratic progress to peoples less favored than we have been, and that we must maintain their belief in us by our policies and our acts.

By the leading part the United States has taken in the United Nations in producing an effective international legal instrument outlawing the world-shocking crime of genocide, we have established before the world our firm and clear policy toward that crime. By giving its advice and consent to my ratification of this Convention, which I urge, the Senate of the United States will demonstrate that the United States is prepared to take effective action on its part to contribute to the establishment of principles of law and justice.

(a) Report of the Acting Secretary of State (Webb) to the President (Truman) on the Convention on the Prevention and Punishment of the Crime of Genocide, Transmitted to the Senate, June 16, 1949.[7]

[EXCERPTS]

I have the honor to transmit to you a certified copy of the convention on the prevention and punishment of the crime of genocide, adopted unanimously by the General Assembly of the United Nations in Paris on December 9, 1948, with the recommendation that it be submitted to the Senate for its advice and consent to ratification.

The convention defines genocide to mean certain acts, enumerated in article II, committed with the intent to destroy, in whole or in part, a national, ethnical, racial, or religious group, as such. These acts are discussed below.

The basic purpose of the convention is the prevention of the destruction of a human group as such. The first resolution of the General Assembly on this subject, 96 (I), adopted unanimously by the members of the United Nations on December 11, 1946, succinctly pointed out that —

> Genocide is a denial of the right of existence of entire human groups, as homicide is the denial of the right to live of individual human beings.

The resolution also pointed out that genocide shocks the conscience of mankind, results in great losses to humanity and is contrary to moral law. Of

---

7 *The Genocide Convention. Hearings before a subcommittee of the Committee on Foreign Relations, United States Senate, Eighty-First Congress, Second Session, on Executive O, The International Convention on the Prevention and Punishment of the Crime of Genocide,* p. 2.

course, homicide also is shocking, results in losses to humanity and is contrary to moral law. The distinction between those two crimes, therefore, is not a difference in underlying moral principles, because in the case of both crimes, moral principles are equally outraged. The distinction is that in homicide, the individual is the victim; in genocide, it is the group.

The General Assembly declared in this resolution that the physical extermination of human groups, as such, is of such grave and legitimate international concern that civilized society is justified in branding genocide as a crime under international law. The extermination of entire human groups impairs the self-preservation of civilization itself. The recent genocidal acts committed by the Nazi Government have placed heavy burdens and responsibilities on other countries, including our own. The millions of dollars spent by the United States alone on refugees, many of them the victims of genocide, and the special immigration laws designed to take care of such unfortunates illustrate how genocide can deeply affect other states. On September 23, 1948, Secretary of State Marshall stated that —

> Governments which systematically disregard the rights of their own people are not likely to respect the rights of other nations and other people and are likely to seek their objectives by coercion and force in the international field.

It is not surprising, therefor, to find the General Assembly of the United Nations unanimously declaring that genocide is a matter of international concern.

Thus, the heart of the convention is its recognition of the principle that the prevention and punishment of genocide requires international cooperation. However, the convention does not substitute international responsibility for state responsibility. It leaves to states themselves the basic obligation to protect entire human groups in their right to live. On the other hand it is designed to insure international liability where state responsibility has not been properly discharged.

. . . .

Genocide is a crime which has been perpetrated by man against man throughout history. Although man has always expressed his horror of this heinous crime, little or no action had been taken to prevent and punish it. The years immediately preceding World War II witnessed the most diabolically planned and executed series of genocidal acts ever before committed. This time there was to be more than mere condemnation. A feeling of general repulsion swept over the world, and following the war manifested itself in the General Assembly's resolution of December 1946. It is this resolution to which the Legal Committee gave full content by providing the General Assembly with a legal instrument designed not only to prevent genocidal acts but also to punish the guilty.

. . . .

On December 2, 1948, in voting in favor of the genocide convention, the representative of the United States made the following statement before the Legal Committee of the General Assembly:

I wish that the following remarks be included in the record verbatim:

Article IX provides that disputes between the contracting parties relating to the interpretation, application, or fulfillment of the present convention, including those relating to the responsibility of a state for genocide or any of the other acts enumerated in article III, shall be submitted to the International Court of Justice. If 'responsibility of a state' is used in the traditional sense of responsibility to another state for injuries sustained by nationals of the complaining state in violation of principles of international law and similarly, if 'fulfillment' refers to disputes where interests of nationals of the complaining state are involved, these words would not appear to be objectionable. If, however, 'responsibility of a state' is not used in the traditional sense and if these words are intended to mean that a state can be held liable in damages for injury inflicted by it on its own nationals, this provision is objectionable and my Government makes a reservation with respect to such an interpretation.

In view of this statement, I recommend that the Senate give its advice and consent to ratification of the convention "with the understanding that article IX shall be understood in the traditional sense of responsibility to another state for injuries sustained by nationals of the complaining state in violation of principles of international law, and shall not be understood as meaning that a state can be held liable in damages for injuries inflicted by it on its own nationals."

．　．　．　．　．　．　．

It is my firm belief that the American people together with the other peoples of the world will hail United States ratification of this convention as another concrete example of our repeatedly affirmed determination to make the United Nations the cornerstone of our foreign policy and a workable institution for international peace and security.

2. FREEDOM OF INFORMATION AND OF THE PRESS

[See *Documents, X, 1948,* p. 438.]

In February the United Nations Economic and Social Council approved a resolution continuing until December 31, 1952, the existence of the Subcommission on Freedom of Information and of the Press.[8] On April 11 the Commission on Human Rights elected the twelve members of the subcommission, who were to serve in their individual capacities, among them the United States nominee, Carroll Binder, editorial editor of the *Minneapolis Tribune.*[9] At the third session of the subcommission, which met at Lake Success from May 31 to June 14, Mr. Binder stated that the subcommission should first inform itself on the general problem of the "adequacy of news" currently available throughout the world and then study existing barriers to the free flow of information. The subcommission adopted a proposal of Mr. Binder to the effect that the Secretary-General solicit additional information from those governments which had not replied or had supplied incomplete information in answer to a request for information based on the provisional agenda of the United Nations Conference on Freedom of Information of March–April 1948.[10] The subcommission, in considering means by which it might receive information concerning current legislation and practices in the field of its competence, recommended that the Secretary-General be authorized to request governments to submit lists of nongovernmental organizations through which information or opinions relevant to the objectives of the subcommission might be obtained.[11]

Mrs. Eleanor Roosevelt and Erwin D. Canham represented the United States

8 United Nations Economic and Social Council, Document E/SR.249, February 24, 1949, p. 18.
9 *Ibid.,* Document E/CN.4/SR.82, April 13, 1949, p. 3.
10 *Ibid.,* Document E/CN.4/Sub.1/SR.55, June 8, 1949, p. 5.
11 *Ibid.,* Document E/CN.4/Sub.1/SR.49, June 10, 1949, p. 9.

on the Social, Cultural and Humanitarian Committee of the General Assembly during the second part of its third session in April and May, at which time the committee examined the draft Convention on the Gathering and International Transmission of News and the draft Convention on the Institution of an International Right of Correction, adopted in 1948 by the United Nations Conference on Freedom of Information at Geneva.[12] The United States announced that it would prefer no validation of peacetime censorship in the amalgamated draft which the committee adopted by merging the two conventions. The United States opposed the placing of restrictions on the activities of overseas correspondents and took the view that if peacetime censorship were unavoidable, it should be rigidly restricted to situations directly relating to the protection of national security or defense. The committee was informed that the United States would not sign the convention if, pursuant to a Mexican proposal, it was required that signatories take measures to insure distribution by their information agencies and correspondents of any corrections issued by foreign governments.

On May 13 the General Assembly approved the Convention on the International Transmission of News and the Right of Correction — the world's first treaty affecting freedom of the press and providing for an international right of correction.[13] This convention was not to be opened for signature until the completion of the supplementary Convention on Freedom of Information. Consideration of the second convention had been deferred by the third session of the Assembly because of great divergence in views of members; and, at the Assembly's fourth session, no agreement proved possible on an acceptable draft text. A joint United States-United Kingdom-Netherlands resolution was adopted by the Assembly in October recommending that the Commission on Human Rights include adequate provisions on freedom of information in the draft International Covenant on Human Rights and postponing action on the draft Convention on Freedom of Information to the fifth session of the General Assembly.[14]

(1) *Statement by the Representative of the United States to the United Nations General Assembly (Canham) on the Draft Convention on the International Transmission of News and the Right of Correction, May 13, 1949.*[15]

[EXCERPTS]

The United Nations General Assembly is about to undertake an unprecedented step. It is about to write into international law, for the first time, a charter of liberties for the gathering and the international transmission of news. It is also about to establish, for the first time, an international right of correction. What is the real significance of these steps?

.   .   .   .

The basic significance of the decisions reached in the Third Committee, and, I hope, about to be affirmed here, is that a vast majority of the United Nations has refused to take even the first step down the long road that leads to totalitarianism and the police state. The Assembly is here reaffirming its belief in freedom. It is here rejecting the most dangerous of all state controls: the effort to control ideas. On the contrary, this convention widens the channels down which factual information may flow: it strengthens the interchange of ideas. And by contributing this to a better informed world, it contributes to a more peaceful and stable world.

12 For a summary of the United Nations Conference on Freedom of Information held at Geneva in March and April, 1948, see *Documents, X, 1948*, p. 438.
13 United Nations General Assembly, Document A/P.V.211, May 13, 1949, p. 236.
14 *Ibid.*, Document A/P.V.232, October 20, 1949, p. 81.
15 *Ibid.*, Document A/P.V.210, May 13, 1949, p. 22.

The convention which is before the General Assembly for adoption is simple, precise, concrete, and wisely limited in its applications. It does not guarantee the millenium overnight. But it is based on sound principles. It is a good beginning. It sets standards which will enable higher goals to be reached through practical experience in the future.

What does the convention actually provide? First, it defines "news materials," "news despatch," "information agency," and "correspondent" in such a way as to include adequately all international transmission and operation of these elements. One of the most difficult differences of opinion arose over the definition of "correspondent." This difficulty, in the view of my delegation, springs really from a misunderstanding. We are convinced that after governments have given the matter more careful legal study, their difficulties on this score will diminish and disappear. But some delegations have felt that no national of a contracting state should be defined as a correspondent in his own state, even though he is engaged in the gathering and international transmission of news for an information agency of another contracting state.

Delegations which have sought to remove nationals from the operation of this convention in their own state have feared it might set up a special kind of citizenship, a discrimination in favor of such nationals, which would enable them to flout the laws of their country. That such a fear can have absolutely no basis in fact is abundantly proved in article III of the convention which states categorically that —

> correspondents and information agencies must conform to the laws in force in the countries in which they are operating.

Further, in article XII, the convention especially affirms that —

> Nothing in the present Convention shall be construed as depriving a Contracting States of its right to make and enforce laws and public regulations for the protection of national security and public order.

I would point out that in the amendment we have presented, paragraph 8 of article XII would read:

> Nothing in the present Convention shall oblige a Contracting State to consider one of its own nationals employed by a foreign information agency operating in its territory as a correspondent, except when he is functioning in behalf of that information agency and then only to the extent required to enable that information agency fully to enjoy the benefits of this Convention;

Then we add the following words:

> provided, however, that no provision of this Convention shall be construed as entitling another Contracting State to intercede on behalf of such national with his government, as distinguished from interceding on behalf of the information agency by which he is employed.

This provision gives a government absolute protection against any kind of special treatment of its own nationals. No foreign government could make any protest to another government on behalf of that government's own nationals. Any protection accorded by this convention is in behalf of the information agency. It does not set up a special kind of citizenship, and it does not sanction discriminatory treatment of any kind. It leaves no room for any national to seek the protection of a foreign government, and it permits no information agency to defy the laws and regulations of the state where it operates.

This convention positively defines and establishes certain basic rights of the information agency and correspondent. These rights are nothing new. They reflect practices regarding correspondents and news material already observed in more democratic countries.

The convention requires contracting states to expedite, in a manner consistent with their respective laws and regulations, the administrative procedures necessary for the entry into, residence in, travel through and egress from their respective territories of correspondents of other contracting states. It provides against discriminatory restrictions on such correspondents. It protects them against expulsion on account of any lawful exercise of their right to collect and report news material. It guarantees access to news and the admission of news dispatches on a nondiscriminatory basis.

In respect to censorship, this convention makes a notable and unprecedented advance. It provides — for the first time in international law, I think — that news material shall leave the territory of contracting states without censorship, editing, or delay, provided that each contracting state may make and enforce regulations relating directly to national defense. That means that the only possible grounds of censorship — and we hope there will be no censorship at all — must be related directly to national defense. The only existing international law on the subject, in the telecommunication conventions, permits much more widespread and dangerous censorship. The limitations on censorship set up by the convention we are discussing today would, of course, prevail among the contracting states which sign and ratify this later convention.

•   •   •   •   •   •   •

The United States delegation is most gratified that the provisions on the international right of correction, originally propounded by the delegation of France, have been included in this convention. Those provisions set up a channel by means of which a contracting state may make sure that the correction of a dispatch it considers false or injurious reaches the information agency in another contracting state which was responsible for such a dispatch.

The machinery is clear, simple, swift. It does not provide for the compulsory publication of such corrections because, in the deep-rooted conviction of many countries, such compulsion is contrary to basic freedoms. The real difficulty, of course, lies in the possibly subjective character of correction. When is a correction a genuine correction, and when is it merely the propaganda of some national regime? The difference would be impossible to guarantee. Therefore, this convention does not introduce the element of compulsion, but it follows what is already the well-established professional practice of responsible newspapers and information agencies. As a matter of course, they publish or transmit well-founded corrections, but they have to remain the ultimate judges — short of laws of libel and slander — of what constitutes a valid correction. We have high hopes that the correction provisions of this convention will provide a useful channel which, above all, will utilize the sense of professional responsibility of newspapermen themselves.

I have said that this convention does not go beyond the existing practices in more democratic countries. Of course, we should like to see it extend the light into the censorship-darkened areas of the world. But it is chimerical to hope that, in the present world climate, the convention would be signed and ratified by such nations as the Soviet states. The representatives of these nations have voted against practically every provision of the convention at the Geneva conference and at this session of the General Assembly. They have given us abundant warning that they will not extend its provisions in their territories.

.   .   .   .

There is another fact, finally, that I want to make clear. The American press has never asked its government for special privileges, and the American Government does not ask special privileges for the press in this convention. There is only one thing the press asks for, and only one thing that the American Government requests internationally on behalf of the press. That is the right to report. The so-called privileges of the press, the so-called freedom of the press, are not privileges or freedom that are the possession of the press. Least of all are they the possession of the publisher. These are rights of the people. They are the duty the press owes the people. It is the duty of the press to report the news of the world and to seek to explain its meaning as accurately, as fearlessly, and as objectively as is possible in a world of imperfect humanity.

.   .   .   .

This convention sets up no special privileges for the press. It does reaffirm the right of the people to know, and it seeks to protect the press in the fulfillment of its duty to report the facts. American newspapermen, I will tell the Assembly frankly, have observed with some misgivings this intervention not of one government but of many governments into the international areas of news gathering and transmission. Newspapermen have learned that most governments instinctively crave power. They have learned that many governments seek to conceal rather than to reveal many of the facts that the people need to know. So they have naturally asked whether this intervention of government into a new field will turn out in the interest of more freedom or of more limitation.

The text of the convention which is before the General Assembly should help to resolve these doubts. By the adoption of this convention today the General Assembly — if it takes that course — will give added strength to agreed principles based on the right of the people to know. No longer, among the nations prepared to accept and apply these principles, will the function of correspondents be subject to the shifting tactics of regimes. They will rest on the firm foundation of law. This convention can prevent any regression of present good practices, if and as a tendency towards greater governmental controls sets in. Recognition of this convention as international law cannot help but influence additional governments to observe the more liberal practices included therein through the pressure of world opinion and the psychological compulsion on all individuals, peoples, and nations to observe law. It is through these beginning steps that we hope the observance of the principles of the convention will ultimately be extended to all parts of the world.

$$\cdot \quad \cdot \quad \cdot \quad \cdot \quad \cdot \quad \cdot \quad \cdot \quad \cdot \quad \cdot$$

3. PROTECTION OF MINORITIES

The United Nations Subcommission on the Prevention of Discrimination and the Protection of Minorities, meeting for its second session from June 13 to 27 at Lake Success, approved a proposal of the United States member, Jonathan Daniels, recommending a four-point procedure for the handling of petitions to the subcommission regarding urgent problems of discrimination.[16] In presenting this proposal Mr. Daniels explained that it was intended to make available to the subcommission the most complete documentation possible, without prejudicing the way in which it would be used in drawing up resolutions and recommendations. The subcommission approved a second proposal submitted by Mr. Daniels to the effect that the General Assembly recommend to all states that they enable recognized minority groups to maintain their cultural heritage by providing adequate facilities for the use of minority languages in schools and courts.[17] These resolutions were subject to approval by the Commission on Human Rights and the Economic and Social Council which took no action on the proposals during the remainder of 1949.

C. World Health Problems

[See *Documents, VIII, 1945–1946,* p. 732; *IX, 1947,* p. 503; *X, 1948,* p. 439.]

The United States was represented by Leonard A. Scheele, Surgeon General, United States Public Health Service, at the second session of the World Health Assembly, which met in Rome from June 13 to July 2.[1] The United States expressed its satisfaction that environmental sanitation had retained the high priority given to it by the first session of the World Health Assembly. Dr. Scheele recommended adoption of the committee's mental health program, involving the expenditure of $943,000 in 1950, on the ground that it was of vital importance to all other health projects of WHO.[2] In committee discussion of the problem of supplies Dr. Scheele explained that in the opinion of the United States the procurement of supplies was an economic and not a technical problem. He felt that it would be dangerous for WHO to undertake a large-scale supply program direct to governments, because this would neutralize the constructive efforts of the organization toward continuing improvement of the health of peoples throughout the world, would not be feasible within the funds available for 1950, and might cause political disruption within the organization.[3]

The Assembly approved a supplemental operating budget of $10,624,410 for 1950 to be used for a United Nations cooperative program of technical assistance for economic development of underdeveloped areas and a regular budget of $7,501,500, 36 percent of which was to be contributed by the United States.[4] The United States was again elected to designate a member to the Executive Board.

During the year under review the United States was represented at the follow-

16 United Nations Economic and Social Council, Document E/CN.4/Sub.2/SR.35, June 27, 1949, p. 15.
17 *Ibid.,* p. 11.
1 World Health Organization, Document A/VR/7, June 16, 1949, p. 1.
2 For congressional action approving United States membership in the World Health Organization, see *Documents, X, 1948,* p. 440.
3 World Health Organization, Document A2/Prog/Min/18, June 25, 1949, p. 7.
4 *Ibid.,* Document A2/110, June 30, 1949, p. 44.

ing meetings sponsored by WHO: the first session of the Expert Committee on Maternal and Child Health, Geneva, January 24; the first session of the Expert Committee on Habit-Forming Drugs, Geneva, January 24; the Committee on Administration and Finance of the WHO Executive Board, Geneva, February 16; the fourth session of the Executive Board of WHO, Geneva, February 21; the third session of the Joint Committee on Health Policy of the United Nations International Children's Emergency Fund and WHO, Geneva, April 12; the fourth session of the Expert Committee on the Unification of Pharmacopoeias, Geneva, April 20; the third session of the Expert Committee on Biological Standardization, London, May 2; the first session of the Expert Committee on Insecticides, Cazliani (Sardinia), May 10; the first session of the Expert Committee on Health Statistics, Geneva, May 23; the fourth session of the Expert Committee on Tuberculosis, Copenhagen, July 26; the third session of the Expert Committee on Malaria, Geneva, August 10; the first session of the Expert Committee on Mental Health, Geneva, August 29; the first session of the Expert Committee on Environmental Sanitation, Geneva, September 12; the first session of the Expert Committee on Plague, Geneva, September 19; the third session of the Expert Committee on Venereal Infection, Washington, October 10; the Joint Food and Agriculture Organization-WHO Expert Committee on Nutrition, Geneva, October 24; and the second session of the Expert Committee on International Epidemiology and Quarantine, Geneva, December 5.

On May 24, the Director General of the World Health Organization, Dr. Brock Chisholm, signed an agreement with Dr. Fred L. Soper, Director of the Pan American Sanitary Office, by the terms of which the Pan American Sanitary Bureau in Washington, D. C., became the regional WHO office for the western hemisphere.[5]

(1) Statement by the United States Representative to the Second World Health Assembly (Scheele) on United States Aid and Participation in International Activities, Made before the Assembly, Rome, Italy, June 16, 1949.[6]

[EXCERPTS]

. . . .

I wish to express my great pleasure at being here and having the opportunity of becoming acquainted with the many distinguished delegates who have played such an important role, not only in the development of the World Health Organization, but in public health progress in their many nations. And I might add that I am very happy to be back with many of my old friends with whom I have worked for many years.

As you are aware, the United States has taken an active part in the development of the World Health Organization as a permanent source of good in the world community. The United States looks forward to the progressive growth and development of the World Health Organization through the years ahead. We are proud of the role that the United States has played, is playing and expects to play in the whole movement for social and economic advancement of which the World Health Organization is such an important part. We appreciate the tributes that previous speakers have paid to the participation of the United States in this movement. Through UNRRA, the International Children's Emergency Fund, the Institute of Inter-American Affairs, the Economic Co-operation Administration, and through special rehabilitation programmes in areas of pressing need, the United States has

5 For congressional action approving United States membership in the World Health Organization, see *Documents, X, 1948*, p. 440.
6 World Health Organization, Document A2/VR/7, June 16, 1949, p. 1.

proved its determination to help in the great task of world-wide social and economic development. Some of our great private organizations, also, are contributing extensively to this task.

We call attention to this aid and assistance which has come from our hearts as well as from our substance, to demonstrate that there is no basis for any charge that the United States has failed people in need anywhere. As the President of the United States stated in his inaugural message in January of this year, the United States intends to continue to contribute to the work for the benefit and improvement of mankind, especially in under-developed areas. We look to the World Health Organization as one means of accomplishing this great objective, by pooling the medical and health resources of all the world for the benefit of each and everyone of us.

In view of the record of the United States, we are disturbed that a question has been raised before this Assembly concerning the motives of our country. I wish to assure this Assembly that the motives of the United States in its programmes of aid and participation in international activities are identical with the principles of the Constitution of the World Health Organization. When matters of misunderstanding, criticism or disagreement arise, as they are bound to from time to time in any great Assembly, the answers can be derived only from the desire for frank discussion. This must be based on the assumption that we all seek the best means of steadily advancing the high objectives that we share together.

I agree fully with the delegate from Czechoslovakia that the World Health Organization and this Assembly should not become an arena for political discussions or activity. It has been said that the refusal of export licences for certain apparatus has jeopardised human life. I wish to deny this charge on behalf of the Government of the United States.. A specific piece of equipment has been mentioned. It was implied that this equipment is necessary in the production of penicillin. This is not the case. The highest grade crystalline penicillin can be produced and is being produced commercially today in the United States without this equipment. A specific charge has been made, therefore, which cannot be substantiated.

. . . .

Of course, it is unlikely that any nation is entirely satisfied with the programme of the World Health Organization at this early stage. We expect this Assembly and each succeeding Assembly to improve its administrative structure, to simplify its operations and to recommend more useful programmes. However, we believe that all criticisms should be constructive and lead to the improvement of this young organization.

We hope to see the World Health Organization increase its activities in the field of technical assistance. We hope that it can help all nations to find the most effective ways of accomplishing their tasks in public health. We, on our part, look to the World Health Organization for help and advice in finding these ways. The United States is particularly impressed with the need for decentralization, through which the usefulness of the Organization would be increased and its work brought closer to the Member States and their peoples.

The United States will continue to play an active role in the World Health Organization, helping the Organization to build a better, healthier world. We will continue to do this in the belief that we are helping to build permanent peace and happiness by advancing the ideals stated in the Preamble of the Constitution of the World Health Organization.

D. Narcotic Drug Control

[See *Documents, VIII, 1945–1946,* p. 724; *IX, 1947,* p. 503; *X, 1948,* p. 450.]

The United States was represented by Harry J. Anslinger at the fourth session of the United Nations Commission on Narcotic Drugs, which met at Lake Success from May 16 to June 3, 1949. The commission adopted a resolution recommending that the Secretary-General accept, if desirable, the laboratory facilities which the United States had offered to place at the disposal of the United Nations for research into the origin of opium, the coordination of research activities by other governments in this field, the maintenance of a center for the distribution and exchange of samples of opium to scientists and scientific institutions designated by governments participating in the Economic and Social Council's joint program of research into the origin of opium.[1] A United States resolution to the effect that the Economic and Social Council request the Secretary-General to transmit to governments the recommendations of the WHO Expert Committee that each government apply provisions placing drugs of a particular chemical nature under control until they had been shown not to be habit-forming was unanimously adopted.[2] At the ninth session of the Economic and Social Council the United States emphasized the importance of the draft resolution of the fourth session of the Commission on Narcotic Drugs relating to the unification of existing international instruments on narcotics. The Council adopted both the commission's resolution on methods of determining the origin of opium by chemical and physical means and a United States proposal that all states increase their efforts to detect and suppress illicit production of opium, coca leaves and other raw narcotics materials and the illicit manufacture of narcotic drugs, apply stringent control measures to the trade in narcotic drugs and strengthen measures for apprehending and punishing offenders.[3]

On March 3 President Truman transmitted to the Senate for its advice and consent to ratification of the draft protocol opened for signature at Paris on November 19, 1948 and signed for the United States on that date, bringing under international control drugs outside the scope of the Convention of July 31, 1931, as amended by the protocol signed at Lake Success on December 11, 1946, limiting the manufacture and regulating the distribution of narcotic drugs.[4] No further action was taken on the draft protocol during the year under review.

E. Relief and Rehabilitation

Following the official liquidation in March 1949 of the United Nations Relief and Rehabilitation Administration, the United States appropriations for participation in the UNRRA expired for expenditure purposes on June 30; at this time the unexpended balance of $2,642,209.08 remaining under the United States appropriations reverted to the surplus fund in the Treasury.[1]

1. CHILDREN'S RELIEF

[See *Documents, X, 1948,* p. 461.]

At a meeting of the Executive Board of the International Children's Emergency Fund in March the United States opposed a proposal to cut by one-half United

---

[1] United Nations Economic and Social Council, Document E/1361, June 7, 1949, p. 49.
[2] *Ibid.,* p. 55.   [3] *Ibid., Official Records* (4th year, 9th session), p. 35.
[4] *Congressional Record,* 95, p. 1805 (Daily edition, March 3, 1949). For action resulting in approval of this protocol by the United Nations General Assembly in October 1948, see *Documents, X, 1948,* p. 451.
[1] House Document 437, 81st Cong., 2d sess.

Nations child-feeding programs in Poland, Czechoslovakia, Rumania and Bulgaria. Following rejection of this proposal, the board approved a United States recommendation that modified slightly the $13,500,000 spending program for Europe in 1950.[1]

In December the United Nations General Assembly appealed to official and private international organizations for further contributions to the ICEF and congratulated the Fund for its "great humanitarian effort" in Europe and the Middle East and for expanding its operations to Asia, Latin America and Africa.[2] No information was forthcoming as to whether or not the Fund was to become a permanent agency. In supporting the resolution embodying this appeal and these congratulations the United States stressed the fact that it regarded the Fund as having been established to meet emergency needs arising out of the war and emphasized that the permanent needs of children throughout the world should be determined on the basis of a study undertaken as a result of resolutions approved by the fourth session of the Social Commission and by the Executive Boards of the ICEF and the WHO in July 1949.[3]

During consideration by the fifth session of the Social Commission of a preliminary report on the continuing needs of children prepared by a working party appointed as a result of the resolutions adopted by the above three organizations, the United States representative (Hyde) declared that the United States was aware of the increasing importance of the needs of children that could be met realistically within the United Nations and that it was convinced that the emergency for which the Fund had been created was coming to a close. The United States felt that some form of long-range planning for children was required.[4]

During the year under review bills were introduced into the Congress (H.R.2785 and S.1754) providing for further contributions to ICEF. The essential difference between the two bills was that S.1754, in addition to extending the time limit, would alter the matching formula so as to match United States contributions against both public and private contributions of other countries.[5] The Senate Committee on Foreign Relations failed to act on S.1754 and reported favorably H.R. 2785, explaining that the mixing of public and private contributions in a matching formula of the kind envisaged in S.1754 would set an undesirable precedent in connection with the financing of United Nations.[6] After amendment by the Senate Committee to eliminate the necessity for a separate bill reappropriating funds already appropriated by the Congress, H.R.2785 passed the Senate.[7] With presidential approval of H.R.2785 on July 14 United States participation in the ICEF was extended until June 30, 1950, with a balance of $17,305,681.32 of previously appropriated funds available.

(1) *Letter from the Secretary of State (Acheson) to the Secretary-General of the United Nations (Lie) on United States Participation in the United Nations Appeal for Children, April 4, 1949.*[8]

I have the honor to acknowledge the receipt of your note dated February 28, 1949 in which you indicate a desire to be advised of the intention of the United States Government with regard to General Assembly Resolution No. 215 III in which it was decided to continue the United Nations Appeal for Children. You also request information as to whether the United Nations International Children's Emergency Fund should maintain contact with the

1 *New York Times,* March 11, 1949, p. 15. For action by the United Nations General Assembly in December 1948 transferring the program of the United Nations Appeal for Children to the administration of the ICEF, see *Documents, X, 1948,* p. 461.
2 United Nations General Assembly, Document A/1195, December 3, 1949.
3 *Ibid.,* Document A/P.V.264, December 2, 1949, p. 66.
4 United Nations Economic and Social Council, Document E/CN.5/SR.109, December 20, 1949, p. 19.
5 *Congressional Record,* 95, p. 1305 (Daily edition, February 16, 1949) and p. 5484 (Daily edition, May 2, 1949).
6 Under the terms of the Foreign Assistance Act of 1948 United States contributions were made on a 72–28 matching ratio, with the United States contributing $72 against each $28 contributed by other governments.
7 *Ibid.,* p. 8910 (Daily edition, June 30, 1949).
8 Department of State, *Bulletin,* XX, p. 515.

Campaign organization which functioned in the United States in 1948 or whether other channels of communication are to be followed.

The United States Government and the American people have a deep concern for the plight of needy children of the world. They have shown this concern from the outbreak of World War II and continuously in the years since, through the provision of funds by the Congress and through voluntary private contributions. The United States Government has appropriated $75,-000,000 to be made available to the United Nations International Children's Emergency Fund under a matching formula of 72% from the United States Government and 28% from other governments. In addition it has provided funds for a free school lunch program for children in Germany and has made a number of other appropriations for foreign relief, a large part of which has been of benefit to children.

In addition to Government appropriations, extensive contributions have been made by the American people through voluntary relief agencies largely for the welfare of children. These gifts are estimated to approximate $1,-000,000 in value since 1939 and in the current year will amount to over $150,000,000.

In the light of the interest in the Fund already demonstrated by the United States and in view of the continuing needs of the children of the world plans are being developed for informing the American people of these needs and of the work of the Fund and for giving them full opportunity to contribute to it. These plans are as follows:

1. Responsibility for informing and enlisting the interest of the public in the work of the Fund will be vested in the United States Committee for the United Nations International Children's Emergency Fund under the Chairmanship of Mrs. Oswald Lord. The Committee will also maintain liaison with American voluntary agencies to assist in coordinating their child welfare programs in countries where the Fund operates, with programs of the Fund. The activities of this Committee will be carried on under policies developed with the advice of the Department of State and the United States Representative on the Executive Board of the Fund.

2. The United States Committee will direct its activities especially toward

(a) keeping the American people informed through such media as the press, radio, magazines and public addresses, of the needs of children and of the operations of the Fund,

(b) encouraging and coordinating efforts by groups and organizations which may undertake to make or obtain contributions for the work of the Fund, and

(c) acting as the agency in the United States through which contributions from volunatry sources will be channeled to the Fund.

3. In order to carry out its functions the United States Committee will form an advisory group which will include representatives of business, labor, farm, professional, religious, patriotic and men's and women's clubs and associations. It will also employ a small salaried staff.

Official relationship between the Fund and this Government should continue to be carried on through normal governmental channels. However, it would greatly facilitate the work of the United States Committee if advice and informational material could be provided by the Fund to the Committee and it is hoped that the Fund will maintain close informal relationships with the Committee for this purpose.

F. Refugees and Displaced Persons

1. INTERNATIONAL REFUGEE ORGANIZATION

[See *Documents, VIII, 1945–1946*, p. 343; *IX, 1947*, p. 141; *X, 1948*, p. 460.]

The United States was represented by George L. Warren at the second, third (special) and fourth sessions of the General Council of the International Refugee Organization, which met in Geneva from March 29 to April 8, June 28 to July 8 and October 11 to 20, respectively. The United States was of the opinion that every effort should be made to speed up the processing of refugees and to achieve the maximum of resettlement possible from available financial resources before June 30, 1950, the original date for completion of IRO's mission.[1] The United States representative felt that this could be accomplished by better coordination of the activities of procurement of supplies, care and maintenance, and resettlement; he joined other members in urging more intensive study of the problem of the anticipated residual group of refugees unable to qualify for resettlement in each area. The General Council, at the suggestion of the United States, requested the Director General (Tuck) to revise the tentative plans for the termination of IRO services. During council examination of the Director General's revised proposals for termination of IRO's services and future international action for the protection of refugees and displaced persons, the United States again played a prominent role in pressing IRO to integrate and hasten its liquidation program, urging the organization to get prompt information on the probable size of its overseas shipping problem in order to obtain a clear idea of its future task. The council decided that IRO would discontinue 1) registration of displaced persons and refugees on August 31, 1949, with certain exceptions; 2) admissions to IRO assembly centers after December 31, 1949; and 3) all care and maintenance activities by June 30, 1950, with certain exceptions.[2] The United States again urged the best possible presentation of financial reports, and careful control and administration by IRO to insure the most economic use of available resources.[3] When it became apparent that IRO's task could not be completed by the target date, the council determined to continue IRO for a period of nine months after June 30, 1950. This was decided after the United States assured the council that it would ask the Congress for funds to support extension.[4] In order to provide for the non-resettleable refugees and to complete the movement the council adopted a total budget of $55,165,446 for operations in this period.[5]

Mr. Warren also represented the United States at the third, fourth, fifth and sixth meetings of the IRO executive committee in Geneva during 1949. An important problem considered by the committee was the resumption by IRO of payment for the movement of eligible Jewish refugees from central Europe to Palestine, with the United States pressing the view that payment should be resumed as recommended by the Director General (Tuck) within the budgetary limits of the current fiscal year.

On July 31 John Donald Kingsley, assistant administrator of the United States Federal Security Administration, succeeded William H. Tuck as Director General of IRO.[6]

---

[1] International Refugee Organization, Document GC/SR/25, April 21, 1949, p. 16. For information on the coming into existence of IRO, see *Documents, X, 1948*, p. 460.
[2] International Refugee Organization, Documents GC/SR/49, July 7, 1949, p. 3 and GC/89/Rev.1, July 7, 1949.
[3] *Ibid.*, Document GC/SR/54, October 25, 1949, p. 4.
[4] *Ibid.*, Document GC/SR/61, October 21, 1949, p. 3.
[5] *Ibid.*, Document GC/121, October 13, 1949.
[6] *Ibid.*, Document GC/SR/50, July 8, 1949, p. 9.

On December 3 the United Nations General Assembly adopted a resolution establishing as of January 1, 1951 the office of High Commissioner for Refugees to provide protection for refugees and stateless persons after the termination of IRO.[7]

(1) Report of the Subcommittee on Relations with International Organizations of the Senate Committee on Expenditures in the Executive Departments on the International Refugee Organization, June 8, 1949.[8]

[EXCERPT]

·   ·   ·   ·   ·   ·   ·   ·

F. SUMMARY AND CONCLUSIONS

1. FINDINGS

With respect to the operations of the IRO, the subcommittee found:

(1) After almost 2 years of IRO operations, over 700,000 displaced persons and refugees still remain in and out of camps in western Germany, Austria, and Italy, the majority of whom are in the United States zone of Germany.

(2) Between July 1, 1947, when the IRO commenced operations, and March 31, 1949, approximately 442,000 persons were resettled and 63,000 were repatriated. Of the number resettled, the IRO participated in the movement of approximately 269,500 persons, according to its own estimates.

(3) By June 30, 1950, the original target date for the termination of its activities, the IRO will have spent between $375,000,000 and $400,000,000 in carrying out its mission.

(4) The IRO will not be able to complete its mission by June 30, 1950, and plans must be made for at least one additional year of operations.

(5) The operations of the IRO have been substantially hindered by internal conflicts, resulting from insufficient staff consultation and lack of coordination; a tendency on the part of some of its officials to take a national rather than an international viewpoint; and a tendency on the part of some of its officials to prolong the life and mission of the Organization.

(6) The IRO's health, care, and maintenance program has been substantially successful.

With respect to the governments of the world, the subcommittee found:

(1) Only 18 nations have joined the IRO, indicating a failure upon the part of many of the governments of the world to assume their full responsibility with respect to displaced persons.

(2) The governments of the world have failed to assume their proportionate share of responsibility for the resettlement of refugees and displaced persons by failing to accept an adequate number for permanent immigra-

---

[7] For the United States position on measures to be taken following the termination of IRO's activities during consideration of the problem by the fourth session of the General Assembly, see *International Organization*, IV, p. 89.

[8] Senate Report 476, 81st Cong., 1st sess.

tion. The situation has resulted largely from rigid adherence to high standards of selectivity, inherent in existing immigration laws, and the application of rules of selectivity with respect to race, occupation, and status.

With respect to United States participation, the subcommittee found:

(1) Participation in the IRO will have cost the United States over $200,-000,000 by June 30, 1950, constituting in excess of 50 percent of the total contributions received by the Organization.

(2) When the IRO terminates its activities, the United States may find itself faced with the necessity of expending large sums of money for the care and maintenance of those displaced persons and refugees who still remain in the United States zone of Germany.

(3) Since the end of the war, the United States has accepted for permanent resettlement only 72,500 persons. Of these, 44,000 were admitted by Executive authority under existing law, prior to the enactment of the Displaced Persons Act of 1948; 28,500 have been admitted under the act as of May 1, 1949.

(4) Under the terms of the Displaced Persons Act of 1948, there is some doubt as to whether this Government can accomplish the resettlement of the 205,000 called for by the statute, by June 30, 1950.

2. CONCLUSIONS

The subcommittee is fully mindful of the fact that the task of the IRO has been and still is one of the most difficult international undertakings in history. The subcommittee is also aware of the fact that some of the internal conflicts referred to are not necessarily indigenous to the IRO, but are rather endemic to many international organizations. However, it would seem that the Organization should bear in mind that it was established only as the instrument whereby the refugee and displaced persons problems created by World War II are to be liquidated. Accordingly, the subcommittee feels that the Organization should make every effort to eliminate internal conflicts and difficulties with a view to accomplishing its mission and liquidating itself at the earliest possible time.

In the opinion of the subcommittee, censure for the delay in effecting the resettlement of displaced persons and refugees cannot properly be placed upon the IRO alone. The accomplishment of its mission has been substantially hampered by the failure of the nations of the world to assume their full responsibility for the solution of the displaced persons and refugee problems created by World War II. They must face these problems realistically and they must realize that contributing a sum of money, however large, to an international organization neither relieves them of their obligations nor constitutes a solution of the problem.

With respect to the United States, the problem is particularly acute. This Government has been contributing the major portion of actual contributions to the IRO. In addition, cessation of the Organization's activities may well result in considerable additional expenditure in connection with the care and maintenance of those displaced persons who will remain in the United States zone of Germany when the IRO's responsibilities cease. The subcommittee suggests that this problem will only be solved by facing the situation realistically. If our Government is to maintain leadership in this vital matter, it must carry out its declared policy by effective measures aimed at liberalizing the admission of displaced persons.

Until the nations of the world, including the United States, are ready and willing to meet these problems — in the only manner in which they can be met — by eliminating certain restrictions with respect to immigration, this problem will never be solved.

· · · · · · ·

2. ADMISSION OF DISPLACED PERSONS TO THE UNITED STATES

[See *Documents, VIII, 1945–1946,* p. 406; *IX, 1947,* p. 145; *X, 1948,* p. 451.]

Numerous bills to amend the Displaced Persons Act of 1948 were introduced into the Congress during the year under review. The administration-sponsored McGrath-Neely bill (S.311) introduced into the Senate on January 10,[1] was designed to raise to 400,000 the number of displaced persons eligible to come to the United States from displaced persons camps in Germany, Austria and Italy, and closely followed the recommendations contained in the first semiannual report of the Displaced Persons Commission, submitted to the Congress on February 1, 1949. The report recommended nine major changes in the Act, six of them being requests for deletions of discriminations and priorities.[2] On May 9, Rep. Emanuel Celler (New York) introduced into the House a second bill (H.R.4567) to amend the Act.[3] A second bill (H.R.4567) which would allow as many as 339,000 displaced persons, including those who had already entered under the Act, to enter the United States until July 1, 1951, represented a compromise with the President's request for admission of 400,000 displaced persons. The deadline when refugees must have entered the European occupied zones of Italy to qualify for admission to the United States was moved from December 22, 1945, to January 1, 1949, thus making eligible those who fled eastern Europe. On June 2 the House passed the bill with an amendment requiring displaced persons to take a non-communist oath on arrival in the United States and sent it to the Senate.[4] The bill remained in the Senate Judiciary Committee until October 12; after three days of Senate debate, it was recommitted to the committee by a vote of 36 approving and 30 opposing recommittal.[5] No further action was taken before the adjournment of the Congress.

As a result of numerous complaints received by the committee and the great amount of legislation introduced, the House on June 21 authorized the Committee on the Judiciary to conduct, within or without the United States, studies, hearings and investigations pertaining to current immigration and naturalization problems.[6] The committee appointed a subcommittee to carry out the provisions of the House resolution and submitted its subcommittee's report on January 20, 1950 to the Committee of the Whole House on the State of the Union.

1 *Congressional Record,* 95, p. 114 (Daily edition, January 10, 1949). For information on the Displaced Persons Act of 1948, see *Documents, X, 1948,* p. 451.
2 Displaced Persons Commission. *Six Months of Operation, July 1 through December 31, 1948,* Washington, 1949.
3 *Congressional Record,* 95, p. 6030 (Daily edition, May 9, 1949).
4 *Ibid.,* p. 7344 (Daily edition, June 2, 1949).
5 *Ibid.,* p. 14981 (Daily edition, October 15, 1949).
6 *Ibid.,* p. 8233 (Daily edition, June 21, 1949).

(1) *Report of a Special Subcommittee of the Committee on the Judiciary of the House of Representatives on Displaced Persons in Europe and their Resettlement in the United States, January 20, 1950.*[7]

[EXCERPT]

. . . .

XIV. CONCLUSIONS AND RECOMMENDATIONS

(a) Although over 120,000 displaced persons have been admitted to the United States by January 1, 1950, under the terms of the Displaced Persons Act of 1948, the great majority of them have, to date, spent only a few months in the country of their new residence. It appears to this subcommittee that the time has not yet arrived when a broad and general judgment could be passed on the extent to which the unprecedented resettlement program inaugurated by the passage of Public Law 774, Eightieth Congress has been successful.

However, the results of studies, investigations, and inquiries conducted by this subcommittee show even at this early stage of the displaced persons resettlement operation that:

(1) The economy of this country has absorbed the new immigrants without noticeable difficulty;

(2) No dangerous or disturbing elements have been injected into our body politic;

(3) The Nation as a whole has welcomed the destitute people and with true American ingenuity is making good use of their capabilities, while simultaneously offering them remarkable opportunities for rehabilitation.

(b) The geographical distribution of the displaced persons over the 48 States is far from being satisfactory. The concentration of over one-third of the new immigrants in the already congested areas of three States, to wit, New York, Pennsylvania, and New Jersey presents potential economic and social dangers and the subcommittee wishes to recommend most urgently that the Displaced Persons Commission, in cooperation with State and private agencies, make a most serious and determined effort to remedy this situation.

(c) With regard to the overseas administration of the 1948 act, particularly in its selection and screening aspects, the subcommittee has already registered in the course of this report its general approval of the methods and safeguards applied. But, once again, the subcommittee wishes to state that as far as the selection of farm workers and skilled agriculturists is concerned, the American sponsor-employer does not receive the kind of dependable service to which he is entitled. Most, if not all, expressions of lack of satisfaction registered with the subcommittee relative to faulty selection of immigrants came from farming areas where agricultural skill was and remains in demand, while fitness of displaced persons sent to those areas is unsatisfac-

7 House Report 1507, 81st Cong., 2d sess.

tory in at least 20 percent of the cases. Although the differences between the European and American farming methods and techniques could provide some explanation of the difficulties, such explanation would justify only partially the evident shortcomings in selection procedure.

The subcommittee recommends that the Displaced Persons Commission, in cooperation with the IRO and voluntary aid agencies in charge of selection, revise and improve their selection methods as they are being applied to unnamed displaced persons to whom farming opportunities are being offered by American sponsors.

(d) The subcommittee was glad to note the high degree of cooperation and mutual understanding existing among the various United States agencies involved in the overseas operation of the displaced persons program. There is one instance, however, where there is room for improvement. The subcommittee has observed at certain consular offices a lack of understanding of congressional intent as evidenced by the passage of Public Law 774, Eightieth Congress.

Certain junior consular officers, most of them in the rank of vice consuls and consuls, seem not to realize adequately what Congress had in mind in enacting this special emergency legislation and appear to be reluctant to accept the necessity of the additional amount of expeditious work required under the terms of the temporary act with its strict but justifiable time limitations. Unnecessary frictions and delays ensuing from this attitude of a small number of young career officers could be easily remedied by prompt and energetic action taken by the Department of State.

(e) The subcommittee finds that a satisfactory solution of the "hard-core" problem could not be reached unless the existing national resettlement programs are extended. The extension of the United States program would have to include: (1) A reasonable increase of the number of displaced persons to whom immigration visas may be issued; (2) change of existing "cut-off dates" and elimination of fixed preference percentages hampering the operation of the program.

The subcommittee does not recommend any relaxation of the other existing legal provisions upon which the admission of displaced persons into this country is predicated.

(f) The subcommittee is of the opinion that the liquidation of the IRO and the cessation of administrative and operational expenditures involved shall definitely occur at the proposed date of March 31, 1951.

(g) The subcommittee recommends full participation and cooperation of the United States Government in the tasks facing the United Nations High Commissioner's Office for Refugees, and it restates its recommendation that the confidential files of the International Tracing Service shall remain in the exclusive custody of a United States agency.

The subcommittee also wishes to recommend at this point that particular care and diligence be applied to the selection of the United Nations High Commissioner for Refugees and his staff. In view of the existing international situation it seems only natural to recommend that such staff be composed solely of nationals of countries recognizing and practicing the democratic concept of the right of asylum and protection for victims of totalitarian processes.

(*h*) The subcommittee recommends that the final report to be submitted by the Displaced Persons Commission at the end of its term, to the President and to the Congress (sec. 8 of Public Law 774, 80th Cong.) shall consider extensively the domestic picture of resettlement of displaced persons in the United States, and that such consideration be based, in part at least, on a survey in which the closest cooperation of State, local, private and public agencies, as well as the participation of institutions of high learning shall be requested.

CHAPTER XII

Cultural Relations

1. UNITED NATIONS EDUCATIONAL, SCIENTIFIC AND CULTURAL ORGANIZATION

[See *Documents, VIII, 1945–1946*, p. 737; *IX, 1947*, p. 508; *X, 1948*, p. 464.]

A. General

(1) Address by the Assistant Secretary of State for Public Affairs (Allen) on United States Foreign Policy and UNESCO, Made before the United States National Commission for UNESCO, Washington, September 9, 1949.[1]

[EXCERPTS]

I think UNESCO has the most difficult task in the world. I also think its task is perhaps the most important which exists today.

Having made about as broad a statement as I can formulate, I shall proceed to examine it.

Some people think that UNESCO has bitten off such a big bite it can't possibly masticate it. UNESCO is trying to mobilize sufficient human sympathy, understanding and friendship among the multifarious and diverse peoples of the world, with their different cultures and languages and their bitterness and enmity, to accomplish world organization sufficiently strong to establish lasting peace.

. . . .

UNESCO, through this seminar of Dr. McKeon's [on ambiguous definitions of "democracy"] is going right to the heart of the problem. It is trying to work out universal concepts regarding the principles on which the UNESCO Charter is based. Those principles center in the word "democracy". The goal of the UNESCO and the goal of the United States are precisely the same. The goal is to achieve world democracy.

. . . .

I'd like to pause for a minute to show how different the job of UNESCO is from the ordinary day-to-day job of any foreign office or State Department. The attitude of the State Department towards any foreign country at any given moment is essentially the attitude of the American people toward that country. This is true in any genuinely democratic country, in our use of the term. This morning at 11:30, what is the attitude of the American people towards Tito, Franco, Peron, Great Britain, France, China, what-have-you?

[1] United States National Commission for UNESCO, Document NC7/17, September 9, 1949.

What goes to make up that attitude which governs the day-to-day workings of the Department of State?

. . . .

In my view, UNESCO is concerned with something over and beyond, and in the long run much more significant, than the temporary changing, ephemeral matters of foreign policy to which I have referred. UNESCO's job, in my mind, is to mobilize, to foster and to encourage the great sentiment for friendship and for peace and for international understanding that exists among peoples everywhere.

I refer to an underlying sentiment which exists among peoples in all countries of the world. I'm certain it exists behind the iron curtain as well as on this side. All of you have had the experience of saying, in any given country, "I perhaps don't like that country very much, but when I get out into the country and talk to the peasants or the farmer and so forth, I find he is really a very fine fellow. He doesn't want war."

I'm certain that if by any good fortune a pronouncement could be broadcast throughout the world tomorrow that peace had been guaranteed for a thousand years, there would be an immediate, simultaneous shout of joy from every farmer in Kansas, every steel worker in Britain, every shepherd in Pakistan, and from peoples behind the iron curtain, too. There is a genuine sentiment among all people to get along together. UNESCO's task is to encourage it and to make it so strong that it will prevail.

The American Government is dedicated to the fullest support of UNESCO in accomplishing its most difficult, yet supremely important and perhaps vital task.

(2) *Address by the Chairman of the United States Delegation to the Fourth General Conference of UNESCO (Allen) before the Plenary Session of the Conference, Paris, September 20, 1949.*[2]

[EXCERPTS]

. . . .

I read with great interest the Director-General's Report on the activities of Unesco during the brief months since he took office. I can well understand the difficulties he has faced and which he describes so well in the first pages of his report. Many of us here in this room have experienced the difficulties of the recruitment of competent staff for our national service; how infinitely more complex are the problems of securing the services of an able secretariat drawn from many countries, to perform new tasks of an international character, requiring knowledge and skills of a different order from those of a national service. We earnestly hope that the problems of recruitment and continuity in the Secretariat will be satisfactorily solved.

Dr. Torres Bodet has given us an enlightened review of the problems of Unesco as he sees them from his vantage point as Director-General of our

2 UNESCO, Document 4C/VR3, September 20, 1949; Department of State, *Bulletin*, XXI, p. 536.

Organization. He has told us that Unesco must simplify its programme, the United States delegation heartily and emphatically agrees. I admit that I find considerable difficulty in understanding all the implications of the bountiful resolutions that we passed in the last session of the Conference in Beirut. I have given considerable study to them, but I am frequently embarrassed by being ask to explain some obscure item which I either have not noticed or not understood. Probably this difficulty rises in part from defects in the way we formulated some of our resolutions, we have not always made them clear or stated precisely what contribution to Unesco's general purpose each project is supposed to make. Nor does our programme as a whole seem to be guided by a central purpose, I have said that I believe it should be. The programme activities of Unesco must be simplified, concentrated and pointed always with certainty towards the development of foundational understanding, needed in the peace-making of the United Nations. I do not wish to be misunderstood on this point, a world community of mind with peace as its central aim will not be developed by a single project or a single programme. Unesco's activities must command the active participation of intellectuals and the masses of the people everywhere. To do this, diversity of effort is required, but I am quite confident that the best results will be obtained — and good results must not be delayed — the best results will be obtained by focussing educational, scientific and cultural co-operation on the issues, concepts and problems crucial to the building of an enduring peace.

.   .   .   .

From what I have already said you will understand that we concur fully in the Director-General's assertion that Unesco's difficulty is not merely one of expressing more clearly and simply what we are trying to do, it goes deeper than that. We have still to agree on basic objectives and a plan of work, we must continued to clarify our aims, but no complete and final definition is likely to be formulated, we admit. Great philosophers continue year after year to try to define the purposes of education, and no-one has ever been completely satisfied by their definitions. But this fact does not absolve us from the responsibility of renewed effort to clarify our goal. Certainly I agree with the Director-General that it is not so much the mere number of activities of Unesco which induces confusion, as it is the absence of one or more clearly designable plans, running through the whole programme. Thus, I hope there will be general agreement at the next session of the Conference on a drastic revision of the programme of Unesco, that it should be presented and organized around the relatively few major projects. We must indeed concentrate and integrate the activities of Unesco. But I trust that we can agree on more than that, for it is not enough to concentrate and integrate in a vacuum, we must firmly establish the frame of reference, the vital purposes within which we concentrate and integrate the Programme.

I venture to make two or three suggestions which I hope will be considered when the Executive Board and the Director-General refashion the programme for our consideration at the next conference. First, let us all recall that while Unesco draws its mandate from the will of the peoples of the world, it must be operated, as I have already said, as a part and parcel of the system of the United Nations.

A world community is needed with sufficient cohesion to enable international justice and an international political organization to function. The United Nations and its Specialized Agencies are the best expression in institutional form which the world now possesses. Unesco exists to strengthen that community and in particular to strengthen the system of the United Nations. How can Unesco best serve the United Nations? I hope that this question will be thoughtfully considered by every delegate who proposes a project to be undertaken by Unesco, or who votes on a budget item during this conference. I hope that the Executive Board and the Director-General will consider how Unesco can best serve the United Nations when they reflect on the future programme of Unesco. Unesco can command to a degree unparalleled by any other organization, the interest and support of educators, scientists and scholars. It can exert an immense influence through the radio, press and films. Would it not be well for the Director-General to invite the Secretary-General of the United Nations and the heads of eight sister agencies of the United Nations to submit, for his consideration, three or four projects which Unesco, as the educational arm of the United Nations might well undertake in order to advance the interests of the whole system? Could he not by such a request at once make clear that Unesco accepts this responsibility to the world community, and at the same time he could ensure the support and co-operation of the other agencies. Unesco is designed as a major agency of the cultural revolution of the twentieth century. This is a revolution like the French revolution, and other great revolutions in history, in the sense that its aim is to spread possession of the instruments of power among all peoples — scholarship, education and art are instruments of power in the modern world. Held closely in the hands of a few fortunate élite, they may be exploited to buttress privilege and block the growth of democracy. But when all the people have access to knowledge and skill and may share in the cultural riches of mankind, tyranny and aggression become increasingly difficult, if not impossible. This cultural revolution, asserting the right of all human beings to education and to the benefits of research and artistic creation is vigorously underway today. Unesco was created to facilitate the revolution as being necessary to the spread of international understanding and the growth of world community. Unesco is not for the few, it is for the many, it is for all. This is why Unesco must proceed with a vigorous and expanded programme of education for the masses of the people of the world. That is why the United States delegation supports an energetic campaign of fundamental education, not only as a part of the programme of Unesco, but also as an essential part of the programme of technical assistance in economic development. That is why too, the U. S. delegation urges that still more effective use be made of the means of mass communication, the radio, films and the printed word.

A great deal has been heard recently about the proposed technical assistance programme for the so-called backward areas of the world. They say that a distinguished member of the American delegation asked recently, "what's to be done about the areas of the world that are going back?" I hope Unesco can assist in reversing that retrograde movement and that all the world can advance together in peace and human dignity. Unesco must cling unflinchingly and firmly to the ideas of free inquiry, freely carried on and freely communicated.

The United States has signed the convention to facilitate the international exchange of audio-visual materials of an educational character. It is our earnest hope that other nations will also sign this convention, which is the first to be negotiated under Unesco's auspices. We hope that it will be rapidly brought into effect — ten signatures are required to bring that Convention into effect. The United States, the first nation to sign it, affixed its signature very shortly after it was opened for signature in Lake Success, about two weeks ago. While we urge the adoption of the present Convention, we also favour continued efforts to enlarge its scope to include other educational materials.

The delegation of the United States reaffirms its faith and confidence in Unesco, we are proud of the efforts which have been made by our National Commission in the United States, to win support for Unesco in our own country. I do not know to what extent we may be considered by the Director-General to have failed to carry out some of the projects in the United States which we have been asked to perform. No doubt we, like other members of the United Nations, may have been remiss to some extent. I wish to give this pledge to the Director-General as the representative of the United States delegation to this Conference, representative of the United States National Commission and representative of the Government of the United States. The United States will, during the coming year, redouble its efforts to bring into the service of Unesco our learned groups, our great civil and cultural organizations and our media of mass communication. We shall welcome recommendations from the Director-General, we shall do all in our power to carry them out. If we are negligent we shall gladly accept his reproof. We shall bear in mind that peace is made in the villages, the towns, in the schools and in the home, and where it lies in our power to build the peace, we will put forward our utmost strength.

．　　　．　　　．　　　．　　　．　　　．　　　．

B. Fourth General Conference

[See Documents, VIII, 1945–1946, p. 743; IX, 1947, p. 508; X, 1948, p. 464.]

The fourth session of the General Conference of the United Nations Educational, Scientific and Cultural Organization met in Paris from September 19 to October 5, 1949. George V. Allen, Assistant Secretary of State for Public Affairs, was chairman of the United States' delegation which included Milton S. Eisenhower, president of Kansas State College and head of the United States National Commission for UNESCO; Luther H. Evans, Librarian of Congress; Martha B. Lucas, president of

Sweet Briar College; and Reinhold Niebuhr, Professor of Applied Christianity at Union Theological Seminary.[3]

Among the major items on the agenda of the Conference were the following: 1) the report of the Director General on the activities of UNESCO during 1949 and the reports of the member states for that year; 2) the report and recommendations of the Executive Board concerning the admission of new members; 3) the duties of states in regard to education, science, and culture for the purpose of insuring a better understanding between peoples, and the practical steps which the state should take to discharge these duties; 4) adoption of the program and budget for 1950; 5) activities of UNESCO in occupied areas; and 6) the election of six members of the Executive Board.[4]

During the fourth session, the extension of the UNESCO program in occupied areas[5] was first debated by the Commission on Official and External Relations. In the commission's discussions, the delegations of Poland, Czechoslovakia, and Hungary protested further continuation of the program launched by the third session of the General Conference, arguing that UNESCO activity encouraged the development of nationalism and militarism in Germany and contributed to the disunity of the German state. When their formal proposal that such activities be terminated was rejected by the commission,[6] the three delegations withdrew from the meeting. In its subsequent report to the General Conference, the commission recommended that UNESCO continue its programs in both Japan and Germany.[7] When the commission's draft resolution to this effect[8] was discussed by the plenary session of the conference, the Polish, Czechoslovakian, and Hungarian representatives again sought to secure the cessation of UNESCO activity in Germany or, failing that, to suspend action on the matter until the fifth session of the General Conference. Both proposals were rejected by the General Conference which approved the commission recommendation on October 4.[9]

When debate rose in the plenary session over the Director General's request for approval of $8,172,000 as the 1950 budget, the United States sought to prevent any division among the member nations on what it considered a "fundamental" matter. The debate was in actuality concerned not with the budget figure but with whether the figure arrived at by the conference should be set as a ceiling beyond which UNESCO activities could not be extended or as a figure by which the annual expenses of the Organization should be generally governed. The United Kingdom, supported by Norway and the Union of South Africa, was the principal advocate of the former proposal. On the final day of the conference, agreement was reached upon a figure of $8 million proposed by the United States as a "general target" at which the budget should aim.[10] As a result of the addition of new members, the United States contribution to UNESCO was reduced from 38.47 percent to 37.04 percent.

The General Conference also considered UNESCO's role in the United Nations program of technical assistance to underdeveloped areas.[11] A draft resolution submitted by the Executive Board outlined UNESCO's participation in the program: "UNESCO's object in entering into the plan launched by the Economic and Social Council will be to furnish under-developed States, territories or areas, at their request, with such advice, technical facilities, study groups, pilot projects, help in establishing technical research institutes and documentary material of various types — all falling within UNESCO's interests as defined by the Constitution — as will enable those States, territories and areas to include in any scheme of economic development undertaken by them such educational, scientific, cultural and informational elements as they may consider essential to the success of that scheme."[12] The Executive Board pointed out that the adoption of this course by the confer-

3 *Ibid.*, p. 397.
4 For the full agenda, see UNESCO, *Journal of the General Conference* (4th session), No. 1.
5 For information concerning Austrian participation in UNESCO, see this volume, p. 165.
6 UNESCO, Document 4C/PRG–OXR/SR.1, September 28, 1949.
7 *Ibid.*, Document 4C/OXR/23, October 3, 1949.
8 *Ibid.*, Document 4C/OXR/16, September 22, 1949.
9 *Ibid.*, Document 4C/55, October 4, 1949.
10 *Ibid.*, *Journal of the General Conference* (4th session), No. 11, p. 96.
11 For further information on technical assistance, see this volume, p. 237.
12 UNESCO, Document 4C/8 (rev.), September 21, 1949.

ence would make necessary a number of supplementary acts which would 1) authorize the Director-General to provide, in consultation with the Executive Board, technical aid to non-member states, 2) empower the Director-General to determine the implementation of a request for assistance to be rendered in each case, and 3) finance UNESCO's contribution from the credit available to the Organization in the Secretary-General's Special Account for Technical Assistance. The conference approved the Executive Board's proposal on October 5.[13]

Seven new members were admitted to UNESCO during 1949. The Director General (Torres Bodet) announced on September 15 that Pakistan and Israel, as members of the United Nations, had become members of UNESCO.[14] In his annual report the Director General announced that Thailand, Switzerland, Burma, and Monaco had filed instruments accepting the Constitution of UNESCO. The application of Ceylon, received on November 8, 1948, and approved by the United Nations Economic and Social Council, awaited action by the fourth session of the General Conference,[15] which unanimously accepted the Executive Board's Recommendation that Ceylon be admitted.[16]

(1) Statement by the Chairman of the United States Delegation to the Fourth General Conference of UNESCO (Allen) on the Continuation of UNESCO Activities in Occupied Areas, Made Before the Plenary Session of the Conference, Paris, October 4, 1949.[17]

[EXCERPT]

. . . .

Mr. President, we have had the sad necessity in this room today to listen to implications that there is evidence that there continues to exist in Germany a spirit of nationalism; that, by implication, those in this room that favour the activities of Unesco in Germany, favour that revival of nazism. That is a most unpleasant implication for anyone to discern, particularly anyone who represents a country which has contributed to the defeat of nazism so very recently. I want to say this to you, in all the genuineness that I can, the German people have brought on a world war twice in the last generation, and I am entirely convinced that, if the German people are so foolish as to bring on another one, the destruction of Germany will be greater than has it ever been before.

There is not the slightest doubt about the fact that, so far as my country is concerned, we are as indelibly opposed to the rise of nazism or aggression in Germany as we are in any other country in the world, and that all the political action which my country has taken is directed against the wiles of fascist-type mentality, or the aggressive nation, it does not make any difference who it is, including Germany. Now let it be thoroughly understood, therefore, that those of us who favour the actions of Unesco in doing what it can in Germany, resist as strongly as we can any implication that that means that we favour any nazi-type of sentiment that may exist in that country.

The question before us today is essentially the heart of Unesco. There are various means by which one can attempt to improve the international organization of the world, to create the international comity which we hope will

13 Ibid., Document 4C/VR15, October 5, 1949; ibid., Document 4C/PRG/14, October 3, 1949.
14 New York Times, September 16, 1949.
15 UNESCO, Document 4C/3, n.d., p. 82–83.
16 Ibid., Document 4C/VR10, September 30, 1949, p. 2.
17 Ibid., Document 4C/VR13, October 4, 1949.

bring lasting peace. There is the military approach — some people are great devotees of that approach, they think that we, in this hall, are wasting our time when we try to bring about international understanding by persuasion. There are many people who say the only way to treat this and that country is by the rule of force, or the only way to treat the whole international situation is by force, the military approach. Unesco's approach is directly opposite to that, it doesn't mean, as I pointed out in my opening remarks, that the American delegation thinks that Unesco by itself will bring about the lasting results that we wish, but Unesco's part in that new world order is an absolutely vital one, bringing along persuasion and international understanding by education. At the same time that other people may be concerned with political, military or economic organizations, Unesco seeks to capture that certain residue of goodwill that exists everywhere, on both sides of every iron curtain and in every country, and that is the purpose for which we believe that Unesco should try to do what it can in Germany — in both sides of Germany if you wish — to work with such elements in Germany as may be willing to integrate their country into the family of nations.

Now there are those who propose the alternative, that Unesco should have nothing whatsoever to do with Germany or the German people, that German should be quarantined, if you wish, the expression has been used this morning. I must say, in all genuineness, that I believe that that is dangerously on the road towards the very principle we detest so strongly in the Nazi régime, namely that of condemning an entire race because of the actions of certain of its people. The suggestion is made that we quarantine the Germans without any distinction, just because they are Germans. Now I submit to you, that that is dangerously close to the theory of genocide, which we all condemn so bitterly. [We] hope very much that Unesco, at this crucial hour in our decision, will not go down the dangerous road that leads towards that philosophy. I think that the resolution as proposed by the Brazilian delegate has done a great deal to take care of the legitimate points and objections which have been raised by the delegates of Poland, Czechoslovakia and Hungary. You will note that the resolution as now presented points very clearly to the fact that we all favour the unity of Germany. It also points out that the actions of Unesco shall be through the Allied Authorities. Now I will read to you to remind you of the purpose for which Unesco has been founded. Let us examine this question from the point of view of whether it fits into the purposes of Unesco. Permit me to remind you of the Preamble of the Organization. There are two or three words in the Preamble that I think are particularly important. "The purpose of the Organization is to contribute to peace and security by promoting collaboration among the nations." Now, that means friendly, peaceful collaboration among all the nations, of all kinds and everywhere. Unesco is the organ which seeks to tempt that desire on the part of people everywhere to collaborate — and it exists. I hope that you will not conclude that the people of any country, and I mean any country, of those represented here and those who are not represented here, shall be condemned to an existence beyond the pale, unworthy of any effort to develop the finer and nobler characteristics of the human being that all of God's creatures are entitled to.

C. United States Participation in Other UNESCO Activities

Luther H. Evans, Librarian of Congress, served in the capacity of an individual member, rather than a governmental representative, on the Executive Board of UNESCO during 1949. The Executive Board held its fifteenth through eighteenth ordinary sessions and one extraordinary session during the year under review. Its work was primarily concerned with 1) approval of the 1949 UNESCO program as adopted by the third session of the General Conference at Beirut,[18] 2) the role of UNESCO in the United Nations expanded program of assistance to underdeveloped areas,[19] 3) preparation of the draft UNESCO program and budget for 1950[20] and 4) preparations for the fourth session of the General Conference.[21] The Executive Board also instructed the Director General to investigate the possibility of establishing liaison with the Council of Europe.[22]

During the year under review, the United States participated in the following major activities sponsored by UNESCO: the International Conference on Adult Education, Elsinore, Denmark, June 16–25; the Inter-American Seminar on Problems of Illiteracy and Education of Adults, Quitandinha, Brazil, July 27–September 3; the International Theater Institute, Zurich, Switzerland, June 27–July 2; the International Conference on Science Abstracting, Paris, France, June 20–25; a meeting of a committee of experts to examine a world-wide comparative study of copyrights, Paris, France, July 4–9; the Twelfth International Conference on Public Education, Geneva, Switzerland, July 4–12; the Committee on Technical Needs in Press, Radio, and Films, Paris, France, July 25–August 3; the International Technical Conference on the Protection of Nature, Lake Success, New York, August 22–September 1; and the International Symposium on High Altitude Biology, Lima, Peru, November 23–30.

For a more comprehensive listing of UNESCO-sponsored conferences in which the United States participated during 1949, see this volume, p. 92.

D. United States National Commission for UNESCO

In order to acquaint the people of the United States with the activities of UNESCO and to stimulate further activity in the United States toward the achievement of UNESCO's objectives, the United States National Commission for UNESCO sponsored the Second National Conference on UNESCO which met in Cleveland, Ohio, from March 31 to April 2, 1949, with some 2,500 representatives of over 800 national organizations in attendance. In addition to the plenary sessions which were addressed by speakers including Milton S. Eisenhower, president of the National Commission, Sir John Maud, member of the UNESCO Executive Board, Mrs. Franklin D. Roosevelt, United States representative to the United Nations Commission on Human Rights, and George V. Allen, Assistant Secretary of State for Public Affairs, the conference in section meetings and small study groups discussed the areas in which the community could promote UNESCO's goals.[23]

The seventh semiannual meeting of the United States National Commission was held in Washington on September 9 and 10. At this meeting, the commission assessed the UNESCO program in the United States for the past year, formulated a program for greater United States participation in UNESCO activities during 1950, prepared the instructions to the United States delegation to the fourth General Conference, and elected a new chairman and Executive Committee.[24] George D. Stoddard was elected chairman of the commission to succeed Milton S. Eisenhower, and Erwin D. Canham, editor of the *Christian Science Monitor* was chosen the commission's new vice chairman. William Benton, Milton S. Eisenhower,

[18] UNESCO, *Courier*, February 1949, p. 3.   [19] *Ibid.*, April 1949, p. 3; *ibid.*, July 1949, p. 2.
[20] *Ibid.*   [21] *Ibid.*, September 1949, p. 14.   [22] *Ibid.*, November 1949, p. 4.
[23] United States National Commission for UNESCO. *2d National Conference: Program and Guide*, Cleveland, n.d.
[24] United States National Commission for UNESCO, *News*, III, August 1949, No. 2, p. 7.

Waldo G. Leland, Rayford W. Logan, Earl J. McGrath, Stanley H. Ruttenberg, and George F. Zook were elected to the Executive Committee.[25]

In the National Commission's program for 1949–1950, five projects were given priority: 1) educational reconstruction, 2) a program of education on human rights, 3) population pressures and food supply, 4) increased understanding of the United Nations system, and 5) improvement of teaching materials.[26]

The Executive Committee of the Commission held three meetings in 1949. The first, held in Washington on February 18 and 19, arranged for the Second National Conference on UNESCO, reviewed the program for 1948, and discussed relations between UNESCO and the United Nations.[27] The second meeting, also held in Washington on June 24 and 25, appraised the national conference, discussed UNESCO participation in the technical assistance program, and considered the agenda for the fourth session of the UNESCO General Conference.[28] At the latter session, the committee heard Willard L. Thorp, Assistant Secretary of State for Economic Affairs, present an outline of the expanded program of technical assistance and conferred with George V. Allen, Assistant Secretary of State for Public Affairs, on plans for the United States delegation to the fourth session of the General Conference.[29] The third session of the Executive Committee to meet during the year was held on November 14 and 15 and was devoted to a discussion of the 1950 program of the National Commission.[30]

2. INTERNATIONAL INFORMATION SERVICE

[See *Documents, VIII, 1945–1946*, p. 752; *IX, 1947*, p. 515; *X, 1948*, p. 474.]

During 1949 the United States, primarily through the strengthening of its "Voice of America" broadcasts, stepped up its overseas information programs. VOA coverage was increased through the establishment of three new transmitting stations; the inauguration of new short-wave studios in Washington;[1] the construction in Tangier, with the permission of the French Government, of six transmitters to augment four relay stations in Munich and five additional stations leased from the British Broadcasting Company;[2] the inception of a high-powered medium-wave relay station in Munich;[3] and the construction, with the cooperation of the Greek Government, of a new medium-wave station in Salonika.[4] The range of broadcast was broadened to provide greater coverage of central Europe and the Soviet Union by doubling the power of the largest transmitter on the east coast, a station located near Boston, Massachusetts, and operated by the World Wide Broadcasting Corporation.[5] To increase the listening audience of VOA additional language broadcasts were added. Iranian-language programs to the middle east were initiated on March 21;[6] programs beamed to China and the far east were transmitted in Cantonese, as well as in Mandarin, Korean, Russian, and English;[7] and on December 12, the Ukrainian language was added to those in which programs were directed to the Soviet Union.[8]

Efforts by the Soviet Union to block reception of all Voice of America broadcasts to its territory resulted in renewed efforts to increase the power of VOA and to develop new techniques for improving reception. An additional appropriation of $11.32 million requested by the Department of State for these purposes[9] and representing an increase of 113 percent was appropriated;[10] and plans were laid to overcome Soviet jamming operations by 1) increasing the efficiency of transmitters in operation, 2) increasing the power of transmission and improving antennae; 3) relocating the transmitters around the perimeter of the broadcasting target; and 4) pouring transmitters in a counter-action of such volume as to match or over-ride Soviet jamming attempts.[11] On April 30, the United States protested to the Inter-

25 *Ibid.*, October 1949, No. 4, p. 3.
26 *Ibid.*, August 1949, No. 2, p. 7.
27 *Ibid., News*, II, March 1949, No. 9, p. 5.
28 *Ibid.*, June 1949, No. 12, p. 6.
29 Department of State, *Bulletin*, XXI, p. 19.
30 United States National Commission for UNESCO, *News*, III, December 1949, No. 6, p. 3.
1 Department of State, *Bulletin*, XX, p. 83.
2 *New York Times*, July 30, 1949, p. 3.
3 Department of State, *Bulletin*, XXI, p. 403.
4 *Ibid.*, p. 829.
5 *New York Times*, July 8, 1949, p. 3.
6 Department of State Press Release 160, March 18, 1949.
7 Department of State, *Bulletin*, XXI, p. 239.
8 *Ibid.*, p. 944.
9 *New York Times*, August 18, 1949, p. 1.
10 Public Law 358, 81st Cong., 1st sess.
11 *New York Times*, August 20, 1949, p. 1.

national Telecommunication Union charging that the Soviet Union had, in jamming VOA reception, violated the Madrid and Atlantic City Telecommunications Conventions and the Cairo and Atlantic City Radio Regulations.[12] When Premier Stalin received the new United States ambassador (Kirk) on August 15, a second protest of the Soviet action as a violation of international telecommunications conventions was presented.[13]

(1) *Address by the Assistant Secretary of State for Public Affairs (Allen) at Duke University, Durham, North Carolina, December 10, 1949.*[14]

[EXCERPTS]

The American public is largely unaware of an important change which has been taking place during the past 15 years in the conduct of foreign relations. Every major foreign office in the world, including the Department of State, is doing things today which it would have considered startling, if not improper, even 10 years ago.

Until recent years, international relations between peoples were conducted by relatively few officials especially selected to live abroad for the purpose of representing one government to another. These officials, called diplomats, were forced by custom and precedent to deal only with an equally limited group of officials in the foreign office of the receiving country. Although diplomats were permitted to establish social contacts with the people among whom they lived, they were not expected to deal on political matters with anyone except the foreign office. Although I do not suggest that this restriction, built up through generations of experience, has been totally discarded today, some rather surprising new methods in conducting foreign relations are being developed, and one wonders where the trend will lead.

· · · · · · ·

But, for better or worse, propaganda as a conscious weapon of diplomacy has increased tremendously during recent years. The technical development of mass communications, by which the greater part of mankind can be reached almost simultaneously by press or radio and the increased numbers of people who can read or understand may prove to have made this new tool as important to diplomacy as the invention of gunpowder was to military science.

I am not particularly concerned with whether either gunpowder or propaganda have benefited or harmed mankind. I merely emphasize, at this point, that propaganda on an immense scale is here to stay. We Americans must become informed and adept in its use, defensively and offensively, or we may find ourselves as archaic as the belted knight who refused to take gunpowder seriously 500 years ago.

· · · · · · ·

At present, the State Department sends out programs over the Voice of America in 22 languages every day, beamed to almost every corner of the world. It is true that we still write diplomatic notes to foreign governments, but we also try our utmost to reach directly into as many foreign homes as we can all over the globe. We talk directly to foreign peoples as well as to their governments. And every other major power is doing the same thing.

Our information, or propaganda, activity is by no means directed solely at peoples behind the Iron Curtain. The Department now maintains 85 information libraries in the leading capitals and important cities throughout the world. These libraries that contain American books and periodicals are usually not located in our Embassies but in separate buildings on busy streets where they will attract the largest numbers of individual foreigners.

· · · · · · ·

We also show American documentary films abroad and sometimes take projectors into the mountain valleys of Central America, Afghanistan, and Ceylon to show movies to anyone who wishes to attend our presentation. We demonstrate democracy in action through scenes of American life.

All this activity is a far cry from the few short years ago when diplomats dealt almost exclusively with foreign offices. Some observers of international affairs, and not alone the gentlemen of the old school, are still shocked by this new activity. Some think the government is in a field that should be left to private industry. Others feel that this direct approach constitutes interference by one country in the internal affairs of another and will come to no good.

After 2 years of experience in this new method of conducting foreign relations, I have reached a few general conclusions. I am convinced that unless the United States continues to utilize this new method, we shall be left at the post by other countries which are becoming skilled in the use of mass media. New methods in government, like new discoveries in science, can be used for good or ill. Direct radio contact with foreign individuals may be taken advantage of to proclaim falsehood as well as truth. But the potentialities of the direct approach are very great in both directions, and we must understand and perfect the techniques to protect and advance our interests. Furthermore, I see no need for the United States to become concerned over a contest in the mass propagation of ideas. We have the best commodity, democracy, to sell, and we are ahead of the world in physical facilities and know-how in mass communications. Our chief problem is to find the proper balance between government and private industry in the field.

I am inclined to think, moreover, that the direct approach in diplomacy will prove, on balance, to be a good development. It is the very opposite to secret diplomacy. If propaganda is deceptive, the glare of world publicity will generally find it out. Lincoln's confidence in the people's wisdom is still apt. Moreover, public debate, openly and honestly conducted, is not interference, in my judgment.

The direct approach, where there is no censorship, is the democratic approach. The Department of State assists friendly foreign governments in presenting their case direct to the American people, and we do not even try to jam unfriendly programs off the air waves.

As Congressman Daniel J. Flood said recently, "If Congress made it illegal for people in this country to listen to foreign broadcasts, 150 million Americans would be listening to them tomorrow, and I'd be one of them." As long as information is free in this country, we need have no fear for our institutions. No dictator ever existed without censorship and no democracy with it. A police state is desperately afraid for its citizens to read and hear directly what foreign governments have to say. Hence the frantic jamming of the Voice of America by the Soviet Union.

I am convinced that eventually, world government of some sort will be accomplished, but it can be brought about only through the assistance of the direct approach to peoples. Propaganda, when based on truth, can be an unequalled force for good.

As Dr. Reinhold Niebuhr points out, the peoples of the world must develop a much greater sense of world community before any form of international political structure can be developed strong enough to keep the peace. To develop a world community, peoples must establish more direct contacts with each other across international boundaries. UNESCO, the United Nations Educational, Scientific and Cultural Organization, is making significant progress in this direction.

In the efforts now being made by governments to reach foreign peoples direct, we may be witnessing an important movement toward the establishment of a world community. At any rate, the American Government will do everything it can to hasten the time when peoples speak directly to peoples in a thousand tongues calling for peace.

3. CULTURAL AND EDUCATIONAL EXCHANGE

[See *Documents, VIII, 1945–1946*, p. 757; *IX, 1947*, p. 523; *X, 1948*, p. 476.]

The list of nations participating in the educational exchange program under the Fulbright Bill was increased in 1949 by the inclusion of the following agreements: Netherlands, May 17, 1949, making the equivalent of $5,000,000 available for educational exchange in the Netherlands, Surinam, and the Netherlands West Indies;[1] Norway, May 25, 1949, making a total of $1,250,000 available at not less than $250,000 a year;[2] Iran, September 1, 1949, making 10,000,000 rials[3] available;[4] Egypt, November 3, 1949, making $300,000 available;[5] Australia, November 26, 1949, making between $5,000,000 and $7,000,000 available.[6]

Under all government programs for educational exchange, 618 students from the United States went abroad in 1949 and 125 foreign students came to this country; 116 teachers were sent abroad from this country while 125 came here to teach; 46 professors from United States universities and colleges went abroad and 102 foreign professors came here; 170 research scholars from this country went abroad and 111 foreign research scholars came to this country.

1 Department of State, *Treaties and Other International Acts Series* 1946.
2 *Ibid.*, 2000.   3 Approximately $310,000.
4 Department of State, *Treaties and Other International Acts Series* 1973.
5 Department of State, *Bulletin*, XXI, p. 831.
6 Department of State, *Treaties and Other International Acts Series* 1994.

(1) *Second Semiannual Report of the United States Advisory Commission on Educational Exchange Concerning Activities Conducted under the United States Information and Educational Exchange Act of 1948 (Public Law 402, 80th Congress) Covering the Period from January 1 to June 30, 1949.*[7]

[EXCERPTS]

. . . .

IV. RECOMMENDATIONS TO THE SECRETARY OF STATE AND ACTION TAKEN

During the past year the Commission on Educational Exchange made a number of recommendations to the Secretary of State in connection with the Public Law 402 program and such allied activities as the point 4 program. The Secretary of State has regularly concurred with these suggestions and has undertaken to put them into effect.

The Commission's recommendations and the Secretary's replies are presented below, together with statements on action taken by the Department of State.

PUBLIC LAW 402 ACTIVITIES AND THE PRESIDENT'S POINT 4 PROGRAM

The Commission made the following recommendations to the Secretary of State:

One of the oldest and most well-developed forerunners of the President's point 4 program is the scientific and technical program of cooperation with the other American Republics now being conducted under the authority of Public Law 402 of the Eightieth Congress but initiated a decade ago as a part of the good-neighbor policy. Other forerunners are the 9-year-old projects of the Institute of Inter-American Affairs and, more recently, certain activities of the Economic Cooperation Administration * * * there are certain principles and suggestions arising from the scientific and technical program of Public Law 402 which the Secretary should have in mind in charting the expanded program.

In the first place, it is clear that the educational, cultural, scientific, and technical programs are interrelated and should be closely coordinated. A detailed examination of all Latin-American educational and technical activities of Public Law 402, country by country, gives a clear picture of these interrelationships. It is not so obvious in the Eastern Hemisphere, since for this part of the world funds were appropriated (for 1948–49 under Public Law 402) for a skeleton program only.

. . . .

Second, the President has emphasized the cooperative, nonimperialistic approach for point 4. From this standpoint, the Commission wishes to comment on this Government's experience with the Latin-American program. It

---

[7] United States Advisory Commission on Educational Exchange, *Second Semiannual Report on Educational Exchange Activities,* Washington, January 3, 1950.

has been basically cooperative in nature. Most of the projects have been on a bilateral basis with each nation sharing the responsibilities and the benefits. The results have been very satisfactory. The willingness of the other nations to join the United States in carrying out this program is evidenced by their substantial and increasing contributions as shown in the accompanying graph.[8]

It has been the experience of the Department of State and the other agencies conducting the program under Public Law 402 that it is not only valuable but indispensable to consult with other governments at every stage of planning and executing a project. Further, it is of benefit to the program to utilize more nationals of other governments than United States visiting consultants. Sometimes great benefits can be derived for the program by compromising on standards and efficiency in order to show deference to the wishes of the host government. This again is a program in which we receive as well as give; officials of each country cooperate on a basis of equality. The Commission believes that this is the only basis upon which technical assistance can succeed under point 4.

There will be many instances where nations other than the United States can take the lead in assisting countries to develop industrial and scientific techniques. The United States should encourage such leadership. Although not a widely used procedure of the scientific and technical program under Public Law 402, this plan has been used extensively and effectively by the Economic Cooperation Administration.

Third, the Commission wishes to recommend a technique used in Public Law 402 program and others to overcome difficulties sometimes resulting from the instability of governments and their personnel. This technique is applied where the United States and another Latin-American government undertake to develop a public service cooperatively, for example, an agricultural station. An agreement is negotiated which requires that any change in annual programs and local personnel must be approved in writing by the appropriate cabinet-level official of the other country and the chief of the United States field party. Proof of effectiveness is found in instances where precipitate changes of government resulted in sweeping changes or upheavals in public programs and personnel of ministries, but where, at the same time, cooperative programs of the country and the United States, solidly based upon concrete agreement, have continued without appreciable modification.

Finally, this Commission finds a great need for broadening the technical training which is now being carried out under Public Law 402. The existing program is too specialized to have wide impact upon the development of a given country.

.   .   .   .

The following is the text of the Department's reply to the Commission's recommendations concerning the point 4 program:

8 Not reprinted here.

The Department is in hearty accord with the Commission's four recommendations that concern point 4, and will follow them in carrying out its responsibilities under the point 4 program.

The Commission's first recommendation stresses the importance of coordination of international technical exchange activities. There will, of course, be close coordination between point 4 technical assistance activities and other activities in the educational, cultural, and scientific fields in each stage — policy, program planning, budgeting, and operations. This will be facilitated if, as proposed in pending legislation, the primary responsibility for direction of point 4 activities is lodged in the Secretary of State. Within the Department of State, this coordination will be achieved by daily working liaison between officers of the point 4 office, the Office of Educational Exchange, and the new regional bureaus. Some of the specific ways in which this coordination will be achieved are:

1. Budgeting for both kinds of activities will be based on clearly defined criteria and lines of demarcation, worked out with the Bureau of the Budget.

2. Officers of the five recently established regional bureaus, where the primary responsibility for coordination and direction of policy programing and international activities on a country-area basis rests, will work together on planning and programing for both point 4 technical assistance and educational, cultural, and scientific programs under Public Law 402, as they affect particular countries.

3. The United States Ambassador will be responsible for coordination and general direction of official United States activities within his country. This responsibility includes point 4 technical assistance and all other educational, cultural, and scientific exchange activities.

4. There will continue to be an interdepartmental advisory committee on point 4 technical assistance, representing the major Federal agencies which will be carrying on both point 4 technical assistance and Public Law 402 scientific and educational activities. Papers of a policy, program, and administrative nature prepared for this committee will receive the customary review and approval by all interested offices of the State Department, including the Office of Educational Exchange, assuring a unified and coordinated departmental position. The secretariat of this committee, as well as other point 4 general manager staff, will be working cooperatively with other committee secretariats, and in particular, with the secretariat for the United States Advisory Commission on Educational Exchange.

The Commission makes the second recommendation that the point 4 program be based on cooperation between contributing and recipient governments and between different contributing governments. The Department's policy is that point 4 activities should be undertaken only in response to the requests of other governments and in cooperation with them. It may be noted that, in requesting the Congress to authorize the Export-Import Bank to make certain guaranties to private American investors abroad, Under Secretary Webb pointed out that guaranties would not be made if the other government concerned disapproved of the investment proposed. The Department will seek to develop a cooperative framework with each other country for the technical exchange activities carried on directly by the United States.

It is anticipated that most of the technical exchange activities in which the experts or skills are supplied from some country other than the United States will be carried out under the auspices of the United Nations or some other intergovernmental body. It is anticipated that even under direct United States programs certain of the experts utilized will be supplied from other countries. It is also planned to utilize institutions and training facilities in

Puerto Rico and Hawaii for the training of students from countries having related cultures and technical problems.

The third recommendation of the Commission favors the use of the servicio technique. This technique is already being used extensively by the United States Government, and the Department plans that it should be used even more widely under the point 4 program. This would be true both of servicios where the United States participation is administered by regular government departments or agencies, and where it is administered by the Institute of Inter-American Affairs or by an analogous institute empowered to operate outside the Western Hemisphere.

The Commission's fourth recommendation is that much wider (and less advanced) technical training be undertaken under point 4 than was possible under Public Law 402. The Department agrees that, if the point 4 program is to achieve results as early and as widespread as possible, it will be necessary to aid educational and training programs in many areas that provide less advanced technical skills than those usually acquired by the specialists brought to the United States for technical training under Public Law 402. Aid in the establishment of vocational training schools, fundamental education, agricultural education, and other technical institutions is planned as an important part of the point 4 program. The Department considers it of great importance to try to bring improved techniques to a substantial part of the populations of underdeveloped areas. This can only be done if there is local institutions, which will provide such training to students in or near their own homes, and which will relate it directly to the work that these students are performing and can be expected to continue to perform.

· · · · · · ·

CHAPTER XIII

Western Hemisphere

1. GENERAL STATEMENTS

(1) *Address by the Secretary of State (Acheson) before the Pan American Society of New York, New York, September 19, 1949.*[1]

[EXCERPTS]

. . . . . .

Before discussing specific policies, it seems well to restate once more the basic principles on which our policy in this Hemisphere must rest. They are:

Our essential faith in the worth of the individual.

The preservation of our way of life without trying to impose it on others.

The observance by all governments of ethical standards based on justice and respect for freely accepted international obligations.

Protection of the legitimate interests of our people and government, together with respect for the legitimate interests of all other peoples and governments.

The juridical equality of all the American republics.

Non-intervention in the internal or external affairs of any American republic.

The stimulation of private effort as the most important factor in political, economic and social purposes.

Freedom of information and the development of free exchanges in all fields.

The perfection, with the other American countries, of regional and universal arrangements for maintaining international peace.

The promotion of the economic, social and political welfare of the people of the American republics.

These then are our guiding principles. A statement of the specific policies which rest on these principles can best be made in conjunction with a review of our long-term objective.

The primary objective of any government is necessarily the security of its territory and people. The Monroe Doctrine is an acknowledgement that the security of this Hemisphere is indivisible. With the development of the inter-American system our countries have jointly created an effective security organization consistent with the Charter of the United Nations.

The Rio de Janeiro Treaty of 1947 provides that in case of armed attack on an American republic, each party pledges itself to assist in meeting the attack.

[1] Department of State Press Release 700, September 15, 1949; Department of State, *Bulletin*, XXI, p. 467.

One of the foremost policies of our country in foreign affairs is to fulfill its obligations under the Rio Treaty and to seek the maximum cooperation among the American nations in achieving the objective of a secure and peaceful continent.

.   .   .   .   .   .

We, the nations of this Hemisphere, have a responsibility not only to ourselves but to the rest of the world to live together in peace and harmony. Together we have played an important part in creating the United Nations. We must live up to the responsibilities which we have thus assumed towards the other member nations. This means, among other things, that we must abide by our regional commitments and maintain peace in our own midst. If all of the countries of the Hemisphere proceed along these lines, as we in this country intend to do, there is no reason why any nation in the Hemisphere should fear aggression.

What I have said, however, should not be construed as blind adherence to the status quo. We oppose aggression; we do not oppose change. Indeed, we welcome and encourage change where it is in the direction of liberty and democracy. We have worked long and persistently in common with our neighbors toward this end.

We would like to see a world in which each citizen participates freely in determining periodically the identity of the members of his government. This is an objective for which we will continue to work, subject always to our common policy of non-intervention.

In the Americas we have had periods of high hope and periods of bitter discouragement as we have seen democratic institutions flourish in some countries, only to see them subverted in others. We always deplore the action of any group in substituting its judgment for that of the electorate. We especially deplore the overthrow by force of a freely elected government. In such situations we do not cease to hope that the people will regain the right to choose their leaders.

We realize, however, that the attainment of the democratic ideal in any country depends fundamentally upon the desires and efforts of the people of that country. The nature of democracy is such that it can be achieved only from within.

Democracy as we endeavor to practice it is a continuing development toward political maturity — not a formula to be imposed upon a nation by a self-appointed ruling class, as is the case with certain other forms of government. Its attainment is essentially a spiritual and personal problem to be solved by the people of each country for themselves.

We are encouraged in our purpose by the realization that the strength of democratic institutions throughout the Hemisphere today is measurably greater than a generation ago. In spite of occasional disappointments, we note a steady forward progress. The spirit of democracy is alive and bearing fruit.

Our policy with respect to recognizing new governments in the hemisphere is not inconsistent with our encouragement of democracy. We maintain diplomatic relations with other countries primarily because we are all on the same planet and must do business with each other. We do not establish an embassy or legation in a foreign country to show approval of its government. We do so to have a channel through which to conduct essential governmental relations and to protect legitimate United States interests.

When a freely elected government is overthrown and a new and perhaps militaristic government takes over, we do not need to recognize the new government automatically and immediately. We can wait to see if it really controls its territory and intends to live up to its international commitments. We can consult with other governments, as we have often done.

But if and when we do recognize a government under these circumstances, our act of recognition need not be taken to imply approval of it or its policies. It is recognition of a set of facts, nothing more. We may have the gravest reservations as to the manner in which it has come into power. We may deplore its attitude toward civil liberties. Yet our long-range objectives in the promotion of democratic institutions may, in fact, be best served by recognizing it and thus maintaining a channel of communication with the country involved. In this way we are also able to discharge our basic function of protecting the interests of our Government and our citizens there. Since recognition is not synonymous with approval, however, our act of recognition need not necessarily be understood as the forerunner of a policy of intimate cooperation with the government concerned.

The economic field offers the greatest opportunity for constructive action. Two sets of problems arise. The first are derived largely from the disruptions of the war, and we hope may be described as short-run problems. The second result from the fact that in wide areas the standard of living is still miserably low. This is a long-run problem, although no less urgent.

It was apparent that the war would be followed by a period of economic stress. In some areas the effectiveness of the economic machine had been destroyed. The effect of the war on various relationships which previously had been the basis of world trade — for example, the reduction in earnings on overseas investment by European countries — raised new issues with respect to achieving equilibrium. Although the heaviest initial impact of this problem fell on Europe, the fundamental disequilibrium has now extended around the world so that for every country the maintenance of trade and the balance of payments has become a major problem of foreign relations. It was obvious in its initial stage that there could be no real recovery in trade without the revival of production in Europe. Therefore, the European Recovery Program must be regarded not merely as a program to meet the individual problems of the European countries but also to revive the flow of goods to and from Europe. We are all aware of the serious character of the present balance of payments problem and it is one to which we must direct our thoughts in the most constructive way possible.

While material well-being is no guarantee that democracy will flourish, a healthy and prosperous people is a far more fertile field for the development of democracy than one which is undernourished and unproductive. That is why we are and must be preoccupied with the long-term problem of economic development.

The record of our economic cooperation in this Hemisphere is substantial. It is one of such proven soundness that it forms the precedent and the basis for the more constructive labor ahead.

.   .   .   .

These then are our three major objectives — the security of our nation and of the Hemisphere; the encouragement of democratic representative institutions; and positive cooperation in the economic field to help in the attainment of our first two objectives.

If I have said nothing new tonight, it may well be because, in a family of nations as in families of individuals we should expect nothing more sensational than growth.

We can take satisfaction in the stability of our policy in the Hemisphere. The Good Neighbor Policy as we practice it today is, for us, an historic, bipartisan, national policy. It has been wrought by democrats at both ends of Pennsylvania Avenue — President Roosevelt, Secretary Hull and Senator Connally, and also by Republicans at both ends of the Avenue — President Hoover, Secretary Stimson and Senator Vandenberg. And this by no means exhausts the distinguished list who have contributed to this great policy.

It is the firm intention of President Truman, as it is of myself as Secretary of State — of the entire personnel of my Department and, I believe, of the people of my country — to work for ever closer relations between the nations of this Hemisphere. We seek by positive good will and effort to strengthen the Organization of American States, within the more extensive design of the United Nations, as the most effective expression of law and order in this Hemisphere.

We and the other American republics have determined and pledged ourselves to carry on our common policy of the Good Neighbor as a living and constantly growing reality.

2. INTER-AMERICAN SYSTEM

A. General

United States participation in the activities of the Organization of American States continued during the year under review. Of the total budget of $2.03 million approved for the operation of OAS for the fiscal year ending June 30, 1950, the United States contribution was set at $1,247,122.61.[1] During the year the Council also gave its approval to a draft bilateral agreement with the United States Government concerning the privileges and immunities of the Organization.[2] Paul C. Daniels served as the representative of the United States on the OAS Council during the year under review.

---

[1] Council of the Organization of American States, Document C–sa–14–E, January 19, 1949.
[2] Organization of American States, *Annals,* I, p. 205. For the text of the agreement, see *ibid.*, p. 274.

(1) Statement by the Secretary of State (Acheson) on the Occasion of the Referral of the Charter of the Organization of American States to the Senate. Department of State Press Release, February 2, 1949.[3]

Made public on January 13, 1949, the Charter of the Organization of American States was transmitted to the Senate for advice and consent with respect to ratification on February 2, 1949. No further action was taken toward the ratification of the Charter during 1949.

The treaty-document that is here submitted for the advice and consent of the Senate to ratification is the proposed legal constitution of the regional inter-American organization. The question that it raises, however, is hardly whether there shall be such an organization. The organization has already proved its value over some 60 years of existence, during which the United States has continuously taken an active part in its development. The constitutional instrument before you represents simply a culmination of this long and successful process. It signifies that our organized inter-American community of good neighbors has been readjusted to serve more adequately the needs of its member states in the contemporary world.

Two factors have combined to make it advisable that our inter-American system now be endowed with a single written charter. The first is the growth in its size, in the scope of its activities, and in its importance to all the American republics during recent years. The second is the establishment of the United Nations, which has given it a new context, giving it the character of a regional agency of the world system in addition to its long-established role as a distinct association of American states.

There are great advantages, where time allows, to building an organization gradually, adding to its structure piece by piece in the light of experience with its operation. The first of the Pan American Conferences, which convened in Washington at the call of the United States in 1889, established the first piece of the inter-American organization, a small permanent office that grew over the years into the present Pan American Union. New pieces were added by successive conferences, which generally met every five years. In the 1930's, when the rise of aggressive dictatorships in Europe and Asia menaced the entire world, the American states undertook a relatively rapid development of their organization to strengthen their common security. The war and the events leading up to it gave impetus to the expansion, the elaboration, and the strengthening of that organization. During those years it grew so rapidly that it threatened, so to speak, to outgrow its old clothes.

With the conclusion of the war, therefore, the American states took stock of all the organizational machinery that had developed within their system, and decided that a general consolidation and codification was called for. At the Mexico City conference in 1945, they proceeded to lay down the lines for such a reorganization. The Governing Board of the Pan American Union was charged with the main preparatory work, and the final decisions emerged from the Bogotá conference of 1948 in the form of the present charter that is now presented for your consideration.

3 Department of State, *Bulletin*, XX, p. 198.

The Mexico City conference took place shortly after the Dumbarton Oaks conversations when the main outlines of the new United Nations structure had already emerged. The conferees at Mexico City were alive to the necessity of developing a constructive relationship between the inter-American system and the United Nations Organization, when it should be set up, so that each would constitute an element of strength for the other. This consideration, too, argued the necessity of giving our regional system a more orderly and clearly defined form.

The United Nations had been established at San Francisco, of course, by the time the American states got down to the work of drafting an inter-American charter. Written into the San Francisco Charter, with the strong support of the American states, was chapter VIII on regional arrangements, and article 51 recognizing the inherent right of individual and collective self-defense if an armed attack occurs. The San Francisco Charter has, in turn, exerted a significant influence in shaping the new forms of our hemisphere system as embodied in this Bogotá charter.

Rather than burden this committee with a lengthy oral statement analyzing the provisions of the Bogotá charter in detail, I propose to recommend to your attention the pertinent chapter of the report of the United States Delegation to the Bogotá conference, and to confine myself, here, to general outlines and the points of principal significance.

As the broad purpose of the United Nations is to achieve world peace and security and to promote human welfare, so the broad purpose of the Organization of American States, explicitly set forth in chapter I of this charter, is to strengthen the peace and security of the continent and to further the economic, social, and cultural progress of the Americas.

The organizational machinery established for these purposes consists principally of three sorts of institutions: (1) the conferences; (2) the Council of the Organization and the Pan American Union; and (3) the specialized organizations.

The conferences themselves are of three kinds:

The Inter-American Conference, which is a new name for the International Conference of American States that has met more or less regularly, generally at five-year intervals, since 1889. This is "the supreme organ of the Organization".

The meeting of Consultation of Ministers of Foreign Affairs does not meet at fixed intervals, but only when problems of an urgent nature require a meeting of top-level representatives. The three meetings of Foreign Ministers held during the past war have shown what an effective device this is for dealing with emergencies. Its agenda is limited, it can meet quickly, and it can act decisively. This conference or "meeting" also serves as the "Organ of Consultation", under the Rio treaty of reciprocal assistance with which you gentlemen are familiar. As such it has the assistance of an Advisory Defense Committee, which meets only in connection with meetings of the Organ of

Consultation and is composed of the highest military authorities of the participating states.

The third category consists of specialized conferences, like conferences on agriculture or public health, most of which are sponsored by specialized organizations. Their purpose is "to deal with special technical matters or to develop specific aspects of inter-American cooperation."

The second group of agencies within the general Organization of American States is represented by the Council of the Organization and the Pan American Union. The Council replaces the former Governing Board of the Pan American Union. However, its scope has been increased under the present charter to embrace activities of the entire Organization, with specified political, advisory, and coordinating functions. It is composed of one representative from each member state and is established permanently in Washington. Under the reciprocal defense treaty of Rio de Janeiro, it is the provisional Organ of Consultation pending the convening of the Foreign Ministers when the treaty is invoked. Tied in with this Council are three specialized councils on economic and social affairs on juridical matters, and on culture matters respectively.

The Pan American Union, which has been undergoing an internal reorganization and strengthening, is the "general secretariat" of the Organization and a focal point for the continuing conduct of the Organization's varied business in the economic and social, the juridical, and the cultural fields.

The specialized organizations constitute the third and final group within the general Organization. They are autonomous technical agencies "having specific functions with respect to technical matters of common interest to the American states". The Pan American Sanitary Bureau and the Inter-American Institute of Agricultural Sciences are examples.

That, in broad outline, is the Organization of American States, as set forth in this charter.

I have mentioned that the Organization of American States, under this charter, has a dual capacity: (1) as an independent regional association of states; and (2) as a regional arrangement under the United Nations, all the American states being also members of the United Nations. In its first capacity, its actions are and must be consistent with the United Nations Charter. In the second capacity, its purpose is to strengthen and support the larger efforts of the United Nations, serving, particularly in the security and pacific settlement fields, as agent for the latter. The relationship with the United Nations in the field of security is defined in various articles of the Rio treaty of reciprocal assistance. Both the Rio treaty and the Bogotá charter contain articles stating that none of their provisions shall be construed as impairing the rights and obligations of the states under the United Nations Charter.

The Bogotá charter contains additional directives to the inter-American agencies for collaboration with the United Nations. One of the duties of the Council of the Organization is to promote and facilitate such collaboration.

Its three technical councils are specifically enjoined to establish, in agreement with the Council, "cooperative relations with the corresponding organs of the United Nations". Finally, the dual character of the Organization is specifically reflected in the provision (art. 100) that the specialized agencies, "In concluding agreement with international agencies of a world-wide character, . . . shall preserve their identity and their status as integral parts of the Organization of American States, even when they perform regional functions of international agencies."

By and of itself, this organizational structure would be merely so much inert machinery. What gives it purpose and effectiveness, what animates it, is a set of aspirations and principles that the American states have in common. These aspirations and principles are familiar to us. They are essentially the aspirations and principles of democratic and peace-loving peoples throughout the world, the aspirations to strengthen peace, security, justice, social progress, and economic well-being, the principles based on respect for the rights of others. They are, specifically, the traditional aspirations and principles of the American states and of the international system through which they take common action for their achievement.

These purposes and principles are also written into the Bogotá charter. I may cite as characteristic of them, references to the juridical equality of states, to respect for international law and observance of treaties, to nonintervention in the affairs of individual countries, and to the importance of democracy to the aims of the American states. Certain of these principles are expressed in the form of rights and duties of states, the texts of which are drawn largely from previous inter-American agreements. The charter moreover stresses the necessity for peaceful settlement of inter-American disputes and incorporates the fundamental obligations of the treaty of Rio de Janeiro regarding solidarity in the face of threats or acts of aggression.

This completes my very general outline of what the Bogotá charter is and what it contains. Let me add just this. It is not all-embracing, by any means, with respect to the detailed procedures of the organized relations among the twenty-one American states. The main security provisions, for example, are to be found in the Rio treaty of reciprocal assistance, which tied into the Bogotá charter by reference. This applies, as well, to other matters such as the pacific settlement of disputes and economic cooperation, which are also the subject of other formal inter-American agreements.

This Bogotá charter is, however, the central constitutional document, the equivalent for our regional organization of the San Francisco Charter for the United Nations. It defines the organization as a whole, establishes the framework within which it can continue to grow and to serve, ever more effectively, the common purposes, not only of the inter-American community, but of the United Nations as well. It is the product of more than half a century of evolution during which the organization has increasingly demonstrated its value to the member countries. I commend it wholeheartedly to this Committee's favorable consideration.

(2) *Statement by the President (Truman) before a Meeting of the Ambassadors to the Organization of American States, October 12, 1949.*[4]

Columbus Day provides a fitting opportunity for me to meet in a friendly and informal way with my distinguished neighbors, the Ambassadors on the Council of the Organization of American States. This organization is an outstanding example of effective international cooperation. The United States Government supports it wholeheartedly. The success of the inter-American system should encourage the peoples of other parts of the world to persevere in their efforts to solve common problems by mutual trust and helpfulness.

We have demonstrated how much can be accomplished when nations temper their national aspirations with concern for the interests of all. This is evident in the work of the American Republics for economic and social development. With increasing emphasis, we are striving to make possible a better life not only for people today but for generations still unborn. Our desire for security, in fact, is not primarily in order that our lives may remain unchanged, but that we may progressively realize our vast possibilities.

It is this spirit which motivates the growing exchange of technical knowledge and skill that has been taking place among our countries. We look forward to even more vigorous technical cooperation through all available channels, including the United Nations and its specialized agencies. We intend increasingly to help one another in the efforts of each to help himself.

We look to the Organization of American States for support of programs to raise living standards and to foster balanced economic development throughout the hemisphere. And since material improvement would be sterile without cultural and intellectual growth, we should make every effort to intensify cultural and intellectual cooperation.

The organization has a great responsibility for strengthening the peace and security of the Americas and for inducing governments to respect their freely accepted international obligations. We in the inter-American system subscribe fully to the principle of nonintervention in the internal or external affairs of any American Republic. At the same time, we are definitely committed to the proposition that our solidarity and high aims are fostered by the exercise of representative democracy in the American states. I am confident that you will continue to provide inspiring leadership toward the achievement of these aims.

As for this government, Secretary Acheson stated recently before the Pan American Society in New York that the good-neighbor policy is for us a firmly established national policy. I fully support the principles and objectives outlined by him on that occasion.

The United States is honored and happy to be the host country of the Organization of American States. We want you to feel most welcome and entirely at home among us as you continue your invaluable work in behalf of all the peoples of the American Republics.

4 *Ibid.*, XXI, p. 664.

B. Political Solidarity and Defense

Two political disputes of major proportions involving the American republics were brought for solution before the appropriate organs of the Organization of American States. The first of these involved charges presented by Costa Rica against Nicaragua, alleging that an armed invasion of the former's territory had been accomplished by forces originating in Nicaragua. The second involved a charge of "moral aggression" on the part of the Dominican Republic against Haiti. Inter-American legal machinery promoted during the year involved preparations for the first meeting of the Inter-American Council of Jurists. The Inter-American Defense Board was the primary instrumentality in planning for hemispheric defense, while individual American republics received unilateral military assistance from the United States in the form of military, naval, and air missions, and advisors.

1. COSTA RICAN–NICARAGUAN SITUATION

Following a meeting of the OAS Council acting as the Provisional Organ of Consultation on January 5, 1949, the United States Ambassador to the Council (Daniels) was designated to a committee to study the dispute between Costa Rica and Nicaragua which had first been brought before the Council on December 11, 1948.[1] In addition, the committee was to prepare for consideration by the Council a draft protocol of settlement which would restore peaceful relations between the two republics.[2] Settlement of the dispute under the direction of the Council was announced on February 19[3] and was followed on February 22 by the signature by representatives of both disputants of a Pact of Amity in Washington, resolving the differences between the two governments. The results of the Council's consideration of the situation were communicated to the United Nations Security Council on February 23.[4]

2. CARIBBEAN SITUATION

On February 15, 1949, the Government of Haiti requested that the Council consider a charge of "moral aggression" against the Dominican Republic, alleging that a former officer of the Haitian army with the knowledge and approval of the Dominican Government was conspiring to overthrow the Haitian Government.[5] After a special committee recommended that the Council acting as the Provisional Organ of Consultation not consider the dispute since early settlement of differences and reestablishment of peaceful relations between the two governments seemed possible,[6] the Inter-American Committee on Methods for the Peaceful Settlement of Conflicts consisting of the ambassadors of Mexico, Brazil, Cuba, Argentina, and the United States met to seek a satisfactory solution to the conflict. A special committee, composed of representatives of the United States, Argentina, and Mexico, was dispatched at the end of May to Haiti and the Dominican Republic to give further study to the question. One week later, the special committee reported the formulation of a basis of agreement between the two governments which was subsequently on June 9, 1949, formally incorporated into a joint declaration by which the two governments 1) reiterated their adherence to the "principles and provisions contained in the Treaties in force between the two Countries and in the American diplomatic Instruments that they have accepted"; 2) disavowed toleration in their respective territories of the activities of any persons or groups conspiring to disturb the domestic peace of either country; and 3) declared their conviction that the faithful observance of these principles would eliminate the causes of conflicts between the two governments.[7]

On August 3, 1949, the Inter-American Peace Committee (formerly the Inter-

---

1 For further information regarding the Costa Rica–Nicaraguan situation, see *International Organization*, III, p. 169, 368.
2 Council of the Organization of American States, Document C–sa–18–E, January 24, 1949; *ibid.*, Document C–sa–20–E, n.d.
3 *New York Times*, February 20, 1949.
4 United Nations Security Council, Document S/1268, February 25, 1949.
5 Council of the Organization of American States, Document C–sa–18–E, January 24, 1949.
6 *Ibid.*, Document C–sa–20–E, n.d.
7 Organization of American States, *Annals*, I, p. 326.

American Committee on Methods for the Peaceful Settlement of Conflicts) met to give general consideration to "the situation in the Caribbean area which has resulted in conflicts and international tension over a considerable period of time." At that time, the committee decided to request of all the American governments information and suggestions pertinent to the situation. The United States memorandum was presented on August 18, 1949, by the United States member of the committee (Daniels).[8] The conclusions of the committee were transmitted to the Secretary-General of the United Nations (Lie) on September 15, 1949.[9]

In December 1949, the committee was asked to take action with regard to a dispute between the Dominican Republic and Cuba. Although no action was taken on this question during the year under review, the United States, through the Secretary of State (Acheson), commented that it deplored "the action of the Government of the Dominican Republic in having brought up the possibility of the use of armed force for the purpose of 'war'." Mr. Acheson pointed out that, in the view of the United States, "proper procedures exist within the inter-American system for dealing with situations which threaten the peace and for repelling aggression against any of the American Republics from any source." Referring to his statement of September 19, 1949,[10] Mr. Acheson concluded that: "Aggression or plotting against any nation of this hemisphere is of concern to us" and stated that wherever aggression might occur or threaten, the United States would use its strongest efforts "to oppose it and to defend the peace of the hemisphere."[11]

(1) *United States Memorandum on the Caribbean Situation, Presented by the United States Ambassador to the Organization of American States (Daniels) to the Inter-American Peace Committee, August 18, 1949. Released September 2, 1949.*[12]

The situation existing in the political areas of the Caribbean, on which the Inter-American Peace Committee has requested information and suggestions from all of the American states, contains a number of elements which warrant close examination by that Committee, in order that it shall fulfill its continuing responsibility, under Resolution XIV of the Second Meeting of Ministers of Foreign Affairs, of keeping constant vigilance to insure that states between which any dispute exists or may arise may solve it as quickly as possible. Furthermore, this study deserves the full cooperation of all of the American governments which are in a position to contribute to the success of the Committee's work.

Although a few striking and well-publicized incidents have attracted general attention, long-continued tensions and evidences of political unrest have threatened to produce, or have actually produced, conflicts which have a deeper significance than would appear from the surface manifestations of isolated instances of plotting or revolutionary activity.

In the period since the cessation of hostilities of World War II, citizens of one or another of the countries in the Caribbean area have engaged in preparations for, and have participated in, movements whose purpose has been to accomplish by intimidation or armed invasion political changes in governments of the area. Despite the exercise of vigilance by the Government of the United States to prevent the violation of applicable United States laws, citi-

---

8 Department of State, *Bulletin*, XXI, p. 450.
9 United Nations Security Council, Document S/1407, October 13, 1949.
10 For excerpts from Secretary Acheson's statement of September 19, 1949, see this volume, p. 497.
11 Department of State, *Bulletin*, XXI, p. 990. 12 *Ibid.*, p. 450.

zens of the United States have from time to time been involved in activities aimed at other governments. These movements have been inspired and carried on, at least in part, by political exiles whose aim is to return, by force if necessary, to active political life in the countries of their origin. Whatever may be the motivation of these individuals, some of whom declare that the cause of their exile is the absence of democratic practices in their home countries, the methods they have chosen may involve violation by established governments of their international obligations with consequent disruption of friendly relations among the countries in the area.

In some instances, the real, apparent or rumored threat of revolutionary activities has served to create international tensions, and there have even been open accusations from government to government. Three times, within a period of a year, the procedures of inter-American peaceful settlement have been called upon to deal with situations thus created. While the success of these instruments in improving the atmosphere for amicable negotiation, or in actually achieving pacific settlement of the specific situations which gave rise to the use of inter-American machinery, has been conspicuous, other situations have continued or new ones have appeared which indicate that all tensions have not been removed, and that means must still be sought for achieving a renewal of international confidence and a feeling of security among members of the American community.

The unfortunate results of these conditions cannot fail to be a matter of concern to the states involved as well as to all the American nations. It is obvious that recurring suspicion and lack of confidence among governments do not provide a proper climate for those mutually beneficial relationships, including economic relationships, which are of importance to the fullest development of the American states. Some of the governments concerned have found the situation sufficiently disturbing to cause them to acquire considerable amounts of armament, which they feel to be necessary for their self-defense, as well as to institute rigorous measures of internal control. Heavy expenditures for armaments for these purposes hinder economic improvement in the area and contribute to an accentuation of discord. The proper functioning of the Organization of American States and the effort to realize the ideals and principles to which all have subscribed in the charter require that methods be found for getting at, and eliminating if possible, the causes of international friction and discord.

In searching for these methods, the Inter-American Peace Committee has wisely chosen to seek full information on those matters which will contribute to its better appreciation of the problem. In fulfillment of its desire to cooperate with the Committee in every appropriate way, the Government of the United States herewith furnishes certain items of information which relate to the activities of its citizens or which have come to its attention in the course of official investigations of activities alleged to have been carried on by its citizens or within its jurisdiction. If further pertinent information which the United States is able to make available is developed, this will be furnished to the Committee.

Early in 1947 the theft of certain United States Government-owned arms was discovered. United States citizens Edward Browder and Karl J. Eisenhardt subsequently pleaded guilty to the theft. Browder received 18 months in prison and Eisenhardt was fined 10 thousand dollars. During the investigation and court proceedings in this case it was brought out that the arms in question were destined for revolutionary purposes in the Caribbean area, particularly against the then Government of Venezuela; and that the movement was financed in considerable part by foreign sources. It was also publicly asserted during these proceedings that a Dominican consular officer in the United States was involved in the movement. The officer concerned was subsequently recalled by his government.

In connection with the revolutionary expedition organized in Cayo Confites in Cuba in July–August–September 1947 against the Dominican Republic, the United States Government took the following action:

1. Revocation in August 1947 of the export license granted for the export of the *LCI Patria* to one Cruz Alonzo in Cuba, when it became known that the ship was destined for the use of the revolutionaries.

2. Recommendation by the United States Embassy in Habana in September 1947 to American pilots recruited to participate in the revolution that they abandon this undertaking and return to the United States.

3. Statements to the United States press on August 2 and September 20, 1947, of the intention of the United States Government to meet its international obligations in connection with revolutionary activities in other countries. This included a statement that as early as January 1947 the appropriate law-enforcing agencies of this government had been taking special precautions to prevent violation of United States neutrality and export control statutes with reference to possible revolutionary activity in the Caribbean.

4. Indictment by a Federal grand jury in Florida on November 25, 1947, of Manolo Castro (who was the then Cuban Government Director of Sports), Miguel Angel Ramirez (Dominican), Hollis B. Smith (American), and two American fliers, on a charge of conspiracy to violate the export control act. Manolo Castro was killed in Habana before the trial began; Miguel Angel Ramirez has never returned to the United States to stand trial; Hollis B. Smith was given a 2-year suspended sentence and put on probation for 3 years by a Federal court in Jacksonville, Florida, in March 1948.

5. On another charge of conspiracy to violate the export control laws in connection with the export of arms to Cuba during the Cayo Confites activity, Reinaldo Rosell (Cuban), and United States citizens Louis Dell, Frank Adkins, and Luis Bordas were given 2-year suspended sentences and were placed on probation for 3 years by a Federal court in Miami, Florida, in May 1948.

Hurst, a United States Air Force pilot during the recent World War, arrived in Guatemala City on January 1, 1948, in a war surplus bombing plane which he had flown out of the United States without obtaining an export license as required by law. In the investigation it was brought out that the plane had been purchased by him with funds made available from foreign sources for use in connection with plans for a revolution against the Government of Nicaragua. In response to a request of the United States Embassy, the Guatemalan Government impounded the bomber, which was later returned to the United States. In May 1949, Hurst was found guilty of violation of Section 452, Title 22, United States Code (Neutrality Act). He was sentenced to 2 years in the penitentiary and fined one thousand dollars. The penitentiary sentence was suspended for a period of 5 years to be conditioned on Hurst's good behavior.

In January 1948, two military aircraft were illegally flown out of the United States by Snow, Mason, and three other United States citizens to Puerto Cabezas, Nicaragua. Investigation revealed that Browder, who, as reported above, had previously been involved in the theft of United States Government property in connection with a revolutionary plot against the Venezuelan Government, was attempting in January 1948 to engage pilots to fly "to an unknown spot" outside the United States to load bombs and then to fly to Venezuela to bomb the city of Caracas. The American pilots stated to investigating authorities that, upon their arrival at the Nicaraguan airport, they were met by 33 Venezuelan citizens who had arrived that same week from the Dominican Republic. In addition to the Venezuelan citizens who had arrived from the Dominican Republic, subsequent investigation revealed that other individuals connected with the same movement had arrived in Nicaragua during January 1948, from Costa Rica, Panama, and the United States.

Following urgent action by United States Embassy officials in Nicaragua, the American airmen were transferred from their hotel in Managua to the United States Air Force Base at Managua and returned at an early date to the Canal Zone and the United States. Legal action was promptly taken against them in the United States Federal courts. Browder pleaded guilty to separate indictments involving organizing a military expedition and violating the United States Neutrality Act. He was sentenced to 18 months imprisonment on each charge, the sentences to run concurrently. Snow, Mason, and the other individuals involved pleaded either guilty or *nolo contendere* to one or both of the above charges and received appropriate sentences.

Paul Warren, a citizen of the United States, has for sometime resided in Costa Rica, where he has engaged in the business of obtaining animals for sale in the United States. In 1948, Mr. Warren became a vigorous partisan of the Caribbean Legion and an active participant in certain of its activities. On various occasions during September, October and November 1948, Warren made trips to Cuba, Guatemala and Honduras. In response to questions of United States authorities, he indicated that his travels were connected with activities of the Caribbean Legion. United States obligations under the Habana convention of 1928 and information as to certain United States statutes were communicated by United States officials to Warren. When it proved difficult to dissuade Warren from his activities, the United States Embassy at San José was directed to take up Warren's passport and inform him that it would be made valid only for his return to the United States. It was made clear to Warren that this government did not object to his remaining in Costa Rica for the carrying on of legitimate business but that the United States is strongly opposed to interference by its citizens in the internal political affairs of other nations.

The invasion of Costa Rica from Nicaraguan territory in December 1948 and the resulting action by the American states is a matter of recent record.[13] This government supported wholeheartedly the inter-American action taken in solution of that controversy and is of the opinion that the course followed in connection with the Costa Rican–Nicaraguan incident offers a valuable precedent for problems of a similar nature. In that connection, the resolution of the Provisional Organ of Consultation of December 24, 1948, is considered by this government to have pertinence to the current problem. The United States has been happy to note the improved relations which have existed between Costa Rica and Nicaragua since the signing by the two governments on February 21, 1949, of the pact of friendship which terminated the incident, and which has subsequently been ratified by both governments.

Information available to this government indicates that on the night of June 19, 1949, a PBY Catalina aircraft bearing United States registration No. N–1096–M was destroyed at Luperon on the north coast of the Dominican Republic after the persons on board endeavored to disembark munitions and attack the local authorities. All 15 persons aboard were either killed or captured. Of those killed, three were identified as American citizens, namely, John W. Chewning, Habet Joseph Maroot, and George R. Scruggs. The plane was registered in the United States in the name of Jesse A. Vickers of Miami Springs, Florida, who had applied for a license in May to export it to Mexico. This application was not approved by the United States Government. On June 4, however, the plane departed for Vera Cruz, and the circumstances surrounding the departure are now under investigation by the proper agencies of the United States Government to obtain information as to possible violations of United States statutes in this connection.

Reports received by United States officials in the course of this investigation indicate that other aircraft landed in Yucatan on June 18 and 19, destined for the Dominican Republic. According to these reports, two of these, which landed in Yucatan on June 18, were transports of Mexican registry, C–46 XB–HUV and C–47 XA–HOS. They are known to have been at the Air Force Base at San José, Guatemala, for several weeks prior to June 19, their presence there having been confirmed by the Guatemalan Government in a note to the United States Embassy. Two other aircraft, which landed on

[13] For information on the Costa Rica–Nicaraguan dispute, see this volume, p. 506.

June 19, were Guatemalan army transports T–1 and T–2; they were reported to have returned to Guatemala on June 26.

The Chief of the Guatemalan Air Force subsequently informed the press that Air Force plane T–1 had not been outside Guatemala and that T–2 had just returned from Houston, Texas. Official United States Government records disclose that T–2 did not have permission to enter the United States, nor was it reported at or in the vicinity of Houston during this period.

The reports also indicate that there were disembarked from these planes in Yucatan some 50 armed persons, several of whom made statements that they were destined for the Dominican Republic to overthrow the Dominican Government. Among the persons disembarked were two individuals who said they were United States citizens and gave their names as Marion R. Finley and Earl G. Adams. Also disembarked were the reported leaders of the expedition, Juan Rodriguez Garcia and Miguel Angel Ramirez (Dominicans), and Eufemio Fernandez (Cuban). Action by Mexican Government officials in taking into custody these armed men and military equipment prevented further movement of this group.

The formulation of recommendations for methods of dealing with the situation in the Caribbean area which fall within the duties and competence of the Inter-American Peace Committee would appear to depend to a very large extent upon the results of its study of the information which will be received in response to its request for cooperation from the American governments.

In the meantime, however, this government calls attention to the relevance to this situation of inter-American and other international agreements on non-intervention, and, specifically, to the 1928 Convention on the Rights and Duties of States in the Event of Civil Strife. It is suggested that the Committee may wish to give consideration to the question of whether obligations assumed in the 1928 convention and other agreements are being observed with sufficient positiveness by all states which have ratified them. It may wish also to consider whether a recommendation should be made that all states which have signed pertinent international agreements should take the steps necessary to complete their ratification. Such suggestions might also include reference to the desirability of there being domestic laws and enforcement machinery adequate to insure compliance with international obligations.

In view of the lapse of time and on the basis of experience regarding its applicability over intervening years, it is conceivable that the terms of the 1928 Convention may not be sufficiently clear or precise to cover situations to which it was intended to apply, or situations of a kind which could not have been fully foreseen when that Convention was negotiated. The Committee may, therefore, wish to consider the desirability of recommending that the Convention should be reviewed, with a view to its being clarified and strengthened, as necessary, or to determining whether a new convention should be drafted.

It is pertinent to recall that, during consideration of the Costa Rican–

Nicaraguan case by the Coas, acting as Provisional Organ of Consultation, the Committee of Information designated by that body presented a report which included, among other conclusions, the following which are particularly relevant to the broader problem:

7. The existence of active military centers of international agitation constitutes, as it is natural to suppose, a justifiable ground for preoccupation on the part of the Governments affected.

8. This situation, which is abnormal and dangerous for American international peace, explains why the majority of the Central American and Caribbean Republics have been living in an atmosphere of mutual distrust, constant anxiety, and open hostility for some time.

9. The situation is all the more regrettable since, because of the characteristics which we have pointed out, the international relations of the republics involved must, of necessity, become more strained each day, as the fear of the intentions of one neighboring country obliges the other to take the precautions which it considers necessary, with serious detriment to its own economy and with grave danger to institutional life.

Furthermore, the Provisional Organ of Consultation approved, on December 24, 1948, a resolution which contains the following particularly relevant articles:

IV. To request both Governments very earnestly to observe loyally by all means in their power the principles and rules of non-intervention and solidarity contained in the various Inter-American instruments signed by them.

VI. To recommend to all American Governments that they actively collaborate for the better fulfilment of the principles by which this Resolution is inspired.

It is suggested that the Committee may wish to invite the attention of all of the American states to the action which was taken at that time.

(2) Conclusions of the Inter-American Peace Committee Regarding the Caribbean Situation, Transmitted to the United Nations Secretary-General (Lie), September 15, 1949.[14]

The Inter-American Peace Committee, convoked at the initiative of the Representative of the United States to consider the situation that certain lamentable events have shown to exist in the political areas of the Caribbean, has given that delicate problem due attention and has studied carefully the various aspects of the situation with the valuable collaboration of those Governments that were good enough to send observations and suggestions.

The Committee believes that its duty in this matter is limited to the solemn reaffirmation of certain standards and principles that are basic for American peace and solidarity, principles and standards whose proper observance would, in the opinion of the Committee, not only keep such a situation as the one under consideration from arising, but avoid even the slightest symptom of disturbed relations among the American States.

With the intention, then, of using to full advantage this occasion for once more calling to the attention of the American conscience the lofty and indis-

14 United Nations Security Council, Document S/1407, October 13, 1949; Department of State, Bulletin, XXI, p. 665.

pensable postulates of our international relationships, the Committee believes it pertinent to formulate the following Conclusions:

1. To reiterate the necessity that all the Member States of the American community continue to be guided in their international conduct by the principle of non-intervention, which is the basic principle of the Organization of American States and hence of Pan-Americanism, solemnly set forth in the "Additional Protocol relative to Non-Intervention" signed at the Inter-American Conference for the Maintenance of Peace (Buenos Aires, 1936), and the latest and definitive expression of which is to be found in article 15 of the Bogotá Charter, in the following words:

> No State or group of States has the right to intervene, directly or indirectly, for any reason whatever, in the internal or external affairs of any other State. The foregoing principle prohibits not only armed force but also any other form of interference or attempted threat against the personality of the State or against its political, economic and cultural elements.

2. To recall, in connection with the foregoing, that the desire to avoid intervention in the internal or external affairs of other States and, even more, the duty of each State to prevent its territory from being used for the preparation or initiation of aggression toward one or more States with which it is at peace, led the American States to sign the Convention on the Rights and Duties of States in the Event of Civil Strife, in 1928; and that, in line with these ideas, the Second Consultative Meeting of Foreign Ministers in Resolution VII, recommended to the Governments of the American Republics some fundamental rules with respect to civil strife, applicable to the situation under study.

3. To express the fervent hope of the Committee that the aforementioned Convention on the Rights and Duties of States be ratified as promptly as possible by the American countries that have not yet done so; and also that it be clarified and perfected at some future inter-American meeting, if this should be considered necessary.

4. To consider the Resolution approved on December 24, 1948, by the Council of the Organization, acting provisionally as Organ of Consultation, with special emphasis on the paragraph in which the Council referred to the need (which might apply to any Government) of taking "adequate measures to rid its territory of groups of nationals or foreigners, organized on a military basis with the deliberate purpose of conspiring against the security of other sister Republics, and of preparing to fight against their Governments."

5. To express, likewise, the desirability that the American nations make every effort, within the limits of their constitutional powers, to avoid any systematic and hostile propaganda, whatever its medium of expression, against other countries of the Continent or their respective Governments.

6. To consider the desirability of the maintenance, as far as possible and in consonance with Resolution XXXV of the Bogotá Conference, of continuity of close and cordial diplomatic relations among the American States, since, as the preamble of the said Resolution states, "the development of the activi-

ties and the full benefits of inter-American cooperation can be realized more effectively if continuous and friendly relations are maintained among the States."

7. To point out that a common denominator of American political life is the adherence, within the sovereignty of each State and in accordance with the characteristics of its own people, to the principles and the exercise of democracy, expressed formally in solemn American obligations (Declaration XXVII of the Inter-American Conference for the Maintenance of Peace, Buenos Aires, 1936; Recommendation LXXII of the Eighth International Conference of American States, Lima, 1938; Resolution VII of the Second Meeting of Consultation, Habana, 1940; Charter of Bogotá, 1948; Resolution XXXII of the Bogotá Conference), outstanding among which is the statement in paragraph (d) of article 5 of the Bogotá Charter, which reads as follows:

> The solidarity of the American States and the high aims which are sought through it require the political organization of those States on the basis of the effective exercise of representative democracy.

8. To make public its aspiration that the Charter of the Organization of American States, which, as provided for in Resolution I and XL of the Bogotá Conference, is the basic instrument of continental solidarity and is at present the means of determining the organization of the system and its component parts, receive definitive confirmation through ratification by all the Governments, so that the juridical and political structure of the Continent will be as complete and permanent as could be desired.

9. To repeat also its equally firm belief that at all times, and especially in the critical atmosphere that characterizes the present international situation, American solidarity should be strengthened even more, if possible, so as to overcome opportunely, through the unity of our peoples, any threat to world peace that might arise.

10. To state the Committee's belief that, to carry out the foregoing conclusion, it will be of great help if each American Government disseminates among all its inhabitants the fullest possible information as to the international obligations assumed by the American States, particularly in matters of non-intervention and of rights and duties of states in the event of civil strife.

11. To express its opinion that the effective application, by the American Governments, of the points to which the Bogotá Conference Resolution XXXII, on Preservation and Defense of Democracy in America, refers will result in establishing democratic institutions still more strongly in this hemisphere.

12. To offer once more the continuing willingness of the Inter-American Peace Committee to lend its services (within the limits of Resolution XIV of the Second Meeting of Consultation) for the pacific and friendly settlement of any conflict or difference that at any moment might arise between two or more American States.

13. To point out likewise, that, in addition to the services that the Inter-

American Peace Committee is ever ready to offer, there are in the inter-American system, and concretely in the Organization, various means of recourse, the proper application of which is a guarantee of a reasonable settlement of any conflict that might arise between them: that is, the methods of pacific settlement that appear in the Pact of Bogotá and in other inter-American instruments, and also the Meeting of Ministers of Foreign Affairs, either in accordance with article 40 of the Charter or as Organ of Consultation in accordance with the provisions of the Inter-American Treaty of Reciprocal Assistance.

14. To state that the foregoing conclusions do not apply exclusively, in the opinion of the Committee, to the situation referred to in the preamble of these conclusions, but to all the American Republics without exception.

3. HEMISPHERIC DEFENSE

On March 31, 1949, the Inter-American Defense Board met in plenary session at Washington. The United States was represented by Lt. General Willis D. Crittenberger, United States Army. The purpose of the meeting was to study the necessary measures for the defense of the continent and to make appropriate recommendations to the governments of the American republics.[15]

An agreement between the United States and Haiti signed and entered into force on January 4, 1949, established for four years a United States Air Force Mission to cooperate with the Secretary of State for National Defense and with the personnel of the Haitian Air Forces "with a view to contributing to the development of the Air Force of the Republic of Haiti."[16] A similar agreement to last two years was signed and entered into force on July 5 between the United States and Mexico.[17] An agreement extending and amending the agreement of December 12, 1940, between the United States and Ecuador for a military mission to that country was effected by an exchange of notes on March 23 and May 17, 1949.[18] On April 14 an agreement for a naval mission to Haiti for a period of four years was signed and entered into force,[19] and the December 12, 1940, agreement on a naval mission to Ecuador was amended and extended by an exchange of notes on January 27 and February 4, 1949.[20] Two agreements on army missions were signed: between the United States and Colombia on February 21, 1949;[21] and between the United States and Peru on June 20, 1949.[22] Both agreements entered into force on the day they were signed and both missions were to remain in the respective countries for a period of four years.

C. Economic and Social Cooperation

For information concerning the activities of the United Nations Economic Commission for Latin America, see this volume, p. 197. For information on United States economic relations with various Latin American countries through the Export-Import Bank of Washington, see *ibid.*, p. 409.

During the year under review, the United States Government continued to participate in a number of inter-American agencies operating in the economic and social fields. Among these were the Inter-American Economic and Social Council, the American International Institute for the Protection of Childhood, the Inter-American Institute of Agricultural Sciences, the Inter-American Commission of Women, the Pan American Sanitary Organization, the Inter-American Indian Institute, and the Inter-American Statistical Institute. The United States was also represented at various inter-American technical conferences in the economic, social, and cultural fields including the Third Inter-American Travel Congress and the Fourth Inter-American Radio Conference.

[15] Organization of American States, *Annals*, I, p. 316.
[16] Department of State, *Treaties and Other International Acts Series* 1863.
[17] *Ibid.*, 1947.   [18] *Ibid.*, 1942.   [19] *Ibid.*, 1907.
[20] *Ibid.*, 1944.   [21] *Ibid.*, 1937.   [22] *Ibid.*, 1892.

The Institute of Inter-American Affairs, a government-owned corporation rather than an intergovernmental agency, continued during 1949 its efforts to promote the health and welfare of the inhabitants of the American republics. Due to cease operations in June 1950, IIAA was extended for a five-year period with a budget of $35 million.[1] During the year under review, the Institute concluded six five-year cooperative agreements with other American states: health and sanitation programs with Venezuela,[2] Haiti,[3] Brazil,[4] and Honduras;[5] a food production program with Costa Rica[6] and an education program in Paraguay,[7] bringing to 25 the number of such programs in operation and to sixteen the number of American Republics participating in IIAA's activities.[8]

D. Dependent Territories

For information on United States participation in the Caribbean Commission, see this volume, p. 374.

On February 2, 1949, the Council of the Organization of American States convened the American Committee on Dependent Territories established by the Ninth International Conference of American States.[1] Prior to the meeting of the committee on March 4, 1949, the Department of State announced:

> The Government of the United States has grave doubts that the American Committee on Dependent Territories can fulfill the tasks thus assigned to it[2] without endangering principles which all American States have accepted in inter-American agreements or in the Charter of the United Nations. It is this Government's view that problems resulting from the status of the territories referred to, which exist or may develop, can and should be settled under procedures which do not involve the risk of violating these principles and for which adequate provision is made in the Charter of the United Nations. The United States, therefore, does not plan to appoint a representative to the Committee on Dependent Territories. . . . In view of the important questions of principle involved, the United States may wish to express its views when the reports [of the committee] are transmitted to it.[3]

The committee devoted a large portion of its discussions during its first meeting to the status of Puerto Rico. It was agreed after debate that, without suspending consideration of the question, members of the Council of OAS should be asked "whether or not Resolution XXXIII of the Bogotá Conference authorized the American Committee on Dependent Territories to study the situation of an American Territory under the sovereignty and effective jurisdiction of any American State." In so deciding, the committee declared that "in view of the present economic, political, and social situation in Puerto Rico, the Committee hopes that this nation will have an opportunity to express itself definitely and freely so as to decide its own destiny."[4] In answer to the committee's request, affirmative answers were received from Costa Rica, Cuba, and Guatemala; negative replies were submitted by Bolivia, Colombia, the Dominican Republic, El Salvador, Honduras, Mexico, Paraguay, Peru, the United States, and Venezuela. As of July 21, 1949, no replies had been received from the remaining states.[5]

1 Public Law 283, 81st Cong., 1st sess.
2 Department of State, *Treaties and Other International Acts Series* 1974.
3 *Ibid.*, 1977.   4 *Ibid.*, 1996.   5 *Ibid.*, 1939.   6 *Ibid.*, 1986.   7 *Ibid.*, 1991.
8 House Report 1123, 81st Cong., 1st sess.
1 Council of the Organization of American States, Document C–sa–17–E, February 2, 1949. See *Documents, X, 1948*, p. 503.
2 The committee's task was to centralize information on, study the situation of, and prepare reports on territories in the Americas which were under the jurisdiction of extra-continental powers.
3 Department of State Press Release 123, March 4, 1949.
4 Pan American Union, *Congress and Conference Series* 60.
5 *Ibid.*, p. 7.

(1) *Statement by the Alternate Representative of the United States to the Council of the Organization of American States (Sanders) on the Competence of the American Committee on Dependent Territories, Made before the Council, April 21, 1949.*[6]

I have no comments to make on the procedure suggested by the Chairman to refer these subjects to the appropriate Committees of the Council, but in the thought that it might be of some interest, I should like to express a few views on the second subject, namely, the Resolution of the Committee of Havana in regard to the subject of Puerto Rico. The immediate question put before the Council by virtue of the resolution adopted by the American Committee on Dependent Territories is whether the Council believes that Resolution XXXIII of the Bogotá Conference should be interpreted so as to authorize the Committee to study and report on the situation in Puerto Rico.

There is considerable doubt, I believe, as to whether the Council itself is authorized to render to the Committee — which is not linked to it by any direct connection — an interpretation of a resolution of an Inter-American Conference. It is my impression that, in the absence of any provision to the contrary, only the parties to such a resolution can determine its intent. For the Council to formulate a reply to the Committee would, therefore, require referral of the matter to the governments for their decision.

It is doubtful whether the problem is important enough to warrant such formal and time-consuming attention.

For my Government, I can say that at no time did our Delegation at Bogotá believe that Resolution XXXIII contemplated that the Committee which it established would investigate the situation in Puerto Rico. The Secretary of State of the United States made clear the position of this Government at Bogotá concerning the questions raised under the agenda item of "European Colonies in America," which gave rise to Resolution XXXIII. Had the question of Puerto Rico been discussed, I am sure the United States Delegation would also have made its position in this respect clear at the time.

The policy of my Government toward Puerto Rico is well known and does not require any exposition here. We have consistently favored the increasing self-government of Puerto Rico. The Puerto Rican people now not only elect their own legislature, but also their own governor. They, therefore, enjoy a greater measure of self-government than any territory of the United States, outside the 48 states of the Union. President Truman has publicly stated the view that the people of Puerto Rico should be given full opportunity to choose any one of four types of political status, including full independence.

The situation in Puerto Rico, including the views of its people and the policy of the United States Government, is an open book which the United States is entirely happy to have anyone read. In conformity with the pertinent provisions of the United Nations Charter, full information on economic, social and educational conditions in that territory has been submitted to the

6 Council of the Organization of American States, Document C–a–27/49, n.d. p. 865.

General Assembly. Although not required to do so by the Charter, the United States has also furnished information on the political status of Puerto Rico. These reports are available to all members of the United Nations.

A few days ago, the elected representatives of the people of Puerto Rico, on their own initiative, expressed their view in regard to the possible investigation of their situation by the Committee in Habana. The Honorable Members of this Council are no doubt familiar with the resolution which was approved unanimously by both Houses of the Puerto Rican Legislature on April 15th and 16th. In this resolution, the Legislature, while appreciating any expression of friendly feeling for its people, very clearly stated that it did not welcome any intervention of any type or for whatever motive in the political, economic or social relations of the Puerto Rican people with those of the United States.

It is a fundamental part of the policy of my Government not to attempt to influence the Puerto Rican people in the determination of their preferences regarding their future political status. Nor do we feel that any other state or group of states should attempt to exert such influence. In accordance with this policy, and having in mind particularly the very clear opinion expressed by the entire legislature of Puerto Rico, my Government perceives no need for the Habana Committee, however well-intentioned may be its motives to pursue this question any further.

3. RELATIONS WITH PARTICULAR COUNTRIES OF LATIN AMERICA

A. Argentina

On May 16, 1949, the United States announced the formation of a joint United States–Argentine commission to study business and commercial problems involved in the widening of trade between the two countries.[1] As a result of subsequent discussions between the Argentine Ambassador (Remorino) and Department of State officials, the commission commenced consultations later in the month. The United States section of the commission was headed by Rollin S. Atwood, acting chief of the Division of River Plate Affairs, Department of State; Dr. Juan Scarpati, Economic Counselor of the Argentine embassy, served as chief of the Argentine section.[2] Three new Argentine advisers joined the discussions in July in an attempt to facilitate the work of the commission toward a definite resolution of the two countries' long-standing commercial difficulties.[3] Members of the commission informed the press on November 1 that a completely modernized basis for trade relations would be agreed upon within the next month as a result of the commission's work. The press reported that the understanding would parallel the lines of the Treaty of Friendship, Economic Development and Commerce which was under negotiation with Uruguay.[4] In an interview with the press on December 15, the Assistant Secretary of State for American Republic Affairs (Miller) informed reporters that, under the new accord, trade with Argentina could increase by 75 percent during 1950.[5] The report of the commission's work was submitted to the Argentine Government on December 24, 1949. No further action on the matter was reported during the year.[6]

1 New York Times, May 18, 1949, p. 17.
2 Department of State Press Release 398, May 27, 1949.
3 New York Times, July 16, 1949, p. 5.
4 Ibid., November 2, 1949, p. 17. For further information on the treaty with Uruguay, see this volume, p. 522.
5 New York Times, December 16, 1949, p. 17.
6 Ibid., December 25, 1949, p. 16.

B. Brazil

On March 16, 1949, the report of the Joint Brazil–United States Technical Commission was submitted to President Truman by John Abbink, chairman of the United States section of the commission. The commission established in 1948 to "analyze the factors in Brazil which are tending to promote or to retard the economic development of Brazil," completed and approved its report in Rio de Janeiro on February 7, 1949. The commission reported that "Brazil, in common with the rest of the world, has experienced the impact of unprecedented postwar difficulties in addition to being faced with the complex economic problems which confront a growing, developing country," and analyzed the general problems faced by Brazil in this connection: the need for greater economic development, balance of payments difficulties in the financing of essential imports, and the detrimental effects of inflationary tendencies upon the rapid development of a balanced economy. The report also discussed the development needs in the major sectors of the Brazilian economy and the broad problems of financing economic development.[7]

United States – Brazilian relations were the subject of discussions between President Truman and the Brazilian President Enrico Gaspar Dutra during the latter's state visit to the United States in May 1949. After addressing a joint session of the Congress, President Dutra and the Brazilian Minister of Foreign Affairs (Fernandes) conferred with President Truman and officials of the Department of State on such problems as 1) United States investments in Brazil and their treatment, 2) the economic development of Brazil, 3) arrangements to release frozen credits for the accounts of United States exporters, 4) the application of the technical assistance program, and 5) technical assistance from the United States to stimulate agricultural, industrial, transport, and hydroelectric developments in Brazil.[8] At the conclusion of the discussions a joint statement released by the White House announced that after a discussion of the report of the Joint Brazil–United States Technical Commission it was suggested that technical discussions on the report might later be held with officials of the Brazilian Ministry of Finance, and that instructions had been issued by the two Presidents calling upon technical experts to commence the negotiation of an appropriate treaty which would stimulate the flow of United States private capital into Brazil. Agreement was also reached on the desirability of a joint study of tax relations between the two countries and on the possibility of negotiating a treaty for the elimination of joint taxation. Presidents Truman and Dutra, in a later statement, announced that they had given approval to the negotiation of a cultural convention designed to encourage and stimulate cultural exchange between the two countries.[9] As a preparatory measure for the joint study of tax relations, the Department of State on June 9 requested interested persons to communicate their views and recommendations on that study to the Commissioner of Internal Revenue.[10]

C. Colombia

On October 17, 1949, the Department of State announced that by an identical exchange of notes the United States–Colombian Trade Agreement of September 13, 1935, had been terminated as of December 1, 1949. In a note to the Colombian Ambassador (Zuleta-Angel), the Assistant Secretary of State for American Republic Affairs (Miller) referred to the unsuccessful trade negotiations undertaken by the two governments at Annecy, France, under the General Agreement on Tariffs and Trade,[11] and stated that, since the treaty of 1935 had been entered into "when economic, monetary and fiscal conditions were substantially different from what they are today," the United States delegation at Annecy had recommended the termination of the agreement by mutual consent. With the termination of that agreement and pending the conclusion of new arrangements, commercial relations between the United States and Colombia would be subject to the provisions of the Treaty of Peace, Amity, Navigation, and Commerce signed by the United States

---

7 For the text of the Joint Commission's report, see Department of State Publication 3487.
8 New York Times, May 20, 1949, p. 5.
9 Department of State, Bulletin, XX, p. 696.
10 Department of State Press Release 432, June 9, 1949.
11 For further information on these negotiations, see this volume, p. 407.

and the Republic of New Granada at Bogotá on December 12, 1846.[12] The termination of the 1935 agreement was subsequently proclaimed by President Truman on November 5, 1949.[13]

D. Mexico

Following the abrogation in October 1948 of the agreement of February 21, 1948, regarding farm labor migration arrangements between the United States and Mexico,[14] the two governments announced early in January 1949 their intention to initiate conversations leading to the adoption of a revised agreement covering conditions under which Mexican agricultural workers might be employed for seasonal farm work in the United States. Discussions commenced in Mexico City on January 17, 1949; the United States negotiating body was led by Leslie A. Wheeler, Counselor of the United States Embassy in Mexico.[15] Agreement was reached between the two governments on August 1 when Mr. Wheeler and the Acting Minister of Foreign Affairs of Mexico (Tello) approved arrangements for the employment of Mexican agricultural workers when, in the view of the United States Employment Service, an inadequate supply of such domestic labor existed. The agreement specifically provided that Mexican nationals could not be employed to replace domestic workers nor to depress prevailing wage rates.[16]

E. Panama

As a climax to several days of rioting in Panama, the President of Panama (Chiari) as a result of pressure exerted by the National Police was forced on November 24, 1949, to resign his office in favor of Dr. Arnulfo Arias, defeated presidential candidate in the 1948 elections. Although both the National Assembly and the Supreme Court of Panama had confirmed the Vice President (Chanis) as Mr. Chiari's successor, the National Election Jury, following Dr. Arias' assumption of office, reversed its previous decision by which Domingo Diaz Arosemana had been declared winner of the 1948 elections and announced that Dr. Arias had in fact received a majority of the votes cast at that time.[17] In a statement to the press on November 25, the Assistant Secretary of State for American Republic Affairs (Miller), expressing "profound shock" at political developments in Panama, announced that the United States, without withdrawing its ambassador to Panama (Davis), would withhold recognition from the new regime pending consultations with the other American republics as soon as the situation had been clarified.[18] Secretary Acheson confirmed Mr. Miller's statement on November 30.[19] The resumption of diplomatic relations was announced by Secretary Acheson on December 14.

(1) Statement by the Secretary of State (Acheson) on the Recognition of the Arias Government of Panama. Department of State Press Release, December 14, 1949.[20]

The United States today is renewing diplomatic relations with Panama. This is being done by means of a note which Ambassador Monnett B. Davis has been instructed to deliver to the Government of Panama in reply to a note addressed to this government by Foreign Minister Carlos N. Brin on December 10, 1949.

The decision of this government to take this action was reached after an exchange of views with the other American Republics. It followed upon

12 Department of State Press Release 800, October 17, 1949.
13 Proclamation 2863; *Federal Register*, XIV, p. 6765.
14 For the text of the agreement of February 21, 1948, see *Documents, X, 1948,* p. 533.
15 Department of State Press Release 24, January 12, 1949.
16 Department of State, *Bulletin*, XXI, p. 313.
17 *New York Times*, November 26, 1949, p. 1.
18 *Ibid.;* Department of State, *Bulletin*, XXI, p. 910.
19 *Ibid.*   20 *Ibid.*, p. 990.

receipt of assurances that the government of Arnulfo Arias accepts and will fulfill the international obligations of Panama and upon determination that it is actually in control of the machinery of government and the national territory of Panama and is generally accepted by the populace. There has been no evidence that any intervention or other interference by any foreign government was brought to bear in effecting recent changes in the Government of Panama.

In accordance with my policy statement on Latin America of September 19, 1949, this act of recognition does not constitute approval of the manner in which the present government came into power. We have in fact publicly deplored the means by which the political changes in Panama since November 19 were effected. It is the hope of this government, however, that, with diplomatic relations thus reestablished, the cordial friendship and mutual respect which traditionally have existed between Panama and the United States will continue.

F. Paraguay

Following the resignation of J. Natalicio Gonzalez as President of Paraguay, Dr. Felipe Molas Lopez in a note of March 2, 1949, to the United States Ambassador at Asunción (Warren) announced that on February 27 he had assumed the presidency. Mr. Warren replied to the Paraguayan note on April 13, acknowledging the statement of the Lopez regime that it was in control of the entire country, was furnishing security and guarantees to its people, proposed to achieve institutional normalization by means of free elections, and would continue to respect Paraguay's international commitments. Mr. Warren's reply was stated by the Department of State to constitute the resumption of normal diplomatic relations between the United States and Paraguay.[21] On September 12, the Paraguayan Government informed the United States Chargé d'Affaires in Paraguay (Randolph) that, "in accordance with the pertinent provisions of the national constitution," Federico Chaves had been elected provisional President of Paraguay. In a reply of the same date, Mr. Randolph informed the new Paraguayan Foreign Minister that the United States intended to continue normal diplomatic relations with his government and reiterated its desire to "extend and strengthen the bonds of friendship" between the two nations. The Department of State announced that this decision was taken in accordance with the policy of recognition enunciated by Secretary Acheson in an address before the Pan American Society of New York on September 19, 1949.[22]

G. Uruguay

(1) Treaty of Friendship, Commerce, and Economic Development between the Governments of the United States and Uruguay, Signed at Montevideo, November 23, 1949.[23]

The following agreement, illustrative of the type of treaty envisaged under Article 12 of the Charter of the International Trade Organization, was the first such treaty to be signed by the United States with one of the Latin American states.

The United States of America and the Oriental Republic of Uruguay, desirous of strengthening the bonds of peace and friendship traditionally existing between them and of encouraging closer cultural, economic, and commercial

---

[21] Department of State Press Release 242, April 13, 1949.
[22] Department of State, *Bulletin*, XXI, p. 558. For the text of Secretary Acheson's statement of September 19, see this volume, p. 197.
[23] Department of State Press Release 916, November 23, 1949.

relations between their peoples, and being cognizant of the contributions which may be made toward these ends by arrangements which facilitate and encourage, on bases mutually advantageous, cultural interchange, industrial and economic development, financial and technical cooperation, the investment of capital, and commercial intercourse, have resolved to conclude a Treaty of Friendship, Commerce and Economic Development, based in general upon the principles of national and of most-favored-nation treatment unconditionally accorded, and for that purpose have appointed as their Plenipotentiaries,

The President of the United States of America:

Christian M. Ravndal, Ambassador Extraordinary and Plenipotentiary of the United States of America to the Oriental Republic of Uruguay; and

The President of the Oriental Republic of Uruguay:

Cesar Charlone, Minister of Foreign Affairs;

Who, having communicated to each other their full powers, found to be in due form, have agreed upon the following Articles:

ARTICLE I
(Entry and Basic Personal Rights)

1. Nationals of either High Contracting Party shall be permitted to enter the territories of the other Party and to remain therein: (a) for the purpose of carrying on trade between the territories of the two Parties and for the purpose of engaging in related commercial activities; and (b) for other purposes, subject to the immigration laws.

2. Nationals of either Party, within the territories of the other Party, shall be permitted: (a) to travel therein freely, and to reside at places of their choice; (b) to enjoy liberty of conscience; (c) to hold both private and public religious services; and (d) to gather and to transmit material for dissemination to the public abroad, and otherwise to communicate with other persons inside and outside such territories by mail, telegraph and other means open to general public use.

3. For the purpose of strengthening the friendly relations and understanding between the two countries by encouraging mutual contacts between their peoples, the best facilities practicable shall be made available for travel by tourists, for the distribution of information for tourists, and with respect to the entry, sojourn and departure of visitors.

4. The provisions of the present Article and of Article XVII shall be subject to the right of either Party to apply measures that are necessary to maintain public order and necessary to protect the public health, morals and safety.

ARTICLE II
(Protection of Persons)

1. The nationals of either High Contracting Party within the territories of the other Party shall receive the most constant protection and security, and shall be accorded, in like circumstances and conditions, treatment, protection and security no less favorable than are accorded to the nationals of such other Party for the protection of their persons, rights, and property. This rule shall be applicable also to institutions, juridical persons, and associations.

2. If, within the territories of either Party, a national of the other Party is accused of crime and taken into custody, he shall: (a) receive reasonable and humane treatment; (b) be formally and immediately informed of the accusations against him; (c) be brought to trial promptly, with due regard to the necessary preparation of his defense; and (d) enjoy all means reasonably necessary to his defense, including the services of competent counsel.

ARTICLE III
(Workmen's Compensation and Social Security)

1. Nationals of either High Contracting Party shall be accorded national treatment in the application of laws and regulations within the territories of the other Party that establish a pecuniary compensation, or other benefit or service, on account of disease, injury or death arising out of and in the course of employment or due to the nature of employment.

2. In addition to the rights and privileges provided in paragraph 1 of the present Article, nationals of either Party shall, within the territories of the other Party, be accorded national treatment in the application of laws and regulations establishing systems of compulsory insurance, under which benefits are paid without an individual test of financial need: (a) against loss of wages or earnings due to old age, unemployment, sickness or disability, or (b) against loss of financial support due to the death of father, husband or other person on whom such support had depended.

ARTICLE IV
(Promotion of Investments)

Each High Contracting Party shall at all times accord equitable treatment to the capital of nationals and companies of the other Party. Neither Party shall take unreasonable or discriminatory measures that would impair the legally acquired rights or interests of such nationals and companies in the enterprises which they have established or in the capital, skills, arts or technology which they have supplied. Neither Party shall without appropriate reason deny opportunities and facilities for the investment of capital by nationals and companies of the other Party; nor shall either Party unreasonably impede nationals and companies of the other Party from obtaining on equitable terms the capital, skills, modern techniques and equipment it needs for its economic development.

ARTICLE V
(Activities of Persons and Companies)

1. Nationals and companies of either High Contracting Party shall be accorded, within the territories of the other Party, national treatment with respect to:

(a) engaging in commercial, manufacturing, processing, financial, construction, publishing, scientific, educational, religious, philanthropic and professional activities;

(b) obtaining and maintaining patents of invention, and rights in trade marks, trade names, trade labels and industrial property of all kinds; and

(c) having access to the courts of justice and to administrative tribunals and agencies, in all degrees of jurisdiction, both in pursuit and in defense of their rights.

2. Nationals and companies of either Party shall further be accorded, within the territories of the other Party, in cases in which national treatment cannot be granted, most-favored-nation treatment with respect to:

(a) exploring for and exploiting mineral deposits;

(b) engaging in fields of economic and cultural activity in addition to those enumerated in sub-paragraph (a) of paragraph 1 of the present Article or in sub-paragraph (a) of the present paragraph;

(c) organizing, participating in and operating companies of such other
    Party.

3. Nationals of either Party admitted into the territories of the other Party
for limited purposes shall not, however, enjoy rights to engage in gainful occu-
pations in contravention of limitations expressly imposed, according to law,
as a condition of their admittance.

4. Nationals and companies of either Party shall be permitted to engage,
within the territories of the other Party, technical experts, executive personnel, attorneys, agents and other specialized employees of their choice,
regardless of nationality. Technical experts so engaged shall be permitted,
among other functions, to make examinations, audits and technical investigations exclusively for, and to render reports to, such nationals and companies in connection with the planning and operation of their enterprises and
enterprises in which they have a financial interest within the territories of
such other Party, regardless of the extent to which such experts may have
qualified for the practice of a profession within such territories.

ARTICLE VI
(Operating through Local Companies)

1. Nationals and companies of either High Contracting Party shall be accorded within the territories of the other Party the right to organize companies for engaging in commercial, manufacturing, processing, construction,
mining, financial, educational, philanthropic, religious and scientific activities,
and to control and manage enterprises which have been lawfully established
by them within such territories for the foregoing and other purposes.

2. Companies, controlled by nationals and companies of either Party and
constituted under the applicable laws and regulations within the territories
of the other Party for engaging in the activities listed in paragraph 1 of the
present Article, shall be accorded national treatment therein with respect to
such activities.

ARTICLE VII
(Property Rights)

1. Nationals and companies of the Oriental Republic of Uruguay shall be
accorded, within the territories of the United States of America:

(a) national treatment with respect to leasing land, buildings and other
    real property appropriate to the conduct of commercial, manufactur-
    ing, processing, financial, construction, publishing, scientific, educa-
    tional, religious, philanthropic and professional activities and for resi-
    dential and mortuary purposes and with respect to occupying and using
    such property; and
(b) other rights in real property permitted by the applicable laws of the
    states, territories and possessions of the United States of America.

2. Nationals and companies of the United States of America shall be accorded, within the territories of the Oriental Republic of Uruguay, national
treatment with respect to acquiring by purchase, or otherwise, and with respect to owning, occupying and using land, buildings and other real property.
However, in the case of any such national domiciled in, or any such company
constituted under the laws of, any state, territory or possession of the United
States of America that accords less than national treatment to nationals and
companies of the Oriental Republic of Uruguay in this respect, the Oriental
Republic of Uruguay shall not be obligated to accord treatment more favor-

able in this respect than such state, territory or possession accords to nationals and companies of the Oriental Republic of Uruguay.

3. Nationals and companies of either High Contracting Party shall be permitted freely to dispose of property within the territories of the other Party with respect to the acquisition of which through testate or intestate succession their alienage has prevented them from receiving national treatment, and they shall be permitted a term of at least five years in which to effect such disposition.

4. Nationals and companies of either Party shall be accorded within the territories of the other Party:

(a) most-favored-nation treatment with respect to acquiring, by purchase or otherwise, and with respect to owning and possessing all kinds of personal property, both tangible and intangible; and

(b) national treatment with respect to disposing of property of all kinds.

ARTICLE VIII
(Protection of Property)

1. The dwellings, offices, warehouses, factories and other premises of nationals and companies of either High Contracting Party located within the territories of the other Party shall receive, with respect to entry and other interventions, the full protection of the measures and procedures established by law and of the standards and principles expressed in Article II of the present Treaty. Official searches and examinations of such premises and their contents, when necessary, shall be made with careful regard for the convenience of the occupants and the conduct of business.

2. Property of nationals and companies of either Party shall receive the most constant protection and security within the territories of the other Party. The taking of property legally acquired by the nationals and companies of either Party within the territories of the other Party shall be subject to procedures and conditions no less favorable than those legally applicable in the case of the taking of the property of nationals of such other Party. Any expropriation shall be made in accordance with the applicable laws, which shall at least assure the payment of just compensation in a prompt, adequate and effective manner.

3. Nationals and companies of either Party shall in no case be accorded, within the territories of the other Party, less than national treatment with respect to the matters set forth in the present Article. Moreover, enterprises in which nationals and companies of either Party have a substantial interest shall be accorded, within the territories of the other Party, not less than national treatment in all matters relating to the taking of privately owned enterprises into public ownership and the placing of such enterprises under public control.

ARTICLE IX
(Taxation of Persons and Companies)

1. Nationals of either Party residing within the territories of the other Party, and nationals and companies of either Party engaged in trade or business or in scientific, educational, religious or philanthropic activities within the territories of the other Party, shall not be subject to the payment of taxes, fees or charges imposed upon or applied to income, capital, transactions, activities or any other object, or to requirements with respect to the levy and collection thereof, within the territories of such other Party, more burdensome than those borne by nationals and companies of such other Party.

2. With respect to nationals of either Party who are not resident or who are not engaged in trade or business within the territories of the other Party, and with respect to companies of either Party which are not engaged in trade or business within the territories of the other Party, most-favored-nation treatment shall apply.

3. In the case of companies of either Party engaged in business within the territories of the other Party, and in the case of nationals of either Party engaged in business within the territories of the other Party but not resident therein, such other Party shall not impose or apply any internal tax, fee or charge upon any income, capital or other similar basis in excess of that which corresponds to the business carried on or the capital invested in its territories, or grant deductions and exemptions less than those reasonably allocable or apportionable, on a similar basis, to its territories. A like rule shall apply also in the case of companies organized and operated exclusively for scientific, educational, religious or philanthropic purposes.

4. Each Party, however, reserves the right to: (a) extend specific advantages as to taxes, fees and charges to nationals, residents and companies of all foreign countries on the basis of reciprocity; (b) accord to nationals, residents and companies of a third country special advantages by virtue of an agreement with such country for the avoidance of double taxation or the mutual protection of revenue; and (c) accord to its non-resident nationals and to residents of contiguous countries more favorable exemptions of a personal nature than are accorded to other non-resident persons.

ARTICLE X
(Commercial Travelers)

Commercial travelers representing nationals and companies of either High Contracting Party engaged in business within the territories thereof shall, upon their entry into and departure from the territories of the other Party and during their sojourn therein, be accorded most-favored-nation treatment in respect of customs and other rights and privileges, including, subject to the exceptions in paragraph 3 of Article IX, taxes and charges applicable to them, their samples and the taking of orders.

ARTICLE XI
(Entry of Goods)

1. Each High Contracting Party shall accord most-favored-nation treatment to products of the other Party, from whatever place and by whatever type of carrier arriving, and to articles destined for exportation to the territories of such other Party, by whatever route and by whatever type of carrier, in all matters relating to customs duties and other charges, internal taxation, sale, storage, distribution, and use, and with respect to all other regulations, requirements and formalities imposed on or in connection with imports and exports.

2. Neither Party shall impose any prohibition or restriction on the importation of any product of the other Party, or on the exportation of any article to the territories of the other Party, that:

(a) if imposed on sanitary or other customary grounds of a non-commercial nature or in the interest of preventing deceptive or unfair practices, arbitrarily discriminates in favor of the importation of the like product of, or the exportation of the like article to, any third country;

(b) if imposed on other grounds, does not apply equally to the importation of the like product of, or the exportation of the like article to, any third country; or

(c) if a quantitative regulation involving allotment to any third country with respect to an article in which such other Party has an important interest, fails to afford to the commerce of such other Party a share proportionate to the amount by quantity or value supplied by or to such other Party during a previous representative period, due consideration being given to any special factors affecting the trade in the article.

3. As used in the present Treaty the term "products of" means "articles the growth, produce or manufacture of." The provisions of the present Article shall not apply to advantages accorded by either Party:

(a) to products of its national fisheries;
(b) to adjacent countries in order to facilitate frontier traffic; or
(c) by virtue of a customs union of which either Party, after consultation with the other Party, may become a member.

ARTICLE XII
(Customs Administration)

1. Each High Contracting Party shall promptly publish laws, regulations and administrative rulings of general application pertaining to rates of duty, taxes or other charges, to the classification of articles for customs purposes, and to requirements or restrictions on imports and exports or the transfer of payments therefor, or affecting their sale, distribution or use; and shall administer such laws, regulations and rulings in a uniform, impartial and reasonable manner. As a general practice, new administrative requirements affecting imports, with the exception of requirements imposed on grounds of sanitation or public safety, shall not go into effect before the expiration of 30 days after publication, or, alternatively, shall not apply to articles en route at time of publication.

2. Each Party shall provide some administrative or judicial procedure under which nationals and companies of the other Party, and importers of products of such other Party, shall be able to obtain prompt review and correction, if necessary, of administrative action relating to customs matters, including the imposition of fines and penalties, confiscations, and rulings on questions of customs classification and valuation by the customs authorities.

The Parties shall afford to importers reasonable opportunity to obtain advice from the competent authorities regarding classification, valuation and duties on merchandise.

ARTICLE XIII
(Internal Treatment of Goods)

1. Products of either High Contracting Party shall be accorded, within the territories of the other Party, national treatment in all matters affecting internal taxation, sale, storage, distribution and use.

2. Articles produced by nationals and companies of either Party within the territories of the other Party, or by companies of the latter Party controlled by such nationals and companies, shall be accorded therein treatment no less favorable than that accorded to like articles of national origin by whatever person or company produced, in all matters affecting exportation, taxation, sale, distribution, storage and use.

ARTICLE XIV
(State Trading)

1. Each High Contracting Party undertakes (a) that enterprises owned or controlled by its Government, and that monopolies or agencies granted ex-

clusive or special privileges within its territories, shall make their purchases and sales involving either imports or exports affecting the commerce of the other Party solely in accordance with commercial considerations, including price, quality, availability, marketability, transportation and other conditions of purchase or sale; and (b) that the nationals, companies and commerce of such other Party shall be afforded adequate opportunity, in accordance with customary business practice, to compete for participation in such purchases and sales.

2. Each Party shall accord to the nationals, companies and commerce of the other Party fair and equitable treatment, as compared with that accorded to the nationals, companies and commerce of any third country, with respect to: (a) the governmental purchase of supplies, (b) the awarding of concessions and other government contracts, and (c) the sale of any service sold by the Government or any monopoly or agency granted exclusive or special privileges.

3. The two Parties agree that business practices which restrain competition, limit access to markets or foster monopolistic control, and which are engaged in or made effective by one or more private or public commercial enterprises or by combination, agreement or other arrangement among such enterprises may have harmful effects upon commerce between their respective territories. Accordingly, each Party agrees upon the request of the other Party to consult with respect to any such practices and to take such measures as it deems appropriate with a view to eliminating such harmful effects.

ARTICLE XV
(Exchange Control)

1. Financial transactions between the territories of the two High Contracting Parties shall be accorded by each Party treatment no less favorable than that accorded to like transactions between the territories of that Party and the territories of any third country. Without prejudice to the provisions of paragraph 4 of the present Article, each Party, however, reserves the rights and obligations it may have under the Articles of Agreement of the International Monetary Fund.

2. Nationals and companies of either Party shall be accorded by the other Party national and most-favored-nation treatment with respect to financial transactions between the territories of the two Parties or between the territories of such other Party and of any third country.

3. In general, any control imposed by either Party over financial transactions shall, subject to the reservations set forth in paragraph 1 of the present Article, be so administered as not to influence disadvantageously the competitive position of the commerce or investment of capital of the other Party in comparison with the commerce or the investment of capital of any third country.

4. Nationals and companies of either Party shall be permitted freely to introduce capital funds into the territories of the other Party and to withdraw therefrom by obtaining exchange in the currency of their own country earnings, whether in the form of salaries, interest, dividends, commissions, royalties or otherwise, and funds for amortization of loans, for transfers of compensation for property referred to in paragraph 2 of Article VIII, and funds for capital transfers. If more than one rate of exchange is in force, such withdrawal shall be at an effective rate of exchange, inclusive of any taxes or surcharges on exchange transfers, that is just and reasonable. However, a Party shall retain the right in periods of exchange stringency to apply exchange restrictions to assure the availability of foreign exchange for payments for

goods and services essential to the health and welfare of its people. In the event that either Party applies such restrictions it shall within a period of three months make reasonable and specific provision for the withdrawals referred to, giving consideration to special needs for other transactions, and shall afford the other Party adequate opportunity for consultation at any time regarding such provision and other matters affecting withdrawals. Such provision shall be reviewed in consultation with the other Party at intervals of not more than twelve months.

5. The treatment prescribed in the present Article shall apply to all forms of control of financial transactions, including (a) limitations upon the availability of media necessary to effect such transactions, (b) rates of exchange, and (c) prohibitions, restrictions, delays, taxes, charges and penalties on such transactions; and shall apply whether a transaction takes place directly, or through an intermediary in another country. As used in the present Article, the term "financial transactions" means all international payments and transfers of funds effected through the medium of currencies, securities, bank deposits, dealings in foreign exchange or other financial arrangements, regardless of the purpose or nature of such payments and transfers.

ARTICLE XVI

1. Between the territories of the two High Contracting Parties there shall be freedom of commerce and navigation.

2. Vessels under the flag of either Party, and carrying the papers required by its law in proof of nationality, shall be deemed to be vessels of that Party both on the high seas and within the ports, places and waters of the other party.

3. Vessels of either Party shall have liberty, on equal terms with vessels of the other Party and on equal terms with vessels of any third country, to come with their cargoes to all ports, places and waters of such other Party open to foreign commerce and navigation. Such vessels and cargoes shall in all respects be accorded national and most-favored-nation treatment within the ports, places and waters of such other Party; but each Party may reserve exclusive rights and privileges to its own vessels with respect to the coasting trade, inland navigation and national fisheries.

4. Vessels of either Party shall be accorded national and most-favored-nation treatment by the other Party with respect to the right to carry all articles that may be carried by vessel to or from the territories of such other Party; and such articles shall be accorded treatment no less favorable than that accorded like articles carried in vessels of such other Party, with respect to: (a) duties and charges of all kinds, (b) the administration of the customs, and (c) bounties, drawbacks and other privileges of this nature.

5. Vessels of either Party that are in distress shall be permitted to take refuge in the nearest port or haven of the other Party, and shall receive friendly treatment and assistance.

6. The term "vessels", as used herein, means all types of vessels, whether privately owned or operated, or publicly owned or operated; but this term does not, except with reference to paragraph 5 of the present Article, include fishing vessels or vessels of war.

ARTICLE XVII
(Transit)

There shall be freedom of transit through the territories of each High Contracting Party by the routes most convenient for international transit:

(a) for nationals of the other Party, together with their baggage;
(b) for other persons, together with their baggage, en route to or from the territories of such other Party; and
(c) for articles en route to or from the territories of such other Party.

Such persons and articles in transit shall be exempt from transit, customs and other duties, and from unreasonable charges and requirements; and shall be free from unnecessary delays and restrictions. They shall, however, be subject to measures referred to in paragraph 4 of Article I, and to non-discriminatory regulations necessary to prevent abuse of the transit privilege.

ARTICLE XVIII
(General Exceptions)

1. The present Treaty shall not preclude the application of measures:

(a) regulating the importation or exportation of gold or silver;
(b) relating to fissionable materials, to radioactive by-products of the utilization of processing thereof or to materials that are the source of fissionable materials;
(c) regulating the production of or traffic in arms, ammunition and implements of war, or traffic in other materials carried on directly or indirectly for the purpose of supplying a military establishment.
(d) necessary to fulfill the obligations of a High Contracting Party for the maintenance or restoration of international peace and security, or necessary to protect its essential security interests;
(e) denying to any company in the ownership or direction of which nationals of any third country or countries have directly or indirectly a controlling interest, the advantages of the present Treaty, except with respect to recognition of juridical status and with respect to access to courts.

2. Without prejudice to the obligations of either Party under any other existing or future international agreement, the most-favored-nation provisions of the present Treaty shall not apply: (a) to advantages accorded by the United States of America or its territories and possessions, irrespective of any future change in their political status, to one another, to the Republic of Cuba, to the Republic of the Philippines, to the Trust Territory of the Pacific Islands or to the Panama Canal Zone; and (b) to the advantages accorded by the Oriental Republic of Uruguay exclusively to the Republic of Bolivia or to the Republic of Paraguay, provided such advantages are not extended to a third country.

3. The provisions of the present Treaty relating to the treatment of goods shall not preclude action by either Party which is required or specifically permitted by the General Agreement on Tariffs and Trade or the Havana Charter for an International Trade Organization during such time as such Party is a contracting party to the General Agreement or is a member of the International Trade Organization. Similarly, the most-favored-nation provisions of the present Treaty shall not apply to special advantages accorded by virtue of the aforesaid Agreement or Charter.

4. The present Treaty does not accord any rights to engage in political activities.

5. No enterprise of either Party which is publicly owned or controlled shall, if it engages in commercial manufacturing, processing, shipping or other business activities within the territories of the other Party, claim or enjoy, either for itself or for its property, immunity therein from taxation, suit, exe-

cution of judgment or other liability to which privately owned and controlled enterprises are subject therein.

ARTICLE XIX
(Definitions)

1. The term "national treatment" means treatment accorded within the territories of a High Contracting Party upon terms no less favorable than the treatment accorded therein, in like situations, to nationals, companies, products, vessels or other objects, as the case may be, of such Party.

2. The term "most-favored-nation treatment" means treatment accorded within the territories of a Party upon terms no less favorable than the treatment accorded therein, in like situations, to nationals, companies, products, vessels or other objects, as the case may be, of any third country.

3. As used in the present Treaty, the term "companies" means corporations, partnerships, companies and other associations, whether or not with limited liability and whether or not for pecuniary profit. Companies constituted under the applicable laws and regulations within the territories of either Party shall be deemed companies thereof and shall have the rights which pertain to them as juridical persons recognized within the territories of the other Party. It is understood that the recognition of such rights does not of itself confer rights upon companies to engage regularly in the business activities for which they are organized.

4. National treatment accorded under the provisions of the present Treaty to companies of the Oriental Republic of Uruguay shall, in any state, territory or possession of the United States of America, be the treatment accorded therein to companies created or organized in other states, territories and possessions of the United States of America.

ARTICLE XX
(Territorial Application)

Except as may be otherwise provided, the territories to which the present Treaty extends shall comprise all areas of land and water under the sovereignty or authority of either of the High Contracting Parties, other than the Panama Canal Zone, and other than the Trust Territory of the Pacific Islands except to the extent that the President of the United States of America shall by proclamation extend provisions of the Treaty to such Trust Territory.

ARTICLE XXI
(Settlement of Disputes)

1. Either of the High Contracting Parties shall at any time grant to the other Party adequate opportunity for consultation with respect to the matters dealt with in the present Treaty.

2. Any dispute between the Parties as to the interpretation or application of the present Treaty, not satisfactorily adjusted by diplomacy or other pacific means, shall be submitted to the International Court of Justice.

ARTICLE XXII
(Ratification and Termination)

1. The present Treaty shall be ratified, and the ratifications thereof shall be exchanged at Washington as soon as possible.

2. The present Treaty shall enter into force on the day of exchange of ratifications. It shall remain in force for ten years from that day and shall continue in force thereafter until terminated as provided herein.

3. Either High Contracting Party may, by giving one year's written notice to the other Party, terminate the present Treaty at the end of the initial ten-year period or at any time thereafter.

IN WITNESS WHEREOF the respective Plenipotentiaries have signed the present Treaty and have affixed hereunto their seals.

DONE in duplicate, in the English and Spanish languages, both equally authentic, at Montevideo, this twenty-third day of November, one thousand nine hundred forty-nine.

PROTOCOL

At the time of signing the Treaty of Friendship, Commerce and Economic Development between the United States of America and the Oriental Republic of Uruguay, the undersigned Plenipotentiaries, duly authorized by their respective Governments, have further agreed on the following provisions, which shall be considered integral parts of the aforesaid Treaty:

1. Rights and privileges with respect to commercial, manufacturing and processing activities accorded, by the provisions of the Treaty, to privately owned and controlled enterprises of either High Contracting Party within the territories of the other Party shall extend to rights and privileges of an economic nature granted to publicly owned or controlled enterprises of such other Party, in situations in which such publicly owned or controlled enterprises operate in fact in competition with privately owned and controlled enterprises. The preceding sentence shall not, however, apply to subsidies granted to publicly owned or controlled enterprises in connection with: (a) manufacturing or processing goods for government use, or supplying goods and services to the government for government use; or (b) supplying, at prices substantially below competitive prices, the needs of particular population groups for essential goods and services not otherwise practically obtainable by such groups.

2. With reference to paragraph 1 of Article I of the Treaty, so long as the United States of America permits the entry into its territories of nationals of the Oriental Republic of Uruguay upon terms substantially as favorable as those applicable upon the date of signature of the Treaty, the Oriental Republic of Uruguay undertakes to permit nationals of the United States of America freely to enter its territories, subject to measures necessary to maintain public order and to protect the public health, morals and safety.

3. The term "mineral", as used in Article V, paragraph 2 (b), refers to petroleum as well as to other mineral substances.

4. The term "financial" as used in Article V and VI shall not extend to banking that involves a trust or fiduciary function, or that involves receiving deposits except as may be incidental to international or foreign business of the banking enterprise.

5. Without prejudice to the obligations of either Party under any other international agreement, the provisions of the present Treaty shall not be construed to restrict the utilization by a Party of accumulated inconvertible currencies.

6. The provisions of Article XIV, paragraph 2 (b) and (c), and of Article XVI, paragraph 4, shall not apply to postal services.

7. The Uruguayan tax system applicable to absentee land-holders (established by Law No. 5377 of January 14, 1916) shall not be affected by the provisions of the Treaty.

8. Nothing in the Treaty shall be construed to limit or restrict in any way the advantages accorded by the Convention Facilitating the Work of Traveling Salesmen signed at Washington August 27, 1918.

9. Article XX does not apply to territories under the authority of either Party solely by reason of temporary military occupation.

10. It is understood that the second sentence of paragraph 1 of Article XII shall not apply to requirements necessary to protect the balance of payments of either Party.

11. It is understood that for the purposes of paragraph 1 of Article XV availability of means of payment is considered to be a commercial consideration.

IN WITNESS WHEREOF the respective Plenipotentiaries have signed this Protocol and have affixed hereunto their seals.

DONE in duplicate, in the English and Spanish languages, both equally authentic, at Montevideo, this twenty-third day of November, one thousand nine hundred forty-nine.

ADDITIONAL PROTOCOL

At the time of signing the Treaty of Friendship, Commerce and Economic Development between the United States of America and the Oriental Republic of Uruguay, the undersigned Plenipotentiaries, duly authorized by their respective Governments, have further agreed upon the following provisions, which shall be considered integral parts of the aforesaid Treaty:

1. The provisions of paragraphs 2 (b) and 2 (c) of Article XI of the Treaty shall not obligate either High Contracting Party with respect to the application of quantitative restrictions on imports and exports:

(a) that have effect equivalent to exchange restrictions authorized in conformity with section 3 (b) of Article VII of the Articles of Agreement of the International Monetary Fund;

(b) that are necessary to secure the equitable distribution among the several consuming countries of goods in short supply; or

(c) that have effect equivalent to exchange restrictions permitted under section 2 of Article XIV of the Articles of Agreement of the International Monetary Fund.

2. Restrictions applied by either Party pursuant to sub-paragraph (c), paragraph 1, of the present Protocol shall, comformable with a policy designed to promote the maximum development of non-discriminatory multilateral trade and to expedite the attainment of a balance of payments position which will obviate the necessity of such restrictions, depart no more than necessary from the provisions of paragraph 2 (b) and 2(c) of Article XI of the Treaty.

IN WITNESS WHEREOF the respective Plenipotentiaries have signed this Protocol and have affixed hereunto their seals.

DONE in duplicate, in the English and Spanish languages, both equally authentic, at Montevideo, this twenty-third day of November, one thousand nine hundred forty-nine.

4. RELATIONS WITH CANADA

For further information on United States relations with Canada during the year under review, see this volume as follows: on tripartite atomic energy discussion, p. 271; on economic and financial problems, p. 382.

A. Joint Defense

On April 12, 1949, a Joint United States-Canada Industrial Mobilization Committee was created by an exchange of notes between the two governments.[1] Dr. John R. Steelman, acting chairman of the National Security Resources Board, and Donald F. Carpenter, chairman of the Munitions Board, represented the United States on the committee; Harry J. Carmichael, chairman of the Industrial Defense Board, and S. D. Pierce, associate deputy minister in the Department of Trade and Commerce, served as the Canadian members of the joint committee.[2] The functions of the committee were outlined as follows:

(i) Exchange information with a view to the coordination of the plans of the United States and Canada for Industrial Mobilization;

---

[1] Department of State, *Treaties and Other International Acts Series* 1889.
[2] Department of State, *Bulletin*, XX, p. 725.

(ii) Consider what recommendations in the field of Industrial Mobilization planning, in areas of common concern, should be made to each Government;

(iii) Be empowered to organize Joint Sub-Committees from time to time to facilitate the discharge of its functions;

(iv) Be responsible for cooperation with the Permanent Joint Board of Defense on matters of Industrial Mobilization.[3]

B. Proposed St. Lawrence Seaway

[See *Documents, IX, 1947,* p. 562; *X, 1948,* p. 540.]

During 1949, seven resolutions urging approval of the Canadian-United States agreement for a St. Lawrence seaway were introduced into the Congress; none was reported from committee. On March 2, 1949, a comprehensive report on the question prepared by various interested government agencies for a Senate foreign relations subcommittee was issued. Questions raised in the course of debate in the 80th Congress (2d session) were analyzed for the benefit of the subcommittee members.[1]

[3] *Ibid.,* p. 537.

[1] For the text of the report to the subcommittee dealing with cost estimates, potential Canadian traffic on the proposed seaway, cost estimates of the Barnhart Island project and the International Rapids project, and the controlling of depths and levels of water at selected ports along the seaway, see *The St. Lawrence Seaway and Power Project. Reports Prepared by Government Agencies for a Subcommittee of the Senate Foreign Relations Committee on Questions Raised during the Debate on S. J. Res. 111 (80 Cong., 2d Sess.), March 2, 1949.* (Committee print.) Washington, 1949.

CHAPTER XIV

Eastern Asia and the Pacific Area

For information on United States economic policy toward eastern Asia and the Pacific area as illustrated through participation in the United Nations Economic Commission for Asia and the Far East, see this volume, p. 187.

1. GENERAL STATEMENTS OF POLICY

(1) *Statement by the Secretary of State (Acheson) on the Basic Principles of Far Eastern Policy, Department of State Press Release, August 5, 1949.*[1]

As you are all aware, the United States is confronted by a situation in China which will test to the full our unity of purpose, our ingenuity, and our adherence to the basic principles which have for half a century governed our policy toward China. The background of that situation and the extensive and persistent efforts of the United States during the past 5 years to assist the Chinese people are fully described in the document which the Department is issuing on August 5. They are summarized in my letter of transmittal to the President. Secretary Marshall in February 1948 confidentially told the Senate Foreign Relations Committee and the House Foreign Affairs Committee in executive session many of the facts which are now being published as well as the conclusions drawn from those facts. He made it clear why public disclosure at that time seemed inadvisable, and I have pointed out in my letter to the President why we feel the information should be made public now. As I also said in that letter, the strength of our system of government is based on an informed and critical public opinion, and it is in order that our people may be fully informed in regard to the background of our Far Eastern policy that this record is now being published.

The situation in China serves to emphasize a vital factor in connection with the question of United States aid to foreign nations — that is, that, while the United States can with the best of intentions contribute substantial aid to a foreign government, it cannot guarantee that that aid will achieve its purpose. The achievement of that purpose must, in the final analysis, depend upon the degree to which the recipient government and people make wise use of our assistance and take effective measures of self-help. Without such action by the recipient, no amount of American aid can avail. This is no less true in China than in other parts of the world.

Our traditional policy of assisting the Chinese people to resist domination by a foreign power or powers is now faced by the gravest difficulties. On the one hand, there is in China a Communist regime which, while in fact serving the imperialist interests of a foreign power, has for the present been able to

[1] Department of State, *Bulletin*, XXI, p. 236.

persuade large numbers of Chinese that it is serving their interests and has been able to extend its sway in constantly widening circles. On the other hand, there is the National Government of China which has been unable to rally its people and has been driven out of extensive and important portions of the country, despite very extensive assistance from the United States and advice from eminent American representatives which subsequent events proved to be sound.

This means that United States policy toward China is confronted by a situation in which alternatives are very sharply limited. We must not base our policy on illusions or wishful thinking. I am convinced however that the basic elements of our traditional policy toward the Far East remain valid now as in the past, and I should like to state certain basic principles by which we should continue to be guided. These are:

1. The United States desires to encourage in every feasible way the development of China as an independent and stable nation able to play a role in world affairs suitable for a great and free people.

2. The United States desires to support the creation in China of economic and political conditions which will safeguard basic rights and liberties and progressively develop the economic and social well-being of its people.

3. The United States is opposed to the subjection of China to any foreign power, to any regime acting in the interest of a foreign power, and to the dismemberment of China by any foreign power, whether by open or clandestine means.

4. The United States will continue to consult with other interested powers, in the light of conditions in the countries concerned and in the Far East as a whole, on measures which will contribute to the continuing security and welfare of the peoples of that area.

5. The United States will encourage and support efforts of the United Nations to achieve these objectives and particularly to maintain peace and security in the Far East.

It is obvious that these basic principles require specification and elaboration in the light of the existing situation in order to be effectively carried out. At the direction of the President, we are taking several concrete steps to this end. The officers of the Department charged with Far Eastern matters are engaged in a comprehensive survey of the impact of developing conditions on our basic policy. In addition, I have enlisted the services in a consultative capacity of Raymond Fosdick, former president of the Rockefeller Foundation, and Everett Case, president of Colgate University, who in collaboration with Ambassador at Large Philip C. Jessup, will advise me and my staff in the Department of State. Mr. Fosdick will be here on Monday [Aug. 8], and Mr. Case will arrive in the Department later this month. We shall be prepared to draw on other assistance as we go along. We shall of course continue to maintain the closest liaison with the National Security Council and the National Military Establishment in working on these problems. On economic and financial matters we shall have the benefit of the experience and knowledge of the Department of the Treasury and of the Economic Cooperation Administration. Throughout all of our study of this problem, we shall maintain contact and close consultation with the members of the Senate Committee on Foreign Relations and the House Committee on Foreign Affairs. All of these steps are designed to bring to bear the united wisdom and resourcefulness of our government in meeting the present situation and any future developments in Asia and the Far East.

Until the thorough review of our Far Eastern policy, which I have just outlined has made substantial progress, I shall wish to restrict my comment on particular aspects of that policy, since any detailed comments now might prejudge the conclusions of our review. I can assure you, however, that the work is being and will be pressed with the greatest possible speed. In the meantime, we will take every opportunity in the day-to-day conduct of our foreign policy to support the five principles I have stated to you. Although I have indicated the seriousness of the situation, I do not in any degree share the defeatist attitude which some current comments reflect. The Chinese Communists, in attempting to establish a totalitarian domination over the Chinese people in the interests of a foreign power and in basing this attempt on a willfully distorted concept of world realities, are committing themselves deeply on the basis of unproved assumptions as to the extent of their own strength and the nature of the reactions which they are bound to provoke in China and elsewhere. The United States, for its part, will be prepared to work with the people of China and of every other country in Asia to preserve and to promote their true interest, developed as they choose and not as dictated by any foreign imperialism.

2. RELATIONS WITH PARTICULAR COUNTRIES IN EASTERN ASIA

A. China

1. GENERAL

On May 1, 1949, communist authorities in China issued a demand that the United Kingdom, France, and the United States withdraw their armed forces from Chinese territories. At the same time, the communist leaders announced their willingness to enter into formal diplomatic relations with foreign states as the effective government of China.[1] Shortly thereafter, the press carried reports that the United States and the United Kingdom had agreed upon the coordination of their policies towards the eventual recognition of the communist government and had further decided to enlist the cooperation of other north Atlantic and Asiatic countries in their planning.[2] Later news reports indicated that the United States had consulted with other non-communist governments in an effort to encourage a common front vis-à-vis the communist regime, to discourage hasty recognition of the communist government,[3] and to coordinate trade policies in order to prevent the future flow of strategic materials into the communist-held areas of Asia.[4] In July the Department of State announced the appointment of special consultants, headed by Ambassador-at-Large Philip C. Jessup, to conduct a general review of United States policy in the far east, with particular reference to China, the Malay states, Indonesia, Burma, Indo-China, Thai-

---

1 *New York Times*, May 1, 1949, p. 1.   2 *Ibid.*, May 19, 1949, p. 11.
3 *Ibid.*, May 26, 1949, p. 4.   4 *Ibid.*, July 2, 1949, p. 1.

land, and India. Other consultants designated were Raymond B. Fosdick, former president of the Rockefeller Foundation, and Everett Case, president of Colgate University.[5] The special consultants did not report on their findings during the year under review.

On August 5, 1949, the Department of State published a "white paper" on United States relations with China. The paper, compiled at the request of President Truman, was accompanied by the following letter of transmittal from the Secretary of State (Acheson).

(1) Letter from the Secretary of State (Acheson) to the President (Truman) Transmitting the Report on United States Relations with China, July 30, 1949. Released by the Department of State, August 5, 1949.[6]

[EXCERPTS]

. . . .

The interest of the people and the Government of the United States in China goes far back into our history. Despite the distance and broad differences in background which separate China and the United States, our friendship for that country has always been intensified by the religious, philanthropic and cultural ties which have united the two peoples, and has been attested by many acts of good will over a period of many years, including the use of the Boxer indemnity for the education of Chinese students, the abolition of extraterritoriality during the Second World War, and our extensive aid to China during and since the close of the war. The record shows that the United States has consistently maintained and still maintains those fundamental principles of our foreign policy toward China which include the doctrine of the Open Door, respect for the administrative and territorial integrity of China, and opposition to any foreign domination of China. It is deplorable that respect for the truth in the compilation of this record makes it necessary to publish an account of facts which reveal the distressing situation in that country. I have not felt, however, that publication could be withheld for that reason.

The record should be read in the light of conditions prevailing when the events occurred. It must not be forgotten, for example, that throughout World War II we were allied with Russia in the struggle to defeat Germany and Italy, and that a prime object of our policy was to bring Russia into the struggle against Japan in time to be of real value in the prosecution of the war. In this period, military considerations were understandably predominant over all others. Our most urgent purpose in the Far East was to defeat the common enemy and save lives of our own men and those of our comrades-in-arms, the Chinese included. We should have failed in our manifest duty had we pursued any other course.

In the years since V-J Day, as in the years before Pearl Harbor, military considerations have been secondary to an earnest desire on our part to assist the Chinese people to achieve peace, prosperity and internal stability. The decisions and actions of our Government to promote these aims necessarily

[5] Department of State, *Bulletin*, XXI, p. 279.   [6] Department of State Publication 3573.

were taken on the basis of information available at the time. Throughout this tragic period, it has been fully realized that the material aid, the military and technical assistance, and the good will of the United States, however abundant, could not of themselves put China on her feet. In the last analysis, that can be done only by China herself.

. . . .

In contrast also to the unity of the people of China in the war against Japan were the divided interests of the leaders of the Kuomintang and of the Chinese Communists. It became apparent in the early forties that the leaders of the Government, just as much as the Communist leaders, were still as preoccupied with the internal struggle for power as they were with waging war against Japan. Once the United States became a participant in the war, the Kuomintang was apparently convinced of the ultimate defeat of Japan and saw an opportunity to improve its position for a show-down struggle with the Communists. The Communists, for their part, seemed to see in the chaos of China an opportunity to obtain that which had been denied them before the Japanese war, namely, full power in China. This struggle for power in the latter years of the war contributed largely to the partial paralysis of China's ability to resist.

It was precisely here that two of the fundamental principles of United States policy in regard to China — noninterference in its internal affairs and support of its unity and territorial integrity — came into conflict and that one of them also conflicted with the basic interests of the Allies in the war against Japan. It seemed highly probable in 1943 and 1944 that, unless the Chinese could subordinate their internal interests to the larger interest of the unified war effort against Japan, Chinese resistance would become completely ineffective and the Japanese would be able to deprive the Allies of valuable bases, operating points and manpower in China at a time when the outcome of the war against Japan was still far from clear. In this situation and in the light of the paramount necessity of the most vigorous prosecution of the war, in which Chinese interests were equally at stake with our own, traditional concepts of policy had to be adapted to a new and unprecedented situation.

After Pearl Harbor we expanded the program of military and economic aid which we had inaugurated earlier in 1941 under the Lend-Lease Act. That program, described in chapter I of the attached record, was far from reaching the volume which we would have wished because of the tremendous demands on the United States from all theaters of a world-wide war and because of the difficulties of access to a China all of whose ports were held by the enemy. Nevertheless it was substantial.

Representatives of our Government, military and civilian, who were sent to assist the Chinese in prosecuting the war soon discovered that, as indicated above, the long struggle had seriously weakened the Chinese Government not only militarily and economically, but also politically and in morale. The reports of United States military and diplomatic officers reveal a growing conviction through 1943 and 1944 that the Government and the Kuomintang had apparently lost the crusading spirit that won them the people's loyalty during the early years of the war. In the opinion of many observers they had sunk into corruption, into a scramble for place and power, and into reliance on the United States to win the war for them and to preserve their own domestic supremacy. The Government of China, of course, had always been a one-party rather than a democratic government in the Western sense. The stresses and strains of war were now rapidly weakening such liberal elements as it did possess and strengthening the grip of the reactionaries who were indistinguishable from the war lords of the past. The mass of the Chinese people were coming more and more to lose confidence in the Government.

It was evident to us that only a rejuvenated and progressive Chinese Government which could recapture the enthusiastic loyalty of the people could and would wage an effective war against Japan. American officials repeatedly brought their concern with this situation to the attention of the Generalissimo and he repeatedly assured them that it would be corrected. He made, however, little or no effective effort to correct it and tended to shut himself off from Chinese officials who gave unpalatable advice. In addition to a concern over the effect which this atrophy of the central Chinese administration must have upon the conduct of the war, some American observers, whose reports are also quoted in the attached record, were concerned over the effect which this deterioration of the Kuomintang must have on its eventual struggle, whether political or military, with the Chinese Communists. These observers were already fearful in 1943 and 1944 that the National Government might be so isolating itself from the people that in the postwar competition for power it would prove itself impotent to maintain its authority. Nevertheless, we continued for obvious reasons to direct all our aid to the National Government.

This was of course the period during which joint prosecution of the war against Nazi Germany had produced a degree of cooperation between the United States and Russia. President Roosevelt was determined to do what he could to bring about a continuance in the postwar period of the partnership forged in the fire of battle. The peoples of the world, sickened and weary with the excesses, the horrors, and the degradation of the war, shared this desire. It has remained for the postwar years to demonstrate that one of the major partners in this world alliance seemingly no longer pursues this aim, if indeed it ever did.

When Maj. Gen. Patrick J. Hurley was sent by President Roosevelt to Chungking in 1944 he found what he considered to be a willingness on the part of the National Government and the Chinese Communists to lay aside their differences and cooperate in a common effort. Already they had been making sporadic attempts to achieve this result.

Previously and subsequently, General Hurley had been assured by Marshal Stalin that Russia had no intention of recognizing any government in

China except the National Government with Chiang Kai-shek as its leader. It may be noted that during the late war years and for a time afterwards Marshal Stalin reiterated these views to American officials. He and Molotov expressed the view that China should look to the United States as the principal possible source of aid. The sentiments expressed by Marshal Stalin were in large part incorporated in the Sino-Soviet treaty of 1945.

From the wartime cooperation with the Soviet Union and from the costly campaigns against the Japanese came the Yalta Agreement. The American Government and people awaited with intense anxiety the assault on the main islands of Japan which it was feared would cost up to a million American casualties before Japan was conquered. The atomic bomb was not then a reality and it seemed impossible that the war in the Far East could be ended without this assault. It thus became a primary concern of the American Government to see to it that the Soviet Union enter the war against Japan at the earliest possible date in order that the Japanese Army in Manchuria might not be returned to the homeland at the critical moment. It was considered vital not only that the Soviet Union enter the war but that she do so before our invasion of Japan, which already had been set for the autumn of 1945.

At Yalta, Marshal Stalin not only agreed to attack Japan within two or three months after V-E Day but limited his "price" with reference to Manchuria substantially to the position which Russia had occupied there prior to 1904. We for our part, in order to obtain this commitment and thus to bring the war to a close with a consequent saving of American, Chinese and other Allied lives, were prepared to and did pay the requisite price. Two facts must not, however, be lost sight of in this connection. First, the Soviet Union when she finally did enter the war against Japan, could in any case have seized all the territories in question and considerably more regardless of what our attitude might have been. Second, the Soviets on their side in the Sino-Soviet Treaty arising from the Yalta Agreement, agreed to give the National Government of China moral and material support and moreover formalized their assurances of noninterference in China's internal affairs. Although the unexpectedly early collapse of Japanese resistance later made some of the provisions of the Yalta Agreement seem unnecessary, in the light of the predicted course of the war at that time they were considered to be not only justified but clearly advantageous. Although dictated by military necessity, the Agreement and the subsequent Sino-Soviet Treaty in fact imposed limitations on the action which Russia would, in any case, have been in a position to take.

For reasons of military security, and for those only, it was considered too dangerous for the United States to consult with the National Government regarding the Yalta Agreement or to communicate its terms at once to Chungking. We were then in the midst of the Pacific War. It was felt that there was grave risk that secret information transmitted to the Nationalist capital at this time would become available to the Japanese almost immediately. Under no circumstances, therefore, would we have been justified in incurring the security risks involved. It was not until June 15, 1945, that General Hurley was authorized to inform Chiang Kai-shek of the Agreement.

In conformity with the Russian agreement at Yalta to sign a treaty of friendship and alliance with Nationalist China, negotiations between the two nations began in Moscow in July 1945. During their course, the United States felt obliged to remind both parties that the purpose of the treaty was to implement the Yalta Agreement — no more, no less — and that some of the Soviet proposals exceeded its provisions. The treaty, which was signed on August 14, 1945, was greeted with general satisfaction both in Nationalist China and in the United States. It was considered that Russia had accepted definite limitations on its activities in China and was committed to withhold all aid from the Chinese Communists. On September 10, however, our embassy in Moscow cautioned against placing undue confidence in the Soviet observance of either the spirit or letter of the treaty. The subsequent conduct of the Soviet Government in Manchuria has amply justified this warning.

When peace came the United States was confronted with three possible alternatives in China: (1) it could have pulled out, lock, stock and barrel; (2) it could have intervened militarily on a major scale to assist the Nationalists to destroy the Communists; (3) it could, while assisting the Nationalists to assert their authority over as much of China as possible, endeavor to avoid a civil war by working for a compromise between the two sides.

The first alternative would, and I believe American public opinion at that time so felt, have represented an abandonment of our international responsibilities and of our traditional policy of friendship for China before we had made a determined effort to be of assistance. The second alternative policy, while it may look attractive theoretically and in retrospect, was wholly impracticable. The Nationalists had been unable to destroy the Communists during the 10 years before the war. Now after the war the Nationalists were, as indicated above, weakened, demoralized, and unpopular. They had quickly dissipated their popular support and prestige in the areas liberated from the Japanese by the conduct of their civil and military officials. The Communists on the other hand were much stronger than they had ever been and were in control of most of North China. Because of the ineffectiveness of the Nationalist forces which was later to be tragically demonstrated, the Communists probably could have been dislodged only by American arms. It is obvious that the American people would not have sanctioned such a colossal commitment of our armies in 1945 or later. We therefore came to the third alternative policy whereunder we faced the facts of the situation and attempted to assist in working out a *modus vivendi* which would avert civil war but nevertheless preserve and even increase the influence of the National Government.

· · · · · · · ·

As the signs of impending disaster multiplied, the President in July 1947, acting on the recommendation of the Secretary of State, instructed Lt. Gen. Albert C. Wedemeyer to survey the Chinese scene and make recommendations. In his report, submitted on September 19, 1947, the General recommended that the United States continue and expand its policy of giving aid to Nationalist China, subject to these stipulations:

1. That China inform the United Nations of her request for aid.

2. That China request the United Nations to bring about a truce in Manchuria and request that Manchuria be placed under a Five-Power guardianship or a trusteeship.

3. That China utilize her own resources, reform her finances, her Government and her armies, and accept American advisers in the military and economic fields.

General Wedemeyer's report, which fully recognized the danger of Communist domination of all China and was sympathetic to the problems of the National Government, nevertheless listed a large number of reforms which he considered essential if that Government were to rehabilitate itself.

.   .   .   .

The reasons for the failures of the Chinese National Government appear in some detail in the attached record. They do not stem from any inadequacy of American aid. Our military observers on the spot have reported that the Nationalist armies did not lose a single battle during the crucial year of 1948 through lack of arms or ammunition. The fact was that the decay which our observers had detected in Chungking early in the war had fatally sapped the powers of resistance of the Kuomintang. Its leaders had proved incapable of meeting the crisis confronting them, its troops had lost the will to fight, and its Government had lost popular support. The Communists, on the other hand, through a ruthless discipline and fanatical zeal, attempted to sell themselves as guardians and liberators of the people. The Nationalist armies did not have to be defeated; they disintegrated. History has proved again and again that a regime without faith in itself and an army without morale cannot survive the test of battle.

The record obviously can not set forth in equal detail the inner history and development of the Chinese Communist Party during these years. The principal reason is that, while we had regular diplomatic relations with the National Government and had the benefit of voluminous reports from our representatives in their territories, our direct contact with the Communists was limited in the main to the mediation efforts of General Hurley and General Marshall.

Fully recognizing that the heads of the Chinese Communist Party were ideologically affiliated with Moscow, our Government nevertheless took the view, in the light of the existing balance of forces in China, that peace could be established only if certain conditions were met. The Kuomintang would have to set its own house in order and both sides would have to make concessions so that the Government of China might become, in fact as well as in name, the Government of all China and so that all parties might function within the constitutional system of the Government. Both internal peace and constitutional development required that the progress should be rapid from one party government with a large opposition party in armed rebellion, to the participation of all parties, including the moderate non-communist elements, in a truly national system of government.

None of these conditions has been realized. The distrust of the leaders of both the Nationalist and Communist Parties for each other proved too deep-seated to permit final agreement, notwithstanding temporary truces and apparently promising negotiations. The Nationalists, furthermore, embarked in 1946 on an over-ambitious military campaign in the face of warnings by General Marshall that it not only would fail but would plunge China into economic chaos and eventually destroy the National Government. General Marshall pointed out that though Nationalist armies could, for a period, capture Communist-held cities, they could not destroy the Communist armies. Thus every Nationalist advance would expose their communications to attack by Communist guerrillas and compel them to retreat or to surrender their armies together with the munitions which the United States has furnished them. No estimate of a military situation has ever been more completely confirmed by the resulting facts.

The historic policy of the United States of friendship and aid toward the people of China was, however, maintained in both peace and war. Since V-J Day, the United States Government has authorized aid to Nationalist China in the form of grants and credits totaling approximately 2 billion dollars, an amount equivalent in value to more than 50 percent of the monetary expenditures of the Chinese Government and of proportionately greater magnitude in relation to the budget of that Government than the United States has provided to any nation of Western Europe since the end of the war. In addition to these grants and credits, the United States Government has sold the Chinese Government large quantities of military and civilian war surplus property with a total procurement cost of over 1 billion dollars, for which the agreed realization to the United States was 232 million dollars. A large proportion of the military supplies furnished the Chinese armies by the United States since V-J Day has however, fallen into the hands of the Chinese Communists through the military ineptitude of the Nationalist leaders, their defections and surrenders, and the absence among their forces of the will to fight.

It has been urged that relatively small amounts of additional aid — military and economic — to the National Government would have enabled it to destroy communism in China. The most trustworthy military, economic, and political information available to our Government does not bear out this view.

A realistic appraisal of conditions in China, past and present, leads to the conclusion that the only alternative open to the United States was full-scale intervention in behalf of a Government which had lost the confidence of its own troops and its own people. Such intervention would have required the expenditure of even greater sums than have been fruitlessly spent thus far, the command of Nationalist armies by American officers, and the probable participation of American armed forces — land, sea, and air — in the resulting war. Intervention of such a scope and magnitude would have been resented by the mass of the Chinese people, would have diametrically reversed our historic policy, and would have been condemned by the American people.

It must be admitted frankly that the American policy of assisting the Chinese people in resisting domination by any foreign power or powers is now confronted with the gravest difficulties. The heart of China is in Communist hands. The Communist leaders have foresworn their Chinese heritage and have publicly announced their subservience to a foreign power, Russia, which during the last 50 years, under czars and Communists alike, has been most assiduous in its efforts to extend its control in the Far East. In the recent past, attempts at foreign domination have appeared quite clearly to the Chinese people as external aggression and as such have been bitterly and in the long run successfully resisted. Our aid and encouragement have helped them to resist. In this case, however, the foreign domination has been masked behind the façade of a vast crusading movement which apparently has seemed to many Chinese to be wholly indigenous and national. Under these circumstances, our aid has been unavailing.

The unfortunate but inescapable fact is that the ominous result of the civil war in China was beyond the control of the government of the United States. Nothing that this country did or could have done within the reasonable limits of its capabilities could have changed that result; nothing that was left undone by this country has contributed to it. It was the product of internal Chinese forces, forces which this country tried to influence but could not. A decision was arrived at within China, if only a decision by default.

And now it is abundantly clear that we must face the situation as it exists in fact. We will not help the Chinese or ourselves by basing our policy on wishful thinking. We continue to believe that, however tragic may be the immediate future of China and however ruthlessly a major portion of this great people may be exploited by a party in the interest of a foreign imperialism, ultimately the profound civilization and the democratic individualism of China will reassert themselves and she will throw off the foreign yoke. I consider that we should encourage all developments in China which now and in the future work toward this end.

In the immediate future, however, the implementation of our historic policy of friendship for China must be profoundly affected by current developments. It will necessarily be influenced by the degree to which the Chinese people come to recognize that the Communist regime serves not their interests but those of Soviet Russia and the manner in which, having become aware of the facts, they react to this foreign domination. One point, however, is clear. Should the Communist regime lend itself to the aims of Soviet Russian imperialism and attempt to engage in aggression against China's neighbors, we and the other members of the United Nations would be confronted by a situation violative of the principles of the United Nations Charter and threatening international peace and security.

Meanwhile our policy will continue to be based upon our own respect for the Charter, our friendship for China, and our traditional support for the Open Door and for China's independence and administrative and territorial integrity.

2. MILITARY AND FINANCIAL AID

[See *Documents, X, 1948*, p. 569.]

During February 1949 the Economic Cooperation Administration ordered the closing of its offices in Peiping and Tientsin, both cities in communist-held areas of China. Thereafter, no further shipments were made to cities within the communist-controlled sections of the country and no stockpiles of supplies were accumulated in cities under the threat of communist capture.[7] During 1949, economic and military assistance to the Chinese Nationalist Government was the subject of various bills introduced in the Congress. One such measure (S.1063), introduced by Senator Pat MacCarran (Nevada) and providing for economic assistance in the amount of $1.5 billion, was strongly opposed by the Department of State. A letter from the Secretary of State (Acheson) to the chairman of the Senate Committee on Foreign Relations (Connally) pointed out, with reference to S.1063, that there was no evidence leading the Department to believe that "the furnishing of additional military material would alter the pattern of current developments in China."[8] No final action was taken during the year on S.1063 nor on two similar measures (H.R.5916 and H.R.5922) introduced in the House of Representatives by Rep. John D. Lodge (Connecticut) and Rep. Francis E. Walter (Pennsylvania) calling for a minimum aid program of $200 million.

The economic cooperation agreement with China, signed on July 3, 1948,[9] was amended by an exchange of notes at Canton on March 26 and 31, 1949. The amended agreement entered into force on March 31. [10]

(1) *Letter from the Secretary of State (Acheson) to the Chairman of the Senate Committee on Foreign Relations (Connally) Concerning Economic and Military Aid to China, March 15, 1949.*[11]

The following comments on S.1063 are offered in response to your request as conveyed by Mr. O'Day, Clerk of the Committee on Foreign Relations, in his letter of February 28, 1949. It is the Department's view that the Bill proposes aid of a magnitude and character unwarranted by present circumstances in China.

Despite the present aid program authorized by the last Congress, together with the very substantial other aid extended by the United States to China since V-J Day, aggregating over $2 billion, the economic and military position of the Chinese Government has deteriorated to the point where the Chinese Communists hold almost all important areas of China from Manchuria to the Yantze River and have the military capability of expanding their control to the populous areas of the Yangtze Valley and of eventually dominating south China. The National Government does not have the military capability of maintaining a foothold in south China against a determined Communist advance. The Chinese Government forces have lost no battles during the past year because of lack of ammunition and equipment, while the Chinese Communist have captured the major portion of military supplies, exclusive of ammunition, furnished the Chinese Government by the United States since V-J Day. There is no evidence that the furnishing of additional military material would alter the pattern of current developments in China. There is, however, ample evidence that the Chinese people are weary of

7 *New York Times*, February 8, 1949, p. 14.   8 Department of State Publication 3573, p. 1052.
9 See *Documents, X, 1948*, p. 569.
10 For the text of the exchange of notes, see Department of State, *Treaties and Other International Acts Series* 1923.
11 Department of State Publication 3573, p. 1053.

hostilities and that there is an overwhelming desire for peace at any price. To furnish solely military material and advice would only prolong hostilities and the suffering of the Chinese people and would arouse in them deep resentment against the United States. Yet, to furnish the military means for bringing about a reversal of the present deterioration and for providing some prospect of successful military resistance would require the use of an unpredictably large American armed force in actual combat, a course of action which would represent direct United States involvement in China's fratricidal warfare and would be contrary to our traditional policy toward China and the interests of this country.

In these circumstances, the extension of as much as $1.5 billion of credits to the Chinese Government, as proposed by the Bill, would embark this Government on an undertaking the eventual cost of which would be unpredictable but of great magnitude, and the outcome of which would almost surely be catastrophic. The field supervision of United States military aid, the pledging of revenue of major Chinese ports in payment of United States aid, United States administration and collection of Chinese customs in such ports, and United States participation in Chinese tax administration, all of which are called for by the Bill, would without question be deeply resented by the Chinese people as an extreme infringement of China's sovereignty and would arouse distrust in the minds of the Chinese people with respect to the motives of the United States in extending aid. While the use of up to $500 million in support of the Chinese currency, as proposed in the Bill, would undoubtedly ease temporarily the fiscal problem of the Chinese Government, stabilization of the Chinese currency cannot be considered feasible so long as the Government's monetary outlays exceed its income by a large margin. After the first $500 million had been expended, the United States would find it necessary to continue provision of funds to cover the Chinese Government's budgetary deficit if the inflationary spiral were not to be resumed. That China could be expected to repay United States financial, economic and military aid of the magnitude proposed, which the Bill indicates should all be on a credit basis, cannot be supported by realistic estimates of China's future ability to service foreign debts even under conditions of peace and economic stability.

The United States has in the past sought to encourage the Chinese Government to initiate those vital measures necessary to provide a basis for economic improvement and political stability. It has recognized that, in the absence of a Chinese Government capable of initiating such measures and winning popular support, United States aid of great magnitude would be dissipated and United States attempts to guide the operations of the Chinese Government would be ineffective and probably lead to direct involvement in China's fratricidal warfare. General Marshall reflected these considerations when he stated in February 1948 that an attempt to underwrite the Chinese economy and the Chinese Government's military effort represented a burden on the United States economy and a military responsibility which he could not recommend as a course of action for this Government.

Despite the above observations, it would be undesirable for the United States precipitously to cease aid to areas under the control of the Chinese Government which it continues to recognize. Future developments in China, including the outcome of political negotiations now being undertaken, are uncertain. Consideration is being given, therefore, to a request for Congressional action to extend the authority of the China Aid Act of 1948 to permit commitment of unobligated appropriations for a limited period beyond April 2, 1949, the present expiration date of the Act. If during such a period, the situation in China clarifies itself sufficiently, further recommendations might be made.

3. THREATS TO THE POLITICAL INDEPENDENCE AND TERRITORIAL INTEGRITY OF CHINA

Following the proclamation of the People's Republic of China by communist leaders on September 21, 1949, the representative of the Chinese Nationalist Government to the United Nations General Assembly (Tsiang), denouncing the communist leaders as Soviet puppets, requested on September 29 that the General Assembly place upon the agenda of its fourth session an additional item concerning "Threats to the political independence and territorial integrity of China and to the peace of the Far East resulting from violations by the Soviet Union of the Treaty of Friendship and Alliance concluded on 14 August 1945 between the Republic of China and the Union of Soviet Socialist Republics,[12] and from violations by the Soviet Union of the Charter of the United Nations."[13] The item, with the support of the representative of the United States (Austin), was subsequently adopted for inclusion by a vote of 45 to 6 with 5 abstentions[14] and referred to the Assembly's Political and Security Committee for consideration. In committee, Australia, Mexico, Pakistan, the Philippines, and the United States introduced a joint resolution calling upon all states to 1) respect the political independence of China and apply the principles of the United Nations charter in their relations with China; 2) have regard for the right of the Chinese people to choose their own political institutions and to maintain a government free of foreign control; 3) observe the provisions of existing treaties relating to China; and 4) refrain from efforts to acquire spheres of influence, to create regimes controlled by foreign powers, or to obtain special privileges in China.[15] The resolution was approved by the committee and adopted in plenary session on December 8, 1949, by a vote of 32 to 5 with 17 abstentions.[6] A second resolution adopted on December 9 referred the question of threats to Chinese independence to the Interim Committee of the General Assembly for "continuous examination and study" in the light of the first resolution.[17]

(1) *Statement by the United States Representative to the United Nations General Assembly (Jessup) on Threats to the Political Independence and Territorial Integrity of China, Made before the Plenary Session of the General Assembly, December 7, 1949.*[18]

[EXCERPTS]

One thing which stood out clearly in the debates in the First Committee on the item which now engages our attention was the strong friendship of the overwhelming majority of nations for China and their concern for its wel-

12 For the text of the treaty of 1945, see *Documents, VIII, 1945–1946*, p. 826.
13 United Nations General Assembly, *Official Records* (4th session), p. 96.
14 *Ibid.*, p. 102.
15 *Ibid.*, Document A/C.1/552, November 28, 1949.
16 *Ibid., Official Records* (4th session), p. 571. For the text of the resolution, see *ibid., Resolutions*, p. 13.
17 *Ibid.*, p. 14.
18 *Ibid.*, Document A/P.V.272, December 7, 1949.

fare and the welfare of the people of China. Those debates also revealed the determination of the overwhelming majority of the delegations represented, as shown in the adoption of the resolution on the promotion of the stability of international relations in the Far East, to do their part to maintain China's integrity and independence.

In sharp contrast to that attitude of the vast majority of the delegations in the First Committee was the attitude of the delegation of the Soviet Union and of the small group of delegations following its lead. The attitude of those delegations was the direct opposite of that which I have described. That attitude strengthens the justified suspicions of other nations regarding the Soviet policy and intentions toward China. That attitude revealed especially two things: First, a callous disregard for the interests of China and the Chinese people; and secondly, a renewed indication of the most regrettable Soviet unwillingness to co-operate in the work of the United Nations and to carry into effect the principles of our Charter. I think it is appropriate to review the actions of the delegation of the Soviet Union on the item which we are now considering.

The first action which it took was to oppose the placing of this item on the agenda, thus seeking to deprive the General Assembly of an opportunity even to study the matter. The second action, which it has repeated today, was an attempt to deny the right of the duly accredited representative of China to speak in the General Assembly. I think it has been the experience of all of us that the delegation of the Soviet Union is not unaware of the existence of the rules of procedure of the General Assembly. It has, on frequent occasions, invoked those rules.

.   .   .   .   .   .

In the third place, the Soviet Union has failed to respond to the expressed willingness of the Chinese delegation to refer certain questions involved in this case to the International Court of Justice. In the fourth place, the Soviet Union refused to participate in the debates in the First Committee and, this afternoon, has said that it refuses to participate in the debates in this plenary meeting of the General Assembly.

.   .   .   .   .

Let us look at the votes of the Soviet Union delegation on the resolutions which came before the First Committee. The vote on the resolution to promote the stability of international relations in the Far East is most revealing. When this question was put to the vote, the Polish delegation – which, it is fair to say, more often than not reflects the view of the Soviet Union delegation – called for a separate vote on the title. And let me repeat the title: "to promote the stability of international relations in the Far East". Five negative votes were cast against the title. One can interpret those five negative votes only to mean the opposition of five delegations to stability in the Far East. Perhaps we should not be surprised, for such an attitude is indeed in accordance with their communistic creed of promoting turmoil and unrest. The five negative votes on the rest of the resolution to promote the stability of international relations in the Far East must raise more questions in our minds:

Can it be that the Soviet Union does not intend or wish to respect the political independence of China? Can it be that the Soviet Union does not intend or wish to respect the right of the Chinese people freely to choose their own political institutions or to maintain a government independent of foreign control? Do they not intend or wish to respect their treaties relating to China? Do they not intend or wish to refrain from seeking spheres of influence or the creation of puppet regimes, or from obtaining special monopoly rights in China?

These are the things which are set forth in this resolution which we call upon all States to adopt. These are the principles which are opposed by the Soviet Union delegation, and the four other delegations.

In my opening statement before the First Committee, I said that the failure to endorse this resolution might well be interpreted as indicating an intention to profit by the present situation in China for purposes of imperialist aggrandisement. What other conclusion can the world draw from the five votes cast against these fundamental principles?

Let us look on the affirmative side at the merits of this resolution. The very fact of the Soviet opposition attests indeed to its importance. That opposition is conclusive proof that this resolution is not, as one representative feared in his statement in the First Committee, a mere "song to the moon". The Soviet opposition is proof that the Soviet Union understands perfectly that this resolution, far from condoning the past actions of Soviet Russia in China, is occasioned by those very actions and reflects the acute fears of the international community of this Soviet Russian continuation of Czarist Russian imperialism in the Far East. This resolution is addressed to the real root of the international problem, to the real concern that the international community has regarding this situation.

The representative of Chile pointed out in the First Committee that the General Assembly is not now dealing with the question of the justice or injustice of the civil strife now raging in China. This resolution does not seek to deal with that issue. It does deal in an integral manner with the international aspects of this problem. This resolution is constructive because it is forward-looking. While it does not ignore the past, it does not content itself with a mere sifting of past events. It is a clear statement of the principles to which all nations must adhere at all times.

. . . .

In my statement before the First Committee, I pointed out that the conscience of the world has expressed itself in the past in multipartite declarations which have played a real part in the history of China's struggle for its integrity. The reality of these declarations has been proved, even though from time to time they have been flouted by aggressors. The enunciation by the Government of the United States in 1900 of the policy of promoting the maintenance of the independence and integrity of China served as a restraining influence on the conduct of all the powers in the ensuing years, despite the continuance of unsettled conditions on China. These principles were written into the Nine Power Treaty of 1922, which the representative of China himself stated gave to his country the opportunity for constructive development.

If the nations of the world had not, during the past fifty years, recorded these self-denying ordinances the devouring waves of Russian and Japanese imperialism might well have totally engulfed China. The proper place today for the reaffirmation of these principles is the General Assembly of the United Nations. The vote in the First Committee shows that the conscience of the world will again speak in the interests of China and the people of China.

I wish to point out also that the debate on the item which we are now considering is in reality a continuation of the debate which resulted in the adoption of the resolution on essentials of peace by a vote of 53 Members of the United Nations. The general charges made against the policies and activities of the Soviet Union in that debate find a further specific application in the matter we are now considering. Although our attention is now focussed upon one geographic area, the fundamental problem is unchanged. It is the problem of maintaining an independent, unified and free country against the aggressive encroachments of a foreign power. The resolution on essentials of peace applies to China as well as to all other parts of the world. That resolution and the resolution which is now before us to promote the stability of international relations in the Far East are closely linked. Together they constitute a code of conduct regarding the Far East. The United States pledges itself to abide by that code of conduct, and it expects all other nations to do likewise.

In joining with other delegations in sponsoring the resolution on the stability of international relations in the Far East the paramount consideration of my delegation and of my Government has been to promote the interests of the people of China. This is not a new policy of the United States. The record shows that this has consistently been our policy. That policy has received only one challenge, and that challenge was made by Mr. Vyshinsky when he was seeking to prevent the General Assembly from discharging its duty to discuss this item which had been placed on the agenda. Mr. Vyshinsky then charged that the proposal of this item was instigated by the United States for imperialistic reasons. It was not instigated by the United States. Moreover, the United States, unlike the Union of Soviet Socialist Republics, has no imperialistic designs on China.

I wonder where are the evidences of the United States imperialism in China which Mr. Vyshinsky may have had in mind. Surely they are not monopolistic agreements of the type which the Soviet Union has been concluding in China, for the United States has neither sought nor obtained such rights. I do not hesitate to say that the Chinese people will agree that there is nothing imperialistic in the continuation of our historic policy of aiding Chinese students and scholars by the allocation in recent years of 200 million dollars for the programme of exchanging students and teachers between the United States and China. I do not think that the Chinese people believe that it was a sign of American imperialism to distribute some 400,000 tons of rice and 180,000 tons of wheat and flour in Shanghai and Canton during the past two years. Nor will they maintain that it was American imperialism which led to the supplying of cotton to keep the textile mills of China in operation so that the workers would not be unemployed and so that they would have wages with which to buy food and clothing.

Charges of United States imperialism can hardly be levelled against the joint United States–Chinese rural reconstruction programme, which was launched in 1948 and continued as long as possible in Szechuan and Cheki-ang, to improve rural living conditions, increase foreign output, and improve the social and educational position of the Chinese farmer. We neither desire nor claim any monopoly in extending help to the people of China; we have not been alone in extending help. But not only in the last year and a half, but on earlier occasions, when the people of China were hungry the people of the United States have sent food. The rice alone which we sent in 1948 and 1949 meant that 10,000,000 Chinese had their rice bowls filled daily during that period. In view of the vast problems of that great population, what we have been able to do has been little enough, but in view of current food short-ages in China, I submit that it contrasts favourably with the barter agreement recently concluded by the Soviet Union with local authorities in Manchuria, under which food would be taken from the rice bowls of the Chinese people for shipment to the Soviet Union.

We shall not cease our efforts on behalf of the people of China, nor shall we cease, in the field of international relations and through the United Nations, to work for the real interests of China itself, for its independence and its integrity.

The draft resolution on the promotion of the establishment of international relations in the Far East will unite the peoples of the free world in the promotion of this common objective.

B. India and Pakistan

[See Documents, X, 1948, p. 580.]

The United Nations Commission for India and Pakistan met at Lake Success early in January 1949 following the announcement by both India and Pakistan that, in accordance with their acceptance of the commission's proposals of December 11, 1948, they had agreed to order a cease-fire effective as of January 1, 1949.[1] In a report submitted to the Security Council on January 10, the commission transmitted a unanimous resolution to the effect that 1) the future status of Jammu-Kashmir would be determined by a free, impartial plebiscite; 2) the plebiscite would be held when, in the opinion of the commission, the cease-fire and truce arrangements called for in its resolution of August 13, 1948,[2] had been rendered effective; 3) the United Nations Secretary-General, in consultation with the commission, would appoint an administrator to organize and conduct the plebiscite; and 4) after the commission had satisfied itself as to the restoration of peaceful conditions, the commission and

1 For a summary of the commission's work since its inception, see Documents, X, 1948, p. 580. For a summary of the resolution of December 1948, see ibid., p. 581.
2 For a summary of the resolution of August 1948, see ibid.

the plebiscite administrator, after discussions with the Indian Government, would determine the final disposition of the forces of India and Jammu-Kashmir.[3] During Security Council discussion of the report the United States paid tribute to the work of the commission. On March 21, the Secretary-General (Lie) announced the appointment of Chester W. Nimitz, Fleet Admiral of the United States Navy, as plebiscite administrator.[4]

Joint meetings were held in New Delhi in March between representatives of India and Pakistan and of the commission. After further conversations and exchanges of views between the commission and the two governments, the commission on April 28 presented "truce terms" designed to implement that section of its August 1948 resolution calling for the withdrawal of troops from Jammu-Kashmir and the formulation of a truce arrangement.[5] Replies to the "truce terms" revealed that great differences of opinion remained to be resolved between India and Pakistan. In July both governments accepted the commission's invitation to attend a joint meeting in Karachi for the purpose of demarcating a cease-fire line in accordance with the Commission's resolution of August 1948. An agreement establishing such a line was signed between representatives of India and Pakistan on July 27. The agreement specified a line of approximately 800 miles, leaving both sides free to adjust their defensive positions behind that line.[6] Following the successful outcome of the Karachi conference, the commission on August 9, 1949, invited the two governments to meetings on the ministerial level to discuss the political aspects of the truce. However, continued conflicts of views made it impossible to reach agreement on the agenda for the proposed meetings.

At the end of August 1949 President Truman addressed a message to the Prime Ministers of India (Nehru) and Pakistan (Ali Khan) urging that they accept a recommendation of the Commission for India and Pakistan for arbitration of differences outstanding between them.[7] When this course of action was accepted by Pakistan but rejected by India, the commission decided that it could no longer continue in effective mediation of the dispute without broader terms of reference. It so reported to the Security Council in December, recommending that the Council appoint a single representative possessing broad authority to attempt to bring the two governments together on all unresolved issues and that the Council consult with India and Pakistan as to the powers of this representative, particularly on his authority to arbitrate issues impeding the creation of conditions for holding the plebiscite.[8] After consulting informally with both governments, the president of the Security Council (McNaughton) submitted proposals which were based on the principle accepted by both disputants that the future of Jammu-Kashmir be settled in a plebiscite and were designed to provide a basis for a process of demilitarization which would precede the plebiscite.[9]

For a detailed summary of the work of the Security Council and the United Nations Commission for India and Pakistan in dealing with the Jammu-Kashmir question during 1949, see *International Organization*, III, p. 300; *ibid.*, IV, p. 110, 268.

(1) Statement by the United States Representative on the United Nations Security Council (Jessup), Made before the Security Council, January 13, 1949.[10]

[EXCERPT]

. . . .

In the opinion of my Government, the Governments of India and Pakistan have gained the respect and admiration not only of this Council but of the peoples of the United Nations by their statesmanlike action in accepting the

[3] United Nations Security Council, Document S/1196, January 10, 1949.
[4] Department of State, *Bulletin*, XX, p. 382.
[5] For the full text of the commission's resolution of August 1948, see United Nations Security Council, Document S/1430, December 9, 1948, p. 26.
[6] *Ibid.*, Document S/1430, December 9, 1949, p. 38.   [7] Department of State, *Bulletin*, XXI, p. 143.
[8] United Nations Security Council, Document S/1430, December 9, 1949, p. 45.
[9] *Ibid.*, *Official Records* (4th year), No. 54, p. 54.   [10] *Ibid.*, No. 3, p. 7.

proposals of the Commission [for India and Pakistan] and, in particular, in promptly effecting cease-fire arrangements on their own initiative, without awaiting formal action by the Commission. By their actions, they have shown their firm and constant support of the principles embodied in the United Nations Charter, which their representatives have again reiterated this afternoon, and they have thus given the world a convincing demonstration of the manner in which progress can be made in the settlement of international disputes by peaceful means.

The Security Council's Commission should also receive, as it has, the warm commendation of members of this Council for the part it has played in contributing to this happy result. An auspicious start has been made toward a peaceful, friendly and just solution of the Kashmir dispute. On the part of my Government, I can say that we offer our sincere encouragement to all concerned in attaining this objective in the near future.

C. Indonesia

For information concerning the action of the United Nations on the Indonesian question and the coming into existence of the United States of Indonesia, see this volume, p. 515.

D. Korea

1. GENERAL

On January 1, 1949, the United States extended full recognition to the Government of the Republic of Korea; John J. Muccio was named the first United States Ambassador to that government.[1] The Korean Republic on January 19, 1949, submitted a formal application for membership in the United Nations.[2] The application was considered by the United Nations Security Council on February 15 following rejection of a Soviet proposal to delete consideration of the matter from the Council's agenda. Although supported by the United States in both the Committee on the Admission of New Members[3] and in the Council, the application failed of approval when opposed by the Soviet Union.[4]

According to an announcement of April 18 conversations were held between representatives of the United States and the south Korean government, as well as with members of the United Nations Commission on Korea, concerning the final withdrawal of United States occupation forces pursuant to the United Nations General Assembly resolution of December 12, 1948.[5] By June 29 all occupation troops had been withdrawn by the United States, military equipment and material had been transferred to the south Korean security forces, and a group of about 500 military personnel remained as a military advisory mission to the south Korean Government.[6] The Soviet Union announced that all occupation forces had been withdrawn from the northern section of Korea in September 1948.

(1) Statement by the Department of State Concerning United States Policy in Korea. Department of State Press Release, June 8, 1949.[7]

On January 1 of this year the United States Government extended full recognition to the Government of the Republic of Korea. In so doing, the United

---

[1] Department of State Press Release 168, March 21, 1949.
[2] United Nations Security Council, Document S/1238, February 1, 1949.
[3] For the text of the report of the Committee on the Admission of New Members, see *ibid.*, Document S/1281, March 9, 1949.
[4] *Ibid., Official Records* (4th year), No. 26.
[5] *New York Times*, May 24, 1949, p. 7. For the text of the resolution of December 12, 1948, see *Documents, X, 1948,* p. 178.
[6] *New York Times*, June 17, 1949, p. 9.   [7] Department of State, *Bulletin*, XX, p. 781.

States welcomed into the community of free nations a new republic, born of the efforts of the United Nations, and of the United States as a principally interested power, to give effect to the urgent and rightful claims of the Korean people to freedom and national independence.

The United States Government, inspired by its historic ties of friendship with the Korean people and by its sincere interest in the spread of free institutions and representative government among the peoples of the world, entertains a particularly deep and sympathetic concern for the welfare of the Republic of Korea. As evidence of this concern, the United States is currently carrying out in Korea a program of economic and technical assistance designed to provide the economic stability without which political stability would be impossible. A request for authorization to continue and to strengthen this program during the coming fiscal year has already been submitted to the Congress. The United States has, moreover, maintained in Korea a military training mission whose function it has been to advise and assist the Government of the Republic of Korea in the development of its own security forces, in consonance with the United Nations General Assembly's resolution of November 14, 1947, and has transferred to that government for those forces substantial amounts of military equipment and supplies under the authority of the Surplus Property Act. The transfer of such equipment and supplies is continuing, while the military training mission has recently been placed on a more formal basis with the establishment of a United States Military Advisory Group to the Republic of Korea. Other forms of assistance, such as that in the fields of education and vocational training, also have been and are being given to the Republic of Korea by the United States Government.

In pursuance of the recommendation contained in the General Assembly's resolution of December 12, 1948, to the effect that the occupying Powers should "withdraw their occupation forces from Korea as early as practicable," the United States Government will soon have completed the withdrawal of its occupation forces from that country. As is clear from the broad program of assistance outlined above, this withdrawal in no way indicates a lessening of United States interest in the Republic of Korea, but constitutes rather another step toward the normalization of relations with that republic and a compliance on the part of the United States with the cited provision of the December 12 resolution of the General Assembly.

While the United States has given unstintingly of its material assistance and political support in order that the Republic of Korea might grow and prosper, this government recognizes that the Korean problem remains one of international concern and that it is only through continued support by the entire community of nations to which that republic owes its existence that the security and stability of this new nation can be assured during the critical months and years that lie ahead. So long as the authority of the Republic of Korea continues to be challenged within its own territory by the alien tyranny which has been arbitrarily imposed upon the people of north Korea, the need for such support will be a vital one.

The United States Government has already pledged its support to the United Nations Commission on Korea in its efforts to assist the Korean people toward the goal of a free and united Korea. It believes, however, that this goal can be achieved only through the continued strengthening of the freely elected and democratic Government of the Republic of Korea as an embodiment of the hopes and aspirations of all Koreans to the freedom and independence for which they have worked and waited so long.

(2) Letter from the United States Ambassador to Korea (Muccio) to the President of the Republic of Korea (Rhee) Concerning the Establishment of a United States Military Advisory Group in Korea, May 2, 1949.[8]

I have the honor to refer to your request for a United States military and naval mission and to recent references thereto in our discussions looking towards setting a date for the early withdrawal of United States occupation forces.

As you know, there has been in existence on a provisional basis for more than eight months a United States military mission known as the Provisional Military Advisory Group whose function it has been to advise and assist the Korean Government in the development and training of its own security forces. It is the judgment of my Government that, due in no small part to the spirit of eager cooperation which has been shown by the Korean Government and its responsible officials, the work of the Provisional Military Advisory Group has contributed significantly to raising the capabilities of the security forces of the Republic of Korea. This judgment would seem to be substantiated by your own recent statement to the effect that Korean defense forces "are now rapidly approaching the point at which our security can be assured, provided the Republic of Korea is not called upon to face attack from foreign sources".

In order to assure the continuance of this progress without further dependence upon the presence of United States occupation forces in Korea, my Government has decided to establish an augmented Korean Military Advisory Group to function as a part of the American Mission in Korea, with responsibility for the training mission heretofore undertaken by the Provisional Military Advisory Group. Under my overall direction as Ambassador, the Korean Military Advisory Group will be headed by Brigadier General W. L. Roberts, presently Commanding General, United States Army Forces in Korea, and Commanding Officer of the Provisional Military Advisory Group. Further details concerning the composition of the new Military Advisory Group will be discussed at an appropriate time with the proper officials of your Government.

2. ECONOMIC ASSISTANCE

With the 1948 program of economic assistance to Korea due to end officially on June 30, 1949, President Truman on June 7 requested that the Congress appropriate $150 million for continuation of the program through the forthcoming fiscal year.[9]

8 Department of State Press Release 428, June 8, 1949.
9 *Christian Science Monitor,* June 8, 1949, p. 19.

In a statement before a closed session of the Foreign Affairs Committee of the House of Representatives, the Secretary of State (Acheson) reportedly declared the opinion of the Department of State that, if the Congress should refuse to continue the program, the Republic of Korea would fall within a period of three months. Secretary Acheson was also reported to have told the committee that "If you do not take this step it seems to me that it is a public declaration that we are not going to do anything in the Far East."[10] The House committee formally approved implementing legislation (H.R.5330) on June 30, 1949, and reported the bill on July 1.[11] After hearings befors the Senate Committee on Foreign Relations, Senator Tom Connally (Texas) introduced a Senate measure for aid to Korea (S.2319) on July 22.[12] The latter bill was passed by the Senate by a vote of 48 to 13 on October 12.[13] No further action was taken on either measure during 1949.

(1) Message from the President (Truman) to the House of Representatives on Economic Assistance to the Republic of Korea, June 7, 1949.[14]

I recommend that the Congress authorize the continuation of economic assistance to the Republic of Korea for the fiscal year ending June 30, 1950.

The United States is now providing relief and a small amount of assistance in rehabilitation to the Republic of Korea under Public Law 793, Eightieth Congress. The continuation of that assistance is of great importance to the successful achievement of the foreign policy aims of the United States. The authority of the present act extends only until June 30, 1949. For this reason legislation is urgently needed and I am hopeful that the Congress may give it early consideration.

The people of the United States have long had sympathetic feelings for the Korean people. American missionaries, supported by American churches of many denominations, brought spiritual guidance, education, and medical aid to the Korean people during their 40 years of Japanese bondage. All Americans who have come to know the Korean people appreciate their fierce passion for freedom and their keen desire to become an independent nation.

Early in the war with Japan, it was resolved that Korea should be liberated. In the Cairo Declaration of December 1943, the United States joined with the United Kingdom and China to express their determination that in due course Korea should become free and independent. This pledge was reaffirmed in the Potsdam Declaration of July 26, 1945, with which the Soviet Union associated itself upon its entrance into the war against Japan in the following month. With our victory over Japan, it was hoped that the Korean Nation would be reborn. Unfortunately, however, only the people of Korea south of the 38° parallel have thus far attained their freedom and independence.

The present division of Korea along the 38° parallel was never intended by the United States. The sole purpose of the line along the 38° parallel was to facilitate acceptance by the Soviet and United States forces of the surren-

10 New York Times, July 2, 1949, p. 1.
   11 House Report 962, 81st Cong., 1st sess.; Congressional Record, 95, p. 8978 (Daily edition, July 1, 1949).
   12 Ibid., p. 10171 (Daily edition, July 22, 1949).
   13 Ibid., p. 14623 (Daily edition, October 12, 1949).
   14 House Document 212, 81st Cong., 1st sess.

der of Japanese troops north and south of that line. Immediately after the completion of the Japanese surrender the United States through direct negotiations with the Soviet Union sought to restore the unity of Korea.

For 2 years these efforts were rendered unavailing by the attitude of the Soviet Union. When it became apparent that further delay would be injurious to the interests of the Korean people, the United States submitted the matter to the General Assembly of the United Nations, in the hope that the United Nations could assist the people of Korea to assume their rightful place as an independent, democratic nation.

By vote of an overwhelming majority, the General Assembly adopted a resolution on November 14, 1947, calling for an election, under the observation of a United Nations Temporary Commission on Korea, to choose a representative national assembly for the purpose of drafting a democratic constitution and establishing a national government. The Soviet Union refused to permit the United Nations Commission to enter its zone. Consequently, the right of the Korean people to participate in a free election to establish a free government was confined to south Korea. As a result of this election, the Government of the Republic of Korea was inaugurated August 15, 1948.

The General Assembly of the United Nations at its next session considered the report of its Commission and in December 1948 adopted a resolution holding the Government of the Republic of Korea to be the validly elected, lawful government of the area in which elections were held under the Commission's observation, and the only such government in Korea. The General Assembly established a reconstituted Commission to consult with the occupying powers on the withdrawal of their forces and to continue to work for the unification of Korea under representative government.

The United States terminated its military government in Korea upon the inauguration of the Government of the Republic of Korea and recognized the new Government on New Year's Day, 1949.

The December 1948 resolution of the General Assembly called on the occupying powers to withdraw their forces as soon as practicable. The United States has thus far retained a small number of troops in Korea at the request of the Government of the Republic to give the Republic an opportunity to establish forces adequate to protect itself against internal disturbances and external attacks short of an aggressive war supported by a major power. A military advisory group requested by the Korean Government for training purposes will be retained in Korea after the withdrawal of United States troops.

The debilitated state in which the Korean economy was left by the Japanese has been accentuated by the separation of the hydroelectric power, coal and metal, and fertilizer industries of the north from the agricultural and textile industries of the south and by the effects of continuing communist agitation. The United States has furnished the people of south Korea with basic relief during the period of military government. Despite such assistance, however, the Republic is still far short of being able to support itself, even at the present modest standard of living of its people. It is in urgent need of further assistance in the difficult period ahead until it can stand on its own feet economically.

The aid now being provided to Korea is essentially for basic relief. Without the continuation of such relief, its economy would collapse, inevitably and rapidly. Bare relief alone, however, would not make it possible for the Republic to become self-supporting. The Republic would remain dependent upon the continuation of relief from the United States at a costly level into the indefinite future, and subject to the same inevitable collapse at any time the relief should be withdrawn. For these reasons the aid granted should be not for mere relief but for recovery. The kind of program which is needed is the kind which the Congress has authorized for the countries of western Europe and under which those countries have achieved such rapid progress toward recovery during the past year. Full advantage should be taken of the broad and successful experience in western Europe by continuing responsibility for the administration of the Korean aid program in the Economic Cooperation Administration, which has been administering aid to Korea since January 1 of this year.

Prior to January 1 of this year, aid to Korea was administered by the Army as a part of its program for government and relief in occupied areas. The budget which I submitted to the Congress in January contemplated that economic assistance to Korea would be continued outside of the Army's program for government and relief in occupied areas. The needs of the Republic of Korea for economic assistance have been carefully studied in the light of the latest available information. I am convinced that the sum of $150,000,000 is the minimum aid essential during the coming year for progress toward economic recovery.

Such a recovery program will cost only a relatively small amount more than a bare relief program. Yet a recovery program — and only a recovery program — will enable the Republic of Korea to commence building up the coal production, electric-power capacity, and fertilizer production which are fundamental to the establishment of a self-supporting economy and to the termination of the need for aid from the United States. Aid in the restoration of the Korean economy should be less costly to the United States in the end than a continued program of relief.

The recovery program which is recommended is not only the soundest course economically but also the most effective from the standpoint of helping to achieve the objectives of peaceful and democratic conditions in the Far East.

Korea has become a testing ground in which the validity and practical value of the ideals and principles of democracy which the Republic is putting into practice are being matched against the practices of communism which have been imposed upon the people of north Korea. The survival and progress of the Republic toward a self-supporting, stable economy will have an immense and far-reaching influence on the people of Asia. Such progress by the young Republic will encourage the people of southern and southeastern Asia and the islands of the Pacific to resist and reject the Communist propaganda with which they are besieged. Moreover, the Korean Republic, by demonstrating the success and tenacity of democracy in resisting communism, will stand as a beacon to the people of northern Asia in resisting the control of the Communist forces which have overrun them.

The Republic of Korea, and the freedom-seeking people of north Korea held under Soviet domination, seek for themselves a united, self-governing and sovereign country, independent of foreign control and support and with membership in the United Nations. In their desire for unity and independence, they are supported by the United Nations.

The United States has a deep interest in the continuing progress of the Korean people toward these objectives. The most effective practical aid which the United States can give toward reaching them will be to assist the Republic to move toward self support at a decent standard of living. In the absence of such assistance, there can be no real hope of achieving a unified, free, and democratic Korea.

If we are faithful to our ideals and mindful of our interest in establishing peaceful and prosperous conditions in the world, we will not fail to provide the aid which is so essential to Korea at this critical time.

3. UNITED NATIONS COMMISSION ON KOREA

[See *Documents, IX, 1947,* p. 119; *X, 1948,* p. 169.]

Established by a United Nations General Assembly resolution of December 12, 1948,[15] the United Nations Commission on Korea, composed of representatives of Australia, China, El Salvador, France, India, the Philippines, and Syria, reported on July 28, 1949, on its work since its inception. The committee reported that its task had been made difficult and nearly impossible by the complete lack of cooperation from the authorities in northern Korea and by the refusal of the Soviet Union to use its good offices to promote greater cooperation from those quarters. The commission's task had also been hindered by the refusal of the south Korean Government to consider participation in discussions with the northern government; the former government based its refusal on the fact that the northern regime had not been recognized by the General Assembly and stated its belief that "the [United Nations] Commission, like the [south Korean] Government, ought to refrain from dealing with it." The commission's report continued:

> There is much military posturing on both sides of the [38th] parallel. This holds a serious danger of provoking open military conflict. Military conflict in Korea would mean a most barbarous civil war. . . . The Government is hastening the pace of its military preparations and is pressing the United States for military aid beyond that already received. United States military personnel advise and assist in the training of the Republic's forces, as on the other side of the parallel military personnel of the USSR reportedly perform such services for the northern forces . . . From the United States, the Government of the Republic expects, as a matter of obligation, military and economic aid for defense against the menace of aggression and invasion from the north.

The report concluded with the statement that "the relations between the USSR and the United States continue to be the largest single, and perhaps decisive, factor contributing to the growing hardening of relations between north and south" and

15 For further information on the establishment of the United Nations Commission on Korea, see *Documents, X, 1948,* p. 178.

that "without a new effort by those Powers to reach agreement on the question of Korea, no substantial progress toward the achievement of unification on the basis of the principles approved by the General Assembly can be made."[16]

During discussions of the commission's report in the Ad Hoc Political Committee of the General Assembly, a Philippine proposal to invite the participation of the delegation of the Republic of Korea was adopted over the opposition of the Soviet Union; at the same time, the latter's proposal to invite representatives of the Democratic People's Republic of Korea was defeated.[17] In committee, the United States, supported by other delegations, proposed that the commission continue its work with broadened powers which would permit it to observe and report on developments leading to open conflict, to facilitate the removal of barriers to economic and social relations between the northern and southern sectors of Korea, and to offer its consultation in the development of a representative government. Although opposed by the Soviet Union and the eastern European nations which wished to terminate the commission's work, the United States resolution, introduced jointly with China, Australia, and the Philippines, was adopted after amendment in the committee by a vote of 44 to 6 with 5 abstentions.[18] The General Assembly approved the proposal in plenary session by a vote of 48 to 6 with 3 abstentions.[19]

(1) Statement by the United States Representative to the United Nations General Assembly (Fahy) on the Problem of the Independence of Korea, Made before the Plenary Session of the General Assembly, October 20, 1949.[20]

The General Assembly is fulfilling its highest function when it speaks or acts on behalf of the independence of peoples and of governments. This is the present case, the case of Korea. The *Ad Hoc* Political Committee, as the first action of this session of an important political matter, overwhelmingly resolved that the United Nations Commission on Korea should continue. The United States urges that the General Assembly now affirm the action of the Committee.

It is approximately 2 years since the General Assembly adopted its resolution of November 14, 1947, designed to bring about the creation of a government in Korea representing the people of that country, who were promised liberation and freedom as a consequence of the defeat of Japan. In the part of Korea south of the 38th Parallel, under United Nations observation, a free election was held. The Government of the Republic of Korea was established. American occupation forces were withdrawn. The lawful character of the new government was acknowledged by the Third General Assembly, at Paris, and that government has since been recognized by more than 20 member states of the United Nations.

No free election was permitted north of the 38th Parallel. There one-third of the people and one-half of the area of the country are behind a barrier erected by a puppet government, supported by the Soviet Union. The representatives of the United Nations are excluded and the authority of the General Assembly is flouted. A vast propaganda campaign is waged against the representative government chosen freely by the people in the area opened to United Nations observation south of the 38th Parallel.

16 United Nations General Assembly, *Official Records* (4th session), Supplement No. 9.
17 *Ibid.*, Document A/AC.31/SR.3, September 29, 1949.
18 *Ibid.*, Document A/AC.31/SR.6, October 3, 1949.
19 *Ibid.*, *Official Records* (4th session), p. 130.   20 Department of State, *Bulletin,* XXI, p. 694.

The United Nations Commission on Korea, established at the third session of the General Assembly, has made a comprehensive report. It points out the threat of conflict, of explosive incidents, of the continuation of social, economic, and political barriers, of lack of unification. There is danger of a cruel civil war growing out of the bellicose manifestations of those who dominate north Korea.

The present resolution was adopted by the *Ad Hoc* Political Committee to continue a United Nations Commission in Korea in aid of maintaining peace and furthering the unification and independence of Korea. So long as there exists in Korea the spirit of incitement to armed combat, and so long as upon occasion such conflict in fact occurs, the purpose of the General Assembly to bring about the unification and complete independence of Korea under a single national government, set up under the scrutiny of the Assembly's Commission, is endangered, as is also the safety and well-being of the Republic of Korea, and that of all its inhabitants. It is for this reason that the Committee resolution provides that the new Commission shall observe and report any developments which might lead to or otherwise involve military conflict in Korea. It is our view that a commission empowered to act in this field will serve as an important stabilizing and deterrent influence, and that in the event conflict should occur, the United Nations would have at hand testimony from a duly constituted agency regarding its nature and origin, and regarding the responsibility for its occurrence.

There remains also the important task of working toward the realization of unity and independence for all Korea. The Committee resolution provides means whereby, in case the threat of military conflict should be suspended or mitigated, the Commission may assist in the establishment of a single national government over an undivided country. The Commission is to seek to facilitate the removal of barriers to friendly intercourse in Korea, and to make its good offices available and be prepared to assist, whenever in its judgment a favorable opportunity arises, in bringing about the unification of Korea in accordance with the principles endorsed by the General Assembly. Its authority to utilize the services and good offices of persons whether or not representatives on the Commission, is designed to give it the broadest possible facilities in carrying out these functions.

We believe that a commission having these powers will be able to contribute substantially, in a manner appropriate in the light of present conditions in Korea, to the final solution of the problem of the independence of that country, through the establishment of a national government acting by, and on behalf of, the will of a united people. We accordingly support the Committee resolution, and of course shall vote against the Soviet draft resolution which was rejected in Committee by an overwhelming vote. We strongly recommend the Committee resolution to the favorable consideration of other delegations as an expression of the purpose of the General Assembly to promote the independence of a long-suffering and valiant people whom we should aid to achieve what so many of us enjoy — freedom and independence.

E. Philippines

(1) Statement on the Joint Discussions between the President of the United States (Truman) and the President of the Philippine Republic (Quirino). White House Press Release, August 11, 1949.[1]

In August 1949, Elpidio Quirino, President of the Republic of the Philippines, paid a state visit to the United States at the invitation of President Truman. In the course of President Quirino's visit, the two Presidents discussed a number of matters of common and continuing interest to their governments. The following statement was released by the White House at the conclusion of the joint discussions.

The President of the Republic of the Philippines and the President of the United States have met in Washington and have discussed at length problems of common interest to the two nations. The spirit of these conversations has reflected the historic and unique relationship between the two countries. As in the past it was the aim of the United States that the Philippines should assume its rightful position as a free and self-reliant member of the world community, so today the United States looks forward to the preservation and strengthening of the position the Philippine Republic has achieved in order that it may make its full contribution to that community.

It is recognized that the capacity of the Philippine Republic to live up to the high hopes which events of the past three years have kindled must depend in part upon its economic situation. The two Presidents have discussed measures for the reinforcement and development of Philippine economy in terms of the recommendations of the report of the Joint Philippine-American Finance Commission issued in 1947, being convinced that the economic progress of the Philippines will be not only in the immediate interests of the two countries but will contribute vitally to the determination of free peoples to resist those forces which seek their enslavement so long as that menace shall threaten. The two Presidents are agreed that this resistance will be most effective in areas where the material well-being of the people allow a full appreciation of the meaning of freedom, and that conversely it is among peoples who have abandoned hope of individual betterment that the least resistance will be offered to those perverted forces which would destroy the ideals to which the two nations are dedicated.

The President of the Philippines has expressed the determination of his country to pursue with vigor the courses of action which offer the greatest promise; the President of the United States has reiterated the desire and intention of the United States to render all feasible assistance. The United States will continue to watch sympathetically the efforts of the peoples of Asia to forge stronger ties of economic cooperation and collaboration, to hasten the progress of self-government, and to preserve their freedom.

[1] Department of State, *Bulletin*, XXI, p. 277.

3. RELATIONS WITH EUROPEAN COUNTRIES IN THE FAR EAST

A. The Netherlands

[See *Documents, IX, 1947*, p. 594; *X, 1948*, p. 575.]

For information concerning United States economic assistance to the Netherlands East Indies, see this volume, p. 212.

(1) *Statement by the Deputy United States Representative to the United Nations Security Council (Jessup) on the Situation in Indonesia, Made before the Council, January 11, 1949.*[1]

[EXCERPTS]

In a statement to the Security Council, the representative of the Netherlands (van Roijen) reported to the Council that military action begun by Dutch troops against the Indonesian republican forces on December 19, 1948, would cease by December 31, 1948, on Java, and by January 5, 1949, on Sumatra, with the exception of "action against roving groups, bands or individuals who attempt to cause unrest" and "against disturbing elements who either individually or collectively endanger public security or interfere with or prevent supply of food and other essential commodities to the needy population."[2] During the Council's discussion of Mr. van Roijen's report, the United States deputy representative (Jessup) made the following statement.

My delegation has taken into account, as the President suggested, the statements which were made before the Security Council at our last meeting. My Government still can find no adequate justification for the military action taken by the Netherlands in Indonesia.

In many important respects the reasons justifying their action put forth by the Netherlands representative at the 389th meeting of the Security Council on 22 December in Paris, and again here last Friday, are not supported by the reports of the Committee of Good Offices.

In our view, the Netherlands military action is in conflict with the *Renville* Agreement [*S/649, Appendix XI*] and with the Security Council Resolution of 1 August [*S/459*] and 1 November 1947 [*S/597*]. As the delegation of the United States has frequently made clear, it is our opinion that these two Security Council resolutions were adopted under the provisions of Article 40, Chapter VII of the Charter, and that therefore, in accordance with Article 25 of the Charter, the Netherlands Government was and is under obligation to comply with their provisions.

On the initiative of the United States [*S/1128*], the Security Council was called into session in Paris to consider the emergency created by the military action of the Netherlands authorities.

·   ·   ·   ·   ·   ·   ·

The Netherlands representative has assured the Security Council that his Government has complied with the cease-fire demand and with the release of prisoners ordered by the Security Council. Neither my Government nor the Committee of Good Offices considers that the Netherlands has done so. In that connexion, I should like to read from the report of the Committee of Good Offices [*S/1189*] which has been distributed to us. In the conclusions of the report the Committee says:

1 United Nations Security Council, *Official Records* (4th year), No. 2, p. 2.
2 *Ibid.*, No. 1, p. 5.

12. The Committee is not in a position to report that there has been satisfactory compliance with sub-paragraph (a) of the resolution of 24 December, which called on the parties to cease hostilities.

(A) The telegram dispatched to territorial commanders in Java by the Chief of Staff of the Royal Netherlands Indonesian Army at 1700, 29 December 1948 is, according to its terms, for information and cannot be construed as an order to "cease hostilities forthwith". The dissemination of the order of the Commander-in-Chief to territorial commanders in Java which confirmed the fact that hostilities in Java had ended at 2400 of 31 December was begun at 1845, Batavia time, 2 January. In Sumatra where a "special emergency situation" existed, the parallel order disseminated late on 4 January had an effective time of 1200, 5 January 1949.

(B) It is noted that these orders were issued at a time when the "operational phase" of military activities presumably had been completed. The orders noted respectively that hostilities had terminated on 31 December 1948 in Java and on 5 January 1949 in Sumatra, but charged the troops to "carry out action against roving groups, bands or individuals, who attempt to cause unrest or, as was stated by our representative to the Security Council", — this is in terms of the Netherlands statement — "to act against disturbing elements, who either individually or collectively endanger public security or interfere with or prevent the supply of food and other essential commodities to the needy population". The orders permit the continuation of the very type of military action that would be required against the guerrilla resistance likely to be offered by regular or irregular Republican forces.

(C) As a result of the immobilization of its military observers, the Committee has no first-hand information as to the effect of the orders discussed above.

I might interpolate that the lack of information of the Committee was due to the fact that the military observers were not allowed at that time to move out into the field for purposes of observation. The report continues:

(D) The Committee is of the opinion that these orders issued more than a week after the adoption of the resolution of 24 December, and expressed as they were, cannot be looked upon as satisfactory compliance with sub-paragraph (a) of the resolution.

(E) There is no channel available to the Committee for dissemination of the resolution of 24 December to the Government or to the commanders of the Republican Army.

13. Sub-paragraph (b) of the Security Council's resolution of 24 December calling for the immediate release of the President of the Republic and other political prisoners has not been implemented. So far as the Committee is aware, President Soekarno, Vice-President Hatta, and the other members of the Republican Government who were captured by Netherlands forces on 19 December are still under detention . . . .

15. Despite the statements made to the Security Council by the Netherlands representative on 27 and 29 December, the Committee has not been in a position to make independent investigations of any kind in the field for the purpose of carrying out its functions under the resolution of 24 December. It has been heard unofficially and informally that certain military and naval liaison officers attached to some of the consular officials in Batavia took advantage of a Netherlands offer to conduct them on a tour of some of the military areas on 5 and 6 January. These officers are not the military observers of the Committee of Good Offices and their observations are not available to the Committee, even if their tour was the type of field investigation and observation required by the functions of the Committee.

I believe it is fair to say that, in a situation of this kind, the Security Council must place reliance on the report of its own agency in the field, particularly if it conflicts with a report from one of the parties to the dispute.

The continuance of military action of the Netherlands authorities after the adoption of the Security Council resolution of 24 December was clearly an act of defiance on the part of the Netherlands authorities. No excuses offered by the Netherlands Government can conceal the fact that it has failed to comply with the Security Council demands both in refusing to order a cease-fire immediately and in refusing to release the political prisoners immediately.

In the opinion of the Government of the United States, the representative of the Netherlands has failed to relieve his Government from the serious charge that it has violated the Charter of the United Nations.

The purpose of the Security Council cease-fire resolution of 24 December was to stop the fighting in Indonesia immediately so that the dispute could be settled not by force but by the processes of peaceful settlement enjoined on Member States by the Charter. Even though members of the Security Council were well aware that it was the Netherlands authorities which had initiated the resumption of military action, the resolution of the Security Council called on both parties to order a cease-fire. In such situations as those which existed at that time, this is an appropriate form of Security Council resolution, since the cessation must be mutual, no matter who is responsible for starting the fighting. It must be assumed that, in ordering a cease-fire, the Security Council could only have intended that such an order would apply equally and simultaneously to both sides. The Council could not have expected one side to comply unilaterally while the other considered itself free to comply at such a time and in such a way as it saw fit. The continuance of military action by the Netherlands forces until all military objectives had been taken cannot be regarded as compliance with the cease-fire order. Certainly the reservation of the right by one side to use its own forces in the territory of the other to eliminate the armed resistance of that other side which may thus far have escaped destruction, cannot be regarded as compliance with the cease-fire resolution.

Taking these factors into account, I am sure that the Security Council has no intention of approving action consolidating military victories which themselves were gained as a result of open defiance of an order of the Security Council.

Probably the most striking and clearest disregard of the orders of the Security Council is to be found in the refusal of the Netherlands authorities to release President Soekarno, Prime Minister Hatta and the other leading officials of the Government of the Republic of Indonesia. Quite aside from the disregard of the Security Council resolution of 28 December [S/1164] which required that these prisoners should be released within twenty-four hours, there is the present fact these persons are still not at liberty. The Security Council cannot be expected to accept the view of the Netherlands Government that these prisoners have been released because they are given a certain liberty of movement on the island of Bangka. In an archipelago comprising thousands of islands, liberty of movement which is restricted to a single island, and one which, I might add, was under Netherlands control even under the *Renville* Agreement, cannot be regarded as being in conformity with the Security Council resolution of 24 and 28 December.

I have just seen document S/1199 containing a further report from the Committee of Good Offices concerning the question of the detention of President Soekarno, Prime Minister Hatta and other leading officials of the Republic of Indonesia.

It appears from this document that there is some question as to the present whereabouts of these officials, but I find nothing in the text of the letter from the Netherlands delegation of 11 January, which is reproduced in that document, to alter the essential facts and the conclusions from those facts which I have just drawn.

The clear intent of the resolutions of the Security Council on this point was that the high officials of the Republican Government should be restored to a position in which they would be free to exercise their governmental authority. The minimum which would seem to be called for at this moment is that the President and other interned officers of the Republic should be allowed to return to their capital and to exercise their appropriate functions there, free from the constraint of any occupying army. They should be free to establish and maintain contact with other officials of their Government. They should also be free to provide their own forces for the maintenance of law and order in Jogjakarta.

Further, my Government, in considering the Netherlands-Indonesian dispute, cannot but recall a history of non-co-operation on the part of the Netherlands in the work of the Committee of Good Offices in Indonesia. The failure to achieve a political settlement and the protracted negotiations which followed the signing of the *Renville* Agreement in January 1948 brought about in Indonesia an increased tension between the Netherlands and the Republic, with a consequent increase in provocative incidents which sorely strained the truce. The bill of particulars for these acts over a period of months is recorded in the reports of the Committee of Good Offices to the Security Council. From these reports it appears that even prior to the resumption of military action against the Republic, the Netherlands pursued a policy which had the effect of weakening the Republic, working unnecessary hardship on the population, isolating the Republican Government economically and politically, and presenting it with a prefabricated interim administration for Indonesia with which it was to associate itself but which it had no part in forming.

My Government considers these acts and the failure of the Netherlands to enter into *bona fide* negotiations since May of last year to be indicative of a reluctance to utilize the procedure for pacific settlement made available by the United Nations, and to be in conflict with both the spirit and the letter of the Linggadjati and the *Renville* Agreements. From a purely pragmatic point of view, it should be pointed out that the quick military successes of the Netherlands forces will not effect a solution of the Indonesian problem. My Government cannot associate itself with any aspect of the Netherlands military action. The use of force in this situation makes the solution of the problem far more complex and difficult. The problem remains a matter of international concern with which the Security Council must continue to deal. It cannot be solved if we begin on the basis of acceptance of the fruits of the illegal use of force.

The Republic of Indonesia represents the largest single political factor in the projected federation and should therefore have a voice in the formation of the federation. The Republic has a two-fold nature. First, it is a political entity; secondly, it is the heart of Indonesian nationalism. This latter attribute cannot be eliminated by any amount of military force. The Netherlands Government may find that, far from assuring law and order in the Indies, the course upon which it has embarked may instead let loose forces of terror, chaos and sabotage. It may well be that the only victory will be that of the forces of anarchy.

My Government is of the opinion that real peace in Indonesia can be expected only if there is a settlement of the political issues on the basis of the principles and procedures agreed to by the parties in the Linggadjati and *Renville* Agreements [*S/649, Appendices VIII and XIII*] and under the auspices of the United Nations. The responsibility for the future rests in the first instance of the Netherlands authorities. The Security Council has a right to assume that the Netherlands Government will, in accordance with its obligations, bring to an end its defiance of the Security Council and give its full co-operation towards reaching a fair and reasonable solution of the Indonesian question.

My Government has, over a substantial period of time, devoted serious thought to this problem and to its proper solution. Our views are contained in the plan which our representative on the Committee of Good Offices submitted to the two parties on 10 September of last year and which was accepted by both of them as a basis for the resumption of negotiations. If Indonesian leaders were restored to their rightful position as the responsible representatives of the Republic of Indonesia, free to conduct the affairs of their Government and to negotiate freely with the Netherlands Government concerning the future of Indonesia, and if these two Governments could proceed to negotiate on the basis of this proposal in accordance with their earlier undertakings, this would be a notable contribution to the ultimate solution of the Indonesian problem.

A first and fundamental step in this direction should be the fixing of a definite date for the holding of elections throughout all Indonesia with a view to establishing the foundations of the United States of Indonesia. Secondly, and also of fundamental importance, is the fixing of a firm date for the transfer of sovereignty from the Kingdom of the Netherlands to the United States of Indonesia. The elections should be held for the purpose of choosing an assembly to represent the people of Indonesia as a provisional legislature and, at the same time, as a constituent assembly for the purpose of drawing up a constitution. The elections should be held by secret ballot with all the safeguards necessary to ensure a vote free from any coercion. Freedom of assembly, speech and publication must be guaranteed, as provided in the *Renville* Agreement.

This programme contemplates a termination of the type of military occupation of the country which has been brought about by Netherlands military action. The withdrawal of the Netherlands armies should begin at the earliest possible date and as rapidly as the need for the preservation of law and order permits. The occupation must be completely terminated before an effective transfer of sovereignty can take place. My Government believes that the length of time which should elapse between the present moment and the date when the elections should take place, and also the date of transfer of sovereignty, should be calculated in terms of months, not in terms of years. As soon as elections have been held and a provisional regime set up, authority should be turned over progressively to the new regime by the Netherlands Government, and the transfer should have been completed by the time at which sovereignty is assumed by the United States of Indonesia.

As I stated earlier, the problem of Indonesia remains a matter of international concern with which the Security Council must continue to deal. The carrying out of the steps necessary for the ultimate transfer of the sovereignty of the United States of Indonesia should, we believe, be accomplished under the auspices of the United Nations and with the help of the machinery it affords. The Committee of Good Offices, in its report of 7 January [S/1189], has appropriately pointed out that "it does not wish to be put in a position of seeming to approve by its participation or even its authentication, any settlement based on force rather than on true negotiation".

The Committee of Good Offices was created originally as an instrument to further free negotiations between the parties. The action of the Netherlands has temporarily suspended the Committee's ability to carry out that function, but the Council's agencies in the field remain in existence, ready to carry out any task assigned to them by the Security Council. No temporary suspension of the functioning of an agency of the Security Council can operate to remove an established interest of the United Nations in dealing with a situation to which the Security Councl [sic] has already addressed itself.

In this connexion it is necessary to call attention to the report of the Committee of Good Offices which indicates that the Netherlands authorities took upon themselves the authority to question whether the military observers were reporting to the Consular Commission or to the Committee of Good Offices. The account of this is to be found in document S/1189, in a letter of 4 January 1949 from the Netherlands delegation addressed to the Committee of Good Offices. This is not a question which concerns the Netherlands authorities. The Security Council can utilize any agency which it considers appropriate, and it is the obligation of a Member of the United Nations to co-operate with any and all agencies operating under Security Council instructions. It cannot be denied that despite the efforts of some Governments of States which are members of the Scurity [sic] Council, this body has not yet succeeded in overcoming the obstacles which have been placed in the path of achieving a peaceful settlement in Indonesia. The responsibility of the Netherlands Government for this lack of success has already been made clear. Another obstacle has been created by the action of a Member of the United Nations which has, in many parts of the world, sought to obstruct the successful operation of the United Nations. I refer to the Union of Soviet Socialist Republics.

When this question of Indonesia was being discussed in the Security Council in Paris, the Soviet Union, speaking both through its own representative and through the representative of the Ukrainian Soviet Socialist Republic, followed its familiar procedure of endeavouring to cloak its own improper actions by seeking to place the blame on someone else. The representative of the USSR [391st meeting] and the representative of the Ukrainian SSR [393rd meeting] both insinuated that the Government of the United States was in some way responsible for the action of the Netherlands in resorting to hostilities against the Indonesian Republic. It thus becomes necessary to point out again certain salient facts.

In the first place, it was the Government of the United States which took the initiative in convening an urgent meeting of the Security Council when it became apparent that the Netherlands was resorting to military action in Indonesia [S/1128]. It was the Government of the USSR which endeavoured to prevent the Security Council from acting promptly by insisting that the Council meeting should be deferred for three days. Every other member of the Council attended the 387th meeting on 20 December except the two Soviet representatives.

The United States also took the initiative, in conjunction with the representatives of Colombia and Syria, in proposing a resolution [S/1142] to the Security Council to deal with the situation, but the USSR representative refused to support this resolution [392nd meeting]. He later tried to cover up this further attempt to block Security Council action by introducing a resolution of his own [S/1148 and S/1148/Corr. 1] which he knew could not be adopted by the Council. More fundamental, however, than these obstructionist tactics in the Security Council, is the fact that the USSR is fundamentally opposed to the Government of the Republic of Indonesia and has itself, through the Communist Party — which is, of course, its mouthpiece throughout the world — sought to undermine and overthrow this Government.

No one doubts that the communists in Indonesia like the communists throughout the world are responsive to and act in accordance with instructions from Moscow. The communist revolt against the Government of President Soekarno and Premier Hatta was itself an effort on the part of the Government of the USSR to overthrow the Indonesian Republic. Furthermore, when the resumption of hostilities by the Netherlands Government against the Indonesian Republic took place, the official Communist Party line, as printed in the communist Press, instead of deploring this action, openly gloated that it was a punishment for the Government of President Soekarno and Premier Hatta, which had successfully put down a communist revolt.

The communist line which, I repeat once more, means the line of the Soviet Government, accused that distinguished statesman of the Indonesian Republic, Mr. Hatta, of being a traitor to his country. At the very time when editorials were appearing to this effect in the Communist Party organs in Paris, the USSR representative on the Security Council sought to cover up the actual policy of his Government by identifying himself with the Council's endeavours to secure the release of Mr. Hatta and other political prisoners [392nd meeting].

These are the facts, which are on the record and known to the world, and which reveal that the Government of the USSR is not interested in supporting the Government of the Indonesian Republic or in restoring peace to Indonesia. On the contrary, it is following its familiar tactics which it has used in Korea, in Greece, in Berlin and again, now, in Indonesia, and which have been described in the speeches of many representatives at the last session of the General Assembly — namely, seeking to overthrow a lawful democratic Government and to undermine its authority. But the USSR does not want an independent Indonesia: it wants an Indonesia under the domination and control of a communist minority taking its orders from Moscow. Anywhere in the world when a communist government climbs in through the window, independence is kicked out of the door.

The Government of the United States, on the contrary, has viewed with admiration the efforts of the Indonesian people, both in the Republic and elsewhere, to gain their independence, and it has steadfastly sought to support them. The Government of the United States still takes that position, and it is for this reason that it has taken the lead in endeavouring in the Security Council and in the Committee of Good Offices to bring about a peaceful adjustment of the difficulties between the Indonesian Republic and the Netherlands Government, and to establish the United States of Indonesia as one of the fully sovereign and independent peoples of the world.

(2) Statement by the Deputy United States Representative to the United Nations Security Council (Jessup) on the Four-Power Draft Resolution on the Indonesian Question, Made before the Council, January 21, 1949.[3]

[EXCERPT]

The United States deputy representative (Jessup) made the following statement in support of a draft resolution on the Indonesian question introduced by the United States, China, Cuba, and Norway on January 21, 1949.

·   ·   ·   ·   ·   ·   ·   ·

In my statement to the Council on 11 January [398th meeting], I expressed the views of my government regarding what has happened in Indonesia. It

3 Ibid., No. 6, p. 6.

is unnecessary to repeat those views today. In the same statement, I also expressed my Government's opinion that the time had come for the Council to take appropriate action designed to help bring about a just and lasting settlement of the Indonesian dispute. We believe that, although the questions with which the Council is now confronted are incredibly complicated, the Council nevertheless has an obligation to find a balanced and a constructive answer to these questions. With this in mind, we have been consulting with various members of the Council over the past few days in an effort to arrive at a considered long-term approach to the problem. In the course of these consultations, as the representative of Cuba has pointed out, a determined effort has been made to wrestle with each of the essential elements in the problem before us. In our opinion, the consultations have resulted in a fundamentally sound answer to the situation with which the Council is confronted.

We have joined with the representatives of China, Cuba and Norway in working out the text of a draft resolution which represents the considered views of all of us regarding the most effective and productive way of dealing with the present situation in Indonesia. Each sponsoring delegation will, of course, state its own point of view, and we have already heard one of the sponsoring delegations do so. I have recognized, as I am sure all members of the Council will have recognized, that the representative of Cuba has well pointed out the fact that this joint resolution is the result of a joint negotiation and represents an attempt to meet many different points of view. I should like, for our part, to elaborate on what we consider the major premises upon which this draft resolution is based, for we believe it is only on these premises that a real solution can be found.

In the first place, we are convinced that there is no question but that the Council must continue to concern itself with the Indonesian question. My delegation is not able to accept the jurisdiction of the Council which has just been so eloquently stated by the representatives of Belgium. We agree with the recent statement *[400th meeting]* of the representative of the United Kingdom that in the light of recent events we now have a situation in which the Security Council must feel compelled to make recommendations. As matters stand, I think the majority of the members of the Council will agree that we have an obligation to continue our efforts to assist in arriving at a solution as a whole. The time has passed for a piecemeal approach.

A second basic premise of ours is that there were and are two parties before us. Discussions concerning the legal inequality in their status have not at any point prevented the Council from dealing with them as parties. The fact that they both in good faith signed an agreement under the auspices of our agency is sufficient, apart from any other consideration, to establish both as parties with which we can legitimately concern ourselves, as we have done hitherto. As we understand the factual situation at the moment, however, it is necessary for the Council to seek to re-establish the position of one of the parties to a point where it can resume *bona fide* negotiations with the other. Naturally, the Council cannot accept the contention that, in its present situation, the Government of the Republic is able to enter upon negotiations in any real sense of the word. Clearly, it must be enabled to negotiate with the Netherlands freely and thus have a voice in the discussion of the future of Indonesia.

In the third place, we do not believe that the Security Council can place the seal of its approval on the results of the recent military action. We all know that the Dutch troops will have to be withdrawn if the ultimate goal of creating a sovereign United States of Indonesia is to be achieved. We do not understand that the Netherlands Government has any intention or desire to maintain its troops in occupation indefinitely. The problem before us is not whether the troops should be withdrawn; the real problem is the method of timing of withdrawal, worked out in such a way as not to create other and perhaps even greater difficulties.

In solving a problem of this nature, we all recognize that there are local conditions which must be taken into account. Practical matters such as the maintenance of order and the supply and delivery of food and other every-day necessities are vital to the success of an operation of this character. For example, as the records of the Committee of Good Offices will show, the problems of providing for the well-being of local populations require long and tedious efforts. The destruction of a single railroad bridge, the burning of a single sugar refinery, can mean that the population of a particular area is cut off from vital sources of supply. There may be many communities whose daily supply of rice depends on access to areas from which, for all we know, they are now completely cut off. Where a local population might have to depend on delivery of grain by oxcart, a blown-up bridge can lead to the severest deprivation unless such factors are provided for. We believe the only way they can be provided for is to approach the problem of withdrawal realistically and painstakingly.

If we overlook such factors as these, we are simply not living up to our primary responsibilities. Accordingly, we recognize that these factors must be brought into balance after full consideration of each one of them. This balance is reflected in the preamble of our draft resolution. In the operating clauses, we have directed the commission to take them all into account before recommending to the parties the circumstances under which withdrawal should take place. The Security Council itself, if its authority is invoked in the matter, should also take these considerations into account.

We all recognized that in our draft resolution we have placed a heavy burden on the commission. We have not, on the other hand, sought to give it any power which the Security Council cannot delegate. In the final analysis, the responsibility rests with the Council. We are convinced, however, that it is necessary to give our agency on the spot sufficient authority in the first instance to enable it to meet the new situation there.

In the fourth place, we consider that the negotiations should be assisted by an agency of the Security Council. Both parties have heretofore accepted such assistance; we assume they will continue to accept it. We believe, however, that eighteen months' experience has shown that a goal must be set for the consummation of negotiations; a protraction of them will not serve the interests of either party. As the reports of the Committee of Good Offices will show, most of the basic issues have already been thoroughly explored. In some matters, there has been a large measure of agreement. It now remains to bridge the gap between these areas, and we believe that with the assistance of the commission, as described in the draft resolution, the gap can be bridged.

The parties have been negotiating intermittently over a period of **three** years. They have not yet arrived at an agreement on the political issues between them. It is clear to all of us, however, that it is only through negotiation of these political issues that there can be a just and durable settlement of the Indonesian question. Fortunately, the negotiations which have taken place so far have produced some measure of agreement on the really fundamental issues. There are certain basic principles which have been incorporated in the Linggadjati and *Renville* Agreements which undoubtedly will form a part of any final settlement. Both these instruments, for example, contemplate the creation and establishment of a federal, sovereign and independent United States of Indonesia. Both contemplate the inclusion of the

Republic as a State within the United States of Indonesia. Both contemplate a union in which the Kingdom of the Netherlands and the United States of Indonesia will be equal partners.

In addition to the measure of agreement reached in these instruments, the parties have also explored, as the reports of the Committee of Good Offices indicate, a considerable number of important issues regarding the interim period between the present and the time when the sovereignty is transferred. We believe that future negotiations should take advantage of the fact that much ground has already been covered, and we have sought to reflect this in the joint draft.

Finally, I think we all realize that it is essential to any workable settlement in Indonesia that it should be the result of agreement on the part of those concerned; we do not believe a political settlement should or could be successfully imposed by one of the parties, or for that matter, through outside intervention. We consider that not only must a final settlement be negotiated, but that, since a final settlement will necessarily affect the future of Indonesia as a whole, the negotiations must take into account the full interests of all parts of Indonesia. For this reason, we believe the representatives of non-Republican parts of Indonesia should have an opportunity to participate in the negotiations.

The draft resolution as a whole is an effort to promote settlement, firstly, by seeking to establish conditions under which free and *bona fide* negotiations can take place; secondly, by allowing all concerned to reach whatever freely negotiated settlement they wish; thirdly, by preserving certain basic points of agreement already reached; and, fourthly, by making certain provisions against the possibility of an impasse. Finally, the resolution provides a time schedule which, we believe, corresponds in all essentials to the achievement of the goals which both parties have again and again declared they desire to achieve.

We believe that this joint resolution meets the various elements in the problem before us which the majority of the members of the Security Council consider must be taken into account. We realize that there are some who would like to see certain elements dealt with in more detail; others would like to see them dealt with less elaborately. The tabling of this draft resolution moves the discussions in the Council into a stage of concrete examination of a text. A full exchange of views on the text should lead to a complete understanding of its intent. If other suggestions are made, my delegation will study them carefully and will be prepared to exchange views in regard to them. We also reserve our right to discuss particular provisions of the draft resolution which has now been tabled if questions are raised regarding them.

We hope that approach made in the joint drafting of this resolution will be recognized by all concerned as an earnest and conscientious attempt to help reach a solution in Indonesia. We hope also that, when the Council expresses its view through the adoption of a resolution, that resolution will command the full support and co-operation of both parties, without which this or any other attempt could not succeed.

(3) *Resolution on the Indonesian Question, Adopted by the United Nations Security Council, January 28, 1949.*[4]

In a paragraph-by-paragraph vote taken on January 28, the four-power resolution introduced on January 21 was approved by the Security Council. Certain sections of the preamble were adopted by a vote of 10 to 0 with 1 abstention (France)

4 *Ibid.*, Document S/1234, January 28, 1949.

while the sections referring to the functions and powers of the United Nations Commission for Indonesia were accepted by a vote of 7 to 0 with 4 abstentions (Argentina, France, the Ukrainian Soviet Socialist Republic, and the Soviet Union).[5]

THE SECURITY COUNCIL,

RECALLING its resolutions of 1 August 1947, 25 August 1947, and 1 November 1947, with respect to the Indonesian Question:

TAKING NOTE with approval of the Reports submitted to the Security Council by its Committee of Good Offices for Indonesia;

CONSIDERING that its resolutions of 24 December 1948 and 28 December 1948 have not been fully carried out;

CONSIDERING that continued occupation of the territory of the Republic of Indonesia by the armed forces of the Netherlands is incompatible with the restoration of good relations between the parties and with the final achievement of a just and lasting settlement of the Indonesian dispute;

CONSIDERING that the establishment and maintenance of law and order throughout Indonesia is a necessary condition to the achievement of the expressed objectives and desires of both parties;

NOTING with satisfaction that the parties continue to adhere to the principles of the Renville Agreement and agree that free and democratic elections should be held throughout Indonesia for the purpose of establishing a constituent assembly at the earliest practicable date, and further agree that the Security Council should arrange for the observation of such elections by an appropriate agency of the United Nations; and that the representative of the Netherlands has expressed his government's desire to have such elections held not later than 1 October 1949;

NOTING also with satisfaction that the Government of the Netherlands plans to transfer sovereignty to the United States of Indonesia by 1 January 1950, if possible, and, in any case, during the year 1950;

CONSCIOUS of its primary responsibility for the maintenance of international peace and security, and in order that the rights, claims and position of the parties may not be prejudiced by the use of force;

1. CALLS upon the Government of the Netherlands to insure the immediate discontinuance of all military operations, calls upon the Government of the Republic simultaneously to order its armed adherents to cease guerrilla warfare, and calls upon both parties to co-operate in the restoration of peace and the maintenance of law and order throughout the area affected.

2. CALLS UPON the Government of the Netherlands to release immediately and unconditionally all political prisoners arrested by them since 17 December 1948 in the Republic of Indonesia; and to facilitate the immediate return of officials of the Government of the Republic of Indonesia to Jogjakarta in order that they may discharge their responsibilities under paragraph 1 above and in order to exercise their appropriate functions in full freedom, including administration of the Jogjakarta area, which shall include the city of Jogjakarta and its immediate environs. The Netherlands authorities shall afford to the

5 *Ibid.*, Document S/P.V.406, January 28, 1949.

Government of the Republic of Indonesia such facilities as may reasonably be required by that Government for its effective function in the Jogjakarta area and for communication and consultation with all persons in Indonesia.

3. RECOMMENDS that, in the interest of carrying out the expressed objectives and desires of both parties to establish a federal, independent, and sovereign United States of Indonesia at the earliest possible date, negotiations be undertaken as soon as possible by representatives of the Government of the Netherlands and representatives of the Republic of Indonesia with the assistance of the Commission referred to in paragraph 4 below on the basis of the principles set forth in the Linggadjati and Renville Agreements, and taking advantage of the extent of agreement reached between the parties regarding the proposals submitted to them by the United States representative on the Committee of Good Offices on 10 September 1948; and in particular, on the basis that:

(a) The establishment of the Interim Federal Government which is to be granted the powers of internal government in Indonesia during the interim period before the transfer of sovereignty shall be the result of the above negotiations and shall take place not later than 15 March 1949;

(b) The elections which are to be held for the purpose of choosing representatives to an Indonesian Constituent Assembly should be completed by 1 October 1949; and

(c) The transfer of sovereignty over Indonesia by the Government of the Netherlands to the United States of Indonesia should take place at the earliest possible date and in any case not later than 1 July 1950;

Provided that if no agreement is reached by one month prior to the respective dates referred to in sub-paragraphs (a), (b), and (c) above, the Commission referred to in paragraph 4 (a) below or such other United Nations agency as may be established in accordance with paragraph 4 (c) below, shall immediately report to the Security Council with its recommendations for a solution of the difficulties.

4. (a) The Committee of Good Offices shall henceforth be known as the *United Nations Commission for Indonesia*. The Commission shall act as the representative of the Security Council in Indonesia and shall have all of the functions assigned to the Committee of Good Offices by the Security Council since 18 December, and the functions conferred on it by the terms of this resolution. The Commission shall act by majority vote, but its reports and recommendations to the Security Council shall present both majority and minority views if there is a difference of opinion among the members of the Commission.

(b) The Consular Commission is requested to facilitate the work of the United Nations Commission for Indonesia by providing military observers and other staff and facilities to enable the Commission to carry out its duties under the Council's resolutions of 24 and 28 December 1948 as well as under the present resolution, and shall temporarily suspend other activities.

(c) The Commission shall assist the parties in the implementation of this resolution, and shall assist the parties in the negotiations to be undertaken under paragraph 3 above and is authorized to make recommendations to them or to the Security Council on matters within its competence. Upon agreement being reached in such negotiations the Commission shall make recommendations to the Security Council as to the nature, powers, and functions of the United Nations agency which should remain in Indonesia to assist in the implementation of the provisions of such agreement until sovereignty is transferred by the Government of the Netherlands to the United States of Indonesia.

(d) The Commission shall have authority to consult with representatives of areas in Indonesia other than the Republic, and to invite representatives of such areas to participate in the negotiations referred to in paragraph 3 above.

(e) The Commission or such other United Nations agency as may be established in accordance with its recommendation under paragraph 4 (c) above is authorized to observe on behalf of the United Nations the elections to be held throughout Indonesia and is further authorized, in respect of the Territories of Java, Madura and Sumatra, to make recommendations regarding the conditions necessary (a) to ensure that the elections are free and democratic, and (b) to guarantee freedom of assembly, speech and publication at all times, provided that such guarantee is not construed so as to include the advocacy of violence or reprisals.

(f) The Commission should assist in achieving the earliest possible restoration of the civil administration of the Republic. To this end it shall, after consultation with the parties, recommend the extent to which, consistent with reasonable requirements of public security and the protection of life and property, areas controlled by the Republic under the Renville Agreement (outside of the Jogjakarta area) should be progressively returned to the administration of the Government of the Republic of Indonesia, and shall supervise such transfers. The recommendations of the Commission may include provision for such economic measures as are required for the proper functioning of the administration and for the economic well-being of the population of the areas involved in such transfers. The Commission shall, after consultation with the parties, recommend which if any Netherlands forces shall be retained temporarily in any area (outside of the Jogjakarta area) in order to assist in the maintenance of law and order. If either of the parties fails to accept the recommendations of the Commission mentioned in this paragraph, the Commission shall report immediately to the Security Council with its further recommendations for a solution of the difficulties.

(g) The Commission shall render periodic reports to the Council, and special reports whenever the Commission deems necessary.

(h) The Commission shall employ such observers, officers and other persons as it deems necessary.

5. REQUESTS the Secretary-General to make available to the Commission such staff, funds and other facilities as are required by the Commission for the discharge of its function.

6. CALLS UPON the Government of the Netherlands and the Republic of Indonesia to co-operate fully in giving effect to the provisions of this resolution.

(4) *Statement by the United States Representative to the United Nations Security Council (Austin) Concerning the Implementation of the Council's Resolution of January 28 on the Indonesian Question, Made before the Council, March 10, 1949.*[6]

In the immediate period following the passage of the Council's resolution of January 28, little progress was made toward its implementation. On February 11, a Netherlands spokesman announced his government's willingness to accept the timetable established by the resolution and leading toward the creation of a United States of Indonesia.[7] Again on February 16, the Netherlands Government indicated that it would comply "in principle" with the Council resolution.[8] An official policy statement subsequently issued by the Netherlands stated its intention to effect the transfer of sovereignty before July 1, 1950, the date established by the January 28 resolution, and proposed a round table conference to convene at The Hague on March 12.[9] On February 28, 1949, Indonesian republican officials rejected the invitation to the discussions at The Hague, stating that they would "never take part in any action evading implementation of the Security Council's resolution."[10]

I should like to state that the United States Government continues to believe that the Security Council's resolution of 28 January represents a sound and practical basis for a just and lasting solution of the Indonesian question, and we continue to support it fully.

Five weeks have passed since the Security Council adopted this resolution. During those five weeks, it must be admitted, little progress has been made in the implementation of the provisions of the Council's resolution. There has been neither actual nor complete cessation of hostilities in Indonesia, and active warfare, both guerilla and organized, is continuing to a variable extent in different areas. This has been reported to us by the United Nations Commission's Military Executive Board in the Commission's report of 1 March.

It is true that the Netherlands has decided to lift the restrictions on the freedom of movement of the leaders of the Republic of Indonesia and that the Netherlands has stated that the lifting of these restrictions is not dependent on the Republican leaders' participation in the proposed conference at The Hague. We have yet to see, however, the practical results of this decision and the leaders of the Republic are, as far as is known, still in residence at Bangka and Prapat. In the Netherlands' Memorandum III contained in Appendix E of the Commission's report of 1 March it is stated that the Republican leaders will be subject to the same restrictions as everybody else, or, in other words, that they will be permitted the same freedom as other civilians enjoy in the areas under Netherlands control. It does not appear, however, that they are free to visit their own territory under Republican control or to have contact with their adherents in those areas. It is apparent that the Dutch have not offered the unconditional freedom which was contemplated in the Council resolution. For instance, the Republican leaders are not allowed to return to Jogjakarta.

6 *Ibid., Official Records* (4th year), No. 19, p. 30.
7 *New York Times*, February 21, 1949, p. 1.
8 *Ibid.*, February 17, 1949, p. 3.
9 *Ibid.*, February 27, 1949, p. 3.
10 *Ibid.*, March 1, 1949, p. 1.

Furthermore, the Netherlands has indicated that it is not prepared to restore the Government of the Republic to its capital at Jogjakarta, as provided in the Councils' resolution of 28 January.

We are unable to understand the attitude of the Government of the Netherlands on this question, for two reasons: first, the provisions of the Security Council resolution in this respect are intrinsically sound and reasonable; secondly, the proposed accelerated transfer of sovereignty would give the Republic the power to restore the capital at Jogjakarta.

We have lisetned [sic] today to what the representative of the Netherlands had to say, and, among other things, he said the following: "It is hoped that by a supreme concerted effort of all parties it should be possible for such a conference to reach an agreement in about six weeks on the main principle for the subjects I have mentioned before. After that, another six weeks will probably be needed, as far as the Netherlands are concerned, for the ratification of the agreements, after which the transfer of sovereignty could take place. From that moment onward, responsibility for the affairs of Indonesia would rest with the Indonesians; they would be responsible for the elections, the maintenance of law and order etc. We shall be prepared to continue to render them assistance for a short while, but only if expressly requested to do so."

I now ask whether the Republicans would be competent to maintain law and order in twelve weeks, as stated. Is it clear that they are not competent to do so now? Again, is it clear that the anarchy described to us in this address would follow on restoration if it were effected now instead of twelve weeks later?

The Security Council resolution of 28 January considers the earliest practicable date for that transfer of sovereignty, but it puts the deadline off until 1 July 1950; that is to say, admittedly a year later, a year after that accelerated deadline. Therefore, the serious question arises whether the dangers spoken of here as probable aftermaths of the restoration of the Republic to power at its capital in Jogjakarta, are real. In other words, does not this address to which we have listened admit that they are not, that they are merely fancied dangers?

What were the reasons which led the Security Council to order the restoration of the Government of the Republic to its former seat of authority? My Government believed at the time of the adoption of the resolution, and continues to believe now, that military action cannot be permitted to eliminate one of the parties before the Council. We continue to believe that until the Republican Government can resume governmental responsibility at Jogjakarta, it cannot be expected to assume the responsibilities which negotiation for a just and lasting political settlement require and entail. For the Republican leaders to take part in any negotiations which are meaningful, must they not have the opportunity to assemble as a government in their own territory, to re-establish the contact of that government with its members who are dispersed by the military action, and to be able to represent accurately the wishes of political adherents?

This is not a question of form or rhetoric; it is a vital question. We have always understood, as has the Netherlands, that any agreement for a settlement of the political future of Indonesia would have to be reached with the Government of the Republic. The Linggadjati and *Renville* Agreements amply bear out this point. I am glad also to note that the Netherlands has confirmed its point of view in this respect in connexion with the proposed conference at The Hague. There would be little of permanent value in any plan which would fail to take this central fact into account.

In order to negotiate an agreement with the Government of the Republic, there must be responsible heads of an organized Republican Government with whom to deal. An agreement resulting from negotiations undertaken without reference to such requirements seems necessarily doomed to futility. For these reasons it was apparent to my Government, and I believe to the majority of the members of the Security Council, when we were considering this matter in January, that a necessary first step in the solution of the Indonesian question was the re-establishment of the Republican Government at Jogjakarta. Unfortunately, this provision of the resolution of 28 January has not been carried out, as the Commission informed us in its report, which states: "The Netherlands Government has not complied with the basic pre-requisites of further action under the resolution". The basic factor in the present political deadlock in Indonesia is the refusal of the Netherlands Government to permit the re-establishment of the Republican Government at Jogjakarta.

In the second memorandum submitted by the Netherlands to the Commission the Netherlands maintains that to allow the return of the Republican Government to Jogjakarta would be tantamount to precluding the possibility of achieving the speedy transfer of sovereignty as envisaged by the Netherlands because with the Republican Government restored to Jogjakarta, the maintenance of law and order by the Netherlands would be impossible. But they also say here that it would be possible within twelve weeks after this accelerated transfer of sovereignty.

This seems to be a very extreme position. I believe that the records of the Committee of Good Offices during the past year indicate that unstable conditions in Indonesia were not the result of the Republican Government's existence at Jogjakarta, but were directly attributable to the fact that the negotiations for a political settlement failed to produce any concrete results.

The extensive guerrilla warfare now being carried on in Indonesia is the direct consequence of the Netherlands' abandonment of negotiations in favour of military action. Is it entirely consistent to propose, as the Netherlands proposes, the transfer of sovereignty three or four months hence to an Indonesian Government which will include the Republic as a member State while at the same time maintaining that the immediate restoration of the Republic in the limited area of Jogjakarta would result in chaos?

It seems to my Government that if Indonesia is to receive early independence, as envisaged by the Netherlands plan, a beginning must be made now by the re-establishment of the Republic. Since the Security Council last considered this matter [410th meeting], the Netherlands Government has made a new proposal that a round table conference be held at The Hague to discuss the conditions for and the means by which the earliest possible transfer of sovereignty could be effectuated, with simultaneous establishment of the Netherlands-Indonesian Union and arrangements for the transition period, including the setting up of a federal interim government, these provisions being considered in their relation to the accelerated transfer of sovereignty.

The Netherlands has issued invitations to the President of the Republic, to other non-Republican Indonesian leaders and to the United Nations Commission for Indonesia to attend this conference. Some information on the Netherlands proposal was given by the United Nations Commission in its report of 1 March and also in a letter to the President of the Security Council from the Netherlands representative dated 2 March. This proposal is in general terms and is regarded by our Commission as a counter-proposal or as a substitute for the provisions of the resolution of 28 January. Our Commission has asked for instructions as to what its position should be towards the invitation which has been extended to it.

We are also informed by the supplementary report of the Commission [S/1270/Add. 1] that the President of the Republic, Mr. Soekarno, has indicated to the Netherlands authorities that he is not at present in a position to accept the invitation. He has, however, stated that he could agree in principle with the purpose of such a conference, and that if certain prior conditions were fulfilled his Government might be prepared to send a delegation. The principal condition is the restoration of the Republican Government at Jogjakarta in accordance with the provisions of the Security Council's resolution. There is an indication in the second appendix to the Commission's supplementary report [S/1270/Add. 1] that the non-Republican Indonesian leaders represented in the Federal Assembly for Consultation are in agreement with the President of the Republic on the necessity for the restoration of the Republican Government at Jogjakarta in accordance with the Security Council's resolution.

The second prerequisite for the acceptance by the Republican Government of the invitation to attend the conference at The Hague is that the position of the United Nations Commission as provided in the resolution of 28 January should not be prejudiced thereby. It is our understanding that the Netherlands has invited the participation of the Commission in accordance with the terms of the Council's resolution, and there would, therefore, appear to be no difficulty on this point. It would be unfortunate, in our view, if agreement could not be reached by the parties concerned on the preliminary step, the restoration of the Government of the Republic to Jogjakarta in accordance with the provisions of the Security Council's resolution, in order to remove an obstacle to further free negotiations between the parties.

If the parties came to such an agreement on the terms and conditions for holding the proposed conference at The Hague, we believe that negotiations between them at such a conference would be consistent with the basic purposes and objectives of the Council's resolution of 28 January which, of course, would remain in full force and effect. We believe that it would be appropriate for the Security Council's Commission to consult with the representatives of the Netherlands, the Government of the Republic and the leaders of the Federal Assembly for Consultation, and to assist them in reaching such agreement. If agreement were reached and the conference held, our Commission could participate therein in accordance with its terms of reference.

(5) Statement by the Alternate United States Representative to the United Nations Security Council (Gross) on the Canadian Draft Resolution on The Hague Round Table Conference, Made before the Council, December 13, 1949.[11]

Pursuant to a Canadian-sponsored resolution, the Security Council on March 23 directed the Commission for Indonesia to assist the Netherlands Government and the Republican leaders in Indonesia to reach agreement with regard to the restoration of the Republican capital of Jogjakarta and the time and conditions for the holding of the proposed round table conference at The Hague. The vote was 8 to 0, with France, the Soviet Union, and the Ukraine abstaining.[12] The United States representative (Austin) supported the resolution as "it clearly opens the door for the entry of both parties to that kind of an agreement in which neither of them loses dignity or has to make any conditions that are derogatory."[13] The Netherlands

---

11 United Nations Security Council, *Official Records* (4th year), No. 52, p. 15.
12 *Ibid.*, No. 24, p. 25.
13 *Ibid.*, p. 23; Department of State, *Bulletin*, XX, p. 382.

Government had previously stated its support of such a meeting;[14] the Republicans had agreed to participation on the condition that initial discussions concern the restoration of the republican government at Jogjakarta.[15] On April 14, discussions began at Batavia, resulting on May 7, in agreement by the Republican delegation 1) to issue an order to Republican armed adherents to cease guerrilla warfare, 2) to cooperate in the restoration of peace and in the maintenance of law and order, and 3) to participate in a round table conference at The Hague with a view to accelerating the unconditional transfer of real and complete sovereignty to the United States of Indonesia. The Netherlands delegation at the same meeting agreed to establish joint committees under the auspices of the United Nations Commission for Indonesia to prepare for the return of the republican government to Jogjakarta and to study and advise on the measures to be taken to cease guerrilla warfare; to release immediately and unconditionally all political prisoners seized since December 17, 1948; to take part in the proposed round table discussion at The Hague to be held as soon as possible after the return of the republican government to Jogjakarta.[16] The United States Government expressed its wholehearted approval of this preliminary agreement.[17] Dutch troops began their evacuation of Jogjakarta on June 24,[18] and on August 1 formal cease-hostilities orders were sent out.[19]

The round table conference, meeting at The Hague from August 23 to November 2, resulted in the signing of the provisional constitution of the United States of Indonesia on October 29,[20] and The Hague Statute of Union on November 2.[21] On November 2, the two parties also signed the document transferring sovereignty over Indonesia "unconditionally and irrevocably" to the United States of Indonesia although this agreement was not to go into effect until December 30. The United Nations Commission for Indonesia reported to the Security Council great satisfaction with the results of the conference.[22] On December 7, the General Assembly approved a message of congratulations to the parties of The Hague agreement by a vote of 44 to 5 with 2 abstentions.[23] A similar resolution failed of passage in the Security Council on December 13 when one of the permanent members, the Union of Soviet Socialist Republics, voted against it.[24] On December 28, the United States extended recognition to the United States of Indonesia and appointed H. Merle Cochran as first United States ambassador.[25]

I believe that the settlement reached last month at The Hague should be regarded as a substantial contribution to the advancement of the purposes and principles of the Charter. It is a striking example of a way in which the primary purpose of this Organization can be carried into action.

The issues which had divided the Netherlands and Indonesia were resolved by peaceful means and in conformity with the principles of justice and law. But settlement concluded at The Hague represents more than an application of the methods of pacific settlement which every signatory of the Charter has agreed to use. In addition, the conferees at The Hague agreed on a new constitutional relationship between the Netherlands and Indonesia by which the legitimate aspirations of the peoples of Indonesia for independence can immediately be fulfilled. By thus acting in accordance with the spirit of the Charter, the parties were expressing and materially extending certain ideals; that should encourage all those Members of the United Nations who seek to promote social progress and better standards of life and larger freedom. For that reason, my Government believes that what occurred at The Hague between 23 August and 2 November has a significance for all Members of the United Nations. At the Conference two peoples, one an Administering Power

14 United Nations Security Council, *Official Records* (4th year), No. 21, p. 24; *New York Times*, March 15, 1949, p. 18.
15 Department of State, *Bulletin*, XX, p. 492.   16 *Ibid.*, p. 653.
17 Department of State Press Release 338, May 9, 1949.
18 *Christian Science Monitor*, June 22, 1949, p. 1.   19 Department of State, *Bulletin*, XXI, p. 181.
20 *New York Times*, October 30, 1949, p. 28.   21 *Ibid.*, November 3, 1949, p. 4.
22 United Nations Security Council, Document S/1416, November 10, 1949.
23 United Nations General Assembly, *Official Records* (4th session), p. 563.
24 United Nations Security Council, *Official Records* (4th year), No. 52, p. 34.
25 Department of State, *Bulletin*, XXII, p. 55.

and the other a nation emerging from colonial status, met, and, with the help of an organ of the Security Council, peacefully negotiated a settlement of the political differences between them. The Netherlands, which, for more than three centuries, had exercised sovereignty in the Indonesian archipelago, voluntarily agreed to transfer sovereignty immediately to the people of Indonesia.

In looking back over developments leading towards the independence of Indonesia, it is well to remember that as long ago as 1942 the Queen of the Netherlands promised that the 70 million people of Indonesia should be free. After the war, the Governments of the Netherlands and the Republic of Indonesia agreed at Linggadjati on certain broad principles which would govern the way in which Indonesia would achieve its independence. In the *Renville* Agreement those principles were re-stated and a truce was worked out under which it was hoped a final settlement could be reached. Last January [*406th meeting*] this Council itself adopted a resolution which took into account the expressed desires of both parties to establish a federal, independent and sovereign United States of Indonesia at the earliest possible date. In that resolution the Council recommended that the Government of the Netherlands and the Government of the Republic, with the assistance of the United Nations Commission for Indonesia, should undertake negotiations looking towards the transfer of sovereignty over Indonesia. In February the Netherlands Government proposed that the parties, together with the Commission, should meet at a round table conference at The Hague. In March [*421st meeting*] the Council accepted a suggestion put forward by the representative of Canada whereby the objectives of the Council's January resolution [*S/1234*] and the proposal for a round table conference at The Hague were harmonized. Finally, at the Round Table Conference in which the representatives of the Netherlands, the Republic of Indonesia, the Federal Consultative Assembly and the United Nations Commission participated, the documents which we now have before us were drawn up and agreed to.

My Government is happy to have been associated with the majority of the Members of the United Nations who have, at each of these important stages in the history of Indonesia's emergence as a sovereign State, given their hearty approval and support to the policies which have now led to success. The peoples of the Netherlands and of Indonesia recognize that, by following the principles laid down in the Charter, they have avoided for themselves, and perhaps for others, much anguish and chaos. They realize also that these principles not only provided orderly processes by which to bring about the goal they have both sought so long but, in addition, provided an ideal towards which to strive, an ideal which all free people in the community of nations respect.

I would join with the representative of Norway [*455th meeting*] in recognizing what he termed the moderation and flexible statesmanship of the Netherlands Government. In an area where its vital interests have been concerned, the Government of the Netherlands is pursuing a policy of co-operation with Indonesia which is based upon the complete independence of that country. In reaching the preliminary arrangements last May at Batavia and again at the Round Table Conference at The Hague, the Government of the Netherlands has fulfilled the obligations for pacific settlement of disputes which it undertook when it subscribed to the Charter at San Francisco.

The Indonesians, likewise, deserve the respect of the international community. We have only to consider the difficulties which often attend the struggle of a people for independence to be struck with the restraint and maturity of judgment which the Indonesians have exhibited in accepting the orderly processes urged upon them by the Security Council. In proving themselves to be conscious of responsibilities to the international community, and in demonstrating again and again a readiness to accept the obligations of pacific settlement provided in the Charter, the Indonesians have shown that they are a people qualified to take their place along with other peace-loving nations in the United Nations.

The settlement reached at The Hague is an example of the constructive role which mediation can play in helping the parties to help themselves in the solution of disputes. The report of the Commission shows how the parties turned to it for help. The Commission's proposals, reached by unanimous decision, were requested by the parties and often helped them to agree on several difficult issues facing the Conference. The Commission based its recommendations on unanimous decisions, although it was not obliged to do so under its terms of reference. Through the concerted effort of the parties and of the Commission, the Conference achieved agreement on the unconditional and irrevocable transfer of complete sovereignty over Indonesia from the Netherlands to the independent and sovereign Republic of the United States of Indonesia.

As the Commission says in the conclusion of its special report to the Council dated 10 November 1949, the new relationship between the peoples of the Netherlands and Indonesia can evolve to the mutual advantage of the partners of the Netherlands-Indonesian Union. In so doing, it will help fulfil the desire of all of us to see the peoples of these two countries, long bound together in another relationship, continue to co-operate with each other in the period following the transfer of sovereignty.

This is an occasion when it is appropriate for the Security Council to record its gratification at the events which have occurred this year in the relations between the Netherlands and Indonesia. The settlement at The Hague, which consummated these events, was what almost all of us wanted. The Indonesians wanted it. The Dutch wanted it. Last week 44 Members of the United Nations recorded in the General Assembly that they were gratified that agreement had been reached. When the fundamental principles and purposes of our Organization have been so well served, it would not be unreasonable to expect that every Member would be eager to join in congratulating the parties on having reached agreement, in welcoming the forthcoming establishment of the Republic of the United States of Indonesia as an independent sovereign State, and in commending the United Nations Commission for Indonesia for the contributions it has rendered in assistance to the parties.

Judging from what was said last week in the General Assembly, and again here yesterday and today in the Council, I can only conclude that certain representatives are distressed to see that an agreement has been reached between the parties. A few States appear reluctant to witness the promotion of social progress and better standards of living in larger freedom for 70 million people in Indonesia. It is difficult to understand this, especially in the light of the fact that the agreement at The Hague was reached through the voluntary action of the parties themselves. It was not a settlement imposed upon them. They had certain standards to go by, to be sure, the standards laid down in the Charter of the United Nations, but the settlement was not dictated to them. We must also remember that the agreement reached at The Hague provides that Indonesia will be a free and independent State, in the fullest sense, before this month is out. This means that the people of Indonesia are free to choose their own form of government and their own people to man their government. How can the representatives of the Ukrainian SSR and the USSR be opposed to this?

While the United Nations has been striving to make a positive contribution to the development of a beneficial relationship between the Netherlands and Indonesia, the Soviet Union has so far been seeking to thwart the efforts of the parties to reach agreement, and has sought to vilify the leaders of the Indonesian people. Soviet Union opposition to this settlement has been expressed in an incessant stream flowing from the propaganda organs of the Soviet Union itself, from Radio Moscow, and in articles appearing in *Bolshevik*, in *Izvestya*, and in *Red Star*.

All of us have seen how the representative of the USSR in the General Assembly and the representative of the Ukrainian SSR in the Council yesterday, and again today, have tried to twist the meaning of the documents which comprise the agreement reached at The Hague. They know, of course, that the meaning of the documents cannot be twisted for anyone who has actually read them. They know also that this meaning cannot be twisted for the people who themselves will soon be benefiting from these great instruments. As we all know, the record of the efforts of the majority of the Members of the United Nations to foster the peaceful development of the Indonesian people toward independence is already quite clear, and anyone is free to consult it at length. That record will also show the constructive contribution made at a conference at New Delhi early this year by Indonesia's neighbours along with a number of other States having close cultural ties with Indonesia. The representative of the Republic of Indonesia has ably characterized agreements of The Hague as instruments ensuring complete independence for Indonesia.

One way in which the United Nations has contributed toward the settlement of the Indonesian question has been through the resolutions which have been adopted from time to time by a majority of the members of the General Assembly and the Security Council. Thus far, the Soviet Union has not been willing to support any of the resolutions of the General Assembly or of the Council looking toward the development of Indonesia as a free and independent people.

I regret that the Soviet Union apparently does not find it possible, even at this stage of the consideration of the Indonesian question, to join with the majority of the Members of the United Nations in making a positive contribution. It is regrettable that the delegations of the Ukrainian SSR and the Soviet Union would seek to terminate the continuing authority of the Commission, as the last paragraph of the Ukrainian SSR draft resolution [S/1433] suggests. I can only assume that the Soviet Union is trying desperately hard to hide a fact which, essentially, cannot be hidden. That simple fact is that an agreement has been reached between the leaders of the Netherlands and of Indonesia, by which the people of Indonesia will be free within a matter of days.

A year ago it appeared to some that the problem of Indonesia was not susceptible of peaceful solution. The action of the parties since that time has proved the contrary. As the Commission's report dated 10 August [S/1373] shows, the Republican Government was returned to Jogjakarta and a cease-fire effectuated as the result of agreement reached at Batavia on 7 May. The assertions of the representative of the Ukrainian SSR that hostilities between the Dutch and the Indonesians are continuing are patently untrue. There may indeed be sporadic outbursts from certain extremist elements. This would not be any more surprising now than it was a year ago last September when, in the midst of one of Indonesia's most tense periods in its fight for freedom, the communists chose to revolt against the Government of the Republic of Indonesia. It may well be that the communists in Indonesia, who have always opposed a negotiated settlement, will find it difficult to accept the fact that Indonesia's independence has been achieved by peaceful means.

Following the arrangements in Batavia last May for a cease-fire and the return to Jogjakarta, negotiations were started between the Federal Consultative Assembly and the Republic on a constitution for the Republic of the United States of Indonesia. Agreement was reached by them on a draft constitution prior to their departure for The Hague. Although it is not the concern of the Security Council to pass on the constitutional instrument of a State, we may certainly be permitted to congratulate the representatives of the Federal Consultative Assembly and the Republic of Indonesia on the fact that they have reached agreement on a draft constitution [S/1417/Add.1, appendix VI]. A glance at the draft constitution shows that it is an instrument of a free people.

At The Hague the parties agreed on a Union Statute [S/1417/Add.1, appendix IX] which provides that co-operation between them will be continued through the medium of the Netherlands-Indonesian Union. This Union, far from prejudicing the status of either member as an independent sovereign State, enhances it. It is a voluntary Union which permits unlimited co-operation between the parties on a basis of equality.

Although the question of New Guinea was not finally settled at The Hague, the decision to postpone the question was a wise one in view of the important factors to be taken into account and in view of the desirability of concluding the Conference successfully within the agreed time limit. It is important that the parties now proceed to ratify the agreements of The Hague so that the implementation of the broader agreements may begin immediately. I have no doubt that, as contemplated within the settlement at The Hague, a satisfactory solution for the problem of New Guinea will be reached within the year.

As we are considering the Indonesian question in the Security Council, the parties are engaged in the process of ratifying the agreements reached at The Hague. Such ratification, of course, must come before the agreements themselves can come into operation.

We must not conclude that the work in Indonesia is done. As the Canadian draft resolution recognizes, certain tasks remain for the Commission by virtue of its terms of reference under the 28 January resolution, as well as by virtue of the request of the parties themselves. It is therefore suitable for the Security Council to note its approval of the Commission's intention to continue exercising its responsibilities. This it may properly do under the resolution of 28 January and the letter of 23 March, and I have already expressed our regret that the representatives of the Ukrainian SSR and the Soviet Union apparently seek to terminate that continuing authority.

Specifically, the Commission has before it the task of recommending whether a plebiscite should be held in a particular territory, and of assisting the parties in arrangements for the withdrawal of Netherlands forces and of observing the implementation of the agreements of The Hague. Both parties have requested the Commission to stay to assist in those phases of the work still to be done in Indonesia, and the Commission itself has stated its intention, under the authority of the January resolution, to aid the parties in these matters. The Commission is able, under its present terms of reference, to continue the task it has handled so successfully thus far.

When the Security Council was considering this case in March of this year, it was a suggestion of the representative of Canada which led to agreement on a message which the Council sent to the Commission for Indonesia. The Commission reported that this letter of 23 March was of some help to it.

The draft resolution which the representative of Canada has now put before us formulates in a felicitous manner an attitude which my Government warmly supports. I shall vote in favour of the draft resolution. I think the Council may properly thank the representative of Canada for his deep interest in this case which has been embodied in the draft resolution now before us.

The draft resolution submitted by the Ukrainian SSR has a familiar look. Substantially the same resolution was proposed in the Security Council a year ago [S/1148], almost to a day, by the Soviet Union. The identical resolution was submitted to the *Ad Hoc* Political Committee and re-introduced in the General Assembly only last week. The United States Government has not altered the opinion which it expressed in the General Assembly that this draft resolution adds nothing to our consideration of the problem and that it in no way reflects the developments and progress of the past year.

CHAPTER XV

Europe, Africa and Western Asia

1. GENERAL

For information concerning economic cooperation with Europe, see this volume, p. 200.

(1) Statement by the Secretary of State (Acheson) on United States Policy toward Western Europe, Made before the Committee on Foreign Relations of the Senate, February 8, 1949.[1]

[EXCERPTS]

When the President signed the Foreign Assistance Act of 1948 he said, "Our program of foreign aid is perhaps the greatest venture in constructive statesmanship that any nation has undertaken. It is an outstanding example of cooperative endeavor for the common good."

At that time, almost three years had passed since the end of hostilities. The nations with which we are here concerned had made heroic efforts to restore the production upon which recovery must be predicated and to achieve economic, social and political stability. They had been through six years of the exhaustion of war and many had suffered the disintegrating effects of enemy occupation. Nature added difficulties and it had become apparent that without further aid they could not achieve their goal.

The Senate Committee on Foreign Relations enumerated in its report the following reasons why Europe was in need:

> Economic nationalism, political tensions and uncertainty, war devastation, the prolonged interruption of international trade, the loss of foreign income and dollar funds, internal financial disequilibrium, shortage of supplies from Southeast Asia, the wartime movement of peoples to certain areas of western Europe, and a ten percent increase of population have all contributed to economic breakdown in Europe. Germany, a focal point in the European economy, is paralyzed. Inflation is rampant. Subversive elements are hampering recovery and engineering social chaos.

In determining to add our assistance to the joint efforts of these nations, the Congress was acutely conscious that the countries of Western Europe were of key importance to both international security and recovery.

Before the end of the war a framework for collective security through the United Nations had been evolved. However, success under the Charter depended not only on the solution of the political problems concerning the enemy states, but also upon the recovery and reinvigoration of the nations which had suffered disruption and destruction in the war. In this effort, the

1 Department of State Press Release 74, February 8, 1949.

continuance of the nations of Western Europe as vigorous and virile communities was essential to the maintenance of a free world of free states for which the war had been fought, as well as for the economic recovery and development of such states.

Thus, a strong United Nations, composed of free member nations, in turn composed of free men, depended upon the avoidance of disintegration both in the international and in the national lives of its member countries. This the Congress rightly believed could only be achieved by the nations with which we are here concerned joining in a great group effort and by the United States adding its aid to their efforts. It was for this purpose that the European Recovery Program was devised and enacted.

The reason for our assistance was stated in the report of the House Committee on Foreign Affairs in the following words:

> It is unnecessary to paint the picture of the alternative with which this country would be faced, should the few great critical barriers to the march of communism disappear. Past and present sacrifices of an economic character would be small indeed compared to the burden which this Nation would have to assume in such a world. The very survival of the United States would be more seriously at stake than at any other time in its history. Faced with this prospect, there can be but one choice: to extend the aid necessary in both economic and military spheres. A calculated risk, it has been called. But such a risk is no risk, compared to the grim certainty of the alternative.

But to leave the matter there is to give only a partial impression. Nations cannot be thought of as abstractions or mere personified collective nouns. They are composed of people. And it is in terms of people that this program must find its success in the reinvigoration of the life of nations.

. . . .

Our moving purpose is not material; it is to make it possible for peoples who want to live a decent, orderly, and just and free life to do so again. To help them, as individuals, as members of families, as citizens of great states to be their true selves again, after two great wars.

. . . .

Events have proved that the hopes reposed in this program, both here and abroad, have not been misplaced.

The 16 nations which were willing and able to meet together to act upon this suggestion are all still to be counted in the ranks of the democracies. There has been no advance in totalitarianism on the continent of Europe.

It cannot be claimed, and I shall not attempt to do so, that this result is solely due to the Recovery Program. But, without it, the situation would have been very different. As it is, the free community of Europe has not only held its own, but it has, during this period, made great strides forward.

The situation today on that continent is vastly more encouraging than it was two years ago. Within the participating countries there has been a rebirth of faith in the vitality of the democratic system and its ability to deal with their postwar problems.

In every important election held in these countries since the inception of this program of recovery, the people have more vigorously reaffirmed their adherence to the principles of individual freedom and governments based on constitutional restraints. Those elements within the countries who, by deliberate choice or foreign inspiration, sought — in the words of Secretary Marshall — "to perpetuate human misery in order to profit therefrom politically", have been checked and forced into retreat.

There is, however, one aspect of increasing strength and confidence on the part of the participating countries which I want to mention.

There have been definite advances made in Europe in the field of collective security.

The Brussels Pact is a striking manifestation of the resolve of the signatory countries to defend their independence and freedoms against external aggression. It has already had an important effect in increasing the sense of security so essential to the achievement of recovery. This pact was warmly welcomed by this country as an important contribution to recovery and a heartening indication of returning strength and confidence to Western Europe. In both of these purposes we are deeply interested.

I believe that no one can fail to see the connection between the revival of the national life of a group of countries and the ability to protect the fruits of their labors. It is for this reason and for the furtherance of the security of the United States that we are now considering how best we can assist in furthering the sense of security in Europe.

I believe that we have recognized here, from the very beginning, and so have the participating countries, that the greater the unity, both economic and political among the free nations of Europe, the greater the progress towards the restoration of those conditions of economic health, social tranquility, political freedom and security which represents our common goal.

In the economic field, the outstanding development towards joint action is found in the Organization for European Economic Cooperation which was established last April by the countries participating in the Recovery Program to coordinate their national recovery efforts. Sixteen sovereign countries, together with the Western zones of Germany and Trieste, meet in this organization to develop, through mutual agreement, the steps necessary to achieve recovery. More and more there has grown the practice of joint effort, of the accommodation of separate national interests to the good of the whole. This Organization already has a record of achievement and gives great promise for the future.

Progress towards closer political association will, of necessity, take time. Impatience for speedy results will not help in its ultimate achievement. Here, I think, we must realize the obstacles which have to be overcome before this great objective is achieved. There have, however, been significant steps toward the eventual development of a closer political union.

The Brussels Pact, to which I have already referred, is considerably more than a military association. It deals with collaboration, in many of the other fields — social, cultural, economic as well as political.

A Council of Europe is soon to be established in which the leading nations of Western Europe will find a forum for the consideration of their common problems.

The form and nature of these developments along economic and political lines must, if they are to be strong and lasting, come from the people of Europe themselves. Only they themselves can work out their own salvation through their own efforts. Our role, as the Congress has already determined, must be to encourage and support these efforts.

.   .   .   .

(2) *Address by the Commanding General of the First Army (Smith) on Europe as a Bulwark of Peace, Delivered before the Conference of Governors, Colorado Springs, Colorado, June 20, 1949.*[2]

[EXCERPTS]

.   .   .   .

The turn of events since the end of the war has placed upon the United States, as the citadel of freedom and the strongest of the free nations, the major responsibility for world recovery, world peace, and world progress, and at the same time has confronted this nation with potentially the gravest challenge ever offered to our principles and our way of life. This situation results from the decision of the leaders of Soviet Russia to turn away from the cooperation which we hoped would prevail after the war, and instead to seek to impose Communism upon the world. The consequent resistance of the free peoples of the world to subjugation and enslavement has brought about the world-wide struggle in which we are now engaged.

.   .   .   .

Regardless of from what direction one approaches the problem, he must inevitably arrive at the conclusion that the best assurance of peace is our determination and strength to support our convictions. It is not sufficient only to have strength to defend ourselves by military means if necessary. The potential must exist and by its very existence it serves its highest purpose, which is in preventing war. We all know now that while victory in war saves us from the imposition of solutions we are determined to reject, victory itself raises grave new problems in turn. As one who has seen war, I am earnestly concerned with the creation of conditions that will assure peace.

This is the object of this nation's policies in foreign affairs. As a member of the United Nations, we are pledged to the settlement of international disputes by pacific means. We are conscientiously trying to strengthen the United Nations as an effective instrument for preserving the peace. We are energetically working, both inside and outside the United Nations, to promote the economic and social conditions throughout the world that will minimize conflicts and remove the causes of wars. If we continue to pursue these policies vigorously and steadfastly we will succeed in throwing back the challenge of Communism and at the same time preserving the peace.

2 Department of State Publication 3570.

One of the fundamental measures for achieving that purpose is the European Recovery Program, an essential and effective means of assuring peace. No one who has been in Europe for any length of time since the war can help but be profoundly impressed by the great change that has taken place since the Marshall Plan has been in operation. Little more than a year ago, Western Europe was disorganized economically, depleted physically, and depressed spiritually. The position of its free nations was precarious. It was a situation of crisis in which anything might happen. The prospects for peace were anything but promising.

The contrast between conditions in Europe then and today is remarkable. The free nations of Western Europe have literally taken a new lease on life. They are working together as never before. The people have been given more than new hope, as important as that is. They have been given something to work with, and their production record proves that they not only are eager to work but that they also have the skill and the determination to reestablish themselves in the world. The Marshall Plan has not been the only factor in effecting this transformation, but it has been the major force in the stabilization of Europe. I am certain that history will confirm President Truman's judgment that the Marshall Plan marked the turning point.

.   .   .   .

The recovery of Europe is a primary requisite for the maintenance of the free way of life and the preservation of peace. But even European recovery is only part of a larger design. The economic revival of Western Europe is necessary to make the peoples of that continent self-supporting and to enable them to resume their proper place in world affairs. Economic recovery also will provide them in time with the strength to assume their own security. But they do not have that strength at present.

All the nations of Western Europe that engaged in the recent war, with the exception of Great Britain, emerged from that conflict practically defenseless. Since VE-day they have begun rebuilding their defenses, but it is a slow, laborious process, particularly since economic recovery has priority. The knowledge of their inadequate defenses, in the face of the aggressive and expansive tendencies of the Soviet Union, has contributed to a pervading sense of insecurity that weighs heavily on Western Europe. Even while putting forth their utmost effort for recovery, the people have been haunted by the fear that they might be rebuilding only to have the fruits of their labor again usurped by an occupying army.

The sense of insecurity arising from these circumstances is in itself a serious detriment to recovery, stability, and peace. In order to achieve our objectives in Europe, the United States must use its own strength to shield the free nations of Europe from aggression while they rebuild their defenses, just as we are using our material resources to enable the people of Western Europe to revive their economies. This is the purpose of the North Atlantic Treaty, which the Foreign Relations Committee of the Senate has unanimously recommended for ratification, and the legislation for military assistance, which the Administration is now preparing to submit to the Congress.

The treaty, which is a pact for the mutual defense of the North Atlantic area against armed attack from any source, commits the 12 signatory countries to help each other to maintain and develop their individual and collective capacity to resist aggression. It is in partial fulfillment of that obligation that the Administration proposes to provide 1 billion, 130 million dollars of military assistance to the European members of the treaty during the next fiscal year.

The purpose of this measure is to accelerate the rebuilding of the defenses of Western Europe, both to increase the faith of the free peoples of Europe in their own ability to resist aggression and to make more effective their pledge to contribute to the mutual defense of the North Atlantic area. The promise that all of the 12 nations signing the treaty naturally including the United States will come promptly to the aid of any one of them which is attacked is in itself a strong deterrent to aggression. From what we know of the nature of Soviet Communism, it is obvious that the effectiveness of that deterrent will be increased in proportion to the known ability of all 12 nations to resist and defeat an aggressor.

The great, the priceless benefit we expect to gain from this treaty is peace. We seek that benefit by making clear in advance our determination and that of our partners in the treaty resolutely to resist armed attack with all the strength available to us all. Determination is not enough; it must be backed by strength.

If war should nevertheless come, the advantages of this arrangement would not by any means accrue solely to the European members of the treaty. With the experience of two World Wars in mind, I think it is clearly apparent that there are tremendous advantages to the United States in having strong and loyal friends on the continent of Europe. In the event of war, these advantages are greatly increased if our associates in Europe are able to maintain their position until we are able to join our forces with theirs on the continent. Therefore, our assistance in strengthening the ability of our Atlantic pact associates successfully to resist aggression in Europe is equivalent to strengthening the defenses of the United States.

The conclusive reason for military assistance to the free nations of Europe is that it materially enhances the prospects for peace. The greatest single achievement leading to the creation of conditions that would assure lasting peace in the world would be the reestablishment in Europe of a group of strong, free, virile and progressive states, living together in harmony and cooperating closely in political, economic, and social matters for the good of their own people and the people of the world. This kind of Europe, no longer dependent on the United States or fearful of attack from the East, would be a stabilizing force with great influence in world affairs.

This kind of Europe would contain a population greater than that of Russia, much further advanced in science and technology, with resources much better developed and an industrial organization much more efficient and productive. Such a Europe would be able effectively to resist the encroachments of Communism. By providing a living, dynamic demonstration of the superior values of the free way of life over totalitarian, such a Europe would inevitably exert a profound attraction for the repressed and impoverished peoples under the Communist yoke.

Above all, the kind of Europe envisioned as resulting from our present policies would be a great constructive force for peace. The free nations of Europe share our aversion for war. That aversion has been intensified by the tragic experiences of recent years. Strength in the hands of the free peoples of Europe will be strength dedicated to the defense of peace. We can make no better investment for peace than the restoration of the strength of the free nations of Europe.

We can help make Europe a bulwark of peace by doing three things: First, continuing the European Recovery Program in full force until we have finished the job and attained the objective we set ourselves in the beginning. Second, entering fully and wholeheartedly into the North Atlantic Treaty for the mutual defense of the vital centers of Western civilization. Third, providing military assistance as an effective step toward reconstituting the strength of Western Europe as a positive force for peace.

.   .   .   .   .

We have made a good start on a policy that has achieved a considerable measure of success. We need to keep at it. Hesitancy or delay at this time would only hearten the enemies of democracy and weaken the confidence of the free peoples in the leadership of the United States which has brought the world thus far along the road to recovery and peace. We can't march up the hill one day and down again the next. We must go forward, step by step, to world peace and security. Only in such a world can our own peace and security be assured.

2. MILITARY COOPERATION WITH WESTERN EUROPE

A. North Atlantic Treaty

[See *Documents, X, 1948*, p. 588.]

In his inaugural address of January 20, 1949, President Truman, stating that the United States would "strengthen freedom-loving nations against the danger of aggression," reported that negotiations were in progress with "a number of countries" with a view to the conclusion of a "joint agreement designed to strengthen the security of the North Atlantic area."[1] Although conversations concerning the agreement had been initiated in Washington during the summer of 1948, press reports indicated that, at the time of the President's address, the geographic scope of the proposed treaty had not as yet been defined. French attempts to include French North African territories in the defense area were reported in February;[2] and discussions continued as to the desirability of bringing the Scandinavian countries, Italy, Switzerland, and Portugal into the pact. The possibility of Swiss participation was, however, precluded in a press statement issued by the Swiss Foreign Minister (Petitpierre) in Paris on February 19.[3] A Norwegian representative (Munthe de Morgenstierne) participated in drafting discussions for the first time on March 4.[4] The text of the draft completed by representatives of Canada, France, Belgium, the Netherlands, Luxembourg, Norway, the United Kingdom, and the United States was made public on March 18, 1949. These governments as well as Denmark, Italy, Iceland, and Portugal formally approved the text on April 2,[5] following their rejection of a Soviet memorandum of March 31 protesting the "aggressive aims" of the pact and its contradiction of the "principles and aims of the United Nations organization and the commitments which the Governments of the United States of America, Great Britain and France have assumed under other treaties and agreements."[6] Formal signing of the pact took place in Washington on April 4, 1949.[7]

The text of the North Atlantic Treaty was transmitted by the President to the Senate for advice and consent with respect to ratification on April 12.[8] Hearings were held by the Senate Committee on Foreign Relations during which both administration witnesses[9] and private witnesses[10] presented testimony from April 27 to May 18. The committee unanimously reported the treaty on June 6 and recommended that the Senate consent to its ratification by the President.[11] Senate consent was indicated by a vote of 82 to 13 taken on July 21 and ratification followed on July 25. The pact entered into force on August 24, 1949.[12]

---

1 For the text of the President's inaugural address, see this volume, p. 7.
2 *New York Times*, February 14, 1949, p. 6.
3 *Ibid.*, February 21, 1949, p. 6.
4 *Ibid.*, March 5, 1949, p. 3.   5 Department of State Press Release 216, April 2, 1949.
6 *New York Times*, April 2, 1949, p. 5. For the text of the statement of the signatories to the treaty regarding the Soviet memorandum, see Department of State, *Bulletin*, XX, p. 457.
7 For the proceedings of signature, see Department of State Publication 3497.
8 Senate Document, Executive L, 81st Cong., 1st sess.
9 *North Atlantic Treaty. Hearings before the Committee on Foreign Relations, United States Senate, 81st Congress, 1st Session* . . . , Part 1.
10 *Ibid.*, Parts 2 and 3.   11 Senate Executive Report 8, 81st Cong., 1st sess.
12 Department of State, *Treaties and Other International Acts Series 1964.*

The Council established under Article 9 of the North Atlantic Treaty met in Washington in its first session on September 17, 1949, to provide for its own future operation and to create a Defense Committee and "such other subsidiary bodies as are deemed necessary to assist the Council" in implementing the treaty.[13] The Defense Committee subsequently met for its first session in Washington on October 5 and for its second session in Paris on December 1.[14] The second session of the North Atlantic Council met in Washington on November 18, at which meeting it approved the creation of a Defense Financial and Economic Committee and confirmed the action of the Defense Committee at its first session in establishing a Military Production and Supply Board.[15]

(1) *Address by the United States Ambassador-at-Large (Jessup) on the North Atlantic Treaty and the Bases of United States Foreign Policy, Delivered before the National Conference on American Foreign Policy, Washington, March 17, 1949.*[16]

It seems to me we always have certain stages in the formation of a foreign policy. One would perhaps begin with an interest in the problem, an interest which may grow into what the Quakers call a concern. As the problem develops, the interest or concern may develop into a need, a need for actually deciding how the United States is going to deal with a particular problem.

Now, that may involve a very broad consideration of a relation to a very broad subject. Again, it may be something relatively narrow. But so far as the broader implications of policy are concerned, I think sometimes that all of us who look at the Department of State from the outside have had too much of a tendency to feel that foreign policy on each particular point ought to be reduced in the Department of State to an entry on a regular library card. Then should someone ask "What is the policy on Germany"? you merely thumb through the cards to "G," and pull out a card, read a few sentences, and you know what the policy is. Obviously, of course, it is not so simple as that. Nevertheless, there are certain principles which I think are rather constant, certainly over very long periods of time. They go into the formation, not only of broad policies but also of many policies in detail.

Policies, of course, are not born. There is not a certain instant when a policy comes into being. It evolves. All policies have backgrounds of shorter or longer periods of time, and they have contributing to them a great many factors and a great many influences.

I believe that in the formation of a foreign policy or in the evolution of a foreign policy there are two factors which always have to be kept in mind: one is a sense of direction, and the other is the choice of method. In the sense of direction in terms of our general over-all policy, I would pick out perhaps four things that seem to be pretty well-fixed in our foreign policy as giving that sense of direction. The first one can be suggested by repeating again the old saying that "War is Hell," and we don't want this country to go to war.

If I may carry that to its obvious conclusion, the maintenance and the perfection of peace is a basic sense of direction. Secondly, and of course related to it, is the question of security. There, it seems to me that our sense of direction in this period is one which recognizes that security is a mutual and not a unilateral concept. The third, it seems to me, is that the same goes for the question of general prosperity, welfare, and economic growth and the possibilities of the evolution and development and improvement of international trade to the mutual advantage of all concerned. Again, it is a mutual and not a unilateral direction. Finally, it seems to me that we have, as part of our

13 Department of State, *Bulletin*, XXI, p. 469.   14 *Ibid.*, p. 948.
15 *Ibid.*, p. 819.   16 *Ibid.*, XX, p. 393.

sense of direction, consideration of the position of the individual in society. There, it seems to me, it is very interesting to reflect on the difference between our way of handling the concept and the way in which the Russians handle it.

I don't suppose a very large proportion of the American people could give you a well-reasoned and detailed statement of their innate conviction that the individual is important. It is the kind of thing, the kind of concept, that we have in our Declaration of Independence and which appears again in Woodrow Wilson's 14 points. It also appears in the Atlantic Charter. Further, it is reflected in the Charter of the United Nations. But I am sure that every American, though he could not match a Marxist in a debate on a reasoned philosophical outline of his theory of the importance of the individual, would have a very strong innate conviction that there was something inside himself, and he knew what it meant. It was not necessary to state it, but he knew what it was, and to him it is very important. I think it is very important and that it marks one of the characteristics, not a unique characteristic of American policy, but yet a characteristic of American policy in the nature of one of these senses of direction to which I have referred.

On the choice of method, I believe that it is perfectly clear at the present time that we have chosen the collective approach to the goals which we have in mind in various aspects of our foreign policy; and specifically in that collective approach, we have chosen the United Nations as an instrument through which we intend to operate for the achievement of what we think is desirable from our point of view, and from the point of view of the world. We have not had in the history of the United States a large number of what might be referred to as basic foreign policies of a long-term character and of supreme importance. Traditionally, we have always referred to the Monroe Doctrine and the policy of neutrality. I think that in retrospect, as the historians write the history of this modern period, the present policy of international cooperation (which certainly has taken the place of the essence of our traditional policy of neutrality from the beginning of our period up through the nineteenth century and the earlier part of this century) certainly the principle of international cooperation needs to be listed in the long-range history of the United States as something of great consequence and of lasting validity. I don't think it is a short-term approach. When we think, however, of this field of international cooperation, we do find in current American thinking some disagreement as to the nature of that process of international cooperation. A lot of people think of it in universal terms; at one high point on one side, the extreme terms of world government, world federalism, whatever form it may take; at a lower extreme, but still within the field of international cooperation, a concept of attending meetings of various bodies of the United Nations but without any real sense of participating in an organization which is actually doing and accomplishing various things. I would suggest that there is a very broad middle ground between the concept of universality and the concept of unilateralism — unilateralism which at certain periods was identical with isolationism. It is in that broad middle group, the middle ground which the United Nations itself occupies now, because the United Nations is far from universal, that the United States is operating.

Coming down to the application of foreign policy, not yet in terms of the handling of a specific issue in a specific place, but along broad lines, I think we have a very clear indication in the President's inaugural address in which he laid down the four points of cooperation with the United Nations, of continuing economic assistance, of providing security, and the bold new program of development of underdevolped areas through our technical know-how and other forms of assistance; these points represent a general line of policy to which the United States is committed and which the United States is following. Against that concept of those four points I would like to speak briefly about a subject for which I know is in the minds of everyone. It is the pending peace pact for the Atlantic community.

As the Secretary told you this morning, the text of the pact is to be published very shortly. Obviously, it isn't appropriate for me to discuss the text just before it is published. However, I would like to deal with it again in the light of its relationship to general, broad, long-term considerations of policy.

It has, as you all know, a rather immediate background in terms of the Brussels pact, the Vandenberg resolution and the Rio pact. I would like to suggest that there is a fundamental conception embodied in the so-called Atlantic pact which goes far back in our history and which, as a matter of fact, is so inherent both in individual human nature and in the nature of a nation, of a state, that it is bound to be present in any foreign policy which is formulated or evolved at any particular period. I refer to the idea of self-defense. That concept of self-defense was certainly at the root of the formulation of the Monroe Doctrine. You remember Monroe referred to those things which would affect, in our opinion, our "peace and safety." In official authoritative declaration many times since that policy was announced in 1820, we have expressly said that it is based on the right of self-defense and the right of self-preservation. We have justified it upon those grounds.

Now, in terms of the world in which the United States lived in 1820, that concept of defense seemed to us, and I think properly, limited to this hemisphere. But the limitation to the hemisphere in the terms of the Monroe Doctrine wasn't a geographical concept essentially. It was a political concept illustrated in terms of geography, because the geography at that time under those conditions, served to bring out the reality of the political situation. But spaced [sic] in international affairs is obviously of political importance only in terms of the facility or difficulty of transversing that space. It isn't the thing in itself which is of consequence. The boundaries of our security, the boundaries of our "peace and safety," as the term is used by Monroe, certainly are not lines which are fixed upon a map. If you choose to chart them any day on a map, you may find you must revise that map on any subsequent day. Clearly those boundaries of our security, of our peace and safety, necessarily change with changing conditions from year to year. The evolution of that conception of ours of the boundaries of our security and of the needs of our defense was, [sic] as stated in 1820, have [sic] many details which can be filled in. I would like to point to a few relatively recent highlights.

Obviously, in the history of the Monroe Doctrine there were many cases of specific application. Carrying the idea on, one comes to the period when Woodrow Wilson was talking about a Monroe Doctrine for the world, which was a concept of mutual defense, getting away from the original unilateralism and merging into the modern period of multilateralism or universalism. One finds in our whole inter-American development from that original period when we were announcing the Monroe Doctrine unilaterally and maintaining it unilaterally, a steady trend reaching to the point of a general universalization and the broadening out of the Monroe Doctrine in terms of a general concept of the American continent. That development, it seems to me, reached a climax in the conclusion of the Rio pact. This pact was based again on the theory of self-preservation, self-defense, of the realization of a community or group of states that they have certain interests in common, and they are entitled to preserve those interests and to preserve themselves against injury to their very life and welfare. That same concept is carried on into article 51 of the Charter with its recognition of the inherent right of individual or collective self-defense. It forms an integral part of the Charter and of the system of the United Nations.

The amount of defense preparation in which a nation wants to engage at any time is, I think, in direct ratio to the sense of insecurity which it may have at that period, or which any group may have. That sense of insecurity in turn is directly related to their anticipation of some possible attack upon their peace and safety. Throughout history, whether it has been phrased officially in terms of self-defense, one has seen individual states or groups of states responding to that inner urge for protecting their peace and safety through some kind of defensive arrangement. Of course, one has seen in history at the same time measures on the other side which have been productive of that sense of insecurity.

Now, inevitably when you consider that whole field of endeavor, one gets back into the traditional argument which shook the League of Nations throughout the period of its discussion of the disarmament problem, as to which is the chicken and which is the egg; whether you can have disarmament before security in order to have security, or whether you must have security in order to permit the possibility of disarmament. That is a problem upon which I suppose people will dispute time without end. I think that the policy of the United States on the matter of disarmament, particularly, as illuminated by the discussions of the General Assembly in Paris last fall, shows a reasonable and intelligent attitude.

You are all familiar with the general position of the United States in regard to the proposals for the control of atomic energy. You are all familiar with the fact that at Paris the Russians put forward their proposal for disarmament. The reaction of the world, as represented in the United Nations including the United States, was one which immediately rejected the idea that disarmament could proceed as long as one of the main military powers of the world refused to allow anyone else to ascertain what it was doing. It was an unwillingness to accept merely the statement of the Soviet Union that it had disarmed or that it was proceeding to disarm, a demand grew for some kind of check, for some kind of knowledge out of which security could develop. Out of that one gets the resolution of the General Assembly looking toward the elaboration of some means of securing the information, because without the information you don't possibly create that sense of security which makes further action in the disarmament field possible.

I think the relation of the pact of the North Atlantic community to the four points stated in the President's program is perfectly clear. One of the things which has concerned a great many people has been the effect of the conclusion of such a treaty upon the United Nations. As I said, I can't go into a textual discussion now, but I believe that as you read the text you will find those anxieties are set at rest. The treaty is very definitely and very extensively geared into the Charter and the machinery of the United Nations. There is nothing there which weakens in the slightest degree that provision in article 103 of the Charter which reads that if any state is a party to any treaty the terms of which are inconsistent with the Charter, then the terms of the Charter shall prevail. There is nothing in this new treaty which will weaken the structure of the United Nations, or will conflict in any way with the responsibility of the United Nations, particularly the Security Council, which has the primary responsibility for international peace and security.

The relationship of a pact of this kind to the question of the continuance of the economic recovery program is also, I think, clear. Economic recovery in itself, or aid in terms of financial and economic measures does not do the trick of putting a country or an area back on its feet economically unless one creates in that area a fundamental sense of safety and removes from over their heads the type of fear which exists in Western Europe. It is very difficult for us to realize how that fear gets into the very bones, for instance, of the people of France, Belgium, and Holland. If you don't eradicate that fear, there is no incentive to proceed with any general program of economic recovery.

Of course, the relationship of the pact to the third point, that of providing security, is very clear. The President himself brought it out in his inaugural message.

On the fourth point, it seems to me that any bold new program, with all that is inherent in it in terms of possibility of the improvement of the welfare of individuals throughout the world, is quite impossible unless we have a world which is secure.

I firmly believe that the conclusion of this treaty for the security of the peace and safety of the Atlantic community will prove in retrospect one of the major contributions to the development of the work of the United Nations; and to the development of a general program for the welfare of the individual and of the world. These are and will continue to be cardinal points of policy of the United States.

(2) Radio Address by the Secretary of State (Acheson) on the North Atlantic Treaty, March 18, 1949.[17]

The text of the proposed North Atlantic Pact was made public today. I welcome this opportunity to talk with my fellow citizens about it. It has taken many months to work out this text with the representatives of the other nations involved. First Mr. Lovett and then I met with the Ambassadors of Canada, Britain, France, Belgium, the Netherlands and Luxembourg. Recently the Ambassador of Norway joined in these discussions. These talks had to be conducted in private and in confidence, so that each of us could speak frankly and fully on matters of vital importance to our countries. It is for this compelling reason that public discussion of the text of the Pact by your representatives has not been possible up to this time.

That restraint no longer applies. The treaty and its implications can now be fully discussed. Public opinion can now be formed on the basis of complete information. Only in this way can your government have what former Secretary of State Stimson has termed "the understanding support . . . of the American people", which is essential to the success of any policy.

I think the American people will want to know the answers to three principal questions about the Pact: How did it come about and why is it necessary? What are its terms? Will it accomplish its purpose?

The paramount purposes of the Pact are peace and security. If peace and security can be achieved in the North Atlantic area, we shall have gone a long way to assure peace and security in other areas as well.

The achievement of peace and security means more than that in the final outcome we shall have prevented war and brought about the settlement of

17 *Ibid.*, p. 384; Department of State Press Release 159, March 18, 1949; Department of State Publication 3489; *New York Times*, March 19, 1949, p. 4.

international disputes by peaceful means. There must be conviction of people everywhere that war *will* be prevented and that disputes *will* be settled peacefully. In the most practical terms, true international peace and security require a firm belief by the peoples of the world that they will not be subjected to unprovoked attack, to coercion and intimidation, to interference in their own affairs. Peace and security require confidence in the future, based on the assurance that the peoples of the world will be permitted to improve their conditions of life, free from fear that the fruits of their labor may be taken from them by alien hands.

These are goals of our own foreign policy which President Truman has emphasized many times, most recently in his inaugural address when he spoke of the hope that we could help create "the conditions that will lead eventually to personal freedom and happiness for all mankind." These are also the purposes of the United Nations, whose members are pledged "to maintain international peace and security" and to promote "the economic and social advancement of all peoples."

These purposes are intimately related to the origins of the United Nations. As the second World War neared its end, the peoples who bore the brunt of the fighting were sick of the horror, the brutality, the tragedy of war. Out of that revulsion came the determination to create a system that would go as far as humanly possible in insuring international peace and security.

The United Nations seeks to maintain peace and security by enjoining its members from using force to settle international disputes. Moreover, it insists that they acknowledge tolerance and cooperation as the guiding principles for the conduct of nations.

The members are expected to settle differences by the exercise of reason and adjustment, according to the principles of justice and law. This requires a spirit of tolerance and restraint on the part of all the members.

But, as in any other institution which presupposes restraint, violence or obstruction can be used to defeat the basic undertaking. This happens in personal relations, in families, communities, churches, politics, and everywhere in human life. If the system is used in ways it was not intended to be used, there is grave danger that the system will be disrupted.

That applies to the United Nations. The system is not working as effectively as we hoped because one of its members has attempted to prevent it from working. By obstructive tactics and the misuse of the veto, the Soviet Union has seriously interfered with the work of the Security Council in maintaining international peace and security.

But the United Nations is a flexible instrument. Although the actions of the Soviet Union have disturbed the work of the United Nations, it is strong enough to be an effective instrument for peace. It is the instrument by which we hope world peace will be achieved. The Charter recognizes the importance of regional arrangements consistent with the purposes and principles of the Charter. Such arrangements can greatly strengthen it.

The Atlantic Pact is a collective self-defense arrangement among the countries of the North Atlantic area. It is aimed at coordinating the exercise of the right of self-defense specifically recognized in Article 51 of the United Nations Charter. It is designed to fit precisely into the framework of the United Nations and to assure practical measures for maintaining peace and security in harmony with the Charter.

It is the firm intention of the parties to carry out the Pact in accordance with the provisions of the United Nations Charter and in a manner which will advance its purposes and principles.

Already one such arrangement under the Charter has been established with U.S. participation. The twenty-one American republics in reorganizing their regional system have specifically brought it within the framework of the United Nations Charter. We are now joining in the formation of a second arrangement, pertaining to the North Atlantic area, likewise within the framework of the United Nations.

It is important to keep in mind that the really successful national and international institutions are those that recognize and express underlying realities. The North Atlantic community of nations is such a reality. It is based on the affinity and natural identity of interests of the North Atlantic powers.

The North Atlantic treaty which now formally unites them is the product of at least three hundred and fifty years of history, perhaps more. There developed on our Atlantic coast a community, which has spread across the continent, connected with Western Europe by common institutions and moral and ethical beliefs. Similarities of this kind are not superficial, but fundamental. They are the strongest kind of ties, because they are based on moral conviction, on acceptance of the same values in life.

The very basis of western civilization, which we share with the other nations bordering the North Atlantic, and which all of us share with many other nations, is the ingrained spirit of restraint and tolerance. This is the opposite of the communist belief that coercion by force is a proper method of hastening the inevitable. Western civilization has lived by mutual restraint and tolerance. This civilization permits and stimulates free inquiry and bold experimentation. It creates the environment of freedom, from which flows the greatest amount of ingenuity, enterprise and accomplishment.

These principles of democracy, individual liberty and the rule of law have flourished in this Atlantic community. They have universal validity. They are shared by other free nations and find expression on a universal basis in the Charter of the United Nations; they are the standards by which its members have solemnly agreed to be judged. They are the elements out of which are forged the peace and welfare of mankind.

Added to this profoundly important basis of understanding is another unifying influence — the effect of living on the sea. The sea does not separate people as much as it joins them, through trade, travel, mutual understanding and common interests.

For this second reason, as well as the first, North America and Western Europe have formed the two halves of what is in reality one community, and have maintained an abiding interest in each other.

It is clear that the North Atlantic Pact is not an improvisation. It is the statement of the facts and lessons of history. We have learned our history lesson from two world wars in less than half a century. That experience has taught us that the control of Europe by a single aggressive, unfriendly power would constitute an intolerable threat to the national security of the United States. We participated in those two great wars to preserve the integrity and independence of the European half of the Atlantic community in order to preserve the integrity and independence of the American half. It is a simple fact, proved by experience, that an outside attack on one member of this community is an attack upon all members.

We have also learned that if the free nations do not stand together, they will fall one by one. The stratagem of the aggressor is to keep his intended victims divided, or better still, set them to quarreling among themselves. Then they can be picked off one by one without arousing unified resistance. We and the free nations of Europe are determined that history shall not repeat itself in that melancholy particular.

As President Truman has said: "If we can make it sufficiently clear, in advance, that any armed attack affecting our national security would be met with overwhelming force, the armed attack might never occur."

The same thought was expressed by the Foreign Relations Committee of the Senate last year in its report recommending approval of Senate Resolution 239. "The Committee is convinced," the report said, "that the horrors of another world war can be avoided with certainty only by preventing war from starting. The experience of World War I and World War II suggests that the best deterrent to aggression is the certainty that immediate and effective counter-measures will be taken against those who violate the peace." That resolution, adopted by an overwhelming vote of the Senate, expressly encourages the development of collective self-defense and regional arrangements within the United Nations framework and the participation of the United States in these arrangements.

What are the principal provisions of the North Atlantic Pact? I should like to summarize them.

First, the Pact is carefully and conscientiously designed to conform in every particular with the Charter of the United Nations. This is made clear in the first Article of the Pact, which reiterates and reaffirms the basic principle of the Charter. The participating countries at the very outset of their association state again that they will settle all their international disputes, not only among themselves but with any nation, by peaceful means in accordance with the provisions of the Charter. This declaration sets the whole tone and purpose of this treaty.

The second Article is equally fundamental. The associated countries assert that they will preserve and strengthen their free institutions and will see to it that the fundamental principles upon which free institutions are founded are better understood everywhere. They also agree to eliminate conflicts in their economic life and to promote economic cooperation among themselves. Here is the ethical essence of the treaty — the common resolve to preserve, strengthen and make understood the very basis of tolerance, restraint and freedom — the really vital things with which we are concerned.

This purpose is extended further in Article 3, in which the participating countries pledge themselves to self-help and mutual aid. In addition to strengthening their free institutions, they will take practical steps to maintain and develop their own capacity and that of their partners to resist aggression. They also agree to consult together when the integrity or security of any of them is threatened. The treaty sets up a council, consisting of all the members, and other machinery for consultation and for carrying out the provisions of the Pact.

Successful resistance to aggression in the modern world requires modern arms and trained military forces. As a result of the recent war, the European countries joining in the Pact are generally deficient in both requirements. The treaty does not bind the United States to any arms program. But we all know that the United States is now the only democratic nation with the resources and the productive capacity to help the free nations of Europe to recover their military strength.

Therefore, we expect to ask the Congress to supply our European partners some of the weapons and equipment they need to be able to resist agression. We also expect to recommend military supplies for other free nations which will cooperate with us in safeguarding peace and security.

In the compact world of today, the security of the United States cannot be defined in terms of boundaries and frontiers. A serious threat to international peace and security anywhere in the world is of direct concern to this country. Therefore it is our policy to help free peoples to maintain their integrity and independence, not only in Western Europe or in the Americas, but wherever the aid we are able to provide can be effective. Our actions in supporting the integrity and independence of Greece, Turkey and Iran are expressions of that determination. Our interest in the security of these countries has been made clear, and we shall continue to pursue that policy.

In providing military assistance to other countries, both inside and outside the North Atlantic Pact, we will give clear priority to the requirements for economic recovery. We will carefully balance the military assistance program with the capacity and requirements of the total economy, both at home and abroad.

But to return to the Treaty, Article 5 deals with the possibility, which unhappily cannot be excluded, that the nations joining together in the Pact may have to face the eventuality of an armed attack. In this Article, they agree that an armed attack on any of them, in Europe or North America, will be considered an attack on all of them. In the event of such an attack, each of them will take, individually and in concert with the other parties, whatever action it deems necessary to restore and maintain the security of the North Atlantic area, including the use of armed force.

This does not mean that the United States would be automatically at war if one of the nations covered by the Pact is subjected to armed attack. Under our Constitution, the Congress alone has the power to declare war. We would be bound to take promptly the action which we deemed necessary to restore and maintain the security of the North Atlantic area. That decision would be taken in accordance with our Constitutional procedures. The factors which would have to be considered would be, on the one side, the gravity of the armed attack; on the other, the action which we believed necessary to restore and maintain the security of the North Atlantic area. That is the end to be achieved. We are bound to do what in our honest judgment is necessary to reach that result. If we should be confronted again with a calculated armed attack such as we have twice seen in the Twentieth Century, I should not suppose that we would decide any action other than the use of armed force effective either as an exercise of the right of collective self-defense or as necessary to restore the peace and security of the North Atlantic area. That decision will rest where the Constitution has placed it.

This is not a legalistic question. It is a question we have frequently faced, the question of faith and principle in carrying out treaties. Those who decide it will have the responsibility for taking all appropriate action under the treaty. Such a responsibility requires the exercise of will — a will disciplined by the undertaking solemnly contracted to do what they decide is necessary to restore and maintain the peace and security of the North Atlantic area. That is our obligation under this Article 5. It is equally our duty and obligation to the security of our own country.

All of these provisions of the Pact are subject to the overriding provisions of the United Nations Charter. Any measures for self-defense taken under the treaty will be reported to the Security Council of the United Nations. These measures will continue only until the Security Council, with its primary responsibility, takes the necessary action to restore peace and maintain security.

The treaty has no time limit, but after it has been in effect twenty years any member can withdraw on one year's notice. It also provides that after it has been in existence ten years, it will be reviewed in the circumstances prevailing at that time. Additional countries may be admitted to the Pact by agreement of all the parties already signatories.

These are the principal provisions of the treaty.

Will the Pact accomplish its purpose?

No one can say with certainty. We can only act on our convictions. The United States Government and the governments with which we are associated in this treaty are convinced that it is an essential measure for strengthening the United Nations, deterring aggression, and establishing the sense of security necessary for the restoration of the economic and political health of the world.

The nations joining in the Pact know that war does not pay. Others may not be as deeply convinced of this as we are. The North Atlantic treaty should help convince them also that war does not pay.

It seems absurd that it should be necessary, in this era of popular education and highly developed communications, to deal with allegations which have no relation to the truth and could not stand even the crudest test of measurement against realities. Nevertheless, the power and persistence with which the lie is today employed as a weapon of international policy is such that this cannot always be avoided.

I refer here to the allegations that this treaty conceals aggressive designs on the part of its authors with respect to other countries. Any one with the most elementary knowledge of the processes of democratic government knows that democracies do not and cannot plan aggressive wars. But for those from whom such knowledge may have been withheld I must make the following categoric and unequivocal statement, for which I stand with the full measure of my responsibility in the office I hold:

> *This country is not planning to make war against anyone. It is not seeking war. It abhors war. It does not hold war to be inevitable. Its policies are devised with the specific aim of bridging by peaceful means the tremendous differences which beset international society at the present time.*

Allegations that aggressive designs lie behind this country's signature of the Atlantic Pact can rest only on a malicious misrepresentation or a fantastic misunderstanding of the nature and aims of American society. It is hard to say which of these attitudes is more irresponsible and more dangerous to the stability of international life. For misunderstanding on a question so vital to world progress and so easily susceptible of clarification could only be willful or the product of a system that imprisons the human mind and makes it impervious to facts. It is the duty of all those who seriously and realistically wish for peace to refuse to be misled by this type of falsehood and to prevent it from poisoning the atmosphere in which the quest of a happier world must be conducted.

This treaty is designed to help toward the goal envisioned by President Truman when he said:

> . . . As our stability becomes manifest, as more and more nations come to know the benefits of democracy and to participate in growing abundance, I believe that those countries which now oppose us will abandon their delusions and join with the free nations of the world in a just settlement of international differences.

To bring that time to pass, we are determined, on the one hand, to make it unmistakably clear that immediate and effective counter measures will be taken against those who violate the peace, and on the other, to *wage peace* vigorously and relentlessly.

Too often peace has been thought of as a negative condition — the mere absence of war. We know now that we cannot achieve peace by taking a negative attitude. Peace is positive, and it has to be waged with all our thought, energy and courage, and with the conviction that war is *not* inevitable.

Under the leadership of President Truman, the United States is waging peace with a vigor and on a scale without precedent. While the war was being fought, this country took the initiative in the organization of the United Nations and related agencies for the collective and cooperative conduct of international affairs. We withdrew our military forces, except those required for occupation duties, and quickly reduced our military establishment to about one-tenth its wartime size. We contributed generously to postwar relief and rehabilitation.

When events called for firmness as well as generosity the United States waged peace by pledging its aid to free nations threatened by aggression, and took prompt and vigorous action to fulfill that pledge. We have actively sought and are actively seeking to make the United Nations an effective instrument of international cooperation. We proposed, and with the eager cooperation of sixteen other nations, put into effect a great concerted program for the economic recovery and spiritual reinvigoration of Europe. We joined the other American republics, and we now join with Western Europe, in treaties to strengthen the United Nations and insure international peace and security.

The United States is waging peace by promoting measures for the revival and expansion of world trade on a sound and beneficial basis. Continuance of the Reciprocal Trade Agreements program and ratification by the United States of the Charter of the International Trade Organization are essential to the success of our foreign trade policies. We are preparing to carry out an energetic program to apply modern skills and techniques to what President Truman has called the "primitive and stagnant" economies of vast areas, so that they will yield a better and richer life for their people.

The United States is waging peace by throwing its full strength and energy into the struggle, and we shall continue to do so.

We sincerely hope we can avoid strife, but we cannot avoid striving for what is right. We devoutly hope we can have genuine peace, but we cannot be complacent about the present uneasy and troubled peace.

A secure and stable peace is not a goal we can reach all at once and for all time. It is a dynamic state, produced by effort and faith, with justice and courage. The struggle is continuous and hard. The prize is never irrevocably ours.

To have this genuine peace we must constantly work for it. But we must do even more. We must make it clear that armed attack will be met by collective defense, prompt and effective.

That is the meaning of the North Atlantic Pact.

(3) Memorandum of the Government of the Soviet Union on the North Atlantic Treaty, April 1, 1949.[18]

On March 18 the State Department of the United States published the text of the North Atlantic treaty which the Governments of the United States of America, Great Britain, France, Belgium, the Netherlands, Luxembourg and Canada intend to sign within the next few days.

The text of the North Atlantic treaty fully confirms what was said in the declaration of the Ministry of Foreign Affairs of the U.S.S.R. on January 29 this year, which is being attached hereto, both as regards the aggressive aims of this treaty and the fact that the North Atlantic treaty contradicts the principles and aims of the United Nations organization and the commitments which the Governments of the United States of America, Great Britain and France have assumed under other treaties and agreements.

The statements contained in the North Atlantic treaty that it is designated for defense and that it recognizes the principles of the United Nations organization serve aims which have nothing in common either with the tasks of self-defense of the parties to the treaty or with real recognition of the aims and principles of the United Nations organization.

Such great powers as the United States, Great Britain and France are parties to the North Atlantic treaty.

Thus the treaty is not directed either against the United States of America, Great Britain or France.

Of the great powers only the Soviet Union is excluded from among the parties to this treaty, which can be explained only by the fact that this treaty is directed against the Soviet Union.

The fact that the North Atlantic treaty is directed against the U.S.S.R. as well as against the countries of peoples' democracy was definitely pointed out also by the official representatives of the United States of America, Great Britain and France.

To justify the conclusion of the North Atlantic treaty, references are being made to the fact that the Soviet Union has defensive treaties with the countries of peoples' democracy.

These references, however, are utterly untenable.

All the treaties of the Soviet Union on friendship and mutual assistance with the countries of peoples' democracy are of a bilateral nature, and they are directed solely against the possible repetition of German aggression of which danger no single peace-loving state can be unaware.

The possibility of interpreting them as treaties which are in any degree aimed against the Allies of the U.S.S.R. in the late war, against the United States or Great Britain or France, is absolutely precluded.

Moreover, the U.S.S.R. has similar treaties against the repetition of German aggression not only with the countries of peoples' democracy, but also with Great Britain and France.

In contradiction to this, the North Atlantic treaty is not a bilateral, but a multilateral treaty, which creates a closed grouping of states and, what is particularly important, absolutely ignores the possibility of a repetition of German aggression, not having consequently as its aim the prevention of a new German aggression.

And in as much as of the great powers which comprised the anti-Hitlerite coalition only the U.S.S.R. is not a party to the treaty, the North Atlantic treaty must be regarded as a treaty directed against one of the chief Allies of the United States, Great Britain and France in the late war against the U.S.S.R.

Participants in the North Atlantic treaty are effecting extensive military measures which can in no way be justified by the interests of self-defense of these countries.

The extensive military measures carried out by the United States in cooperation with Great Britain and France under the present peacetime conditions, including the increase in all types of armed forces, the drafting of a plan for the utilization of the atomic weapon, the stockpiling of atom bombs, which are purely an offensive

18 *Ibid.,* April 2, 1949, p. 5. The text is that reported by Tass and distributed in London by the Soviet monitor.

weapon, the building of a network of air and naval bases, etc. — by no means bear a defensive character.

The preservation in Washington of the combined Anglo-American Staff organized during the second World War, the recent establishment of the military staff of the so-called Western Union in Fontainebleau (France), as well as the intention immediately to set up the defense committee envisaged by the North Atlantic treaty, are by no means an indication of the peace-loving or defensive aims of the participants of the treaty, but, together with other numerous military preparations, contribute to intensifying anxiety and alarm and to the whipping up of war hysteria in which all sorts of instigators of a new war are so interested.

The North Atlantic pact is designed to daunt the states which do not agree to obey the dictate of the Anglo-American grouping of powers that lay claim to world domination, though the untenability of such claims was once again affirmed by the second World War which ended in the debacle of Fascist Germany, which also had laid claim to world domination.

Among the participants in the North Atlantic treaty are also countries whose governments expect to benefit at the expense of the richer parties to this treaty and make various plans with regard to obtaining new credits and other material advantages.

At the same time one cannot but see the groundlessness of the anti-Soviet motives of the North Atlantic treaty, inasmuch as it is known to all that the Soviet Union does not intend to attack anyone and in no way threatens the United States of America, Great Britain or the other parties to the treaty.

The conclusion of the North Atlantic treaty and establishment of a new grouping of powers is motivated by the weakness of the United Nations organization.

It is perfectly evident, however, that the North Atlantic treaty does not serve the cause of consolidating the United Nations organization but on the contrary leads to the undermining of the very foundation of this international organization because establishment of the above grouping of powers is far from corresponding to the aims and principles of the United Nations organization and runs counter to the Charter of this organization.

Parties to the North Atlantic treaty maintain that this treaty allegedly represents a regional arrangement envisaged by Article 52 of the United Nations Charter. But such references are utterly groundless and untenable. There can be no question whatsoever of any regional character of this treaty inasmuch as the union provided for by this treaty embraces states located in both hemispheres of the globe and has not as its aim settlement of any regional issues.

This is also confirmed by the fact as has already been announced that states which are not members of the United Nations organization (Italy and Portugal) are being drawn into participation in the North Atlantic treaty through Article 52 of the United Nations Charter [which] has in view conclusion of regional arrangements only among members of the United Nations organization.

Nor can establishment of a North Atlantic grouping of states be justified by the right of each member of the United Nations to an individual or collective self-defense in conformity with Article 51 of the Charter. Suffice it to say such a right under the Charter of the United Nations can arise only in case of an armed attack against a member of the organization; yet as is known to all neither the United States of America, Britain, France, nor other parties to the pact are threatened by any armed attack.

It is clear references to Articles 51 and 52 of the United Nations Charter are untenable and designed merely to cover up the real aggressive aims of a military grouping of states which are being set up by the conclusion of the North Atlantic treaty.

No one can deny that the North Atlantic treaty and, first and foremost, Article 5 of this treaty directly contradicts the Charter of the United Nations organization. The text of Article 53 of the Charter which speaks of enforcement actions under regional arrangements, states directly that "no enforcement action shall be taken under regional arrangements or by regional agencies without the authorization of the Security Council," with the exception of special measures provided with regard to former enemy states. This notwithstanding Article 5 of the North Atlantic pact envisages employment of armed force by the parties to the treaty without any authorization of the Security Council.

Thus, even if the North Atlantic treaty were to be considered a regional arrangement, Article 5 of this treaty is incompatible with the United Nations Charter.

This shows once more how unfounded are all references of the North Atlantic treaty to the recognition of the principles and aims of the Charter of the United Nations organization.

On the basis of the above-said the Soviet Government arrives at the following conclusions:

1. The North Atlantic treaty has nothing in common with the aims of self-defense of states who are parties to the treaty, who are threatened by no one, whom no one intends to attack. On the contrary this treaty has an obviously aggressive character, is aimed against the U.S.S.R. which fact is not concealed even by the official representatives of the states-parties to the treaty in their public pronouncements.

2. The North Atlantic treaty not only does not contribute to the consolidation of peace and international security which is the duty of all members of the United Nations organization, but it directly runs counter to the principles and aims of the United Nations Charter and leads to the undermining of the United Nations organization.

3. The North Atlantic treaty runs counter to the treaty between Great Britain and the Soviet Union signed in 1942 under which both states assumed the obligation to cooperate in the maintenance of peace, international security and "not to conclude any alliances and not to participate in any coalitions directed against the other high contracting party."

4. The North Atlantic treaty runs counter to the treaty between France and the Soviet Union signed in 1944 under which both states assumed an obligation to cooperate in the maintenance of peace and international security and "not to conclude any alliance and not to take part in any coalition directed against one of the high contracting parties."

5. The North Atlantic treaty runs counter to agreements between the Soviet Union, the United States of America and Great Britain concluded at the Yalta and Potsdam conferences as well as at other conferences of representatives of these powers held both during and after the second World War under which the United States of America and Great Britain like the Soviet Union assumed the obligation to cooperate in consolidation of general peace and international security and to the consolidation of the United Nations organization.

(4) *Address by the President (Truman) at the Signing of the North Atlantic Treaty, Washington, April 4, 1949.*[19]

On this historic occasion I am happy to welcome the Foreign Ministers of the countries which, together with the United States, form the North Atlantic community of nations.

The purpose of this meeting is to take the first step toward putting into effect an international agreement to safeguard the peace and prosperity of this community of nations.

It is altogether appropriate that nations so deeply conscious of their common interests should join in expressing their determination to preserve their present peaceful situation and to protect it in the future.

What we are about to do here is a neighborly act. We are like a group of householders, living in the same locality, who decide to express their community of interests by entering into a formal association for their mutual self-protection.

---

[19] Department of State Publication 3497, p. 33.

This treaty is a simple document. The nations which sign it agree to abide by the peaceful principles of the United Nations, to maintain friendly relations and economic cooperation with one another, to consult together whenever the territory or independence of any one of them is threatened, and to come to the aid of any one of them which may be attacked.

It is a simple document, but if it had existed in 1914 and in 1939, supported by the nations which are represented here today, I believe it would have prevented the acts of aggression which led to two world wars.

The nations represented here have known the tragedy of those two wars. As a result, many of us took part in the founding of the United Nations. Each Member of the United Nations is under a solemn obligation to maintain international peace and security. Each is bound to settle international disputes by peaceful means, to refrain from the threat or use of force against the territory or independence of any country, and to support the United Nations in any action it takes to preserve the peace.

That solemn pledge — that abiding obligation — we reaffirm here today.

We rededicate ourselves to that obligation and propose this North Atlantic Treaty as one of the means to carry it out.

Through this treaty we undertake to conduct our international affairs in accordance with the provisions of the United Nations Charter. We undertake to exercise our right of collective or individual self-defense against armed attack, in accordance with article 51 of the Charter, and subject to such measures as the Security Council may take to maintain and restore international peace and security.

Within the United Nations, this country and other countries have hoped to establish an international force for the use of the United Nations in preserving peace throughout the world. Our efforts to establish this force, however, have been blocked by one of the major powers.

This lack of unanimous agreement in the Security Council does not mean that we must abandon our attempts to make peace secure.

Even without that agreement, which we still hope for, we shall do as much as we can. And every bit that we do will add to the strength of the fabric of peace throughout the world.

In this treaty we seek to establish freedom from aggression and from the use of force in the North Atlantic community. This is the area which has been at the heart of the last two world conflicts. To protect this area against war will be a long step toward permanent peace in the whole world.

There are those who claim that this treaty is an aggressive act on the part of the nations which ring the North Atlantic.

This is absolutely untrue.

The pact will be a positive, not a negative, influence for peace, and its influence will be felt not only in the area it specifically covers but throughout the world. Its conclusion does not mean a narrowing of the interests of its members. Under my authority and instructions, the Secretary of State has recently made it abundantly clear that the adherence of the United States to this pact does not signify a lessening of American concern for the security and welfare of other areas, such as the Near East. The step we are taking today should serve to reassure peace-loving peoples everywhere and pave the way for the world-wide stability and peaceful development which we all seek.

Twice in recent years nations have felt the sickening blow of unprovoked aggression. Our peoples, to whom our Governments are responsible, demand that these things shall not happen again.

We are determined that they shall not happen again.

In taking steps to prevent aggression against our own peoples, we have no purpose of aggression against others. To suggest the contrary is to slander our institutions and defame our ideals and our aspirations.

The nations represented here are bound together by ties of long standing. We are joined by a common heritage of democracy, individual liberty, and the rule of law. These are the ties of a peaceful way of life. In this pact we merely give them formal recognition.

With our common traditions we face common problems. We are, to a large degree, industrial nations, and we face the problem of mastering the forces of modern technology in the public interest.

To meet this problem successfully, we must have a world in which we can exchange the products of our labor not only among ourselves but with other nations. We have come together in a great cooperative economic effort to establish this kind of world.

We are determined to work together to provide better lives for our people without sacrificing our common ideals of justice and human worth.

But we cannot succeed if our people are haunted by the constant fear of aggression and burdened by the cost of preparing their nations individually against attack.

In this pact we hope to create a shield against aggression and the fear of aggression — a bulwark which will permit us to get on with the real business of government and society, the business of achieving a fuller and happier life for our citizens.

We shall, no doubt, go about this business in different ways. There are different kinds of governmental and economic systems, just as there are different languages and different cultures. But these differences present no real obstacle to the voluntary association of free nations devoted to the common cause of peace.

We believe that it is possible for nations to achieve unity on the great principles of human freedom and justice and at the same time to permit, in other respects, the greatest diversity of which the human mind is capable.

Our faith in this kind of unity is borne out by our experience here in the United States in creating one nation out of the variety of our continental resources and the peoples of many lands.

This method of organizing diverse peoples and cultures is in direct contrast to the method of the police state, which attempts to achieve unity by imposing the same beliefs and the same rule of force on everyone.

We believe that our method of achieving international unity through the voluntary association of different countries dedicated to a common cause is an effective step toward bringing order to our troubled world.

For us, war is not inevitable. We do not believe that there are blind tides of history which sweep men one way or the other. In our own time we have seen brave men overcome obstacles that seemed insurmountable and forces that seemed overwhelming. Men with courage and vision can still determine their own destiny. They can choose slavery or freedom — war or peace.

I have no doubt which they will choose. The treaty we are signing here today is evidence of the path they will follow.

If there is anything certain today, if there is anything inevitable in the future, it is the will of the people of the world for freedom and peace.

(5) *North Atlantic Treaty, Signed at Washington, April 4, 1949. Ratified by the President (Truman), July 25, 1949. Entered into Force, August 24, 1949.*[20]

The Parties to this Treaty reaffirm their faith in the purposes and principles of the Charter of the United Nations and their desire to live in peace with all peoples and all governments.

They are determined to safeguard the freedom, common heritage and civilization of their peoples, founded on the principles of democracy, individual liberty and the rule of law.

They seek to promote stability and well-being in the North Atlantic area.

They are resolved to unite their efforts for collective defense and for the preservation of peace and security.

They therefore agree to this North Atlantic Treaty:

ARTICLE 1

The Parties undertake, as set forth in the Charter of the United Nations, to settle any international disputes in which they may be involved by peaceful means in such a manner that international peace and security, and justice, are not endangered, and to refrain in their international relations from the threat or use of force in any manner inconsistent with the purposes of the United Nations.

ARTICLE 2

The Parties will contribute toward the further development of peaceful and friendly international relations by strengthening their free institutions, by bringing about a better understanding of the principles upon which these institutions are founded, and by promoting conditions of stability and well-being. They will seek to eliminate conflict in their international economic

20 Department of State, *Treaties and Other International Acts Series* 1964.

policies and will encourage economic collaboration between any or all of them.

ARTICLE 3

In order more effectively to achieve the objectives of this Treaty, the Parties, separately and jointly, by means of continuous and effective self-help and mutual aid, will maintain and develop their individual and collective capacity to resist armed attack.

ARTICLE 4

The Parties will consult together whenever, in the opinion of any of them, the territorial integrity, political independence or security of any of the Parties is threatened.

ARTICLE 5

The Parties agree that an armed attack against one or more of them in Europe or North America shall be considered an attack against them all; and consequently they agree that, if such an armed attack occurs, each of them, in exercise of the right of individual or collective self-defense recognized by Article 51 of the Charter of the United Nations, will assist the Party or Parties so attacked by taking forthwith, individually and in concert with the other Parties, such action as it deems necessary, including the use of armed force, to restore and maintain the security of the North Atlantic area.

Any such armed attack and all measures taken as a result thereof shall immediately be reported to the Security Council. Such measures shall be terminated when the Security Council has taken the measures necessary to restore and maintain international peace and security.

ARTICLE 6

For the purpose of Article 5 an armed attack on one or more of the Parties is deemed to include an armed attack on the territory of any of the Parties in Europe or North America, on the Algerian departments of France, on the occupation forces of any Party in Europe, on the islands under the jurisdiction of any Party in the North Atlantic area north of the Tropic of Cancer or on the vessels or aircraft in this area of any of the Parties.

ARTICLE 7

This Treaty does not affect, and shall not be interpreted as affecting, in any way the rights and obligations under the Charter of the Parties which are members of the United Nations, or the primary responsibility of the Security Council for the maintenance of international peace and security.

ARTICLE 8

Each Party declares that none of the international engagements now in force between it and any other of the Parties or any third state is in conflict with the provisions of this Treaty, and undertakes not to enter into any international engagement in conflict with this Treaty.

ARTICLE 9

The Parties hereby establish a council, on which each of them shall be represented, to consider matters concerning the implementation of this Treaty. The council shall be so organized as to be able to meet promptly at any time. The council shall set up such subsidiary bodies as may be necessary; in particular it shall establish immediately a defense committee which shall recommend measures for the implementation of Articles 3 and 5.

ARTICLE 10

The Parties may, by unanimous agreement, invite any other European state in a position to further the principles of this Treaty and to contribute to the security of the North Atlantic area to accede to this Treaty. Any state so invited may become a party to the Treaty by depositing its instrument of accession with the Government of the United States of America. The Government of the United States of America will inform each of the Parties of the deposit of each such instrument of accession.

ARTICLE 11

This Treaty shall be ratified and its provisions carried out by the Parties in accordance with their respective constitutional processes. The instruments of ratification shall be deposited as soon as possible with the Government of the United States of America, which will notify all the other signatories of each deposit. The Treaty shall enter into force between the states which have ratified it as soon as the ratifications of the majority of the signatories, including the ratifications of Belgium, Canada, France, Luxembourg, the Netherlands, the United Kingdom and the United States, have been deposited and shall come into effect with respect to other states on the date of the deposit of their ratifications.

ARTICLE 12

After the Treaty has been in force for ten years, or at any time thereafter, the Parties shall, if any of them so requests, consult together for the purpose of reviewing the Treaty, having regard for the factors then affecting peace and security in the North Atlantic area, including the development of universal as well as regional arrangements under the Charter of the United Nations for the maintenance of international peace and security.

ARTICLE 13

After the Treaty has been in force for twenty years, any Party may cease to be a party one year after its notice of denunciation has been given to the Government of the United States of America, which will inform the Governments of the other Parties of the deposit of each notice of denunciation.

ARTICLE 14

This Treaty, of which the English and French texts are equally authentic, shall be deposited in the archives of the Government of the United States of America. Duly certified copies thereof will be transmitted by that Government to the Governments of the other signatories.

In witness whereof, the undersigned Plenipotentiaries have signed this Treaty.

Done at Washington, the fourth day of April, 1949.

(6) *Communiqué Issued by the North Atlantic Council at the Conclusion of Its First Session, Held in Washington, September 17, 1949. Released to the Press, September 17, 1949.*[21]

I.

The Council established by Article 9 of the North Atlantic Treaty held its first session in Washington on September 17, 1949. Representatives of the Parties to the Treaty attending this first session were: For Belgium, the Minister of Foreign Affairs, M. Paul van Zeeland; for Canada, the Secretary of State for External Affairs, Mr. Lester B. Pearson; for Denmark, the Minister of Foreign Affairs, Mr. Gustav Rasmussen; for France, the Minister of Foreign Affairs, M. Robert Schuman; for Iceland, the Minister to the United States, Mr. Thor Thors; for Italy, the Minister of Foreign Affairs, Count Sforza; for Luxembourg, the Minister of Foreign Affairs, Mr. Josef Bech; for the Netherlands, the Minister of Foreign Affairs, Mr. Dirk U. Stikker; for Norway, the Minister of Foreign Affairs, Mr. Halvard M. Lange; for Portugal, the Minister of Foreign Affairs, Mr. José Caeiro da Matta; for the United Kingdom, the Secretary of State for Foreign Affairs, Mr. Ernest Bevin; for the United States, the Secretary of State, Mr. Dean Acheson.

The task of the Council is to assist the Parties in implementing the Treaty and particularly in attaining its basic objective. That objective is to assist, in accordance with the Charter, in achieving the primary purpose of the United Nations—the maintenance of international peace and security. The Treaty is designed to do so by making clear the determination of the Parties collectively to preserve their common heritage of freedom and to defend themselves against aggression while emphasizing at the same time their desire to live in peace with all governments and all peoples.

It is in this spirit that the Foreign Ministers of the Parties have met in Washington and have taken steps to implement the Treaty. The meetings of the Council showed that all parties are united in their resolve to integrate their efforts for the promotion of lasting peace, the preservation of their common heritage and the strengthening of their common defense.

The main purpose of the Council during this first session was to provide for its own future operation and, in accordance with Article 9, to establish a Defense Committee and such other subsidiary bodies as are deemed necessary to assist the Council in considering matters concerning the implementation of the North Atlantic Treaty.

II. Organization

The Council is the principal body in the North Atlantic Treaty Organization. In accordance with the Treaty, the Council is charged with the responsibility of considering all matters concerning the implementation of the provisions of the Treaty. Such subsidiary bodies as are set up under Article 9 of the Treaty are subordinate to the Council.

21 Department of State, *Bulletin*, XXI, p. 469.

The organization established under the North Atlantic Treaty should be operated with as much flexibility as possible and be subject to review from time to time. The establishment of this machinery does not preclude the use of other means for consultation and cooperation between any or all of the Parties on matters relating to the Treaty.

III. Council

As regards its own organization, the Council agreed as follows:

As decided on April 2, the Council will normally be composed of Foreign Ministers. Should the latter be unable to attend, their places shall be taken by plenipotentiary representatives designated by the Parties. To enable the Council to meet promptly at any time the diplomatic representatives in Washington of the Parties shall be empowered to act as their Government's representatives whenever necessary.

Terms of Reference

The North Atlantic Treaty shall constitute the terms of reference of the Council.

Time and Frequency of Sessions

The Council shall be convened by the Chairman and shall meet in ordinary session annually and at such other times as may be deemed desirable by the majority of the Parties. Extraordinary sessions under Articles 4 and 5 of the Treaty may be called at the request of any Party invoking one of these Articles.

Location of the Council Sessions

The location of each session of the Council shall be determined by the Chairman after consultation with the other members of the Council. For general convenience the ordinary annual session should normally be held at about the same time and in the same general geographical area as the annual session of the General Assembly. Other ordinary sessions should whenever practicable be held at some convenient location in Europe.

Chairmanship

Chairmanship shall be held in turn by the Parties according to the alphabetical order in the English language beginning with the United States. Each Party shall hold the office from the beginning of one ordinary annual session until the appointment of the new Chairman at the following ordinary annual session. If any Party does not wish to accept the Chairmanship, it shall pass to the next Party in alphabetical order.

Languages

English and French shall be the official languages for the entire North Atlantic Treaty Organization.

Permanent Coordination

Additional political bodies shall not be established unless and until experience has demonstrated their need. However, the existing informal arrangement for consultation between representatives in Washington of the Parties shall be maintained.

IV. Defense Committee

The Council established a Defense Committee.

The Council reaffirmed that ensuring the security of the North Atlantic area is a primary objective of the North Atlantic Treaty and is vital to the security of each of the Parties. It is therefore of paramount importance that the Parties, separately and jointly, by means of continuous and effective self-help and mutual aid, maintain and develop their individual and collective capacity to resist armed attack. The Defense Committee should therefore immediately take the requisite steps to have drawn up unified defense plans for the North Atlantic area.

As regards the organization of the Defense Committee, the Council agreed as follows:

The Defense Committee will be composed of one representative from each Party. These representatives will normally be Defense Ministers. In any case where this is not possible, another representative may be designated.

Terms of Reference

The Defense Committee shall recommend measures for the implementation of Articles 3 and 5 in accordance with general policy guidance given by the Council.

Time and Frequency of Sessions

The Defense Committee shall be convened by the Chairman and shall meet in ordinary session annually and at such other times as it may be requested to meet by the Council or as may be deemed desirable by the majority of the members of the Defense Committee.

Location

The location of each session of the Defense Committee shall be determined by the Chairman in consultation with the members of the Committee.

Chairmanship

Chairmanship shall be held in turn by the Parties according to the alphabetical order in the English language beginning with the United States. Each Party shall hold the office from the beginning of one ordinary annual session until the appointment of the new Chairman at the following ordinary annual session. If any Party does not wish to accept the Chairmanship, it shall pass to the next Party in alphabetical order.

The Council suggested to the Defense Committee the general outline of those subsidiary military bodies which it considered appropriate for the task of aiding the Defense Committee in recommending measures for the implementation of Articles 3 and 5 of the Treaty. The Defense Committee was invited, among other things, to consider the question of these subsidiary bodies in detail and to elaborate on the general provisions suggested by the Council for each body.

V. Military Committee

The Council suggested in general terms that the military organization should include the following:

The Defense Committee should establish a Military Committee composed of one military representative from each Party. These representatives should be Chiefs of Staff or their representatives. (Iceland, having no military establishment, may, if it so desires, be represented by a civilian official.)

Terms of Reference

The Military Committee should:

provide general policy guidance of a military nature to its Standing Group;
advise the Defense Committee and other agencies on military matters as appropriate;
recommend to the Defense Committee military measures for the unified defense of the North Atlantic area.

Location

The Military Committee should normally meet in Washington.

Standing Group

In order to facilitate the rapid and efficient conduct of the work of the Military Committee, there should be set up a sub-committee of that body to be known as the "Standing Group". The Standing Group should be composed of one representative each of France, the United Kingdom, and the United States.

Terms of Reference

The Standing Group, in accordance with general policy guidance provided by the Military Committee, should provide such specific policy guidance and information of a military nature to the Regional Planning Groups and any other bodies of the organization as is necessary for their work.

To achieve the unified defense of the North Atlantic area, the Standing Group should coordinate and integrate the defense plans originating in the Regional Planning Groups, and should make appropriate recommendations thereon to the Military Committee.

The Standing Group should recommend to the Military Committee those matters on which the Standing Group should be authorized to take action in the name of the Military Committee within the framework of approved policy.

It is recognized that it is the responsibility of individual governments to provide for the implementation of plans to which they have agreed. It is further recognized that it is the primary responsibility of the Regional Planning Groups to prepare plans for the defense of their respective regions. Subject to these principles, it is understood that before the Standing Group makes recommendations on any plan or course of action involving the use of forces, facilities, or resources of a Party not represented on the Standing Group, going beyond or differing from arrangements previously agreed by the Party concerned, the Party should have the right to participate in the Standing Group in the work of formulating such recommendations. It is also understood that when communicating their regional plans to the Standing Group, the Regional Planning Groups should be entitled to have their plans presented and explained by any one of their members and not necessarily by a member of the Standing Group.

Time and Frequency of Sessions

The Standing Group should be so organized as to function continuously.

Location

The permanent site of the Standing Group should be in Washington.

Permanent Representation

In order to maintain close contact with the Standing Group, a Party not represented thereon may appoint a special representative to provide permanent liaison with the Standing Group.

VI. Regional Planning Groups

In order to ensure speedy and efficient planning of the unified defense of the whole North Atlantic area there should be established Regional Planning Groups on a geographical basis. It should be provided that:

(1) before any Regional Planning Group makes any recommendations affecting the defense of the territory or involving the use of forces, facilities, or resources of any Party not a member of that Group, that Party should have the right to participate in the Group in the work of formulating such recommendations;

(2) any Group which considers that a Party not a member of the Group can contribute to the defense planning of that Group's region, can call upon that Party to join in the planning as appropriate.

Composition

NORTHERN EUROPEAN REGIONAL PLANNING GROUP

Denmark, Norway, and the United Kingdom.

The United States has been requested and has agreed to participate actively in the defense planning as appropriate.

Other Parties may participate under the provisions listed above.

WESTERN EUROPEAN REGIONAL PLANNING GROUP

Belgium, France, Luxembourg, the Netherlands, and the United Kingdom.

Canada and the United States have been requested and have agreed to participate actively in the defense planning as appropriate.

Other Parties may, and in particular Denmark and Italy will, participate under the provisions listed above.

SOUTHERN EUROPEAN–WESTERN MEDITERRANEAN REGIONAL PLANNING GROUP

France, Italy, and the United Kingdom.
The United States has been requested and has agreed to participate actively in the defense planning as appropriate.
Other Parties may participate under the provisions listed above.
It is recognized that there are problems which are clearly common to the defense of the areas covered by the three European regional groups. It is therefore important that arrangements be made by the Defense Committee with a view to ensuring full cooperation between two, or if the need arises, all three groups.

CANADIAN–UNITED STATES REGIONAL PLANNING GROUP

Canada and the United States.
Other Parties may participate under the provisions listed above.

NORTH ATLANTIC OCEAN REGIONAL PLANNING GROUP

Belgium, Canada, Denmark, France, Iceland, the Netherlands, Norway, Portugal, the United Kingdom and the United States.
The responsibilities for planning the defenses in the North Atlantic Ocean cannot be shared equally by all members of the Group. On the other hand, these responsibilities can to some extent be divided along functional lines and allocated to those Parties who are best able to perform the respective defense functions. Therefore, the North Atlantic Ocean Regional Planning Group, when it meets, should establish a series of planning sub-groups related to specific functions of defense. The Group should determine on which sub-group or sub-groups each Party should sit, and the arrangements necessary to ensure coordination between these sub-groups in the interest of speedy and effective planning.

Terms of Reference

Each Regional Planning Group should:

develop and recommend to the Military Committee through the Standing Group plans for the defense of the region;
cooperate with the other Regional Planning Groups with a view to eliminating conflict in, and ensuring harmony among, the various regional plans.

Location

The Defense Committee should consider the question of the location of the Regional Planning Groups.

VII.

The Council recognizes that the question of military production and supply is an integral part of the whole problem of the defense of the North Atlantic area. Consequently, there shall be established as soon as possible appropriate machinery to consider these matters. The details of organization of this machinery, terms of reference, etc., shall be studied forthwith by a working group which shall submit recommendations to the Defense Committee or to the Council.

VIII.

The Council recognizes the importance of economic and financial factors in the development and implementation of military plans for the defense of the North Atlantic area. Consequently, there shall be established as soon as possible appropriate machinery to consider these matters. The details of organization of this machinery, terms of reference, etc., shall be studied forthwith by a working group which shall submit recommendations to the Council.

B. Mutual Defense Assistance Program

On April 8, 1949, the Department of State made public copies of communications exchanged between the Department and the Brussels Treaty powers, Norway, Denmark, and Italy concerning the provision by the United States of military assistance to those governments.[1] In releasing the text of this correspondence, the Department revealed that it had been, for some time, preparing a program of foreign military assistance based upon informally submitted estimates of the urgent military needs of certain of the western European governments. Despite the fact that these various requests had been received within a matter of days after the signing of the North Atlantic Treaty, the Department pointed out that the requests were not "a product of the Pact" but demonstrated that "even without the existence of the North Atlantic Pact, the need for assistance and the recommended response of this Government would be the same."[2] On July 25, the President (Truman) in a message to the Congress urged the enactment of legislation authorizing military aid to the nations of western Europe.[3] The position of the administration on the proposed Mutual Defense Assistance Program was further clarified by an exchange of correspondence between Rep. John Davis Lodge (Connecticut) and the Secretary of State (Acheson).[4] The draft legislation proposed by the administration envisaged an expenditure of $1.45 billion, of which approximately $1.1 billion would be devoted to aid to the North Atlantic Treaty Countries, and approximately $3.5 million would be spent for aid to other countries, such as Greece, Turkey, Korea, the Philippines, and Iran.[5]

On August 5, 1949, Rep. John Kee (West Virginia) introduced in the House of Representatives H.R.5895, a bill "to promote the foreign policy and provide for the defense and general welfare of the United States by furnishing military assistance to foreign nations."[6] The bill was favorably reported with amendments by the Committee on Foreign Affairs on August 15.[7] The House began debate on August 17 and passed H.R.5895 with amendments the following day.[8] On August 19, the House-approved measure was referred jointly to the Senate Committee on Foreign Affairs and the Committee on Armed Services which, on September 12, after also considering a Senate bill (S.2388), recommended that the Senate amend H.R.5895 by striking out all after the enacting clause and substituting the final committee version of S.2388.[9] Senate debate on H.R.5895 opened on September 19 and concluded on September 22 with the passage of the bill as amended.[10] The report of the conference between the two Houses was approved by the House and Senate on September 28[11] and the bill was signed by the President on October 6, 1949.[12]

(1) Message from the President (Truman) to the Congress Transmitting Recommendations for the Enactment of Legislation Authorizing Military Aid to the Nations of Western Europe, July 25, 1949.[13]

To continue and strengthen our program for world peace and national security, I recommend that the Congress enact legislation authorizing military aid to free nations to enable them to protect themselves against the threat of aggression and contribute more effectively to the collective defense of world peace.

---

1 For the text of the correspondence with the Brussels Treaty powers, see Department of State Press Release 228, April 8, 1949; for correspondence with the Italian Government, see *ibid.*, 229, April 8, 1949; for correspondence with the Danish Government, see *ibid.*, 231, April 8, 1949; and for correspondence with the Norwegian Government, see *ibid.*, 230, April 8, 1949. The requests for assistance were dated April 5, April 6, April 7 and April 7, respectively.

2 *Ibid.*, 232, April 8, 1949.
3 House Document 276, 81st Cong., 1st sess.
4 Department of State, *Bulletin*, XXI, p. 476.
5 *New York Times*, July 26, 1949, p. 3.
6 *Congressional Record*, 95, p. 11090 (Daily edition, August 5, 1949).
7 House Report 1265, 81 st Cong., 1st sess.; *ibid.*, p. 11745 (Daily edition, August 15, 1949).
8 *Ibid.*, p. 12037 (Daily edition, August 18, 1949).
9 Senate Report 1068, 81st Cong., 1st sess.; *ibid.*, p. 13012 (Daily edition, September 12, 1949).
10 *Ibid.*, p. 13420 (Daily edition, September 22, 1949).
11 *Ibid.*, p. 13657, 13716 (Daily edition, September 28, 1949).
12 Public Law 329, 81st Cong., 1st sess.
13 House Document 276, 81st Cong., 1st sess.; Department of State, *Bulletin*, XXI, p. 186; *New York Times*, July 26, 1949, p. 2.

Such legislation is an essential part of our efforts to create an international structure capable of maintaining law and order among nations. Our prosperity and security as well as that of other free nations depend upon our success in establishing conditions of international order. Increased assurances against the danger of aggression are needed to support our international economic programs and, in particular, the European recovery program, which are so vital to the building of a stable world.

Under the Charter of the United Nations each member nation is bound to settle international differences by peaceful means, and to refrain from the threat or use of force against the territory of any country. Thus, in joining the United Nations, the nations have given their assent to the basic principles of international peace and security.

We have, however, learned the unfortunate truth that this obligation, by itself, is not sufficient at the present time to eliminate the fear of aggression and international violence. The record of world events since 1945 offers us no certainty that all members of the United Nations will uphold these principles of peace in actual practice. Indeed, there is proof to the contrary, proof that in the pursuit of selfish ends some nations have resorted and may again resort to the threat or use of force. The fear created by this experience haunts the world and creates conditions of insecurity and instability which stand in the way of economic and social progress.

To reduce this danger and to allay these fears, we have taken additional steps to reinforce the obligations of the Charter. Under the Pact of Rio de Janeiro and in the North Atlantic Treaty, we are creating a framework of mutual obligation to prevent international violence in the Western Hemisphere and in the North Atlantic area. These treaties provide support for the principles of the Charter of the United Nations.

Furthermore, even in the absence of such compacts, we have refused to tolerate assaults on the integrity of peace-loving nations whose conduct conforms to the principles of the Charter. We have given military as well as diplomatic aid directly to nations threatened by aggression. Through our aid to Greece and Turkey we have recognized the fact that, if the principles of international peace are to prevail, free nations must have the means as well as the will to resist aggression.

So long as the danger of aggression exists, it is necessary to think in terms of the forces required to prevent it. It is unfortunate that this is true. We cannot, however, achieve our goal of permanent peace by ignoring the difficult and unpleasant tasks that lie in the way. We need to show the same firmness and resolution in defending the principles of peace that we have shown in enunciating them. The better prepared the free nations are to resist aggression, the less likelihood there is that they will have to use the forces they have prepared. The policemen in our communities seldom have to use their weapons, but public peace would be greatly endangered if they did not have them.

The preparation of the military means for keeping the peace is necessary not only to the security of the United States but also to building a safe and prosperous world society.

Helping free nations to acquire the means of defending themselves is an obligation of the leadership we have assumed in world affairs. Within the practical limits of our resources we must strive to act with foresight and precision, so that our strength and the collective strength of the free peoples associated with us will be most effective.

To be effective, the aid which we supply to other nations for defending themselves must be planned ahead. It must not be wasted. It must be carefully allocated to meet the realities of our own security. Above all, it is urgent to initiate a program of aid promptly if we are not to lose the momentum already gained toward recovery and political stability.

These general requirements are given sharp emphasis by consideration of the specific cases where aid is needed. Many anxious governments have requested our military assistance. Among these requests there can be no more meaningful appeals than those which have come from the countries of western Europe. It is entirely logical that these governments should turn to us and that we should help them. Their defense is our defense and is of deep concern to us. Twice in one generation we have found that we had to join with them in fighting against aggressor nations in order to preserve our freedom and the freedom of other democratic countries.

The principal task of the free nations of western Europe in the last 4 years has been to restore their war-shattered economies. The inherent difficulties of this task have been aggravated by the foreign policy of the Soviet Union, which has done its utmost to prevent European recovery. Full economic recovery requires peaceful conditions and the assurance that the work of labor, industry, and agriculture will not be swept away in an outburst of international violence. In place of these conditions the Soviet Union, with its violent propaganda, its manipulation of the conspiratorial activities of the world Communist movement, and its maintenance of one of the largest peacetime armies in history, has deliberately created an atmosphere of fear and danger.

In the face of what has occurred in Greece, and in Berlin, in the face of the threats and pressures to which Iran and Turkey have been exposed, in the light of the suppression of human liberty in countries under Communist control, the nations of western Europe have not been able to ignore the necessity of a military defense for themselves. They have seen what the Soviet Union has done to nations for which it professed friendship and with which it was recently allied. They have observed how a Communist coup d'état, operating in the shadow of the massed military might of the Soviet Union, can overthrow, at one stroke, the democratic liberties and the political independence of a friendly nation.

As a consequence of that experience, and in the light of the fact that the two most devastating wars in history originated in Europe, they realize that they must have a shield against aggression to shelter their political institutions and the rebirth of their own economic and social life.

The nations of western Europe have addressed themselves in all seriousness to the task of providing such a shield. In the Treaty of Brussels five nations of western Europe established joint measures for their own defense. In support of that treaty they have coordinated both their defensive strategy and their plans to produce necessary military supplies.

Those five nations, together with Norway, Denmark, and Italy, have undertaken annual military expenditures equivalent to about 5½ million dollars. This is the maximum amount they are able to spend without seriously interfering with the civilian production necessary for their economic recovery. This amount is not, however, enough to furnish these nations the protection they need. Concentrating, as they are, on restoring their economic stability, they are unable to spare the plants and the materials required to bring their defense establishments up to the necessary levels. Furthermore, there are certain items essential for their defense which they are not equipped to provide for themselves. They have, therefore, come to us with urgent requests for assistance in providing the necessary margin of arms and equipment which will make them better able to repel aggression and mitigate the anxieties of their peoples.

I recommend that we supply these countries with assistance of three types: First, a limited amount of dollar aid to enable them to increase their own production of military items without impairing their efforts for economic recovery; second, the direct transfer of certain essential items of military equipment; and, third, the assistance of experts in the production and use of military equipment and the training of personnel. Such a program will enable these countries to acquire the elements necessary to their defense without hampering their recovery.

The military assistance which we propose for these countries will be limited to that which is necessary to help them create mobile defensive forces. Our objective is to see to it that these nations are equipped, in the shortest possible time, with compact and effectively trained forces capable of maintaining internal order and resisting the initial phases of external aggression.

At the present time the military power which is the greatest deterrent to aggression is centered in the United States, 3,000 miles away from Europe. It must be made clear that the United States has no intention, in the event of aggression, of allowing the peoples of western Europe to be overrun before its own power can be brought to bear. The program of military assistance now proposed is a tangible assurance of our purpose in this regard.

Outside of western Europe we are already engaged in a program of military assistance to Greece and Turkey. This program has been in effect since May 1947. The Communist effort in Greece, in the form of a guerrilla war supported from abroad, has been condemned by the General Assembly of the United Nations. Our aid to Greece has checked this attempt to overthrow the political independence of a free nation. It is important that present gains against the guerrillas be maintained and that the operations be pressed to a successful conclusion. Only if this is done, can the economic reconstruction of Greece be accomplished.

In Turkey our aid has lessened the burden of military preparedness which the threatening pressure of the Soviet Union had imposed on a primarily agrarian economy. Although the Turkish defense system has been improved, additional equipment and maintenance parts are needed for the modernization of certain Turkish defense units.

We are also confronted by the necessity of making military assistance available in other areas of the world outside Europe.

In Iran the use of surpluses of United States military equipment has aided in improving the defensive effectiveness of the Iranian Army and the maintenance of internal order. It is now necessary to provide certain additional items to round out this program, and thereby to strengthen the ability of Iran to defend its independence.

The new Republic of Korea, established as a result of free elections held under the auspices of the United Nations, is menaced by the Communist regime in the northern part of the country. With the advice and assistance of the United States, the Korean Government has established a small force to protect its internal security and defend itself against outside aggression short of a full-scale war. Equipment has been requested from the United States for minimum army and coast-guard forces. It is essential to the survival of the Korean Republic that this assistance be made available.

In addition, it is necessary to continue our program of limited aid to the Republic of the Philippines, which was originated under the act of June 26, 1946.

In this hemisphere we have assumed obligations of mutual defense with the other American Republics under the Pact of Rio de Janeiro. Our northern neighbor, Canada, is a party with us to the North Atlantic Treaty. It is important under the terms of these two treaties that we should assist Canada and the American Republics to establish adequate defenses properly coordinated with our own.

In view of our limited resources, it is impossible for us to assist on a grant basis all countries whose defense is related to our own. We can afford to bear the cost of military aid only with respect to those countries vital to our national security where the danger is greatest, and where the ability to pay for military equipment is least. With respect to such countries as Canada and the American Republics, therefore, I recommend that our assistance be limited to the use of the facilities of our Government to procure defense equipment for them at their own expense.

All these various requirements for military assistance should obviously be handled in a unified program, adaptable in its administration to the operation of our foreign policy.

The sum which will be needed in new appropriations for the fiscal year 1950 for all the grant programs now contemplated, together with a margin for emergencies, is approximately $1,450,000,000. The bulk of the supplies to be procured under these programs will be delivered over the next 2 years. Of this total $50,000,000 has recently been requested for the interim continuation of our program of military aid to Greece and Turkey under existing authorizations. New authorization will be required for $1,400,000,000.

The major portion of the total is to be devoted to the needs of the western European nations. It is not proposed that specific sums be committed in advance to particular countries. Rather, the President should be able to make allocations as circumstances require.

The aid we provide will constitute only a minor fraction of what these countries will spend themselves. Agreements will be executed with the recipients, to provide for mutual assistance and to assure proper use of the equipment furnished. The recipient nations will be required to limit the use of the items supplied to the defense of agreed geographic areas, and will not be permitted to transfer them to other nations without the consent of the United States. The President should be authorized to terminate our aid at any time. Aid will be terminated in the event that a recipient acts in a manner inconsistent with the policies and purposes of the program or with its obligations under the charter of the United Nations.

The recommended program covers the most pressing current needs for military aid. How long it may be necessary to continue military aid depends on many unpredictable factors. Our burden will undoubtedly lessen as our program for peace brings its returns. Advancing economic recovery will enable the free nations to sustain a larger share of the expense of their own defense measures. Progress toward a peaceful settlement of international differences will reduce the threat of violence, and lighten the cost of preparedness. Ultimately, when the peaceful principles of the United Nations are fully realized, the protection of the peace may be assigned to the security forces of that organization.

If this program of military aid is to succeed, we must prosecute it promptly and vigorously. Our policies for peace are having the desired effect. We cannot afford to lose the momentum we have already gained.

One need only look back to the situation with which we were confronted 2½ years ago to be convinced of the rightness of our course of action. At that time the free nations of Europe were not only exposed and defenseless, but they were also caught in an economic impasse which threatened the existence of their democratic forms of government. Europe, with its great storehouse of skills and its heritage of free institutions, seemed about to disintegrate and to fall piece by piece under the sway of totalitarian control.

The fact that such a disaster has been averted should inspire us with confidence in the ultimate triumph of the cause of peace and freedom not only in Europe but elsewhere in the world.

Like the North Atlantic Treaty, this program of military aid is entirely defensive in character. By strengthening the defense establishments of the free nations, it will increase the confidence of the peoples of the world in a peaceful future and protect the growth of world recovery.

I would not suggest that this program alone will bring present international tensions to an end. It will, however, preserve the initiative which the free nations of the world now have, and help to create a world structure so firm economically and militarily as to convince any potential aggressor nation that its own welfare lies in the direction of mutual tolerance and peaceful foreign relations.

(2) An Act to Promote the Foreign Policy and Provide for the Defense and General Welfare of the United States by Furnishing Military Assistance to Foreign Nations, Approved October 6, 1949.[14]

Be it enacted by the Senate and House of Representatives of the United States of America in Congress assembled, That this Act may be cited as the "Mutual Defense Assistance Act of 1949".

FINDINGS AND DECLARATION OF POLICY

The Congress of the United States reaffirms the policy of the United States to achieve international peace and security through the United Nations so that armed force shall not be used except in the common interest. The Congress hereby finds that the efforts of the United States and other countries to promote peace and security in furtherance of the purposes of the Charter of the United Nations require additional measures of support based upon the principle of continuous and effective self-help and mutual aid. These measures include the furnishing of military assistance essential to enable the United States and other nations dedicated to the purposes and principles of the United Nations Charter to participate effectively in arrangements for individual and collective self-defense in support of those purposes and principles. In furnishing such military assistance, it remains the policy of the United States to continue to exert maximum efforts to obtain agreements to provide the United Nations with armed forces as contemplated in the Charter and agreements to achieve universal control of weapons of mass destruction and universal regulation and reduction of armaments, including armed forces, under adequate safeguards to protect complying nations against violation and evasion.

The Congress hereby expresses itself as favoring the creation by the free countries and the free peoples of the Far East of a joint organization, consistent with the Charter of the United Nations, to establish a program of self-help and mutual cooperation designed to develop their economic and social well-being, to safeguard basic rights and liberties and to protect their security and independence.

The Congress recognizes that economic recovery is essential to international peace and security and must be given clear priority. The Congress also recognizes that the increased confidence of free peoples in their ability to resist direct or indirect aggression and to maintain internal security will advance such recovery and support political stability.

TITLE I

NORTH ATLANTIC TREATY COUNTRIES

SEC. 101. In view of the coming into force of the North Atlantic Treaty and the establishment thereunder of the Council and the Defense Committee which will recommend measures for the common defense of the North Atlantic area, and in view of the fact that the task of the Council and the Defense Committee can be facilitated by immediate steps to increase the integrated defensive armed strength of the parties to the treaty, the President is hereby authorized to furnish military assistance in the form of equipment, materials, and services to such nations as are parties to the treaty and have heretofore requested such assistance. Any such assistance furnished under this title shall be subject to agreements, further re-

14 Public Law 329, 81st Cong., 1st sess.

ferred to in section 402, designed to assure that the assistance will be used to promote an integrated defense of the North Atlantic area and to facilitate the development of defense plans by the Council and the Defense Committee under article 9 of the North Atlantic Treaty and to realize unified direction and effort; and after the agreement by the Government of the United States with defense plans as recommended by the Council and the Defense Committee, military assistance hereunder shall be furnished only in accordance therewith.

SEC. 102. There are hereby authorized to be appropriated to the President for the period through June 30, 1950, out of any moneys in the Treasury not otherwise appropriated, for carrying out the provisions and accomplishing the policies and purposes of this title, not to exceed $500,000,000, of which not to exceed $100,000,000 shall be immediately available upon appropriation, and not to exceed $400,000,000 shall become available when the President of the United States approves recommendations for an integrated defense of the North Atlantic area which may be made by the Council and the Defense Committee to be established under the North Atlantic Treaty. The recommendations which the President may approve shall be limited, so far as expenditures by the United States are concerned, entirely to the amount herein authorized to be appropriated and the amount authorized hereinafter as contract authority.

SEC. 103. In addition to the amount authorized to be appropriated under section 102, the President shall have authority, within the limits of specific contract authority which may be hereafter granted to him in an appropriation Act, to enter into contracts for carrying out the provisions and accomplishing the policies and purposes of this title in amounts not exceeding in the aggregate $500,000,000 during the period ending June 30, 1950, and there are hereby authorized to be appropriated for expenditure after June 30, 1950, such sums as may be necessary to pay obligations incurred under such contract authorization. No contract authority which may be granted pursuant to the provisions of this section shall be exercised by the President until such time as he has approved recommendations for an integrated defense of the North Atlantic area which may be made by the Council and the Defense Committee to be established under the North Atlantic Treaty.

SEC. 104. None of the funds made available for carrying out the provisions of this Act or the Act of May 22, 1947, as amended, shall be utilized (a) to construct or aid in the construction of any factory or other manufacturing establishment outside of the United States or to provide equipment or machinery (other than machine tools) for any such factory or other manufacturing establishment, (b) to defray the cost of maintaining any such factory or other manufacturing establishment, (c) directly or indirectly to compensate any nation or any governmental agency or person therein for any diminution in the export trade of such nation resulting from the carrying out of any program of increased military production or to make any payment, in the form of a bonus, subsidy, indemnity, guaranty, or otherwise, to any owner of any such factory or other manufacturing establishment as an inducement to such owner to undertake or increase production of arms, ammunition, implements of war, or other military supplies, or (d) for the compensation of any person for personal services rendered in or for any such factory or other manufacturing establishment, other than personal services of a technical nature rendered by officers and employees of the United States for the purpose of establishing or maintaining production by such factories or other manufacturing establishments to effectuate the purposes of this Act and in conformity with desired standards and specifications.

TITLE II

GREECE AND TURKEY

SEC. 201. In addition to the amounts heretofore authorized to be appropriated, there are hereby authorized to be appropriated, out of any moneys in the Treasury not otherwise appropriated, not to exceed $211,370,000 to carry out the provisions of the Act of May 22, 1947, as amended, for the period through June 30, 1950.

TITLE III

OTHER ASSISTANCE

Sec. 301. The President, whenever the furnishing of such assistance will further the purposes and policies of this Act, is authorized to furnish military assistance as provided in this Act to Iran, the Republic of Korea, and the Republic of the Philippines.

Sec. 302. There are hereby authorized to be appropriated to the President for the period through June 30, 1950, out of any moneys in the Treasury not otherwise appropriated, for carrying out the provisions and accomplishing the purposes of section 301, not to exceed $27,640,000.

Sec. 303. In consideration of the concern of the United States in the present situation in China, there is hereby authorized to be appropriated to the President, out of any moneys in the Treasury not otherwise appropriated, the sum of $75,-000,000 in addition to funds otherwise provided as an emergency fund for the President, which may be expended to accomplish in that general area the policies and purposes declared in this Act. Certification by the President of the amounts expended out of funds authorized hereunder, and that it is inadvisable to specify the nature of such expenditures, shall be deemed a sufficient voucher for the amounts expended.

TITLE IV

GENERAL PROVISIONS

Sec. 401. Military assistance may be furnished under this Act, without payment to the United States except as provided in the agreements concluded pursuant to section 402, by the provision of any service, or by the procurement from any source and the transfer to eligible nations of equipment, materials, and services: *Provided,* That no equipment or materials may be transferred out of military stocks if the Secretary of Defense, after consultation with the Joint Chiefs of Staff, determines that such transfer would be deterimental to the national security of the United States or is needed by the reserve components of the armed forces to meet their training requirements.

Sec. 402. The President shall, prior to the furnishing of assistance to any eligible nation, conclude agreements with such nation, or group of such nations, which agreements, in addition to such other provisions as the President deems necessary to effectuate the policies and purposes of this Act and to safeguard the interests of the United States, shall make appropriate provision for —

(a) the use of any assistance furnished under this Act in furtherance of the policies and purposes of this Act;

(b) restriction against transfer of title to or possession of any equipment and materials, information or services furnished under this Act without the consent of the President;

(c) the security of any article, service, or information furnished under this Act;

(d) furnishing equipment and materials, services, or other assistance, consistent with the Charter of the United Nations, to the United States or to any among other eligible nations to further the policies and purposes of this Act.

Sec. 403. (a) Any funds available for carrying out the policies and purposes of this Act, including any advances to the United States by any nation for the procurement of equipment and materials or services, may be allocated by the President for any of the purposes of this Act to any agency, and such funds shall be available for obligation and expenditure for the purpose of this Act in accordance with authority granted hereunder or under the authority governing the activities of the agency to which such funds are allocated.

(b) Reimbursement shall be made by or to any agency from funds available for the purpose of this Act for any equipment and materials, services or other assistance furnished or authorized to be furnished under authority of this Act from, by, or through any agency. Such reimbursement shall include expenses arising from or incident to operations under this Act and shall be made by or to such agency in an amount equal to the value of such equipment and materials, services (other than salaries of members of the armed forces of the United States) or other assistance and such expenses. The amount of any such reimbursement shall be credited as reimbursable receipts to current applicable appropriations, funds, or accounts of such agency and shall be available for, and under the authority applicable to, the purposes for which such appropriations, funds, or accounts are authorized to be used, including the procurement of equipment and materials or services, required by such agency, in the same general category as those furnished by it or authorized to be procured by it and expenses arising from and incident to such procurement.

(c) The term "value", as used in subsection (b) of this section, means —

(1) with respect to any excess equipment or materials furnished under this Act, the gross cost of repairing, rehabilitating, or modifying such equipment or materials prior to being so furnished;

(2) with respect to any nonexcess equipment or materials furnished under this Act which are taken from the mobilization reserve (other than equipment or materials referred to in paragraph (3) of this subsection), the actual or the projected (computed as accurately as practicable) cost of procuring for the mobilization reserve an equal quantity of such equipment or materials or an equivalent quantity of equipment and materials of the same general type but deemed to be more desirable for inclusion in the mobilization reserve than the equipment or materials furnished;

(3) with respect to any nonexcess equipment or materials furnished under this Act which are taken from the mobilization reserve but with respect to which the Secretary of Defense has certified that it is not necessary fully to replace such equipment or materials in the mobilization reserve, the gross cost to the United States of such equipment and materials or its replacement cost, whichever the Secretary of Defense may specify; and

(4) with respect to any equipment or materials furnished under this Act which are procured for the purpose of being so furnished, the gross cost to the United States of such equipment and materials.

In determining the gross cost incurred by any agency in repairing, rehabilitating, or modifying any excess equipment furnished under this Act, all parts, accessories, or other materials used in the course of such repair, rehabilitation, or modification shall be priced in accordance with the current standard pricing policies of such agency. For the purpose of this subsection, the gross cost of any equipment or materials taken from the mobilization reserve means either the actual gross cost to the United States of that particular equipment or materials or the estimated gross cost to the United States of that particular equipment or materials obtained by multiplying the number of units of such particular equipment or materials by the average gross cost of each unit of that equipment and materials owned by the furnishing agency.

(d) Not to exceed $450,000,000 worth of excess equipment and materials may be furnished under this Act or may hereafter be furnished under the Act of May 22, 1947, as amended. For the purposes of this subsection, the worth of any excess equipment or materials means either the actual gross cost to the United States of that particular equipment or materials or the estimated cost to the United States of that particular equipment or materials obtained by multiplying the number of units of such particular equipment or materials by the average gross cost of each unit of that equipment or materials owned by the furnishing agency.

Sec. 404. The President may exercise any power or authority conferred on him by this Act through such agency or officer of the United States as he shall direct, except such powers or authority conferred on him in section 405 and in clause (2) of subsection (b) of section 407.

Sec. 405. The President shall terminate all or part of any assistance authorized by this Act under any of the following circumstances:

(a) If requested by any nation to which assistance is being rendered;

(b) If the President determines that the furnishing of assistance to any nation is no longer consistent with the national interest or security of the United States or the policies and purposes of this Act; or

(c) If the President determines that provision of assistance would contravene any decision of the Security Council of the United Nations, or if the President otherwise determines that provision of assistance to any nation would be inconsistent with the obligation of the United States under the Charter of the United Nations to refrain from giving assistance to any nation against which the United Nations is taking preventive or enforcement action or in respect of which the General Assembly finds the continuance of such assistance is undesirable.

(d) Assistance to any nation under this Act may, unless sooner terminated by the President, be terminated by concurrent resolution by the two Houses of the Congress: *Provided,* That funds made available under this Act shall remain available for twelve months from the date of such termination for the necessary expenses of liquidating contracts, obligations, and operations under this Act.

SEC. 406. (a) Any agency may employ such additional civilian personnel without regard to section 14 (a) of the Federal Employees Pay Act of 1946 (60 Stat. 219), as amended, as the President deems necessary to carry out the policies and purposes of this Act.

(b) Nothwithstanding the provisions of Revised Statutes 1222 (U. S. C., title 10, sec. 576), personnel of the armed forces may be assigned or detailed to noncombatant duty, including duty with any agency or nation, for the purpose of enabling the President to furnish assistance under this Act.

(c) Technical experts and engineering consultants, not to exceed fifteen persons at any one time, as authorized by section 15 of the Act of August 2, 1946 (U. S. C., title 5, sec. 55a), required for the purposes of this Act, may, if the President deems it advantageous for the purposes of this Act and if in his opinion the existing facilities of the agency concerned are inadequate, be employed by any agency performing functions under this Act, and individuals so employed may be compensated at rates not in excess of $50 per diem.

(d) Service of any individual employed as a technical expert or engineering consultant under subsection (c) of this section shall not be considered as service or employment bringing such individual within the provisions of sections 281, 283, and 284 of United States Code, title 18, of section 190 of the Revised Statutes (U. S. C., title 5, sec. 99), or of any other Federal law imposing restrictions, requirements, or penalties in relation to the employment of persons, the performance of services, or the payment or receipt of compensation in connection with any claim, proceeding, or matter involving the United States, except insofar as such provisions of law may prohibit any such individual from receiving compensation in respect of any particular matter in which such individual was directly involved in the performance of such service.

(e) For the purpose of carrying out the provisions of this Act, there may be employed not to exceed three persons at a rate of compensation not to exceed $15,000 and one person at a rate of compensation not to exceed $16,000. Any person so employed shall be appointed by the President, by and with the advice and consent of the Senate.

SEC. 407. (a) Nothing in this Act shall alter, amend, revoke, repeal, or otherwise affect the provisions of the Atomic Energy Act of 1946 (60 Stat. 755).

(b) The President may perform any of the functions authorized under section 401 of this Act without regard to (1) the provisions of title 10, United States Code, section 1262 (a), and title 34, United States Code, section 546 (e); and (2) such provisions as he may specify of the joint resolution of November 4, 1939 (54 Stat. 4), as amended.

SEC. 408. (a) Notwithstanding any other provision of law, the Reconstruction Finance Corporation is authorized and directed, until such time as appropriations shall be made under the authority of this Act and the Act of May 22, 1947, as amended, to make advances not to exceed in the aggregate $125,000,000 to carry out the provisions of this Act and the Act of May 22, 1947, as amended, in such manner, at such time, and in such amounts as the President shall determine, and no interest shall be charged on advances made by the Treasury to the Reconstruction Finance Corporation for this purpose. The Reconstruction Finance Corporation shall be repaid without interest for advances made by it hereunder from funds made available for the purposes of this Act and the Act of May 22, 1947, as amended.

(b) Funds made available for carrying out the provisions of title I shall be available for the expenses of administering the provisions of this Act and of the Act of May 22, 1947, as amended. Whenever possible the expenses of administration of this Act shall be paid for in the currency of the nation where the expense is incurred, as provided in subsection (d).

(c) Whenever he determines that such action is essential for the effective carrying out of the purposes of this Act, the President may from time to time utilize not to exceed in the aggregate 5 per centum of the amounts made available for the purposes of any title of this Act for the purposes of any other title. Whenever the President makes any such determination, he shall forthwith notify the Committee on Foreign Relations of the Senate, the Committees on Armed Services of the Senate and of the House of Representatives, and the Committee on Foreign Affairs of the House of Representatives.

(d) Upon approval by the President, any currency of any nation received by the United States for its own use in connection with the furnishing of assistance under this Act may be used for expenditures for essential administrative expenses of the United States in any such nation incident to operations under this Act and the amount, if any, remaining after the payment of such administrative expenses shall be used only for purposes specified by Act of Congress.

(e) The President may, from time to time, in the interest of achieving standardization of military equipment and in order to provide procurement assistance without cost to the United States, transfer, or enter into contracts for the procurement for transfer of, equipment, materials or services to nations designated in title I, II, or III of this Act, or to a nation which has joined with the United States in a collective defense and regional arrangement: *Provided,* That, prior to any such transfer or the execution of any such contracts, any such nation shall have made available to the United States the full cost, actual or estimated, of such equipment, materials, or services, and shall have agreed to make available forthwith upon request any additional sums that may become due under such contracts.

(f) Any equipment or materials procured to carry out the purposes of title I of this Act shall be retained by, or transferred to, and for the use of, such department or agency of the United States as the President may determine in lieu of being disposed of to a nation which is a party to the North Atlantic Treaty whenever in the judgment of the President of the United States such disposal to a foreign nation will not promote the self-help, mutual aid, and collective capacity to resist armed attack contemplated by the treaty or whenever such retention is called for by concurrent resolution by the two Houses of the Congress.

SEC. 409. That at least 50 per centum of the gross tonnage of any equipment, materials, or commodities made available under the provisions of this Act, and transported on ocean vessels (computed separately for dry bulk carriers and dry cargo liners) shall be transported on United States flag commercial vessels at market rates for United States flag commercial vessels in such manner as will insure a fair and reasonable participation of United States flag commercial vessels in cargoes by geographic areas.

SEC. 410. The President, from time to time, but not less frequently than once every six months, while operations continue under this Act, shall transmit to the Congress reports of expenditures and activities authorized under this Act, except information the disclosure of which he deems incompatible with the security of the United States. Reports provided for under this section shall be transmitted to the Secretary of the Senate or the Clerk of the House of Representatives, as the case may be, if the Senate or the House of Representatives, as the case may be, is not in session.

SEC. 411. For the purpose of this Act —

(a) The terms "equipment" and "materials" shall mean any arms, ammunition or implements of war, or any other type of material, article, raw material, facility, tool, machine, supply, or item that would further the purposes of this Act, or any component or part thereof, used or required for use in connection therewith, or required in or for the manufacture, production, processing, storage, transportation, repair, or rehabilitation of any equipment or materials, but shall not include merchant vessels.

(b) The term "mobilization reserve", as used with respect to any equipment or materials, means the quantity of such equipment or materials determined by the Secretary of Defense under regulations prescribed by the President to be required to support mobilization of the armed forces of the United States in the event of war or national emergency until such time as adequate additional quantities of such equipment or materials can be procured.

(c) The term "excess", as used with respect to any equipment or materials, means the quantity of such equipment or materials owned by the United States which is in excess of the mobilization reserve of such equipment or materials.

(d) The term "services" shall include any service, repair, training of personnel, or technical or other assistance or information necessary to effectuate the purposes of this Act.

(e) The term "agency" shall mean any department, agency, establishment, or wholly owned corporation of the Government of the United States.

(f) The term "armed forces of the United States" shall include any component of the Army of the United States, of the United States Navy, of the United States Marine Corps, of the Air Force of the United States, of the United States Coast Guard, and the reserve components thereof.

(g) The term "nation" shall mean a foreign government eligible to receive assistance under this Act.

SEC. 412. Whoever offers or gives to anyone who is now or in the past two years has been an employee or officer of the United States any commission, payment, or gift, in connection with the procurement of equipment, materials, or services under this Act, and whoever, being or having been an employee or officer of the United States in the past two years, solicits, accepts, or offers to accept any such commission, payment, or gift, shall upon conviction thereof be subject to a fine of not to exceed $10,000 or imprisonment for not to exceed three years, or both.

SEC. 413. If any provision of this Act or the application of any provision to any circumstances or persons shall be held invalid, the validity of the remainder of the Act and applicability of such provision to other circumstances or persons shall not be affected thereby.

C. Brussels Pact Machinery

[See *Documents, X, 1948*, p. 584.]

On January 7, the press reported that Ambassador Lewis W. Douglas, United States Ambassador to the United Kingdom, had been appointed as "observer" on the Military Supply Board, a subsidiary body of the Consultative Council of Western Powers created by the Brussels Pact of March 17, 1948.[1]

On March 14, the Consultative Council met in London, six weeks ahead of its scheduled meeting, to consider the integration of the Brussels Pact machinery into the framework of the proposed North Atlantic Treaty.[2] No details were released as to the decisions taken in the course of this secret meeting. Signature of the North Atlantic Treaty by the five governments was effected on April 2, 1949; and on April 5, the five signatories addressed a request for military assistance to the United States Government. In reply of April 6, the Department of State indicated a willingness to "recommend to the United States Congress that the United States provide military assistance to countries signatory to the Brussels Treaty, in order to assist them to meet the matériel requirements of their defense program."[3] The Defense Ministers of the five powers on April 8 agreed on a general plan for the defense of western Europe and on the means for putting the plan

[1] *New York Times*, January 8, 1949, p. 4. For the text of the Brussels Pact, see *Documents, X, 1948*, p. 585.

[2] *New York Times*, March 14, 1949, p. 12. For further information on the North Atlantic Treaty, see this volume, p. 594.

[3] Department of State, *Bulletin*, XX, p. 494. For further information on the Mutual Defense Assistance Program in which aid to the Brussels Pact powers was ultimately incorporated, see this volume, p. 620.

into effect. Representatives of the United States and Canadian general staffs attended the defense discussions as observers. Details of the plan were left for formulation by the Chiefs of Staff Committee and the Military Supply Board.[4] Agreement in principle on the distribution of the costs of joint defense was reportedly reached by the Defense Ministers on July 15, 1949;[5] and agreement by the Defense Ministers on a unified plan of arms production and service supply was announced on July 16.[6]

For information on the Consultative Council and the Council of Europe, see this volume, p. 637.

For detailed summary of the activities of the Brussels Pact bodies during 1949, see *International Organization*, III, p. 365, 550, 726; *ibid.*, IV, p. 148.

(1) *Address by the Permanent United States Representative to the United Nations (Austin) on the United States and the Brussels Pact, Delivered before the Vermont Historical Society, February 24, 1949.*[7]

[EXCERPT]

Today, the greatest obstacle in the way of recovery is fear. We in the United States have never known the kind of fear that pervades the daily lives of the people of Western Europe. The efforts of workers, businessmen, and farmers are crippled by its cold grip. Their plans for the future are weighed against the fear that foreign armies will again sweep across their land, destroying or carrying away the fruits of their labor. This sense of insecurity robs them of a vital ingredient in the recipe for recovery — confidence in the future.

These fears often are exaggerated, but they are by no means groundless. In the four years since the end of the war, the Western Europeans have seen the Red Army used as the instrument for establishing Moscow-directed Communist dictatorships in country after country. It was just a year ago this month that Czechoslovakia's free, democratic Government was swept aside by a Communist coup. Then began the efforts to drive the Western allies from Berlin. The culminating provocation — the land blockade of Berlin — is clearly recognized by Europeans as a threat to the peace. That threat still exists. The men flying the airlift through winter fog can tell us how much value to place in so-called peace offensives conducted only through public statements and newspaper interviews.

After the fall of Czechoslovakia, the Governments of the United Kingdom, Belgium, France, the Netherlands, and Luxembourg acted. They met in Brussels to consider what kind of action they could take for their common security. Out of this meeting came the treaty signed at Brussels last March. The provisions of that treaty have a special importance to us now. The agreement provided for:

Sweeping plans for closer economic, social and cultural cooperation;

Settlement of disputes among the signatories by peaceful means;

Guarantees of full military and other mutual aid in the event of an armed attack upon a member nation, in accordance with the United Nations Charter;

And, finally, the treaty provided for permanent consultative machinery to

4 *New York Times*, April 9, 1949, p. 4.   5 *Ibid.*, July 16, 1949, p. 5.
6 *Ibid.*, July 17, 1949, p. 6.   7 Department of State Publication 3463.

achieve its defense purposes. While we were in Paris, the combined military planning staff appointed pursuant to this treaty established its headquarters at Fontainebleau.

The Brussels treaty has advanced the strength and unity of Western Europe. But the determination and sincerity of purpose behind it are not adequate to lessen fear and insecurity in Europe. The reason is simple. The combined resources of the Brussels pact nations cannot at this time provide enough military strength to assure effective resistance to aggression. As a consequence, their combined strength is not adequate to discourage aggression. We must help if the potential promise of the Brussels treaty as an instrument of peace is to be realized.

Three months after the signing of the Brussels treaty, the Senate of the United States gave strong support, in principle, to its objective.[8] The people of Western Europe believed, and I believe correctly, that the Vandenburg resolution was a direct and encouraging response to the project they had undertaken. That resolution, adopted by a vote of 64 to 4, recommended in paragraphs 2, 3, and 4 that the United States should —

First, encourage the progressive development of collective security arrangements in keeping with the principles of the United Nations Charter;

Second, associate itself with such arrangements when they are based on full self-help and mutual aid and when they affect the security of this country; and

Third, make clear, in advance, that any armed attack upon another nation which affects the security of the United States will be resisted by the United States in the exercise of our inherent right of self-defense.

This declaration of purpose by the Senate of the United States was an important victory in the campaign against fear. It was a reaffirmation of our determination to take an active part in world affairs to insure peace and our own security.

But now we are faced with the problem of attaining the objectives so clearly stated in the Vandenberg resolution. We must decide what measures we will undertake to help Western European nations build a military establishment strong enough to assure their collective self-defense and to discourage aggression which jeopardizes our common security.

*   *   *   *   *   *   *

(2) Statement on Behalf of the Department of State Concerning the Status of Western Union Development, Read into the Record of the Committee on Foreign Affairs of the House of Representatives, August 2, 1949. Department of State Press Release, August 17, 1949.[9]

The most significant, and the first legal move toward the European unity which so many have talked about for so long, came about a little over 1 year ago with the signing of the Brussels treaty. Under the treaty, Belgium, France, Luxembourg, the Netherlands, and the United Kingdom have agreed to co-

---

8 For the text of the Senate resolution of June 11, 1948, see *Documents, X, 1948*, p. 583.
9 Department of State, *Bulletin*, XXI, p. 295.

operate among themselves to strengthen their economic, social, and cultural ties.

Because of the uncertain political situation in Western Europe and the fact that the continuation of a free, independent Western Europe seemed in jeopardy, there were written into the treaty important measures for collective self-defense. It was considered essential to take steps toward guaranteeing military security. Remarkable progress toward this goal has been made in 1 year.

It was recognized first that the five powers individually would be totally unable to hold off an all-out act of aggression. The central concept has been therefore to construct a unified military instrument able to offer effective resistance to any such threat.

To develop the program, The Western Union Defense Committee was established. This consists of the five Ministers of Defense, and holds the over-all responsibility of preserving the territorial and military integrity of Western Europe. To carry out the decisions of the Defense Committee, two other groups were set up, The Western Union Chiefs of Staff Committee and the Western Union Military Supply Board.

The former includes the chiefs of staff of the land, sea, and air forces, although normally each country is represented by only one chief of staff. This group is responsible for advising on every aspect of Western European defense.

The Supply Board advises the Defense Committee on all questions relating to military supplies, and consists of high ranking members from each of the five powers.

In addition, a Finance and Economic Committee was established to deal with the financial problems of these two groups.

To study the technical and tactical questions of Western European defense, the Brussels treaty governments appointed a Commanders-in-Chief Committee in 1948. The members of this committee are:

Chairman — Field Marshal Viscount Montgomery of Alamein
Commander-in-Chief — Land Forces, General D'Armes Jean de Lattre de
    Tassigny
Commander-in-Chief — Air Forces, Air Chief Marshal Sir James Robb
Flag Officer, Western Europe — Vice Admiral Robert Jaujard

This committee holds in its hands the responsibility for preparing the plans for Western European defense and is responsible to the Western Union Chiefs of Staff. If aggression should occur, the committee would assume command of such forces of the Western Union countries as would be put at its disposal.

In considering how Western Europe can best be defended, the primary emphasis has been on mutual aid. The five powers now have a common organization for the use of their military forces; they have made estimates as to what each member should contribute in case of war; they know approximately what equipment will be necessary, and they are using what equipment they presently have on a mutual basis. In addition, each of the Brussels treaty powers has compulsory military training to maintain adequate reserves.

Great progress has already been made in many fields of defense planning. A complete program for such defense has been drawn up, including the use of land, naval, and air forces. Already communication systems are operating among the participating nations.

To coordinate their defense plans, warships have been loaned from one Western Union country to another; jet aircraft are being provided until production can be increased in the recipient nations, military equipment which is surplus in one country has been distributed to others needing it; progress has been made in standardizing military equipment by a system of licensing; and technical and scientific knowledge in the field of military production has been pooled.

This exchange has carried over from the field of supplies into the field of personnel. Officers and men are being increasingly exchanged to attend military courses, and common training is also under consideration.

In this connection, of particular interest have been the joint air defense exercises at the end of June carried on by the British RAF with active contributions by the air arms of the Netherlands, Belgium, and France; and the more recent naval maneuvers, which carried out large-scale combined exercises. During these maneuvers, the combined fleets, together with the air forces, gave special attention to cooperating in the fields of defense of convoys against submarines and air attack, and also to joint minesweeping.

It is clear that the Western Union countries realize that adequate land, sea, and air forces be maintained. Under article four of the Brussels treaty, they have agreed to give to any member which is attacked all military and other aid and assistance in their power. Under the Atlantic pact, they have given further emphasis to this responsibility by agreeing to "continuous and effective self-help" and to expand their "capacity to resist armed attack."

In all these joint operations and in planning for Western European defense the major handicap is lack of equipment. For instance, to allow for the necessary expansion of the military structure in case of war, it is necessary to equip not only the peacetime forces but also to build up an adequate reserve of military supplies in case of emergency. This has not been possible thus far.

They are tremendously hindered by the fact that they do not have adequate supplies or the capacity to produce such supplies. Occupation by the enemy and/or the effect of 5 years of war on the normal process of maintaining, expanding, and improving their capital equipment played havoc with production. Further, a thoroughly agreed-on principle in the field of the rearmament of Western Europe is that economic recovery takes precedence over military production.

They are therefore unable to restore their military production to the necessary level, although they now possess the framework of a military instrument able to absorb such production. They are, moreover, faced with the fact that the lack of capital equipment is hindering production increase, and the fact that their inadequate production is hindering the supply of capital equipment.

Much emphasis is being laid on the importance of standardizing arms and equipment to aid joint operations. Toward the end of the war many of the Western European nations were provided with American equipment with which they have made a start toward rebuilding their military forces. This in itself has meant a considerable standardization between the Western Union countries. With limited economic resources, however, replacement of existing equipment has been largely impossible by new production. Standardization therefore can only be thought of in long-range terms. Along these lines, much work has been done, and much progress been made in the fields of research and development.

Joint operations are being extended into every phase of military planning. The Western Union countries have agreed on common operational plans and codes in the field of tactics, including the common use of maps and charts; tactical and technical manuals are being exchanged on a mutual basis; and the mutual solving of operational problems has extended beyond into the field of logistics. These joint efforts extend to details such as providing and issuing trilingual glossaries and the translation of manuals into three languages.

It is now obvious that Western Union is no longer a mere plan on paper. It is grown into an operating unit, which has made real progress during its 1 year of existence. Its members have made and are making great sacrifices to a common cause. The mere fact of Western Union has had a great effect on the will of the peoples to resist aggression. Cooperation among the five powers is increasing steadily.

Despite tremendous strides made in the field of economic production, however, the chief problem remains that of supply. It seems impossible that this problem can be solved without United States military assistance.

3. COUNCIL OF EUROPE

[See *Documents, X, 1948,* p. 589.]

(1) *Communiqué Issued by the Consultative Council of the Brussels Pact Powers on the Establishment of the Council of Europe. Released to the Press, January 28, 1949.*[1]

The fourth meeting of the Consultative Council took place in London on January 27 and 28.

The Council took note with satisfaction of the work accomplished under the Brussels Treaty in the social and cultural spheres. A detailed statement on social and cultural matters is attached.[2]

After considering the most valuable preparatory work accomplished in Paris by the Committee for the Study of European Unity, the Council agreed that there should be established a Council of Europe, consisting of a ministerial committee meeting in private and consultative body meeting in public.

The permanent commission was instructed to study the detailed application of the decisions of principle taken by the Council.

1 *New York Times,* January 29, 1949, p. 2.   2 Not reprinted here.

The Council decided to invite other European countries to take part in negotiations for the establishment of the Council of Europe.

The Council also considered a report on matters relating to defense and there was useful interchange of views on certain outstanding political matters.

As regards Palestine, there was general agreement that the stage had now been reachd at which de facto recognition could be given the Government of Israel.

(2) Statement by the Secretary of State (Acheson) on the Signing of the Statute of the Council of Europe. Department of State Press Release, May 11, 1949.[3]

Since the inception of the European Recovery Program the United States has recognized the need for a closer degree of unity among the free nations of Europe. During the past few years numerous individual proposals have been advanced with this as their aim. The United States has not specifically endorsed any of these individual proposals, but has given its support in general to the idea of European unity. The United States has maintained the position that it should not endorse unofficial proposals which envisaged a specific form of political unity and that the promotion of unity was primarily a matter for the Europeans themselves.

On May 5, 1949, representatives of Belgium, Denmark, France, Ireland, Italy, Luxembourg, the Netherlands, Norway, Sweden, and the United Kingdom signed the Statute for the Council of Europe.[4] This act on the part of those nations is a welcome step forward toward the political integration of the free nations of Europe. The people of those nations are to be praised for their realization that a free Europe, to remain free and attain a higher degree of well-being, must be a united Europe.

Before World War II, few regarded any step in the direction of political unity as being within the realm of practical politics. But with the cooperation born of conflict and nurtured by collaboration in the economic field since the war, there came the realization that political cooperation was not only desirable but was a natural path leading toward the achievement of common purposes.

The basis of this political cooperation is not intangible. The people of these nations possess a common heritage of free institutions, a love of liberty, a belief in the worth of the individual, and a respect for the rule of laws formulated by free men for their own protection.

The progressively closer political integration of the free nations of Europe will insure that the economic cooperation which has resulted from the European Recovery Program will not wane, but, on the contrary, will become even closer and more enduring.

With the deposit of instruments of ratification by the Governments of Luxembourg, Norway, and Italy, the Statute of the Council of Europe entered into force

3 Department of State Press Release 347, May 11, 1949; Department of State, *Bulletin*, XX, p. 664.
4 For the text of the Statute of the Council of Europe, see *ibid.*, XXI, p. 858a.

on August 3, 1949. Upon the invitation of the Committee of Ministers which met in Strasbourg on August 8, Greece and Turkey became members of the Council, bringing the total membership to twelve.[5] The first session of the Consultative Assembly opened in Strasbourg on August 10 attended by 101 delegates of the member nations.

For a detailed summary of the activities of the Council of Europe and its subsidiary bodies during the year under review, see *International Organization,* III, p. 729; *ibid.,* IV, p. 149.

4. RELATIONS WITH PARTICULAR COUNTRIES OF EUROPE

A. The United Kingdom

Relations between the United States and the United Kingdom for the period under review fall into three general categories: 1) those relating to the functioning of the United Nations and other multilateral agencies; 2) those of a quadrilateral character relating to occupation matters; and 3) those of a less general and/or bilateral nature relating to regional organizations, commodity arrangements and normal diplomatic intercourse. For the most part these have been documented elsewhere in this volume.

In the first category, information on United Kingdom–United States relations within the general framework of the United Nations will be found on p. 306; on the International Trade Organization, p. 398; on the General Agreement on Tariffs and Trade, p. 407; on regulation and reduction of armaments, p. 339; and on the international control of atomic energy, p. 347. Multilateral relations involving both the United Kingdom and the United States in the operation of the European Recovery Program are documented on p. 200; in the conclusion of the North Atlantic Treaty, p. 594; in the Mutual Defense Assistance Program, p. 620; in the operation of the Brussels Pact machinery, p. 632; and in the establishment of the Council of Europe, p. 637. In the second category, information on relations between the two governments in the occupation of Germany will be found on p. 101; of Austria, p. 169; and of Japan, p. 170. Information on United Kingdom–United States relations in the third category will be found as follows: on the Caribbean Commission, p. 374; on the South Pacific Commission, p. 378; and on international commodity agreements and negotiations, p. 437.

1. ECONOMIC AND FINANCIAL RELATIONS

In an address to the House of Commons on July 6, 1949, concerning the economic status of the United Kingdom and the sterling area, the United Kingdom Chancellor of the Exchequer (Cripps) stated that "the most difficult problem with which the sterling area has been faced is in its balance of trade and payments with the dollar area," a situation well demonstrated by "the critical effect of the dollar shortage upon our sterling economy over the past few years." Sir Stafford informed the Commons that two steps would be taken to seek a remedy for the situation: 1) a meeting of the Finance Ministers of the Commonwealth would convene in London on July 13 to devise "mutual cooperative measures" to deal with the dollar shortage problem; and 2) conversations would soon be initiated with the United States Secretary of the Treasury (Snyder) and the Canadian Minister of Finance (Abbott) for a discussion of the whole matter. As an interim measure, a three-month moratorium on all except essential dollar purchases was announced by Sir Stafford.[1] On July 8, this moratorium was extended to cover 36 non-self-governing territories under United Kingdom administration.[2] The results of the exploratory tripartite conversations were summarized and released to the press in a United Kingdom Treasury communiqué of July 10, 1949.[3] The Commonwealth conference adjourned on July 19 and its results summarized in a communiqué issued on that date.[4] In a joint release of August 19, the Department of

---

5 *The Times* (London), August 10, 1949, p. 4.
1 *New York Times,* July 7, 1949, p. 4.   2 *Christian Science Monitor,* July 9, 1949, p. 5.
3 Department of State, *Bulletin,* XXI, p. 197.   4 *New York Times,* July 19, 1949, p. 4.

State and the Department of the Treasury announced that the preliminary three-power economic discussions would be resumed on September 6, following technical and fact-finding discussions scheduled to begin August 27 among representatives of the three governments.[5] Discussions opened in Washington September 7 and concluded on September 12.

On September 18, the United Kingdom announced the devaluation of the pound sterling from $4.03 to $2.80.[6] Approval of this new par value for the British pound was announced by the International Monetary Fund on the same date.[7] Changes in the par values of local currencies during 1949 were subsequently announced, in each case with the concurrence of the Fund, by Australia, Union of South Africa, Norway, India, Denmark, Egypt, Finland, France, Canada, Iceland, the Netherlands, Greece, Iraq, Belgium, Luxembourg, Uruguay, Paraguay, and Austria.

(1) *Communiqué Issued by the Finance Ministers of the Commonwealth on the Dollar Problem, London, July 18, 1949.*[8]

[1]

The final session of the meeting of Commonwealth Finance Ministers was held in London today. At the end of the meeting the representatives from the other Commonwealth countries placed on record their thanks to the Chancellor of the Exchequer for presiding over their meetings.

[2]

The purpose of the meeting was to enable Ministers of the Commonwealth to exchange views on the urgent economic problems at present confronting their countries with particular reference to the fall in the level of the gold and dollar reserves of the sterling area during recent months.

[3]

The representatives of the sterling area countries expressed their pleasure that Canada had been able to be represented at these meetings and to take part in the discussions upon the positive and constructive side in particular. The Canadian representative could not of course take any part in urging dollar cuts which would vitally affect Canada, but fully supported all the constructive recommendations made.

[4]

Attention was also given to the special position of South Africa, which is not a member of the sterling area dollar pool.

[5]

They also recognized with appreciation the contribution to sterling area dollar earnings made by certain colonial territories such as Malaya and the importance of enabling those territories to maintain and if possible increase that contribution.

[6]

Ministers reviewed the economic position of the sterling area, both immediate and long-term. They reaffirmed their conviction that the strength and stability of sterling are essential to the well-being not only of each member of the sterling area but also of the world as a whole.

[7]

Immediate steps necessary to check the continuing heavy drain on the central reserves of the sterling area were discussed, and the Ministers concerned agreed

---

5 *Ibid.*, p. 307.   6 *The Times* (London), September 19, 1949, p. 4.
7 International Monetary Fund Press Release 91, September 18, 1949.
8 *New York Times*, July 19, 1949, p. 4.

to recommend to their Governments action comparable in its results to that already decided upon by the United Kingdom.

[8]

Emergency measures to stem the current drain on the sterling area's reserves are perforce negative and unconstructive. It was recognized that while the immediate action must be to protect the reserves of the sterling area, the problems of the past few months were an aggravation of long-standing difficulties. The meeting, therefore, was pleased to note that discussions had taken place between United Kingdom, Canadian and United States Ministers and agreed with them that the aim must be the achievement of a pattern of world trade in which the dollar and non-dollar countries can operate together within one single multilateral system. The meeting noted with satisfaction that further discussions were being arranged to take place in Washington early in September to consider the action required to carry out this aim.

[9]

The Ministers agreed that the achievement of this aim depended on the establishment of conditions which would make a single multilateral system of world trade and payment practicable. These conditions did not exist at present.

It was agreed that the Governments represented would give consideration in collaboration with other Governments concerned to measures designed to establish these conditions, and that in endeavoring to solve the shorter-term problem care should be taken to concentrate upon measures which would fit into the permanent pattern of world trade.

[10]

It was agreed that a lasting solution of the sterling area's difficulties could not be found without a very substantial expansion of the area's earnings of dollars and the most effective use and development of the resources of each component part. Practical and positive measures designed to this end were discussed and accepted for recommendations to Governments. The Ministers recognized the special position of those countries which are at present in a lesser or greater degree underdeveloped but which, with assistance, might not only improve the standard of living of their people but also make a greater contribution to the resources available to the world.

[11]

These measures to be effective clearly call for close and continuing consultation between Governments, and the Ministers make recommendations for the necessary action to meet this need.

(2) *Joint Communiqué issued by the Governments of the United States, the United Kingdom, and Canada on the Tripartite Economic Discussions, Washington, September 12, 1949.*[9]

1. Representatives of the United States, the United Kingdom, and Canada have met during the past week to examine the trade and financial relationships between the sterling area and the dollar area. The pound and the dollar are the two principal world trading currencies. While the development of a satisfactory balance of payments between the two areas is a matter of fundamental concern to the democratic world, it involves many problems which concern in the first instance the governments which are the centres of these two currency systems. The present discussions were held to examine these problems. It was recognized that the task of working out conditions under which world trade can develop

9 United Kingdom Command Paper 7788; Department of State, *Bulletin*, XXI, p. 473.

steadily and in increasing freedom will require a strenuous and sustained effort, not only on the part of the United States, the United Kingdom, and Canada, but also by all other countries desiring the same objectives.

2. It was agreed that the common aim is to work toward an ultimate solution which will maintain employment and establish equilibrium of international trade on a mutually profitable basis at high levels. These objectives and general course of action have already been set forth in the United Nations Charter, the Bretton Woods Agreements, and the Havana Charter for an International Trade Organization. It was the broad purpose of the present meetings to explore, within this general framework, various specific measures which the three governments might take to prevent a serious breakdown in the dollar-sterling relationships which would have led to a crippling limitation of dollar imports into the sterling area and to hasten the achievement of those objectives.

3. These conversations have carried forward the consultations initiated in London during 8th–10th July. They have resulted in a clear understanding of the character of the difficulties to be faced and an increasing realization that a fully satisfactory solution will necessitate continuing efforts in many directions. In the course of these conversations it has become possible to discuss with complete frankness specific problems and the types of measures which will have to be taken if the three countries are to achieve their common purpose.

4. In the early stages of the discussion, attention was given to the immediate problem confronting the United Kingdom and the rest of the sterling area as a result of the rapid decline of gold and dollar reserves. Note was taken by the three governments of the emergency action which sterling area countries have decided to take to meet this situation. These measures are not pleasant ones; they will cause difficulties and sacrifices for everyone concerned. Nevertheless, they are a temporary necessity, and are recognized as such by all three governments.

5. The Ministers were in complete agreement that no permanent solution to the problem could be found in the emergency steps contemplated. A more fundamental attempt would have to be made by all concerned to expand the dollar earnings of the sterling area and to increase the flow of investment from the North American Continent to the rest of the world, including the sterling area.

6. This more fundamental attempt would involve both separate actions of the three countries operating individually, and joint action by the three acting in cooperation with each other. In approaching these possibilities of individual and joint action on the sterling-dollar problem, there was common agreement that this action should be based on the assumption that extraordinary aid from the North American Continent would have come to an end by the middle of 1952. This would require that the sterling area increase its dollar earnings so as to pay its way by 1952. This would require in the sterling area the creation of appropriate incentives to exporters to the dollar area and a vigorous attack upon costs of production to enhance the competitive position of sterling area products. Maximum efforts would be made to direct exports to the dollar area and build up earnings from tourism and other services. As a part of this export campaign by the sterling area countries, it was recognized that an essential element was the creation of a feeling of confidence on the part of sterling area exporters. They must feel that they will be afforded the opportunity to remain in the markets of the United States and Canada in which they will have gained a place, and that the minimum of difficulties will be placed in their way in entering those markets.

On their part the creditor countries undertook to facilitate, to the greatest extent feasible, an expansion of dollar earnings by debtor countries, including the sterling area. It was agreed that the United States and Canada should reduce obstacles to the entry of goods and services from debtor countries, in order to provide as wide an opportunity as possible for those countries to earn dollars through the export of goods and the provision of services, including tourism. It was recognized that such a policy would be in the interest of producers in the United States and Canada, for only in this way can the future level of trade provide adequately for those sectors of the American and Canadian economies which depend in considerable part upon foreign markets.

7. The discussion of possible individual and joint actions, both long-run and short-run, ranged over a wide field. In addition to the question of dollar earnings of the United Kingdom and the rest of the sterling area, mentioned above, the Ministers gave special attention to the following subjects:

1. Overseas investment.
2. Commodity arrangements and stockpiling.
3. Limitations on items which may be financed under present Economic Cooperation Act (ECA) procedures.
4. Customs procedures.
5. Tariff policy.
6. Liberalization of intra-European trade and payments.
7. Sterling balances.
8. Petroleum.
9. Shipping.
10. Provisions for continuing consultation.

8. A working group on overseas investment reviewed both recent experience and future prospects for the flow of productive investment, both private and public, from North America to overseas areas, especially underdeveloped countries. It was agreed that a high level of such investment could make an important contribution toward reducing the sterling-dollar disequilibrium and that every aspect of this problem should be explored on a continuing basis. In order to initiate this work, the President's Committee for Financing Foreign Trade will be asked immediately to explore possible lines of action in co-operation with corresponding groups of British and Canadian financial and business representatives. While dealing with all aspects of private and public investment, the Committee will be expected to address itself especially to the problem of incentives and of providing a suitable environment for a high level of private investment.

9. A working group on commodity arrangements and stockpiling gave special attention to rubber and tin. The Canadian representatives stated that the Canadian Government was prepared to take steps to increase reserve stocks of tin and rubber in Canada. The United States representatives reported that the United States Government was prepared to open to natural rubber a substantial additional area of competition, including a modification of the Government order relating to the consumption of synthetic rubber. The United States would review its stockpiling programme, with particular reference to rubber and tin.

10. Special attention was given by another group to the practical difficulty being experienced by the United Kingdom in making fully effective use of its ECA aid to cover its dollar deficit. This difficulty arises out of the fact that, although the United Kingdom needs dollars to pay for goods in the United States, to make settlements with other countries, to pay for services, and for other purposes, the types of transactions which may be financed by ECA dollars have been definitely limited. It has been agreed that, in order to carry out the basic purposes of the Economic Cooperation Act, it will be necessary for the United Kingdom to finance with its share of ECA funds a wider range of dollar expenditures than has hitherto been eligible, both within and outside of the United States. After careful examination of the dollar expenditures proposed to be made or authorized by the United Kingdom, it appears that eligibility requirements can be broadened to the extent required within the limits set by the Economic Cooperation Act. This would broaden the use but not increase the amount of ECA funds allocated to the United Kingdom.

11. In the consideration of measures which creditor countries might take to reduce barriers to trade, it was recognized that customs procedures may create obstacles, psychological as well as actual. Technical discussions of this subject disclosed that the United States, through administrative action and proposed legislation, was already contemplating constructive steps in this field. Canadian representatives stated that the Canadian Government would undertake a further review of the administrative operation of its Customs Act in the light of these discussions. As to tariff rates, it was noted that high tariffs were clearly inconsistent with the position of creditor countries. There had already been significant and substantial reductions in U.S. tariffs during the last fifteen years. The policy of the United States Governmnent

was to seek further negotiation of trade agreements through which additional reductions might be made, within the framework of the Reciprocal Trade Agreements Act.

12. There was agreement that one of the ways in which the competitive position of United Kingdom products might be improved was by a widening of the area in which such products competed freely with those of other countries. In this connection as an initial step toward a more general liberalization the United Kingdom delegation outlined its proposals for liberalizing trade with countries with which it did not have balance of payments difficulties, and raised the question whether the provisions of Section 9 of the Anglo-American Financial Agreement, and Article 5 of the Anglo-Canadian Financial Agreement presented an obstacle to such a plan. It was the view of the United States and Canadian delegations that such liberalization of United Kingdom import regulations should be considered since the United Kingdom shortage of dollars should not in itself force the United Kingdom to reduce its purchases from areas with which it does not have a shortage of means of payment. It was agreed that any United Kingdom import regulations as they affect United States and Canadian products would be the subject of continuing review by representatives of the three governments through continuing facilities for consultation.

13. – (a) A further subject which was discussed was the United Kingdom liability represented by the sterling balances of other countries. A large number of countries has been accustomed to hold either all or a part of their foreign exchange reserves in the form of sterling. The existence and availability of such holdings is an integral feature of the widespread multilateral use of sterling for the purpose of financing international trade. One of the problems of the postwar period has been the existence of exceptionally large accumulations of sterling which were built up, mainly during the war, as the result of payments by the United Kingdom for goods and services purchased overseas in furtherance of the common war effort. In June, 1945, these balances amounted to $13½ billion. Since then there have been considerable fluctuations both in the total and in the holdings of individual countries, though the amount outstanding at the end of 1948 was approximately the same as at June, 1945.

(b) In principle the whole of these balances represents a charge on United Kingdom production of goods and services. In practice, however, a substantial proportion will continue to be held as reserves by the countries concerned. To the extent that the balances are liquidated, some proportion of United Kingdom production of goods and services is used to discharge this liability instead of to pay for current imports of goods and services.

(c) This whole problem in its various aspects, including the necessity to provide capital goods for development, was discussed in a preliminary way on the basis of prior technical examination by the experts of the three governments. It was agreed that this was one of the subjects which concerned other countries and would require further study.

14. Investigation of the ways in which the sterling area could move toward a position in which it could earn its own way led to the discussion of other special problems, including petroleum and shipping – two important elements in the sterling area balance of payments picture. The United Kingdom representatives set forth the facts of the very large dollar deficit which the sterling area presently incurs because of oil transactions, and their desire to reduce this deficit to the minimum possible level. It was mutually recognized that the question of oil production and refining, and geographical distribution raised problems of extreme complexity involving the protection of legitimate interests of the major producing countries and companies. The Ministers recognized that these two questions of petroleum and shipping could not be resolved in the short time available to them, and that further study would be required. In the case of petroleum they agreed to appoint representatives to analyse the facts and to provide the basis for subsequent discussions.

15. There has been agreement on the objective toward which policies should be directed and agreement on certain immediate steps which will be taken to bring that objective nearer. There is, however, as has been emphasized, a number of questions requiring closer examination than this short conference has allowed. It is proposed,

therefore, to continue the examinations, initiated during the conference, of questions on which it is hoped that useful understanding can be reached under the direction of the present Ministerial group. These arrangements for continuing consultation — supplementing the usual channels of communication between governments — will be used to keep under review the effectiveness of actions already agreed upon and to prepare, for governmental consideration, measures which could carry further those adjustments which are considered to be necessary. In establishing these arrangements for continuing consultation, the three Governments wish to emphasize that these arrangements underline rather than diminish their interest in the development of economic co-operation within the entire community of western nations. The tripartite arrangements will not in any way encroach upon, or detract from, the area of competence of the Organisation for European Economic Cooperation (OEEC) and other existing organs of international economic collaboration. On the contrary, these arrangements for continuing consultation, by contributing materially to the solution of problems which today adversely affect the working of the entire OEEC group and yet are not susceptible of solution within that group, will facilitate the progress of economic collaboration in the wider field.

16. In summary the Ministers of the three countries concerned are satisfied that a real contribution to the solution of the sterling-dollar difficulties has been made by the conclusions recorded above. They are confident that, with sustained efforts on all sides and with the seizure of every opportunity by sterling area exporters to enter into and remain in dollar markets which are open to them, there is the prospect of reaching a satisfactory equilibrium between the sterling and dollar areas by the time exceptional dollar aid comes to an end.

2. TRIPARTITE ATOMIC DISCUSSIONS

A secret high-level meeting between the President and other ranking government officials, including David A. Lilienthal, chairman of the United States Atomic Energy Commission, and Dwight D. Eisenhower, acting chairman of the Joint Chiefs of Staff, which was held in Washington on July 14, was officially described on July 19 as concerned with the question as to whether the United Kingdom should receive information and materials which would enable that government to produce the atomic bomb.[10] President Truman officially confirmed on July 28 that the discussions of two weeks previously had concerned "certain problems which this country faces in the field of atomic energy." Further discussions were planned, the President announced, which would "explore with the United Kingdom and Canada some of the basic questions underlying any determination of long-range policy in this field."[11] These exploratory conversations were subsequently scheduled to commence on September 20 and were to be conducted by the Combined Policy Committee which supervised tripartite relations in connection with atomic energy developments.[12]

On September 23, 1949, President Truman announced that the United States possessed evidence leading to the conclusion that "within recent weeks an atomic explosion occurred in the U.S.S.R."[13] Similar announcements were made by the Governments of the United Kingdom and of Canada on the same date.[14] In a statement to the press on September 26, the Under Secretary of State (Webb) and the Counselor of the Department of State (Kennan) informed reporters that the disclosure of the Soviet explosion made the tripartite talks "more timely" and would probably put them on a "continuing" basis.[15] A second statement by Mr. Webb pointed out that "this new factor emphasized the need for the most rational and economic utilization of the materials, techniques, and knowledge available to the three countries."[16]

10 *New York Times*, July 20, 1949, p. 1.
11 Department of State, *Bulletin*, XXI, p. 185.
12 *Ibid.*, p. 472. The Combined Policy Committee consisted of the Secretaries of State and Defense and the Chairman of the Atomic Energy Commission, for the United States; the United Kingdom ambassador and minister, for the United Kingdom; and the Minister of Trade and Commerce, for Canada (*ibid.*).
13 *Ibid.*, p. 487.
14 *The Times* (London), September 24, 1949, p. 4.
15 *New York Times*, September 27, 1949, p. 1.
16 Department of State, *Bulletin*, XXI, p. 488.

(1) Statement by the President (Truman) on the Occurrence of an Atomic Explosion in the Soviet Union. White House Press Release, September 23, 1949.[17]

I believe the American people, to the fullest extent consistent with national security, are entitled to be informed of all developments in the field of atomic energy. That is my reason for making public the following information.

We have evidence that within recent weeks an atomic explosion occurred in the U. S. S. R.

Ever since atomic energy was first released by man, the eventual development of this new force by other nations was to be expected. This probability has always been taken into account by us.

Nearly four years ago I pointed out that "Scientific opinion appears to be practically unanimous that the essential theoretical knowledge upon which the discovery is based is already widely known. There is also substantial agreement that foreign research can come abreast of our present theoretical knowledge in time." And, in the Three-Nation Declaration of the President of the United States and the Prime Ministers of the United Kingdom and of Canada, dated November 15, 1945, it was emphasized that no single nation could in fact have a monopoly of atomic weapons.

This recent development emphasizes once again, if indeed such emphasis were needed, the necessity for that truly effective enforceable international control of atomic energy which this Government and the large majority of the members of the United Nations support.

B. Union of Soviet Socialist Republics

For information on Soviet–United States relations within the general framework of the United Nations, see this volume, p. 307, and on the international control of atomic energy, p. 347. Relations with the Soviet Union in the occupation of Germany are dealt with on p. 101; in the occupation of Austria, p. 164; and in the occupation of Japan, p. 170. For information concerning the announcement of an atomic explosion in the Soviet Union, see p. 645. For information concerning United States relations with the Soviet Union and the eastern European countries on navigation of the Danube, p. 422.

1. GENERAL STATEMENTS

(1) Remarks by the Secretary of State (Acheson) on Replies by the Premier of the Soviet Union (Stalin) to Questions Submitted by the European General Manager of the International News Service (Smith). Department of State Press Release, February 2, 1949.[1]

On January 27, 1949, Kingsbury Smith, European general manager of the International News Service submitted to Premier Stalin for reply a series of four questions concerning cooperation between the Soviet Union and the United States in the interests of peace. Premier Stalin replied to these questions on January 30, 1949. In a press conference of February 2, Secretary Acheson commented as follows on Premier Stalin's replies.

17 *Ibid.*, p. 487.
1 Department of State, *Bulletin*, XX, p. 192. The text is a transcription of Secretary Acheson's remarks as released to the press by the Department of State.

I suppose except for the preservation of our nation and of our liberties, there is no matter more fundamental to the American people than the preservation of peace. I say this because it is a matter not only fundamental but also sacred in America, and neither our people nor any of our representatives would play international politics with a matter of this importance. The hopes of hundreds of millions of people throughout the world are pinned on the preservation of peace. No man of conscience would tamper with those hopes or use the raising or the lowering of them as a pawn in any maneuver.

Now, with those observations, I wish to talk about these questions and answers quite candidly but quite realistically.

The first one of them, in the first group, reads as follows:

"Would the Government of the U.S.S.R. be prepared to consider the issuance of a joint declaration with the Government of the United States of America asserting that the respective governments have no intention of resorting to war against one another?"

The answer is that "the Soviet Government would be prepared to consider the issuance of such a declaration."

Now, I confess that I find this answer puzzling. Both the Soviet Union and the United States and all the other members of the United Nations are pledged by the most solemn treaty commitments not to engage in war against one another. I should like to refresh your memory.

Paragraphs three and four of article II of the United Nations Charter provide:

> All Members shall settle their international disputes by peaceful means in such a manner that international peace and security, and justice, are not endangered.
> All Members shall refrain in their international relations from the threat or use of force against the territorial integrity or political independence of any state, or in any other manner inconsistent with the Purposes of the United Nations.

The President of the United States in his inaugural address stated that it was the position of his administration and of the people of the United States to give unfaltering support to the United Nations. He did not say that he was prepared to consider making that statement. He made it. So as I say, this answer is a puzzling one. So far as commitment is concerned, so far as the most solemnly pledged word is concerned, I had thought that we had long passed the point at which this answer seems to stick.

Question no. 2: "Would the Government of the U.S.S.R. be prepared to join with the Government of the United States of America in measures designed to implement this pact of peace such as gradual disarmaments?"

The answer is: "Naturally the Government of the U.S.S.R. would cooperate with the Government of the United States of America in the carrying out of measures designed to implement this pact of peace and leading to gradual disarmament."

Now, "naturally" means, "in the nature of things" and the nature of things in the past three years since the end of hostilities has not been such as to encourage the expectation of the cooperation which is indicated in this answer. The members of the United Nations have considered since the first draft of the Charter that the hope of disarmament required not only the confidence and assurance which would come from peace settlements, which would be enduring because they would be just, but also from the carrying out of the whole system for the preservation of international peace which is contemplated in the United Nations Charter. Indeed, the very structure of the

Charter is based upon these assumptions. The United States so far from hanging back on any even technical application of this assumption led the way by a demobilization after the last war which was not gradual but was precipitant. This country disbanded the greatest assemblage of armed force which had ever been put together in the world before. Not only is this true but this Government, together with all the other governments represented upon the Security Council, with the unhappy exception of the Soviet Union, did its best to implement those paragraphs and articles of the Charter which, first of all, were designed for the peaceful settlement of disputes, and secondly, for the provision of an international armed force which would give authority to the United Nations.

The use of the veto has frustrated the first effort. Obstruction of the U.S.S.R. in the military committees has frustrated the second effort. The United States went still further.

In the Atomic Energy Commission of the United Nations, it led the way in an attempt to put under international control the most destructive weapon and the most destructive force which man has yet devised. Here again these efforts of many nations were frustrated by Soviet action — so patently frustrated that the Commission was forced to report to the General Assembly that it was unable to carry out its task. In the debate which followed in the General Assembly, the Soviet Delegation made it unmistakably clear that it would not participate in any arrangements which would permit an effective international control of atomic energy.

Now, I mention these points not to score in a debate in which I have no interest but to point out that in the nature of things, the other nations have not received and have little reason to expect the cooperation which is indicated in that answer. This is certainly true if the present may be regarded as the outcome of the past.

Now I should like to take up out of order the fourth question because it relates to the first two.

The fourth question is: "Would your Excellency be prepared to confer with President Truman at a mutually suitable place to discuss the possibility of concluding such a pact of peace?"

The answer is: "I have already stated before that there is no objection to a meeting." Now you will notice that the purpose of the meeting has to do with the arrangements of which I have already spoken, that is, considering issuing a declaration regarding a matter which is already the subject of solemn treaty commitment. The White House spokesman reminded you, in answer to questions, of the fact that President Truman has on numerous occasions stated that he would be pleased to have Premier Stalin visit the United States and visit the President in Washington.

Now in this connection I am sure it is clear to you, and if it is not clear to you I should like to make it clear now, that the Government of the United States would not discuss with any nation any matter which was of direct interest to other nations without the participation of the representatives of those other nations. This is not a new or startling doctrine. There have been many statements of it. I have here one made by General Marshall on May 12 of last year when questioned about the confidential interview between Ambassador Smith and Foreign Minister Molotov. There are two or three sentences which bear on this point. Secretary Marshall said:

> General Smith did not ask for any general discussion or negotiation. We have had a long and bitter experience with such efforts. This Government had no intention of entering into bilateral negotiations with the Soviet Government

on matters relating to the interests of other governments. The discussion of any proposals in regard to outstanding issues which the Soviet Government may have in mind must, as a matter of course, be conducted in the body charged with responsibility for these questions.

Now coming back to the discussion about this meeting, this morning we have still a further development. There has been a new question and answer. We gather from that exchange that Premier Stalin is unhappily prevented by the condition of his health from coming to Washington because he cannot travel either by sea or air. He thus seems to be effectively grounded. The implication of this answer perhaps is that the President of the United States for the fourth time should travel half way around the world to meet Premier Stalin and on this occasion to do so for the purpose of talking with him on a matter so tenuous that it defies specific statement. I think that concludes the comment on that question and answer.

Now the third question and answer, which I will deal with last, is as follows: Question: "If the Governments of the United States of America, the United Kingdom and France agreed to postpone establishment of a separate western German state pending a meeting of the Council of Foreign Ministers to consider the German problem as a whole, would the Government of the U.S.S.R. be prepared to remove the restrictions which Soviet authorities have imposed on communications between Berlin and the western zones of Germany?"

Answer: "Provided the United States of America, Great Britain and France observe the conditions set forth in the third question, the Soviet Government sees no obstacles to lifting the transport restrictions on the understanding, however, that transport and trade restrictions introduced by the three powers should be lifted simultaneously."

Now this question and answer is the only one of the four which relates to an issue between the Soviet Government and the Western powers. Therefore, it is the most interesting exchange of the four. I might review very briefly for you this situation out of which it comes.

For more than six months now the protests of the three Western powers against the illegal blockade of Berlin have been the subject of the most earnest discussion. There were discussions in Moscow between the ambassadors and the Soviet authorities. The discussions were then transferred to the military governors in Berlin. Both groups of discussions failed. The matter was then transferred to the Security Council in Paris. There the Security Council proposed a solution to this difficulty, a solution which got 9 of the 11 votes on the Security Council but failed because of the Soviet veto. This matter is still on the agenda of the Security Council.

During all of this time the reasons which were given by the Soviet Government were first of all that there were technical difficulties which interrupted transport. Then the reason was given that the blockade was necessary to protect the economy of the Soviet zone against the results of a monetary reform in the Western zone.

Now it is true that the question of the postponement of the Western German government did arise in the Moscow discussions, but it is of even greater importance, that having arisen it was abandoned by the Soviet Union as a condition to lifting the blockade for the reasons which are so fully set forth in the United States White Paper on that subject.

Last summer when these discussions were going on, the Western German government had not been formed. Its formation was not imminent. In the months which have passed it has still not been formed, and yet during all of this period the blockade has continued. The preparatory work for the formation of this Western German government has continued to go forward and is going forward as necessary work for the accomplishment of the responsibilities of the three Western powers.

The three Western powers have stressed, repeated again and again to the Soviet Union, that their agreements in regard to Western Germany do not in any sense preclude agreement on Germany as a whole. In fact, they have pointed out that this work facilitates agreement upon Germany as a whole and they have, as I have stated, stressed again and again that what they have in mind and what they are doing is purely provisional pending such agreement on Germany as a whole. During all of these months the three Western powers have tried patiently and persistently to solve the difficulties which have been put forward by the Soviet Government as the reasons for the blockade.

As to the second point in this answer made by Premier Stalin — that he would expect that if Soviet restrictions were lifted the Western restrictions would be lifted — that point has been made clear from the start. The Western governments have always stated that if the Soviet Government permits normal communications with and within Berlin their counter measures will, of course, be lifted.

There are many ways in which a serious proposal by the Soviet Government to restore normal interzonal communications and communications with and within Berlin could be made. All channels are open for any suggestions to that end. The United States, together with the other Western occupying powers, would, of course, consider carefully any proposal made to solve the Berlin problem consistent with their rights, their duties, their obligations as occupying powers.

As I say, all of the normal channels are open. I hope you will not take it amiss if I point out that if I on my part were seeking to give assurance of seriousness of purpose I would choose some other channel than the channel of a press interview.

May I end this statement as I began it, by stating that the interest of the United States and of all the hundreds of millions of people throughout the world in peace is so fundamental that the matter of peace cannot be tampered with and cannot be used as an instrument in any international political maneuver. It will not be so used by the United States.

(2) *Statement by the Permanent Representative of the United States to the United Nations (Austin) on the Soviet Proposal for a Five-Power Peace Pact, Made before the United Nations General Assembly Political and Security Committee, November 14, 1949.*[2]

[EXCERPTS]

For information concerning the action by the General Assembly on the Soviet proposal and the United States–United Kingdom counter-proposal on the essentials of peace, see this volume, p. 306.

The representative of the Soviet Union has furnished this Committee with another exhibition of his verbal fireworks. His table thumping has twice inadvertently jarred the name plate of the United States from the table in front of me. All of us, I believe, will acknowledge his facility for creating flash and thunder, but our interest in the display was dulled a little by the number of times we have had to witness it. With only minor variations, the performance has been repeated at four successive General Assemblies.

2 *Ibid.*, XXI, p. 801.

In this General Assembly, the Soviet Union delegation, on the instruction of its government, charges that preparations for a new war are now being conducted in a number of countries and in particular in the United States and the United Kingdom. In its warmongering charges the Soviet Union departs from previous attacks upon "certain circles" and directs its accusations against governments, charging them with organizing aggressive blocs and pursuing aggressive aims. Today, we have listened to the representative of the Soviet Union expressing claims that propaganda for a new war is aided and abetted by the governments of the United States and the United Kingdom. These charges are coupled with a proposal for a new treaty among the five permanent members of the Security Council. The proposal is epitomized in the item on the agenda reading: "Condemnations of the preparations for a new war and the conclusion of a Five Power pact for the strengthening of peace."

The purport of the speech of the representative of the Soviet Union was to offer proof that the United States and the United Kingdom are interested in breaking the peace of the world. All of us deeply regret that the skill and energy employed by the Soviet Union to produce propaganda proposals are not employed in an effort at harmony. Name-calling does not promote constructive collaboration. Provocation does not contribute to friendly cooperation.

. . . .

Under the Charter, the five permanent members of the Security Council have particular responsibility for maintaining peace and security. Their particular responsibility was recognized when they were accorded special voting privileges. The fact that one of these five — the Soviet Union — has ignored that particular responsibility and has abused that special privilege has been the principal barrier to constructive cooperation.

. . . .

Does the Soviet representative contend that a new pact would initiate a reversal of such policies? If it would, then such a pact is unnecessary. If it would not, then such a pact would be a futility.

Confidence in Soviet pledges has been undermined by the experience of the past few years. To find cause for concern, it is not necessary to recall the Friendship Pact with Nazi Germany, or the Soviet nonaggression pacts with Finland, Latvia, Esthonia, and Lithuania. We need only look at the long, unhappy list of broken Soviet pledges that has grown since we have been engaged in the common effort to create the United Nations.

. . . .

Faced with these facts, the peace-loving nations have been compelled to seek other paths toward their goal of peace. They have had to face squarely the problem posed by Soviet insistence that everybody is out of step but the Cominform. The aggressively reactionary Soviet policies that have prevented the Cominform states from cooperating with the rest of the world have forced the rest of the world to promote collective security without them.

These collective efforts to strengthen international peace and security are the real objects of the Soviet Union's attack. You are asked to condemn the United States, the United Kingdom, and an unspecified number of other states because they are partners in such agreements as the Treaty of Rio de Janeiro, the North Atlantic Treaty, and the Mutual Defense Assistance Act. The Soviet Union thus wants you to condemn agreements which seek to advance the objectives of the United Nations. The existence of these agreements is a reassurance to all states having a similar aim and a similar purpose. Their purpose is peace.

None of the safeguards we have erected will ever be used unless there is a clear violation of peace which the Security Council is unable to prevent. None of these safeguards alter our hope that the Soviet Union will sometime join with the other members of the United Nations to strengthen collective security. That has been our hope since the first day we began planning the organization of the United Nations. It remains our hope today.

. . . .

The Soviet proposal is not aimed at building a universal system of collective security within the United Nations. On the contrary, it points toward domination of world affairs by the major powers. This is an old objective of Soviet policy, but it shall not become an objective of United States policy.

We oppose this Soviet proposal because we believe the people of the world want more peace, not more pledges. We regard treaties as instruments of inviolable law and not as instruments of propaganda. We are opposed to treaties that render lip-service to important principles but then provide easy means of escape and evasion.

. . . .

If the Soviet Government wishes to undertake measures for strengthening peace, the means are at its instant command. Stop your campaign of hate against the non-Cominform world. Forsake your doctrine that the non-Cominform world is your enemy. Let your people meet with ours and discuss together our common problems. Lift your iron curtain and you will strengthen peace.

. . . .

2. COUNCIL OF MUTUAL ECONOMIC ASSISTANCE

A communiqué issued in Moscow on January 25, 1949, announced that as a result of an economic conference among representatives of the Soviet Union, Bulgaria, Hungary, Poland, Rumania, and Czechoslovakia, a Council of Mutual Economic Assistance had been created. The task of the council would be the exchange of experience in the economic field and the rendering of technical assistance in regard to raw materials, foodstuffs, machinery, and equipment. The council would reach decisions only with the consent of the government of the country concerned and would meet periodically in the capitals of the member countries.[3] The text of the protocol establishing the council was released on June 3, 1949, and revealed that each member government had agreed to supply the council with full and detailed information and was obligated to accept and follow its advice. To implement the objectives of the council, the final article of the twenty-year protocol called for the establishment of mixed companies between member states.[4]

3. COMMUNIST INFORMATION BUREAU

[See *Documents, IX, 1947*, p. 622.]

(1) *Communiqué Adopted by the Communist Information Bureau, Meeting Somewhere in Hungary. Broadcast by Radio Moscow, November 29, 1949.*[5]

The events of the last two years have fully confirmed the correctness of the analysis of the international situation made by the first conference of the Information Bureau of the Communist and Workers parties in September of 1947.

---

3 Embassy of the Union of Soviet Socialist Republics. *USSR Information Bulletin*, IX, p. 66.
4 *New York Times*, June 4, 1949, p. 1.
5 The text consists of excerpts of the communiqué as transcribed and translated by the Soviet monitor in London from a Moscow radio broadcast. *New York Times*, November 30, 1949, p. 6.

During this period the two lines in world policy have been still more clearly and more sharply revealed:

The line of the democratic anti-imperialist camp headed by the U.S.S.R., the camp which conducts a persistent and consistent struggle for peace among the peoples and for democracy.

And the line of the imperialist anti-democratic camp headed by the ruling circles of the United States, the camp which has for its main aim the forcible establishment of the Anglo-American world domination, the enslavement of foreign countries and peoples, the destruction of democracy and the unleashing of a new war.

The change in the correlation of forces in the international area in favor of the camp of peace and democracy provokes mad fury and rage among the imperialist warmongers.

The Anglo-American imperialists count upon changing the march of historical development by means of a war, to solve their internal and external contradictions and difficulties, to consolidate the position of monopoly capital, and to conquer world domination [sic].

The enslaving Marshall Plan, its direct widening into the Western Union and the North Atlantic military bloc, directed against all peace-loving peoples, the impetuous armaments race in the United States and in the West European countries, the inflation of military budgets and the spreading of the network of American military bases serve this policy.

This policy also finds its expression in the refusal of the Anglo-American bloc to prohibit atomic weapons despite the collapse of the legend of American atomic monopoly, and in the fanning of war hysteria by all possible means.

The maturing economic crisis is bringing still more poverty, unemployment, starvation and fear of the morrow to the working masses.

At the same time the policy of preparing a new war is linked with continuous encroachments by the ruling imperialist circles on the elementary and vital rights and democratic liberties of the masses of the people.

It is necessary to work still more stubbornly for the organizational consolidation and extension of the movement of the supporters of peace, drawing into that movement ever new sections of the population and converting it into a nationwide movement.

Particular attention should be devoted to bringing into the movement the trade unions, women's youth, cooperative, sports, cultural and educational, religious and other organizations, as well as scientists, writers, journalists, workers in the field of culture, parliamentary leaders and other political and social leaders who are in favor of peace and are against war.

The reactionary trade union leaders like Green, Carey and Deakin [William Green, head of the American Federation of Labor; James Carey, secretary of the Congress of Industrial Organizations; Arthur Deakin, president of the British Trades Union Congress], conducting a splitting anti-popular policy, are the bitterest enemies of the working class, the accomplices of the warmongers and lackeys of imperialism, who conceal their betrayal in pseudo-Socialist, cosmopolitan phraseology.

The Communist and Workers parties, continuously fighting for peace, must day by day expose the right-wing Socialist leaders as the bitterest enemies of peace.

It is essential to develop and consolidate to the utmost cooperation and unity of action among the rank and file organizations and the rank and file members of the Socialist parties.

The Communist and Workers parties should . . . make wise use of the new and effective forms of mass struggle for peace which fully justified themselves, such as:

Committees in defense of peace in towns and villages.

The drawing up of petitions and protests.

The ballots among the population which have been widely practiced in France and Italy.

Publication and distribution of literature exposing the war preparations.

The collection of funds for the struggle for peace.

The organization of boycotts of films, newspapers, books, periodicals, radio campaigns and of the institutions and leaders propagating the idea of a new war.

The forces of democracy, the forces of the supporters of peace, considerably exceed the forces of reaction.

In the struggle for working-class unity special attention should be given to the masses of Catholic workers and working people and their organizations, bearing in mind that religious convictions are not an obstacle to working class unity, particularly when this unity is needed to have peace.

For the Communist and Workers parties, the ideological exposure of, and the irreconcilable struggle against all manifestations of opportunism, sectarianism and bourgeois nationalism, and the struggle against the penetration of hostile agents into the party milieu, are of decisive importance.

The lessons which arise from the exposure of the Tito-Rankovitch [Interior Minister Alexander Rankovitch of Yugoslavia] spy clique imperatively demand that the Communist and Workers parties should increase revolutionary vigilance to the utmost.

The agents of the Tito clique are today acting as the bitterest splitters in the ranks of the working class and democratic movements and are carrying out the will of the American imperialists.

For this reason a decisive struggle is necessary against the intrigues of these agents of the imperialists, wherever they try to work in workers and democratic organizations.

Recent events have shown that the Yugoslav Government is completely dependent upon foreign imperialistic circles and has become a tool of their aggressive policy, which has led to elimination of the independence and autonomy of the Yugoslav Republic.

The Yugoslav traitors, carrying out the will of the imperialists, made it their task to create political bands of reactionary nationalists, clerical and Fascist elements in the countries of people's democracy in order, with their support, to bring about a counter-revolutionary coup in these countries, wrench them away from the Soviet Union and the entire Socialist camp and subordinate them to the forces of imperialism.

The Tito clique made Belgrade an American center of espionage and anti-Communist propaganda. . . . The Tito-Rankovitch clique, who climbed to power in the disguise of friends of the U.S.S.R., are, on the instructions of the Anglo-American imperialists, conducting a slanderous and provocative campaign against the U.S.S.R., using the foulest fabrications borrowed from the arsenal of Hitler.

In the field of home policy, the sum total of the work of the traitorous Tito-Rankovitch clique is the liquidation, in effect, of the people's democratic system in Yugoslavia.

As a result of the counter-revolutionary policy of the Tito-Rankovitch clique . . . an anti-Communist police state regime of a Fascist type has been established in Yugoslavia.

Kulaks in the villages and capitalist elements in the towns form the social basis of this regime.

Power in Yugoslavia is actually in the hands of anti-popular reactionary elements.

The central and local bodies are staffed by active leaders of the old bourgeois parties, by kulak and other elements hostile to the people's democracy.

The ruling upper strata are upheld by an excessively inflated military police apparatus, with the aid of which they oppress the people of Yugoslavia, have converted the country into a military camp, destroyed the political rights of the working people and trampled on all free expression of thought.

Thousands of Yugoslav patriots, loyal to communism, are expelled from the party, thrown into prison and concentration camps, and many of them have been tortured and killed in prisons, or shot in the back.

The Yugoslav Communist party is controlled by counter-revolutionary forces, who speak in the name of the party.

It is known that the bourgeoisie have long used the old method of recruiting for themselves spies and provocateurs from the ranks of the party and the working class.

By this same means the imperialists try to demoralize the party from within and subordinate it to themselves. In Yugoslavia they have succeeded in achieving this aim.

The Information Bureau . . . considers that the struggle against the Tito clique, hired spies and assassins is the international duty of all Communist and Workers parties.

It is the duty of the Communist and Workers parties to give the utmost assistance to the Yugoslav working class and working peasantry who are fighting for Yugoslav's return to the camp of democracy and socialism.

C. France

For information concerning particular aspects of United States relations with France during 1949, see this volume as follows: on participation in the European Recovery Program, p. 200; on the occupation of Germany, p. 101; on the occupation of Austria, p. 164; on the settlement of certain lend-lease and mutual-aid accounts, p. 412; on the functioning of the Brussels Pact machinery, p. 632; on participation in the North Atlantic Treaty, p. 594; and on progress toward western European union, p. 637.

The convention for the avoidance of double taxation and the prevention of evasion in the cases of taxes on estates and inheritances, signed between the United States and France in Paris on October 18, 1946, was proclaimed in force by the President (Truman) on October 27, 1949. A supplementary protocol signed at Washington on May 17, 1948, was thereby also made effective.[1]

D. Belgium

For information on United States–Belgian relations as documented elsewhere, see this volume as follows: on the European Recovery Program, p. 200; on the Brussels Treaty machinery, p. 632; on the North Atlantic Pact, p. 594; on the Mutual Defense Assistance Program, p. 620; and on the Council of Europe, p. 637.

E. Bulgaria

1. GENERAL

For information on United States–Bulgarian relations as documented elsewhere in this volume, see as follows: on the Danube Commission, p. 422; on the Communist Information Bureau, p. 652; and on the Council of Mutual Economic Assistance, *ibid*.

2. VIOLATIONS OF THE PEACE TREATIES WITH BULGARIA, HUNGARY, AND RUMANIA

[See *The First Five Peace Treaties. Supplement: Documents, VIII, 1945–1946.*]

(1) *Letter from the United States Representative to the United Nations (Austin) to the Secretary-General of the United Nations (Lie) Concerning the Observance in Bulgaria, Hungary, and Rumania of Human Rights and Fundamental Freedoms, September 20, 1949.*[1]

While the United States during April 1949 was engaged in an exchange of correspondence concerning the implementation of the human rights provisions of the treaties of peace with Bulgaria, Hungary, and Rumania, the United Nations General

---

[1] For the text of the convention, see Department of State, *Treaties and Other International Acts Series, 1982.*

[1] United Nations General Assembly, Document A/985, September 23, 1949.

Assembly at the second part of its third session considered related questions placed before it by Bolivia and Australia and appearing on the agenda as "Having regard to the provisions of the Charter and of the peace treaties, the question of the observance in Bulgaria and Hungary of human rights and fundamental freedoms, including questions of religious and civil liberties, with special reference to recent trials of church leaders."[2] In debate on the item, the United States representative (Cohen), declaring that his government had no intention of interfering in the national affairs of either Bulgaria or Hungary or of favoring any particular political factions in those countries, charged both governments with violations of human rights in a "deliberate, systematic and continuous" manner.[3] Accordingly, the United States supported a resolution adopted by a vote of 34 to 6 with 9 abstentions on April 30 which 1) expressed the Assembly's concern at the "grave" accusations made against Hungary and Bulgaria, 2) noted with satisfaction that steps had already been taken by some of the signatories to the peace treaties regarding the charges, 3) drew the attention of Bulgaria and Hungary to their obligations under the treaties, and 4) retained the question on its agenda for the fourth regular session.[4] The following letter to the United Nations Secretary-General (Lie) traced the steps which were taken by the United States Government toward the implementation of the resolution subsequent to its adoption.

Under instructions from my Government, I have the honor to refer to the General Assembly resolution of 30 April 1949 (272 (III)) on the question of observance in Bulgaria and Hungary of human rights and fundamental freedoms. In this resolution the General Assembly noted with satisfaction that steps had been taken by several signatories of the Treaties of Peace regarding the charges made against the Governments of Bulgaria and Hungary and expressed the hope that measures would be diligently applied, in accordance with the Treaties, in order to ensure respect for human rights and fundamental freedoms. The Assembly drew the attention of the Governments of Bulgaria and Hungary to their obligations under the Peace Treaties, including the obligation to cooperate in the settlement of the question and decided to retain the question on the agenda of the fourth session. On 20 August 1949, the Government of Australia proposed for inclusion on the agenda of the fourth session the question of observance of fundamental freedoms and human rights in Rumania.

As one of the signatories to the Treaties of Peace with Bulgaria, Hungary and Rumania the United States has instituted measures referred to in the above-mentioned resolution of the General Assembly.

1. In its notes of 2 April 1949 (Annexes 1, 2 and 3),[5] the Government of the United States formally charged the Governments of Bulgaria, Hungary and Rumania with violations of the respective clauses of the Peace Treaties obligating them to secure to their peoples the enjoyment of human rights and fundamental freedoms. United States Government requested that remedial measures be taken by the three Governments. The Governments of Hungary, Bulgaria and Rumania replied in notes delivered on 8, 21 and 18 April 1949, respectively (Annexes 4, 5 and 6).[6]

2. Since in these notes the three Governments denied that they had violated the Treaty provisions and indicated their unwillingness to adopt the requested remedial measures, the United States Government informed them that in its view disputes had arisen concerning the interpretation and execution of the respective Treaties of Peace. In the notes delivered by the American Legations in Sofia, Budapest and Bucharest on 31 May 1949 (Annexes

---

2 The primary religious trial here referred to was that of Josef Cardinal Mindszenty, Roman Catholic Primate of Hungary, on charges of treason.
3 Department of State, *Bulletin*, XX, p. 518, 556.
4 United Nations General Assembly, Document A/851, April 30, 1949.
5 For the text of the United States notes to Bulgaria, Hungary, and Rumania, see Department of State, *Bulletin*, XX, p. 450.
6 For the text of the Bulgarian, Hungarian, and Rumanian replies, see *ibid.*, p. 755.

7, 8 and 9),[7] the United States Government invoked the relevant Treaty Articles providing for the settlement of such disputes by the Heads of Diplomatic Missions of the United Kingdom, Soviet Union and United States in the three capitals (Article 36 of the Treaty with Bulgaria, Article 40 of the Treaty with Hungary, Article 38 of the Treaty with Rumania). The United States Chiefs of Mission in the three capitals requested their Soviet and British colleagues to meet with them to consider the disputes, in accordance with the procedure specified in those Articles (Annexes 10, 11, 12, 13, 14 and 15).[8] The Ministers of the United Kingdom expressed their willingness to comply with this request (Annexes 16, 17 and 18).[9] However, the Soviet Government declined, in a note of 11 June 1949, to authorize its representatives to discuss the matter (Annex 19).[10] The Soviet Government rejected a further request by the United States Government to reconsider its position (Annexes 20 and 21).[11] On 27 July 1949, the Government of Bulgaria addressed a note to the United States Government setting forth its view that the settlement procedures provided for in Article 36 of the Peace Treaty with Bulgaria were not applicable (Annex 22).[12]

3. As a result, the Government of the United States found it necessary to invoke the additional Peace Treaty procedure which envisages the establishment of commissions composed in each case of one representative of each party to the dispute and a third member chosen by mutual agreement of the two parties from nationals of a third country. In its notes delivered on 1 August 1949 (Annexes 23, 24 and 25) the Government of the United States requested the Governments of Hungary, Bulgaria and Rumania to join with it in naming these commissions.[13] The three Governments rejected this request in their notes dated 26 August, 1 September and 2 September 1949, respectively (Annexes 26, 27 and 28).[14] On 19 September 1949, the United States addressed further notes to the Governments of Hungary, Bulgaria and Rumania in which it restated its views on the disputed issues (Annexes 29, 30 and 31).[15]

I am attaching in the Annex copies of the notes exchanged in this matter, with a request that you, Mr. Secretary-General, be kind enough to circulate copies of this communication and of the notes to all members of the General Assembly in connection with the impending consideration of this matter in the fourth session of the General Assembly.

(2) Resolution Requesting an Advisory Opinion of the International Court of Justice Concerning the Implementation of the Treaties of Peace with Bulgaria, Hungary, and Rumania, Adopted by the United Nations General Assembly, October 22, 1949.[16]

In accordance with an Australian request, the fourth session of the United Nations General Assembly gave further consideration to the question of human rights in Bulgaria and Hungary, as well as in Rumania. The following, a joint United States–Canadian–Bolivian resolution, was approved by the Assembly by a vote of 47 to 5 with 7 abstentions on October 22.

7 See *ibid.*, p. 758, 759.
8 Not reprinted here. For a statement by the Acting Secretary of State (Webb) on these notes, see *ibid.*, p. 759.
9 Not reprinted here.
10 Not reprinted here. For a statement by the Acting Secretary of State (Webb) on the Soviet reply, see *ibid.*, p. 824.
11 For the text of the Soviet note, see *ibid.*, XXI, p. 29.
12 Not reprinted here.
13 See *ibid.*, p. 238.
14 For a summary of the notes, see *ibid.*, p. 456.
15 See *ibid.*, p. 514.
16 United Nations General Assembly, Document A/1023, October 18, 1949.

Whereas the United Nations pursuant to Article 55 of the Charter shall promote universal respect for, and observance of, human rights and fundamental freedoms for all without distinction as to race, sex, language or religion,

Whereas the General Assembly at the second part of its third regular session considered the question of the observance in Bulgaria and Hungary of human rights and fundamental freedoms,

Whereas the General Assembly, on 30 April 1949, adopted resolution 272 (III) concerning this question in which it expressed its deep concern at the grave accusations made against the Governments of Bulgaria and Hungary regarding the suppression of human rights and fundamental freedoms in those countries; noted with satisfaction that steps had been taken by several States signatories to the Peace Treaties with Bulgaria and Hungary regarding these accusations; expressed the hope that measures would be diligently applied, in accordance with the Treaties, in order to ensure respect for human rights and fundamental freedoms; and most urgently drew the attention of the Governments of Bulgaria and Hungary to their obligations under the Peace Treaties, including the obligation to co-operate in the settlement of the question,

Whereas the General Assembly has resolved to consider also at the fourth regular session the question of the observance in Romania of human rights and fundamental freedoms,

Whereas certain of the Allied and Associated Powers signatories to the Treaties of Peace with Bulgaria, Hungary and Romania have charged the Governments of those countries with violations of the Treaties of Peace and have called upon those Governments to take remedial measures,

Whereas the Governments of Bulgaria, Hungary and Romania have rejected the charges of Treaty violations,

Whereas the Governments of the Allied and Associated Powers concerned have sought unsuccessfully to refer the question of Treaty violations to the Heads of Mission in Sofia, Budapest and Bucharest, in pursuance of certain provisions in the Treaties of Peace,

Whereas the Governments of these Allied and Associated Powers have called upon the Governments of Bulgaria, Hungary and Romania to join in appointing Commissions pursuant to the provisions of the respective Treaties of Peace for the settlement of disputes concerning the interpretation or execution of these Treaties,

Whereas the Governments of Bulgaria, Hungary and Romania have refused to appoint their representatives to the Treaty Commissions, maintaining that they were under no legal obligation to do so,

Whereas the Secretary-General of the United Nations is authorized by the Treaties of Peace, upon request by either party to a dispute, to appoint the third member of a Treaty Commission if the parties fail to agree upon the appointment of a third member,

Whereas it is important for the Secretary-General to be advised authoritatively concerning the scope of his authority under the Treaties of Peace,

THE GENERAL ASSEMBLY

1. *Expresses* its continuing interest in and its increased concern at the grave accusations made against Bulgaria, Hungary and Romania,

2. *Records* its opinion that the refusal of the Governments of Bulgaria,

Hungary and Romania to co-operate in its efforts to examine the grave charges with regard to the observance of human rights and fundamental freedoms justifies this concern of the General Assembly about the state of affairs prevailing in Bulgaria, Hungary and Romania in this respect;

3. *Decides* to submit the following questions to the International Court of Justice for an advisory opinion:

I. Do the diplomatic exchanges between Bulgaria, Hungary and Romania on the one hand and certain Allied and Associated Powers signatories to the Treaties of Peace on the other, concerning the implementation of article 2 in the Treaties with Bulgaria and Hungary and article 3 in the Treaty with Romania, disclose disputes subject to the provisions for the settlement of disputes contained in article 36 of the Treaty of Peace with Bulgaria, article 40 of the Treaty of Peace with Hungary, and article 38 of the Treaty of Peace with Romania?

In the event of an affirmative reply to question I:

II. Are the Governments of Bulgaria, Hungary and Romania obligated to carry out the provisions of the articles referred to in question I, including the provisions for the appointment of their representatives to the Treaty Commissions?

In the event of an affirmative reply to question II and if within thirty days from the date when the Court delivers its opinion the Governments concerned have not notified the Secretary-General that they have appointed their representatives to the Treaty Commissions, and the Secretary-General has so advised the International Court of Justice:

III. If one party fails to appoint a representative to a Treaty Commission under the Treaties of Peace with Bulgaria, Hungary and Romania where that party is obligated to appoint a representative to the Treaty Commission, is the Secretary-General of the United Nations authorized to appoint the third member of the Commission upon the request of the other party to a dispute according to the provisions of the respective Treaties?

In the event of an affirmative reply to question III:

IV. Would a Treaty Commission composed of a representative of one party and a third member appointed by the Secretary-General of the United Nations constitute a commission, within the meaning of the relevant Treaty articles, competent to make a definitive and binding decision in settlement of a dispute?

4. *Requests* the Secretary-General to make available to the International Court of Justice the relevant exchanges of diplomatic correspondence communicated to the Secretary-General for circulation to the Members of the United Nations and the records of the General Assembly proceedings on this question;

5. *Decides* to retain on the agenda of the fifth regular session of the General Assembly the question of the observance of human rights and fundamental freedoms in Bulgaria, Hungary and Romania, with a view to ensuring that the charges are appropriately examined and dealt with.

F. Greece

1. GREEK-TURKISH AID PROGRAM

[See *Documents, IX, 1947,* p. 642; *X, 1948,* p. 632.]

For information concerning the Foreign Aid Appropriation Act, 1950, by which funds were appropriated for aid to Greece and Turkey for the 1949/50 fiscal period, see this volume, p. 221. For information on military aid to Greece, see *ibid.,* p. 627.

(1) Military and Economic Assistance to Greece, Cumulative through June 30, 1949.[1]

The following table reflects the value of military goods and services rendered to Greece from all sources, including the United Kingdom, and of economic assistance rendered by the United States under Public Law 75 (80th Cong.).

	Cumulative by Quarter				
	Military Goods and Services				Economic Aid
Period	Total	Army and Air Force	Navy	Other[1a]	
Quarter ending					
1947					
September	$25,316,888	$23,909,000	$424,126	$983,762	
December	43,067,010	40,190,000	914,639	1,962,371	$21,797,752
1948					
March	77,244,526	71,000,000	2,972,512	3,272,014	69,075,934
June	111,299,628	100,972,533	5,111,838	5,215,257	105,196,401
September	165,581,155	152,468,311	7,897,587	5,215,257	113,268,440
December	225,990,014	210,412,323	10,362,434	5,215,257	115,150,119
1949					
March	264,978,939	246,593,939	12,790,702	5,594,298	119,454,805
June	296,461,606	271,929,587	14,780,931	9,751,088	118,310,849

2. INCIDENTS ON THE GREEK BORDER

[See *Documents, VIII, 1945–1946*, p. 881; *IX, 1947*, p. 688; *X, 1948*, p. 634.]

(1) Statement by the Department of State Concerning Conversations on the Greek Question among Representatives of the Soviet Union, the United Kingdom, and the United States. Department of State Press Release, May 20, 1949.[2]

A *Tass* despatch has referred to conversations on Greece among representatives of the Soviet Union, United Kingdom and the United States during the recent General Assembly. The following is a brief summary of the facts:

On April 26, during the course of informal dinner table conversations at the home of Mr. Trygve Lie, various matters on the agenda of the United Nations were discussed by Mr. Andrei Gromyko, Mr. Hector McNeil and Mr. Dean Rusk. At one point in this conversation Mr. Rusk expressed the hope that the three governments would use their influence to bring about a settlement of the Greek question, in order that the Greek people might concentrate on the reconstruction of their country. Mr. Gromyko commented that if foreign troops were withdrawn the matter would solve itself. Mr. Rusk replied that our military assistance to Greece had become necessary because of conditions created in Greece by armed rebellion against the Greek Government by the guerrillas, directly assisted by Greece's three northern neighbors. Mr. Rusk

---

1 Compiled from Department of State Publication 3674, Tables III and IV, p. 31, 33.
1a Represents value of goods supplied to the military program from aid funds other than those allocated by Treasury warrant to the National Military Establishment.
2 Department of State Press Release 378, May 20, 1949; *New York Times*, May 21, 1949, p. 2.

also called Mr. Gromyko's attention to the efforts being made by the United Nations Special Committee on the Balkans (UNSCOB) and to Mr. Evatt's conciliation efforts at Lake Success. Mr. Gromyko's reaction to these United Nations efforts in the matter followed the same negative lines employed by the Soviet Delegation in the course of the Greek debate in the United Nations.

Shortly thereafter Mr. Gromyko asked to see Mr. McNeil and Mr. Rusk who called upon him on May 4. Mr. Gromyko referred to the previous "vague" conversation and said he wished to discuss the matter further in more concrete terms. Mr. Rusk and Mr. McNeil made it clear that such an informal conversation should imply no change in the forum for discussing the Greek question from existing United Nations channels.

Mr. Gromyko then referred to certain proposals which had been made in Prague by Mr. Porphyroghenis of the Greek guerrilla junta. Mr. Gromyko characterized these proposals as calling for a cease fire, a general amnesty and new elections, in the administration of which the guerrilla forces would participate. Mr. Rusk reiterated that the main issue was the illegal furnishing of assistance across Greece's northern frontier to rebels in Greece and that the United Nations was the appropriate forum for discussion of that issue.

It is of interest to note that on May 7, three days after this conversation, the Greek guerrilla radio broadcast that communications in the foreign press on the guerrilla proposals "do not correspond with the views of the provisional democratic government . . . which has not yet officially expounded anywhere its concrete views on this question".

McNeil and Rusk again saw Gromyko briefly on May 14 at the plenary session of the General Assembly at Flushing Meadows. In this conversation Rusk and McNeil made it clear that while we would welcome the restoration of peace in Greece, we could not negotiate on the matter except in an appropriate international forum which provided for full participation by the Greek Government. Rusk again specifically referred to UNSCOB and to Mr. Evatt's conciliation efforts. He stated further that the main issue was the illegal activities of Greece's northern neighbors, particularly Albania and Bulgaria, in furnishing assistance to rebels in Greece.

At the close of the above conversation, Mr. Gromyko said that he had three other points which had not been mentioned earlier. First, the Soviet Union would be willing to participate with the great powers in the supervision of a new Greek election; second, the Soviet Union would be willing to join with the great powers in a commission to "control" the northern frontier of Greece; and third, all foreign military assistance, both materiel and personnel, would have to be withdrawn from Greece. There have been no further conversations.

In the Department's view, the basic issue in the Greek situation is the violation of Greece's northern frontier by military and other assistance to the rebel forces in Greece. This illegal foreign intervention has been repeatedly exposed by the competent organs of the United Nations and denounced by an overwhelming majority of the General Assembly as endangering the peace and as inconsistent with the purposes and principles of the Charter. The United Nations has had this problem before it since 1946 and has established the means for settling it. The General Assembly elected both the Soviet Union and Poland to membership on the present United Nations Special Committee on the Balkans, but both have refused to take their seats. The action of the Soviet Union in blocking effective action in the Security Council, in refusing to participate in the effort of the General Assembly to bring about a settlement and in lending encouragement to the illegal operations which have disturbed the peace, explain why peace has not yet been achieved.

Internal questions such as an amnesty and elections are matters for determination by the Greek Government. We believe that that Government has made a sincere and genuine effort to settle the matter with the help of the United Nations and in a manner consistent with the security of Greece. United States military assistance became necessary because of the direct threat to the independence and integrity of Greece. It was in direct response to the situation created by the illegal intervention of Greece's northern neighbors. So long as that situation continues, the United States will not relax its determination to assist the Greeks in protecting themselves against this form of aggression. We would, however, welcome a bona fide effort by the Soviet Union to remove the threat to the peace and security of the Greek people, and hope that it will use its influence in full support of the United Nations in seeking a settlement.

At no time during any of the informal conversations referred to above was any suggestion made that the Greek question be discussed in the Council of Foreign Ministers. The United States has consistently taken the view that we are prepared to discuss any matter with the Soviet Union in the proper form; in the case of the Greek question it is the United Nations, in which the Greek Government would have full participation.

(2) *Statement by the United States Representative to the United Nations General Assembly (Cohen) on the Proposed Conciliation Committee for Greece, Made before the Political and Security Committee, September 28, 1949.*[3]

At the opening of general debate in the political and security committee during the fourth regular session of the United Nations General Assembly, the committee unanimously approved an Australian proposal appointing a Conciliation Committee for Greece consisting of the president of the General Assembly (Romulo), the United Nations Secretary-General (Lie), and the chairman (Pearson) and vice-chairman (Sarper) of the Political and Security Committee. The following statement by the United States representative on the committee (Cohen) was made in support of the Australian resolution. The Conciliation Committee was to "endeavor to reach a pacific settlement of existing differences between Greece on the one hand, and Albania, Bulgaria and Yugoslavia on the other."[4] After holding twenty-nine meetings the Conciliation Committee reported that "in spite of its best efforts it was unable to develop a basis of conciliation on which an agreement could be reached between the Governments of Albania, Yugoslavia, Bulgaria and Greece," although "the discussions served a useful purpose in clarifying and in some cases narrowing the points of difference between the Governments concerned."[5]

3 Department of State, *Bulletin*, XXI, p. 542.
4 United Nations General Assembly, Document A/1062, November 5, 1949.

The United States delegation supports the proposal of the Australian delegation that we make a new effort through the principal officers of this Committee and the General Assembly to obtain by conciliation a pacific settlement of the existing differences between Greece and her northern neighbors. It is our hope that this effort may be made before we proceed to discuss the details of the Balkan Committee's report. We hope that the chances of success of the proposed conciliation committee will not be prejudiced by provocative debate on the substantive issues.

Last year's report of the Balkan Committee as well as this year's report of that Committee has fully familiarized us with the issues. Although some of the states concerned continue to ignore the Charter of the United Nations and the recommendations of the Assembly and continue to endanger peace by aiding and fomenting guerrilla activity against the independence and territorial integrity of Greece, thanks to the courage of the Greeks and the support given to Greece by states which do respect the Charter and the recommendations of the Assembly, the danger to peace in the Balkans has been substantially reduced. It is happily becoming apparent that the Charter and the recommendations of the Assembly cannot be treated as if they were mere scraps of paper.

Last year's Assembly President, Mr. Evatt, stated on May 19 that "an early attempt [by the Conciliation Committee] to complete its work might well be successful." The Balkan Committee in its 1949 supplementary report also recommended that during the fourth session of the General Assembly "an effort be made . . . to reach a pacific settlement of existing differences" between Greece and her northern neighbors. Under these circumstances, we believe it is our duty to make another good faith effort to bring about a solution through conciliation. We can trust the principal officers of our Committee and of the Assembly to accomplish this if it is possible and to see that the terms of the settlement carry provisions adequate to insure their observance.

But it is only fair to say that if the states concerned genuinely desire a pacific settlement of their differences, that settlement should be reached without undue delay.

It should not need to be reiterated that the neighbors of Greece have no right to interfere in her internal affairs. Good neighbors do not indulge in civil warmongering. If we really want to give Greece the opportunity to reconstruct in freedom her war-shattered political and economic life, we must see that the external threats which have endangered her security are removed.

Nor should it need to be reiterated that international treaties regulate the boundaries of Greece and her northern neighbors. Under the Charter they are not subject to change by force or threat of force. In our view, it cannot advance the cause of conciliation and peaceful settlement to introduce at this time extraneous territorial issues.

The terms of reference of the conciliation commission proposed by Australia are broad and flexible enough to enable the Commission to fulfill its

5 *Ibid.*, Document A/C.1/503, October 18, 1949.

task if all the states concerned are genuinely desirous of seeing that task fulfilled.

The United States interest in Greece is an interest in peace. The United States has no special interests in Greece which in any way threaten the security of the Balkan countries or any other country.

We certainly shall do all in our power to assist the Conciliation Commission to bring about a peaceful settlement if it is set up by this Committee.

Of course, it is our view that if the Conciliation Commission is unable to effect a pacific settlement within the time proposed in the Australian draft, this Committee should proceed to consider and act upon the Balkan Committee's report. We should not conclude the present session without taking some effective measures to prevent the continued fomenting of guerrilla warfare against Greece in violation of the Charter.

(3) *Resolution on Threats to the Political Independence and Territorial Integrity of Greece, Adopted by the United Nations General Assembly, November 18, 1949.*[6]

The following resolution, in effect confirming the findings of the United Nations Special Committee on the Balkans as reported to the fourth session of the General Assembly, was adopted by the Assembly by a vote of 50 to 6 with 2 abstentions.

THE GENERAL ASSEMBLY

Having considered the reports of the United Nations Special Committee on the Balkans established by General Assembly resolution 109 (II) and continued by General Assembly resolution 193 (III), including the additional facts and the recommendations in its supplementary report of 10 September 1949, and in particular its unanimous conclusions that:
  (i) Albania and Bulgaria have continued to give moral and material assistance to the Greek guerrilla movement, Albania being the principal source of material assistance;
  (ii) There has been an increase in the support afforded to the guerrillas from certain States not bordering upon Greece, particularly Romania,
Having noted the report of the Conciliation Committee established by the First Committee of the General Assembly in its resolution of 29 September 1949;
1. CONSIDERS that the active assistance given to the Greek guerrillas by Albania in particular, by Bulgaria and by certain other States, including Romania, in disregard of the Assembly's recommendations, is contrary to the purposes and principles of the United Nations Charter and endangers peace in the Balkans;
2. CONSIDERS that further foreign assistance to the Greek guerrillas resulting in the launching of new armed action against Greece from adjacent territory would seriously increase the gravity of the danger to the peace and would justify the Special Committee in recommending, pursuant to paragraph 8 of resolution 109 (II), the convocation, as a matter of urgency, of a special session of the General Assembly in order to give consideration to further steps necessary for the removal of this danger to the peace;

6 *Ibid.*, Document A/1117, November 19, 1949; *ibid.*, Document A/1117/Corr.1, November 22, 1949.

3. CALLS UPON Albania, Bulgaria and the other States concerned to cease forthwith rendering any assistance or support to the guerrillas in fighting against Greece, including the use of their territories as a base for the preparation or launching of armed actions;

4. RECOMMENDS to all Members of the United Nations and to all other States:

(a) To refrain from any action designed to assist directly or through any other Government any armed group fighting against Greece;

(b) To refrain from the direct or indirect provision of arms or other materials of war to Albania and Bulgaria until the Special Committee or another competent United Nations organ has determined that the unlawful assistance of these States to the Greek guerrillas has ceased;

(c) To take into account, in their relations with Albania and Bulgaria, the extent to which those two countries henceforth abide by the recommendations of the General Assembly in their relations with Greece;

5. AGAIN CALLS UPON Albania, Bulgaria and Yugoslavia to co-operate with Greece in the settlement of their differences by peaceful means, in accordance with the provisions of Article 2, paragraph 3 of the Charter, and to that end recommends:

(a) That, in view of the existence of diplomatic relations between the Governments of Greece and Yugoslavia, further efforts be made by those Governments through diplomatic channels to resolve the differences between them;

(b) That Albania and Bulgaria on the one hand, and Greece on the other, establish normal diplomatic and good neighbourly relations, and endeavour through diplomatic channels to resolve differences;

(c) That they renew previously operative conventions or conclude new ones providing effective machinery for the regulation and control of their common frontiers and for the peaceful adjustment of frontier incidents;

6. CALLS UPON Albania, Bulgaria and Yugoslavia to co-operate with the Special Committee in enabling it to carry out its functions, in particular the functions in accordance with paragraph 10 (c) of resolution 193 (III) and paragraphs 8, 9 and 11 of the present resolution, and upon Greece to continue to co-operate towards the same end;

7. APPROVES the reports of the Special Committee and continues it in being in accordance with all the terms of reference contained in the present resolution and in General Assembly resolutions 109 (II) and 193 (III), which are hereby continued in effect;

8. AGAIN INSTRUCTS the Special Committee to continue to be available to assist the four Governments concerned in the implementation of the Assembly's resolutions, in particular, to promote the restoration of normal relations between Greece and her northern neighbours and the maintenance of international peace and security in the Balkans, and for this purpose continues the authorization to the Special Committee, in its discretion, to appoint and utilize the services and good offices of one or more persons whether or not members of the Special Committee;

9. NOTES the report of the Special Committee, which states that the Governments of Albania, Bulgaria and Yugoslavia have publicly announced that Greek guerrillas who have entered their respective territories have been disarmed and interned, and calls upon all States harbouring Greek guerrillas to co-operate with the Special Committee or other appropriate international agency for verification of the disarming and disposition of the Greek guerrillas who have entered their respective territories;

10. CALLS UPON all States harbouring Greek nationals as a result of the Greek guerrillas' operations against Greece to facilitate the peaceful repatriation to Greece of all such individuals who desire to return and live in accordance with the law of the land;

11. AUTHORIZES the Secretary-General to arrange, through the Special Committee or other appropriate United Nations or international agency, the extension of any feasible assistance to the Governments concerned in making and carrying out arrangements for the repatriation to Greece or resettlement elsewhere of Greek guerrillas and other Greek nationals who have been involved in the guerrilla warfare.

G. Hungary

For information on United States-Hungarian relations as documented elsewhere in this volume, see as follows: on alleged violations of the Hungarian treaty of peace of 1947, p. 655; on the Danube Commission, p. 422; on the Communist Information Bureau, p. 652; and on the Council of Mutual Economic Assistance, *ibid.*

H. Italy

For further information concerning economic cooperation with Italy under the European Recovery Program, see this volume, p. 200.

1. GENERAL

(1) *Treaty of Friendship, Commerce and Navigation between the Governments of the United States and Italy, Signed at Rome, February 2, 1948, Entered into Force, July 26, 1949.*[1]

The treaty of friendship, commerce, and navigation with Italy, approved by the Senate on June 2, 1948,[2] was ratified by the President (Truman) on June 16, 1949.[3] The treaty entered into force on June 26, 1949 upon the exchange of ratifications by the two governments. This was the first "comprehensive" commercial treaty concluded between the United States and a European country since World War II and marked the resumption of commercial treaty relations with Italy which were interrupted in 1937 when the Treaty of 1871 was terminated by mutual agreement.[4]

The UNITED STATES OF AMERICA and the ITALIAN REPUBLIC, desirous of strengthening the bond of peace and the traditional ties of friendship between the two countries and of promoting closer intercourse between their respective territories through provisions responsive to the spiritual, cultural, economic and commercial aspirations of their peoples, have resolved to conclude a Treaty of Friendship, Commerce and Navigation based in general upon the principles of national and of most-favored-nation treatment in the unconditional form, and for that purpose have appointed as their Plenipotentiaries,

THE PRESIDENT OF THE UNITED STATES OF AMERICA:

Mr. JAMES CLEMENT DUNN, *Ambassador Extraordinary and Plenipotentiary of the United States of America to the Italian Republic,* and,

[1] Department of State, *Treaties and Other International Acts Series* 1965.
[2] See *Documents, X, 1948,* p. 642.
[3] Department of State, *Bulletin, XXI,* p. 114.
[4] *Ibid.,* p. 198.

THE PRESIDENT OF THE ITALIAN REPUBLIC:

The Honorable CARLO SFORZA, *Minister Secretary of State for Foreign Affairs.*

Who, having communicated to each other their full powers found to be in due form, have agreed upon the following Articles:

Article I

1. The nationals of either High Contracting Party shall be permitted to enter the territories of the other High Contracting Party, and shall be permitted freely to reside and travel therein.
2. The nationals of either High Contracting Party shall, within the territories of the other High Contracting Party, be permitted, without interference, to exercise, in conformity with the applicable laws and regulations, the following rights and privileges upon terms no less favorable than those now or hereafter accorded to nationals of such other High Contracting Party:

    (*a*) to engage in commercial, manufacturing, processing, financial, scientific, educational, religious, philanthropic and professional activities except the practice of law;

    (*b*) to acquire, own, erect or lease, and occupy appropriate buildings, and to lease appropriate lands, for residential, commercial, manufacturing, processing, financial, professional, scientific, educational, religious, philanthropic and mortuary purposes;

    (*c*) to employ agents and employees of their choice regardless of nationality; and

    (*d*) to do anything incidental to or necessary for the enjoyment of any of the foregoing rights and privileges.

3. Moreover, the nationals of either High Contracting Party shall not in any case, with respect to the matters referred to in paragraphs 1 and 2 of this Article, receive treatment less favorable than the treatment which is or may hereafter be accorded to the nationals of any third country.
4. The provisions of paragraph 1 of this Article shall not be construed to preclude the exercise by either High Contracting Party of reasonable surveillance over the movement and sojourn of aliens within its territories or the enforcement of measures for the exclusion or expulsion of aliens for reasons of public order, morals, health or safety.

Article II

1. As used in this Treaty the term "corporations and associations" shall mean corporations, companies, partnerships and other associations, whether or not with limited liability and whether or not for pecuniary profit, which have been or may hereafter be created or organized under the applicable laws and regulations.
2. Corporations and associations created or organized under the applicable laws and regulations within the territories of either High Contracting Party shall be deemed to be corporations and associations of such High Contracting Party and shall have their juridical status recognized within the territories of the other High Contracting Party whether or not they have a permanent establishment, branch or agency therein.
3. Corporations and associations of either High Contracting Party shall, within the territories of the other High Contracting Party, be permitted, without interference, to exercise all the rights and privileges enumerated in paragraph 2 of Article I, in conformity with the applicable laws and regulations, upon terms no less favorable than those now or hereafter accorded to corporations and associations of such other High Contracting Party. The preceding sentence, and all other provisions of this Treaty according to corporations and associations of the Italian Republic rights and privileges upon terms no less favorable than those now or hereafter accorded to

corporations and associations of the United States of America, shall be construed as according such rights and privileges, in any state, territory or possession of the United States of America, upon terms no less favorable than those upon which such rights and privileges are or may hereafter be accorded therein to corporations and associations created or organized in other states, territories or possessions of the United States of America.

4. Moreover, corporations and associations of either High Contracting Party shall not in any case, with respect to the matters referred to in this Article, receive treatment less favorable than the treatment which is or may hereafter be accorded to corporations and associations of any third country.

Article III

1. The nationals, corporations and associations of either High Contracting Party shall enjoy, throughout the territories of the other High Contracting Party, rights and privileges with respect to organization of and participation in corporations and associations of such other High Contracting Party, including the enjoyment of rights with respect to promotion and incorporation, the purchase, ownership and sale of shares and, in the case of nationals, the holding of executive and official positions, in conformity with the applicable laws and regulations, upon terms no less favorable than those now or hereafter accorded to nationals, corporations and associations of any third country. Corporations and associations of either High Contracting Party, organized or participated in by nationals, corporations and associations of the other High Contracting Party pursuant to the rights and privileges enumerated in this paragraph, and controlled by such nationals, corporations and associations, shall be permitted to exercise the functions for which they are created or organized, in conformity with the applicable laws and regulations, upon terms no less favorable than those now or hereafter accorded to corporations and associations that are similarly organized or participated in, and controlled, by nationals, corporations and associations of any third country.

2. The nationals, corporations and associations of either High Contracting Party shall be permitted, in conformity with the applicable laws and regulations within the territories of the other High Contracting Party, to organize, control and manage corporations and associations of such other High Contracting Party for engaging in commercial, manufacturing, processing, mining, educational, philanthropic, religious and scientific activities. Corporations and associations, controlled by nationals, corporations and associations of either High Contracting Party and created or organized under the applicable laws and regulations within the territories of the other High Contracting Party, shall be permitted to engage in the aforementioned activities therein, in conformity with the applicable laws and regulations, upon terms no less favorable than those now or hereafter accorded to corporations and associations of such other High Contracting Party controlled by its own nationals, corporations and associations.

Article IV

The nationals, corporations and associations of either High Contracting Party shall be permitted within the territories of the other High Contracting Party to explore for and to exploit mineral resources, in conformity with the applicable laws and regulations, upon terms no less favorable than those now or hereafter accorded to nationals, corporations and associations of any third country.

Article V

1. The nationals of each High Contracting Party shall receive, within the territories of the other High Contracting Party, the most constant protection and security for their persons and property, and shall enjoy in this respect the full protection

and security required by international law. To these ends, persons accused of crime shall be brought to trial promptly, and shall enjoy all the rights and privileges which are or may hereafter be accorded by the applicable laws and regulations; and nationals of either High Contracting Party, while within the custody of the authorities of the other High Contracting Party, shall receive reasonable and humane treatment. In so far as the term "nationals" where used in this paragraph is applicable in relation to property it shall be construed to include corporations and associations.

2. The property of nationals, corporations and associations of either High Contracting Party shall not be taken within the territories of the other High Contracting Party without due process of law and without the prompt payment of just and effective compensation. The recipient of such compensation shall, in conformity with such applicable laws and regulations as are not inconsistent with paragraph 3 of Article XVII of this Treaty, be permitted without interference to withdraw the compensation by obtaining foreign exchange, in the currency of the High Contracting Party of which such recipient is a national, corporation or association, upon the most favorable terms applicable to such currency at the time of the taking of the property, and exempt from any transfer or remittance tax, provided application for such exchange is made within one year after receipt of the compensation to which it relates.

3. The nationals, corporations and associations of either High Contracting Party shall within the territories of the other High Contracting Party receive protection and security with respect to the matters enumerated in paragraphs 1 and 2 of this Article, upon compliance with the applicable laws and regulations, no less than the protection and security which is or may hereafter be accorded to the nationals, corporations and associations of such other High Contracting Party and no less than that which is or may hereafter be accorded to the nationals, corporations and associations of any third country. Moreover, in all matters relating to the taking of privately owned enterprises into public ownership and the placing of such enterprises under public control, enterprises in which nationals, corporations and associations of either High Contracting Party have a substantial interest shall be accorded, within the territories of the other High Contracting Party, treatment no less favorable than that which is or may hereafter be accorded to similar enterprises in which nationals, corporations and associations of such other High Contracting Party have a substantial interest, and no less favorable than that which is or may hereafter be accorded to similar enterprises in which nationals, corporations and associations of any third country have a substantial interest.

4. The nationals, corporations and associations of either High Contracting Party shall enjoy freedom of access to the courts of justice and to administrative tribunals and agencies in the territories of the other High Contracting Party, in all degrees of jurisdiction established by law, both in pursuit and in defense of their rights; shall be at liberty to choose and employ lawyers and representatives in the prosecution and defense of their rights before such courts, tribunals and agencies; and shall be permitted to exercise all these rights and privileges, in conformity with the applicable laws and regulations, upon terms no less favorable than the terms which are or may hereafter be accorded to the nationals, corporations and associations of the other High Contracting Party and no less favorable than are or may hereafter be accorded to the nationals, corporations and associations of any third country. Moreover, corporations and associations of either High Contracting Party which are not engaged in business or in non-profit activities within the territories of the other High Contracting Party shall be permitted to exercise the rights and privileges accorded by the preceding sentence without any requirement of registration or domestication.

Article VI

The dwellings, warehouses, factories, shops, and other places of business, and all premises thereto appertaining, of the nationals, corporations and associations of either High Contracting Party, located in the territories of the other High Contracting Party, shall not be subject to unlawful entry or molestation. There shall not be made any visit to, or any search of, any such dwellings, buildings or premises, nor shall any books, papers or accounts therein be examined or inspected, except under conditions and in conformity with procedures no less favorable than the conditions and procedures prescribed for nationals, corporations and associations of such other High Contracting Party under the applicable laws and regulations within the territories thereof. In no case shall the nationals, corporations or associations of either High Contracting Party in the territories of the other High Contracting Party be treated less favorably with respect to the foregoing matters than the nationals, corporations or associations of any third country. Moreover, any visit, search, examination or inspection which may be permissible under the exception stated in this Article shall made[1] with due regard for, and in such a way as to cause the least possible interference with, the occupants of such dwellings, buildings or premises or the ordinary conduct of any business or other enterprise.

Article VII

1. The nationals, corporations and associations of either High Contracting Party shall be permitted to acquire, own and dispose of immovable property or interests therein within the territories of the other High Contracting Party upon the following terms:

(a) in the case of nationals, corporations and associations of the Italian Republic, the right to acquire, own and dispose of such property and interests shall be dependent upon the laws and regulations which are or may hereafter be in force within the state, territory or possession of the United States of America wherein such property or interests are situated; and

(b) in the case of nationals, corporations and associations of the United States of America, the right to acquire, own and dispose of such property and interests shall be upon terms no less favorable than those which are or may hereafter be accorded by the state, territory or possession of the United States of America in which such national is domiciled, or under the laws of which such corporation or association is created or organized, to nationals, corporations and associations of the Italian Republic; provided that the Italian Republic shall not be obligated to accord to nationals, corporations and associations of the United States of America rights in this connection more extensive than those which are or may hereafter be accorded within the territories of such Republic to nationals, corporations and associations of such Republic.

2. If a national, corporation or association of either High Contracting Party, whether or not resident and whether or not engaged in business or other activities within the territories of the other High Contracting Party, is on account of alienage prevented by the applicable laws and regulations within such territories from succeeding as devisee, or as heir in the case of a national, to immovable property situated therein, or to interests in such property, then such national, corporation or association shall be allowed a term of three years in which to sell or otherwise dispose of such property or interests, this term to be reasonably prolonged if circumstances render it necessary. The transmission or receipt of such property or interests shall be exempt from the payment of any estate, succession, probate or administrative taxes or charges higher than those now or hereafter imposed in like cases of nationals, corporations or associations of the High Contracting Party in whose territory the property is or the interests therein are situated.

3. The nationals of either High Contracting Party shall have full power to dispose of personal property of every kind within the territories of the other High Contracting Party, by testament, donation or otherwise and their heirs, legatees or donees, being persons of whatever nationality or corporations or associations wherever created or organized, whether resident or non-resident and whether or not engaged in business within the territories of the High Contracting Party where such property is situated, shall succeed to such property, and shall themselves or by their agents be permitted to take possession thereof, and to retain or dispose of it at their pleasure. Such disposition, succession and retention shall be subject to the provisions of Article IX and exempt from any other charges higher, and from any restrictions more burdensome, than those applicable in like cases of nationals, corporations and associa-

1 The words "shall made" should read "shall be made".

tions of such other High Contracting Party. The nationals, corporations and associations of either High Contracting Party shall be permitted to succeed, as heirs, legatees and donees, to personal property of every kind within the territories of the other High Contracting Party, left or given to them by nationals of either High Contracting Party or by nationals of any third country, and shall themselves or by their agents be permitted to take possession thereof, and to retain or dispose of it at their pleasure. Such disposition, succession and retention shall be subject to the provisions of Article IX and exempt from any other charges, and from any restrictions, other or higher than those applicable in like cases of nationals, corporations and associations of such other High Contracting Party. Nothing in this paragraph shall be construed to affect the laws and regulations of either High Contracting Party prohibiting or restricting the direct or indirect ownership by aliens or foreign corporations and associations of the shares in, or instruments of indebtedness of, corporations and associations of such High Contracting Party carrying on particular types of activities.

4. The nationals, corporations and associations of either High Contracting Party shall, subject to the exceptions in paragraph 3 of Article IX, receive treatment in respect of all matters which relate to the acquisition, ownership, lease, possession or disposition of personal property, no less favorable than the treatment which is or may hereafter be accorded to nationals, corporations and associations of any third country.

Article VIII

The nationals, corporations and associations of either High Contracting Party shall enjoy, within the territories of the other High Contracting Party, all rights and privileges of whatever nature in regard to patents, trade marks, trade labels, trade names and other industrial property, upon compliance with the applicable laws and regulations respecting registration and other formalities, upon terms no less favorable than are or may hereafter be accorded to the nationals, corporations and associations of such other High Contracting Party, and no less favorable that[2] the treatment now or hereafter accorded to nationals, corporations and associations of any third country.

Article IX

1. Nationals, corporations and associations of either High Contracting Party shall not be subjected to the payment of internal taxes, fees and charges imposed upon or applied to income, capital, transactions, activities or any other object, or to requirements with respect to the levy and collection thereof, within the territories of the other High Contracting Party:

(a) more burdensome than those borne by nationals, residents, and corporations and associations of any third country;

(b) more burdensome than those borne by nationals, corporations and associations of such other High Contracting Party, in the case of persons resident or engaged in business within the territories of such other High Contracting Party, and in the case of corporations and associations engaged in business therein, or organized and operated exclusively for scientific, educational, religious or philanthropic purposes.

2. In the case of corporations and associations of either High Contracting Party engaged in business within the territories of the other High Contracting Party, and in the case of nationals of either High Contracting Party engaged in business within the territories of the other High Contracting Party but not resident therein, such other High Contracting Party shall not impose or apply any internal tax, fee or charge upon any income, capital or other basis in excess of that reasonably allocable or apportionable to its territories, nor grant deductions and exemptions less than those reasonably allocable or apportionable to its territories. A comparable rule shall

2 The word "that" should read "than".

apply also in the case of corporations and associations organized and operated exclusively for scientific, educational, religious or philanthropic purposes.

3. Notwithstanding the provisions of paragraph 1 of the present Article, each High Contracting Party reserves the right to: (a) extend specific advantages as to taxes, fees and charges to nationals, residents, and corporations and associations of all foreign countries on the basis of reciprocity; (b) accord to nationals, residents, and corporations and associations of a third country special advantages by virtue of an agreement with such country for the avoidance of double taxation or the mutual protection of revenue; and (c) accord to its own nationals and to residents of contiguous countries more favorable exemptions of a personal nature than are accorded to other nonresident persons.

Article X

Commercial travelers representing nationals, corporations or associations of either High Contracting Party engaged in business within the territories thereof shall upon their entry into and sojourn within the territories of the other High Contracting Party and on departure therefrom, be accorded treatment no less favorable than the treatment now or hereafter accorded to commercial travelers of any third country in respect of customs and other rights and privileges and, subject to the exceptions in paragraph 3 of Article IX, in respect of all taxes and charges applicable to them or to their samples.

Article XI

1. The nationals of either High Contracting Party shall, within the territories of the other High Contracting Party, be permitted to exercise liberty of conscience and freedom of worship, and they may, whether individually, collectively or in religious corporations or associations, and without annoyance or molestation of any kind by reason of their religious belief, conduct services, either within their own houses or within any other appropriate buildings, provided that their teachings or practices are not contrary to public morals or public order.

2. The High Contracting Parties declare their adherence to the principles of freedom of the press and of free interchange of information. To this end, nationals, corporations and associations of either High Contracting Party shall have the right, within the territories of the other High Contracting Party, to engage in such activities as writing, reporting and gathering of information for dissemination to the public, and shall enjoy freedom of transmission of material to be used abroad for publication by the press, radio, motion pictures, and other means. The nationals, corporations and associations of either High Contracting Party shall enjoy freedom of publication in the territories of the other High Contracting Party, in accordance with the applicable laws and regulations, upon the same terms as nationals, corporations or associations of such other High Contracting Party. The term "information", as used in this paragraph, shall include all forms of written communications, printed matter, motion pictures, recordings and photographs.

3. The nationals of either High Contracting Party shall be permitted within the territories of the other High Contracting Party to bury their dead according to their religious customs in suitable and convenient places which are or may hereafter be established and maintained for the purpose, subject to the applicable mortuary and sanitary laws and regulations.

Article XII

1. The nationals of either High Contracting Party, regardless of alienage or place of residence, shall be accorded rights and privileges no less favorable than those accorded to the nationals of the other High Contracting Party, under laws and regulations within the territories of such other High Contracting Party that (a) establish

a civil liability for injury or death, and give a right of action to an injured person, or to the relatives, heirs, dependents or personal representative as the case may be, of an injured or deceased person, or that (b) grant to a wage earner or an individual receiving salary, commission or other remuneration, or to his relatives, heirs or dependents, as the case may be, a right of action, or a pecuniary compensation or other benefit or service, on account of occupational disease, injury or death arising out of and in the course of employment or due to the nature of employment.

2. In addition to the rights and privileges provided in paragraph 1 of this Article, the nationals of either High Contracting Party shall, within the territories of the other High Contracting Party, be accorded, upon terms no less favorable than those applicable to nationals of such other High Contracting Party, the benefits of laws and regulations establishing systems of compulsory insurance, under which benefits are paid without an individual test of financial need: (a) against loss of wages or earnings due to old age, unemployment or sickness or other disability, or (b) against loss of financial support due to the death of father, husband or other person on whom such support had depended.

Article XIII

1. The nationals of each High Contracting Party shall be exempt, except as otherwise provided in paragraph 2 of this Article, from compulsory training or service in the armed forces of the other High Contracting Party, and shall also be exempt from all contributions in money or in kind imposed in lieu thereof.

2. During any period of time when both of the High Contracting Parties are, through armed action in connection with which there is general compulsory service, (a) enforcing measures against the same third country or countries in pursuance of obligations for the maintenance of international peace and security, or (b) concurrently conducting hostilities against the same third country or countries, the exemptions provided in paragraph 1 of this Article shall not apply. However, in such an event the nationals of either High Contracting Party in the territories of the other High Contracting Party, who have not declared their intention to acquire the nationality of such other High Contracting Party, shall be exempt from service in the armed forces of such other High Contracting Party if within a reasonable period of time they elect, in lieu of such service, to enter the armed forces of the High Contracting Party of which they are nationals. In any such situation the High Contracting Parties will make the necessary arrangements for giving effect to the provisions of this paragraph.

Article XIV

1. In all matters relating to (a) customs duties and subsidiary charges of every kind imposed on imports or exports and in the method of levying such duties and charges, (b) the rules, formalities, and charges imposed in connection with the clearing of articles through the customs, and (c) the taxation, sale, distribution or use within the country of imported articles and of articles intended for exportation, each High Contracting Party shall accord to articles the growth, produce or manufacture of the other High Contracting Party, from whatever place arriving, or to articles destined for exportation to the territories of such other High Contracting Party, by whatever route, treatment no less favorable than the treatment now or hereafter accorded to like articles the growth, produce or manufacture of, or destined for, any third country.

2. With respect to the matters referred to in paragraph 1 of this Article, the nationals, corporations and associations of either High Contracting Party shall be accorded, within the territories of the other High Contracting Party, treatment no less favorable than the treatment which is or may hereafter be accorded to the nationals, corporations and associations of such other High Contracting Party; and with respect to such matters the nationals, corporations and associations, vessels and cargoes of either High Contracting Party shall be accorded, within the territories of the other

High Contracting Party, treatment no less favorable than the treatment which is or may hereafter be accorded to nationals, corporations and associations, vessels and cargoes of any third country.

3. No prohibition or restriction of any kind shall be imposed by either High Contracting Party on the importation, sale, distribution or use of any article the growth, produce or manufacture of the other High Contracting Party, or on the exportation of any article destined for the territories of the other High Contracting Party, unless the importation, sale, distribution or use of the like article the growth, produce or manufacture of all third countries, or the exportation of the like article to all third countries, respectively, is similarly prohibited or restricted.

4. If either High Contracting Party imposes any quantitative regulation, whether made effective through quotas, licenses or other measures, on the importation or exportation of any article, or on the sale, distribution or use of any imported article, it shall as a general rule give public notice of the total quantity or value of such article permitted to be imported, exported, sold, distributed or used during a specified period, and of any change in such quantity or value. Furthermore, if either High Contracting Party allots to any third country a share of such total quantity or value of any article in which the other High Contracting Party has an important interest, it shall as a general rule allot to such other High Contracting Party a share of such total quantity or value based upon the proportion of the total quantity or value supplied by, or in the case of exports a share based upon the proportion exported to, the territories of such other High Contracting Party during a previous representative period, account being taken in so far as practicable of any special factors which may have affected or may be affecting the trade in that article. The provisions of this paragraph relating to imported articles shall also apply in respect of the quantity or value of any article permitted to be imported free of duty or tax, or at a lower rate of duty or tax than the rate of duty or tax imposed on imports in excess of such quantity or value.

5. If either High Contracting Party requires documentary proof of origin of imported articles, the requirements imposed therefor shall be reasonable and shall not be such as to constitute an unnecessary hindrance to indirect trade.

Article XV

1. Laws, regulations of administrative authorities and decisions of administrative or judicial authorities of each High Contracting Party that have general application and that pertain to the classification of articles for customs purposes or to rates of duty shall be published promptly in such a manner as to enable traders to become acquainted with them. Such laws, regulations and decisions shall be applied uniformly at all ports of each High Contracting Party, except as otherwise specifically provided for in statutes of the United States of America with respect to the importation of articles into its insular territories and possessions.

2. No administrative ruling by the United States of America effecting advances in rates of duties or charges applicable under an established and uniform practice to imports originating in the territories of the Italian Republic, or imposing any new requirement with respect to such importations, shall as a general rule be applied to articles the growth, produce or manufacture of the Italian Republic already en route at the time of publication thereof in accordance with the preceding paragraph; reciprocally, no administrative ruling by the Italian Republic effecting advances in rates of duties or charges applicable under an established and uniform practice to imports originating in the territories of the United States of America, or imposing any new requirement with respect to such importations, shall as a general rule be applied to articles the growth, produce or manufacture of the United States of America already en route at the time of publication thereof in accordance with the preceding paragraph. However, if either High Contracting Party customarily exempts from such new or increased obligations articles entered for consumption or withdrawn from warehouse for consumption during a period of thirty days after the date of such publication, such practice shall be considered full compliance by such High Contracting Party with this paragraph. The provisions of this paragraph shall

not apply to administrative orders imposing antidumping or countervailing duties or relating to regulations for the protection of human, animal or plant life or health, or relating to public safety, or giving effect to judicial decisions.

3. Each High Contracting Party shall provide some administrative or judicial procedure under which the nationals, corporations and associations of the other High Contracting Party, and importers of articles the growth, produce or manufacture of such other High Contracting Party, shall be permitted to appeal against fines and penalties imposed upon them by the customs authorities, confiscations by such authorities and rulings of such authorities on questions of customs classification and of valuation of articles for customs purposes. Greater than nominal penalties shall not be imposed by either High Contracting Party in connection with any importation by the nationals, corporations or associations of the other High Contracting Party, or in connection with the importation of articles the growth, produce or manufacture of such other High Contracting Party, because of errors in documentation which are obviously clerical in origin or with regard to which good faith can be established.

4. Each High Contracting Party will accord sympathetic consideration to such representations as the other High Contracting Party may make with respect to the operation or administration of import or export prohibitions or restrictions, quantitative regulations, customs regulations or formalities, or sanitary laws or regulations for the protection of human, animal or plant life or health.

Article XVI

1. Articles the growth, produce or manufacture of either High Contracting Party, imported into the territories of the other High Contracting Party, shall be accorded treatment with respect to all matters affecting internal taxation, or the sale, distribution or use within such territories, no less favorable than the treatment which is or may hereafter be accorded to like articles of national origin.

2. Articles grown, produced or manufactured within the territories of either High Contracting Party in whole or in part by nationals, corporations and associations of the other High Contracting Party, or by corporations and associations of the High Contracting Party within the territories of which such articles are grown, produced or manufactured which are controlled by nationals, corporations and associations of the other High Contracting Party, shall be accorded within such territories treatment with respect to all matters affecting internal taxation, or the sale, distribution or use therein, or exportation therefrom, no less favorable than the treatment now or hereafter accorded to like articles grown, produced or manufactured therein in whole or in part by nationals, corporations and associations of the High Contracting Party within the territories of which the articles are grown, produced or manufactured, or by corporations and associations of such High Contracting Party which are controlled by such nationals, corporations and associations. The articles specified in the preceding sentence shall not in any case receive treatment less favorable than the treatment which is or may hereafter be accorded to like articles grown, produced or manufactured in whole or in part by nationals, corporations and associations of any third country, or by corporations and associations controlled by such nationals, corporations and associations.

3. In all matters relating to export bounties, customs drawbacks and the warehousing of articles intended for exportation, the nationals, corporations and associations of either High Contracting Party shall be accorded within the territories of the other High Contracting Party treatment no less favorable than the treatment which is or may hereafter be accorded to the nationals, corporations and associations of such other High Contracting Party.

Article XVII

1. The treatment prescribed in this Article shall apply to all forms of control of financial transactions, including (a) limitations upon the availability of media necessary to effect such transactions, (b) rates of exchange, and (c) prohibitions, restric-

tions, delays, taxes, charges and penalties on such transactions; and shall apply whether a transaction takes place directly, or through an intermediary in another country. As used in this Article, the term "financial transactions" means all international payments and transfers of funds effected through the medium of currencies, securities, bank deposits, dealings in foreign exchange or other financial arrangements, regardless of the purpose or nature of such payments and transfers.

2. Financial transactions between the territories of the two High Contracting Parties shall be accorded by each High Contracting Party treatment on[3] less favorable than that now or hereafter accorded to like transactions between the territories of such High Contracting Party and the territories of any third country.

3. Nationals, corporations and associations of either High Contracting Party shall be accorded by the other High Contracting Party treatment no less favorable than that now or hereafter accorded to nationals, corporations and associations of such other High Contracting Party and no less favorable than that now or hereafter accorded to nationals, corporations and associations of any third country, with respect to financial transactions between the territories of the two High Contracting Parties or between the territories of such other High Contracting Party and of any third country.

4. In general, any control imposed by either High Contracting Party over financial transactions shall be so administered as not to influence disadvantageously the competitive position of the commerce or investment of capital of the other High Contracting Party in comparison with the commerce or the investment of capital of any third country.

Article XVIII

1. If either High Contracting Party establishes or maintains a monopoly or agency for the importation, exportation, purchase, sale, distribution or production of any article, or grants exclusive privileges to any agency to import, export, purchase, sell, distribute or produce any article, such monopoly or agency shall accord to the commerce of the other High Contracting Party fair and equitable treatment in respect of its purchases of articles the growth, produce or manufacture of foreign countries and its sales of articles destined for foreign countries. To this end, the monopoly or agency shall, in making such purchases or sales of any article, be influenced solely by considerations, such as price, quality, marketability, transportation and terms of purchase or sale, which would ordinarily be taken into account by a private commercial enterprise interested solely in purchasing or selling such article on the most favorable terms. If either High Contracting Party establishes or maintains a monopoly or agency for the sale of any service or grants exclusive privileges to any agency to sell any service, such monopoly or agency shall accord fair and equitable treatment to the other High Contracting Party and to the nationals, corporations and associations and to the commerce thereof in respect of transactions involving such service as compared with the treatment which is or may hereafter be accorded to any third country and to the nationals, corporations and associations and to the commerce thereof.

2. Each High Contracting Party, in the awarding of concessions and other contracts, and in the purchasing of supplies, shall accord fair and equitable treatment to the nationals, corporations and associations and to the commerce of the other High Contracting Party as compared with the treatment which is or may hereafter be accorded to the nationals, corporations and associations and to the commerce of any third country.

3. The two High Contracting Parties agree that business practices which restrain competition, limit access to markets or foster monopolistic control, and which are engaged in or made effective by one or more private or public commercial enterprises or by combination, agreement or other arrangement among public or private commercial enterprises may have harmful effects upon the commerce between their respective territories. Accordingly, each High Contracting Party agrees upon the request of the other High Contracting Party to consult with respect to any such prac-

---

3 The word "on" should read "no".

tices and to take such measures as it deems appropriate with a view to eliminating such harmful effects.

Article XIX

1. Between the territories of the High Contracting Parties there shall be freedom of commerce and navigation.

2. Vessels under the flag of either High Contracting Party, and carrying the papers required by its national law in proof of nationality, shall be deemed to be vessels of that High Contracting Party both within the ports, places and waters of the other High Contracting Party and on the high seas. As used in this Treaty, "vessels" shall be construed to include all vessels of either High Contracting Party whether privately owned or operated or publicly owned or operated. However, the provisions of this Treaty other than this paragraph and paragraph 4 of Article XX shall not be construed to accord rights to vessels of war or fishing vessels of the other High Contracting Party; nor shall they be construed to extend to nationals, corporations and associations, vessels and cargoes of, or to articles the growth, produce or manufacture of, such other High Contracting Party any special privileges restricted to national fisheries or the products thereof.

3. The vessels of either High Contracting Party shall have liberty, equally with the vessels of any third country, to come with their cargoes to all ports, places and waters of the other High Contracting Party which are or may hereafter be open to foreign commerce and navigation.

Article XX

1. The vessels and cargoes of either High Contracting Party shall, within the ports, places and waters of the other High Contracting Party, in all respects be accorded treatment no less favorable than the treatment accorded to the vessels and cargoes of such other High Contracting Party, irrespective of the port of departure or the port of destination of the vessel, and irrespective of the origin or the destination of the cargo.

2. No duties of tonnage, harbor, pilotage, lighthouse, quarantine, or other similar or corresponding duties or charges, of whatever kind or denomination, levied in the name or for the profit of the government, public functionaries, private individuals, corporations or establishments of any kind, shall be imposed in the ports, places and waters of either High Contracting Party upon the vessels of the other High Contracting Party, which shall not equally and under the same conditions be imposed upon national vessels.

3. No charges upon passengers, passenger fares or tickets, freight moneys paid or to be paid, bills of lading, contracts of insurance or re-insurance, no conditions relating to the employment of ship brokers, and no other charges or conditions of any kind, shall be imposed in a way tending to accord any advantage to national vessels as compared with the vessels of the other High Contracting Party.

4. If a vessel of either High Contracting Party shall be forced by stress of weather or by reason of any other distress to take refuge in any of the ports, places or waters of the other High Contracting Party not open to foreign commerce and navigation, it shall receive friendly treatment and assistance and such repairs, as well as supplies and materials for repair, as may be necessary and available. This paragraph shall apply to vessels of war and fishing vessels, as well as to vessels as defined in paragraph 2 of Article XIX.

5. The vessels and cargoes of either High Contracting Party shall not in any case, with respect to the matters referred to in this Article, receive treatment less favorable than the treatment which is or may hereafter be accorded to the vessels and cargoes of any third country.

Article XXI

1. It shall be permissible, in the vessels of either High Contracting Party, to im-

port into the territories of the other High Contracting Party, or to export therefrom, all articles which it is or may hereafter be permissible to import into such territories, or to export therefrom, in the vessels of such other High Contracting Party or of any third country; and such articles shall not be subject to any higher duties or charges whatever than those to which the articles would be subject if they were imported or exported in vessels of the other High Contracting Party or of any third country.

2. Bounties, drawbacks and other privileges of this nature of whatever kind or denomination which are or may hereafter be allowed, in the territories of either High Contracting Party, on articles imported or exported in national vessels or vessels of any third country shall also and in like manner be allowed on articles imported or exported in vessels of the other High Contracting Party.

Article XXII

1. Vessels of either High Contracting Party shall be permitted to discharge portions of cargoes, including passengers, at any ports, places or waters of the other High Contracting Party which are or may hereafter be open to foreign commerce and navigation, and to proceed with the remaining portions of such cargoes or passengers to any other such ports, places or waters, without paying higher tonnage dues or port charges in such cases than would be paid by national vessels in like circumstances, and they shall be permitted to load in like manner, in the same voyage outward, at the various ports, places and waters which are or may hereafter be open to foreign commerce and navigation. The vessels and cargoes of either High Contracting Party shall be accorded, with respect to the matters referred to in this paragraph, treatment in the ports, places and waters of the other High Contracting Party no less favorable than the treatment which is or may hereafter be accorded to the vessels and cargoes of any third coyntry.[4]

2. The coasting trade and inland navigation of each High Contracting Party are excepted from the requirements of national and most-favored-nation treatment.

Article XXIII

There shall be freedom of transit through the territories of each High Contracting Party by the routes most convenient for international transit (a) for persons who are nationals of any third country, together with their baggage, directly or indirectly coming from or going to the territories of the other High Contracting Party, (b) for persons who are nationals of the other High Contracting Party, together with their baggage, regardless of whether they are coming from or going to the territories of such other High Contracting Party, and (c) for articles directly or indirectly coming from or going to the territories of the other High Contracting Party. Such persons, baggage and articles in transit shall not be subject to any transit duty, to any unnecessary delays or restrictions, or to any discrimination in respect of charges, facilities or any other matter; and all charges and regulations prescribed in respect of such persons, baggage or articles shall be reasonable, having regard to the conditions of the traffic. Either High Contracting Party may require that such baggage and articles be entered at the proper customhouse and that they be kept whether or not unde[5] bond in customs custody; but such baggage and articles shall be exempt from all customs duties or similar charges if such requirements for entry and retention in customs custody are complied with and if they are exported within one year and satisfactory evidence of such exportation is presented to the customs authorities. Such nationals, baggage, persons and articles shall be accorded treatment with respect to all charges, rules and formalities in connection with transit no less favorable than the treatment which is or may hereafter be accorded to the nationals of any third country, together with their baggage, or to persons and articles coming from or going to the territories of any third country.

4 The word "coyntry" should read "country".
5 The word "unde" should read "under".

Article XXIV

1. Nothing in this Treaty shall be construed to prevent the adoption or enforcement by either High Contracting Party of measures:

(a) relating to the importation or exportation of gold or silver;

(b) relating to the exportation of objects the value of which derives primarily from their character as works of art, or as antiquities, of national interest or from their relationship to national history, and which are not in general practice considered articles of commerce;

(c) relating to fissionable materials, to materials which are the source of fissionable materials, or to radio-active materials which are by-products of fissionable materials;

(d) relating to the production of and traffic in arms, ammunition and implements of war and to such traffic in other goods and materials as is carried on for the purpose of supplying a military establishment;

(e) necessary in pursuance of obligations for the maintenance of international peace and security, or necessary for the protection of the essential interests of such High Contracting Party in time of national emergency; or

(f) imposing exchange restrictions, as a member of the International Monetary Fund, in conformity with the Articles of Agreement thereof signed at Washington December 27, 1945, but without utilizing its privileges under Article VI, section 3, of that Agreement so as to impair any provision of this Treaty; provided that either High Contracting Party may, nevertheless, regulate capital transfers to the extent necessary to insure the importation of essential goods or to effect a reasonable rate of increase in very low monetary reserves or to prevent its monetary reserves from falling to a very low level. If the International Monetary Fund should cease to function, or if either High Contracting Party should cease to be a member thereof, the two High Contracting Parties, upon the request of either High Contracting Party, shall consult together and may conclude such arrangements as are necessary to permit appropriate action in contingencies relating to international financial transactions comparable with those under which exceptional action had previously been permissible.

2. Subject to the requirement that, under like circumstances and conditions, there shall be no arbitrary discrimination by either High Contracting Party against the other High Contracting Party or against the nationals, corporations, associations, vessels or commerce thereof, in favor of any third country or the nationals, corporations, associations, vessels or commerce thereof, the provisions of this Treaty shall not extend to prohibitions or restrictions:

(a) imposed on moral or humanitarian grounds;

(b) designed to protect human, animal or plant life or health;

(c) relating to prison-made goods; or

(d) relating to the enforcement of police or revenue laws.

3. The provisions of this Treaty according treatment no less favorable than the treatment accorded to any third country shall not apply to:

(a) advantages which are or may hereafter be accorded to adjacent countries in order to facilitate frontier traffic;

(b) advantages accorded by virtue of a customs union of which either High Contracting Party may, after consultation with the other High Contracting Party, become a member so long as such advantages are not extended to any country which is not a member of such customs union;

(c) advantages accorded to third countries pursuant to a multilateral economic agreement of general applicability, including a trade area of substantial size, having as its objective the liberalization and promotion of international trade or other international economic intercourse, and open to adoption by all the United Nations;

(d) advantages now accorded or which may hereafter be accorded by the Italian Republic to San Marino, to the Free Territory of Trieste or to the State of Vatican City, or by the United States of America or its territories or possessions to one another, to the Panama Canal Zone, to the Republic of Cuba, to the Republic of the Philippines or to the Trust Territory of the Pacific Islands; or

(e) advantages which, pursuant to a decision made by the United Nations or an organ thereof or by an appropriate specialized agency in relationship with the United Nations, may hereafter be accorded by either High Contracting Party to areas other than those enumerated in subparagraph (d) of the present paragraph.

The provisions of subparagraph (d) shall continue to apply in respect of any advantages now or hereafter accorded by the United States of America or its territories or possessions to one another irrespective of any change in the political status of any of the territories or possessions of the United States of America.

4. The provisions of this Treaty shall not be construed to accord any rights or privileges to persons, corporations and associations to engage in political activities, or to organize or participate in political corporations and associations.

5. Each High Contracting Party reserves the right to deny any of the rights and privileges accorded by this Treaty to any corporation or association created or organized under the laws and regulations of the other High Contracting Party in the ownership or direction of which nationals of any third country or countries have directly or indirectly a controlling interest.

6. No enterprise of either High Contracting Party which is publicly owned or controlled shall, if it engages in commercial, manufacturing, processing, shipping or other business activities within the territories of the other High Contracting Party, claim or enjoy, either for itself or for its property, immunity therein from taxation, from suit, from execution of judgment, or from any other liability to which a privately owned and controlled enterprise is subject therein.

7. The provisions of this Treaty shall not be construed to affect existing laws and regulations of either High Contracting Party in relation to immigration or the right of either High Contracting Party to adopt and enforce laws and regulations relating to immigration; provided, however, that nothing in this paragraph shall prevent the nationals of either High Contracting Party from entering, traveling and residing in the territories of the other High Contracting Party in order to carry on trade between the two High Contracting Parties or to engage in any commercial activity related thereto or connected therewith, upon terms as favorable as are or may hereafter be accorded to the nationals of any third country entering, traveling and residing in such territories in order to carry on trade between such other High Contracting Party and such third country or to engage in commercial activity related to or connected with such trade.

Article XXV

Subject to any limitation or exception provided in this Treaty or hereafter agreed upon between the High Contracting Parties, the territories of the High Contracting Parties to which the provisions of this Treaty extend shall be understood to comprise all areas of land and water under the sovereignty or authority of either of the High Contracting Parties, other than the Canal Zone, and other than the Trust Territory of the Pacific Islands except to the extent that the President of the United States of America shall by proclamation extend provisions of the Treaty to such Trust Territory.

Article XXVI

Any dispute between the High Contracting Parties as to the interpretation or the application of this Treaty, which the High Contracting Parties shall not satisfactorily adjust by diplomacy, shall be submitted to the International Court of Justice, unless the High Contracting Parties shall agree to settlement by some other pacific means.

Article XXVII

1. This Treaty shall be ratified, and the ratifications thereof shall be exchanged at Rome as soon as possible.

2. This Treaty shall enter into force on the day of the exchange of ratifications, and shall continue in force for a period of ten years from that day.

3. Unless one year before the expiration of the aforesaid period of ten years either High Contracting Party shall have given written notice to the other High Contracting Party of intention to terminate this Treaty upon the expiration of the aforesaid period, the Treaty shall continue in force thereafter until one year from the date on which written notice of intention to terminate it shall have been given by either High Contracting Party.

IN WITNESS WHEREOF the respective Plenipotentiaries have signed this Treaty and have affixed hereunto their seals.

DONE in duplicate, in the English and Italian languages, both equally authentic, at Rome, this second day of February one thousand nine hundred forty-eight.

PROTOCOL

At the time of signing the Treaty of Friendship, Commerce and Navigation between the United States of America and the Italian Republic, the undersigned Plenipotentiaries, duly authorized by their respective Governments, have further agreed on the following provisions, which shall be considered as integral parts of said Treaty:

1. The provisions of paragraph 2 of Article V, providing for the payment of compensation, shall extend to interests held directly or indirectly by nationals, corporations and associations of either High Contracting Party in property which is taken within the territories of the other High Contracting Party.

2. Rights and privileges with respect to commercial, manufacturing and processing activities accorded, by the provisions of the Treaty, to privately owned and controlled enterprises of either High Contracting Party within the territories of the other High Contracting Party shall extend to rights and privileges of an economic nature granted to publicly owned or controlled enterprises of such other High Contracting Party, in situations in which such publicly owned or controlled enterprises operate in fact in competition with privately owned and controlled enterprises. The preceding sentence shall not, however, apply to subsidies granted to publicly owned or controlled enterprises in connection with: (a) manufacturing or processing goods for government use, or supplying goods and services to the government for government use; or (b) supplying, at prices substantially below competitive prices, the needs of particular population groups for essential goods and services not otherwise practicably obtainable by such groups.

3. The concluding sentence of paragraph 1 of Article XVIII shall not be construed as applying to postal services.

4. The provisions of paragraph 2 (a) of Article I shall not be construed to extend to the practice of professions the members of which are designated by law as public officials.

5. The provisions of paragraph 2 of Article XI shall not be construed to affect measures taken by either High Contracting Party to safeguard military secrets.

IN WITNESS WHEREOF the respective Plenipotentiaries have signed this Protocol and have affixed hereunto their seals.

DONE in duplicate, in the English and Italian languages, both equally authentic, at Rome this second day of February one thousand nine hundred forty-eight.

ADDITIONAL PROTOCOL

In view of the grave economic difficulties facing Italy now and prospectively as a result of *inter alia*, the damage caused by the late military operations on Italian soil; the looting perpetrated by the German forces following the Italian declaration of war against Germany; the present inability of Italy to supply, unassisted, the minimum needs of its people or the minimum requirements of Italian economic recovery; and Italy's lack of monetary reserves; at the time of signing the Treaty of Friendship, Commerce and Navigation between the United States of

America and the Italian Republic, the undersigned Plenipotentiaries, duly author-ized by their respective Governments, have further agreed on the following provisions, which shall be considered as integral parts of said Treaty:

1. The provisions of paragraph 3 of Article XIV of the abovementioned Treaty and that part of paragraph 4 of the same Article which relates to the allocation of shares, shall not obligate either High Contracting Party with respect to the appli-cation of quantitative restrictions on imports and exports:

(a) that have effect equivalent to exchange restrictions authorized in con-formity with section 3 (b) of Article VII of the Articles of Agreement of the Inter-national Monetary Fund;

(b) that are necessary to secure, during the early post-war transitional period, the equitable distribution among the several consuming countries of goods in short supply;

(c) that are necessary in order to effect, for the purchase of imports, the utilization of accumulated inconvertible currencies; or

(d) that have effect equivalent to exchange restrictions permitted under section 2 of Article XIV of the Articles of Agreement of the International Monetary Fund.

2. The privileges accorded to either High Contracting Party by subparagraphs (c) and (d), paragraph 1, of the present Protocol, shall be limited to situations in which (a) it is necessary for such High Contracting Party to apply restrictions on imports in order to forestall the imminent threat of, or to stop, a serious decline in the level of its monetary reserves or, in the case of very low monetary reserves, to achieve a reasonable rate of increase in its reserves, and (b) the application of the necessary restrictions in the manner permitted by the aforesaid paragraph 1 will yield such High Contracting Party a volume of imports above the maximum level which would be possible if such restrictions were applied in the manner prescribed in paragraphs 3 and 4 of Article XIV of the Treaty.

3. During the current transitional period of recovery from the recent war, the provisions of Article XVI, paragraph 1, of the Treaty shall not prevent the applica-tion by either High Contracting Party of needed controls to the internal sale, dis-tribution or use of imported articles in short supply, other than or different from controls applied with respect to like articles of national origin. However, no such controls over the internal distribution of imported articles shall be (a) applied by either High Contracting Party in such a manner as to cause unnecessary injury to the competitive position within its territories of the commerce of the other High Contracting Party, or (b) continued longer than required by the supply situation.

4. Neither High Contracting Party shall impose any new restriction under para-graph 1 of the present Protocol without having given the other High Contracting Party notice thereof which shall, if possible, be not less than thirty days in advance and shall not in any event be less than ten days in advance. Each High Contracting Party shall afford to the other High Contracting Party opportunity for consultation at any time concerning the need for and the application of restrictions to which such paragraph relates as well as concerning the application of paragraph 3; and either High Contracting Party shall have the right to invite the International Mone-tary Fund to participate in such consultation, with reference to restrictions to which subparagraphs (a), (c) and (d) of paragraph 1 relate.

5. Whenever exchange difficulties necessitate that pursuant to Article XXIV, paragraph 1 (f), the Italian Government regulate the withdrawals provided for in Article V, paragraph 2, the Italian Government may give priority to applications made by nationals, corporations and associations of the United States of America to withdraw compensation received on account of property acquired on or before December 8, 1934, or, if subsequently acquired:

(a) in the case of immovable property, if the owner at the time of acquisition had permanent residence outside Italy, or, if a corporation or association, had its center of management outside Italy;

(b) in the case of shares of stock, if at the time of acquisition Italian laws and regulations permitted such shares to be traded outside Italy;

(c) in the case of bank deposits, if carried on free account at the time of taking;

(d) in any case, if the property was acquired through importing foreign exchange, goods or services into Italy, or through reinvestments of profits or accrued interest from such imports whenever made.

The Italian Government undertakes to grant every facility to assist applicants in establishing their status for the purposes of this paragraph; and to accept evidence of probative value as establishing, in the absence of preponderant evidence to the contrary, a priority claim.

6. Whenever a multiple exchange rate system is in effect in Italy, the rate of exchange which shall be applicable for the purposes of Article V, paragraph 2, need not be the most favorable of all rates applicable to international financial transactions of whatever nature; provided, however, that the rate applicable will in any event permit the recipient of compensation actually to realize the full economic value thereof in United States dollars. In case dispute arises as to the rate applicable, the rate shall be determined by agreement between the High Contracting Parties.

IN WITNESS WHEREOF the respective Plenipotentiaries have signed this Protocol and have affixed hereunto their seals.

DONE in duplicate, in the English and Italian languages, both equally authentic, at Rome, this second day of February one thousand nine hundred forty-eight.

2. DISPOSITION OF THE FORMER ITALIAN COLONIES

(1) *Statement by the United States Representative to the United Nations General Assembly (Dulles) before the General Assembly Political and Security Committee, April 6, 1949.*[6]

In this matter of the former Italian colonies, the General Assembly exercises an authority which is unique in the history of the United Nations. Normally the Assembly can only make recommendations, which are without binding effect upon the member states. In this case, however, the four states which under the Italian peace treaty were charged with the responsibility of disposing of the colonies have agreed in advance to be bound by this Assembly's recommendations. Therefore, the Assembly in the present instance is acting in effect as the supreme legislative authority.

The responsibility which the Assembly thus assumes is a heavy one. The problem does not lend itself to easy solution. Indeed, if there had been an easy solution, the problem would not now be here. The Council of Foreign Ministers has struggled vainly with the matter ever since its first meeting in September 1945. Not only did its three years of effort fail to produce a solution, but in the course of the effort all the Governments concerned have shifted their positions, thus also demonstrating the close balance of many conflicting factors.

It is, as I say, because the problem has proved baffling, that it has at last come to us here, and what we do with it will not merely affect the destinies of some 3 million people, it will also affect the future of the United Nations itself. Here we are, a body not hampered by the veto, with final authority with respect to a vexing problem which has defied solution by what is commonly referred to as "power politics." If this Assembly proceeds competently to find a just and practical solution, that will add greatly to the prestige of the United Nations. If, on the other hand, the Assembly proves itself impotent, then the result will be that international problems will more and more be

6 Department of State, *Bulletin*, XX, p. 484.

dealt with on the basis of applicable national power, rather than on the basis of high principles internationally applied.

The provisions of the Italian peace treaty represented an act of faith in the Assembly of the United Nations. It devolves upon us to justify that faith.

We are dealing here with non-self-governing territories, and we shall, I assume, want to apply the principles of the Charter, which are found notably in chapter XI. Two basic principles are there laid down. First, the interests of the inhabitants are paramount. Second, regard should be had for international peace and security. On behalf of the United States, I shall indicate briefly and in a preliminary way the conclusions which seem to us to be suggested by the application of these two principles to the three colonial areas in question; namely, Libya, Eritrea, and Italian Somaliland. In this connection, we have relied largely upon the report of the Commission of Investigation, which in 1947 the Four Powers sent to ascertain the wishes of the inhabitants and to gather other pertinent information.

Let us turn first to Libya. The inhabitants seem well advanced toward self-government and independence, and we believe any Assembly decision should put the primary emphasis on achieving early independence.

Also, the relevancy of this area to international peace and security cannot be ignored. Names such as Tobruk and Bengasi have not been forgotten, and Egyptian and other Arab states are entitled to a solution that does not again place them in jeopardy. The future of Libya, indeed, intimately affects the whole strategic position in the Mediterranean and the Near East.

It seems, therefore, that both the welfare of the inhabitants and international peace and security require that Libya should be placed under the trusteeship system and the administration entrusted to the care of a state or states which have demonstrated the capacity and the will to develop independence, in accordance with article 76 of the Charter, and also to assure that the trust territory shall play its part in the maintenance of international peace and security, in accordance with article 84 of the Charter.

In this connection we believe that the Assembly will wish to consider carefully the view of the Government of the United Kingdom and of the other members of the British Commonwealth. Libya was liberated as the result of a great Allied offensive in which British Commonwealth troops bore the brunt of the fighting. Also, the United Kingdom Government is, under the peace treaty, actually administering all of Libya except Fezzan, and such administration, which has now lasted for upwards of five years, has given intimate knowledge from which this Assembly can, no doubt, profit. Furthermore, the United Kingdom has given ample evidence, not merely by word but by deed, that it genuinely believes in the principle of developing non-self-governing areas so as to make them independent. For this reason, we consider that regardless of whether the General Assembly decides to deal with Libya as a whole or in part, the United Kingdom should be invited to undertake the administration of Cyrenaica.

If we turn to Eritrea, we find people who are neither homogeneous nor ready for self-government. However, in the case of much of Eritrea, there is close affinity with the neighboring people of Ethiopia. Also, in the case of this part of Eritrea, there has been a demonstrated relationship to international peace and security. We feel that it is important that the disposition of the territory be such as to insure that it cannot again be used by any nation as a base of operations against Ethiopia. Furthermore, it seems reasonable that Ethiopia should have adequate access to the sea.

These considerations combine to suggest that the eastern portion of Eritrea, including the port of Massawa and the city of Asmara, might be incorporated into Ethiopia, subject to appropriate protection of Italian and other minorities.

In the case of the western province of Eritrea, the affinity of the people is closer with the peoples to the west of them, and it would seem that a separate solution should be found for the future of the inhabitants of the western province.

In the case of Italian Somaliland, it is apparent that the inhabitants are not, and in any predictable period will not be, ready for self-government or independence. For a long time to come, outside assistance and guidance will be required in order to develop the meager resources and to bring about a development of the sparse population so that they can stand by themselves. The area is without major strategic importance from the standpoint of international peace and security.

In view of the revival of democratic government and institutions in Italy since the overthrow of Fascism and the demonstrated willingness and ability of the present government of Italy to assume the obligations of a peace-loving state in accordance with the Charter, we feel that Italy should be invited to undertake the responsibility of administering Italian Somaliland under the United Nations trusteeship system.

In all of these matters we believe that the arrangements should be such as to afford the Italian people an opportunity to participate in the development of their former colonies so far as is consistent with the reasonable wishes of the people and the maintenance of harmonious order. The Italian nation has a surplus population of people who have demonstrated, in many parts of the world, their great capacity to develop waste places into productivity. We believe that the material welfare of the Italian people and the inhabitants of Africa can be advanced by cooperation under sound administration. We hope that this Assembly will approach the matter in that spirit. Let us not allow wrongs of the past, however grievous, and emotions of the past, however justifiable, to dominate our debates and to prescribe permanent barriers to the fruitful intercourse of peoples who can help each other and who, in the words of our Charter should practice tolerance and live together in peace with one another as good neighbors.

I offer the foregoing as an indication of the far-reaching importance of the problem with which we deal, and of the many factors which must be taken into account if we are to reach a just and equitable solution. We look forward to hearing the expression of views of other delegates. My Government has every confidence in the inherent wisdom of this body and in its ability to cope with this problem in a manner commensurate with the important issues involved.

(2) Statement by the United States Representative to the United Nations (Austin) before the Plenary Session of the General Assembly, May 17, 1949.[7]

After six weeks of debate and hearings, the political committee submitted a draft resolution to the General Assembly.[8] The draft resolution had been approved by the Committee by a vote of 34 to 16 with 7 abstentions on May 13.[9] In support of the resolution in the General Assembly, the United States representative made the following speech.

During the last six weeks we have listened attentively to the views of other delegations, of the representative of the Italian Government, and of various representatives of the inhabitants of the former Italian colonies. The effort of the First Committee and of its subcommittee has been devoted to the task of finding its solution to the problem of the disposal of the former Italian colonies.

The First Committee's draft resolution before the Assembly seeks to take into account the various views expressed. It is not possible to find a solution which would completely reconcile all the various suggestions which have been put forward, and that is a postulate. It is possible, however, to apply the trusteeship system of the United Nations to certain territories, to incorporate another territory into an adjoining state with homogeneous population and interests, and under appropriate guaranties for the protection of minorities, to provide for the agreements and instruments designed to settle and stabilize the rights of states and peoples concerned, in accordance with the purposes and principles of the Charter and of the treaty of peace with Italy.

I submit that this is not colonization or colonialism under either its own name or some other name. This is not supporting imperialism. I speak of that only because of the charges made rather recklessly today.

During the last few years most of the members of the United Nations have bent their efforts to restoring suitable peacetime political and economic conditions throughout the world. These efforts have met with considerable success. We have, nevertheless, an obligation to assure to the peoples of these territories a prompt transition from wartime to peacetime administration. The uncertainties regarding their future must be removed. New political institutions are required to prepare them to govern themselves. Their progressive development towards self-government should begin — the earlier the better, now rather than after another assembly. Economic progress is needed to bring them greater benefits and to enable them to lay the necessary foundations for early nationhood, as in Libya, or to play their part, where appropriate, in the development of neighboring nations to whose destinies they may be tied, as in Eritrea.

7 Ibid., p. 713.
8 United Nations General Assembly, Document A/C.1/476, May 13, 1949.
9 Ibid., 1st Committee, Official Records (3d session 2d part), p. 375.

These important considerations indicate the need for prompt action. Our trust will not permit us to indulge in the luxury of prolonging indecision in the hope of agreement on a perfect solution. Our efforts must instead be directed toward the achievement of a formula which, in attaining United Nations major objectives, reconciles to the greatest extent possible the various conflicting views which have been expressed in this General Assembly.

During the consideration of this problem in the First Committee, the representative of the United States on several occasions set forth the views of our delegation on the various aspects of this problem. I do not pretend that the resolution approved by the Committee corresponds fully with those views. Nor does it present a perfect solution. However, it does apply the principles of the Charter, and it is animated by the spirit of the Charter.

In the case of Libya, the resolution paves the way for independence and unity. Independence will be attained in 10 years unless there are very strong reasons to the contrary at that time. Unity is arranged for in the recommendation that the powers charged with the administration of the three territories should take adequate measures to promote coordination of their activities in order that nothing should be done to prejudice the attainment of an independent and unified Libyan state. There again the principles of the Charter govern the action because the Trusteeship Council will be responsible for supervising the execution of this provision. The representative of Poland whimsically calls this a fig leaf. However, the truth is that the formula of the resolution contains ample provision for working out the necessary machinery to achieve a unified state at the time of independence.

The Norwegian delegation's amendment to the subcommittee's draft regarding the independence of Libya is a virtual guarantee now that Libya will be independent. This guaranty would take effect in 10 years unless at that time the General Assembly, by a two-thirds vote, should decide otherwise. The consequent decision, if this provision were adopted, would place the burden of proof heavily upon those — should there be any — who believed 10 years from now that independence should not be granted.

To state it another way, the risk of nonpersuasion — that is, the risk of nonindependence — is not on the Libyans. Under this resolution, it is on the challenger of their independence.

Let me say in passing that the United States delegation will support the amendment proposed by Egypt which would, if adopted, grant Libya independence in 10 years from the adoption of this resolution. I shall refer to this again shortly.

The references to unity are not taken lightly by my delegation. We should expect the trusteeship agreements which would be worked out in order to implement these recommendations further to strengthen the object of unity. I would remind the members of this Assembly, moreover, that these agreements will be submitted to the General Assembly for their approval, and that they will then have a further opportunity to assure themselves that the administrations of the territories do undertake the obligations and do serve the basic objectives of the trusteeship system, with special regard for the interests of the inhabitants. An important principle of the Charter is that the interests of the inhabitants of these territories are paramount. The destiny of human beings — in the language of my distinguished friend General Romulo — will be the highest objective among the provisions of these agreements, to be passed upon under the trusteeship system and by the Trusteeship Council. Let me observe again that the freely expressed wishes of the people will be considered, in connection with other elements of Charter requirements, in formulating those agreements.

I should also like to say something about the importance which my delegation attaches to the advisory council for Tripolitania provided in paragraph 1 (c) of the resolution. We consider the establishment of the advisory council to be one of the most important features of the resolution. The resolution provides that between now and the end of 1951, when the Italian trusteeship over Tripolitania will become effective, there shall be an advisory council consisting of several states and a representative of the people of the country — a representative of the inhabitants. This advisory council would be given the power to determine its own scope and duties in consultation with the administering authority. It would have the broad responsibility under the resolution of assisting the temporary British administration during the interim period. It is our considered view that the advisory council, in so assisting the temporary British administration, will be able to aid substantially the beginning of the process of political, economic, social, and educational development contemplated by the Charter, which must lead and precede independence of the unified Libya in 10 years. We hope that the advisory council will meet as soon as possible to organize itself and to begin discharging its important responsibilities.

In the case of Eritrea, the draft resolution reflects the desire of the majority of the inhabitants of the area to be incorporated within Ethiopia to merge their destiny with that of the Ethiopian people, with whom they are united by race, language, and religion. Is this a Charter principle or not? Is this imperialism? It also satisfies Ethiopia's urgent need for adequate access to the sea by incorporating within Ethiopia the port of Massawa, the only satisfactory port in the area. The proposal, moreover, calls for the protection of minorities and municipal charters for the cities of Asmara and Massawa. This is a reconciliation which in our view protects the interests of Ethiopia as well as those of the minority peoples in that area. The resolution contemplates the implementation of this provision by international instrument or agreement. The contents of these international instruments or agreements will further be agreed on in the Interim Committee before the next session of the General Assembly. That Interim Committee will be acting as the subsidiary organ of the General Assembly in working out these agreements for submission to the fourth session of the General Assembly.

Italian Somaliland would be placed under the international trusteeship system with Italy as the administering authority and with independence as the objective. Here again, transfer of administration would not take place until a trusteeship agreement satisfactory to the General Assembly is approved. In entrusting the administration of these territories of Tripolitania and Somaliland to Italy, we shall be welcoming the Italy of today as a partner in the great task of assisting the people of Africa on the road of political and economic progress.

While this resolution does not contain the perfect answer to the general problem before us, it does contain constructive elements of an answer to the problem, and we urge it upon the General Assembly as the most practicable solution in the circumstances. The United States delegation therefore, supports the resolution as a whole and every part of it.

As I am about to point out, there are certain amendments now on the table to which we would agree. I wish to speak about all of the amendments briefly. My delegation will vote against the proposal of the Soviet Union contained in the document A/881[11] for reasons which were stated by us fully, and I shall not restate them.

With respect to the draft resolution submitted by the delegation of Iraq contained in document A/875,[12] we shall be unable to support it because of our conviction that Libya requires a period of preparation under the trusteeship system. In expressing this conviction, I should like to reiterate our belief that Libya will be able to attain independence after the preparatory period of 10 years. As I have already stated, we will welcome and support the Egyptian amendment in this regard contained in document A/885.[13] We share with the delegation of Liberia the spirit which animated it to introduce an amendment setting a period after which the General Assembly would determine whether the inhabitants have made sufficient progress to warrant independence. We believe, however, that 15 years is too short a period in which to accomplish the difficult task it will involve, and that a period corresponding to about one generation would be more realistic. We are prepared, therefore, to support the amendment offered by the delegations of Argentina, Brazil, and Peru to the Liberian amendment prolonging the time from 15 to 25 years. Of course, you understand that the United States delegation supports the Liberian amendment whether it is amended by this last amendment or not. We also welcome and support the Egyptian amendment on the western province of Eritrea. That amendment corresponds to the position we took in the First Committee on the subcommittee's draft resolution.

---

11 The resolution of the Soviet Union, not reprinted here, proposed that Libya, Italian Somaliland, and Eritrea be placed under the international trusteeship system. In each case the administering authority would be assisted by a special advisory committee of nine members, including the five permanent members of the Security Council and representatives of the indigenous population.

12 The Iraqi proposal, not reprinted here, would have granted immediate independence to Libya.

13 The Egyptian proposal, not reprinted here, would have placed all of Libya under trusteeship with Egypt, France, Saudi Arabia, the United Kingdom, and the United States as administering powers. Italian Somaliland would be administered under a similar system with Egypt, Ethiopia, France, Italy, Pakistan, the United Kingdom, and the United States as administering powers. The Egyptian proposal further stated that the western provinces of Eritrea should be incorporated into the Anglo-Egyptian Sudan.

(3) *Draft Resolution on the Disposition of the Former Italian Colonies, Submitted by the United States to the United Nations General Assembly Political and Security Committee, October 10, 1949.*[14]

When the draft resolution of the political committee was considered by the plenary session of the General Assembly, the proposals regarding Cyrenaica and Fezzan were approved by votes of 36 to 17 with 6 abstentions and 36 to 15 with 7 abstentions. The recommendation that Italy be the administering authority for Tripolitania, however, lacked the necessary two-thirds vote when it received 33 affirmative and 17 negative votes with 8 abstentions. The Argentinian and Uruguayan representatives immediately stated that they and the other Latin American states could not support the resolution as a whole since it had been clearly recognized that the draft resolution had gained the support of Latin American states only by the granting to Italy of trusteeship of Tripolitania. Although the Assembly approved the remaining sections of the draft resolution, the resolution as a whole was defeated when it received 14 affirmative votes and 37 negative votes with 7 abstentions.[15] Further consideration of the question was postponed until the fourth session of the General Assembly.[16] The following resolution presented by the United States was one of six resolutions placed before the political committee in the course of its discussion.

The General Assembly

In accordance with Annex XI, paragraph 3 of the Treaty of Peace with Italy,
Having studied the question of the disposal of the former Italian Colonies,
Having taken note in particular of the Report of the Four Power Commission of Investigation, and having heard spokesmen of organizations representing substantial sections of opinion in the territories concerned,

Recommends

A. With respect to Libya, where conditions already exist for the creation of an independent state,
1. That Libya become independent three years from the date of the adoption of this resolution. During the period prior to independence
(a) The powers now administering the territories of Cyrenaica, Tripolitania and the Fezzan, shall administer them for the purpose of assisting in the establishment of Libyan independence, and shall co-ordinate their activities to this end;
(b) The administering authorities shall co-operate in the formation of governmental institutions and, at a suitable time at least one year prior to the date of independence, shall arrange for representatives of the inhabitants of Cyrenaica, Tripolitania and the Fezzan to meet and consult together to determine the form of government which they desire to establish upon the attainment of independence;
(c) The present administering authorities shall make an annual report to the Secretary-General, for the information of the Members of the United Nations, on steps they have taken to implement sub-paragraphs (a) and (b) above;
(d) There shall be established an Advisory Council consisting of representatives of Egypt, France, Italy, the United Kingdom, the United States and two representatives of the local population, one from Cyrenaica and one from Tripolitania. The Council shall advise the administering authorities as to how assistance might be given to

14 United Nations General Assembly, Document A/C.1/497, October 10, 1949.
15 *Ibid.*, Document A/P.V.218, May 17, 1949.
16 *Ibid.*, Document A/P.V.219, May 18, 1949; *ibid.*, Document A/899, May 18, 1949.

the inhabitants with regard to formation of a government for an independent Libya, and such related problems as common services. The Council shall establish its seat outside of Libya at a place to be determined after consultation with the Secretary-General, and shall be empowered to visit the territory and to obtain, with the co-operation of the administering authorities, such information as it deems necessary to enable it to discharge its functions. The Council shall make an annual report to the Secretary-General, for the information of the Members of the United Nations, on the carrying out of its task.

B. With respect to Eritrea, having regard for the homogeneity of the eastern provinces of that territory with Ethiopia and for the homogeneity of the Western Province of that territory with the adjacent Sudan,

1. That Eritrea, except for the Western Province, be reunited with Ethiopia on condition that the Government of Ethiopia undertake to apply in those areas, the provisions of paragraphs 1, 2 and 4 of Article 19 of the Treaty of Peace with Italy, and that, without prejudice to the sovereignty of Ethiopia, appropriate municipal charters be provided for the cities of Asmara and Massawa.

2. That the economic and financial provisions of the Treaty of Peace with Italy which apply to ceded territories within the meaning of the Treaty shall apply to the territory ceded to Ethiopia.

3. That the Governments of Ethiopia, Italy and the United Kingdom report to the Sixth Regular Session of the General Assembly on the measures taken pursuant to the foregoing provisions on Eritrea.

4. That the Western Province of Eritrea be united with the adjacent Sudan.

5. That the Governments of the United Kingdom, Egypt, and Ethiopia report to the Sixth Regular Session of the General Assembly on the measures taken in this regard, including the progress made in demarcating the permanent boundary between Ethiopia and the Western Province after union with the adjacent Sudan.

6. That the Government of Ethiopia shall consult with the Interim Committee of the General Assembly in preparing municipal charters for Asmara and Massawa, and that these charters shall be submitted for approval by the Fifth Regular Session of the General Assembly.

C. With respect to Italian Somaliland, which requires a substantial period of guidance toward self government for which the international trusteeship system is particularly suitable,

1. That Italian Somaliland be placed under the international trusteeship system with Italy as the Administering Authority. The General Assembly and the Trusteeship Council shall review the progress and development of this territory from time to time with a view to determining whether it is ready for independence.

2. That the Government of Italy negotiate the terms of trusteeship with the Trusteeship Council and that such terms be submitted for the approval of the General Assembly at its Fifth Regular Session.

3. That in respect to the delimitation of the international boundaries of Italian Somaliland, a commission consisting of representatives of Ethiopia and Italy and a third Member to be appointed by the Secretary-General of the United Nations be established to fix such boundaries.

(4) *Resolution on the Disposition of the Former Italian Colonies, Adopted by the United Nations General Assembly, November 21, 1949.*[17]

On November 12, 1949 the political committee of the General Assembly again approved a draft resolution on disposal of the former Italian colonies[18] by a vote of 50 to 8 with no abstentions, on the sections dealing with Libya, 47 to 7 with 4 abstentions, on those dealing with Italian Somaliland, and 47 to 5 with 6 abstentions, on those dealing with Eritrea.[19] The resolution was accepted by the General Assembly on November 21, 1949, by a vote of 48 to 1 (Ethiopia) with 9 abstentions.[20] In accordance with the provisions of the resolution, Adrian Pelt (Netherlands) was approved as United Nations Commissioner for Libya on December 10, 1949.[21] The Trusteeship Council on December 9 appointed a committee of six nations to draft a trusteeship agreement for Somaliland, taking into account any draft which Italy might care to submit. Three non-administering and three administering powers were elected to the committee — the United States, the United Kingdom, France, the Philippines, Iraq, and the Dominican Republic.[22]

The General Assembly,

In accordance with Annex XI, paragraph 3, of the Treaty of Peace with Italy, 1947, whereby the Powers concerned have agreed to accept the recommendation of the General Assembly on the disposal of the former Italian colonies and to take appropriate measures for giving effect to it,

Having taken note of the report of the Four Power Commission of Investigation, having heard spokesmen of organizations representing substantial sections of opinion in the territories concerned, and having taken into consideration the wishes and welfare of the inhabitants of the territories, the interests of peace and security, the views of the interested Governments and the relevant provisions of the Charter,

A. *With respect to Libya, recommends:*

1. That Libya, comprising Cyrenaica, Tripolitania and the Fezzan, shall be constituted an independent and sovereign State;

2. That this independence shall become effective as soon as possible and in any case not later than 1 January 1952;

3. That a constitution for Libya, including the form of the government, shall be determined by representatives of the inhabitants of Cyrenaica, Tripolitania and the Fezzan meeting and consulting together in a National Assembly;

4. That, for the purpose of assisting the people of Libya in the formulation of the constitution and the establishment of an independent Government, there shall be a United Nations Commissioner in Libya appointed by the General Assembly and a Council to aid and advise him;

5. That the United Nations Commissioner, in consultation with the Council, shall submit to the Secretary-General an annual report and such other special reports as he may consider necessary. To these reports shall be added

[17] *Ibid.,* Document A/1124, November 22, 1949.
[18] *Ibid.,* Document A/C.1/546, November 12, 1949; *ibid.,* Document A/C.1/541/Corr.1, November 15, 1949.
[19] *Ibid.,* First Committee, *Official Records* (4th session), p. 260.
[20] United Nations General Assembly Document A/P.V. 250, November 21, 1949.
[21] *Ibid.,* Document A/P.V. 276, December 10, 1949.
[22] Department of State, *Bulletin,* XXI, p. 934.

any memorandum or document that the United Nations Commissioner or a member of the Council may wish to bring to the attention of the United Nations;

6. That the Council shall consist of ten members, namely:

(a) One representative nominated by the Government of each of the following countries: Egypt, France, Italy, Pakistan, the United Kingdom of Great Britain and Northern Ireland and the United States of America;

(b) One representative of the people of each of the three regions of Libya and one representative of the minorities in Libya;

7. That the United Nations Commissioner shall appoint the representatives mentioned in paragraph 6 (b), after consultation with the administering Powers, the representatives of the Governments mentioned in paragraph 6 (a), leading personalities and representatives of political parties and organizations in the territories concerned;

8. That, in the discharge of his functions, the United Nations Commissioner shall consult and be guided by the advice of the members of his Council, it being understood that he may call upon different members to advise him in respect of different regions or different subjects;

9. That the United Nations Commissioner may offer suggestions to the General Assembly, to the Economic and Social Council and to the Secretary-General as to the measures that the United Nations might adopt during the transitional period regarding the economic and social problems of Libya;

10. That the administering Powers in co-operation with the United Nations Commissioner:

(a) Initiate immediately all necessary steps for the transfer of power to a duly constituted independent Government;

(b) Administer the territories for the purpose of assisting in the establishment of Libyan unity and independence, co-operate in the formation of governmental institutions and co-ordinate their activities to this end;

(c) Make an annual report to the General Assembly on the steps taken to implement these recommendations;

11. That upon its establishment as an independent State, Libya shall be admitted to the United Nations in accordance with Article 4 of the Charter;

B. *With respect to Italian Somaliland, recommends:*

1. That Italian Somaliland shall be an independent sovereign State;

2. That this independence shall become effective at the end of ten years from the date of the approval of a Trusteeship Agreement by the General Assembly;

3. That during the period mentioned in paragraph 2, Italian Somaliland shall be placed under the International Trusteeship System with Italy as the Administering Authority;

4. That the Administering Authority shall be aided and advised by an Advisory Council composed of representatives of the following States: Colom-

bia, Egypt and the Philippines. The headquarters of the Advisory Council shall be Mogadiscio. The precise terms of reference of the Advisory Council shall be determined in the Trusteeship Agreement and shall include a provision whereby the Trusteeship Council shall invite the States members of the Advisory Council, if they are not members of the Trusteeship Council, to participate without vote in the debates of the Trusteeship Council on any question relating to this territory;

5. That the Trusteeship Council shall negotiate with the Administering Authority the draft of a Trusteeship Agreement for submission to the General Assembly if possible during the present session, and in any case not later than the fifth regular session;

6. That the Trusteeship Agreement shall include an annex containing a declaration of constitutional principles guaranteeing the rights of the inhabitants of Somaliland and providing for institutions designed to ensure the inauguration, development and subsequent establishment of full self-government;

7. That in the drafting of this declaration the Trusteeship Council and the Administering Authority shall be guided by the annexed text proposed by the Indian delegation;

8. That Italy shall be invited to undertake provisional administration of the territory:

(a) At a time and pursuant to arrangements for the orderly transfer of administration agreed upon between Italy and the United Kingdom, after the Trusteeship Council and Italy have negotiated the Trusteeship Agreement;

(b) On condition that Italy gives an undertaking to administer the territory in accordance with the provisions of the Charter relating to the International Trusteeship System and to the Trusteeship Agreement pending approval by the General Assembly of a Trusteeship Agreement for the territory;

9. That the Advisory Council shall commence the discharge of its functions when the Italian Government begins its provisional administration;

C. *With respect to Eritrea, recommends*:

1. That a Commission consisting of representatives of not more than five Member States, as follows, Burma, Guatemala, Norway, Pakistan and the Union of South Africa, shall be established to ascertain more fully the wishes and the best means of promoting the welfare of the inhabitants of Eritrea, to examine the question of the disposal of Eritrea and to prepare a report for the General Assembly, together with such proposal or proposals as it may deem appropriate for the solution of the problem of Eritrea;

2. That in carrying out its responsibilities the Commission shall ascertain all the relevant facts, including written or oral information from the present administering Power, from representatives of the population of the territory, including minorities, from Governments and from such organizations and

individuals as it may deem necessary. In particular, the Commission shall take into account:

(a) The wishes and welfare of the inhabitants of Eritrea, including the views of the various racial, religious and political groups of the provinces of the territory and the capacity of the people for self-government;

(b) The interests of peace and security in East Africa;

(c) The rights and claims of Ethiopia based on geographical, historical, ethnic or economic reasons, including in particular Ethiopia's legitimate need for adequate access to the sea;

3. That in considering its proposals the Commission shall take into account the various suggestions for the disposal of Eritrea submitted during the fourth regular session of the General Assembly;

4. That the Commission shall assemble at the headquarters of the United Nations as soon as possible. It shall travel to Eritrea and may visit such other places as in its judgment may be necessary in carrying out its responsibilities. The Commission shall adopt its own rules of procedure. Its report and proposal or proposals shall be communicated to the Secretary-General not later than 15 June 1950 for distribution to Member States so as to enable final consideration during the fifth regular session of the General Assembly. The Interim Committee of the General Assembly shall consider the report and proposal, or proposals, of the Commission and report, with conclusions, to the fifth regular session of the General Assembly;

D. *With respect to the above provisions:*

1. *Invites* the Secretary-General to request the necessary facilities from the competent authorities of each of the States in whose territory it may be necessary for the Commission for Eritrea to meet or travel.

2. *Authorizes* the Secretary-General, in accordance with established practice,

(a) To arrange for the payment of an appropriate remuneration to the United Nations Commissioner in Libya;

(b) To reimburse the travelling and subsistence expenses of the members of the Council for Libya, of one representative from each Government represented on the Advisory Council for Somaliland, and of one representative and one alternate from each Government represented on the Commission for Eritrea;

(c) To assign to the United Nations Commissioner in Libya, to the Advisory Council for Somaliland, and to the United Nations Commission for Eritrea such staff and to provide such facilities as the Secretary-General may consider necessary to carry out the terms of the present resolution.

I. Rumania

For information on United States–Rumanian relations, see this volume as follows: on alleged violations of the Rumanian treaty of peace of 1947, p. 655; on the Danube Commission, p. 422; on the Communist Information Bureau, p. 652; and on the Council of Mutual Economic Assistance, *ibid.*

J. Spain

[See *Documents, VIII, 1945–1946*, p. 887; *IX, 1947*, p. 712.]

For the third time, the General Assembly during the second part of its third session considered the question of Franco Spain and the implementation of its resolutions of December 12, 1946,[1] and November 17, 1947.[2] In discussions in the Assembly's political and security committee, a Polish resolution which called upon all Members of the United Nations to stop the export to Spain of strategic materials and to refrain from entering into agreements or treaties with the Franco government, and a joint Bolivian-Colombian-Peruvian-Brazilian resolution which would leave Members full freedom of action in their relations with Spain were considered. The latter resolution, by a vote of 25 to 16 with 16 abstentions was recommended for adoption by the General Assembly at the conclusion of the committee's discussions on May 7.[3] By the same vote in the plenary session of the Assembly on May 16, the joint resolution, since it was not supported by the required two-thirds majority, failed of adoption.[4] The United States abstained from voting on the resolution. The Polish draft resolution in a paragraph-by-paragraph vote was also defeated,[5] with the United States voting against its adoption.

(1) *Statement by the Secretary of State (Acheson) on United States Policy toward Spain. Department of State Press Release, May 11, 1949.*[6]

What I should like to do is to try to put this present matter, which involves a vote in the United Nations as to whether or not the 1946 resolution is to be modified, in its real setting. As you know, the resolution was passed in 1946 by the General Assembly of the United Nations, and it recommended to the member nations that they withdraw their ambassadors from Madrid. At that time the United States did not have an ambassador in Madrid because Mr. Norman Armour, who had been the Ambassador, had resigned and no one had been appointed to take his place. Therefore, in carrying out the spirit of the resolution no one has been since appointed to take Mr. Armour's place.

The argument revolves around the question of whether that resolution should be changed and whether the ambassadors should be restored. Now in the first place, I assume it is everybody's belief that a recommendation by the General Assembly of the United Nations should be followed until it is changed. I do not think there would be any argument about that. Argument might arise about whether we should attempt to change it.

Another preliminary observation: I should like to say that in and of itself this question of whether or not ambassadors, as distinct from chargé d'affaires, are in Madrid is a matter of no real importance at all. This resolution was adopted by the United Nations in the belief that it would lead to certain reforms on the part of Franco which would make the relations with his government by other free governments more happy. It has not had that effect.

Now why was the resolution passed and what are the issues which grow out of it, and what is American policy?

In the first place, let us state what the policy will be on that resolution. Our

1 See *Documents, VIII, 1945–1946*, p. 890.   2 See *ibid., IX, 1947*, p. 712.
3 United Nations General Assembly, 1st Committee, *Official Records* (3d session, 2d part), p. 239.
4 United Nations General Assembly, *Official Records* (3d session, 2d part), p. 501.
5 *Ibid.*, p. 504.
6 Department of State Press Release 349, May 11, 1949.

policy will be to abstain from voting upon that resolution which is to the effect that the question shall be left to the judgment of each individual member of the United Nations. We shall not vote on that. We shall abstain.

Now this question, if it has any importance — and it obviously has, because it arouses a great deal of emotion, both in this country and in other countries — is because it is a symbol of something else. The reason the 1946 resolution was passed is rooted in history. The Franco Government was one which was established with the active support, and only with the active support, of Hitler and Mussolini. The Republican Government in Spain received the support of the Soviet Union. There were charges at the time that the Republican Government was Communist. Those charges were denied. It is unimportant at this point to go into what if any substance they had. The fact of the matter was that a government was established in Spain which was patterned on the regimes in Italy and in Germany and was, and is, a fascist government and a dictatorship.

The importance is not in throwing words around in talking about "fascists", because other people call us fascists, too. We do not get anywhere merely by using that word. The important thing is what goes on in Spain. It is also important what the Western European Governments think of what goes on in Spain because, as I have said, the important matter is not whether we send an ambassador instead of a chargé d'affaires; the important thing is what can be done to bring Spain into the community of free nations in Europe in both the economic and the defense fields. When you think about that you discover at once that the Western European Governments are opposed, and have publicly stated their opposition, to this collaboration with Spain in the economic and military fields.

Now why is that so? I say we get nowhere by using such words as "fascism", but if we look at the situation in Spain, we will see some perfectly simple fundamental facts which cannot be obscured. I presume that the foundation of liberty — individual liberty — is not in great phrases at all but in certain simple procedures and simple beliefs, and I should put first on the list of essentials for individual liberty the writ of habeas corpus and an independent judiciary. One of the things that all dictators do — from the time of the French Revolution and before the French Revolution down to the present time — is to take anyone that they do not like and throw him in the oubliette and there he stays until he dies or until they shoot him or until they take him out. The fundamental protection against that in free countries is the writ of habeas corpus.

Now what does that mean? That means that anybody who is detained against his will may at any time get an order from the court that he shall be produced in person before the court and that those who hold him must justify the fact that they are holding him under the provisions of law. There is nothing more fundamental in the preservation of human liberty than that ancient British tradition which is now incorporated in most of the procedures in the free world. That right does not exist in Spain.

I suppose a second fundamental right, which is useful only if you have the first, is that if you are tried — and, of course, it follows from the writ of habeas corpus that you cannot be sentenced to prison unless you are convicted of some crime — the second right is that in being convicted of a crime you are convicted not by employees of the state but by your own fellow citizens. That is the right of trial by jury. It means that no judge, even though he be independent, certainly no administrative official, can order you put in jail. The only people who can do that are ten in some parts of the world, twelve in others — citizens just like yourself — and if they listen to the testimony and say Joe Doakes goes to jail, then he goes to jail. If they say he does not go to jail, then he does not go to jail. That is fundamental. That right does not exist in Spain.

Then there is the question of religious liberty, which is fundamental to a free exercise of the human personality. That right does not exist in Spain.

Then there is the right of association — association in political activities, association in trade union activities, association in benevolent activities — that right does not exist in Spain.

I could go on, but what I want to draw to your attention is that these certain fundamental basic rights of the individual which make the difference between what we call free Europe and the iron curtain countries — these rights do not exist in Spain, and the Spanish people are prevented from enjoying them by action of the Spanish Government.

It seems perfectly clear to the Western European countries that you cannot have an intimate working partnership with such a regime in the economic field and in the defense field. There must be some move to liberalize that. None of them say, nor do we say, that Spain, which has never been a full-flowered democracy, must become so. But they all say that there must be some move toward that situation because if there isn't, what is the use of having ambassadors? We have someone with a different title. It may raise the prestige of the individual a little bit, but what is the use of it all?

It is important only if it becomes a symbol, and if it becomes a symbol of the fact that after all we don't care much about these rights, then it is a bad symbol. If it ceases to be a symbol it wouldn't make any difference to anyone whether you had an ambassador or whether you didn't.

But the fundamental thing is that American policy is to try to bring Spain back into the family of Western Europe. That is a family matter. You have to convince the Spaniards that they must take some steps toward that end, and you have to convince the Europeans that they have to take some steps. So that it isn't fundamentally a matter which can be brought about by American action, and therefore the policy of the American Government is one which I am quite sure is calculated to please neither group of extremists in the United States — either those who say that we must immediately embrace Franco, or those who say that we must cast him into the outermost darkness. But it is a policy directed toward working with the Spaniards and with the Western Europeans, bringing about a situation where these fundamental liberties do exist in Spain and where the Western Europeans can bring Spain into the community.

I have spoken at some length on this subject because it is so easy to confuse form with substance.

5. RELATIONS WITH PARTICULAR COUNTRIES OF AFRICA AND WESTERN ASIA

A. Israel

[See *Document, X, 1948,* p. 659.]

1. GENERAL

On January 31, following election of a permanent government in Israel, the United States government extended *de jure* recognition to this government.[1] Shortly afterward embassies were established in the respective capitals of the two governments.

Following recommendation by the Security Council that Israel be admitted to membership in the United Nations, the United States, Australia, Canada, Guatemala, Haiti, Panama, and Uruguay sponsored a joint draft resolution embodying this recommendation in the Ad Hoc Political Committee of the General Assembly in May. After bitter debate in committee and plenary session, the General Assembly decided on May 11 to admit Israel to membership in the United Nations by a vote of 37 to 12, with 9 abstentions.[2]

2. THE PALESTINE QUESTION

Following representations by the United States representative in Tel Aviv, James G. McDonald, as to the grave consequences ensuing from the crossing of the Egyptian border by Israeli troops, the government of Israel on January 4 notified the Department of State that its forces had been withdrawn from Egypt. In communications to both the Israeli and Egyptian governments, the United States stressed the hope that both parties would comply with the provisions of the Security Council resolutions of 1948 calling for a cease-fire, cessation of hostilities and prompt negotiation of a permanent armistice.

In accordance with the General Assembly resolution of December 11, 1948 establishing a United Nations Conciliation Commission, the commission established its official headquarters in Jerusalem on January 24. The United States was represented on the commission by Mark F. Ethridge, publisher of the *Louisville Courier-Journal*. After preliminary exchanges of views with Arab governments in Beirut in March and with the Israeli government at Tel Aviv in April, the commission continued its work of conciliation in Lausanne with delegations from Egypt, Syria, Lebanon, Transjordan and Israel.

In June Mr. Ethridge reported to President Truman that the Arab-Israeli negotiations at Lausanne were "deadlocked" and that both Israeli and Arab representatives must adopt "entirely new approaches" if a formal peace were to be reached.[3] Mr. Ethridge attributed the deadlock principally to the question of refugees displaced during the Palestine war and reported that the Arab delegations were in common agreement on this matter, insisting that the Israeli government decide its course of action in this regard before boundaries and more general matters were discussed. On June 13 the Conciliation Commission submitted to the Secretary-General its third progress report in which it concluded that in order to further negotiations, it would be advantageous to link together the refugee question and the territorial question, without neglecting a study of the economic and social problems arising in the middle east.[4] The commission reported no substantial progress on any of the three

1 Department of State, *Bulletin,* XX, p. 205.
2 United Nations General Assembly, Document A/P.V.207, May 11, 1949.
3 Department of State, *Bulletin,* XX, p. 780.
4 United Nations General Assembly, Document A/927, June 21, 1949.

main problems involved — refugees, frontiers and the internationalization of Jerusalem.

In July Paul A. Porter, former head of the United States economic mission to Greece, replaced Mr. Ethridge as United States representative on the commission. After a brief recess in the negotiations at Lausanne, Secretary of State Acheson urged the Israeli and Arab governments to return delegations with "full authority" to negotiate a settlement of all outstanding issues.[5] In August the commission, in order to obtain clarification of the positions of the various delegations, submitted a memorandum setting forth certain questions, notably regarding refugees and the territorial problem. After considering the attitudes revealed in the replies to this memorandum, the commission requested the parties to reexamine certain main points in their replies and submit new proposals on those subjects.[6] A report of the commission issued the following month revealed that it had made sustained efforts in accordance with the General Assembly resolution of December 11, 1948, to bring the interested parties to undertake direct negotiations, but that as to the general negotiations, these efforts had been unsuccessful, owing to the fact that the Arab delegations refused to meet the Israeli delegation and declared themselves satisfied with the present procedure.[7]

The commission reconvened in New York on October 19, with Mr. Ely E. Palmer replacing Mr. Porter as United States representative. The following month the commission was invited to appear before the Ad Hoc Political Committee of the General Assembly, to which the Jerusalem question had been referred. In the *ad hoc* committee the United States generally approved the suggestions of the commission and stressed demilitarization in Palestine and the importance of working out a plan which could be implemented.[8] The commission's proposals provided for establishment of a permanent international regime to exercise "full and permanent authority over the Jerusalem area", with the city and surrounding territory to be split into Arab and Israeli sections. Principal organs of government would include 1) a United Nations Commissioner appointed by and responsible to the General Assembly; 2) a mixed elective council, responsible for zonal coordination; 3) an international tribunal of three judges, constituting the highest judicial authority; and 4) a mixed tribunal of one Arab, one Israeli and one neutral judge, which would handle cases of civil and criminal law involving residents of different zones or property rights cutting across zones.[9] The United States representative, John Ross, stressed the fact that the commission had kept firmly in mind the principle of maximum local autonomy laid down in the Assembly resolution of December 11, 1948, while achieving the international objectives of this resolution as well. He appealed to committee members not to yield to pressure of circumstances in the closing days of the Assembly session to such an extent as to lose sight of the essential objective — the establishment of an international regime for Jerusalem which would take into account both the principle of maximum local autonomy and the interests of the international community.[10]

The United States voted against adoption of recommendations of a subcommittee that the Conciliation Commission reconsider its reports on Jerusalem to bring them into closer harmony with the Assembly resolution of November 29, 1947, calling for the internationalization of Jerusalem as a *corpus separatum* administered through the United Nations Trusteeship Council, and requesting the Trusteeship Council to complete a draft statute for Jerusalem and proceed immediately to its implementation. Following adoption of the subcommittee's proposal by the *ad hoc* committee, the United States, while reaffirming its continued strong support for a permanent international regime for Jerusalem, in plenary session repeated its objection to this proposal and expressed serious doubt as to its practicability. It restated its support of the commission's proposal as offering a workable, middle-ground compromise between all interests involved and pointed out the scant consideration given this proposal.[11] With the United States voting against adoption the committee's proposals were approved on December 9 by the General Assembly.

5 Department of State, *Bulletin*, XXI, p. 148.
6 United Nations General Assembly, Document A/992, September 22, 1949.
7 *Ibid.*   8 *Ibid.*, Document A/AC.31/SR.43, November 24, 1949.
9 *Ibid.*, Document A/973, September 12, 1949.
10 *Ibid.*, Document A/AC.31/SR.43, November 24, 1949.
11 *Ibid.*, Document A/P.V. 274, December 9, 1949.

During the year under review the Palestine question was also considered by the Security Council, which began consideration on August 4 of the report of the acting mediator, Dr. Ralph J. Bunche, on the status of the armistice negotiations and the truce in Palestine. Dr. Bunche reported that now that the practical application of the Security Council's truce had been superseded by effective armistice agreements voluntarily negotiated by Israel with Egypt, Lebanon, Transjordan, and Syria in the transition from truce to permanent peace and the Conciliation Commission was conducting peace negotiations, the mission of the mediator had been fulfilled. The United States supported a resolution proposed by Dr. Bunche declaring that the completion of armistice agreements rendered unnecessary the prolongation of the truce and terminating or transferring the functions of the mediator. The United States representative (Austin) stated that his government did not intend to allow the export of arms which would permit a competitive race in the middle east area. He declared that export of arms to the area should be strictly limited to legitimate security requirements and hoped that all nations would pursue a similar policy.[12] On August 11 the Council adopted a resolution which found that "the armistice agreements constituted an important step toward establishment of permanent peace in Palestine"; declared the agreements superseded the Council's truce; reaffirmed, pending the final peace settlement, the Council's cease-fire order of July 15, 1948; and relieved the acting mediator of any further responsibility under Security Council resolutions.[13]

At a special session of the Trusteeship Council in December the United States abstained from voting on a resolution expressing concern at Israel's removal of certain central government offices to Jerusalem, such action being incompatible with the General Assembly's plan for internationalization of Jerusalem.

(1) Statement by the United States Representative to the United Nations General Assembly Political and Security Committee (Ross) on the Question of Jerusalem, Made before the Committee, November 24, 1949.[14]

[EXCERPTS]

. . . .

The question of protection of the Holy Places in the Jerusalem area and of free access to them is not basically controversial.

This question has received perhaps more attention than any other aspect of the Jerusalem problem. It is right that this is so because millions throughout the world have the deepest and most fundamental attachment to Palestine as a holy land and in particular to Jerusalem as a holy city. The profound religious symbolism of Jerusalem considered as a whole must never be forgotten in our consideration of this problem. The Draft Statute prepared by the Conciliation Commission, in our opinion, deals effectively with these matters in the manner best calculated to preserve the interests of the religious groups concerned while maintaining the principle of maximum local autonomy which was also set forth by the General Assembly last fall.

. . . .

It is the view of my Delegation that these provisions of the Draft Statute should commend themselves to the members of this Committee since they achieve the objectives set forth in the Assembly's resolution of December 11 last year with regard to the Holy Places. It is also our view that these provisions of the Draft Statute should commend themselves to the two states most directly interested in the matter, namely, Israel and Jordan. It should be apparent to those two states that proposals such as those put forward by

---

12 United Nations Security Council, Document S/P.V.434, August 4, 1949.
13 *Ibid.*, Document S/P.V.437, August 11, 1949.
14 United States Delegation to the General Assembly Press Release 756, November 24, 1949.

the Conciliation Commission for the protection of and access to the Holy Places are the minimum which are likely to be acceptable to the international community.

The second objective stated by the General Assembly in its resolution of December 11 was that the Jerusalem area should be placed under effective United Nations control. This objective reflects the fundamental concern of the international community and the responsibility of the United Nations with regard to the peace and security of Jerusalem, bearing in mind that Jerusalem was a focal point of the recent conflict in Palestine. The United Nations does not have at its disposal the armed forces that would be necessary to impose a system of United Nations control on the people of Jerusalem, nor has there ever been any indication that the United Nations would be willing to impose a solution. However, United Nations machinery for conciliation and mediation has proved effective in bringing about a truce in Palestine and assisting the principal parties to enter into armistice agreements . . . In any event, the employment of peaceful methods in this matter will in the long run be more effective in establishing and maintaining United Nations control than the use of armed forces.

It is apparent, therefore, that the first step toward the establishment of effective United Nations control in Jerusalem and the maintenance of peace and security in that area must be the demilitarization of the area. This point was recognized by the General Assembly last year when, in its resolution of December 11, it requested the Security Council to "take further steps to ensure the demilitarization of Jerusalem at the earliest possible date."

.   .   .   .

My Delegation is not unaware of the importance of Jerusalem as a factor in the security of Israel and of Jordan. But we are firmly convinced that, so far as Jerusalem is a factor in the situation, the security of these two states is to be found more surely in the demilitarization of the Jerusalem area under international supervision than by continuing the area in the status of an armed camp. In view of the fact that respective claims to the City on both sides are so deep-seated, deriving from centuries of religious and cultural association, it would seem most appropriate for both parties to agree to withdraw their military and paramilitary forces and stocks of war material from the area and for the United Nations to establish effective procedures to ensure that Jerusalem will remain demilitarized. It is our belief that effective United Nations control can be established in this matter; such control would place neither side in a disadvantageous position.

Thus it seems to my Delegation that the Conciliation Commission's proposals for the demilitarization of Jerusalem should commend themselves not only to the Members of the Assembly but to Israel and Jordan, the two states directly involved. We also feel that these proposals are wholly consistent with the principle of maximum local autonomy and should commend themselves to the Arab and Jewish populations of Jerusalem. They would retain, of course, under the Commission's proposals such municipal police forces as might be necessary for the preservation of law and order and they would above all enjoy the opportunity to live at peace with one another as good neighbors.

The third objective set forth by the General Assembly in its resolution of last December 11 was that a permanent international regime for the Jerusalem area should be established. In order to carry out the objectives of an international character which I have already discussed — protection of the Holy Places under United Nations supervision, and demilitarization of the

Jerusalem area under effective United Nations control — a minimum of international machinery is clearly essential.

But in addition to these objectives there are others which are of international concern because they involve relations between the two major population groups in Jerusalem. These objectives include such matters as the coordination of main public services, principally such public utilities as water and electricity, the coordination of measures for the maintenance of public order, economic relations within the area, the protection of sites and antiquities, and town planning.

. . . .

Mr. Chairman, I have been discussing the question of Jerusalem largely in terms of the proposals made by the Palestine Conciliation Commission. We believe that, within the framework of its instructions the Commission has done a good conscientious job and that its Members and its secretariat should be commended for their work.

If there are those among us who for one reason or another do not find the plan proposed by the Commission altogether to their liking, they should address themselves to the terms of last December's resolution.

. . . .

I have already said that the United States supports the proposals of the Palestine Conciliation Commission as reflecting the intentions and purposes of the General Assembly. In supporting those proposals it is our view that they are consistent with the middle-of-the-road course to which we adhere.

In stating this view I should make it clear that we are prepared to examine on their merits any proposed amendments of the Draft Statute or any new proposals which would facilitate our task of reaching a general agreement.

With regard to the Holy Places in Palestine outside Jerusalem, it will be recalled that the General Assembly in its resolution of December 11, 1948 instructed the Palestine Conciliation Commission to call upon the political authorities of the areas concerned to give appropriate formal guarantees as to the protection of the Holy Places outside Jerusalem, and free access to them. The Commission was also instructed to present these undertakings to the General Assembly for approval.

The Commission has obtained and forwarded to the Assembly a communication concerning these Holy Places from the representative of Israel and a joint communication on the same subject from representatives of Egypt, Jordan, Lebanon, and Syria. (A/1113).

The Arab representatives have made a helpful formal declaration taking as a basis the draft submitted to both parties by the Conciliation Commission. The Israeli Government, while reiterating its readiness solemnly to give formal guarantees concerning the Holy Places in Israeli-controlled territory, considered that it would be preferable to take up the actual formulation of a declaration in the light of the situation arising from the discussions which we are now undertaking.

I do not wish, Mr. Chairman, at this time to deal at any greater length with this subject. It is the hope of the United States Delegation, however, that the successful conclusion of our efforts to find a solution of the problem of Jerusalem will lead us in turn to satisfactory declarations with regard to the Holy Places outside Jerusalem.

. . . .

(2) *Resolution on the Internationalization of Jerusalem, adopted by the United Nations General Assembly, December 9, 1949.*[15]

The General Assembly,

Having regard to its resolutions 181 (II) of 29 November 1947 and 194 (III) of 11 December 1948,

Having studied the reports of the United Nations Conciliation Commission for Palestine set up under the latter resolution,

I. *Decides*

In relation to Jerusalem,

Believing that the principles underlying its previous resolutions concerning this matter, and in particular its resolution of 29 November 1947, represent a just and equitable settlement of the question,

1. To restate, therefore, its intention that Jerusalem should be placed under a permanent international regime, which should envisage appropriate guarantees for the protection of the Holy Places, both within and outside Jerusalem and to confirm specifically the following provisions of General Assembly resolution 181 (II): (1) The City of Jerusalem shall be established as a *corpus separatum* under a special international regime and shall be administered by the United Nations; (2) The Trusteeship Council shall be designated to discharge the responsibilities of the Administering Authority . . .; and (3) The City of Jerusalem shall include the present municipality of Jerusalem plus the surrounding villages and towns, the most eastern of which shall be Abu Dis; the most southern, Bethlehem; the most western, Ein Karim (including also the built-up area of Motsa); and the most northern, Shu'fat, as indicated on the attached sketch-map (annex B);

2. To request for this purpose that the Trusteeship Council at its next session, whether special or regular, complete the preparation of the Statute of Jerusalem (A/118/Rev.2), omitting the now inapplicable provisions, such as articles 32 and 39, and, without prejudice to the fundamental principles of the international regime for Jerusalem set forth in General Assembly resolution 118 (II) introducing therein amendments in the direction of its greater democratization, approve the Statute, and proceed immediately with its implementation. The Trusteeship Council shall not allow any actions taken by any interested Government or Governments to divert it from adopting and implementing the Statute of Jerusalem;

II. *Calls upon* the States concerned, to make formal undertakings, at an early date and in the light of their obligations as Members of the United Nations, that they will approach these matters with good will, and be guided by the terms of the present resolution.

3. RELIEF FOR PALESTINIAN REFUGEES

On March 24 the President signed a Senate joint resolution authorizing a special contribution by the United States of $16,000,000 for the relief of Palestine refugees

[15] United Nations General Assembly, Document A/1251, p. 25, December 28, 1949.

in pursuance of the General Assembly resolution of November 19, 1948 urging all members of the United Nations to make voluntary contributions as soon as possible to a relief fund totaling $32,000,000.[16]

In August the United Nations Palestine Conciliation Commission adopted a United States proposal to send an economic survey mission to the middle east to study the problems involved in the resettlement of Arab refugees and promote the establishment of economic conditions favorable to peace.[17] Gordon R. Clapp, chairman of the board of directors of the Tennessee Valley Authority, was appointed chairman of the survey mission; in addition to the United States, France, Turkey, and the United Kingdom were represented on the mission, which left in September to establish its headquarters in Beirut. In December the report of the mission was considered by the General Assembly. The United States co-sponsored in the Ad Hoc Political Committee with France, Turkey and the United Kingdom a draft resolution giving effect to the recommendations of the mission for a program of relief and public works to improve the productivity of the middle east as well as to employ a large number of refugees. The draft resolution, following recommendations of the mission, proposed establishment of a Near East Relief and Works Agency to supersede the United Nations Relief for Palestine Refugees and of an advisory commission composed of representatives of the governments of France, Turkey, the United Kingdom and the United States to advise the director of the agency. It was estimated that the program would cost $54,900,000 from January 1, 1950 to June 30, 1951.[18] After approval by the *ad hoc* committee the resolution was approved in plenary session on December 8.[19]

B. Turkey

For further information on the Greek-Turkish aid program, see this volume, p. 657.

(1) *Military and Economic Assistance to Turkey, Cumulative through June 30, 1949.*[1]

Period	Cumulative by Quarter				
	Total	Army and Air Force	Navy	Roads[2]	General
Quarter ending:					
1947					
December	$ 905,380	$ 297,120	$ 3,852	$ 604,408	
1948					
March	13,338,237	6,511,269	3,927,596	2,899,014	$ 358
June	37,832,576	26,671,120	7,602,589	3,555,269	3,598
September	59,015,724	45,531,406	9,344,991	4,134,053	5,274
December	73,476,136	57,215,887	11,955,334	4,299,050	5,965
1949					
March	84,680,212	67,378,350	12,796,824	4,493,655	11,383
June	102,439,475	79,100,566	18,323,696	5,000,000	15,213

C. Union of South Africa

The Political and Security Committee of the General Assembly considered the question of the treatment of Indians in the Union of South Africa at its meetings from May 9 to 11, 1949, during the second part of the third session of the Assembly. A draft resolution presented by the Union of South Africa declaring the matter to be

[16] Department of State, *Bulletin*, XX, p. 419.
[17] *New York Times*, August 25, 1949, p. 11.
[18] United Nations General Assembly, Document A/AC.31/SR.51, December 1, 1949.
[19] *Ibid.*, Document A/P.V.273, December 8, 1949.
[1] Department of State Publication 3674, Table VII, p. 39.
[2] Includes $588,731, representing the value of road-construction machinery procured by the Army Corps of Engineers.

essentially one of domestic jurisdiction and not within the competence of the General Assembly[1] was defeated by a vote of 5 to 23 with 12 abstentions.[2] The United States delegate (Cohen) opposed this draft resolution stating that it was doubtful that Article 2 (7) of the United Nations Charter, providing that the United Nations should not intervene in the domestic jurisdiction of any state, was intended to prevent any consideration of such matters by the General Assembly and any expression of opinion in the form of a recommendation designed to assist the parties in reaching a settlement. Mr. Cohen continued by pointing out that the task of the General Assembly in promoting the observance of human rights and fundamental freedoms had already been initiated in the Declaration of Human Rights.[3] An Indian draft resolution which declared the Union of South Africa guilty of violating the Charter and international obligations in connection with the alleged discrimination and called for a three-member commission to study the situation and recommend a solution[4] was accepted by the political committee by a vote of 21 to 17 with 12 abstentions. In voting against the Indian draft, the United States representative (Cohen) stated that while sympathetic with some of its objectives he did not believe that it would contribute to a solution of the problem.[5] The Indian draft was subsequently withdrawn in discussion at the plenary session.[6] The committee also approved a draft resolution proposed by France and Mexico calling upon India, Pakistan, and the Union of South Africa to participate in a round table discussion dealing with the treatment of people of Indian origin in South Africa and taking into consideration the United Nations Charter and the Declaration of Human Rights,[7] by a vote of 39 to 2 with 9 abstentions.[8] The French-Mexican Draft was approved by the plenary session of the General Assembly by a vote of 47 to 1 (Union of South Africa) with 10 abstentions.[9]

1 United Nations General Assembly, Document A/C.1/460, May 10, 1949.
2 Ibid., 1st Committee, Official Records (3d session, 2d part), p. 321.
3 Ibid., p. 293.
4 Ibid., Document A/C.1/461/Rev.1, May 10, 1949.
5 Ibid., 1st Committee, Official Records (3d session, 2d part), p. 322.
6 United Nations General Assembly, Official Records (3d session, 2d part), p. 439.
7 Ibid., Document A/C.1/462/Rev. 1, May 11, 1949.
8 Ibid., 1st Committee, Official Records (3d session, 2d part), p. 324.
9 United Nations General Assembly, Official Records (3d session, 2d part), p. 455.

Index

Compiled by Gordon Bassett